KT-477-215

THE ROUGH GUIDE TO
CHINA

This eighth e**di**

Thomas Bi**r**
David Leff**m**
Charles Yo**u**

15 377 126 9

ROUGH GUIDES

Contents

Introduction to
China

China is a nation on the march. As it accelerates away from its preindustrial cocoon at a rate unmatched in human history, huge new cities with cutting-edge architecture continue to spring up, connected by an ever-expanding high-speed rail network. But look closer and you'll see China's splendidly diverse geographic, ethnic, culinary and social make-up is not lost; modernity conceals a civilization that has remained intact, continually recycling itself, for over four millennia. Chinese script was perfected during the Han dynasty (220 BC–220 AD), and the stone lions that stand sentinel outside skyscrapers first appeared as temple guardians over three thousand years ago. Indeed, it is the contrast between change and continuity that make modern China so fascinating.

The first thing that strikes visitors to this country is the extraordinary density of its population. In much of eastern, central and southern China, villages, towns and cities seem to sprawl endlessly into one another along the grey arteries of busy expressways. Move to the far south or west, however, and the population thins out as it begins to vary; large areas are inhabited not by the "Chinese", but by scores of distinct ethnic minorities, ranging from animist hill tribes to urban Muslims. Here, the landscape begins to dominate: green paddy fields and misty hilltops in the southwest, the scorched, epic vistas of the old Silk Road in the northwest, and the magisterial mountains of Tibet.

Although abundant buses, flights and high-speed trains have made getting around China the easiest it has ever been, to get under the skin of this country is still no simple matter. The main tourist highlights – the Great Wall, the Forbidden City, the Terracotta Army and the Yangzi gorges – are relatively few considering the vast size of the country, and much of China's historic architecture has been deliberately destroyed in the rush to modernize. Added to this are the frustrations of travelling in a land where few people

ABOVE THE GREAT WALL OPPOSITE FROM TOP GIANT PANDAS, SICHUAN; HONG KONG BY NIGHT

speak English, the writing system is alien and foreigners are sometimes viewed as exotic objects of intense curiosity – though overall you'll find that Chinese people, despite a reputation for curtness, are generally hospitable and friendly.

Where to go

As China has opened up in recent years, so the emphasis on tourism has changed. Many well-known cities and sights have become so developed that their charm has vanished, while in remoter regions – particularly Tibet, Yunnan and the Northwest – previously restricted or "undiscovered" places have become newly accessible. The following outline is a selection of both "classic" China sights and less-known attractions, which should come in handy when planning a schedule.

Inevitably, **Beijing** is on everyone's itinerary, and the **Great Wall** and the splendour of the **Forbidden City** are certainly not to be missed; the capital also offers some of the country's best food and nightlife. **Chengde**, too, just north of Beijing, has some stunning imperial buildings, constructed by emperors when this was their favoured retreat for the summer.

South of the capital, the **Yellow River** valley is the cradle of Chinese civilization, where remnants of the dynastic age lie scattered in a unique landscape of loess terraces. The cave temples at **Datong** and **Luoyang** are magnificent, with huge Buddhist sculptures staring out impassively across their now industrialized settings. Of the historic capitals, **Xi'an** is the most obvious destination, where the celebrated

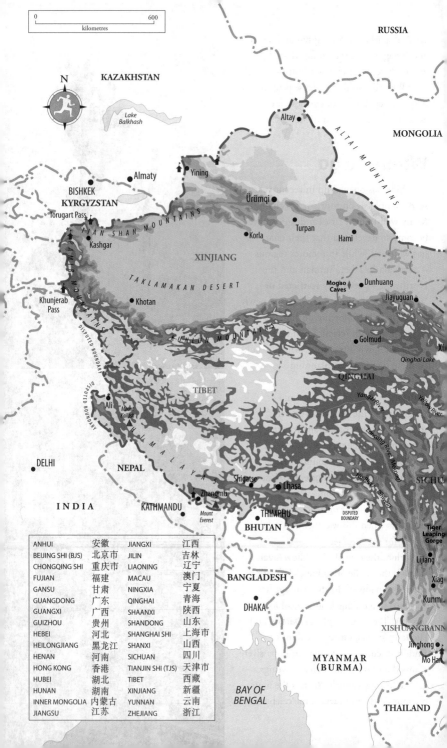

0   600
kilometres

RUSSIA

KAZAKHSTAN

N

Lake Balkhash

MONGOLIA

Altay

A L T A I   M O U N T A I N S

Almaty
Yining

Ürümqi

BISHKEK
KYRGYZSTAN

Torugart Pass

T I A N   S H A N   M O U N T A I N S

Korla
Turpan
Hami

Kashgar

XINJIANG

Mogao   Dunhuang
Caves
Jiayuguan

Khunjerab
Pass

T A K L A M A K A N   D E S E R T

K A R A K O R A M   M O U N T A I N S

Khotan

D I S P U T E D   B O U N D A R Y

K U N L U N   M O U N T A I N S

Golmud

Xi

Qinghai Lake

D I S P U T E D   B O U N D A R Y

QINGHAI

Ali
Mount
Kailash

TIBET

Yangtze River

Yellow River

Lancang River (Mekong)

DELHI

H I M A L A Y A S

NEPAL

Shigatse
Lhasa

SICHU

Zhangmu

I N D I A

KATHMANDU

North Road (G318)

DISPUTED
BOUNDARY

**Tiger
Leaping
Gorge**

Mount
Everest

THIMPHU

BHUTAN

Lijiang

Xiag

ANHUI	安徽	JIANGXI	江西
BEIJING SHI (BJS)	北京市	JILIN	吉林
CHONGQING SHI	重庆市	LIAONING	辽宁
FUJIAN	福建	MACAU	澳门
GANSU	甘肃	NINGXIA	宁夏
GUANGDONG	广东	QINGHAI	青海
GUANGXI	广西	SHAANXI	陕西
GUIZHOU	贵州	SHANDONG	山东
HEBEI	河北	SHANGHAI SHI	上海市
HEILONGJIANG	黑龙江	SHANXI	山西
HENAN	河南	SICHUAN	四川
HONG KONG	香港	TIANJIN SHI (TJS)	天津市
HUBEI	湖北	TIBET	西藏
HUNAN	湖南	XINJIANG	新疆
INNER MONGOLIA	内蒙古	YUNNAN	云南
JIANGSU	江苏	ZHEJIANG	浙江

BANGLADESH

DHAKA

Kunmi

XISHUANGBANN

Jinghong
Mo Han

**MYANMAR
(BURMA)**

**BAY OF
BENGAL**

THAILAND

MARTIAL ARTS

Thousands of **martial arts** have evolved in China, usually in isolated communities that had to defend themselves, such as temples and clan villages. All, though, can be classed into two basic types: **external** ("hard") styles concentrate on building up physical strength to overpower opponents; the trickier **internal** ("soft") styles concentrate on developing and focusing the internal energy known as *qi*. Both styles use forms – prearranged sets of movements – to develop the necessary speed, power and timing; as well as kicks, punches and open palm strikes, they also incorporate movements inspired by animals.

The most famous external style is **Shaolin kung fu**, developed in the Shaolin Temple in Henan province (see box, p.264) and known for powerful kicks and animal styles – notably eagle, mantis and monkey. The classic Shaolin weapon is the staff, and there's even a drunken form, where the practitioner sways and lurches as if inebriated.

But the style that you're most likely to see – it's practised in the open all over the country – is the internal **tai ji quan**. The body is held in a state of minimal tension to create the art's characteristic "soft" appearance. Its emphasis on slow movements and increasing *qi* flow means it is excellent for health, and it's a popular workout for the elderly.

Terracotta Army still stands guard over the tomb of Emperor Qin Shi Huang. Other ancient towns include sleepy **Kaifeng** in Henan, and **Qufu**, the birthplace of Confucius, in Shandong, both offering architectural treasures and an intimate, human scale that's hard to find in the large cities. The area is also well supplied with **holy mountains**, providing both beautiful scenery and a rare continuity with the past: **Tai Shan** is perhaps the grandest and most imperial of the country's pilgrimage sites; **Song Shan** in Henan sees followers of the contemporary kung fu craze making the trek to the Shaolin Temple, where the art originated; and **Wutai Shan** in Shanxi features some of the best-preserved religious sites in the country.

Dominating China's east coast near the mouth of the Yangzi, **Shanghai** is the mainland's most Westernized city, a booming port where the Art Deco monuments of the old European-built Bund – the riverside business centre – rub shoulders with a hypermodern metropolis, crowned with some of the world's tallest skyscrapers. Shanghai's modernity and profit-driven population finds a natural rival in the international commercial hub of **Hong Kong**, off China's south coast. With its colonial heritage and refreshingly cosmopolitan outlook, there's almost nothing Hong Kong cannot offer in the way of tourist facilities, from fine beaches to great eating, drinking and nightlife. Nearby **Macau** is also worth a visit, if not for its casinos then for its Baroque churches and Portuguese cuisine.

In the southwest of the country, Sichuan's **Chengdu** and Yunnan's **Kunming** remain two of China's most easy-going provincial capitals, and the entire region is, by any standards, exceptionally diverse, with landscapes encompassing everything from snowbound summits and alpine lakes to steamy tropical jungles. The karst (limestone peak) scenery is particularly renowned, especially along the Li River between **Yangshuo** and **Guilin** in Guangxi. In Sichuan, pilgrims flock to see the colossal Great Buddha at **Leshan**, and to ascend the holy mountain of **Emei Shan**; to the east, the city of **Chongqing** marks the start of river trips down the **Yangzi**, Asia's longest river, through the **Three Gorges**. As Yunnan and Guangxi share borders with Vietnam, Laos and Myanmar (Burma), and

FACT FILE

• With an **area** of 9.6 million square kilometres, China is the fourth-largest country in the world and the most populous nation on Earth, with around 1.38 billion people. Of these, 92 percent are of the **Han** ethnic group, with the remainder comprising 55 officially recognized minorities such as Mongols, Uyghurs and Tibetans.

• The main **religions** are Buddhism, Taoism, Islam and Christianity, though the country is officially atheist.

• China's longest river is the **Yangzi** (6275km) and the highest peak is Chomolungma – **Mount Everest** (8850m) – on the Nepalese border.

• The **Chinese Communist Party** is the sole political organization, and is divided into Executive, Legislative and Judicial branches. The chief of state (President) and the head of government (Premier) are elected for five-year terms at the National People's Congress.

• Though few **industries** are **state owned** nowadays, the uncontrolled **free-market economy** of recent times is being reigned in by the current administration.

Sichuan rubs up against Tibet, it's not surprising to find that the area is home to dozens of ethnic autonomous regions. The attractions of the latter range from the traditional Bai town of **Dali**, the wild splendor of **Tiger Leaping Gorge** and the Dai villages of **Xishuangbanna** in Yunnan, to the **Khampa heartlands** of western Sichuan, the exuberant festivals and textiles of Guizhou's **Miao** and the wooden architecture of **Dong settlements** in Guangxi's north.

The huge area of China referred to as the **Northwest** is where the people thin out and real wilderness begins. **Inner Mongolia**, just hours from Beijing, is already at the frontiers of Central Asia; here you can follow in the footsteps of Genghis Khan by horseriding on the endless grasslands of the steppe. To the south and west, the old **Silk Road** heads out of Xi'an right to and through China's western borders, via **Jiayuguan**, terminus of the Great Wall of China, and the lavish Buddhist cave art in the sandy deserts of **Dunhuang**.

West of here lie the mountains and deserts of vast Xinjiang, where China blends into old Turkestan and where simple journeys between towns become modern travel epics. The oasis cities of **Turpan** and **Kashgar**, with their bazaars and Muslim heritage, are the main attractions, though the blue waters of **Tian Chi**, offering alpine scenery in the midst of searing desert, are deservedly popular. Beyond Kashgar, travellers face some of the most adventurous routes of all, over the Khunjerab and Torugart passes to Pakistan and Kyrgyzstan respectively.

Tibet remains an exotic destination. Despite 65 years of Chinese rule, coupled with a mass migration of Han Chinese into the region, the manifestations of Tibetan culture are perceptibly intact – the Potala Palace in **Lhasa**, red-robed monks, lines of pilgrims turning prayer wheels, butter sculptures and gory frescoes decorating monastery halls. And Tibet's mountain scenery, which includes **Mount Everest** and **Mount Kailash** is worth the trip in itself, even if opportunities for independent travel are very limited.

When to go

China's climate is extremely diverse. The **south** is subtropical, with wet, humid summers (April–Sept), when temperatures can approach 40°C, and a typhoon season on the southeast coast between July and September. Though it is often still hot enough to swim in the sea in December, the short winters (Jan–March) can be surprisingly chilly.

Central China has brief, cold winters, with temperatures dipping below zero, and long, hot, humid summers: the three Yangzi cities – Chongqing, Wuhan and Nanjing – are proverbially referred to as China's three "furnaces". Rainfall here is high all year round. The **Yellow River basin** marks a rough boundary beyond which central heating is fitted as standard in buildings, helping to make the region's harsh winters a little more tolerable. Winter temperatures in Beijing rarely rise above freezing from December to March, and biting winds off the Mongolian plains add a vicious wind-chill factor, yet summers can be well over 30°C. In **Inner Mongolia** and **Dongbei**, winters are at least clear and dry, but temperatures remain way below zero, while summers can be uncomfortably warm. **Xinjiang** gets fiercely hot in summer, though without the humidity of the rest of the country, and winters are as bitter as anywhere else in northern China. **Tibet** is ideal in midsummer, when its mountain plateaus are pleasantly warm and dry; in winter, however, temperatures in the capital, Lhasa, frequently fall below freezing.

Overall, the **best time to visit** China is spring or autumn, when the weather is at its most temperate.

AVERAGE TEMPERATURES AND RAINFALL

	Jan	Feb	March	April	May	June	July	Aug	Sept	Oct	Nov	Dec
BEIJING												
Max/min (°C)	1/-10	4/-8	11/-1	21/7	27/13	31/18	31/21	30/20	26/14	20/6	9/-2	3/-8
Max/min (°F)	34/14	39/18	52/30	70/45	81/55	88/64	88/70	86/68	79/57	68/43	48/28	37/18
rainfall (mm)	4	5	8	17	35	78	243	141	58	16	11	3
CHONGQING												
Max/min (°C)	9/5	13/7	18/11	23/16	27/19	29/22	34/24	35/25	28/22	22/16	16/12	3/-8
Max/min (°F)	48/41	55/45	64/52	73/61	81/66	84/72	93/75	95/77	82/72	72/61	61/54	37/18
rainfall (mm)	15	20	38	99	142	180	142	122	150	112	48	20
HONG KONG												
Max/min (°C)	18/13	17/13	19/16	24/19	28/23	29/26	31/26	31/26	29/25	27/23	23/18	20/15
Max/min (°F)	64/55	63/55	66/61	75/66	82/73	84/79	88/79	88/79	84/77	81/73	73/64	68/59
rainfall (mm)	33	46	74	137	292	394	381	367	257	114	43	31
KUNMING												
Max/min (°C)	20/8	22/9	25/12	28/16	29/18	29/19	28/19	28/19	28/18	24/15	22/12	20/8
Max/min (°F)	68/46	72/48	77/54	82/61	84/64	84/66	82/66	82/66	82/64	75/59	72/54	68/46
rainfall (mm)	8	18	28	41	127	132	196	198	97	51	56	15
SHANGHAI												
Max/min (°C)	8/1	8/1	13/4	19/10	25/15	28/19	32/23	32/23	28/19	23/14	17/7	12/2
Max/min (°F)	46/34	46/34	55/39	66/50	77/59	82/66	90/73	90/73	82/66	73/57	63/45	54/36
rainfall (mm)	48	58	84	94	94	180	147	142	130	71	51	36

Author picks

Our authors spent several months researching every corner of China, from sprawling Mongolian grasslands to city nightclubs, Tibet's awe-inspiring mountains and Beijing's maze of *hutongs*. These destinations are some of their personal favourites.

High-tech cityscapes For superlative views of glittering urban architecture, head to the Shanghai Tower (p.366) or the Peak in Hong Kong (p.554) – preferably at night – and gaze down across forests of luminous, futuristic towers.

Ethnic minorities Experience China's cultural diversity in Tibetan monastery towns (pp.896–921), Dai and Bai villages (p.685), Uyghur mosques (p.852) and Mongolian nomad tents (p.236).

Epic scenery Drink in dramatic landscapes at Lake Karakul, its fridgid shores grazed by bactrian camels (p.862); Zhangjiajie's spectacular forest of splintered stone pinnacles, wreathed in cloud (p.439); and the grandeur of Meili Xue Shan's frosted summit (p.703).

Chinese cuisine Indulge yourself with a crispy, calorie-laden Peking duck in Beijing (p.108), a simple bowl of beef noodles in Lanzhou (p.801), a bright and noisy *dim sum* breakfast in Hong Kong (p.581), or one of Sichuan's scorching, chilli-laden hotpots (p.730).

Top hikes Wear out your hiking shoes on a two-day trail through Tiger Leaping Gorge (p.697), the 65km-long staircase to the summit of Emei Shan (p.752) or a two-hour leg stretch along Hong Kong's Dragon's Back path (p.559).

Traditional architecture Explore the medieval walled town of Pingyao (p.251), Jokhang Tibetan temple (p.888), domestic buildings at Yixian (p.407), the Dong drum towers and bridges at the Guangxi–Guizhou border (p.626) and Zigong's merchant guildhalls (p.756).

Vanished cultures The country's inhospitable, far western fringes hide remains of long-forgotten civilizations. Try Tibet's all-but-unheard-of Guge Kingdom (p.921) or the haystack-shaped mausoleums of Ningxia's Western Xia rulers (p.225).

> Our author recommendations don't end here. We've flagged up our favourite places – a perfectly sited hotel, an atmospheric café, a special restaurant – throughout the Guide, highlighted with the ★ symbol.

FROM TOP LAKE KARAKUL; THE JOKHANG, LHASA; DONG DRUM TOWER, ZHAOXING

31

things not to miss

It's not possible to see everything that China has to offer in one trip – and we don't suggest you try. What follows is a selective taste of the highlights: natural wonders and outstanding sights, plus the best activities and experiences. All highlights have a page reference to take you straight into the Guide, where you can find out more.

1

1 TERRACOTTA ARMY, XI'AN
Page 212
These 2200-year-old, life-sized warriors protect the tomb of China's first emperor.

2 JIAYUGUAN FORT, GANSU
Page 820
Famously lonely desert outpost, guarding the remote western tail end of the Great Wall.

3 HONG KONG HARBOUR VIEWS
Page 561
Take the Star Ferry to Tsim Sha Tsui to admire one of the world's most spectacular cityscapes.

4 LABRANG MONASTERY, XIAHE

Page 804
Rub shoulders with pilgrims and red-robed clergy at this enormous complex, one of the pivots of Tibetan Lamaism.

5 THE YELLOW RIVER AT SHAPOTOU

Page 221
Witness how "China's Sorrow", the mighty Yellow River, is being used to revegetate desert dunes.

6 TIGER LEAPING GORGE, YUNNAN

Page 697
One of China's great hikes, along a steep-sided canyon, with attractive homestays along the way.

7 KASHGAR'S SUNDAY MARKET

Page 853
Central Asian crowds trade sheep, horses, cattle, camels and more at Xinjiang's premier frontier bazaar.

13

13 CHENGDE
Page 147

The former imperial retreat from the heat of summer holds a string of pretty temples.

14 MOUNT KAILASH, TIBET
Page 920

Make a tough pilgrimage circuit around this striking mountain, considered holy by four different religions.

15 TAI SHAN, SHANDONG
Page 296

A taxing ascent up endless stone staircases is rewarded with some immaculate temples and pavilions.

16 SISTERS' MEAL FESTIVAL
Page 646

Join thousands of locals at Taijiang, Guizhou, during a wild three-day showcase of ethnic Miao culture.

17 HANGING TEMPLE, HENG SHAN
Page 244

Rickety wooden shrines to China's three core faiths, suspended on a cliff-face by flimsy-looking scaffolding.

14

15

16

17

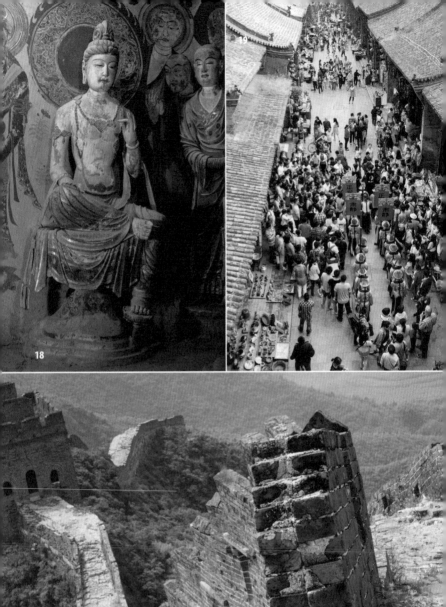

21

22

23

24

26

27

28 LI RIVER
Page 615
Ride a boat or a bamboo raft through the heart of this weird, poetical landscape, past a host of contorted limestone pinnacles.

29 DIM SUM
Page 499
The classic Cantonese breakfast; there's no better place to try it than in Guangzhou.

30 THE BUND, SHANGHAI
Page 352
Watch Chinese holidaymakers queuing up to have their photos taken against Shanghai's luminous, futuristic skyline.

31 GIANT BUDDHA, LESHAN
Page 749
Marvel at the world's largest carved Buddha, hewn into a riverside cliff way back during the Tang dynasty.

Itineraries

China is vast, and you'll barely be able to scratch the surface on a single trip. The following itineraries will, however, give you an in-depth look at some of the country's most fascinating areas – the Grand Tour covers the essentials, while the other suggested routes cover the trip to the deserts of the west, and China's tropical southwestern corner.

GRAND TOUR

This tour ticks the major boxes – historical sights, gorgeous countryside and sizzling cities. Allow two weeks in a hurry, or three at a more leisurely pace.

❶ Beijing The Chinese capital is packed with essential sights, including the Forbidden City, the Summer Palace and the Great Wall. **See p.60**

❷ Pingyao Step back in time inside the walls of this charming, traffic-free Ming-dynasty town, spending the night at a traditional courtyard inn. **See p.251**

❸ Xi'an Dynastic capital for a millennium, Xi'an is filled with treasures, including the enigmatic Terracotta Army, built to guard the tomb of China's despotic first emperor. **See p.197**

❹ Chengdu The Sichuanese capital features traditional teahouses, fire-breathing opera, lively temples and locally bred pandas. **See p.731**

❺ Three Gorges Take a three-day cruise down this impressive stretch of the mighty Yangtze River, between Chongqing and the massive Three Gorges Dam. **See p.768**

❻ Yangshuo Cycle between jagged limestone peaks and brilliant green paddy fields surrounding Yangshuo village, which looks like something straight off a Chinese scroll painting. **See p.617**

❼ Hong Kong Stunning cityscapes, modern conveniences, serious shopping, glorious beaches, wonderful mountain trails and superb cuisine – this bustling territory has it all. **See p.540**

WILD WEST

This three-week-long trip takes you from Beijing to China's Wild West, where you can ride horses across Mongolian grasslands, or soak up Uyghur culture in Xinjiang.

❶ Beijing Before setting out, get a taster of northwestern China in Beijing's Muslim quarter, where street hawkers sell delicious skewers of barbecued lamb. **See p.92**

❷ Datong Cycle around Datong's rebuilt city walls, then bus out to giant Buddhist sculptures at the Yungang caves, and the gravity-defying Hanging Temple. **See p.238**

❸ Grasslands Use pleasant Hohhot, the capital of Inner Mongolia, to explore the never-ending grasslands to the north, preferably on horseback. **See p.236**

❹ Shapotou See the mighty Yellow River flowing smoothly between desert dunes at this tiny, remote resort town in upcountry rural Ningxia – a spellbinding sight. **See p.221**

❺ Lanzhou Slurp down outstanding beef noodles at this former garrison town along the fabled Silk Road, the gateway to China's Muslim Northwest. **See p.797**

ABOVE THE LI RIVER

❻ Jiayuguan The fortress at the Great Wall's western extremity, over 2000km from Beijing, is impressive for its mighty defences, yet dwarfed by the stark desert scenery. **See p.820**

❼ Dunhuang Ride a camel across 300m-high dunes outside this small city, then explore the marvellous galleries of ancient Buddhist sculptures at the Mogao caves. **See p.823**

❽ Turpan Small, relaxed oasis town, with a main street shaded by grape trellises and a surrounding desert packed with historical relics from its former Silk Road heyday. **See p.842**

❾ Kashgar Frontier city where Chinese, Uyghur and Central Asian cultures mix: don't miss the astonishing Sunday Bazaar, crammed with metalwork, spices and livestock traders. **See p.850**

SIGHTS OF THE SOUTHWEST

The southwestern provinces offer spellbinding mountain vistas, karst-dotted rivers and rushing waterfalls, alongside fascinating minority villages and laidback cities.

❶ Emei Shan Join Buddhist pilgrims ascending this forested, temple-studded mountain up seemingly endless flights of stone steps. **See p.751**

❷ Dafo This gigantic Buddha statue was completed in 803 AD and remains one of the world's biggest religious sculptures. **See p.749**

❸ Jiuzhaigou Enchanting alpine valley of calcified waterfalls and lovely blue lakes, all surrounded by magestically forested peaks – get in early to beat the crowds. **See p.773**

❹ Tiger Leaping Gorge Starting from the old Naxi town of Lijiang, make the two-day hike through a stunning landscape of fractured granite mountains and deep river canyons. **See p.695**

❺ Dali Dali's laidback street life and outlying minority villages encourage unplanned long stays. **See p.679**

❻ Kunming The cheery, pleasantly warm Yunnanese capital retains considerable charm despite its modernity. Don't forget to try the famous "Crossing-the-Bridge" noodles. **See p.663**

❼ Kaili Jumping-off point for visiting villages of the Miao minority, famed for their festivals and spectacular embroideries. **See p.643**

❽ Li River Take a cruise down this magical river, lined with karst pinnacles, between Guilin and Yangshuo. **See p.615**

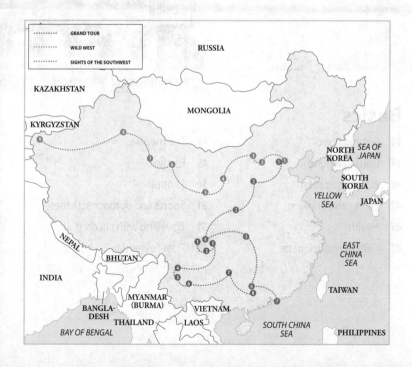

STREET SIGN IN ENGLISH AND CHINESE, SHANGHAI

Basics

Getting there

China's most important long-haul inter-national gateways are Beijing, Hong Kong, Guangzhou and Shanghai, though many other Chinese cities are served by international flights, operated mainly by airlines based in East Asia. There are also well-established overland routes into China – including road and rail links from its Southeast Asian neighbours, as well as the alluring Trans-Siberian Express from Moscow.

Fares to Hong Kong are at their highest during the fortnight before Christmas, the fortnight before Chinese New Year (see p.49) and from June to early October. The cheapest time to fly there is in February (after Chinese New Year), May and November. For Beijing and Shanghai, peak season is generally in the summer. Flying on weekends is slightly more expensive; price ranges quoted below are for midweek travel.

Flights from the UK and Ireland

You can fly **direct** from London Heathrow to Beijing (10hr) with Air China or British Airways; to Hong Kong (12hr) with British Airways, Cathay Pacific or Virgin Atlantic; to Guangzhou with China Southern (12hr) or to Shanghai (13hr) with British Airways, China Eastern or Virgin Atlantic. Other airlines that fly via a change of planes in a hub city include Aeroflot, Air France, KLM, Qatar, Singapore and Thai.

You can also fly direct from London Gatwick to Tianjin with Tianjin Airlines (17hr) and from Manchester to Hong Kong (with Cathay Pacific; 11hr) or Beijing (with Hainan Air; 11hr); a Manchester–Shanghai route might also be in the pipeline. Flying to China from other UK airports or from the Republic of Ireland involves either catching a connecting flight to London or Manchester, or flying via the airline's hub city.

From the UK, the lowest available **fares** to Beijing, Hong Kong or Shanghai start from around £380 in low season, rising to above £900 in high season.

Under a deal struck in 2016, it's possible that the number of direct UK-to-China flights will double in the near future.

Flights from the US and Canada

From North America, there are more flights to **Hong Kong** than to other Chinese destinations, though there's no shortage of flights to Beijing and Shanghai, and there are some direct services to Guangzhou. Airlines flying **direct** include Air Canada, Air China, Cathay Pacific, United and China Eastern. You can also choose to fly to a Chinese provincial city – Chinese, Japanese, Korean and Hong Kong airlines offer services to cities throughout China via their respective hubs. It takes around thirteen hours to reach Beijing from the West Coast; add seven hours or more to this if you start from the East Coast (including a stopover on the West Coast en route). Routes over the North Pole shave off a couple of hours' flying time; these include Air Canada's routes from Toronto, Air China's from New York, United's from Chicago and Continental's flights from Newark to Beijing.

Round-trip fares to Hong Kong, Beijing and Shanghai are broadly comparable: in low season, expect to pay US$750–1200 from the West Coast (Los Angeles, San Francisco, Vancouver), or US$900–1400 from the East Coast (New York, Montréal, Toronto). To get a good fare during high season, buy your ticket as early as possible.

Flights from Australia, New Zealand and South Africa

The closest entry point into China from **Australia** and **New Zealand** is Hong Kong, though from Australia it's also possible to fly direct to Guangzhou, Shanghai and Beijing. It's not a problem to fly elsewhere in China from either country if you catch a connecting flight along the way, though this can involve a layover in the airline's hub city.

From eastern Australia, expect to pay AU$750–1300 to Hong Kong with Cathay Pacific, China Airlines, Air Asia or Virgin Australia/Singapore Airlines;

AU$600–1200 to Shanghai with China Eastern, Xiamen Air, Qantas, Air China or China Southern; and AU$600–1200 to Beijing with Xiamen Air, Air China or China Eastern. Cathay, Qantas, Air China and China Eastern fly direct; other trips require a stopover in the airline's hub city. **From Perth**, fares to the above destinations are around AU$100 more expensive.

Flights **from New Zealand** are limited; the only direct flights are with Hong Kong Airlines, China Southern, Air China or Cathay Pacific/Air New Zealand from Auckland to Beijing, Shanghai or Hong Kong (NZ$800–2000). You might find cheaper deals if you're prepared to stop off en route; try Air Asia (for Beijing or Hong Kong), or China Southern (for Shanghai).

From South Africa, South African Airways have direct flights from Johannesburg to Hong Kong (14hr; from ZAR4500); for Beijing, Shanghai or anywhere else on the mainland you're looking at upwards of ZAR7500 and will have to change planes along the way.

Round-the-World flights

If China is only one stop on a much longer journey, you might want to consider buying a **Round-the-World** (**RTW**) ticket (from around £1000/US$1800). Some travel agents can sell you an "off-the-shelf" RTW ticket that will have you touching down in about half a dozen cities (Beijing and Hong Kong are on many itineraries); others will have to assemble one for you, which can be tailored to your needs but is often more expensive.

Airlines, agents and operators

When booking airfares, the cheapest online deals are often with stock operators such as STA, Trailfinders and Flight Centres, though it's always worth checking airline websites themselves for specials – and, often, a lot more flexibility with refunds and changing dates.

AIRLINES

Aeroflot Ⓦ aeroflot.com/cms/en
Air Asia Ⓦ airasia.com
Air Canada Ⓦ aircanada.com
Air China Ⓦ www.airchina.com.cn/en
Air France Ⓦ airfrance.com
Air New Zealand Ⓦ airnz.co.nz
Alitalia Ⓦ alitalia.com
All Nippon Airways Ⓦ www.anaskyweb.com
American Airlines Ⓦ aa.com
Asiana Airlines Ⓦ flyasiana.com
Austrian Airlines Ⓦ austrian.com
British Airways Ⓦ ba.com

Cathay Pacific Ⓦ cathaypacific.com
China Airlines Ⓦ china-airlines.com
China Eastern Airlines Ⓦ ceair.com
China Southern Airlines Ⓦ csair.com
Delta Ⓦ delta.com
Emirates Ⓦ emirates.com
EVA Air Ⓦ evaair.com
Finnair Ⓦ finnair.com
Hainan Airlines Ⓦ hainanairlines.com
Hong Kong Airlines Ⓦ hongkongairlines.com
Japan Airlines Ⓦ jal.com
Jetstar Ⓦ jetstar.com
KLM Ⓦ klm.com
Korean Air Ⓦ koreanair.com
Lufthansa Ⓦ lufthansa.com
Malaysia Airlines Ⓦ malaysiaairlines.com
Nepal Airlines Ⓦ nepalairlines.com.np
Qantas Airways Ⓦ qantas.com
Qatar Airways Ⓦ qatarairways.com
Royal Brunei Ⓦ flyroyalbrunei.com
Royal Jordanian Ⓦ rj.com
SAS Ⓦ flysas.com
Singapore Airlines Ⓦ singaporeair.com
South African Airways Ⓦ flysaa.com
Swiss Ⓦ swiss.com
Thai Airways Ⓦ www.thaiair.com
Tianjin Airlines Ⓦ tianjinairlines.co.uk/
Turkish Airlines Ⓦ turkishairlines.com
United Airlines Ⓦ united.com
Vietnam Airlines Ⓦ vietnamairlines.com
Virgin Atlantic Ⓦ virgin-atlantic.com
Virgin Australia Ⓦ virginaustralia.com
Xiamen Air Ⓦ xiamenair.com

AGENTS AND OPERATORS

Absolute Asia Can ☎ 1 212 627 1950, Ⓦ absolutetravel.com. Numerous tours, all in first-class accommodation, from six-day tasters to the sixteen-day "Silk Road" expedition.
Adventures Abroad US ☎ 1 800 665 3998, Ⓦ adventures-abroad.com. Small-group specialists with two-week tours from Beijing and Shanghai to Hong Kong, plus interesting Silk Road trips from Uzbekistan to Beijing, and Yunnan/Tibet adventures.
Asian Pacific Adventures US ☎ 1 800 825 1680, Ⓦ asianpacific adventures.com. Numerous tours of China, the most interesting of which focus on southwestern ethnic groups and overlooked rural corners.
Bamboo Trails Taiwan ☎ 886 07 7354945, Ⓦ bambootrails.com. A small travel company specializing in the Chinese world, offering some unique group itineraries (including Movie China and The Bamboo Trail), as well as high-end, tailor-made trips.
Bike Asia China ☎ 0773 8826521, Ⓦ bikeasia.com. Guided bicycle tours ranging from day-long pedals around rural Guangxi to two-week epic rides across southwestern China.
Birdfinders UK ☎ 01258 839066, Ⓦ birdfinders.co.uk. Several trips per year to find rare and endemic species in Sichuan and northeast China.

China Direct UK ☎ 020 7538 2840, ⓦ chinadirect-travel.co.uk. Reliable British agency with more than two decades of experience in China, specializing in small-group and tailor-made tours. Their nine-day "Pandas and Palaces" tour is great for the big draws of Beijing, Xi'an and Chengdu.

China Holidays UK ☎ 020 7487 2999, ⓦ chinaholidays.co.uk. Aside from mainstream packages to the Three Gorges, Shanghai and Guilin, they also run themed tours, including cooking and birdwatching specials.

CTS Horizons UK ☎ 020 7868 5590, ⓦ ctshorizons.com. The China Travel Service's UK branch, offering an extensive range of tours including some cheap off-season hotel-and-flight packages to Beijing, and tailor-made private tours.

Exodus UK ☎ 020 3603 9372, ⓦ www.exodus.co.uk; US ☎ 1844 227 9087, ⓦ exodustravels.com. Some interesting and unusual overland itineraries around China and in the wilds of Tibet, Inner Mongolia and the Northwest, from a week-long whizz around the highlights to a month of walking, hiking and biking expeditions.

Explore Worldwide UK ☎ 01252 760000, ⓦ explore.co.uk. Big range of small-group tours and treks, including Tibet and trips along the Yangzi. Their 21-day "shoestring" tour is particularly popular.

Geographic Expeditions US ☎ 1 888 570 7108, ⓦ geoex.com. Travel among the ethnic groups of Guizhou, Tibet, Yunnan and western Sichuan, as well as more straightforward trips around Shanghai and Beijing.

Insider Journey Aus ☎ 1300 138 755, ⓦ insiderjourneys.com.au. Covers the obvious China sights and a bit more; also arranges visas for Thailand, Laos, Vietnam and Cambodia.

Intrepid Travel UK ☎ 0800 781 1660, Aus ☎ 03 9473 2673; ⓦ intrepidtravel.com. Excellent small-group tours with the emphasis on cross-cultural contact and low-impact tourism; visits some fairly out-of-the-way corners of China.

Mir Corp US ☎ 206 624 7289, ⓦ mircorp.com. Specialists in Trans-Siberian rail travel, for small groups as well as individual travellers.

Mountain Travel Sobek US ☎ 1 888 831 7526, ⓦ mtsobek.com. Adventure tours to Tibet, northern Yunnan and along the Silk Road.

North South Travel UK ☎ 01245 608291, ⓦ northsouthtravel .co.uk. Friendly, competitive travel agency, offering discounted fares worldwide, including to Beijing. Profits are used to support projects in the developing world, especially the promotion of sustainable tourism.

On the Go Tours UK ☎ 020 7371 1113, Aus ☎ 07 3358 3385; ⓦ onthegotours.com. Runs group and tailor-made tours, many tying in with China's most interesting festivals.

Pacific Delight Tours US ☎ 1 800 221 7179, ⓦ pacificdelight tours.com. City breaks, cruises along the Li and Yangzi rivers, plus a range of tours to Tibet, the Silk Road and western Yunnan.

Peregrine Aus ☎ 1300 854 445, ⓦ peregrineadventures.com. Tours to the Silk Road, the Yangzi, Tibet and a complete "China Highlights" package, from two to four weeks.

Regent Holidays UK ☎ 020 7666 1244, ⓦ regent-holidays.co.uk. Offers Trans-Siberian packages for individual travellers in either direction and with different possible stopover permutations, as well as interesting China tours.

The Russia Experience UK ☎ 0845 521 2910, Aus ☎ 1300 654 861; ⓦ trans-siberian.co.uk. Besides detailing their excellent Trans-Siberian packages, their website is a veritable mine of information about the railway.

STA Travel UK ☎ 033 321 0099, US ☎ 800 781 4040, Aus ☎ 134 782, NZ ☎ 0800 474 400, SA ☎ 0861 781 781; ⓦ statravel.co.uk. Worldwide specialists in independent travel; also student IDs, travel insurance, rail passes, and more. Good discounts for students and under-26s. China options include tours from 8 to 21 days, covering Beijing, Shanghai and the Yangzi and Li rivers, among others.

Sundowners UK ☎ 020 8877 7657, Aus ☎ 03 9672 5386, NZ ☎ 0800 770 156; ⓦ sundownersoverland.com. Tours of the Silk Road; also does Trans-Siberian rail bookings.

Trailfinders UK ☎ 020 7368 1200, Ireland ☎ 01 677 7888, Aus ☎ 1300 780 212; ⓦ trailfinders.com. One of the best-informed and most efficient agents for independent travellers. Numerous China options on offer.

Travel CUTS Canada ☎ 1 866 246 9762, US ☎ 1 800 592 2887; ⓦ travelcuts.com. Canadian youth and student travel firm.

Wendy Wu Tours UK ☎ 0800 1445 282, ⓦ wendywutours.co.uk. Long-running operator specializing in China and Southeast Asia; focuses on taking groups to main sights, but also offers less-mainstream packages to Yunnan, Sichuan and the Northwest.

Wild China Beijing ☎ 010 6465 6602, ⓦ wildchina.com. Small group tours to out-of-the-way places, such as minority villages in Guizhou, as well as Tibet tours and tracking pandas in Sichuan.

World Expeditions UK ☎ 0800 074 4135, ⓦ worldexpeditions .co.uk; Aus ☎ 1300 720 000, ⓦ worldexpeditions.com.au; NZ ☎ 0800 350 354, ⓦ worldexpeditions.co.nz. Offers cycling and hiking tours in rural areas, including a Great Wall trek.

Overland routes

China has a number of **land borders** open to foreign travellers, though you'll need to research the current paperwork situation for each (and possibly obtain relevant visas) before leaving home. Remember too that Chinese visas must be used within three months of their date of issue, meaning that on a longer trip, you may have to apply for one en route – something that's becoming increasingly difficult (see p.53).

Via Russia and Mongolia

One of the classic overland routes to China is through Russia **by train** to Beijing. As a one-off trip, the rail journey is a memorable way to begin or end a stay in China; views of stately birch forests, misty lakes and arid plateaus help time pass much faster than you'd think, and there are frequent stops during which you can wander the station platform, purchasing food and knick-knacks – package trips (see p.34) include more lengthy stopovers. The trains are comfortable and clean: second-class compartments contain four berths, while first-class have two and even boast a private shower.

There are actually two rail lines from Moscow to Beijing: the **Trans-Manchurian** (see box, p.188), which runs almost as far as the Sea of Japan before turning south through Dongbei (Manchuria) to

TRANS-SIBERIAN AND TRANS-MONGOLIAN TRAINS

The easiest way to book international **train tickets** to Ulaan Bataar and Moscow and have them delivered to your hotel in China is online through ⓦchinahighlights.com. Alternatively, Beijing's International Train Booking Office (Mon–Fri 8.30am–noon & 1.30–5pm; ☎010 6512 0507) is at the CITS office of the *International Hotel*, 9 Jianguomenwai Dajie, just south of *Chuanban* restaurant (see map, pp.84–85). Out of season, few people make the journey (you may get a cabin to yourself), but in summer there may well not be a seat for months.

Getting **visas** for Russia and/or Mongolia in China can be tricky, since regulations change all the time; it's always best (and, sometimes, essential) to organize them in your own country. If you want to apply in Beijing, check first whether it will be possible; you may need to show proof of inward and onward travel, and possibly hotel bookings and an official invitation too. See Beijing embassy websites and ⓦseat61.com for the latest advice. Trans-Siberian **tours and packages** (see below) cost more than doing it yourself, but will save a world of hassle.

Train #K3, which follows the **Trans-Mongolian route**, leaves every Wednesday from Beijing station and takes five-and-a-half days. A bunk in a second-class cabin with four beds – which is perfectly comfortable – costs around US$770. Trains leave Moscow for Beijing every Tuesday, though in this direction you'll likely have to buy tickets through an agency.

Train #K19, which follows the **Trans-Siberian route**, leaves every Saturday from Beijing Station, takes six days and costs upwards of US$590. Train #K23 to Ulaan Baatur in Mongolia departs every Tuesday and Saturday, takes 27hr and costs around US$260 for one bed in a four-bed berth.

Beijing; and the **Trans-Mongolian** (see above), which cuts through Mongolia from Siberia. The Manchurian train takes about six days, the Mongolian train about five. The latter is more popular with foreigners, a scenic route that rumbles past Lake Baikal and Siberia, the grasslands of Mongolia, and the desert of northwest China, skirting the Great Wall along the way. At the Mongolia/China border, you can watch as the undercarriage is switched to a different gauge.

Meals are geared to which country you're passing through; it's best in China and possibly worst in Russia. In Mongolia, the dining car accepts payment in US dollars, Chinese or Mongolian currency; while in Russia, US dollars or Russian roubles can be used. It's worth having small denominations of US dollars as you can change these on the train throughout the journey, or use them to buy food from station vendors along the way – though experiencing the cuisine and people in the dining cars is part of the fun. Bring some treats and snacks as a backup, and that great long novel you've always wanted to read.

Tickets and packages

Booking tickets needs some advance planning, especially during the popular summer months. Sorting out travel arrangements from abroad is also complex – you'll need a visa for Russia, as well as for Mongolia if you intend to pass through there. It's therefore advisable to use an experienced **travel agent** who can organize all tickets, visas and stopovers (if required), in advance. Visa processing is

an especially helpful time-saver, given the queues and paperwork required for visas along the route. You'll find the best source of current information at ⓦseat61.com.

You can cut complications and keep your costs down by using the online ticket booking system offered by **Real Russia** (ⓦrealrussia.co.uk); they mark up prices by about twenty percent, but save you a lot of hassle. A second-class Moscow–Beijing ticket booked with Real Russia costs £500–700 depending on the time of year; they will then help you sort out your visas for a small fee (as will all other agencies). Note that tours with Russian agencies offer good value for money; try **All Russia Travel Service** (ⓦrusrailtravel.ru) or **Ost West** (ⓦostwest.com). Tailor-made tours from Western companies will be much more expensive, but offer the minimum hassle: the **Russia Experience** (ⓦtrans-siberian.co.uk) has a good reputation. For details of companies at home that can sort out Trans-Siberian travel, check the lists of specialist travel agents (see p.32).

Via the Central Asian republics

You can reach China through several Central Asian countries, though the obstacles can occasionally be insurmountable; contact an in-country agent or Trans-Siberian operator (see p.32) for up-to-date practicalities. Once in the region, crossing into China **from Kazakhstan** is straightforward – there are comfortable trains from Almaty (Tues & Sun) and Astana (Sat) to Ürümqi, which take two nights and cost about US$170 for a berth in a four-berth compartment. Kashgar in the northwestern Chinese province of Xinjiang is an eleven-hour drive **from Bishkek in Kyrgyzstan**, and the two cities are linked by buses in summer months. Foreigners, however, have had difficulties in trying to use these and have usually had to resort to expensive private transport, run by local tour operators, to help them across. You may well be expected to bribe the border guards (a bottle of spirit will often suffice).

From Pakistan and Nepal

The routes across the Himalayas to China are among the toughest in Asia. The first is **from Pakistan into Xinjiang** province via the **Karakoram Highway** (see p.851), along one of the branches of the ancient Silk Road. You need a Chinese visa, but otherwise this route requires no pre-planning, except for the fact that it is open only May–October, and closes periodically due to landslides; at the time of writing, however, most Western governments were advising against travel to Pakistan, due to fundamentalist militants and **attacks on Westerners**.

Another possible route is **from Nepal into Tibet**, but the border is often closed, and, as travel restrictions to Tibet are tight and subject to change, you should check Ⓦ thelandofsnows.com for current information. We cover this in more detail in the Tibet chapter (see p.879).

From India, for political reasons, there are no border crossings to China. For years, authorities have discussed opening a bus route from Sikkim to Tibet, north from Darjeeling, but despite both sides working on the road, the border remains closed.

From Vietnam

Vietnam has three border crossings with China – **Dong Dang**, 60km northeast of Hanoi; **Lao Cai**, 150km northwest; and the little-used **Mong Cai**, 200km south of Nanning. All three are open daily 8.30am–5pm. Officious Chinese customs officials at these crossings occasionally confiscate guidebooks; bury this one at the bottom of your bag.

A direct **train from Hanoi** is advertised as running all the way to **Beijing** (60hr), passing through **Nanning** and **Guilin**. In practice, though, you'll probably have to change trains in Nanning. Alternatively, there are daily trains from Hanoi to Lao Cai, eleven hours away in Vietnam's mountainous and undeveloped northwest (near the pleasant minority hill-resort of Sa Pa), from where you can cross into Yunnan province at Hekou, and catch regular buses to Kunming. From Mong Cai, there are also regular buses to Nanning.

From Laos and Myanmar (Burma)

Crossing into China **from Laos** also lands you in Yunnan, this time at Bian Mao Zhan in the Xishuang-banna region. Formalities are very relaxed and unlikely to cause any problems. It's 220km on local buses north from here to the regional capital, Jinghong. Alternatively, there are also direct daily buses between Luang Namtha in Laos and Jinghong (8hr), and Luang Prabang to Kunming (24hr).

Entering China **from Myanmar** (Burma) is a possibility, too, with the old Burma Road cutting northeast from Rangoon (Yangon) to Lashio and the crossing at Ruili in Yunnan. At present, this border is open only to groups travelling with a tour agency, which will sort out all the necessary paperwork in Yangon. Be aware that border regulations here are subject to change.

By ferry from Korea and Japan

There are a number of **ferry routes** linking China with Korea and Japan. Those **from Korea** take one night, and most depart from Inchon, a coastal city connected to Seoul by subway train; services to Tanggu, near Tianjin, land you closest to Beijing (see p.139), though there are other useful services to Dalian (see p.166), Dandong (see p.169), Qingdao (see p.287) and Yantai (see p.283). Trips take 16–24 hours, services usually run twice a week, and fares and standards are similar across the board; the cheapest tickets (KRW115,000) will get you a berth in a common room (though often closed off with a curtain, and therefore surprisingly private), while paying a little more (from KRW165,000) will get you a bed in a private, en-suite room.

From Japan, there are weekly ferries from Osaka to Shanghai, but these are usually more expensive than flying with budget airlines. The ferry takes a whopping 46 hours, compared with three hours to fly.

Getting around

China's public transport is comprehensive and good value: you can fly to all regional capitals and many cities, the rail network extends to every region, and you can reach China's remotest corners on local buses. It might also be useful to rent a car and driver – you can only drive a vehicle here with a Chinese driving license. Tibet is the one area where there are widespread restrictions on independent travel (see p.879).

However, getting around such a large, crowded country requires planning, patience and stamina, especially if you plan to do everything independently. This is especially true for long-distance journeys, where you'll find that travelling in as much comfort as you can afford saves a lot of undue stress. **Tours** are one way of taking the pressure off, and may be the only practical way of getting out to certain sights (see p.39).

Public holidays – especially the May, October and Spring Festival breaks (see p.49) – are bad times to travel, as half of China is on the move between family and workplace: ticket prices rise (legally by no more than fifteen percent, though often by up to double), bus- and train-station crowds swell insanely, and even flights might become scarce.

By train

China's **rail network** is vast, efficient and reliable. The country invests billions of yuan annually on the network, as the government considers a healthy transport infrastructure essential to economic growth – and political cohesion. The twenty-first century has seen some impressive developments: a rail line over the mountains between eastern China and **Tibet** completed in 2005; the country's first ultra-fast **bullet** trains, which began operation in eastern China in 2007; and an expanding web of **high-speed networks between major cities**.

Food on trains, though expensive and ordinary, is always available, either from trolleys serving snacks and microwaved boxes of rice and stir-fries or in a dedicated restaurant car. You can also buy snacks from vendors at train stations during the longer station stops.

Timetables and tickets

It's easiest to check **train schedules** online (see box below).

Note that you'll need your **passport** when **booking tickets**, whether in person or online. Tickets

---

CHINESE BOOKING SITES

Anyone looking to book their own transport and accommodation in China should check out ⓦ**travelchinaguide .com**, which is best for train bookings; their dedicated **train timetable app** is the most comprehensive available. Another site with an integrated app is ⓦ**ctrip.com**, which also gives better prices on airfares and accommodation.

– always **one-way** – are available sixty days before travel and show the date of departure and destination, along with the train number, carriage, and seat or berth number. **Station ticket offices** are all computerized, and while queues can tie you up for an hour or more of jostling, you'll generally get what you're after if you have some flexibility. At the counter, state your destination, the train number if possible, the day you'd like to travel, and the class you want – have some alternatives handy. If you can't speak Chinese, get someone to write things down for you before setting out, as staff rarely speak English.

In all cities, you might also find **downtown advance purchase offices** – though these seem to be being phased out – where you pay a small commission (¥5/ ticket). It makes sense to try these places first, as train stations – especially for high-speed services – are often located far from city centres. **Agents**, such as hotel travel services, can also book on your behalf for a commission of ¥30 or more per ticket.

The best way to **book tickets online** and then either collect them from the station or, in major cities, have them delivered to your hotel door, is through ⓦtravelchinaguide.com, for a US$5 fee. You can also reserve tickets through other websites such as ⓦctrip.com, but these cannot be picked up by foreigners at in-town railway booking offices, or from the automatic machines at the station (which require a Chinese ID card to use). Instead, you have to queue at a dedicated window at the station, which has been known to take over an hour – so make sure you arrive with plenty of time to spare.

If you've bought a ticket but decide not to travel, you can get most of the fare **refunded** by returning the ticket to a ticket office. The process is called *tuipiao* (退票, tuìpiào), and there's usually a separate window for this at stations.

Types of train

The different **types of train** each have their own code on timetables; these can indicate the difference between a comfortable five-hour cruise and a nineteen-hour nightmare. **China Rail High Speed** (**CRH**; 高速, gāosù) services come with a **C, D or G prefix**, depending on whether they make long-distance or regional journeys. As they travel up to 350km/h, you can now get from Beijing to Guangzhou, for instance (around 2200km) in just eight hours. The aircraft-like carriages are kept in excellent condition, with surprisingly clean Western-style toilets, reclining seats, and a decent enough amount of legroom. CRH trains generally use dedicated high-speed stations, often on the periphery of the cities they serve.

SAMPLE TRAIN FARES

The fares below are for one-way travel on express and high-speed trains. Note that, especially if you book in advance through ⓦ ctrip.com, airfares might only be only slightly more expensive than buying high-speed train tickets.

	HARD SEAT	HARD SLEEPER	SOFT SLEEPER	HIGH SPEED
FROM BEIJING				
Guangzhou	¥250	¥460	¥780	¥860
Hong Kong	-	¥515	¥800	-
Shanghai	¥120	¥325	¥500	¥555
Xi'an	¥155	¥290	¥440	¥515
FROM XI'AN				
Guangzhou	¥240	¥430	¥740	¥815
Turpan	¥265	¥475	¥735	-
Ürümqi	¥275	¥495	¥770	-

Where there are no high-speed services, look for **Z-, T- and K-class trains**, which still travel at a respectable 120–160km/h and all have modern fittings. Z-class generally travel directly between two points; T- and K-class stop at main stations along the route. Toilets are usually Western-style in soft sleeper carriages, and squat elsewhere; the latter can be truly disgusting.

Ordinary trains (普通车, pǔtōng chē) have a four-digit number only and, though they often cruise at around 100km/h, stop pretty much everywhere en route. They range from those with clean carriages to ancient plodders destined for the scrapheap with cigarette-burned linoleum floors and grimy windows. A few busy, short-haul express services, such as the Shenzhen–Guangzhou train, have **double-decker carriages**.

No-smoking rules are vigorously enforced on high-speed trains, though on slower services it's still common to see passengers puffing away between carriages.

Ticket classes

On **high-speed (CRH)** services there are two seat classes, the only real difference between them being a two-two seat arrangement in first, compared to the three-two arrangement in second.

On regular trains, there are **four ticket classes**: soft sleeper, hard sleeper, soft seat and hard seat, not all necessarily available on each train. **Soft sleeper** (软卧, ruǎnwò) costs around the same as flying, and gets you a berth in a four-person compartment with a soft mattress, fan and optional radio. **Hard sleeper** (硬卧, yìngwò), about two-thirds the price of soft sleeper, is the best value. Carriages are divided into twenty sets

of three-tiered **bunks**; the lowest bunk is the largest, but costs more and gets used as communal seating during the day; the upper bunk is cheapest but headroom is minimal. Each set of six bunks has its own vacuum flask of boiled water (topped up from the urn at the end of each carriage) – bring your own mugs and tea. There are fairly spacious **luggage racks**, though make sure you chain your bags securely while you sleep.

In either sleeper class, on boarding the carriage you will have your ticket exchanged for a metal tag by the attendant. The tag is swapped back for your ticket (so you'll be able to get through the barrier at the station) about half an hour before you arrive at your destination, whatever hour of the day or night this happens to be.

Soft seat (软座, ruǎnzuò) is widespread on services whose complete route takes less than a day. Seats cost around the same as express-bus fare, have plenty of legroom and are well padded. More common is **hard seat** (硬座, yìngzuò), which costs around half the soft-seat fare but is only recommended for relatively short journeys, as you'll be sitting on a padded three-person bench, with every available bit of floor space crammed with travellers who were unable to book a seat. In rural areas, you'll be the focus of intense and unabashed speculation from farmers and labourers who can't afford to travel in better style.

Finally, if there's nothing else available, you can buy an **unreserved ticket** (无座, wúzuò; literally "no seat"), which lets you board the hard-seat section of the train – though you might have to stand for the entire journey if you can't upgrade on board.

Boarding the train

Turn up at the station with at least half an hour to spare before your train leaves – or at least an hour if you have to collect a pre-booked ticket from the ticket office. You'll need to show your passport to be allowed into the station; all luggage is then **x-rayed** to check for dangerous goods such as firecrackers. You next need to work out which **platform** your train leaves from – most stations have electronic departure boards in Chinese (high-speed stations have dual-language boards); show your ticket to station staff who will point you in the right direction. Passengers are not allowed onto the platform until the train is almost in, which can result in some mighty stampedes when the gates open. Carriages are **numbered** on the outside, and your ticket is checked by a guard as you board. Once on the train, you can try to **upgrade** any ticket at the controller's booth, in the hard-seat carriage next to the restaurant car (usually #8), where you can sign up for beds or seats as they become available.

By bus and minibus

Buses go everywhere that trains go, and well beyond, usually more frequently but more slowly. Finding the departure point isn't always easy; even small hamlets can have **multiple bus stations**, generally located on the side of town in which traffic is heading.

Bus station **timetables** – except electronic ones – can be ignored; ask station staff about schedules and frequencies, though they generally can't speak English. **Tickets** are easy to buy: ticket offices at main stations are computerized, queues are seldom bad, and – with the exception of backroad routes, which might only run every other day – you don't need to book in advance. Bring your passport when buying tickets. In country towns, you sometimes buy tickets on-board. **Destinations** are always displayed in Chinese characters on the front of the vehicle. Take some **food** along, although buses usually pull up at inexpensive roadhouses at mealtimes. Only the most upmarket coaches have **toilets**; drivers stop every few hours or if asked to do so by passengers (though roadhouse toilets are some of the worst in the country).

Downsides to bus travel include drivers who spend the journey chatting on their mobile phone or coast downhill in neutral, with the engine off; and the fact that vehicles are obliged to use the horn before overtaking anything – earplugs are recommended. **Roadworks** are a near-certainty too, as highways are continually being repaired, upgraded or replaced; in 2010, a 100km-long jam on the Tibet–Beijing highway, blamed on roadworks, took nine days to clear. Appallingly graphic films are currently being played to passengers to encourage them to wear seat belts – after you've seen one, you'll be only too glad to buckle up.

Types of buses

There are various **types of buses**, though there's not always a choice available for particular routes, and, if there is, station staff will assume that as a foreigner you'll want the fastest, most comfortable and most expensive service.

Ordinary buses (普通车, pǔtōng chē) are cheap and basic, with lightly padded seats; they're never heated or air-conditioned, so dress accordingly. Seats can be cramped and luggage racks tiny; you'll have to put anything bulkier than a satchel on the roof or your lap, or beside the driver. They tend to stop off frequently, so don't count on an average speed of more than 30km/h. **Express buses** (快车, kuài chē) are the most expensive and have good legroom, comfy seats that may well recline, air-conditioning and video. Bulky luggage gets locked away in the belly of the bus, a fairly safe option. **Sleeper buses** (卧铺车, wòpù chē) have cramped, basic bunks instead of seats, minimal luggage space and a poor safety record, and are not recommended if there is any alternative. The final option is **minibuses** (小车, xiǎochē; or 包车, bāochē) seating up to twenty people, common on routes of less than 100km or so. They cost a little more than the same journey by ordinary bus, can be extremely cramped, and often circuit the departure point for ages until they have filled up.

By plane

China's **airlines** link all major cities; planes are modern and well maintained and service is fairly good, though delayed departures are common. The main operators are Air China (ⓦ www.airchina.com.cn/en), China Southern (ⓦ csair.com), China Eastern (ⓦ www.flychinaeastern.com) and Hainan Airlines (ⓦ hainanairlines.com). Flying is well worth considering for long distances, especially as prices compare favourably with the cost of upper-tier rail travel – though on shorter routes some services have been pretty much supplanted by high-speed trains (between Chengdu and Chongqing, for instance).

You can **buy tickets** online at competitive rates via the airline websites, ⓦ elong.net or ⓦ english.ctrip.com. You'll need to provide your passport details (make sure you give names exactly as they appear in your passport) and might need to provide a phone number to confirm the booking – your hotel's will do. Book more than 24 hours in advance if using an overseas credit card. Tickets can also be arranged through accommodation tour desks, at downtown airline offices or airport ticket desks.

Fares are based on one-way travel (so a return is the price of two one-way tickets) and include all taxes; **the best deals** are on routes also covered by competitively priced high-speed trains. For example: from Beijing, expect to pay at least ¥550 to Xi'an; ¥600 to Shanghai; ¥900 to Chengdu; ¥1030 to Shenzhen; ¥1200 to Kunming; ¥1780 to Ürümqi; and ¥920 to Hong Kong.

Check-in time for all flights is ninety minutes before departure.

By ferry

Though there are few public **ferries** in China, you can make one of the world's great river journeys down the **Yangzi** between Chongqing and Yichang (see p.768), via the mighty **Three Gorges** – though the spectacle has been lessened by the construction of the giant Three Gorges Dam. Another favourite is the day-cruise down the **Li River** between Guilin and Yangshuo in southwestern Guangxi province, past a forest of pointy pinnacles looking just like a Chinese scroll painting (see p.616). By **sea**, there are **passenger ferries** between Hong Kong and Macau (see p.573), and between Guangxi and Hainan Island (p.632).

Conditions on board are greatly variable, but on overnight trips there's always a choice of **classes** – sometimes as many as six – which can range from a bamboo mat on the floor right through to private cabins. Don't expect anything too impressive, however; many mainland services are cramped and overcrowded, and cabins, even in first-class, are grimly functional.

By bike

China has the highest number of **bicycles** (自行车, zìxíngchē) of any country in the world – about a quarter of the population owns one, despite a rising trend towards mopeds, motorbikes and cars. Few cities have any hills, and some have **bike lanes**, though many of the bigger cities are in the process of banning bicycles from main roads in order to free them up for cars.

Rental shops or booths are common around train stations (¥10–20/day). You will need to leave a deposit (¥200–400) and/or some form of ID, and you're fully responsible for anything that happens to the bike while it's in your care, so check brakes, tyre pressure and gears before renting. Most rentals are bog-standard black rattletraps – the really deluxe models feature working bells and brakes. There are **repair shops** all over the place should you need a tyre patched or a chain fixed up (¥10–30). If the bike sustains any serious damage, it's up to the parties involved to sort out responsibility and payment on the spot. Always use a **bicycle chain** or lock – they're available everywhere – and in cities, leave your vehicle in one of the ubiquitous designated **parking areas**, where it will be guarded by an attendant for a small fee.

An alternative to renting is to **buy a bike**, a sensible option if you're going to be based anywhere for a while. All department stores sell them: a heavy, unsophisticated machine will only set you back about ¥500, whereas a mountain bike will be upwards of ¥900. A **folding bike** (around ¥550) is a great idea, as you can cycle around all day and, when you're tired, put it in the boot of a taxi or take it on a bus. You can also **bring your own bike** into China; international airlines usually insist that the front wheel is removed, deflated and strapped to the back, and that everything is thoroughly packaged. Inside China, airlines, trains and ferries all charge to carry bikes, and the ticketing and accompanying paperwork can be baffling. Another option is to see China on a **specialized bike tour** such as those offered by Bike China (Ⓦbikechina.com), Bike Asia (Ⓦbikeasia.com) or Cycle China (Ⓦcyclechina.com).

On a tour

Local tour operators, who are listed throughout this guide, offer excursions ranging from city coach tours to river cruises and multiday cross-country hikes or horse treks. While you always pay for the privilege, sometimes these tours are good value: travel, accommodation and food – usually plentiful and excellent – are generally included, as might be the services of an interpreter and guide. And in some cases, tours are virtually the only way to see something really worthwhile, saving endless bother organizing local transport and accommodation. In general, **foreign-owned operations** tend to give better service – or at least to understand better what Westerners want when they take a tour.

On the downside, there are disreputable operators who'll blatantly overcharge for mediocre services, foist unhelpful guides on you and spend three days on what could better be done in an afternoon. Bear in mind that many Chinese tour guides are badly paid, and supplement their income by taking tourists to souvenir shops where they'll receive commissions. It always pays to make exhaustive **enquiries** about the exact nature of the tour, such as exactly what the price includes and the departure/return times, before handing any money over.

City transport

All Chinese cities have some form of **public transit system**. An increasing number have (or are building) **light-rail systems** and underground **metros**; elsewhere, the **city bus** is the transport focus. These are cheap and run from 6am–10pm or later, but (Hong Kong's apart) they're usually slow and crowded. Pricier **private minibuses** often run the same routes in similar comfort but at greater speed; they're either numbered or have their destination written up at the front.

Taxis are always available in larger towns and cities; main roads, transit points and tourist hotels are good places to find them. They cost a fixed rate of ¥5–13 within certain limits, and then add from ¥1 per kilometre. You'll also find motorized or cycle-rickshaws known as "**Three Wheelers**" in many towns and cities, whose highly erratic rates are set by bargaining beforehand.

Accommodation

China's accommodation scene continues to improve at pace, with most cities boasting a range of good options from budget to top-end. Luxury hotels (mostly international brands), domestic budget hotel chains and backpacker hostels are as good as similar places in the West, though mid-range hotels are often lacking in character, many of them former state-run behemoths.

Price is not a good indicator of quality. The Chinese hospitality industry remains on a steep learning curve, so new places are often vastly better than old ones.

Security in accommodation is reasonably good, with budget dosshouses and youth hostels the only places where you'll really have to keep an eye on your stuff; the latter usually have places in which you'll be able to lock away valuables.

Finding a room

Booking online is a routine procedure at all but the cheapest local hotels, either direct or via an English-

language **accommodation-booking website** such as elong (Ⓦelong.net) or China Trip (Ⓦenglish.ctrip .com). Those two sites don't require pre-payment for rooms; you simply reserve through the website and pay on arrival (though you might occasionally arrive to find they've given your room to somebody who paid up front). Budget travellers should check out **hostel websites** such as Ⓦhostelworld.com and Ⓦhostelbookers.com.

In some places, however, the concept of booking ahead may be alien, and you won't make much headway without spoken Chinese – though it's a good idea to call (or to ask someone to call for you) to see if vacancies exist before lugging your bag across town. Be aware that **room rates** displayed at reception are almost always just the starting point in negotiations. Staff are generally amenable to **bargaining** and it's normal to get thirty percent off the advertised price, even more in low season or where there's plenty of competition. Always ask to **see the room first**. Rooms usually have either **twin beds** (双人房, shuāngrén fáng) or **single beds** (单人房, dānrén fáng), which often means "one double bed", rather than a small bed; some places also have triples or even quads.

New arrivals at city bus and train stations are often besieged by **touts** wanting to lead them to a hotel where they'll receive a commission for bringing guests in. Chinese-speakers might strike a bargain this way, but you do need to be very clear about how much you're willing to pay before being dragged all over town.

If in some places you find yourself being turned away by every hotel, it's not that they don't like you – they probably haven't obtained **police permission** to take foreigners, and would face substantial fines for doing so. The situation is dependent on the local authorities, and can vary not just from province to province, but also from town to town. Nothing is ever certain in China, however: being able to speak Chinese greatly improves your chances of negotiating a way through these restrictions, as does being able to write your name in Chinese on the register (or having it printed out so the receptionist can do this for you) – in which case the authorities need never know that a foreigner stayed.

Checking in and out

If you've booked ahead – certainly in larger cities – **checking in** generally only involves having your passport photocopied and arranging payment. Otherwise, especially in places that see few foreigners, you'll probably also have to fill in a **form** giving details of your name, age, date of birth, sex and address, where you are coming from and going to, and how many days you intend to stay. Some hotels might only have these forms in Chinese, and might never have seen a foreign passport before – which explains why hotel receptionists can panic when they see a foreigner walk in the door.

You always **pay in advance**, including a **deposit** which may amount to twice the price of the room. Assuming you haven't broken anything – make sure everything works properly when you check in – deposits are refunded; just don't lose the receipt.

In cheaper places, disconnect your **telephone** to avoid being woken by prostitutes calling up through the night.

At most mid-range and high-end hotels, **breakfast** will come as part of your room rate; you'll usually get a coupon for this when you check in. Breakfast is served a little earlier than most foreign travellers would like – some places stop service at 8am, though 7–9am is by far the most common timeframe.

Check-out time is noon, though you can ask to keep the room until later for a proportion of the daily rate. Make sure you arrange this **before** check-out time, however, as staff may otherwise refuse to refund room deposits, claiming that you have overstayed. Conversely, if you have to leave very early in the morning (to catch transport, for instance), you may be unable to find staff to refund your deposit, and might also encounter locked front doors or compound gates.

Hotels

The different Chinese words for hotel are vague indicators of the status of the place. Sure signs of upmarket pretensions are **dajiudian** (大酒店, dà jiǔdiàn), which translates as "big alcohol shop", or, in the countryside, **shan zhuang** (山庄, shān zhuāng) or "mountain resort". **Binguan** (宾馆, bīnguǎn) and **fandian** (饭店, fàndiàn) are more general terms for hotel, covering everything from downmarket lodgings to smart new establishments; reliably basic are **guesthouse** (客栈, kèzhàn), **hostel** (招待所, zhāodàisuǒ) and **inn** (旅馆, lǚguǎn; or 旅舍, lǚshè). Sometimes you'll simply see a sign for "accommodation" (住宿, zhùsù).

Whatever type of hotel you are staying in, there are two things you can rely on: one is a pair of plastic or paper **slippers**, which you use for walking to the bathroom, and the other is a vacuum flask of drinkable **hot water** that can be refilled any time by the floor attendant – though upmarket places tend to provide electric kettles instead.

Upmarket

In the larger cities, you'll find **upmarket** four- or five-star hotels. Conditions in such hotels are comparable to those anywhere in the world, with all the usual **facilities** on offer – such as swimming pools, gyms and business centres – though the finer nuances of service are sometimes lacking. Prices for standard doubles in these places are upwards of ¥1200, with a fifteen percent **service charge** on top; the use of credit cards is routine.

Even if you cannot afford to stay in the upmarket hotels, they can still be pleasant places to escape from the hubbub, and nobody in China blinks at the sight of a stray foreigner roaming around the foyer of a smart hotel. As well as air-conditioning and clean toilets, you'll find cafés and bars (sometimes showing satellite TV), wi-fi and internet facilities, and often ATMs.

Mid-range

Many modern Chinese hotels are **mid-range**, and just about every town in China has at least one hotel of this sort. The quality of mid-range places is the hardest to predict from the price: an old hotel with cigarette-burned carpets, leaking bathrooms and grey bedsheets might charge the same as a sparkling new establishment next door; newer places are generally better, as a rule. In remote places, you should get a twin in a mid-range place for ¥150, but expect to pay at least ¥300 in any sizeable city.

There's been a recent explosion in **urban budget hotels** aimed at money-conscious businessmen, which offer small (but not cramped) clean double rooms with showers, phones, TV and internet portals right in city centres. Some places like Kunming, Chengdu and Shanghai have local brands, but nationwide chains include *7 Days Inn* (🌐 7daysinn.cn), *Home Inn* (🌐 homeinns.com) and *Jinjiang Inn* (🌐 hotels.jinjiang.com). At around ¥300 a double, or even less, they're a very good deal, especially if you're able to take advantage of early-booking promotions (you'll need to speak Chinese for this, and possibly to have a local credit card too).

Cheap hotels

Cheap hotels, where doubles cost less than ¥150, vary in quality from the dilapidated to the perfectly comfortable. In many cities, they're commonly located near the train or bus stations, though they may need some persuading to take foreigners. Where they do, you'll notice that the Chinese routinely **rent beds** rather than rooms – doubling up with one or more strangers, and paying per bed – as a means of saving money. Foreigners are seldom allowed to share rooms with Chinese people, but if there are three or four foreigners together it's often possible for them to share one big room; otherwise single travellers might have to negotiate a price for the whole room.

Hostels and guesthouses

China has a rapidly expanding network of **youth hostels** (青年旅舍, qīngnián lǚshè), many affiliated with the International Youth Hostel Association (IYHA). **Booking ahead** is always advisable – usually easiest on sites such as ⓦhostelworld.com and ⓦhostelbookers.com. At IYHA hostels, members get a small discount, usually ¥10, and you can join at any mainland hostel for ¥60.

Hong Kong, Macau and a few regions of China (mostly in southwestern provinces) also have a number of **privately run guesthouses** in everything from family mansions to Mongolian tents, whose variety comes as a relief after the dullness of mainland accommodation. Prices for double rooms in these guesthouses are generally lower than in hotels.

Camping

Camping is only feasible in Hong Kong – where there are free campsites scattered through the New Territories – and in wilderness areas of Tibet, Sichuan, Yunnan, Qinghai, Xinjiang, Gansu and Inner Mongolia, far away from the prying eyes of thousands of local villagers. Don't bother trying to get permission for it: this is the kind of activity that the Chinese authorities do not have any clear idea about, so if asked they will certainly answer "no".

Eating and drinking

The Chinese love to eat, and from market-stall buns and soup, right through to the intricate variations of regional cookery, China boasts one of the world's greatest cuisines. Meals are considered social events, and the process is accordingly geared to a group of diners sharing a variety of different dishes with their companions. Fresh ingredients are available from any market stall, though unless you're living long term in the country there are few opportunities to cook for yourself.

Ingredients

In the south, **rice** as grain, noodles, or dumpling wrappers is the staple, replaced in the cooler north by **wheat**, formed into buns or noodles. **Meat** is held to be invigorating and, ideally, forms the backbone of any meal. **Pork** is the most common meat used, except in areas with a strong Muslim tradition where it's replaced with mutton or beef. **Fowl** is considered especially good during old age or convalescence; most rural people in central and southern China seem to own a couple of chickens, and the countryside is littered with duck and geese farms. **Fish and seafood** are highly regarded and can be expensive, as are rarer **game** meats.

Eggs – duck, chicken or quail – are a popular nationwide snack, often flavoured by hard-boiling in a mixture of tea, soy sauce and star anise. There's also the so-called "thousand-year-old" variety, preserved for a few months in ash and straw – they look gruesome, with translucent brown albumen and green yolks, but actually have a delicate, brackish flavour. **Dairy products** serve limited purposes in China. Goat's cheese and yoghurt are eaten in parts of Yunnan and the Northwest, but milk is considered fit only for children and the elderly and is not used in cooking.

Vegetables accompany nearly every Chinese meal, used in most cases to balance tastes and textures of meat, but also appearing as dishes in their own right. Though the selection can be very thin in some parts of the country, there's usually a wide range on offer, from leafy greens to water chestnuts, mushrooms, bamboo shoots, seaweed and radish.

Soya beans are ubiquitous in Chinese cooking, being a good source of protein in a country where meat has often been a luxury. The small green beans are sometimes eaten straight in the south, but are more often salted and used to thicken sauces, fermented to produce **soy sauce**, or boiled and pressed to make white cakes of **tofu** (bean curd). Fresh tofu is flavourless and as soft as custard, though it can be pressed further to create a firmer texture, deep-fried until crisp, or cooked in stock and used as a meat substitute in vegetarian cooking. The skin that forms on top of the liquid while tofu is being made is itself skimmed off, dried, and used as a wrapping for spring rolls and the like.

Seasonal availability is smoothed over by a huge variety of **dried**, **salted** and **pickled vegetables**, meats and seafood, which often characterize local cooking styles. There's also an enormous assortment of fresh regional **fruit**.

Breakfast, snacks and street food

Breakfast is not a big event by Chinese standards, more something to line the stomach for a few hours. Much of the country is content with a bowl of rice porridge flavoured with pickles and eaten with plain buns, or sweetened soya milk accompanied by a fried dough stick; dumplings, sometimes in soup, are another favourite. Guangdong and Hong Kong are the exceptions, where the traditional breakfast of **dim sum** (also known as **yum cha**) involves a selection of tiny buns, dumplings and dishes served with tea.

Other **snacks and street food** are served through the day from small, early-opening **stalls** located around markets, train and bus stations. These serve grilled chicken wings; kebabs; spiced noodles; baked yams and potatoes; boiled eggs; various steamed or stewed dishes dished up in earthenware **sandpots**; grilled corn and – in places such as Beijing and Sichuan – countless local treats. Also common are **steamed buns**, which are either stuffed with meat or vegetables (baozi) or plain (mantou, literally "bald heads"). The buns originated in the north and are especially warming on a winter's day; a sweeter Cantonese variety is stuffed with barbecued pork. Another northern snack now found everywhere is the ravioli-like **jiaozi**, again with a meat or vegetable filling and either fried or steamed; **shuijiao** are boiled jiaozi served in soup. Some small restaurants specialize in jiaozi, containing a bewildering range of fillings and always sold by weight.

Restaurants and eating out

The cheapest **hole-in-the-wall canteens** are necessarily basic, with simple food costing a few yuan and often much better than you'd expect from the furnishings. Proper **restaurants** are usually bright, busy places whose preferred atmosphere is renao, or "hot and noisy", rather than the often quiet norm in the West. Prices at these places obviously vary a lot, but even expensive-looking establishments charge only ¥35–70 for a main dish, and servings tend to be generous.

While the cheaper places might have long hours, **restaurant opening times** are early and short: breakfast lasts from around 6–9am; lunch 11am–2pm; and dinner from around 5–9pm, after which the staff will be yawning and sweeping the debris off the tables around your ankles.

Ordering and dining

Pointing is all that's required at street stalls and small restaurants; they'll usually have the fare laid out, ready for cooking or already done. In **proper restaurants**

CHINESE WEIGHTS

Note that dishes such as jiaozi and some seafood, as well as fresh produce, are sold by weight: a **liang** (两, liǎng) is 50g, a **banjin** (半斤, bànjīn) 250g, a **jin** (斤, jīn) 500g, and a **gongjin** (公斤, gōngjīn) 1kg.

you'll be given a **menu** – most likely Chinese-only, unless you're in a tourist area, though many now have pictures, and some are on tablets (more fiddly than useful). Alternatively, have a look at what other diners are eating – the Chinese are often delighted that a foreigner wants to eat Chinese food, and will indicate the best options on their table.

When **ordering**, unless eating a one-dish meal like Peking duck or a hotpot, try to select items with a **range of tastes and textures**; it's also usual to include a soup. In cheap places, servings of noodles or rice are huge, but as they are considered basic stomach fillers, quantities decline the more upmarket you go.

Dishes are all **served** at once, placed in the middle of the table for diners to share. With some poultry dishes you can crunch up the smaller bones, but anything else is spat out on to the table-cloth or floor, more or less discreetly depending on the establishment – watch what others are doing. **Soups** tend to be bland and are consumed last (except in the south where they may be served first or as part of the main meal) to wash the meal down, the liquid slurped from a spoon or the bowl once the noodles, vegetables or meat in it have been picked out and eaten. **Desserts** aren't a regular feature in China, though sweet soups and buns are eaten (the latter not confined to main meals) in the south, particularly at festive occasions.

Resting your chopsticks together across the top of your bowl means that you've **finished** eating. After a meal, the Chinese don't hang around to talk over drinks as in the West, but get up straight away and leave. In canteens, you'll **pay** up front, while at restaurants you ask for the bill and pay either the waiter or at the front till. **Tipping** is not expected in mainland China, though in Hong Kong you generally leave around ten percent.

Western and international restaurants

There's a fair amount of **Western and international food** available in China, though supply and quality vary. Hong Kong, Shanghai and Beijing have the best range, with some excellent restaurants covering everything from Russian to Brazilian cuisine, and there are international food restaurants in every Chinese city of any size, with Korean and Japanese the best represented. Elsewhere, upmarket hotels may have Western restaurants, serving expensive but huge **buffet breakfasts** of scrambled egg, bacon, toast, cereal and coffee; and there's a growing number of **cafés** in many cities, especially ones with large foreign expat populations. **Burger**, **fried chicken** and **pizza** places are ubiquitous, including domestic chains such as *Dicos* alongside *McDonald's*, *KFC* and *Pizza Hut*.

Self-catering

Self-catering for tourists is feasible to a point. **Instant noodles** are a favourite travel food with the Chinese, available anywhere – just add boiling water, leave for five minutes, then stir in the flavourings supplied. Fresh **fruit and veg** from markets needs to be washed and peeled before eating raw; you can supplement things with **dried fruit**, **nuts and seeds**, roast and cured meats, biscuits and all manner of snacks. In cities, these things are also sold in more hygienic situations in **supermarkets**; many provincial capitals also have branches of the international chain **Carrefour** (家乐福, jiālèfú), where you can generally find small caches of Western foods.

Drink

Water is easily available in China, but never drink what comes out of the tap. **Boiled water** is always on hand in hotels and trains, either provided in large vacuum flasks or an urn, and you can buy **bottled spring water** at station stalls and supermarkets in anything from small bottles to 5-litre containers. However, plastic pollution is a problem in China; the best way to avoid contributing to plastic waste is to purify your own water. **Chemical sterilization** using chlorine is completely effective, fast and inexpensive, and you can remove the nasty taste it leaves with neutralizing tablets or lemon juice. Alternatively, you could invest in a purifying filter incorporating chemical sterilization to kill even the smallest viruses.

Tea

Tea has been known in China since antiquity and was originally drunk for medicinal reasons. Over the centuries a whole **social culture** has sprung up around this beverage, spawning **teahouses** that once held the same place in Chinese society that the local pub or bar does in the West. Plantations of neat rows of low tea bushes adorn hillsides across southern China, while the brew is enthusiastically consumed from the highlands of Tibet – where it's mixed with barley meal and butter – to every restaurant and household between Hong Kong and Beijing. Unfortunately, in a land where a pot of tea used to be plonked in front of every restaurant-goer before they'd even sat down, you now usually have to pay for the privilege – and your tea can work out more expensive than the rest of your meal.

Chinese tea comes in red, green and flower-scented **varieties**, depending on how it's processed; only Hainan produces Indian-style **black** tea. Some regional kinds, such as *pu'er* from Yunnan, Fujian's *tie guanyin*, Zhejiang's *longjing* or Sichuan's *zhuye qing*, are highly sought after; indeed, after locals in Yunnan decided that banks weren't paying enough interest, they started investing in *pu'er* tea stocks, causing prices to soar.

The manner in which it's **served** also varies from place to place: sometimes it comes in huge mugs with a lid, elsewhere in dainty cups served from a miniature pot; there are also formalized **tea rituals** in parts of Fujian and Guangdong. When drinking in company, it's polite to top up others' cups before your own, whenever they become empty; if someone does this for you, lightly tap your first two fingers on the table to show your thanks. If you've had enough, leave your cup full, and in a restaurant take the lid off or turn it over if you want the pot refilled during the meal.

Chinese leaf tea is never drunk with milk or sugar, though recently **Taiwanese bubble tea** – Indian-style tea with milk, sugar and sago balls – has become popular in the south. It's also worth trying some **Muslim** *babao cha* (Eight Treasures Tea), which involves dried fruit, nuts, seeds and crystallized sugar heaped into a cup with the remaining space filled with hot water, poured with panache from an immensely long-spouted copper kettle.

Alcohol

The popularity of **beer** in China rivals that of tea, and, for men, is the preferred mealtime beverage (drinking alcohol in public is considered improper for Chinese women, though not for foreigners). The first brewery was set up in the northeastern port of Qingdao by the Germans in the nineteenth century (see p.286); now, though the Tsingtao label is widely available, most provinces produce at least one brand of four percent Pilsner. Sold in 660ml bottles, it's always drinkable, often pretty good, and is actually cheaper than bottled water. Craft beer has recently caught on too, and is becoming available in major cities across the country.

Watch out for the term "**wine**" on English menus, which usually denotes **spirits**, made from rice, sorghum or millet. Serving spirits to guests is a sign of hospitality, and they're always used for toasting at banquets. Local home-made varieties can be quite good, while mainstream brands – especially the expensive, nationally famous Maotai and Wuliangye – are pretty vile to the Western palate. China does have several commercial **wine labels**, the best of which is Changyu from Yantai in Shandong province, and there are ongoing efforts to launch wine as a stylish niche product, with limited success so far.

Western-style bars are found in all major cities. These establishments serve both local and imported beers and spirits, and are popular with China's middle class, as well as foreigners. Mostly, though, the Chinese drink alcohol only with their meals – all restaurants serve at least local brews and spirits. **Imported beers and spirits** are sold in large department stores and in city bars, but are always expensive.

Soft drinks

Canned drinks, usually sold unchilled, include various lemonades and colas. **Fruit juices** can be unusual and refreshing, flavoured with chunks of lychee, lotus and water chestnuts. **Milk** is sold in powder form as baby food, and increasingly in bottles for adult consumption as its benefits for invalids and the elderly become accepted wisdom.

Coffee

Coffee has long been grown and drunk in Yunnan and Hainan, and **coffee** culture has taken off across China, with cafés in every major city across the land. The quality varies widely; it's pretty good in the trendy brunch-houses of Beijing and Shanghai, for example, though pretty wretched in the generic (and huge) local chains.

Health

No vaccinations are required to visit China, except for yellow fever if you're arriving from an area where the disease is endemic. However, it's recommended that you are up-to-date with routine inoculations (such as MMR and tetanus), and vaccinated against Hepatitis A and typhoid, both of which can be contracted through contaminated food or water. You should also consider getting rabies shots if you plan to visit Tibet (see p.883).

Precautions

It's worth taking a first-aid kit with you, particularly if you will be travelling extensively outside the cities, where buying the appropriate medicines might be difficult. Include bandages, plasters, painkillers, oral rehydration salts, medication to counter diarrhoea and antiseptic cream. A sterile set of hypodermics may be advisable, as re-use of needles does occur in China. Note there is widespread ignorance of sexual health issues, and AIDS and STDs are widespread – always practise safe sex.

Intestinal troubles

The most common health hazards in China are the **cold and flu infections** that strike down a large proportion of the population year-round. **Diarrhoea** is also common, usually in a mild form while your stomach gets used to unfamiliar food, but also sometimes with a sudden onset accompanied by stomach cramps and vomiting, which indicates **food poisoning**. In both instances, get plenty of rest, drink lots of water, and in serious cases replace lost salts with **oral rehydration salts** (**ORS**); this is especially important with young children. Take some sachets with you, or make your own by adding half a teaspoon of salt and six of sugar to a litre of cool, previously boiled water. While suffering from diarrhoea, avoid milk, greasy or spicy foods, coffee and most fruit, in favour of bland foodstuffs such as rice, plain noodles and soup. If symptoms persist, or if you notice blood or mucus in your stools, consult a doctor, as you may have **dysentery**.

To avoid stomach complaints, eat at places that look busy and clean, and stick to fresh, thoroughly cooked food. Shellfish is a potential hepatitis A risk, and best avoided. Fresh fruit you've peeled yourself is safe; other uncooked foods may have been washed in unclean water. **Don't drink untreated tap water** – only consume boiled or bottled water, or filter your own (see opposite).

Infectious diseases

Hepatitis A is a viral infection spread by contaminated food and water, which causes an inflammation of the liver. The less common **hepatitis B** virus can be passed on through unprotected sexual contact, transfusions of unscreened blood, and dirty needles. Hepatitis symptoms include yellowing of the eyes and skin, preceded by lethargy, fever, and pains in the upper right abdomen.

Typhoid and cholera are spread by contaminated food or water, generally in localized epidemics; both are serious conditions and require immediate medical help. Symptoms of **typhoid** include headaches, high fever and constipation, followed by diarrhoea in the later stages. The disease is infectious. **Cholera** begins with sudden but painless onset of watery diarrhoea, later combined with vomiting, nausea and muscle cramps. Rapid dehydration rather than the infection itself is the main danger, and cases should be treated immediately and continually with oral rehydration solutions.

Summer outbreaks of **malaria** and **dengue fever** occur across southern China, usually in localized areas. Symptoms are similar – severe headaches, joint pains, fever and shaking – though a rash might also appear with dengue. There's no cure for dengue fever, whereas malaria can be prevented and controlled with medication; both require immediate medical attention to ensure that there are no complications. You can minimize your chances of being bitten by mosquitoes in the first place by wearing light-coloured, full-length clothing and insect repellent in the evenings when mosquitoes are active.

Temperature issues

In tropical China, the **temperature and humidity** can take a couple of weeks to adjust to. High humidity can cause **heat rashes**, **prickly heat** and **fungal infections**. Prevention and cure are the same: wear loose clothes made of natural fibres, wash frequently and dry-off thoroughly afterwards. Talcum or anti-fungal powder and the use of mild antiseptic soap help, too.

Don't underestimate the strength of the sun in the tropics, desert regions such as Xinjiang, or high up on the Tibetan Plateau. Sunscreen is not always easily available in China, and local stuff isn't always of sufficiently high quality anyway. Signs of **dehydration** and **heatstroke** include a high temperature, lack of sweating, a fast pulse and red skin. Reducing your body temperature with a lukewarm shower will provide initial relief.

Plenty of places in China – Tibet and the north in particular – also get very **cold**. Watch out here for **hypothermia**, where the core body temperature drops to a point that can be fatal. Symptoms are a weak pulse, disorientation, numbness, slurred speech and exhaustion. To prevent the condition, wear lots of layers and a hat, eat plenty of carbohydrates, and stay dry and out of the wind. To treat hypothermia, get the victim into shelter, away from wind and rain, give them hot drinks – but not alcohol – and easily digestible food, and keep them warm. Serious cases require immediate hospitalization.

Altitude sickness

High altitude, in regions such as Tibet and parts of Xinjiang, Sichuan and Yunnan, prevents the blood from absorbing oxygen efficiently, and can lead to **altitude sickness**, also known as **AMS** (acute mountain sickness). Most people feel some symptoms above 3500m, which include becoming easily exhausted, headaches, shortness of breath, sleeping disorders and nausea; they're intensified if you ascend to altitude rapidly, for instance by flying direct from coastal cities to Lhasa. Relaxing for the first few days, **drinking** plenty of water, and taking painkillers will ease symptoms. Having acclimatized at one altitude, you should still ascend slowly, or you can expect the symptoms to return.

If for any reason the body fails to acclimatize to altitude, serious conditions can develop including **pulmonary oedema** (characterized by severe breathing trouble, a cough and frothy white or pink sputum), and **cerebral oedema** (causing severe headaches, loss of balance, other neurological symptoms and eventually coma). The only treatment for these is **rapid descent**: in Tibet, this means flying out to Kathmandu or Chengdu without delay. You'll also need to see a doctor as soon as possible.

Getting medical help

Medical facilities in China are best in major cities with large expat populations, where there are often high-standard clinics, and the hotels may even have resident doctors. Elsewhere, larger cities and towns have hospitals, and for minor complaints there are plenty of pharmacies that can suggest remedies, though don't expect English to be spoken.

Chinese hospitals use a mix of Western and Traditional Chinese Medicine approaches. They sometimes charge high prices for simple drugs, and use procedures that aren't necessary, such as putting you on a drip just to administer antibiotics. Always ask for a second opinion from a Western–trained doctor if you're worried (your embassy should be able to recommend one if none is suggested in this guide). In an **emergency**, you're better off taking a cab than waiting for an ambulance – it's quicker and will work out much cheaper. There's virtually **no free health care** in China even for its citizens; expect to pay around ¥500 as a consultation fee.

Pharmacies are marked by a green cross, and if you can describe your ailment or required medication, you'll find many drugs which would be restricted and expensive in the West are easily available over the counter at very low prices. Be wary of **counterfeit drugs**, however; check for spelling mistakes in the packaging or instructions.

Culture and etiquette

The Chinese are, on the whole, pragmatic, materialistic and garrulous. Many of the irritations experienced by foreigners – the occcasional sniggers and unhelpful service – can often be put down to nervousness and the language barrier, rather than hostility. Visitors who speak Chinese will encounter an endless series of delighted and amazed interlocutors wherever they go, invariably asking about their country of origin, their job and the reason they are in China.

If you're **invited** to someone's home, take along a **gift** – a bottle of spirits, some tea or an ornamental trinket are good choices (anything too utilitarian could be considered patronizing) – though your hosts won't impolitely open this in front of you. **Restaurant bills** are not shared out between the guests; instead, individuals will make great efforts to pay the whole amount themselves – even pretending to go to the toilet but actually paying, or resorting to fairly rough-and-tumble tactics at the till. Normally this honour will fall to the person perceived as the most senior, and as a foreigner dining with Chinese you should make some effort to stake your claim, though it is probable that someone else will grab the bill before you do. Attempting to pay a "share" of the bill will embarrass your hosts.

Privacy

There's almost no concept of **privacy in mainland China** – partitions in public toilets barely screen each cubicle, and in some places there are no partitions at all. All leisure activities are enjoyed in large, noisy groups, and the desire of some Western tourists to be "left alone" can be interpreted by locals as eccentric or arrogant.

Exotic foreigners inevitably become targets for **blatant curiosity**. People stare and point, voices on the street shout out "helloooo" twenty times a day, or – in rural areas – people even run up and jostle for a better look, exclaiming loudly to each other, *laowai, laowai* ("foreigner"). This is not usually intended to be aggressive or insulting, though the

cumulative effects of such treatment can prove to be annoying, perhaps even alienating.

Spitting and smoking

Various other forms of behaviour perceived as antisocial in the West are considered perfectly normal in China. The widespread habit of **spitting**, for example, though slowly on the wane, can be observed in buses, trains, restaurants and even inside people's homes. Outside the company of urban sophisticates, it would not occur to people that there was anything disrespectful in delivering a powerful spit while in conversation with a stranger. **Smoking**, likewise, is almost universal among men, and in most of the country any attempt to stop others from lighting up is met with incomprehension – though smoking in enclosed public places (including bars, restaurants and all transport) has been banned in Beijing and Shanghai since 2015.

Clothing

Chinese clothing styles lean towards the casual, though surprisingly for such an apparently conservative-minded country, summertime **skimpy clothing** is common in all urban areas, particularly among women (less so in the countryside). Even in potentially sensitive Muslim areas, many Han Chinese girls insist on wearing miniskirts and see-through blouses. Although Chinese men commonly wear shorts and expose their midriffs in hot weather, Western men who do the same should note that the bizarre sight of hairy flesh in public – chest or legs – will instantly become the focus of giggly gossip. The generally relaxed approach to clothing applies equally when visiting temples, though in **mosques** men and women alike should cover their bodies above the wrists and ankles. As for **beachwear**, bikinis and briefs are in, but nudity has yet to become fashionable.

Casual clothing is one thing, but **scruffy clothing** quite another. If you want to earn the respect of the Chinese – useful for things like getting served in a restaurant or checking into a hotel – you should make some effort. While the average Chinese peasant might reasonably be expected to have wild hair and wear dirty clothes, a rich foreigner doing so will arouse a degree of contempt.

Meeting people

When **meeting people** it's useful to have a **business card** to flash around – Chinese with business aspirations hand them out at every opportunity, and are a little crestfallen if you can't produce one in return. It's polite to take the proffered card with both hands and to have a good look at it before putting it away – though not in your back pocket. If you don't speak Chinese but have your name in Chinese printed on them, they also become useful when checking in to hotels that are reluctant to take foreigners, as the staff can then copy your name into the register.

Nowadays, even more important than a business card is the smartphone app **WeChat** (Ⓦwechat .com). As most foreign social media such as Twitter and Facebook are blocked in China, WeChat is utterly ubiquitous. Texting is free (it can also handle video messaging and internet calls), and people will ask for your WeChat contact details instead of a phone number.

Shaking hands is not a Chinese tradition, though it is fairly common between men. Bodily contact in the form of embraces or back-slapping can be observed between same-sex friends, and these days, in cities, a boy and a girl can walk round arm in arm and even kiss without raising an eyebrow. **Voice levels** in China seem to be pitched several decibels louder than in most other countries, though this should not necessarily be interpreted as a sign of belligerence.

Sex and gender issues

Women travellers in China usually find **sexual harassment** less of a problem than in other Asian countries. Chinese men are, on the whole, deferential and respectful. A more likely complaint is being ignored, as the Chinese will generally assume that any man accompanying a woman will be doing all the talking, ordering and paying. Women on their own visiting remote temples or sights should be on their guard – don't assume that all monks and caretakers have impeccable morals.

Prostitution, though illegal and officially denied, is everywhere in China. Single foreign men are likely to be approached inside hotels; it's common practice for prostitutes to phone around hotel rooms at all hours of the night. Bear in mind that the consequence of a Westerner being caught with a prostitute may be unpleasant.

Homosexuality is increasingly tolerated by the authorities and general public, though open displays may get you in trouble outside the more cosmopolitan cities. There are gay bars in most major cities, especially Beijing and Shanghai.

Dating a local won't raise many eyebrows in these relaxed times, though displays of mixed-race public affection certainly will.

The media

Xinhua is the state-run news agency, and it supplies most of the national print and TV media. All content is Party-controlled and censored, though there is a limited coverage of minor social issues and natural disasters as long as the government is portrayed as successfully combating the problem. However, gone are the days when surprisingly frank stories about corruption and riots occasionally slipped through the censorship net; ever since President Xi Jinping made highly publicized visits to newspaper offices in 2015 to encourage "patriotism" in the press, any journalist or editor who tried to publish such things would find themselves disgraced, dismissed or even imprisoned for "revealing state secrets".

Newspapers and magazines

The national **Chinese-language newspaper** is the *People's Daily* (with an online English edition at Ⓦenglish.peopledaily.com.cn), though all provincial capitals and many major cities produce their own dailies with a local slant. The only national **English-language newspaper** is the *China Daily* (Ⓦchinadaily.com.cn), which is scarce outside big cities. **Hong Kong**'s English-language media includes the locally produced newspapers, the *South China Morning Post* and *The Standard*, published alongside regional editions of *Time*, *Newsweek*, the *Asian Wall Street Journal* and *USA Today*. All these have so far remained openly critical of Beijing on occasion, despite the former colony's changeover to Chinese control.

Most big cities, including Beijing, Shanghai, Kunming, Chengdu and Chongqing, have free **English-language magazines** aimed at expats; the publications contain listings of local venues and events, plus classifieds and feature articles; they're monitored by the authorities, so don't expect anything too controversial.

Television and radio

Chinese **television** comprises a dozen or so channels run by the state television company, **CCTV** (China Central Television), plus a host of regional stations; not all channels are available nationwide. Most of the content comprises news, flirty game shows, travel and wildlife documentaries, soaps, historical dramas and bizarre song-and-dance extravaganzas featuring performers in fetishistic, tight-fitting military outfits entertaining party officials with rigor-mortis faces. **CCTV 17** shows international news in English. The **regional stations** are sometimes more adventurous, with a current trend for frank dating games, which draw much criticism from conservative-minded government factions for the rampant materialism displayed by the contestants.

On the **radio** you're likely to hear the latest soft ballads, or versions of Western pop songs sung in Chinese. For **news from home**, listen via the websites of the **BBC World Service** (W bbc.co.uk /worldservice), **Radio Canada** (W rcinet.ca), the **Voice of America** (W voanews.com) and **Radio Australia** (W abc.net.au/ra).

Festivals

China celebrates many secular and religious festivals, two of which – the Spring Festival (Chinese New Year) and National Day on October 1 – involve major nationwide holidays. Avoid travel during these times, as the country's transport network becomes severely overloaded.

Most festivals take place according to dates in the **Chinese lunar calendar**, in which the first day of the month is the time when the moon is at its thinnest, with the full moon marking the middle of the month. By the Gregorian calendar used in the West, such festivals fall on a different day every year – check online for the latest dates. Most festivals

celebrate the turning of the seasons or auspicious dates, such as the eighth day of the eighth month (eight is a lucky number in China). These are times for gifts, family reunions, feasts and setting off firecrackers. It's always worth visiting temples on festival days, when the air is thick with incense, and people queue up to kowtow to altars and play games that bring good fortune, such as trying to hit the temple bell by throwing coins.

Aside from the following national festivals, China's **ethnic groups** punctuate the year with their own ritual observances, which are described in the relevant chapters of the Guide. In Hong Kong, all the national Chinese festivals are celebrated.

A HOLIDAYS AND FESTIVALS CALENDAR

January/February Two-week-long **Spring Festival** (see box below). Everything shuts down for a national holiday during the first week.

February Tiancang Festival On the twentieth day of the first lunar month, Chinese peasants celebrate Tiancang, or Granary Filling Day, in the hope of ensuring a good harvest later in the year.

March Guanyin's Birthday Guanyin, the Bodhisattva of Mercy, and probably China's most popular deity, is celebrated on the nineteenth day of the second lunar month.

April 4/5 Qingming Festival Also referred to as Tomb Sweeping Day, this is when people visit the graves of ancestors and burn ghost money in honour of the departed.

April 13–15 Dai Water Splashing Festival Anyone on the streets of Xishuangbanna, in Yunnan province, is fair game for a soaking.

May 1 Labour Day A three-day national holiday when everyone goes on the move.

May 4 Youth Day Commemorating the student demonstrators in Tian'anmen Square in 1919, which gave rise to the Nationalist "May Fourth Movement". It's marked in most cities with flower displays.

June 1 Children's Day Most schools go on field trips, so if you're visiting a popular tourist site, be prepared for mobs of kids in yellow baseball caps.

SPRING FESTIVAL (CHINESE NEW YEAR)

The **Spring Festival** is two weeks of festivities marking the beginning of the lunar **New Year**, usually in late January or early February. In Chinese astrology, each year is associated with one of twelve animals, and the passing into a new phase is a momentous occasion. The festival sees China at its most colourful, with shops and houses decorated with good-luck messages. The first day of the festival is marked by a family feast at which *jiaozi* (dumplings) are eaten, sometimes with coins hidden inside. To ward off bad fortune, people dress in red clothes (red is a lucky colour) and eat fish, since the Chinese script for fish resembles the script for "surplus", something everyone wishes to enjoy during the year. Firecrackers are let off almost constantly to scare ghosts away and, on the fifth day, to honour **Cai Shen**, god of wealth. Another ghost-scaring tradition is the pasting up of images of door gods at the threshold. Outside the home, New Year is celebrated at **temple fairs**, which feature acrobats and clouds of smoke as the Chinese light incense sticks to placate the gods. The celebrations end with the **lantern festival**, when the streets are filled with multicoloured paper lanterns. It's customary at this time to eat *tang yuan*, glutinous rice balls stuffed with sweet sesame paste.

June/July Dragon-boat Festival On the fifth day of the fifth lunar month, dragon-boat races are held in memory of the poet Qu Yuan, who drowned himself in 280 BC (see box, p.412). The traditional food to accompany the celebrations is *zongzi* (lotus-wrapped rice packets). Another three-day public holiday.

August/September Ghost Festival The Chinese equivalent of Halloween, this is a time when ghosts from hell are supposed to walk the earth. It's not celebrated so much as observed; it's regarded as an inauspicious time to travel, move house or get married.

September/October Moon Festival Also known as the Mid-Autumn Festival, this is celebrated on the fifteenth day of the eighth month of the lunar calendar. Moon cakes, containing a rich filling of sugar, lotus-seed paste and walnut, are eaten, and plenty of spirits consumed. The public get a further three days off.

September/October Double Ninth Festival Nine is a number associated with *yang*, or male energy, and on the ninth day of the ninth lunar month such qualities as assertiveness and strength are celebrated. It's believed to be a good time for the distillation (and consumption) of spirits.

September 28 Confucius Festival The birthday of Confucius is marked by celebrations at all Confucian temples. It's a good time to visit Qufu, in Shandong province, when elaborate ceremonies are held at the temple there.

October 1 National Day Another week-long holiday when everyone has time off to celebrate the founding of the People's Republic. TV is even more dire than usual, as it's full of programmes celebrating Party achievements.

December 25 Christmas This is marked as a religious event only by the faithful, but for everyone else it's an excuse for a feast and a party.

Shopping

China is a good place to shop for tourist souvenirs, folk art, clothes, household goods and faked designer labels – but not for real designer brands or electronic goods (including mobile phones), which are all cheaper at home or online. Even small villages have markets, while larger cities will also have big department stores, shopping malls and even international supermarket chains.

Prices in stores are fixed, but **discounts** (折扣, zhékòu) are common: they're marked by a number between one and nine and the character "折", indicating the percentage of the original price you have to pay – "8折", for example, means that the item is on sale at eighty percent of its original price. At markets, you're expected to **bargain** for goods unless prices are displayed. If you can speak Chinese, hang around for a while to get an idea what others are paying, or just ask at a few stalls selling the same things; Chinese shoppers usually state the price they're willing to pay, rather than beginning low and working up to it after haggling. Don't become obsessed about saving every last yuan; being charged more than locals and getting ripped off from time to time is inevitable.

Souvenirs popular with foreign tourists include "chops" (stone seals with your name engraved in characters on the base); all manner of reproduction antiques, from porcelain to furniture; mementos of Mao and the Cultural Revolution; T-shirts and "old-style" Chinese clothes; scroll paintings; and ethnic jewellery and textiles. Chinese tourists also look for things like local teas, "purple sand" teapots and bright tack. Pretty much the same selection is sold at all tourist sites, irrespective of relevancy. For **real antiques**, you need specialist stores or markets – some are listed in the Guide – where anything genuine is meant to be marked with a wax seal and requires an export licence to take out of the country. With world prices for Chinese art going through the roof, forgeries abound. Don't expect to find any bargains for the real thing – many dealers are, in fact, beginning to buy their antiques overseas, where they cost less, for resale in China.

Clothes are good value in China, with brand stores such as Giordano, Baleno, Metersbonwe and Raidy Boer selling high-quality smart-casual wear. Fashion-conscious places such as Shanghai and Hong Kong also have **factory outlet** stores, selling last year's designs at low prices, and all major cities have specialist stores stocking outdoor and hiking gear, though it often looks far better than it turns out to be for the price. Silk and other **fabrics** are also good value, if you're into making your own clothes, while **shoes** are inexpensive too. With the Chinese youth racing up in height, finding clothing in large **sizes** is becoming less of an issue.

All bookshops and many market stalls in China sell **CDs** of everything from Beijing punk to Beethoven, plus **DVDs** of domestic and international movies (often subtitled – check on the back). While extremely cheap, many of these are **pirated** (the discs may be confiscated at customs when you get home). Genuine DVD films may be region-coded for Asia, so check the label and whether your player at home will handle them.

Hong Kong is the only place with a comprehensive range of **international goods**; on the mainland, your best bet is to head to provincial capitals, many of which have a branch of **Carrefour** (家乐福, jiālèfú) or **Wal-Mart** (沃尔玛, wòěrmǎ), where you may find small caches of foreign goodies.

Sports and outdoor activities

Since 2008, when China hosted the Olympics, athletic passion has become almost a patriotic duty. But the most visible forms of exercise are timeless; head to any public space in the morning and you'll see citizens going through martial-arts routines, playing ping pong and street badminton, even ballroom dancing. Sadly though, facilities for organized sport are fairly limited.

The Chinese are good at "small ball" games such as squash and badminton, and, of course, table tennis, at which (at the time of writing) they have been consecutive world champions since 2005 in the men's and since 1995 in the women's. Chinese teams aren't known for excelling at "big ball" games, such as **football**. Nevertheless, Chinese men follow foreign football avidly, with games from the European leagues shown on CCTV 5. There's also a national obsession among students for **basketball**, which predates the rise to international fame of NBA star **Yao Ming**, who played for the Houston Rockets.

If China has an indigenous "sport", however, it's the **martial arts** – not surprising, perhaps, in a country whose history is littered with long periods of civil conflict. Today, there are hundreds of Chinese martial-arts styles, often taught for exercise rather than for fighting.

As for **outdoor activities**, hiking for its own sake is slowly catching on, though tourists have plenty of opportunities for step-aerobic-type exercise up long, steep staircases ascending China's many **holy mountains**. Snow sports have become popular in Dongbei, which has several **ski resorts**, while the wilds of Yunnan and Sichuan, along with Qinghai and Tibet, are drawing increasing numbers of adventurous young city-born Chinese – always dressed in the latest outdoor gear – to **mountaineering** and four-wheel-drive expeditions.

Travelling with children

Children in China are, despite the recent abandonment of the one-child policy, usually indulged and pampered. Foreigners travelling with children can expect to receive lots of attention from curious locals – and the occasional admonition that the little one should be wrapped up warmer.

While **formula and nappies** might be available in modern, big city supermarkets, elsewhere you'll need to bring a supply (and any **medication** if required) with you – local kids don't use nappies, just pants with a slit at the back, and when baby wants to go, mummy points him at the gutter. Similarly, changing facilities and baby-minding services are virtually unknown on the mainland outside high-end international hotels.

Hong Kong is the only part of China where children are specifically catered to by attractions such as Ocean World and Disneyland; elsewhere, the way most Chinese tourist sites are decked up like fairground rides makes them attractive for youngsters in any case. Things to watch for include China's poor levels of **hygiene** (keeping infants' and toddlers' hands clean can be a full-time occupation), spicy or just unusual food, plus the **stress levels** caused by the ambient crowds, pollution and noise found in much of the country – though this often seems to affect parents more than children.

Travel essentials

Costs

China is an **expensive** place to visit compared with the rest of Asia. Though food and transport are good value, accommodation can be pricey for what you get, and **entry fees** for temples, scenic areas and historic monuments are becoming high even on an international scale – so much so that the central government is trying to get local authorities to reduce them (with little effect so far). Actual prices vary considerably between **regions**: Hong Kong and Macau are as costly as Europe or the US; the developed eastern provinces are expensive by Chinese standards; and the further west you go, the more prices fall.

By doing everything cheaply and sticking mostly to the less expensive interior provinces, you can survive on £50/US$65/¥400 a day; travel a bit more widely and in better comfort and you're looking at £80/US$105/¥700 a day; while travelling in style and visiting only key places along the east coast, you could run up daily expenses of £250/US$330/¥2200 and above.

Discount rates for pensioners and students are available for many sights, though students may well be asked for a Chinese student card – the practice varies from place to place, even within the same city. Pensioners can often just use their passports to prove they are over 60 (women) or 65 (men).

Crime and personal safety

While the worst that happens to most visitors to China is being pickpocketed on a bus or getting **scammed** (see box opposite), you do need to take care. Carry passports and money (and your phone, if it fits) in a concealed money belt, and keep some foreign notes – perhaps around US$300 – separately from the rest of your cash, together with your insurance policy details and photocopies of your passport and visa. Be wary on **buses**, the favoured haunt of **pickpockets**, and **trains**, particularly in hard-seat class and on overnight journeys.

One of the most dangerous things you can do in China is **cross a road**: marked pedestrian crossings might as well not be there for all motorists pay attention to them; and even when traffic lights flash green to show it's safe to cross, vehicles are still permitted to turn into or out of the road. **Hotel rooms** are on the whole secure, dormitories much less so, though often it's fellow travellers who are the problem here. Most hotels should have a safe, but it's not unusual for things to go missing from these. Wandering around cities late at night is as risky in China as anywhere else; walking alone across the countryside is ill-advised, particularly in remote regions. If anyone does try to rob you, run away, or, if this isn't possible, stay calm and don't resist.

You may see stress-induced **street confrontations**, though these rarely result in violence, just a lot of shouting. Another irritation, particularly in the southern cities, is gangs of **child beggars**, organized by a nearby adult. They target foreigners and can be very hard to shake off; handing over money usually results in increased harassment.

The police

The **police**, known as the **Public Security Bureau** or **PSB**, are recognizable by their dark blue uniforms and caps, though there are a lot more around than you might at first think, as plenty are undercover. They have much wider powers than most Western

SCAMS

A good number of professional **con artists** target tourists – especially in places such as Shanghai, Beijing and Guilin – with variations on the following scam. A sweet-looking young couple, a pair of girls, or perhaps a kindly old man, will ask to practise their English or offer to show you round. Having befriended you – which may take hours – they will suggest some refreshment, and lead you to a teahouse, art gallery or restaurant. After eating or drinking, you will be presented with a bill for thousands of yuan, your new "friends" will vanish, and some large gentlemen will appear – who in some cases force people into handing over their card and PIN and raiding their bank account before letting them go. It's hard to believe just how convincing these scam artists can be: never eat or drink with a stranger unless you have confirmed how much you're expected to pay.

police forces, including establishing the guilt of criminals – trials are used only for deciding the sentence of the accused (though this is changing and China now has the beginnings of an independent judiciary). If the culprit is deemed to show proper remorse, this will result in a more lenient sentence.

The PSB also have the job of looking after foreigners, and you'll most likely have to seek them out for **visa extensions**, reporting theft or losses, and obtaining permits for otherwise closed areas of the country (mostly in Tibet). On occasion, they might seek you out; it's common for the police to call round to your hotel room if you're staying in a remote place – they usually just look at your passport and then move on.

While individual police often go out of their way to help foreigners, the PSB itself has all the problems of any police force in a country where corruption is widespread, and it's best to minimize contact with them.

Offences to avoid

With adjacent opium-growing areas in Burma and Laos, and a major Southeast Asian distribution point in Hong Kong, China has a massive **drug problem**. Heroin use has become fairly widespread in the south, particularly in depressed rural areas, and ecstasy is used in clubs. In the past, the police have turned a blind eye to foreigners with drugs, as long as no Chinese are involved, but you don't want to test this out. In 2009, China **executed** British national Akmal Shaikh for drug trafficking, and annually holds mass executions of convicted drug offenders on the UN anti-drugs day in June.

Visitors are not likely to be accused of **political crimes**, but foreign residents can be expelled from the country for talking about politics or religion. The Chinese people they talk to will be treated less leniently. In Tibet, and at sensitive border areas, censorship is taken extremely seriously; **photographing** military installations (which can include major road bridges), instances of police brutality or gulags is not a good idea.

Electricity

The electricity supply runs on 220 volts, with **plugs** either a triple flat pin or round double prong, except in Hong Kong, where they favour the UK-style square triple prong. Adaptors are widely available from neighbourhood hardware stores.

Entry requirements

Unless you're briefly transiting China via certain key cities (see box, p.54), all foreign nationals require a **visa** to enter mainland China, available worldwide from Chinese embassies and consulates and through specialist tour operators and visa agents, and online. Bear in mind that application requirements have become fairly strict in recent times, and you need to check the latest rules at least three months before you travel; the following information outlines the situation at the time this book went to print. Don't count on being able to extend your visa once in China (see p.54).

By far the most straightforward option is to **apply in your home country** – the country that issued your passport, regardless of your country of residence. You will need to fill out a form with a detailed itinerary of your proposed trip, along with proof of a return ticket and accommodation reservations for every night that you're in China. To get around the last hurdle, find a hotel via Ⓦ ctrip.com that doesn't require your credit card details to make a reservation, book it for the duration, and then cancel the booking once you have your visa. You'll be asked your occupation, and it's not wise to admit to being a journalist, photographer or writer; in such instances, it's best to say "consultant" or similar. Your passport must be valid for at least another six months from your planned date of entry into China, and have at least one blank page.

If you don't apply in your home country, or you fall short of any of the requirements, you'll probably also be asked to provide an official introductory letter from an organization inviting you to China, bank statements and possibly documents proving your annual income and employment record – things that might be impossible to produce if, for instance, you're in the middle of a round-the-world trip. The only solution in this case might be to head to Hong Kong and apply through independent agents there, who charge steeply but can usually wrangle a one-month visa.

Visas must be used **within three months** of issue, and the **cost** varies considerably depending on the visa type, the length of stay, the number of entries allowed, and – especially – your nationality. For example, US nationals pay US$140 for a multi-entry tourist visa with up to ten years validity, whereas UK nationals pay £150 for one lasting two years. **Don't overstay** your visa: the fine is ¥500 a day, along with the possibility that you may be deported and banned from entering China for five years.

Tourist visas (L) are valid for upwards of two months (maximum limits depend on nationality), and can be single- or multiple-entry. **Business** (M) and **Research** visas (F) are valid for upwards of three months; to apply, you'll need an official invitation from a government-recognized Chinese organization. Twelve-month **work visas** (Z) again require an invitation, plus a health certificate.

Students intending to **study** in China for less than six months need an invitation or letter of acceptance from a college there and will be given an F visa. If you're intending study for longer than six months, there is an additional form, and you will also need a health certificate; then you'll be allowed to stay for up to a year (X visa).

You're allowed to **import** into China up to four hundred cigarettes, plus 1.5l of alcohol and up to ¥20,000 cash. Foreign currency in excess of US$5000 or the equivalent must be declared. It's illegal to import printed or filmed matter critical of the country, but this is currently only a problem with Chinese border guards at crossings from Vietnam, who have confiscated guidebooks to China that contain maps showing Taiwan as a separate country (such as this one); keep them buried in the bottom of your bags.

CHINESE EMBASSIES AND CONSULATES

Australia ☎ 02 6273 4780, Ⓦ au.china-embassy.org/eng.
Canada ☎ 1 613 789 3434, Ⓦ ca.chineseembassy.org/eng.
Ireland ☎ 01 269 1707, Ⓦ ie.china-embassy.org/eng.
New Zealand ☎ 04 474 9631, Ⓦ chinaembassy.org.nz.

VISA-FREE TRANSIT

Currently, visitors from the US, Canada, UK and many European countries arriving on international flights at eighteen cities, including Beijing, Shanghai, Xi'an, Guilin, Guangzhou, Chongqing and Chengdu, can spend up to 72 hours in transit **without a visa**. To be eligible, you must have proof of onward travel to a third country (so you can't, for instance, be on a round-trip from Hong Kong). You are also not allowed to leave the relevant city's boundaries during your stay.

South Africa ☎ 012 431 6500, ⓦ chinese-embassy.org.za.
UK ☎ 020 7299 4049, ⓦ chinese-embassy.org.uk.
US ☎ 1 202 495 2266, ⓦ www.china-embassy.org/eng.

Visa extensions

You can apply for a **visa extension** through the nearest **Public Security Bureau** (**PSB**) – the department is normally labelled "Aliens' Entry Exit Section" or similar. Be aware that if the office strictly follows the official rules, you'll need to produce all the paperwork required for your original application. However, in reality, the amount of hassle varies greatly from place to place.

A **first extension**, valid for thirty days, costs ¥160–185, depending on your nationality. You must apply at least seven days before your old visa expires, and provide your passport, passport photos and a receipt from your accommodation proving that you're staying in the town in which you're applying. Processing the application takes seven working days. The worst places to apply (bar Tibet) are Xinjiang, Beijing and Shanghai.

A **second or third extension** is harder to get, and impossible if your visa was originally issued outside your home country. In cities with large foreign populations, use a visa agent (advertised in expat magazines), as the PSB may well reject your application otherwise. However, in small towns you'd be unlucky not to be given some kind of extension. Don't admit to being low on funds.

Insurance

China is a relatively safe place to travel, though traffic accidents, respiratory infections, petty theft and transport delays are all fairly common – meaning that it's sensible to ensure you've arranged some form of **travel insurance** before leaving home (see box below).

Internet

Almost every urban Chinese has a **smartphone** nowadays, and the best way to keep online is to carry one as well, or, failing that, a tablet or laptop. Free **wi-fi** is ubiquitous, from inner-city cafés and tourist areas to airport lounges and just about every form of accommodation (aside from back-country inns). There's only one **social media app** you'll need: WeChat (see opposite).

Internet bars (网吧, wǎngbā) are everywhere in China and charge ¥5–10 per hour; they're invariably full of network-gaming teenagers. You're officially required to show a Chinese ID card before being allowed to use one – obviously impossible for most tourists. In some places this rule is strictly enforced; elsewhere nobody cares, or you'll be handed a fake ID at the front counter which will allow you to sign on.

Censorship is a major headache for anyone wanting to access foreign websites, thanks to the dryly named "**Great Firewall**" or Net Nanny, which blocks sites deemed undesirable by the state. This currently includes anything connected to Google – so no Google Maps, Gmail or YouTube; those with Gmail accounts might want to set up an email account for their trip with Hotmail, Yahoo or similar. All foreign social media is banned, including Twitter and Facebook. To get around the firewall, you need to install a **web proxy** or VPN (Virtual Private Network) on your phone or laptop. This has to be set up before

---

ROUGH GUIDES TRAVEL INSURANCE

Rough Guides has teamed up with WorldNomads.com to offer great **travel insurance** deals. Policies are available to residents of more than 150 countries, with cover for a wide range of adventure sports, 24hr emergency assistance, high levels of medical and evacuation cover and a stream of travel safety information. Roughguides.com users can take advantage of their policies online 24/7, from anywhere in the world – even if you're already travelling. And since plans often change when you're on the road, you can extend your policy and even claim online. Roughguides.com users who buy travel insurance with WorldNomads.com can also leave a positive footprint and donate to a community development project. For more information, go to ⓦ roughguides.com/travel-insurance.

you leave home and costs a few pounds/dollars a month; check online to find the best current option for travelling to China, as they get disabled by Chinese censors fairly regularly. Using a VPN in China is illegal, but just about every foreign business runs one.

Laundry

Big-city hotels and youth hostels everywhere offer a **laundry service** for anything between ¥10 and ¥100; alternatively, some hostels have self-service facilities – every corner store in China sells **washing powder** (洗衣粉, xǐyīfěn). Otherwise, ask for accommodation staff for the nearest laundry, where they usually charge by dry weight. Laundromats are virtually unknown in China.

Living in China

It is fairly easy for foreigners to live in China full time, whether as a student, a teacher or for work. Anyone planning to stay more than six months is required to pass a **medical** examination (from approved clinics) proving that they don't have any venereal disease – if you do have a VD, expect to be deported and your passport endorsed with your ailment.

Many mainland cities – including Beijing, Shanghai, Guangzhou, Kunming and Chengdu – have no restrictions on where foreigners can **reside**, though either you or your landlord must register with the local PSB. **Property rental** is relatively inexpensive if you avoid purpose-built foreign enclaves. The easiest way to find accommodation is to go through an **agent**, who will generally charge one month's rent as a fee; find them online or in expat magazines.

Teaching

There are **schemes** in operation to place **foreign teachers** in Chinese educational institutions – contact your nearest Chinese embassy (see p.53) for details. Some employers ask for a TEFL qualification, though a degree, or simply the ability to speak the language as a native, is usually enough. Most teachers find their students keen, hard working, curious and obedient, and report that it is the contact with them that makes the experience worthwhile. That said, avoid talking about religion or politics in the classroom as this can get the pupils into trouble.

The **teaching salary** for a foreigner – though this depends heavily on your location, and the workload you accept – is around ¥6000 per month for a bachelor's degree, ¥9000 for a master's degree and ¥16,000 for a doctorate. This isn't enough to put much away, but you should also get subsidized on-campus accommodation, plus a fare to your home country – one-way for a single semester and a return for a year's work. The workload is usually fourteen hours a week, and if you work a year you get paid through the winter holiday. You'll earn more – say, ¥20,000 a month with a degree in teaching – in a **private school**, though be aware of the risk of being ripped off by a commercial agency (you might be given more classes to teach than you'd agreed to, for example). Research the institution thoroughly before committing.

Studying

Many universities in China now host substantial populations of **international students**, especially in Beijing, Shanghai and Xi'an. Indeed, the numbers of foreigners at these places are so large that in

---

ESSENTIAL APPS

Make your trip easier with some handy **smartphone apps**: all of the below are free.

Baidu maps Ⓦ map.baidu.com. Chinese-language take on Google Maps (which is blocked in China unless you're running a VPN). Works in a limited way with *pinyin*, but you'll need to input Chinese characters for best results.

Ctrip & Elong Ⓦ elong.net, Ⓦ english.ctrip.com. Useful for booking flights and accommodation; use Travel China Guide (see below) for trains.

Didi Ⓦ xiaojukeji.com. Uber-like Chinese app for taxis in over 350 cities; you offer a pick-up fee and wait for drivers to respond – in auction style. Drivers will take cash too, so there's no need for a domestic bank card. Chinese-language only, but not too hard to get to grips with.

ExploreMetro Ⓦ exploremetro.com. Subway maps for Beijing, Guangzhou, Hong Kong, Shenzhen and Shanghai.

Pandabus Ⓦ pandabus.cn. Uses your phone's GPS to show public bus timetables for your location. Works with English searches, though results are in Chinese.

Pleco & DianHua Ⓦ pleco.com, Ⓦ dianhuadictionary.com. Comprehensive English/*pinyin*/Chinese dictionaries, with free and paid-for versions. Pleco has add-on optical character recognition too, for a fee.

Travel China Guide Ⓦ travelchinaguide.com. The best way to book train tickets online and have them delivered to your hotel room.

Waygo Ⓦ waygoapp.com. Use your phone's camera to scan a Chinese-language menu or transport timetable and get a basic translation. Limited, but surprisingly useful.

WeChat Ⓦ wechat.com. Social media app that's essential for making friends in China (see p.48).

some ways you're shielded from much of a "China experience", and you may find smaller centres offer both a mellower pace of life and more contact with Chinese people outside the campus.

Most foreign students come to China to study **Mandarin**, though there are many additional options available – from martial arts to traditional opera or classical literature – once you break the language barrier. Courses cost from the equivalent of US$2700 a year, or US$900 a semester. Hotel-style campus accommodation costs around US$20 a day; most people move out as soon as they speak enough Chinese to rent a flat.

Your first resource is the nearest Chinese embassy (see p.53), which can provide a list of contact details for Chinese universities offering the courses you are interested in; most universities also have English-language websites. Be aware, however, that promotional material may have little bearing on what is actually provided. Though teaching standards themselves are high at Chinese universities, the administration departments are often confusing or misleading places. Ideally, visit the campus first and be wary of paying course fees up front until you've spoken to a few students.

Working

There is plenty of **work** available for foreigners in mainland Chinese cities, where a whole section of expat society gets by as actors, cocktail barmen, Chinglish correctors, models, freelance writers and so on. To really make any money here, however, you need either to be employed by a foreign company or run your own business.

China's vast markets and WTO membership present a wealth of **commercial opportunities** for foreigners. However, anyone wanting to do business here should do thorough research beforehand. The difficulties are formidable – red tape and shady business practices abound. Remember that the Chinese do business on the basis of mutual trust and pay much less attention to contractual terms or legislation. Copyright and trademark laws are often ignored, and any successful business model will be immediately copied. You'll need to develop your *guanxi* (connections) assiduously, and cultivate the virtues of patience, propriety and bloody-mindedness.

Study and work programmes

AFS Intercultural Programs ⓦ afs.org. Intercultural exchange organization whose China offerings include academic and cultural exchanges that are anywhere from one month to a year long.
Council on International Educational Exchange (CIEE)
ⓦ ciee.org. Leading NGO offering study programmes and volunteer

projects around the world. China options include: an academic semester or year abroad; a gap year (US students only); summer study; and paid teaching for a semester or year.

Maps

Street maps for almost every town and city in China are available from kiosks, hotel shops and bookshops. Most are in Chinese only, showing bus routes, hotels, restaurants and tourist attractions; local bus, train and flight timetables are often printed on the back as well. The same vendors also sell pocket-sized provincial **road atlases**, again in Chinese only.

Some of the major cities and tourist destinations also produce **English-language** maps, available at upmarket hotels, principal tourist sights or tour operators' offices. In Hong Kong and Macau, the local tourist offices provide free maps.

Countrywide maps, which you should buy before you leave home, include the excellent 1:4,000,000 map from GeoCenter, which shows relief and useful sections of all neighbouring countries, and the Collins 1:5,000,000 map. One of the best maps of Tibet is *Stanfords Map of South-Central Tibet; Kathmandu–Lhasa Route Map*.

Also note that, as all **Google** services are blocked in China, you'll need to install a VPN to access Google Maps or use a domestic alternative such as Baidu maps (see box, p.55).

Money

The mainland **Chinese currency** is formally called **yuan** (¥), more colloquially known as **renminbi** (RMB, literally "the people's money") or **kuai**. One yuan breaks down into ten *jiao*, also known as **mao**. **Paper money** was invented in China and is still the main form of exchange, available in ¥100, ¥50, ¥20, ¥10, ¥5 and ¥1 notes, with a similar selection of mao. One mao, five mao, and ¥1 **coins** are increasingly common, though less so in rural areas. China suffers regular outbreaks of **counterfeiting** – many people check their change for watermarks, metal threads, UV ink marks and – crucially – the feel of the paper.

The yuan floats within a narrow range set by a basket of currencies, keeping Chinese exports cheap (much to the annoyance of the US). At the time of writing, the **exchange rate** was approximately ¥6.9 to US$1, ¥8.7 to £1, ¥7.3 to €1, ¥5.2 to CAN$1, ¥5.1 to AU$1, ¥4.9 to NZ$1 and ¥0.5 to ZAR1. For exact rates, check ⓦ xe.com.

Hong Kong's currency is the Hong Kong **dollar** (HK$), divided into one hundred cents, while in **Macau** they use **pataca** (usually written MOP$), in turn broken down into a hundred avos. Both currencies are worth slightly less than the yuan, but while Hong Kong dollars are accepted in Macau and southern China's Special Economic Zones, and they can be exchanged internationally, neither yuan nor pataca is any use outside the mainland or Macau respectively. Tourist hotels in Beijing, Shanghai and Guangzhou also sometimes accept payment in Hong Kong or US dollars.

Banks and ATMs

Banks in major Chinese cities are sometimes open seven days a week, though **foreign exchange** is usually only available Monday to Friday, approximately 9am–noon and 2–5pm. All banks are closed for the first three days of the Chinese New Year, with reduced hours for the following eleven days, and at other holiday times. In Hong Kong, banks are generally open Monday to Friday from 9am to 4.30pm, and 9am to 12.30pm on Saturday, while in Macau they close thirty minutes earlier.

Cirrus, Visa and Plus **cards** can be used to make cash withdrawals from **ATMs** operated by the Bank of China, the Industrial and Commercial Bank of China, China Construction Bank and Agricultural Bank of China, as long as the ATM displays the relevant logo. In major east-coast cities, almost every one of these banks' ATMs will work with foreign cards, but elsewhere it's likely that only the main branch of the Bank of China will have a suitable machine. Your bank back home will charge a **fee** on each withdrawal. You can change your yuan into dollars or sterling at any Bank of China branch.

Credit cards and wiring money

China is basically a cash economy, and **credit cards**, such as Visa, American Express and MasterCard, are only accepted at big tourist hotels and the fanciest restaurants, as well as some tourist-oriented shops; there is usually a four percent handling charge. It's straightforward to obtain cash advances on a Visa card at many Chinese banks, though the commission is a steep three percent. You can also use Visa cards to get cash advances using ATMs bearing the "Plus" logo, and book hotels and the like online.

It's possible to **wire money** to China through Western Union (Ⓦwww.westernunion.cn); funds can be collected from one of their agencies or branches of the Postal Savings Bank of China.

Opening hours

China officially has a **five-day week**, though this only really applies to government offices, which open Monday to Friday approximately 8am–noon and again from 1–5pm. Generalization is difficult, though: post offices open daily, as do many shops, often keeping long, late hours, especially in big cities. Although banks *usually* close on Sundays – or for the whole weekend – even this is not always the case.

Tourist sights generally open every day, usually 8am–5pm and without a lunch break. Most public **parks** open from about 6am. **Museums** tend to have more restricted hours, often closing on Mondays. If you arrive at an out-of-the-way place that seems to be closed, however, don't despair – knocking or poking around will often turn up a drowsy doorkeeper. Conversely, you may find some places locked and deserted when they are supposed to be open. Public holiday dates are covered earlier in this chapter (see p.49).

Phones

Everywhere in China has an **area code** that must be used when phoning from outside that locality; these are given for all telephone numbers throughout this guide. **Local calls** are free from landlines, and **long-distance** China-wide calls are ¥0.3 a minute. International calls cost from ¥3.5 a minute, though much cheaper if you use an IP internet phonecard (see below).

Mobile coverage in China is excellent and comprehensive; they use the GSM system. Assuming your phone is unlocked and compatible, the cheapest deal is to buy a Chinese **SIM card** (SIM卡, SIM kǎ or 手机卡, shǒujīkǎ) for your phone from street kiosks or any China Mobile, China Unicom or China Telecom shop. The regulations state that you have to show a Chinese ID card or foreign passport to buy a SIM card. Depending on where you are, however, you might be sold one without anyone checking, but it's luck of the draw. We recommend downloading several useful apps (see box, p.55).

Basic SIM cards **cost** ¥100, which gets you 300MB download and 100 minutes of talk time; you extend this with prepaid **top-up cards** (充值卡, chōngzhí kǎ) from the same outlets. Making and receiving domestic calls this way costs ¥0.2 per minute, and texts ¥0.1 each; usually, you can't call overseas, though you can text.

If your phone is locked, it could well be cheaper to **buy a new handset** rather than pay your provider's roaming charges; the cheapest (non-smart) phones cost around ¥200. Make sure shop staff change the operating language into English for you.

The cheapest way to call overseas with any phone is to use an **IP card**, which comes in ¥100 units. You dial a local number, then a PIN, then the number you're calling. Rates are as low as ¥2.4 per minute to the US and Canada, ¥3.2 to Europe. IP cards are sold from corner stores, mobile-phone emporiums, and from street hawkers (usually outside the mobile-phone emporiums) all over the country. These cards can only be used in the places you buy them – move to another city and you'll have to buy a new card.

Photography

Photography is a popular pastime among the Chinese, and all big towns and cities have photo stores selling the latest cameras (especially Hong Kong), where you can also download your digital images onto disc for around ¥30, though prints are expensive at ¥1 each. Camera batteries, film and memory cards are fairly easy to obtain in city department stores.

Chinese people are often only too pleased to have their picture taken, though many temples **prohibit photography** inside buildings; and you should avoid taking pictures of anything to do with the military, or that could be construed as having strategic value, including ordinary structures such as bridges in sensitive areas along borders, in Tibet, and so forth.

Post

The Chinese postal service is fast and efficient, with letters taking a day to reach destinations in the same city, two or more days to other destinations in China, and up to several weeks to destinations abroad. **Overseas postage rates** are fairly expensive and vary depending on weight, destination and where you are in the country. The International **Express Mail Service** (**EMS**), however, is unreliable, with items often lost in transit or arriving broken, despite registered delivery and online tracking. **DHL** (Ⓦdhl .com), available in a few major cities, is a safer bet.

Main post offices are open daily, usually from 8am–8pm; smaller offices may keep shorter hours or close at weekends. As well as at post offices, you can post letters in green **post boxes**, though these are rare outside big cities.

To send **parcels**, turn up with the goods you want to send and the staff will sell you a box and pack them up for ¥15 or so. Once packed, but before the parcel is sealed, it must be checked at the customs window and you'll have to complete masses of paperwork, so don't be in a hurry. If you are sending valuable goods bought in China, put the receipt or a photocopy of it in with the parcel, as it may be opened for customs inspection further down the line.

Time

Despite its huge east–west spread, the whole of China occupies a single time zone, 8hr ahead of GMT, 13hr ahead of US Eastern Standard Time, 16hr ahead of US Pacific Time and 2hr behind Australian Eastern Standard Time. There is no daylight saving.

Tourist information

The **internet** is your best source of information before you travel, as Chinese tourist offices overseas mostly sell packages and have little to offer individual travellers. Once you reach the mainland, you'll find the **CITS** (China International Travel Service; 中国国际旅行社, **zhōngguó guójì lǚxíngshè**) and alternatives such as the **CTS** (China Travel Service; 中国旅行社, **zhōngguó lǚxíngshè**) everywhere from large cities to obscure hamlets. However, places with the CITS/CTS logo are individual businesses that have been granted

---

DIALLING CODES

To **call mainland China** from abroad, dial your international access code (Ⓣ00 in the UK and the Republic of Ireland, Ⓣ011 in the US and Canada, Ⓣ0011 in Australia, Ⓣ00 in New Zealand and Ⓣ27 in South Africa), then Ⓣ86 (China's country code), then area code (minus initial zero) followed by the number.

To call **Hong Kong**, dial your international access code followed by Ⓣ852, then the number; and for **Macau**, dial your international access code, then Ⓣ853 and then the number.

PHONING ABROAD FROM CHINA

To **call abroad** from mainland China, Hong Kong or Macau, dial Ⓣ00, then the country code (see below), then the area code minus initial zero (if any), followed by the number.

UK Ⓣ44	Ireland Ⓣ353	Australia Ⓣ61
New Zealand Ⓣ64	US & Canada Ⓣ1	South Africa Ⓣ27

between separate branches. Though they book flight and train tickets, local tours and accommodation, their value to independent travellers is usually pretty low, even on the rare occasions that someone speaks English. Other sources of information on the ground include accommodation staff or tour desks – especially at youth hostels – and backpacker cafés in destinations such as Dali and Yangshuo.

Cities with large expat populations (including Beijing, Shanghai, Chengdu and Guangzhou) have English-language **magazines** with bar, restaurant and other **listings**. These are usually distributed free in bars and upmarket hotels, and often have accompanying websites, listed throughout the Guide.

Hong Kong and Macau both have efficient and helpful tourist information offices, and several free listings magazines (see p.575 & p.600).

CHINESE TOURIST OFFICES ABROAD

Australia and New Zealand 11th Floor, 234 George St, Sydney, NSW 2000 ☎ 02 9252 9838
Canada Ⓦ tourismchina.org
UK Ⓦ cnto.org.uk
US Ⓦ cnto.org

GOVERNMENT WEBSITES

Australian Department of Foreign Affairs Ⓦ dfat.gov.au, Ⓦ smartraveller.gov.au
British Foreign & Commonwealth Office Ⓦ fco.gov.uk
Canadian Department of Foreign Affairs Ⓦ dfait-maeci.gc.ca
Irish Department of Foreign Affairs Ⓦ foreignaffairs.gov.ie
New Zealand Ministry of Foreign Affairs Ⓦ mft.govt.nz
South African Department of Foreign Affairs Ⓦ www.dfa.gov .za/consular/travel_advice.htm
US State Department Ⓦ travel.state.gov

CHINA ONLINE

China Backpacker Ⓦ chinabackpacker.info. Heaps of trekking information for well-known and very off-the-beaten-path areas of China. Dated in parts but still a great resource.
China Bloglist Ⓦ chinabloglist.org. Directory with links to over five hundred blogs about China, most of whose writers claim unique insights into the country, its people and culture.
China Daily Ⓦ chinadaily.com.cn. The official, state-approved version of the news. Not as bad as you'd perhaps think.
China Expat Ⓦ chinaexpat.com. Aimed at foreign residents, but a generally useful English-language resource, with a wide range of China-related articles and plenty of links.
China From Inside Ⓦ chinafrominside.com. Glimpses into China's traditional martial arts, with dozens of English-language articles and interviews with famous masters.
China Trekking Ⓦ chinatrekking.com. Inspiring trekking background; plenty of first-hand details you won't find elsewhere.

Danwei Ⓦ danwei.org. English-language analysis of highbrow and "serious" goings-on in the Chinese media. Thorough and worthy, but could do with an occasional injection of humour.
I am Xiao Li Ⓦ youtube.com/user/iamxiaoli. If David Lynch had designed a Mandarin Chinese course, it would have been like this. Disturbing.
International Campaign for Tibet Ⓦ savetibet.org. An authoritative source of current news from Tibet.
Managing the Dragon Ⓦ managingthedragon.com. Blog commentary on economic subjects from investor-who-lost-millions Jack Perkowski (who has since bounced back).
Middle Kingdom Life Ⓦ middlekingdomlife.com. Online manual for foreigners planning to live and work in China, providing a sane sketch of the personal and professional difficulties they're likely to face.
Shanghaiist Ⓦ shanghaiist.com. Focused on Shanghai, this covers trending domestic news stories with a cruel and trashy tabloid slant – try searching for *tuhao* ("nouveau riche"). Gives a rare insight into the underbelly of contemporary Chinese life.
Travel China Ⓦ travelchinaguide.com. Unusual in covering obscure places and small-group tours, as well as the normal run of popular sites and booking links.
Youku Ⓦ youku.com. One of the many YouTube-style clones in China, with a similar range of content (all in Chinese).
Zhongwen Ⓦ zhongwen.com. A handy online Chinese/English dictionary, though much more academic than similar options such as DianHua (see **p.55**).

Travellers with disabilities

In **mainland China** the disabled are generally hidden away; attitudes are not very sympathetic and little special provision is made. As it undergoes an economic boom, much of the country resembles a building site, with intense crowds and traffic, few ramps and no effort to make public transport accessible. Ribbed paving down every city street is intended to help blind people navigate, but as most Chinese pavements are unevenly surfaced obstacle courses of trees and power poles, parked vehicles, market stalls and random holes, the system is completely useless. Only a few upmarket international hotel chains, such as *Holiday Inn*, have experience in assisting disabled visitors. The situation **in Hong Kong** is considerably better; check out the Hong Kong Tourist Association website (Ⓦ discoverhongkong .com) for extensive Accessible Hong Kong listings.

To help ease your trip, it may be worth considering an organized tour. Take spares of any specialist clothing or equipment, extra supplies of drugs (carried on your person if you fly), and a prescription including the generic name (in English and Chinese characters) in case of emergency. If there's an association representing people with your disability, contact them early on in the planning process.

Beijing and around

北京

THE SUMMER PALACE

1

Beijing and around

By turns brash, gaudy, elegant, charming, polluted and historic, the Chinese capital of Beijing leaves an indelible impression on each and every traveller who passes through – this city is never, ever dull. It is one of China's longest surviving capitals: for a full millennium, the drama of China's imperial history was played out here, with the emperor enthroned at the centre of the Chinese universe in the Forbidden City, now one of Asia's most famous draws. Beijing was, according to some accounts, the first city in the world to hit a population of one million; as such, despite the setbacks which plagued the first decades of communist stronghold, it should come as little surprise to see the remote control of urbanity stuck on permanent fast-forward here. Crisscrossed by freeways, spiked with high-rises and soaked in neon, this vivid metropolis is China at its most dynamic.

First impressions of Beijing are of an almost inhuman vastness, conveyed by the sprawl of apartment buildings, in which most of the city's population of 21.5 million are housed, and the eight-lane freeways that slice it up. It's a notion that's reinforced on closer acquaintance, from the magnificent **Forbidden City**, with its impressive wealth of history, the concrete desert of **Tian'anmen Square** and the gargantuan buildings of the modern executive around it, to the rank after rank of office complexes that line its mammoth roads. Outside the centre, the scale becomes more manageable, with parks, narrow alleyways and historic sites such as the **Yonghe Gong**, the **Observatory** and, most magnificent of all, the **Temple of Heaven**, offering respite from the city's oppressive orderliness and rampant, continual reconstruction. In the suburbs beyond, the two **summer palaces** and the **Western Hills** have been favoured retreats since imperial times. Unexpectedly, some of the country's most pleasant scenic spots also lie within the scope of a day-trip, and, just to the north of the city, another of the world's most famous sights, the long and lonely **Great Wall**, winds between mountaintops.

Beijing is an invaders' city, the capital of oppressive foreign dynasties – the Manchu and the Mongols – and of a dynasty with a foreign ideology: the communists. As such, it has assimilated a lot of outside influence, and today has an international flavour reflecting its position as the capital of a major commercial power. As the front line of China's grapple with **modernity**, the city is being continually ripped up and rebuilt, a factor responsible for the strange lack of cohesion, despite its scale and vibrancy; there's rarely anything unexpectedly interesting to uncover between the sights. And despite the

THE FORBIDDEN CITY

Highlights

❶ Forbidden City Imperial magnificence on a grand scale and the centre of the Chinese universe for six centuries. **See p.70**

❷ Temple of Heaven This classic Ming-dynasty building, a picture in stone of ancient Chinese cosmogony, is a masterpiece of architecture and landscape design. **See p.89**

❸ Summer Palace Escape the city in this serene and elegant park, dotted with imperial architecture. **See p.95**

❹ 798 Art District This huge complex of galleries and studios provides the focus for a thriving contemporary arts scene. **See p.98**

❺ Peking duck A real Beijing classic, and worthy of its fame, as long as you can find the right place to eat it. **See p.108**

❻ Showtime Beijing's various shows are hugely popular with visitors, especially the breathtaking acrobatic displays. **See p.113**

❼ The Great Wall One of the world's most extraordinary engineering achievements, the old boundary between civilizations is China's must-see. **See p.119**

❽ Tianyi Tomb Out in the Western Hills, this offbeat museum gives a fascinating insight into the life of palace eunuchs. **See p.127**

HIGHLIGHTS ARE MARKED ON THE MAPS ON P.64 & PP.68–69

1

islands of historic architecture dotted throughout the centre, rising incomes have created a brash consumer-capitalist society that Westerners will feel very familiar with: students in the latest fashions while away their time in cafés, hip-hop has overtaken the clubs, boutique bars are integrating the back lanes, and schoolkids carry mobile phones in their lunchboxes. Even so, you'll still see large groups of the older generation assembling in the evenings to perform the Maoist *yangkou* (loyalty dance), once universally learned; and in the *hutongs*, the city's twisted grey stone alleyways, men sit with their pet birds and pipes, as they always have done.

Brief history

It was in Tian'anmen, on October 1, 1949, that Chairman Mao Zedong hoisted the red flag to proclaim officially the **foundation of the People's Republic**. He told the crowds that the Chinese had at last stood up, and defined liberation as the final culmination of a 150-year fight against foreign exploitation. The claim, perhaps, was modest. Beijing's recorded **history** goes back a little over three millennia, to beginnings as a trading centre for Mongols, Koreans and local Chinese tribes. Its predominance,

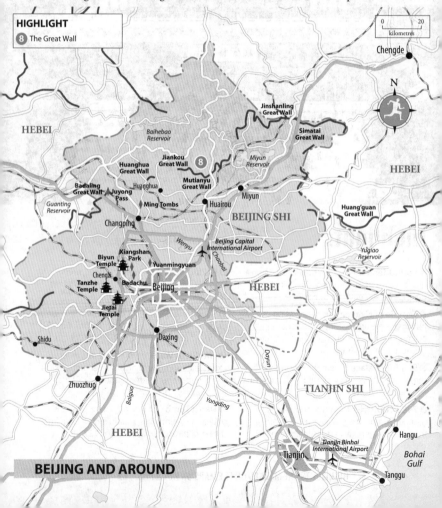

HIGHLIGHT

8 The Great Wall

BEIJING AND AROUND

WHEN TO VISIT BEIJING

If the Party had any control over it, no doubt Beijing would have the best climate of any Chinese city; as it is, it has one of the worst. The **best time to visit** is in autumn, between September and October, when it's dry and clement. In winter, it gets very cold, down to -20°C, and the mean winds that whip off the Mongolian plains feel like they're freezing your ears off. Summer (June–Aug) is muggy and hot, often above 30°C with bouts of torrential rains, and the short spring (April & May) is dry but windy, with dust often blowing in from the northwestern deserts – you'll see it covering cars.

however, dates to the mid-thirteenth century, and the formation of **Mongol China** under Genghis and later Kublai Khan.

The Khans

It was Kublai who took control of the city in 1264, and who properly established it as a capital – then named **Khanbalik** – replacing the earlier power centres of Luoyang and Xi'an. Marco Polo visited him here, working for a while in the city, and was clearly impressed with the level of sophistication; he observed in *The Travels*:

So great a number of houses and of people, no man could tell the number... I believe there is no place in the world to which so many merchants come, and dearer things, and of greater value and more strange, come into this town from all sides than to any city in the world.

The **wealth** came from the city's position on the Silk Road, and Polo described "over a thousand carts loaded with silk" arriving "almost each day", ready for the journey west out of China. And it set a precedent in terms of style and grandeur for the Khans, later known as emperors, with Kublai building himself a palace of astonishing proportions, walled on all sides and approached by great marble stairways.

The Ming dynasty

When the **Ming dynasty** defeated the Mongols in 1368, they emphasized their new regime by initially abandoning Beijing (literally, "**Northern Capital**"), with its frontier location and foreign associations, in favour of establishing themselves in the Chinese heartlands at Nanjing ("**Southern Capital**"). However, the second Ming emperor, Yongle, returned to Beijing, building around him prototypes of the city's two greatest **monuments** – the Imperial Palace and Temple of Heaven. It was in Yongle's reign, too, that the basic **city plan** took shape, rigidly symmetrical, extending in squares and rectangles from the palace and inner-city grid to the suburbs, much as it is today.

The Qing dynasty

Post-Ming history is dominated by the rise and eventual collapse of the Manchus, northerners who ruled China as the **Qing dynasty** from 1644 to the beginning of the twentieth century. Beijing, as the Manchu capital, was at its most prosperous in the first half of the eighteenth century, the period which saw the construction of the Jesuit-designed **Summer Palace** – the world's most extraordinary royal garden, with two hundred pavilions, temples and palaces, and immense artificial lakes and hills – to the north of the city. With the central Imperial Palace, this was the focus of endowment and the symbol of Chinese wealth and power. However, in 1860, the **Opium Wars** brought British and French troops to the walls of Beijing, and the Summer Palace was first looted and then razed to the ground by Anglo-French forces.

While the imperial court lived apart from the squalor of the world inside their Forbidden City, conditions for the civilian population, in the capital's suburbs, were starkly different. Kang Youwei, a Cantonese political reformer visiting in 1895, described this dual world:

1

No matter where you look, the place is covered with beggars. The homeless and the old, the crippled and the sick with no one to care for them, fall dead on the roads. This happens every day. And the coaches of the great officials rumble past them continuously.

This official indifference spread from the top down. From 1884, using funds meant for the modernization of the nation's navy, the Empress Dowager Cixi had begun building a new Summer Palace of her own. The empress's project was the last grand gesture of **imperial architecture** and patronage – and like its model was also badly burned by foreign troops in the aftermath of the Boxer Rebellion in 1900. By this time, with successive waves of occupation by foreign troops, the empire and the imperial capital were near collapse. The **Manchus abdicated** in 1912, leaving Beijing to be ruled by warlords. In 1928, it came under the military dictatorship of Chiang Kai-shek's Guomindang, who once again moved the national capital south to Nanjing and renamed the city **Beiping**.

The communist era

Restored to capital status after World War II, Beijing was taken by the **communists** in January 1949, nine months before Chiang Kai-shek's flight to Taiwan assured final victory. The **rebuilding of the capital** was an early priority, since the city that Mao Zedong inherited for the Chinese people was in most ways primitive. Imperial laws had banned the building of houses higher than the official buildings and palaces, so virtually nothing was more than one storey high. The new plans aimed to reverse this but retain the city's sense of ordered planning, with Tian'anmen Square at its heart – unsurprisingly, the communists' initial inspiration was Soviet, with an emphasis on heavy industry and poor-quality high-rise housing programmes.

In the zest to be free from the past, much of **Old Beijing** was destroyed, or co-opted: the Temple of Cultivated Wisdom became a wire factory and the Temple of the God of Fire produced electric lightbulbs. In the 1940s, there were 8000 temples and monuments in the city; by the 1960s, there were only around 150. Even the city walls and gates, relics mostly of the Ming era, were pulled down and their place taken by ring roads and avenues.

More destruction was to follow during the **Cultural Revolution** (see p.936), when few of the capital's remaining ancient buildings escaped desecration. Things improved with the death of Mao and the accession of pragmatic Deng Xiaoping and his fellow moderates, who embraced capitalism – though not, as shown by the massacre at Tian'anmen Square and the surrounding events of 1989, freedom (see p.938).

MODERN ARCHITECTURE IN BEIJING

Since dynastic times, Beijing has been an image-conscious city – anxious to portray a particular face to its citizenry, and to the world at large. In the early days of communist rule, Soviet functionality predominated, though from the 1990s onwards Beijing underwent the kind of urban transformation usually only seen after a war. Esteemed architects from across the globe were roped in for a series of *carte blanche* projects and, though the overall results have been hit and miss, some of their buildings are truly astounding. The best include the fantastic **Olympic venues** from 2008 (the "Bird's Nest" and "Water Cube"); Paul Andreu's **National Theatre** (the "Egg"); and, perhaps most striking of all, the **CCTV headquarters** (the "Twisted Doughnut") by Dutch architect Rem Koolhaas, which appears to defy gravity with its intersecting Z-shaped towers.

However, the rise to power of the culturally conservative Xi Jinping as China's president in 2012 has since seen a rejection of anything deemed as pandering to foreign tastes, and this includes architecture: in 2016, a **formal ban** was announced on any further "bizarre, oversized, xenocentric and weird" building projects. On the positive side, perhaps this might see Beijing's surviving courtyard houses modernized, rather than torn down.

1

BEIJING ORIENTATION, OPENING HOURS AND SECURITY

There's no doubt that Beijing's initial culture shock owes much to the artificiality of the city's **layout**. The main streets are huge, wide and dead straight, aligned east–west or north–south, and extend in a series of widening rectangles across the whole thirty square kilometres of the inner capital. The pivot of the ancient city was a north–south road that led from the entrance of the Forbidden City to the city walls. This remains today as **Qianmen Dajie**, though the main axis has shifted to the east–west road that divides Tian'anmen Square and the Forbidden City and, like all major boulevards, changes its name every few kilometres along its length.

Note that most government-run sights – including the Forbidden City, main museums and even many of the larger temples – are **closed on Mondays**. Note too, that following several incidents blamed on Muslim separatists, security in the capital verges on paranoia; there are **bag scans** at all subway stations, main sights, and to enter the barriers surrounding Tian'anmen Square.

Recent history

In 2008 Beijing succeeded in putting on a spectacular **Olympic Games**; this was the city's grand coming-out party, and no expense was spared to show that the capital – and China – could hold its own on the world stage. The city's infrastructure was vastly upgraded, a process which continues today. Some US$12bn has been spent on green projects, including a 125km tree belt around the city to curb the winter sandstorms that rage in from the Gobi Desert. Parks and verges have been prettified, fetid canals cleaned, and public facilities are better than anywhere else in China. Historic sites have also been renovated – or, it sometimes appears, invented.

The city gleams like never before, but what little antique character Beijing had has disappeared along with the widespread demolition of old city blocks and *hutongs*. Today, the city's main problems are the pressures of **migration**, **pollution** and **traffic congestion**: car ownership has rocketed, and the streets are nearing gridlock.

Beijing

北京, běijīng

BEIJING is a city that almost everyone enjoys. For new arrivals, it provides a user-friendly introduction to the country, with a sizeable foreign community and plenty of English-language signage and speakers on hand; and for travellers who've been roughing it round rural China, the creature comforts on offer are a delight.

The place to start exploring is **Tian'anmen Square**, geographical and psychological centre of the city, where a cluster of important sights can be seen in a day, although the **Forbidden City**, at the north end of the square, deserves a day, or even several, all to itself. Heading north brings you to a city section with a more traditional and human feel, with some magnificent **parks, palaces and temples**, some of them in the *hutongs*. To the east, the **Sanlitun** area is a ghetto of expat services including some good upscale restaurants and plenty of bars; heading south will bring you to **Qianmen**, an important shopping area which ends in style with one of the city's highlights, the **Temple of Heaven** in Tiantan Park. An expedition to the outskirts is amply rewarded by the **Summer Palace**, the best place to get away from it all.

Beijing requires patience and planning to do it justice – because of the frankly alienating scale of the place, wandering aimlessly around without a destination in mind will rarely be rewarding. This is also an essentially private city, whose surface is difficult to penetrate; sometimes, it seems to have the superficiality of a theme park. To delve deeper, meander what's left of the labyrinthine *hutongs* – plenty of these residential warrens survive, though in nothing like their original extent – and check out the little antique markets, the residential shopping districts, the smaller, quirkier sights, and the parks; the latter are some of the best in China, and you'll see Beijingers performing *tai*

1

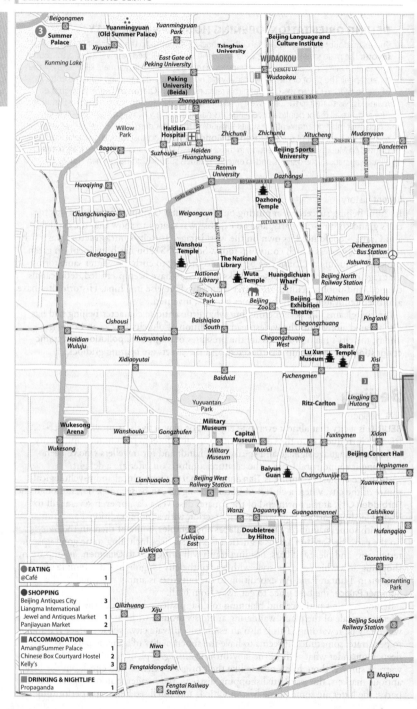

Beigongmen

Yuanmingyuan
(Old Summer Palace)

Yuanmingyuan
Park

**3 Summer
Palace**

1 Xiyuan

Kunming Lake

Tsinghua
University

**Beijing Language and
Culture Institute**

East Gate of
Peking University

WUDAOKOU

CHENGFU LU

1 Wudaokou

**Peking
University
(Beida)**

Zhongguancun

FOURTH RING ROAD

Willow
Park

**Haidian
Hospital**

HAIDIAN LU

Zhichunli

Zhichunlu

Xitucheng

Mudanyuan

ZHIEHUN LU

Jiandemen

Bagou

Suzhoujie

Haiden
Huangzhuang

**Beijing Sports
University**

Renmin
University

BEISANHUAN XILU

Dazhongsi

THIRD RING ROAD

Huoqiying

THIRD RING ROAD

Changchunqiao

Weigongcun

**Dazhong
Temple**

XUEYUAN NAN LU

Chedaogou

**Wanshou
Temple**

**The National
Library**

National
Library

**Wuta
Temple**

**Huangdichuan
Wharf**

Zizhuyuan
Park

Beijing
Zoo

**Beijing
Exhibition
Theatre**

Deshengmen
Bus Station

Jishuitan

**Beijing North
Railway Station**

Xizhimen

Xinjiekou

Cishousi

Baishiqiao
South

Chegongzhuang

Ping'anli

**Haidian
Wuluju**

Huayuanqiao

Chegongzhuang
West

**Lu Xun
Museum**

**Baita
Temple**

2 Xisi

Xidiaoyutai

Baiduizi

Fuchengmen

3

Yuyuantan
Park

Ritz-Carlton

Lingjing
Hutong

**Wukesong
Arena**

Wanshoulu

Gongzhufen

**Military
Museum**

**Capital
Museum**

Fuxingmen

Xidan

Wukesong

Military
Museum

Muxidi

Nanlishilu

Beijing Concert Hall

Hepingmen

Lianhuaqiao

**Beijing West
Railway Station**

**Baiyun
Guan**

Changchunjie

Xuanwumen

Wanzi

Daguanying

Guanganmennei

Caishikou

Hufangqiao

Liuliqiao
East

**Doubletree
by Hilton**

Liuliqiao

Taoranting

Taoranting
Park

Qilizhuang

Xiju

Niwa

Fengtaidongdajie

Fengtai Railway
Station

**Beijing South
Railway Station**

Majiapu

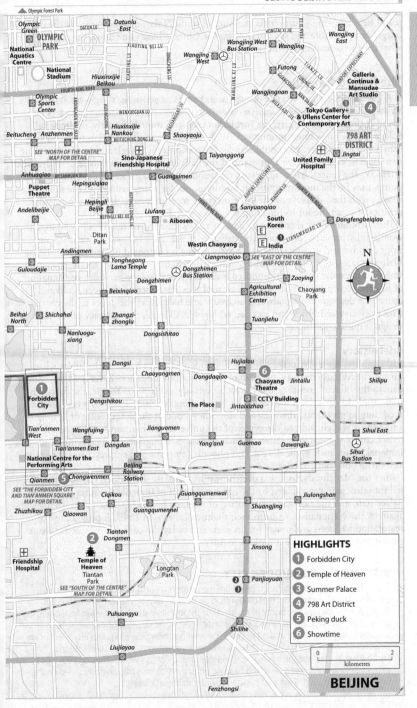

▲ Olympic Forest Park

HIGHLIGHTS

1 Forbidden City
2 Temple of Heaven
3 Summer Palace
4 798 Art District
5 Peking duck
6 Showtime

0   kilometres   2

BEIJING

1

ji and hear birdsong – just – over the hum of traffic. Take advantage, too, of the city's burgeoning nightlife and see just how far the Chinese have gone down the road of what used to be called spiritual pollution.

The Forbidden City

故宫, gùgōng • Tues–Sun: April–Oct 8.30am–5pm; Nov–March 8.30am–4.30pm; plus Mon June 1–Aug 31 • April–Oct ¥60; Nov–March ¥40; audio-guide ¥40 • ⓦ www.dpm.org.cn • Subway line #1 to Tian'anmen East, Exit A or Tian'anmen West, Exit B

Lying at the heart of the city, the **Forbidden City** – or, more accurately, the **Imperial Palace** – is Beijing's finest monument. To do it justice, you should plan to spend at least a whole day here; you could wander the complex for a week and keep discovering new aspects, especially now that many of the halls are doubling as museums of dynastic artefacts. The central halls, impressive for demonstrating the sheer scale of imperial pomp, may be the most magnificent buildings, but for many visitors it's the side rooms, with their displays of the more intimate accoutrements, that bring home the realities of court life for its inhabitants.

The Forbidden City is encased by a moat and, within the turreted walls, employs a wonderful symmetry and geomantic structure to achieve a balance between *yin* and *yang*: positive and negative energy. The city's spine is composed of eleven south-facing Halls or Gates, all colossal, exquisite and ornate. Branching off from this central vertebrae are more than eight hundred buildings that share the exclusive combination of imperial colours: red walls and yellow roof tiles. Elsewhere, jade green, gold and azure blue decorate the woodwork, archways and balconies. The doors to the central halls are heavy, red, thick and studded with gold. All in all, the intricacy of the city's design is quite astonishing.

Brief history

Although the earliest structures on the Forbidden City site began with Kublai Khan during the Mongol dynasty, the **plan** of the palace buildings is essentially Ming. Most date to the fifteenth century and the ambitions of the Emperor Yongle, the monarch responsible for switching the capital back to Beijing in 1403. The halls were laid out according to geomantic theories, and since they stood at the exact centre of Beijing, and Beijing was considered the centre of the universe, the harmony was supreme. The palace complex constantly reiterates such references, alongside personal symbols of imperial power such as the dragon and phoenix (emperor and empress) and the crane and turtle (longevity of reign).

After the Manchu dynasty was overthrown in 1912, the Forbidden City began to fall into disrepair, exacerbated by the quiet selling-off of imperial treasures by former palace staff, and the not-so-subtle looting of artefacts by the Japanese in the 1930s and again by the Nationalists, prior to their flight to Taiwan, in 1949. A programme of **restoration** has been under way for decades, and today the complex is in better shape than it was for most of the twentieth century.

VISITING THE FORBIDDEN CITY

The Forbidden City can only be entered from the south; the north, east and west gates are all exits only. There's a maximum of 80,000 visitors allowed in daily; this sounds enormous but during public holidays and pretty much any time through July and August you'd be lucky to get in after 1pm. Visitors have freedom to wander most of the site, though not all of the buildings; crowds gravitate around the main halls, with smaller side wings and less-well-known exhibitions far quieter. If you want detailed explanations of everything you see, take the **audio tour**, available at the main gate. If you take this option, it's worth retracing your steps afterwards for an untutored view, and heading off to the side halls that aren't included on the tour. Note that you will need your passport in order to buy a ticket.

1

SEX AND THE FORBIDDEN CITY

The emperors rarely left the Forbidden City – perhaps with good reason. Their lives were governed by an extraordinarily developed taste for **luxury and excess**. It is estimated that a single meal for a Qing emperor could have fed several thousand of his impoverished peasants, a scale obviously appreciated by the last influential occupant, the Empress Dowager Cixi (see box, p.96), who herself would commonly order preparation of 108 dishes at a single sitting. **Sex**, too, provided startling statistics, with the number of Ming-dynasty concubines approaching ten thousand. At night, the emperor chose a girl from his harem by picking out a tablet bearing her name from a pile on a silver tray. She would be delivered to the emperor's bedchamber naked but for a yellow cloth wrapped around her, and carried on the back of a servant, since she could barely walk with her bound feet.

The Wumen

午门, wǔmén

The **Wumen** (Meridian Gate) itself is the largest and grandest of the Forbidden City gates and was reserved for the emperor's sole use. From its vantage point, the Sons of Heaven would announce the new year's calendar to their court and inspect the army in times of war. It was customary for victorious generals returning from battle to present their prisoners here for the emperor to decide their fate. He would be flanked, on all such imperial occasions, by a guard of elephants, the gift of Burmese subjects.

Jinshui He and Taihemen

North through the Wumen you find yourself in a vast paved court, cut east–west by the **Jinshui He** (金水河, jīnshuǐ hé), the Golden Water Stream, with its five marble bridges, decorated with carved torches, a symbol of masculinity. Beyond is a further ceremonial gate, the **Taihemen** (太和门, tàihémén), Gate of Supreme Harmony, its entrance guarded by a magisterial pair of lions, and beyond this a still greater courtyard where the principal imperial audiences were held. Within this space the entire court, up to one hundred thousand people, could be accommodated. They would have made their way in through the lesser side gates – military men from the west, civilian officials from the east – and waited in total silence as the emperor ascended his throne. Then, with only the Imperial Guard remaining standing, they kowtowed nine times.

Taihe Dian

太和殿, tàihédiàn

Raised on a three-tiered marble terrace, the **Taihe Dian** (Hall of Supreme Harmony) is the tallest and most spectacular of the three main **ceremonial halls**. This was used for the most important state occasions, such as the emperor's coronation or birthdays, and the nomination of generals at the outset of a campaign; it last saw action in an armistice ceremony in 1918. A marble pavement ramp, intricately carved with dragons and flanked by bronze incense burners, marks the path along which the emperor's chair was carried. His golden dragon throne stands within the hall.

Zhonghe Dian

中和殿, zhōnghédiàn

Beyond the Taihe Dian, you enter the **Zhonghe Dian**, Hall of Central Harmony, another throne room, where the emperor performed ceremonies of greeting to foreigners and addressed the imperial offspring (the product of his multitude of wives and concubines). The hall was used, too, as a dressing room for the major Taihe Dian events, and it was here that the emperor examined the seed for each year's crop.

1

Baohe Dian

保和殿, bǎohédiàn

The **Baohe Dian**, Hall of Preserving Harmony, was used for state banquets and imperial examinations, graduates from which were appointed to positions of power in China's bureaucratic civil service. Its galleries, originally treasure houses, display various finds from the site, though the most spectacular, a vast block carved with dragons and clouds, stands at the rear of the hall. This is a Ming creation, reworked in the eighteenth century, and it's among the finest carvings in the palace. It's certainly the largest – a 250-tonne chunk of marble transported here from faraway, by flooding the roads in winter to form sheets of ice.

Imperial living quarters

To the north of the Baohe Dian, paralleling the structure of the ceremonial halls, are the three principal palaces of the **imperial living quarters**. Again, the first chamber, the **Qianqing Gong** (乾清宫, qiánqīnggōng), Palace of Heavenly Purity, is the most extravagant. It was originally the imperial bedroom – its terrace is surmounted by incense burners in the form of cranes and turtles (symbols of immortality) – though it later became a conventional state room. Beyond, echoing the Zhonghe Dian in the ceremonial complex, is the **Jiaotai Dian** (交泰殿, jiāotàidiàn), Hall of Union, the empress's throne room.

FORBIDDEN CITY EXHIBITIONS

The buildings spreading out from the Forbidden City's central axis house a variety of exhibitions of Chinese and international historical artefacts and treasures (check what's on at ⓦ dpm.org.cn); you'll find a map showing their location on the back of your entrance ticket. While exploring this maze of smaller halls and courtyards is an excellent way of experiencing a more intimate side of the Forbidden City, it has to be said that many of the older displays are badly captioned and unimaginative, and that some of the finest imperial treasures were looted by foreign forces and the Chinese Nationalists during the twentieth century. The exception is the recently-opened area in the northeastern side of the complex, whose halls display some impressive imperial artworks.

The Treasure Gallery (¥10). In buildings surrounding the Hall of Supremacy. Gold, silver, pearl and jade items demonstrating the wealth, majesty and luxury of imperial life.

Hall of Clocks (¥10). This hall, always a favourite, displays the result of one Qing emperor's passion for liberally ornamented Baroque timepieces, most of which are English and French, though the rhino-sized water clock by the entrance is Chinese. There's even one with a mechanical scribe who can write eight characters. Some clocks are wound to demonstrate their workings at 11am and 2pm.

Ceramics Gallery Hall of Literary Brilliance (free). A wonderful, air-cooled selection of fine pots, statues and porcelain treasures; keep an eye out for the Ming and Qing vases.

Dafo Tang (free). Buddhist artwork, but not what you'd expect: a room full of exquisite miniatures in coloured hardstone, some set with tiny jewels; look for the slightly comical set of eighteen *luohans*, Buddha's disciples.

Painting and Calligraphy Gallery Hall of Martial Valour (free). Pieces demonstrating the art, skill and beauty of artists and literary aesthetics.

Jade Gallery Palace of Accumulated Purity (free). A selection of intricate jade objects from the Imperial Court.

Gold and Silver Gallery Palace of Great Brilliance (free). Precious religious, decorative, dress and sacrificial items.

Opera Gallery Hall for Viewing Opera (free). Fascinating display of all the finery of the Chinese opera.

Palace of Compassion and Tranquillity (free). Sculpture gallery featuring Tang-dynasty camels, Song wooden Bodhisattvas showing a heavy Indian influence, and life-sized ceramic *arhats* from the Ming dynasty.

Kunning Gong
坤宁宫, kūnnínggōng

Kunning Gong, the Palace of Earthly Tranquillity, is where the emperor and empress traditionally spent their wedding night. By law the emperor had to spend the first three nights of his marriage, and the first day of Chinese New Year, with his wife. The palace is a bizarre building, partitioned in two. On the left is a large sacrificial room with its vats ready to receive offerings (1300 pigs a year under the Ming). The wedding chamber is a small room, off to one side, painted entirely in red, and covered with decorative emblems symbolizing fertility and joy. It was last pressed into operation in 1922 for the child wedding of Pu Yi, the last emperor, who, finding it "like a melted red wax candle", decided that he preferred the Yangxin Dian (see below).

Yangxin Dian
养心殿, yǎngxīndiàn

The **Yangxin Dian**, or Mind Nurturing Palace, is one of a group of palaces west of the living quarters, where emperors spent most of their time. Several of the palaces retain their furniture from the Manchu times, most of it eighteenth century; in one, the **Changchungong** (Palace of Eternal Spring), is a series of paintings illustrating the Ming novel, *The Dream of Red Mansions*.

Palace of Longevity and Health
寿康宫, shòukāng gōng

The auspiciously-named **Palace of Longevity and Health** complex was built for Qianlong's mother in 1736; the centrepiece is a red sandalwood throne from 1771, made by Suzhou craftsmen to celebrate her eightieth birthday. The pleasantly small-scale adjoining apartments, with their carpets, tasteful hangings and screens, are a relief from the rest of the Forbidden City; there's a feeling you could actually live a normal life here, not just as a pawn in some vast gilded cage. A few select treasures are on display in a side wing, including scroll painting and copy of the *Heart Sutra* by Qianlong, the latter in gold ink on blue paper – he was a much finer calligrapher than artist.

The Imperial Garden

From the Inner Court, the Kunningmen (Gate of Terrestrial Tranquillity) opens north onto the **Imperial Garden**, by this stage something of a respite from the elegant buildings. There are a couple of **cafés** here amid a pleasing network of ponds, walkways and pavilions, designed to be reminiscent of southern Chinese landscapes. In the middle of the garden, the **Qin'an Dian**, or Hall of Imperial Tranquillity, was where the emperor came to worship a Taoist water deity, Xuan Wu, who was responsible for keeping the palace safe from fire. You can exit here into Jingshan Park, which provides an overview of the complex (see p.79).

Tian'anmen Square

天安门广场, tiān'ānmén guǎngchǎng • Daily sunrise–sunset • Free • Subway line #1 to Tian'anmen East, Exit D or subway line #2 to Qianmen, Exit A

For many Chinese tourists, gigantic **Tian'anmen Square** is a place of pilgrimage. Crowds flock to gaze at Chairman Mao's **portrait** on Tian'anmen gate, then head south to see the fellow himself (maybe) in his **mausoleum**, quietly bowing their heads by the **Monument to the People's Heroes** en route. The square itself is plain, searingly hot in summer and rather dull considering its colourful recent history (see box, p.76). It's worth popping by at **sunrise** or **sunset**, when the national flag at the northern end of the square is raised in a military ceremony. Crowds are usually large for both. Be aware that security barriers surround the square, and all bags have to be scanned at gateways; you might also be body-searched or have to show ID.

1

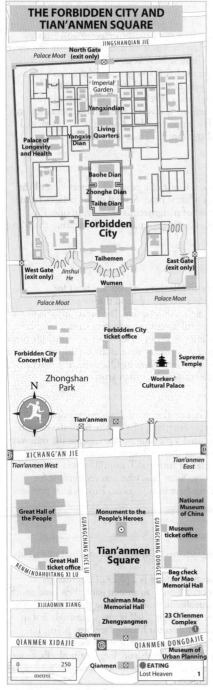

THE FORBIDDEN CITY AND TIAN'ANMEN SQUARE

Tian'anmen

天安门, tiānānmén • Daily 8.30am–4.30pm • ¥15 • Buy tickets from the Forbidden City ticket office (see p.70)

Tian'anmen, the "Gate of Heavenly Peace", was once the main entrance to the Forbidden City. The boxy gatehouse is familiar across the world, and occupies an exalted place in Chinese communist iconography, appearing on banknotes, coins, stamps and indeed virtually any piece of state paper you can imagine. As such, it's a prime object of pilgrimage, with many visitors milling around waiting to be photographed in front of the large **portrait of Mao** (one of the very few still on public display), which hangs over the central passageway.

Reviewing Platform

From the **Reviewing Platform** above Tian'anmen, Mao delivered the liberation speech on October 1, 1949. For the entrance fee you can climb up to this platform yourself, where security is tight – all visitors have to leave their bags, are frisked and have to go through a metal detector before they can ascend. Inside, the fact that most people cluster around the souvenir stall selling official certificates of their trip reflects the fact that there's not much to look at.

The parks

Tian'anmen is flanked by two **parks**: Zhongshan to the west, and the grounds of the Workers' Cultural Palace to the east. These are great places to escape the rigorous formality of Tian'anmen Square, not to mention the crowds of the Forbidden City.

Zhongshan Park

中山公园, zhōngshān gōngyuán • Entrances on Xichang'an Jie and Nanchang Jie • **Park** Daily 6am–9pm • ¥3 • **Flower exhibition and Huifang Garden** Daily 9am–4.30pm • ¥5 • Subway line #1 to Tian'anmen West

The delightful **Zhongshan Park** boasts the ruins of the **Altar of Land and Grain**, a site of biennial sacrifice during the Qing and Ming dynasties. It was built during Yongle's reign in 1420, and hosts harvest-time events closely related to those of the Temple of Heaven (see p.89). You'll have to pay extra for the **flower exhibition** and the **Huifang Garden**; the former is a greenhouse full of so-so blooms, while the latter is a beautiful, bamboo-strewn section of the park.

Workers' Cultural Palace

劳动人民文化宫, láodòng rénmín wénhuàgōng • Entrances on Dongchang'an Jie and Nanchizi Dajie • Daily 6.30am–7.30pm • ¥2, or ¥15 including Front Hall • ⓦ www.bjwhg.com.cn • Subway line #1 to Tian'anmen East

The **Workers' Cultural Palace** is far smaller than the Forbidden City, but also far more manageable, infinitely less crowded, and equally lovely in parts – proof of sorts is provided by its status as Beijing's number-one venue for wedding photos. The park is centred on the **Supreme Temple** (太庙, tài miào), today a sort of Forbidden City annexe; this is a stupendously beautiful place, though you'll need an extra ticket to peek inside the first of its three halls (the other two are, sadly, closed off). Surrounding these are a number of exhibition halls, often worth checking out for their temporary art shows.

Monument to the People's Heroes

人民英雄纪念碑, rénmín yīngxióng jìniànbēi

Towards the northern end of Tian'anmen Square is the **Monument to the People's Heroes**, a 38m-high **obelisk** commemorating the victims of the revolutionary struggle. Its foundations were laid on the October 1, 1949, the day that the establishment of the People's Republic was announced. Bas-reliefs illustrate key scenes from China's revolutionary history; one of these, on the east side, shows the Chinese burning British opium (see p.931) in the nineteenth century. The calligraphy on the front is a copy of Mao Zedong's handwriting and reads "Eternal glory to the Heroes of the People". The platform on which the obelisk stands is guarded, and a prominent sign declares that commemorative gestures, such as the laying of wreaths, are banned.

Chairman Mao Memorial Hall

毛主席纪念堂, máozhǔxí jìniàntáng • Sept–June Tues–Sun 8am–noon; July & Aug daily 7–11am • Free (bring ID) • Bag & camera deposit on the east side of Tian'anmen Square (¥2–15, depending on size) • No photography

At the centre of the centre of China lies a corpse that nobody dare remove.

Tiziano Terzani, *Behind the Forbidden Door*

Chairman Mao Memorial Hall, Mao's **mausoleum**, was constructed in 1977 by an estimated million volunteers. It's an ugly building that looks like a drab municipal facility and contravenes the principles of Chinese geomancy – presumably deliberately – by interrupting the line from the palace to Qianmen and by facing north. Mao himself wanted to be cremated, and the erection of the mausoleum was apparently no more than a power play by his would-be successor, Hua Guofeng. In 1980 Deng Xiaoping, then leader, said it should never have been built, although he wouldn't go so far as to pull it down.

Much of the interest of a visit here lies in witnessing the sense of awe of the Chinese confronted with their former leader and architect of modern China, who was accorded an almost god-like status during his life. Whatever you might think of Mao personally, the atmosphere inside is of an eerily silent, respectful reverence; you can even buy flowers at the entrance to leave in memoriam (deposit them in the first hall).

Viewing the Chairman

After depositing your bag and camera at the bag check across the road to the east, join the orderly queue of Chinese – almost exclusively working-class out-of-towners – on the northern side. The queue advances surprisingly quickly, and takes just a couple of minutes to file through the chambers. Mao's **corpse**, looking bizarrely sun-tanned and draped in a red flag within a crystal coffin, appears unreal, which it may well be; a wax copy was made in case the preservation went wrong. Mechanically raised from a freezer

1

DISSENT IN TIAN'ANMEN SQUARE

Blood debts must be repaid in kind – the longer the delay, the greater the interest.

Lu Xun, writing after the massacre of 1926

Chinese history is about to turn a new page. Tian'anmen Square is ours, the people's, and we will not allow butchers to tread on it.

Wu'er Kaixi, student, May 1989

It may have been designed as a space for mass declarations of loyalty, but in the twentieth century **Tian'anmen Square** was as often a venue for expressions of popular dissent; against foreign oppression at the beginning of the century, and, more recently, against its domestic form. The first mass protests occurred here on May 4, 1919, when three thousand students gathered in the square to protest at the disastrous terms of the **Versailles Treaty**, in which the victorious allies granted several former German concessions in China to the Japanese. The Chinese, who had sent more than a hundred thousand labourers to work in the supply lines of the British and French forces in Europe, were outraged. The protests of **May 4**, and the movement they spawned, marked the beginning of the painful struggle of Chinese modernization. In the turbulent years of the 1920s, the inhabitants of Beijing again occupied the square, first in 1925, to protest over the **massacre in Shanghai** of Chinese demonstrators by British troops, then in 1926, when the public protested after the government's capitulation to the Japanese. Demonstrators marched on the government offices and were fired on by soldiers.

In 1976, after the death of popular premier Zhou Enlai, thousands of mourners assembled in Tian'anmen without government approval to voice their dissatisfaction with their political leaders, and again in 1978 and 1979 groups assembled here to discuss new ideas of **democracy and artistic freedom**, triggered by writings posted along Democracy Wall on the edge of the Forbidden City. In 1986 and 1987, people gathered again to show solidarity for the **students** and others protesting at the Party's refusal to allow elections.

But it was in **1989** that Tian'anmen Square became the venue for a massive expression of **popular dissent**, when, from April to June, nearly a million protesters demonstrated against the slow pace of reform, lack of freedom and widespread corruption. The government, infuriated at being humiliated by their own people, declared martial law on May 20, and on **June 4** the military moved in. The killing was indiscriminate; tanks ran over tents and machine guns strafed the avenues. No one knows how many died in the massacre – certainly thousands. Hundreds were arrested afterwards and many are still in jail. The event remains a taboo topic; look out for droves of undercover police on the massacre's anniversary.

every morning, it is said to have been embalmed with the aid of Vietnamese technicians who had previously worked on the body of Ho Chi Minh. Apparently, 22 litres of formaldehyde went into preserving his body; rumour has it that not only did the corpse swell grotesquely, but that Mao's left ear fell off during the embalming process, and had to be stitched back on.

Zhengyangmen

正阳门, zhèngyángmén • Daily 8.30am–4pm • ¥20 • Subway line #2 to Qianmen, Exit A

For an overview of Tian'anmen Square, ascend its south gate, **Zhenyangmen**. Similar to Tian'anmen to the north, and 40m high, it gives a good idea of how much more impressive the square would look if Mao's mausoleum hadn't been stuck in the middle of it.

Great Hall of the People

人民大会堂, rénmín dàhuìtáng • Entrance off Tian'anmen Square • Daily when not in session: April–June 8.15am–3pm; July & Aug 7.30am–4pm; Sept–Nov 8.30am–3pm; Dec–March 9am–2pm • ¥30 (bring ID) • Subway line #1 to Tian'anmen West, Exit C or line #2 to Qianmen, Exit C

Taking up almost half the west side of Tian'anmen Square is the **Great Hall of the People**. This is the venue of the National People's Congress, and hundreds of black limos with tinted windows are parked outside when it's in session. When it isn't, it's

OPPOSITE CCTV BUILDING >

1

open to the public: what you see on the mandatory route is a selection of the 29 reception rooms – all looking like the lobby of a Chinese three-star hotel, with badly fitted red carpet and armchairs lined up against the walls.

National Museum of China

中国历史博物馆, zhōngguó lìshǐ bówùguǎn · Entrance off Tian'anmen Square · Tues–Sun 9am–5pm, last ticket 3.30pm · Free (bring ID) · Subway line #1 to Tian'anmen East, Exit D

The monumental building to the east of Tian'anmen Square is now home to the world's largest museum, the **National Museum of China**. Head straight to the lower ground floor, which packs the whole of Chinese history into an exhaustively thorough collection featuring thousands of hard-hitting exhibits; you could easily spend half a day here, though a couple of hours will probably be enough.

Ancient China exhibition

The museum's main attraction is the engrossing **Ancient China exhibition** in the basement, which traces China's history from Neolithic to pre-communist times, heading through the various dynasties in a spellbinding succession of relics. Archeology from just about every province is represented, and it's easy to become overwhelmed; things to look out for include bronze wine vessels from the Western Zhou, a jade shroud and mini terracotta army from the Liao, and a bronze acupuncture statue (and, inevitably, some great porcelain vases) from the Ming.

The other floors

Forget the ironically tiring **Road of Rejuvenation** exhibit on the second floor – a collection of bombastic national messages, paintings of Japanese imperial evil and innumerable photos of red-tied delegations; this one's aimed squarely at the locals. Instead, head upstairs to the third and fourth floors, where you'll find small exhibitions on bronze, jade, porcelain, fans, money and more.

Qianmen

前门, qiánmén · Subway line #2 to Qianmen, Exit C

Just south of Tian'anmen Square is one of Beijing's most famous **gates** – **Qianmen**, an imposing, double-arched edifice dating back to the fifteenth century. Before the city's walls were demolished, this controlled the entrance to the inner city from the outer, suburban sector, and in imperial days the shops and places of entertainment banned from the interior city were concentrated around here.

Museum of Urban Planning

规划博物馆, guīhuà bówùguǎn · Qianmen Dong Dajie · Tues–Sun 9am–5pm · ¥30 · ⓦ www.bjghzl.com.cn · Subway line #2 to Qianmen, Exit B

The quirky **Museum of Urban Planning** is little visited; for some reason, displays on solid waste management and air quality have failed to galvanize the public. Given its focus on the future, it's also laughably old-fashioned – and, on occasion, unintentionally hilarious – but there are definite highlights in three excellent, and very different, mapping exhibits.

The maps

First, and visible on a wall from the escalator, is a fascinating **bronze model** showing the city as it used to look in imperial times, back when every significant building was part of an awesome, grand design. Then comes another TV screen, which slowly spools through a digitized version of an **ancient scroll**, heading through Old Beijing from south wall to north wall, via the Forbidden City. The star attraction, though, is an enormous and fantastically detailed underlit **model of the city** that takes up the entire top floor. At a scale of 1m:1km it covers more than three hundred square metres, and illustrates what the place will look like once it's finished being ripped up and redesigned by 2020.

1

North of the centre

The area **north of the Forbidden City** has a good collection of sights you could happily spend days exploring. Just outside the Forbidden City are **Jingshan and Beihai parks**, two of the finest in China; north of here, the peripheries of the **Shicha Lakes** – Qianhai and Houhai – are filled with bars, restaurants and cafés. These continue east to **Nanluogu Xiang**, an artsy, renovated *hutong* area that has proven wildly popular with young locals out for a stroll; it's somewhere to people-watch over a coffee, and boasts several places to stay.

Around the lakes you'll also find a somewhat older *hutong* district, perhaps the last major one left in the city, and once the home of princes, dukes and monks. Its alleys are a labyrinth, with something of interest around every corner; some regard them as the final outpost of a genuinely Chinese Beijing. Buried deep within them is **Prince Gong's Palace**, with the **Bell and Drum towers**, once used to mark dawn and dusk, standing on the eastern edge of the district.

Jingshan Park

景山公园, jǐngshān gōngyuán • Across from the north gate of the Forbidden City • Daily: April–Oct 6.30am–9pm; Nov–March 6.30am–8pm • ¥2 • Subway line #6 or #8 to Nanluoguxiang, Exit A

Jingshan Park is a natural way to round off a trip to the Forbidden City. An artificial mound, it was created by the digging of the palace moat, and served as a windbreak and a barrier to malevolent spirits (believed to emanate from the north) for the imperial quarter of the city. Its history, most momentously, includes the suicide of the last Ming emperor, **Chong Zhen**, in 1644, who hanged himself here from a locust tree after rebel troops broke into the imperial city. The spot, on the eastern side of the park, is easy to find as it is signposted everywhere, though the tree that stands here is not the original.

As the highest point in all downtown Beijing – though only a tiddly 46m – it's the **views** from the top of the hill that make this park such a compelling target: they take in the whole extent of the Forbidden City – giving a revealing perspective – and a fair swath of the city outside, a deal more attractive than at ground level. To the west is Beihai with its bulbous white stupa and fat, snaking lake; in the north, Gulou and Zhonglou (the Drum and Bell towers); and to the northeast, the Yonghe Gong.

Beihai Park

北海公园, běihǎi gōngyuán • South gate accessed by Wenjin Jie; north gate via Di'anmen Xi Dajie • Daily: April–Oct 6.30am–9pm; Nov–March 6.30am–8pm; sights close 5pm • ¥10; ¥20 including all buildings • Ten-person cruise boats ¥580/hr, or ¥60pp/hr; pedaloes ¥40/hr • Subway line #6 to Beihai North, Exit D, for the north entrance

Over half of **Beihai Park** is water – the lake, stretching over 1km from south to north, is one of the most renowned places in all China to view summertime lotus flowers (only Hangzhou's West Lake is reputedly better), and is Beijing's favourite ice-skating spot in the winter months. The park was supposedly created by Kublai Khan, long before any of the Forbidden City structures were conceived, and its scale is suitably ambitious: the lake was man-made, an island being created in its midst with the excavated earth. Emperor Qianlong oversaw its landscaping into a classical garden, and Mao's widow, the ill-fated Jiang Qing, was a frequent visitor. Today, its willows and red-columned galleries make it a grand place to retreat from the city and recharge.

The Round

Just inside the main gate, which lies on the park's southern side, the **Round**, an enclosure of buildings behind a circular wall, has at its centre a courtyard, where there's a large jade bowl said to have belonged to Kublai Khan. The white-jade Buddha in the hall behind was a present from Burmese Buddhists.

1

NORTH OF THE CENTRE

■ ACCOMMODATION	
Bamboo Garden	1
Courtyard 7	5
Downtown Backpackers	6
The Orchid	3
Peking Youth Hostel	7
Red Lantern House	4
Shatan	9
Sitting on the Walls Courtyard House	8
Sleepy Inn	2

● SHOPPING	
C Rock	1
Plastered T-Shirts	3
Soul Art Shop	2
Three Stone	4

■ DRINKING & NIGHTLIFE	
Dusk Dawn Club (DDC)	5
Great Leap	4
Mao Mao Chong	4
Modernista	1
Pass By Bar	3

● EATING	
Alley Café	7
Café Sambal	1
Café Zarah	4
Dali Courtyard	3
Nuage	6
Shuxiangju	2
Xiao Beijing Jiaozi	5

0   500
metres

Sogo Department Store

Anhuaqiao   THIRD RING ROAD   BEISANHUAN ZHONG LU

Puppet Theatre

N

WAIGUANXIE JIE

GULOU WAI DAJIE

ANDINGMEN WAI DAJIE

QINGNIANGOU LU

Liuyin Park

HUANGSI JIE

HEPINGLI BEI JIE

Rendinghu Park

ANDELI BEI JIE

ANDELI BEI JIE

Qingnianhu Park

Qingnianhu Lake

ANDINGMEN WAI DAJIE

Ditan Swimming Pool

Ditan Park

LINJIA HUTONG

ANDELI NAN JIE

JIUGULOUWAI DAJIE

QINGNIANHU XILUE

JIAOCHANGKOU JIE   LIUPUKANG JIE

GULOU NEI DAJIE

LIUPUKANG NAN HUTONG

Deshengmen Bus Station

DAJING HUTONG

ANDE LU   ANDE LU   ANDE LU

DESHENGMEN DONG BINHE LU

DESHENGMEN DONG DAJIE   ANDINGMEN XI DAJIE

Xu Beihong Museum

XIHAI BEIYAN

Xihai

XIHAI NANYAN

Guloudajie

ZHONGTAO HUTONG   DONGTAO HUTONG   Andingmen   WUDAOYING HUTONG

XITAO HUTONG

Song Qingling's Former Residence

DASHIQIAO HUTONG

XIAOSHIQIAO HUTONG

YONGHENG HUTONG

Confucius Temple

GUOZI JIAN

SHALUO HUTONG

GUOXING HUTONG   JINGTU HUTONG

ANDINGMEN NEI DAJIE

CHENJIANDIAN HUTONG

XIEJIA HUTONG

FANGJIA HUTONG

GULOU XIDAJIE

Wine Museum

DOUFUCHI HUTONG   HUAFENG HUTONG

HOUHAI BEIYAN

Houhai   SHICHA LAKES

JIUGULOU DAJIE

Bell Tower

BAOCHAO HUTONG

BEILUOGU XIANG

JIAODAOKOU

HOUHAI BEIYAN

Drum Tower

GULOU DONGDAJIE

DESHENGMENNEI DAJIE

YANGFANG HUTONG

HOUHAI NAN YAN

YINDING BRIDGE

QIANGULOUYUAN HUTONG   JU'ER HUTONG   XIANG'ER HUTONG

ZHENGJUE HUTONG

DASHIBEI HUTONG   HONGSHAN HUTONG

LIUHAI HUTONG

HOUHAI NAN YAN

YIN DING XIE JIE

HOEYUANENSI HUTONG

SHAJING HUTONG   QIANYUAN'ENSI HUTONG

QIANHAI XI JIE

DAXINKAI HUTONG

JINGYANG HUTONG   QINLAO HUTONG

BEIBINGMASI HUTONG

DI'ANMEN WAI DAJIE

MAO'ER HUTONG

LIUYIN JIE

JIE CHENGXIANG

Prince Gong's Palace

DINGFU JIE

QIANHAI BEIYAN

Qianhai

QIANHAI NANYAN

YU'ER HUTONG   DONGMIANHUA HUTONG

BANCHANG HUTONG

CHAODOU HUTONG

FU XUE HUTONG

HUGUOSI JIE

XINGHUA HUTONG

LONGTOUJING JIE

QIANHAI XIJIE

Shichahai

FUXIANG HUTONG

Penghao Theatre

Beihai North

DI'ANMEN XIDAJIE   DI'ANMEN DONG DAJIE   ZHANGZI ZHONG LU

Nine Dragon Screen

Nanluoguxiang   XIEZUD. HUTONG

BEIHE HUTONG   SHANLAO HUTONG

Five Dragons Pavilion

XI HUANGCHENGGEN BEI JIE

AIMIN JIE

DONGGUANDAO JIE

BEIHAIBEIJIA QIAO

HUANGHUAMEN KIE

DONGHUANGCHENGGEN BEIJIE

BEI HEYAN HUTONG

MEISHUGUAN HOUJIE

YUQUN HUTONG

Beihai Park

XISHIKU DAJIE

NAFU HUTONG

JINGSHAN HOU JIE

SANYANJING HUTONG

National Art Museum of China

DIANMEN

WANGFUJING DAJIE

The Round

Dagoba

Jingshan Park

JINGSHAN XI JIE

JINGSHAN DONG JIE

SHATAN HOUJIE

WUSI DAJIE

Xishiku Church

XI'ANMEN DAJIE

WENJIN JIE

Zhongnanhai (out of bounds)

North Gate (exit only)   JINGSHAN HOU JIE   JINGSHANQIAN JIE

Capital Theatre

DONGCHANG HUTONG

Forbidden City

The island

From the Round, a walkway provides access to the **island**, which is dotted with buildings – including the **Yuegu Lou**, a hall full of steles (stone slabs carved with Chinese characters); and the giant white **dagoba** (a dumpy Tibetan-style pagoda) sitting on the crown of the hill, built in the mid-seventeenth century to celebrate a visit by the Dalai Lama. It's a suitable emblem for a park that contains a curious mixture of religious constructions, storehouses for cultural relics and imperial garden furniture. Nestling inside the dagoba is a shrine to the demon-headed, multi-armed Lamaist deity, Yamantaka.

North of the lake

On the **north side** of the lake stands the impressive **Nine Dragon Screen**, built in 1402 by the Ming – who were just re-establishing the city after moving the capital to Nanjing (see p.308) – to ward off evil spirits. An ornate wall of glazed tiles, depicting nine stylized, sinuous dragons in relief, it's one of China's largest at 27m in length, and remains in good condition. Nearby are the **Five Dragon Pavilions**, supposedly in the shape of a dragon's spine. Even when the park is crowded at the weekend, the gardens and rockeries near here remain tranquil and soothing – it's easy to see why the area was so favoured by Qianlong. It's popular with courting couples today, some of whom like to dress up for photos in period costume (there's a stall outside the Nine Dragon Screen) or take boats out on the lake.

The Shicha Lakes

24hr • Free • Pedaloes from docks around the lake ¥120/hr • Subway line #8 to Shichahai, Exit A1, or #2 to Jishuitan, Exit B

Just north of Beihai Park are the twin **Shicha Lakes** (什刹海, shíchà hǎi), an appealing, easy-going area protected from city traffic by a narrow belt of *hutongs*. It was once something of an imperial pleasure ground and home to a number of high officials and distinguished eunuchs, with several of their **old mansions** now open to the public (and the sites of many more marked by plaques). Having been dredged and cleaned up in recent times, the lakeshore has become a drinking and dining hotspot, though be warned that the bars and restaurants here are overpriced and their staff rather pushy; it can be more relaxing to rent a pedal-boat and have a drink on that instead. Look too for the hardy locals who swim in the lakes every day; it may be tempting to join in, but foreigners who do so often end up getting sick.

Qianhai and Houhai

Smaller of the two Shicha Lakes, southerly **Qianhai** (前海, qiánhǎi) is joined to elongated **Houhai** (后海, hòuhǎi) by a narrow isthmus spanned by the cute, humpback **Yinding Bridge**; it's not high but from the top you can see the Western Hills on (very rare) clear days. The web of short alleys east of here – especially **Yandai Xie Jie** (烟袋斜街, yāndài xiéjiē) – are packed with little jewellery and trinket shops, somewhere to look for contemporary souvenirs.

Prince Gong's Palace

恭王府, gōngwáng fǔ • Qianhai Xi Jie • Daily: April–Oct 8am–5pm; Nov–March 9am–4pm • ¥40 • Subway line #6 to Beihai North, Exit B, turn left up Sanzuoqiao Hutong, then left at the crossroads

The charming **Prince Gong's Palace** was once the residence of the influential Prince Gong Yixing, brother of Emperor Xianfeng, unwilling signatory to the humiliating Peking Convention of 1860 which ended the Second Opium War, and instigator of a palace coup the following year that brought Empress Dowager Cixi to power. Its many courtyards, joined by covered walkways, have been restored to something like their former elegance. In the very centre is the **Yin'an Dian**, a hall where the most important ceremonies and rites were held; keep a lookout for the sumptuously painted ceiling of **Xi Jin Zhai**, used as a studio by Prince Gong. The northern boundary of the courtyard area is marked by a 151m-long wall; sneak around this and you'll be on the southern cusp of a gorgeous **garden** area, set around an attractive lake.

1

Song Qingling's Former Residence

宋庆龄故居, sòngqìnglíng gùjū • 46 Houhai Beiyan • Daily 9am–4.30pm • ¥20 • Subway line #2 to Jishuitan, Exit B

On the northern shore of Houhai, **Song Qingling's Former Residence** is a Qing mansion with an agreeable, spacious garden. The wife of Sun Yatsen, who was leader of the short-lived republic that followed the collapse of imperial China (see p.932), Song Qingling commands great respect in China, and the exhibition inside details her busy life. The collection of her personal effects, including letters and cutlery, is pretty dry, but check out the revolver Sun Yatsen (obviously not a great romantic) gave his wife as a wedding gift. More interesting is the building itself, whose interior gives a glimpse of a typical Chinese mansion from the beginning of the twentieth century – all the furnishings are pretty much as they were when she died.

Xu Beihong Museum

徐悲鸿纪念馆, xúbēihóng jìniànguǎn • 53 Xinjiekou Bei Dajie • Tues–Sun 9am–noon & 1–5pm • ¥5 • ⑩ www.xubeihong .org/English/museum.htm • Subway line #2 to Jishuitan, Exit C

Just west of the Shicha Lakes, but easily combined with a visit, is the **Xu Beihong Museum**. The son of a wandering portraitist, Xu (1895–1953) did for Chinese art what his contemporary Lu Xun did for literature – modernize an atrophied tradition. Following the death of his father, Xu had to look after his entire family from the age of 17 and spent much of his early life labouring in semi-destitution and obscurity before receiving the acclaim he deserved. His extraordinary talent is well in evidence here in seven halls, which display a huge collection of his works. These include many ink paintings of **horses**, for which he was most famous, and **Western-style oil paintings**, which he produced while studying in France (and that are now regarded as his weakest works); the large-scale **allegorical images** also on display allude to tumultuous events in modern Chinese history. However, the pictures that are easiest to respond to are his delightful sketches and studies, in ink and pencil, often of his infant son.

The Drum and Bell towers

Junction of Gulou Xi Dajie, Gulou Dong Dajie and Di'anmen Wai Dajie • Daily 9am–5pm • ¥20 per tower, or ¥30 combined ticket • Subway line #8 to Shichahai, Exit A2, or line #2 or #8 to Guloudajie, Exit G

These two monstrous, architecturally stunning towers stand directly to the north of the Forbidden City, providing yet more evidence that Beijing was once laid out according to a single, great scheme. Today's city planners have, belatedly, decided to go for something similar; the surrounding area has recently been gentrified, tidying up (and sadly thinning out) the adjoining mesh of *hutongs* – though a wander through the remainder will uncover an unusual **museum** dedicated to Chinese grain spirits, *baijiu*.

Drum Tower

鼓楼, gǔlóu • Drumming hourly 9.30–11.30am & 1.30–4.45pm

The formidable two-storey **Drum Tower**, a squat, wooden, fifteenth-century Ming creation set on a red-painted stone base, is the southern member of the pair. In every city in China, drums were banged to mark the hours of the day, and to call imperial officials to meetings. Nowadays, at regular intervals throughout the day, a troupe of drummers in traditional costume whack cheerfully away at the giant drums inside. They're not, to be blunt, terribly artful, but seeing them in action is still an impressive sight; as is the working replica of an ancient Chinese water clock, a *kelou*. Views from the top are fantastic, particularly after the steep slog up, but unfortunately only the southern end – the one facing the Bell Tower – is open.

Bell Tower

钟楼, zhōnglóu

The **Bell Tower**, at the other end of the small plaza from the Drum Tower, is somewhat different in appearance, being made of stone and a bit smaller. The original structure was of Ming vintage, though the tower was destroyed by fire and rebuilt in the eighteenth century. It still, however, boasts its original iron bell, which, until 1924, was rung every evening at 7pm to give an indication of the time. A sign by the bell relates the legend of its creation: the bell-maker was under threat of execution for being unable to cast such a complex artefact, when at the last moment his daughter, **Hua Xian**, jumped into the molten mix – with added girl, the bell cast perfectly. The unobstructed panoramas from the top are even better than those from the Drum Tower – again, it's a short but tough pant up.

Wine Museum

北京乾鼎老酒博物馆, běijīng gāndǐng lǎojiǔ bówùguǎn • 69 Zhaofu Jie, Zhangwang Hutong • Daily 9am–4.30pm • ¥29 • ⏰ www.dwwine.cn • Subway line #8 to Shichahai, Exit A2

Despite being tucked away down a side street you can't miss the eccentric **Wine Museum**, given its side wall studded in metre-high wine jars. Inside, the whole single-floor display is crammed with glass cabinets of **Chinese grain spirits**, *baijiu*, all arranged by province. Foreigners find *baijiu* something of an acquired taste – aside from its sheer strength (often 50° proof or above), it has a distinctively raw aroma – but famous labels like Maotai or Wuliangye are essential for toasts at any Chinese banquet. Most bottles here date from the 1980s, but one is eighteenth century and a couple – they're the earthenware bottles in the Guizhou cabinet – are from the Ming dynasty (before 1644).

Nanluogu Xiang

南锣鼓巷, nánluógǔ xiàng • Subway line #6 to Nanluoguxiang, Exit E

There aren't, to be frank, too many streets in Beijing that could be called attractive, but the pedestrianized north–south *hutong* of **Nanluogu Xiang** is an exception. Lined with trees, dotted with cafés, boutiques and restaurants, it has become a prime strolling street for teenagers and the city's bright and beautiful young things, partly because there's a drama school just around the corner. Unfortunately, Nanluogu Xiang's crushing popularity might be its downfall: in the evenings it's hard to walk from one end of the street to the other in less than half an hour, tour groups have already been banned and there's talk of putting in gates to limit the numbers of visitors. You might want to explore the alleys shooting off to the east and west instead, where there are enough open-air mahjong games, rickety family-owned stores, and old men sitting out with their caged birds to maintain that ramshackle, backstreet Beijing charm.

East of the centre

Beijing's **eastern districts** are the most cosmopolitan and fashionable parts of the city. Just east of Tian'anmen, the madcap shopping district of **Wangfujing** buzzes by day and evening, while the pretentious bars and restaurants of **Sanlitun**, to the northeast, crackle until a far later hour. Although the best places to see contemporary Beijing in action, neither areas have much in the way of traditional sights, so step forward **Yonghe Gong** and the **Confucius Temple**, Beijing's two most attractive religious complexes. Yet even here there are plenty of eating and drinking options: the lanes either side of these temples – the most obvious of which is up-and-coming **Wudaoying Hutong** – are dotted with boutique cafés and low-key bars.

Yonghe Gong

雍和宫, yōnghé gōng • Yonghegong Bei Dajie • Daily: April–Oct 9am–4.30pm; Nov–March 9am–4pm • ¥25 • Subway line #2 or #5 to Yonghegong Lama Temple, Exit C

You won't see many bolder or brasher temples than **Yonghe Gong**, built towards the end of the seventeenth century as the residence of Prince Yin Zhen. In 1723, when the prince became Emperor Yong Zheng and moved into the Forbidden City, the temple was retiled in imperial yellow and restricted thereafter to religious use. It became a

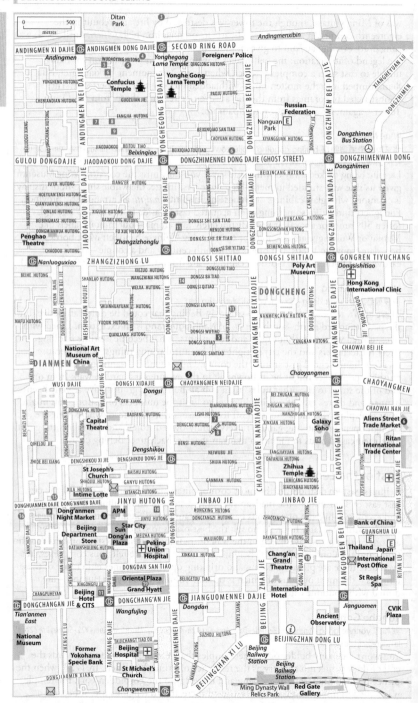

Map labels

Century Theatre
Westin Chaoyang Hotel
Liangmaqiao
LIANGMAQIAO LU
International SOS Clinic
XINDONG LU
XINYUAN NAN LU
Lufthansa Centre
International Medical Center
Shuizhui Lake
LIANGMA QIAO LU
Liangma River
Landmark Towers
Chaoyang Park
WAI XIEJIE
DONGZHIMEN WAI XIAO JIE
Kazakhstan
British Council library
3.3 Mall
Kyrgyzstan
NONGZHANGUAN BEI LU
SANLITUN BEI LU
DONGSANHUAN BEI LU
MAIZIDIAN JIE
South Africa
Nali Mall
SANLITUN NANLU
Australia
Canada
Sanlitun Village Complex
DAJIE
Lao
Myanmar
Agricultural Exhibition Centre
Agricultural Exhibition Center
Tai Koo Li South
THIRD RING ROAD
GONGREN TIYUCHANG BEILU
XINFUCUN ZHONGLU
SEE INSET RIGHT FOR DETAILS
3.3 Mall
SANLITUN
Nali Mall
Sanlitun Village Complex
Tai Koo Li South
Beijing Chaoyang Golf Club
Nanhu Lake
Bodhi Spa
Yashow Clothing Market
Tuanjiehu
BEILU
NONGZHANGUAN NAN LU
GONGREN TIYUCHANG XILU
Workers' Stadium
Sanlitun Soho
SANLITUN NANLU
NANSANLITUN LU
DONGSANHUAN NAN LU
GONGREN TIYUCHANG DONGLU
BAIJIAZHUANG LU
GONGREN TIYUCHANG NAN LU
Tuanjiehu Park
Dongyue Temple
Dongdaqiao
Hujialou
WAI DAJIE
CHAOYANG BEI DAJIE
GUANDONGDIAN BEI JIE
CHAOWAI NAN JIE
Chaoyang Theatre
CHAOYANGMEN WAIDAJIE
NANYINGFANG HUTONG
FANCAODI BEI HUTONG
North Korea
JINGHUA BEI JIE
ZHAOFENG JIE
Jintaixizhao
SHENLU LU
RITAN LU
JINTONG XI LU
JINTONG DONG LU
New Zealand
Central Park
JINGHUA DONG LU
Ritan Park
RITAN DONG LU
The Place
JINGHUA NAN JIE
CCTV Headquarters
United Kingdom
GUANGHUA LU
DONGSANHUAN ZHONG LU
GUANGHUA LU
HEZHENLU
Mongolia
XIUSHUI BEI JIE
Ireland
China World Trade Centre
LeCool
China World Hotel
Wanda Cineplex
JIANHUA LU
XIUSHUI DONG JIE
Silk Market
Friendship Store
JIANGUOMENWAI DAJIE
Yang'anli
Guomao
JIANGUO LU
Dawanglu
LG Towers
Park Hyatt
TONGHUIHE BEI LU
TONGHUIHE BEI LU
Sihui Bus Station
N
EAST OF THE CENTRE
Shuangjing Subway

Inset (3.3 Mall area)
Shuizhui Lake
3.3 Mall
Nali Mall
SANLITUN NANLU
Sanlitun Village Complex
Tai Koo Li South
GONGREN TIYUCHANG BEILU

● SHOPPING
Aliens Street Market	6
Bookworm	4
Daxin Textiles	5
Dong Liang Studio	7
Foreign Language Bookstore	8
Huashiweiye DVD	1
Jixiangzhai	2
Laos	3
Silk Market	9

■ ACCOMMODATION
Beijing	11
Côte Cour	8
Double Happiness Courtyard Hotel	5
Fly By Knight Courtyard Hostel	7
Ibis Beijing Dongdaqiao	6
Jianguo	12
Kapok	9
Opposite House	1
Park Hyatt	13
Peninsula Palace	10
Red Hotel	3
Sanlitun Youth Hostel	4
Yoyo	2

■ DRINKING & NIGHTLIFE
Arrow Factory	6
Atmosphere	17
Cuju	15
Destination	11
Distillery	8
First Floor	4
Hot Cat Club	8
Jing A Taproom	13
Mesh	1
Migas	3
Modernsky Lab	16
Ramo	7
School Bar	5
Slow Boat Taproom	14
Tiki Bungalow	9
Tree	2
Vics	12

● EATING
Bellagio	1
Bookworm	10
Chuanban	18
Crescent Moon	11
Crystal Jade	2
Dongzhimennei Dong Dajie (Ghost Street)	6
Foodie Town	9
HA (High Altitude Coffee)	7
He Kitchen & Co	5
Jin Ding Xuan	3
Jingzun	8
Justine's	20
Lime	13
Made in China	19
Malacca Legend	14
Qin Tang Fu	12
Renhe	15
Siji Minfu	16
Veggie Table	4
Xiaochi Jie Night Market	17

1

lamasery in 1744, housing monks from Tibet and Inner Mongolia. The temple has supervised the election of the Mongolian Living Buddha (the spiritual head of Mongolian Lamaism), who was chosen by drawing lots out of a gold urn. After the civil war in 1949, Yonghe Gong was declared a national monument and closed for the following thirty years. Remarkably, it escaped the ravages of the Cultural Revolution, and today again serves as a functioning centre for **Tibetan Buddhism**.

The halls

There are five main **prayer halls**, arranged in a line from south to north, and numerous side buildings housing Bodhisattva statues and paintings. The statues in the **Yonghe Hall** (雍和殿, yōnghédiàn), the second one along, are gilded representations of the past, present and future Buddhas, respectively standing to the left, centre and right.

Buddhas of longevity and medicine stand in the third hall, the **Pavilion of Eternal Blessings** (永佑殿, yǒngyòudiàn), though they're far less interesting than the *nandikesvras*, representations of Buddha having sex, in a side room. Once used to educate emperors' sons, the statues are now covered by drapes. The chamber behind, the **Hall of the Wheel of Law**, has a gilded bronze statue of Gelugpa, the founder of the Yellow Hats (the largest sect within Tibetan Buddhism) and paintings that depict his life, while the thrones at its side are for the Dalai Lama (each holder of the post used to come here to teach).

In the last, grandest hall, the **Wanfu Pavilion** (万福殿, wànfúdiàn), stands an 18m-high statue of the Maitreya Buddha, the world's largest carving made from a single piece of wood – in this case, the trunk of a Tibetan sandalwood tree. Gazing serenely out, the giant reddish-orange figure looms over you; details, such as his jewellery and the foliage fringing his shoulders, are beautifully carved. It took three years for the statue, a gift to Emperor Qianlong from the seventh Dalai Lama, to complete its passage to Beijing.

Confucius Temple

孔庙, kǒngmiào • Guozijian Jie • Tues–Sun 8.30am–5pm • ¥30 • Performances April–Oct 10am, 11am, 2pm, 3pm & 4pm • Subway line #2 or #5 to Yonghegong Lama Temple, Exit D

Entered on a quiet *hutong* lined with shops selling incense, images and tapes of religious music, **Confucius Temple** is one of Beijing's most pleasant sights, somewhere to sit on a bench in the peaceful courtyard among the ancient, twisted trees, and enjoy the silence – though there's plenty to look at inside, too. The complex is split into two main areas: the temple proper to the east, and the easy-to-miss, but equally large, old Imperial College to the west.

The temple complex

Constructed in 1306, the **temple** is a charming place filled with red-lacquered halls and gnarled cypresses, some of which are over 700 years old. The buildings themselves are pretty ancient, too; parts of the colossal **Dacheng Hall** date back to 1411. Aside from a courtyard at the back, where you can catch performances of Confucian music, the most popular sight is the long hall containing the **Qianlong stone scriptures**, the Thirteen Classics of the Confucian cannon, consisting of 630,000 characters carved on giant stone steles between 1726 and 1738.

The Imperial College

国子监, guózǐ jiàn

To the west of the temple complex is the old **Imperial College**, the temple's junior by only two years and equally beautiful. After walking through the gigantic main gate, you'll be confronted by the **Memorial Arch**, clad with orange and green tiles and featuring the calligraphy of Emperor Qianlong. Behind this is the **Biyong Hall**, set in a circular lake filled with carp; Qianlong used to give speeches here, backed by an elaborate folding screen. The side halls are now employed as **museums**, covering a diverse range of subjects – it's worth tracking down the Imperial Examination exhibition, which includes a metre-long ribbon covered in microscopic characters, smuggled into the examination cell as a crib sheet by a former candidate.

Ditan Park

地坛公园, dìtán gōngyuán • Main entrance at Guanghua Lu • Daily 6am–9.30pm • ¥2, extra ¥5 for altar and museum • Subway line #2 or #5 to Yonghegong Lama Temple, Exit A

Around 100m north from the Yonghe Gong, **Ditan Park** is more interesting as a place to wander among the trees and spot the odd martial arts performance than for its small **museum** holding the emperor's sedan chair and the enormous **altar** at which he performed sacrifices to the earth.

Dongyue Temple

东岳庙, dōngyuè miào • Chaoyangmen Wai Dajie • Tues–Sun 8am–5pm • ¥40 • Subway line #6 to Dongdaqiao, Exit A

The intriguingly bizarre Dongyue Temple features a large central courtyard holding around thirty annexes, each of which deals with a different aspect of Taoist life, the whole making up a sort of surreal spiritual bureaucracy. There's the "Department of Suppressing Schemes", "Department of Wandering Ghosts", even a "Department for Fifteen Kinds of Violent Death". In each, a deity statue holds court over brightly painted figures, many of demons with monstrous animal heads. Look too for the truly **ancient trees** swamped in auspicious red ribbons in the temple courtyards, dedicated to the patron deity of literature, Wenchang; and also a bronze sculpture of Wenchang's trusty steed, the "Wonder Mule".

Poly Art Museum

保利大厦博物馆, bǎolì dàshà bówùguǎn • Floor 9, Poly Plaza, Dongzhimen Nan Dajie • Mon–Sat 9.30am–4.30pm • ¥50 • ☎ 010 65008117, ⊕ en.polypm.com.cn/english/bwge.php • Subway line #2 to Dongsishitiao, Exit D

Within the **Poly Plaza**, a boring-looking office block, lies the small **Poly Art Museum**, which has one of the most select collections of **antiquities** in the capital. In the hall of ancient bronzes you'll find four of the twelve bronze animals that were **looted from the Old Summer Palace** (see p.97); the pig, tiger, ox and monkey were bought in the West by patriotic businessmen, and their return was much heralded. Another two were returned in 2013, and now take pride of place in the National Museum of China (see p.78); the four here may follow in due course. The second hall displays ancient Buddha statues.

Sanlitun

三里屯, sānlǐtún • Subway line #10 to Tuanjiehu, exits A or D

The most famous **nightlife district** in Beijing, if not all China, **Sanlitun** has come a long way since its first few watering holes opened up on "Bar Street". It's now full to the brim with fancy boutiques and shopping malls, a wonderfully cosmopolitan array of excellent cafés and restaurants, and some of Beijing's trendiest bars. The area is centred on **Tai Koo Li** (太古里, tài gǔ lǐ), a visually splendid mix of upper-class shops, bars and restaurants formally known as "The Village", and still often referred to as such. To the southwest is the **Workers' Stadium** (工人体育场, gōngrén tǐyùchǎng), colloquially known as "Gongti" to Beijingers, and itself surrounded by bars and clubs.

Ritan Park

日坛公园, rìtán gōngyuán • 24hr • Free • Subway line #1 to Yong'anli, Exit A1, or line #6 to Dongdaqiao, Exit D

Just south of the Sanlitun area, and part of Beijing's Central Business District (CBD), is **Ritan Park**, one of the imperial city's original four. Each park was the location for a yearly sacrificial ritual performed by the emperor, but today's Ritan Park is popular with embassy staff and courting couples, who make use of its numerous secluded nooks. It's a very attractive place, with paths winding between groves of cherry trees, rockeries and ponds.

1

The diplomatic district

The **diplomatic district** surrounding Ritan Park has a casual, affluent, cosmopolitan atmosphere thanks to its large contingent of foreigners, many of them staff from the **Jianguomenwai diplomatic compound**, an odd place with neat buildings in ordered courtyards, and frozen sentries on plinths. Though their embassy lies elsewhere, you'll see plenty of Russians (and Cyrillic writing); many have set up shop in this area, most notably in the weird **Ritan International Trade Center** (most of whose shops have closed doors and no customers, and seem to be fronts).

Zhihua Temple

智化寺, zhìhuà sì • 5 Lumicang Hutong • Tues–Sun 8.30am–4.30pm • ¥20, first 200 people free on Wed • Music performances 10am & 3pm • Subway line #2 or #6 to Chaoyangmen, exits G or H

Though a bit dusty and desolate, and hidden away down an obscure back lane, **Zhihua Temple** constitutes the largest collection of wooden Ming-dynasty structures in Beijing. It was founded in 1444 as the family temple of eunuch **Wang Zheng**, a domineering imperial favourite; the original complex was vast, though only four halls now survive along what would have been the central axis. Aside from antique roof beams and a mural of *Dizang and the Ten Kings of Hell* in the main hall, make sure you catch the haunting 15min-long performances of **religious music**, with an orchestra of monks playing gongs, woodwind and bells – a tradition handed down from the Ming dynasty and only recently revived.

Ancient Observatory

古观象台, gǔguānxiàngtái • 2 Dongbiaobei Hutong • Tues–Sun 9am–5pm • ¥20 • ☎ 010 65269468 • Subway line #1 or #2 to Jianguomen, Exit C

The **Ancient Observatory**, an unexpected survivor marooned amid concrete expressways and high-rises, comes as a delightful surprise. Founded in the thirteenth century on the orders of Kublai Khan, it was subsequently staffed by Muslim astronomers until they were displaced by Jesuit missionaries during the Ming dynasty, who astonished the emperor and his subjects by making a series of precise astronomical forecasts. The Jesuits re-equipped the observatory and remained in charge until the 1830s.

The squat, unadorned observatory building – looking much like an isolated section of city wall – was built in 1442 and features eight Qing-dynasty bronze **astronomical instruments** on the top, designed by polymath Ferdinand Verbiest: stunningly sculptural armillary spheres, theodolites and the like, all beautifully ornamented with entwined dragons, lions and clouds. There's also a small **museum** at ground level displaying pottery decorated with star maps, and a courtyard featuring busts of famous **Chinese astronomers**, such as Zhang Heng (who invented the armillary sphere) and Zu Chongzhi (mathematician and plotter of the equinoxes).

Wangfujing

王府井, wángfǔjǐng • Subway line #1 to Wangfujing, exits B, C1 or C2

Wangfujing district is where the capital gets down to the business of **shopping** in earnest. The haunt of quality stores for over a century, it was called Morrison Street before the communist takeover. There are some giant malls here, including the **Oriental Plaza**, which stretches east for nearly a kilometre; sadly the infamous **Donghuamen night market** – which served up scorpions, testicles and the like to generations of disbelieving tourists – closed in 2016.

National Art Museum of China

中国美术馆, zhōngguó měishùguǎn • 1 Wusi Dajie • Daily 9am–5pm • Free (bring ID); charges for special exhibitions • ☎ 010 84033500, ⓦ namoc.org • Dongsi subway (lines #5 & #6)

Bar the shopping, there's little to see in the Wangfujing area except the **National Art Museum of China**, a huge exhibition hall showcasing state-approved artworks. It's not as

1

stuffy as it sounds, now embracing modern trends such as installation and video art, and as there's no permanent display you need to check the website for current offerings; past subjects have included ethnic embroidery from southwestern China, seal carving, and Socialist Realist propaganda posters.

South of the centre

Visitors usually head **south of Tian'anmen Square** for one main reason: the glorious **Temple of Heaven**, a visually arresting ancient building that counts as one of Beijing's must-see sights. However, there's plenty to distract you on your way: of most interest is the earthy, old-fashioned *hutong* area surrounding the famed **Dashilan shopping street** (大栅栏路, dàshílàn lù), which has been Beijing's prime backpacker base for decades, and remains a good area for aimless browsing, snacking and wandering. Forming a neat counterpoint is **Qianmen Dajie**, a shopping street stretching immediately south of Qianmen – a brand-new, though pleasing, pastiche of dynastic styles.

Temple of Heaven

天坛, tiāntán • **Park** Daily 6am–9pm • ¥15 • **Temple** Daily 8am–6pm • ¥35, including park entry • ⓦ en.tiantanpark.com • Subway line #5 to Tiantandongmen, Exit A1

Set 2km south of Tian'anmen, in large, tranquil Tiantan Park, which is full of trees, lawns and wild corners, the **Temple of Heaven** is widely regarded as the pinnacle of Ming design. For five centuries it was at the very heart of imperial ceremony and symbolism, and for many modern visitors its architectural unity and beauty remain more appealing – and on a much more accessible scale – than the Forbidden City.

The temple is easiest to access via the park's east gate, which is the only one close to a subway station. Walking, cycling or coming by bus, you're more likely to enter the park from the north or west. Exiting via the park's west gate, you can head a little north to the Museum of Natural History (see p.92).

Altar of Heaven

The main pathway leads straight to the circular **Altar of Heaven**, consisting of three marble tiers representing (from the top down) heaven, earth and man. The tiers are comprised of blocks in various multiples of nine, cosmologically the most powerful

---

TIANTAN: BETWEEN HEAVEN AND EARTH

Construction of the Temple of Heaven was begun during the reign of Emperor Yongle, and completed in 1420. The temple complex was conceived as the prime meeting point of earth and heaven, and symbols of the two are integral to its design. **Heaven** was considered round, and the **earth** square; thus the round temples and altars stand on square bases, while the park has the shape of a semicircle beside a square. The intermediary between earth and heaven was, of course, the **Son of Heaven** – the emperor, in other words.

The temple was the site of the most important ceremony of the imperial court calendar, when the emperor prayed for the year's harvests at the **winter solstice**. Purified by three days of fasting in the huge, recently restored **Palace of Abstinence**, he made his way to the park on the day before the solstice, accompanied by his court in all its magnificence. On arrival at Tiantan, the emperor would meditate in the Imperial Vault, ritually conversing with the gods on the details of government, before spending the night in the Hall of Prayer for Good Harvests. The following day he sacrificed animals before the Altar of Heaven. It was forbidden for commoners to catch a glimpse of the great annual procession to the temple, and they were obliged to bolt their windows and remain, in silence, indoors. Indeed, the Tiantan complex remained sacrosanct until it was thrown open to the people on the first Chinese National Day of the Republic, in October 1912.

The last person to perform the rites was **General Yuan Shikai**, the second president of the Republic, on December 23, 1914. He planned to declare himself emperor but died a broken man, his plans thwarted by opponents, in 1916.

SOUTH OF THE CENTRE

ACCOMMODATION
365 Inn	1
Leo Hostel	2

SHOPS
Beijing Curio City	4
Neiliansheng Shoes	3
Panjiayuan Market	5
Ruifuxiang	2
Ten Fu	1

EATING
Deyuan	5
Goubuli	4
Liqun	2
Quanjude	3
Starbucks	1

DRINKING
365 Inn	1

number, symbolizing both heaven and emperor. The centre of the altar's bare, roofless top tier, where the Throne of Heaven was placed during ceremonies, was considered to be the middle of the Middle Kingdom – the very centre of the earth. Various acoustic properties are claimed for the altar; from this point, it is said, all sounds are channelled straight upwards to heaven. To the east of the nearby **fountain**, which was reconstructed after fire damage in 1740, are the ruins of a group of buildings used for the preparation of sacrifices.

Imperial Vault of Heaven

Directly north of the Altar of Heaven, the **Imperial Vault of Heaven** is an octagonal structure made entirely of wood, with a dramatic roof of dark blue, glazed tiles. It is

preceded by the so-called **Echo Wall**, said to be a perfect whispering gallery, although the unceasing cacophony of tourists trying it out makes it impossible to tell.

Hall of Prayer for Good Harvests

At the north end of the park, the **Hall of Prayer for Good Harvest**, the principal temple building of the entire complex, amply justifies all this build-up. Made entirely of wood, without the aid of a single nail, the circular structure rises from a tiered marble terrace and has three blue-tiled roofs. Four compass-point pillars, representing the seasons, support the vault, enclosed in turn by twelve outer pillars (one for each month of the year and hour of the day). The dazzling colours of the interior, surrounding the central dragon motif on the coffered ceiling, give the hall an ultramodern look; it was in fact

1

rebuilt, faithful to the Ming design, after the original was destroyed by lightning in 1889. The official explanation for this appalling omen was that it was divine punishment meted out on a sacrilegious caterpillar, which was on the point of crawling to the golden ball on the hall's apex when the lightning struck. Thirty-two court dignitaries were executed for allowing this to happen.

Museum of Natural History

自然博物馆, zìrán bówùguǎn • Tianqiao Nan Dajie • Tues–Sun 10am–5pm • Free • ☎ 010 67020733, ⓦ bmnh.org.cn • Subway line #7 to Zhushikou, Exit C

Just north of Tiantan Park's east gate, the **Museum of Natural History** is highly popular with local and foreign kids alike – they never fail to be impressed by the **dinosaur skeletons**, set amid an array of local fossils. On the upper levels of the building, China's prodigious wealth of animal life is portrayed in stuffed form, while sharks, manta rays and the like zip above your head in the basement **aquarium**.

Museum of Architecture

古代建筑博物馆, gǔdài jiànzhù bówùguǎn • Dongjing Lu, south of Nanwei Lu (look for the red arch) • Tues–Sun 9am–5pm • ¥15, first 200 visitors free on Wed • ☎ 010 63172150, ⓦ bjgjg.com • Subway line #7 to Zhushikou, Exit C

One of Beijing's most underrated attractions, the **Museum of Architecture** is housed in the former **Xiannong Temple**. The temple was founded in 1420, and was where the emperor ritually ploughed a furrow to ensure a good harvest (Xiannong being the Ancestral Farmer) – you can see the gold-plated plough he used in the Hall of Worship. The Hall of Jupiter has a fantastically ornate ceiling and cutaway models of famous buildings from all over the country. Anyone who has ever wondered how a *dougong* works – those ornate interlocking brackets seen on temples – can satisfy their curiosity here. There's also a side wing dedicated to Beijing's *siheyuan* courtyard houses, and a great model of the city as it appeared in 1949, before the communists ripped it up.

Niu Jie Mosque

牛街清真寺, niújiē qīngzhēnsì • Niu Jie • Daily from first to last prayers • ¥10, free for Muslims • Subway line #7 to Guang'anmennei, Exit D, or bus #6 from the north gate of Temple of Heaven Park

Some 3km southwest of Qianmen, **Niu Jie** (Ox Street) is a congested thoroughfare alive with butchers, steamy little restaurants and hawkers selling fried dough rings, rice cakes and *shaobing*, Chinese-style muffins with a meat filling. This is the city's **Muslim quarter**, populated by the **Hui minority** – of which there are nearly 200,000 in the capital – with a focus in the **mosque** on its eastern side, an attractive, colourful marriage of Chinese and Islamic design, with abstract and flowery decorations and text in Chinese and Arabic over the doorways. You won't get to see the handwritten, Yuan-dynasty copy of the Koran without special permission, or be allowed into the main prayer hall if you're not a Muslim, but you can inspect the courtyard, where a copper cauldron, used to cook food for the devotees, sits near the graves of two Persian imams who came here to preach in the thirteenth century. Also in the courtyard is the "tower for viewing the moon", which allows imams to ascertain the beginning and end of Ramadan, the Muslim period of fasting and prayer.

West of the centre

The area **west of the Forbidden City** is rarely visited by Western tourists, partly because Beijing's best restaurants and places to stay lie elsewhere. However, there's enough tucked away here to entertain the curious. Tourism drops off sharply west of the Forbidden City, partly because the attractions are widely scattered, but mostly because this is Beijing's financial district, and first impressions are of oversized main roads, glistening office blocks and alienating acres of concrete paving. However, there's enough tucked away here to entertain the curious for a few days: a number of wonderful temples, a fine museum and a pair of appealing parks, as well as the city's principal zoo and aquarium.

National Centre for Performing Arts

中国国家大剧院, zhōngguó guójiā dàjùyuàn • 2 Xichang'an Jie • ☎ 010 66550000, Ⓦ en.chncpa.org • Subway line #1 to Tian'anmen West, Exit C

Immediately west of the Great Hall of the People (see p.76) lies the **National Centre for the Performing Arts**, which opened up in 2007. Designed by French architect Paul Andreu and nicknamed – for obvious reasons – the "Egg", this glass and titanium dome houses a concert hall, two theatres and a 2500-seat opera house (see p.113).

Capital Museum

首都博物馆, shǒudū bówùguǎn • Fuxingmenwai Dajie • Tues–Sun 9am–5pm • Free (bring ID) • ☎ 010 63370491, Ⓦ en.capitalmuseum.org.cn • Subway line #1 to Muxidi, Exit C1

The gigantic **Capital Museum** is a real beauty, both inside and out. Its most interesting feature is a massive bronze cylinder, which shoots diagonally down through the roof as if from heaven. It's a huge place, and walking between the various exhibits will take some time, but despite this the layout is actually quite simple: Beijing exhibition halls are in the **cube**, cultural relics in the **cylinder**. If you're short on time or energy, skip the cube and head for the rarer pieces in the cylinder instead.

The cylinder: galleries

The ground-floor **gallery** in the **cylinder** holds Ming and Qing paintings, mostly landscapes. The calligraphy upstairs can be safely missed unless you have a special interest, but the bronzes on level three are pretty interesting: a sinister third-century-BC owl-headed dagger, for example, or the strangely modern-looking three-legged cooking vessels decorated with geometrical patterns – which are more than three thousand years old. The display of jade on the fourth floor is definitely worth lingering over; some astonishing workmanship has gone into the buckles, boxes and knick-knacks here, and the white quail-shaped vessels are particularly lovely.

The cube: exhibition halls

The **cube of exhibition halls** on the building's west side can be travelled around rather faster than those in the cylinder. The bottom level hosts a confusing show on the history of Beijing – there aren't enough English captions to make any sense of the exhibition – while the models of historical buildings on the next level up can be skipped in favour of the exhibition of old Beijing's folk traditions and artistry on Floor 5, with life-sized mock-ups of entire houses, and lively dioramas of street life and festival processions.

Baiyun Guan

白云观, báiyún gùan • Off Baiyun Lu • Daily 8.30am–4.30pm • ¥10 • Subway line #1 to Muxidi, C1

Once the most influential Taoist centre in the country, **Baiyun Guan**, the White Cloud Temple, has been extensively renovated after a long spell as a military barracks and is now the headquarters for the influential Quanzhen (Complete Reality) Sect. There are thirty resident monks, and it's become a popular place for pilgrims, with a busy, thriving feel to it. Among a few unusual features, check out the three gateways at the entrance, symbolizing the worlds of Taoism – Desire, Substance and Emptiness – and three monkeys depicted in relief sculptures around the temple. It's said to be lucky to find all three: the first is on the gate, easy to spot as it's been rubbed black, and the other two are in the first courtyard. The place is at its most colourful during the New Year temple fair (see p.49).

1

Military Museum

军事博物馆, jūnshì bówùguǎn • Fuxing Lu • Tues–Sun 8.30am–5pm • ¥8 • ☏ 010 66866244, ⊕ eng.jb.mil.cn • Subway line #1 or #9 to Military Museum, Exit A

The almost brutally old-fashioned **Military Museum** – full of big, bad communist art and politically laboured captions such as "Hall of Agrarian Revolutionary War" – was undergoing a total facelift at the time of writing, though should have reopened by the time you read this. In the meantime, hangars have been set up in the courtyard where you can see tanks, fighter jets and even a couple of small gunboats, mostly of Cold War vintage.

Baita Temple

白塔寺, báitǎ sì • Fuchengmennei Dajie • Tues–Sun 9am–5pm • ¥20 • Subway line #2 to Fuchengmen, Exit B, or line #4 to Xisi, Exit A

The massive white **dagoba** of this famous temple is visible from afar, rising over the rooftops of the labyrinth of *hutongs* that surround it. Shaped like an upturned bowl with an inverted ice-cream cone on top (the work of a Nepali architect), the 35m-high dagoba was built in the Yuan dynasty; it's a popular spot with Buddhist pilgrims, who ritually circle it clockwise. The temple's main sight is the collection of thousands of small statues of Buddha – mostly Tibetan – housed in one of its halls, very impressive en masse. Another hall holds bronze *luohans* (Buddha's original group of disciples), including one with a beak; small bronze Buddhas; and other, outlandish Lamaist figures.

Lu Xun Museum

鲁迅博物馆, lǔxùn bówùguǎn • 19 Gongmenkou Er Tiao, off Fuchengmennei Dajie • Tues–Sun 8am–5pm • Free (bring ID) • ⊕ www.luxunmuseum.com.cn • Subway line #2 to Fuchengmen, Exit B

A large and extensively renovated courtyard house, this museum was once home to **Lu Xun** (1881–1936), widely accepted as the greatest Chinese writer of the modern era. He gave up a promising career in medicine to write books, with the aim, so he declared, of curing social ills with his pithy, satirical stories. Lu Xun bought this house in 1924, but as someone who abhorred pomp, he might feel a little uneasy here nowadays. His possessions have been preserved like treasured relics, giving a good idea of what Chinese interiors looked like at the beginning of the twentieth century, and there's a photo exhibition lauding his achievements. Unfortunately there are no English captions, though a bookshop on the west side of the compound sells English translations of his work, including his lauded *The True Story of Ah Q*.

Beijing Zoo

动物园, dòngwùyuán • Xizhimenwai Dajie • Daily: April–Oct 7.30am–6pm; Nov–March 7.30am–5pm • ¥15, or ¥18 including pandas, children under 1.2m free • ☏ 010 68390274, ⊕ www.bjzoo.com • Subway line #4 to Beijing Zoo

Beijing Zoo is most worth visiting for its panda house. Here you can join the queues to have your photo taken sitting astride a plastic replica of the creature, then push your way through to glimpse the living variety – kept in relatively palatial quarters and familiar through the much-publicized export of the animals to overseas zoos for mating purposes. There are other Chinese rarities too – bar-headed geese, golden monkeys – plus tigers, otters and a children's zoo, with plenty of farmyard animals and ponies to pet. While many of the cages are relatively drab, there are far worse zoos both in China and outside.

Wuta Temple (aka Zhenjue Temple)

五塔寺, wútǎ sì, 真觉寺, zhēnjué sì • Wutasi Lu, off Zhongguancun Nan Dajie • Daily 9am–4.30pm • ¥20, free to first 300 visitors on Wed • Subway line #4 or #9 to National Library subway, Exit C

Canal-side **Wuta Temple** boasts a central hall radically different from any other sacred building you'll see in the capital. Completed in 1424, it's a stone cube decorated on the outside with reliefs of animals, Sanskrit characters, and Buddha images – each has a different hand gesture – and topped with five layered, triangular spires. It's visibly Indian in influence, and is said to be based on a temple in Bodhgaya, where Buddha gained enlightenment. There are 87 steps to the top, where you can inspect the spire

1

carvings at close quarters – including elephants and Buddhas, and, at the centre of the central spire, a pair of feet. The new halls behind the museum are home to statues of bulbous-eyed camels, docile-looking tigers, puppy-dog lions and the like, all collected from the spirit ways of tombs and long-destroyed temples.

Wanshou Temple

万寿寺, wànshòu sì • Guangyuanzha Lu • Daily 9am–4pm • ¥20, free to first 300 visitors on Wed • Subway line #4 or #9 to National Library, Exit A

A Ming construction that was once a favourite of the Dowager Empress Cixi (see box, p.96), **Wanshou Temple** is the last survivor of the several dozen places of worship which once lined the canal-sides all the way up to the Summer Palace. It's now a small museum of ancient art, with five exhibition halls of Ming and Qing relics, mostly ceramics – not something to cross town for, but it's certainly worth popping by if you're in the area.

The far north

Beijing's far northern quarters are home to a number of attractions. In the city's northwest corner is the wonderful **Summer Palace**, an imperial retreat which has retained the charm of centuries gone by; Beijing's main **university district** lies nearby, and exudes a somewhat different atmosphere. Heading east will bring you to the **Olympic area**, a touch neglected since the heady summer of 2008. East again, and on the way to the airport, is the **798 Art District**, once the cradle of China's contemporary art scene, though now rather commercial.

The Summer Palace

颐和园, yíhé yuán • Several entrances, but most commonly accessed from the north or east • Daily 8am–7pm; buildings close at 5pm • Park ¥20; plus buildings ¥60 • Subway line #4 to Xiyuan C2 (east) or Beigongmen, Exit D (north); also accessible by boat (see box below)

One of Beijing's must-see attractions, the **Summer Palace** is a lavish imperial playground whose grounds are large enough to have an almost rural feel. During the hottest months of the year, the court would decamp to this perfect location, the site surrounded by hills, cooled by the sizeable Kunming Lake and sheltered by judicious use of garden landscaping. Today it functions as a lovely public park.

The palace buildings, many connected by a suitably majestic gallery, are built on and around **Wanshou Shan** (Longevity Hill), north of the lake and west of the main gate. Many of these edifices are intimately linked with **Empress Dowager Cixi** – anecdotes about whom are the stock output of the numerous tour guides – but to enjoy the site, you need know very little of its history: like Beihai (see p.79), the park, its lake and pavilions form a startling visual array, akin to a traditional Chinese landscape painting brought to life.

Brief history

There have been imperial summer pavilions at the Summer Palace since the eleventh century, although the present park layout is essentially eighteenth-century, created by the Manchu Emperor Qianlong. However, the key character associated with the palace is Cixi, who ruled over the disintegrating Chinese empire from 1861 until her death in

---

BY BOAT TO THE SUMMER PALACE

The fastest route to the Summer Palace is by subway, but there's also a **boat service** from Huangdichuan wharf (皇帝船码头, huángdìchuán mǎtóu; departures hourly 10am–4pm; ¥40), tucked away behind the Beijing Exhibition Centre just east of Beijing Zoo, that takes the old imperial approach along the now dredged and prettified Long River. Your vessel is either one of the large, dragon-shaped cruisers or a smaller speedboat holding four people, passing the Wuta Temple, Zizhuyuan Park, and a number of attractive bridges and willow groves en route.

1

EMPRESS DOWAGER CIXI

Born in 1835 to a minor Manchu official, Cixi entered the imperial palace at 15 as Emperor Xianfeng's **concubine**, quickly becoming his favourite and bearing him a son. When the emperor died in 1861, she became regent, ruling in place of her boy for the next 25 years through a mastery of intrigue and court politics. When her son died of syphilis, she installed her nephew as puppet regent, imprisoned him, and retained her authority. Her fondness of extravagant gestures (every year she had ten thousand caged birds released on her birthday) drained the state's coffers, and her deeply conservative policies were inappropriate for a time when the nation was calling out for reform.

With foreign powers taking great chunks out of China's borders through the latter part of the nineteenth century, Cixi was moved to respond by supporting the xenophobic **Boxer Movement** (see p.932). After the Boxers laid siege to Beijing's foreign legation quarter – an act that saw Beijing invaded and then looted by foreign armies – Cixi and the emperor Guangxu disguised themselves as peasants and fled to Xi'an, where they stayed for two years. On her return, Cixi clung to power, attempting to delay the inevitable fall of her dynasty. One of her last acts before she died in 1908 was to arrange for Guangxu's murder.

1908. The Summer Palace was very much her pleasure ground; it was she who resurrected the site in 1888 after the Old Summer Palace (see opposite) had been destroyed by Western forces during the Opium Wars.

The palaces

The **palaces** are built to the north of the lake near the **East Gate**, on and around Wanshou Shan, and many remain intimately linked with Cixi. The main compound includes the **Renshou Dian**, a majestic hall where the empress gave audience. It contains much of the original nineteenth-century furniture, including an imposing throne. Beyond, to the right, is the **Dehe Yuan** (Palace of Virtue and Harmony), dominated by a three-storey **theatre**, complete with trap doors for the appearances and disappearances of the actors. Theatre was one of Cixi's main passions and she sometimes took part in performances, dressed as Guanyin, the goddess of mercy. The next major building along the path is the **Yulan Tang** (Jade Waves Palace), where the emperor Guangxu was kept in captivity for ten years at Cixi's orders. Just to the west is the dowager's own principal residence, the **Leshou Tang** (Hall of Joy and Longevity), which houses Cixi's hardwood throne, and the table where she took her infamous 108-course meals. The chandeliers were China's first electric lights, installed in 1903 and powered by the palace's own generator.

The Long Corridor and Kunming Lake

Boats for hire at any of the jetties ¥40/hr • Winter ice skate hire at the main entrance ¥10 per hour

From Leshou Tang, the **Long Corridor** runs to the northwest corner of **Kunming Lake**. Flanked by various temples and pavilions, the corridor is actually a 700m covered walkway, its inside walls painted with more than eight thousand images of birds, flowers, landscapes and scenes from history and mythology. Near the west end of the corridor is Cixi's ultimate flight of fancy, a magnificent lakeside pavilion in the form of a 36m-long **marble boat**, boasting two decks. Constructed using funds intended for the Chinese navy, it was regarded by Cixi's acolytes as a characteristically witty and defiant snub to her detractors, though her misappropriations caused China's heavy naval defeats during the 1895 war with Japan. Close to the marble boat is a **jetty** – the tourist focus of this part of the site – with rowing boats for hire. In winter, the Chinese **skate** on the lake here – a spectacular sight, as some of the participants are really proficient.

The south of the park

It's a pleasant fifteen-minute walk from the marble boat to the southern part of Kunming Lake, where the scenery is wilder and the crowds thinner. Should you need a destination, the main attraction to head for is the white **Seventeen-Arch Bridge**, 150m long and topped with 544 cute, vaguely canine lions, each with a slightly different posture. The bridge leads to **South Lake Island**, where Qianlong used to review his navy, and which holds a brace of fine halls, most striking of which is the **Yelu Chucai Memorial Temple**.

Yuanmingyuan (Old Summer Palace)

圆明园, yuánmíng yuán • Qinghua Xilu • Daily 8am–6pm; buildings close at 5pm • Park ¥10, all-inclusive ticket ¥25 • Subway line #4 to Yuanmingyuan, Exit B

Beijing's original **summer palace**, the elegant, European-style **Yuanmingyuan** was designed by Jesuit architects during the early eighteenth century for the Qing Emperor Kangxi. Once nicknamed China's Versailles, the palace boasted the largest royal gardens in the world, containing some two hundred pavilions and temples set around a series of lakes and natural springs.

Today the extensive landscaped gardens remain, but the entire palace complex was destroyed by British and French troops in 1860, in retaliation for mistreatment of prisoners during the Opium Wars (see p.931). The troops had previously spent twelve days looting the imperial treasures, an unedifying history described in inflammatory terms on signs all over the park. Still, don't let that put you off, as the overgrown ruins are rather appealing and unusual.

There are actually three sections to the park, centred around Fuhai Lake; all together this forms an absolutely gigantic area, but the most impressive ruins, **Xiyanglou** (西洋楼, xīyáng lóu), are about 1.5km from the entrance up in the northeastern section. The stone and marble fragments hint at how fascinating the original must once have been, with its marriage of European Rococo decoration and Chinese motifs.

Dazhong Temple

大钟寺, dàzhōng sì • Beisanhuan Xi Lu • Tues–Sun 8.30am–4.30pm • ¥15 • Subway line #13 to Dazhongsi, Exit A

The **Dazhong Temple** houses one of Beijing's most interesting little exhibitions, showcasing several hundred **bronze bells** from temples all over the country. These are considerable works of art, their surfaces enlivened with embossed texts in Chinese and Tibetan, abstract patterns and images of storks and dragons. The odd, scaly, dragon-like creature shown perching on top of each bell is a *pulao*, a legendary animal supposed to shriek when attacked by a whale (the wooden hammers used to strike the bells are carved to look like whales). The shape of Chinese bells dampens vibrations, so they only sound for a short time and can be effectively used as instruments: you can buy CDs of the bells in action.

King of Bells

The Dazhong Temple derives its name from the enormous bell hanging in the back (*dazhong* means big bell); this Ming creation, known as the **King of Bells**, is as tall as a two-storey house. Hanging in the back hall, it is, at fifty tonnes, the biggest surviving bell in the world, and can reputedly be heard up to 40km away. You can climb up to a platform above it to get a closer look at some of the 250,000 Chinese characters on its surface, and join visitors in trying to throw a coin into the small hole in the top.

Olympic Park

奥林匹克公园, àolínpǐkè gōngyuán • Subway line #8 or #15 to Olympic Park, Exit A2, or line #8 to Forest Park South Gate, exits A or B

China used the 2008 Olympics to make an impact on the world stage, and facilities built for the occasion were accordingly lavish. The **Olympic Park** – a 1.5km-long strip of concrete paving with the **National Stadium** and **Aquatics Center** at one end, and the entrance to the **Forest Park** at the other – was placed on the city's north–south axis, to be bang in line with the Forbidden City. In addition, subway line #8 (eight being a highly auspicious number in China) was built for the occasion.

1

National Stadium

奥林匹体育馆, àolínpǐkè tǐyùguǎn • Daily: April–Oct 8.30am–7pm; Nov–March 9am–5.30pm • General entry and museum ¥50, full ticket ¥110

The 90,000-seater **National Stadium**, nicknamed the "Bird's Nest" on account of its exterior steel lattice, was built at a cost of over US$400m by Herzog & de Meuron, with input from Ai Weiwei. It made a grand stage for many memorable events, including the spectacular opening display, but since the Olympics it hasn't seen much use, hosting a couple of concerts and football games, and a winter theme park; it's eventually expected to become part of a larger shopping and event complex.

National Aquatics Center

国家游泳中心, guójiā yóuyǒng zhōngxīn • Daily: April–Oct 9am–8pm; Nov–March 9am–5.30pm • ¥30 • Swimming pool Mon–Fri 12.30–5.30pm, Sat & Sun 9am–5.30pm, 2hr maximum stay • ¥60

Next door to the National Stadium, the **National Aquatics Center** quickly became known as the Water Cube, thanks to its bubble-like exterior membrane. Part of it is now occupied by the **Beijing Watercube Waterpark** which, though expensive, is a lot of fun; it holds several pools, with wave machines, water slides, diving and an Olympic-sized competition pool.

Forest Park

奥林匹克森林公园, àolínpǐkè sēnlín gōngyuán • Daily: March 15–Nov 15 6am–9pm; Nov 16–March 14 6am–8pm • Free • Subway line #8 to Forest Park South Gate, exits A or B

North from the sports facilities along the sterile, blazing concrete corridor lies **Forest Park**, a real oasis of picturesque calm: 680 hectares of recently landscaped woodland, lakes and cheerful flowerbeds, divided into north and south sections by the Fifth Ring Road. You could spend a pleasant few hours wandering around the footpaths here – there are marked walking circuits of 3–10km in length; and, as very few people get past the entrance area, it's easy to have a quiet time.

798 Art District

798艺术区, qījiǔbā yìshùqū • Daily 24hr • Free • Subway line #14 to Jiangtai, Exit B, then walk north for 15min

Though it's way out on the way to the airport, the **798 Art District** is a hotspot for Beijing's arty crowd. Originally this huge complex of Bauhaus-style buildings was an electronics factory, built by East Germans; when that closed down in the 1990s, artists moved in and converted the airy, light and, above all, cheap spaces into studios. As the Chinese art market blossomed, **galleries** followed, then **boutiques** and **cafés** – a process of gentrification that would take fifty years in the West, but happened here in about five. The city government – terrified of unfettered expression – initially wanted to shut the area down, but now that 798's emphasis is ever more commercial, the future of the place looks secure.

Visiting 798

The 798 district has the feel of a campus, with a grid of pedestrianized, tree-lined streets dotted with wacky sculptures – a caged dinosaur, a forlorn gorilla – and the gnarliness of the industrial buildings (those in "Power Square" are particularly brutal) softened by artsy graffiti. It's surprisingly large, but there are maps throughout. **Exhibitions** open every week, and every art form is well represented – though with such a lot of it about, it varies in quality. Many galleries close on Monday. Note that, unlike all other Beijing sites, it's actually better on the weekend, when there's a real buzz about the place; on weekdays it can feel a little dead.

ARRIVAL AND DEPARTURE

BEIJING

Beijing's arrival points are well connected to the city's transport network, with the **airport** and major **train stations** all on the subway system. Not all **bus stations** or accommodation are so conveniently located, however, so you could well end up

1

AIRPORT TRANSPORTATION

By taxi You'll be pestered in the arrivals hall by charlatan taxi drivers; ignore them and use the official ranks outside. A taxi between the airport and city centre will cost ¥70–150, and takes 50min–1hr 30min, depending on traffic.

By subway The "Airport Express" light rail runs from T3 and stops at T2 (connected by a walkway and free shuttle bus to T1); it then hits Sanyuanqiao (on line #10), before terminating at Dongzhimen (on lines #2 and #13). The ride from the airport to Dongzhimen takes about 30min from T3, and 20min from T2; tickets cost ¥25. The trains run every 15min, 6.30am–10.30pm. If you want to continue your journey from Dongzhimen by taxi, note that drivers at the Dongzhimen exit commonly gouge new arrivals, so walk a little way and hail a taxi from the street.

By bus Airport buses (¥16) to the city depart from T3, stopping at T2 and T1 on the way; buy tickets from desks inside the terminals. They leave regularly on eleven routes; the most useful are line #1 for Guomao, and line #3 for Dongzhimen and the main train station. The same routes return to the airport from the city. Journeys take at least 1hr each way.

taking a **taxi**: walking to your hotel isn't really an option, as distances are always long, exhausting at the best of times and unbearable with luggage. Leaving Beijing, you can get just about anywhere in China via the extensive air and rail systems, though you'd be advised to buy a ticket a few days in advance, especially during the summer or around Spring Festival (and note that you need a Tibet permit before buying **tickets to Lhasa** – see p.878). Few visitors travel long-distance by bus, though it has the advantage that you can usually just turn up and get on, as services to major cities are frequent.

BY PLANE

Beijing Capital International Airport (北京首都机场, běijīng shǒudū jīchǎng; ⓦen.bcia.com.cn) sits 29km northeast of the centre, serving both international and domestic flights from its three terminals (T1, T2 and T3) – if you're departing, make sure you know which you need before heading to the airport. There are banks and ATMs here; get some small change if you're planning to take any buses.

Destinations Baotou (1hr 30min); Changchun (2hr); Changsha (2hr 30min); Chengdu (3hr); Chongqing (3hr); Dalian (1hr 20min); Dandong (1hr 40min); Fuzhou (3hr); Guangzhou (3hr 15min); Guilin (3hr 10min); Guiyang (3hr 15min); Haikou (3hr 45min); Hangzhou (2hr 10min); Harbin (1hr 25min); Hefei (2hr); Hohhot (1hr 10min); Hong Kong (3hr 20min); Huangshan (2hr); Ji'nan (1hr 10min); Kunming (3hr); Lanzhou (2hr 30min); Lhasa (4hr); Luoyang (1hr 55min); Nanchang (2hr 30min); Nanjing (2hr); Nanning (3hr 30min); Qingdao (1hr 15min); Qiqihar (2hr); Sanya (4hr); Shanghai (1hr 55min); Shenyang (1hr 30min); Shenzhen (3hr 20min); Taiyuan (1hr 15min); Ürümqi (4hr); Wenzhou (2hr 25min); Wuhan (2hr 15min); Wuyishan (2hr 30min); Xiamen (2hr 50min); Xi'an (2hr); Xining (2hr 35min); Yinchuan (2hr); Zhangjiajie (3hr); Zhengzhou (1hr 50min).

BY TRAIN

Beijing has four useful train stations: Beijing, North, West and South, with the latter two hosting the most high-speed services. Tickets can be bought at the stations or, with a small surcharge, from hotels, travel agents and rail ticket outlets; as always, you'll need your passport to book

and board. The stations are all large, busy and have poor signage; arrive with plenty of time to spare, especially if buying tickets or collecting pre-paid tickets. All stations have left-luggage offices and are within taxi range of central accommodation.

Beijing (北京站, běijīng zhàn) is just southeast of the city centre on subway line #2. It handles relatively slow services to northeastern China and Shanghai – aside from Shanhaiguan and Chengde, there's almost nowhere you can't get to faster from another station – and international routes to Moscow and Ulaan Baatar (see p.34 for details).

Destinations Baotou (7 daily; 8hr–14hr); Beidaihe (many daily; 2–6hr); Changchun (many daily; 6hr 15min–16hr); Chengde (4 daily; 4hr 30min–6hr 30min); Dalian (9 daily; 6hr 30min–14hr); Dandong (2 daily; 14–22hr 30min); Harbin (many daily; 7hr 30min–21hr); Hohhot (7 daily; 6hr 30min–11hr 15min); Shanghai (3 daily; 15–22hr); Shanhaiguan (many daily; 2hr 35min–7hr 15min); Shenyang (many daily; 5–11hr).

Beijing North (北京北站, běijīng běi zhàn) is a minor terminal northwest of the centre, near Xixhimen subway station (lines #2, #4 & #13), with a useful service to Badaling on the Great Wall (see p.120) and a slow one to Hohhot.

Destinations Badaling (many daily; 1hr 15min); Hohhot (3 daily; 8hr 15min–11hr 40min).

Beijing South (北京南站, běijīng nán zhàn) is a modern terminus southwest of the centre on subway lines #4 and #14, handling the majority of high-speed trains to eastern China, including frequent departures to Tianjin and Shanghai.

Destinations Fuzhou (6 daily; 8–11hr); Hangzhou (14 daily;

5hr–6hr 40min); Ji'nan (many daily; 1hr 30min–2hr 30min); Nanjing (many daily; 3hr 40min–9hr 30min); Qingdao (13 daily; 4hr 30min–5hr 10min); Qufu (many daily; 2–3hr); Shanghai (many daily; 4hr 45min–12hr); Tai'an (22 daily; 2hr); Tianjin (many daily; 34–50min); Xiamen (3 daily; 11hr).

Beijing West (北京西站, běijīng xī zhàn) is west of the centre on subway lines #7 and #9, and handles normal and high-speed services to southern, central and western destinations – including direct trains to Hong Kong (book at least six days in advance) and Lhasa.

Destinations Baotou (5 daily; 12–17hr); Changsha (many daily; 5hr 40min–22hr); Chengdu (6 daily; 14–31hr); Chongqing (5 daily; 12–31hr); Datong (4 daily; 6hr); Guangzhou (9 daily; 8–30hr); Guilin (4 daily; 10hr 40min–29hr); Guiyang (8 daily; 8hr 45min–33hr); Hohhot (7 daily; 6hr 35min–10hr); Hong Kong (1 daily; 11–24hr); Kunming (2 daily; 34–45hr); Lanzhou (6 daily; 17–28hr); Lhasa (daily; 40hr 30min); Luoyang (many daily; 4–12hr); Nanchang (8 daily; 8–19hr); Nanning (5 daily; 13–31hr); Taiyuan (many daily; 2hr 30min–13hr); Ürümqi (1 daily; 31hr 30min); Wuhan (many daily; 4hr 15min–17hr 30min); Xi'an (many daily; 4hr 25min–18hr); Zhengzhou (many daily; 2hr 30min–9hr).

BY BUS

Beijing has many long-distance bus stations, each one serving only a few destinations. However, there's little point travelling far from Beijing by bus; even where there's no direct high-speed trains to your destination, it's often quicker to take one to the nearest city, and a local bus from there. The most useful options are listed below; if you arrive at any other station, it's generally best to catch a taxi to the nearest subway.

Dongzhimen (东直门公共汽车站, dōngzhímén gōnggòng qìchēzhàn) is a station northeast of the centre on subways lines #2 and #13, and is of most use for buses to Chengde.

Sihui (四惠公共汽车站, sìhuì gōnggòng qìchēzhàn) is in the southeast on subway line #1, and is good for buses to Chengde (3hr 30min–4hr).

GETTING AROUND

Beijing's scale militates against taking "bus number 11" – Chinese slang for walking – almost anywhere. The **bus and subway systems** are extensive, though you need to be wary of pickpockets and many visitors quickly tire of the heaving rush-hour crowds and take rather more taxis than they'd planned – they're still cheap. A **transport card** (¥20 deposit, plus a minimum ¥20 charge-up), available at all subway stations, can be used on the subway, airport express, public buses and even a few taxis; you get fifty percent off bus fares.

BY SUBWAY

Clean, efficient and very fast, the subway (see map, p.102) currently numbers nineteen lines and is by far the most convenient method of public transport – but come prepared for poor signage (it helps to know the next station or terminus in the direction you're heading) and lengthy hikes between interchange platforms. It operates daily from 5.30am–11pm, and entrances are marked by a logo of a square inside a "G" shape; you're obliged to pass bags through an airport-style scanner on entry, and you might be body scanned at some stations. Tickets cost ¥2 per journey from station ticket offices, or when using a transport card. All stops are marked in English or *pinyin*, and announced in English after Chinese.

BY BUS

Services generally run 5.30am–11pm every day, though some operate 24hr. Routes are efficiently organized, though none is marked in English at the stops or on the buses – unless you speak Chinese, or can find an English-speaker, you may have to rely on luck, or instructions from your hotel or a tourist office.

City bus and trolleybus Even though the city's 200-plus bus and trolleybus services run extremely regularly, you'll find getting on or off at busy times hard work (rush hours are 7–9am & 4.30–8pm). The fare for ordinary buses is ¥2, or an incredibly cheap ¥1 when using a travel card. Buses numbered #201–215 only provide night services.

Tourist bus These look like ordinary buses but have their numbers written in green and operate April–Oct, several

---

BIKING AROUND BEIJING

Chinese cycling pace is **sedate**, and with good reason. Chinese roads are unpredictable and at times fairly lawless, with aggressive trucks that won't get out of the way, impatient taxi drivers in the cycle lane, buses veering suddenly towards the pavement, and jaywalkers aplenty. Still, riding around Beijing is less daunting than riding around many Western cities, as there are bike lanes on all main roads; you'll be in the company of plenty of other cyclists. **Ringing your bell** is sometimes the only way of letting someone know you're there, even if they can actually see you. At junctions, cyclists cluster together and then cross en masse when strength of numbers forces other traffic to give way. If you feel nervous, just dismount and walk the bike across.

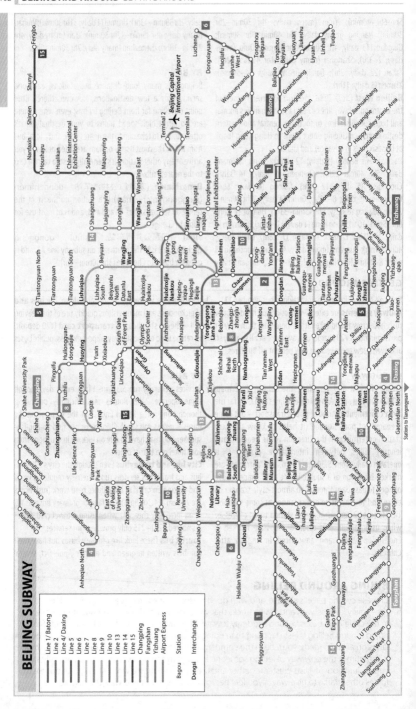

BEIJING SUBWAY

Line 1/ Batong
Line 2
Line 4/ Daxing
Line 5
Line 6
Line 7
Line 8
Line 9
Line 10
Line 13
Line 14
Line 15
Changping
Fangshan
Yizhuang
Airport Express

Bagou ○ Station
Dongsi ◉ Interchange

times an hour 9am–5pm, between the city centre and certain attractions. Routes #1 and #2 (¥15) circuit via Tian'anmen, the Forbidden City, Beihai Park, Dazhilan and elsewhere around the centre; while Route #3 (¥15) heads out to the Drum Tower, National Stadium, Yuanmingyuan and the Summer Palace.

BY TAXI

Taxis cost ¥2.3 per kilometre, with a minimum fare of ¥13. Using a taxi after 11pm will incur a surcharge of twenty percent. Drivers are generally honest (except the ones who hang around transport links); the main problem is getting one at all during rush hour, downpours or in popular nightspots like Sanlitun – see p.55 for useful phone apps.

BY BIKE

As a positive alternative to relying on public transport, it's worth renting a bike at a daily charge of ¥20–50 and a deposit of ¥200–500 – if the nearest hostel can't help out, try the operators below. You can also buy used bikes for

about ¥400 from shops all over town; a good bet is the strip of bike shops on the south side of Jiaodaokou, just west of the Ghost Street restaurants (see p.109). See p.39 for general cycling advice.

Alley Coffee 寻常巷陌, xúncháng xiàng mò. 61 Shatan Hou Jie, just east of Jingshan Park ☏010 84047228. Backpacker-friendly café with good bikes for rent by the day.

Bike Beijing 康多自行车店, kāngduō zìxíngchē diàn. 81 Beiheyuan Da Jie, not far from the Forbidden City or Wangfujing ☏010 65265857, ⓦbikebeijing .com. Guided tours in and around the city; mountain biking through the Fragrant Hills and trips to the Great Wall (cycle there, then hike). Helpful, with good English spoken. Rental ¥100 per day.

Natooke 固定齿轮自行车, gùdìng chǐlún zìxíngchē. 19-1 Wudaoying Hutong, near the Lama and Confucius temples ☏010 84026925, ⓦnatooke .com. Bike repairs, sales and rental, either by the hour (¥20) or ¥80 per day.

INFORMATION

Tourist information Hostels are generally the best source of information, even putting many top hotels to shame in this regard. However, the city's official website (ⓦwww.ebeijing.gov.cn) is also surprisingly informative.

Magazines and newspapers The *China Daily* (¥2), available from higher-end hotels, has a listings section detailing cultural events. Much more useful are the free magazines aimed at the large expat community, which contain up-to-date and fairly comprehensive event, entertainment and restaurant listings. Look for *The Beijinger* (ⓦthebeijinger.com), *That's Beijing*

(ⓦthatsmags.com/beijing), *City Weekend* (ⓦcityweekend .com.cn/beijing) and *Time Out* (ⓦtimeoutbeijing.com), all of which give addresses in *pinyin* and Chinese; you can pick up copies in most bars and other expat hangouts.

Maps In these days of mobile phone apps and good subway connections, maps are less vital than before. There is, however, a wide variety available from hotels and bookshops, while street vendors also sell (mostly Chinese) maps too.

Travel agents CITS (ⓦcits.net) are at 103 Fuxingmen Nei Dajie (☏010 66011122); also in the *Beijing Hotel*, 33

CITY TOURS

Organized tours of the city and its outskirts run by accommodation or generic agents such as CITS offer a painless way of seeing the main sights quickly; the price will include lunch and a tour guide and start around ¥460 per person. The following offer quirkier alternatives:

Beijing Sideways (ⓦbeijingsideways.com). Dash around Beijing in a side-car, its adjoining motorbike driven by a local expat. Plenty of options available, including *hutong* tours, night tours, and trips to the Great Wall.

Bike Beijing (ⓦbikebeijing.com). Offers some excellent bicycle tours of Beijing and its surrounding area, from half-day *hutong* trips to 15-day grassland journeys.

China Culture Center (ⓦchinaculturecenter.org). Varied schedule, including guided tours around obvious sights, themed excursions and occasional limited-number day-trips to remoter places like Cuandixia (see p.129).

The China Guide (ⓦthechinaguide.com). In addition to China-wide tours, they also run Great Wall and tailor-made city excursions lasting 1–4 days.

Granite Studio (ⓦgranitestudio.org). Works with The Hutong (see below), but also organizes private guided walks and themed discussions around the city.

★**The Hutong** (ⓦthehutong.com). This excellent outfit runs some interesting tours, including informative culinary and tea-market trips.

Tours By Locals (ⓦtoursbylocals.com). Worldwide network of tours guided by local residents, with over sixty listings for Beijing.

1

Dongchang'an Jie (☎010 65120507), and the *New Century Hotel* (☎010 68491426), opposite the zoo. They offer expensive tours, a tour guide and interpreter service, and advance ticket booking for trains, planes and ferries (the latter from Tianjin). Travel Stone (☎010 56707485, ⓦtravel-stone.com) are a recommended independent agent, and about the only place in Beijing where you can buy plane tickets with cash.

ACCOMMODATION

Unlike many cities in China, Beijing offers plenty of atmospheric, memorable **places to stay**, whatever your budget – especially those inside *siheyuan* courtyard houses, mostly scattered through the *hutong* district north of the centre. The city's cheapest beds are, of course, in **hostel dormitories**, though note that private rooms inside ordinary **urban hotels** are often cleaner, more comfortable and cheaper than a hostel double. Most of the **mid-range and high-class hotels** are east of the centre, strung out along the international shopping streets of Wangfujing and Jianguomen or clustered around subway stations. Further north, the Sanlitun district has some good accommodation options too, with plenty of places to eat and drink nearby.

HOSTELS

Beijing has a tremendous wealth of hostels, most of them clean and professionally run. You can expect them to feature a lounge with a TV and a few DVDs, self-service laundry (¥15 or so), and bike rental (around ¥20 a day). They will also offer tours to sights outside the city such as the Great Wall, and will arrange train and plane tickets for a small commission (¥40 at most). Don't be put off if you don't fit the backpacker demographic; there are a few slightly pricier options in which you won't hear Bob Marley or see tables filled with empty Qingdao bottles.

NORTH OF THE CENTRE

Downtown Backpackers 东堂青年旅舍, dōngtáng qīngnián lǚshè. 85 Nanluogu Xiang ☎010 84002429, ⓦbackpackingchina.com; subway line #6 or #8 to Nanluoguxiang, Exit E; map p.80. Long-time backpacker favourite, located among the artsy boutiques of Beijing's trendiest – and most overcrowded – *hutong*; you won't be short of eating and nightlife options. There are a couple of single rooms and doubles, some with balconies (¥320), which get rapidly booked up. Dorms **¥70**, doubles **¥260**

Peking Youth Hostel 北平国际青年旅舍, běipíng guójì qīngnián lǚshè. 113-2 Nanluogu Xiang ☎010 84039098, ⓦpeking.hostel.com; subway line #6 or #8 to Nanluoguxiang, Exit E; map p.80. Purpose-built hostel with immaculate rooms (including a women-only dorm for ¥10 extra); there's some great people-watching to be enjoyed from the rooftop café, the downstairs component of which is extremely popular with passers-by. Difficult to justify the steep price though. Dorms **¥130**, doubles **¥500**

★**Red Lantern House** 红灯笼客栈, hóngdēnglong kèzhàn. 5 Zhengjue Hutong ☎010 83285771, ⓦredlanternhouse.com; subway line #4 to Xinjiekou, Exit C; map p.80. A converted courtyard house in an engaging market area, close to Houhai. The main building offers reception, restaurant/bar and dorms; these open straight on to the social area and can be noisy. A separate building about 250m west has simple, airy and spotless en-suite doubles with floral wallpaper; it's much quieter

overall and there's a small courtyard to sit around in. Dorms **¥85**, doubles **¥300**

Sitting on the Walls Courtyard House 城墙客栈, chéngqiáng kèzhàn. 57 Nianzi Hutong ☎010 64027805, ⓦwww.beijingcitywalls.com; subway line #6 to Nanluoguxiang, Exit A; map p.80. Converted courtyard house that offers a bit of character, friendly staff, pets and dodgy plumbing. It's very central, just behind the Forbidden City, though a little tough to find first time; most taxi drivers won't know where it is. Wend your way through the alleyways, following the signs. Dorms **¥100**, doubles **¥420**

Sleepy Inn 丽舍什刹海国际青年旅店, lìshè shíshàhǎi guójì qīnnián lǚdiàn. 103 Deshengmennei Dajie ☎010 64069954; subway line #2 to Jishuitan, Exit B; map p.80. This homely place has a great (if tricky-to-find) location, beside a canal just off Xihai Lake, and is probably the most laidback of Beijing's hostels. A good terrace, pleasant café and helpful staff make up for slightly overpriced rooms; the dorms are good value, though. Dorms **¥100**, doubles **¥380**

EAST OF THE CENTRE

Fly By Knight Courtyard Hostel 夜奔北京四合院客栈, yèbēn běijīng sìhéyuàn kèzhàn. 6 Dengcao Hutong ☎010 41095935; subway line #5 or #6 to Dongsi, Exit C; map pp.84–85. Superb courtyard hostel, tucked into an atmospheric *hutong* area east of the Forbidden City. It's a small, boutiquey place, and thus gets booked up early; those lucky enough to bag a room or bed will benefit from a relaxed atmosphere, punctuated with occasional martial arts lessons. Dorms **¥180**, doubles **¥550**

Sanlitun Youth Hostel 三里屯青年旅舍, sānlìtún qīngnián lǚshè. Off Chunxiu Lu ☎010 51909288, ⓦsanlitun.hostel.com; subway line #2 to Dongsishitiao, Exit B; map pp.84–85. Most notable for being the closest hostel to Sanlitun, this is a friendly place that boasts a good bar of its own. The only problem for most backpackers is its distance from the nearest subway station. Dorms **¥55**, doubles **¥250**

SOUTH OF THE CENTRE

365 Inn 365 安怡之家宾馆, 365 ānyí zhījiā bīnguǎn. 55 Dazhalan Xijie ☎010 63085956, ⓦchina365inn.wixsite.com/365inn; subway line #2 to Qianmen, Exit C; map pp.90–91. Highly popular place on the bustling Dazhalan strip. Its warren of rooms are cheery and relatively spacious, though guests tend to spend more time in the street-facing restaurant, which morphs into a busy bar come evening. Dorms **¥80**, doubles **¥270**

★**Leo Hostel** 广聚园青年旅舍, guǎngjùyuán qīngnián lǔshè. 52 Dazhalan Xijie ☎010 63031595, ⓦleohostel.com; subway line #2 to Qianmen, Exit C; map pp.90–91. The best hostel on Dazhalan, and particularly popular with younger backpackers on account of its cheap bar and fun vibe. Leafy and attractive communal spaces make up for rooms that are slightly tatty round the edges; some of the dorms can be a bit cramped. It's easy to find, and a short walk from Tian'anmen Square and the Forbidden City. Dorms **¥75**, doubles **¥380**

WEST OF THE CENTRE

Chinese Box Courtyard Hostel 团圆四合院客栈, tuányuán sìhéyuàn kèzhàn. 52 Xisi Beiertiao ☎010 66186768, ⓦchinesebox.hostel.com; subway line #4 to Xisi, Exit A; map pp.68–69. Charming little family-run courtyard hotel, hidden behind a sturdy red door in a *hutong*. It only has a couple of rooms, so you'll certainly need to book ahead; the dorms are pricey, but the incongruously luxurious double rooms are among the best in their range. There are daily events such as musical performances, tea tastings and "dumpling parties". Small breakfast included. Dorms **¥150**, doubles **¥550**

★**Kelly's** 凯丽家, kǎilì jiā. 25 Xiaoyuan Hutong ☎010 66118515, ⓦkelly'scourtyard.com; subway line #4 to Xisi, Exit D; map pp.68–69. Sympathetically restored courtyard home with friendly management, right at the end of a quiet *hutong* cul-de-sac. The comfortable en-suite rooms – arranged around a warm, glassed-in terrace – are just a little on the small size, but this is the only quibble and it's good value for the price. **¥446**

HOTELS
NORTH OF THE CENTRE

Bamboo Garden 竹园宾馆, zhúyuán bīnguǎn. 24 Xiaoshiqiao Hutong ☎010 58520088, ⓦbbgh.com.cn; subway line #2 or #8 to Guloudajie, Exit E; map p.80. A quiet courtyard hotel in a *hutong* close to the Drum and Bell towers featuring charming, bamboo-filled gardens. It was converted from the residence of a Qing official, and most rooms boast a smart mix of contemporary and classical Chinese decor, though the cheapest options are rather small. **¥780**

Courtyard 7 秦唐府客栈七号院, qíntángfǔ kèzhàn qīhàoyuàn. 7 Qiangulouyuan Hutong ☎010 64060777, ⓦcourtyard7.com; subway line #8 to Shichahai, Exit C; map p.80. Rooms in this courtyard hotel off Nanluogu Xiang might be on the small side for the price – and the few "economic" options (¥560) are also windowless – but they are all elegantly furnished, with four-poster beds and colourful, tiled bathrooms. **¥900**

The Orchid 65 Baochao Hutong ☎010 84044818, ⓦtheorchidbeijing.com; subway line #8 to Shichahai, Exit C; map p.80. Located on newly popular Baochao *hutong*, this is one of the best boutique hotels in the whole city. Its modern, minimalist rooms, all dark wooden floors and crisp white walls, are arranged around a delightful courtyard; their rooftop area offers superlative sunset views, and staff will encourage you to drink one of their delicious house cocktails up there. **¥1200**

Shatan 沙滩宾馆, shātān bīnguǎn. 28 Shatan Hou Jie ☎010 84026688, ⓦshatanhotel.com; subway line #6 or #8 to Nanluoguxiang, Exit A; map, p.80. Absolutely ordinary mid-range Chinese hotel, but it's well-located at the edge of a *hutong* district close to Jingshan Park, rooms are large, comfortable and clean, and online rates are better than hostel doubles – though their cheapest rooms lack windows. **¥450**

EAST OF THE CENTRE

Beijing 北京饭店, běijīng fàndiàn. 33 Dongchag'an Jie ☎010 65137766, ⓦwww.chinabeijinghotel.com .cn; subway line #1 to Wangfujing, Exit C2; map pp.84–85. Beijing's most central hotel, just east of Tian'anmen Square, and one of the most recognizable buildings in the city, with a ludicrously over-decorated entranceway. There's a huge pool, smart but bland rooms, and unbeatable views over the Forbidden City from the top floors of the west wing. **¥1200**

Côte Cour 演乐宾馆, yǎnyuèbīnguǎn. 70 Yanyue Hutong ☎010 65237981, ⓦhotelcotecourbj.com; subway line #5 or #6 to Dongsi, Exit C; map pp.84–85. Fourteen-room courtyard-style boutique hotel, in the middle of the city but in a quiet *hutong*. Skilfully decorated in oriental chic, it's a place to consider for style and character rather than lavish facilities. Call in advance and they'll arrange a taxi to pick you up, though drivers sometimes won't go down the alley – meaning a 5min walk. **¥1268**

Double Happiness Courtyard Hotel 阅微庄宾馆, yuèwēizhuāng bīnguǎn. 37 Dongsi Sitiao ☎010 64007762, ⓦhotel37.com; subway line #5 or #6 to Dongsi, Exit B; map pp.84–85. Located down a narrow, bustling alley, this courtyard hotel has larger rooms than most, with wooden floors and the usual traditional Chinese carved and lacquered decor. The courtyards are attractive, with red lanterns and plenty of foliage. **¥990**

Ibis Beijing Dongdaqiao 宜必思酒店, yíbìsī jiǔdiàn. 30 Nansanlitun Lu ☎010 65088100,

1

w accorhotels.com; subway line #6 to Dongdaqiao, Exit B; map pp.84–85. A reliably cheap option, whose sparsely-furnished rooms are surprisingly large and comfortable for the price. Sanlitun's bars and restaurants are only 10min up the road. **¥380**

Jianguo 建国饭店, jiànguó fàndiàn. 5 Jianguomenwai Dajie ☏010 65002233, w hotel jianguo.com; subway line #1 to Yong'anli, Exit B; map pp.84–85. Well run and good-looking, though not overly ostentatious, with many of the rooms arranged around cloistered gardens. The restaurant, *Justine's* (see p.109), has some of the best French food in the city, and the Silk Market is close by. Many walk-in rates only include breakfast for one. **¥1000**

★**Kapok** 木棉花酒店, mùmiánhuā jiǔdiàn. 16 Donghuamen Dajie ☏010 65259988, w kapokhotel beijing.com; subway line #1 to Wangfujing, Exit C2; map pp.84–85. Swish boutique hotel just east of the Forbidden City, with clean lines, glass walls and a bamboo theme giving it a distinctive, modish look. It's quite a walk to the nearest subway, but overall it's chic, well located and good value. **¥700**

Opposite House 瑜舍, yúshè. Sanlitun Lu ☏010 64176688, w www.theoppositehouse.com; subway line #10 to Tuanjiehu; map pp.84–85. This trendy modern hotel is filled with modern Chinese art, thanks to its connections with UCCA (see p.115). Rooms offer minimalist chic with no stinting on comfort; bathrooms have oakwood tubs and waterfall showers. It's just around the corner from Sanlitun, so there's no shortage of restaurants and nightlife in the area. There's no sign on the outside – look for the green building next to the 3.3 Mall. **¥2300**

Park Hyatt 柏悦酒店, bóyuè jiǔdiàn. 2 Jianguomenwai Dajie ☏010 85671234, w beijing .park.hyatt.com; subway line #1 or #10 to Guomao, Exit D; map pp.84–85. One of the most architecturally masterful hotels in the city, set atop a toy-like series of blocks illuminated rather beautifully at night. Rooms here offer all the pared-down luxury you'd expect of the chain, and there are stupendous views from all sides. There's a great bar and restaurant up top, and *Xiu* bar down below. **¥1700**

Peninsula Palace 王府饭店, wángfǔ fàndiàn. 8 Jingyu Hutong ☏010 85162888, w peninsula .com; subway line #5 to Dengshikou, Exit A; map pp.84–85. Discreet local representative of this famous upmarket Hong Kong chain, within walking distance of the Forbidden City. Clever use of space means the Deluxe rooms – barely more expensive than their base rate – have the feeling of a suite. **¥2400**

Red Hotel 红驿栈, hóngyìzhàn. 10B Taiping Zhuang, Dongzhimenwai Dajie, Chunxiu Lu ☏010 64171066, w www.red-hotel.com; subway line #2 to Dongsishitiao, Exit B; map pp.84–85. Modern, clean, friendly budget hotel surrounded by inexpensive restaurants, whose rooms and whole ambience are a cut above what you'd expect at this price. Not much English spoken. **¥350**

Yoyo 优优客酒店, yōuyōu kè jiǔdiàn. Due east of 3.3 Building ☏010 64173388, w www.yoyohotel.cn; subway line #10 to Tuanjiehu, Exit A; map pp.84–85. A lovely little boutique-style hotel, located just a hop, skip and jump from Sanlitun on a (surprisingly) quiet alley. Rooms may be minuscule, but considering the location you won't do any better for the price. **¥399**

THE FAR NORTH

Aman@Summer Palace 安缦颐和, ānmàn yíhé. 1 Gongmenqian Jie ☏010 59879057, w aman.com; subway line #4 to Xiyuan, Exit C2; map pp.68–69. About as close as you'll be able to stay to the Summer Palace, both in terms of location (it's just outside the East Gate) and feel – parts of the complex are centuries old, with contemporary rooms decked in period timber. This is a place to get away from it all; the restaurants, pool and spa facilities are top-notch, and there's even a secret gate into the palace, which can be opened at night for a crowd-free stroll. **¥6300**

EATING

Nowhere else on the Chinese mainland can compete with the culinary wealth of Beijing: splurging in classy **restaurants** is a great way to spend your evenings, as prices in even the most luxurious places are a lot more affordable than their equivalent in the West. Every style of Chinese food is available, but among this abundance it's sometimes easy to forget that Beijing has its own culinary tradition – specialities well worth trying are **Peking duck** (see box, p.108) and the often overlooked **Mongolian hotpot**, very different from the ubiquitous spicy Sichuanese version. Other Asian cuisines, including Japanese and Malay, are also widely available; Western food is easy to find too, with a few good **cafés** and brunch places dotted around the city's trendier areas.

FAST FOOD AND STREET FOOD

Street food is everywhere in Beijing (see box opposite), but if you're at a loss you can do worse than head for the nearest **shopping mall**: all have (air-conditioned) food courts with local and international fast-food chains, smart-casual restaurants and snack bars. The status of Wangfujing's tourist **night markets**, once infamous for their stalls selling impaled chicken hearts, sparrows, crickets, silkworm pupae, scorpions and sheep testicles, is uncertain; one has definitely closed, and the other is perhaps on borrowed time.

BEIJING SNACKS AND STREET FOOD

Most Beijingers kick off the day at the nearest streetside stall or hole-in-the-wall serving steamer-fuls of ravioli-like **jiaozi** or **baozi** stuffed buns; **mung-bean milk** known as *douzhi* (豆汁, dòuzhī), a real local favourite despite its greyish tinge and faintly repulsive, sour smell; or **jianbing** (煎饼, jiānbǐng), a savoury crêpe cooked on a circular hotplate and seasoned with chilli bean paste and spring onions, all folded around a crispy biscuit – a wonderfully warming winter breakfast. In a country where dairy products are a rarity, Beijing **yoghurt** (老北京酸奶, lǎo běijīng suānnǎi) is also worth trying; sold in cute clay pots, it has a delicious, honey-like taste.

If you need something to fill a gap as you wander, try heavily spiced barbecued meat **kebabs** (串, chuàn, though pronounced *"chuar"* in Beijing's pirate-like accent), often served up by Uyghurs from China's northwest. Lamb skewers (羊肉串, yángròu chuàn) are the de facto choice, though there are usually various cuts of chicken to choose from too. A sweet alternative are skewers of **toffee haws** (糖葫芦, táng húlu; also made with grapes, strawberries etc), which were originally sold by street hawkers.

Some restaurants around town specialize in **local snacks**, many of which have entertaining names: there's "rolling donkey" (驴打滚, lǘ dǎgǔn), steamed sweet soya-bean rolls dusted in toasted flour; "sweet ears" (糖耳朵, táng ěrduo), sugary, jelly-soft twists of cooked dough; "door-stud" buns (门钉肉饼, méndīng ròubǐng), stuffed with various fillings and fried to golden perfection; and "seasoned millet mush" (面茶, miàn chá), hot millet-flour porridge with sesame sauce floating on top. Then there are rice cakes with sweet fillings (艾窝窝, ài wōwō); blocks of syrup-coated flour noodles (沙琪玛, sàqímǎ); "stir-fried" liver (炒肝, chǎo gān), actually a tonic soup flavoured with garlic and ginger; and fried noodles with fermented soya bean paste (炸酱面, zhájiàng miàn).

SNACK CHAINS

Huguosi 护国寺小吃店, hùguósì xiǎochī diàn. Muslim canteen serving a range of Beijing snacks (including "rolling donkey"), restaurant dishes and freshly-made, takeaway pastries and breads (try their *shaobing* sesame buns). Daily 5.30am–9pm.

Longfusi 隆福寺小吃店, lóngfúsì xiǎochī diàn. Full run of traditional Beijing street food and snacks in relatively smart surroundings; nerve yourself to slurp a bowl of millet mush or *douzhi*. Daily 7am–9pm.

Qinfeng Steamed Dumpling 庆丰包子铺, qìngfēng bāizipù. *Baozi* specialist, founded in the 1940s but doubly famous after Xi Jinping was recently seen sampling their wares. A fraction of the cost of better-known Tianjin rival, *Goubuli*. Daily 6.30am–9pm.

Yonghe King 永和大王, yǒnghé dàwáng. Breakfast chain recognized for its *youtiao* (fried dough sticks) and cheap noodle dishes. Daily 6am–10.30pm.

NIGHT MARKET

Xiaochi Jie 小吃街, xiǎochī jiē. Xiagongfu Jie; subway line #1 to Wangfujing, Exit C2; map pp.84–85. This pedestrianized alley is lined with stalls selling xiǎo chī – literally, "little eats" – from all over China. Though vendors are pushy, it's atmospheric and has tables to sit down at with an ice-cold glass of beer. Daily 10am–midnight.

CAFÉS

Coffee culture has thoroughly infiltrated Beijing, though as the preserve of foreigners and well-to-do locals, prices are high. Note that some bars are also great spots to linger over

a cappuccino; and that some of the places below do decent Western-style light meals and cakes.

@Café 798 Art District ☎010 64387264; subway line #14 to Jingtai, Exit B; map pp.68–69. The best café in the 798 District, with good coffee (surprisingly cheap for the area, at ¥20–30) and a nice range of meals. Try the pasta dishes (from ¥40), some of which use fresh, handmade spaghetti. Daily 11am–6pm.

★**Alley Café** 寻常巷陌, xúncháng xiàng mò. 61 Shatan Hou Jie ☎010 84047228; subway line #10 to Tuanjiehu, Exit A; map p.80. Close to Jingshan Park and Forbidden City exits, Shatan Hou Jie is crowded with mediocre places to eat, of which this informal backpacker-style option is the exception. Decent coffee (¥25), Western-style set breakfasts, good *jiaozi* (¥32) and fairly average rice-and-curry meals. Attractive courtyard patio and very friendly English-speaking staff, plus bike hire too. Daily 8am–8pm.

Bookworm 老书虫, lǎo shūchóng. 4 Sanlitun Nan Jie ☎010 65869507, ⓦbeijingbookworm.com; subway line #10 to Tuanjiehu, Exit D; map pp.84–85. Hugely popular place for an espresso-and-laptop session with Beijing's expat crowd, largely on account of its excellent book selection (see p.116), and regular literary events and lectures. Check the website for details. Daily 9am–2am.

Café Zarah 飒哈, sàhā. 42 Gulou Dong Dajie ☎010 84039807, ⓦcafezarah.com; subway line #5 to Beixinqiao or line #6 to Nanluoguxiang, Exit E; map p.80. Cosy, attractively converted courtyard house serving good continental breakfasts (from ¥45) and plenty of snacks, including tasty home-made ice cream and a few

1

PEKING DUCK

Originally a Muslim dish, but now absorbed into Chinese cuisine, succulent **roast duck** is Beijing's big culinary hitter. Every restaurant has a different preparation technique, but once the duck has been brought to your table and carved, or vice versa, the routine is always the same: slather some dark, tangy bean sauce onto elastic, paper-thin pancakes, pop in a few scallions, add shreds of duck, duck skin (crisp and rich) and cucumber, roll it up and eat. Nothing is wasted; the duck's entrails are usually made into a soup or separate dish of their own, then served up alongside the meat.

Prices vary depending on where you go and whether you'd like side dishes served with the duck; some places advertise low prices but then charge extra for the sauce, pancakes and scallions. These days it's tough to find a whole duck for under ¥170, while at the city's more famous establishments you can expect to pay at least double this price. Recommended places include *Liqun* (see p.110), *Jingzun* (see opposite) and *Quanjude* (see p.110).

cakes plonked, rather unfairly, on the counter. Wed–Mon 10am–midnight.

★**HA (High Altitude Coffee)** 高海拔咖啡, gāohǎibá kāfēi. 84 Dongsi Bei Dajie; subway line #5 to Beixinqiao, Exit C, or Zhangzizhong, Exit B; map pp.84–85. They roast their own coffee; you can choose generic (¥25) or pay more for Ethiopian, Central American or Kenyan beans (from ¥45). Stylish grey brick and concrete space on two levels, with heavy wooden tables downstairs and comfy sofas above. Their cheesecake is great too. Daily 10am–8pm.

He Kitchen & Co. 48 Wudaoying Hutong; subway line #10 to Yonghegong, Exit D; map pp.84–85. Many things recommend this café: the sophisticated space, the hocks of Spanish ham hanging from the ceiling, the craft beer, the decent coffee... but not, sadly, most of their attempts at Western-style salads and sandwiches. Daily 9am–11pm.

★**Soloist** 39 Yangmeizhu Xie Jie, Dazhalan; subway line #10 to Qianmen, Exit C; map pp.90–91. There aren't many cafés down this way, which makes this excellent two-storey place, with its "antique industrial" exposed red-brick interior, doubly welcome – even if it is a haven for coffee snobs. They roast their own beans, and the very chic range includes high-end Kenyan and Hawaiian brews (¥45–100). Daily 10.30am–10pm.

RESTAURANTS

Visitors to Beijing will be amazed by how many restaurants the city has – not just on every corner, but everywhere between them too. Their nature changes as you shift around: Sanlitun and the Drum Tower/Yonghe Gong areas are trendy and cosmopolitan; Wangfujing caters to the masses with its series of shopping-mall chain restaurants; you'll find good duck south of Qianmen, and Muslim food everywhere (though especially around Niu Jie Mosque). Expect to eat earlier than you would in Western cities: restaurants start serving lunch from 11.30am, while dinner begins around 6pm. Few places stay open much after 10pm.

THE FORBIDDEN CITY & TIAN'ANMEN SQUARE

★**Lost Heaven** 花马天堂, huāmǎ tiāntáng. 23 Ch'ienmen complex, 23 Qianmen Dong Dajie ☎010 85162698, �🌐lostheaven.com.cn; subway line #2 to Qianmen, Exit B; map p.74. At the northeast corner of the former US Legation compound, this elegant restaurant features almost romantically subdued lighting, heavy Southeast Asian furniture, stylish crockery and a range of Yunnanese and Burmese curries, spicy salads flavoured with fresh herbs and tropical fruits, taro spring rolls and tamarind juice drinks. ¥150 a head. Daily noon–2pm & 5pm–1am.

NORTH OF THE CENTRE

Café Sambal 桑芭, sāng bā. 43 Doufuchi Hutong ☎010 64004875, ⓦcafesambal.com; subway line #8 to Shichahai, Exit A2; map p.80. Authentic Malay food in a laidback courtyard restaurant, tucked away down a *hutong* and quite easy to miss. There's a good set lunch of *bak ku teh* sparerib soup, sweet milky tea and dessert (¥68); otherwise, mains are around ¥45. Daily 10am–11pm.

Dali Courtyard 大理院子, dàlǐ yuànzi. 67 Xiaojingchang Hutong ☎010 84041430; subway line #5 to Beixinqiao subway; map p.80. Charming courtyard restaurant with no menu – you simply turn up, pay the fixed price (¥128, or ¥200 for a few extra dishes), then the chef gives you whatever Yunnanese food he feels like cooking; dishes are generally rice-based, and all sets will have a fish course. Reservations recommended. Daily noon–2.30pm & 6–10.30pm.

Nuage 庆云楼, qìngyún lóu. 22 Qianhai Dongzhao ☎010 64019581; subway line #8 to Shichahai, Exit A2; map p.80. Decent Vietnamese food served in a smart upstairs bar-restaurant. Try the steamed garlic prawns and battered squid, and finish with super-strong Vietnamese coffee if you don't intend to sleep in the near future. You'll spend upwards of ¥120 per head. Daily 11am–2pm & 5.30–10.30pm.

Shuxiangju 蜀乡居家常菜, shǔxiāngjū jiāchángcài. 2 Weikang Hutong, though entrance is on Xinjiekou Dong Jie; look for the "My Home Welcome" sign ☎010 53693353; subway line #2 to Jishuitan, Exit C; map p.80. Friendly, fast-food-style restaurant with Sichuanese name, staff and menu: fish-flavoured pork shreds, dry-fried beans, twice-cooked pork, *mapo doufu*, and even the rarely-seen smoked duck. Great value at around ¥50 a head. Daily 24hr.

Xiao Beijing Jiaozi 小北京饺子, xiǎo běijīng jiǎozi. 52 Di'anmen Wai Dajie ☎010 84014598; subway line #8 to Shichahai, Exit C; map p.80. Within spitting distance of touristy Qianhai and the Drum Tower, yet bright, cheerful, reasonably-priced food from around ¥20 a serving: prawn and cucumber dumplings, cold side dishes like lotus root in syrup, bashed cucumber, and "sesame tofu" (actually buckwheat and soya bean mash flavoured with chilli and Sichuan pepper). Daily 10.30am–10pm.

EAST OF THE CENTRE

Bellagio 味千拉面, wèiqiānlāmiàn. Level 3, Tai Koo Li complex, Sanlitun ☎010 64177040; subway line #10 to Tuanjiehu, Exit A; map pp.84–85. Busy Taiwanese chain, with typically generous portions, heavy sauces, plenty of chilli and sugar and some specialities such as *migao* (steamed glutinous rice flavoured with shrimp and mushroom) and *caipu dan* (a turnip omelette). Daily 11.30am–9pm.

★**Chuanban** 川办餐厅, chuānbàn cāntīng. Inside the Sichuan Provincial Government office, 5 Gongyuan Toutiao, north off Jianguomen Dajie ☎010 65122277; subway line #1 or #2 to Jianguomen, Exit A; map pp.84–85. Catering to Sichuanese office workers, this is one restaurant in which staff don't ask if you can eat chilli: if you can't, you're in the wrong place. Big range of snacks and dishes served among faux-antique teahouse decor: *lazi ji*, cold spicy noodles, steamed spareribs in rice flour, tea-smoked duck; slow-simmered soups are a speciality. Large portions; around ¥75 a head. Mon–Fri 11am–2pm & 5–9.30pm, Sat & Sun 11am–9.30pm.

Crescent Moon 弯弯月亮, wānwān yuèliàng. 16 Dongsi Liutiao ☎010 64005281; subway line #5 or #6 to Zhangsizhonglu, Exit C; map pp.84–85. Uyghur place done up in green and yellow paint with Islamic-style domes on the roof. Inside, it's unusually clean and orderly: order a roast leg of lamb smothered with cumin (¥130), plus a couple of vegetable dishes, pilau and naan, and you

have a substantial meal for two. Surprisingly for a Muslim restaurant, they also stock Xinjiang Black Beer. The dining hall is relatively small but there are private rooms at the rear. Daily 11am–10pm.

Crystal Jade 翡翠酒家, fěicuì jiǔjiā. Level 3, Tai Koo Li complex, Sanlitun ☎010 64166858, ⓦcrystaljade .com; subway line #10 to Tuanjiehu, Exit A; map pp.84–85. Bright and modern Shanghai-style chain known for its excellent *xiaolongbao* dumplings (¥25 for four) and generously-sized *lamian* noodle soups (¥45). Cold side dishes are good too, especially tofu with preserved eggs, pickled white radish in syrup, and wood-ear fungus with vinegar dressing. Around ¥75 a head. Daily 11am–3pm & 5–9pm.

Foodie Town 美食城, měishí chéng. At the foot of Soho Tower, Sanlitun; subway line #10 to Tuanjiehu, Exit D; map pp.84–85. Tasty fast food from across China eaten off plastic tables and trays in a noisy, rapid-turnover environment – you're here to fuel up, not dine. Infinitely cheaper than most local restaurants, so in demand with local shop staff. Daily 7am–7pm.

★**Jin Ding Xuan** 金鼎轩, jīn dǐng xuān. 77 Hepingli Xi Jie ☎010 64978978; subway line #2 or #5 to Yonghegong Lama Temple, Exit A; map pp.84–85. A stone's throw from Ditan Park, this four-storey, antique-style place has food from right across China. Choices include shrimp and pork dumplings (¥19), Sichuan noodles (¥12), wonton soup (¥16) and breakfast-style dough sticks (¥5). Leave room for the mango pudding (¥8). It's excellent value and, despite being open around the clock, is always packed – expect to take a ticket and wait for space. Daily 24hr.

★**Jingzun** 京尊烤鸭店, jīngzūn kǎoyā diàn. 6 Taiping Nan Li, Chunxiu Lu ☎010 64174075; subway line #2 to Dongsishitiao, Exit B; map pp.84–85. Despite being packed with expats and close to a *Holiday Inn*, this comfortable, informal place isn't the tourist rip-off you might expect: a whole roast duck is just ¥168, and you'll pay about ¥100 a head in a group for duck with plenty of side dishes and beer. There's also a front terrace for sitting out in good weather. Daily 11am–10pm.

Justine's Inside Jianguo Hotel (建国饭店, jiànguó fàndiàn). 5 Jianguomenwai Dajie ☎010 65002233; subway line #1 to Yong'anli, Exit B; map pp.84–85. Beijing's oldest French restaurant is suitably fancy

GHOST STREET

Nicknamed "Ghost Street" (鬼街, guǐ jiē), a 1km-long stretch of **Dongzhimen Nei Dajie** is lined with hundreds of restaurants, all festooned with red lanterns and neon – a colourful and boisterous scene, particularly on weekends. Note that staff in these restaurants will probably speak little or no English; few places will have an English menu, but plenty have a picture menu. It's an atmospheric place, for sure, though when the crowds arrive in the evening the whole street can resemble a car park.

1

– super-plush carpets, giant mirrors, golden chandeliers and stained glass. The menu switches around with pleasing regularity; try the lobster soup or grilled lamb. Service is attentive. Around ¥350 per person. Daily 6.30am–10.30am, noon–2pm & 6–10pm.

Lime 青柠, qīng níng. Building 15, Central Park ☎010 65970887; subway line #10 to Jintaixizhao, Exit A; map pp.84–85. A friendly Thai venue serving fairly authentic food for ¥40–65 per dish. Their outdoor seats are the best place from which to gaze over Central Park, a cosmopolitan residential area hidden from the surrounding main roads. Daily 11am–10pm.

★Made in China 东方君悦大酒店, dōngfāng jūnyuè dàjiǔdiàn. Grand Hyatt, 1 Dongchang'an Jie ☎010 65109024; subway line #1 to Wangfujing, Exit A; map pp.84–85. One of the swankiest places in town, and the Chinese-with-a-twist food is reliably excellent; their signature menu goes for ¥498 per person (minimum two), but à la carte items are around ¥120. Daily 11.30am–2.30pm & 5.30–10.30pm.

Malacca Legend 马六甲傳奇, mǎliùjiǎ chuánqí. The Place, North Building, 9 Guanghua Lu ☎010 65871393; subway line #6 to Dongdaqiao, Exit D; map pp.84–85. Small place serving Nyonya Malay dishes, pleasantly informal despite the starched tablecloths and straight-backed chairs. Choose from dry curry *rendang*, *pie tee*, crab or seafood, with *es kachang* (a mountain of shaved ice and sweet syrup) to cool off on a hot day. Lunch sets of curry, rice, prawn crackers, egg *sambal* and *pandan* pancakes are good value (¥50). Daily 11am–10pm.

Qin Tang Fu 秦唐府, qíntángfǔ. 69 Chaoyangmen Nanxiao Jie ☎010 65598135; subway line #5 or #6 to Dongsi, Exit C; map pp.84–85. The best place in town for the famous Xi'an dish *yangrou paomo* (羊肉泡馍, yángròu pāomó) – tiny bread cubes in a spicy lamb broth. Not somewhere to cross the city for, but it's fun and backpacker-friendly at just ¥32. Daily 11am–11pm.

Renhe 仁和酒家, rénhé jiǔjiā. 19 Donghuamen Dajie; subway line #1 to Tian'anmen East subway, Exit B; map pp.84–85. A short walk from the Forbidden City's east gate, this is a cut above the area's other (mostly horrendous) restaurants. Here you're far less likely to be ripped off or served yesterday's rice; in fact, the food is rather good, especially their tasty tofu dishes (from ¥32). Its outdoor seats are also a good place for evening beers. Daily 6am–1am.

★Siji Minfu 四季民福, sìjì mínfú. 11 Nanchizi Jie ☎65267369; subway line #1 to Tian'anmen East subway, Exit B; map pp.84–85. Smart, modern Beijing restaurant specializing in succulent roast duck, with the open brick ovens and sweating chefs in starched white uniforms as part of the floor show. Try to grab a table at the back overlooking the Forbidden City moat; touristy but

easily the best restaurant in the area. No bookings, so get here early or expect to wait. Around ¥150 a head. Daily 11am–9pm.

Veggie Table 吃素的, chīsù de. 19 Wudaoying Hutong ☎010 64462073; subway line #2 or #5 to Yonghegong Lama Temple, Exit D; map pp.84–85. Top-notch organic vegan menu, featuring couscous, curries and meze (including superb hummus and falafel). Pride of place goes to their famed mushroom burger (¥62); tasty enough even for non-vegetarians. Mon–Fri 11.30am–3.30pm & 5.30–10.30pm, Sat & Sun 11.30am–11.30pm.

SOUTH OF THE CENTRE

Deyuan 德缘烤鸭店, déyuán kǎoyā diàn. 57 Dazhalan Xi Jie ☎010 63085371; subway line #2 to Qianmen, Exit C; map pp.90–91. Elaborate antique-style frontage alive with golden phoenixes, where they advertise a whole Peking duck for just ¥138 – though as they add ¥20 for carving, ¥14 for pancakes etc, you won't see much change from ¥200. Good quality though, and still the cheapest in the district. Daily 10am–2pm & 5–9pm.

★Dong Lai Shun 东来顺, dōngláishùn. 7 Dazhalan Dong Jie, inside and upstairs at the tourist market – look for the entranceway Lucky Rabbit god statuette ☎010 63165836; subway line #2 to Qianmen, Exit C; map pp.90–91. Founded in 1903 and now with branches all over China, this features Beijing's own – non-spicy – Muslim hotpot. Order clear stock and platters of thinly-sliced lamb, vegetables, mushrooms, glass noodles and dipping sauce, and cook your selection in a copper-funnelled "Mongolian" hotpot. You definitely need a group; expect ¥100 a head and don't be cajoled by staff into over-ordering. Daily 11am–9pm.

Liqun 利群烤鸭店, liqún kǎoyādiàn. 11 Beixiangfeng Hutong ☎010 67025681; subway line #2 to Qianmen, Exit B or line #7 to Qiaowan, Exit A; map pp.90–91. Famous but downright grungy roast duck specialist – possibly doomed, as gentrification of the adjoining *hutong* district edges closer. Quality remains high, however; it's ¥265 for a whole duck with accompaniments, or ¥365 with a host of side dishes as well. Expect to queue even after you've made a reservation (essential, in any case). Daily 11am–10pm.

Quanjude 全聚德, quánjùdé. 30 Qianmen Dajie ☎010 67011379; subway line #2 to Qianmen, Exit C; map pp.90–91. Beijing's most famous duck restaurant by far; reservations are not vital, but be advised if you don't want to spend ages in the queue. The duck (¥365) is everything you'd expect: rich, juicy and with meltingly crisp copper-coloured skin. Daily 11am–1.30pm & 4.30–8pm.

DRINKING AND NIGHTLIFE

Beijing's **bars** are split between Sanlitun's obvious scene, and the small, boutique venues hidden among the maze of *hutongs* spreading eastwards from the Bell Tower area. "Hidden" is the word; some of these places don't even have signs outside, so you'll have to check house numbers as you go. Most serve a range of imported ales and spirits, but the big thing at the moment is locally brewed **craft beer** – including excellent IPA at around ¥40 a pint – and the major breweries are *Arrow Factory*, *Slow Boat*, *Jing A* and *Great Leap*. Otherwise, Beijing's local pilsner is *Yanjing*, which can be cheaper than bottled water if bought in a shop, though a 350ml bottle at a bar will cost ¥20–40. Drinks aside, bars often serve some of the best Western-style fast food in the city – burgers, fish and chips, pizza and the like. Chinese **clubs** are quite slick these days, with hip-hop and house music proving crowd-pleasers. For up-to-the-minute reviews, check the expat magazines.

BARS

NORTH OF THE CENTRE

★**Great Leap** 大跃啤酒, dàyuè píjiǔ. 6 Doujiao Hutong ⓦ greatleapbrewing.com; subway line #5 to Shichahai, Exit C; map p.80. Hidden behind a wall at the corner of a square, this restaurant comprises a pleasantly shaded courtyard garden, bar with exposed beams, heavy wooden furniture and a brick floor. East City Porter and Little General IPA are good, but the thing to try is Edmund Backhouse Pilsner, named after the infamous Sinologist and literary forger (see *Hermit of Peking*, p.968). Tues–Thurs 5–10.30pm, Fri 5–11pm, Sat 2–11pm, Sun 2–10pm.

Mao Mao Chong 毛毛虫, máomao chóng. 12 Banchang Hutong ⓣ 1584 2719052; subway line #6 or #8 to Nanluoguxiang, Exit F; map p.80. Renowned for its locally-themed cocktails at ¥40–60: Bloody Mao, Chong Collins, pandan daiquiri and their signature Mala Mule – lime, ginger beer and chilli-infused vodka. It's a tiny space but the bar staff are cool, there's a jazz soundtrack, and the pizza is good. Mon–Thurs 6pm–midnight, Fri & Sat 4pm–late.

Modernista 44 Baochao Hutong, cnr of Baochao and Wangzuo ⓣ 1369 1425744; subway line #2 or #8 to Guloudajie, Exit G; map p.80. Art Deco, 1930s-feel interior with red velvet curtain for the stage, floor tiles in domino checks and geometric lines everywhere. French-heavy clientele, tapas (and full meals in the evening) plus Prohibition-era cocktail menu (¥40–75), reconstructing several "lost" recipes. Live music with jazz/funk bias most weekends. Mon–Fri 4pm–2am, Sat & Sun 11am–2am.

Pass By Bar 过客酒吧, guòkè jiǔbā. 108 Nanluogu Xiang; subway line #6 to Nanluoguxiang, Exit E; map p.80. A renovated courtyard turned comfortable bar/restaurant, popular with backpackers and students. There are lots of books and pictures of China's far-flung places to peruse, and well-travelled staff to chat to. Daily 9am–4am.

EAST OF THE CENTRE

★**Arrow Factory** 箭厂啤酒, jiànchǎng píjiǔ. 9 Jianchang Hutong ⓣ 010 64076308, ⓦ www .arrowfactorybrewing.com; subway line #2 or #5 to Yonghegong Lama Temple, Exit D; map pp.84–85. Slightly downbeat exterior, with their *Stuff'd* restaurant at the front (go for the home-made sausages) and bar – decked

in requisite bare-concrete-and-timber decor – tucked away to the side. Current pick of their beers is the English Archer and aptly-named Seeing Double. Mon–Thurs 5pm–1am, Fri 5pm–2am, Sat 11.30am–2am, Sun 11.30am–1am.

Atmosphere 云酷酒吧, yúnkù jiǔbā. 80F World Trade Center ⓣ 010 85716459; subway line #1 or #10 to Guomao, Exit E2; map pp.84–85. Dress up (no shorts or slippers), catch the lift inside the *Shangri-la* hotel's east entrance, and step out eighty floors up at Beijing's loftiest bar. Come prepared for some shocking prices and (on clear days) stunning views. Book ahead for a window seat. Mon–Fri 2pm–2am, Sat & Sun noon–2am.

Cuju 蹴鞠洛哥餐吧, cùjū luògē cānbā. 28 Xiguan Hutong ⓣ 010 64079782, ⓦ cujubeijing.com; subway line #5 to Zhangzizhonglu, Exit A; map pp.84–85. Eclectic rum selection, including some home-made infusions in medicine bottles behind the bar (try Pirates' Delight, flavoured with cinnamon and *gouqi*). Dampen the effects with filling Moroccan food, such as the Totale (¥68), a plate of sausage slathered in a spicy sauce. Despite lack of space, they've installed two TVs for catching soccer games live. Opens at all hours if there's an international game on, otherwise daily 6am–midnight.

★**Distillery** 23 Xinsi Hutong ⓣ 010 64093319, ⓦ capitalspiritsbj.com; subway line #5 to Zhangzizhonglu, Exit B; map pp.84–85. Beijing's first boutique distillery occupies the front part of an old *siheyuan*, decked downstairs in spartan-chic concrete and timber; upstairs there's a mellow lounge overlooking grey-tiled rooftops. Produces its own vodka and gin in the copper still at the rear – try a G&T with the juniper-heavy house special, "Uncle Karl" (¥50) – plus there are forty-odd commercial varieties to choose from, alongside a substantial collection of American whiskies. Mon–Sat 7pm–midnight.

First Floor 壹楼, yī lóu. Tongli Building, behind Tai Koo Li, Sanlitun ⓣ 010 64130587, ⓦ firstfloorbj.com; subway line #10 to Tuanjiehu, Exit A; map pp.84–85. Generally horrible staff, but decent draft beer and pub food; streetside tables make it a favourite with expats watching the endless parade of bohemian Beijingers outside. Gets busier and sleazier as the night progresses. Daily 11am–midnight.

Jing A Taproom 京A, jīng A. 1949 Complex, 4 Gongti Bei Lu, Sanlitun ⓣ 010 65018883, ⓦ jingabrewing .com; subway line #10 to Tuanjiehu, Exit D; map

1

pp.84–85. Brick-walled compound hidden at the back of an entertainment complex, with outdoor tables, spacious bar and smart junior executives as clientele. Try their Flying Fist ale. Mon–Wed 5pm–midnight, Thurs 4pm–midnight, Fri 4pm–2am, Sat 11am–2am, Sun 11am–midnight.

Mesh At the Opposite House (瑜舍, yúshè). 11 Sanlitun Lu ☎ 010 64105220, ⓦ theoppositehouse.com; subway line #10 to Tuanjiehu, Exit A; map pp.84–85. Cosy, classy lounge bar in the basement of a chic hotel, attracting a trendy, international crowd. Dress up, order a cocktail (from ¥80), and try to look sophisticated. Daily 5pm–2am.

Ramo 64 Fangjia Hutong ☎ 010 84035004; subway line #5 to Beixinqiao, Exit A; map pp.84–85. Quiet spot to chill over a range of imported boutique bottled beers after exhausting yourself touring the nearby temples. Also serves light bar meals – pizza by the slice (¥20), chicken croquettes (¥28) and burger and chips (¥40). When the weather's right, there are tables out front for watching *hutong* life. Daily 9.30am–11pm.

Slow Boat Taproom 悠航鲜啤, yōu háng xiān pí. 56 Dongsi Ba Tiao ☎ 010 65385537, ⓦ slowboat brewery.com; subway line #5 to Zhangzizhonglu, Exit C; map pp.84–85. Cramped concrete box, tiled white on the inside (the rumour is that it was indeed once a toilet block) jam-packed with communal wooden tables and benches. You usually end up standing but the excellent beer – try Monkey's Fist IPA – more than compensates. Filling bar meals too. Mon–Thurs 5pm–midnight, Fri 5pm–1am, Sat 2pm–1am, Sun 11.30am–10pm.

★ **Tiki Bungalow** 34 Jiaodaokou San Tiao; subway line #5 to Beixinqiao, Exit A; map pp.84–85. Quirky place for a Beijing backstreet: there's a Great White shark called Wilson hanging from the ceiling, a palm frond-fringed bar, Tiki mugs, an affable manager in a Hawaiian shirt and the biggest wall of rum you could ever hope to lay eyes on. If you like your spirits straight, try one of the less usual brands – Burmese, Japanese, even Scottish – otherwise all your favourites are here, plus a long list of cocktails (including a classic Mai Tai). Mon–Sat 7pm–2am.

Tree 树酒吧, shù jiǔbā. Behind 3.3 Mall, Sanlitun ☎ 010 64151954; subway line #10 to Tuanjiehu, Exit A; map pp.84–85. Relaxed and unassuming little bar, with a selection of Belgian white beers and decent pizza; if you'd like to mix things up a bit, they've a great sister bar within stumbling distance. Daily midday–late.

CLUBS

Destination 目的地, mùdìdì. 7 Gongti Xi Lu ⓦ bjdestination.com; subway line #2 to Dongsishitiao, Exit C; map pp.84–85. Beijing's biggest and most popular gay club by far, with two floors full of half-naked men (mainly local), as well as women who'd rather avoid non-gay fellas for the night. Entry ¥60. Daily 8pm–late.

Migas 那里花园, nàlǐ huāyuán. 6F Nali Patio ⓦ migasbj.com; subway line #10 to Tuanjiehu, Exit A; map pp.84–85. The upstairs bar at this Spanish restaurant has long been a favourite with Beijing's young-and-well-heeled set; views from here are simply superb, and there's barely room to wiggle your butt during the weekend DJ sets. Weekdays are a different story, with lounge music pulsing over a nattering crowd, all seated on funky furniture. Daily 6pm–late.

Propaganda East Gate, Huaqing Jiayuan; subway line #13 to Wudaokou, Exit B; map pp.68–69. "Oh god, *that* place…" is the stock reaction when mentioning this bar to someone who's been in Beijing for a while. This infamous Wudaokou student club is a shameless meat market, whose ¥50 all-you-can-drink nights (every Wed) are crazily popular. The spirits are dodgy for sure, though; stick to the beer. Daily 8pm–late.

Vics 威克斯, wēikèsī. Workers' Stadium north gate; subway line #2 to Dongsishitiao, Exit C; map pp.84–85. One of many unapologetically trashy clubs in the area, this long-running hip-hop place features a sweaty dancefloor filled with enthusiastic booty grinders. The low cover charge and cheapish drinks (bottled beer is ¥25) make it popular with students and embassy brats. ¥50 on weekends, free Mon–Thurs. Daily 9.30pm–2am.

BEIJING OPERA

Beijing opera (京戏, jīng xì) is the most celebrated of China's 350 or so regional operatic styles – a unique combination of song, dance, acrobatics and mime. Highly stylized, to the outsider the performances can often seem obscure and wearying, as they are punctuated by a succession of crashing gongs and piercing, discordant songs. But it's worth seeing once, especially if you can acquaint yourself with the story beforehand. Most of the plots come from historical or mythological romances – the most famous, which any Chinese will explain to you, are *Journey to the West*, *The Three Kingdoms*, *Madame White Snake* and *The Water Margin* – and full of moral lessons. Offering an interesting, if controversial, variation on the traditions are those operas that deal with contemporary themes – such as the struggle of women to marry as they choose. The **colours** used on stage, from the costumes to the make-up on the players' faces, are highly symbolic: red signifies loyalty; yellow, fierceness; blue, cruelty; and white, evil. Many hostels offer **opera tours**, including entry and one-way transport, for ¥200.

ENTERTAINMENT

Most visitors to Beijing make a trip to see Beijing **opera** and the superb Chinese **acrobatics** displays – both of which remain timeless arts. In contrast, the contemporary **theatrical and live music scenes** continue to develop apace, while Western **classical music** can be heard at any of the concert halls.

TRADITIONAL OPERA

A trip to see Beijing's famous opera (see box opposite) is one of the most popular diversions for international travellers. If the regular shows seem too long, you could visit a teahouse to get your fix – such performances are short and aimed at foreigners.

★**Chang'an Grand Theatre** 长安大戏院, cháng'ān dàxìyuàn. 7 Jianguomennei Dajie ☎010 65101308; subway line #1 or #2 to Jianguomen, Exit A; map pp.84–85. A modern, central theatre seating 800 and putting on a wide range of performances throughout the day – it's probably the most popular place in town for Beijing opera. From ¥180.

Huguang Guildhall 湖广会馆, húguǎng huìguǎn. 3 Hufangqiao Lu ☎010 63045396; subway line #7 to Hufangqiao, Exit C; map pp.90–91. The appeal of this place is its age – the building dates to 1807, and though heavily restored, the traditional wooden stage and teahouse setting makes for a superb atmosphere. Seats ¥180–380. Performances nightly at 6.30pm.

Lao She Teahouse 老舍茶馆, lǎoshě cháguǎn. 3F Dawancha Building, 3 Qianmen Xidajie ☎010 63036830; subway line #2 to Qianmen, Exit C; map pp.90–91. Teahouse theatre that puts on shadow puppet, folk music and Peking opera performances on separate floors. Free 10min shadow puppet shows through the day; otherwise performance timetables are posted in the lobby. Seats from ¥180 depending on view of the stage. Daily 10am–2pm & 5–8.30pm.

Liyuan Theatre 梨园剧场, líyuán jùchǎng. 1F Qianmen Jianguo hotel (前门建国饭店), qiánmén jiànguó fàndiàn), 175 Yong'an Lu ☎010 63016688, ⓦqianmenhotel.com; subway line #7 to Hufangqiao, Exit B; map pp.90–91. Perhaps the most accessible place to see opera; as you go in you pass the actors putting on their make-up – a great photo op. The opera itself is a visitor-friendly bastardization, lasting an hour and jazzed up with some martial arts and slapstick. Tickets can be bought from the office in the front courtyard of the hotel (daily 9–11am, noon–4.45pm & 5.30–8pm; ¥90–280). Performances nightly at 7.30pm.

National Centre for the Performing Arts 国家大剧院, guójiā dàjùyuàn. 2 Xichang'an Jie ☎010 66550000; subway line #1 to Tian'anmen West, Exit C; map pp.68–69. This is one venue you can't miss: it's that giant egg west of Tian'anmen Square. The opera hall seats over 2000, with fantastic acoustics and lighting; tickets start from ¥180 (box office opens daily from 9.30am, or ring to reserve). Performances nightly at 7.30pm.

Zhengyici Theatre 正义祠剧场, zhèngyìcí jùchǎng. 220 Qianmen Xiheyanjie ☎010 63189454; subway line #2 to Hepingmen, Exit C2; map pp.90–91. A genuinely old wooden opera stage, grander than that at the Huguang Guildhall and worth a visit just to check out the architecture. Tickets from ¥280. Performances nightly at 8pm.

DRAMA AND DANCE

Most evenings you can catch Chinese song and dance simply by turning on the TV, though there's plenty of opportunity to see it live. Some venues stage performances in the original language, which, with tickets at ¥50–100, are a lot cheaper to watch here than at home.

Beijing Exhibition Theatre 北京展览馆剧场, běijīng zhǎnlǎnguǎn jùchǎng. 135 Xizhimenwai Dajie ☎010 68354455; subway line #4 to Beijing Zoo, Exit C2; map pp.68–69. This giant hall, containing nearly 3000 seats, stages classical ballet, folk dance and large-scale song-and-dance revues.

Capital Theatre 首都剧场, shǒudū jùchǎng. 22 Wangfujing Dajie ☎010 65121598, ⓦbjry.com; subway line #5 or #6 to Dongsi, Exit G; map p.80 & pp.84–85. Look out for the People's Art Theatre company here – their photo archive, documenting their history, is displayed in the lobby. Tickets generally start at ¥120. Most performances are in Chinese.

Penghao Theatre 蓬蒿剧场, pénghāo jùchǎng. 35 Dongmianhua Hutong ☎010 64006452, ⓦpenghaotheatre.com; subway line #6 to Nanluoguxiang, Exit E; map p.80 & pp.84–85. In a *hutong* just behind the Central Academy of Drama, this intimate, privately run theatre set in a beautifully converted courtyard house also has a rather nice rooftop bar. Check website for performance prices.

Puppet Theatre 中央木偶剧院, zhōngyāng mù'ǒu jùyuàn. Cnr of Anhua Xili & Third Ring Road ☎010 64254798, ⓦpuppetchina.com; subway line #8 to Anhuaqiao, Exit D1 – but bizarrely there is no road crossing at this exit, leaving you in the middle of a busy road; map p.80. Once as important for commoners as opera was for the elite, Chinese puppetry usually involves hand puppets and marionettes. Shows here, both live and recorded, are aimed at kids, involve Beijing opera, short stories and Western fairy tales; tickets from ¥100. Five shows daily 10am–3pm.

ACROBATICS AND MARTIAL ARTS

Beijing Workers' Club 北京工人俱乐部, běijīng gōngrén jùlèbù. 7 Hufang Lu ☎010 63528910,

1

ⓦthelegendofjinsha.com; subway line #7 to Hufangqiao, Exit B; map pp.90–91. Popular for its "Legend of Jinsha" show, which adds a few interesting quirks to the old acrobatic routines – silk-rope dancing, water cannon, and some zany motorbike stunts. Tickets from ¥110. Daily 3.50pm & 5.30pm.

★**Chaoyang Theatre** 朝阳剧场, cháoyáng jùchǎng. 36 Dongsanhuan Beilu ⓣ010 65072421, ⓦchaoyangtheatre.com; subway line #6 or #10 to Hujialou, Exit C1; map pp.84–85. If you want to see acrobatics, come to one of the shows here. At the end, the Chinese tourists rush off as if it's a fire drill, leaving the foreign tour groups to do the applauding. There are plenty of souvenir stalls in the lobby – make your purchases after the show rather than during the interval, as prices reduce at the end. Tickets from ¥180. Daily 7.15–8.30pm.

Red Theatre 红剧场, hóng jùchǎng. 44 Xingfu Dajie ⓣ010 67142473, ⓦredtheatre.cn; subway line #5 to Tiantandongmen, Exit B; map pp.90–91. A lively kung fu routine, featuring smoke, fancy lighting and some incredible action. Tickets from ¥180. Daily 5.15pm & 7.30pm.

LIVE MUSIC VENUES

Beijing has a glut of places in which to see music – everything from stadiums for superstars to small indie rock bars.

Beijing Concert Hall 北京音乐厅, běijīng yīnyuètīng. 1 Beixinhua Jie ⓣ010 66057006; subway line #1 or #4 to Xidan, Exit D; map pp.68–69. This hall seats 1000 people and hosts regular concerts of Western classical and Chinese traditional music by Beijing's resident orchestra and visiting orchestras from the rest of China and overseas. Tickets from ¥80.

Century Theatre 世纪剧院, shìjì jùyuàn. Sino-Japanese Youth Centre, 40 Liangmaqiao Lu ⓣ010 64663311; subway line #10 to Liangmaqiao, Exit C; map pp.84–85. An intimate venue for soloists and small ensembles. Mostly Chinese modern and traditional classical compositions. ¥120–150. Evening performances.

Forbidden City Concert Hall 北京中山公园音乐堂, běijīng zhōngshān gōngyuán yīnyuètáng. Zhongshan Park, Xichang'an Jie ⓣ010 65598285, ⓦfcchbj.com; subway line #1 to Tian'anmen West, Exit C; map p.74. A stylish hall, with regular performances of Western and Chinese classical music, and occasionally jazz

too. Tickets from ¥80.

★**National Centre for the Performing Arts** 国家大剧院, guójiā dàjùyuàn. 2 Xichang'an Jie ⓣ010 66550000; subway line #1 to Tian'anmen West, Exit C; map pp.68–69. The giant egg-shaped structure just west of Tian'anmen Square hosts the best international performances in its huge concert hall. Note that you can't bring a camera.

Workers' Stadium 工人体育场, gōngrén tǐyùchǎng. Off Gongti Beilu ⓣ010 65016655; subway line #2 to Dongsishitiao, Exit C; map pp.84–85. This is where giant gigs are staged, mostly featuring Chinese pop stars, though the likes of Björk have also played here (though, given her views on Tibet, that'll never happen again).

INDIE ROCK BARS

Dusk Dawn Club (DDC) 14 Shanlao Hutong; subway line #6 or #8 to Nanluoguxiang, Exit B; map p.80. Small-scale venue hosting live jazz, folk and indie bands; it's aimed at young, arty, upwardly-mobile Chinese and many come as much for the bar and funky ambience than for the music. Tues–Sun 1pm–2am.

Hot Cat Club 热力猫, rèlì māo. 46 Fangjia Hutong ⓣ010 64007868; subway line #5 to Beixinqiao, Exit A; map pp.84–85. Perfect venue – it always feels just a bit too small – and mainstay of Beijing's live music scene, hosting foreign and domestic bands hammering out blues, rock, reggae and indie. Mon–Thurs Tiger beer is just ¥10, Wed is Comedy Club night, Thurs has open-mic music, with Beijing bands Fri–Sun. Daily 10am–late.

Modernsky Lab 摩登天空, módēng tiānkōng. Floor B1, Building D, Galaxy Soho; subway line #2 or #6 to Chaoyangmen, Exit G; map pp.84–85. Chinese indie record label and music festival organizer now has its own live venue, though it's surprisingly low-key and barely advertised – check free weekly listings magazines to see what's on.

School Bar 53 Wudaoying Hutong; subway line #2 or #5 to Yonghegong Lama Temple, Exit D; map pp.84–85. Underground bar vibe with vivid red walls, a sometimes angry young crowd and strong punk and grunge bias. Beer is cheap at ¥25 a bottle. Daily 8pm–late.

FILM

There are scores of cinemas in Beijing showing Chinese and dubbed Western films, many of them on the top floor of

---

THE MIDI FESTIVAL

The **Midi Rock Music festival** (ⓦwww.midifestival.com) started as a student bash in Haidan Park, and has since grown to a China-wide extravaganza, with Beijing's event now attended by thousands and held out in the countryside. It has always been controversial, banned in 2008 and with foreign acts occasionally refused permission to play. Still, plenty of local talent is on display, and the audience is enthusiastic. You can even camp, for the full-on "Chinese Glastonbury" experience. Check the website for dates, venue and ticket prices.

shopping malls. Foreign movies will either be dubbed into Chinese or shown in the original language with subtitles; Ⓦwww.247cinema.cn is an invaluable English-language booking site, as it tells you which perfomances are in English. Tickets cost around ¥80.

CONTEMPORARY ART

Beijing is the centre for the vigorous **Chinese arts scene** and there are plenty of interesting new **galleries** opening up, particularly in the 798 Art District (see p.98). Galleries in the city centre are rather more commercial than those in the suburban artsy areas; they tend to focus on selling paintings rather than making a splash with a themed show.

798 ART DISTRICT

Galleria Continua 常青画廊, chángqīng huàláng. ☎010 64361005, Ⓦgalleriacontinua.com; map pp.68–69. Shows international and home-grown art stars across three floors' worth of space – head up to the top for a nuts-and-bolts view (literally) of this former factory. They tend to choose artists "with something to say", and rotate exhibitions 3–5 times per year. Tues–Sun 11am–6pm.

Mansudae Art Studio 万寿台创作社美术馆, wànshòutái chuàngzuòshè měishùguǎn. ☎010 59789317, Ⓦmansudaeartstudio.com; map pp.68–69. Small studio displaying North Korean painting – every bit as fascinating as you might imagine, with a range from misty mountain scenes to brave Socialist Realism. There's also a small shop on site, where you can buy North Korean goodies. Tues–Sun 10am–6pm.

Tokyo Gallery+ 东京艺术工程, dōngjīng yìshùgōngchéng. ☎010 84573245, Ⓦtokyo-gallery .com; map pp.68–69. The first gallery to set up shop here, and still one of the best, with a large elegant space for challenging shows. Tues–Sun 10am–5.30pm.

Ullens Centre for Contemporary Art 尤伦斯当代艺术中心, yóulúnsī dāngdài yìshùzhōngxīn. ☎010 64386675, Ⓦucca.org.cn; map pp.68–69. This huge nonprofit space is more of a museum than a gallery; no artwork is for sale and it is the only space that charges an entrance fee. There are three exhibition halls and a programme of regular events, which mainly focus on Asian artists. ¥30. Daily 10am–7pm.

CITY-CENTRE GALLERIES

National Art Museum of China 中国美术馆, zhōngguó měishùguǎn. 1 Wusi Dajie ☎010 84033500, Ⓦnamoc.org/en; subway line #5 or #6 to Dongsi, Exit E; map p.80 & pp.84–85. This grand building usually holds a couple of shows at once. There's no permanent display; past exhibitions have included specialist women's and minority people's exhibitions, and even a show of Socialist Realist propaganda. Free (bring ID); occasional charges for special exhibitions. Daily 9am–5pm.

Red Gate Gallery 红门画廊, hóngmén huàláng. Dongbianmen watchtower, Chongwenmen Dong Dajie ☎010 65251005, Ⓦredgategallery.com; subway line #1 or #2 to Jianguomen, Exit C; map pp.84–85. Commercial gallery, run by a Western curator, inside one of the last remnants of the old city wall. A little more adventurous than other Beijing galleries, it has a good reputation overseas. Daily 10am–5pm.

SHOPPING

Beijing has some great **shopping** – the best choice of **souvenirs** and **consumables** in the country is on sale here – and its collection of intriguing little **markets** offers an appealing and affordable alternative to the new giant **malls**. **Clothes** are particularly inexpensive; there's also a wide choice of **antiques** and **handicrafts**, but don't expect to find any bargains or particularly unusual items as the markets are well picked over.

ANTIQUES, CURIOS AND CARPETS

There's no shortage of antique stores and markets in the capital, offering opium pipes, jade statues, porcelain Mao figurines, mahjong sets, Red Guard alarm clocks, Fu Manchu glasses, and all manner of bric-a-brac. While you're not likely to unearth anything valuable, not all "antiques" are reproductions (or, if you like, fakes): small pieces, such as hairpins, wood carvings, embroideries and prints may indeed be real – though often expensive by international standards.

SHOPS

Rongbaozhai 荣宝斋, róngbǎozhāi. Liulichang Xi Jie Ⓦrongbaozhai.cn; subway line #2 or #4 to Xuanwumen, Exit H; map pp.90–91. Beijing's most famous supplier of anything to do with traditional calligraphy and painting: brushes, paper, inkstones, water droppers, scroll weights, brush rests and ink sticks. The rest of the street is full of similar shops with lower prices, as is most of nearby Nanxinhua Jie. Daily 9am–5.30pm.

Soul Art Shop 创艺无限, chuàng yì wúxiàn. 97 Nanluogu Xiang Ⓦruantao.com; subway line #6 or #8 to Nanluoguxiang, Exit E; map p.80. Fun and colourful acrylic models of animals, plants and deities – including Beijing's own Rabbit god – based on traditional dough sculptures. Cheerful and creative souvenirs. Daily 10am–8pm.

★**Three Stone** 三石斋风筝坊, sāndànzhāi fēngzhengfǎng. 25 Di'anmen Xi Dajie Ⓦcnkites.com;

subway line #6 to Nanluoguxiang, Exit E; map p.80. A specialist kite shop with a rich history – the ancestors of the current owner once made kites for the Qing royals. Though there are plenty of fancy designs here, they also sell a fair few cheapies. Daily 9am–8pm.

Xuhua Zhai 旭华斋, xùhuá zhài. 120 Liulichang Xi Jie ☎ 1355 2698708; subway line #2 or #4 to Xuanwumen, Exit H; map pp.90–91. Small, dark store with affable owner and small, dark glass-fronted cases stuffed with trinkets. You won't find any rare Ming vases here, but worth a browse for low-key, genuinely old curios. Bargain hard. Daily 10am–6pm.

MARKETS

Baoguo Temple 报国寺, bàoguó sì. Subway line #7 to Guanganmennei, Exit B, turn left and you're there; map pp.90–91. Deconsecrated temple whose halls are now full of curio dealers – coins, old books, wood carvings, prints and bric-a-brac. Individual dealers keep their own hours, but Saturday mornings are best overall. Daily from 9am.

Beijing Antique City 北京古玩城, běijīng gǔwánchéng. Huawei Nanlu; subway line #10 to Panjiayuan, Exit C2; map pp.68–69. A giant cube of a building housing more than 400 stalls; tourist souvenirs downstairs, a warren of antique dealers on the three remaining floors. Best visited on a Sunday. Daily 9.30am–6.30pm.

Liangma International Jewel and Antiques Market 亮马国际珠宝古玩城, liàngmǎ guójì zhūbǎo gǔwán chéng. 27 Liangmaqiao Lu; subway line #10 to Sanyuanqiao, Exit B; map pp.68–69. Two floors of jade and jewellery, with curios and carpets on the third floor. If you know what you're after, there are some interesting pieces here, from Tibetan and Mongolian woollen rugs to antique militaria. Daily 10am–6pm.

Panjiayuan Market 潘家园市场 pānjiāyuán shìchǎng. Panjiayuan Lu; subway line #10 to Panjiayuan, Exit B; map pp.68–69. Beijing's biggest antique market. Some appealing stuff if you strike lucky at the small stalls inside the entrance, but otherwise mostly trinket wholesalers with vast stocks of whatever "old" things are in vogue at the moment – polished stones, Song-style ceramics, bronze teapots etc. Busiest at the weekends. Mon–Fri 8am–6pm, Sat & Sun 6am–6pm.

BOOKS

Beijing can claim a better range of English-language literature than anywhere else in China. If you're starting a trip of any length, stock up here. Higher-end hotels sell copies of foreign newspapers and magazines, such as *Time* and *Newsweek*, for around ¥50.

★**Bookworm** 老书虫书吧, lǎoshūchóng shūbā. 4 Sanlitun Nan Jie ☎ 010 65869507, ⓦ beijingbookworm.com; subway line #10 to Tuanjiehu, Exit D; map pp.84–85. There are plenty of English-language books, both used and new, on sale in this popular café, which also hosts regular literary events and lectures. Daily 9am–2am.

Cathay Bookshop 中国书店, zhōngguó shūdiàn. Liulichang Xi Jie ⓦ zgsd.net; subway line #2 to Hepingmen, Exit D2; map pp.90–91. There are several branches of this art-focused store across the city but this is the biggest and best: mostly new books downstairs in the front, with secondhand to the rear, and a huge stock of antique volumes and prints – not just Chinese either – upstairs. As usual in China, anything vaguely collectable is expensive. Daily 9am–5.30pm.

Foreign Language Bookstore 外文书店, wàiwén shūdiàn. 218 Wangfujing Dajie ⓦ bpiec.com.cn; subway line #1 to Wangfujing, Exit C2; map pp.84–85. This dowdy store has the biggest selection of foreign-language books in mainland China: fiction, art books, textbooks on Chinese medicine, translations of Chinese classics, and imported fiction. Daily 8am–5pm.

Page One 叶壹堂, yèyī táng. Tai Koo Li (south mall), Sanlitun Lu ☎ 010 64176626; subway line #10 to Tuanjiehu, Exit A; map pp.84–85. Big Beijing branch of this Singapore chain, with a wide selection of English-language books, including travel guides, novels and artsy stuff. Daily 10am–10pm.

CLOTHES

SHOPS

Dong Liang Studio 栋梁, dòngliáng. 102, 2-Building, Central Park, Jinghua Lu ☎ 010 84047648, ⓦ dongliangchina.com; subway line #10 to Jintaixizhao, Exit A; map pp.84–85. Chic, elegant and affordable clothes by local designers; look out for beautiful dresses by JJ, Ye Qian and Shen Ye. Mon–Sat 9am–5pm.

Jixiangzhai 吉祥斋, jíxiáng zhāi. 3.3 Building, shop 1017, Tai Koo Li, Sanlitun ☎ 010 51365330, ⓦ www .jixiangzhai.cn; subway line #10 to Tuanjiehu, Exit A; map pp.84–85. High-end, very stylish Chinese silk dresses, rich in colour and embroidery, with definite "ethnic" leanings. Daily 11am–11pm.

Mr King Tailor Shop 金先生裁缝店, jīn xiānsheng cáiféng diàn. 90 Dazhalan Xi Jie ☎ 010 63180990; subway line #2 to Qianmen, Exit C; map pp.90–91. If you want handmade clothes but prices at the larger stores east down towards Qianmen make your eyes water, check out this small, one-man operation, with a surprisingly good range of Chinese and Western styles and fabrics. Daily 9am–10pm.

Neiliansheng Shoes 内联升布鞋, nèiliánshēng bùxié. 34 Dazhalan ☎ 010 63013041, ⓦ nls1853.com; subway line #2 to Qianmen, Exit C; map pp.90–91. Look out for the giant shoe in the window. All manner of handmade flat, slip-on shoes and slippers in traditional designs, starting from ¥200 or so – they make great gifts. Daily 9am–8pm.

Plastered T-Shirts 创可贴T恤, chuàngkětiē tīxù. 61 Nanluogu Xiang ⓦ plasteredtshirts.com; subway line #6 to Nanluoguxiang, Exit E; map p.80. Hipster T-shirts and sweatshirts whose witty designs reference everyday Beijing life – subway tickets, thermoses and so on. It's a standard ¥180 per shirt. Daily 9am–7pm.

Ruifuxiang Store 瑞蚨祥丝绸店, ruìfúxiáng sīchóudiàn. 5 Dazhalan, off Qianmen Dajie ☎ 010 63035313, ⓦ refosian.com; subway line #2 to Qianmen, Exit C; map pp.90–91. Silk and cotton fabrics and a good selection of shirts and dresses, with a tailor specializing in made-to-measure qipaos. You should aim to barter a little off the quoted price. Daily 9.30am–8.30pm.

MARKETS

Aliens Street Market 老番街, lǎofān jiē. Yabao Lu, north of Ditan Park; subway line #2 or #6 to Chaoyangmen, Exit A; map pp.84–85. This bustling warren of stalls has a vast range of (cheap) goods, but it's particularly worth picking over for clothes and accessories; take a close look at the stitching before you hand over your cash. Daily 9.30am–7pm.

Daxin Textiles 大新纺织品东四市店, dàxīn fǎngzhīpǐn dōngsìshì diàn. 227 Chaoyangmennei Da Jie; subway line #5 or #6 to Dongsi, Exit B; map pp.84–85. Dozen or more booths under one roof selling silk and cloth by the metre; tailors here can make suits, qipaos etc. About twenty percent cheaper than other dealers in town. Daily 9am–7.30pm.

Silk Market 秀水市场, xiùshuǐ shìchǎng. Off Jianguomenwai Dajie; subway line #1 to Yong'anli, Exit A; map pp.84–85. This huge six-storey tourist-heavy mall has electronics, jewellery and souvenirs, but its main purpose is to profit through flouting international copyright laws, with hundreds of stalls selling fake designer labels. You'll need to haggle hard. Daily 9.30am–9pm.

TEA

There are teashops all over the city, with Zhang Yiyuan and Ten Fu the two biggest chains; you'll find branches all over the city, but perhaps the best are the two facing each other across Qianmen Dajie (see map, p.91), where English is spoken.

CDS AND DVDS

C Rock 99 Gulou Dong Dajie; subway line #2 to Nanluoguxiang, Exit E; map p.80. One of the best places in the city to go hunting for CDs by local bands; the friendly owner will be pleased to make recommendations, and give you a listen to a few choice tracks. Hours vary; generally 11am–5pm.

Huashiweiye DVD In the pedestrian street behind Tai Koo Li; subway line #10 to Tuanjiehu, Exit A; map pp.84–85. Forget the name of this place, since even the proprietors aren't sure; it's marked from the outside as "CD DVD SHOP", and that's what they sell; thanks to a wide selection of films, they've a regular base of expat customers. Daily 8am–5pm.

SPORTS AND ACTIVITIES

During the **2008 Olympics**, a passion for athletic activity became a patriotic duty. Now the dust has settled, the legacy of the Games includes a range of good **sports facilities** across the capital, from the outdoor workout machines placed in every neighbourhood to the showpiece stadiums themselves. However, the most visible kinds of exercise need no fancy equipment; head to any **park** in the morning and you'll see citizens going through all sorts of martial arts routines, walking backwards, chest slapping, and tree hugging.

SPECTATOR SPORTS

Beijing's football team, Guo'an, plays at the massive Workers' Stadium in the northeast of the city (see map, pp.84–85). There's a timetable outside the ticket office, which is just east of the north gate of the stadium. Tickets cost around ¥50, though you'll likely have to get them on the day from a tout. Basketball is almost as popular; the Beijing Ducks play at the superb Wukesong Arena (tickets ¥50), built for the Olympics.

SWIMMING

Avoid swimming pools at the weekends, when they're full of teenagers doing just about everything but swimming. As well as the pools listed below, bear in mind that some hotels open their lavish pools and gym facilities to non-guests; most impressive are those at the Westin Chaoyang (1 Xinyuan Nan Lu; ☎ 010 59228888; ¥250 for a weekend pass), the

Ritz-Carlton (1 Jinchengfang Dong Jie; ☎ 010 66016666; ¥220/weekend) and the Doubletree by Hilton (168 Guang'anmen Wai Dajie; ☎ 010 63381888; ¥150/weekend).

Ditan Swimming Pool 8 Hepingli Zhong Jie ☎ 010 64264483; subway line #5 to Hepinglibeijie; see map p.80. If you just want a cheap swim, try this place, open year-round (entry ¥30). In the summer, there are outdoor pools open for the same price at nearby Qingnian Lake.

Olympic Water Cube Since the Games, this famous Olympic venue (otherwise known as the National Aquatics Center; see p.98) has reopened as a water theme park, featuring spas, slides and a wave pool. ¥60. Daily 10am–9.30pm.

MASSAGE & SPA

Beijing is full of dodgy massage joints, but plenty of reliable venues do exist. Prices are rising, but are still less than you'd pay in most Western countries.

1

Bodhi 菩提, pútí. 17 Gongti Beilu, opposite Workers' Stadium ☎010 64130226, ⓦwww.bodhi.com.cn; subway line #2 to Dongsishitiao. Ayurvedic and Thai massages are among the many options available at this Southeast Asia-styled clinic. Ayurvedic massage ¥288 for 1hr. Daily 11am–12.30pm.

Chi Shangri-La Hotel, 29 Zizhuyuan Lu ☎010 68412211; subway line #9 or #4 to National Library, Exit A. Therapies at this luxurious New Age spa claim to use the five Chinese elements – metal, fire, wood, water and earth – to balance your yin and yang. It might look like a Tibetan temple, but there can't be many real Tibetans who could afford to darken its doors; a Chi

Balance Massage costs ¥1430, a Himalayan Healing Stone Massage ¥1700 (and there's a 15 percent service charge). Daily 10am–midnight.

Dragonfly 悠庭, yōutíng. ⓦdragonfly.net.cn. This well-reputed Shanghai chain has opened two centres in the capital – check the website for locations. Their classic Chinese massage (60min; ¥188) is always popular, as are the foot massages. Daily 10am–11pm.

Taipan 东方大班, dōng fāng dà bān. 6 Ritan Lu ☎010 65025722, ⓦtaipan.com.cn. A popular chain, with branches all over the city – no frills, but clean and cheap. ¥228 for a 75min foot massage or a 60min body massage.

DIRECTORY

Courier service DHL (ⓦcn.dhl.com) has a handful of depots in the metropolitan area; check the website for locations.

Embassies Visa departments open for a few hours every weekday morning (contact them for times and to ask what you'll need; some only accept US dollars). Remember that they'll take your passport from you, and it's impossible to buy train tickets or check in at a new hotel without it. You can get passport-size photos from machines all over town. Most embassies are either around Sanlitun in the northeast or in Jianguomenwai compound, north of and parallel to Jianguomenwai Dajie: **Australia**, 21 Dongzhimenwai Dajie ⓦchina.embassy.gov.au; **Canada**, 19 Dongzhimenwai Dajie ☎010 51394000; **India**, 5 Liangmaqiao Bei Jie ⓦindianembassy.org.cn; **Ireland**, 3 Ritan Donglu ⓦembassyofireland.cn; **Japan**, 7 Ritan Lu ☎010 85319800; **Kazakhstan**, 9 Sanlitun Dongliu Jie ☎010 65326182; **Kyrgyzstan**, 2-4-1 Tayuan Compound ⓦkyrgyzstanembassy.net; **Laos**, 11 Sanlitun Dongsi Jie ☎010 65321224; **Mongolia**, 2 Xiushui Bei Jie ☎010 65321203; **Myanmar (Burma)**, 6 Dongzhimenwai Dajie ⓦmyanmarembassy.com; **New Zealand**, Sanlitun Dongsan Jie ⓦmfat.govt.nz; **Pakistan**, 1 Dongzhimenwai Dajie ⓦpakbj.org.pk; **Russian Federation**, 4 Dongzhimen Beizhong Jie ⓦrussia.org.cn; **South Africa**, 5 Dongzhimenwai Dajie ☎010 85320000; **South Korea**, 20 Dongfang Dong Lu ☎010 85310700; **Thailand**, 40 Guanghua Lu ⓦthaiembbeij.org; **UK**, 11 Guanghua Lu ⓦgov.uk/government/world/china; **US**, 55 Anjialou Lu ⓦbeijing.usembassy-china.org.cn; **Vietnam**, 32 Guanghua Lu ⓦvnemba.org.cn/en.

Hospitals and clinics Most big hotels have a resident medic. The following two hospitals have foreigners' clinics where some English is spoken: **Peking Union Medical College Hospital**, 1 Shuaifuyuan, Wangfujing (Mon–Fri 8am–4.30pm; the foreigner unit is south of the inpatient building; ☎010 69159180, ⓦpumch.ac.cn); and the **Sino-Japanese Friendship Hospital**, in the northeast of the city just beyond Beisanhuan Dong Lu (daily 8–11.30am & 1–4.30pm with a 24hr emergency unit; ☎010 64222952, ⓦzryhyy.com.cn). At each of the above you will have to pay a consultation fee of around ¥200. For services run by and for foreigners, try the **Beijing International SOS Clinic**, Suite 105, Kunsha Building, 16 Xinyuanli (daily 24hr; ☎010 64629112, ⓦrafflesmedicalgroup.com); the **International Medical and Dental Centre**, S111 Lufthansa Centre, 50 Liangmaqiao Lu (☎010 64651561, ⓦimcclinics.com); the **Hong Kong International Clinic**, 3F, Swissôtel Hong Kong Macau Centre, Dongsishitiao Qiao (daily 9am–9pm; ☎010 65532288, ⓦhkclinic.com); or the **United Family Hospital**, 2 Jingtai Lu (appointment ☎4008 919191, emergency ☎010 59277120, ⓦbeijing.ufh.com.cn). Expect to pay at least ¥500 for a consultation.

Internet There's free wi-fi everywhere in Beijing: at cafés, restaurants, shopping malls, hotel lobbies, hostels, and even at some tourist sights. If you need access to a terminal, try hotel business centres (expensive), youth hostels (cheap or free, at least for guests), or net bars, which are only marked in Chinese and where you might be asked to show your passport or even a Chinese ID card (see p.54).

Kids If you need child-specific distractions, check out ⓦbeijing-kids.com, which has an excellent "Things to Do" menu, covering places to eat, places to play, and local events. Many of Beijing's tourist sights are free for children under 1.2m high.

Language courses You can do short courses (from two weeks to two months) in Mandarin Chinese at **Beijing Foreign Studies University** (ⓦlb.bfsu.edu.cn); or at the **Bridge School** (ⓦbridgeschoolchina.com), which offers evening classes. For courses in Chinese lasting six months to a year, apply to **Peking University** (ⓦenglish.pku.edu.cn); or **Beijing Normal University** (ⓦenglish.bnu.edu.cn). Expect to pay around US$1500 in tuition fees per semester.

Libraries The **National Library of China** (Mon–Fri 8am–5pm; ⓦwww.nlc.cn/newen), 39 Baishiqiao Lu, just north of Zizhuyuan Park, is one of the largest in the world, with more than ten million volumes, including manuscripts from the Dunhuang Caves and a Qing-dynasty encyclopedia. The oldest texts are Shang-dynasty inscriptions on bone. To take books out, you need to be a

Beijing resident, but a day-pass lets you look around. The British Council Library, 4F Landmark Building, 8 Dongsanhuan Bei Lu, has a wide selection of books and magazines; anyone can wander in and browse.

Pharmacies There are large pharmacies stocking both Western and Chinese medicines at 136 Wangfujing and 42 Dongdan Bei Dajie. The famous Tongrentang Medicine Store has its flagship store on Dazhalan, which also has a doctor for on-the-spot diagnosis.

Post office The International Post Office is just north of the intersection of Jianguomen Dajie and Yabao Lu (Daily 8am–6.30pm).

Visa extensions Apply at least 7 days before your visa expires at the Foreigners' Police, 2 Andingmen Dong Dajie (Mon–Fri 8am–noon & 1.30–4pm; ☎010 84015292); a 30-day extension costs ¥160. See p.54 for what you're likely to need. The process takes a week, so make sure you won't need your passport during this time.

Around Beijing

No visit to Beijing would be complete without a trip to the **Great Wall**, whether at one of the more easily accessible sections – perhaps taking in the **Ming Tombs**, another remnant of imperial glory, along the way – or by hiking around the wall's remoter, ruinous, wilder stretches. For an invigorating breather from the city, the densely wooded **Western Hills** – and, further out, **Jietai** and **Tanzhe temples** – shouldn't be overlooked; while either the ancient **Marco Polo Bridge** or **Tianyi Tomb**, home to the unique **Eunuch Museum**, can easily be covered in a half-day trip from downtown Beijing. Alternatively, the distant village of **Cuandixia** has seemingly changed little over the last century, and makes for an intriguing overnight stay.

The Great Wall

长城, chángchéng

This is a Great Wall and only a great people with a great past could have a great wall and such a great people with such a great wall will surely have a great future. Richard M. Nixon

The practice of building walls along China's northern frontier began in the fifth century BC and continued until the sixteenth century, creating a discontinuous array of fortifications, which came to be known as **Wan Li Changcheng** – "**the Great Wall**" for

---

GREAT WALL, LONG HISTORY

The Chinese have walled their cities throughout recorded history, and during the Warring States Period (around the fifth century BC) simply extended the practice to separate rival territories. The Great Wall's origins lie in these fractured lines of fortifications and in the vision of the first emperor **Qin Shi Huang** who, having unified the empire in the third century BC, joined and extended the disparate sections to form one continuous defence against barbarians.

Under subsequent dynasties, whenever insularity rather than engagement drove foreign policy, the wall continued to be maintained; in response to shifting regional threats, it grew and changed course. It lost importance under the Tang, when borders were extended north, well beyond it. The Tang was, in any case, an outward-looking dynasty that kept the barbarians in check far more cheaply by fostering trade and internal divisions. With the emergence of the insular Ming, however, the wall's upkeep again became a priority; from the fourteenth to the sixteenth century, military technicians worked on its reconstruction. The Ming wall is the one that you see today.

The 7m-high, 7m-thick wall, with its 25,000 battlements, served to bolster Ming sovereignty for a couple of centuries. It restricted the movement of the nomadic peoples of the distant, non-Han minority regions, preventing plundering raids. Signals made by gunpowder blasts, flags and smoke swiftly sent news of enemy movements to the capital. In the late sixteenth century, a couple of huge Mongol invasions were repelled, at Jinshanling and Badaling. But a wall is only as strong as its guards, and it was one of these – Wu Sangui (see p.144) – who allowed the Manchu armies through at the end of the Ming dynasty. Disdained by the Qing, the wall slowly crumbled away, and it wasn't until the 1950s that the first stretches were restored and opened up to tourists.

1

GREAT WALL TOURS

Just about all accommodation can organize a day-trip to Badaling, Mutianyu or Simatai sections of the wall, sometimes with a trip to the Ming Tombs thrown in, for ¥250–450 per person. The cost depends on the section involved, whether lunch is included or not, and whether you spend half the trip at souvenir markets along the way (many low-paid guides top up their wages with commissions). Trips are either in a taxi or small minibus (probably with a minimum of two passengers), or you'll be packed off with an agency tour. Some hostels also offer **hiking** and overnight camping trips to less-visited sections from about ¥340, or contact Beijing Hikers (✆beijinghikers.com), who are expensive individually but might be able to tack you on to an existing tour.

If you're just here for the day, it's best to avoid high on-site prices by bringing your own food and drink. At all the less touristy places, each tourist or group of tourists will be followed along the wall by a villager selling drinks, for at least an hour; if you don't want to be pestered, make it very clear from the outset that you are not interested in anything they are selling – though after a few kilometres you might find that ¥5 can of Coke very welcome.

English-speakers. Today, the line of the wall can be followed from Shanhaiguan, by the Yellow Sea (see p.144), to Jiayuguan in the northwestern deserts (see p.820), a distance of around three thousand kilometres (or, according to a recent survey taking in all the disconnected sections, over 20,000km) – an astonishing feat of engineering.

As a symbol of national pride, the wall's restored sections are now besieged daily by rampaging hordes of tourists, while its image adorns all manner of products, from wine to cigarettes. Yet even the most over-visited section at **Badaling** is still easily one of China's most spectacular attractions. **Mutianyu** is somewhat less crowded, distant **Simatai** much less so, and far more beautiful; you'll get more out of these sections by walking away from the arrivals area. To see the wall in its crumbly glory, head out to **Jinshanling**, **Jiankou** or **Huanghua**, as yet largely untouched by development. For other trips to other unreconstructed sections, check out ✆wildwall.com.

Badaling

八达岭, bādálǐng • Daily 7am–6pm • ¥45 • Cable car ¥80

The best-known section of the wall is at **Badaling**, 70km northwest of Beijing. Here the wall is 6m wide, with regularly spaced watchtowers dating from the Ming dynasty. It follows the highest contours of a steep range of hills, forming a formidable defence, so much so that this section was never attacked directly but instead taken by sweeping around from the side after a breach was made in the weaker, low-lying sections.

As the easiest part of the wall to reach from Beijing, Badaling is also the most packaged, and you're greeted on arrival by a giant tourist circus of restaurants and souvenir stalls selling "I climbed the Great Wall" T-shirts. One thing worth a browse here is the **Great Wall Museum** (included in the main ticket), with plenty of aerial photos, models and construction tools. Otherwise it's hard to feel that there's much genuine about the experience; indeed, the wall itself is hardly original here, as the "restorers" basically rebuilt it wholesale on the ancient foundations.

ARRIVAL AND DEPARTURE   BADALING

Many tours arrive in the early afternoon (when the place is at its busiest), spend an hour or two on site and then return, which really gives you little time for anything except the most cursory of jaunts. It's just as easy, and cheaper, to travel under your own steam; note that you can also get to/from the Ming Tombs (and Beijing's subway network) from here.

By bus From Deshengmen station in Beijing, near the Jishuitan subway stop, catch bus #877 (1hr; ¥12). From (and to) the Ming Tombs, catch bus #879 (50min; ¥8).
By train From Beijing North station (13 daily; 1hr 15min);

the wall entrance is a 2km walk from Badaling station. Services depart Beijing 6am–9.30pm, and from Badaling 8.20am–9.30pm.

ACCOMMODATION

Cao's Courtyard 曹家四合院客栈 cáojiā sìhéyuàn kèzhàn. 18 Chadao village, Yanqing ☎1851 4663311. Pleasant, low-key compound-style hotel with simple but comfortable en-suite rooms – and, of course, a courtyard terrace. It's only a short walk from the train station, and about 10min from the wall. **¥280**

Commune by the Great Wall 长城脚下的公社 chángchéngjiǎo xiàde gōngshè. By the Shuiguan

Great Wall, 4km east of Badaling ☎010 81181888, ⓦcommunebythegreatwall.com. Each of the eleven striking buildings was designed by a different architect (the complex won an architectural award at the 2002 Venice Biennale) and is run as a small boutique hotel. It's an incredible setting, though for this price the food is average and the complex itself is looking a little tired throughout. **¥2600**

Juyong Pass

居庸关, jūyōng guān • Daily 8am–5pm • ¥45

The closest section to Beijing, the wall at **Juyong Pass**, only fifteen minutes' bus ride south of the Badaling section, has been rather over-restored by enthusiastic builders. That said, it's not too popular, and thus not too crowded. Strategically, this was an important stretch, guarding the way to the capital, just 50km away. From the two-storey gate, the wall climbs steeply in both directions, passing through modern copies of the mostly Ming fortifications. The most interesting structure, and one of the few genuinely old ones, is the intricately carved stone base of a long-vanished stupa just beyond here. Access to unreconstructed sections is blocked, but you can walk for about an hour in either direction.

ARRIVAL AND DEPARTURE   JUYONG PASS

By bus From Deshengmen bus station in Beijing, near Jishuitan subway stop, catch bus #345, #670 or others to Shahe, then catch a Chang #68 bus to Juyong (altogether 2hr; ¥12).

By train Take a Badaling train from Beijing North station (see p.100), then a Juyong shuttle bus from Badaling station.

Huanghua

黄花长城, huánghuā chángchéng • Daily 8am–4.30pm • ¥45

The section of the wall at **Huanghua**, 60km north of Beijing, dates to 1404 and is a good example of Ming defences, with wide ramparts, intact parapets and beacon towers. It climbs both sides of a steep, V-shaped valley, with its central section submerged by a small reservoir; on arrival, you'll be dropped off on a road that cuts through the wall. The section to the left is too hard to climb, but the section on the right, past the reservoir, shouldn't present too many difficulties for the agile; indeed, the climb gets easier as you go, with the wall levelling off along a ridge.

The wall here is attractively ruined – so watch your step – and its course makes for a pleasant walk through some lovely countryside. Keep walking for about 2km, to the seventh tower, and you'll reach some steps that lead south down the wall and onto a stony path. Follow this path down past an ancient barracks to a pumping station, and you'll come to a track that takes you south back to the main road, through a graveyard and orchards. When you hit the road you're about 500m from where you started; head north and after 150m you'll come to a bridge where taxis and buses to Huairou congregate.

ARRIVAL AND DEPARTURE   HUANGHUA

By bus Take bus #916 from Dongzhimen bus station in Beijing to Huairou (怀柔, huáiróu; ¥12), and then bus

#H21 to the reservoir (小西湖, xiǎo xīhú; ¥10). The last bus from Huairou to Beijing is at 7pm.

ACCOMMODATION AND EATING

There are a couple of restaurants in the village by the wall, though nothing to get too excited about.

Guesthouses Locals rent out spare rooms in their houses, with the usual spartan facilities: hard beds, bare furnishings

and only cold water on tap which they might be able to heat up for you. Bargain hard over the rates. **¥50–100**

1

Mutianyu Great Wall

慕田峪, mùtiányù • Daily 7am–6pm • ¥45 • Bus from service centre to cable-car station ¥10 • Cable car up ¥80; Slideway down ¥40; combined ¥100

Mutianyu Great Wall, 90km northeast of the city, is the second most popular section, with a huge service centre some 3km from the base of the wall where all transport terminates. However, Mutianyu is geared towards families rather than tour buses and is relatively quiet, with superb ridge-top views of lush, undulating hills crowned by the wall; well endowed with guard towers, it was built in 1368 and renovated in 1983.

From the entrance, steep steps lead up to the wall; you can get a cable car up (and the toboggan-like Slideway down), though it's not far to walk. The stretch of wall you can walk here is about 3km long, with barriers in both directions to stop you continuing any further.

ARRIVAL AND DEPARTURE   MUTIANYU

However you reach Mutianyu, returning by other means shouldn't be a hassle, provided you do so before 6pm; plenty of minibuses wait in the car park to take people back to the city. If you can't find a minibus back to Beijing, get one to the town of Huairou (怀柔, huáiróu) from where you can get regular bus #916 back to the capital – the last bus leaves at 6.30pm.

By bus Take bus #916 from Dongzhimen to Huairou (1hr; ¥12); get off at Mingzhu Square, where you can catch a shuttle bus (¥5) or minibus (¥50 per person) to the wall.

ACCOMMODATION AND EATING

★ Brickyard Retreat 瓦厂, wǎ chǎng. The Schoolhouse, 12 Mutianyu village ☎ 010 61626506, ⓦ brickyardatmutianyu.com. Former schoolhouse and tile factory now converted into a charming restaurant and boutique guesthouse; the comfortable rooms feature industrial-chic brick and tile decor, plus big windows with views of mountains and the (distant) Great Wall. No TV or phones in rooms. The restaurant serves hearty Chinese and Western dishes, made largely with home-grown ingredients. ¥1600

Goose and Duck Ranch 鹅和鸭农庄, éhéyā nóngzhuāng. In Qiaozi, near Huairou ☎ 010 64353778, ⓦ www.gdclub.net.cn. This chirpy family holiday camp has plenty of outdoor pursuits on offer, including archery, go-karting and horseriding. You'll have to book three days in advance. Weekend all-inclusive package ¥700

Shambhala at the Great Wall 新红资避暑山庄, xīnhóngzī bìshǔ shānzhuāng. Xiaguandi village, near Huairou, about 2hr north of Beijing ☎ 010 84018886, ⓦ shambhalaserai.com. This former hunting lodge is now an idyllic boutique hotel, set in attractive countryside. Each of the ten traditional courtyard buildings was constructed from local materials, with a mix of Chinese, Tibetan and Manchu themes; the rooms, all protected by a stone animal, feature Qing-style carved beds. There's also an on-site spa for some serious pampering, and the place is a short walk from the Great Wall. ¥850

Jiankou

箭扣, jiànkòu • Daily 7am–5pm • No official entry fee; villagers charge ¥20 for visitors to enter the drop-off hub at Xizhai village (see opposite)

A fairly intrepid destination is **Jiankou**, about 30km northwest of Huairou town (怀柔, huáiróu), itself north of Beijing. The wall here is white, as it's made of **dolomite**, and there is a **hikeable** and very picturesque section that winds through thickly forested mountain. Don't make the trip without a local guide; much of the stonework is loose on the wall, which is a little tricky to find in the first place. You really need to watch your step, and some nerve-racking sections are so steep that they have to be climbed on all fours.

Hiking Jiankou

You need to be in good shape to **hike** the full 20km track at Jiankou; also be aware that the path has been **blocked off** at one of the watchtowers and that edging around this is extremely dangerous, with a long drop if you slip. The far western end of the hike starts at **Nine Eye Tower**, one of the biggest watchtowers on the wall, and named after its nine peepholes. It's a tough 12km from here to the **Beijing Knot** – a watchtower where three walls come together (and incidentally the flattest area to set up a tent). Around here the views are spectacular, and for the next kilometre or so the hiking is easier, at least until you reach a steep section called "Eagle Flies Vertically". Though theoretically you can scale this, then carry on for another 10km to Mutianyu, it is not recommended; the hike gets increasingly dangerous and includes some almost vertical climbs, such as the notorious "sky stairs".

ARRIVAL AND DEPARTURE   JIANKOU

While Jiankou is just about feasible as a day-trip from Beijing, realistically you'll need to either camp up on the wall, or stay to the north at the transit point of Xizhai village (西栅子, xīzhàzi), where you can pick up guides.

By bus The cheapest way is to catch bus #867 or #936 from Dongzhimen to Yujiayuan (于家园, yújiā yuán; ¥13), from where there are two buses daily to Xizhai (¥8), at 11.30am & 4.30pm.

ACCOMMODATION

Jiankou Zhao's Hostel 箭扣赵家, jiànkòu zhào jiā. Near the car park in Xizhai village ☏010 89696677. Plenty of local farmers rent out rooms, but it's recommended that you call in at this spartan but clean hostel. Mr Zhao is full of information on the hike, and will either guide you himself or sort out someone else to do it. The home-cooked food, incidentally, is excellent – ask if he has any trout. Dorms ¥15, rooms ¥70

Simatai

司马台, sīmǎtái • Daily 8am–4pm & 6–9pm • ¥40 • Cable car ¥20 • Gubei old town ¥180

Some 110km northeast of Beijing, **Simatai** fulfils most visitors' expectations of the Great Wall: a pale ribbon snaking across purple hills, with crumpled blue mountains in the distance. It mostly dates back to the Ming dynasty, and sports a few late innovations such as spaces for cannon, with the inner walls at right angles to the outer wall to thwart invaders who breached the first defence. A rather more modern intrusion is the construction of waterside **Gubei** (古北水镇, gǔběi shuǐ zhèn), also known as W Town, a generic – though surprisingly convincing – "old town" which serves as the gateway to Simatai.

From Gubei, a winding path takes you up to the wall, where most visitors turn right. Regularly spaced watchtowers allow you to measure your progress uphill along the ridge. If you're not scared of heights you can take the cable car to the eighth tower. The walk over the ruins isn't an easy one, and gets increasingly precipitous – but with better views – after about the tenth watchtower. After the fourteenth tower (2hr on), the wall peters out and the climb becomes quite dangerous – don't go any further.

Note that because of the new lake and the blocking-off of one of the towers en route, you can **no longer hike to Jinshanling**.

ARRIVAL AND DEPARTURE   SIMATAI

The journey out from the capital to Simatai takes about 3hr by private transport. It's easiest to arrange a tour all the way from Beijing; you can travel here independently, but this is only worth doing if you want to stay for a night or two.

By bus Take bus #980 from Dongzhimen to Miyun (密云, mìyún; ¥15), and then bus Mi37, Mi50 or Mi51 to Simatai village; alternatively, a taxi from Miyun costs over ¥100 return.

By taxi A rented taxi will cost about ¥850 return, including a wait.

ACCOMMODATION AND EATING

For food, head to one of the nameless places at the side of the car park, where the owners can whip up some very creditable dishes; if you're lucky, they'll have some locally caught wild game in stock.

Dongpo 东坡农家乐园, dōngpō nóngjiā lèyuán. 250m north of the wall ☏1361 3143252 (no English spoken and erratic mobile signal). One of many similar "farmhouse"-style options run by locals, with simple facilities; one room has a traditional *kang* (heated brick bed), and there's a shared bathroom with solar hot water. Ask about the short hike from the guesthouse to Wangjing tower. They also offer free pickup from the Jinshanling service centre (see p.124). Book in advance. ¥300

1

Jinshanling

金山岭长城, jīnshānlǐng chángchéng • Daily 8am–5pm • ¥65 • Cable car ¥40

Jinshanling, about 135km from Beijing and not far west of Simatai, is one of the least visited and best preserved parts of the wall, with jutting obstacle walls and oval watchtowers, some with octagonal or sloping roofs.

Turn left along the wall and you soon encounter a largely unreconstructed section, allowing you to experience something of the wall's magnitude; a long and lonely road that unfailingly picks the toughest line between peaks. Take the hike seriously, as you are scrambling up and down steep, crumbly inclines, and you need to be sure of foot. Eventually you reach a **blocked watchtower**, where you'll have to turn back; note that in any case the new lake makes it impossible to reach Simatai – a once-popular hike.

Alternatively, if you head right when you get onto the wall at Jinshanling, you quickly reach an utterly abandoned and overgrown section. After about four hours' walk along here, you'll reach a road that cuts through the wall, and from here you can flag down a passing bus back to Beijing. This route is only recommended for the intrepid.

ARRIVAL AND DEPARTURE   JINSHALING

By bus From outside Wangjing West subway station in Beijing (line #13 or #15), catch a bus to Luanping (滦平, luánpíng; every 40min 7am–4.30pm; ¥32) and get out at the Jinshanling service centre. There are a handful of free shuttle buses daily from the service centre to the wall, or simply hike 2km.

Ming Tombs

十三陵, shísān líng • Subway line #8 to Zhuxinzhuang and then catch the Changping line to the Ming Tombs station, from where take a shuttle bus for the final 4km • To reach Badaling from the tombs, catch bus #879 (50min; ¥8)

After their deaths, all but three of the sixteen Ming-dynasty emperors were entombed in giant underground vaults in a valley 50km northwest of Beijing. The site – known in English as the **Ming Tombs** – was chosen by the third Ming emperor, Yongle, for its beautiful scenery of gentle hills and woods, still one of the loveliest landscapes around the capital. Two of the tombs, Chang Ling and Ding Ling, were restored in the 1950s, and the site is marked above ground by grand halls, platforms and a spirit way.

That said, there's very little to actually see here, and unless you've a strong historical bent a trip probably isn't worth making for its own sake – although the area is a nice place to picnic, and easy to reach by subway from the city. To get the most out of a visit, consider spending a full day here, hiking around the smaller tombs further into the hills (you should be able to buy a map of them at the site). Alternatively, make use of the bus connection to tie in a tomb trip with the Great Wall at Badaling (see p.120).

Spirit Way

神道, shéndào • Daily 7am–7pm • ¥35

The approach to the Ming Tombs, the 7km-long **Spirit Way**, is the site's most exciting feature, well worth backtracking along from the ticket office. The road commences with the **Dahongmen** (Great Red Gate), a triple-entranced triumphal arch, through the central opening of which only the emperor's dead body was allowed to be carried. Beyond, the road is lined with colossal stone statues of animals and men. Alarmingly larger than life, they all date from the fifteenth century and are among the best surviving examples of Ming sculpture. Their precise significance is unclear, although it is assumed they were intended to serve the emperors in their next life. The animals depicted include the mythological *qilin* (a reptilian beast with a deer's antlers and a cow's tail) and the horned, feline *xiechi*; the human figures are stern, military mandarins. Animal statuary reappears at the entrances to several of the tombs, though the structures themselves are something of an anticlimax.

1

Chang Ling

长陵, cháng líng • Daily 8.30am–5pm • ¥50

At the end of the Spirit Way stands the tomb of Yongle himself: **Chang Ling**, the earliest at the site. There are plans to excavate the underground chamber – an exciting prospect since the tomb is contemporary with some of the finest buildings of the Forbidden City in the capital. At present, the enduring impression above ground is mainly one of scale – vast courtyards and halls, approached by terraced white marble. Its main feature is the Hall of Eminent Flowers, supported by huge columns consisting of individual tree trunks which, it is said, were imported all the way from Yunnan province in China's southwest.

Ding Ling

定陵, dìng líng • Daily 8.30am–5pm • ¥65

The main focus of the Ming Tombs area is **Ding Ling**, the underground tomb-palace of the Emperor Wanli, who ascended the throne in 1573 at the age of 10. Reigning for almost half a century, he began building his tomb when he was 22, in line with common Ming practice, and hosted a grand party within on its completion. The mausoleum, a short distance east of Chang Ling, was opened up in 1956 and found to be substantially intact, revealing the emperor's coffin, flanked by those of two of his empresses, and floors covered with scores of trunks containing imperial robes, gold and silver, and even the imperial cookbooks. Some of the treasures are displayed in the tomb, a huge musty stone vault, undecorated but impressive for its scale; others – having deteriorated after their excavation in 1956, thanks to the poor preservation techniques available at the time – have been replaced by replicas.

Western Hills

西山, xīshān

Thanks to their coolness at the height of summer, Beijing's rugged **Western Hills** are somewhere to escape urban life for a while; long favoured as a restful retreat by religious men, intellectuals, and even politicians – Mao lived here briefly, and the Politburo assembles here in times of crisis.

The hills are divided into three parks, the nearest to the centre being the **Botanical Gardens**, 3.5km northwest of the Summer Palace. Two kilometres farther west, **Xiangshan** is the largest and most impressive of the parks, but just as pretty is **Badachu**, its eight temples strung out along a hillside 2.5km to the south of Xiangshan. The hills take roughly an hour to reach from Beijing on public transport, and each park really deserves a day to itself.

Botanical Gardens

植物园, zhíwù yuán • Daily 7.30am–6pm • ¥10; including conservatory and temple ¥50 • ⊕ www.beijingbg.com

The huge **Botanical Gardens**, just over 5km west of the Summer Palace as the crow flies, feature over 2000 varieties of trees and plants arranged in formal gardens (and usually labelled in English). They're at their prettiest in summer, though the terrain is flat and the landscaping is not as original as in the older parks. The impressive **conservatory** has desert and tropical environments and a lot of fleshy foliage from Yunnan. Behind the **Wofo Temple** is a bamboo garden, from which paths wind off into the hills; one heads northwest to a pretty cherry valley, just under 1km away, where Cao Xueqing is supposed to have written *The Dream of Red Mansions* (see p.969).

Wofo Temple

卧佛寺, wòfó sì • Daily 8.30am–4pm • ¥5, or free with Botanical Gardens through ticket (see above)

The gardens' main path leads after 1km to the **Wofo Temple**, whose main hall houses a huge reclining Buddha, more than 5m in length and cast in copper. With two giant feet protruding from the end of his painted robe, and a pudgy baby-face, calm in repose, he

1

looks rather cute, although he is not actually sleeping but dying – about to enter nirvana. Suitably huge shoes, presented as offerings, are on display around the hall.

ARRIVAL AND DEPARTURE	THE BOTANICAL GARDENS

By bus Bus #331 from outside the Yuanmingyuan (see p.97) travels via the north gate of the Summer Palace to the Western Hills. Bus #360 also heads this way from the zoo.

By subway Take line #4 to Beigongmen; outside Exit A, catch bus #563 or #331 to the gardens.

Xiangshan Park

香山公园, xiāngshān gōngyuán • Daily 6am–6pm • ¥10 • Cable car ¥60 • ⓦ xiangshanpark.com

Around 2km west of the Botanical Gardens lies **Xiangshan Park**, a range of hills dominated by Incense Burner Peak in the western corner. It's at its best in the autumn (before the sharp November frosts), when the leaves turn red in a massive profusion of colour. Though busy at weekends, the park is too large to appear swamped, and is always a good place for a hike and a picnic. Take the path up to the peak (1hr) from where, on clear days, there are magnificent views down towards the Summer Palace and as far as distant Beijing. You can hire a horse to take you down again for ¥30, cheaper than the cable car.

Zhao Miao

昭庙, zhāo miào • Daily 7am–4pm • Free with park entry

Right next to the north gate of the park is the **Zhao Miao** (Temple of Brilliance), one of the few temples in the area that escaped vandalism by Western troops in 1860 and 1900. It was built by Qianlong in 1780 in a Tibetan style, designed to make visiting Lamas feel at home.

Biyun Temple

碧云寺, bìyún sì • Daily 8am–5pm • ¥10

About 400m west of the park's north gate is the superb **Biyun Temple**. A striking building, it's dominated by a bulbous, north Indian-style dagoba and topped by extraordinary conical stupas. Inside, rather bizarrely, a tomb houses the hat and clothes of Sun Yatsen – his body was held here for a while before being relocated to Nanjing in 1924. The giant main hall is now a maze of corridors lined with *arhats*, five hundred in all, and it's a magical place. The benignly smiling golden figures are all different; some have two heads or sit on animals, and one is even pulling his face off.

ARRIVAL AND DEPARTURE	XIANGSHAN PARK

By bus Bus #331 heads from outside the Yuanmingyuan (see p.97) via the north gate of the Summer Palace, both of which are also on subway line #4. Bus #360 also travels this way from the zoo.

By subway Take line #4 to Beigongmen; outside Exit A, catch bus #696 or #331 to the park.

ACCOMMODATION

Fragrant Hills Hotel 香山饭店, xiāngshān fàndiàn. Close to the main entrance of Xiangshan Park ☏ 010 62591166, ⓦ www.xsfd.com. This hotel makes a good base for a weekend escape and some in-depth exploration of the Western Hills. A startlingly incongruous sight, the light, airy hotel looks like something between a Tibetan temple and an airport lounge. It was designed by I.M. Pei, also responsible for Hong Kong's Bank of China tower. **¥988**

Badachu

八大处, bādàchù • Daily 6am–6.30pm • ¥10; cable car up ¥50; sled down ¥60 • Bus #347 from the zoo; or subway line #1 to Pingguoyuan, Exit C, then bus #972

A forested hill 10km south of Xiangshan Park, **Badachu** (Eight Great Sites) derives its name from the presence of eight temples here. Fairly small affairs, lying along the path that curls around the hill, the temples and their surroundings are nonetheless quite attractive, at least on weekdays; don't visit at weekends when the place is teeming.

At the base of the path is a pagoda holding what's said to be **one of Buddha's teeth**, which once sat in the fourth temple, about halfway up the hill. The third temple is a nunnery, and is the most pleasant, with a relaxing teahouse in the courtyard. There's a statue of the rarely depicted, boggle-eyed thunder deity inside the main hall. The other temples make good resting points as you climb up the hill.

Tianyi Tomb

田义墓, tiányì mù • 80 Moshikou Da Jie • Daily 9am–4pm • ¥8 • Subway line #1 to Pingguoyuan, then taxi 3km to the tomb (about ¥15)

Hidden at the back of a crowded street market around 20km west of the city, the **Tianyi Tomb** is that of the influential Ming-dynasty palace **eunuch** and power-broker who became a favourite of the emperor Wanli. He was buried here, at the foot of auspiciously south-facing hills, after 63 years of faithful service to the imperial household; there's a small spirit way flanked by civil and military guardian statues, plus a host of impressive steles outlining Tianyi's life story and achievements. The tomb itself, marked by a concreted-over mound at the back of the complex, is unimpressive, but you can descend into the vault beneath where a heavy stone door and vacant platform are all that remain after the site was looted in 1911. Back near the entrance, a courtyard holds further steles and stone guardian animals, plus surrounding halls form a small **Eunuch Museum** (宦官博物馆, huànguān bówùguǎn), featuring gruesome photos and models, a castration knife, and the mummified body of another Qing-dynasty eunuch who was buried at the site.

Sino-Japanese War Museum and Marco Polo Bridge

Subway line #14 to Dawayao, then a taxi or three-wheeler (¥10) for the final 2km; or it's an unpleasant 30min walk around a complex traffic flow

Some 15km southwest of Beijing, a remnant of the old Imperial Highway crosses the Yongding River over the twelfth-century arches of the **Marco Polo Bridge**, an infamous site in China, where the Japanese launched their attack on the capital in 1937 – an event seen by some as the opening battle of the World War II, and commemorated here at the **Sino-Japanese War Museum**. The bridge is intriguing, and the museum – enclosed inside the 8m-high reconstructed walls of the Ming-dynasty **Wanping Fortress** (宛平城, wǎnpíng chéng) – is perhaps less bombastic than you'd expect, though horrifically graphic at times.

EUNUCHS

In a practice dating back at least to the Han dynasty, China's ruling houses employed **eunuchs** as staff – 20,000 once lived in the Forbidden City – not least to ensure the authenticity of the emperor's offspring. In daily contact with the royals, they often rose to considerable **power**, but this was bought at the expense of their dreadfully low standing in the public imagination. As palace bureaucrats, they were inevitably **despised** (often with good reason) for being utterly corrupt and scheming; Confucianism also held that disfiguration of the body impaired the soul, and eunuchs were buried apart from their ancestors in special graveyards outside the city. In the hope that they would still be buried "whole", they kept and carried around their testicles in bags hung on their belts. They were usually recruited from the poorest families – attracted by the rare chance of amassing wealth other than by birth. Eunuchry was finally banned in 1924 and the remaining 1500 eunuchs were expelled from the palace. An observer described them "carrying their belongings in sacks and crying piteously in high-pitched voices".

Sino-Japanese War Museum

中国人民抗日战争纪念馆, zhōngguó rénmín kàngrìzhànzhēng jìniànguǎn • Daily 9am–4.30pm • Free

The enormous **Sino-Japanese War Museum** is usually packed with school groups being given an education in national outrage. Eight themed halls lay out the conflict's history, which reach back to Japan's occupation of northeastern China after the original Sino-Japanese War of 1894–95. Japan went on to annex Manchuria and finally sparked all-out war by attacking the Wanping Fortress here, outside Beijing, on September 18, 1937. Cases of spears, sabres and chain whips illustrate how ill-equipped Chinese guerrilla forces were to tackle a modern army – and also, perhaps, how brave. One surprising aspect is how inclusive the museum is: British, US, Russian and even Guomindang campaigns against Japan are all given space, painting a picture of an international effort to save China from the invaders. One hall is devoted to Japanese atrocities, such as the notorious Nanjing Massacre (see box, p.312); yet the exhibition's captions are relatively muted: an exhaustive documentation of China's case against Japan, rather than an attempt to browbeat visitors with dogma.

Marco Polo Bridge

卢沟桥, lúgōu qiáo • April–Oct 7am–8pm; Nov–March 7am–6pm • ¥20

Head out through the western gate of the Wanping Fortress, and it's a short walk to where the eleven granite arches of the 266m-long **Marco Polo Bridge** span a vestigial stretch of river, recently dammed upstream. Built in 1192, the bridge was seen by the great traveller some seventy years later, who wrote that "there is not a bridge in the world to compare to it" – though the version here today, its parapets lined with a parade of stone lions, mostly dates to 1698. A plaza at the eastern end sports life-sized bronze statues of camel trains, a memento of the trade artery that once was the Imperial Highway, which stretched west from here through Xi'an and Lanzhou to distant Xinjiang, Tibet and Mongolia. A section of impressively rutted flagstones run down the centre of the bridge, deeply grooved by baggage carts. For the best photographs, get here around sundown.

Jietai and Tanzhe temples

Due west of Beijing, the splendid **Jietai and Tanzhe temples** sit in wooded, hilly countryside beyond the hazy industrial zone that rings the city. Getting there and back can be time-consuming, so take a picnic and enjoy the clean air, peace and solitude.

Jietai Temple

戒台寺, jiètái sì • Daily 8am–5pm • ¥45, ¥85 combined ticket with Tanzhe Temple

Sitting on a hillside 35km west of Beijing, **Jietai Temple** looks more like a fortress, surrounded as it is by forbiddingly tall, red walls. First constructed during the Sui dynasty (581–600), it's an extremely atmospheric, quiet place, made slightly spooky by its venerable but eccentric-looking **pine trees**, all growing in odd directions. In the main hall is an enormous tenth-century platform of white marble at which novice monks were ordained. At 3m high, it's intricately carved with figures – monks, monsters (beaked and winged) and saints. Another, smaller side hall holds a beautiful wooden altar that swarms with dragon reliefs.

Tanzhe Temple

潭柘寺, tánzhè sì • Daily 8am–4.30pm • ¥55, ¥85 combined ticket with Jietai Temple

Twelve kilometres beyond Jietai, **Tanzhe Temple** has the most beautiful and serene location of any temple near the city. It's also one of the oldest, having been constructed during the Jin dynasty (265–420), and one of the largest too. Although there are no longer any clergy living or working here, it once housed a thriving monastic community; these days, a terrace of stupas provides the final resting place for a number of eminent monks.

The temple complex

Wandering through the complex, past the stupas, you reach an enormous central courtyard, with an ancient, towering gingko tree at its heart that's over a thousand years old. Across the courtyard, a second, smaller gingko was once supposed to produce a fresh branch every time a new emperor was born. From here you can take in the other buildings, arrayed on different levels up the hillside, or look around the lush gardens, whose bamboo is supposed to cure all manner of ailments.

ARRIVAL AND DEPARTURE   JIETAI AND TANZHE TEMPLES

By public transport For either temple, first take subway line #1 to its western terminus at Pingguoyuan. From here, bus #948 goes to Jietai; bus #931 also travels via Jietai and terminates at Tanzhe Temple (this bus has two routes, so make sure the driver knows where you're going). A taxi between the two temples costs around ¥35.

By taxi A taxi to visit both temples should cost around ¥400 from the city centre.

Cuandixia

爨底下, cuàndǐxià, also known as 川底下, chuāndǐxià · ¥35

Around 90km west of Beijing, **Cuandixia** village has some of this part of the country's finest surviving Ming- and Qing-dynasty residential architecture. It's a splendid setting: fanning downhill from a ridge, against a backdrop of the rugged Jingxi mountains, the village forms a tight cluster of eighty-odd traditional, grey-tiled courtyard houses built on stone terraces. Cuandixia sits close to one of the old imperial post roads – now Highway #109 – which explains the village's one-time, now faded, prosperity; many of the houses are decorated with auspicious murals, and feature carvings in stone and wood. A local oddity is that almost everyone in the village is surnamed **Han**, after the original clan which migrated here from Shanxi province some five centuries ago. A few small temples and viewpoints above the village make for some easy hikes, and if you're enjoying the experience you might want to check out similar villages nearby: Huanglingxi (黄岭西村, huánglǐngxī cūn), Shaungshitou (双石头村, shuāngshítou cūn) and the old garrison town of Baiyu (柏峪村, bǎiyù cūn).

ARRIVAL AND DEPARTURE   CUANDIXIA

By public transport Take subway line #1 to Pingguoyuan, then walk 150m west to the bus station; there are 2 buses daily direct to Cuandixia at 7.30am & 12.40pm. Return buses depart Cuandixia at 10.30am & 3.30pm. The journey takes 2–3hr in total from downtown Beijing.

On a tour Several Beijing tour operators offer private excursions to Cuandixia, but these are expensive for solo travellers: try ⓦ thechinaguide.com or ⓦ chinaculturecenter .org, who might be able to tack you on to an existing tour.

ACCOMMODATION

Unless on a tour, you'll have to spend the night at Cuandixia, and though there's little to see or do as such, it's a refreshing break from the capital. Many places have signs up offering basic **homestay accommodation** (¥150) and meals, though be aware that nobody in the village speaks English.

Hebei and Tianjin

河北 / 天津

CHENGDE, PUTUO ZONGCHENG TEMPLE

2

Hebei and Tianjin

A somewhat anonymous region, Hebei has two great cities at its heart – Beijing and Tianjin – both of which long ago outgrew the province and struck out on their own as separate municipalities. In the south, a landscape of flatlands is spotted with heavy industry and mining towns – China at its least glamorous – which are home to the majority of the province's seventy million inhabitants. The sparsely populated tableland to the north, rising from the Bohai Gulf, holds more promise. For most of its history this marked China's northern frontier and, as a buffer zone protecting the nation from barbarian invasion, the area has long been heavily militarized. It was here that the first sections of the Great Wall were built in the fourth century AD, along the Hebei–Shanxi border, in an effort to fortify China's borders against her aggressive neighbours.

The parts of this barrier visible today, however, are the remains of the much younger and more extensive Ming-dynasty structure, begun in the fourteenth century as a deterrent against the Mongols. You can see the wall where it meets the sea at **Shanhaiguan**, a fortress town only a few hours by train from Beijing. Just south down the coast from here, the seaside resort of **Beidaihe** hosts busy throngs of happy holidaymakers throughout the summer months, a good place to experience how the Chinese like their holiday spots the way they like their restaurants – *renao* (literally "hot and noisy"). Well north of the wall, the town of **Chengde** is the province's most visited attraction, an imperial base set amid the wild terrain of the Hachin Mongols and conceived on a grand scale by the eighteenth-century emperor Kangxi, with temples and monuments to match. Given their popularity and easy access from Beijing, it's worth arranging trips to all three destinations as far ahead as possible, as accommodation and – especially – transport can get booked out long in advance.

   Tianjin, Beijing's one-time port and former Concession town with a reputation for antiques markets, is worth a day-trip from Beijing to explore its hodgepodge of colonial architecture, visit an unusual museum and to make an evening river cruise through the city centre.

Tianjin

天津, tiānjīn

The third-largest city in China after the capital and Shanghai, **TIANJIN** is generally ignored by Western travellers – even those who enter or exit China via the nearby port of **Tanggu**. One reason is that Beijing, with its infinitely more famous sights, is just 130km to the northwest, a mere thirty minutes away by high-speed train. However, this also brings Tianjin within easy day-trip range of the capital, and while the city has few specific attractions – best of which are its **antiques market**, the excellent **Yangliuqing Woodblock Printing Museum**, and a fun **river cruise** – Tianjin does have its own very definite

COLONIAL ARCHITECTURE, TIANJIN

Highlights

❶ **Tianjin** Glimpse dilapidated colonial architecture, browse antiques markets and take a river cruise. **See p.132**

❷ **Beidaihe beachfront** Once the pleasure preserve of colonists, then communists, the summer sands are now chock-a-block with the bikini-clad masses. **See p.142**

❸ **Shanhaiguan** A dusty relic of a walled city on the Bohai Gulf, where you can follow the Great Wall until it disappears dramatically into the sea. **See p.144**

❹ **Chengde** The summer playground of emperors, whose many palaces and temples have been restored, to the delight of Beijing day-trippers. **See p.147**

HIGHLIGHTS ARE MARKED ON THE MAP ON P.134

character. Much of this derives from the extensive central core of ageing nineteenth- and early twentieth-century European-style **streetscapes**, even if elsewhere Tianjin has become a massive construction site, with mushrooming flocks of brand-new skyscrapers rearing up against the skyline. But thanks to a campaign by noted writer and local resident **Feng Jicai**, much of the old colonial quarter has been listed as historic – look for the distinctive plaques on the relevant buildings. This hasn't necessarily protected antique architecture from overzealous renovation, however, and in places contemporary Tianjin presents an unwieldy fusion of Beijing's bustle and Shanghai's Bund.

HEBEI & TIANJIN

0	100

kilometres

INNER MONGOLIA

HEBEI

Jining

Zhangjiakou

Xuanhua

Datong

Sanggan River

SHANXI

BEIJING SHI

BEIJING

Luan River

4 Chengde

LIAONING

Great Wall

Qinglong

Shanhaiguan

Qinhuangdao

2 **3**

Beidaihe

Tangshan

Bohai Gulf

Tianjin **1**

Baoding

Renqui

TIANJIN SHI

Tanggu

Dalian, Kobe & Incheon

Ziya River

Shijiazhuang

Cangzhou

Hengshui

Dezhou

SHANDONG

SHANXI

Xingtai

Handan

Ji'nan

Mongolia

N

Taiyuan

HIGHLIGHTS
1 Tianjin
2 Beidaihe beachfront
3 Shanhaiguan
4 Chengde

TIANJIN ORIENTATION

The majority of Tianjin's colonial buildings are clustered in the grid of streets on the southern side of the **Hai River** (海河, hǎi hé), whose gentrified banks are great for ambling. From the main train station, you can approach the old town via **Jiefang Bridge**, built by the French in 1903, which leads south along heavily restored and developed **Jiefang Bei Lu**, an area given an oddly Continental feel by the pastel colours and wrought-iron scrollwork balconies of the French Concession. This is at its most appealing around the glorified roundabout known as **Zhongxin Park**, which marks the southeastern end of the main shopping district. Rising above all of this are the **skyscrapers** of new Tianjin, tallest of which is currently the 337m-high Tianjin World Financial Center; the Goldin Finance 117 and the Rose Rock IFC, two near-600m-tall beasts (though plagued by construction hiccups), are scheduled to bring Tianjin into the world's select 100-storey-plus club around 2018.

2

Brief history

Though today the city is given over to industry and commerce, it was as a **port** that Tianjin first gained importance. When the Ming emperor Yongle moved the capital from Nanjing to Beijing, Tianjin became the dock for vast quantities of rice paid in tribute to the emperor and transported here from all over the south via the Grand Canal. In the nineteenth century, the city's strategically useful location caught the attention of the seafaring Western powers, not least during the First Opium War (see p.931): with well-armed gunboats, the invaders were assured of victory, and the **Treaty of Tianjin**, signed in 1858, gave the Europeans the right to establish nine treaty ports on the mainland, from which they could conduct trade and sell opium.

Tianjin's own **Concessions**, along the banks of the Hai River, were separate, self-contained, European fantasy worlds (see below). The Chinese were discouraged from intruding, except for servants, who were given pass cards. Tensions between the indigenous population and the foreigners exploded in the **Tianjin Massacre** of 1870, when a Chinese mob attacked a French-run orphanage, killing nuns, priests and the French consul in the belief that the Chinese orphans had been kidnapped and were merely awaiting the pot. The city had its genteel peace interrupted again by the **Boxer Rebellion** in 1900 (see p.932), after which the foreigners levelled the walls around the old Chinese city to enable them to see in and keep an eye on its residents.

Central Tianjin

The city centre is home to a few sights, all within fairly easy walking distance of the train station. Here you'll find the bulk of Tianjin's **colonial architecture**: running from west to east along the north bank of the river were the Austrian, Italian, Russian and Belgian Concessions, though most of the old buildings here have been destroyed. Unmistakeable are the chateaux of the French Concession, which now make up the downtown district south of the river, down to Nanjing Lu, and the haughty mansions the British built east of here. Farther east again, the architecture of an otherwise unremarkable district has a sprinkling of stern German constructions.

The most appealing clutch of old lanes and facades lie either side of **Binjiang Dao** and **Heping Lu**, two pedestrianized, over-restored shopping streets lined with upmarket international boutiques. It's a good place just to wander around and maybe sample some of Tianjin's street snacks, but as a specific target the **antiques market** is, perhaps, of most interest to visitors.

China Porcelain House Museum

中国瓷房子博物馆, zhōngguó cífángzi bówùguǎn • Chifeng Dao • Daily 9am–6pm • ¥35 • Metro line #3 to Heping Lu

While most people won't feel the need to go inside, the **China House Museum** is a must-see for its (frankly insane) premises – a colonial mansion clad entirely in broken pottery, replete with extensive additional curlicues. This is the work of Zhang Lianzhi, a Tianjin native who purchased the house in 2002; he has since gone on to fill it with thousands of porcelain pieces, mainly from the Qing dynasty, though some go back to the Tang (618–907). A couple of rooms at the front of the property function as small shops, though prices verge on the extortionate.

The antiques market

旧货市场, jiùhuò shìchǎng • Daily 8am–5pm • Metro line #3 to Heping Lu

On a busy day Tianjin's **antiques market**, centred around the intersection of Shenyang and Shandong roads, is a great attraction even if you have no intention of buying. The side-alleys here are lined with dark, poky shops, pavement vendors with their wares spread out in front of them on yellowed newspapers and stallholders waving goods in the faces of passers-by. Expect a range of jade jewellery, ceramic teapots, fans and perfume bottles, Russian army watches, opium pipes, snuffboxes, ornate playing cards, old photographs, rimless sunglasses, and a whole slew of nineteenth-century bric-a-brac such as gilt buttons, hairpins and even rusty militaria.

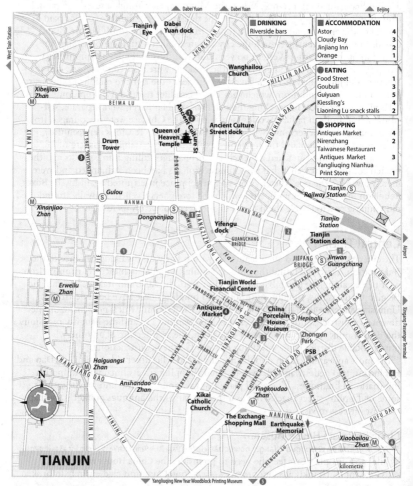

DRINKING
Riverside bars — 1

ACCOMMODATION
Astor — 4
Cloudy Bay — 3
Jinjiang Inn — 2
Orange — 1

EATING
Food Street — 1
Goubuli — 3
Guiyuan — 5
Kiessling's — 4
Liaoning Lu snack stalls — 2

SHOPPING
Antiques Market — 4
Nirenzhang — 2
Taiwanese Restaurant Antiques Market — 3
Yangliuqing Nianhua Print Store — 1

TIANJIN

The market expands and contracts according to the time of year (small in winter, big in summer), but it's always at its largest on Thursdays and Saturdays.

Xikai Catholic Church

西开教堂, xīkāi jiàotáng • Daily 5.30am–4.30pm • English-language Mass Sun 11am • Metro lines #1 or #3 to Yingkou Dao

At the southern end of Binjiang Dao, this **Catholic church** is a useful landmark and one of the most distinctive buildings in the city. Dedicated to St Joseph, it was built by the French in 1917. With an odd facade of horizontal brown and orange brick stripes topped with three green domes, it has a pleasing interior, if less interesting than the exterior.

Tangshan Earthquake Memorial

抗震纪念碑, kàngzhèn jìniànbēi • Metro lines #1 or #3 to Yingkou Dao

The diffuse zone of unremarkable buildings east of the Catholic church, around Nanjing Lu, is notable only for the **Earthquake Memorial** opposite the *Friendship Hotel*. More tasteful than most examples of Chinese public statuary, this hollow pyramid commemorates the 250,000 people who died in the **1976 Tangshan earthquake**, northeast of Tianjin – one of the world's worst ever natural disasters, and one which many Chinese believe foretold the subsequent death of Chairman Mao.

Northwest of the centre

There's a clutch of sights to the north and west of central Tianjin, an area bisected by the prettified Hai River; you can use its banks as a pleasant means of access from the train station, or **cruise** the area by boat (see box, p.138). Off the east bank are two interesting places of worship, the Buddhist **Dabei Yuan** and the Christian **Wanghailou Church**. To the west of the river lies the mildly diverting **Ancient Culture Street**, and the **Drum Tower** area, both of which have been over-renovated in faux-dynastic style.

Dabei Yuan

大悲院, dàbēi yuàn • Tianwei Lu, off Wuma Lu • Daily 9am–4pm • ¥5 • Dabei Yuan ferry dock or metro line #3 to Jinshiqiao

Tianjin's major Buddhist temple, **Dabei Yuan**, is located on a narrow lane off Zhongshan Lu in the northern part of the city. Large bronze vessels full of water stand outside the buildings, a fire precaution that has been in use for centuries. Outside the first hall, which was built in the 1940s, the devout wrap their arms around a large bronze incense burner before lighting incense sticks and kowtowing. In the smaller, rear buildings – seventeenth-century structures extensively restored after the Tangshan earthquake – you'll see the temple's resident monks, while small antique wood and bronze Buddhist figurines are displayed in a hall in the west of the complex.

Tianjin Eye

天津之眼, tiānjīn zhīyǎn • On Jingang Bridge • Daily 9.30am–9.30pm • ¥70 • Dabei Yuan ferry dock or metro line #3 to Jinshiqiao

The 120m-tall **Tianjin Eye** is perched west of the Dabei Yuan, right over the Hai River on Jingang Bridge. Eight-seater pods carry passengers up to the skyline on a 30min cycle, providing superlative views of the river and an ever more modern cityscape.

Wanghailou Church

望海楼教堂, wànghǎilóu jiàotáng • Junction of Shizilin Dajie and Haihe Dong Lu • Open during services only (times vary) • Dabei Yuan ferry dock or metro line #3 to Jinshiqiao

The stern **Wanghailou Church** stands not far south of Dabei Yuan, over Shizilin Dajie on the north bank of the river. Built in 1904, it has an austere presence thanks to the use of dark stone. It's the third church to stand on this site – the first was destroyed in the massacre of 1870 (see p.135), a year after it was built, and the second was burnt down in 1900 during the Boxer Rebellion. It's possible to visit during the week, but the Sunday-morning Chinese-language services (7am) make a stop here much more interesting.

2

Ancient Culture Street

古文化街, gǔwénhuà jiē • Between Beima Lu and Shuige Lu • Ancient Culture Street ferry dock or metro line #2 to Dongnanjiao

Every city in China worth its salt has an antique-style district, often no more than a few years old. Tianjin's incarnation, **Ancient Culture Street**, runs just west of the river, its entrance marked by colourful arches. There are a few genuinely old structures here (including a section of Ming-dynasty cobbled road) but – despite all the curling, tiled roofs, carved balconies and red-and-green wooden shopfronts – not much in the way of venerable atmosphere or culture. Part of the problem is the overload of souvenir stalls, and one has to wonder how on earth *Doraemon* keyrings, ceramic snowmen and butt-wiggling dog dolls can be representative of "old Tianjin".

Queen of Heaven Temple

天后宫, tiānhòu gōng • Daily 9am–5pm • ¥10

One actual piece of culture on Ancient Culture Street is the heavily restored **Queen of Heaven Temple**, originally built in 1326 and supposedly the oldest building in Tianjin. It's dedicated to the southern Chinese deity Tian Hou (also known as Matsu), protector of sailors and fishermen, and the imported cult is evidence of Tianjin being an important port as far back as the Yuan dynasty. An exhibition of local crafts fills the side halls.

Yangliuqing New Year Woodblock Printing Museum

杨柳青木版年画博物馆, yángliǔqīng mùbǎn niánhuà bówùguǎn • 111 Donghou Sanhe Li/Binguan Lu • Tues–Sun 9am–4.30pm • Free • Metro line #3 to Wujiayao

Hidden down an obscure lane 2km southwest of the city centre, the **Yangliuqing New Year Woodblock Printing Museum** is sadly under-visited despite its outstanding collection of these colourful folk art pictures, traditionally pasted up outside homes to usher in luck over the coming year. Though there were many centres for the craft across China, Yangliuqing – a village in Tianjin's western suburbs – became famous during the Qing dynasty, when a host of family-run studios competed to produce prints of folk tales, deities, fat babies, and scenes from daily life. Naturalistic and technically complex, they were often unusually large (some measure over a metre across) and typically used hand-painted colours over a block-printed outline.

A century of civil war devastated the industry, however, and by the 1950s many of the old designs had been lost, the woodblocks converted into chopping boards. The museum's archive has gathered together over 1300 survivals, with a broad range on display on two floors; look for the cheery Mao-era illustrations, promising happiness

---

TIANJIN BY BOAT

A fun way to view Tianjin's old city is aboard the **ferries and cruises** along a short section of the Hai River, between the train station and Tianjin Eye. The area was demarcated into national zones, and each section today retains a hint of its old flavour in the many (reconstructed) colonial-era facades finished in the French, British and Italian styles – interspersed, of course, with some eye-catching blocks of contemporary riverside architecture. There are many notable **bridges** too, not least the plank-and-steel-girder Jiefang Bridge opposite the station, and the impressively heavy-looking stone Guangcheng Bridge, complete with gilded Neoclassical statues, which could have been transplanted from London.

PRACTICALITIES

Haihe Cruises ☎022 58306789, ⓦ www.haihetour .com. Runs 50min cruises from Tianjin Station dock daily, on the hour 9am–5pm (¥80) and 7.30pm & 8.30pm (¥100). The journey takes you nonstop upstream to Dabei Yuan dock at the Tianjin Eye before returning.

By ferry Regular ferries travel from the station via docks at Ancient Culture Street, Yifengu and Dabei Yuan; they depart every 30min, 9am–4.30pm. A 1-day pass costs ¥100.

and prosperity for all; and the four large "Tale of White Snake" prints, each showing successive stages in the printing process.

ARRIVAL AND DEPARTURE

TIANJIN

By plane Binhai International Airport (天津滨海国际机场, tiānjīn bīnhǎi guójì jīchǎng) lies 15km east of Tianjin; it has connections to every major city in China, as well as multiple international destinations. Shuttle buses serve various parts of the city; most useful for travellers are those to the main train station (every 30min 6am–7.30pm; 20min; ¥15).

Destinations Changsha (2hr 20min); Chengdu (3hr); Dalian (1hr); Fuzhou (3hr 50min); Guangzhou (3hr 10min); Guilin (2hr 45min); Haikou (4hr 50min); Hangzhou (1hr 50min); Harbin (3hr); Hong Kong (3hr 30min); Kunming (3hr 50min); Lanzhou (2hr 10min); Nanjing (1hr); Qingdao (1hr 15min); Shanghai (1hr 55min); Shenyang (2hr); Shenzhen (3hr 15min); Taiyuan (1hr 15min); Wuhan (2hr 30min); Xiamen (2hr 50min); Xi'an (2hr).

By train Tianjin's main train station (天津站, tiānjīn zhàn), centrally located on the north bank of the river at the nexus of metro lines #2, #3 and #9, mostly handles high-speed services between Beijing and eastern China. A few high-speed trains also depart from the West station (火车西站, huǒchē xīzhàn; metro line #1).

Destinations Beidaihe (many daily; 1hr–5hr 45min); Beijing (every 20min; 35–90min); Guangzhou (7 daily; 25hr); Harbin (31 daily; 6hr 15min–19hr); Shanghai (many daily; 4hr 45min–20hr); Shanhaiguan (many daily; 1–6hr); Shenyang (many daily; 3hr 30min–12hr).

By bus There is no point in using buses to get to or from Tianjin: the city's train connections are faster and more numerous, while its confusing profusion of bus stations are all outside the centre.

By ferry Tianjin Xingang Passenger Terminal (天津新港客运站, tiānjīn xīngǎng kèyùn zhàn), around 60km east of central Tianjin, has connections to Dalian, as well as international services to Inchon in South Korea. Tickets can be purchased from travel agents all over Tianjin (ask your hostel/hotel for the closest one; many even sell tickets themselves), or at the port itself. There are frequent minibuses between the port and Tianjin's main train station (¥10), and some shuttle services direct to Beijing (¥70); alternatively, it's ¥100–120 for a taxi from the port to central Tianjin, and you'll easily find others to share the cost if necessary.

Destinations Dalian (March–Oct daily; rest of year every other day; 12–15hr); Inchon (2 weekly; 25hr).

GETTING AROUND

Downtown and the old Concession areas are just about small enough to explore on foot; for river ferry services, see box opposite.

By metro Tianjin's useful metro system (from ¥2 per journey) currently comprises subway lines #1, #2, #3, and the Jinbing light rail #9 (though this isn't of any use for visitors). More lines are under construction.

By bus Buses run 5am–midnight, with fares a standard ¥1.5 throughout the city centre. The most useful route, by far, is the #600, which starts behind the main train station, then heads out on a circular route past (or close to) all the main city sights.

By taxi Cabs are plentiful – flag fall is ¥9, and ¥15 is sufficient for most journeys around town.

ACCOMMODATION

Astor 利顺德大饭店, lìshùndé dà fàndiàn. 33 Tai'er Zhuang Lu ☎ 022 58526888, ⓦ starwoodhotels.com. A charming hotel, and the only one in the city that exudes any colonial-era vibes whatsoever, this is located in a former British mansion dating back to 1863. Modern but still featuring elegant colonial panelling, antique-style light fittings, polished wooden floors and woollen carpets, this remains one of the most stylish places to stay in Tianjin. ¥900

Cloudy Bay 云雾之湾国际青年旅舍, yúnwùzhīwān guójì qīngnián lǚshě. 120 Ha'erbin Lu ☎ 022 27230606, ⓦ yhachina.com. Welcoming youth hostel featuring slightly fuddled staff, clean rooms with bright paint jobs and a great roof terrace-bar. Look for a blue-and-white building just south of the Xinhua Dao intersection. Dorms ¥70, doubles ¥300

Jinjiang Inn 锦江之星火车站店, jǐnjiāng zhīxīng huǒchēzhàn diàn. 17 Jinbu Dao ☎ 022 58215018. A cheap chain hotel, conveniently located close to the station (150m from south exit #4), with clean, unexciting, motel-like rooms. It's often full – book ahead if possible. ¥210

Orange 桔子酒店北安桥店, júzi jiǔdiàn běi'ān qiáo diàn. 7 Xing'an Lu ☎ 022 27348333. Decent cheapie down an alley by the riverside, with rooms that are a notch above those of other budget chains. Try to nab a room with a river view; those from the upper levels are good. Note that it's quite difficult to access the hotel, especially from the riverside itself. ¥300

2

EATING

For **local snacks** – such as deep-fried squid, *erduoyuan* (rice cakes fried in sesame oil; the name means "ear hole") or *mahua* (fried dough twists) – try **Liaoning Lu**, west off pedestrianized Binjiang Dao. **Food Street** (食品街, shípǐn jiē) on Qinghe Dajie, east of Nanmenwai Dajie, comprises an indoor eating area crammed with restaurants to suit all budgets.

Goubuli 狗不理包子铺, gǒubùlǐ bāozi pù. 77 Shandong Lu ☎022 27302540. Famed as much for its name (meaning "Dogs Wouldn't Touch It") as for its food, this Tianjin stalwart serves succulent – if very expensive – *baozi* dumplings, as well as a host of standard restaurant dishes. Always crowded despite poor service. Expect to pay ¥60 for a plate of *baozi* in the downstairs canteen, or around ¥80 for a main in the upstairs restaurant. Daily 10am–9pm.

★**Guiyuan** 桂园餐厅, guìyuán cāntīng. 103 Chengdu Dao, across from the intersection with Guangxi Lu ☎022 23397530. Slightly shabby, very busy place on three floors, serving Tianjin specialities; expect to share a table with strangers unless you want a long wait.

Everyone orders "eight-treasure tofu" (mostly braised seafood) and "black garlic beef", a Chinese take on French pepper steak. No English signage or menu. Daily 11am–2pm & 5–9pm.

Kiessling's 起士林西式餐厅, qǐshìlín xīshì cāntīng. 333 Zhejiang Lu, just off Nanjing Lu. Hidden behind the domed, columned concert hall, and formerly Austrian-owned, this restaurant has been around for nearly 100 years, and still serves Western food: breaded fish fillets, mashed potatoes, pasta and so forth, all around ¥50–100 per dish. The beer hall and dining room on the top level is worth a stop, if only for its home-brewed dark beer (¥25). Restaurant daily 11am–2pm & 5–9pm.

DRINKING

For drinking, it's hard to beat the small curl of bars on the **river bank** opposite the train station; many sell draught beer from just ¥8, and their outdoor terraces are glorious places to sit on a sunny day.

SHOPPING

Nirenzhang 泥人张, nírénzhāng. Ancient Culture St. Brightly-painted clay figurines are a traditional Tianjin folk art, though among fairly crude models of simpering deities are some really fine pieces of famous figures and ordinary people engaged in their daily activities – but prices are steep. Daily 10am–7pm.

Taiwanese Restaurant Antiques Market 台湾菜馆, táiwān càiguǎn. West of the Drum Tower on Chengxiang Zhong Lu. Though tourists flock to the Shenyang Dao market (see p.136), more serious collectors target this subterranean, rather more upmarket den, where you're likely to find far more gaudy (and possibly genuine) items. Thurs is the busiest day. Market daily 10am–5pm, though individual dealers keep their own hours.

Yangliuqing Nianhua Print Store 杨柳青年画店, yángliǔqīng niánhuà diàn. Ancient Culture St. The

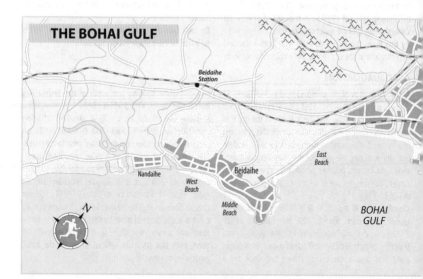

best available range of these bold, eye-catching posters, though sadly that's not saying much: nowadays the industry seems keen on churning out lurid images of fat babies. The museum (see p.138) has a similar selection, but also books (some in English). Daily 10am–7pm.

DIRECTORY

Banks and exchange The main Bank of China (daily 8am–5pm) is at 80 Jiefang Bei Lu, on the corner of Datong Dao.

Post The post office (daily 9am–6.30pm) is just east of Tianjin Station.

2

The Bohai Gulf

On the **Bohai Gulf**, 300km east of Beijing, lies the rather bizarre seaside resort of **Beidaihe**. The coastline, reminiscent of the Mediterranean – rocky, sparsely vegetated, erratically punctuated by beaches – was originally patronized a hundred years ago by European diplomats, missionaries and businessmen, who built villas and bungalows here, and reclined on verandas sipping cocktails after indulging in the new bathing fad. Most of Beidaihe's visitors nowadays are ordinary, fun-loving tourists, usually relatively well-heeled Beijingers; in high season (May–Aug), when the temperature hovers around the mid-20s Celsius and the water is warm, it's a fun place to spend the day. Only 25km or so to the northeast, historic attractions at **Shanhaiguan** have year-round appeal, and include some fine sturdy fortifications within the town, and remnants of the **Great Wall** outside.

Note that, this close to Beijing, high-speed trains to both Beidaihe and Shanhaiguan are typically **booked out** weeks in advance throughout the summer (July & Aug); at these times you might have more luck travelling via Tianjin.

Beidaihe

北戴河, běidàihé

China doesn't have a long history of beach culture, but little **BEIDAIHE** has become a well-established retreat for Beijingers seeking an escape from the capital's cloying summer humidity and pollution. As a sign of how attitudes are relaxing, it wasn't so long ago that dark swimsuits were compulsory to avoid the illusion of nudity, though

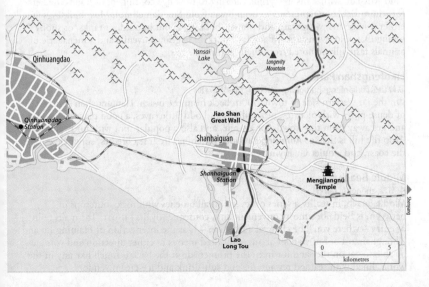

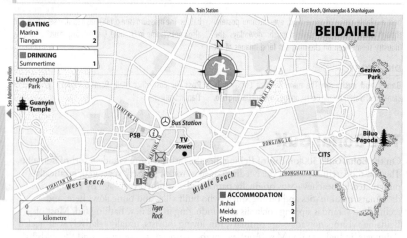

these days bright, skimpy bikinis are *de rigueur* on the town's three main beaches, while the streets by the shore are as gaudy and kitschy as any busy seaside resort. Away from the sea, up the hill, the tree-lined streets are much quieter, and the majority of the town seems to consist of nondescript compounds hosting guesthouses, **villas** and sanatoriums, some open to paying guests and others set aside for the Party, PLA or state-run companies who reward favoured members with trips to the seaside.

Note that much of Beidaihe shuts down during colder months; the streets along the seafront are at their liveliest from May to August.

Haining Lu

Beidaihe's central area is the southern stretch of **Haining Lu**, a busy stretch of hotels, seafood restaurants and tourist shops which runs down to the beach as **Bao'er Lu**. This central area has been given a colonial German facelift, with older buildings restored and newer ones fitted out with timber-frame cladding; the overall flavour, however, is Sino-Russian, with signs in Cyrillic catering to the huge contingent of holidaymakers for whom Beidaihe represents a cheap break from Siberian climes. Most buildings are either restaurants, with crabs and prawns bobbing about in outdoor tanks, or shops selling Day-Glo swimsuits, inflatables, snorkelling gear, souvenirs and a menagerie of animals tastefully sculpted from shells and raffia.

Lianfengshan Park

联峰山公园, liánfēngshān gōngyuán • Daily 7am–5pm • ¥20

On the far western side of town, 500m back from the beach, **Lianfengshan Park** is a hill of dense pines with picturesque pavilions and odd little caves, a good place to wander and get away from the crowds for a while, and also a popular spot with birdwatchers. Atop the hill is the **Sea Admiring Pavilion**, which has fresh sea breezes, super views of the coast, and a quiet Guanyin Temple.

Middle Beach

中海滩, zhōnghǎi tān • ¥8

Middle Beach, in reality a series of several small beaches with rocky outcrops in between, is Beidaihe's most convenient and, consequently, its busiest. The main point of entry – where you'll be charged admission – is at the intersection of Haining Lu and Zhonghaitan Lu, but wander about a hundred metres in either direction and you may be able to get on the sand for free. The promenade at the back is much like any in the world, lined with seafood restaurants and soft-drink and ice-cream vendors.

East Beach

东海滩, dōnghǎi tān • Daily 24hr • Free • Bus #1 or #34 from bus station

Stretching 15km to the industrial rail hub of Qinhuangdao is **East Beach**, a more sedate location than Middle Beach, thanks to its popularity with cadres and sanatorium patients. The beach is long enough for you to be able to find a spot where you can be alone, though much of the muddy shoreline isn't very attractive. At low tide its wide expanse is dotted with seaweed collectors in rubber boots.

Geziwo Park

鸽子窝公园, gēziwō gōngyuán • ¥12 • Bus #1 or #34 from bus station

At the southern tip of East Beach is **Geziwo Park**, a 20m-high rocky outcrop named for the seagulls fond of perching here, presumably by someone who wasn't skilled in bird identification – the name means "Pigeon's Nest". It's a good spot for watching the sunrise. Mao sat here in 1954 and wrote a poem, *Ripples sifting sand: Beidaihe*, which probably loses something in translation.

ARRIVAL AND DEPARTURE
BEIDAIHE

By train Beidaihe train station (北戴河站, běidàihé zhàn), with high-speed connections to Beijing, Tianjin, Shenyang and Shanhaiguan, is 5km west of town; catch bus #5 (¥1; last bus around 8pm) to the central bus station. A taxi will cost around ¥40.
Destinations Beijing (many daily; 1hr 50min–7hr); Shanhaiguan (many daily; 30min–1hr); Shenyang (many daily; 2hr 50min–7hr); Tianjin (many daily; 2hr 40min–7hr).
By bus Beidaihe bus station (北戴河汽车站, běidàihé

qìchē zhàn) is off Haining Lu, a 15min walk from Middle Beach. It's useful for getting to and from Shanhaiguan (1hr 30min), though you'll need to change buses halfway along in the gritty regional "capital" of Qinhuangdao (秦皇岛, qínhuángdǎo): from Beidaihe, take the #34 (¥2) and let the bus attendant know you're going to Shanhaiguan, then they'll set you down in Qinhuangdao, at the nexus with the #33 route (¥2), which you should take the remainder of the way – not a nice journey.

GETTING AROUND

By taxi Cabs around town cost ¥10, but once down by the beach Beidaihe is small enough to get around easily on foot.

By bicycle Stands at the beaches rent bicycles at ¥20–40/hr, plus ¥300 deposit.

ACCOMMODATION

Beidaihe's accommodation is busiest between May and August; out of season room prices are often slashed by half. Most of the budget hotels (some of which are pretty dodgy) are not licensed to accept foreigners, though hunt around a bit and you're sure to find one who'll take you, legally or otherwise.

Jinhai 金海宾馆, jīnhǎi bīnguǎn. 13 Bao'er Lu, off Zhonghaitan Lu ☎0335 4030048. With an easy-to-find location next to the beach, and good sea views from many rooms, this is the best choice in its price range – as droves of visiting Russians will attest. **¥350**
Meidu 美都饭店, měidū fàndiàn. Xijing Lu ☎0335 4030053. The most reliable of Beidaihe's cheaper options – fairly basic at the lower price range but clean, tidy, and

nowhere near as institutional or noisy as similar options. No breakfast. **¥230**
Sheraton 华贸喜来登酒店, huámào xǐláidēng jiǔdiàn. 16 Binhai Lu ☎0335 4281111. If you're in the market for a smart, international-style business hotel with all facilities – including a pool and gym – then this is the best choice in town, though not right on the sea front (but it's not far to East Beach either). **¥820**

EATING

Beidaihe is noted for its crab, cuttlefish and scallops. Try one of the innumerable small seafood places on Haining Lu, where you order by pointing to the tastiest-looking thing scuttling or slithering around the bucket.

Marina 玛丽娜西餐厅, mǎlìnà xīcāntīng. Bao'er Lu. The best of the town's several Russian restaurants – they've tried hard to make Russian visitors at home with the lighting and seating. Simple Russian salads and stews available from ¥15–30 and borshch for ¥8, plus a range of

acceptable Chinese food. Daily 9am–10pm.
Tiangan 天干海鲜大排档, tiāngān hǎixiān dàpái dàng. 8 Bao'er Lu. The most consistently popular of the seafood barbecue restaurants heading down Haining Lu. They'll grill you up shrimp, tofu, squid and other seafood

2

for ¥5–15 a skewer, while bottles of beer are ¥5. You can also drop by in the morning for some cheap-as-chips

Chinese breakfast: a variety of goods, mostly pickled, from ¥2 per saucer. Daily 8am–late.

DRINKING

The seafood shacks along Haining Lu are also the best places to drink; in summer, many stay open until after midnight.

Summertime 夏令咖啡, xiàlìng kāfēi. Haining Lu. A relaxed café serving decent coffee (from ¥20), as well as pizza and waffles. There's free wi-fi too, making this a great place to check your emails over breakfast. Daily 9.30am–11pm.

Shanhaiguan

山海关, shānhǎiguān

A town at the northern tip of the Bohai Gulf, **SHANHAIGUAN** – "the Pass Between the Mountains and the Sea" – was originally built during the Ming dynasty as a fortress to defend the eastern end of the **Great Wall**. The wall crosses the Yanshan mountains to the north, forms the east wall of the town and meets the sea a few kilometres to the south. Far from being a solitary castle, Shanhaiguan originally formed the centre of a network of defences: smaller forts, now nothing but ruins, existed to the north, south and east, and beacon towers were dotted around the mountains. The town's tourist potential is now being tapped, and extensive demolition and reconstruction continues within the city walls as the tide of tourist buses visiting the town grows ever larger. It's obvious that not much money has made its way into the town outside the battlements, and aside from the reconstructed streets (now given over to tourist shops and restaurants) the *hutongs* of the old town are squalid and crumbling. That said, Shanhaiguan is still arranged along its original plan of straight boulevards following the points of a compass, intersected with a web of alleys, and the odd courtyarded gem makes Shanhaiguan a good place to explore on foot, as well as an excellent base for visiting the Great Wall sites of **Lao Long Tou** (see p.146) and **Jiao Shan** (see p.146).

First Pass Under Heaven

天下第一关, tiānxià dìyī gūan • Daily 7.30am–5pm • ¥40

Dominating the town is a fortified gatehouse in the east wall, the **First Pass Under Heaven**, which for centuries was the entrance to the Middle Kingdom from the barbarian lands beyond. An arch topped by a two-storey tower, the gate makes the surrounding buildings look puny: one can only imagine how formidable it must have looked when first built in 1381, with a wooden drawbridge over a moat 18m wide, and three outer walls for added defensive strength. Yet it all proved useless: in 1644, the disaffected Ming general **Wu Sangui** opened the gates to the Manchu armies, ushering in China's final imperial dynasty, the Qing (though, to be fair to Wu, he needed their help: the last Ming emperor had committed suicide and Wu's father and concubine were being held hostage by rebels). It last served as an active military base during the first Sino-Japanese War of 1894, and finally became redundant after Dongbei was incorporated into provincial China in 1907, which shifted the national frontier far to the northeast.

These days, the gate is overrun by hordes of marauding tourists, and is at its best in the early morning before most of them arrive; there are several **entrances**, with the main one west of the gate, another by the battlements to the south, and another way down the wall by the southeastern corner of the old town.

The gateway and wall

The gateway's name is emblazoned in huge red characters above the archway, calligraphy attributed to **Xiao Xian**, a Ming-dynasty scholar who lived in the town. A steep set of steps leads up from Dong Dajie to the impressively thick wall, nearly 30m wide. The tower on top, a two-storey, 10m-high building with regularly spaced arrow slits along its walls, is now a **museum** containing weapons, armour and costumes, as

Jiao Shan (11km)

SHANHAIGUAN

ACCOMMODATION	
Jingshan	1
Shanhai Holiday	2
Super 8	3

DONG DAJIE

BEI DAJIE

First Pass Under Heaven

Old Bell Tower

NAN DAJIE

XI DAJIE

CHANGCHEN XI LU

Great Wall Museum

Bank of China

Bus Stop

GUANCHENG NANLU

NANGUAN DAJIE

LAOLONGTOU LU

Train Station

N

0 — 500
metres

Qinhuangdao & Beidaihe

Menglionghai Miao

2

Lao Long Tou

well as pictures of the nobility, who are so formally dressed they look like puppets. It's possible to stroll a little way **along the wall** in either direction; the walk is scattered with pay-per-view telescope and binocular stands, which afford a view of tourists on the Great Wall at Jiao Shan several kilometres to the north (see p.146), where the wall zigzags and dips along vertiginous peaks before disappearing over the horizon.

The Great Wall Museum

长城博物馆, chángchéng bówùguǎn • Daily 8am–5pm • Free

Follow the city wall south from the gate and you come to the **Great Wall Museum**. Its eight halls showcase the history of the region in chronological order from Neolithic times, and the history of the wall from its beginnings. In addition to the tools used to build the wall, the vicious weaponry used to defend and attack it is also on display, including mock-ups of siege machines and broadswords that look too big to carry, let alone wield. The last three rooms contain dioramas, plans and photographs of local historic buildings. Inside the final room is a **model** of the area as it looked in Ming times, giving an idea of the extent of the defences, with many small outposts and fortifications in the district around.

ARRIVAL AND DEPARTURE
SHANHAIGUAN

By train The train station, with high-speed services to Beijing, Tianjin, Beidaihe and Shenyang, is a few hundred metres south of the city wall – easily walkable through a park-like area, though cabbies will try to persuade you otherwise (it's ¥5 if you're tempted).

Destinations Beidaihe (many daily; 25–45min); Beijing (many daily; 2hr 5min–7hr 30min); Shenyang (many daily; 2hr 10min–6hr 45min); Tianjin (many daily; 1hr 20min–5hr 30min).

By bus The only useful bus links Shanhaiguan with Beidaihe.

You'll need to change buses halfway along in messy Qinhuangdao (秦皇岛, qínhuángdǎo); take the #33 (¥2) from points along Guancheng Nan Lu (there's a stop just outside the southern city gate), then change in Qinhuangdao for the #34 (¥2), which drops off at Beidaihe's bus station. All in all, it'll take at least 90min to get between the two cities.

ACCOMMODATION AND EATING

It's best to visit Shanhaiguan on a day-trip if possible, as services are limited: most hotels are Chinese-only, and while there are plenty of places to snack or get a basic stir-fry, there are no notable restaurants in town.

Fulinmen 福临门酒店, fúlínmén jiǔdiàn. Guancheng Xi Lu ☎0335 5260777. Decent standard budget option right outside the old walls, with firm (rather than rock-hard) beds, reasonably-sized rooms and 24hr hot water – and it's just a 15min walk from the train station. Some of the staff speak English too. **¥280**

Shanhai Holiday 山海假日酒店, shānhǎi jiàrì jiǔdiàn. Beima Lu ☎0335 5352888. This antique-style complex with stone courtyards, wooden gates and temple-like eaves, lies within an entire Qing-styled part of town,

west of the Drum Tower – the restaurant here, though pricey, is also good. Some find it pleasing, others rather tacky, but the hotel itself is one of the town's few comfortable places to stay. **¥400**

Yihe 谊合宾馆, yìhé bīnguǎn. 4 Nanhai Xi Lu, about 1.5km southeast along the road to Lao Long Tou ☎0335 5939777. An out-of-town option, which looks pretty basic on the outside and has functional rooms – tiled floors, whitewashed walls – but it's surprisingly clean and has no qualms about taking foreigners. **¥250**

The Great Wall beyond Shanhaiguan

Walk around Shanhaiguan's old town, and you'll be pestered continuously for rides to a series of nearby sights. It's well worth heading to a couple, especially the (reconstructed) sections of **Great Wall** to the north and south – the latter is where the wall finally runs into the sea, while the former marks its first steep rise into the mountains. Intrepid hikers could try and make it to **Yansai Lake** (燕塞湖, yànsài hú), up in the mountains directly north of Shanhaiguan, or to **Longevity Mountain** (长寿山, chángshòu shān), a hill of rugged stones east of the lake, where many of the rocks have been carved with the character *shou* (longevity).

Lao Long Tou

老龙头, lǎolóng tóu • Daily 7am–7.30pm • ¥80 • Bus #25 from Laolongtou Lu • ¥20 by taxi from Shanhaiguan

Follow the remains of the Great Wall south from Shanhaiguan and after 4km you'll reach **Lao Long Tou** (Old Dragon Head, after a large stone dragon's head that used to look out to sea here), the point at which the wall hits the coast – literally jutting out into the water. A miniature fortress with a two-storey temple in the centre stands right at the end of the wall. Unfortunately everything here has been so reconstructed it all looks brand new, and is surrounded by a rash of tourist development. The rather dirty beaches either side of the wall are popular bathing spots.

Walk for a few minutes past the restaurants west of Lao Long Tou and you'll come to the old British Army **barracks**, on the right; this was the beachhead for the Eight Allied Forces in 1900, when they came ashore to put down the Boxers. A plaque here reminds visitors to "never forget the national humiliation and invigorate the Chinese nation".

Jiao Shan

角山, jiāo shān • Daily 8am–6.30pm • ¥30 • Cable car ¥30 one-way, ¥50 return • ¥20 by taxi from Shanhaiguan

A couple of kilometres to the north of Shanhaiguan lies **Jiao Shan**, a partially-reconstructed section of the Great Wall. The ticket office is an easy walk from the town's north gate; from here, a steep path takes you through some dramatic scenery into the Yunshan mountains, or you can cheat and take the cable car.

The further along the wall you go the better it gets – the crowds peter out, the views become more dramatic, and once the reconstructed section ends past the third watchtower, you're left standing beside – or on top of – the real, crumbly thing. Head a few kilometres further east and you'll discover a trio of passes in the wall, and a beacon tower that's still in good condition. You can keep going into the mountains for as long as you like, so it's worth getting here early and making a day of it.

Mengjiangnü Temple

孟姜女庙, mèngjiāngnǚ miào • Daily 8am–4pm • ¥30 • ¥20 by taxi from Shanhaiguan

Some 6.5km northeast of town is **Mengjiangnü Temple**, dedicated to a legendary woman whose husband was press-ganged into one of the Great Wall construction squads. He died from exhaustion, and she set out to search for his body to give him a decent burial, weeping as she walked along the wall. So great was her grief, it is said, that the wall crumbled in sympathy, revealing the bones of her husband and many others who had died in its construction. The temple is small and elegant, with good views of the mountains and the sea. Statues of the lady herself and her attendants sit looking rather prim inside.

Chengde

承德, chéngdé

Around 250km northeast of Beijing, unassuming **CHENGDE** boasts a highly colourful history: though the town itself is bland, on its fringes lie some of the most magnificent examples of imperial architecture in China, remnants from its glory days as the **summer retreat** of the Manchu emperors. Gorgeous temples punctuate the cabbage fields around town, and a palace-and-park hill complex, **Bishu Shanzhuang**, covers an area to the north nearly as large as Chengde itself. Farther north and to the east, on the west side of the **Wulie River** – more of a reservoir, thanks to a series of weirs – stands a further set of imposing **temples**. Today Chengde has once more become a summer haven, justly popular with weekending Beijingers escaping the capital.

The majority of Chengde's one-million-strong population live in a semirural suburban sprawl to the south of the centre, leaving the city itself fairly small scale – the new high-rises on its traffic-clogged main artery, **Nanyingzi Dajie**, are yet to obscure the view of distant mountains and fields.

Brief history

Originally called "Rehe", the site was discovered by the Qing emperor **Kangxi** at the end of the seventeenth century. Attracted by the cool summer climate and rugged landscape, he built small lodges here from which he could indulge in a fantasy Manchu lifestyle, hunting and hiking like his northern ancestors. **Construction** began in 1703, involving craftsmen from all over China, and within a decade there were 36 palaces, temples, monasteries and pagodas set in a great walled park, its ornamental pools and islands dotted with beautiful pavilions and linked by bridges.

THE BRITISH AT CHENGDE

The first **British Embassy** to China, under Lord Macartney, visited Qianlong's court in 1793 hoping to negotiate for open trade agreements and permission to establish a permanent trading post along the coast. Having sailed up the river to Beijing in a ship whose sails were painted with characters reading "Tribute bearers from the vassal king of England", they were somewhat disgruntled to discover that the emperor had decamped to Chengde for the summer. However, they made the journey there, in impractical European carriages, where they were well received by the emperor, though the visit was hardly a success. Macartney caused an initial stir by **refusing to kowtow** (though he did kneel), while Qianlong was **unimpressed** with the gifts the British had brought and, with Manchu power at its height, rebuffed all the British requests, remarking: "We possess all things. I set no value on objects strange or ingenious, and have no use for your country's manufactures." His letter to the British monarch concluded, magnificently, "O king, Tremblingly Obey and Show No Negligence!"

2

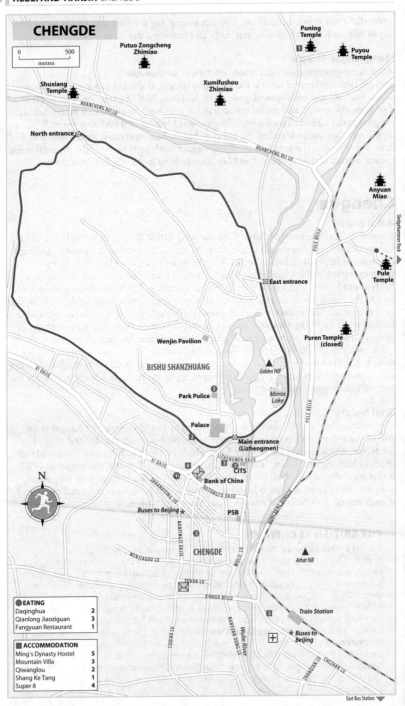

CHENGDE

0 ——— 500
metres

Puning Temple

Puyou Temple

Putuo Zongcheng Zhimiao

Xumifushou Zhimiao

Shuxiang Temple

HUANCHENG BEI LU

North entrance

HUANCHENG BEI LU

Anyuan Miao

Sledgehammer Rock

PULE BEI LU

Pule Temple

East entrance

Wenjin Pavilion

BISHU SHANZHUANG

Golden Hill

Puren Temple (closed)

Park Police

Mirror Lake

PULE BEI LU

Palace

Main entrance (Lizhengmen)

XI DAJIE

LIZHENGMEN DAJIE

CITS

Bank of China

DUTONGFU DAJIE

@

BUCHENG DONGLU

SHAANXIYING JIE

NANYINGZI DAJIE

Buses to Beijing

PSB

CHENGDE

WENJIAGOU LU

Arhat Hill

YUHUA LU

XINHUA BEILU

NANYUAN DONG LU

Train Station

Wulie River

Buses to Beijing

DONGDAQIAO LU

TIANJIAN LU | CHEZHAN LU

East Bus Station

EATING
Daqinghua	2
Qianlong Jiaoziguan	3
Fangyuan Restaurant	1

ACCOMMODATION
Ming's Dynasty Hostel	5
Mountain Villa	3
Qiwanglou	2
Shang Ke Tang	1
Super 8	4

The complex expanded further as it became diplomatically useful for the Qing emperors to spend time north of Beijing, forging closer links with the troublesome Mongol tribes, whose princes were wowed with splendid audiences, hunting parties and impressive military manoeuvres. Kangxi's grandson, **Qianlong** (1736–96), added another 36 imperial buildings during his reign, which was considered to be the heyday of Chengde.

The city gradually lost imperial popularity when it came to be seen as unlucky after emperors Jiaqing and Xianfeng died here in 1820 and 1861 respectively. The buildings were left empty and neglected for most of the twentieth century, but largely escaped the ravages of the Cultural Revolution. Ongoing restorations, in the interests of tourism, began in the 1980s.

2

Bishu Shanzhuang

避暑山庄, bìshǔ shānzhuāng • Daily 8am–5.30pm • April 16 to Oct 15 ¥145; Oct 16 to April 15 ¥90 • Bus #1, #5, #15 or #30 from Chengde

Surrounded by a 10km-long wall, the enormous **Bishu Shanzhuang** (Bishu Mountain Resort) occupies the northern third of the town's area. This is where, in the summer months, the Qing emperors lived, feasted, hunted and occasionally dealt with affairs of state. The palace buildings just inside the main entrance are unusual for imperial China as they are low, wooden and unpainted – simple but elegant, in contrast to the opulence and grandeur of Beijing's palaces. It's said that Emperor Kangxi wanted the complex to reflect a Manchurian encampment, to show his disdain for fame and wealth – it was often described as the "Temporary Palace" – though with 120 rooms and several thousand servants he wasn't exactly roughing it.

The same principle of idealized naturalness governed the design of the park. With its twisting paths and streams, rockeries and hills, it's a fantasy re-creation of the rough northern terrain and southern Chinese beauty spots that the emperors would have seen on their tours. Lord Macartney noted its similarity to the "soft beauties" of an English manor park of the Romantic style.

Covering the whole park and its buildings takes at least a day, and an early start is recommended; it's at its nicest in the early morning anyway. The park is simply too big to get overcrowded, and if you head north beyond the lakes, you're likely to find yourself alone.

The Palace

The **main gate**, Lizhengmen, is in the south wall, off Lizhengmen Dajie. The **palace quarter**, just inside the complex to the west of the main gate, is built on a slope, facing south, and consists of four groups of dark wooden buildings spread over an area of 100,000 square metres. The first, southernmost group, the Front Palace, where the emperors lived and worked, is the most interesting, as many of the rooms have been restored to their full Qing elegance, decked out with graceful furniture and ornaments. Even the everyday objects are impressive: brushes and inkstones on desks, ornate fly whisks on the arms of chairs, little jade trees on shelves. Other rooms house displays of ceramics, books and exotic martial-art weaponry. The Qing emperors were fine calligraphers, and examples of their work appear throughout the palace.

Front Palace

There are 26 buildings in this group, arranged south to north in nine successive compounds, which correspond to the nine levels of heaven. The main gate leads into the **Outer Wumen**, where high-ranking officials waited for a single peal of a large bell, indicating that the emperor was ready to receive them. Next is the **Inner Wumen**, where the emperor would watch his officers practise their archery. Directly behind, the **Hall of Frugality and Sincerity** is a dark, well-appointed room made of cedarwood, imported at great expense from south of the Yangzi River by Qianlong, who had none of his grandfather Kangxi's scruples about conspicuous consumption. Topped with a curved roof, the hall has nine bays, and patterns on the walls include symbols of longevity and good luck. The **Four Knowledge Study Room**, behind, was where the emperor worked, changed his clothes and rested. A vertical scroll on the wall outlines the knowledge required of a gentleman: he must be aware of what is small, obvious, soft and strong.

Rear Palace

The main building in the **Rear Palace** is the **Hall of Refreshing Mists and Waves**, the living quarters of the imperial family, and beautifully turned out in period style. It was in the west room here that Emperor Xianfeng accepted the humiliating Treaty of Peking in 1860, giving away more of China's sovereignty and territory after their defeat in the Second Opium War. The **Western Apartments** are where Cixi, better known as the Empress Dowager (see box, p.96), lived when she was one of Xianfeng's concubines. A door connects the apartments to the hall, and it was through here that she eavesdropped on the dying emperor's last words of advice to his ministers, intelligence she used in her rise to power.

Outer complexes

The outer two complexes are much smaller than the inner. The **Pine and Crane Residence**, a group of buildings parallel to the front gate, is a more subdued version of the Front Palace, home to the emperor's mother and his concubines. In the **Myriad Valleys of Rustling Pine Trees**, to the north of here, Emperor Kangxi read books and granted audiences, and Qianlong studied as a child. The group of structures southwest of the main palace is the **Ahgesuo**, where male descendants of the royal family studied during the Manchurian rule; lessons began at 5am and finished at noon. A boy was expected to speak Manchu at 6, Chinese at 12, be competent with a bow by the age of 14 and marry at 16.

The lake

Boats rented from behind the palace, on the lakeshore • ¥60/hr

Renting a **rowing boat** is the best way to get around the **lake area** of the park – a network of pavilions, bridges, lakes and waterways – though you can easily walk. Much of the architecture here is a direct copy of southern Chinese buildings. In the east, the **Golden Hill**, a cluster of buildings grouped on a small island, is notable for a hall and tower modelled after the Golden Hill Monastery in Zhenjiang, Jiangsu province. The **Island of Midnight and Murmuring Streams**, roughly in the centre of the lake, holds a three-courtyard compound which was used by Kangxi and Qianlong as a retreat, while the compound of halls, towers and pavilions on **Ruyi Island**, the largest, was where Kangxi dealt with affairs of state before the palace was completed.

Wenjin Pavilion

文津阁, wénjīn gé

Just beyond the lake area, on the western side of the park, is the grey-tiled **Wenjin Pavilion**, surrounded by rockeries and pools for fire protection. Originally this served as an imperial library housing a complete edition of the *siku quanshu*, an eighteenth-century encyclopedia of all Chinese knowledge, comprising an enormous 36,381 volumes. From the outside, the structure appears to have two storeys; in fact there are three – a central section is windowless to protect the books from the sun. Sadly, the building is closed to the public.

Grassland and hills

A vast expanse of **grassland** extends from the north of the lake area to the foothills of the mountains, comprising Wanshu Yuan (Garden of Ten Thousand Trees) and Shima Da (Horse Testing Ground). The **hilly area** in the northwest of the park has a number of rocky valleys, gorges and gullies with a few tastefully placed lodges and pagodas. The deer, which graze on tourist handouts, were reintroduced after being wiped out by imperial hunting expeditions.

2

The temples

The **"Eight Outer Temples"** in the foothills of the mountains around Chengde – in fact there were originally twelve of them, though only six are now open to the public – were built in the architectural styles of different ethnic nationalities, so that wandering among them is rather like being in a religious theme park. This isn't far from the original intention, as they were constructed less to express religious sentiment than as a way of showing off imperial magnificence, and also to make envoys from anywhere in the empire feel more at home. Though varying in design, all the temples share **Lamaist features** – Qianlong found it politically expedient to promote Tibetan and Mongolian Lamaism as a way of keeping these troublesome minorities in line.

Puning Temple

普宁寺, pǔníng sì • Daily 8am–5.30pm • April–Oct ¥80; Nov–March ¥60 (joint ticket with adjacent Puyou Temple) • Bus #6 from Lizhengmen Dajie

Puning Temple – also known as the "Big Buddha Temple" after the statue in its Mahayana Hall – was built in 1755 to commemorate the Qing victory over the Mongolian Junggar rebels at Yili in northwest China, and is based on the oldest Tibetan monastery, the Samye. Like traditional Tibetan buildings, it lies on the slope of a mountain facing south. This is the only working temple in Chengde, with shaven-headed Mongolian monks manning the altars and trinket stalls, and though the atmosphere is not especially spiritual – it's usually clamorous with day-trippers – the temple and its grounds exude undeniable charm.

Hall of Heavenly Kings and East Hall

In the **Hall of Heavenly Kings**, the statue of a fat, grinning monk holding a bag depicts Qi Ci, a tenth-century character with a jovial disposition, believed to be a reincarnation of the Buddha. In the **East Hall**, the central statue, flanked by *arhats*, portrays Ji Gong, a Song-dynasty monk who was nicknamed Crazy Ji for eating meat and being almost always drunk, but who was much respected for his kindness to the poor.

Mahayana Hall

The rear section of the temple, separated from the front by a wall, comprises 27 Tibetan-style rooms laid out symmetrically, with the **Mahayana Hall** in the centre. Some of the buildings are actually solid (the doors are false), suggesting that the original architects were more concerned with appearances than function. The hall itself is dominated by the 23m-high gilded **wooden statue of Guanyin**, the Goddess of Mercy. She has 42 arms with an eye in the centre of each palm, and three eyes on her face, which symbolize her ability to see into the past, present and future. The hall has two raised entrances, and it's worth looking at the statue from these upper viewpoints as they reveal new details, such as the eye sunk in her belly button, and the little Buddha sitting on top of her head.

SEEING THE TEMPLES

The temples are now in varying states of repair, having been left untended for decades. Of the original twelve, two have been destroyed and another three are dilapidated; the remaining seven stand in two groups: a string of five just beyond the northern border of Bishu Shanzhuang; and two more to the east of the park. If you're short on time the **Puning Temple** is a must, if only for the awe-inspiring statue of Guanyin, the largest wooden statue in the world.

A good itinerary is to see the northern cluster in the morning, return to town for lunch, and in the afternoon head for the Pule Temple and Sledgehammer Rock, a bizarre protuberance that dominates the eastern horizon of the town (see p.154).

Xumifushou Temple

须弥福寿之庙, xūmífúshòuzhī miào • Daily 8am–5.30pm • April–Oct ¥80; Nov–March ¥60 (joint ticket with Putuo Zongcheng Temple) • Bus #118 from Lizhengmen Dajie

Recently restored, the **Xumifushou Temple**, just southwest of Puning Temple, was built in 1780 in Mongolian style for the ill-fated sixth Panchen Lama when he came to Beijing to pay his respects to the emperor (see box, p.154) – indeed, it's a near-copy of Tashilunpo Monastery in Shigatse, the Lama's home town in Tibet (see p.911). Though he was lavishly looked after – contemporary accounts describe how Qianlong invited the Lama to sit with him on the Dragon Throne – he went home in a coffin (see box, p.154).

The temple centrepiece is the **Hall of Loftiness and Solemnity**, its finest features the eight sinuous gold dragons sitting on the roof, each weighing over 1000kg.

Putuo Zongcheng Temple

普陀宗乘之庙, pǔtuó zōngchéngzhī miào • Daily 8am–5.30pm • April–Oct ¥80; Nov–March ¥60 (joint ticket with Xumifushou Temple) • Bus #118 from Lizhengmen Dajie

Next door to the Xumifushou Temple, the magnificent **Putuo Zongcheng Temple** (Temple of Potaraka Doctrine) was built in 1771 and is based on the Potala Palace in Lhasa. Covering 220,000 square metres, it's the largest temple in Chengde, with sixty groups of halls, pagodas and terraces. The grand terrace forms a Tibetan-style facade screening a Chinese-style interior, although many of the windows on the terrace are fake, and some of the whitewashed buildings around the base are merely filled-in shapes. The roof of the temple has a good view over the surrounding countryside.

The West Hall

Inside Putuo Zongcheng, the **West Hall** is notable for holding a rather comical copper statue of the Propitious Heavenly Mother, a fearsome woman wearing a necklace of skulls and riding side-saddle on a mule. According to legend, she vowed to defeat the evil demon Raksaka, so she first lulled him into a false sense of security – by marrying him and bearing him two sons – then swallowed the moon and in the darkness crept up on him and turned him into a mule. The two dancing figures at her feet are her sons; their ugly features betray their paternity.

Other halls

The **Hall of All Laws Falling into One**, at the back, is worth a visit for the quality of the decorative religious furniture on display. Other halls hold displays of Chinese pottery and ceramics and Tibetan religious artefacts, an exhibition slanted to portray the gorier side of Tibetan religion and including a drum made from two children's skulls.

Pule Temple

普乐寺, pǔlè sì • Daily 8.30am–4.30pm • ¥50 (joint ticket with Anyuan Temple) • Bus #10 from Lizhengmen Dajie

Due east of Bishu Shanzhuang, the **Pule Temple** (Temple of Universal Happiness) was built in 1766 by Qianlong as a place for Mongol envoys to worship, and its style is an odd mix of Han and Lamaist elements. The Lamaist back section, a triple-tiered terrace and hall, with a flamboyantly conical roof and lively, curved surfaces, steals the show from the more sober, squarer Han architecture at the front. The ceiling of the back hall is a wood-and-gold confection to rival the Temple of Heaven in Beijing. Glowing at its centre is a **mandala of Samvara**, a Tantric deity, in the form of a cross. The altar beneath holds a Buddha of Happiness, a life-size copper image of sexual congress; more cosmic sex is depicted in two beautiful mandalas hanging outside. Outside the temple, the view from the car park is spectacular, and just north is the path that leads to Sledgehammer Rock and the cable car.

2

THE PANCHEN LAMA AT CHENGDE

In 1786, the **Panchen Lama** was summoned from Tibet by Qianlong for his birthday celebrations. This was an adroit political move to impress the followers of Lamaist Buddhism. The Buddhists included a number of minority groups who were prominent thorns in the emperor's side, such as Tibetans, Mongols, Torguts, Eleuths, Djungars and Kalmucks. Some accounts (notably not Chinese) tell how Qianlong invited the Panchen Lama to sit with him on the Dragon Throne, which was taken to Chengde for the summer season. He was certainly feted with honours and bestowed with costly gifts and titles, but the greatest impression on him and his followers must have been made by the replicas of the Potala and of his own palace, constructed at Chengde to make him feel at home – a munificent gesture, and one that would not have been lost on the Lamaists. However, the Panchen Lama's visit ended questionably in Beijing when he succumbed to smallpox, or possibly poison, and his coffin was returned to Tibet with a stupendous funeral cortege.

Anyuan Temple

安远庙, ānyuǎn miào • Daily 8.30am–4.30pm • ¥50 (joint ticket with Pule Temple) • Bus #10 from Lizhengmen Dajie

Anyuan Miao (Temple of Appeasing the Borders) lies within walking distance to the north of the Pule Temple, and is decidedly less appealing, though enjoys a delightful setting on the tree-lined east bank of the Wulie River. It was built in 1764 for a community of 12,000 Mongolian prisoners of war who were relocated to Chengde by Qianlong after his victorious campaign against them at Ili.

Sledgehammer Rock

棒锤山, bàngzhōng shān • ¥50 • 2km walk from the Pule Temple, or cable car (¥50 return) • Bus #10 from Lizhengmen Dajie

Of the scenic areas around Chengde, the one that inspires the most curiosity is **Sledgehammer Rock**. Thinner at the base than at the top, the towering column of rock is more than 20m high, and skirted by stalls selling little models and Sledgehammer Rock T-shirts. According to legend, the rock is a huge dragon's needle put there to plug a hole in the peak, which was letting the sea through. The rock's obviously phallic nature is tactfully not mentioned in tourist literature, but is acknowledged in local folklore – should the rock fall, it is said, it will have a disastrous effect on the virility of local men.

ARRIVAL AND DEPARTURE   CHENGDE

Unlike anywhere else in northeast China, it's usually quicker to reach Chengde by **bus**; the fastest trains stopping here are only K-class, and there are plenty of slow plodders along the line too. Onward train tickets and local tours can be booked from CITS on Lizhengmen Dajie (☎ 0314 2027483), with similar services available at most hotels.

By train Chengde train station is southeast of town on a spur-line between Beijing and Dongbei; from Beijing you'll chug through rolling countryside, with a couple of Great Wall vistas on the way. Tickets are easy to buy at the station, though there's a helpfully located ticket office just east of the *Mountain Villa* hotel.

Destinations Beijing (7 daily; 4hr 30min–10hr 30min); Dandong (1 daily; 16hr); Shenyang (2 daily; 12–13hr).

By bus Chengde has at least two long-distance bus

stations, both with departures daily 6am–6pm for Dongzhimen and Sihui bus stations in Beijing: 4km to the north is Sifang Station (四方长途汽车客运站, sìfāng chángtúqìchē kèyùn zhàn); while the East bus station (汽车东站, qìchē dōng zhàn) lies 7km to the south of town on bus #118 route. There's also a depot of sorts immediately in front of the train station.

Destinations Beijing (3–5hr); Tianjin (1 daily; 4hr).

GETTING AROUND

Getting around Chengde can be slow going – at peak hours during the summer the main roads are so congested that it's quicker to **walk**. The town itself is just about small enough to cover on foot, and it's easy to walk or **cycle** between the two westernmost temples, and even on to Puning Temple, though this last section is busy, tedious and best navigated by **taxi**.

By bus Local buses are infrequent and always crammed. Buses #5 and #11, which go from the train station to Bishu Shanzhuang; bus #6 from here to the Puning Temple; and bus #118 to the northern temples are the most useful.

By taxi Taxis are easy to find, but drivers don't use their meters – a ride into town from transit points shouldn't cost more than ¥20.

By minibus Hotels will be able to help with chartering a minibus for around ¥350 a day (bargain hard).

ACCOMMODATION

There are plenty of **hotels** in Chengde town itself, plus a couple of expensive places on the fringes of Bishu Shanzhuang. Unfortunately, as with elsewhere in Hebei, strict enforcement of local government rules means foreigners are barred from **cheaper accommodation**; if you're really slumming it, try the flophouses in the side-alleys opposite the *Super 8*. On the plus side, rates at approved hotels are highly negotiable and off-peak discounts of up to two-thirds are possible.

★**First Met Hostel** 初见客栈, chūjiàn kèzhàn. Block 4, Yuhua Business Centre, 106 Yuhua Lu ☎0314 7014117. Hidden among modern apartment blocks, this is a good option, especially for budget travellers. Rooms are plain but kept nice and clean with security lockers in the dorms, there's an outdoor terrace for sunny days, and staff are helpful. Bike rental too. Dorms **¥60**, twins **¥150**

Huilong 会龙大厦酒店, huìlóng dàshà jiǔdiàn. 2 Chezhan Lu ☎0314 2085369. One of the more inexpensive proper hotels that foreigners are allowed to stay in, with rooms ranging from the cheap-and-simple to relatively plush varieties. Not much atmosphere, but perfectly comfortable and convenient for the train station too. **¥300**

Mountain Villa 山庄宾馆, shānzhuāng bīnguǎn. 127 Xiaonanmen (entrance on Lizhengmen Dajie) ☎0314 2025588. This grand, well-located complex has huge rooms, high ceilings and a cavernous lobby, and is extremely popular with tour groups. The large rooms in the main building are nicer but a little more expensive than those in the ugly building round the back. Service can be surly but the Chinese buffet breakfast is good. **¥550**

Qiwanglou 绮望楼宾馆, qǐwànglóu bīnguǎn. 1 Bifengmen Dong Lu ☎0314 2024385. Well-run hotel with imitation Qing-style buildings (though rooms are of modern design), just moments from the Bishu Shanzhuang main entrance. Its flowery grounds make for a pleasant walk even if you're not staying here. Service is excellent, and the staff among the few people in Chengde who speak English. **¥1400**

Shang Ke Tang 普宁寺上客堂大酒店, pǔníng sì shàngkètáng dàjiǔdiàn. Puning Temple ☎0314 2058888. This interesting hotel's staff wear period clothing and braided wigs befitting the adjoining Puning Temple, and glide along the dim bowels of the complex to lead you to appealingly rustic rooms. You're a little away from the action here, though this is not necessarily a negative, and there are a few cheap restaurants in the area. **¥550**

EATING

Chengde doesn't offer much in the way of culinary adventure. There are plenty of restaurants catering to tourists on **Lizhengmen Dajie**, around the main entrance to the Bishu Shanzhuang; on summer evenings, rickety tables are put on the pavement outside, and plenty of diners stay on drinking well into the evening.

Daqinghua 大清花, dàqīnghuā. 21 Lizhengmen Dajie ☎0314 2082222. Pine-walled dumpling restaurant that's the best option in the area around the Bishu Shanzhuang entrance. Their dumplings (¥12–20) are great, though there's a full menu of tasty northeastern dishes – including delicious stewed pork hocks, grilled ribs and toffee potatoes at around ¥45 a dish. Daily 11.30am–8.50pm.

Fangyuan 芳园居, fāngyuánjū. Inside Bishu Shanzhuang ☎0314 2161132. This snazzy restaurant serves imperial cuisine, including such exotica as "Pingquan Frozen Rabbit"; prices are pretty high, however, and you won't get much change from ¥150 per person, even without drinks. Daily 11am–5pm.

Qianlong Jiaoziguan 乾隆饺子馆, qiánlóng jiǎoziguǎn. Just off Centre Square, a park at the heart of the shopping district ☎0314 2076377. The best *jiaozi* in town are served here, and far more besides – the menu is full of Chinese staples, with a few more interesting items such as sauerkraut with lung, braised bullfrog in soy, and battered venison. The more adventurous mains clock in at ¥60–100, though penny-pinchers will appreciate the spicy Sichuan noodles (¥12). Daily 11am–9pm.

DRINKING

The best place for a drink is busy **Shaanxiying Jie**, a streamside street stretching west of Nanyingzi Dajie; there are a few quieter places across the road to the east.

Dongbei

东北

CRANES AT ZHALONG NATURE RESERVE

Dongbei

Dongbei (东北, dōngběi) – or, more evocatively, Manchuria – may well be the closest thing to the "real" China that visitors vainly seek in the well-travelled central and southern parts of the country. Not many foreign tourists get up to China's northernmost arm, however, due to its reputation as an inhospitable wasteland: "Although it is uncertain where God created paradise", wrote a French priest when he was here in 1846, "we can be sure he chose some other place than this." Yet, with its immense swaths of fertile fields and huge mineral resources, Dongbei is metaphorically a treasure house. Comprising Liaoning, Jilin and Heilongjiang provinces, as well as part of Inner Mongolia, it is economically and politically among the most important regions of China, and, for much of its history, the area has been fiercely contested by Manchus, Nationalists, Russians, Japanese and Communists. With 4000km of sensitive border territory alongside North Korea and Russia, Dongbei is one of China's most vulnerable regions strategically.

In addition, economic pressures have made it prone to internal unrest, with worker protests common and a widening gap between the haves and have-nots that is threatening to become a chasm. Redressing this imbalance is **tourism**, a good portion of it domestic, which has become the leading growth industry. The region is cashing in on its colourful history, seen most vividly in the preservation of long-ignored Russian and Japanese colonial architecture, some of which you can actually stay in. The region's food is heavily influenced by neighbouring countries, and every town has a cluster of Korean, Japanese and, up north, Russian restaurants. The local specialities are also quite diverse, ranging from fresh crabs in Dalian and river fish in Dandong, to silkworms in the countryside.

Furthest south of the Dongbei provinces, **Liaoning** boasts the busy port of **Dalian**; the provincial capital **Shenyang**, home to China's "other" Forbidden City; and Dandong, which sits right on the North Korean border. Moving north is **Jilin** province, whose capital **Changchun** sports the Puppet Emperor's Palace, home to Puyi during his reign as "emperor" of the Japanese state Manchukuo. Lastly, and hogging most of China's border with Russia, is **Heilongjiang**: the province's capital and major city, **Harbin**, is a thoroughly likeable place, and world-renowned for its amazing Ice Festival – in winter it is very, very cold, with temperatures as low as -30°C, combined with howling gales. Summer, conversely, is very pleasant across the region, and Dongbei can be a lovely escape from the rest of China, sweltering away down south.

Brief history

The history of Manchuria proper begins with **Nurhaci**, a tribal leader who in the sixteenth century united the warring tribes of the Northeast against the corrupt central

PUPPET EMPEROR'S PALACE, CHANGCHUN

Highlights

❶ Old Yalu Bridge, Dandong Walk halfway to North Korea on this structure, bombed by the US during the Korean War. **See p.168**

❷ The Imperial Palace, Shenyang Pre-empting Beijing's Forbidden City, this was the historical seat of the Manchus before they seized the capital. **See p.171**

❸ Puppet Emperor's Palace, Changchun The second act of the "last emperor" Puyi's life was played out here, where he was installed by the Japanese as leader of Manchuria. **See p.176**

❹ Changbai Shan The Northeast's loveliest nature reserve – see the crater lake and root around for wild ginseng, though beware of North Korean border guards. **See p.178**

❺ Winter ice festivals Most Manchurian metropolises have one, but Harbin's is the biggest and best, with illuminated ice sculptures that tower higher by the year. **See p.185**

❻ Russian architecture, Harbin Harbin's a great summertime destination, too, with local beer guzzled by the truckload around the city's beautiful Russian buildings. **See p.185**

HIGHLIGHTS ARE MARKED ON THE MAP ON P.160

rule of Ming-dynasty Liaoning. He introduced an **alphabet** based on the Mongol script, administered Manchu law and, by 1625, had created a firm and relatively autonomous government that was in constant confrontation with the Chinese. Subsequently, **Dorgun** was able to go a stage further, marching on Beijing with the help of Wu Sangui, a Ming general who surrendered to the Manchus because the warlord Li Zicheng (whose assault on Beijing had driven the last Ming emperor to suicide) had captured his concubine.

DONGBEI

0 — 250
kilometres

- - - - High Speed Rail line

HIGHLIGHTS

1 Old Yalu Bridge, Dandong

2 The Imperial Palace, Shenyang

3 Puppet Emperor's Palace, Changchun

4 Changbai Shan

5 Winter ice festivals

6 Russian architecture, Harbin

The Qing dynasty

In 1644, the **Qing dynasty** was proclaimed, and one of Nurhaci's grandsons, **Shunzhi**, became the first of a long line of Manchu emperors, with his uncle Dorgun as regent. Keen to establish the Qing over the whole of China, the first **Manchu emperors** – Shunzhi, Kangxi and Qianlong – did their best to assimilate Chinese customs and ideas. They were, however, even more determined to protect their homeland, and so the whole of the northeast was closed to the rest of China. This way they could guard their monopoly on the valuable **ginseng trade** and keep the agricultural Han Chinese from ploughing up their land, a practice that often resulted in the desecration of the graves of the Manchus' ancestors. But isolationism was a policy that could not last forever, and the eighteenth century saw increasing migration into Manchuria. By 1878, these laws had been rescinded, and the Chinese were moving into the region by the million, escaping the flood-ravaged plains of the south for the fertile northeast.

Foreign occupation

All this time, Manchuria was much coveted by its neighbours. The **Sino-Japanese War** of 1894 left the Japanese occupying the Liaodong Peninsula in the south of Liaoning province; alarmed by Japan's victory and the quantity of Chinese territory it had taken, European nations forced the Japanese to hand Liaodong back to China, which then turned to **Russia**, also hungry for influence in the area. The deal was that the Russians be allowed to build a **rail line** linking Vladivostok to the main body of Russia, an arrangement that in fact led to a gradual and, eventually, complete occupation of Manchuria by the imperial Russian armies. This was a bloody affair, marked by atrocities and brutal reprisals, and was followed in 1904 by a Japanese declaration of war in an attempt to usurp the Russians' privileges for themselves.

Manchukuo

The **Russo-Japanese War** concluded in 1905 with a convincing Japanese victory, though Japan's designs on Manchuria didn't end there. Japan's population doubled between 1872 and 1925, creating the perceived need to expand its territories; this, coupled with a disastrous economic situation at home and an extreme militaristic regime, led to their invasion of the region in 1932, establishing the puppet state of **Manchukuo**. This regime was characterized by horrific and violent oppression – not least the secret germ-warfare research centre in **Pingfang** (see p.185), where experiments were conducted on live human subjects. Rice was reserved for the Japanese, and it was a crime for the locals to eat it. Japan's defeat at the end of World War II finally drew a line under all of this, although it was some time (and in spite of a vicious campaign backed by both Russia and the US against the Communists) before Mao finally took full control of the northeast.

Recent history

Relations with Russia dominate recent history. In the brief romance between the two countries in the 1950s, Soviet experts helped the Chinese build efficient, well-designed factories and workshops in exchange for the region's agricultural products. These factories laid the foundation for China's automobile industry: the **First Automobile Works** (FAW) in Changchun, for example, began production then, and now has a joint venture with VW and Audi. In the 1960s, relations worsened, the Soviets withdrew their technical support and bitter **border disputes** erupted, notably around the Wusuli (Ussuri) River, where hundreds of Russian and Chinese troops died fighting over an insignificant island in the world's first military confrontation between communist states. An extensive network of nuclear shelters was constructed in northeastern cities. Following the collapse of the Soviet Union, military build-ups around the border areas and state paranoia have lessened, and the shelters have been turned into underground shopping malls. Russian faces can again be seen on the streets, often **traders** buying up consumer goods to take over the border.

3

DONGBEI'S MINORITY COMMUNITIES

After forcing **minority communities** to embrace official communist culture during the 1950s and 60s, the Chinese government now takes a more enlightened – if somewhat patronizing – approach to the peoples of the north. The **Manchu** people, spread across Inner Mongolia and Dongbei, are the most numerous and assimilated; having lived so long among the Han, they are now almost identical, though Manchu tend to be slightly taller, and their men have more facial hair.

In the inhospitable northern margins of Dongbei live communities such as the **Hezhen**, one of the smallest minority nations in China with under 5000 members. Inhabiting the Russian border region where the Songhua, Heilong and Wusuli (Ussuri) rivers converge (and slightly more numerous in Russia itself), they're known to the Han Chinese as the "Fish Tribe", and their culture and livelihood centre around fishing. Indeed, they're the only people in the world to make clothes out of fish skin: the fish is gutted, descaled, then dried and tanned and the skins sewn together to make light, waterproof coats, shoes and gloves.

More numerous are the Mongolic **Daur**, 120,000 of whom live along the Nen River near Qiqihar. They are fairly seamlessly assimilated these days, but still retain distinctive marriage and funerary traditions, and have a reputation for being superb at hockey, a form of which they have played since the sixth century.

However, perhaps the most distinctive minority are the **Oroqen**, a tribe of around 8000 nomadic hunters living in patrilineal clan communes called *wulileng*, split fairly evenly between the sub-Siberian wildernesses of Inner Mongolia and Heilongjiang. Although they have recently adopted a more settled existence, their main livelihood still comes from deer-hunting, while household items, tools and canoes are made from birch bark by Oroqen women. Clothes are fashioned from deer hide, and include a striking hat made of a roe deer head, complete with antlers and leather patches for eyes, which is used as a disguise in hunting.

Last, but not least, are the **Koreans**, who number around 2.5 million in China. Ethnic Koreans with Chinese citizenship are known as Chosonjok, and count for around 2 million of the total – around half of these live in an autonomous prefecture around Yanji, a city in which Chinese and Korean food, customs and language coexist in a quite fascinating fashion.

Liaoning

辽宁, liáoníng

Of the Dongbei provinces, **LIAONING** has the most to see; there's also a pleasing amount of variety to proceedings. The thriving port of **Dalian** sports cleaned-up beaches, a cliffside drive, and restored Russian and Japanese neighbourhoods. Whoosh north by high-speed train and you'll soon arrive in Liaoning's capital, **Shenyang**, home to China's second Forbidden City – the restored **Manchu Imperial Palace** – and the tombs of the men who established the Qing dynasty. Head southeast and you'll eventually hit **Dandong**, the country's window on North Korea, which features a promenade on the Yalu River and a fascinating Korean War museum.

Dalian

大连, dàlián

Few visitors to **DALIAN** – a sprawling, modern city on the Yellow Sea – leave with a negative impression of the place. It is, quite simply, one of the most agreeable urban areas in China, boasting swathes of colonial architecture, proximity to some good beaches, and some excellent seafood. It's also one of China's most cosmopolitan cities, partly because it has changed hands so often – in the years around the turn of the twentieth century, it found itself under Japanese, then Russian, then Japanese, then Soviet occupation. The "foreign devils" are still here, though they're now invited: Dalian has been designated a Special Economic Zone, one of China's "open-door" cities, with regulations designed to attract overseas investment. Unlike most Chinese metropolises, the city boasts green spaces and an excellent traffic control system, both the handiwork of the high-flying former mayor turned national commerce minister and Politburo member Bo Xilai – since found guilty of corruption and sentenced to life imprisonment.

Dalian has plenty in the way of sightseeing. The city centre is a pleasant and peaceful enough place to simply stroll around, with interesting former **Russian** and **Japanese quarters**, though you'll have to head south for the best beaches, as well as the **zoo**, **aviary** and **theme parks**.

Brief history

As the only ice-free port in the region, Dalian was eagerly sought by the foreign powers that held sway over China in the nineteenth century. The Japanese took the city in 1895 yet soon ceded it back to China, who then allowed the Russians to build a rail line here – Moscow saw Dalian as an alternative to ice-bound Vladivostok. In 1905, after decisively defeating the Russian navy, the Japanese wrested it back and remained in control for long enough to complete the construction of the port facilities and city grid – still visible in the many traffic circles and axial roads. After World War II, the Soviet Union occupied the city for ten years, finally withdrawing when Sino-Soviet relations improved.

The city centre

The city's hub is **Zhongshan Square** (中山广场, zhōngshān guǎngchǎng), really a circle, whose spokes are some of the most interesting streets in the city, dotted with Russian and Japanese buildings, and today home to an even more cosmopolitan air. To the west is **Renmin Square** (人民广场, rénmín guǎngchǎng), which is large, grassy and lit with floodlights at night.

The old Russian quarter

老俄罗斯风景区, lǎo éluósī fēngjǐngqū

Just over 1km northwest of Zhongshan Square is the **old Russian quarter**. This neighbourhood used to house Russian gentry, though today each peeling mansion is

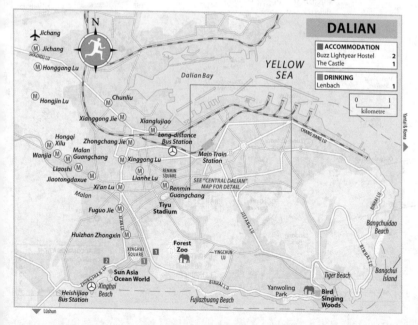

home to several families. The pedestrianized main street takes you past restored pistachio-coloured facades and street vendors selling Russian cigarettes, lighters, vodka and Soviet pins. Easy on the eye, and surprisingly calm, it's one of the most appealing parts of the city to base yourself in (see p.166).

The Japanese quarter

老日本风景区, lǎo rìběn fēngjǐngqū

South of the train station is the former **Japanese quarter**, its hub (both then and now) the Japanese-designed **Laodong Park** (劳动公园, láodòng gōngyuán). A hilly zone with some great walking trails, it's a pleasant escape from urbanity. **Nanshan** (南山, nánshān), the neighbourhood across the street east of the park, was once home to the Japanese community; now, the cream-coloured, red-roofed villas are being renovated by nouveau riche Chinese. The most attractive street hereabouts is **Fenglin Jie**, home to a couple of cool cafés (see p.167).

South of the centre

The coastline **south of the centre** is quite spectacular, with a series of good **beaches**, all free, and rocky outcrops; these are hugged by Dalian's most scenic road, **Binhai Lu**

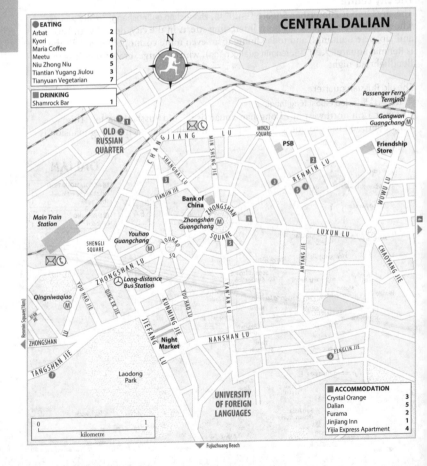

CENTRAL DALIAN

● EATING	
Arbat	2
Kyori	4
Maria Coffee	1
Meetu	6
Niu Zhong Niu	5
Tiantian Yugang Jiulou	3
Tianyuan Vegetarian	7

■ DRINKING	
Shamrock Bar	1

■ ACCOMMODATION	
Crystal Orange	3
Dalian	5
Furama	2
Jinjiang Inn	1
Yijia Express Apartment	4

(滨海路, bīnhǎi lù), which winds past the villas of Party bigwigs and local sports stars. The turquoise sea stretches before you to the south, while the north side of the road is green year-round with trees and new grass. Attractions here include the **Dalian Forest Zoo**, a wonderful **aviary**, and two hugely expensive **theme parks**.

Sun Asia Ocean World

圣亚海洋世界, shèngyà hǎiyáng shìjiè • Daily 9am–5pm • ¥110, Polar World ¥80 • Taxi from the city ¥20–30

The giant theme park of **Sun Asia Ocean World** is located just off **Xinghai Beach** (星海公园浴场, xīnghǎi gōngyuán yùchǎng). Its main feature is a 118m-long underwater tunnel, reputedly the longest in Asia, which affords close-up views of 10,000 fish of over 200 species – though you'd have a tough job counting them all. The park's polar section is also fun, and is home to polar bears, penguins and the like. Xinghai Beach itself features the usual fairground rides, souvenir stands and restaurants.

Dalian Forest Zoo

森林动物园, sēnlín dòngwùyuán • Daily 8.30am–5pm, panda pavilion 8.30am–4pm • ¥120, children under 1.3m free • Taxi from the centre ¥20–30 • Buses #5, #501 & #702, and also hourly tourist buses from Tiger Beach

Dalian Forest Zoo is hugely popular with local kids. Naturally, the stars of the show here are the pandas, with both giant and smaller red varieties represented; there's also a caged "safari" area, a reptile pavilion, and an area for parrot performances. Opposite the entrance is a cable-car station, allowing an easy ascent of the small neighbouring peak; there are superlative views of city and sea from the top.

Yanwoling Park

燕窝岭公园, yànwōlǐng gōngyuán • Daily dawn–dusk • Free • Hourly tourist buses from Tiger Beach or the zoo

The entrance to **Yanwoling Park** is marked by a statue – made from shells – of a little boy with seagulls. From here, a profusion of maintained trails and stairs takes you down precipitous slopes to the sea. One particularly nice hike, signed in English, ends up at Sunken Boat Rock, a cove where starfish cling to rocks and the only sounds are those of the waves. Strong currents make swimming here dangerous, however.

Bird Singing Woods

鸟语林, niǎoyǔ lín • Daily 7.30am–5pm • ¥40 • Hourly tourist buses from Tiger Beach or the zoo • Bird shows 1.30am, 1.30pm & 2.40pm • Parrot performances 10am, 11.30am, 1pm, 2.10pm, 3.20pm & 4.30pm

Just south of Tiger Beach, **Bird Singing Woods** is one of the most enjoyable sights in Dalian, and far better value than the zoo. Few of the birds actually sing – the ostriches and crested cranes near the entrance merely race over to stare at you, while the fowl in the hilly area beyond cluck and squawk to get at your food, available in ¥5 packs. The same price will buy some fish for the highly comical spoonbills, though seagulls will try to snatch it away first. The shows are surprisingly entertaining; peacocks fly (or rather fall) in from the upper reaches of the park, pelicans save football penalties, and parrots perform their usual tricks.

Tiger Beach

老虎滩, lǎohǔ tān • Ocean Park daily 7.30am–5.30pm, ¥210 • Bus #2, #4, #30, #402 or #801

At **Tiger Beach**, the funfair of **Ocean Park** seems to cover the entire bay area. A mind-boggling array of combination tickets covers attractions inside the park, such as the dolphin show and coral hall. The coastal setting is lovely, though the place is often full to bursting, especially on weekends.

ARRIVAL AND DEPARTURE

DALIAN

BY PLANE

Dalian Zhoushuizi airport (大连周水子国际机场, dàlián zhōushuǐzǐ guójì jīchǎng) is 12km northwest of the city; there are services to most major cities in China, as well as flights to Japan, Russia, Singapore and both Koreas. A taxi should cost ¥30–50, and it's also a stop on metro line #2.

Destinations Beijing (1hr 10min); Changchun (3 daily; 1hr); Harbin (1hr 25min); Hong Kong (1 daily; 3hr 25min); Shanghai (1hr 30min); Shenyang (50min).

BY TRAIN

Main train station (大連站, dàlián zhàn). The main train station is an easy walk from Zhongshan Square, just 1km to the east. Tickets are easy enough to buy here (though there'll be a queue), or at a number of ticket offices around town.

Destinations Beijing (4 daily; 6hr–15hr); Dandong (1 daily; 2hr); Harbin (8 daily; 10hr–12hr 30min); Shenyang (2–3 hourly; 1hr 55min–6hr).

Dalian North station (大連北站, dàlián běizhàn). With advance planning you should be able to avoid heading to Dalian North station, located 20km from the centre (best on the metro), though it handles most of the high-speed services – including all of the ones to Harbin. Destinations Beijing (4 daily; 4hr 50min–6hr 30min);

Dandong (hourly; 1hr 45min–3hr 45min); Harbin (1–2 hourly; 3hr 35min–4hr 35min); Shenyang (2–5 hourly; 1hr 30min–5hr).

BY BUS

It's hard to know which bus station you'll pitch up at in this vast city, though many services arrive around the main train station. With high-speed trains to all major cities in Dongbei, and decent sleepers to Beijing, you probably won't be needing them anyway.

BY FERRY

Dalian's **passenger-ferry terminal** is 1km northeast of Zhongshan Square. Ferries to Yantai are a full day faster than the train, and cheaper (4–6 daily; 4–7hr; ¥250–800). Tickets can be bought in advance from the passenger-ferry terminal, or from one of the many windows both at and around the train station. A twice-weekly service also runs to Inchon in South Korea (18hr; from ¥1020).

GETTING AROUND

By bus Tourist buses (hourly; ¥10) from the train station circle the entire town, serving all sights and beaches to the south. You can hop on and off with your ticket, though hard-sell conductors will do their best to make you buy theme-park tickets too. Buses for specific sights are given in the main text.

By taxi As the city centre is compact, the minimum ¥8 fare will get you to most places. A taxi from the city centre to beaches is around ¥40.

By tram There are a couple of tram lines in the centre (¥1;

pay on board); one runs north–southwest roughly along Zhongshan Lu, beginning in the shopping area around the north end of Xi'an Lu, a couple of kilometres west of the train station, before passing Xinghai Square and terminating at Heishijiao.

By metro There were three lines in service at the time of writing (¥2–5), connecting both train stations, the airport and the south coast – a highly useful means of transport.

By bike Tandem and mountain bikes are available to rent at the beaches for around ¥20/hr.

ACCOMMODATION

Dalian is choked with **five-star hotels** – *Holiday Inn*, *Ramada*, *Swissotel*, *Kempinski* and *Shangri-La* can all be found here – but **budget options** open to foreigners are scarce. The good news is that, as in many beach towns, off-season rates are usually half those of summer.

CITY CENTRE

★**Crystal Orange** 桔子水晶酒店, júzi shuǐjīng jiǔdiàn. 50 Youhao Lu ☎0411 82806767, ⓦorange hotel.com.cn; map p.164. Fantastic, modern boutique-style hotel, a short walk from the old Russian quarter. Rooms are phenomenal value, with a black-white-silver colour scheme, electronically powered Venetian blinds, iPhone speaker units, and Rubik cubes to play with. Head on up to the lobby on the 16th floor. **¥449**

Dalian 大连宾馆, dàlián bīnguǎn. 4 Zhongshan Square ☎0411 82633111, ⓦdl-hotel.com; map p.164. A stylish old place, built by the Japanese in 1927 – check out the ornate entrance, built almost like a Paris metro station. Bar occasionally indifferent service, it's a decent hotel, with an excellent sushi restaurant on the ground floor. **¥498**

Furama 富丽华大酒店, fùlìhuá dàjiǔdiàn. 60 Renmin Lu ☎0411 82630888, ⓦfurama.com.cn; map

p.164. Set in the very heart of the city, this upscale Japanese hotel's gargantuan lobby is a luxury mall of sorts, featuring palatial rooms and every facility you'd expect of a quality five-star. **¥780**

Jinjiang Inn 锦江之星, jǐnjiāng zhīxīng. 20 Laoleluosi Jie ☎0411 88105588; map p.164. The pan-China budget chain has this branch in the old Russian quarter. This colonial-era structure is beautiful from the outside (local tourists stop just to take pictures of it), and the minimalist rooms aren't bad either; the ones in the basement are cheapest, and some actually do get a little natural light. **¥259**

★**Yijia Express Apartment** 易嘉公寓式酒店, yìjiā gōngyùshì jiǔdiàn. 90 Luxun Lu ☎0411 82317722; map p.164. For something a little different, give one of Dalian's apartment complexes a try – this one is central, boasts rooms as big as most hotel suites, and costs around the same as the budget chains. The entrance is on the pedestrian arcade north of Luxun Lu. **¥198**

SOUTH COAST

Buzz Lightyear Youth Hostel 巴斯光年青年旅舍, bāsī guāngnián qīngnián lǚshè. 16 Haiwan Lu ☏0411 66896167; map p.163. Nice new hostel option, located in an alley opposite the main entrance to Sun Asia Ocean World. The dorms are overpriced (private rooms less so, though you'll have to book ahead for these), but you're paying for the location, in a quiet neighbourhood

yet an easy walk to the beach. Ten out of ten for the name, too. Dorms **¥80**, rooms **¥250**

The Castle 一方城堡豪华精选酒店, yīfāng chéngbǎo háohuá jīngxuǎn jiǔdiàn. 600 Binhai Xi Lu ☏0411 86560000; map p.163. If you head to Xinghai Square, you won't be able to miss this place – a gargantuan, castle-like affair which absolutely dominates the area. Swanky exteriors don't always translate into plush interiors in China, but this one doesn't disappoint – the common areas radiate luxury, and the same goes for the indoor pool. **¥1680**

EATING

RESTAURANTS

Arbat 阿尔巴, āěrbā. Russia Customs St ☏0411 82347758; map p.164. It took a little while, but a Russian restaurant has finally opened up in Russia-town. It's not bad, either, with goodies such as borshch (¥25) or herring, potatoes and onion (¥25) available in modern surroundings. Russian beer on offer, too. Daily 11am–10pm.

Kyori 鄉里, xiāng lǐ. 1 Wanmin Jie ☏0411 66669087; map p.164. A bit of a leftfield suggestion, maybe, but this place does a good job of showing what a semi-seedy Japanese *izakaya* is like – very authentic, right down to the fried chicken (¥38), *katsudon* (¥40), and shots of tasty *shochu* (from ¥40). Daily 11am–2.30pm & 4–11pm.

★**Niu Zhong Niu** 牛中牛, niúzhōngniú. Just off Renmin Lu ☏0411 82651006; map p.164. This fancy-looking venue is a great place in which to try Korean food; barbecue some beef (from ¥30 per portion), go for a *bibimbap* (veggies on rice in a sizzling-hot bowl; ¥20), or try some cold *naengmyeon* noodles (¥16). Daily 11am–11pm.

★**Tiantian Yugang Jiulou** 天天渔港酒楼, tiāntiānyúgǎng jiǔlóu. 10 Renmin Lu ☏0411 84549111; map p.164. For seafood away from the beaches, don't miss one of Dalian's branches of *Tiantian*; come dinnertime, they're usually packed with people

enjoying draught beer and fresh steamed crab. They've eschewed the usual picture menu for foreigner-friendly wax versions of their dishes. Expect to pay around ¥100 per head. Daily 10am–10pm.

Tianyuan Vegetarian 天缘素食店, tiānyuán sùshídiàn. Tangshan Jie ☏0411 83673110; map p.164. Vegetarians should head straight for this out-of-the-way restaurant, near the small but colourful Songshan Temple. They have the usual mix of cheap, meat-like tofu dishes (most priced at ¥24), though the menu is in Chinese only – have a look at what others are eating, if necessary. Daily 9am–9pm.

CAFÉS

Maria Coffee 玛丽亚咖啡, mǎliyà kāfēi. 4-2 Russia Customs St ☏138 89616147; map p.164. The best of the cafés on "Russia Road", with great coffee made by the owner, using her decades-old roaster. It's an amiable place in which you'll be encouraged to practise your Chinese. Daily 8.30am–9.30pm.

Meetu 原木餐厅, yuánmù cāntīng. 21 Fenglin Jie ☏0411 82815858; map p.164. Spacious, artsy affair on Fenglin Jie, the most attractive street in the whole city. The coffee's good, if a little pricier than the norm, and Western-style food is available too. Daily 8.30am–9.30pm.

DRINKING

Dalian has lots of bars, though the ones in the centre can be a little tame; the ones on Longquan Jie can get busy on weekends, and there are some good *izakaya* (Japanese-style bars, also serving food) tucked in around *Niu Zhong Niu* restaurant.

Lenbach 兰巴赫, lán bā hè. South of Xinghai Square ☏0411 39829230; map p.163. German-style bar-restaurant with an enviable location, overlooking the waves towards the offshore bridge – walk past the funfair to get here. The food's okay, with German sausage, sauerkraut and the like on offer, and there's plenty of good draught beer to pick from. Daily 11.30am–11.30pm.

Shamrock Bar 爱尔兰酒吧, àiěrlán jiǔbā. 2 Luxun Lu ☏0411 82100750; map p.164. Any purportedly cosmopolitan city needs an Irish bar, and this is Dalian's own offering – the usual mix of foreign beers, cocktails, western food and occasional music, it's extremely popular with local expats. Daily 11am–midnight, sometimes later.

DIRECTORY

Post office The post office (Mon–Sat 8am–6pm) is next to the main train station, on Changjiang Lu.

Visa extensions The PSB is centrally located at 18 Shiji Jie

(daily 8am–4.30pm; ☏0411 82804361). One of Dongbei's better bets for visa extensions.

Dandong

丹东, dāndōng

Once an obscure port tucked away in the corner of Liaoning province at the confluence of the **Yalu River** and the Yellow Sea, **DANDONG** is now a popular weekend destination for Chinese and South Koreans, who come to gaze across the river at the listless North Korean city of Sinuiju. Foreigners from further afield are also drawn to the massive memorial and museum dedicated to the defence of China's communist neighbour against imperialists during the Korean War. All in all, Dandong makes a worthwhile weekend trip out of Beijing or a stopover while touring the sooty northeast, as well as a convenient departure point for Changbai Shan (see p.178).

Dandong remains small enough to feel human in scale, and the tree-lined main streets are uncrowded, clean and prosperous. A strong influence can be felt from across the border, with vendors along the riverfront promenade selling North Korean banknotes and stamps – the latter bear slogans such as "Become human gun bombs!", while the former are actually illegal for foreigners to use in North Korea itself. Additionally, North Korean TV is on view in some Dandong hotels.

The Chinese side of the Yalu is a boomtown compared with what you can see of Sinuiju. The most scenic area is by the bridges, full of strolling tourists, particularly in the early evening – best is **Yalu River Park** (鸭绿江公园, yālùjiāng gōngyuán), where you can drive bumper cars and eat street snacks.

Old Yalu Bridge

鸭绿江断桥, yālùjiāng duànqiáo • Daily 7am–6pm • ¥30

On foot, the nearest you can get to North Korean soil without a visa is halfway across the river, on **Old Yalu Bridge**, the "broken" bridge in the south of town, next to the new bridge. The Koreans have dismantled their half but the Chinese have left theirs as a memorial, complete with thirty framed photos of its original construction by the Japanese in 1911, when the town was called Andong. The bridge ends at a tangled mass of metal that resulted from American bombing in 1950 during the Korean War. Several viewing platforms are on site, along with pay-telescopes trained on Sinuiju on the far bank. There isn't much to see on Sinuiju's desultory shore, save for some rusting ships and curious civilians – unlike the Chinese side, on which the riverfront is the focal point of town, North Koreans aren't really encouraged to look over the water, lest they feel motivated to get out for good.

The Museum to Commemorate Aiding Korea Against US Aggression

抗美援朝纪念馆, kàngměi yuáncháo jìniànguǎn • Daily 8am–4.30pm • Free with ID • Buses #1, #3, #4 or #5 from station to sports stadium, then a 5min walk north • Taxis ¥10–15

Built in 1993, the huge, macabre **Museum to Commemorate Aiding Korea Against US Aggression** feels like a relic of the Cold War – though note the Coca-Colas for sale at

---

A NORTH KOREAN PLEASURE CRUISE

From 8am, **boats** set out from all along Dandong's promenade, by the bridge, on 30min trips across the river (costing ¥60 in a large boat that leaves when full, or ¥100 per person for a zippy six-seater). The boats take you into North Korean waters to within a few metres of shore, where you can do your part for international relations by waving at the soldiers shouldering automatic rifles – some will happily wave back. Photography is allowed, and bring along binoculars if possible, for a good look at the bombastic Communist slogans adorning many buildings (in Korean text only, of course). On the boats they're usually piping one of two songs – *Pangapsumnida*, a North Korean song of welcome; and *Arirang*, a traditional folk song enjoyed in both Koreas. If you've an interest in actually visiting Sinuiju and Pyongyang far beyond, try Koryo Tours (ⓦ koryogroup.com).

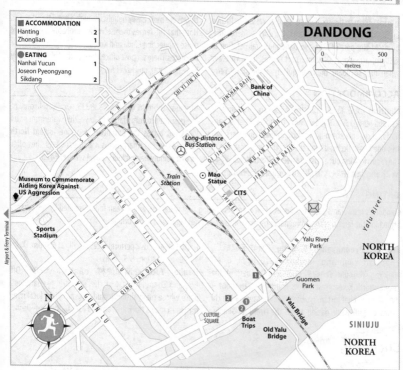

3

the entrance, next to Jiang Zemin's plaque swearing eternal North Korean-Sino friendship. It has nine exhibition halls on the Korean War, full of maps, dioramas, machine guns, hand grenades, photographs (mostly captioned in English), and sculptures of lantern-jawed Chinese and Korean soldiers. A few large plaques in each hall spell out the basic theme of each room – tending to be along the lines of "the Americans were terrible aggressors, China heroically won the war after stepping in to help its Korean brothers and sisters". The trifling details that the North kicked off the war by invading the South, and that at best the conflict (which has never officially ended) was a draw, are conspicuous by their absence.

ARRIVAL AND INFORMATION
DANDONG

Arriving at Dandong train station, or at the long-distance bus station just to the north, puts you right in the centre of town – a gleaming, marble-paved square featuring a Mao statue, about 1km north of the Yalu River.

By plane Dandong's small airport (丹东浪头机场, dāndōng làng tóu jīchǎng) is 14km southwest of town; take a shuttle bus into town (¥10) or a taxi (about ¥50).
Destinations Beijing (6hr 25min); Shanghai (2hr 20min).
By train Dandong is well connected to the rest of northeast China, though journey times can be long if you're not on one of the high-speed services. Tickets are easy enough to get from the train station, which sits right in the centre of town.
Destinations Beijing (4 daily; 6hr 15min–22hr); Changchun (6 daily; 3hr–8hr 30min); Dalian (hourly;

2–4hr); Shenyang (2–3 hourly; 1hr 10min–5hr 30min); Tonghua (2 daily; 6hr 40min–12hr 30min).
By bus The long-distance bus station is handily located in the thick of the action, very close to the train station. If you're planning to head off to the Changbai Shan Nature Reserve, you'll need to get an early-morning bus to Tonghua (通化, tōnghuà), from where it's another 3hr by bus; buy a ticket the night before travel.
Destinations Dalian (hourly; 3hr 30min); Shenyang (2 hourly; 3hr); Tonghua (2 daily; 4hr 30min).
By ferry Dandong's ferry terminal (丹东港, dāndōng

gǎng), 38km to the southwest, handles vessels to Inchon in South Korea (3 weekly; 20hr). On days of departure, buses to the port (¥25) leave Dandong's train station at 1.30pm; arriving at Dandong port, buses to town leave when full, so board them as quickly as possible. Ferry

tickets are most easily bought through a hotel travel agent. Note that the ferries themselves are probably the worst of those connecting China and Korea.

Services There's a post office close to the Yalu Park (daily 8am–5.30pm), on Liuwei Jie.

ACCOMMODATION

Hanting 汉庭酒店, hàntíng jiǔdiàn. Building 5, Fangba ☎ 0415 2583666. Most branches of this pan-national cheapie chain now refuse to take foreigners, but this one is still licensed – all the better if you score one of the rooms looking out across the river to North Korea. ¥240

★ **Zhonglian** 中联大酒店, zhōnglián dàjiǔdiàn. 62

Binjiang Zhonglu ☎ 0415 2333333, ☜ zlhotel.com.cn. The poshest accommodation in town, this waterfront hotel looks out across the bombed-out bridge toward North Korea. As well as smart rooms with great views, they offer an exceedingly helpful lobby travel service. ¥478

EATING

Dandong's restaurants cater to masses of weekenders craving freshwater fish and Korean food, supplied by restaurants stretching the length of the promenade; there are also a few cafés here, west of the bridge.

Joseon Pyeongyang Sikdang 朝鲜平壤饭店, cháoxiǎn píngrǎng fàndiàn. 42 Building E, off Binjiang Zhonglu ☎ 0415 3120198. The best of the several North Korean restaurants lining the waterfront – eat your raw beef tartare (*yukhoe*; ¥58) or savoury kimchi pancake (¥30) while gazing across the river into Sinuiju.

North Korean music performances nightly at 6.30pm. Daily 10.30am–1.30pm & 5–9pm.

Nanhai Yucun 南海渔村, nánhǎi yúcūn. Off Binjiang Zhonglu, west of the Yalu Bridge. Garrulous place whose many dishes include the *luzi yu*, a local river fish; most mains clock in at around ¥30. Daily 9am–9pm.

Shenyang

沈阳, shěnyáng

Capital of Liaoning province and unofficial capital of the northeast, **SHENYANG** is a railway junction and banking centre that has served as host to the Manchus, Russians, Japanese, Nationalists and then Communists. The city draws domestic tourists from all over the northeast of China, and their primary focus is all too obvious: as any cabbie here will delight in telling you, Shenyang has the only other **Imperial Palace** in China. This was constructed by Manchus before their takeover of the Ming dynasty; many visitors find it far more user-friendly than its (much larger) counterpart in Beijing.

Though you're unlikely to need more than a couple of days in Shenyang, there are **other notable sights** dotted around this fast-moving city, including a stunning monument to Chairman Mao built during the frenzied height of the Cultural Revolution; the tombs of two former emperors; and architecture left over from Japan's occupation, including a real gem of a hotel. You'll have to time it right to enjoy another amusement: from December to February, the town hosts the **Shenyang International Ice and Snow Festival**. Held at Qipanshan, 17km northeast of town, it's lower-key than Harbin's festivities (see p.185), but increasingly popular.

Brief history

Though well known in China as an important power base for the more radical hardline factions in Chinese politics (Mao's nephew, Yuanxin, was deputy Party secretary here until he was thrown in jail in 1976), Shenyang had its real heyday in the early seventeenth century. Nurhaci declared the city (then known as Mukden) the first capital of the expanding Manchu empire. He died in 1626, as work on his palace was just beginning, and was succeeded by his eighth son, **Abahai**, who consolidated and extended Manchu influence across northern China. When the Manchus, having defeated the resident Ming, moved to Beijing in 1644 and established the Qing dynasty, Shenyang declined steadily in importance. The city began to take on its modern, industrial role with the arrival of the Russians in the nineteenth century, who made it the centre of their rail-building programme. Years later, the puppets of the Japanese state also set up shop here, exploiting the resources of the surrounding region and building an industrial infrastructure whose profits and products were sent home to Japan.

Zhongshan Square

中山广场, zhōngshān guǎngchǎng

Shenyang has some great examples of uncompromising Soviet-style constructions, the most eye-catching of which is the giant **Mao statue** in **Zhongshan Square**. Erected in 1969 at the height of the Cultural Revolution, it comprises a pastiche of Communist iconography, its base lined with strident, blocky peasants, Daqing oilmen, PLA soldiers and students (though the Little Red Books the latter were waving have mostly been chipped off). Above them, the monolithic Mao stands wrapped in an overcoat, a superman whose raised hand makes him look as if he's directing traffic.

The Imperial Palace

沈阳故宫, shěnyáng gùgōng • Daily: April–Oct 8.30am–5.30pm; Nov–March 8.30am–4.30pm • ¥60 • Metro to Zhong Jie

Begun in 1626, the wonderful complex of the **Imperial Palace** is essentially a vastly scaled down replica of Beijing's Forbidden City. Entering from the south, you'll first come across

3

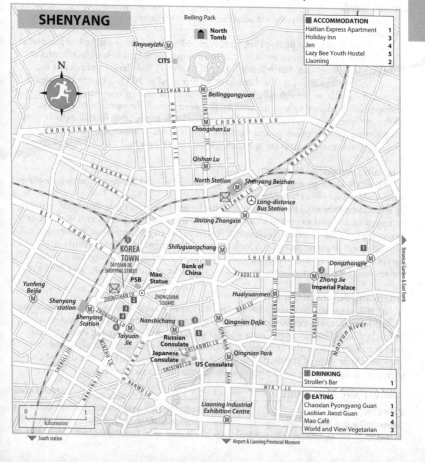

SHENYANG

ACCOMMODATION
Haitian Express Apartment	1
Holiday Inn	3
Jen	4
Lazy Bee Youth Hostel	5
Liaoning	2

DRINKING
Stroller's Bar	1

EATING
Chaoxian Pyongyang Guan	1
Laobian Jiaozi Guan	2
Mao Café	4
World and View Vegetarian	3

the **Cong Zhen Dian**, a low, wooden-fronted hall where the Qing dynasty was proclaimed and which was used by ministers to discuss state affairs. Beyond here, in the second courtyard, stands the Phoenix Tower, most formal of the ceremonial halls, and the Qingning building, which housed bedrooms for the emperor and his concubines.

Da Zheng Dian

In the eastern section of the complex, the **Da Zheng Dian** is a squat, octagonal, wooden structure in vivid red and lacquered gold, with two pillars cut with writhing golden dragons in high relief. Here, the Emperor Shunzhi was crowned before seizing Beijing – and the empire – in 1644. Colourful, dynastic-style performances take place just outside on the hour.

Shi Wang Ting

Just in front of the Da Zheng Dian stand the **Shi Wang Ting**, ten square pavilions once used as offices by the chieftains of the Eight Banners (military divisions) of the Empire, and now housing a collection of bizarrely shaped swords and pikes. Take time to wander away from the groups amid the side palaces, and note the Manchu dragons in bas-relief, unique to this palace.

North Tomb

北陵, běi líng • Daily 7am–5pm • park entry ¥6; park plus tomb ¥50 • metro to Beilinggongyuan for south entrance, or Lingxi for west entrance

Located inside spacious **Beiling Park** (北陵公园, běilíng gōngyuán) – itself a fun place where families pedal boats around its various lakes in summer, and build snow sculptures or ice-skate in winter – the **North Tomb** is that of **Abahai** (1592–1643), founder of the Qing dynasty. The well-preserved complex, constructed in 1643, is entered through a gate to the south, either side of which are pavilions; the easternmost was for visiting emperors to wash and refresh themselves, the westernmost for sacrifices of pigs and sheep. A "spirit way" flanked with animal statues leads to the **Long En Hall**, which contains an altar for offerings and the spirit tablets of the emperor and his wife. Their tree-covered burial mounds are at the rear, where you'll also find a fine dragon screen.

Liaoning Provincial Museum

辽宁省博物馆, liáoníngshěng bówùguǎn • Tues–Sun 9am–5pm • Free (bring ID) • ⓦ lnmuseum.com.cn • On the #108 and #130 bus routes, or a tram ride from Baitahelu metro

The **Liaoning Provincial Museum** is one of the largest museums in the northeast, though it upped sticks from its central location in 2015, and moved way out south of the river – annoyingly for the traveller, it's almost 20km from the city centre. If you've the time, it's still worth popping along for a look at the well-arranged exhibits of paintings, copperware, pottery and porcelain. Perhaps most interesting are the fragments of oracle bones used for divination, featuring some of the earliest examples of written Chinese.

Shenyang Botanical Garden

沈阳世博园, shěnyáng shìbó yuán • Daily 9am–5pm • ¥50 • Bus #168 from a stop one block northeast of the Imperial Palace

A half-hour bus ride outside town, **Shenyang Botanical Garden** is a vast area featuring formal gardens from all over China and the world, as well as various species of plant and tree from all over the Dongbei region. Some of the attempts at foreign gardens may be a little wide of the mark, but it makes for a great escape from the dust of the city, particularly on the strolling paths which encircle the pleasant lake.

ARRIVAL AND DEPARTURE   SHENYANG

BY PLANE

Shenyang Taoxian International Airport (沈阳桃仙 国际机场, shěnyáng táoxiān guójì jīchǎng), 20km south of the city, is the busiest in the Northeast; aside from a great number of domestic destinations, there are also flights to Thailand, Japan, Germany, Singapore, Canada, and both

Koreas. Getting into town is as easy as boarding an airport bus (¥15) to the train station; taxis will start the bidding at ¥150, though you can haggle this down. Taxis are cheaper heading back to the airport, as drivers will agree to use the meter (¥90); a seat in a shared cab costs ¥25 per person.

Destinations Beijing (1hr 15min); Changbai Shan (50min); Dalian (50min); Harbin (1hr); Hong Kong (4hr 35min); Shanghai (2hr).

BY TRAIN

There are three main stations in town – the old **main station** (沈阳站, shěnyáng zhàn), and the high-speed **North** (北站, běizhàn) and **South** (南站, nánzhàn) stations. The South station is pretty far (almost 25km from the centre), so be sure to book tickets to one of the other two; they both host high-speed services, are connected to the city metro, and are even within walking distance of the central sights.

Main train station destinations Beijing (16 daily; 4–15hr); Changchun (1–4 hourly; 1hr 15min–4hr 45min); Dalian (2–5 hourly; 1hr 45min–6hr); Dandong (1–5 hourly; 1hr 15min–5hr); Harbin (1–3 hourly; 2hr 15min–8hr); Jilin (12 daily; 2hr 10min–8hr); Tonghua (6 daily; 6hr 30min–9hr); Yanji (5 daily; 4–14hr).

Shenyang North station destinations Beijing (1–3 hourly; 4–14hr); Changchun (2–5 hourly; 1–4hr); Dalian (1–2 hourly; 1hr 30min–2hr 15min); Dandong (4 daily; 1hr 30min); Harbin (1–5 hourly; 2–8hr); Jilin (15 daily; 2–8hr); Tonghua (3 daily; 8hr 30min); Yanji (7 daily; 4–14hr).

BY BUS

The gleaming, futuristic **long-distance bus station** (快速客运站, kuàisù kèyùnzhàn), near the North station, is little used by foreigners since Shenyang is so well connected by train. To get to the centre from here, catch one of the many minibuses plying the route, or take a taxi (¥10).

Destinations Changchun (3hr); Dalian (5hr); Harbin (6hr); Jilin (4hr).

GETTING AROUND

By taxi Cabs are widely available and start at ¥8 for 3km; getting to the farther-flung sights could cost over ¥60 each way.

By bus The extensive local bus system (tickets ¥1) is not too crowded; bus maps can be bought outside all stations for about ¥5.

Metro Shenyang's metro system consists of two lines: one north–south, and one east–west. It's handy for getting across town from either of the train stations, and there are stops just a short walk from the Imperial Palace, Beiling Park and some other sights. Tickets cost ¥2–4, depending upon the number of stations travelled, and run 5am–11pm.

ACCOMMODATION

Haitian Express Apartment 海天快捷短租公寓中街店, hǎitiān kuàijié duǎnzū gōngyù zhōngjiē diàn. D2 Dayue City, 9-2 Xiaodong Lu ☏ 133 24037337. Dongbei is full of attractive apartment options – particularly useful for budget travellers, since so few of the city's cheapies accept foreigners. This one sports large rooms with decor ranging from boutique hotel to love motel in style – good value, in any case. It's a bit far east of the centre, though a short walk from Dong Zhongjie metro station. **¥168**

Holiday Inn 假日饭店, jiàrì fàndiàn. 204 Nanjing Beilu ☏ 024 23341888, ⌨ holidayinn.com. Modern high-rise in the heart of town, with health club attached; the entrance is just off Nanjing Lu. It's a popular place, and you're advised to book ahead in season; conversely, rates may be slashed in winter. **¥480**

Jen 今旅酒店, jīnlǚ jiǔdiàn. 68 Zhonghua Lu ☏ 024 23412288, ⌨ hoteljen.com. Formerly the *Traders*, this is one of the most luxurious places to stay in central Shenyang,

and it remains very competitively priced. The opulence of the lobby is matched by that of the rooms, and the professionalism of the largely English-speaking staff. **¥680**

★**Lazy Bee Youth Hostel** 懒蜂窝国际青年旅舍, lǎnfēngwō guójì qīngnián lǚshè. 16 Dongwei Lu ☏ 024 66985997. The best of Shenyang's surprisingly modest array of hostel options, with sturdy (if slightly pricey) dorm beds, an attractive café-restaurant, an artsy yet cosy air, and a pleasingly central location. Dorms **¥85**, doubles **¥230**

★**Liaoning** 辽宁宾馆, liáoníng bīnguǎn. 97 Zhongshan Lu ☏ 024 23839104, ⌨ liaoninghotel.com. This historic lodging, constructed by the Japanese in 1927, overlooks the Chairman Mao statue on Zhongshan Square. Rooms are spacious and light, and can even go for under ¥200 if you book online. Stop over if only for a look at how things were almost a century ago – some of the fittings and furnishings are remarkably well preserved. **¥388**

EATING

Chaoxian Pyongyang Guan 朝鲜平壤馆, cháoxiǎn píngrǎng guǎn. 106 Xita Jie ☏ 024 23478802. The giant flag on the front gives the game away: this is a North Korean restaurant. Staff are no refugees; they're here with the blessing of the government in Pyongyang, and at 7pm

some of them perform a surreal medley of music from the world's most secretive state. The food's good too; try the cold *naengmyeon* noodles (¥30), the savoury *jeon* pancakes, or even treat yourself to North Korean Taedonggang beer. Daily 11am–10pm.

★**Laobian Jiaozi Guan** 老边饺子馆, lǎobiān jiǎoziguǎn. 6 Zhong Jie ☎024 24315666. Shenyang's most famous restaurant is a super-busy dumpling house on the city's main shopping drag – any local will be able to point you here. The food is utterly superb for the price: rounds of dumplings go from ¥18, with intriguing fillings including sauerkraut, sea cucumber and chicken-and-mushroom. Then there's the non-dumpling selection; try spicy battered shrimp (¥55), goose stewed in beer (¥68), or even some donkey meat. Daily 10am–9.30pm.

Mao Café 猫咖啡, māo kāfēi. 222 Nanjing Bei Jie, no phone. Among a fair few cafés within walking distance of the main train station, this little number is the most appealing – unless you're averse to cats, for there are several stalking the premises. Daily 11am–10pm.

World and View Vegetarian 宽巷子素菜馆, kuānxiàngzi sùcàiguǎn. 202 Shiyi Weilu ☎024 22848678. This curiously titled place is where to go if meat is off your menu; as with most such places, they try as hard as they can to show vegetarians what they're missing, with fake-meat dishes such as sausage and Peking duck. Dishes range around the ¥25 mark. Daily 10am–10pm.

DRINKING

Stroller's Bar 流浪者酒吧, liúlàngzhě jiǔbā. 36 Bei Wujing Jie, near the junction with Shiyi Weilu ☎024 22876677. The best pub choice in the centre, with a vast range of beers: eleven German and seventeen Belgian ones at the last count, as well as draught Guinness (¥60). The food's great too, with goulash, lasagne, moussaka and other dishes – most cost precisely ¥68. Daily 11.30am–2am.

DIRECTORY

Consulate Russia, 31 Shisiwei Lu, in the south of the city (Mon–Fri 9am–noon; ☎024 23223927). It's better to apply in Beijing for your Russian visa, though it's always best to get one in your own country.

Post office Shenyang's main post office is at 32 Zhongshan Lu (Mon–Fri 8am–6pm).

Visa extensions The relevant PSB is on Taishan Lu, by the entrance to the North Tomb (Mon–Fri 8am–5pm; ☎024 86901116).

Jilin

吉林, jílín

JILIN must go down as one of China's least-visited provinces, and its two main cities have an air of neglect about them (as even locals will confess). The region bore the brunt of Japanese, Russian and Chinese communist planning more than anywhere in China: during the twentieth century, Jilin's vast deposits of coal and iron ore transformed the area into a network of sprawling industrial hubs.

Today, things are on the up: roads have been improved, the rail network is thorough and easy to use, most hotels are delighted to see foreigners, and winter brings low-cost skiing and sledding. The provincial capital, **Changchun**, boasts the Puppet Emperor's Palace memorializing Puyi's reign as "emperor" of the Japanese state Manchukuo; while **Jilin city** is famed for the ice-coated trees that line its riverfront in winter, and ski resorts on the outskirts of town. Popular with both domestic and South Korean tourists is the **Changbai Shan Nature Reserve**, a swath of mountain and forest scenery along the North Korean border in the far east of the province; for independent foreign travellers, however, the area is a little tricky (and costly) to get around. Lastly, new high-speed rail connections are enabling travellers to hit **Yanji**, capital of an autonomous Korean prefecture.

Changchun

长春, chángchūn

CHANGCHUN has historical notoriety from its role as **Hsinking**, capital of Manchukuo, the Japanese-controlled state that, from 1932 to 1945, had the former Manchu princeling Xuantong (better known as Puyi) as its emperor. Now a huge, sprawling, industrial city, it's also renowned for its many colleges, its movie studio and the

Number One Automobile Factory. The city retains its imperial architecture and design, with straight boulevards and squares throughout.

If you're short on time, or just don't feel like staying in Changchun (nobody would blame you), it's perfectly possible to rock up on a train in the morning or early afternoon, take a subway train to the **Puppet Emperor's Palace** – the city's most memorable sight – and then head off again in the evening.

The Puppet Emperor's Palace

伪皇宫, wěihuáng gōng • Daily 8.30am–4pm • ¥80, museum free • Metro to Weihuanggong

Changchun's only truly notable attraction is the **Puppet Emperor's Palace**, in the east of the city. Like its former occupant Puyi (see box opposite), the palace is really just a shadow of Chinese imperial splendour; in its defence, it does boast a swimming pool and horse-racing track. This luxurious retreat was only meant to be temporary, until his grand abode proper was completed south of Changchun's train station at Wenhua Square (the second-largest square in the world after Tian'anmen) – plans that led to nothing.

Inside the palace grounds, the **Museum of North East China's Occupation by Japan** documents Japan's brutal invasion and rule. On a lighter note, be sure to see the restored Japanese garden, one of Changchun's most tranquil spots.

ARRIVAL AND DEPARTURE   CHANGCHUN

By plane Changchun Longjia airport (长春龙嘉国际机场, chángchūn lóngjiā guójì jīchǎng), 10km northwest of town, is connected to every major city in China, plus Seoul in South Korea. Airport buses (40min; ¥20) head to a few points in town, including Renmin Square.
Destinations Beijing (1hr 30min); Changbai Shan (50min); Dalian (1hr 10min); Shanghai (2hr 30min).

By train The surprisingly attractive train station (长春站, chángchūn zhàn) lies to the north of the centre on the subway line, and has frequent connections – including a fair few high-speed services – to the rest of the northeast. Tickets are easy to buy at the station (it's near-deserted at night).

Destinations Beijing (15 daily; 6–18hr); Dandong (4 daily; 3–9hr); Harbin (1–5 hourly; 1–4hr); Jilin (2–5 hourly; 40min–2hr); Shenyang (1–6 hourly; 1hr 20min–8hr); Tonghua (2 daily; 7hr); Yanji (1–3 hourly; 2–10hr).

Most high-speed services now run to the West station (西站, xī zhàn), though since this is around 15km from the centre (on plenty of bus routes), try to get a ticket to the main station instead.

By bus The main station is just to the south of the train station. With Changchun's excellent rail connections, the only services worth bothering with are those to Baihe, near the northern gate of Changbai Shan (2 daily; 6hr).

INFORMATION

Tours You can organize tours to Changbai Shan through most hotels, though you'll save a little by going to CITS. There are a few branches around town, including one at

1323 Xi'an Dajie (☎0431 88929311); there was a more convenient one by the train station's south exit, but this entire area was under reconstruction at the time of writing.

GETTING AROUND

By taxi Taxi fares begin at ¥5; most rides in town will be under ¥10. It can be tough to find a cab around the train station.

By subway Changchun's rather sloppy subway system

currently has two lines (confusingly numbered #3 and #4); one runs above ground, and despite the fact that it's essentially brand-new, some stations have already fallen into disrepair. Tickets cost ¥2–4, depending upon distance travelled.

BACKCHAT

Jilin province is famous for **er ren zhuan** – loosely translated as "Repartee for Two" – a form of theatre closer to vaudeville than Beijing opera, incorporating dancing, singing, baton-twirling, costume changes and soliloquies. A typical performance sees a man and woman regaling the audience with a humorous tale of their courtship and love. CDs of the genre are available at stores, and you may be able to get into a performance with translation via CITS, or you could just ask a cabbie or local to point you to a theatre.

THE LAST EMPEROR

In 1908, at the age of 2, **Puyi** ascended to the imperial throne in Beijing, at the behest of the dying Dowager Cixi. Although forced to abdicate four years later by the Republican government, he retained his royal privileges, continuing to reside as a living anachronism in the Forbidden City. Outside, the new republic was coming to terms with democracy and the twentieth century, and Puyi's life, circumscribed by court ritual, seems a fantasy in comparison. In 1924, he was **expelled** by Nationalists who were uneasy at what he represented, but the Japanese eventually found a use for him in Changchun as someone who could lend a symbolic legitimacy to their rule. After the war, he was re-educated by the Communists and lived the last years of his life as a gardener. His story was the subject of Bernardo Bertolucci's lavish film *The Last Emperor*.

ACCOMMODATION AND EATING

Chunyi Hotel 春谊宾馆, chūnyí bīnguǎn. South of the station plaza ☎0431 82096888. Built in 1909 by the Japanese, the province's oldest inn is hardly beautiful, but good value for cleanliness, location and price (often just over half the rack rate). It also has a good hotpot buffet restaurant on the second floor of its newer VIP wing – stuff your face for just ¥78 per person. ¥580

International Hotel 国际大厦酒店, guójì dàshà jiǔdiàn. 568 Xi'an Dalu ☎0431 88485116. Though its prices hint at budget-chain mediocrity, this is actually a comfortable and more than adequate business hotel, with rooms that are excellent value for the location. ¥288

Shangri-La 香格里拉饭店, xiānggélǐlā fàndiàn. 569 Xi'an Dalu ☎0431 88981818, ⊛shangri-la.com. In the centre of the new commercial district, this is the city's five-star option – if a rather expensive one. As you'd expect for the price, service is excellent, and the rooms extremely plush. ¥1000

★**Xiangyangtun** 向阳屯饭馆, xiàngyángtún fànguǎn. 433 Dong Chaoyang Lu, off Tongzhi Jie ☎0431 88982876. Changchun's best place to eat, by a long way. It's a traditional Dongbei restaurant – most things here are still cooked on wood-fired stoves. They have a picture menu, though nothing is written in English; try the *zheng jidan jiang* (蒸鸡蛋酱, zhēng jīdànjiàng; ¥14), a spicy egg dish served in a metal bowl, or one of the many tofu, cured meat or mushroom dishes. And all this with Mao overlooking affairs – you can't miss him. Daily 11am–11pm.

Jilin

吉林, jílín

Known as Kirin during the Manchukuo time, **JILIN** is split in two by the Songhua River, with the downtown area spread along its northern shore. There's nothing as such to see here, but the waterside promenade makes for a pretty walk – there's a pretty Catholic church here, and during the winter the riverside trees get coated in frost (a phenomenon resulting from condensation from the hydroelectric dam at Songhua Lake). It's Jilin's claim to fame, along with an **ice festival** in January and neighbouring parks for skiing and sledding. The city also makes a potential jumping-off point for Changbai Shan.

Beishan Park

北山公园, běishān gōngyuán • Taxi from town about ¥15 • **Yuhuangge** ¥1

To the west of town, **Beishan Park** is filled with pathways and temples, the most interesting of which is **Yuhuangge** (Jade Emperor's Temple), where rows of fortune-tellers gather out front. The small lake at the base of the mountain is also a pleasant place to hang out on a hot day – the usual pedalo-rides are available, and children will get the chance to inject their parents with jealousy by zorbing.

Zhuque Shan

朱雀山, zhūquè shān • Daily 8am–5pm • ¥30 • Buses #9 and #33 from Jilin Dajie, one big block west of the train station; or taxi from town about ¥60, then 1km walk to park

Fourteen kilometres southeast of Jilin, **Zhuque Shan** park is known for its hiking and temples, but is primarily the closest winter ski area to town. There are two small slopes, one for skiing and one for sledding. The sleds are actually two downhill skis nailed together with a piece of raised plywood, and they really fly if you get a running start and bellyflop. A good restaurant on-site seats guests on a *kang*, a heated raised platform that provides a nice vantage point over the hill. Foreigners are a rarity, and the staff and patrons a lot of fun.

Songhua Lake

松花湖, sōnghuā hú • Bus #33 from Jilin Dajie (see p.177), or taxi from town about ¥80

Beyond Zhuque Shan, 20km southeast of Jilin, is **Songhua Lake**, a deep expanse very attractively surrounded by forested hills. Unlike most Chinese scenic attractions, the lake seems big enough to absorb all its visitors, and even on weekends it's possible to find some peaceful spots. At the Songhua's southern end is the huge **Fengman Dam**, a source of great local pride, though something which could one day subject the city to catastrophic flooding.

ARRIVAL AND DEPARTURE   JILIN

By train The train station is right in the centre of town, around 2km north of the river. It receives quite a few high-speed services, too.
Destinations Beijing (6 daily; 7–17hr); Changchun (2–5 hourly; 40min–2hr); Dalian (11 daily; 4–14hr); Harbin (6 daily; 1hr 40min–2hr 20min); Shenyang (1–4 hourly; 2–9hr).

By bus The bus station is in the centre of town, very close to the train station. As with much of Dongbei, good train connections render the buses near useless; the only exceptions are services to Baihe (2 daily; 5hr), near the northern gate of Changbai Shan.

ACCOMMODATION AND EATING

Chuanren Baiwei 川人百味, chuānrén bǎiwèi. 101 Chongqing Lu ☎0432 62568858. By far the most attractive restaurant in Jilin, and just down the road from the station, this serves a mix of Sichuanese and Dongbei cuisine in a pleasingly attractive environment – all charming lights and floor-tiles. Most mains ¥20–40, though the cheapest noodle dishes go for next to nothing. Daily 8am–10pm.

Elephant Café 大象咖啡, dàxiàng kāfēi. More of a bar than a café, this friendly little venue near the church is good for both caffeine and alcohol fixes. They've taken the elephant motif to something approaching the extreme, but it somehow still comes across as stylish – especially so for Jilin. Daily 2pm–midnight.

Jilin International 吉林国际大酒店, jílín guójì dàjiǔdiàn. 20 Zhongxing Jie ☎0432 66571888. A comfortable, affordable place, right in front of the train station – you can't miss it. The rooms feel a wee bit dated after heading up from the relatively snazzy lobby, but they're absolutely fine for the price, and there are grand views from the upper floors. ¥230

World Trade Winning 世贸万锦大酒店, shìmào wànjǐn dàjiǔdiàn. 2 Jiangwan Lu ☎0432 62222666. Charlie Sheen and his hashtags would be quite at home in this new, ritzy hotel, overlooking a particularly scenic bend of the river. There's a pool and fitness centre on site, and rooms come with plush carpets and large bathrooms. ¥580

DIRECTORY

Post office Also just north of one of the main river bridges, on Jilin Dajie; Mon–Sat 9am–5pm.
Travel agents There's a travel agency inside the *Jilin International*, offering regular tours to and around

Changbai Shan; figure on a minimum of ¥380 per person for the transport and accommodation, though this can go up if you need single occupancy, and will start to hit ¥1000 once entry tickets and the like are factored in.

Changbai Shan

长白山, chángbái shān • ¥125

The **Changbai Shan** ranges run northeast to southwest for more than 1000km along the Chinese–North Korean border. With long, harsh winters and humid summers, this is the only mountain range in East Asia to possess alpine tundra, and its highest peak, Baitou Shan (2744m), is the tallest mountain on the eastern side of the continent. **Changbai Shan Nature Reserve**, with its jagged peaks emerging from swaths of lush pine forests, is one of the highlights of Dongbei, not least for its stunning lake, **Tian Chi**, which actually straddles the international border.

Despite Changbai Shan's remote location, both domestic and South Korean tourists come here in great numbers; a village has grown up on the mountain, and the scenery

---

JILIN'S SKI RESORTS

Jilin has two first-class **ski resort areas**, which are considerably more expensive and better equipped – as well as vastly more professional – than those at Zhuque Shan.

Beida Lake Huaxue Chang (北大湖滑雪场, běidàhú huáxuěchǎng) ☏0432 4202168. 56km southeast of Jilin; in winter months hourly buses make the trip (1hr 30min; ¥20), or charter a taxi (up to ¥200).

Songhua Lake Huaxue Chang (松花湖滑雪场, sōnghuā hú huáxuěchǎng) ☏0432 4697666. 26km east of Jilin; take bus #9 or #33 to the small district of Fengman (丰满, fēngmǎn; 30min) and continue by taxi, or get a taxi all the way from Jilin city for about ¥100.

---

and atmosphere are somewhat marred by litter, souvenir stalls and hawkers. The reserve averages around 10,000 visitors a day in summer – as you're herded from one spot to the next, it's easy to feel the outdoors experience has been diluted a bit, and getting away from the crowds is the key to a rewarding visit. You need to come well prepared with all-weather gear, whatever the time of year.

Northern route

Open 24hr • Park buses 8.30am–about 3pm, ¥85

A huge, alpine-style hut marks Changbai Shan's northern entrance. From here, regular buses head along the **northern route** through gorgeous, forested surrounds towards Tian Chi, though you'll need to hike or get a 4WD for the last section of the route. On your way up this flank of the mountain, you may care to stop by the **Underground Forest** (地下森林, dìxià sēnlín), an extremely attractive tree-filled canyon; **Small Tian Chi** (小天池, xiǎo tiānchí), a lake that's almost laughable when compared to its larger sibling; and a **hot spring** area in which the gushing, steaming water is used to boil eggs and corn (both ¥5). There are paths ascending from the spring area to Tian Chi, a journey of well over one thousand steps.

Western route

Open 24hr • Park buses 8.30am–about 3pm, ¥85

Changbai Shan's **western route** is less interesting and less beautiful than its northern counterpart, though you'll have far fewer people to deal with. Buses stop by at a couple of **gardens** (only really worth visiting in warmer months), and a deep, rocky canyon. There is, as yet, no road for the last section up to Tian Chi, though it's possible to hike.

Tian Chi

天池, tiān chí • 4WD to lake from north or west "changing centres", where buses terminate, ¥80; walkable in good weather

It is surely only a matter of time before **Tian Chi**, a dramatic volcanic crater lake 5km across, encircled by angular crags, gushing waterfalls and snowcapped peaks, takes its place alongside China's must-see wonders. As long as the irascible weather cooperates, the effort of climbing the thousand or so concrete steps to reach the lake, not to mention all the trouble of getting to the reserve in the first place, is forgotten as you cross the boulder-strewn snow field to what must be one of the most spectacular views anywhere in the world.

Head off on your own and you can quickly be swallowed up in the wilderness, but be careful around Tian Chi, since the lake straddles the **Chinese–North Korean border** – if you stray across, you're subject to arrest and charges of espionage. At the height of the Cultural Revolution, Chairman Mao ordered that the line be demarcated, but it isn't clearly visible on the ground.

ARRIVAL AND DEPARTURE   CHANGBAI SHAN

Despite Changbai Shan's remote location, there are good **train**, **bus** and **plane** links. The vast majority of visitors are on a tour of some kind – it's tough to get around independently, though possible with a modicum of patience. You might not save any money though, as prices for tickets, transport and accommodation stack up quickly.

3

GINSENG

Ginseng has been collected as a medicinal plant for millennia, and the first Chinese pharmacopoeia, written in the first century, records its ability to nourish the five internal organs, sharpen intelligence, strengthen *yin* (female energy) and invigorate *yang* (male energy).

It is the ginseng root that is prized. Plants are rare and the hunt for them is shrouded in **superstition**. The roots are said to be guarded by snakes and tigers, and legend has it that if a hunter should dream of a laughing, white-bearded man or a group of dancing fairies, he must get up, remain silent, and walk off into the forest. His colleagues must follow without speaking to him, and he will lead them to a root.

Changbai ginseng is regarded as the finest in China. Ginseng hunters here work in summer, when the plant can be spotted by its red berries. One way to find it is to listen for the call of the Bangchui sparrow, which becomes hoarse after eating ginseng seeds. When a ginseng is found, a stick is planted in the ground and a red cloth tied to it: according to tradition, the cloth stops the ginseng child – the spirit of the root – from escaping.

Ginseng generally grows in the shade of the Korean pine, and it is said that a plant of real medicinal value takes fifty years to mature. The plants are low-growing, with their roots pointing upwards in the topsoil. Digging one out is a complex, nail-biting operation, because if any of the delicate roots are damaged, the value of the whole is severely diminished. Roots are valued not just by weight, but by how closely their structure resembles a human body, with a head and four limbs. If you find a wild root, you're rich, as Changbai ginseng sells for over ¥1000 a gram. Artificially reared ginseng is worth a fraction of this.

By plane Cute little Changbai Shan airport (长白山机场, chángbáishān jīchǎng) is close to the park's western entrance, and can save hours over catching a bus or train to the park. In theory, airport buses connect the airport with the west entrance (¥5) or Baihe town (¥28); unfortunately, bus timetables are out of kilter with flight schedules, and it's not unknown for services to rock up at the airport 5min after the planes have left. To reach the airport from Baihe, buses depart from the *Jinhuishe International Hotel* (金水鹤国际酒店, jīnshuǐhè guójì jiǔdiàn), which sits in an inconvenient, isolated spot between Baihe train station and Erdao Baihe. There are also airport buses from the west gate. Taxis from the airport charge around ¥50 to the west gate, or ¥250 to Baihe – they're fine with you splitting the fare with other arriving passengers, if you can find any willing to do so.

Destinations Beijing (1hr 50min); Changchun (50min); Shenyang (50min).

By train Baihe train station (白河站, báihé zhàn) is the most useful jump-off point for independent visitors to Changbai Shan, though services hitting this station are all clunkers, and often full; to get anywhere bar Dandong and Shenyang, you may have to change in Tonghua (通化, tōnghuà).

Destinations Dandong (1 daily; 17hr); Shenyang (3 daily; 13hr 30min); Tonghua (6 daily; 6–7hr).

By bus Baihe bus station is handily located just across the road from Baihe train station. Again, it's not terribly busy, though far faster than the trains for Changchun (2 daily; 6hr) and Jilin (5 daily; 5hr).

TOURS

Changbai Shan is most easily reached on a three-day, **two-night tour** arranged through CITS in Jilin (see p.178). These cost over ¥1000 per person, including park entrance fees and accommodation, and covers all the must-see sights, including Tian Chi.

INFORMATION

ACCESS

Changbai Shan has two main entrances, both of which eventually converge on Tian Chi, the focal point of pretty much every visitor to the park. Shoddy Changbai Shan maps are available at both entrances.

Northern entrance The northern entrance is easiest to access for independent travellers via the scruffy mountain town of Baihe (白河, báihé) 20km away, the main base of operations with plenty of accommodation, as well as the area's main train and bus stations. The route to Tian Chi is also prettier and more rewarding from the northern entrance.

Western entrance Changbai Shan's western entrance is

far less developed, though the new Changbai Shan airport nearby is becoming an increasingly popular option for tour operators and independent travellers alike.

WEATHER

Bear in mind that the weather in the region is not kind, and can change very suddenly. Summer brings torrential rain; winter snows can close roads; and year-round cloud and mist can make it impossible to see 10m ahead. The best chance for decent weather is between June and September. Conditions are posted at both park entrances, though your hotel should also be able to let you know how Tian Chi is looking at any given time.

GETTING AROUND

By bus From Baihe, there are a couple of morning buses (45min; ¥10) to the park's north entrance, and more through the day in summer. The last buses return to Baihe around 4pm. For buses between Baihe and the west gate, you'll need to board the irregular airport services (see opposite).

By taxi Given the awful state of public transport in Baihe, you're almost inevitably going to need a taxi at some point. Rides start at ¥5, though it'll be more like ¥60 to the north gate. If you'll be descending late, it may be a good idea to grab your driver's business card for the return trip – if you miss the last bus, you'll otherwise be reliant upon the kindness of whichever tour groups are yet to head back down from the park. Those descending before 3pm should find it easy to share a cab (¥20 per person) down to Baihe.

ACCOMMODATION AND EATING

Most visitors stay at **Baihe**, a town 20km from the park's northern entrance. There are a few grubby accommodation options in the immediate vicinity of the train and bus stations, though most prefer to head into the main commercial area, **Erdao Baihe** (二道白河站, èrdào báihé zhàn), around 4km to the south; it's ¥5 by taxi, though you'll have to haggle it down from ¥10. More pleasant than this scruffy area is the zone surrounding the *Changbai Shan* hotel, which is around 4km southwest of the station (again ¥5 by taxi); this also has better (though not really good) **restaurants** than those in Erdao Baihe. An amazing number of places to eat specialize in dog meat – if in any doubt when ordering, ask if your dish features *gou rou* (狗肉, gǒuròu). Lastly, there are a few upmarket places to stay around both main **park gates**.

BAIHE

Changbai Shan Hostel 长白山国际青年旅舍, chángbáishān guójì qīngnián lǚshè. Just south of the train station ☎0433 5710800, ⓦyhachina.com. Probably the best-organized place in the area, in terms of the service they offer independent travellers – as well as running shuttle buses to both park entrances, they're able to organize overnight stays on the mountain. It's in an ugly part of town, though just a short walk from the train station – turn right when you hit the main road. Dorms ¥45, twins ¥200

Changbaishan 长白山大厦, chángbáishān dàshà. 50 Tongchang Lu ☎0433 5723333. This long-standing hotel in Baihe's most appealing quarter is a large place popular with tour groups, though they are more than happy to take independent travellers. Rooms are fine, if a little dated, and service is courteous. ¥500

Singie Art Hotel 星际艺术之家酒店, xīngjì yìshù zhījiā jiǔdiàn. Erdao Baihe ☎0433 5750222. At the northern end of Baihe's main commerical district, this hotel is good value for money – even if the designers focused exclusively on the trendy-looking lobby, rather than the somewhat mediocre rooms. ¥350

NORTH GATE

Athletes Village 运动员村宾馆, yùndòng yuáncūn bīnguǎn. ☎0433 5746066. Marked as it is with the Olympic rings, it's hard to tell what other connection this alpine-styled hotel has to the world of athletics, bar a decent swimming pool and fitness centre. Though inevitably overpriced, the rooms are rather nice, and you'll get the chance to bathe in hot spring water too. It's a short walk from the north gate. ¥680

WEST GATE

Days Hotel Landscape Resort 蓝景戴斯度假酒店, lánjǐng dàisī dùjià jiǔdiàn. ☎0439 6337999. Attractive lodge-style resort, located just down the road from the west gate. As well as wonderfully attractive rooms and forest surroundings, they've by far the best restaurants in the Changbai Shan area. ¥1200

Tianci Travel Village 天瑅旅游度假村, tiāncì lǚyóu dùjiǎcūn. ☎0439 6598555. Relatively cheap complex between the airport and the west gate. The fixtures and fittings in the lobby may look suspiciously old, but rooms (some of which are carpeted) are more modern in appearance, and pretty large too; the on-site restaurant comes in handy, considering the remote location. Discounts usually available outside weekends. ¥390

Yanji

延吉, yánjí

Sitting almost within visible range of the North Korean border (though please don't try walking there), amiable little **YANJI** is a good example of how high-speed rail is facilitating travel in China – previously accessible only on pricey flights or trains which took forever to arrive, it's now relatively straightforward to get to on the *gao tie*, with this sudden competition also driving flight ticket prices down. Most are here to see the fascinating intermingling of cultures that result from its status as the seat of the **Yanbian Korean Autonomous Prefecture** – *hangeul* vies with Chinese characters for supremacy all across town, and those with an ear for such things will often hear the local Chosonjok (ethnic Koreans) switching languages mid-sentence. Other than the frequent roars of military jets patrolling the sensitive border area, Yanji gives off a pleasantly relaxed vibe; coupled with richly forested surroundings perfect for hiking or biking, it appears destined to attract international travellers in ever greater numbers.

Mao'er Shan

帽儿山, màoér shān · Daily 24hr · Free · Taxi from town about ¥60

Look south from town, and you'll see what looks like a forested boob poking from the horizon. This is **Mao'er Shan**, a small mountain (or large hill) topped by a pagoda – every single person in Yanji has been here, most probably quite a few times. Views of the city and its mountain environs are quite lovely, and it's a simple ninety-minute walk to the top and back down along a well-made path.

ARRIVAL AND DEPARTURE   YANJI

BY PLANE

The tiny **airport** is just southwest of the centre, and has pricey international services to and from South Korea, as well as a modest range of flights to nearby Chinese destinations.

Destinations Beijing (2hr); Chang Baishan (50min); Changchun (40min); Dalian (2hr); Shenyang (1hr 15min).

BY TRAIN

Main train station (延吉站, yánjí zhàn). The main train station is south of the centre of town, around 2km south of the river, though few international visitors tend to arrive here.

Destinations Changchun (3 daily; 8hr); Jilin (7 daily; 5hr 30min–7hr); Shenyang (5 daily; 13hr).

Yanji West station (延吉西站, yánjí xī zhàn). You're more likely to pitch up at the high-speed-only West station out in the sticks a ¥30 cab-ride from the centre.

Destinations Beijing (1 daily; 9hr); Changchun (1–2 hourly; 2hr 20min); Dalian (2 daily; 6hr); Harbin (2 daily; 4hr); Jilin (1–2 hourly; 1hr 40min); Shenyang (7 daily; 4hr).

ACCOMMODATION AND EATING

Fengmao 丰茂, fēng mào. Henan Jie ☎ 0433 2252666. Surprisingly attractive for a Yanji restaurant, this super place sells sticks of meat to be barbecued at the table (¥40 should be enough to fill you up), as well as a range of Korean dishes. The waitresses are Pyongyang girls chosen mainly for their beauty – no photos allowed, for security reasons, but if you pretend it's your birthday, you might just get an absorbing serenade about Marshall Kim. Daily 11am–2pm & 5–10pm.

Ryugyong 柳京饭店, liǔjīng fàndiàn. 124 Xinxing Jie ☎ 0433 2912211. Good-value, Japanese-owned hotel near the town centre and the university quarter. The restaurant behind the lobby also makes a great (if usually empty) place to eat North Korean grub, while watching North Korean music or news – the cold *naengmyeon* noodles really hit the spot, though try to save room for their delectable fried kimchi balls. ¥230

INTO FORBIDDEN NORTH KOREA

A smattering of foreigners are making their way into **North Korea** from Yanji into Rason, the DPRK's official Special Economic Zone – a back-door route into a back-door country, and a chance to earn some real travel kudos. You'll need to join a tour, and some of those available head all the way down to Pyongyang – try Koryo Tours (ⓦ koryogroup.com) or Paektu Cultural Exchange (ⓦ paektuculturalexchange.org).

Heilongjiang

黑龙江, hēilóngjiāng

The province of **HEILONGJIANG** has always been considered a little remote to the Chinese – a perception that remains intact, even in these days of high-speed trains and cheap flights. "Black Dragon River" is a land of extremities: this is home to China's northernmost and easternmost points, as well as its coldest. Winter temperatures regularly plummet below -30°C, though this is high season in the provincial capital **Harbin**, which hosts a world-famous annual **Ice Festival**. Though the winter cold makes it hard to truly enjoy the city itself, in summer it's one of the most pleasant in the land.

Beyond Harbin, Dongbei's northeast is little visited by Western tourists, with the main draw being the **Zhalong Nature Reserve**, near Qiqihar. If you're journeying any further, it's likely you'll be on the **Trans-Manchurian train** and on your way to Russia, via Hailar and Manzhouli, both in **Inner Mongolia** (see p.227).

Harbin

3

哈尔滨, hā'ěrbīn

The capital of Heilongjiang province and laid out on the southern bank of the Songhua River, **HARBIN** is most famous for its wonderfully photogenic winter **Ice Festival**. While visiting at this time is highly recommended, it's certainly worth popping by in a warmer month too, for this is one of the few northern cities with a distinctive character. A few roads near Harbin's centre are lined with gorgeous colonial-era structures. In fact, the city used to be nicknamed "Little Moscow", and though much of the old architecture has been replaced with sterile blocks and skyscrapers, corners of Harbin still look like the last threadbare outpost of imperial Russia – leafy boulevards are lined with European-style buildings painted in soothing pastel shades, and bulbous onion domes dot the skyline (albeit with the skyscrapers of modern China as a backdrop). There are several **Russian restaurants**, and the locals have picked up on some of their neighbour's customs: as well as a taste for ice cream and pastries, the residents have a reputation as the hardest drinkers in China.

Brief history

Harbin was a small fishing village on the Songhua River until world history intervened. In 1896, the Russians obtained a contract to build a rail line from Vladivostok through Harbin to Dalian, and the town's population swelled to include 200,000 foreigners. More Russians arrived in 1917, this time White Russian refugees fleeing the Bolsheviks, and many stayed on. In 1932, the city was captured by Japanese forces invading Manchuria, then in 1945 it fell again to the Russian army, who held it for a year before Stalin and Chiang Kai-shek finally came to an agreement to return Harbin to China. Things haven't been totally peaceful since; Harbin was the scene of fierce factional fighting during the Cultural Revolution, and when relations with the Soviet Union deteriorated, the inhabitants looked anxiously north as fierce border skirmishes took place.

Zhongyang Dajie

中央大街, zhōngyāng dàjiē

Better than any of Harbin's actual sights is a walk down **Zhongyang Dajie**, the city's most charming road. Many shops along this pedestrianized stretch have been restored, with plaques out front detailing, in English, their past lives as colonial homes and stores. Make sure you go in the **department store at no. 107**, if only to see its spectacular skylight, as well as a rendition of a section from Michelangelo's Sistine Chapel mural, which hangs on the back wall. There are good restaurants and bars along the numbered streets running off the main road, which are paved with cobblestones and closed to cars and bicycles. In winter, ice sculptures line the street, while summer sees pavement cafés and bars set up.

3

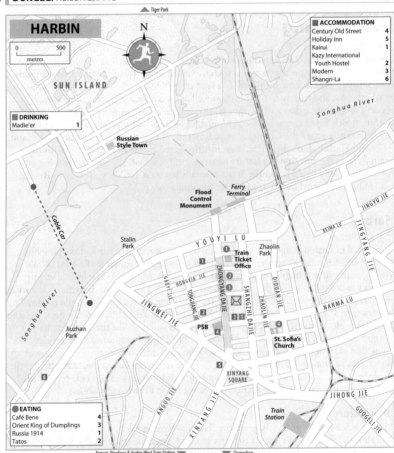

HARBIN

0   500
metres

SUN ISLAND

■ DRINKING
Madie'er   1

■ ACCOMMODATION
Century Old Street   4
Holiday Inn   5
Kairui   1
Kazy International
  Youth Hostel   2
Modern   3
Shangri-La   6

Tiger Park

N

Songhua River

Russian
Style Town

Cable Car

Flood
Control
Monument

Ferry
Terminal

JINGYU JIE

JINGYANG JIE

BEIMA LU

Stalin
Park

Songhua River

Jiuzhan
Park

Y O U Y I L U

Zhaolin
Park

Train
Ticket
Office

HONGXIA JIE

GANYI JIE

LONGJIANG JIE

ZHONGYANG DAJIE

SHANGZHI DAJIE

ZHAOLIN JIE

DIDUAN JIE

NANMA LU

JINGWEI JIE

PSB

St. Sofia's
Church

ANGUO JIE

XINYANG JIE

XINYANG
SQUARE

JIHONG JIE

GUOGELI JIE

Train
Station

● EATING
Café Bene   4
Orient King of Dumplings   3
Russia 1914   1
Tatos   2

Airport, Pingfang & Harbin West Train Station ▼   ▼ Changchun

St Sophia's Church

哈尔滨建筑艺术馆, hā'ěrbīn jiànzhù yìshùguǎn • Daily 8.30am–5pm • ¥15

The most interesting formal sight in Harbin has to be **St Sophia's Church** (哈尔滨建筑艺术
馆, hā'ěrbīn jiànzhù yìshùguǎn), a Russian Orthodox cathedral built in 1907. Set in its own
square and restored to all its onion-domed glory, the cathedral now houses the **Harbin
Architecture and Art Centre**, with a photographic survey of Harbin's history as a Russian
railway outpost. On summer evenings, the area around the cathedral comes alive with
impromptu badminton games, ladies displaying their fan-dancing skills and – the
highlight – a well-choreographed display from the square's fountains. They are roped off,
but it is never long before someone charges into the maelstrom. The cathedral itself is
illuminated from sunset until around 10pm – a truly enchanting sight.

Stalin Park

斯大林公园, sīdàlín gōng yuán

The river-bank area is a worthwhile district to explore, starting from the **Flood Control
Monument** (防洪纪念碑, fánghóng jìniànbēi) at the bottom of Zhongyang Dajie. Built in
1958, the monument commemorates the many thousands who have died in the
Songhua floods, and has been updated to mark floods from the summers of 1989

and 1998. The square here is a popular hangout for local people, who gather to walk dogs, fly kites and send paper lanterns into the night-time sky. Stretching along the river banks from the monument is **Stalin Park**, particularly lively on weekends, when people come to meet, chat and drink. Some even bathe in the river – not a good idea, as levels of pollution are so high that fish can no longer survive. Others cluster around palm-readers and storytellers who relate old Chinese folk legends.

Sun Island

太阳岛, tàiyáng dǎo • Ferries from near Flood Control Monument ¥10 return, from a stop further east ¥2 • Cable car ¥50 one-way, ¥80 return; Sightseeing bus ¥15; Tandem bikes ¥50 per hour, ¥200 deposit • **Sun Island Park** Daily 9am–5pm • ¥30 • **Russia-Style Town** Daily 9am–5pm, ¥20 • **Tiger Park** Daily 9am–4pm • ¥90

Across from the city on the Songhua River's northern bank is the busy resort and sanatorium village of **Sun Island**. In summer you can catch a ferry; in winter, the Songhua freezes solid and you can ride a horse carriage, rent a go-kart or walk across – the ice is so thick it will support a fully loaded bus or lorry, and it gets used as a road.

Sun Island Park is an enormous leisure complex (taking up the northern two-thirds of the island) with lakes for boating, swimming pools and fairground rides. Nearer the river is the small, and rather twee, **Russia-Style Town**, whose faux-colonial buildings are perhaps less impressive than the real ones south of the river. If none of these attractions floats your boat, it's pleasurable, not to mention free, simply to walk around the generous swath of the island that abuts the river.

Pingfang: Unit 731

平方731部队, píngfāng 731 bù duì • Xinjiang Dong Lu • Tues –Sun 9–11.30am & 1–3.30pm • ¥20 • Bus #343 from the main train station, or a short walk from Xinjiang Dajie, the southernmost stop on metro line #1

Harbin's most notorious location lies a forty-minute bus journey southwest of the centre at **PINGFANG**. This was the home of a secret Japanese research establishment during World War II, now open to the public as a **museum**. Here, prisoners of war were subjected to horrendous torture – being injected with deadly viruses, dissected alive, and frozen or heated slowly until they died – under the pretence of scientific experimentation. More than three thousand people from China, Russia and Mongolia were murdered by troops from unit 731 of the Japanese army. After the war, the Japanese tried to hide all evidence of the base, and its existence only came to light through the efforts of Japanese investigative journalists. It was also discovered that, as with scientists in defeated Nazi Germany, the Americans gave the Japanese scientists immunity from prosecution in return for their research findings.

HARBIN ICE FESTIVAL

In compensation for Harbin's cruel winter weather, the annual **Ice Festival** (冰灯节, bīngdēng jié), centred on Zhaolin Park, is held from January 5 to February 5 – though with the influx of tourists, the dates extend each year (most recently, things were running into early March). Sculptors, some of them teenagers, work twelve-hour days in -20°C December weather to help transform the park into a fairy-tale landscape: the magnificent ice sculptures they create are sometimes entire buildings, complete with slides, stairways, arches and bridges. Carved with chainsaws and picks, the creations often have coloured lights inside to heighten the psychedelic effect. Highlights of past festivals have included detailed replicas of St Paul's Cathedral and life-size Chinese temples, though these days cartoon characters outnumber more traditional Chinese subject matter.

The festivities take place in various places around the city, though the two largest exhibitions are over the river on Sun Island. Here you'll find the Snow Sculpture Art Expo (8am–8pm; ¥240) and the Ice & Snow World (11am–9.30pm; ¥330) – the latter is the biggie, and the one in which most of the coolest photos of the festival are taken. Back in central Harbin, there's the smaller Ice Lantern Garden Party (2–9.30pm; ¥60) in Zhaolin Park. At all venues, festival's end is marked with fireworks and pickaxes; visitors are encouraged to destroy the icy artwork by hand.

Most of the museum's exhibits are photographs taken here during the war; looking at these, and a painting of bound prisoners being used as bomb targets, you can begin to understand why Chinese antipathy towards Japan runs so deep.

ARRIVAL AND DEPARTURE

BY PLANE

Harbin airport (哈尔滨太平国际机场, hā'ěrbīn tàipíng guójì jīchǎng) is 50km southwest of the town and served by an airport bus (every 20min; 1hr or more; ¥20), which drops you near the *Holiday Inn*. A taxi will cost ¥120.
Destinations Beijing (1hr 50min); Dalian (1hr 20min); Hong Kong (1 daily; 4hr 40min); Shanghai (2hr 40min); Shenyang (55min).

BY TRAIN

Main train station (哈尔滨站, hā'ěrbīn zhàn). Harbin's main train station lies a short walk from the centre of town.
Destinations Beijing (11 daily; 8–21hr); Changchun (1–3 hourly; 1hr 30min–4hr); Hailar (6 daily; 10–14hr); Heihe (2 daily; 10hr–11hr 30min); Jilin (1 daily; 2hr 30min); Manzhouli (3 daily; 12hr 30min–14hr); Qiqihar (1–3 hourly; 1hr 30min–11hr); Shenyang (1–3 hourly; 3–8hr); Suifenhe (3 daily; 5hr 40min–7hr 30min); Yabuli (9 daily; 2hr 30min).

Harbin West station (哈尔滨西站, hā'ěrbīn xīzhàn). Almost all high-speed services pitch up at Harbin West, a typically huge, gleaming entity isolated some 10km from the centre – one of the many places in China piping the same Kenny G sax track through their PA system, 24 hours a day. Taxis from the west station cost around ¥30, though a metro connection was nearing completion at the time of writing.
Destinations Beijing (4 daily; 7–8hr); Changchun (1–3 hourly; 55min–2hr 30min); Jilin (5 daily; 2hr–2hr 30min); Shenyang (1–5 hourly; 2–7hr).

BY BUS

The long-distance bus station is on Songhuajiang Jie, across from the main train station. You can pretty much ignore it, though; distances from Harbin are long, and train connections almost always far faster.

GETTING AROUND

By bus The most useful bus is #103, which runs between Zhongshan Lu and Zhaolin Park (兆林公园, zhàolín gōng yuán) just east of Zhongyang Dajie.
By taxi Taxi fares around the city start at ¥8 for the first 3km; Harbin has lots of one-way streets, so don't panic if it

seems your driver is lapping the block.
By subway The new Harbin metro system was still a one-line-only affair at the time of writing, though more were on the way, including line #3 to Harbin West train station.

ACCOMMODATION

★**Century Old Street** 百年老街酒店, bǎinián lǎojiē jiǔdiàn. 32 Zhongyang Dajie ☏ 0451 84699969. This is probably the best-value accommodation in Dongbei, a baby blue-painted Russian beauty whose rooms almost live up to the expectations generated by the gorgeous exterior. Cheapest rooms lack windows, but their larger "luxury" options (just ¥30 more) are still a steal. ¥198
Holiday Inn 万达假日饭店, wàndájiàrì fàndiàn. 90 Jingwei Jie ☏ 0451 84887205, ⓦ holidayinn.com. One

of the town's top choices, with a good location at the head of Zhongyang Dajie, and very helpful English-speaking staff. Rooms are pleasantly decorated, and extremely comfortable, but it's hard to get around the fact that they're well overpriced. ¥858
Kairui 凯瑞酒店, kǎiruì jiǔdiàn. 28 Shangyou Jie ☏ 0451 87099888. A decent new boutique option, located on a quiet side-street off Zhongyang Dajie – rooms are elegant affairs with pleasing decorative flourishes, and

---

CROSSING INTO SIBERIA

From northern Heilongjiang, there are a number of crossing points into **Siberia**, of which Heihe, a large border town that sees a lot of traffic with the Russian town of Blagoveshchensk, is the best option. There are direct overnight trains from Harbin to Heihe; upon arrival, Russia is a mere few strides and a mountain of paperwork away. A rail connection also exists between Harbin and Suifenhe, from where it's a 4hr bus ride to Vladivostok. By far the simplest way to get into Russia from Dongbei is to hop on the Trans-Siberian train to Moscow (see box, p.34), which passes through Harbin every Sunday afternoon on its way west to the border at Manzhouli.

The biggest problem with crossing from Dongbei into Siberia is getting a **visa**, which is always easiest – and often essential – to sort out in your home country. It may also be possible in Beijing; if you're very lucky indeed, you may get one from the Russian consulate in Shenyang (see p.174).

some have truly huge bathrooms. However, it's only worth booking if you can get half of the rack rate, which is most of the time, bar the Ice Festival. **¥880**

Kazy International Youth Hostel 卡兹国际青年旅舍, kǎzī guójì qīngnián lǚshè. 27 Tongjiang Jie ☏ 0451 87654211, ⓦ yhachina.com. Formerly in an old synagogue, this hostel moved to a grubby courtyard – it's at ground level, despite a misleading HI sign hinting that it's up the fire escape. Staff are lethargic and the obligatory café-bar area a little staid, but private rooms are particularly good value. Dorms **¥40**, private rooms **¥120**

Modern 马达尔宾馆, mǎdá'ěr bīnguǎn. 89 Zhongyang Dajie ☏ 0451 84884199, ⓦ hotel.hrbmodern .com. The name is a misnomer, as this place was built in 1906 and is Harbin's oldest hotel. An elegant building on one of the city's busiest streets, it's bursting with character. Enter via a ground-floor restaurant. **¥680**

Shangri-La 香格里拉大饭店, xiānggélǐlā dàfàndiàn. 555 Youyi Lu ☏ 0451 84858888, ⓦ shangri-la.com. A five-star hotel overlooking Stalin Park, Zhongyang Dajie and Zhaolin Park, making rooms here hard to come by during the Ice Festival – book early. Some rooms are simply gigantic, and all exude the luxury you'd expect from this upper-class chain. **¥1200**

EATING

Influenced by Russian cuisine, local cooking is characterized by the exceptionally heavy use of garlic, and *lots* of potato and fungi – a favourite local dish is *xiaoji dunmogu* (chicken and stewed mushrooms).

Café Bene 咖啡陪你, kāfēi péinǐ. North side of church square. The coffee at this Korean chain is just so-so, but the views out over the church from the upper floor are rather special – a lovely morning view. Daily 10am–9pm.

★**Orient King of Dumplings** 东方饺子王, dōngfāng jiǎozi wáng. 81 Zhongyang Dajie ☏ 0451 84855111. A real Harbin institution – there are no fewer than eighteen branches of this dumpling chain in town. This one is by far the most attractive, a two-storey affair with photos of old Harbin on the walls. The dumplings themselves are simply superb, with intriguing fillings such as cucumber-and-shrimp and egg-and-courgette; they're also amazing value at ¥12–38 per portion. Daily 9am–9pm.

Russia 1914 俄罗斯一九一四, éluósī yījiǔyīsì. 59 Xi Toudao Jie. Also known as *Russia Coffee & Food*, this is the perfect place for afternoon tea, with atmosphere to match – evoking the early 1900s. Main meals are also served, but it's hard to beat a cup of Russian tea (¥12) with Russian bread and jam (¥10). Daily 10am–midnight.

★**Tatos** 华梅饭店, huáméi fàndiàn. 127 Zhongyang Dajie ☏ 0451 84688855. The best Russian restaurant in town, if only for the atmosphere – in this lavishly decorated basement venue, it's easy to forget that you're still in China. Most mains are in the ¥30–50 range, with the shashlik particularly recommended if you can spare the 40min it takes to cook them. They also have yummy Baltika beer (¥25), with the dark #6 variety particularly rare in China. Daily 11am–11pm.

DRINKING

In summer and during the busy winter periods, tented areas resembling outdoor German beer halls spring up on the fringes of Zhongyang Dajie – though much of a muchness with little to choose between them, they're great spots to enjoy piping-hot barbecued skewers and a stein or two of ice-cold Harbin beer (¥35 for a 2000ml jug).

Madie'er 马迭尔, mǎ dié'ěr. 39 Xibaodao Jie ☏ 0451 86713333. Perennially popular indoor bar located amid all the outdoor ones, with tasty Czech-style draught beer from ¥20 (a little more for their IPA), and good pub grub. Daily 11am–11pm.

DIRECTORY

Post office There's a big post office just east of Zhongyang Dajie, on Xishisidao Jie (Mon–Sat 8am–6pm).

Visa extensions The PSB's visa section is on Jingweitou Daojie (Mon–Fri 8–11am & 2–5pm; ☏ 0451 89537122).

Yabuli

亚布力, yàbùlì • Ski season Nov–March

Regarded as the premier ski destination in China, **YABULI** resort's 3800m of piste spreads across the southern slopes of Guokui Shan (1300m), literally Pot-Head Mountain, 194km southeast of Harbin. Six lifts shuttle an average of 10,000 skiers per day during the winter months. Although popular, the pistes are nowhere near as good as those in Europe, North America or Japan, nor are they cheap to ski. If you're after a proper skiing holiday, this is not really the place, and the slopes cropping up outside most northern cities offer much better value for money and are easier to get to. Nevertheless, a trip can still be good fun if expectations are kept in check.

ARRIVAL AND INFORMATION   YABULI

Packages covering travel, accommodation and skiing can be booked at travel agents in Harbin and throughout China, but it's fairly easy (and much cheaper) to organize your own trip independently.

By train Yabuli's main station (亚布力站, yàbùlì zhàn) has services to Harbin, Dalian and even distant Beijing; in season, shuttle buses (¥60) run to the resort entrance. Yabuli South station (亚布力南站, yàbùlì nánzhàn) is located far closer to said entrance; most of the year there's just the one daily service to Harbin (3hr 30min), but there are more during the ski season, so think about booking your tickets to this one instead.

TO RUSSIA ON THE TRANS-MANCHURIAN

For those with time and a little bit of patience to spare, the evocatively named **Trans-Manchurian railway** is one of the best ways to enter or exit China. The line barrels northeast out of Beijing, eventually crossing the Russian border to connect with its far more illustrious sibling, the Trans-Siberian. Indeed, once a week **direct trains** run the route all the way between Beijing and Moscow, avoiding Mongolia and thus the necessity of acquiring an extra visa. The trip takes around six days, starting almost simultaneously in both Moscow and Beijing each Saturday evening; trains are comfortable, with private rooms and restaurant cars. **Visas** must be arranged in advance both ways, and the difficulty of acquiring a Russian one – not to mention that of buying the ticket itself – means that many choose to organize the trip through a travel agency (see p.32 for recommended operators). Prices vary enormously depending upon whether you go through an agency or do things by yourself; for the latter, there's a wealth of reliable, up-to-date information on Seat 61 (W seat61.com).

With a little advance planning, it'll be possible to visit other Russian cities before hitting Moscow, with the Siberian city of Irkutsk a favourite thanks to its proximity to Lake Baikal, the world's largest body of fresh water. Easier to organize are stops at Chinese cities on the way: Shenyang (see p.170), Changchun (see p.174) and Harbin (see p.183) all have their merits, and new high-speed services have cut travel times considerably. From Harbin, the train cuts through **Inner Mongolia** (see p.227 for more on this province's history and attractions) before hitting the Russian border, passing through the pleasant towns of Hailar and Manzhouli.

HAILAR

With rail connections as well as an airport, **Hailar** (海拉尔, hǎilā'ěr) is the main transport hub of the region, and a centre for grassland visits. The town itself is of minimal interest – the chief reason most visitors come to Hailar is to see the **Hulunbuir grasslands** (呼伦贝尔草原, hūlúnbèi'ěr cǎoyuán), an apparently limitless rolling land of plains and low grassy mountains. As elsewhere in Inner Mongolia, there are the CITS-approved villages of Mongol herders; though you could try to strike off independently, it's worth noting that the grassland **tours** here don't attract hordes of people. A day-trip from Hailar to eat a traditional mutton banquet on the grasslands, for a group of four people, costs around ¥450 each, or a little under double that to stay the night; you can book at most hotels in town.

MANZHOULI

A few hours to the west of Hailar is **Manzhouli** (满洲里, mǎnzhōulǐ), a bustling centre for cross-border commerce whose wholesale demolition, renovation and development – much of which has involved the surreal addition of Versailles-inspired facades to communist tower blocks – has left it with little atmosphere. It's worth a visit for trips to the surrounding countryside, as well as air fresher than you may have experienced elsewhere in China. There are plenty of **hotels** in town, and **eating** is a treat if you love Russian food. Those staying the night may care to visit the great **Dalai Lake** (达赉湖, dálài hú; Hulun Nur in Mongolian), a shallow expanse of water set in marshy grazing country where flocks of swans, geese, cranes and other migratory birds come to nest. In June and July, the grasslands in this region are said to be the greenest in all Mongolia, and coming here may be the most rewarding – and least expensive – way to see the region's grasslands. A taxi from town will cost from ¥300 round-trip.

Main station destinations Beijing (1 daily; 17hr); Dalian (2 daily; 16hr); Harbin (9 daily; 3hr).
Information Few Chinese possess their own ski gear, so it should come as no surprise that you'll be able to rent everything you need at the resort entrance. Their pricing structure is in a constant state of flux; lift tickets will end up costing around ¥280/day, and equipment another ¥200 or so.

ACCOMMODATION

Sun Mountain Resort 阳光度假村, yángguāng dùjiàcūn. ☎0451 53458888, ⓦyabuliski.com. Though overpriced (surprise, surprise), Yabuli's first hotel remains its best, and renovations have ensured it's still a quality place. Ski lifts are a stone's throw away, rooms are large and well appointed, and the restaurants are decent enough. **¥1200**

Yunding 云鼎宾馆, yúndǐng bīnguǎn. ☎0451 51679970. The best "cheapie" on the slopes, with a mix of carpeted and wooden-floored rooms, all of a decent size, and all en suite; some also have internet-ready computers, with the usual sticky keyboards. Ski equipment rental is also available here. **¥600**

Qiqihar

齐齐哈尔, qíqíhā'ěr

A four-hour bus ride west of Harbin, **QIQIHAR** is one of the northeast's oldest cities, and still a thriving industrial centre. Alas, it's more fun to say the city's name aloud than to stay here for more than a day, and the sole reason to visit is the **Zhalong Nature Reserve**, 30km southeast of town.

Zhalong Nature Reserve

扎龙自然保护区, zhālóng zìrán bǎohùqū • July–March 8am–4pm; April–June 8am–6pm • ¥50 • Best from April–June, though viewing season extends through September • Bus #306 from Qiqihar (1hr; ¥20); taxis from ¥150 one-way (grab the driver's business card for the return journey)

The marshy plain of **Zhalong Nature Reserve** abounds in shallow reedy lakes and serves as the summer breeding ground of thousands of species of bird, including white stork, whooper swan, spoonbill, white ibis and – the star attractions – nine of the world's fifteen species of crane. Most spectacular of these is the endangered **red-crowned crane**, a lanky black-and-white bird over 1m tall, with a scarlet bald patch. It has long been treasured in the East as a paradigm of elegance and is a popular symbol of longevity, living up to sixty years. The birds mate for life, and the female only lays one or two eggs each season, over which the male stands guard.

Walking around the reserve, although not forbidden, is not encouraged by the keepers – or by the murderous swarms of mosquitoes. Come prepared, and bring binoculars if you can, too. Dedicated ornithologists might like to spend a few days here, but for most people an afternoon crouched in the reed beds will be enough.

ARRIVAL AND DEPARTURE

QIQIHAR

By plane Qiqihar's small airport (齐齐哈尔三家子机场, qíqíhā'ěr sānjiāzǐ jīchǎng) is 10km to the south of town. Buses (¥10) meet the few planes, or it's ¥25 to the centre by taxi.
Destinations Beijing (1hr 50min); Shanghai (2hr 50min).
By train Qiqihar's main station (齐齐哈尔站, qíqíhā'ěr zhàn) is 3km east of the city centre, and now has some high-speed services; there are more from the South station

(齐齐哈尔南站, qíqíhā'ěr nánzhàn), 10km further down the line. Plenty of buses head into town from both stations, though it's far easier by taxi.
Main station destinations Beijing (5 daily; 15–26hr); Hailar (8 daily; 9hr); Harbin (1–5 hourly; 1hr 35min–9hr).
South station destinations Beijing (2 daily; 9hr 30min); Harbin (1–3 hourly; 1hr 25min–1hr 45min).

ACCOMMODATION

Ibis 宜必思酒店, yíbìsī jiǔdiàn. 2 Bukui Lu ☎0452 2430000. A great addition to Qiqihar, close to the station (take a cab) and acceptable for travellers of all budgets. If you've stayed at an *Ibis* before, you know what the rooms will be like: not too big, but clean and quiet. Discounts are not uncommon. **¥279**

3

The Yellow River
黄河

YUNGANG CAVES, DATONG

The Yellow River

From its lofty source on the Tibetan plateau, the famed Yellow River (黄河, huánghé) runs for almost 5500km before emptying into the Yellow Sea, making it China's second-longest waterway after the Yangzi, and the sixth longest in the world. The river's name stems from the vast quantities of loess it carries, a fertile yellow silt which has done much to benefit the region's agricultural potential over the millennia. However, the river's popular nickname, "China's Sorrow", hints at the regular floods and changes of course that have repeatedly caused devastation – the waterway is often likened to a dragon, a reference not just to its sinuous course, but also to its uncontrollable nature, by turns benign and malevolent. On the flipside, it provides much-needed irrigation to areas otherwise arid and inhospitable, and has created some of China's most distinctive landscapes, barrelling past colossal sand dunes before sliding along pancake-flat loess plains scarred with deep, winding crevasses.

4

Such is the length of the Yellow River that the first and last major cities it hits – Lanzhou and Ji'nan – are actually covered in other chapters (see p.797 & p.289). In between, the river flows through **Ningxia**, **Inner Mongolia**, **Shanxi**, **Shaanxi** and **Henan**, and has played a vital role in the history, geography and fortunes of each province – though sadly its capricious nature makes river travel impossible in the region.

The most famous sight in the Yellow River's catchment area is actually some distance from the river itself: the city of **Xi'an** is one of China's biggest tourist destinations, with as many temples, museums and tombs as the rest of the region put together, and with the **Terracotta Army** deservedly ranking as one of China's premier sights. Xi'an is also home to a substantial **Muslim** minority, whose cuisine is well worth sampling. East of the city, and also within **Shaanxi** province, is the spectacular **Hua Shan** range, whose temple-studded slopes offer superb – if occasionally terrifying – hiking opportunities.

Heading northwest into **Ningxia**, a tiny province with a substantial Hui minority, you can witness the river's mighty waters running between desert sand dunes at the resort of **Shapotou**. Still a relatively exotic, tourist-free zone, Ningxia also offers quiet, attractive cities, while the provincial capital of **Yinchuan** is a base for fascinating sights

SHAPOTOU DUNES

Highlights

❶ The Terracotta Army No visit to China is complete without a peek at these warrior figurines, guarding the tomb of Qin Shi Huang near Xi'an. **See p.212**

❷ Hiking Hua Shan Within day-trip distance of Xi'an, this spectacular mountain range encourages a longer stay, and begs to be hiked around. **See p.216**

❸ Shapotou Perhaps the most photogenic stretch of the Yellow River, with the waters sliding past hefty desert dunes. **See p.221**

❹ The Hanging Temple If you've a fear of heights, stay away from this incredibly photogenic temple, perched on stilts on a cliffside south of Datong. **See p.244**

❺ Pingyao An intact Ming-era walled city, home to winding back alleys and a number of atmospheric hotels and guesthouses. **See p.251**

❻ Longmen Caves Walk along a riverside promenade past caves peppering limestone cliff faces, containing more than 100,000 Buddhist carvings. **See p.259**

HIGHLIGHTS ARE MARKED ON THE MAP ON PP.194–195

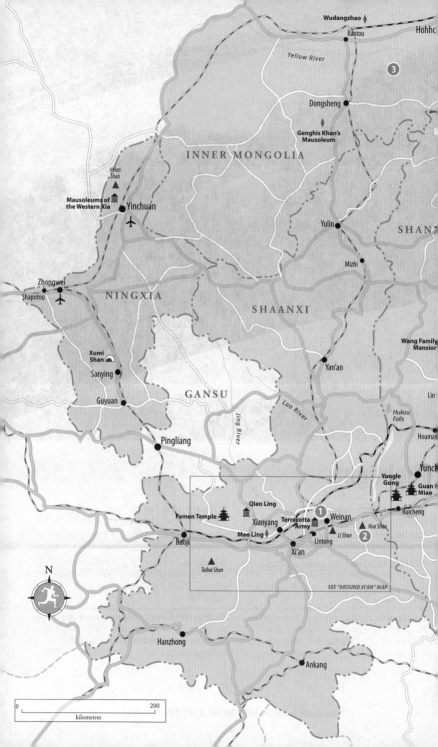

Wudangzhao

Baotou

Hohho

Yellow River

③

Dongsheng

Genghis Khan's
Mausoleum

INNER MONGOLIA

Helan
Shan

Mausoleums of
the Western Xia

Yinchuan

Yulin

SHAN

Mizhi

Zhongwei

NINGXIA

Shapotou

SHAANXI

Xumi
Shan

Sanying

Yan'an

Guyuan

GANSU

Wang Family
Mansior

Jing River

Luo River

Lin

Pingliang

Hukou
Falls

Houma

Yunc

Yongle
Gong

Guan
Miao

Qian Ling

Famen Temple

Xianyang

Terracotta
Army

①

Weinan

Ruicheng

Mao Ling

②

Hua Shan

Baoji

Lintong

Li Shan

Xi'an

Taibai Shan

SEE "AROUND XI'AN" MAP

N

Hanzhong

Ankang

0   200

kilometres

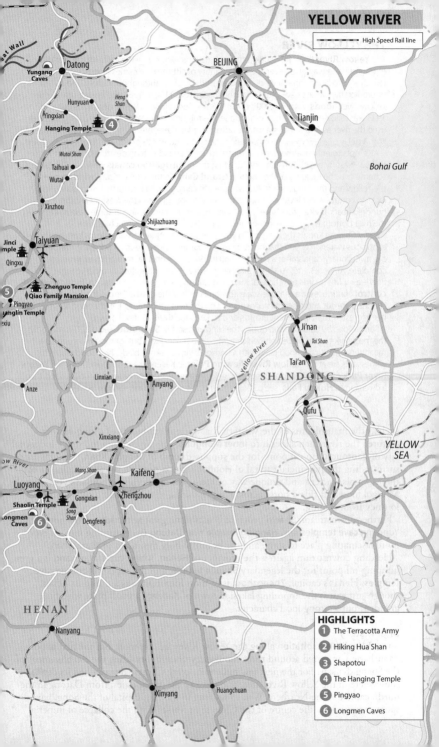

YELLOW RIVER

High Speed Rail line

Great Wall

Yungang Caves

Datong

BEIJING

Tianjin

Bohai Gulf

Hunyuan

Heng Shan

Yingxian

Hanging Temple ④

Wutai Shan

Taihuai

Wutai

Xinzhou

Shijiazhuang

Jinci Temple

Taiyuan

Qingxu

⑤

Zhenguo Temple

◆ **Qiao Family Mansion**

▷ Pingyao

Jiexiu

Jianlin Temple

Yellow River

Ji'nan

Tai Shan

Tai'an

SHANDONG

Linxian

Anyang

Qufu

Xinxiang

YELLOW SEA

low River

Mang Shan

Kaifeng

Luoyang

Gongxian

Zhengzhou

Shaolin Temple

Song Shan

Longmen Caves ⑥

Dengfeng

HENAN

Nanyang

Xinyang

Huangchuan

HIGHLIGHTS

① The Terracotta Army

② Hiking Hua Shan

③ Shapotou

④ The Hanging Temple

⑤ Pingyao

⑥ Longmen Caves

THE YELLOW RIVER

The **Yellow River** flows for 5500km through nine provinces, making it one of the world's mightiest waterways. However, the vast quantity of **silt** the river carries along its twisted length – 1.6 billion tonnes a year – has confused its course throughout history, and its unpredictable swings have often brought chaos. From 1194 to 1887, there were fifty major Yellow River **floods**, with 300,000 people killed in 1642 alone. Another disastrous event in 1933 was followed in 1937 by further tragedy – this time man-made – when Chiang Kai-shek used the river as a weapon against the advancing Japanese, breaching its dykes to cut the rail line. A delay of a few weeks was gained at the cost of hundreds of thousands of Chinese lives.

Attempts to enhance the river's potential for creation rather than destruction began very early, at least by the eighth century BC, when the first **irrigation canals** were cut. The largest scheme was the building of the 1800km **Grand Canal** in the sixth century, which connected the Yellow and the Yangzi rivers and was used to carry grain to the north. It was built using locks to control water level, an innovation that did not appear in the West for another four hundred years. **Dykes**, too, have been built since ancient times, and in some eastern sections the river bottom is higher than the surrounding fields, often by as much as 10m.

Every Chinese knows the story of Da Yu, the legendary figure responsible for battling the capricious waters. It is said that he mobilized thousands of people to dredge the riverbed and dig diversionary canals after a terrible flood in 297 BC – work that took thirteen years to complete. At work's end, Yu sank a talismanic bronze ox in the waters, in order to tame the flow – a replica guards the shore of Kunming Lake in Beijing's Summer Palace. Today, **river control** continues on a massive scale. To stop flooding, the riverbed is dredged, diversion channels are cut and reservoirs constructed on the river's tributaries. Land around the river has been forested to help prevent erosion and so keep the river's silt level down.

Surrounded by colossal sand dunes, the Ningxia resort of **Shapotou** (see p.221) is probably the most spectacular place from which to view the Yellow River, but for most of its course it meanders across a flat flood plain with a horizon sharp as a knife blade. Two good places to witness this are at the **Yellow River Viewing Point** in Kaifeng (see p.273) and from the **Yellow River Park** outside Zhengzhou (see p.268). To see the river in a more tempestuous mood, take a diversion to **Hukou Falls** (see p.256), farther north on the Shaanxi–Shanxi border.

such as the mausoleums of the Western Xia, ancient reminders of a long-extinct culture. The river then slides into **Inner Mongolia**, passing through the super-industrial city of **Baotou**, jump-off point for the supposed **tomb of Genghis Khan**. The grasslands surrounding the provincial capital of **Hohhot** make it possible to catch a glimpse of the Mongols' ancient and unique way of life – you can sleep in a nomad's yurt, sample Mongol food and ride a horse across the grasslands, all within half a day's train journey from Beijing.

Further downstream, **Shanxi** province boasts some great attractions, most notably the **Yungang cave temples** and **Hanging Temple** near **Datong** (itself turning into an ever more fascinating place to stay), and the beautiful holy mountain of **Wutai Shan**.

Heading downstream again is the province of **Henan**, whose capital **Luoyang** is a great jumping-off point for the legendary **Shaolin temple**, and the superb **Longmen cave temples**. Henan's capital, **Zhengzhou**, is of most importance as a transport nexus, though just east is the appealing lakeside town of **Kaifeng**, a small place with little grandeur but a strong local character.

Brief history

Sites of **Neolithic habitation** along the Yellow River are common, but the first major conurbation appeared around three thousand years ago, heralding the establishment of the Shang dynasty. For the next few millennia, every Chinese dynasty had its **capital** somewhere in the Yellow River area, and most of the major cities, from Datong in the north, capital of the Northern Wei, to Kaifeng in the east, capital of the Song, have spent some time as the centre of the Chinese universe. With the collapse of imperial

China, the area sank into provincialism, and it was not until late in the twentieth century that it again came to prominence. The old capitals have today found new leases of life as industrial and commercial centres, and thus present two sides to the visitor: a rapidly changing, and sometimes harsh, modernity; and a static history, preserved in the interests of tourism. This latter feature contrasts strongly with, for instance, southwestern China, where temples might double as tourist attractions but are also clearly functional places of worship; here, most feel much more like museums – even if they seldom lack grandeur.

Shaanxi

陕西, shǎnxī

SHAANXI province is dusty, harsh and unwelcoming, with a climate of extremes: in winter, strong winds bring yellow dust storms, while summer is hot and wet. However, it's remarkable for the depth and breadth of its history, best exemplifed in the provincial capital, **Xi'an**: famed for the renowned **Terracotta Army** to the east, it was used as a dynastic capital over the course of two thousand years. Mysterious terracotta figures aside, there's other evidence of the city's former glories, in the shape of the tomb of the great emperor Qin Shi Huang, and a host of nearby temples and museums; it's a far bigger, busier place than many visitors expect, and perhaps the country's most cosmopolitan city outside the eastern seaboard.

Shaanxi, however, is more than just Xi'an. If you've had enough of the relics of ancient cultures, head east to **Hua Shan**, a spectacular mountain range offering superb, easy-to-access hikes.

4

Xi'an

西安, xī'ān

Silk Road stopover, seat of ancient empires, and home to one of the world's most perplexing archeological riddles – **XI'AN** tingles with intrigue, and counts as one of China's must-sees. To many, it's synonymous with the mysterious **Terracotta Army**, standing in inscrutable silence just to the east, but these are merely the most famous remnant from Xi'an's extraordinarily long history – between 1000 BC and 1000 AD, it served as the **imperial capital** for no fewer than eleven dynasties. As such, it should come as no surprise that the place is filled with, and surrounded by, a wealth of hugely important sites and relics. The list of newly discovered treasures grows with each passing decade; in addition to the Terracotta Army, highlights include **Neolithic Banpo**, and the Han and Tang **imperial tombs**. In the city itself, you'll find the Tang-dynasty

---

XI'AN ORIENTATION

Central Xi'an is bounded by city walls, with a bell tower marking the crossroads of the four main streets. Getting around this area is a doddle, since the street layout closely follows the ordered **grid plan** of the ancient city; the only exception is the **Muslim Quarter**, northwest of the Bell Tower, around whose unmarked winding alleys it's easy (and not necessarily unpleasurable) to get lost.

 Downtown Xi'an, inside the walls, is just about compact enough to get around on foot, with enough sights to fill a busy day. To the southeast you'll find the **Beilin Museum**, which holds a massive collection of steles, next to the **city walls**, imposing remnants of Imperial China.

 The area south of the Ming-dynasty city walls is scattered with architecture from the Han and Tang dynasties. The excellent **Shaanxi History Museum** and the small **Daxingshan Temple** sit between the two **Goose pagodas** and their temples, which are some of Xi'an's oldest buildings, and certainly the most distinctive.

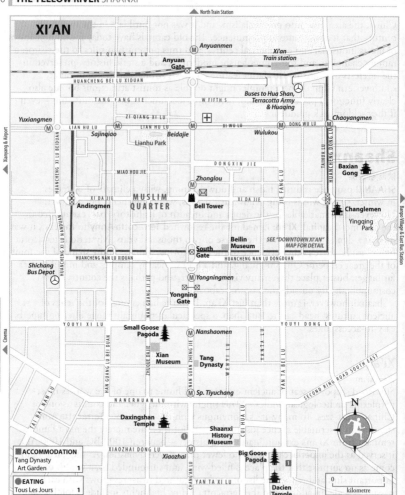

XI'AN

North Train Station

ZI QIANG XI LU

Anyuanmen

Anyuan Gate

Xi'an Train station

HUANCHENG BEI LU XIDUAN

TANG FANG JIE

W FIFTH S

Buses to Hua Shan, Terracotta Army & Huaqing

ZI QIANG XI LU

XI WU LU

Chaoyangmen

Yuxiangmen

LIAN HU LU

LIAN HU LU

DONG WU LU

Sajinqiao

Beidajie

Wulukou

Lianhu Park

DONGXIN JIE

MIAO HOU JIE

Zhonglou

Baxian Gong

XI DA JIE

MUSLIM QUARTER

Bell Tower

XI DA JIE

Changlemen

Andingmen

Yingqing Park

Beilin Museum

SEE "DOWNTOWN XI'AN" MAP FOR DETAIL

South Gate

HUANCHENG NAN LU XIDUAN

HUANCHENG NAN LU DONGDUAN

Shichang Bus Depot

Yongningmen

Yongning Gate

YOUYI XI LU

YOUYI DONG LU

Small Goose Pagoda

Nanshaomen

Xian Museum

Tang Dynasty

NANERHUAN LU

Sp. Tiyuchang

N

Daxingshan Temple

Shaanxi History Museum

SECOND RING ROAD SOUTH EAST

XIAOZHAI DONG LU

Xiaozhai

Big Goose Pagoda

■ ACCOMMODATION
Tang Dynasty Art Garden   1

● EATING
Tous Les Jours   1

YAN TA XI LU

Dacien Temple

0   1
kilometre

Bell and Drum towers and the Ming city walls, as well as two excellent museums holding a treasury of relics from the most fabled chapters of Chinese history.

However, visitors are also advised to prepare for a modicum of disappointment. Historically significant though it may be, today's Xi'an is a manufacturing metropolis of five million inhabitants, filled with traffic and prone to heavy pollution – issues that can make trips to the outlying sights a bit of a chore. Yet most travellers are able to see past these failings, perhaps best evidenced by a large foreign community, many of whom come to study, since the colleges are regarded as some of the best places outside Beijing to learn Chinese.

Brief history

Some three thousand years ago, the western Zhou dynasty, known for their skilled bronzework, built their capital at Fenghao, a few kilometres west of Xi'an. When Fenghao was sacked by northwestern tribes, the Zhou moved downriver to Luoyang and, as their empire continued to disintegrate into warring chiefdoms, the nearby Qin kingdom expanded. In 221 BC, the larger-than-life **Qin Shi Huang** united the Chinese in a single empire, the Qin, with its capital at **Xianyang**, just north of Xi'an. The underground **Terracotta Army**, intended to guard his tomb, are this tyrant's inadvertent gift to today's tourist prosperity.

The Han

The Qin dynasty's successors, the **Han**, ruled from 206 BC to 220 AD, building themselves a new, splendid and cosmopolitan capital a few kilometres northwest of Xi'an, which they called **Chang'an** – Eternal Peace. Its size reflected the power of their empire, and records say that its walls were 17km round with twelve great gates. Chang'an was the start of the **Silk Road**, along which, among many other things, Chinese silk was carried to dress Roman senators and their wives at the court of Augustus. There was also a brisk trade with south and west Asia; Han China was an outward-looking empire.

When the dynasty fell, Chang'an was destroyed, though the imperial **tombs** remain, including Emperor Wu's mound at **Mao Ling**. It was not until 589 that the **Sui** dynasty reunited the warring kingdoms into a new empire, but their dynasty hardly lasted longer than the time it took to build a new capital near Xi'an, called **Da Xingcheng** – Great Prosperity.

The Tang

The **Tang**, who replaced the Sui in 618, overlaid their new capital in a rational grid plan that became the model not only for many other Chinese cities, but also the contemporary Japanese capital Hei'an (now Kyoto). During this time, the city became one of the biggest in the world, with over a million inhabitants. The Tang period was a **golden age** for China's arts, and ceramics, calligraphy, painting and poetry all reached new heights. Its sophistication was reflected in its religious tolerance – not only was this a great period for **Buddhism**, with monks busy translating the sutras that the adventurous monk **Xuan Zong** had brought back from India, but the city's **Great Mosque** dates from the Tang, and one of the steles in the Provincial Museum bears witness to the founding of a chapel by Nestorian Christians.

Decline

After the fall of the Tang, Xi'an went into a long **decline**. It was never again the imperial capital, though the Ming emperor Hong Wu rebuilt the city as a gift for his son; today's great walls and gates date from this time. Occasionally, though, the city did continue to provide a footnote to history. When the Empress Dowager Cixi had to flee Beijing after the Boxer Rebellion, she set up her court here for two years. In 1911, during the uprising against the Manchu Qing dynasty, the Manchu quarter in Xi'an was destroyed and the Manchus massacred. And in 1936, Chiang Kai-shek was arrested at Huaqing Hot Springs nearby in what became known as the Xi'an Incident (see box, p.212).

Inside the wall

The **Bell Tower** stands at the centre of the traffic circle where Xi'an's four main streets converge. North of the **Drum Tower** just to the west, you'll find narrow alleys lined with cramped, half-timbered, two-storey buildings – this is the **Muslim Quarter**, for centuries the centre of Xi'an's substantial Hui population; numbering around 30,000 today, they're said to be descended from eighth-century Arab soldiers. **Beiyuanmen**, the street that runs north from the Drum Tower gate, is flagstoned and lined with Muslim restaurants, all packed out and lively in the evening.

Heading south from the Bell Tower along Nan Dajie, you'll soon come to the **Yongning gate**, the huge south gate. A turn east takes you along **Shuyuanmen**, a pleasant, cobbled street of souvenir shops, art stores and antique shops traversing the heart of Beilin, a touristy artists' quarter, and home to a superb **museum**.

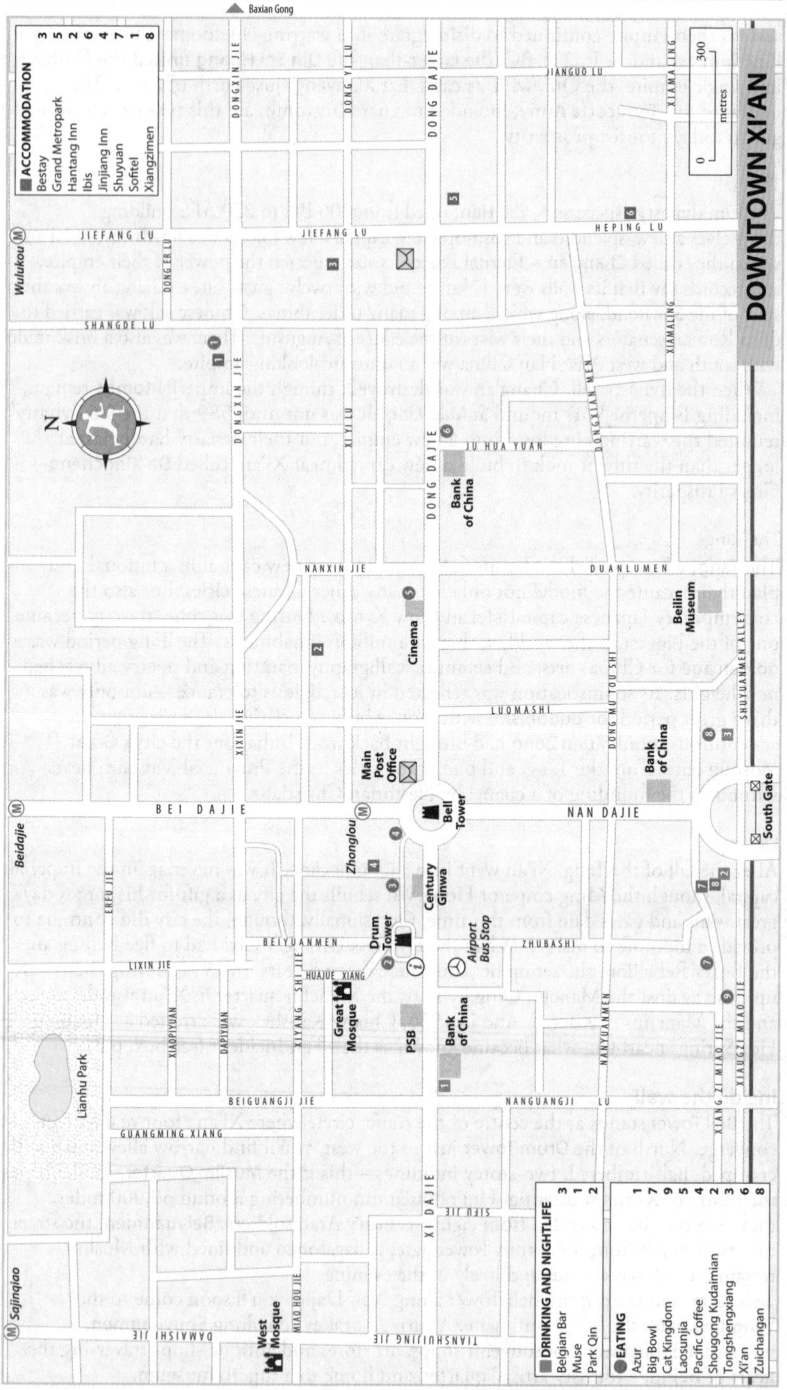

4

▲ Baxian Gong

DOWNTOWN XI'AN

■ ACCOMMODATION	
Bestay	3
Grand Metropark	5
Hantang Inn	6
Ibis	4
Jinjiang Inn	7
Shuyuan	1
Sofitel	8
Xiangzimen	

Streets and locations:

DONGXIN JIE
DONG YI LU
DONG DAJIE
JIANGUO LU
XIAMALING

JIEFANG LU — Wulukou (M)
JIEFANG LU
DONG ER LU
HEPING LU
XIAMALING

SHANGDE LU

DONGXIN JIE

N

XI YI LU

NANXIN JIE
DONGSHAN MEN

DONG DAJIE
JU HUA YUAN
Bank of China

DUANLUMEN

Cinema
Beilin Museum

XIXIN JIE
LUOMASHI
DONG MU TOU SHI
SHUYUANMEN ALLEY

Main Post Office
Bank of China

BEI DAJIE — Beidajie (M)
Zhonglou
Bell Tower
NAN DAJIE
South Gate

EREU JIE
Century Ginwa
Drum Tower
Airport Bus Stop
ZHUBASHI

BEIYUANMEN
LIXIN JIE
XIYANG SHI JIE
HUAJUE XIANG
NANYUANMEN

Lianhu Park

XIAOPIYUAN
DAPIYUAN
Great Mosque
PSB
Bank of China
XIANG XI MIAO JIE
XIANGZI MIAO JIE

BEIGUANGJI JIE
NANGUANGJI LU

GUANGMING XIANG

XI DAJIE
SIFU JIE

MIAO HOU JIE

West Mosque — Sajiqiao (M)

DAMAISHI JIE
TIANSHUIJING JIE

■ DRINKING AND NIGHTLIFE	
Belgian Bar	3
Muse	1
Park Qin	2

● EATING	
Azur	1
Big Bowl	7
Cat Kingdom	9
Laosunjia	5
Pacific Coffee	4
Shougong Kudaimian	2
Tongshengxiang	3
Xi'an	6
Zuichangan	8

0 — 300 metres

The city walls

西安城墙, xī'ān chéngqiáng • Daily: Dec–Feb 8am–7pm • ¥54 • Electric shuttle ¥50 for circuit, or ¥5 per station; bike rental ¥45 for 2hr 30min, plus ¥200 deposit • **City Wall Park** Daily 6am–10pm • Free • Boat rental ¥30 for 15min

Imposing enough to act as a physical barrier between the city centre and the suburbs, Xi'an's **city walls** were originally built in the Tang dynasty, though they took their modern form in 1568, when they were faced with brick. Recently restored, the walls are the most distinctive feature of the modern city, forming a 12m-high rectangle whose perimeter is nearly 14km in length. Some 18m wide at the base, they're capped with crenellations, a watchtower at each corner and a fortress-like gate in the centre of each side. Surrounding the wall is a small moat – once a further line of defence, but now lined by pleasant strips of parkland, which you can also tour on a short **boat ride**. You can **ascend** the wall from the **four main gates** (the southern one being the most common entry point), then explore on foot, by pushbike, or on an **electric shuttle bus**. If prepared with food and drinks, you can spend the better part of a day up here.

The Bell Tower

钟楼, zhōng lóu • Daily: April–Oct 8.30am–8.30pm; Nov–March 8.30am–5.30pm • ¥35, or ¥50 including Drum Tower • Enter via Zhonglou subway station (line #2)

Though located in the very centre of modern-day Xi'an, the **Bell Tower** was first raised two blocks west of here in 1384, at the centre of the Tang-dynasty city; the present triple-eaved wooden structure, standing on a brick platform, was built in 1582 and restored in 1739. Inside is an exhibition of chimes and a bronze bell (not the original). A wraparound balcony provides a good view of the city's traffic; if you'd rather see the tower from the outside instead, try *Pacific Coffee* to the northwest (see p.207).

4

The Drum Tower

鼓楼, gǔlóu • Off Xi Dajie • Daily: April–Oct 8.30am–8.30pm; Nov–March 8.30am–5.30pm • ¥35, or ¥50 including the Bell Tower • A short walk west of Zhonglou subway station (line #2)

Just west of the Bell Tower is the **Drum Tower**, a triple-eaved wooden building atop a 50m-long arch. You enter up steps on the eastern side, to find a row of drums that used to be banged at dusk, a complement to the bell in the Bell Tower, which heralded the dawn.

The Great Mosque

清真大寺, qīngzhēn dàsì • Off Huajie Xiang • Daily 8am–5.30pm • April–Oct ¥25, Nov–March ¥15

Just north of the Drum Tower, the narrow, covered alley of **Huajue Xiang** – essentially one long line of tourist tat – heads to the **Great Mosque**; a more interesting approach can be made on the small roads running up the western and northern sides of the complex. The largest mosque in China, it was originally established in 742, then rebuilt in the Qing dynasty and heavily restored. An east–west-facing complex that integrates Arabic features into a familiar Chinese design, it's a calm place, untouched by the hectic atmosphere of the streets outside.

Beilin Museum

碑林博物馆, bēilín bówùguǎn • Sanxue Jie • Daily 8.30am–6.30pm • March–Oct ¥75, Nov–Feb ¥50 • Southeast of Zhonglou subway station (line #2)

About 500m east of the Yongning gate, near an access point for the city walls, is the **Beilin Museum**, a converted Confucian temple. Aside from an annexe on the west side, which holds an exhibition of chronologically arranged **Buddhist images** where you can follow the evolution of styles over the centuries, the museum's main focus is six halls containing more than a thousand **steles**.

The **first hall** contains the twelve Confucian classics – texts outlining the Confucian philosophy – carved onto 114 stone tablets, a massive project ordered by the Tang emperor Wenzong in 837 as a way of ensuring the texts were never lost or corrupted by copyists' errors. The **second hall** includes the **Daqing Nestorian tablet**, on the left as you go in, recognizable by a cross on the top, which records the arrival of a Nestorian priest in Chang'an in 781 and gives a rudimentary description of Christian doctrine.

In the **third hall**, one stele is inscribed with a **map of Chang'an** at the height of its splendour, when the walls were extensive enough to include the Big Goose Pagoda within their perimeter. Among the steles in the **fourth hall** is an image called the "God of Literature Pointing the Dipper", with the eight characters that outline the Confucian virtues – regulate the heart, cultivate the self, overcome selfishness and return propriety – cleverly made into the image of a jaunty figure. "To point the dipper" meant to come first in the exams on Confucian texts, which controlled entry to the civil service.

Outside the wall

The area to the south, **outside the city wall** contains more of historical merit than the entire interior – two lofty **pagodas**, a couple of excellent **temples**, and reams of dynastic booty in the city and provincial **museums**. If you've still time and energy for more, the **Baxian Gong**, a charming Taoist temple, sits just to the east of the walls.

The Small Goose Pagoda

小雁塔, xiǎoyàn tǎ • Youyi Xi Lu, southwest of the Yongning gate • Daily 9am–5.30pm • ¥30 • Just west of Nanshaomen subway (line #2)

The delicate, 45m-high **Small Goose Pagoda** was founded during the Tang dynasty in 707 to store sutras brought back from India, and sits in what remains of the Jianfu Temple. Two of the pagoda's original fifteen storeys were damaged in an earthquake, leaving a rather abrupt jagged top to the roof, to which you can ascend for a view of the city. A shop at the back of the complex sells Shaanxi folk arts.

Xi'an Museum

西安博物馆, xī'ān bówùguǎn • Zhuque Dajie • Wed–Mon 9am–5pm • Free (bring ID) • Visitor numbers limited to 3000 per day

Sited adjacent to the grounds of the Small Goose Pagoda, the **Xi'an Museum** compares favourably with the more illustrious, and far more crowded, Shaanxi Museum (see below). Its design echoes the ancient Chinese concept of a round heaven surrounding a square earth, and over 130,000 relics are on display across its three floors. Best of all is the **underground hall** which, rather appropriately, shows objects unearthed from in and around Xi'an – take time to linger around the superb Han-dynasty pottery. Up on the **first floor** you'll find Buddhist regalia and an interesting "virtual" display, while the **second floor** has dedicated halls for jades, seals, paintings and the like.

Daxingshan Temple

大兴善寺, dàxīngshàn sì • Xingshan Xijie • Daily 8am–5pm • Free • Just northwest of Xiaozhai subway (line #2)

The **Daxingshan Temple** is usually overlooked by visitors, but the absence of teeming crowds makes a visit even more worthwhile – this is one of the calmest, most pleasant places in noisy Xi'an. It's also the only functional Buddhist temple in the city; destroyed during the late Tang's persecution of the religion, today's buildings are mainly Qing, and the eaves have been repainted with consummate care. If your time is short, make a beeline for the main hall, which features a giant sandalwood statue of Guanyin.

Shaanxi History Museum

陕西历史博物馆, shǎnxīlìshǐ bówùguǎn • Tues–Sun 8am–5pm • Free, though you can cheat the queues by buying a ¥20 ticket • Visitor numbers limited to 4000 per day • Just east of Xiaozhai subway (line #2)

One of the city's major highlights, and often full to bursting point, the **Shaanxi History Museum** is an impressive modern building within walking distance of the Daxingshan

Temple and the Big Goose Pagoda. The exhibition halls are spacious, well laid out, and have English captions, displaying to full advantage a magnificent collection of more than three thousand relics.

The **lower floor**, which contains a general survey of the development of civilization until the Zhou dynasty, holds mostly weapons, ceramics and simple ornaments – most impressive is a superb set of Western Zhou and Shang bronze vessels covered in geometric designs suggestive of animal shapes, used for storing and cooking ritual food. The **western hall** holds bronzes and ceramics, in which the best-looking artefacts are Tang. Large numbers of ceramic funerary objects include superbly expressive and rather vicious-looking camels, guardians and dancers. The **eastern hall** features a display of Tang gold and silver, mainly finely wrought images of dragons and tiny, delicate flowers and birds, and an exhibition of Tang costume and ornament. Highlights of the two **upstairs galleries** include the Han ceramic funerary objects, particularly the model houses.

Dacien Temple

大慈恩寺, dàcí'ēn sì • Daily 8am–6.30pm • ¥50, plus ¥30 to climb Big Goose Pagoda • A short walk south of Dayanta subway (line #3), a ¥10–15 taxi ride from the city walls, or on numerous bus routes • Fountain shows Wed–Mon noon & 8.30pm, Sat & Sun also 2pm, 4pm & 6pm

The **Dacien Temple**, 4km south of the city walls at the end of Yanta Lu, is the largest temple in Xi'an. The original, destroyed during the fall of the Tang dynasty in 907, was even bigger: founded in 647, it had nearly two thousand rooms, and a resident population of more than three hundred monks. The surrounding area is a bit of a circus nowadays, with the armies of souvenir sellers dwarfed by a crowd-pulling **musical fountain**, arranged in steps, which fills the northern approach to the temple. The entrance, however, is to the south, and inside the walls the atmosphere is much calmer, though still oriented towards tourism rather than worship, even though there are resident monks here.

The most famous person associated with the temple is **Xuanzang**, the Tang monk who made a pilgrimage to India and returned with a trove of sacred Buddhist texts (see box, p.844). At his request, the **Big Goose Pagoda** (大雁塔, dàyàn tǎ) was built of brick at the centre of the temple grounds as a fireproof store for his precious sutras. More impressive than its little brother (see opposite), the seven-storey pagoda is sturdy and angular, square in plan, and more than 60m tall. As you go in, look for a famous **tablet** on the right showing Xuanzang dwarfed by his massive bamboo backpack.

Baxian Gong

八仙宫 • bāxiān gōng • ¥3 • Within walking distance of Kangfu Lu subway (line #1)

The **Baxian Gong**, Xi'an's largest Taoist temple, lies in a shabby area east of the city walls. It's said to be sited over the wine shop where **Lü Dongbin**, later one of the Eight Immortals, was enlightened by Taoist master Han Zhongli. Containing an important collection of steles, including pictures of local scenic areas and copies of complex ancient medical diagrams of the human body, the temple is the setting for a popular **religious festival** on the first and fifteenth day of every lunar month. However, it is probably of most interest to visitors for the **antiques market** that takes place outside (see box, p.206).

ARRIVAL AND DEPARTURE
XI'AN

BY PLANE
Xi'an Xianyang airport (西安咸阳国际机场, xī'ān xiányáng guójì jīchǎng; ⓦ www.xxia.com.cn), 40km northwest of the city, is connected to town by regular airport buses (6am–8pm; ¥25; 1hr), which terminate at eight locations around town; the most useful are the

Rainbow Hotel (just south of the Drum Tower), the Grand Metropark hotel (see p.205), and the main train station. A taxi costs ¥100–120 for the vehicle, or ¥25–30 per person if you share.
Destinations Beijing (2hr); Hong Kong (22hr 30min); Shanghai (2hr).

BY TRAIN

Train tickets are annoying to get at the station; either use your accommodation (usually around ¥40 a ticket), an app such as Ctrip (¥20 a ticket), or one of several advance-ticket offices scattered around (¥5; ask at your accommodation for the closest one to you).

Main station (西安站, xī'ān zhàn) The busy main train station, just outside the north wall, is a major stop on slow routes from Zhengzhou, Beijing, Chengdu and Lanzhou. It will, by 2018, be on metro line #4; for now, umpteen buses will get you to the Bell and Drum tower area from the south exit, while taxis congregate here too.

Destinations Beijing (10 daily; 11hr–13hr); Datong (1 daily; 16hr 30min); Guangzhou (8 daily; 22hr–30hr); Hua Shan (many daily; 1hr 30min); Lanzhou (many daily; 7hr–8hr 30min); Lhasa (2 daily; 32hr); Luoyang (many daily; 4hr 30min–5hr 30min); Shanghai (12 daily; 15hr–20hr); Taiyuan (6 daily; 8hr 30min–12hr); Ürümqi

(14 daily; 28–34hr); Xining (17 daily; 9hr 15min–12hr); Zhengzhou (many daily; 6hr–7hr 30min).

Xi'an North station (西安北站, xī'ān běizhàn) The high-speed station lies a full 15km north of the city walls; from here, the city centre is easily accessible on metro line #2 (30min).

Destinations Beijing (11 daily; 4hr 40min–6hr); Guangzhou (7 daily; 8hr 40min); Hua Shan (14 daily; 30min); Luoyang (21 daily; 1hr 30min–2hr); Shanghai (1 daily; 11hr); Taiyuan (17 daily; 3hr–4hr); Zhengzhou (many daily; 2hr–2hr 30min).

BY BUS

Xi'an is so well connected by train that fewer and fewer people are arriving by bus. The only services you'll really need are those to Hua Shan (2hr), which depart from an area to the east of the main train station's south exit.

GETTING AROUND

By bus The largest concentration of city buses (normal ones ¥1, with a/c ¥2) is found outside the train station, at the northern end of Jiefang Lu. There are other clusters just outside the Yongning Gate, and at the southern end of Yanta Lu (just north of the Big Goose Pagoda). Bus #610 (labelled as tourist bus #8 in Chinese) is particularly useful, as it links many of the sights: it runs from the train station via Bei Xin Jie, Bei Dajie, the Bell and Drum towers, then south off Xi Dajie down Guangji Jie to Small Goose Pagoda, Daxingshan Temple, the History Museum and on to the Big Goose Pagoda.

By metro Xi'an's new metro system provides a welcome relief from the city's crowded, congested buses. Line #1 crosses the city east–west, line #2 runs north–south, and

line #3 squiggles northeast to southwest; line #4 should open up in 2018, and there are plenty more in the planning stage. Fares cost ¥2–4, depending upon the distance travelled.

By taxi Cabs are plentiful, though drivers here are even more berserk than those in other Chinese cities, and such is demand that taxis can be hard to pick up at rush hour. Rides start at ¥9, and ¥15 should be enough to get you almost anywhere within the city walls, or down to the southern sights.

By bicycle As Xi'an's streets are wide and flat, and the main roads have cycle lanes, controlled at major intersections by officials with flags. Hostels rent bikes for around ¥20 per day, with a deposit of up to ¥200.

INFORMATION

Tours All hostels can book you on local tours (see box, p.209 for prices and routes), and some act as agents for Yangzi ferries, too; you don't have to be staying with them either. Hotels and motels also have tour desks, though

you're more likely to be bundled in with Chinese-speaking groups if you use them. The best of the city's information offices is located just west of the Drum Tower, off Xi Dajie (daily 9am–8.30pm; ☎ 029 87630166).

ACCOMMODATION

Xi'an is firmly on the tourist itinerary, and **accommodation** abounds for all budgets. As plenty of options are located within the city walls, close to the most interesting bits of Xi'an and with easy access to the tourist sights, there seems little point in staying outside, in the drabber, more modern parts of town.

HOSTELS

★**Hantang Inn** 汉唐旅舍, hàntáng lǚshè. 7 Nanchang Xiang ☎ 029 87287772; map p.200. The most pleasant hostel in the city, with a fun bar downstairs, decent rooms, and a ping-pong table, sunbeds (which feel quite luxurious) and a small sauna up on the roof. Rooms are comfortable too. Their sister operation just up the road, *Hantang House*, offers much

the same but is marginally cheaper, flashier and noisier. Daily events are shared across the two hostels. Dorms **¥50**, twins **¥220**

Shuyuan 书院旅舍, shūyuàn lǚshè. Shuncheng Xi Xiang ☎ 029 87287721; map p.200. Owned by the *Hantang* team, who may or may not have plans to commandeer the whole city, this is an appealingly ramshackle hostel facing the city walls. The building is based on a traditional courtyard plan, and rooms are generally fine, if occasionally a little musty; there's also a great bar downstairs (the *Park Qin*, p.207). Dorms **¥50**, rooms **¥220**

Xiangzimen 湘子门国际青年旅舍, xiāngzǐmén guójì qīngnián lǚshè. 16 Xiangzimiao Jie ☏029 62867888, ⓦyhachina.com; map p.200. Beautiful old courtyard mansion hostel with wooden fittings – there's nothing else like this closer than Pingyao. The downstairs doubles are decent but windowless and claustrophobic; better to try rooms in the new wing. Dorms **¥55**, doubles **¥240**

HOTELS

Bestay 百时快捷酒店, bǎishí kuàijié jiǔdiàn. 110 Jiefeng Lu ☏029 87436868, ⓦwww.bestay.com.cn; map p.200. Cheapie on a quiet, atmospheric road featuring umpteen restaurants. They've gone for artsy decoration in the common areas, though rooms themselves are, mercifully, kept simple. All in all, a good budget choice for those who'd rather not join the backpackers at a hostel; note, however, that there's no elevator. **¥189**

Grand Metropark 维景国际大酒店, wéijǐng guójì dàjiǔdiàn. 158 Dong Dajie ☏029 87691234, ⓦhkctshotels.com; map p.200. Little changed since its previous incarnation as the *Hyatt*, including the signature pyramidal atrium. Rooms are well appointed, and suitably popular with tour groups and business folk. **¥625**

Ibis 宜必思酒店, yíbìsī jiǔdiàn. 59 Heping Lu ☏029 87275555, ⓦibis-cn.accorhotels.com; map p.200. Blocky and unadventurous it may appear from the outside, but rooms here are decent value, even if they're a little bit small. Staff speak English and score good service marks. **¥428**

Jinjiang Inn 锦江之星旅馆, jǐnjiāng zhīxīng lǚguǎn. 110 Jiefang Lu ☏029 87452288, ⓦwww .jinjianginns.com; map p.200. Exactly what you'd expect of a *Jinjiang Inn*: low rates, smartly furnished modern rooms and efficient service. Right in the thick of things, too, though on a relatively calm street. **¥229**

★**Sofitel** 索菲特国际饭店, suǒfēitè guójì fàndiàn. 319 Dongxin Jie ☏029 87928888, ⓦsofitel .com; map p.200. Part of a large complex of high-class hotels, the twin *Sofitel* buildings boast scented lobbies, intricately designed interiors, and plush rooms, presided over by a young and energetic staff; rates usually drop to around the ¥1000 mark. Their restaurants are also excellent; try *Azur* (see below), or *Churrasco* for Brazilian barbecue. **¥1700**

Tang Dynasty Art Garden 大唐博相府, dà táng bó xiāng fǔ. 6-1 Furong Dong Lu ☏029 85563333, ⓦtangdynastyartgardenhotel.com; map p.198. If you're in the mood for something different, you could do worse than hunting down this mellow, dynastic-era-themed hotel, whose rooms are arrayed around a series of tranquil courtyards just west of the Dacien Temple. Forget the rack rate – you'll usually get a room here for ¥900. **¥2680**

EATING

RESTAURANTS

Azur 319 Dongxin Jie, in the east wing of the Sofitel ☏029 87928888; map p.200. Entered through a panoply of hanging cuboid lanterns, this is perhaps the most stylish venue in town, blending the cuisines of North Africa, southern Europe and the eastern Mediterranean. The lunch

---

XI'AN FOOD

Xi'an is a great place to eat, though the best of the **local food** is fairly rough and ready, and most enjoyably consumed in the Muslim Quarter's hectic, open-fronted restaurants. Here you'll find **liáng fěn** (凉粉; cold, translucent noodles shaved off a block of beanstarch jelly and served with a spicy sauce); **miànpí** (面皮; flat noodles made of refined wheat dough); and **kùdài miàn** (裤带面; super-thick "belt" noodles, served in a spicy sauce). The latter are usually sold alongside the similar *biang biang mian*, famed for employing the most complicated Chinese character still in use – it can't be written onto most menus, or indeed books such as this. You'll also find huge rounds of flat bread, which make an excellent accompaniment to a handful of grilled mutton skewers (羊肉 串, yángròu chuàn); **sweets** such as steamed "eight treasure pudding" (glutinous rice cooked in a tiny wooden pot and dusted with sugar and sesame); and preserved fruits heaped on plates.

The most widely touted Xi'an dish, however, is *paomo*, and it would be a shame to leave the city without having given it a try. It's basically a meat soup – there are both lamb (羊肉泡馍, **yángròu pàomó**) and beef (牛肉泡馍, **niúròu pàomó**) versions – poured over a bowlful of tiny bread cubes. At many restaurants, diners are given discs of bread and encouraged to do the cubing themselves. Most foreigners seem to prefer the taste and texture of larger chunks – this will likely be met with a scornful look from your waitress, since locals take their time with this process, producing something almost akin to breadcrumbs. The bowl is then taken to the kitchen and piled with shredded meat and noodles, and it's all served with cloves of pickled garlic and chilli paste for you to tip in as required.

4

(¥188) and dinner buffets (¥288) are immaculate, if pricey, though there's a cheaper *à la carte* selection (pastas from ¥95). It's also a good place to drop in for an evening tipple. Daily 11.30am–10.30pm.

Big Bowl 老碗, lǎo wǎn. 55 Xiangzimiao Jie ☎029 68893666; map p.200. Cheap yet highly attractive choice in Xi'an's most important backbacker base, this is a long, skinny restaurant so popular that people have to queue at mealtimes. Noodle dishes from ¥12, with some Shaanxi specials; see the English menu for details. Daily 11.30am–9.20pm.

★**Laosunjia** 老孙家, lǎosūnjiā. Corner of Nanxin Jie and Dong Dajie, 5F of Go Go Happy Building ☎029 87421858; map p.200. No list of Xi'an restaurants is complete without this *yangrou paomo* venue, whose fame is such that every second restaurant in the Muslim quarter has appropriated the name. This one is the real deal; they've been in business since 1898, though recently relocated to a modern venue. *Paomo* goes from ¥28 a bowl; for a bit more, you can have it with decidedly non-traditional ingredients such as ostrich and deer. Daily 9am–9pm.

Shougong Kudaimian 手工裤带面, lǎosūnjiā kùdài miàn. Behind Drum Tower; map p.200. Reliable, earthy choice for *kudai mian*, Xi'an's famous "belt" noodles (so named on account of their thickness), served luke-warm in a spicy, oily sauce; or *biang biang mian*, a similar dish using the most complicated Chinese characters in existence (take a picture of them on the outdoor signs).

SHOPPING IN XI'AN

Xi'an is an excellent place to pick up souvenirs and antiques, which are generally cheaper and more varied than in Beijing, though prices require haggling and the standard of goods, especially from tourist shops, is sometimes shoddy. Shopping is also an enjoyable evening activity, since the markets and department stores are open until 10pm – the Muslim Quarter and Beilin make for an entertaining stroll under the stars, where the nocturnal hawkers sell everything from dinner to souvenir silk paintings.

ARTWORK

Xi'an has a strong artistic pedigree, and the **paintings** available here are much more varied in style than those you see elsewhere in China. As well as the widespread line-and-wash paintings of legendary figures, flowers and animals, look for bright, simple **folk paintings**, usually of country scenes. A traditional Shaanxi art form, appealing for their decorative, flat design and lush colours, these images were popular in China in the 1970s for their idealistic, upbeat portrayal of peasant life. A good selection is sold outside the Banpo Museum (see p.209). For **rubbings** from steles, much cheaper than paintings and quite striking, try the Big Goose Pagoda and Shuyuanmen, especially around the Beilin Museum, which is also a great area to find **calligraphy and paintings**. The underground pedestrian route at the South Gate includes an interesting diversion down an old bomb shelter tunnel to Nan Shang Jie, where **papercuts** are for sale.

Strong competition means you can pick up a painting quite cheaply if you're prepared to **bargain**. Beware the bright young things who introduce themselves as art students whose class happens to be having an exhibition. They're essentially touts who will lead you to a room full of mediocre work at inflated prices.

SOUVENIRS

Beiyuanmen and Huajue Xiang, the alley that runs off to the Great Mosque, are the places to go for **small souvenirs**, engraved chopsticks, teapots, chiming balls and the like. Clusters of stalls and vendors swarm around all the tourist sights, and are often a nuisance, though the stalls around the Great Mosque are worth checking out – you'll see curved Islamic **shabaria** knives among the Mao watches and other tourist knick-knacks.

For a personalized souvenir, try the **seal engravers** along Shuyuanmen, where you'll also find a variety of calligraphy sets and other **artists' materials**.

ANTIQUES

Antiques abound in Xi'an, but be aware that many – however dusty and worn – are reproductions. The best place to go is the market outside **Baxian Gong**, which is biggest on Wednesdays and Sundays; many vendors are villagers from the outlying regions who look as if they are clearing out their attics. You can find some unusual items here, such as books and magazines dating from the Cultural Revolution containing rabid anti-Western propaganda, Qing vases, opium pipes and even rusty guns.

Both go for ¥15, or ¥25 including more meat and vegetables. Daily 8am–11pm.

Tongshengxiang 同盛祥, tóngshèngxiáng. 5 Xi Dajie ☎ 029 87233480; map p.200. Set in an elaborately styled building between the Drum and Bell towers, this multistorey Muslim place is famous for its *paomo* (from ¥32), as well as its *tangbao* (soup buns). Head to the upper levels, rather than the canteen-like ground floor. Daily 7.30am–10pm.

Xi'an 西安饭庄, xī'ān fànzhuāng. 2F 298 Dong Dajie ☎ 029 87680880; map p.200. A restaurant famed as the place where the plotters of the Xi'an Incident (see p.212) formulated their plan to kidnap Chiang Kai-shek. The modern incarnation isn't all that pretty, but the food here is top-notch, a winning mix of banquet dishes such as gourd-shaped chicken (¥98) and hot-and-sour meatballs (¥58), and some incredibly cheap noodle dishes. Daily 11am–2pm & 5–9pm.

★**Zuichangan** 醉長安, zuìchángān. 56 Shuyuanmen ☎ 029 87281828; map p.200. A little hard to find (you may have to ask around), this super little restaurant is well worth hunting down. It serves affordable Shaanxi specialities from a menu sadly devoid of English or pictures – try the tofu and onions, served on a sizzling platter. Grab a table out in the courtyard, if you can – gentle zither music is played here every evening. Daily 11am–9.30pm.

CAFÉS

Cat Kingdom 猫国度, māo guó dù. 56 Xiangzimiao Jie ☎ 029 87288631; map p.200. China has gone gaga for cutesey-poo cat cafés of late, and this is a great example, filled with amiable felines to stroke and play with – some of them have emerged victorious at cat beauty pageants. Daily 11am–1pm.

Pacific Coffee 太平洋咖啡, tàipíngyáng kāfēi. Off northwest corner of Bell Tower ☎ 029 87230096; map p.200. Western-style café serving adequate coffee (¥30 or so), though most notable for its stunning views of the Bell Tower. Daily 8am–11pm.

Tous Les Jours 多乐之日, duō lè zhī rì. 92 Changan Zhong Lu ☎ 029 88322262; map p.198. Korean chain-café whose various pastries, cakes, coffees and smoothies can be just the treat if you're pounding around the sights south of the wall – it's just around the corner from Daxingshan Temple. Daily 8am–11pm.

DRINKING AND NIGHTLIFE

Xi'an has a large student population and general prosperity that make it more exciting at night than many other Chinese cities. The easiest place to start is the bar street area on *Defu Xiang*, just north of the *Xiangzimen* hostel, which is lined with Western-style **pubs** – none are particularly remarkable, but since all can be peeked inside from the street it's easy to find the best venue. Alternatively, all of the **hostels** listed here (see p.204) have great bars, in which it's easy to round up fellow travellers for an extended night out elsewhere.

Belgian Bar East of the South Gate ☎ 029 87264019; map p.200. A far more appealing venue than those you'll find on Bar Street, just to the west. Authentic Belgian beer from ¥40 per pint of draught; cheaper Chinese beer is also available. Happy hour from 3–8pm. Daily 3pm–midnight.

Muse Corner of Xi Dajie and Nanguangji Lu; map p.200. The most popular club in town, at the time of writing. The music, generally of the hip-hop variety, is typically overloud, though the wiggling bodies inside don't seem to care – perhaps because there's almost never a cover charge to get in. Daily 8pm–5am.

★**Park Qin** Shuncheng Xi Xiang ☎ 029 87287721; map p.200. This snazzy subterranean den is so much more than a regular hostel bar – backpackers are usually totally outnumbered by locals, guzzling down beer and some fun-looking cocktails (including a fair few house specialities). There's live music every night, too. Daily 7pm–3am.

ENTERTAINMENT

Tang Dynasty 唐乐宫, tánglè gōng. 75 Chang'an Beidajie ☎ 029 87822222, ⊕ xiantangdynasty.com. Theatre-restaurant with performances of traditional song and dance – too gaudy for most tastes, though some seem to enjoy the show. Nightly ninety-minute performances ¥500 with banquet dinner; some hotels and hostels sell tickets at a discounted rate and provide transport.

DIRECTORY

Cinema Few cinemas in Xi'an show foreign films, and even those that do usually dub rather than subtitle. One occasional exception is the Qu Jiang International Cinema on Dong Dajie – tickets go from ¥66.

Hospital Xi'an Central Hospital is on Xi Wu Lu (☎ 029 87212380), just west of Bei Dajie metro station.

Post office The central post office (8am–8pm) faces the Bell Tower at the intersection of Bei Dajie and Dong Dajie.

Visa extensions The PSB is at 138 Xi Dajie (Mon–Sat 8am–noon & 3–5pm). Xi'an being such a popular place, many travellers try to extend their visa here, usually without too much bother.

4

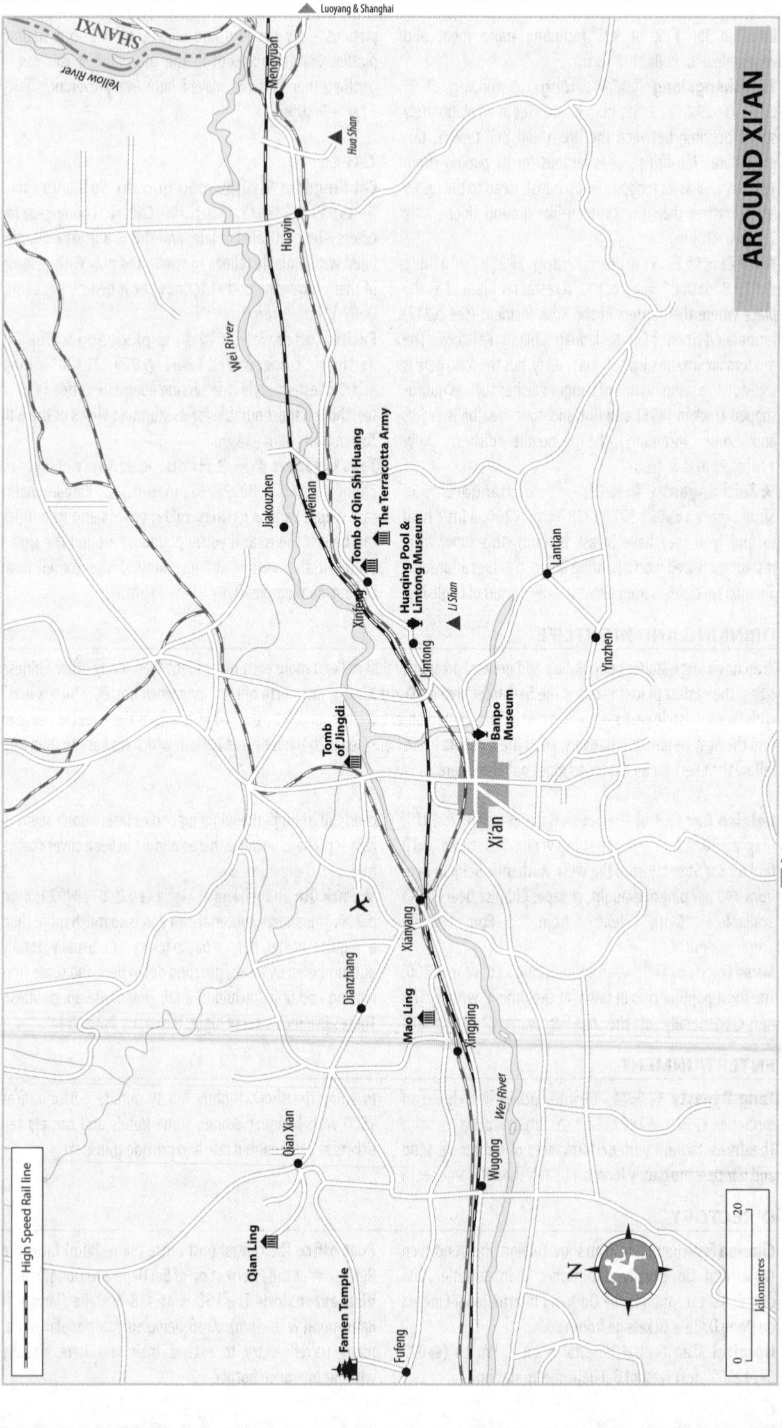

4

AROUND XI'AN

Luoyang & Shanghai

SHANXI

Yellow River

Mengyuan

Hua Shan

Huayin

Wei River

Jiakouzhen

Weinan

Tomb of Qin Shi Huang

The Terracotta Army

Huaqing Pool &
Lintong Museum

Xinfeng

Li Shan

Lintong

Lantian

Yinzhen

Tomb of Jingdi

Banpo
Museum

Xi'an

Foping

Xianyang

Dianzhang

Mao Ling

Xingping

Wei River

Qian Xian

Wugong

Qian Ling

Famen Temple

Fufeng

High Speed Rail line

N

0   20
kilometres

TOURS AROUND XI'AN

The easiest way to see the sights around Xi'an is to get up early and take one of the many **tours** on offer. Most hotels, and all hostels, can arrange such tours, sometimes even with no advance notice; the hostels are usually both the cheapest and most reliable, though you should still ask about exactly what you're getting (prices below include entrance tickets), and expect to be taken to some shops on the way. Most tours leave by 8am.

THE EASTERN ROUTE

The popular **eastern route** covers one or more of Huaqing Pool, the Terracotta Army, the Tomb of Qin Shi Huang and the Banpo Museum. Prices start at around ¥270 for the Terracotta Army plus the Tomb of Qin Shi Huang, rising to ¥380 including either the Banpo Museum or Huaqing Pool. You can visit all of these places fairly easily by yourself, going at your own pace and avoiding the dreaded shop visits, but tours make more sense if you'd like to see more than a couple of sights.

THE WESTERN ROUTE

The **western route**, going to the Imperial Tombs and sometimes as far as the Famen Temple, is less popular as it's longer and more expensive, and guidance tends to be in Chinese only – it's also harder to find anyone running it off season. A tour including one of the tombs and Famen Temple will cost from ¥380, while those only interested in Jingdi can knock it down to ¥250 per person in a group of four. Also available are tours hitting Jingdi and the Terracotta Army – more like ¥550 per person.

FURTHER AFIELD

Xi'an also functions as a base for a host of farther-flung sights. Most popular is Hua Shan (see p.216), a mountain range to the east – a day-trip will be around ¥450, including the cable car. The mighty **Hukou waterfalls** (see box, p.256) are beyond easy day-trip distance, but it'll be around ¥450 for this too, including a night's accommodation. One unusual option offered by the hostels is a full-day trip southwest to a **panda reserve** at Foping in the Qingling mountains (¥200–300), where you can see captive animals and tour the research centre. Lastly, hostels can also book you on **Yangzi River ferries** from Chongqing to Yichang (see p.768) from ¥620, not including transport from Xi'an.

4

Around Xi'an

You could spend days on excursions **around Xi'an**. People swarm to see the **Terracotta Army** and **Banpo Museum**, and if your stay in Xi'an is short then the army is still the must-see sight. However, with a little more time, recommended attractions off the main tour-group itinerary include the **Famen Temple**, with a superb museum attached, which is a little too remote for most visitors; and the **Tomb of Jingdi**, which has become extremely popular with backpackers.

Banpo Museum

半坡博物馆, bànpō bówùguǎn • Daily 8am–5.30pm • March–Nov ¥65, Dec–Feb ¥45 • A short walk from Banpo subway (line #1) • Also accessible on tours (see box above)

The **Banpo Museum**, 8km east of the city centre, sits over the excavated site of a **Neolithic village** occupied between around 4500 BC and 3750 BC. Discovered in 1953, it constitutes the biggest and best-preserved site so far found of **Yangshao culture**, and is named after the village near the eastern bend of the Yellow River where the first relics of this type were found.

The covered excavation area is a lunar landscape of pits, craters and humps, navigated on raised walkways, and it can be hard to relate these to the buildings and objects described on the signs in whimsical English. Outside the museum, the **Culture Village** is a crude attempt to bring the prehistoric settlement to life – it's basically a Neolithic theme park.

> ## XUAN ZONG AND YANG GUIFEI
>
> The tale of Emperor Xuan Zong and his concubine Yang Guifei is one of the great Chinese **tragic romances**, the equivalent to the Western Antony and Cleopatra, and is often depicted in art and drama, most famously in an ode by the great Tang poet Bai Juyi. Xuan Zong took a fancy to Yang Guifei – originally the concubine of his son – when he was over 60, and she was no spring chicken. They fell in love, but his infatuation with her, which led to his neglect of affairs of state, was seen as harmful to the empire by his officials, and in part led to the rebellion of the disgruntled general, **An Lushan**. As An Lushan and his troops approached the capital, the emperor and his retinue were forced to flee southwest into Sichuan; along the way, his army mutinied and demanded Yang Guifei's **execution**.

Huaqing Pool

华清池, huáqīng chí · Daily 8am–5pm · March–Nov ¥150, Dec–Feb ¥120 · Cable car up Li Shan ¥35 up, ¥30 down · Buses from east side of train station square: minibuses #914 and #915 (¥7; 1hr), or larger bus #306 (¥6; 1hr 10min); both continue to Terracotta Army (¥3) · Also accessible on tours (see box, p.209)

Huaqing Pool is at the foothills of Li Shan, 30km east of Xi'an on the road to the Terracotta Army. Its **springs**, with mineral-rich water emerging at a constant and agreeable 43°C, have been attracting people for nearly 2500 years. Qin Shi Huang had a residence here, as did the Han emperors, but its present form, a complex of **bathing houses and pools**, was created during the Tang dynasty. It was under the reign of the second Tang emperor, **Xuan Zong** – who spent much of the winter here in the company of his favourite concubine, **Yang Guifei** (see box above) – that the complex reached its height of popularity as an imperial pleasure resort.

The complex

Huaqing's collection of classical buildings is usually unromantically thronged with day-trippers. The old **imperial bathhouses**, at the back of the complex, must once have looked impressive, but today you'll find little to get your teeth into – visitors take plenty of pictures and chuck coins in for luck, but mainly because there's not a lot else to do. The largest bath is the **Lotus Pool**, more than 100m square, and once reserved for the use of Xuan Zong; a little smaller is **Crabapple Pool**, for concubine Yang. There are also a few halls, now housing souvenir shops, and a small **museum**, where fragments of Qin and Tang architectural detail – roof tiles and decorated bricks – hint at past magnificence. A marble boat, at the edge of Jiulong Pond, on the left as you enter, was constructed in 1956.

The bathhouse

Private rooms from ¥280, footbath ¥50

The **hot spring bathhouse**, set in a building directly up from the main entrance, offers you the chance to bathe in the waters – at a cost that has ballooned since a recent renovation of the complex. More affordable is the **footbath section** to the right of the entrance; you'll be given a flannel and soap, and are likely to emerge with very pink, water-plumped feet.

The Lintong Museum

临潼博物馆, líntóng bówùguǎn · Daily 8am–6pm · Free · 150m from the main Huaqing Pool entrance

Small though it may be, the **Lintong Museum** provides a rewarding diversion while visiting Huaqing Pool, with a collection that includes silver chopsticks and scissors, a bronze jar decorated with human faces, a crossbow and numerous Han funerary objects. The most captivating exhibit is a **Tang reliquary** unearthed nearby – inside a stone stupa about 1m high, decorated with images of everyday life, was

OPPOSITE CENTRAL STREET AND TOWER, PINGYAO (P.251) >

THE XI'AN INCIDENT

Huaqing Pool's modern claim to fame is as the setting for the **Xi'an Incident** in 1936. As Japanese troops continued to advance into China, Chiang Kai-shek virtually ignored them, concentrating instead on pursuing his policy of national unification – meaning the destruction of the Communists before all else. In December 1936, he flew to Xi'an, which was then under the control of **Marshal Zhang Xueliang** and his Manchurian troops. Although GMD supporters, they, like many others, had grown weary of Chiang's policies, fuelled by the fact that their Manchurian homeland was now occupied by the Japanese. In secret meetings with Communist leaders, Zhang had been convinced of their genuine anti-Japanese sentiments, and so, on the morning of December 12, Nationalist troops stormed Chiang's headquarters at the foot of Li Shan, capturing most of the headquarters staff. The great leader himself was eventually caught halfway up the slope in a house at the back of the complex, behind the pools – a neo-Grecian pavilion on the lower slopes of the mountain marks the spot. Still in his pyjamas and without his false teeth, he had bolted from his bed at the sound of gunfire. Chiang was forced to pay a heavy ransom but was otherwise unharmed, his captors allowing him to remain in control of China – provided that he allied with the Communists against the Japanese. Today, tourists line up here to don GMD uniforms and have their pictures taken.

found a tiny silver coffin, fussily ornamented with silver spirals, strings of pearls and gold images of monks. Inside this, an even tinier gold coffin held a glass jar with a handful of dust at the bottom. These delicate relics, and the dust, optimistically labelled "ashes of the Buddha", are actually more interesting than anything at Huaqing Pool.

The Terracotta Army

兵马俑 • bīngmǎ yǒng • Daily 8am–5pm • March–Nov ¥150, Dec–Feb ¥120; includes entry to Tomb of Qin Shi Huang • Photography permitted, but not tripods or flash • Buses from east side of train station square: minibuses #914 and #915 (¥8; 1hr 20min), or larger bus #306 (¥7; 1hr 30min) • Also accessible on tours (see box, p.209)

No historical records exist of the **Terracotta Army**, which was set to guard **Qin Shi Huang's tomb** over two thousand years ago, and was only discovered accidentally by peasants sinking a well 28km east of Xi'an in 1974. Three rectangular vaults were found, constructed of earth with brick floors and timber supports. Today, hangars have been built over the excavated site so that the ranks of soldiers – designed never to be seen, but now one of the most popular tourist attractions in China – can be viewed *in situ*.

The army is probably the highlight of any trip to Xi'an, so don't be discouraged by what greets arrivals: a vast car park and a tourist complex of industrial proportions whose main purpose seems to be to channel visitors through a kilometre-long gauntlet of overpriced, mediocre restaurants and souvenir stalls.

Vault 1

Vault 1 is the largest, and has so far yielded more than a **thousand figures** (out of an estimated eight thousand) ranked in battle formation and assembled in a grid of 6m-deep corridors. Facing you as you enter the hangar, this is one of the most memorable sights in China; you can inspect the static soldiers at closer range via raised walkways running around their perimeter. Averaging 1.8m in height, the figures are hollow from the thighs up; head and hands were modelled separately and attached to the mass-produced bodies. Each soldier has **different features** and expressions and wears marks of rank; some believe that each is a portrait of a real member of the ancient Imperial Guard. Their hair is tied in buns and they are wearing knee-length battle tunics; some figures wore leather armour, now decayed, and traces of **pigment** show that their monochrome grey dress was once bright yellow, purple and green.

A central group of **terracotta horses** is all that remains of a set of chariots. These wore harnesses with brass fittings and have been identified as depicting a breed from Gansu and Xinjiang. Each has six teeth, an indication that they are in their prime.

Vault 2

Vault 2 is a smaller, L-shaped area, still under excavation; it's thought to hold more warriors than vault 1. The four groups here – crossbowmen, charioteers, cavalry and infantry – display more variety of posture and uniform than the figures in the main vault, though a large number of smashed and broken figures make the scene look more like the aftermath of a battle than the preparation for one. **Four exceptional figures** found here are exhibited at the side: a kneeling archer, a cavalryman leading a horse, an officer with a stylish goatee and the magnificent figure of a general, 2m tall, wearing engraved armour and a cap with two tails. Also on show are some of the weapons discovered at the site (including a huge bronze battle-axe); made of sophisticated alloys, some were still sharp after two thousand years underground. At times, you'll find a half-blind peasant signing postcards in the shop at vault 2; this is **Yang Zhifa**, the man who discovered it all in 1974.

Vault 3

The much smaller **vault 3**, where over seventy figures and a chariot have been found, seems to have been battle headquarters. Armed with ceremonial *shu*, a short bronze mace with a triangular head, the figures are not in battle formation but form a guard of honour. Animal bones found here provide evidence of ritual sacrifices, which a real army would have performed before going into battle. A photo exhibition of plaster replicas gives some idea of how the figures would have been painted.

QIN SHI HUANG

4

As a silkworm devours a mulberry leaf, so Qin swallowed up the kingdoms of the Empire.
The first-century-BC historian Sima Qian

Though only 13 when he ascended the throne of the western state of Qin in 246 BC, within 25 years **Qin Shi Huang** had managed to subjugate all the quarrelsome eastern states, thus becoming the first emperor of a unified China. During his eleven years as the sole monarch of the Chinese world, Qin Shi Huang set out to transform it, hoping to create an empire that his descendants would continue to rule for "ten thousand years". His reign was marked by centralized rule, and often **ruthless tyranny**. As well as standardizing weights and measures (even the width of cartwheels) and ordering a unified script to be used, the First Emperor decreed that all books, except those on the history of the Qin and on such practical matters as agriculture, be destroyed, along with the scholars who produced them. It was only thanks to a few Confucian scholars, who hid their books away, that any literature from before this period has survived.

As well as overseeing the construction of roads linking all parts of the empire, mainly to aid military operations, Qin Shi Huang began the construction of the **Great Wall**, a project that perhaps – more than any of his harsh laws and high taxes – turned the populace, drummed into constructing it, against him. Ambitious to the end, Qin Shi Huang died on a journey to the east coast seeking the legendary island of the immortals and the secret drug of longevity they held. His entourage concealed his death – easy to do as he lived in total seclusion from his subjects – and on their return installed an easily manipulated prince on the throne. The empire soon disintegrated into civil war, and within a few years Qin Shi Huang's capital at Xianyang had been destroyed, his palace burnt and his tomb ransacked.

It is possible that Qin Shi Huang, seen as an archetypal tyrant, has been harshly judged by history, as the story of his reign was written in the Han dynasty, when an eastern people whom he subjugated became ascendant. They are unlikely to have been enamoured of him, and the fact that the Terracotta Army faces east, the direction from where Qin Shi Huang thought threats to his empire would come, indicates the animosity that existed. The outstanding artistry of the terracotta figures has revised the accepted view of the Qin dynasty as a time of unremitting philistinism, and his reign has been reassessed since their discovery. Mao Zedong, it is said, was an admirer of his predecessor in revolution.

The museums

At the side of vault 2 is a small **museum** where two magnificent **bronze chariots**, found in 1982 near Qin Shi Huang's tomb, are displayed in glass cases. They're about half actual size. The front one, depicting the Imperial Fleet leader's chariot, has four horses and a driver, and is decorated with dragon, phoenix and cloud designs, with a curved canopy and a gold-and-silver harness. Behind the driver is a large compartment featuring a silver door-latch and windows that open and close. The chariot at the back was the emperor's and has seats and beds in the rear. Both chariots were made with astonishing attention to detail; even the driver's knuckles, nails and fingerprints are shown. Another museum holds small artefacts found around the area, including a skull with an arrowhead still embedded in it, and a few kneeling pottery attendants, the only **female figures** depicted.

The Tomb of Qin Shi Huang

秦始皇陵, qínshǐhuáng líng • Daily 8am–5pm • Same ticket as Terracotta Army, and accessible on free shuttle buses

The **Tomb of Qin Shi Huang** is now no more than an artificial hill, nearly 2km west of the Terracotta Army. The burial mound was originally at the southern end of an inner sanctuary with walls 2.5km long, itself the centre of an outer city, none of which remains. The tomb has yet to be excavated and there's not much to see here; hassled at every step by souvenir sellers, you can walk up stone steps to the top of the hill, where you have a view of fields scraped bare for agriculture. According to accounts by **Sima Qian** in his *Historical Records*, written a century after the entombment, 700,000 labourers took 36 years to create a subterranean imperial city, full of wonders: the heavens were depicted on the ceiling of the central chamber with pearls, and the geographical divisions of the earth were delineated on a floor of bronze, with the seas and rivers represented by pools of mercury and made to flow with machinery. Automatic crossbows were set to protect the many gold and silver relics. Abnormally high quantities of **mercury** have been found in the surrounding soil, suggesting that at least parts of the account can be trusted.

The Tomb of Jingdi

汉阳陵, hànyánglíng • Daily 8.30am–6pm • ¥90 • Hostel tours from ¥160 (transport only)

The **Tomb of Jingdi** (188–141 BC) has recently become one of the most popular out-of-town excursions with Xi'an hostel-goers, and deservedly so – especially since it's still largely off the tour-bus circuit. This is the tomb of the sixth emperor of the great Han dynasty; Jingdi is recognized as one of its main drivers, having centralized control and put down the rebellions threatening to tear the nascent dynasty apart.

The **tomb** here is, as with so many sights in Xi'an, still being excavated; you'll be able to see some of this for yourself at close range, with the aid of glass floor panels and well-placed lighting – an atmospheric experience. Some of the relics unearthed here, including a wide range of terracotta figures, are on display in a superb on-site **museum**.

EMPRESS WU ZETIAN

The rise to power of **Empress Wu Zetian** is extraordinary. Originally the **concubine** of Emperor Gao Zong's father, she emerged from her mourning to win the affections of his son, bear him sons in turn, and eventually marry him. As her husband ailed, her power over the administration grew until she was strong enough, at his death, to usurp the throne. Seven years later she was declared empress in her own right, and ruled until being forced to abdicate in favour of her son shortly before her death in 705 AD. Her reign was notorious for intrigue and bloodshed, but even her critics admit that she chose the right ministers for the job, often solely through merit. The heavy negative historical criticism against her may be solely because she was a woman, as the idea of a female in a position of authority is entirely contrary to Confucian ethics (her title was "Emperor", there being no female equivalent for so exalted a position). For more about Wu Zetian, see also p.746.

The Tomb of Mao Ling

茂陵, màolíng • Daily 8am–5pm • March–Nov ¥80, Dec–Feb ¥60 • Best accessed by tour (see box, p.209), or take bus from Xi'an long-distance terminal to Xianyang, then a taxi

Located 40km west of Xi'an, the **Tomb of Mao Ling** is the resting place of the fifth Han emperor, Wu Di (157–87 BC), and is the largest of the twenty Han tombs in the area. It's a great green mound against the hills, which took more than fifty years to construct and contains, among many treasures, a full **jade burial suit** – jade was believed to protect the corpse (and the soul) from decay. A dozen **smaller tombs** nearby belong to the emperor's court and include those of his favourite concubine and his generals, including the brilliant strategist Huo Qubing who fought several campaigns against the northern tribes and died at the age of 24. A small **museum** displays some impressive relics, including many massive stone sculptures of animals that once lined the tombs' spirit ways, simplified figures that look appealingly quirky; look for the frogs and a cow, and the horse trampling a demonic-looking barbarian with its hooves, a macabre subject made to look almost comical.

The Tomb of Qian Ling

乾陵, qiánlíng • Daily 8am–5pm • March–Oct ¥122, Nov–Feb ¥82 • Best accessed by tour (see box, p.209), or take bus from Xi'an train station (8am, returning 3pm; 3hr)

Qian Ling is 80km northwest of Xi'an, and usually the second tomb toured after Mao Ling. This hill tomb, on the slopes of Liang Shan, is where **Emperor Gao Zong** and his empress **Wu Zetian** (see box opposite) were buried in the seventh century.

The **Imperial Way** leading to the tombs is formed from two facing rows of carved stone figures of men and flying horses, and with two groups of (now headless) mourners – guest princes and envoys from tribute states, some with their names on their backs. The tall stele on the left praises Gao Zong; opposite is the uninscribed **Wordless Stele**, erected by the empress to mark the supreme power that no words could express.

Tomb of Prince Zhang Huai

章怀幕, zhānghuái mù • Entry with Qian Ling ticket

Seventeen **lesser tombs** are contained in the southeast section of Qian Ling. Among the five excavated since 1960 here is the **tomb of Prince Zhang Huai**, second son of Gao Zong, forced to commit suicide by his mother Wu Zetian during one of her periodic purges of those opposing her rise to power. At this tomb you walk down into a vault frescoed with army and processional scenes, a lovely tiger with a perm in the dip on either side. One fresco shows the court's welcome to visiting foreigners, with a hook-nosed Westerner depicted. There are also vivid frescoes of polo playing and, in the **museum** outside, some Tang pottery horses.

Tomb of Princess Yong Tai

永泰幕, yǒngtài mù • Entry with Qian Ling ticket

The **tomb of Yong Tai** is the finest at Qian Ling – no surprise, considering the fact that she was the emperor's granddaughter. Niches in the wall hold funeral offerings, and the vaulted roof still has traces of painted patterns. The passage walls leading down the ramp into the tomb are covered with murals of animals and guards of honour. The court ladies are still clear, elegant and charming after 1300 years, displaying Tang hairstyles and dress. At the bottom is the great tomb in black stone, lightly carved with human and animal shapes. Some 1300 gold, silver and pottery objects were found here and are now in Xi'an's Shaanxi Museum. At the mouth of the tomb is the traditional **stone tablet** into which the life story of the princess is carved – according to this, she died in childbirth at the age of 17, but some records claim that she was murdered by her grandmother, the Empress Wu Zetian.

Famen Temple

法门寺, fǎmén sì • Daily 8am–6pm • March–Oct ¥120, Nov–Feb ¥90 • Best accessed by tour (see box, p.209), or take bus from Xi'an train station (8am, returning 3pm; 3hr)

The extraordinary **Famen Temple**, 120km west of Xi'an, home of the finger bone of the Buddha, and the nearby **museum** containing an unsurpassed collection of Tang-dynasty relics, are worth the long trip it takes to get out here.

Brief history

In 147 AD, King Ashoka of India, to atone for his warlike life, had precious **Buddhist relics** (*sarira*) distributed throughout Asia. One of the earliest places of Buddhist worship in China, the Famen Temple was built to house his gift of a **finger**, in the form of three separate bones. During the Tang dynasty, these were ceremonially removed every thirty years; the bones would be taken to the court at Chang'an at the head of a procession, and when the emperor had paid his respects, they'd be closed back up in the **crypt** underneath the temple stupa, together with a lavish collection of offerings. After the fall of the Tang, the vault was forgotten about until the stupa above collapsed in 1981, revealing the most astonishing array of precious objects, and at the back, concealed inside box after box, the legendary finger of the Buddha.

The stupa and crypt

Today, the temple is a popular place of pilgrimage. The **stupa and crypt** have been rebuilt, with a **shrine** holding the finger at the crypt's centre. A praying monk is always in attendance, sitting in front of the finger, next to the safe in which it is kept at night (if it's not being exhibited elsewhere, as happens periodically). Indeed, the temple's monks are taking no chances, and the only entrance is protected by a huge metal door of the kind usually seen in a bank. You can look into the original crypt – at 21m long, the largest of its kind ever discovered in China – though there's not much to see now.

The museum

Don't miss the **museum** west of the temple, which houses the well-preserved Tang relics found in the crypt. Exhibits are divided into sections according to their material, with copious explanations in English. On the lower floor, the **gold and silver** are breathtaking for the quality of their workmanship: especially notable are a silver incense burner with an internal gyroscope to keep it upright; a silver tea basket, the earliest physical evidence of tea-drinking in China; and a gold figure of an elephant-headed man. Some unusual items on display are twenty **glass plates and bottles**, some Persian with Arabic designs, some from the fifth-century Roman Empire. Glassware, imported along the Silk Road, was more highly valued than gold at the time, as none was made in China.

At the centre of the main room is a gilded **silver coffin**, which held one of the finger bones, itself inside a copper model of a stupa, inside a marble pagoda. Prominent upstairs is a gold-and-silver **monk's staff**, which, ironically, would have been used for begging alms, but the main display here is of the **caskets** that the other two finger bones were found in – finely made boxes of diminishing size, of silver, sandalwood, gold and crystal, which sat inside each other, while the finger bones themselves were in tiny jade coffins.

Hua Shan

华山, huáshān • March–Nov ¥180, Dec–Feb ¥100; ticket valid for two days • **West Peak** Bus to Donggoukou for cable car; cable car ¥140 one-way March–Nov, ¥120 one-way Dec–Feb • **North Peak** Bus to Waimiaogou for cable car ¥20; cable car ¥80 one-way March–Nov, ¥40 one-way Dec–Feb • **"Danger Trail"** ¥30

The five peaks of **Hua Shan** provide some of the best mountain scenery in China – crowded though their trails may be, they make for thoroughly enjoyable hiking nonetheless. They rise in a series of rugged, occasionally tree-dappled granite crags from the plains 120km east of Xi'an; here you can choose your desired level of energy expenditure, from low (cable car) to medium (a hike up the North Peak), to hard (a terrifying hike along the "Danger Trail"). Though the summits aren't that high, the gaunt rocky cliffs, twisted pines and rugged slopes certainly look like genuine mountains as they swim in and out of the misty trails.

Hua Shan was originally known as Xiyue (Western Mountain), because this is the westernmost of the five sacred **Taoist** mountains. It's always been a popular place for pilgrimage, though these days people puffing up the steep, narrow paths or enjoying the dramatic views from the peaks are more likely to be tourists – or the astonishingly hardy porters who shuttle up and down the mountain, often several times a day, to deliver supplies.

Ascending Hua Shan

There's a Chinese saying, "There is one path and one path only to the summit of Hua Shan", meaning that sometimes the hard way is the only way. These days the saying is redundant, since the **North Peak** and **West Peak of Hua Shan** are accessible by cable car; however, anyone in decent health will be able to make it up this far on foot. The original, arduous **old route** begins at the west gate and **Yuquan Temple** (玉泉院, yùquán yuàn), dedicated to the tenth-century monk Xiyi, who lived here as a recluse. From here, every few hundred metres you'll come across a wayside refreshment place offering stone seats, a burner, tea, soft drinks, maps and souvenirs – the higher you go, the more attractive the knobbly walking sticks on sale seem. In summer, you'll be swept along in a stream of Chinese, mostly young couples, dressed in their fashionable (but often highly impractical) holiday finest, sometimes including high-heeled shoes.

To the North Peak

Known as the **Eighteen Bends**, the deceptively easy-looking climb up the gullies in fact winds for about two hours before reaching the series of stone steps that ascend to the first summit, **North Peak** (1615m). At one point there's a (poorly signed) fork in the path; go left and the steps continue, go right and the path gets so steep that you'll have to drag your way up (or, if you're even more unfortunate, down) part of the way along a series of chains. On the way you'll pass plenty of small **temples**, some of which can be peeked inside – a chance, at least, to get your breath back. All in all, it'll take from two-and-a-half to four hours to get up to the peak, depending upon your level of fitness, and the weather.

The Middle Peak and beyond

Many people turn back at the North Peak, although you can continue to **Middle Peak** next, then East, South and West peaks (each at around 2000m), which make up an **eight-hour circuit trail**. If you're going to do this in a single day, you'll likely need to get the cable car up to the North Peak first. Some people arrive in the evening and climb by moonlight in order to see the **sunrise** over the Sea of Clouds from Middle or East Peak; if you plan to climb at night, be sure to take some warm clothes and a flashlight with spare batteries.

The Danger Trail

Of most interest to daredevil travellers is the **Danger Trail** near the South Peak. The going is rough in places and you'll need a head for heights (and, preferably, a bit of rock-climbing experience), with chain handrails, wooden galleries and rickety ladders attached at difficult points. The most nerve-racking stretch traverses a cliff-hugging wooden boardwalk perched above a sheer 1000m drop, after which you'll need to use a harness with chain-links to complete the walk.

As Hua Shan lies between Xi'an and Luoyang, you can take in the mountain en route between the two cities, or as an excursion from Xi'an.

BY TRAIN

Hua Shan station (华山站, huáshān zhàn). Near the park's east gate, and around ¥10 by taxi from the west gate and surrounding accommodation.

Destinations Beijing (3 daily; 12–14hr); Luoyang (1–2 hourly; 3hr 30min); Xi'an (1–2 hourly; 1hr 30min).

Hua Shan North station (华山北站, huáshān běizhàn). The new high-speed station is 10km away; take any bus departing here (¥2) and they'll tell you where to transfer to another bus for the west gate; it'll be around ¥25 by taxi.

Destinations Beijing (4 daily; 5hr); Luoyang (12 daily; 1hr–1hr 40min); Xi'an (hourly; 35min).

BY BUS

Buses (2hr; ¥36 one-way, ¥60 return) go from the east side of Xi'an train station concourse to Hua Shan's east gate. The last buses back to Xi'an leave at around 7.30pm.

TOURS

Day-tours organized by hostels in Xi'an (see p.209), including transport, cable car, entry and occasionally a light breakfast, cost around ¥450 per person. Do check, before you sign up, exactly what is included, as you don't want to be stung unexpectedly once you're here.

ACCOMMODATION AND EATING

Most visitors stay in the motley selection of **hotels** downhill from the west gate; if you're doing so, the most enjoyable place to eat in the area is the line of **restaurants** on the other side of the main road (Yuquan Jie), which have pleasant outdoor seating in warmer months (note that it can get very windy). There are also a few places to stay on and **around the peaks** themselves, though the nicest thing to be said about the food on the mountain – available from tiny path-side restaurants – is that it's palatable. It's also more expensive the higher you go; if you're on a tight budget, stock up beforehand.

WEST GATE AREA

★**Huashan** 华山客栈, huáshān kèzhàn. 2 Yuquan Dongjie ☎ 0913 4658008. The classiest place to stay near the west gate, with attentive staff and moderately plush rooms. Try to bag one that faces south – away from the main road and, more importantly, towards the mountains. The small garden area behind the main building is a pleasant place to nab a beer. **¥380**

Huashan Gehui 华山戈辉宾馆, huáshān gēhuī bīnguǎn. Yuquan Zhong Jie ☎ 0913 4363361. The best of the many budget places around the west gate – unlike some of the competition, they're licensed to accept foreign guests, and you may be able to wangle a train-station pick-up. Private rooms can work out almost as cheap as the dorm beds, which are usually male-only. Dorms from **¥45**, private rooms **¥128**

ON THE MOUNTAIN

Dongfeng 东峰宾馆, dōngfēng bīnguǎn. East

Peak. This is the best place from which to see the sunrise; rooms are spartan but they've a great restaurant that isn't too much of a rip-off, considering the location. Dorms from ¥145, doubles ¥440

Yuntai 云台饭店, yúntái fàndiàn. North Peak

☎ 1571 9136466. A hop, skip and jump from the North Peak, this is a popular base from which to embark upon a morning bash around the peak circuit. Rooms are nothing special, but the little café-restaurant comes in handy. Dorms from ¥95, doubles ¥380

Ningxia

宁夏, níngxià

Squeezed between Inner Mongolia, Gansu and Shanxi, **Ningxia** is the smallest of China's provinces, and an autonomous region for the **Hui** minority (see box opposite). Geographically, the area is dominated by coalfields and the **Yellow River**, without which the hilly south of the province, green and extremely beautiful, would be barren and uninhabitable desert. In the west of the province, however, the river does actually run past desert dunes at **Shapotou**, near the city of **Zhongwei** – one of the most visually arresting sights in China. Other sights include the capital **Yinchuan**, which makes a pleasant stopover, and one relic from an obscure northern branch of the Silk Road, the delightful **Xumi Shan Grottoes**, located well away from the Yellow River in the southern hills.

Despite a certain degree of industrialization in modern times, Ningxia remains an underdeveloped area. For visitors, the rural scenes provide the charm of the place, but this province is one of the poorest in the country.

Brief history

Historically, the area within what is now Ningxia has never been a secure one for the Chinese: almost every dynasty built its section of **Great Wall** through here and, in the nineteenth century, the Hui people played an active part in various Muslim rebellions, which were subsequently put down with great ferocity by the Qing authorities. Until recent times, Ningxia's very existence as a separate zone remained an open question; having first appeared on the map in 1928, the region was temporarily subsumed by Gansu in the 1950s before reappearing again in 1958. It appears that the authorities of the People's Republic could not make up their minds whether the Hui population was substantial enough to deserve its own autonomous region, in the same way as the Uyghurs and the Mongols.

Unsurprisingly, the science of **irrigation** is at its most advanced here: two thousand years ago the great founding emperor of China, Qin Shi Huang, sent a hundred thousand men here to dig irrigation channels. To those ancient systems of irrigation, which are still used to farm cereal crops, have now been added ambitious reforestation and desert reclamation projects.

Guyuan

固原, gùyuán

Located in the remote, impoverished southern part of Ningxia province, the town of **GUYUAN** is itself of no special interest. Aside from a ruinous stretch of the **Great Wall** 5km north, built in the Qin dynasty, Guyuan's main tourist function is as a base for visiting the Buddhist grottoes at **Xumi Shan**, a major relic of the Silk Road, curiously marooned far to the north of the favoured route from Lanzhou to Xi'an. In addition, the great Taoist complex of **Kongtong Shan** at Pingliang in Gansu (see p.796) is also only two hours from Guyuan, another possible day-trip.

The Xumi Shan grottoes

须弥山, xūmí shān • Daily 9am–5pm • ¥50

The dramatic **Xumi Shan grottoes** lie about 55km northwest of Guyuan. No fewer than 138 caves have been carved out from the rusty red sandstone cliff-face on five adjoining hillsides, and a large number of statues – primarily from Northern Wei, Sui and Tang dynasties – survive, in a somewhat diminished state. With a beautifully secluded natural backdrop, the grottoes occupy a huge site, the red cliffs and shining tree-covered slopes commanding panoramic views. The last stage of the journey there takes you through one of the remotest corners of rural China where, at the height of summer, you can occasionally see the golden wheat being cut by hand, then spread out over the road to be threshed by passing vehicles.

The caves

The site covered by the **caves** takes at least two hours to walk around. After entering the cliffs area, bear left first for Cave 5 and the **Dafo Lou**, a statue of a giant 20m-high Maitreya Buddha facing due east. Originally this Buddha was protected by a wall that has long since fallen away. Head back to the entrance and you'll see the five hillocks lined up along an approximate east–west axis, each with one key sight and a cluster of caves.

After the Dafo Lou, the second major sight you come to is the **Yuanguang Temple**, a temple housing caves 45, 46 and 48, where statues were built during the North Zhou and Tang dynasties. You'll need to ask the nun to open the caves. Looking at their smoky-coloured surface today, it is hard to imagine that all Buddha statues were once coated in gold. From here you have to cross a bridge and bear left to reach **Xiangguo Temple**, centred around the magnificent Cave 51 with its 5m-high Buddha seated around a central pillar. Returning to the bridge, walk underneath it and up the dry riverbed towards the cliff, to reach **Taohua Dong** (Peach Blossom Cave).

ARRIVAL AND DEPARTURE — GUYUAN

By train Guyuan's train station (固原站, gùyuán zhàn), on the Zhongwei–Baoji line, is on the northeastern edge of town. Note that it can be hard to buy tickets for the single overnight sleeper to Xi'an at short notice; if you're planning on doing this, arrange your departure from Guyuan before you arrive.
Destinations Lanzhou (1 daily; 10hr); Xi'an (4 daily; 7hr 30min–8hr 30min); Yinchuan (7 daily; 5hr 30min–7hr);

Zhongwei (9 daily; 3hr–4hr 30min).
By bus The long-distance bus station is in the west of town but, with the exception of Yinchuan, trains are far more convenient.
Destinations Lanzhou (2 daily; 8hr); Sanying (hourly; 1hr); Xi'an (5 daily; 7hr); Yinchuan (every 30min; 5hr); Zhongwei (3 daily; 4hr).

GETTING AROUND

By bus Bus #1 (¥1) links the train station and the bus station in town. There's one daily direct bus to Xumi Shan, but at the wretchedly inconvenient time of 2pm – you'd have to stay the night. To make a day-trip of it, head from Guyuan to the small town of Sanying (三营, sānyíng),

and tell the driver that you want to see the grottoes. From the drop-off point in Sanying, hire transport for the thirty-minute drive to the caves; a return trip (including 2hr wait while you look around) should cost about ¥100.
By taxi Taxis start at ¥5, and rarely cost much more than that.

ACCOMMODATION AND EATING

There's plenty of **accommodation**, mostly rather insalubrious, outside Guyuan's bus and train stations; and don't expect anything wonderful in terms of **places to eat**. At Xumi Shan, there's a drinks and snacks kiosk at the grottoes' car park, plus basic accommodation if you need to stay the night.

Hongbao 红宝宾馆, hóngbǎo bīnguǎn. 231 Zhongshan Nanlu ☎0954 2066866. Though nothing to write home about, moderately plush rooms make this one

of the more reliable choices in Guyuan, and walkable from the train station if your luggage is light. Mercifully, the noise from the on-site KTV doesn't carry up to the rooms. **¥230**

Zhongwei and around

中卫, zhōngwèi

ZHONGWEI – a mini-city based around a simple crossroads, with a traditional **drum tower** (鼓楼, gǔlóu) at the centre – lies right alongside one of the most curious stretches of the **Yellow River**. Just west of town at **Shapotou**, the waterway can be seen roaring past an expanse of **sand dunes**, providing a rare opportunity to see a river of such size in desert terrain; it's a splendid sight and is definitely worth a visit if you are in the area. The Yellow River has essentially moulded the Zhongwei of today: historically, the old walled city was said to have had no north gate, simply because there was nothing more to the north of here. It remains in a potentially awkward location, between the fickle river to the south and the sandy **Tenger Desert** to the north, but today's Zhongwei is surrounded by a rich belt of irrigated fields, set in a chequerboard grid of straw thatch implanted to hold the sands in place and provide irrigation.

Gao Miao

高庙, gāomiào • A short walk north of the Drum Tower • Daily 8am–7pm • ¥30

Zhongwei itself has one intriguing sight, the **Gao Miao**, a quite extraordinary temple catering for a number of different religions, including Buddhism, Confucianism and Taoism. Originally constructed in the early fifteenth century, and rebuilt many times, the temple is now a magnificent jumble of buildings and styles. From the front entrance you can see dragon heads, columns, stairways and rooftops spiralling up in all directions; the left wing contains vivid sculptures of five hundred *arhats*, while the right wing is a mock hell. Altogether, there are more than 250 temple rooms, towers and pavilions.

Yellow River viewing area

黄河宫, huáng hé gōng • **Viewing area** 24hr • Free • **Museum** Daily 9am–6pm • ¥20 • Taxi from town around ¥15

Closer to the city than Shapotou, and far cheaper to visit, the **Yellow River viewing area** is a fine little escape from central Zhongwei, and a particularly popular sunset-watching spot for local youth. A structure resembling a blue flame sits atop a so-so museum, showcasing relics (the interesting ones are mostly replicas) from sites around the river's course.

Shapotou

沙坡头 • shāpōtóu • ¥100; optional activities extra • Minibus from central Zhongwei (¥5), or taxi ¥30–40; also direct buses from Yinchuan (5 daily; 3hr)

By the banks of the Yellow River 16km west of Zhongwei, **SHAPOTOU** is a tourist resort whose main pleasure is in the contrast between the leafy, shady banks of the river, and the harsh desert that lies just beyond. The resort is a pleasant enough place, with various activities on hand – ferry rides, ziplines over the river, sand-sledding and camel rides. There's very little shade, so bring a hat and sunscreen. There are two main entrances, one to the south, and another high up to the north – the latter is preferable if arriving by taxi, since from here you can slide down a huge sand dune to get to the main resort area. That dune is traversible by cable car, though you can hike up and run down (surprisingly easy) for free. Most people come to Shapotou on a day-trip, but you can easily spend an enjoyable night here at the nearby *Shapo Holiday* (see p.222).

ARRIVAL AND DEPARTURE
ZHONGWEI AND AROUND

By plane Little Zhongwei-Shapotou airport (中卫沙坡头机场, zhōngwèi shāpōtóu jīchǎng) is 9km north of the centre; a taxi into town will cost around ¥25, including the ¥5 fee drivers need to pay to enter the airport complex.
Destinations Beijing (2hr); Xi'an (1hr).

By train Zhongwei's train station (中卫站, zhōngwèi zhàn) is just off the north arm of the city's crossroads, off Renmin Square; most trains on the main Lanzhou–Beijing

rail line call here, while there are also services to Xi'an.
Destinations Guyuan (9 daily; 3hr 20min–4hr 30min); Hohhot (6 daily; 10–13hr); Lanzhou (10 daily; 5–6hr); Wuwei (7 daily; 3hr 30min–6hr 30min); Yinchuan (15 daily; 2hr 15min–3hr).

By bus The long-distance bus station (中卫汽车站, zhōngwèi qìchē zhàn) is 3km east of the centre; walkable, though you can take bus #1 (¥1) or a taxi (¥7). Yinchuan services run frequently, either regular buses or more expensive express coaches that utilize the new highway; there are also five daily direct services linking Yinchuan and Shapotou, which makes it possible to bypass Zhongwei entirely.

Destinations Guyuan (3 daily; 4hr); Wuwei (3 daily; 4hr); Yinchuan (every 30min; 2hr 30min).

GETTING AROUND

By taxi Zhongwei's centre is small enough to walk everywhere, although plenty of taxis – all recently given a desert-yellow makeover – are available to ferry you around. Flag fall is ¥6, and it'll cost at least ¥30 to get to Shapotou.

By minibus Minibuses to Shapotou (¥5) depart when fullish from a point on Changcheng Xijie, just southwest of the train station.

ACCOMMODATION AND EATING

The train station square in **Zhongwei** is alive most evenings with stands peddling barbecued meat; this is the city's most pleasant and atmospheric place to eat, as you sit on a plastic chair overlooking a small stream. Such is the popularity of **Shapotou** that many establishments are fully booked on weekends.

ZHONGWEI

★**East Business** 东商务宾馆, dòng shāngwù bīnguǎn. Changcheng Donglu ☏0955 7033977. This well-run little hotel is superb value for money, its clean rooms a welcome change from the grotty neighbouring options available for similar prices – no wonder it's often fully booked. Cross the square in front of the train station, then turn left before you cross the stream; it's right there. **¥128**

North By Northwest 北偏北国际青年旅舍, běipiān běi guójì qīngnián lǚshè. Xinglong Bei Jie ☏0955 7635060. So-so hostel option with a lobby bar, tolerably clean rooms, and English-speaking staff who can organize trips out into the Tenger Desert. There's a great place for *jianbing* pancakes (¥6) just down the road – lovingly made, they're some of the best in China. Dorms **¥45**, private rooms **¥138**

Qiaoxifu Mianguan 巧媳妇面馆, qiǎoxífù miànguǎn. Changcheng Donglu. One of the first restaurants you'll hit when exiting the train station – it's on the left at the first crossroads – this friendly spot is also one of the only places in town with an English menu (sometimes Spanish has been used instead). This does not include their many excellent noodle dishes, which are on the wall in Chinese only, but does feature a load of tasty local staples – you can fill up for under ¥20, easy peasy. Daily 9.30am–11pm.

Zhongwei 中卫大酒店, zhōngwèi dàjiǔdiàn. Bei Dajie ☏0955 7028444. Plush place offering generous discounts out of season, with fair-sized rooms and decent beds. It's more or less opposite the entrance to the Gao Miao. **¥428**

SHAPOTOU

★**Shapo Holiday** 沙坡头假日酒店, shāpōtóu jiàrì jiǔdiàn. Shapotou ☏0955 7689073. Delightful hotel in a cool and pleasant location near the Shapotou tourist complex, with gardens full of trees and vine trellises. It has well-designed doubles with bath and, despite the tourist draw just down the road, is rarely busy; given the remote location, its tiny, simple restaurant is a pleasant relief. Only open April–Oct, and usually overpriced on accommodation booking engines. **¥388**

Yinchuan

银川, yínchuān

The capital of Ningxia, **YINCHUAN** is a bland modern city possessing little of essential interest bar the Islamic designs incorporated into many of its buildings, some of which pulse with green neon at night. From 1038, however, Yinchuan was capital of the **Western Xia kingdom**, an independent state which survived for less than two hundred years (see box, p.225). It was virtually forgotten about until the early twentieth century, when archeological remains started being recognized for what they were; a visit to their weathered **mausoleums**, some 20km outside the city, is highly recommended.

Yinchuan is frustratingly spread out, and divided into three parts from east to west, though almost everything of interest – bar the excellent regional museum – is in **Xingqing district** (兴庆区, qìngxīng qū), the de facto city centre. The best place to start exploring is around the eastern part of Jiefang Dong Jie, which is dominated by a couple of well-restored, traditionally tiered Chinese towers guarding the main intersections. In time, Yinchuan's main area of interest may shift westwards towards the train station – an area richer and more manicured than Xingqing, but presently a little devoid of focal points.

Yuhuang Pavilion

玉皇阁, yùhuáng gé • Southern end of Yuhuangge Bei Jie; enter from north side • Daily 9am–5pm • Free

The more interesting of the two traditional towers on Jiefang Jie is the 400-year-old **Yuhuang Pavilion**, which can be climbed for pleasant views over the city centre; poke around and you'll also find a two-floor exhibition room, though it contains little of note. The small plaza to the north occasionally hosts music and dance in the evenings.

Nanguan Grand Mosque

南关清真寺, nánguān qīngzhēn sì • Off Yuhuangge Nanlu • Daily 8am–7pm • ¥10, free to Muslims

Nanguan Grand Mosque, the biggest mosque in Yinchuan, is one of the few places in town you'll find Hui in any appreciable numbers. Founded in 1915, it was rebuilt in 1981 after years of damage and neglect during the Cultural Revolution, but now looks something like a leisure centre with minarets. It's located a short walk south of the Yuhuang Pavilion.

Chengtiansi Pagoda

承天寺塔, chéngtiānsì tǎ • Daily 9am–5pm • ¥5, plus ¥20 to climb pagoda

The **Chengtiansi Pagoda**, also known as the West Pagoda, stands in a pleasant, leafy courtyard in the west of Xingqing. A place of worship for Buddhists, this classic Chinese twelve-storey tower was first built around 1050 during the time of the Western Xia; the top six storeys were rebuilt during the Qing dynasty. You can climb the octagonal tower right to the top for excellent views.

4

Ningxia Museum

宁夏博物馆, níngxià bówùguǎn • East side of Renmin Guangchang • Daily 9am–5pm • Free (bring ID) • Bus #102 from Xingqing or train station, or a ¥15 taxi ride from either

Plonked next to Renmin Square, halfway between Xingqing district and the train station, Ningxia's brand-new **Provincial Museum** is a great place to get a handle on Hui culture. A typically huge affair, it has been designed with Islamic motifs aplenty – in fact, when you first sight it over the large concourse, it may well appear to be some kind of large, Brutalist mosque. It contains some interesting English-labelled exhibitions, including relics from the Xia mausoleum (see opposite), a superb display of rock art, and pottery dating back to Silk Road times.

ARRIVAL AND DEPARTURE YINCHUAN

By air Yinchuan's little airport (银川河东国际机场, yínchuān hédōng guójì jīchǎng) lies 15km southeast of Xingqing. Airport buses (¥20) depart from outside the *Ningxia Argent Hotel* on the hour; a taxi into Xingqing will cost more like ¥50.

Destinations Beijing 2hr); Shanghai (3hr 30min); Xi'an (50min).

By train The beautiful, Islamically styled train station (银川站, yínchuān zhàn) is inconveniently sited at the west end of Jinfeng district; a taxi for the 12km run to Xingqing will cost ¥20–30, or take bus #102. Buy tickets in Xingqing at the booking office on Xinhua Xi Jie (daily 9am–6pm), or the office by the airport bus departure point.

Destinations Baotou (8 daily; 6hr); Beijing (6 daily; 12–19hr); Guyuan (7 daily; 6hr 30min–9hr); Hohhot (9 daily; 8–10hr); Lanzhou (5 daily; 7hr –9hr 30min); Xi'an (6 daily; 12–15hr); Zhongwei (15 daily; 2–3hr).

By bus The main long-distance station (银川长途汽车站, yínchuān chángtú qìchēzhàn) is around 5km south of central Xingqing, from where a taxi into town will cost about ¥15–20. It's only really worth heading out this way for express services to Guyuan (every 30min; 5hr), Zhongwei (every 30min; 2hr 30min) and Shapotou (5 daily; 3hr); the bus journey to Xi'an (4 daily; 10hr) is faster than the train, but it's a long haul.

GETTING AROUND

By taxi Taxis start at ¥6, though the city is so spread out that rides can easily hit the ¥20–30 level.

Tours Your accommodation will probably be able to organize tours to Helan Shan and the Western Xia Mausoleums, though one solid bet is the Ningxia Tourism office next to Yuhuang Ge (☏ 0951 7881592), who can get you on a Chinese-language tour to the rock carvings and West Film Studio for ¥328, or the mausoleums and a nearby lake for the same price.

ACCOMMODATION

Accommodation in Yinchuan can be amazingly tight in midsummer: Chinese tourists flock here, and you may end up doing a lot of traipsing around to find a room. It's best to stay in Xingqing district – all places listed below are located in this part of the city.

7 Days Inn 7天连锁酒店, 7 tiān liánsuǒ jiǔdiàn. 27 Limin Jie ☏ 0951 5134555. One of the few chain-cheapies accepting foreigners in central Yinchuan, with a nice location near Chengtiansi Pagoda – you can actually see it from some south-facing rooms, which have the added advantage of being quieter. **¥134**

Hey Traveller Hostel 你好旅人青年旅舍, nǐhǎo lǚrén qīngnián lǚshè. Off Huimin Nanlu, which is itself off Jiefang Dongjie ☏ 0951 2010678. Yinchuan now has plenty of hostels, but this is one of the few in Xingqing. It's a winner, too, with super-low prices, comfy-enough rooms, and a bunch of cool restaurants on the same alley. Dorms **¥50**, twins **¥98**

Holiday Inn 假日酒店, jiàrì jiǔdiàn. 141 Jiefang Xijie ☏ 0951 7800000, ⊚ holidayinn.com. By far the best hotel in central Yinchuan, a modern affair with an airy lobby and stylish rooms, some of which feature music docks and speakers. There's a swimming pool on site, too, and the price is fair. **¥700**

Yinquan 银泉大酒店, yínquán dàjiǔdiàn. 157 Shengli Jie ☏ 0951 3999888. A good-value place near the mosque. Rooms are quiet, and there's a rather excellent hotpot restaurant on the ground floor. **¥288**

EATING

Yinchuan's culinary scene is pretty poor. Your best bet is probably finding a **hotpot restaurant**, though there's plenty of **fast food** – Chinese and Western – on Gulou Nanjie, a mainly pedestrianized road running south of the drum tower.

THE WESTERN XIA KINGDOM

The ancient **Western Xia kingdom** (1038–1227 AD) encompassed a vast expanse of land, overlapping regions of what is now Ningxia, Gansu and Shaanxi provinces. Established by the nomadic Dangxiang clan of Qiang ancestry, the kingdom had twelve kings and developed its own **written language**, which combines influences from Mongolian, Tibetan and Chinese. The Western Xia territory survived prior to independence by playing off the Song or Liao dynasties against each other. In 1038, **Li Yuanhao**, leader of Western Xia, was militarily powerful enough to oppose Song jurisdiction and thus this third kingdom was created. A prosperous period ensued as the kingdom benefited from controlling the trade routes into Central Asia. The new era saw a time of great **cultural development**, a state academy was erected, and future officials took Confucian examinations. Less emphasis, however, was placed on military matters, and in 1227 the Western Xia were obliterated by the Mongol empire of **Genghis Khan**.

Café Bene 咖啡陪你, kāfēi péinǐ. Jiefang Xijie. Korean café chains are huge business in China at the moment, even this far into the hinterland – good coffees, large (and slightly odd-looking) desserts, free wi-fi and a mellow atmosphere make this a nice place to while away an hour. Daily 10am–10pm.

★**Ningxia Labour Union Hotel** 宁夏工会大厦, níngxià gōnghuì dàshà. Zhongshan Nanjie ☎0951 5162222. Hotpot restaurants can be a little tricky for those unable to read Chinese, so hooray for this buffet venue, which allows you to simply grab whatever you want – it's all pretty high quality, too. It costs ¥49 for lunch and ¥59 for dinner, plus a ¥20 deposit refundable to those able to finish what they've taken. Daily 11.30am–2pm & 5.30–9pm.

Pizza and Steak 比格比萨, bǐgé bǐsà. Gulou Nanjie ☎0951 5111117. There's no shame indulging in some Western food if you've made it as far as Ningxia. This restaurant is better value than the *Pizza Hut* down the road; it's ¥55 per person for a pizza-and-salad-bar buffet, and around the same to have a large pizza made fresh. Daily 10am–2pm & 5–10pm.

★**Zen Theme** 吾悠需, wú yōu xū. Zhongshan Nanjie ☎0951 7885188. An astonishingly attractive restaurant, standing proud like a gem in gritty Xingqing – despite the presence of Yinchuan's best-dressed waitresses, you can still fill up for under ¥20 if you really want to. The food on the picture menu is best described as contemporary Chinese – try some of the silky tofu dishes, or opt for one of the many veggie choices. Daily 9.30am–9.30pm.

Western Xia Mausoleums

西夏王陵, xīxià wánglíng • Daily 8am–6pm • ¥95

The **Western Xia Mausoleums**, about 10km west of Yinchuan's sprawl and thus around 40km west of Xingqing district, stand as monuments to the nine kings of Western Xia (see box above). The site is spectacular and atmospheric, with towering, haystack-shaped piles of brown mud bricks, slowly disintegrating and punctuating the view around the Helan Mountain range. The entrance fee includes transport within the complex to the museum, figure gallery and the biggest mausoleum of the nine. Interesting items in the museum include the original pieces of the Lishi pillar support and some terracotta bird ornaments with human faces.

ARRIVAL AND DEPARTURE ‖ WESTERN XIA MAUSOLEUMS

By minibus and taxi Getting here from Yinchuan's Xingqing district is either expensive or difficult. If you favour the expensive option, just grab a cab – drivers will start the bidding at ¥200 (or more) one-way, though you should be able to get them down to ¥250 return, including waiting time. Alternatively, green and red buses (no number, though with Xixia written on the front) run from a stop just east of Nanmen Square; these cost just ¥2, though they take up to 2hr to reach the tombs. Finally, you could split the difference and take a bus to Xixia district (1hr; ¥1), from which it's a far cheaper taxi-ride to the ruins (around ¥25 each way).

Helan Shan

贺兰山, hèlán shān

The rugged **Helan Shan** range rises up behind the Western Xia Mausoleums, and races away to the north, where there are a number of sights on and around the eastern (ie,

---

YELLOW RIVER MERLOT

Although beer and *bai jiu* are still the national drinks of choice, China's wine market has ballooned in recent years – the country is already the world's largest consumer of **red wine**, with locals throwing back almost two billion bottles per year. A high proportion of those come from the established Old World and New World wine countries, but China is rapidly fashioning a new New World market sector. At first glance, there appear to be few similarities between Ningxia and Napa Valley, but the eastern slopes of Helan Shan are now pumping out some of Asia's best wines – there are over two hundred wineries in Ningxia province, and it's somewhat dizzying to think that this is merely the beginning.

Yinchuan-facing) slopes. Of most interest here is a series of wonderful **rock carvings**, while there's also ample opportunity for **hiking** in a couple of park areas. Sights listed here run north to south, from the mountain range's main access point; Yinchuan starts about 20km to the southeast, and the Xingqing district another 20km further along.

The rock carvings

贺兰山岩画, hèlánshān yánhuà · Daily 8am–6pm · ¥70, including ride from entrance

The **rock carvings** here date back to the early Neolithic period – some have been dated to just under 10,000 years of age. There are over 1500 here, set in a pretty valley, though only a few are on view to tourists; the images of hunting, animals and Neolithic faces are quite wonderful, and the mind boggles at how many generations have passed since their creation.

Suyukou National Park

苏峪口国家公园, sūyùkǒu guójiā gōngyuán · April–Oct ¥60, Nov–March ¥40 · Cable car ¥30 each way

About 7km south of the rock art galleries is **Suyukou National Park**, an expanse of pine trees that's home to the Helan range's best hiking trails – swaths of pine forest, with wonderful vistas of the flat Yinchuan area to the east. You can hike way up to the peak of Helan Shan, though these days most prefer to take the cable car.

Baisikou Shuang Ta

拜寺口双塔, bàisìkǒu shuāng tǎ · Daily 8am–5pm · ¥10

Located 14km south of Suyukou are the **Baisikou Shuang Ta**, a pair of 12m-high pagodas guarding a pass. You won't stay here for too long, but the towers – set a short distance away from each other – are highly photogenic, jutting from the ground like giant pencils with the Helan Shan range rippling away behind.

West Film Studio

镇北堡西部影视城, zhènběibǎo xībù yǐngshìchéng · Daily 8am–6pm · ¥100 · Bus #16 from Nanmen Square, or #17 from train station

East of the Helan mountain range, and easily visited on the way back, is the **China West Film Studio** where the film *Red Sorghum*, directed by Zhang Yimou, was shot (see box, p.962). The stunning film depicts village life in northwest China during the period leading up to World War II – in part a rural idyll, in part a brute struggle to survive. The scenes of dry, dusty hillsides alternating with the lush fields of sorghum are a fair record of how parts of Ningxia still look today. The studio itself is immensely popular with Chinese tourists, who flock to take pictures of each other in and around faux-dynastic buildings.

ARRIVAL AND DEPARTURE HELAN SHAN

By bus and taxi Bus #16 from Nanmen Square, or #17 from train station, only go as far as the film studios. You could board one of these, then try to cab it from there to the other sights – it'll save you a bit of money. From Xingqing it'll cost at least ¥350 to hire a driver for a half-day.

Inner Mongolia

内蒙古, nèi měnggǔ

Mongolia is an almost total mystery to the outside world, its very name synonymous with remoteness. Landlocked between the two Asian giants of Russia and China, it seemed to have been doomed to obscurity, trapped in a hopeless environment of fleeting summers and interminable, bitter winters. And yet, seven hundred years ago the people of this benighted land suddenly burst out of their frontiers, and for a century subjugated and terrorized almost all of the Eurasian landmass.

Visitors to the **Inner Mongolia Autonomous Region** will not necessarily find many signs of this today. The modern-day heirs of the Mongol hordes are not only placid – quietly going about their business of shepherding, herding horses and entertaining tourists – but, even here, are vastly outnumbered by the Han Chinese (by almost nineteen million to fewer than four million). In addition, this is, and always has been, a sensitive border area, and there are still restrictions on the movements of tourists in some places.

Nevertheless, traces of the "real" Mongolia remain, in terms of both landscape and people – and not just the **Mongol script**, a vertical rarity in global terms, used

KUBLAI KHAN

In Xanadu did Kubla Khan
A stately pleasure-dome decree…   Samuel Taylor Coleridge

4

Immortalized not only in the poetry of Coleridge but also in the memoirs of Marco Polo, **Kublai Khan** (1215–94) – known to the Chinese as Yuan Shizu – is the only emperor popularly known by name to the outside world. And little wonder: as well as mastering the subtle statecraft required to govern China as a foreigner, this grandson of Genghis Khan commanded an **empire** that encompassed the whole of China, Central Asia, southern Russia and Persia – a larger area of land than perhaps anyone in history has ruled over, before or since. And yet this king of kings had been born into a nomadic tribe which had never shown the slightest interest in political life, and which, until shortly before his birth, was almost entirely illiterate.

From the beginning, Kublai Khan had shown an unusual talent for politics and government. He managed to get himself elected **Khan of the Mongols** in 1260, despite considerable opposition from the so-called "steppe aristocracy" who feared his disdain for traditional Mongolian skills. He never learned to read or write Chinese, yet after audaciously establishing himself as **Emperor of China**, proclaiming the Yuan dynasty in 1271, he soon saw the value of surrounding himself with advisers steeped in Confucianism. This was what enabled him to set up one hundred thousand Mongols in power over perhaps two hundred million Chinese. As well as **reunifying China** after centuries of division under the Song, Kublai Khan's contributions include establishing **paper money** as the standard medium of exchange, and fostering the **development of religion**, Lamaist Buddhism in particular. Above all, under his rule China experienced a brief period of **cosmopolitanism** which saw not only foreigners such as Marco Polo promoted to high positions of responsibility, but also a final flowering of the old Silk Road trade, as well as large numbers of Arab and Persian traders settling in seaports around Quanzhou in southeastern China.

Ironically, however, it was his admiration for the culture, arts, religion and sophisticated bureaucracy of China – as documented so enthusiastically by Marco Polo – that aroused bitter hostility from his own people, the Mongols, who despised what they saw as a betrayal of the ways of Genghis Khan. Kublai Khan was troubled by skirmishing nomads along the Great Wall just as much as his more authentically Chinese predecessors, forcing the abandonment of **Xanadu** – in Inner Mongolia, near the modern city of Duolun – his legendary summer residence immortalized in Coleridge's poem *Kubla Khan*. Today virtually nothing of the site remains.

alongside Chinese throughout the province. Dotting the region are enormous areas of **grassland**, gently undulating plains stretching to the horizon and still used by nomadic peoples as pastureland for their horses. Tourists are able to visit the grasslands and even stay with the Mongols in their yurts, though the only simple way to do this is on an **organized tour** out of the regional capital **Hohhot** – an experience rather short on authenticity. If you don't find what you are looking for in the Hohhot area, however, a whole vast swath of Mongol territory lies across the border in Dongbei province, much of it untouched by Western tourists (see p.188).

Brief history

One man's name is synonymous with unleashing Mongol armies on an unsuspecting world: the great **Genghis Khan** (1162–1227), under whose rule much of China and pretty much the whole of Central Asia were conquered (see p.929). After his immediate successors had wrested control of eastern Europe, Mongol forces were poised in 1241 to make the relatively short final push across Europe, when a message came from deep inside Asia that the invasion was to be cancelled. The decision to spare western Europe cleared the way for the **final conquest of China** instead.

The Yuan dynasty

By 1271 the Mongols had established their own dynasty in China – the **Yuan**. It was the first time the country had come under foreign rule, and the Yuan is still an era about which Chinese historians can find little good to say, though the empire was expanded considerably by incorporating Yunnan and Tibet for the first time. The magnificent zenith of the dynasty was achieved under **Kublai Khan** (see box, p.227), as documented in Marco Polo's *The Travels* (see p.966). Ironically, however, the Mongols were able to sustain their power only by becoming Sinicized, and abandoning the traditional nomadic Mongol way of life. Kublai Khan and his court soon forgot the warrior skills of their forefathers, and in 1368, after less than a century on the imperial throne, the Yuan were **driven out of China** by the rising Ming dynasty. The Mongols returned to Mongolia, and reverted to their former ways, hunting, fighting among themselves and occasionally skirmishing with the Chinese down by the Wall.

Post-Khan decline

Thereafter, Mongolian history moves gradually downhill, though right into the eighteenth century they maintained at least nominal control over many of the lands won by Genghis Khan. These included **Tibet**, from where **Lamaist Buddhism** was imported to become the dominant religion in Mongolia. Over the years, as well, came **settlers** from other parts of Asia: there is now a sizeable Muslim minority in the region, and under the Qing many Chinese settlers moved in too, escaping overpopulation and famine at home, a trend that has continued under the Communists. The incoming settlers tried ploughing up the grassland with disastrous ecological results – wind and water swept the soil away – and the Mongols withdrew to the hills. Only recently has a serious programme of land stabilization and reclamation been established.

Recent history

Sandwiched between two imperial powers, Mongolia found its independence constantly threatened. The Russians set up a protectorate over the north, while the rest effectively came under the control of China. In the 1930s, Japan occupied much of eastern Inner Mongolia as part of Manchukuo, and the Chinese Communists also maintained a strong presence. In 1945 Stalin persuaded Chiang Kai-shek to recognize the independence of **Outer Mongolia** under Soviet protection as part of the Sino-Soviet anti-Japanese treaty, effectively sealing the fate of what then became the Mongolian People's Republic. In 1947, **Inner Mongolia** was designated the first autonomous region of the People's Republic of China.

Baotou and around

包头, bāotóu

Tell a Chinese that you're off to **BAOTOU**, and you'll most likely receive a wide-eyed *"wei shenme!?"* ("why on earth?") in response. Inner Mongolia's biggest and bleakest city, it has long been famed as China's nerve centre for iron and steel production, and many travellers – even those just passing through on a train – have been enthralled by the sight of satanic fires burning in the great blast furnaces. Things have improved in recent years, with many of those furnaces being moved out of town, and a significant reduction in the purple and green sunsets often produced by a sky full of metallic particulate matter. The city has been hard at work tidying itself up – while much of Baotou still exudes a Soviet ugliness, and there's still precious little to actually see or do, the area around the almost absurdly large **A'erding Square** has recently been subject to mall-and-café gentrification, and looks quite attractive.

The city's best use for the traveller, however, remains its springboard status to a couple of distant sights – **Wudangzhao**, an attractive Tibetan-style monastery, and the purported mausoleum of **Genghis Khan**.

Inner Mongolia Museum

内蒙古博物馆, nèi měnggǔ bówùguǎn • A'erding Dajie • Tues–Sun 9am–5pm • Free • Bus #1 from train station, or an easy walk from A'erding Square

Compared with other provincial museums, most of which are giant, gleaming structures, the **Inner Mongolia Museum** is decidedly shabby – nevertheless, and despite a total absence of English captioning, it still constitutes the most worthwhile sight in Baotou. The first floor features Yuan-dynasty relics from the nearby site of Yanjialing, and local treasures from other nearby areas; a few pieces feature designs which, if not conclusively Mongolian, are at least not distinctively Chinese. The second floor, and part of the first, feature temporary exhibition halls; frustratingly for travellers to the region (and perhaps a fair few locals), they're usually used to showcase the delights of other, non-Mongolian, Chinese minority groups.

The Yellow River

黄河, huáng hé • Bus #18 (¥2) from Baotou East station; taxi from Baotou station ¥20

The main sight in the immediate vicinity of Baotou (about 8km away) is the **Yellow River**, worth having a look at, if only to ruminate on its historical significance; as seen from the park-like viewing point, the river here is around 1km wide, shallow, sluggish and chocolate brown. When the Chinese built the Great Wall far to the south, the area between the Inner Mongolian loop of the Yellow River and the Wall became known as the **Ordos**, and remained the dominion of the nomad. To the Chinese, however, the Yellow River seemed like the logical northern limit of China. The Qing eventually decided matters once and for all not only by seizing control of the Ordos, but also by moving north of the river into the heart of Mongolia. Today, the whole Yellow River region, from Yinchuan in Ningxia province up to Baotou and across to Hohhot, is thoroughly irrigated and productive land – without the river, it would be pure desert.

BAOTOU ORIENTATION

A colossal city, Baotou comprises three main areas: **Donghe** (东河, dōnghé), the ramshackle, oldest part of town, to the east; west lies the pleasant shopping and residential area of **Qingshan** (青山, qīngshān); and, further west again, the iron- and steelworks at **Kundulun** (昆都仑, kūndūlún). Qingshan is bisected by A'erding Jie, a wide road which zooms straight as an arrow to A'erding Square – empty, with little of note on its periphery and vast to the point of ridicule, it's beautiful in a very strange way.

Wudangzhao

五当召, wǔdāng zhào • Daily 8am–5pm • ¥60 • Bus #7 (¥10) from East train station to Shiguai (石拐, shíguǎi), then taxi (¥100 return) for the final 25km; round-trip taxi hire from Baotou about ¥400 • Tours from Baotou around ¥240 per person

Set in a pretty, narrow valley about 70km northeast of Baotou, **Wudangzhao** is the best-preserved Lamaist monastery still functioning in Inner Mongolia, one of the results of the Mongolian conquest of Tibet in the thirteenth century. For centuries afterwards, the roads between Tibet and Mongolia were worn by countless pilgrims and wandering monks bringing Lamaist Buddhism to Mongolia. This particular monastery, of the Yellow Sect, was established in 1749 and at its height housed 1200 lamas. Seven generations of Living Buddhas were based here, the ashes of whom are kept in one of the halls. Today, however, the few remaining monks are greatly outnumbered by tourists from Baotou, and sadly their main duties now seem to involve hanging around at the hall entrances to check tourists' tickets.

Beyond the monastery you can hike off into the surrounding hills and, if you're keen, you should be able to **stay** in the pilgrims' hostel in the monastery as well.

Genghis Khan's Mausoleum

成吉思汗陵园, chéngjísīhàn língyuán • Daily 8am–7pm • ¥120 • Early bus or train from Baotou to Dongsheng (东胜, dōngshèng), then bus to mausoleum (1hr)

The first thing to be said about **Genghis Khan's Mausoleum** – around 150km south of Baotou – is that it's not all it's cracked up to be: it probably isn't the tomb of Genghis Khan, and it isn't a particularly attractive place anyway, but nonetheless it provides a fascinating insight into the modern cult of the famous warrior.

Special **sacrificial ceremonies** take place here four times a year on certain days of the lunar calendar – the fifteenth day of the third lunar month, the fifteenth day of the fifth lunar month, the twelfth day of the ninth month and the third day of the tenth month. On these occasions, Mongolian monks lead solemn rituals that involve piling up cooked sheep before the statue of the Khan. The ceremonies are attended not only by local

GENGHIS KHAN

Genghis Khan (1162–1227) was born, ominously enough, with a clot of blood in his hand. Under his leadership, the Mongols erupted from their homeland to ravage the whole of Asia, butchering millions, razing cities and laying waste to all the land from China to eastern Europe. It was his proud boast that his destruction of cities was so complete that he could ride across their ruins by night without the least fear of his horse stumbling.

Even before Genghis exploded onto the scene, the nomadic Mongols had long been a thorn in the side of the city-dwelling Chinese. Construction of the **Great Wall** had been undertaken to keep these two fundamentally opposed societies apart. But it was always fortunate for the Chinese that the early nomadic tribes of Mongolia fought as much among themselves as they did against outsiders. Genghis Khan's achievement was to weld together the warring nomads into a fighting force the equal of which the world had never seen: the secret of his success was skilful **cavalry tactics**, acquired from long practice in the saddle on the wide-open Mongolian plains. Frequently his armies would rout forces ten or twenty times their size.

Led by Genghis, the Mongols unleashed a massive onslaught on China in 1211. The Great Wall proved no obstacle, and with two hundred thousand men in tow Genghis cut a swath across northwest China towards Beijing. It was not all easy progress, however – so great was the destruction wrought in northern China that **famine and plague** broke out, afflicting the invader as much as the invaded. Genghis Khan himself died (of injuries sustained in falling from his horse) before the **capture of China** had been completed. His body was carried back to Mongolia by a funeral cortege of ten thousand, who murdered every man and beast within 16km of the road so that news of the Great Khan's death could not be reported before his sons and viceroys had been gathered from the farthest corners of his dominions. The whereabouts of his **tomb** is uncertain, though according to one of the best-known stories his ashes are in the mausoleum outside Dongsheng (see above).

people, but also by pilgrims from the Republic of Mongolia itself – whatever the truth about the location of his burial place, the popular view among Mongolians is that this is a holy site. The side halls, all very pretty, have ceremonial yurts, altars, burning incense, hanging paintings and Mongolian calligraphy, and offerings as though to a god.

Some history

Genghis Khan is known to have died in northern China, but while his funeral cortege may have passed through this region on its way back to Mongolia, the story that the wheels of his funeral cart got stuck in the mud here, resulting in his burial on the spot, is almost certainly apocryphal. At best, scholars believe, the site contains a few of the warrior's relics. The real tomb is thought to be on the slopes of Burkhan Khaldun, in the Hentei mountains, not far to the east of Ulaan Baatar in Outer Mongolia. The reason it came to be so strongly believed that the Khan was buried here in China appears to be that the tribe who were charged with guarding the real sepulchre eventually drifted down across the Yellow River to the Ordos – but continued to claim the honour of being the official guardians of the tomb.

The mausoleum

The main part of the cement mausoleum is formed by halls shaped like Mongolian yurts. The connecting corridors are adorned with bizarre murals supposedly depicting the life of Genghis Khan – though note the women in Western dress (1890s-style). In the middle of the main hall stands a 5m-high marble **statue** of Genghis before a map of his empire.

The museum and relics

There's a small, free **museum** by the mausoleum ticket office with a few alleged **relics**, which have a murky political history. Several times they have been removed, and later returned, the most recent occasion being during World War II, when the Japanese seized them. Apparently the Japanese had plans to set up a puppet Mongol state, centred around a Genghis Khan shrine. They even drew up plans for an elaborate mausoleum to house them – plans that were then commandeered by the Chinese Communists who, having safely returned the relics from a hiding place in Qinghai, built the mausoleum for themselves in 1955 as a means of currying favour with the Mongolian people.

ARRIVAL AND DEPARTURE

BAOTOU AND AROUND

By air Baotou's airport (包头机场, bāotóu jīchǎng) is just 2km south of Baotou East train station. Taxis will take you into town for ¥20–40, but it can be hard to persuade drivers to use the meter.

Destinations Beijing (55min); Shanghai (2hr 25min); Xi'an (1hr 15min).

By train There are two major train stations: Baotou station (包头站, bāotóu zhàn) to the west, and Baotou East (包头东站, bāotóu dōngzhàn) over 20km down the line. Almost all through-trains stop at both stations (times given here are from the main station), and there's now a

high-speed service to Hohhot. Train ticket booking offices can be found all around town.

Destinations Beijing (13 daily; 8–14hr); Dongsheng (11 daily; 1hr 10min); Hohhot (2–4 hourly; 1–2hr); Lanzhou (3 daily; 15hr); Yinchuan (7 daily; 6–7hr).

By bus The city's main bus station (包头长途汽车站, bāotóu chángtú qìchēzhàn) is within walking distance of the East train station; you'll only really need this station to get to Dongsheng (every 30min; 1hr 30min) for Genghis Khan's Mausoleum, or Shiguai (hourly; 1hr) for Wudangzhao.

GETTING AROUND AND TOURS

By bus The three parts of the city are well connected by frequent buses (¥2), which take 30–40min to travel between Donghe and Kundulun.

By taxi Fares begin at ¥6.5 for the first 3km, charging ¥1.5 per additional kilometre. Traversing Baotou, this can add up quickly.

Tours Most hotels can get you on a tour to Wudangzhao or the mausoleum, but staff at the *Header* hotel (see p.232) are usually easiest to deal with, and their prices are fair – about ¥260 per person (minimum of two) to either, or a little more for trips including a short desert tour.

ACCOMMODATION AND EATING

Of the two ends of town, **Donghe** is the more convenient place to stay for trips to Genghis Khan's mausoleum, though sadly there isn't much choice here. **Kundulun** has far more choice, and makes a more appealing place to stay. Baotou isn't famous for its cuisine, and **restaurants** here are average to say the least.

DONGHE

West Lake 西湖宾馆, xīhú bīnguǎn. 10 Nanmenwai Dajie ☎0472 4187101. The best of the limited options in this part of town. From the train station, walk straight up Nanmenwai Dajie; the hotel is on the right, before the intersection with Bayan Tala Dajie. **¥248**

KUNDULUN

Donghao 东皓酒店, dōnghào jiǔdiàn. Building 36, Hualijiazu ☎0472 5359999. Good-value cheapie near the museum. Don't be fooled by the drab exterior, since the rooms here are a cut above those you'll usually find at this price level, with warm tones, tidy bathrooms and a kettle for making your morning cup of green tea. **¥138**

★**Haide** 海德酒店, hǎidé jiǔdiàn. 56 Gangtie Dajie ☎0472 5365555, ⓦhd-hotel.com.cn. Sometimes known as the *Header*, this is an upmarket option with a high standard of service and facilities – sauna, spa and pool included. There's now substantial competition at the higher end in Baotou, so prices here are about half of what they should be; you'll most likely pay over the odds if using an international booking engine. **¥400**

Little Sheep Hot Pot 小肥羊, xiǎoféiyáng. Off southeast corner of A'erding Square. One of the only notable places to eat in the centre of town, this hotpot place is hugely busy at mealtimes, despite the over-high prices. You'll end up paying up to ¥100 per person for meat, tofu, veg and noodles. Daily 11am–11pm.

Shenhua International 神华国际大酒店, shénhuá guójì dàjiǔdiàn. 17 Shaoxian Lu ☎0472 5368888. A tall edifice a block to the southeast of A'erding Square, a professionally run outfit with its own pool, sauna and gym. Rooms are quite lovely, with soft duvets and good carpets – after you've settled in for a couple of hours here it can be quite a surprise to see the ugly city lurking out of the window. **¥450**

Hohhot

呼和浩特, hūhéhàotè

By far the most interesting and liveable city in Inner Mongolia, **HOHHOT** just about manages to live up to its Mongolian name – "green city" – with a series of tree-lined roads and boulevards. Founded under the khanate in the sixteenth century, its population has ballooned to almost three million, almost 90 percent of them Han Chinese. You won't find too much Mongolian culture here, but there are some charming historical buildings in the southwestern part of the city centre – an area recently subject to extensive gentrification along dynastic lines, though already falling into disrepair.

Brief history

There has been a settlement at Hohhot since the Ming dynasty, though it did not become the capital of Inner Mongolia until 1952. Until relatively modern times, it was a small town centred on a number of **Buddhist temples**. The temples are still here, and it's also worthwhile tracking down the vanishing **Mongol** districts, not least to try some of their distinctive food. The other reason for visiting Hohhot is its proximity to some of the famous Mongolian **grasslands** within a 100km radius of the city.

> ### NAADAM IN HOHHOT
>
> Summer is a good time to be in Hohhot, coinciding as it does with Mongolia's famed **Naadam festival**. Shows of horsemanship, wrestling and other games take place at the gigantic **Inner Mongolia horse racecourse**, 2km north of the train station; built in the shape of two circular Mongolian yurts, adjacent and connected to each other to form the elongated shape of a stadium, it's the biggest racecourse in China by far. The dates vary, but Naadam usually falls between late July and early August. Outside the holiday, displays of Mongolian riding and dancing sometimes take place here too.

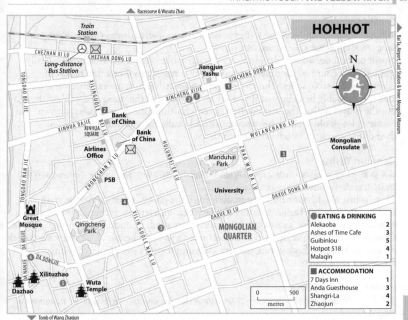

Dazhao

大召, dàzhāo • Da Nanjie; entrance on south side of complex • Daily 8am–6.30pm • ¥35 • Bus #6, #7 or #8 from the train station; taxi around ¥25

Constructed in 1579, and recently the subject of a typically gaudy renovation, the **Dazhao** temple was dedicated in the late seventeenth century to the famous Qing emperor Kangxi – a gold tablet with the words "Long Live the Emperor" was set before the silver statue of Sakyamuni, and in the main hall murals depicting the visit of Kangxi can still be seen.

Xilituzhao

席力图召, xílìtúzhào • Da Nanjie; entrance on south side of complex • Daily 8am–6.30pm • ¥30 • Bus #6, #7 or #8 from the train station; taxi around ¥25

East of Dazhao, and a temple of similar scale and layout, **Xilituzhao** dates from the same era, though it too has been restored. The dagoba is interesting for featuring Sanskrit writing above Chinese dragons above Tibetan-style murals. Since 1735 this has been the official residence of the reincarnation of Hohhot's Living Buddha, who is in charge of Buddhist affairs in the city.

Wuta Temple

五塔寺, wǔtǎ sì • Wutasi Qianjie; entrance on south side of complex • Daily 8.30am–5.30pm • ¥35

Around 1km east of the Dazhao temple, the **Wuta Temple** was built in 1727, in an Indian style, and remains Hohhot's most attractive piece of architecture. This composite of five pagodas originally belonged to the Ci Deng Temple, which no longer exists. It's relatively small, but its walls are engraved with no fewer than 1563 Buddhas, all in slightly different postures. Currently stored inside the pagoda building is a rare, antique Mongolian cosmological map that marks the position of hundreds of stars.

Great Mosque

清真大寺, qīngzhēn dàsì • Zhongshan Lu • Open from first to last prayers • Free • Only Muslims allowed inside prayer halls • Bus #6, #7 or #8 from the train station, or around ¥20 by taxi

North of the Dazhao temple, Hohhot's attractive black-brick **Great Mosque** is easily spotted on account of its minaret, topped with a pagoda roof in a fine fusion of Chinese and Arabic styles. The Hui people who worship here are extremely friendly, and will probably be delighted if you ask to look around the mosque complex (though not the prayer halls). The surrounding streets constitute the Muslim area of town, and besides a lot of old men with wispy beards and skullcaps, you'll find a good – if dwindling – array of noodle and kebab shops.

Jiangjun Yashu

将军衙署, jiāngjūn yáshǔ • Xincheng Xijie • Daily April–Oct 8am–7pm; Nov & March, 9am–5pm; Dec–Feb 9am–3pm • ¥25 • Bus #3 (¥1) from the train station, or around ¥10 by taxi

There is just one historic building marooned in the part of town east of the train station: the **Jiangjun Yashu**, a former military headquarters, even though it looks like a temple. Now it's a tiny museum with some bizarre modern Buddhist art mingling with Qing office furniture at the back. The best reason to come here is to see the scale model of ancient Hohhot, back before the city walls and temples were replaced with boulevards and banks.

Inner Mongolia Museum

内蒙古博物馆, nèiménggǔ bówùguǎn • Off Xinhua Donglu • Tues–Sun 9am–5pm • Free (bring ID) • Bus #3; taxi from train station ¥25

Some 6km east of the Jiangjun Yashu, the new **Inner Mongolia Museum** is infinitely better than its counterpart in Baotou (see p.229). Even before you get in, you'll be struck by the space-age architecture's swooping roofs, with a small tract of grassland (the Mongol connection) racing up to meet them. The museum's curators are still experimenting with the layout, though the pick of the exhibits includes a tremendous display of **ethnic Mongolian items**, such as costumes, saddles, long leather coats and cummerbunds, as well as hunting and sporting implements, including hockey sticks and balls. There's also a good **paleontology** display, with complete fossils of a woolly rhinoceros and a sizeable dinosaur. Then there are the halls dedicated to the **Khans**, with interesting maps and objects outlining the exploits of Genghis Khan and the huge Mongol empire of the thirteenth century.

ARRIVAL AND DEPARTURE | HOHHOT

By air Hohhot's Baita airport (呼和浩特白塔国际机场, hūhéhàotè báitǎ guójì jīchǎng) lies 35km east of the city, and airport bus route #1 (30min; ¥15) drops arriving passengers outside the *Zhaojun Hotel* (see opposite). A taxi costs around ¥50.

Destinations Beijing (1hr 10min); Shanghai (2hr 30min); Xi'an (1hr 30min).

By train Hohhot's station (呼和浩特站, hūhéhàotè zhàn), to the north of the city centre, has good connections east and west, as well as trains across the border to Ulaan Baatar in Outer Mongolia (see box, p.236). The station ticket office is often hideously crowded (and the whole area plain hideous), but dedicated rail offices around town can procure tickets for a ¥5 commission; ask at your hotel for the nearest. There's also an East station (呼和浩特东站,

hūhéhàotè dōngzhàn) 12km up the track; though this will be of little use to travellers until high-speed services commence, some trains only stop here, so be careful when purchasing your ticket to Hohhot.

Main station destinations Baotou (many daily; 1–2hr); Beijing (10 daily; 6–11hr); Datong (10 daily; 3hr 30min–4hr 30min); Taiyuan (2 daily; 10hr); Xi'an (5 daily; 13–15hr); Yinchuan (2 daily; 8hr 30min).

By bus The main long-distance station (呼和浩特长途汽车站, hūhéhàotè chángtú qìchēzhàn), right outside the train station exit on the west, is useful for services to Datong (every 30min; 2hr 30min), which are faster than the train, and Xilamuren (hourly; 2hr) for the grasslands. Coming into town, you may also rock up at one of two depots off the main road to the west.

GETTING AROUND AND TOURS

By bus The local bus network is a bit of a nightmare, but the #1, #6, #7 or #8, which head from the train station area to sights in the west part of town, can be useful.

By taxi The minimum fare is ¥8, though traffic and distance mean that the meter regularly ticks over the ¥20 level.

Tours There are numerous travel agents in town, mostly dealing in grassland tours. However, you're advised to go with *Anda* hostel (see below), who not only have fair prices with no hidden add-ons, but run tours tailored to foreign, rather than domestic, tourists.

ACCOMMODATION

7 Days Inn 7天连锁酒店, 7 tiān liánsuǒ jiǔdiàn. 24 Xinhua Lu ☏ 0471 6655077. Few of Hohhot's cheap chain hotels accept foreigners, but this one does and has a highly convenient location to boot, a short cab-ride from the train station and surrounded by good restaurants. ¥129

★**Anda Guesthouse** 安达宾馆, āndá bīnguǎn. Qiaokou Xijie ☏ 0471 6918039, ⓦ andaguesthouse .com. Friendly little youth hostel, with cheap dorm beds and pleasant private rooms. The Mongolian owner is a fountain of local knowledge, and will be able to rustle up a tailor-made grasslands trip in no time. The hostel is almost impossible to find independently – call ahead for a free train station pick-up. Dorms ¥60, rooms ¥180

★**Shangri-La** 香格里拉酒店, xiānggélǐlā jiǔdiàn. Xilinguole Nanlu ☏ 0471 3366888, ⓦ shangri-la.com. You'll have to travel for hundreds of kilometres to find better rooms – this is Hohhot's plushest hotel, with superb standards of service, a scented lobby, and great views from the higher floors. ¥1288

Zhaojun 昭君大酒店, zhāojūn dàjiǔdiàn. 69 Xinhua Dajie ☏ 0471 6668850. A well-organized and comfortable place in the centre of town, diagonally across from Xinhua Square. The travel service in the lobby has information in English on their grassland and Genghis Khan Mausoleum tours. ¥320

EATING

The highlight of eating in Hohhot is dining on **Mongolian food**, best experienced in the Mongolian quarter south of the university. For an excellent breakfast or lunch, order a large bowl of sugary milk tea, along with *chaomi* (buckwheat), *huangyou* (butter), *nailao* (hard white cheese) and *naipi* (a sweetish, biscuit-like substance formed from the skin of boiled milk). Toss everything into the tea, and eat it with chopsticks – it's surprisingly delicious.

Alekaoba 阿乐烤吧, ālè kǎobā. Xincheng Xijie ☏ 0471 6967510. Occasionally raucous restaurant serving a mix of Chinese and Korean food. There's meat to barbecue from ¥30 per portion, *bibimbap* (veggies on rice) for ¥15, and *kimbap* (California rolls) for ¥20. Daily 24hr.

Ashes of Time Cafe 时光简影咖啡馆, shíguāng jiǎnyǐng kāfēi guǎn. Daxue Xilu ☏ 0471 6937399. A thoroughly pleasant café selling a range of coffees and teas for ¥30 and up. It's highly popular with students from the nearby university. Daily 11am–11pm.

Guibinlou 贵宾楼, guìbīnlóu. Xincheng Xijie ☏ 0471 2527522. An excellent choice close to the sights – look for the temple-style entrance. A copper burner full of meat and other goodies can be yours for ¥138, but perhaps more suitable for lunch are the succulent lamb dumplings (¥20), or the aubergine, potato and coriander (served cold; ¥18). Daily 6am–2pm & 5–9pm.

★**Hotpot 518** 快乐518火锅, kuàilè 518 huǒguō. Da Dongjie ☏ 0471 6301933. A brilliant hotpot for dummies: gone is the regular menu full of indecipherable ingredients, replaced here with a supermarket-style aisle where you select your food from colour-coded dishes. Also gone is the copper boiler; instead, you eat from an electric hob. It's still great, and the young staff occasionally perform odd dance numbers. ¥80 should be enough to fill you up. Daily 10am–11pm.

★**Malaqin** 马拉沁饭店, mǎlāqìn fàndiàn. Xincheng Xijie ☏ 0471 6926685. The most famous restaurant in town, with a menu bursting with Chinese goodies, many of a notably Mongolian bent. Try your mutton in a potato stew (¥78), or heavily seasoned then served on a sizzling platter (¥98). All can be followed up with mashed yam with blueberry sauce (¥18), or washed down with Mongolian tea (¥10). Daily 11am–2.30pm & 5.30–9pm.

DIRECTORY

Consulate The Republic of Mongolia consulate (Mon, Tues & Thurs 8.30am–noon; ☏ 0471 4923819) is in the east of the city, at 5 Dongying Nanlu. Visas are fairly easy to obtain, and cost ¥290 for a month; you can get one the next day for ¥500. Note that Mongolian entry requirements have a habit of changing – ask your own embassy for the latest advice.

Post office The main post office (daily 8am–6pm) is on the northeastern corner of the train station square.

Visa extensions The PSB can be found in the government building to the south of the junction between Zhongshan Xi Lu and Xilin Guole Lu. It can be surprisingly useful for a PSB in an autonomous province, and there are usually no problems with visa extensions – don't rely on it, though, if your visa is close to expiry.

4

Around Hohhot

Hohhot has become a pleasant place to hunker down in for a few days, and there are a few sights nearby to keep you occupied – these include the Tang-dynasty **Tomb of Wang Zhaojun**, beautiful **Wusutu Zhao** temple, and the **Bai Ta** pagoda. Bar the pagoda, all are easily accessible on public transport, though taxis are pretty cheap for small groups.

The grasslands

Mongolia isn't all one giant steppe, but three areas in the vicinity of Hohhot are certainly large enough to give the illusion of endlessness. These are **Xilamuren** (希拉穆仁草原, xīlāmùrén cǎoyuán), which begins 80km north of Hohhot; **Gegentala** (格根塔拉草原, gégēntǎlā cǎoyuán), 70km further north; and **Huitengxile** (辉腾锡勒草原, huīténgxīlè cǎoyuán), 120km northeast of Hohhot. It's hard to differentiate between them, except that Xilamuren – the only one of the three that can feasibly be reached independently – is the most visited and Gegentala the least.

Most people visit by taking one of the **grassland tours**, which Westerners rarely enjoy but domestic tourists seem to love. The tours all follow the same pattern, with visitors based at a site comprising a number of **yurts** (蒙古包, ménggǔ bāo) – these are circular felt tents with floor rugs as the only furniture, horsehair blankets, a stove for warmth, and outside toilets, though said tents are increasingly being replaced with ugly concrete iterations. Transport, meals and accommodation are all included in the price, while various unconvincing "Mongolian entertainments" – wrestling and horseriding are the two most common – can cost a lot extra. Watch out for the local firewater, *baijiu*, which you're more or less forced to drink when your Mongolian hosts bring silver bowls of the stuff round to every table during the evening banquet; this can be followed by a fairly degenerate evening of drinking, dancing and singing.

If you accept the idea that you are going on a tour of the grasslands to participate in a bizarre social experience, then you'll get much more out of it. Besides, it is perfectly possible to escape from your group by hiring your own horse, or heading off for a hike. If your stay happens to coincide with a bright moon, you could be in for the most hauntingly beautiful experience of your life.

GETTING AROUND AND TOURS   **THE GRASSLANDS**

From Hohhot Travelling independently to the Xilamuren grassland can work out cheaper than taking a tour, though it involves jumping through a few hoops. Store your luggage at your hotel in Hohhot, and catch a bus from the long-distance bus station (5–6 daily; 90min; ¥25); these set down adjacent to the grassland. When you get off you will be accosted by people offering to take you to their yurts – try to negotiate an all-inclusive daily rate of about ¥200 for the yurt, including a meal or two, before you accept any offer. You aren't exactly in the wilderness here, but you can wander off into the grass and soon find it. Return buses run to Hohhot, though if they're already full they won't even pass through town. If this occurs (which it often does), enterprising taxi drivers will take carfuls of

---

ON TO OUTER MONGOLIA

Should you require them, visas for the Republic of Mongolia, otherwise known as **Outer Mongolia**, are available in Hohhot (see p.235) and Beijing (see p.119). Aero Mongolia (ⓦ aeromongolia.mn) run direct flights from Hohhot to the Outer Mongolian capital, Ulaan Baatar, though many travellers prefer to make the run by train – there are two weekly departures, with trains leaving Hohhot at 9.30pm Mon & Fri, and arriving in Ulaan Baatar two mornings later (sleeper tickets from ¥1100).

Alternatively, you can save a fair bit by doing the journey in stages: the first leg is to get to the curious, bustling border town of **Erlianhot** (二连浩特; èrlián hàotè), shortened to Erlian on timetables – one train leaves Hohhot at 10am (8hr 30min; from ¥54), and another just before midnight (7hr; sleepers from ¥146). There's plenty of cheap accommodation in Erlian, if you need it. After crossing the border (figure on at least ¥50 by taxi), you should have plenty of time to kill before the evening train on to Ulaan Baatar (18hr).

people to the scruffy mid-point town of Wuchuan (武川, wǔchuān), then buy your onward ticket and pop you on the bus for Hohhot – meaning that you don't usually spend any more than you would have done for the direct bus.

Tours A two-day tour (with one night in a yurt) is definitely enough – in a group of four or five people, this should come to around ¥480 each. Some travel services can tack smaller parties onto existing groups. Bear in mind that you may find yourself sleeping crushed into a small yurt with six others who don't speak your language, and that the tour may not be in English, even if you've requested that it should be; *Anda* hostel (see p.235) runs excellent foreigner-centred tours (Chinese friends are allowed, of course), spending a night in an authentic yurt, and offering freebies such as archery and cowpat-collecting – the latter remains a necessity in these parts, and is not as grim as it sounds.

Tomb of Wang Zhaojun

昭君墓, zhāojūn mù • Daily 8am–6pm • ¥65 • Minibus #44 (¥1.5) from Hohhot train station

The **Tomb of Wang Zhaojun**, about 8km to the south of Hohhot, is the burial site of a Tang-dynasty princess, sent from present-day Hubei to cement Han–Mongol relations by marrying the king of Mongolia. It isn't spectacular – a huge mound raised from the plain and planted with gardens, in the centre of which is a modern pavilion – but the romantic story it recalls has important implications for modern Chinese politics, signifying the harmonious marrying of the Han with the minority peoples. In the rose garden, among pergolas festooned with gourds, is a little museum devoted to Zhaojun, containing some of her clothes, including a tiny pair of shoes, plus jewels, books and a number of steles.

Wusutu Zhao

乌素图召, wūsùtúzhào • Daily 8am–6pm • ¥25 • Taxi from town around ¥60 one-way; buses from various parts of town

Well worth the effort to reach, the **Wusutu Zhao** complex is the only temple in Mongolia to have been designed and built solely by Mongolians. Boasting Mongolian, Tibetan and Han architectural styles, it lies 12km northwest of Hohhot, south of the Daqing Shan ranges and in attractive countryside separated from the city by an expressway. There are still few souvenir stands or gaudy refurbishments, so take the time to scour the Ming-era murals within and the ornate woodcuts attached to sticks at the base of the Buddhas. The surrounding grasslands and trails into the mountains make for a relaxing day out.

Bai Ta

白塔, bái tǎ • Daily 8.30am–5.30pm • ¥25 • Taxi from town around ¥100 return, including waiting time

The **Bai Ta**, or White Pagoda, lies about 17km east of the city along Xincheng Xi Jie – it's a possible stop on the way to the airport, which was named after it. An attractive, 55m-high wood-and-brick construction erected in the tenth century, it's covered in ornate carvings of coiling dragons, birds and flowers on the lower parts of the tower.

Shanxi

山西, shānxī

With an average height of 1000m above sea level, **Shanxi province** is effectively one huge highland plateau. Its name, not to be confused with Shaanxi (home to Xi'an; see p.197), means "west of the mountains", though rocky peaks indeed stream happily throughout the province, ending abruptly at all borders bar its northeast and southwestern corners. Provincial tourism staff call it a "museum above the ground", a reference to the many unrestored but still intact **ancient buildings** that dot the region, some from dynasties almost unrepresented elsewhere in China.

Just outside the coal-mining city of **Datong** lie the **Yungang cave temples** – one of China's major Buddhist art sites – and the gravity-defying **Hanging Temple**. To the south lies Shanxi's major mountain drawcard: the beautiful, if seasonally inaccessible, **Wutai Shan** range. South again, past the uninteresting provincial capital, **Taiyuan**, is a host of

CAVE HOUSES

A common sight among the folds and fissures of the dry loess plain of northern Shanxi (and neighbouring Shaanxi) are **cave dwellings**, a traditional form of housing that's been in use for nearly two thousand years. Hollowed into the sides of hills terraced for agriculture, they house more than eighty million people, and are eminently practical – cheap, easy to make, naturally insulated and long-lasting. In fact, a number of intact caves in Hejin, on the banks of the Yellow River in the west of the province, are said to date back to the Tang dynasty. Furthermore, in a region where flat land has to be laboriously hacked out of the hillside, caves don't take up land that could be cultivated.

The **facade** of the cave is usually a wooden frame on a brick base. Most of the upper part consists of a wooden lattice – designs of which are sometimes very intricate – faced with white paper, which lets in plenty of light, but preserves the occupants' privacy. Tiled eaves above protect the facade from rain damage. Inside, the **single-arched chamber** is usually split into a bedroom at the back and a living area in front, furnished with a *kang*, whose flue leads under the bed and then outside to the terraced field that is the roof – sometimes, the first visible indication of a distant village is a set of smoke columns rising from the crops.

Such is the popularity of cave homes that prosperous cave dwellers often prefer to build themselves a new courtyard and another cave rather than move into a house. Indeed, in the suburbs of towns and cities of northern Shaanxi, new concrete apartment buildings are built in imitation of caves, with three windowless sides and an arched central door. It is not uncommon even to see soil spread over the roofs of these apartments with vegetables grown on top.

little places worth a detour, the highest profile of which is **Pingyao**, an old walled town preserved entirely from its Qing-dynasty heyday as a banking centre. Southwest of here and surprisingly time-consuming to reach, the Yellow River presents its fiercest aspect at **Hukou Falls**, as its chocolate-coloured waters explode out of a short, tight gorge.

Brief history

Strategically important, bounded to the north by the Great Wall and to the south by the Yellow River, Shanxi was for centuries a buffer territory against the northern tribes. Today, the significance is economic: this is China's most **coal-rich** province, with 500 million tonnes mined here annually, a quarter of the national supply. Physically, Shanxi is dominated by the proximity of the Gobi Desert, and wind and water have shifted sand, dust and silt right across the province. The land is farmed, as it has been for millennia, by slicing the hills into steps, creating a plain of ribbed hillocks that look like the realization of a cubist painting. Erosion and increasing desertification are serious problems, presently being combated by extensive tree-planting and dune stabilization projects.

Datong

大同, dàtóng

Those who visited **DATONG** any time before 2010 would be absolutely astonished by what the city looks – and smells – like today. Its very name was once synonymous with **coal**: the sooty stench from umpteen surrounding **mines** would instantly invade the nostrils of anybody who stepped off the train here, and those who made their way into the city centre would find a pleasantly gritty but harrowingly impoverished place. While there are still plenty of mines in the vicinity, the city centre has recently been the subject of one of China's biggest urban makeovers, courtesy of assertive major **Geng Yanbo** – the realization of his vision has resulted in a fair bit of controversy.

Whether or not the ends have justified the means, the casual visitor will find today's Datong an attractive place with plenty to see. The knobbly remains of the earthen **ramparts** that once bounded the old city have been replaced with gigantic, imposing walls; inside these bulky ramparts, and spreading east and west of a centrally located

Ming-dynasty **Drum Tower** (鼓楼, gǔlóu), you'll also find a series of new Qing-style districts. Plenty of unrestored parts of town do remain, and you should check these out too – they exude a rugged atmosphere that those who don't have to live here might just find appealing, and a good number of small temples and old monuments are hidden away in the backstreets. Many visitors also use the city as a springboard to outlying sights, especially the **Yungang Caves** (see p.242) and **Hanging Temple** (see p.244).

Brief history

The Turkic **Toba** – a non-Han people from Central Asia – took advantage of the internal strife afflicting central and southern China to establish their own dynasty, the **Northern Wei** (386–534 AD), taking Datong as their capital in 398 AD. Though the period was one of discord and warfare, the Northern Wei became fervent Buddhists and commissioned a magnificent series of **cave temples** at Yungang, just west of the city. Over the course of almost a century, more than a thousand grottoes were completed, containing over fifty thousand statues, before the capital was moved south to Luoyang, where construction began on the similar Longmen Caves (see p.259).

A second period of greatness came with the arrival of the Mongol **Liao dynasty**, also Buddhists, who made Datong their capital in 907. Their rule lasted two hundred years, leaving behind a small legacy of statuary and some fine temple architecture, notably in the **Huayan** and **Shanhua temples** in town, and a **wooden pagoda**, the oldest in China, in the nearby town of Yingxian. Datong remained important to later Chinese dynasties for its strategic position just inside the Great Wall, south of Inner Mongolia, and the tall **city walls** date from the early Ming dynasty.

Nine Dragon Screen

九龙壁, jiǔlóng bì • South side of Da Dongjie • Daily 8am–6.30pm • ¥10

Northeast of the Drum Tower, the **Nine Dragon Screen** is the largest of several similar Ming-dynasty screens around the city: a lively 45m-long relief of nine sinuous dragons depicted in 426 multicoloured glazed tiles, rising from the waves and cavorting among suns. The only other dragon screens of this age are in Beijing, the main difference being that Datong's are four-clawed, indicating the dwelling of a prince, not an emperor (whose dragons had five claws). Originally, the screen stood directly in front of a palace, destroyed in the fifteenth century, as an unpassable obstacle to evil spirits, which, it was believed, could only travel in straight lines. A long, narrow pool in front of the screen is meant to reflect the dragons and give the illusion of movement when you look into its rippling surface.

Huayan Temple

华严寺, huáyán sì • Accessible from Huayuan Jie • Daily 8.30am–6pm • ¥64, covers both complexes

A short walk west of the drum tower are the remaining buildings of the large

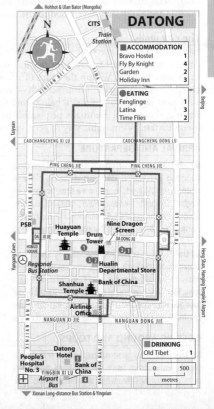

Hohhot & Ulan Bator (Mongolia)

DATONG

N

CITS

Train Station

■ ACCOMMODATION
Bravo Hostel 1
Fly By Knight 4
Garden 2
Holiday Inn 3

● EATING
Fengling 1
Latina 3
Time Flies 2

Taiyuan

XINJIAN BEI LU

XIMA LU

CAOCHANGCHENG XI LU

CAOCHANGCHENG DONG LU

PING CHENG JIE

PING CHENG JIE

DA BEI LU

XINJIAN BEI LU

YU HE XI LU

PSB

DA XI JIE

Huayuan Temple

Drum Tower

Nine Dragon Screen

DA DONG JIE

HONGQI SQUARE

Yungang Caves

Regional Bus Station

Hualin Departmental Store

Shanhua Temple

Bank of China

Airlines Office

XINJIAN NAN LU

NANGUAN XI JIE

NANGUAN DONG JIE

NANGUAN NAN JIE

Datong Hotel

People's Hospital No.3

Bank of China

Airport Bus

YINGBIN XI LU

Xinnan Long-distance Bus Station & Yingxian

Beijing

Heng Shan, Hanging Temple & Airport

■ DRINKING
Old Tibet 1

0   500
metres

Huayan Temple, originally dating to 1062 AD during the Liao dynasty and now forming two complexes. The **Upper Temple**, the first one you come to, is a little shabby, but its twelfth-century **Main Hall** is one of the largest in China, and is unusual for facing east – it was originally built by a sect that worshipped the sun. The roof is superb, a Tang-style design with two vertical "horns" fashioned to look like lions doing handstands. The cavernous interior has some wonderful Ming statuary including twenty life-size guardians, gently inclined as if listening attentively, but the main draw is the Qing-dynasty **frescoes** completely covering the walls, depicting Buddha's attainment of nirvana.

The Lower Temple

Turn right out of the entrance to this complex and you come to the **Lower Temple**, notable for its rugged-looking hall, a rare Liao-dynasty construction from 1038, complete with contemporary statues. Halls surrounding the front courtyard form a **museum** of regional discoveries spanning the Liao, Jin, Khitan and Yuan eras.

Shanhua Temple

善化寺, shànhuà sì · Da Nanjie · Daily 8am–6.30pm · ¥40

South of the Drum Tower lies the **Shanhua Temple**, a pretty place of solace in which birdsong replaces traffic noise. Founded during the Tang dynasty, what you see is a Ming restoration of a Jin structure. The buildings have a solid presence very different from the delicate look of later Chinese temples, and are impressive for their obvious age alone – one dates from 1154. The Jin-era statues in the main hall, five Buddhas in the centre with 24 *lokapalas* (divine generals) lined up on either side, are exceptionally finely detailed. One of the outlying courtyards sports a **five-dragon screen**, relocated from a monastery that once stood to the south of the city.

The city walls

Daily 8am–9pm · ¥30 · Golf buggies ¥10 per ride · Accessible via all gates, and several points between

Anyone who visited Datong prior to 2011 will be astonished by what has happened to its old **city walls**. Within the space of a few years, more or less the whole 10km circumference was rebuilt from scratch – no mean feat, even for a city long associated with hard work. Work was still being conducted on the western side at the time of writing, though it'll eventually be possible to cycle clean around the perimeter, making for an extremely enjoyable way to get a view of the city.

ARRIVAL AND DEPARTURE   DATONG

By air Datong's tiny airport (大同云冈机场, dàtóng yúngāng jīchǎng) is 15km east of the city centre. A shuttle bus (¥15) heads to and from a departure point on Yingbin Lu, opposite the *Datong Hotel* (大同宾馆, dàtóng bīnguǎn; see map, p.239). Alternatively, a taxi costs ¥50.
Destinations Beijing (1hr); Shanghai (2hr 10min); Xi'an (1hr 40min).

By train The train station (大同站, dàtóng zhàn) – on an extremely slow line to Beijing – is on the city's northern edge, on several bus routes, or a ¥15–20 taxi ride from town. High-speed services to Xi'an may have started by the time you read this, and a line to Beijing was still under construction at the time of writing; they'll use the new

Datong East station (大同东站, dàtóng dōng zhàn). Main station destinations Beijing (10 daily; 6–8hr); Hohhot (12 daily; 3–4hr); Taiyuan (10 daily; 3–6hr); Xi'an (1 daily; 16hr).

By bus Xinnan bus station (新南站, xīnnán zhàn), south of the centre on the #30 bus route (which also links with the train station), is Datong's main long-distance depot. There's a more central Regional bus station (长途汽车站, chángtú qìchēzhàn), off Xinjian Beilu just west of the walled city; both serve similar destinations, so ask at your accommodation for the best one to use.
Destinations Beijing (hourly, 4hr); Hohhot (hourly; 3hr 30min); Taiyuan (hourly; 3hr 30min); Wutai Shan (2 daily; 5hr).

GETTING AROUND AND TOURS

By bus Datong has numerous bus services (¥1), though ongoing reconstruction means that you should check routes on arrival. Currently, #4 heads from the train station into town.

By taxi Flag fall is ¥7, and a ride within town should be under ¥20.

Tours The helpful CITS office is based at the *Taijia* hotel

(6.30am–4pm; ☏ 130 08088454), in a compound just out and to the right of the station exit. They offer day-trips from ¥100/person (transportation only; more if fewer than 5 people) to Yungang Caves and the Hanging Temple; you can add the Wooden Pagoda for ¥100/group. Note that they're not beyond giving false public transport information in order to get you onto a tour. Similar tours are offered by hotels and hostels around town.

ACCOMMODATION

★**Bravo Hostel** 子鼠丑牛国际青年旅舍, zǐshǔ chǒuniú guójì qīngnián lǔshè. 34 Gulou Dongjie ☏ 186 35571010. New hostel in one of the newest and nicest parts of central Datong. Set around a mellow courtyard which occasionally doubles as a live music space, the rooms are just fine, and the English-speaking owner is adept with helping international travellers get to know the city. Dorms **¥35**, doubles **¥138**

Fly By Knight 夜奔客栈, yèbēn kèzhàn. 22F 15 Yinbin Lu ☏ 186 11914348, ⓦ flybyknightdatong.com. Another addition to the chain, this is quite different to the traditional guesthouses in Beijing (see p.104) and Pingyao (see p.254). Instead, it's set in a large, spacious, squeaky-clean upper-floor apartment, boasting wonderful views out over the walled city. A little hard to find by yourself, since there's no sign – give them a call on arrival. Dorms **¥100**, doubles **¥280**

Garden 花园大饭店, huāyuán dàfàndiàn. 59 Da Nanjie ☏ 0352 5865825, ⓦ gardenhoteldatong.com. The city centre's top-end option, with good service, crisp linen on the beds and an excellent location. There's also a Brazilian buffet (see below). You'll never pay the full rack rate – ¥350 is more likely. **¥1080**

★**Holiday Inn** 假日酒店, jiàrì jiǔdiàn. Off Yingbin Lu ☏ 0352 2118888, ⓦ holidayinn.com. Now the top place to stay in town, this immaculately designed hotel lies just to the south of the city wall, beyond a pleasingly grubby area that's great for street eats. Rooms are spick and span, and there are excellent restaurants on site, as well as a lovely swimming pool. **¥588**

EATING

Datong is far enough north for **mutton hotpot** to figure heavily in the local cuisine, along with potatoes, which you can buy, processed into a starchy jelly and seasoned with sauces, from street stalls. Other **typically northern dishes** available are *zongzi* (glutinous rice dumplings) and *yuanxiao* (sweet dumplings).

★**Fenglinge** 风临阁, fēnglíngé. Gulou Xijie ☏ 0352 2059699. Datong's most attractive restaurant by far, with temple-style woodwork, silky cushions and smartly dressed staff. It's set in a (totally rebuilt) venue said to be over 500 years old – they claim to have provided food to Dowager Cixi (see box, p.96) on her flight from the Allied Forces in 1900. Try the *shaomai* dumplings (¥18–45 per portion), of which the "flower" varieties are the best. There are some very cheap dishes on the menu, and it's possible to eat for under ¥30 per person – all in all, the best restaurant for hundreds of kilometres around. Daily 11.30am–2pm & 5.30–8.30pm.

Latina 59 Da Nanjie ☏ 0352 5865866. This *Garden Hotel* restaurant (see above) serves Brazilian barbecue – incongruous in dusty Datong, but quite a pleasant surprise – for a princely ¥198 per person. There's suitably samba-style music performed each evening. Daily 11.30am–2pm & 6–9pm.

★**Time Flies** 西藏往事 时光与水, shíguāng yǔshuǐ. Gulou Dongjie ☏ 186 03526110. On the city's trendiest street (at the time of writing), you'll need an eagle eye to spot this café's sign – it's well worth the hunt, though, for once through the door you'll emerge into a surprisingly swanky-looking place with chandeliers and

4

TOURING AROUND DATONG

There's public transport to the separate sights around Datong (see individual accounts for details), though many visitors choose to go with a tour (see opposite). It's usually ¥435 per person (including tickets) for the Yungang Caves, the Hanging Temple and Heng Shan. If you want to rent your own vehicle, a **taxi** for a day-trip to the Yungang Caves and the Hanging Temple will cost around ¥300, though you may be able to haggle this down slightly; while ¥250 will cover a round-trip to the Hanging Temple and Wood Pagoda. Add an extra ¥100 to either for adding on Heng Shan too; and another ¥50 if you'd like to continue to Wutai Shan rather than head back to Datong afterwards.

Note that there are also regular public buses through the day between Hunyuan (for the Hanging Temple and Heng Shan) and Yingxian (for the Wood Pagoda), and plenty of cheap hotels and restaurants in either should you feel like staying the night – though Yingxian is more appealing by far.

wooden eaves overhead, and soft mood music on the sound system. The coffee's pricey but tasty, and be sure to leave room for the creamy durian cheesecake. Daily 10am–11pm.

DRINKING

Old Tibet 西藏往事, xīzàng wǎngshì. 2 Huayuan Jie. Tucked down inside a shop and popular with the city's few expats, this great little basement bar's pleasing, Tibetan-style interior encourages casual conversation rather than raucous drinking. Can be a little smelly, though. Beers from ¥10. Daily noon–2am.

DIRECTORY

Hospital People's Hospital No. 3 is in the south of the city on Yingbin Xi Lu, just west of the crossroads with Xinjian Nanlu.
Post office The city's main post offices are inconveniently located, but there's one by the train station, and another in the centre on Xiaonan Jie (daily 8am–6pm).
PSB The police station (Mon–Sat 8.30am–noon & 2.30–6pm) is on Xinjian Beilu, 200m north of the post office.

Around Datong

Datong is the main jumping-off point for two of northern China's most spectacular sights: the phenomenal **Yungang Caves** and the gravity-defying **Hanging Temple**, which can both be seen in a single day. The latter can also be combined with a visit to **Heng Shan**, one of the five holy mountains of Taoism, or as a stop on the way to **Wutai Shan** (see p.246). Roads are sometimes bumpy and often blocked in winter, when transport times can double, but at least journeys are enlivened by great views: the lunar emptiness of the fissured landscape is broken only occasionally by villages whose mud walls seem to grow out of the raw brown earth. Some of the villages in the area still have their **beacon towers**, left over from when this really was a wild frontier.

Yungang Caves

云冈石窟, yúngāng shíkū • Daily 8am–6.30pm • ¥125 • Bus #3 from Xinjian Nanlu in Datong (¥1, up to 1hr); taxi ¥50 each way (off the meter)

Just 16km west of Datong, the monumental **Yungang Caves**, a set of Buddhist grottoes carved into the side of a sandstone cliff, are a must. Carved out around 400 AD at a time of religious revival, the caves were the first and grandest of the three major Buddhist grottoes, the other two being the Longmen Caves in Luoyang (see p.259) and the Mogao Caves in Gansu (see p.826). These are the best preserved by far, and recent renovations have made the surrounding coal mines a little less visible.

Caves 1–4

The easternmost caves are slightly set apart from, and less spectacular than, the others. **Caves 1 and 2** are constructed around a single square central pillar, elaborately carved in imitation of a wooden stupa but now heavily eroded, around which devotees perambulated. **Cave 3**, 25m deep and featuring a 10m-tall Maitreya statue, is the largest in Yungang and may once have been used as a lecture hall – while **cave 4**, eroded and inaccessible, has a central pillar carved with images of Buddha.

Cave 5

After crossing the small stream from cave 4 (it's also possible to scramble uphill to a small temple here), you'll find that the subsequent caves have somewhat more elaborate entrances. First up is **cave 5**, inside which you'll suddenly be confronted and dwarfed by a huge, 17m-high Buddha, his gold face shining softly in the half-light – a humbling experience. Other Buddhas of all sizes, a heavenly gallery, are massed in niches that honeycomb the grotto's gently curving walls, and two Bodhisattvas stand attentive at his side. This cave was closed to visitors at the time of writing.

Cave 6

At the spectacular **cave 6**, a wooden facade built in 1652 leads into a high, square chamber dominated by a thick central pillar carved with Buddhas and Bodhisattvas in deep relief, surrounded by flying Buddhist angels and musicians. The vertical grotto walls are alive with reliefs depicting incidents from the **life of the Buddha** at just above head height, which form a narrative when read walking clockwise around the chamber. Easily identified scenes at the beginning include the birth of the Buddha from his mother's armpit, and Buddha's father carrying the young infant on an elephant. Buddha's first trip out of the palace, which is depicted as a schematic, square Chinese building, is shown on the east wall of the cave, as is his meeting with the grim realities of life, in this case a cripple with two crutches.

Caves 7–15

Caves 7 and 8 are a pair, both square, with two chambers, and connected by an arch lined with angels and topped with what looks like a sunflower. The figures here, such as the six celestial worshippers above the central arch, are more Chinese in style than their predecessors.

The columns and lintels at the entrances of **caves 9, 10 and 12** are awash with sculptural detail in faded pastel colours: Buddhas, dancers, musicians, animals, flowers, angels and abstract, decorative flourishes bearing a resemblance to Persian art. Parts of cave 9 are carved with imitation brackets to make the interior resemble a wooden building.

The outstretched right arm of the 15m-high Buddha inside **cave 13** had to be propped up for stability, so his sculptors ingeniously carved the supporting pillar on his knee into a four-armed mini-Buddha. The badly eroded sculptures of **caves 14 and 15** are stylistically some way between the massive figures of the early western caves and the smaller reliefs of the central caves.

4

BUILDING THE YUNGANG CAVES

Construction of the Yungang Caves began in 453 AD, when Datong was the capital of the Northern Wei dynasty, and petered out around 525, after the centre of power moved to Luoyang. The caves were made by first hollowing out a section at the top of the cliff, then digging into the rock, down to the ground and out, leaving two holes, one above the other. As many as forty thousand craftsmen worked on the project, coming from as far as India and Central Asia, and there is much **foreign influence** in the carvings: Greek motifs (tridents and acanthus leaves), Persian symbols (lions and weapons), and bearded figures, even images of the Hindu deities Shiva and Vishnu, are incorporated among the more common dragons and phoenixes of Chinese origin. The soft, rounded modelling of the **sandstone figures** – China's first stone statues – lining the cave interiors has more in common with the terracotta sculptures of the Mogao Caves near Dunhuang in Gansu, begun a few years earlier, than with the more linear features of Luoyang's later limestone work. In addition, a number of the seated Buddhas have sharp, almost Caucasian, noses.

The caves' present condition is misleading, as originally the cave entrances would have been covered with wooden facades, and the sculptures would have been faced with plaster and brightly painted; the larger ones are pitted with regular holes, which would once have held wooden supports on which the plaster face was built. Over the centuries, some of the caves have inevitably suffered from weathering, though there seems to have been little vandalism, certainly less than at Luoyang.

Today a 1km-long fragment of the original array survives, arranged in **three clusters** (east, central and west) and numbered east to west from 1 to 51. The earliest group is caves 16–20, followed by 7, 8, 9 and 10, then 5, 6 and 11 – the last to be completed before the court moved to Luoyang. Then followed 4, 13, 14 and 15, with the caves at the eastern end – 1, 2 and 3 – and cave 21 in the west, carved last.

The western caves

Compared to the previous caves, the figures in the **western caves**, the earliest ones of the complex, are simpler and bolder, though they are at least as striking. Constructed between 453 and 462 AD, under the supervision of the monk Tan Hao, all are in the same pattern of an enlarged niche containing a massive Buddha flanked by Bodhisattvas. The **giant Buddhas**, with round faces, sharp noses, deep eyes and thin lips, are said to be the representations of five emperors.

The Buddha in **cave 16**, whose bottom half has disintegrated, has a knotted belt high on his chest, Korean-style. The Buddhas were carved from the top down, and when the sculptors of the Buddha in **cave 17** reached ground level they needed to dig down to fit his feet in. The same problem was solved in **cave 18** by giving the Buddha shortened legs. The 14m-high Buddha in **cave 20**, sitting open to the elements in a niche that once would have been protected by a wooden canopy, is probably the most famous, and certainly the most photographed.

The small and unspectacular caves 21–51 are not much visited, but the ceiling of **cave 50** is worth a look for its flying elephants, and in **caves 50 and 51** there are sculptures of acrobats.

The museum

Housed in an impressive new building, the site **museum** also has copious empty space and silly modern displays. However, it's worth popping in, if only for the chance to see some of the cave relics at closer quarters – most of what you see here was unearthed in the mammoth digs of the early 1980s.

The Hanging Temple

悬空寺, xuánkōng sì • Daily 7am–6pm • ¥130 • Summertime minibuses from outside Datong train station; bus from Datong to Hunyuan (浑圆, húnyuán) and then a taxi (¥20, after haggling) • See p.240 for tours

Clinging to the side of a sheer cliff-face in a gorge some 80km southwest of Datong, the **Hanging Temple** is one of the most visually arresting sights in all China. It's not, however, an attraction for those nervous of heights – literally translating as "Temple Suspended in the Void", its buildings are anchored by wooden beams set into the rock.

There's been a temple on this site since the Northern Wei, though the buildings were periodically destroyed by the flooding of the Heng River (now no longer there, thanks to a dam upstream), occasioning the temple to be rebuilt higher and higher each time. Your first glimpse of it will be spectacular enough, but things get a great deal more atmospheric once you're inside the rickety, claustrophobic structure. Tall, narrow stairs and plank walkways connect the six halls – natural caves and ledges with wooden facades – in which shrines exist to Confucianism, Buddhism and Taoism, all of whose major figures are represented in nearly eighty statues in the complex, made from bronze, iron and stone.

Heng Shan

恒山, héngshān • Daily 8am–6pm • ¥130 • Return cable car to Hengzong Temple ¥60; bus from Datong to Hunyuan (浑圆, húnyuán) and then take a taxi (¥30) • See p.240 for tours

The Hanging Temple sits on the valley road that runs up to **Heng Shan**, a range of peaks that constitutes one of China's five main Taoist mountains – its history as a religious centre stretches back more than two thousand years, and plenty of emperors have put in an appearance here to climb the highest peak, Xuanwu (2000m), a trend begun by the very first emperor, Qin Shi Huang. From the base of the mountain, an easy climb takes you to Heng Shan's main place of worship, **Hengzong Temple**, via switchbacking paths through other smaller temples, about a thirty-minute walk up and twenty minutes down. Heng Shan's peak lies another forty minutes uphill from Hengzong Temple, and might be the quietest place left on the mountain.

FROM TOP HUA SHAN (P.216); TERRACOTTA WARRIORS, XI'AN (P.212) >

The Wood Pagoda

应县木塔, yìngxiàn mùtǎ • Daily: April–Oct 7.30am–7pm; Nov–March 8am–5.30pm; ¥50 • Bus to Yingxian then taxi (¥5) •
Tours from Datong are available (see p.240)

At the centre of the small town of **YINGXIAN** (应县, yìngxiàn), 75km south of Datong,
the stately **Wood Pagoda**, built in 1056 in the Liao dynasty, is one of the oldest wooden
buildings in China, a masterful piece of structural engineering that looks solid enough
to stand here for another millennium – however, it's not possible to ascend. During a
recent renovation, a cache of **treasures** was found buried underneath the pagoda,
including Buddhist sutras printed using woodblocks dating back to the Liao.

The pagoda

The tower reaches nearly 70m high and is octagonal in plan with nine internal storeys,
though there are only six layers of eaves on the outside. The first storey is taller than the
rest with extended eaves held up by columns forming a cloister around a mud-and-
straw wall. The original pagoda was constructed without nails, though there are now
plenty in the floors. Originally, each storey had a statue inside, but now only one
remains, an 11m-tall Buddha with facial hair and stretched-out earlobes – characteristic
of northern ethnic groups, such as the Khitan, who came to power in Shanxi during
the Liao dynasty (916–1125 AD).

Wutai Shan

五台山, wǔtái shān • ¥168; extra fees apply for temples

One of China's four Buddhist mountains, the five flat peaks of **Wutai Shan** – the name
means "Five-terrace Mountain" – rise around 3000m in the northeastern corner of
Shanxi province, near the border with Hebei. Its main base, the village of **Taihuai**,
lies on a backroads route linking Datong and Taiyuan, and it's possible to access the
mountains from either of those cities. The long bus ride here is rewarded with fresh
air, superb scenery, some fascinating temple architecture and a spiritual (if not always
peaceful) tone. Though increasingly accessible, many of Wutai Shan's forty temples
have survived the centuries intact and remain functioning, full of resident clergy.

Despite a surprising number of ordinary Chinese people here as **pilgrims** – thumbing
rosaries and prostrating themselves on their knees as they clamber up the temples' steep
staircases – it has to be said that intense summertime tourism at Wutai Shan can put
paid to feelings of remoteness, and might make you regret the effort taken to reach
here. Crowds fade away between October and April, though during this period you
will have to come prepared for some low temperatures and possible blizzards. Note that
all temples are **open** daily from sunrise to sunset.

Brief history

Wutai Shan was an early bastion of Buddhism in China, a religious centre at least since the
reign of Emperor Ming Di (58–75 AD). At that time, a visiting Indian monk had a vision
in which he met **Wenshu** (Manjusri), the Buddhist incarnation of Wisdom, who is usually
depicted riding a blue lion and carrying a manuscript (to represent a sutra) and a sword to
cleave ignorance. By the time of the Northern Wei, Wutai Shan was a prosperous Buddhist
centre, important enough to be depicted on a mural at the Dunhuang Caves in Gansu.

> ### DOUGONGS
>
> The ceilings and walls of the Wood Pagoda's spacious internal halls are networks of beams held
> together with huge, intricate **wooden brackets**, called *dougongs*, of which there are nearly
> sixty different kinds. Interlocking, with their ends carved into curves and layered one on top of
> another, these give the pagoda a burly, muscular appearance, and as structural supports they
> perform their function brilliantly – the building has survived seven earthquakes.

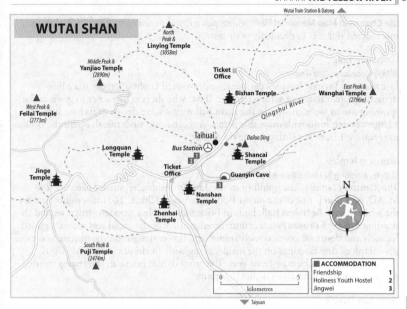

The mountain reached its height of popularity in the Tang dynasty, when there were more than two hundred temples scattered around its peaks. In the fifteenth century, the founder of the **Yellow Hat order**, now the dominant Buddhist sect in Tibet, came to the area to preach; Manjusri is particularly important in Tibetan and Mongolian Buddhism, and Wutai Shan remains an important pilgrimage place for Lamaists.

Taihuai
台怀, táihuái

The monastic village of **TAIHUAI**, a strip of tourist facilities and temples spread along about 1km of road, sits in a depression at the centre of the Wutai area, surrounded by the five holy peaks. Orientation is easy: uphill along the road is north, with the main batch of temples jammed alongside one another immediately to the west, and a smaller group of pavilions studding the steep hillside to the east across a river. Many visitors stay for only one night, but the relaxed atmosphere – together with the physical exertion of climbing the hills – may encourage a longer stay.

Tayuan Temple
塔院寺, tǎyuàn sì • Daily 6.30am–6.30pm • ¥10; Mao hall ¥2 extra

Easily visible west of the main road, and first on most itineraries, is the 50m-tall, Tibetan-style **White Stupa** of the **Tayuan Temple**. The stupa is a staggering sight against the temple's dark grey roofs, a bulbous, whitewashed peak hung with 250 bells whose chiming can be heard across the valley on a windy day. The largest of many such bottle-shaped pagodas on Wutai Shan, it testifies to the importance of the mountain to Lamaism, which is also represented by the tall **wooden poles** with bronze caps standing inside many of the temple's entrances.

Inside a hall behind the pagoda, a Ming-dynasty, two-storey library was built to house a bizarre and beautiful revolving **wooden bookcase**, much older than the rest of the complex. Its 33 layers of shelves, split into cubbyholes and painted with decorative designs, hold volumes of sutras in Tibetan, Mongolian and Chinese. Not far from **Shanhai Lou**, the chunky main gate of the temple – which you can climb for views – is the **Chairman Mao Memorial Hall**, whose placement at the heart of one of Buddhism's most sacred sights is in decidedly poor taste.

Luohou Temple

罗喉寺, luóhóu sì · 24hr · Free

Just north of Tayuan Temple's entrance, under-visited **Luohou Temple** is a Ming-dynasty reconstruction of a Tang temple. Those who do pop by gather to gawk at the spinning round wooden altar in the main hall with a wave design at its base supporting a large wooden lotus with moveable petals. A mechanism underneath opens the petals to reveal four Buddhas sitting inside the flower.

Xiantong Temple

显通寺, xiǎntōng sì · Daily 6.30am–6.30pm · ¥10

The **Xiantong Temple**, just uphill from the Tayuan Temple, reputedly dates back to 68 AD, and if so is one of the oldest Buddhist sites in China. The main sights here are the whitewashed **Beamless Hall**, built in brick to resemble a wooden structure; and the dazzling 5m-high **Bronze Palace**, constructed entirely of the metal and recently gilded. Its walls and doors are covered with animal and flower designs on the outside and rank upon rank of tiny Buddhas on the inside, along with an elegant bronze Manjusri Buddha sitting on a human-faced lion. The grounds also house an interesting sundial, which uses zodiac animals to depict the hours.

Yuanzhao Temple

圆照寺, yuánzhào sì · Daily 6.30am–6.30pm · ¥10

Sitting on the hill behind Luohou Temple, via a splendid statue of Manjusri surrounded by *arhats* and clouds at the **Yuanzhao Temple**, and atop a stone staircase of 108 steps, is the **Pusa Ding**. This Ming and Qing complex once accommodated emperors Kangxi and Qianlong, hence the yellow roof tiles and dragon tablet on the stairway, both indicating imperial patronage. This is a great destination for a first day in town, as it affords an aerial view of the valley and is a good way to warm up for longer hikes to higher temples.

Dailuo Ding

黛螺顶, dàiluó dǐng · Daily 7am–7pm · ¥8 · Cable car April–Oct ¥50 one-way, ¥85 return; Nov–March ¥40 one-way, ¥70 return

Dailuo Ding, the hillside overlooking the town to the east, offers the most accessible hiking in the Taihuai area, and provides superb vistas of the town below and mountains beyond. You can walk up the steep stone staircase in about twenty minutes, or take a cable car most of the way. At the top is **Shancai Temple** (山财寺, shāncái sì), a tiny but beautiful temple with unpretentious halls dedicated to Wenshu.

ARRIVAL AND INFORMATION TAIHUAI

Note that Taihuai is also known as "Wutai Shan" (but not just "Wutai", which is another township) on transport timetables.

By train Wutai Shan station (五台山站, wǔtáishān zhàn) is 20km north at Shahe town, on the Beijing–Taiyuan line. It's connected through the day to Taihuai by taxis and shuttle buses (1hr 30min). There's nowhere to buy tickets in Taihuai itself, though you can get them online easily enough (see box, p.36).
Destinations Beijing (3 daily; 6–7hr); Pingyao (2 daily; 5hr 40min–7hr 20min); Taiyuan (7 daily; 3hr 30min–6hr).
By bus Taihuai's bus station is a few kilometres south of the main temple clutch. Note that the Datong road crosses a high pass, which can see it closed at short notice by snow.

Buy tickets at the station, and on all park bus routes.
Destinations Beijing (3 daily; 6hr); Datong (2 daily; 5hr); Pingyao (1 daily; 4hr); Taiyuan (hourly; 3hr 30min).
By taxi Note that if you're coming to Wutai Shan by taxi from elsewhere, you'll also have to pay the park entry fee for your driver. It's usually cheaper to leave your driver at the gate, and head into town with a local cab; they typically ask for ¥50. Alternatively, it's a nice walk in fair weather.

Services The Bank of China in Taihuai has an ATM which works with foreign cards, but it's wise to arrive with enough yuan to last the duration of the visit.

OFF THE TRAIL IN WUTAI SHAN

There's some decent **hiking** in the area south of Taihuai; whatever the time of year, don't head off into the hills without some warm, weatherproof gear, food and water, and a torch, even though in good weather the trails here present no special difficulties. Allow plenty of time for hikes, as the paths are hard to find in the dark and even in summer the temperature drops sharply at sundown.

GETTING AROUND AND TOURS

By taxi Taxis have been clogging up the Wutai Shan roads for years – especially since the free tour buses around the area were ditched in 2015, following protests about the ¥50 fee it added to the Wutai Shan ticket price.

You may well end up paying a lot more than that to taxi drivers (and local chancers) anyway, if you're planning to see lots of temples – ¥10 is the minimum they'll ask, even for a short trip.

ACCOMMODATION AND EATING

The number of **hotels** in Taihuai has increased steadily in recent years, and even in peak season it shouldn't be hard to find a place to stay. Few stand out in any way; you're best off looking at the area west of the main road to the south of Taihuai, near the Nanshan Temple turn-off. Taihuai's **restaurants** are plentiful, bar the area around the main temples, which only has a couple; however, as you'd expect with a trapped market, the food is mediocre and about double what you'll pay in most cities. Fortunately, there are a few **supermarkets** around, and some places doing breakfast sets for as little as ¥10 – ask around.

Friendship 友谊宾馆, yǒuyì bīnguǎn. West of the main road, south of the bus station ☎ 0350 6586666. Clean, safe and quiet, this hotel is a reliably comfortable choice in an area with few reliably comfortable choices, and not too expensive. There's a good restaurant and small café on site. You'll usually get a few hundred lopped off the rack rate. **¥1080**

Holiness Youth Hostel 善斋青年旅馆, shànzhāi qīngnián lǚguǎn. West of the main road, south of the bus station ☎ 180 13141900, ⓦ holinessyouthhostel .com. One of the cheapest places in town, and a little hard to find on account of its alley location, this simple guesthouse has made an effort to tart itself up in hostel

style. The owners speak very little English, but try their best to help out with travel queries. **¥128**

Jingwei 经委大酒店, jīngwěi dàjiǔdiàn. Across the river between Nanshan Temple and the Guanyin Temple ☎ 0350 6542129. For something different, try this hotel, tucked on a nameless road on the other side of Dailuo Ding from Taihuai. Unless there's a group staying, there's an eerie (though pleasant) feel to the large, empty corridors – and more than half taken off the rack rate. Positives are that the rooms and on-site restaurant are just fine, and that you'll be well away from the crowds. The main Taihuai road is less than a fifteen-minute walk away, as are the wonderful Nanshan and Guanyin temples. **¥680**

South of Taihuai

Few tourists get very far out of Taihuai; it's certainly worth the effort, however, as not just the temples, but also the views and the scenery, are gorgeous. All of the following temples can be accessed in a single day, using the park buses to cut distances. Taxi drivers will be glad to drive you around; you'll pay around ¥100 for a simple tour of the following sights.

Nanshan Temple

南山寺, nánshān sì • 24hr • Free

The **Nanshan Temple** sits in a leafy spot halfway up Yangbai Shan, a hilltop 5km south of Taihuai. It's approached by a steep flight of stairs, with the entrance marked by a huge screen wall of cream-coloured brick. Decorated brickwork, including fake brackets and images of deities in flowing robes, is the temple's most distinctive feature. Ming images of *luohans* in the main hall are lifelike and expressive; one gaunt figure is sleeping with head propped up on one knee, his skin sagging over his fleshless bones. Come here in the late afternoon, if possible – the sunset views are out of this world, the vista centring on two bucolic valleys, which barrel into the mountains beyond.

Guanyin Cave

观音洞, guānyīn dòng · ¥5 · Daily 7am–6pm

The small temple around **Guanyin Cave**, a twenty-minute walk east up the road from Nanshan Temple, is an unexpected delight. It's free from tourists generally, and many of those who do pop by are Tibetan pilgrims. Steep staircases make their way between various buildings to the cave itself; there are great mountain views all the way down. If you fancy a countryside walk, take the road heading to the left of the temple as you exit.

Zhenhai Temple

镇海寺, zhènhǎi sì · Daily 7am–6pm · ¥5

About 2km southwest of Nanshan Temple, the **Zhenhai Temple**, sitting at an altitude of 1600m just off the road, seems an odd place to build a temple celebrating the prevention of floods, although legend has it that Wenshu tamed the water of the spring that now trickles past the place. During the Qing dynasty, a monk called **Zhang Jia**, reputed to be the living Buddha, stayed here; he is commemorated with a small pagoda south of the temple.

Longquan Temple

龙泉寺, lóngquán sì · Daily 24hr · Free

The **Longquan Temple** is on the west side of the Qingshui River, 5km southwest of Taihuai, just off the main road. Its highlight is the decorated **marble entranceway** at the top of 108 steps, whose surface is densely packed with images of dragons, phoenixes and foliage. The rest of the temple seems sedate in comparison, though the Puji Pagoda inside is a similar confection – a fat stupa carved with guardians, surmounted by a fake wooden top and guarded by an elaborate railing. Both structures date from the beginning of the twentieth century.

Taiyuan

太原, tàiyuán

Industrial powerhouse and the capital of Shanxi province, sprawling **TAIYUAN** is a victim of its own excellent transport connections – with Pingyao (see opposite) so close, and Beijing just a few hours away, there's no real need to stay the night here. If you've time, however, it's definitely worth setting aside half a day to visit the **Jinci Temple**, southwest of the city, a large complex with some unexpectedly venerable architecture.

Shuangta Temple

双塔寺, shuāngtǎ sì · Shuangta Beilu · Daily 8am–6pm · ¥30 · Bus #820 from train station

No tour of the city's ancient buildings would be complete without a look at the two 50m-tall pagodas of the **Shuangta Temple**, south of the train station. These were built by a monk called Fu Deng in the Ming dynasty, under the orders of the emperor, and today have become a symbol of the city. You can climb the thirteen storeys for a panoramic view of Taiyuan.

Jinci Temple

晋祠寺, jìncí sì · Daily 8am–6pm · ¥70 · Bus #804 from train station

About 25km southwest of Taiyuan, **Jinci Temple** contains perhaps the finest Song-dynasty buildings in the country, though the complex is oriented towards tourism rather than worship. A temple has stood on the site since the Northern Wei, and today's buildings are a diverse collection from various dynasties. The **Hall of the Holy Mother** is the highlight, its facade a mix of decorative flourishes and the sturdily functional, with wooden dragons curling around the eight pillars that support the ridge of its upward-curving roof.

ARRIVAL AND DEPARTURE TAIYUAN

BY PLANE

Taiyuan's **airport** (太原武宿国际机场, tàiyuán wǔsù guójì jīchǎng) is 15km southeast of the city, a ¥60 taxi ride away; shuttle buses (¥16) link the airport to both train stations.

Destinations Beijing (1hr); Shanghai (1hr 55min); Xi'an (2–4 daily; 1hr).

BY TRAIN

Main station (太原站, tàiyuán zhàn). Taiyuan's main station is at the eastern end of Yingze Dajie. It hosts some express services.

Destinations Beijing (10 daily; 4hr 30min–11hr); Datong (10 daily; 3hr–5hr 30min); Luoyang (2 daily; 12hr); Pingyao (12 daily; 1hr 15min–2hr 30min); Xi'an (8 daily;

8–12hr); Zhengzhou (4 daily; 10hr 30min–12hr).

Taiyuan South station (太原南站, tàiyuán nánzhàn). Most high-speed trains use the new South station, located on several bus routes, and a ¥20 cab ride from the centre.

Destinations Beijing (1–3 hourly; 2hr 30min–3hr); Pingyao (1–2 hourly; 40min); Xi'an (hourly; 3hr–3hr 45min); Zhengzhou (2 daily; 3hr 45min).

BY BUS

The only place you're likely to arrive by bus is the small **East bus station** (东客站, dōng kèzhàn), 1.5km east of the train station on Wulongkou Jie, which handles Wutai Shan services (hourly; 3hr 30min); take a taxi to the train station for ¥8, or walk.

ACCOMMODATION

Haiyue 海悦酒店, hǎiyuè jiǔdiàn. 9 Pingyang Lu ☎0351 7778869. This smart little hotel has rooms which are extremely good value – spacious, stylish and modern. Throw in a good location, and free bicycles for guest use, and you're onto a winner. **¥238**

On The Road Youth Hostel 在路上青年客栈, zàilùshàng qīngnián kèzhàn. 103C Zhongzheng Garden, off Qinxian Lu ☎186 36813425. Good hostel option a short way south of the centre. It's a mite more

attractive than regular Chinese hostels, though a little hard to find – it's advisable to call ahead of your arrival. Dorms **¥45**, twins **¥100**

Yingze 迎泽宾馆, yíngzé bīnguǎn. 189 Yingze Dajie ☎0351 8828888. This stylish four-star hotel has its own café, bookshop and tour company, and is thick with visiting dignitaries and upmarket domestic tourists. Not to be confused with another, much less presentable, *Yingze* just to the east. **¥800**

EATING

★**Tianyigong** 天一宫, tiān yī gōng. 99 Yingze Dajie. Most restaurants in town are much of a muchness, but for something a little different head to this place, at the base of an unmissable Oriental-tower hotel – there's an almost colonial air to proceedings, with stained-glass windows,

wooden furnishings and fancy chairs. Poke around on the tablet menu and you'll find plenty of Chinese staples and Shanxi specialities; the cold buckwheat noodles, served with flecks of meat and spice, are a tasty treat (¥38). Daily 9.30am–10pm.

Pingyao

平遥, píngyáo

Though relatively minuscule for a Chinese town (a mere half-a-million inhabitants), **PINGYAO** is now firmly ensconced on the Chinese backpacker trail, and for good reason: not only does it form a logical stopover point between Beijing and Xi'an, but its wall-bound core – the majority of which is filled with traditional eighteenth- and

PINGYAO TICKETS

Entry to Pingyao itself is free, but to visit the attractions you have to buy an **all-inclusive ticket** (¥130), which covers nineteen of the city buildings, plus the walls. Sold at most places it's used to gain entry to, along with an English-language audio-guide (¥40, plus ¥100 deposit; bring ID too), it's valid for two days.

nineteenth-century buildings – provides a step back in time. This is one of the most authentic old-town areas in China, with lanterns outnumbering LEDs, and slate roofing all over the place. Night-time can be a magical experience, both outside and back at your pad – most local guesthouses are set in charismatic old courtyard mansions, and many provide travellers with the chance to sleep on traditional Shanxi beds (*kang*), raised up on platforms. Take a few steps away from the restaurants and souvenir stands of the pedestrianized main streets, and you're in another world – few urban areas across the country are more pleasurable for an aimless wander. Throw in a couple of fine rural **temples** and some impressive **fortified clan villages**, all within day-trip distance, and staying overnight becomes a pleasurable necessity, rather than a possibility. Pingyao is one of those places that can be very hard to leave.

Of course, this being China, it's not all perfect. Recent years have seen some truly baffling additions to the main pedestrianized streets (including a decidedly non-dynastic space simulator), while many bars kindly boom their music into the ears of passers-by through hefty streetside speakers. Many locals are justifiably angry with this, and the police occasionally perform minor crackdowns – here's hoping that local officials are able to maintain the air that has made many a visitor fall for little Pingyao.

Brief history

Pingyao reached its zenith in the Ming dynasty, when it was a prosperous **banking centre**, one of the first in China, and its wealthy residents constructed luxurious **mansions**, adding massive **city walls** to defend them. In the course of the twentieth century, however, the town slid rapidly into provincial obscurity, which kept it largely unmodernized. Inside the walls, Pingyao's narrow streets, lined with elegant Qing architecture, are a revelation, harking back to the town's nineteenth-century heyday. This is especially true at night, when the glow from nearby houses shows the way – though small kids stay off the street after dark, haunted by their parents' tales of returning Ming-era **ghosts** who, it's said, navigate the unchanged alleys with ease. Few buildings in the walled city are higher than two storeys; most are small shops much more interesting for their appearance than their wares, with ornate wood-and-painted-glass lanterns hanging outside, and intricate wooden latticework holding paper rather than glass across the windows.

The town walls

Daily 8am–6.30pm • On city sight ticket (see box above)

From various access points around their 6km length, steps lead up to Pingyao's Ming **town walls**, 12m high and crenellated, and punctuated with a watchtower every 50m or so. You can walk all the way around them in two hours, and get a good view into some of the many courtyards inside the old town. A belt of sculpted **parkland** has been created to the south and east, and it's the corresponding walls that provide the best views. The structures where the wall widens out are *mamian* (literally, horse faces), where soldiers could stand and fight. At the southeast corner of the wall, the **Kuixing Tower** (奎星楼, kuíxīnglóu), a tall, fortified pagoda with a tiled, upturned roof, is a rather flippant-looking building in comparison to the martial solidity of the battlements. It was also, until recently, possible to climb the **City Tower** (市楼, shìlóu) on Pingyao's central crossroads – it's worth asking at your accommodation whether this charming little building has once again opened its creaky doors to tourists.

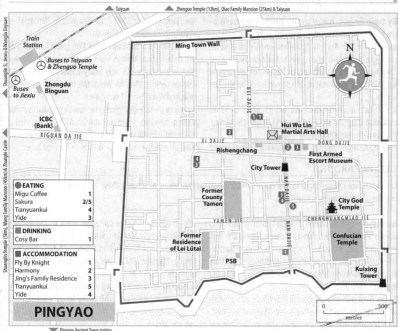

Pingyao Ancient Town station

Rishengchang

日升昌, rìshēngchāng • Western end of Dong Dajie • Daily 9am–5pm • On city sight ticket (see box opposite)

Rishengchang, established in 1824, was China's first bank and one of the first places in the world where cheques were used. During the Qing, more than four hundred financial houses operated in Pingyao, handling over eighty million ounces of silver annually. After the Boxer Rebellion, Dowager Empress Cixi came here to ask for loans to pay the high indemnities demanded by the Eight Allied Forces. Soon after, the court defaulted, then abdicated, and the banks dried up. Hong Kong and Shanghai took over Pingyao's mantle, rendering the city an isolated backwater.

Town museums

Daily, most 8am–6pm • On city sight ticket (see box opposite)

There are many, many **museums** in town, but after visiting a few you'll find the exhibits are repetitive and nowhere near as interesting as the buildings themselves, which are probably much like your accommodation in any case. Still, they give a good excuse to wander, and some – like the two **armed escort museums** and former **Hui Wu Lin martial arts training hall** (汇武林博物馆, huìwǔlín bówùguǎn) – are, given the need to protect the city's financial reserves from banditry, also relevant to Pingyao's history. Worthwhile options include the **Former County Yamen** (平遥县衙门, píngyáoxiàn yámén), a massive complex on Yamen Jie, which housed the town's administrative bureaucracy (the prisons here were in use until the 1960s); the **Former Residence of Lei Lütai** (雷撸汰故居, léilǔtài gùjū), Rishengchang's founder; the ramshackle **City God Temple** (城隍庙, chénghuáng miào) on Chenghuang Miao Jie; and the large **Confucian Temple** (文庙, wénmiào), also on Chenghuang Miao Jie.

ARRIVAL AND INFORMATION PINGYAO

Pingyao is most easily accessed by **train**, though there are also plentiful **bus** connections with Taiyuan, also home to the nearest airport (see p.251). Traffic is restricted in town, and it's a 15–30min walk to accommodation from arrival points, but if your bags are heavy a swarm of bicycle rickshaws and electric buggies will offer to carry you – ¥10–15 is a decent fare.

By train Pingyao is now receiving high-speed trains on the new Taiyuan–Xi'an line; they stop at the confusingly-named Pingyao Ancient Town station (平遥古城站; píngyáo gǔchéng zhàn), set in the countryside a full 7km from the city, though easy by bus (¥1) or taxi (around ¥20). The tiny main station is just northwest of the city walls.

Main station destinations Beijing (3 daily; 9–13hr); Linfen (11 daily; 2hr 30min); Taiyuan (12 daily; 1hr 30min); Xi'an (4 daily; 8hr 30min–10hr).

Pingyao Ancient City station destinations Beijing (3 daily; 4hr); Linfen (hourly; 50min); Taiyuan (hourly; 35min); Xi'an (6 daily; 2hr 40min–3hr 15min).

By bus There's a small bus depot 1km to the northeast of the train station, though most buses will set you down outside the latter. It's only really useful for services to Taiyuan (hourly; 2hr), for which the train is better in any case, and Wutai Shan (1 daily; 4hr).

Services Amazingly, given the town's popularity with foreign travellers, there are still no ATMs in the centre accepting international cards. The nearest is a branch of ICBC, about a five-minute walk outside the west gate.

GETTING AROUND

Cars are banned from Pingyao's few main streets, though at the height of summer these are usually congested with bicycles and pedestrians instead.

By bicycle Cycling around Pingyao's interior perimeter road is almost as much fun as walking around the wall itself, providing views of Pingyao at its most attractive. Bikes are available from some of the guesthouses, and from agencies with English signs along Xi Dajie (from ¥10 per day, plus ¥100 deposit).

Tours Most hotels, including all listed here (see below), will be able to offer tours of surrounding sights. Most will bundle groups into a car or minibus, though you'll have to rely on others going the same way – exceptions include the Wang Family Mansion, which can be visited for ¥50 per person (or ¥80 including Zhangbi Castle), and Qiao Family Mansion (¥120 per person). It's possible to organize a carful to the Wang mansion and Shuanglin Temple for ¥350, or ¥450 including Zhangbi Castle; lastly, it'll be around ¥400 for a visit to the Mianshan mountain range. Note that none of the prices listed here include entry tickets.

ACCOMMODATION

Staying overnight in Pingyao is a must: all of the following places are housed in atmospheric **mansions** with stone courtyards, wooden window screens, traditional furniture and *kang* to sleep on. Although offering much the same in the way of decor, **prices** vary quite a lot – you'll pay most along Xi Dajie, since that's where Chinese groups tend to head. Lodgings can fill up quickly – especially at weekends or during holidays – so it's best to book in advance.

★**Fly By Knight** 夜奔客栈, yèbēn kèzhàn. 16 Bei Dajie ☎0354 5685289, ⓦflybyknightpingyao.com. Sister hostel to those in Beijing (see p.104) and Datong (see p.241), this is another winner, with comfortable rooms set around a courtyard that's up there with the most peaceful in Pingyao. The English-speaking staff are adept at organizing tours or providing information about the town. Dorms ¥70, doubles ¥160

★**Harmony** 和议昌客栈, héyìchāng kèzhàn. Off Xi Dajie ☎0354 5684952. Presided over by a cheery, English-speaking local couple, this is a tremendous place whose rooms, arrayed around the courtyards of an old mansion, are the equal of some far more expensive alternatives, decorated with silk drapes and carved bed-heads. The excellent facilities include bike rental and free train station pick-up. ¥250

★**Jing's Family Residence** 锦宅, jǐn zhái. 16 Dong Dajie ☎0354 5841000, ⓦjingsresidence.com. This courtyard mansion started life as a silk merchant's home in the early eighteenth century, and has been lovingly renovated as a smart boutique hotel. Rooms boast decorative lacquered bed screens (bar the jaw-dropping master suite) and expensive beauty products in the bathrooms, while the charming courtyards are dotted with lanterns. You'll also be able to indulge in a spa session, or be served afternoon tea. The breakfasts are delicious, too. ¥1750

Tianyuankui 天元奎客栈, tiānyuánkuí kèzhàn. 73 Nan Dajie ☎0354 5680069, ⓦpytyk.com. This is the liveliest of the central guesthouses, and for good reason. Accessible through labyrinthine, lantern-strewn courtyards, their immaculate rooms will make you want to whip out your camera before putting your bag down. The on-site restaurant (see opposite) is great too, and staff are fonts of local knowledge. ¥300

Yide 一得客栈, yídé kèzhàn. 16 Sha Xiang, just south off Xi Dajie ☎0354 5685988, ⓦwww.yide-hotel .com. Eighteenth-century building hidden at the end of a quiet lane, and surrounded by several other courtyard homes. Rooms are cosy, and the restaurant is a good place to dine even if you're not staying (see opposite). You'll usually save a little by booking online. ¥520

EATING

Eating in Pingyao is fun, with a score of tasty, well-presented **local dishes**. Umpteen **restaurants** serve these, though prices are tourist-inflated, and portions not always that large – you're best off heading to one of the **hotels**. Things to look for include salted, five-spiced beef; wild greens; yams; flat "mountain noodles" (served on their edges in a steamer); and "cat's ear noodles" (triangular flecks of dough flicked into boiling water). For **cheap Chinese staples**, head to the western end of Xi Dajie, or to the streets between the West Gate and the train station.

Migu Coffee 16 Bei Dajie ☎ 0354 5685765. The best of the town's new glut of cafés, with good coffee, soft music and a pleasing modern interior full of books – interestingly, they usually have a few Chinese-language Rough Guides (genuine, too) to look through. Daily 10am–9pm.

Sakura 6 Dong Dajie ☎ 134 85468281. Part of a foreigner-focused chain that stretches way into the Chinese wild west, this is the city's best option for Western food, if that's what you're after – lasagne (¥50), pizzas (from ¥65) and the like. After sundown it morphs into a popular bar, replete with shisha smoke (¥50); there's another location, often rowdier, on Nan Dajie. Daily 10am–11pm.

★**Tianyuankui** 73 Nan Dajie. The lobby restaurant at this hotel (see opposite) is one of the best in the city, and prices are backpacker-friendly. Staff have been drilled well,

and know what foreigners like and dislike. Local specialities (see above) have been marked with stars on the menu, and their *kao lao lao* is the best in town (¥28); alternatively, try their special "fried and juicy" aubergine dish (¥38), which arrives on your table looking more like a dressed fish. Daily 7.30am–11pm.

★**Yide** 16 Sha Xiang. Yet another excellent hotel restaurant (see opposite), and one of the best places in which to sample Pingyao specialities. Amazingly, despite the luxurious appearance, their dishes (at ¥15–50 each) are hardly any more expensive than those at the motley shack-restaurants lining the main roads – and in some cases, they're cheaper. There's also Western breakfast fare and good coffee, extremely inexpensive rice and noodle dishes, and yummy caramel-dipped yam for dessert (¥35). Daily 7am–10pm.

DRINKING

Cosy Bar 165 Nan Dajie ☎ 0354 5684952. One of Pingyao's most backpacker-friendly bars, eschewing the usual KTV noise for a chilled-out atmosphere, and

occasional live music. Cheap beers and good cocktails (¥35 and up) round out the picture. Daily 4pm–midnight.

Around Pingyao

You could easily spend a couple of days in the countryside around Pingyao, though you'd only need a few hours to visit either of two nearby **temples** – one full of superb statues, the other interesting for its age. Further afield, a couple of Ming-dynasty **fortified mansions** standing starkly among the surrounding hills would be even more impressive if you hadn't seen Pingyao first, but are anyway worth the effort it takes to reach them. Most visitors hit these sights as part of a tour (see opposite for an idea of prices), but some are easily accessible independently.

Shuanglin Temple

双林寺, shuānglín sì • Daily 8am–6pm • ¥40 • Within cycle range of Pingyao; bus to Jiexiu (介休, jièxiū; ¥6) and get off en route; round-trip by taxi ¥40 or so, after haggling

The fortress-like **Shuanglin Temple** stands 5km southwest of Pingyao, just off the main road to Jiexiu. Originally built in the Northern Wei, the present buildings, ten halls arranged around three courtyards, are Ming and Qing. Once you're inside, the fine architecture pales beside the contents of the halls, a treasury of 1600 coloured terracotta and wood **sculptures** dating from the Song to the Qing dynasties. They're arranged in tableaux, with backgrounds of swirling water or clouds, turning the dusty wooden halls into rich grottoes. Some of the figures are in bad shape but most still have a good deal of their original paint, although it has lost its gaudy edge. It's worth hiring a **guide** (ask at your accommodation), as each hall and each row of statues have intriguing histories attached.

The halls

The horsemen dotted in vertical relief around the **Wushung Hall**, the first on the right, illustrate scenes from the life of Guandi, the god of war, but the figures in most of the

HUKOU FALLS

Isolated way out in Shanxi's western backblocks, **Hukou Falls** (壶口瀑布, húkǒu pùbù; ¥91) are the Yellow River at its most impressively turbulent. Flowing north, the river's span approaches 400m at this point, yet it suddenly finds itself forced through a gap only 20m wide – the resultant torrent is predictably fierce, and predictably loud. The falls are regarded by the Chinese as one of their premier beauty spots, though you may question whether reaching them is worth the effort: they're accessed via **Linfen** (汾纷, línfén), a stop on the high-speed line from Pingyao or Xi'an, from which you can take a bus (1hr 30min) to the falls. Tour agents in Xi'an (see p.209) run overnight trips to the falls, while from Pingyao you can usually get a day-trip for ¥240.

halls are depictions of Buddha or saints and guardians. The **eighteen arhats** in the **second hall**, though unpainted, are eerily lifelike, and somewhat sinister in the gloom with their bulging foreheads, long tapering fingernails and eyes of black glass that follow you round the room. In the **third hall**, the walls are lined with elegant 20cm-high Bodhisattvas inclined towards a set of larger Buddha figures at the centre like so many roosting birds. The statue of **Guanyin** – sitting in a loose, even provocative, pose – is probably a reflection of the confidence and pride Pingyao enjoyed during its economic heyday.

Zhenguo Temple

镇国寺, zhènguó sì · Daily 8am–6pm · ¥30 · Bus #9 from train station

Out in the fields 12km northeast of Pingyao, **Zhenguo Temple** is a quiet, forgotten place, fronted by gnarled old trees. It's surprising then to find one of China's **oldest wooden buildings** here: the Wanfo Hall was built in 963 AD and looks like it hasn't been touched since, with an amazingly complex system of brackets holding the roof up and full of contemporary, Indian-influenced statuary. At the rear, the upper hall has some Qing frescoes of the life of Buddha, all set in a Chinese context, while the Ming-dynasty **Dizang Hall** is a riot of paintings of the King of Hell and his demons handing out punishments to sinners.

The Wang Family Mansion

王家大院, wángjiā dàyuàn · Daily 8am–5pm · ¥55 · Bus from Pingyao's bus depot to Jiexiu (介休, jièxiū; 50min; ¥10), then minibus #11 to the mansion (30min, ¥4) · See p.254 for tours

Some 45km southwest of Pingyao, the **Wang Family Mansion** is more like a huge, fortified castle than a private residence. Set among stark brown hills, the location, enormous scale and – especially – the details of the mansion buildings are all astounding, with high brick walls surrounding an intricate and vast collection of interconnected Qing-dynasty courtyards, halls (around a thousand), gardens, galleries, triumphal archways and screens, all built in carved grey stone along a rigidly symmetrical plan. The Wangs settled here at the end of the Mongol dynasty and built this complex in the early nineteenth century, after the family struck it rich not only in commerce but also political appointments; the infamous **Empress Dowager Cixi** stayed a night here in 1900 while fleeing to Xi'an after the Boxer Rebellion. The complex is in two sections, joined by a stone bridge over a gully, and you could easily spend half a day here getting lost among the architecture.

The Qiao Family Mansion

乔家大院, qiáojiā dàyuàn · Daily 8am–5pm · ¥72 · See p.254 for tours

The comfortably scaled **Qiao Family Mansion** lies 25km northeast of Pingyao near the hamlet of **Leguan Zhen**. An enchanting maze of attractive details including carved screens and tiled roofing, the mansion was used as a setting by Zhang Yimou for his film *Raise the Red Lantern*, in which the labyrinthine layout of the place symbolizes just how restricted life was for women in classical China.

Zhangbi Castle

张壁古堡, zhāngbì gǔbǎo • ¥60 including guide • See p.254 for tours

About 40km southwest of Pingyao, **Zhangbi Castle** was built at the beginning of the seventh century, yet was only recently added to Shanxi's litany of tourist sights. Though pleasant enough on the surface, the castle is more famed for its network of **underground tunnels**, most of which were added by the Sui dynasty for protection against Tang invasion. The Tang themselves later added a few tunnels of their own, and explorations of the resultant warren – a multilayered maze which dives over 20m beneath the surface – are thoroughly enjoyable. The labyrinthine nature of the tunnels makes hiring a guide all but essential, even more so since doing so will also get you a tour of **Zhangbi Village**, a pleasing, ramshackle hotchpotch of Yuan, Ming and Qing buildings.

Henan

河南, hénán

China's third most populous province, **HENAN**'s modern-day industrial trappings conceal a rich history watered by the great **Yellow River**. The wonderful **Longmen Caves** lie due south of **Luoyang**, an ancient dynastic capital thought by the Chinese of antiquity to be the centre of the universe – it may, at one time, have been the largest city on earth. Luoyang also makes a good jumping-off point for one sight whose name, at least, is familiar to many Westerners: **Shaolin Temple**, home to the famed fighting monks. Henan's modern capital, **Zhengzhou**, is unremarkable, but further to the east is the old city of **Kaifeng**, which wears its history rather better than others in the province – particularly in the form of the ancient wall still enclosing its centre.

4

Luoyang and around

洛阳, luòyáng

LUOYANG, to many Chinese, is synonymous with peonies – distinctive little pink flowers which pop up here each spring (see box below), they're used as a motif all over the city, livening up what is, in reality, a rather drab and industrial place. This modern overlay conceals a rich history – Luoyang has been occupied since Neolithic times, and served as China's capital at various points from the Zhou dynasty through to 937 AD. Confucius once studied here, and this is where Buddhism first took root in China in 68 AD.

Most visitors are here to see the famed **Longmen Caves**, one of China's three major rock art galleries, which lie just south of the city's sprawl – however little you know about Buddhism or about sculpture, you'll be impressed by the scale and complexity of the work here and by the extraordinary contrast between the power of the giant figures and the intricate delicacy of the miniatures. On the way to the caves you can also visit **Guanlin Miao**, a memorial temple to Three Kingdom hero Guan Di. The other major

---

LUOYANG'S PEONIES

It's said that in 800 AD the Tang Empress Wu Zetian, enraged that the **peonies**, alone among flowers, disobeyed her command to bloom in the snow, banished them from her capital at Chang'an. Many were transplanted to Luoyang (the secondary capital) where they flourished, and have since become one of the city's most celebrated attractions, the subject of countless poems and cultivation notes. Luoyang now boasts over 150 varieties of peony, which have found their way onto every available patch or scrap of ground – including central Wangcheng Park (王成公园, **wángchéng gōngyuán**; ¥55 during the April Peony Festival) – a splendid sight when they flower in spring. The peony motif is also everywhere in the city, from trellises to rubbish bins.

sight is the Buddhist **Baima Temple**, which lies east of the city centre; and there's also an interesting, if not very well presented, **Museum of Ancient Tombs** northwest of Luoyang, where you can see the interiors of the mounds that dot the local fields. All these can be visited on various **buses** from Luoyang, and you could pack the lot into one very busy day. In addition, the city is within striking distance of several important religious complexes, including **Shaolin Temple** (see p.263).

Luoyang Old Town

老城, lǎochéng • On plenty of bus routes; taxi from the city centre ¥20 or so

Just east of the centre, the city's **old town** area has been spruced up of late. Inside its surrounding wall and moat you'll find several old mansions, though none are particularly notable – head instead to the **Drum Tower** (鼓楼, gǔlóu), near the end of a largely pedestrianized street which fires east from the **West Gate**, itself an impressive fortification. Maroon-and-gold banners flutter from the various establishments on this drag, while the earthy side-streets are well worth poking around – all in all, a nice little excursion.

Luoyang Museum

洛阳博物馆, luòyáng bówùguǎn • Nietai Lu • Tues–Sun 9am–4.30pm • Free (bring ID) • Bus #77 from train station; taxi from the city centre ¥20–25

The absolutely gigantic **Louyang Museum**, slightly inconveniently located south of the Luo River, is worth a visit on account of its well-laid-out profusion of extraordinary treasures, most of which date from Luoyang's days as the capital of eight dynasties.

LUOYANG

The main halls

One of the first halls you'll come across is a huge exhibit of **ancient stone carving**, an amazing collection of statues, steles and the like from various points in Luoyang's history. On the upper level are halls dedicated to **Han and Tang pottery** and **Qing-dynasty relics**. Given Luoyang's history, the former is by far the more interesting; look out for a glazed incense burner of Eastern Han vintage (25–220 AD), found in Wangcheng Park in 2004. A side-hall features a dedicated display on **funerary pottery** from throughout the dynasties – pay attention to the stylistic shifts, essentially moving from simple to decorative, from the Han to the Tang. The latter are more eye-catching; look out for multicoloured, expressive camels and several hook-nosed, pointy chinned foreigners.

Luoyang Ancient Treasure Hall

In the **Luoyang Ancient Treasure Hall** you'll find all sorts of goodies. The area around Luoyang entered the Bronze Age before the rest of China, so the

■ ACCOMMODATION		● EATING	
Christian's	1	Lao Luoyang Mian Guan	3
Dongshan	5	Tudari	1
Ease House	4	Wangfu Yuhuayuan	2
Heartland Youth Hostel	3		
Peony	2	■ DRINKING	
		Party House	1

Shang bronzes are especially extensive; look, too, for an endearing **jade tiger** from the Zhou, as well as some Indian-influenced **Wei statuary**, and a model farm from a Han tomb, with a sow and her row of piglets. Lastly, ornate **gold and silver** from the Tang shows the influence of Persian and Roman styles.

The Longmen Caves

龙门石窟, lóngmén shíkū • Daily 8am–5.30pm • ¥100 • English-speaking guide ¥100 for 40min, ¥240 for 90min • Shuttle buses ¥10, boats ¥25 • Bus #81 from Luoyang train station or #99 from opposite Wangcheng Park entrance (¥1); taxi ¥30–50 from city centre

A UNESCO World Heritage Site, the **Longmen Caves** are a spectacular parade of Buddhist figurines and reliefs only 12km south of central Luoyang – they start just after the city sprawl starts to thin out. Caves pockmark the cliffs lining a meandering river, hosting figures ranging in size from the miniature to the monumental; they're all accessible on a series of staircases and elevated paths, which zigzag their way across the cliff face. This is an extremely popular place in the summer, though even the teeming crowds can't lessen the spectacle; try to visit early on in the day, if you're here in summer, as the exposed site can be rather hot.

Longmen's roadhead is almost 2km short of the caves, and there's another on the opposite side of the river; if you don't fancy paying extra for a shuttle bus, head down to the river and follow it to the main entrance, which is on the west side of the river. Starting from the northern end and moving south down the group, the following are the most important carvings, which stand out due to their size.

The Bingyang Caves

The three **Bingyang Caves** are among the earliest at the site; the central one, commissioned by Emperor Xuan Wu to honour his parents, supposedly took 800,000 men working from 500 to 523 AD to complete. The Buddha statues here show northern characteristics – long features, thin faces, splayed fishtail robes – and traces of Greek influence. The side caves, completed under the Tang, are more natural and voluptuous, carved in high relief.

The Cave of Ten Thousand Buddhas

Just south of the Bingyang Caves you'll find **Wanfo**, the Cave of Ten Thousand Buddhas. Creaetd in 680 by Gao Zong and his empress Wu Zetian, it contains not ten but fifteen thousand Buddhas carved in tiny niches, each one different and the smallest just 2cm high.

CREATING THE LONGMEN CAVES

Over the years, 1350 caves, 750 niches and 40 pagodas containing 110,000 statues were carved out of the limestone cliffs bordering the Yi River to create the Longmen Caves. Stretching more than 1km in length, the carvings were **commissioned** by emperors, the imperial family, other wealthy families wanting to buy good fortune, generals hoping for victory, and religious groups. The Toba Wei began the work in 492 AD, when they moved their capital to Luoyang from Datong, where they had begun the Yungang Caves (see p.242). At Longmen, they adapted their art to the different requirements of a harder, limestone surface. Three sets of caves, Guyang, Bingyang and Lianhua, date from this early period. Work continued for five hundred years and reached a second peak under the Tang, particularly under Empress Wu Zetian, a devoted adherent of Buddhism.

There's a clearly visible progression from the early style brought from Datong, of simple, rounded, formally modelled holy figures, to the complex and elaborate, but more linear, Tang carvings, which include women and court characters. In general, the Buddhas are simple, but the sculptors were able to show off with the attendant figures and the decorative flourishes around the edges of the caves.

Other caves

Lianhua (Lotus Flower Cave) is another early one, dating from 527, and named after the beautifully carved lotus in its roof; while at **Moya Sanfo** you can see an incomplete trinity, abandoned when the Tang dynasty began to wobble. But by far the most splendid is **Fengxian** (Ancestor Worshipping Cave), where an overwhelming seated figure of Vairocana Buddha, 17m high with 2m-long ears, sits placidly overlooking the river, guarded by four enormous warrior attendants (though the southern two are heavily damaged) who are grinding malevolent spirits underfoot.

The **Medical Prescription Cave**, built in 575, details several hundred cures for everything from madness to the common cold. **Guyang** is the earliest collection of all, begun in 495, where you can still see traces of the vivid paintwork that originally gave life to these carvings. There's a central Buddha and nineteen of the "Twenty Pieces", important examples of ancient calligraphy.

Guanlin Miao

关林庙, guānlín miào • Daily 8am–5pm • ¥40 • On various bus routes from the city centre

Some 7km south of Luoyang and easily combined with a trip to the Longmen Caves, the red-walled **Guanlin Miao** is a temple complex dedicated to **Guan Di** – also known as Guang Gong and Guan Yu – the famously loyal Three Kingdoms general (see box, p.396). Guan Di was captured and executed by the King of Wu, who then sent the head to Cao Cao, the King of Wei; Cao Cao neatly sidestepped this grisly game of pass-the-parcel by burying the head with honour in a tomb behind the temple, now a wooded, walled mound. Since his death, Guan Di has become the patron saint of martial virtue, worshipped by the military, police and the criminal underworld.

The temple and grounds

Despite its military theme, the temple is beautiful and rather peaceful, the elegant Ming buildings highly carved and richly decorated. Especially fine are the carved stone lionesses lining the path to the Main Hall. Each has a different expression and a different cub, some riding on their mother's back, some hiding coyly behind her paws. In the first hall, look carefully at the eaves for rather comical images of Guan Di fighting – he's the one on the red horse, a faithful animal called **Red Hare** – and leading an army engaged in sacking a city engulfed by carved wooden flames. Inside stands a 7m-tall statue of the general, resplendent in technicolour ceremonial robes with a curtain of beads hanging from his hat.

The Baima Temple

白马寺, báimǎ sì • Daily 7.30am–7pm • ¥50; Bus #56 from main train station (¥1.50); taxi around ¥25 • Also visited on some Shaolin Temple tours (see p.263)

Historic, leafy **Baima Temple** (White Horse Temple), 12km east of Luoyang, was founded in 68 AD, and has some claim to being the first Buddhist temple in China. Home to a thriving monastic community, the Baima Temple is primarily a place of worship, and over-inquisitive visitors are tactfully but firmly pointed away from closed buildings. Inside the temple, you'll find this a placid place, its silence only pricked by the sound of gongs or the tapping of stonemasons carving out a stele.

Brief history

Legend says that the Emperor Mingdi of the Eastern Han dreamed of a golden figure with the sun and moon behind his head, and so sent two monks westwards to find out what his dream meant. They reached India and returned, riding white horses with two Indian monks in tow, laden down with Buddhist sutras. Baima Temple was built to honour them, and its layout is in keeping with the legend: there are two stone horses, one on either side of the entrance, and the tombs of the two monks, earthen mounds ringed by round stone walls, lie in the first courtyard.

The Main Hall

Beyond the Hall of Celestial Guardians, the **Main Hall** holds a statue of Sakyamuni flanked by the figures of Manjusri and Samantabhadra. Near the Great Altar is an ancient bell weighing more than a tonne; as in the days when there were over ten thousand Tang monks here, it is still struck in time with the chanting. The inscription reads: "The sound of the Bell resounds in Buddha's temple causing the ghosts in Hell to tremble with fear".

The Cool Terrace

Behind the Main Hall is the **Cool Terrace** where, it is said, the sutras brought back from India were translated. Offerings of fruit on the altars, multicoloured cloths hanging from the ceilings and lighted candles in bowls floating in basins of water, as well as the heady gusts of incense issuing from the burners in the courtyards, indicate that, unlike other temples in the area, this is the genuine article.

The Museum of Ancient Tombs

洛阳古墓博物馆, luòyáng gŭmù bówùguăn • Daily 9am–5pm • ¥20 • Bus #83 from main train station

In a patch of open land around 6km northwest of Luoyang, the **Museum of Ancient Tombs** contains the relocated brick interiors of two dozen tomb mounds from the area, dating from the Western Han to Northern Song periods. Most had been robbed in antiquity, and the museum is neglected, but, compared with Longmen's overwhelming scale, it does give a more human view of the times.

The tombs

The tombs are arranged underground around a central atrium, into which you descend from beside souvenir stalls (there are no signs, but the helpful stallholders will point the way). Each is entered through a short tunnel, and is very small – you can barely stand in a couple – but decorated brickwork and frescoes liven the whole thing up. Best, however, is **Jing Ling**, the tomb of Xuan Wu of the Northern Wei, which stands just outside the museum grounds – again, there's no sign but you can't miss the huge earth hillock. This hasn't been relocated, and you descend a 50m-long ramp into Xuan Wu's tomb chamber – guarded by two sneering demons – where his sarcophagus remains.

ARRIVAL AND DEPARTURE

LUOYANG AND AROUND

By air Luoyang's airport (洛阳北郊机场, luòyáng běijiāo jīchăng) lies 20km north of town; from here, bus #83 will bring you to the train station, or it's around ¥35 by taxi.

Destinations Beijing (1hr 30min); Shanghai (1hr 30min).

By train Luoyang has two train stations. The main station (洛阳站, luòyáng zhàn) is just north of the city centre, while the huge Longmen station (洛阳龙门站, luòyáng lóngmén zhàn), which handles high-speed services only, is 10km south. Both stations are on innumerable bus routes; it costs up to ¥30 to get to or from Longmen station by taxi. Advance-purchase offices all over town charge a ¥5 fee per ticket – particularly handy for booking services from far-flung Longmen station.

Main station destinations Beijing (8 daily; 7hr 30min–11hr); Hua Shan (20 daily; 3hr 45min); Ji'nan (5 daily; 9–12hr); Kaifeng (18 daily; 2–3hr); Shanghai (9 daily; 10–17hr); Xi'an (1–2 hourly; 4hr 45min); Zhengzhou (2 hourly; 1hr 30min–2hr).

Longmen station destinations Beijing (7 daily; 4hr); Hua Shan (hourly; 1hr–1hr 30min); Shanghai (1 daily; 9hr); Xi'an (1–2 hourly; 1hr 45min); Zhengzhou (1–3 hourly; 40min).

By bus There are bus stations either side of the main train station, both serving similar destinations.

Destinations Shaolin Temple (every 30min; 1hr 30min); Xi'an (several daily; 4hr); Zhengzhou (every 30min; 1hr 30min).

GETTING AROUND AND TOURS

By bus The train station area is also the place to pick up city buses, including those to Baima Temple and the Longmen Caves (see accounts for details), while touts for buses to Shaolin Temple (see p.263) hang around outside the main bus station, and are not shy of grabbing customers. City buses usually cost ¥1.

By taxi Taxis are plentiful, and have a ¥5 flag fare; Luoyang is big, meaning that you may end up paying more than ¥20

for a ride, especially if travelling to or from the Longmen Caves or the high-speed station.

Tours Your accommodation will be able to help with standard day-tours of sights in the vicinity of town. For standard day-trips including Baima Temple and Shaolin Temple (excluding entry tickets), costs start at around ¥140 per person.

ACCOMMODATION

Basing yourself in one of the **budget options** near Luoyang's train station isn't such a bad idea, as there are good connections to the sights and transport out once you've finished; just to the south, the centre of town is cleaner, and the accommodation more upmarket. On online booking engines you'll find plenty of options in the new area **south of the river**; though it's spread out and rather dull, it's fine if you're just using the high-speed station and visiting the **Longmen Caves**. There's also an option out near the caves themselves.

THE CITY CENTRE

★**Christian's** 克丽司汀酒店, kèlìsītīng jiǔdiàn. 56 Jiefang Lu ☎0379 63266666, ⍩www.5xjd.com. Chic hotel with friendly, young staff, and a shark patrolling its tank in the lobby. Rooms have been designed with rare attention, with internet-ready computers in each, and plush carpets; each floor has been given a theme, meaning that you can stay in European, Chinese or even Balinese style. Note that the bathrooms are rather visible from a few of the bedrooms – check first – and that rates usually drop to more like ¥800. **¥1999**

★**Ease House** 颐舍酒店, yíshè jiǔdiàn. Junction of Guanlin Lu and Yongtai Jie ☎0379 69986000. If you're going to stay south of the river, this is a great choice, with rooms which look pretty sophisticated for the price, excellent buffet breakfasts, complimentary fruit and yoghurt, and free transfer to the high-speed station. **¥430**

Heartland Youth Hostel 中原驿国际青年旅舍, zhōngyuányì guójì qīngnián lǚshè. Off Zhongzhou Zhonglu, 200m east of Peony Hotel ☎0379 64856485. The best, and best-located, of Luoyang's new clutch of hostels. Staff are helpful and speak English, the dorms are cosy (ie, a bit cramped), and the private rooms are excellent value. They also run a sister hostel out in the Old Town. Dorms **¥40**, doubles **¥90**

Peony 牡丹大酒店, mǔdāndà jiǔdiàn. 15 Zhongzhou Xilu ☎0379 3944668, ⍩peonyhotel.net. Tall hotel whose drab lobby doesn't do justice to rooms which are perfectly acceptable – those facing north have nicer views. The breakfasts are fine, and there are usually discounts available from the rack rate. **¥550**

LONGMEN CAVES

Dongshan Hotel 东山宾馆, dōngshān bīnguǎn. Longmen Caves ☎0379 64686000, ⍩www.lydongshanhotel.cn. On a hilltop overlooking the Longmen Caves, this resort-style hotel boasts almost a hundred elegant rooms, a free gym and a few interesting quirks, such as piped spring water and a superb night-time view of the caves from a fourth-floor bar. The downside of its remote location is that you're almost obliged to dine on site. **¥880**

EATING AND DRINKING

It's a shame that Luoyang's famous **water-feast meals** (水席, shuǐxí) are so hard to find; so named because they're largely soup-based, they can be extremely expensive too. For cheap **noodles and dumplings**, try the snack stalls near the main station.

EATING

★**Lao Luoyang Mian Guan** 老洛阳面馆, lǎo luòyáng miànguǎn. 17 Wangcheng Lu, just south of Wangcheng Park ☎0379 62209260. This is the place to go for *shuixi* meals; though instead of an expensive banquet, which is the usual way to go, you'll be able to select individual dishes from a picture menu. Dishes cost around ¥26 per bowl, though don't order too many as servings are absolutely gigantic. Regular Chinese staples also available at single-figure prices. Daily 11am–2.30pm & 5–9.30pm.

Tudari 土大力, tǔdàlì. Off Jiefang Lu. This Korean restaurant, sitting on the northern cusp of a shopping precinct just east of *Christian's* hotel, serves up tasty portions of *naengmyeon* (cold noodles; ¥24), *bibimbap* (veggies on rice; from ¥28), and various Japanese *yakitori* sticks (from ¥18 for four). Daily 11am–11.30pm.

Wangfu Yuhuayuan 王府御花园, wángfǔ yùhuāyuán. 445 Zhongzhou Zhong Lu. Decent roast-duck restaurant with smart antique-style furnishings, but not especially expensive – a whole duck, plus the pancakes, veg, and sauce is only ¥118. Daily 9.30am–2pm & 5–9pm.

DRINKING

Party House 枫吧, fēng bā. Mudan Guangchang ☎138 03799755. The best bar of the half-dozen or so huddled together at the east end of Mudan Park (a fun area to go for drink, at least on weekends), and the one at which you're least likely to be deafened by the house band), with a global range of beer (including the lesser-spotted Beer Lao; ¥25), an excellent pool table, and a swanky interior. They often show English Premier League games on weekend evenings. Daily 7pm–3am.

DIRECTORY

Post office The post office (Mon–Sat 8am–6pm) is on the north side of Zhongzhou Zhong Lu, near the junction with Jinguyuan Lu.

Visa extensions The PSB is at 1 Kaixuan Xi Lu (Mon–Sat 8am–noon & 2–6pm).

Song Shan

嵩山, sōng shān

Halfway between Luoyang and Zhengzhou lie the seventy-odd peaks of the **Song Shan** range – quite a modest little chain, with its tallest summits around 1500m above sea level. When Luoyang became the Zhou capital in 771 BC, these hills were considered to be at the axis of the **five sacred Taoist mountains**, with Hua Shan to the west, Tai Shan to the east, Heng Shan to the south and another Heng Shan to the north. Given the importance to Taoism, it's ironic that the busiest sight around Dengfeng today is the **Shaolin Temple**, a Buddhist complex famed not just as one of the earliest dedicated to the Chan (Zen) sect, but also where **Chinese kung fu** is said to have originated. A major Taoist temple survives, however, in the **Zhongyue Miao**, and there are some other worthwhile sights nearby.

Shaolin Temple

少林寺, shàolín sì • Daily 7.30am–6pm • ¥100 • Kung fu shows daily 10am–4pm, included in ticket price

Shaolin Temple is a place of legends. This is the temple where the sixth-century founder of Buddhism's Chan (Zen) sect, **Bodhidharma**, consolidated his teachings in China, and also where – surprisingly, given Buddhism's peaceful doctrines – **Chinese kung fu** is said to have originated. Today, it's a tourist black spot, packed with noisy groups and commercial enterprises, and a complete non-starter if you're seeking any form of spiritual enlightenment – though as an entertaining look into modern China's kung fu cult, it's a lot of fun. In autumn, the place is particularly busy, filling up with martial-arts enthusiasts from all over the world who come to attend the international **Wushu Festival** in nearby Zhengzhou.

Brief history

The original Shaolin Temple was built in 495 AD. Shortly afterwards, the Indian monk **Bodhidharma** (known as **Da Mo** in China) came to live here after visiting the emperor in Nanjing, then crossing the Yangzi on a reed (depicted in a tablet at the temple). As the temple has been burned down on several occasions – most recently in 1928, by the warlord Shi Yousan – the buildings you see here today are mostly reconstructions in the Ming style, built over the last twenty years. Despite this, and the incredible density of tourists, the temple and surroundings are beautiful, and the chance to see some impressive martial-art displays here makes it well worth the trip.

The kung fu show hall

Once through the gates, the road passes two huge open areas packed in the morning and afternoons with hundreds of **martial-arts students** in tracksuits, arranged in small groups and practising jumps, throws, kicks and weapons routines. Just on from here and to the right is the **kung fu show hall**, with performance times posted outside. The half-hour performance is a cut-down version of the stage show that regularly tours the world, with demonstrations of Shaolin's famous stick fighting and animal-style kung fu, all pretty electrifying if you haven't seen it before. You may care to sit on the upper level – foreigners on the lower level sometimes get pushed into showing off their (usually awful) kung fu skills for a delighted audience.

The temple

The **temple entrance** is about 200m further up the path from the show hall, and inside you should look for trees whose bark has been drilled with holes by kung fu practitioners' fingers. At the end of the entranceway is a boxy pavilion housing two

SHAOLIN KUNG FU

Kung fu was first developed at the Shaolin Temple as a form of gymnastics to counterbalance the immobility of meditation. The monks studied the movement of animals and copied them – the way snakes crawled, tigers leapt and mantises danced – and coordinated these movements with meditational breathing routines. As the temple was isolated it was often prey to bandits, and gradually the monks turned their exercises into a form of self-defence.

The monks owed their strength to rigorous **discipline**. From childhood, monks trained from dawn to dusk, every day. To strengthen their hands, they thrust them into sacks of beans, over and over; when they were older, into bags of sand. To strengthen their fists, they punched a thousand sheets of paper glued to a wall; over the years, the paper wore out and the young monks punched brick. To strengthen their legs, they ran around the courtyard with bags of sand tied to their knees, and to strengthen their heads, they hit them with bricks.

Only after twenty years of such exercises could someone consider themselves proficient in kung fu, by which time they were able to perform incredible **feats**, examples of which you can see illustrated in the murals at the temple and in photographs of contemporary martial-arts masters in the picture books on sale in the souvenir shops. Apart from breaking concrete slabs with their fists and iron bars with their heads, the monks can balance on one finger, take a sledgehammer blow to the chest, and hang from a tree by their neck. Their **boxing routines** are equally extraordinary, their animal qualities clearly visible in the vicious clawing, poking, leaping and tearing that they employ. One comic-looking variation that requires a huge amount of flexibility is **drunken boxing**, where the performer twists, staggers and weaves as if inebriated – useful training given that Shaolin monks are allowed alcohol.

Yet the monks were not just fighters; as many hours were spent **meditating and praying** as in martial training. They obeyed a moral code, which included the stricture that only fighting in self-defence was acceptable, and killing your opponent was to be avoided if possible. These rules became a little more flexible over the centuries as emperors and peasants alike sought their help in battles, and the Shaolin monks became legendary figures for their interventions on the side of righteousness.

The monks were at the height of their power in the Tang dynasty, though they were still a force to be reckoned with in the Ming, when **weapons** were added to their discipline. However, the temple was sacked during the 1920s and again in the 1960s during the Cultural Revolution, when Shaolin's monks were persecuted and dispersed. Things picked up again in the 1980s, when, as a result of Jet Li's enormously popular first film *Shaolin Temple*, there was a **resurgence** of interest in the art. The old masters were allowed to teach again, and the government realized that the temple was better exploited as a tourist resource than left to rot.

Evidence of the popularity of kung fu in China today can be seen not just at the tourist circus of the Shaolin Temple, but in any cinema, where **kung fu films**, often concerning the exploits of Shaolin monks, make up a large proportion of the entertainment on offer. Many young Chinese today want to study kung fu, and to meet demand numerous **schools** have opened around the temple. Few of them want to be monks, though – the dream of many is to be a movie star.

Inevitably, such attention and exploitation has taken its toll on Shaolin Temple's original purpose as a Buddhist monastery. The temple's primary drive today seems less towards the spiritual and more about the travelling shows and protecting commercial interests – they are currently pursuing efforts to trademark the name "Shaolin", in order to capitalize on its use by everything from martial-arts outfits to beer companies. For a good account of what it's like to live and train here, and the challenges that the modern temple faces, read *American Shaolin* by Matthew Polly (see p.966).

fearsome demon statues that tower overhead, fists raised. On the right in the courtyard beyond are two large glassed-in tablets from 728 AD, raised by the Emperor **Taizong** after thirteen of Shaolin's monks had aided him against the rebel Wang Shichang; in gratitude, he passed an edict allowing monks at the temple to eat meat and drink wine. The temple's halls are quite small and simple, but two at the rear of the complex are worth attention: **Qianfo Hall**, whose brick floor is dented from where the monks used to stamp during their kung fu training; and the **White Robe Hall**, where Ming-dynasty **murals** covering two walls depict Taizong being saved by the monks.

Ta Lin

塔林, tǎlín

The **Ta Lin**, 200m up the hill past the temple entrance, is where hundreds of stone pagodas, memorials to past monks, are tightly grouped together in a "forest". Up to 10m tall, and with stepped, recessed tops, these golden stone structures are visible from a wooden walkway that circles the area; they look particularly impressive against the purple mountain when snow is on the ground. The earliest dates to 791 AD and commemorates a monk named Fawan, while the forest is still being added to as monks die.

The mountains

Songyang cable car ¥50; Shaolin cable car ¥60

The mountains beyond Ta Lin can be ascended by cable car or stone steps. There are two main routes to choose from, with the **Songyang** route the more popular; this heads up Shaoshi Shan, the highest peak in the area at 1512m, past a cave where Bodhidharma supposedly passed a nine-year vigil, sitting motionless facing a wall in a state of enlightenment. There are some spectacular views of rugged hills from these lofty paths, though on busy days crowds can dampen the effect somewhat. The Songyang cable car is most popular, but far fewer people take the new **Shaolin** cable car, which starts a little further along the path from Ta Lin and heads up a neighbouring mountain; views here are just as good.

Dengfeng

登封, dēngfēng

More or less equidistant from Zhengzhou and Luoyang – though you'll have to take the high road, rather than the low – little **Dengfeng** is the major town in the Song Shan area, and boasts a rather pleasing array of sights on its periphery, including the **Zhongyue Miao**, a spectacular Taoist temple complex. Dengfeng itself, though, is a messy place which doesn't really encourage an overnight stay, and you can see most of the regional attractions on day-trips from Luoyang or Zhengzhou.

4

Zhongyue Miao

中岳庙, zhōngyuè miào • Daily 8am–6pm • ¥80 • Bus #2 from Dengfeng

The **Zhongyue Miao**, on the eastern edge of Dengfeng, is a huge Taoist temple founded as long ago as 220 BC, though the buildings here today date from the Ming. Inside, the spacious, wooded courtyards and brilliantly coloured buildings stand out against the muted green of the mountain behind. If you've just come from crowded Shaolin, the calm atmosphere of this working Taoist monastery is particularly striking.

A series of gateways, courtyards and pavilions leads to the **Main Hall** where the emperor made sacrifices to the mountain. The Junji Gate, just before the hall, has two great sentries, nearly 4m high, brightly painted and flourishing their weapons. The courtyard houses gnarled old cypresses, some of them approaching the age of the temple itself, and also features four Song-dynasty **iron statues** of guardian warriors in martial poses. The **Bedroom Palace** behind the Main Hall is unusual for having a shrine that shows a deity lying in bed. Contemporary worshippers tend to gravitate to the back of the complex, where you may see people burning what look like little origami hats in the iron burners here, or practising *qi gong*, exercises centring around control of the breath.

Songyang Academy

嵩阳书院, sōngyáng shūyuàn • Daily 8am–6pm • ¥30 • Buses #2 or #6 from Dengfeng

At the top end of Songshan Lu 3km north of Dengfeng, the **Songyang Academy** consists of a couple of lecture halls, a **library** and a memorial hall, founded in 484 AD, which was one of the great centres of learning under the Song. Many famous scholars from history lectured here, including Sima Guang and Cheng Hao. In the courtyard are two enormous cypresses said to be over 4000 years old, as well as a stele from the Tang dynasty.

Songyue Temple Pagoda

嵩岳寺塔, sōngyuèsì tǎ · Daily 7am–6pm · ¥80 · Buses #2 and #6 from Dengfeng

The path beyond the Songyang Academy climbs to Junji Peak and branches off to the **Songyue Temple Pagoda**, 5km north of Dengfeng. Built at the beginning of the sixth century by the Northern Wei, this 45m-tall structure is both the oldest pagoda and the oldest complete brick building in China, rare for having twelve sides.

ARRIVAL AND TOURS   SONG SHAN

If you're only interested in the Shaolin Temple, it's not worth making a point of stopping in Dengfeng – catch a direct bus or tour from either Luoyang or Zhengzhou.

By bus Dengfeng's small bus station (登封汽车站, dēngfēng qìchēzhàn) is southeast of town; the last buses from Dengfeng depart around 6pm. Buses from Zhengzhou can drop you off at Shaolin Temple on the way, and some terminate at the temple itself, though there's no actual terminal – when leaving, search out direct buses to Luoyang or Zhengzhou here, or catch one of the white minibuses to Dengfeng and change there.
Dengfeng destinations Luoyang (every 30min; 1hr

30min); Zhengzhou (every 30min; 1hr 30min).

Tours More or less any hotel in Luoyang can get you on a tour bus to Shaolin Temple (see p.263); from Zhengzhou you may have to try a few places, but it's still perfectly possible. Hotels in both Luoyang and Zhengzhou are able to organize taxi tours of the Song Shan area; figure on ¥600–900 for the day. Those with a decent command of Chinese can cut this down considerably by negotiating directly with taxi drivers.

GETTING AROUND

By bus All sights in this area can be accessed by bus from Dengfeng's bus station, though it can be tricky to track them down – even locals get confused, though you'll soon find people willing to help out. Most buses operate from

the main road in front of Dengfeng's bus station; white minibuses to Shaolin Temple (¥5) use the station itself.
By taxi Taxis are useful for accessing sights or accommodation around Dengfeng; the basic fare is ¥7.

ACCOMMODATION AND EATING

Dengfeng's **accommodation** is OK, though the town itself is grubby and functional and you might be tempted to stay out at Shaolin Temple instead – you'll be offered rooms as soon as you step off the bus – and there's a decent hotel within the grounds. For **eating**, there are numerous dumpling places scattered around Dengfeng; in the temple complex, a large building near the kung fu hall offers Western fast food and cheap Chinese staples.

SHAOLIN TEMPLE
Kungfu Hostel 功夫旅舍, gōngfū lǚshè. Behind the kung fu hall ☎ 0371 62748889. Neat hostel option within a ten-minute walk of the temple. They've made a little effort with decorations of the rooms and dorms, and staff run occasional meditation and kung fu classes for guests. One other plus point – the country air here can come as a pleasant change if you've been staying in urban China for a little while. Dorms ¥70, twins ¥220
Zen International 禅居国际饭店, chánjū guójì fàndiàn. Behind the kung fu hall ☎ 0371 62745666. Located within the grounds of the temple itself, this is an

upmarket hotel – if a somewhat ageing one. There's a decent on-site restaurant, offering huge (and mostly vegetarian) lunch buffets at ¥38 a head. Ignore the rack rates, as you can usually halve these. ¥680

DENGFENG
Very Pear 梨花酒店, líhuā jiǔdiàn. 1 Shaolin Dadao ☎ 0379 62900000. A ten-minute walk from the bus station, this place is not bad, considering the weird name: it's a modern place with decent rooms, though nothing in the way of facilities. ¥280

Zhengzhou

郑州, zhèngzhōu

Close to the south bank of the Yellow River, **ZHENGZHOU** lies almost midway between Luoyang to the west and Kaifeng to the east. The walled town that existed here 3500 years ago was probably an early capital of the Shang dynasty, and excavations have revealed bronze foundries, bone-carving workshops and sacrificial altars. Today's Zhengzhou, however, is an entirely modern city, rebuilt virtually from scratch after heavy bombing in the war against Japan. Despite the resultant dearth of historical sights (especially for those daring to wear flip-flops), and the industrial trappings inevitably springing from a position atop China's two main rail routes, Zhengzhou is pleasant enough, its broad, leafy avenues lined with shopping malls and boutiques.

Erqi Pagoda

二七塔, èrqī tǎ · Daily 9am–5pm · Free · No flip-flops

The hub of downtown Zhengzhou is the **Erqi Pagoda**, made up of two conjoined nine-storey towers. It was built to commemorate those killed in a 1923 Communist-led rail strike that was put down with great savagery by the warlord Wu Pei Fu. You can climb up for a great view over central Zhengzhou.

The city walls

Daily 24hr · Free

East of the Erqi Pagoda, there's a remnant of old Zhengzhou in its ancient **city walls**, rough earthen ramparts 10m high, originally built more than two thousand years ago. Most Chinese cities have reconstructed their old fortifications along grand, Great

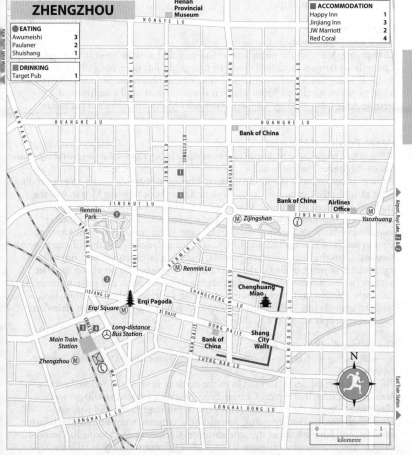

Wall-style lines, but in reality many of them were mere earthen barriers – bless Zhengzhou for keeping it real (at least, for now). There are paths along and around the walls, and you can walk for about 3km by the south and east sections (the west section has been destroyed by development), descending to cross the main roads along the way. Planted with trees, the walls are now used by the locals as a shortcut and a park, full of courting couples, kids who slide down the steep sides on metal trays, and old men who hang their cage birds from the trees and sit around fires cooking sweet potatoes – a historical monument, yet part of the fabric of everyday life.

Ruyi Lake

如意湖, rúyì hú • Daily 24hr • Free

Just to the east of central Zhengzhou, **Ruyi Lake** is a pretty new development flanked by some adventurous architecture – a series of golden "eggs" which contain the occasionally diverting **Henan Art Centre**, plus the city's **concert** and **opera halls**. Encircling the lake are 45 stone pillars, each with individual golden headwear – look carefully and you'll spy everything from a Roman soldier's helmet to a Chinese Liberation Army cap (if you're curious, there's a key on a golden plaque near the steps). Also here are the *JW Marriott* hotel (see opposite) and *Paulaner* bar-restaurant (see p.270).

Chenghuang Miao

城隍庙, chénghuáng miào • Daily 9am–5pm • Free • No flip-flops

Chenghuang Miao, on the north side of Shangcheng Lu, is the most interesting of Zhengzhou's temples, with well-observed images of birds decorating the eaves of the first hall, underneath roof sculptures of dragons and phoenixes. Murals in the modern Main Hall owe much to 1950s socialist realism, and surround a sculpture of a stern-looking Chenghuang, magisterial defender of city folk, who sits flanked by two attendants.

Henan Provincial Museum

河南省博物院, hénánshěng bówùyuàn • Northern end of Jingqi Lu • Daily 8.30am–6.15pm • Free (bring ID); English audioguide ¥30 • Bus #32 from the main train station

A giant stone pyramid, the modern **Henan Provincial Museum** boasts an outstanding collection of relics unearthed in the region, dating back to when Henan was the cradle of Chinese civilization. As you move clockwise, each hall covers a particular stage of regional history, beginning with the Stone Age: look for **oracle bones** inscribed with the ancestors of modern Chinese script unearthed from **Anyang**, 200km north of Zhengzhou, site of China's Shang-dynasty capital; and some superb **bronzes**, from the Shang to Tang periods, including large tripods and tiny animal figures used as weights. By far the most interesting pieces, however, are the **Han pottery**, with scale models of houses showing defensive walls and towers, models of domestic animals, and huge numbers of human figurines – dancers, musicians, soldiers, court ladies – all leaving the impression that the Han were an articulate, fun-loving people who liked to show off.

The Yellow River Scenic Area

黄河公园, huánghé gōngyuán • Daily 8am–6pm • ¥60 • Bus #16 (¥5) from Minggong Lu, just outside Zhengzhou's train station

The Yellow River slides by just 28km to the north of town at the **Yellow River Scenic Area**, really a stretch of typical Chinese countryside incorporating villages and allotments. Despite the dusty environs, parts of this large, semi-wild park are surprisingly verdant, incorporating forested hills, crumbly temple buildings, lakeside pavilions and large statues of dynastic emperors (including one Mount Rushmore-like design). You can spend an afternoon here walking, **horse-trekking** or taking a speedboat ride along the river. From the hilltops you have a good view over the river and the plain of mud either side of it. It's hard to imagine that in 1937, when Chiang Kai-shek breached the dykes 8km from the city to prevent the Japanese capturing the rail line, the Yellow River flooded this great plain, leaving more than a million dead and countless more homeless.

ARRIVAL AND DEPARTURE   ZHENGZHOU

By plane Zhengzhou airport (郑州新郑国际机场, zhèngzhōu xīnzhèng guójì jīchǎng) lies well to the east of the city; a taxi into the centre should cost around ¥100, while airport buses (every 30min; ¥20) head to several destinations around town, including the Aviation Building at 3 Jinshui Lu.
Destinations Beijing (1hr 10min); Hong Kong (2hr 35min); 1hr 10min); Shanghai (1hr 40min).

By train Tickets can be hard to buy at the main station due to the overwhelming crowds, and the East station is a bit far away – there are advance-booking booths dotted around town, all charging a ¥5 fee per ticket. Zhengzhou's main station (郑州站, zhèngzhōu zhàn) is well located, just to the southwest of the city centre. Most high-speed services run from the smart, new East station (郑州东站, zhèngzhōu dōngzhàn), 6km to the east – a ¥30 cab-ride, or jump on the subway.
Main station destinations Beijing (1–3 hourly; 3hr 40min–9hr); Guangzhou (1–3 hourly; 5hr 30min–17hr);

Kaifeng (1–4 hourly; 45min); Luoyang (1–4 hourly; 40min–2hr); Qufu (3 daily; 5–7hr); Shanghai (20 daily; 7–15hr); Taiyuan (4 daily; 12hr); Xi'an (1–2 hourly; 2hr 15min–7hr).
Zhengzhou East station destinations Beijing (2–4 hourly; 2hr 30min–3hr 20min); Guangzhou (14 daily; 6hr); Luoyang (8 daily; 40min); Taiyuan (2 daily; 3hr 30min); Xi'an (13 daily; 2hr 15min–3hr).

By bus The long-distance bus station (郑州长途站, zhèngzhōu chángtú zhàn) is opposite the train station, though there is also the usual run of other depots scattered around the city's edges. Bus tickets to all major regional destinations are easy to get at the horde of windows surrounding the main bus station. In addition, day-trips to Shaolin leave from in front of the train station around 8–11am, when you'll find minibuses lined up.
Destinations Dengfeng (1hr 30min); Kaifeng (1hr 30min); Luoyang (2hr 30min); Shaolin Temple (1hr 45min).

4

GETTING AROUND

By bus The main city bus terminuses lie either side of the train station plaza. Routes can be hard to ascertain for non-Chinese-speakers; maps in Chinese with details of bus routes are available outside the train station. Fares cost ¥1–2.
By subway At the time of writing, Zhengzhou had one subway line up and running, another ready to open, and

four more in the works. Line #1 (¥2–4) is already useful for getting between the two train stations, though oddly, there's no entrance from the train station plaza – you'll have to walk to the nearest station at Erqi Ta.
By taxi Cabs have an ¥8 minimum charge, though Zhengzhou is a big city – you could be looking at fares of up to ¥30.

ACCOMMODATION

If you've only come to Zhengzhou in transit, it makes sense to stay around the **train station area**, where there's plenty of inexpensive, decent accommodation, though it can get noisy. There are also a couple of **motel and upmarket hotel options** further out, in less crowded settings.

★**Happy Inn** 喜鹊家旅馆, xīquèjiā lǚguǎn. 9 Jingliu Lu ☎0371 87559666. This boutique hotel is a lovely surprise, full of neat little touches: cartoon shows are projected behind reception, which features a small magazine library and DVDs laid out for rent. The rooms are quiet and clean, and the place is located on Zhengzhou's most appealing street for nightlife. **¥359**
Jinjiang Inn 锦江之星旅馆, jǐnjiāng zhīxīng lǚguǎn. 77 Erma Lu ☎0371 66932000, ⓦjinjianginns .com. An easy walk from the main train station or the Erqi Pagoda, this is one of the only foreign-friendly cheapies in the area, and is perfectly adequate for the price. **¥169**
JW Marriott 绿地JW万豪酒店, lǜdì JW wànháo

jiǔdiàn. 2 CBD ☎0371 88828888, ⓦjwmarriott zhengzhou.com.cn. The most appealing of Zhengzhou's many five-star hotels, occupying the 38th–55th floors of an Oriental-style skyscraper, poking out of the newly-created Henan Art Center zone. Every room has splendid views, while service standards and the on-site restaurants are also top-notch. **¥1020**
Red Coral 红珊瑚酒店, hóngshānhú jiǔdiàn. 20 Erma Lu ☎0371 66652226. The best of the motley crew of mid-rangers outside the train station, with large, comfortable rooms, a filling breakfast buffet, helpful staff – and Kenny G, the original epic sax man, playing 24hr in the lift. **¥398**

EATING

Zhengzhou has abundant **eating** options, though you'll likely want to escape the train station area, which is as crowded with fast-food eateries as it is with people.

Awumeishi 阿五美食, āwǔ měishí. 10 Minzhu Lu ☎0371 86515555. The best place in town for the local speciality, *liyu beimian* (鲤鱼焙面), a real Henan favourite consisting of a whole carp covered with a tangy brown sauce (¥99) and noodles (an extra ¥39) – tasty as hell, but watch out for the many bones. There are other great items on the picture menu, including mashed aubergine with minced garlic (¥25). Daily 10am–10pm.

Paulaner CBD ☎0371 87506999. For something a little different, head to this smart-looking German restaurant-bar under the *JW Marriott* – Bavarian dishes include a peppery goulash (¥45), *Schweinshaxen* (¥128) and sausage, sauerkraut and mash (¥98). Draught beer available too, of course. Daily 10.30am–1.30am.

★**Shuishang** 水上餐厅, shuǐshàng cāntīng. 100 Beierqi Lu ☎0371 66249599. Straddling a small river, this is a delightful, old-fashioned venue serving Hong Kong-style *dim sum*. There's a menu, but you may not need it – waitresses will soon bus their trolleys over to your table with rounds of succulent goodies, most of which cost ¥13–18 per plate. Daily 7am–2pm & 5pm–5am.

DRINKING

Target Pub 目标酒吧, mùbiāo jiǔbā. 10 Jingliu Lu ☎138 03857056. Get your fill of Guinness and darts at this deliberately ramshackle-looking pub, in the best street for bars, and which is popular with expats and some of Zhengzhou's more colourful locals. Daily 7pm–3am, sometimes later.

DIRECTORY

Post office The principal post office (Mon–Fri 8am–8pm) is next to the train station, on the south side of the concourse.
Visa extensions The PSB's visa section is east of the centre at 90 Huanghe Nan Lu (Mon–Fri 8.30am–noon & 3–6pm; ☎0371 69625990), a short walk south of Huanghenanlu metro station.

Kaifeng

开封, kāifēng

Located on the alluvial plains in the middle reaches of the Yellow River 70km east of Zhengzhou, **KAIFENG** is an ancient capital with a history stretching back over three thousand years. However, unlike other ancient capitals in the region, the city hasn't grown into an industrial monster, with most of its sights in a pleasingly compact area within the **town walls**, which enclose a 5km-long rectangle. These tamped-earth ramparts have been heavily damaged and there's no path along them, but they do present a useful landmark. The town is also crisscrossed by **canals**, part of a network that connected it to Hangzhou and Yangzhou in ancient times. While not especially attractive, Kaifeng's low-key ambience and sprinkling of older temples and pagodas encourage a wander, and in all, this is a worthwhile place to spend a couple of days, especially if you've grown weary of the scale and pace of most Chinese cities.

At the very centre of town, and the best place from which to kick off a tour of the city's sights, lies **Shudian Jie** (书店街; Bookshop Street), a scruffy run of two-storey

---

KAIFENG'S JEWS

A number of families in Kaifeng trace their lineage back to the **Jews**, though their origins remain a mystery. It's likely that their ancestors arrived from Central Asia around 1000 AD, when trade links between the two areas were strong. The community was never large, but it seems to have flourished until the nineteenth century, when – perhaps as a result of disastrous floods, including one in 1850 that destroyed the synagogue – the Kaifeng Jews almost completely died out. However, following the atmosphere of greater religious tolerance in contemporary China, many Jews have begun practising their faith again. You can see a few relics from the synagogue in the museum, including three steles that once stood outside it, but most, such as a Torah in Chinese now in the British Museum, are in collections abroad.

imitation Qing buildings with fancy balconies. Many shops here do indeed sell books, from art monographs to pulp fiction with lurid covers, while it's a great place to grab a night-time snack (see p.274). Also ask about the opening of the new **Kaifeng Museum** – the old one, home to a series of **steles** recording the history of Kaifeng's Jewish community, and one of the only remnants of the old synagogue (see box opposite) – had just closed its doors at the time of writing.

Brief history
Kaifeng had its heyday during the Song dynasty between 960 and 1127 AD, when the city became the political, economic and cultural centre of the empire. A famous 5m-long

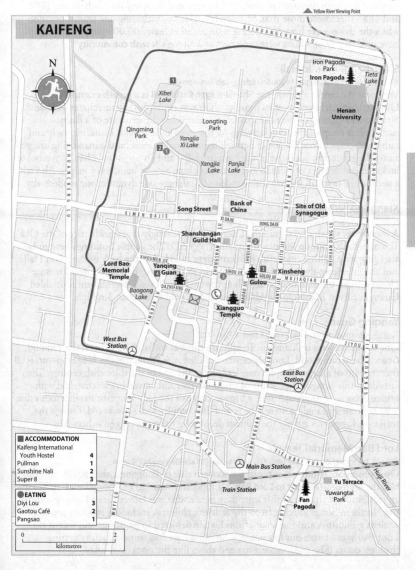

KAIFENG

N

▲ Yellow River Viewing Point

BEIHUANGCHENG LU

Iron Pagoda Park
Iron Pagoda
Tieta Lake

Xibei Lake

Longting Park

Qingming Park

Yangjia Xi Lake

Yangjia Lake

Panjia Lake

Henan University

BEIMEN DAJIE

DONGGUANCHENG LU

XIHUANCHENG LU

Song Street

Bank of China

Site of Old Synagogue

XIMEN DAJIE

XI DAJIE

DONG DAJIE

BEIDAWEN JIE

Shanshangan Guild Hall

SHIDIAN JIE

DONG DAJIE

BEITO JIE

NEIHUAN DONG LU

XIHOUMEN JIE

ZHONGSHAN LU

Lord Bao Memorial Temple

Yanqing Guan

DAZHIFANG JIE

SIHOU JIE

MADAO JIE

NANTU JIE

Xinsheng

MUJIAQIAO JIE

Gulou

Baogong Lake

YINGBIN LU

Xiangguo Temple

ZIYOU LU

West Bus Station

ZIYOU LU

GONGYUAN LU

BINHE LU

East Bus Station

WULI LU

WUFU XI LU

ZHONGSHAN LU

XINMENGUAN JIE

WUFU LU

TIELUBEI YUAN

Hujji River

Main Bus Station

POTA LU JIE

Yu Terrace

Train Station

Fan Pagoda

Yuwangtai Park

■ ACCOMMODATION	
Kaifeng International Youth Hostel	4
Pullman	1
Sunshine Nali	2
Super 8	3

● EATING	
Diyi Lou	3
Gaotou Café	
Pangsao	1

0 ———— 2
kilometres

horizontal **scroll** by Zhang Azheduan, *Qingming Shang He* (*Qingming Festival Along the River*), now in the Forbidden City in Beijing, unrolls to show views of the city at this time, teeming with life, crammed with people, boats, carts and animals. It was a great age for painting, calligraphy, philosophy and poetry, and Kaifeng was famed for the quality of its textiles and embroidery, and for its production of ceramics and printed books. It was also the home of the first mechanical timepiece in history, Su Song's **astronomical clock tower** of 1092, which worked by the transmission of energy from a huge water wheel.

Kaifeng's Golden Age ended suddenly in 1127 when Jurchen invaders overran the city. Just one royal prince escaped to the south, to set up a new capital out of harm's reach beyond the Yangzi at Hangzhou, though Kaifeng itself never recovered. What survived has been damaged or destroyed by repeated **flooding** since – between 1194 and 1887 there were more than fifty severe incidents, including one fearful occasion when the dykes were breached during a siege and at least 300,000 people are said to have died, many of whom were members of Kaifeng's **Jewish community**.

Shanshangan Guild Hall

陕山甘会馆, shǎnshāngān huìguǎn • Xufu Jie • Daily 8am–6pm • ¥25

Very near the centre of town, the **Shanshangan Guild Hall** is a superb example of Qing-dynasty architecture at its most lavish. It was established by merchants of Shanxi, Shaanxi and Gansu provinces as a social centre and has the structure of a flashy, ostentatious temple. The woodcarvings on the eaves are excellent, including lively and rather wry scenes from the life of a travelling merchant – look for the man being dragged along the ground by his horse in the Eastern Hall – and groups of gold bats (a symbol of luck) beneath images of animals and birds frolicking among bunches of grapes. Also take a peek in the first hall for two scale models of Kaifeng – one dynastic, one modern-day.

Xiangguo Temple

相国寺, xiàngguó sì • Ziyou Lu • Daily 8am–6pm • ¥45

A short walk south of the guild hall, across an appealingly ramshackle part of the Old Town, is the **Xiangguo Temple**, founded in 555 AD. The simple buildings here today are Qing style, with a colourful, modern frieze of *arhats* at the back of the Main Hall, and an early Song-dynasty bronze Buddha in the Daxiong Baodian (Great Treasure House). In an unusual octagonal hall at the back you'll see a magnificent four-sided Guanyin carved in ginkgo wood and covered in gold leaf, about 3m high.

Yanqing Guan

延庆观, yánqìng guān • Ziyou Lu • Daily 8.30am–6.30pm • ¥30

One kilometre west of Xiangguo Temple, on the way to Baogong Lake, is the **Yanqing Guan**, whose rather odd, knobbly central building, the **Pavilion of the Jade Emperor**, is all that remains of a larger temple complex built at the end of the thirteenth century. The outside of this octagonal structure of turquoise tiles and carved brick is overlaid with ornate decorative touches; inside, a bronze image of the Jade Emperor sits in a room that is by contrast strikingly austere. The rest of the complex looks just as old, though the images of kangaroos among the animals decorating the eaves suggest otherwise.

Lord Bao Memorial Temple

包公祠, bāogōng cí • Daily 8am–6pm • ¥25 • **Boats to Yangjia Lake** ¥35 one-way, ¥50 return

On a promontory jutting out into the western side of Baogong Lake (包公湖, bāogōng hú), the **Memorial Temple to Lord Bao** is a modern imitation of a Song building holding an exhibition of the life of this legendary figure who was Governor of Kaifeng during the Northern Song. Judging from the articles exhibited, including modern copies of ancient guillotines and the scenes from his life depicted in paintings and waxworks, Lord Bao was a harsh but fair judge, who must have had some difficulty getting through doors if he really wore a hat and shoes like the ones on display.

Yangjia Lake

杨家湖, yángjiā hú · Daily 8am–6pm · ¥80 · **Boats to Lord Bao Memorial Temple** ¥35 one-way, ¥50 return

Taking up much of the northern part of central Kaifeng, **Yangjia Lake** was originally part of the imperial gardens, but now forms the centre of a large warren of carnival-like tourist traps arranged around the lakeshore. You'll only have to pay the ticket price to enter the park areas – not really worth it, to be honest, as the lake is pretty enough from the free-to-visit stretches. In addition, the canal leading south from Yangjia Lake and Qingming Park to Baogong Lake has been newly gentrified along Qing lines, and is Kaifeng's best place for an evening stroll (unless you hate bats or mosquitoes, of which there are plenty); with views of bamboo, lotus flowers, moon bridges and quaint pavilions, it's actually more pleasant than many of Kaifeng's pay-to-enter parks.

Qingming Park

清明上河园, qīngmíng shànghéyuán · Daily 9am–6pm · ¥100, extra for additional attractions

At **Qingming Park**, a kitschy theme park west of Yangjia Lake, you can walk through a realized version of *Qingming Shang He*, wandering to your heart's content past costumed courtesans and ingratiating shopkeepers. It's a good place for families, and perhaps those who want an interesting (though expensive) window into China's current means of packaging history for local consumption.

Iron Pagoda Park

铁塔公园, tiětǎ gōngyuán · Accessible only off Beimen Dajie · Daily 8am–6pm · ¥60, plus ¥35 to climb the tower · Buses #1 and #3 from the centre of town

The northeastern corner of walled Kaifeng is occupied by **Iron Pagoda Park**. At its centre you'll find the 13-storey, 56m-high pagoda that gives it its name, a striking Northern Song (1049 AD) tower so named because its surface of glazed tiles gives the building the russet tones of rusted iron – especially beautiful when fired up by the setting sun. Its base, like all early buildings in Kaifeng, is buried beneath a couple of metres of silt deposited during floods. Most of the tiles hold relief images, usually of the Buddha, but also of Buddhist angels, animals and abstract patterns. Behind the pagoda is a large lake, and it's quite possible to kill a few hours wandering around its circumference, and the rest of the park.

The Fan Pagoda

繁塔, fán tǎ · 7am–7pm · ¥30 · Taxi from train station ¥10

The dumpy, hexagonal **Fan Pagoda** pokes out of a labyrinthine maze of alleyways, about 3km southeast of the city centre. Built in 997 AD, and the oldest standing building in Kaifeng, it was once 80m tall and had nine storeys; three remain today. It's set in a scruffy, semi-derelict park, and receives precious few visitors – you may have to wake up the staff in order to buy your ticket.

Yuwangtai Park

禹王台公园, yǔwángtái gōngyuán · Daily 7am–7pm · ¥30 · Taxi from train station ¥10

East of the Fan Pagoda, **Yuwangtai Park** surrounds the **Yu Terrace**, an earthen mound now thought to have been a music stage that was once the haunt of Tang poets. The park, dotted with pavilions and commemorative steles, is pleasant in summer when the many flower gardens are in bloom – it's overpriced, though.

Yellow River Viewing Point

黄河公园, huánghé gōngyuán · Daily 24hr · Free, charges apply for various activities · Bus #6 (¥1) from Beimen Dajie, by entrance to Iron Pagoda Park, or about ¥45 by taxi

It's worth catching a bus to the **Yellow River Viewing Point**, 11km north of town, especially if you haven't seen the river before. From a pavilion near the road (still a little far from the river), you can look out onto a plain of silt that stretches to the horizon, across whose dramatic emptiness the syrupy river meanders. Beside the pavilion is an **iron ox**, which once stood in a now submerged temple. It's a cuddly-looking beast with a horn on its head that makes it look like a rhino sitting on its hind legs. An inscription on the back reveals its original function – as a charm to ward off floods, a tradition begun by the legendary flood-tamer Da Yu. There are now various activities such as jet-skiing and horseriding on and around the river itself, but it's perhaps simply more pleasurable to kick your footwear off and let the mighty river ooze slowly past your feet.

ARRIVAL AND DEPARTURE
KAIFENG

By plane The nearest airport to Kaifeng is at Zhengzhou (see p.269).

By train Kaifeng's small train station (开封站, kāifēng zhàn) sits 2km south of the old town, and receives services from all over the area. You can buy tickets here, though there are several booking offices in the centre, including a convenient one diagonally across from the hostel. At the time of writing, a new high-speed station was being constructed to the north – by the time you read this, it should be handling services on the Xi'an–Xuzhou line.

Destinations Beijing (2 daily; 13hr); Luoyang (22 daily; 2hr 30min); Qufu (1 daily; 3hr 40min); Shanghai (11 daily; 6hr 30min); Xi'an (19 daily; 7–9hr); Zhengzhou (many daily; 45min).

By bus The main long-distance station (开封汽车站, kāifēng qìchē zhàn) is in front of the train station to the east, though you might also wind up at the smaller west or east bus stations, near the southern walls. The only notable destinations are Zhengzhou (hourly; 1hr 30min) and Luoyang (hourly; 2hr 30min).

GETTING AROUND

By bus City buses cost ¥1 and are useful for arrival points – numbers #1 and #9 head into town from the station – though taxis are more convenient elsewhere.

By taxi Taxis are cheap; flag fall is ¥5, and ¥15 will get you almost anywhere you need to go. Note that drivers waiting at the station will likely refuse to use their meters; head to the main road and pick up a cruising cab.

By boat It's possible to take a boat ride between Yangjia

Lake and the Lord Bao Memorial Temple – a highly pleasurable experience, especially by night, though perhaps get a one-way ticket (¥35) rather than a return (¥50), since the canal also makes for a delightful walk.

By bicycle Surprisingly few places rent out bikes; try the hostel, which will give you one for ¥20 per day (¥200 deposit).

ACCOMMODATION

Despite Kaifeng's small size, it has several good-value **budget hotels**; pickings are somewhat slimmer at the upper end of the scale.

Kaifeng International Youth Hostel 开封天福国际青年旅舍, kāifēng tiānfú guójì qīngnián lǚshè. 30 Yingbin Lu ☏0378 23153789, ⊕yhachina.com. Kaifeng's sole hostel option is a bit grubby around the edges: rooms could do with a clean, and beds are a bit creaky. Well worth it if you're after a dorm bed and some travel company. Dorms **¥100**, doubles **¥298**

★**Pullman** 铂尔曼酒店, bóěrmàn jiǔdiàn. Longting Beilu ☏0378 23589999, ⊕pullmanhotels .com. By far the classiest place in town, set away from the action on the shores of a pleasant lake. All of the rooms, without exception, have been lovingly designed, with all sorts of quirky flourishes, as well as thick pile carpets. The pool is a lovely place to splash around, and the on-site

eateries are great too. **¥758**

Sunshine Nali 阳光纳里, yángguāng nàlǐ. Building 5, off Longting Xilu ☏0378 22382222. Part of a new "old-style" development, one of the nicest areas in town, staff and owners at this hotel still seem to be learning the ropes – the rooms look inviting (though many have no view), the parasol-filled courtyard is a pretty place to hang out, but service standards are next to nonexistent. Room for improvement. **¥468**

Super 8 速8酒店, sù bā jiǔdiàn. Gulou Jie ☏0378 28888588. The best, and most usefully located, of Kaifeng's chain-hotel cheapies. Rooms aren't bad at all for the price, even if the bathrooms can be a little wee – get a room facing west towards the Drum Tower, if you can. **¥228**

EATING

Kaifeng's best place to eat is the **night market** in the area between Shudian Jie and Sihou Jie, where the food, as well as the ambience, is fun. You'll find *jiaozi*, made in front of you; skewers of mutton cooked by Uyghur peddlers; and shock-the-folks-back-home favourites like sparrow, snails and silkworm.

★**Diyi Lou** 第一楼, dìyīlóu. 43 Sihou Jie ☎0378 25998688. This smart spot is famous for Kaifeng's own take on the humble *baozi*; flat and circular, they look a little like wagon wheels. The ones served here (¥25 per round) are utterly delectable, though often take up to 30min to prepare; there are six different varieties available, of which the seafood (海米, hǎimǐ) are the tastiest. Dumplings aside, there's a full menu of Chinese staples to choose from; try the fried veggie balls (¥20). Daily 11.30am–2pm & 5–8.30pm.

Gaotou Café 高头书咖, gāotóu shūkā. 78 Shudian Jie. Finally, a decent café on Shudian Jie! There have been several botched attempts in the recent past, but this little place – entered via a spectacle shop, and filled with books – actually makes good coffee. The soft music also makes a nice escape from the noise outside. Daily 8am–8.30pm.

Pangsao 胖嫂拉面, pàngsǎo lāmiàn. 43 Sihou Jie ☎0371 23231717. The only reliable place to have opened up so far in the newly Qing-ified development to the south of Qingming Park, serving their signature handmade noodles for ¥12, either cold and spicy or in a hot soup. There's plenty of other choice on the picture menu too, or swing by in the evening for some lamb kebabs – best washed down with a half-litre of draught Qingdao (three-litre towers also available if you're with friends, or extremely thirsty). Daily 10am–2pm & 5–10pm.

DIRECTORY

Post office There's a post office (Mon–Fri 8am–noon & 2.30–6pm) on Dazhifang Jie, and plenty of other branches around town.

PSB The PSB is at 86 Zhongshan Lu (daily 9am–noon & 3–5pm; ☎0378 5322242).

Shopping Kaifeng is a good place to find paintings and calligraphy, among the best buys in China. The obvious thing to pick up is a full-size reproduction of the *Qingming Shang He* scroll, which shouldn't set you back more than ¥150, or renowned New Year woodblock prints produced at the nearby town of Zhuxian. Try the shops on Song Jie and Shudian Jie.

4

The eastern seaboard

山东 / 江苏 / 浙江

SUZHOU

5

The eastern seaboard

Encompassing the provinces of Shandong, Jiangsu and Zhejiang, China's eastern seaboard stretches for almost 2000km between the mouths of the Yellow and Yangzi rivers. These waterways have played a vital part in the cultural and economic development of China for the last two thousand years, and the area today remains one of the country's economic powerhouses. Including Shanghai, a city flanked by Jiangsu and Zhejiang, the eastern seaboard is home to nearly 250 million people – meaning that, if somehow cleaved from China, it would be the world's fourth most populous country. This makes for great transport infrastructure: comfortable, modern buses run along the many inter-city expressways, while the area has the country's highest concentration of high-speed rail routes. Yet, however modernized the eastern seaboard might be, with cities which rank among the most sophisticated in the land, there's plenty of visible history to get your teeth into as you journey around the region.

Shandong province is home to some small and intriguing places: the coastal city of **Qingdao**, which offers a couple of beaches, swaths of colonial architecture, lots of beer and seafood; **Ji'nan**, a large city in which you can go swimming in a *hutong* spring; **Tai Shan**, one of the major pivots of the Taoist religion; and **Qufu**, the birthplace of Confucius, with its giant temple and mansion. Over in Jiangsu province there's **Nanjing**, China's large but likeable "southern capital", and wonderful **Suzhou**, whose centre is crisscrossed by gorgeous canals, and dotted with classically designed gardens. Heading further south to Zhejiang province it would be unthinkable to bypass **Hangzhou**, which Marco Polo termed "the most beautiful and magnificent city in the world"; its Xi Hu (West Lake), still recognizable from classic scroll paintings, is deservedly rated as one of the most scenic spots in China. The same can be said of the enchanting island of **Putuo Shan**, which juts out of the sea just east of the mainland.

The region's prosperity means that its **accommodation** is on the expensive side, though there are excellent youth hostels in almost all tourist centres. The **climate** varies a fair bit from north to south: Shandong's is similar to that of Beijing; while the Yangzi River region, despite being low-lying and far from the northern plains, is unpleasantly cold and damp in winter, yet also unbearably hot and sticky during the summer –

QINGDAO

Highlights

① Qingdao Seafood, beer, beaches and colonial-era architecture are the most prominent draws of this affable coastal city. **See p.284**

② Wangfu Chizi, Ji'nan Swim with China's fittest pensioners at this open-air pool, fed by spring water. **See p.291**

③ Tai Shan Ascend one of China's holiest peaks – a calf-busting climb which has drawn pilgrims from Shandong and beyond for centuries. **See p.296**

④ Qufu Delve into the world of Confucius in the sage's charming home town. **See p.300**

⑤ Suzhou A striking medley of tree-lined canals, ramshackle homes, old stone bridges and traditional Chinese gardens. **See p.318**

⑥ Xi Hu, Hangzhou You will get great vistas from this beautiful lake, best appreciated by cycling the area. **See p.327**

⑦ Moganshan An old colonial hill resort that has become fashionable as a summer retreat – it's a great spot for a brisk hike. **See p.334**

⑧ Shaoxing Charismatic backwater once home to writer Lu Xun, whose elegant mansion – now a museum – offers a glimpse into a vanished world. **See p.335**

HIGHLIGHTS ARE MARKED ON THE MAP ON P.280

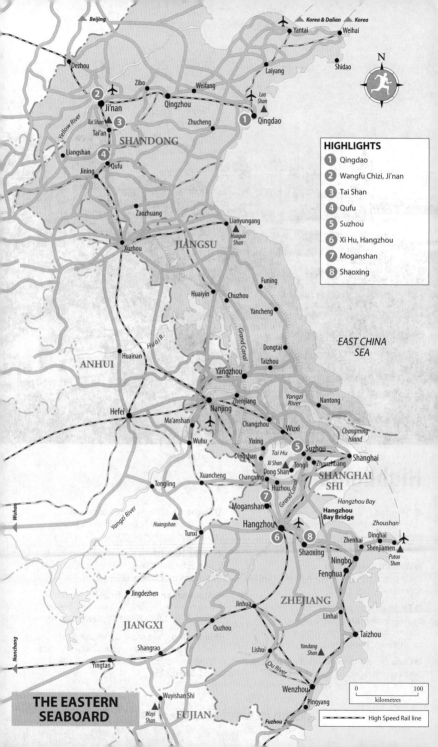

HIGHLIGHTS

1. Qingdao
2. Wangfu Chizi, Ji'nan
3. Tai Shan
4. Qufu
5. Suzhou
6. Xi Hu, Hangzhou
7. Moganshan
8. Shaoxing

THE EASTERN
SEABOARD

High Speed Rail line

5

Nanjing's reputation as one of the "three furnaces" of China is well justified. If possible, try to visit in spring (mid-April to late May), during which a combination of rain showers, sunshine and low humidity gives the terrain a splash of green as well as putting smiles on the faces of residents emerging from the harsh winter.

Brief history

The murky Yellow River oozes slowly across Shandong province and into the sea, and its dusty basin provided China with its original heartland – human settlements have existed in Shandong for more than six thousand years, with Neolithic remains indicating a sophisticated agricultural society. In the Warring States Period (720–221 BC), Shandong included the states of Qi and Lu, and the province is well endowed with ancient tombs and temples, not least thanks to the efforts of its most illustrious son, Confucius (see box, p.303).

The Yangzi basin

It was the lower Yangzi basin, however, which provided the power base for China's first empire. As early as the sixth century BC, the basin's flat terrain, large crop yield and superb communications offered by coastal ports and navigable waterways enabled the principal towns of the area to develop quickly into important trading centres. These presented an irresistible target for the expanding Qin dynasty, and in 223 BC the region was annexed, immediately developing into one of the empire's economic hubs. After the end of the Han dynasty in the third century AD, several regimes established short-lived capitals in southern cities; however, the real boost for southern China came when the Sui (589–618 AD) extended the Grand Canal to link the Yangzi with the Yellow River and, ultimately, to allow trade to flow freely between here and the northern capitals. With this, China's centre of gravity took a decisive shift south. Under later dynasties, Hangzhou and then Nanjing became the greatest cities in China, each serving as capital of the country at some point, and acting as counterweights to the bureaucratic tendencies of Beijing since its own accession to power.

Recent history

The area's recent history, though, has been dominated by foreign influence and its ramifications. The Treaty of Nanking, which ceded Hong Kong to Britain, was signed in Nanjing in 1842, after which the city itself became a treaty port. In 1897, the Germans arrived in Shandong, occupying first the port of Qingdao and then the capital, Ji'nan, their influence spreading further as they built a rail system across the province. Resentment at this interference, exacerbated by floods and an influx of refugees from the south, combined at the turn of the twentieth century to make Shandong the setting for the Boxer Rebellion (see p.932). Moving on a few decades, Nanjing was to suffer one of the world's worst ever massacres, with an estimated 300,000 civilians killed by Japanese soldiers in what is now known as the Rape of Nanking (see box, p.312).

Shandong

山东, shāndōng

Shandong province, encompassing a fertile plain through which the Yellow River completes its journey, was once one of the poorest regions of China, overpopulated and at the mercy of the river, whose course has continually shifted, bringing chaos with every move. Times have changed, and it is now one of the most **prosperous** provinces in the land. Visitors may also remark upon the friendliness of the people, who are proud of their reputation for hospitality. That tradition goes right back to **Confucius**, a Shandong native who declared in *The Analects*, "Is it not a great pleasure to have guests coming from afar?"

5

Despite Shandong's new-found wealth, some of its most appealing attractions are as old as the hills. One actually *is* a hill, albeit a rather large one – **Tai Shan**, China's holiest Taoist mountain, and a favourite with hikers and temple-hunters alike. Also popular is little **Qufu**, formerly home to Confucius, and where a magnificent temple complex stands in his honour. The coast is lined with colossal cities, of which **Qingdao** proves the most attractive to visitors.

Yantai

烟台, yāntái

On the Yellow Sea in northern Shandong, **YANTAI** is a large, bustling city with a giant port. Tourist sights are thin on the ground, however – the main reason to visit the area is to hang out by the beach, and utilize the **ferry** connections to Dalian, or even Korea (see box opposite). Away from the transit points along scruffy Beima Lu, Yantai is a modern, agreeable place, with a busy shopping district south of the port on **Nan Dajie**. Things take a pleasant turn for the scruffy in the area around **Yantaishan Park**, which boasts a few colonial-era buildings, and a whole bunch of places serving excellent seafood.

Yantai Folk Museum

烟台民俗博物馆, yāntái mínsú bówùguǎn • 2 Yulan Jie • Tues–Sun 8am–4.30pm • Free (bring ID)

Yantai folk museum is housed in a beautiful old guildhall, set up around the turn of the nineteenth century by Fujianese merchants and ship owners. It remains most notable for its architecture; the main building here is the **Tian Hou Miao**, a temple to the southern Chinese sea goddess, whom sailors trust to guide ships to safety. The temple itself was brought from Fujian by ship in 1864 and is a good example of southern architecture, with its richly carved wooden roof beams, eaves and panels illustrating historical scenes, and sweeping, pronged roofline fancifully ornamented with mythical figures in wood, stone and glazed ceramics. The whole temple complex is set in a little garden with pools and a stage – the goddess is said to have been fond of plays.

Wine Culture Museum

张裕酒文化博物馆, zhāngyù jiǔwénhuà bówùguǎn • Off Beima Lu; entrance on west side of complex • Daily 9am–5.30pm • ¥50, or from ¥80 including wine tasting

Yantai's **Wine Culture Museum** is worth a look, not so much for the humdrum historical exhibits but because – rarely for China – they produce a grape wine that is actually drinkable. Make sure you descend into the vast **cellar** where, sitting proud and beribboned among lesser casks, are the three-century-old "Barrel Kings", each holding

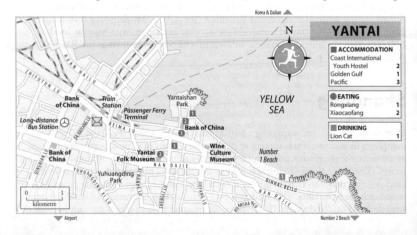

FERRIES TO KOREA

In addition to services from Qingdao (see p.287), two other Shandong ports – Yantai and Weihai – offer ferry connections to **Inchon** in South Korea, only one hour from Seoul by subway train. **Tickets** can be bought in advance from travel agencies, or at the terminals themselves. There are several classes on each vessel, with gradations in price as you move down the scale. You will also have to pay a **departure tax** and **fuel surcharge**, totalling around ¥60.

Ferries leave **Yantai** on Monday, Wednesday and Friday; the journey takes sixteen hours and tickets start at ¥1040. Tickets can be bought easily enough at the terminal. From **Weihai** (威海, wēihǎi), 80km east of Yantai, ferries leave on Tuesday, Thursday and Sunday; the journey takes fourteen hours, and tickets start at ¥820.

fifteen tonnes. You can have a go at bottling in cellar 4, or make your way straight to the **bar** in cellar 5 for your samples – the 12-year-old red is excellent, as is their brandy, both of which are on sale in the museum shop.

Yantaishan Park

烟台山公园, yāntáishān gōngyuán • Daily 7am–6pm • ¥55

Yantaishan Park, marking the eastern edge of the port area, features a steep hill where the locals used to keep an eye out for pirates, all latticed with twisting paths, pavilions, a couple of former consulates and an old Japanese military camp. It's overpriced, though.

The seafront

The city's **seafront** is pleasant on a good day. There are two **beaches** east of Yantaishan Park, but they're not great – littered, windy and hemmed in by unattractive buildings. Number 2 beach is the farther and more preferable of the two, though the water can be very polluted. For better swimming and a more pleasant environment, you'll have to head further south to the shorefront east of Yantai University – around 9km from the old city centre.

ARRIVAL AND INFORMATION   YANTAI

By air Yantai's airport (烟台莱山国际机场, yāntái láishān guójìjīchǎng) is a whopping 70km west of the city; shuttle buses (¥20) run from here to the bus station, or a taxi will cost around ¥170.

Destinations Beijing (1hr 15min); Hong Kong (2 weekly; 3hr 30min); Ji'nan (50min); Nanjing (1hr 20min); Shanghai (1hr 30min).

By train The station (烟台站, yāntái zhàn) is handily located just to the west of the centre, and receives some high-speed services.

Destinations Beijing (5 daily; 5hr 30min–15hr); Ji'nan (1–2 hourly; 3hr 45min–8hr); Qingdao (1 daily; 4hr 30min).

By bus Yantai's main bus station (汽车总站, qìchē zǒngzhàn) is about 1km west of the train station on

Qingnian Lu, though sometimes you get dropped in the train station forecourt. The only connections you're likely to need are those to Qingdao (every 30min; 3hr 30min), since there's still only one daily train connecting the two cities.

By ferry The port (烟台港, yāntái gǎng), just east of the train station, handles international services to Korea (see box above), as well as domestic ferries to Dalian (4–6 daily; 4–7hr; ¥250–800); some of the latter run overnight, in which case you're advised to book a sleeper berth. There are ticket offices in the terminal – you'll have to run between the various companies' booths to find the service you need – and several more around the train station.

Post office The post office (Mon–Fri 8am–6pm) is on Beima Lu, near the corner of Da Haiyang Lu.

ACCOMMODATION

Coast International Youth Hostel 海岸国际青年旅馆, hǎi'àn guójì qīngnián lǚguǎn. 41 Chaoyang Jie ☎180 53588599, ⓦyhachina.com. Surrounded by bars, this hostel is more or less the only decent budget choice in town, fronted by a café section and featuring rooms which are nothing to write home about, but adequate for the price. Dorm beds ¥40, doubles ¥140

Golden Gulf 金海湾酒店, jīnhǎiwān jiǔdiàn. 34 Hai'an Jie ☎0535 6636999, ⓦgoldengulfyantai.com. You can't miss this large, spacious place, abutting Yantaishan Park at the northern end of the strand. For some reason it's only ever busy when a group or conference is in town – the place can give off a *Shining* feel at other times, though service is pleasant and both rooms and common

5

areas well appointed. ¥630

Pacific 太平洋大酒店, tàipíngyáng dàjiǔdiàn. 74 Shifu Jie ☎0535 6588866. Have a look online for great rates at this towering, faintly classy edifice – they can be super cheap, and if you can score a room for ¥200 or so, you've got yourself a bargain. Rooms are large, if a little dated, and do note that the swimming pool has been mothballed. ¥440

EATING

For cheap eating, you can try the **street stalls** in the back lanes between Beima Lu and Nan Dajie. There are more on Chaoyang Jie, the street heading up to Yantaishan Park.

★**Rongxiang** 荣祥海鲜房, róngxiáng hǎixiānfáng. 25 Fumin Jie ☎155 06633177. This seafood place may be hard to find, but it's so worth it – the fact that it's packed out every single lunch- and dinnertime is proof that the locals respect its super-fresh fare, and prices aren't all that different to the shacks outside. There's no menu, so just point at whatever you like and ask for the price – the steamed oysters are a bargain at ¥25 for a bowlful, or go for the scallops, served with veggies for ¥68. Daily 11am–2pm & 4.30–9pm.

Xiaocaofang 小草房, xiǎo cǎo fáng. 87 Huamao Jie. If seafood's not your thing and you just feel like a decent Chinese meal, give this simple place a try – the picture menu is full of tasty staples, including fried egg and tomato, and excellent "Japanese" tofu, from around ¥20. Daily 10am–2pm & 5–9pm.

DRINKING

Chaoyang Jie has a huge range of bars – none truly stand out, though a simple walk up and down will help you decide on a favourite.

Lion Cat 狮猫啤酒, shīmāo píjiǔ. Off Binhai Beilu. For something a little different to the Chaoyang Jie bars, head to this little shack, which serves craft beer in litre-sized cans – comically huge things emblazoned with the words "my beer, my rules", they go for ¥40, and you'll most likely feel an odd sense of pride strolling down the beach with one in your hand. Give the IPA a whirl. Daily 9am–9pm.

Qingdao

青岛, qīngdǎo

There's a lot to like about **QINGDAO** – and not just on account of its status as the home of **Tsingtao**, China's most famous beer. Relatively fresh and modern for a Chinese city, Qingdao enjoys a charming, windswept location right next to the famed **Yellow Sea**, and here you can chomp down superb seafood, hunt down a nearby beach, or prise sea creatures from their shells at low tide. It's also surprisingly cosmopolitan for a provincial Chinese city, the result of its former status as a German military base; take time to wander amid the red-roofed **Bavarian architecture** of the hilly old city centre. Modern Qingdao remains an important **port**, the fourth largest in the land; the city is connected by ferry to both Japan and South Korea, and is highly recommended as an introduction, or full stop, to a trip around China.

For all Qingdao's colourful history, its progress is relentlessly modern. The **2008 Olympics**, whose sailing events were held here, accelerated the rate of change, most evident in the skyscraper-filled new city sprouting to the east. For tourists, most places of interest are within the walkable, compact **old German town**; exceptions include a series of **beaches** dotted along the shoreline, and day-trips east to the famous peak of **Lao Shan**.

Brief history

Qingdao sprang to prominence in 1897, after two German missionaries were murdered here in a prelude to the **Boxer Rebellion** (see p.932). Following a hysterical speech by Germany's **Kaiser Wilhelm** (which coined the phrase "Yellow Peril"), the feeble Manchu court ceded the territory for 99 years, along with the right to build the Shandong rail lines. Qingdao made an ideal deep-water base for the German navy, and while they were here they established a **brewery** producing the now world-famous Tsingtao beer

("Tsingtao" being the old transliteration of Qingdao). However, the city was forcibly taken from Germany in 1914 by the **Japanese** and later gifted to Japan at the Treaty of Versailles, an event that led to nationwide demonstrations which eventually saw Qingdao returned to China in 1922.

The churches

Both daily 8am–5pm • ¥10

Anchoring the old German town is the fine **St Michael's Church** (天主教堂, tiānzhǔ jiàotáng), whose distinctive double spires can be seen from all over the western parts of the city; it's a favourite with those taking wedding photos. Poke down the streets east of here – some are cobbled affairs lined with pink buildings, whose black iron balconies overlook the street. Farther east on Jiangsu Lu, there's the 1908 **Gospel church** (基督教堂, jīdū jiàotáng), built of solid stone and with a dark-blue tin clock tower; you can climb up for a closer look at the various cogs and pulleys.

Qingdao Museum

青岛市博物馆, qīngdǎoshì bówùguǎn • Daxue Lu • Tues–Sun 9am–4.30pm • Free

The **Qingdao Museum** is housed in a beautiful, temple-like building, which in the 1930s was the headquarters of the sinister-sounding Red Swastika Association, a welfare institute. There's a collection of paintings here from the Yuan through to Qing dynasties, and four large **Buddhas** dating back to 500–527 AD – slim striking figures with bulbous, smiling heads, one hand pointing upward to heaven, the other down to the earth. Some halls double as space for contemporary art exhibits.

5

Tsingtao Brewery and Museum

青岛啤酒博物馆, qīngdǎo píjiǔ bówùguǎn • 56 Dengzhou Lu • Daily 8.30am–4.30pm • ¥50 • ☎ 0532 83833437

For a great many visitors to Qingdao – Chinese as well as foreign – one essential city sight is the **Tsingtao brewery**, a pretty red-brick affair built in 1903 (see box below). Ignore the small, rather tame, **Tsingtao Brewery Museum** that takes up "Section A" of the site, and head instead to the actual brewery area, which comes across as something like a boozy version of Willy Wonka's chocolate factory: men clad in matching overalls supervise production, knocking pipes with spanners, adjusting valves and the like, while bottles and cans – both empty and full – rifle along in their thousands. There are a few nice little surprises on your way around, not least the "raw", untreated beer included with your ticket – it's absolutely superb. Later on you'll have a chance to drag yourself through the "drunkenness simulator" – merely a tilted, enclosed room, though it may bring to mind certain sensations that your sober mind has tried to forget. You'll exit into the on-site bar, where your free glass of draught awaits – quite a come-down after the raw one.

The beaches

Qingdao's **beaches**, with fine white sand, are busy places in the summer, when holidaymakers come to promenade or just slump and look out to sea against a backdrop of pine trees. **Kite flying** is popular, too – some of the country's highest-quality kites are made at the nearby city of Weifang. Closest to the old town, **Number 6 beach** is at the bottom of Zhongshan Lu; it's small but has the liveliest social scene, with crowds promenading along **Zhanqiao Pier** and numerous little stalls lining Taiping Lu selling gaudy swimsuits and cheap souvenirs.

Naval Museum

海军博物馆, hǎijūn bówùguǎn • Off Laiyang Lu • Daily 8am–5pm • ¥50

The quirky **Naval Museum** is easily visible from the southern boundary of the old town – its halls comprise one **submarine** and one **destroyer** which, though decommissioned long ago, still bob up and down in the water. The submarine is the more interesting of the two, its narrow, dark rooms arrayed with masses of chunky old valves, dials, levers and knobs, many of them bearing Russian markings.

Number 1 beach

The old town ends abruptly with a flurry of high-rises and paved plazas at **Number 1 beach**, which is the best in town – and the longest too, at over 580m. In season, it's packed with ice-cream vendors, trinket stalls and a rash of photographers. There are beachball-shaped changing huts, showers, multicoloured beach umbrellas, and

---

TSINGTAO BEER

Many a Western traveller arrives in Qingdao with a nagging sense of familiarity regarding the city's name: this is the home of **Tsingtao**, China's undisputed number-one beer. The confusion stems from its non-*pinyin* romanization, which can be directly attributed to the brewery's age; it was started way back in 1903 (when Chinese used the Wade-Giles transliteratory system) as a German-British joint venture, before coming under **Japanese** control during their occupation of Qingdao. The Japanese ramped up production and essentially transformed Tsingtao from a pumped-up microbrewery to a national success story. During the first decades of **Communist control**, Tsingtao beer was pretty much the only product exported from China.

As in the rest of China, bottles of Tsingtao can be bought all over the city. However, it would be a shame to leave Qingdao without buying the unpasteurized **draught** version, sold from the roadside in plastic bags – getting the nectar into the bag without spillage is something of an art form. Tsingtao also takes pride of place during the August **International Beer Festival** (see ⓦ thatsqingdao.com for information), which is held at the International Beer City, way out to the east of town.

designated swimming areas marked out with buoys and protected by shark nets. The water, however, is like Chinese soup – murky and warm, with unidentifiable things floating in it – so swimming is not recommended.

ARRIVAL AND DEPARTURE QINGDAO

By air Liuting International Airport (青岛流亭国际机场, qīngdǎo liútíng guójì jīchǎng) links Qingdao with Germany, Japan, Singapore, South Korea and Taiwan, as well as many domestic destinations. It lies 30km to the northeast of the centre, the intervening distance spanned by taxis (¥100) or airport buses (¥20; 1hr). There are three bus lines to choose from: take the one heading to Zhongshan Lu, which drops off outside an airlines office (☎0532 2895577). To head to the airport, the most convenient stop is just up the road from the *KFC* (see map, p.285); the buses leave at 40 minutes past the hour.

Destinations Beijing (1hr 15min); Hangzhou (1hr 30min); Hong Kong (3hr); Nanjing (1hr); Shanghai (1hr 15min).

By train Qingdao Station (青岛站, qīngdǎo zhàn), built along German architectural lines, is conveniently located in the area of greatest tourist interest. For now, most high-speed trains still stop here, though services will start to shift to the new North station (青岛北站, qīngdǎo běizhàn), on plenty of bus routes into town, or about ¥40 by taxi.

Main station destinations Beijing (12 daily; 4hr 40min–5hr); Ji'nan (2–5 hourly; 2hr 30min–5hr 30min); Qufu (2 daily; 3hr 20min); Shanghai (4 daily; 6hr 40min);

Tai'an (11 daily; 3–7hr); Xi'an (3 daily; 21hr); Yantai (1 daily; 4hr 45min).

Qingdao North station destinations Beijing (1 daily; 9hr); Ji'nan (13 daily; 2hr 30min–4hr 30min); Qufu (2 daily; 3hr 20min); Shanghai (4 daily; 6hr 40min); Tai'an (11 daily; 3–7hr); Xi'an (3 daily; 21hr); Yantai (1 daily; 4hr 45min).

By bus Qingdao's main bus terminal (青岛汽车站, qīngdǎo qìchē zhàn) is over 6km north of town; bus #5 runs from here down to the seafront at Taiping Lu, or it's about ¥30 by taxi. The most useful services are to Yantai (2 hourly; 3hr 30min).

By ferry The passenger-ferry terminal (大港客运站, dàgǎng kèyùnzhàn) hosts ferries from Japan and South Korea. It's located just north of the old town – bus #303 heads to the train station area and #8 to Zhongshan Lu, though it'll only cost around ¥15 by taxi. The cheapest tickets buy comfy capsule-like berths with dividing curtains; paying a bit more gets you a berth in a private room, in which instance you'll likely be bundled in with another foreigner. In addition to the ticket, expect to pay around ¥60 in fuel and port surcharges.

Destinations Inchon, Korea (Mon, Wed & Fri; 16hr; from ¥870); Shimonoseki, Japan (Mon & Thurs; 36hr; from ¥1250).

GETTING AROUND AND INFORMATION

By bus Qingdao has a decent bus system, but you may not need to use it – the city centre is compact, and actually quite interesting to walk around (if, on occasion, a little hilly).

By taxi Flagfall is ¥9, and you should be able to get anywhere in the centre for under ¥20; note that some "luxury" taxis start at ¥12 instead, and rise in price far more quickly.

By subway The first line of the new Qingdao Metro system

– line #3 – commenced operations in late 2015; the section heading to the new town is still under construction, though eventually it'll all be linked to the old centre too.

Magazines There's plenty of information on the *Red Star* website (ⓦmyredstar.com), though it's aimed more at expats than tourists – the focus is on the New Town to the east, rather than the old centre.

ACCOMMODATION

Qingdao's old town has abundant accommodation and, though the city's newest, flashest places are much further east, there's a good range here.

25° Four Seasons Youth Hostel 25度四季青年旅舍, 25 dùsìjì qīngnián lǚshè. 303 Yunnan Lu ☎186 60285080. Good, new hostel option set in a pleasant neighbourhood, within easy walking distance of the sights. Rooms are a little bare, but they're clean and functional, and there's a pool table and bar in the lobby area. Dorms from ¥45, doubles ¥240

Huiquan Dynasty 汇泉王朝大酒店, huìquán wángcháo dàjiǔdiàn. 9 Nanhai Lu ☎0532 82999888, ⓦhqdynasty.com. A well-located five-star hotel – the beach is directly opposite, and there's a nice indoor pool if you fancy cleaner water to swim in. Many rooms have fantastic

views, as does the nifty revolving restaurant way up on top, which serves a mix of local and international food. ¥850

★Kaiyue Youth Hostel 凯越国际青年旅馆, kǎiyuè guójì qīngnián lǚguǎn. 31 Jining Lu ☎0532 82845450, ⓦyhaqd.com. Situated near some of the town's older colonial quarters, and inside what was once a church, this recently renovated hostel is a lovely place to stay, and the staff can organize all watersports plus kite-flying activities. The basement restaurant-bar is also hugely popular (see p.288). Dorms from ¥45, doubles ¥230

Sam APH 山姆的家, shānmǔde jiā. 20 Fushan Lu ☎186 61622266, ⓦsamhostel.com. This splendid homestay-like option is proving popular both domestic and overseas visitors to Qingdao, largely on account of its setting in a colonial villa – a real antique with some highly atmospheric quarters, augmented by decidedly modern accoutrements such as a sun deck. Very close to the newly trendy area around Qingdao Museum. **¥470**

Zhanqiao Prince 栈桥宾馆, zhànqiáo bīnguǎn.
31 Taiping Lu @0532 82888666, @www .zhanqiaoprincehotel.com. Elderly hotel with heaps of character from the wood-panelled lobby upwards, and featuring the excellent *Zhanqiao Old House* restaurant on the lobby floor (see below). Sun Yatsen stayed here once, too, though he probably didn't have to pay ¥130 extra for a sea view. **¥628**

EATING

Qingdao has ample **restaurants** to choose from. The speciality is **seafood**; mussels and crabs here are particularly good, and there are plenty of small, noisy and busy seafood places in the streets leading down to the coast, where competition means standards are high, and, with some exceptions, **costs** are reasonably low. The area west of the museum has recently been prettified, and a slew of trendy **cafés** have opened up – well worth a wander.

RESTAURANTS

Chuanweiju 川味居, chuān wèi jū. 26 Hunan Lu @0532 82875388. There are plenty of seafood places on and around the south section of Henan Lu, though this is a slight cut above – picture menu, pleasant interior, and an outdoor patio. Try the slightly odd seafood tofu (¥38), washed down with a mug of Tsingtao (¥15). Daily 9am–9pm.

Chunhelou 春和楼饭店, chūnhélóu fàndiàn. 146 Zhongshan Lu @0532 82824346. Dating back to 1891, this is one of Qingdao's most famous eateries, and is suitably heaving in the evenings – head up to the top floor for generous portions of spiced chicken (¥68), or delectable shrimp dumplings (¥36 per round). Daily 11am–3pm & 5–10pm.

★**Zhanqiao Old House** 栈桥宾馆, zhànqiáo bīnguǎn. 31 Taiping Lu @0532 82888666. Surprisingly reasonable prices at this restaurant, which sits pretty in the bowels of the *Zhanqiao Prince* hotel, and offers shimmery ocean views. Fish is the speciality, best taken in the form of a giant shellfish platter (¥88, feeds two), but simple mains

(¥20 or so) and goodies such as shrimp balls (¥32) are on offer for those who want a promenade view without breaking the bank. The sour-and-spicy seafood soup (¥20) is also highly recommended. Daily 10am–10pm.

CAFÉS

★**1899 Café** 爱爾1899, ài ěr 1899. 15 Zhejiang Lu @0532 82891919. Right by St Michael's Church, this is the most appealing of the many, many, many café options to have opened up recently in this neck of the woods – those taking (and starring in) the wedding photos outside the church need something to drink. The seats are comfy, the atmosphere is artistic, and there's nothing wrong with the coffee. Daily 9.30am–9pm.

Qiusuo Shushe 求索书社, qiúsuǒ shūshè. 31 Taiping Lu @0532 82888666. The largest and most pleasant café in the glut which have opened up behind the *Cool Cat* bar – there's no English-language sign, but keep an eye out for a large hall overlooked by distinctive cuboid lanterns. Daily 10am–9pm.

DRINKING

In the old centre, you'll see umpteen bars and restaurants selling **draught Tsingtao** from large outdoor barrels, sometimes in takeaway plastic bags which are very hard to drink from; some places also offer a tasty stout version. **Nightlife** isn't as exciting in the Old Town as you'll find out east in the new town (see @myredstar.com for up-to-date listings information).

★**Cool Cat** 酷猫美术啤酒, kùmāo měishù píjiǔ. 10 Daxue Lu, opposite the museum @0532 85639843. Previously referred to as the *SAW House*, this microbrewery pumps out rounds of delectable bitter, coffee stout, pale ale, and whatever else they've been brewing; they go for ¥35 a glass (cheap for Chinese craft beer), and for a little more you can have them served with a German sausage. Mon–Fri 4pm–2am, Sat & Sun noon–midnight.

Kaiyue Youth Hostel 凯越国际青年旅馆, kǎiyuè guójì qīngnián lǚguǎn. 31 Jining Lu @0532 82845450. The basement restaurant-bar in this hostel (see p.287) is extremely popular with travellers, young locals and elements of the Qingdao expat crowd. Pizzas (from ¥50) are the pick of the food choices; beer runs from ¥18 a bottle, and is best enjoyed with new friends, over the pool or table football. Daily 8am–midnight.

DIRECTORY

Post office The main post office (Mon–Sat 8am–6pm) is about halfway along Zhongshan Lu.

Visa extensions The PSB (Mon–Sat 8am–noon & 2–7pm) is at 29 Hubei Lu, not far from the train station.

5

Lao Shan

崂山, láo shān • ¥130

The **Lao Shan** area, 400 square kilometres of rugged, mountainous coast 40km northeast of Qingdao, makes an easy day-trip from the city. It's a good place to **hike** around, dotted with caves, springs and waterfalls amid striking scenery, among which it's possible to lose the crowds and trinket stalls. Writers have been inspired by the landscape for centuries – *Strange Tales from a Chinese Studio* by the Qing-dynasty author **Pu Songling** (see p.969) was written here – and have left noble graffiti in the form of poems and sage reflections cut into rocks all around the area. Jiushui Valley here is also the source of **Lao Shan mineral water**, which is purported to give Tsingtao beer its special taste.

Ju Feng

巨峰, jù fēng • Cable car ¥40 each way

Rising 1133m above sea level, **Ju Feng** is Lao Shan's apex. From the bus drop-off point a pathway of stone steps, constructed a century ago by the enterprising German Lao Shan Company to cater for their compatriots' weakness for alpine clambering, runs all the way to the summit and then back down a different route on the other side. The **path** climbs past gullies and woods, streams and pools, and the ascent should take around three hours; you're able to shorten this with a cable-car ride from the base. There's a temple halfway up, where you can fortify yourself with fruit and tea for the final haul. At the **summit**, a ruined temple now houses a meteorological station. The view is great, and gets even better as you descend by the alternative route back to the village.

Taiqing Gong

太清宫, tàiqīng gōng • Temple ¥20 • Cable car ¥35 one-way, ¥60 return

Taiqing Gong, a temple to the south of Lao Shan, is the oldest and grandest of local temples, consisting of three halls set amid old trees – some dating back to the Han and Tang dynasties – and gardens. Outside the first hall are two camellias about which Pu Songling wrote a story. There are nine other temples nearby, which are peaceful places.

ARRIVAL AND GETTING AROUND   LAO SHAN

By bus Public bus #304 (¥8; 1–2hr) leaves frequently from the east side of the train station, dropping you at Yakou (哑口, yǎkǒu), the easternmost part of the Lao Shan area. Plenty of other buses come here from other parts of Qingdao.

On a tour Almost alll of Qingdao's hostels, and most hotels, run tours to Lao Shan from around ¥200 per person, including transport and entry tickets; some make annoying shopping stops on the way there and back, so ask about these when booking.

Shuttle buses Shuttle buses run between the various sights in each area of the park, and these will be included within the price of your ticket.

Ji'nan

济南, jǐnán

The Shandong capital of **JI'NAN** is regularly ranked among China's most liveable cities, a fact not lost on its proud denizens. There's a rather literal underlying factor at work, for Ji'nan is famed nationwide for its **natural springs**, a series of clear blue upwellings set among several urban parks. Within walking distance of each other and connected by

JI'NAN BY BOAT

You can explore parts of Ji'nan by **boat**, with regular departures heading clockwise around the city's waterways (¥10 per person per stop; ¥100 for the whole trip); they stop at ten stations on this 7km route, including Wulong Tan Park, Baotu Spring, Black Tiger Spring and Daming Lake. The recent drought has affected services, but hopefully they'll be up and running again by the time you read this.

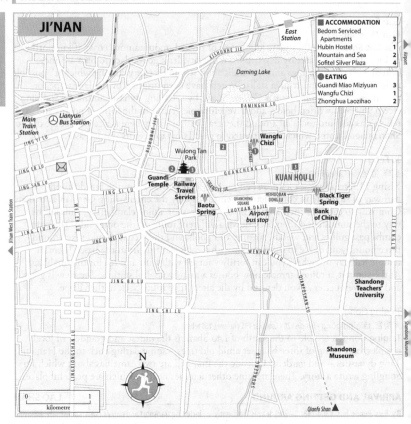

boat (see box, p.289), the springs have suffered of late from a protracted drought – the lower flow has decreased the quality of what was once probably the cleanest water to be found in any Chinese city, and all fingers are crossed that such clarity will soon return.

The city itself is a maze of gleaming high-rises, wide boulevards and umpteen flyovers, making it hard to believe that this is the site of one of China's **oldest settlements**, inhabited for the last four thousand years – such history is best taken in at the **provincial museum**, or the Buddhist relics on the steep hillside of **Qianfo Shan**, respectively to the east and south of the city centre. Most of the modern action is centred around **Quancheng Square** (泉城广场, quánchéng guǎngchǎng), while just to its east, the new **Kuan Hou Li** (宽厚里, kuān hòu lǐ) development of faux-dynastic buildings is a fun place to poke around.

Wulong Tan Park

五龙潭公园, wǔlóngtán gōngyuán • Gongqingtuan Lu • Daily 7am–6pm • ¥5

In the city centre, **Wulong Tan Park** is a family favourite, with goldfish-filled ponds, flower-scented paths, and local kids spraying each other with pipe-like water-shooters; in the summer, it is tempting to take off your shoes and wade with them through the shallower ponds. The **Wulong Tan Springs** have some serious pedigree – they were mentioned in the *Spring and Autumn Annals*, government texts of 694 BC. In the east of the park is a modern hall to one of China's most famous female poets, **Li Qingzhao**, who was born in 1084 in Ji'nan – it contains extracts from her work and paintings by well-known contemporary artists.

5

Guandi Temple

关帝庙, guāndì miào • Gongqingtuan Lu • Daily 7am–7pm • Free

Just outside Wulong Tan's south gate is a tiny **Guandi Temple**, noted as the site where eunuch An Dehai, manipulative confidant of the Qing Empress Dowager Cixi, was executed by governor Ding Baozhen in 1869 after making an outrageously pompous, imperial-style tour of the nearby countryside. If you're peckish, try the wonderful *Guandi Miao Miziyuan* restaurant next door (see p.294).

Baotu Spring

趵突泉, bàotū quán • Luoyuan Lu • Daily 7am–6pm • ¥40

South of Wulong Tan Park, Ji'nan's celebrated **Baotu Springs** is set in a captivating park full of shaded walkways, intricate flower gardens, delicate bridges and charming pagodas; elderly gents hone their calligraphy skills on the floor with spring water. However, despite the park's undoubted splendour, it's worth noting that the Wulong Tan Springs (see opposite) are almost as good, and far cheaper to visit.

Black Tiger Spring

黑虎泉, hēihǔ quán • 24hr • Free

Behind a wall on Heihuquan Dong Lu, the **Black Tiger Spring** rises from a subterranean cave and emerges through tiger-headed spouts into a canal that once formed the old city's moat. People come here to fill up jerrycans from the spring and play in the water.

Daming Lake

大明湖, dàmíng hú • Daily 6am–6pm • ¥30

Large and handsome, and just north of the city centre, **Daming Lake** is surrounded by some quaint gardens, pavilions and bridges, edged with willow trees and sprinkled with water lilies; it makes a nice counterpoint to the city's springs, especially when accessed by boat (see box, p.289). Note that you don't need a ticket to explore most of the lakeshore, with the south bank a particularly calm, relaxing place to drink some wine or beer in the evening.

Qianfo Shan

千佛山, qiānfó shān • Daily 8am–6pm • ¥30 • Bus routes include the #K51; taxi from the centre ¥20

A scenic spot worth a trip is **Qianfo Shan**, about 5km south of the city centre. Most of the original Buddha and Bodhisattva statues that once dotted the slopes of this

---

JI'NAN'S SECRET SPRING

Ji'nan is justly famed for its springs, but very few outsiders are aware of the quirkiest one in town – possibly the best-kept travel secret in the whole of Shandong. You won't find **Wangfu Chizi** (王府池子, wángfǔ chízi) on any tourist maps, and the pool's location at the centre of a labyrinthine tangle of alleyways makes it doubly difficult to track down, but your efforts will not go unrewarded. Edged with grey *hutong* buildings, this is essentially an **open-air swimming pool**, and the fact that it remains such an integral part of local life makes for quite a spectacle – lines of elderly men bob up and down on their daily laps, housewives engage in casual conversation while local youths whoop and shout as they scrub themselves clean on the western bank. The water quality isn't superb – spit, cigarette butts and ice-cream wrappers are inevitable – but it's hard to resist the temptation to join in the fun, even more so when being persuaded by a gaggle of bronzed and finely chiselled pensioners.

There's also a bit of **history** in the air – as may be inferred from its name, which roughly translates as "King's Abode Pool". Wangfu Chizi was once the property of a local prince, and the family still living on the north bank are descendants of former royal bodyguards. The pool maintains a temperature of around 16°C (ie, pretty cold) throughout the year, making for an ethereal effect in the winter, when mist rises from the waters and makes silhouettes of the swimmers. It's also worth dropping by in the late evening, when locals drain draught beer on the south bank while listening to the gentle lapping of waves.

5

"Thousand Buddha Mountain" were destroyed by Red Guards, but new ones are being added, largely paid for by donations from Overseas Chinese. The mountainside is leafy and tracked with winding paths, the main one lined with painted opera masks; it's quite a climb to the summit (2hr), but the sculptures, and the view, get better the higher you go. Behind the **Xingguo Temple** near the top, you'll find some superb sixth-century Buddhist carvings.

Shandong Museum

山东博物馆, shāndōng bówùguǎn • Jingshiyi Lu • Tues–Sun 9am–5pm • Free (bring ID) • Bus routes include the #18, #62 & #63; taxi from the centre ¥20 • Ⓦ sdmuseum.com

East of the centre, the modern, beautifully designed **Shandong Museum** portrays the long history of Ji'nan city, and Shandong province as a whole. Exhibits are arranged over three large floors; the upper levels are of greatest interest, particularly the exhibits from excavations at Longshan and Dawenkou, two nearby Neolithic sites noted for the delicate black pottery unearthed there; the remains date back to 5000–2000 BC. Elsewhere are a number of fine Buddhist carvings, Han **pictorial tomb reliefs**, Tang-dynasty tombstones, and a 22m-long Ming-dynasty **wooden boat**; the latter was excavated from the marshes southwest near Liangshan, the setting for China's Robin Hood epic, *Outlaws of the Marsh*.

ARRIVAL AND INFORMATION JI'NAN

BY PLANE

Yaoqiang International Airport (济南遥墙国际机场, jǐnán yáoqiáng guójì jīchǎng). Boasting international connections to Japan, South Korea and Hong Kong, the airport is 40km northeast of the city. A taxi ride will set you back at least ¥100, while airport shuttles (6am–7pm; ¥20; hourly; 1hr) pick up and drop off just west of the *Sofitel Silver Plaza* hotel.

Destinations Beijing (1hr); Nanjing (1hr); Shanghai (1hr 20min); Yantai (50min).

BY TRAIN

Train tickets are not hard to get at the stations; alternatively, there are ticket offices strewn across the city, including one opposite Wulong Tan Park (daily 8.30am–5pm; ☎ 0531 81817171).

Main station (济南站, jǐnán zhàn). Ji'nan's main train station is just to the northwest of the city centre and receives some high-speed services.

Destinations Beijing (1–3 hourly; 2–6hr); Qingdao (1–3 hourly; 2hr 20min–5hr); Qufu (12 daily; 40min–2hr

20min); Shanghai (17 daily; 4–14hr); Taishan (1–2 hourly; 25min–1hr); Yantai (10 daily; 6hr–7hr 30min).

West station (济南西站, jǐnán xīzhàn). For other services you'll have to head to the West station, from which a number of bus routes (¥1) head into the centre; it's also around ¥20 by taxi from a surprisingly orderly rank.

Destinations Beijing (2–5 hourly; 1hr 30min–2hr); Qufu (1–3 hourly; 30–50min); Shanghai (2–5 hourly; 3hr 20min–4hr 40min); Tai'an (for Taishan; 17 daily; 20min).

BY BUS

Ji'nan is so well connected by train that the only buses you may need are those to Tai'an (1hr 30min) or Qufu (2hr); you can take them from the small terminal in front of the train station.

INFORMATION

Services Ji'nan's main post office (8am–4.30pm) is a red-brick building on Jing Er Lu, just west of Wei Er Lu, though there are plenty around the city.

GETTING AROUND

By bus Many of the city's bus routes (¥1) begin from the train station, though given the layout of the city it's generally far easier to get a cab to your accommodation.

By taxi Taxis start at ¥9, and nowhere in the centre is

more than ¥20 away.

By metro The city's first metro line should open by 2019, though it will be of little use to travellers. line #2, which will connect the two main stations, will follow by 2023.

ACCOMMODATION

★**Bedom Serviced Apartments** 拜登盛邸服务公寓, bàidēng shèngdǐ fúwù gōngyù. Building D, 26 Quancheng Lu ☎ 0531 5557677. Not a hotel, but a series of rather fancy apartments, all of which are suite-style affairs which are surprisingly large for the price. Comfy

beds, power showers and some splendid views – highly recommended, at least for a break from the norm. ¥318

Hubin Hostel 湖滨国际青年旅舍, húbīn guójì qīngnián lǚshè. Block 2, Lufeng Paper Art Zone, off Shaonian Lu ☎ 0531 88629238, Ⓦ yhachina.com. Set in

OPPOSITE BAMBOO GROVE, MOGANSHAN (P.334) >

5

a fascinating old factory area, this hostel may be hard to find, but it's worth it – decent rooms, plus those Chinese hostel common-room staples of pool table and cheap beer, with which to enjoy the evening. Dorm beds ¥45, private rooms ¥168

Mountain and Sea 山与海文化酒店, shānyǔhǎi wénhuà jiǔdiàn. 1 Xiyundouyu Jie ☎ 0531 81187171, ⓦ sofitel.com. A nice little find, if you can find it, hiding away in the atmospheric *hutong* area. The European castle-kitsch decor is curious, to say the least, though the rooms

are excellent value, especially if you can land one of the duplexes. ¥238

Sofitel Silver Plaza 索菲特银座大酒店, suǒfēitè yínzuò dàjiǔdiàn. 66 Luoyuan Dajie ☎ 0531 86068888, ⓦ sofitel.com. The pinnacle of luxury in Ji'nan, right in the heart of the city with views of Quancheng Square – they're especially good from the breakfast area up top. The fittings here are quite superb, with huge bathrooms featuring Lanvin smellies, and rates are often discounted by up to half. ¥900

EATING

The train station area is surrounded by the usual local and international chains, though there are far more appealing options in the city centre. The trendiest area at the time of writing – at least in a studenty, snack-style sense – was **Furong Jie**, an alley north of Quancheng Lu, and immediately west of the Wangfu Chizi spring (see p.291). Slightly more upmarket are the attractive restaurants around the new **Kuan Hou Li** development (see p.290), though nothing here really stands out.

★**Guandi Miao Miziyuan** 关帝庙 蜜脂园, guāndì miào mìzhīyuán. Gongqingtuan Lu, near Wulong Tan Park ☎ 0531 86011251. Connected to the Guandi Temple (see p.291), though the door is sometimes closed, this is the city's best place in which to sample local Lu cuisine, all served up in a ramshackle courtyard filled with bamboo, carp and caged birds. Top picks from the helpful picture menu include tofu made with local spring water, and battered shrimp (both ¥48). Daily 10am–2pm & 5–10pm.

Wangfu Chizi 王府池子, wángfǔ chízi. The no-name snack shack at the Wangfu Chizi is the most atmospheric place to eat in town, with old men in bathing suits

dropping by for snails, peanuts, barbecued shrimp and the like between swims, and occasionally somersaulting into the pool from above your head. Also a grand place for beer in the evening – the local draught uses water from the Baotu Springs. Daily 9am–11pm.

Zhonghua Laozihao 中华老字号, zhōnghuá lǎozìhào. Puli Jie, just west of Wulong Tan Park's southern entrance. This decades-old dumpling restaurant is something of a local institution, and handily located. They've a few different varieties (the pork and shrimp ones are usually best), each costing around ¥18 per portion; order and collect from the counter. Daily 8.30am–8.30pm.

Tai'an

泰安, tài'ān

Though one million visitors pass through scruffy **TAI'AN** each year, almost none of them is interested in the town itself – they're all here to see **Tai Shan**, the hulking mountain just to the north (see p.296). Tai'an has, for centuries, served as a base for pilgrims, and on certain holy days ten thousand people at one time might be making their way up the crowded path to the peak.

Before heading off to join them, however, you should definitely visit **Dai Miao**, an important and ancient temple at Tai'an's centre. Just to the north of this temple are some busy **market streets** selling medicinal herbs that grow on the mountain, such as ginseng, the tuber of the multiflower knotweed and Asian puccoon, along with strange vegetables, bonsai trees and potted plants.

Dai Miao

岱庙, dài miào • Dongyue Lu • Daily 8am–5.30pm • ¥30

Dai Miao, the temple where emperors once made sacrifices to Tai Shan, is the traditional starting point for the procession up the mountain. It's a magnificent complex, with yellow-tiled roofs, red walls and towering old trees; there's a blend of buildings from different belief systems here, with veneration of the mountain as the only constant factor – the peak is, suitably, visible from many parts of the temple. Be sure to head up the steps by the north or south entrances; whether you're looking inside the halls or out to the mountains, the view from the perimeter path is quite spectacular.

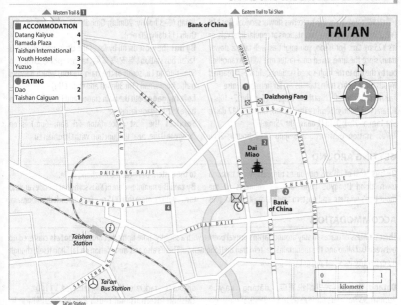

ACCOMMODATION

Datang Kaiyue	4
Ramada Plaza	1
Taishan International Youth Hostel	3
Yuzuo	2

EATING

| Dao | 2 |
| Taishan Caiguan | 1 |

Tiankuang Dian

Tiankuang Dian (Hall of the Celestial Gift) is matched in size only by halls in the Forbidden City and at Qufu. Construction started as early as the Qin dynasty (221–206 BC), though expansion and renovation have gone on ever since, particularly during the Tang and Song dynasties. Inside, three of the murals are covered by a huge **mural**, a Song-dynasty masterpiece depicting the Emperor Zhen Zong as the God of Tai Shan on an inspection tour and hunting expedition. The mural is fairly worn overall, but you can still see thousands of figures, each rendered in painstaking detail. There is also a **statue** of the God of Tai Shan, enthroned in a niche and dressed in flowing robes, holding the oblong tablet that is the insignia of his authority. The five sacrificial vessels laid before him bear the symbols of the five peaks.

The courtyards

The surrounding **courtyards**, halls and gardens are used as a museum for **steles**; the oldest, inside the **Dongyuzuo Hall**, celebrates the visit of Emperor Qin and his son in the third century BC. Many of the great calligraphers are represented here and even the untrained Western eye can find something to appreciate. Charcoal rubbings of the steles can be bought from the mercifully discreet souvenir shops inside the temple complex. The courtyards are also well wooded with cypresses – including five supposedly planted by the Han emperor Wu Di – ginkgos and acacias.

Temple of Yanxi

In a side courtyard at the back of the complex is the **Temple of Yanxi**. A Taoist resident on the mountain, Yanxi was linked with the mountain cult of the Tang dynasty. A separate hall at the rear is devoted to the Wife of the Mountain, a deity who seems somewhat of an afterthought, appearing much later than her spouse.

ARRIVAL AND INFORMATION   TAI'AN

By train Tai'an has two stations, and it's important to note which one you'll be using. Tai'an station (泰安站, tài'ān zhàn) is a high-speed-only affair over 10km to the west of the centre; the central station, confusingly called Taishan

5

(泰山站, tàishān zhàn), receives slower services. Bus #18 (¥2; 25min) connects the two stations at regular intervals, or it's ¥25 by taxi. For Ji'nan, you might as well take a slower train, since the time saved on a faster one will be cancelled out by the trip to the high-speed station; Qufu is best reached by bus, since Qufu's train stations are far from the centre.

Taishan station destinations Beijing (5 daily; 7–10hr); Ji'nan (1–3 hourly; 50min–1hr 30min); Qingdao (12 daily; 5hr 15min–7hr); Qufu (4 daily; 1hr 25min).

Tai'an station destinations Beijing (1–3 hourly; 2hr); Ji'nan (2–3 hourly; 20min); Qingdao (8 daily; 3hr 15min); Qufu (13 daily; 20min).

By bus The most useful by far of the city's many depots is Tai'an bus station (泰安汽车站, tài'ān qìchē zhàn) on Sanlizhuang Lu, south of the train station, which handles traffic from Ji'nan (1hr 30min) and Qufu (1hr).

Left luggage Both the train station and Tai'an bus station have left-luggage facilities.

Services The post office (Mon–Fri 8am–6pm) is on Dongyue Dajie, near the junction with Qingnian Lu.

GETTING AROUND

By bus Most of Tai'an's city buses run east–west through town along Dongyue Dajie: bus #3 connects to the mountain's western and eastern trailheads; #14 also goes to the eastern trailhead via Daizhong Dajie.

By taxi The minimum fare of ¥6 is sufficient for rides around town, with no more than ¥15 required to reach the mountain.

ACCOMMODATION

There's a mess of places to stay around Tai'an's arrival points, with a slightly more upmarket group of **hotels** clustered up between Dai Miao and the mountain's eastern trail on Hongmen Lu. There's also accommodation on Tai Shan itself, though it's expensive for what you get (see p.300).

Datang Kaiyue 大堂凯悦酒店, dàtáng kǎiyuè jiǔdiàn. 53 Dongyue Dajie ☎ 0538 8169999. Surprisingly plush for the price, this hotel has corridors lined with carpets of brown and gold, leading to well-appointed rooms with flatscreen televisions. If you're in luck, you'll be able to swipe half off the rack rate. ¥480

Ramada Plaza 东尊华美达大酒店, dōngzūnhuá měidá dàjiǔdiàn. 16 Yingsheng Dong Lu ☎ 0538 8368666, ⓦ ramadaplazataian.com. This superlative five-star resort basks in a stupendous location amid Tai Shan's rocky foothills. Decorated with the chain's signature gold and dark reds, its rooms are little havens of comfort, and most provide stunning mountain views. It's a little outside town, but the on-site restaurants are the only upscale places to eat in Tai'an in any case. Ask about discounts – rack rates are regularly halved. ¥1160

Taishan International Youth Hostel 泰山国际青年旅舍, tàishān guójì qīngnián lǚshè. 8 Fuqian Lu ☎ 0538 6285196, ⓦ yhachina.com. Handily located a short walk from Dai Miao, this is a bit of a treat, with friendly staff and pine-clad dormitories. It's tucked away in a small alley behind a covered shopping arcade; turn through the tunnel at 65 Tongtian Jie. Dorm beds ¥70, doubles ¥188

Yuzuo 御座宾馆, yùzuò bīnguǎn. 50 Daimiao Bei Lu ☎ 0538 8269999, ⓦ yuzuo.cn. This quality, low-rise hotel could scarcely be better located – it's within the Dai Miao complex itself. Rooms are calm and opulently appointed, and staff try hard to hide the fact that they don't have many foreigners to deal with, though be warned that the breakfast is a little odd. ¥560

EATING

Tai'an cuisine can be exquisite, particularly red-scaled **carp**, fresh from pools on the mountain and fried while it's still alive. In reality, few places now serve such delicacies, and the town is one of those places where you're best off hunting down a street shack for kebabs and beer – try the alleys south of the youth hostel.

Dao 道, dào. Dongyue Lu ☎ 0538 8204232. A lovely recent addition to the city centre, particularly during breakfast time – an oasis of calm in which you can have decent coffee, and pick from a selection of sugary baked treats. Daily 8am–10pm.

Taishan Caiguan 泰山菜馆, tàishān càiguǎn. Hongmen Lu ☎ 0538 6267777. A short walk north of the centre, this cheery restaurant is perhaps the best and most reliable place to eat in town – not that this is saying very much. They specialize in tofu dishes: for ¥28 a serve, try the stupendous fried tofu balls (豆腐丸子 dòufu wánzi). Daily 9am–11pm.

Tai Shan

泰山, tàishān • Feb–Nov ¥125, Dec–Jan ¥100

Tai Shan is not just a mountain, it's a god. It's the easternmost and holiest of China's five major Taoist peaks (the other four being Hua Shan, the two Heng Shans and Song

Shan), and has been worshipped by the Chinese throughout recorded history: the ascent is engrossing and beautiful – and very hard work.

Once host to emperors and the devout, Tai Shan is now Shandong's biggest tourist attraction, a religious theme park whose paths are thronged with a constant procession of tourists – and genuine **pilgrims**. There are photo booths, souvenir stalls, soft-drinks vendors and teahouses; halfway up, there's a **bus station** and **cable car**. Yet the temples and the mountain itself are magnificent enough to survive their trivialization.

The account here follows the **eastern trail**. The traditional ascent actually begins from **Daizhong Fang**, a stone arch to the north of the Dai Miao in Tai'an, though most start their ascent at the **First Heavenly Gate** (一天门, yītiān mén), which is followed by a Ming arch said to mark the spot where Confucius began his climb. The best way down – and the one less likely to make jelly of your legs – is along the **western trail**, which is longer, quieter and has some impressive views. It diverges from the east trail at Zhongtianmen, then loops round and joins the main trail back at the base of the mountain.

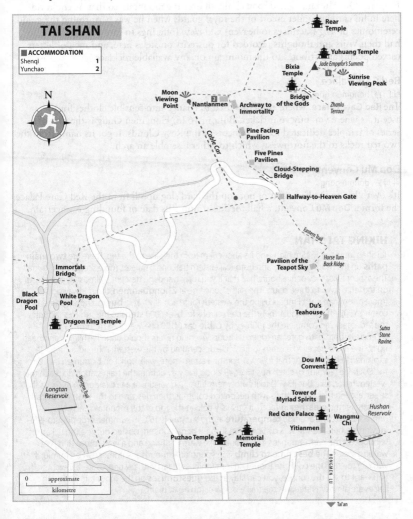

TAI SHAN

ACCOMMODATION
Shenqi	1
Yunchao	2

Rear Temple
Yuhuang Temple
Jade Emperor's Summit
Bixia Temple
Sunrise Viewing Peak
Moon Viewing Point
Nantianmen
Archway to Immortality
Bridge of the Gods
Zhanlu Terrace
Cable Car
Pine Facing Pavilion
Five Pines Pavilion
Cloud-Stepping Bridge
Halfway-to-Heaven Gate
Eastern Trail
Pavilion of the Teapot Sky
Horse Turn Back Ridge
Immortals Bridge
Black Dragon Pool
White Dragon Pool
Dragon King Temple
Du's Teahouse
Sutra Stone Ravine
Dou Mu Convent
Western Trail
Longtan Reservoir
Tower of Myriad Spirits
Red Gate Palace
Wangmu Chi
Yitianmen
Hushan Reservoir
Puzhao Temple
Memorial Temple
HONGMEN LU

0   approximate   1
kilometre

Tai'an

5

TAOISM AT TAI SHAN

Taoism, after a long period of communist proscription, is again alive and flourishing at Tai Shan, and you're more than likely to see a bearded Taoist monk on the way up. Women come specifically to pray to **Bixia Yuan Jun**, the Princess of the Rosy Clouds, a Taoist deity believed to be able to help childless women conceive. Tai Shan also plays an important role in the **folk beliefs** of the Shandong peasantry (tradition has it that anyone who has climbed Tai Shan will live to be 100).

Brief history

More so than any other holy mountain, Tai Shan was the haunt of **emperors**, and owes its obvious glories – the temples and pavilions along its route – to the patronage of the imperial court. From its summit, a succession of emperors surveyed their empires, made sacrifices and paid tribute. Sometimes, their retinues stretched right from the top to the bottom of the mountain, 8km of pomp and ostentatious wealth. In 219 BC, Emperor Qin Shi Huang had **roads** built all over the mountain so that he could ride here in his carriage under escort of the royal guards when he was performing the grand ceremonies of *feng* (sacrifices to heaven) and *chan* (offerings to earth). Emperors also had their visits and thoughts recorded for posterity on steles here, and men of letters carved poems and tributes to the mountain on any available rockface.

Red Gate Palace

红门宫, hóngmén gōng

The **Red Gate Palace**, where emperors used to change into sensible clothes for the ascent, is where you buy your ticket. Built in 1626, Hongmen Gong is the first of a series of temples dedicated to the Princess of the Rosy Clouds. It got its name from the two red rocks to the northwest, which together resemble an arch.

Dou Mu Convent

斗母宫, dǒumǔ gōng

It's over 2km to the first sight of note on the hard slog uphill from the Red Gate Palace: the former **Dou Mu Convent**, a hall for Taoist nuns. Its date of founding is uncertain,

HIKING TAI SHAN

Tai Shan looms at 1545m high, and it's about 8km from the base to the top. There are **two main paths** up the mountain: the grand historical eastern trail, and a quieter, more scenic western trail. The ascent takes four or five hours, half that if you rush it, and the descent – almost as punishing on the legs – two to three hours. The paths converge at **Zhongtianmen**, the midway point (more often than not, climbers using the western route actually take a **bus** to Zhongtianmen, costing ¥30). After Zhongtianmen, the path climbs for over 6000 **steps** to the summit, though the sedentary can complete the journey by **cable car** (¥100 one-way, ¥200 return).

Officially, both path gates are open 24 hours; evening hikers should bring flashlights and head up by the more travelled eastern route while descending by the western route (the circuit explained in the account that follows). For the eastern route, walk uphill on Hongmen Lu from the Dai Miao (20min), or catch bus #3 or #9 along the way or from the train station. To reach the western route, take bus #3 (¥1) to its other terminus, Tianwaicun, or a taxi (around ¥8). Cross the street, ascend the stairs dotted with decorated columns, then descend to the shuttle-bus park.

Whatever the **weather** in Tai'an, it's usually cold at the top of the mountain and always unpredictable. The average **temperature** at the summit is 18°C in summer, dropping to -9°C in winter, when the sun sets by 5pm. The summit conditions are posted outside the ticket windows at the park entrances. You should take warm clothing and a waterproof, and wear walking shoes. The **best time to climb** is in spring or autumn, for summer can be humid; if you can tolerate the cold, the mountain is magnificent (and virtually untouristed) in winter. If you want to see the sunrise, you can stay at the **guesthouses** on the mountain – though prices are almost as steep as the trail – or risk climbing at night.

but it was reconstructed in 1542. Today, there are three halls, a drum tower, a bell tower and an ancient, **gnarled tree** outside, which is supposed to look like a reclining dragon. Like all the temple buildings on the mountain, the walls are painted with a blood-red wash, here interspersed with small grey bricks.

Sutra Stone Ravine
经石谷, jīngshí gǔ
North of Dou Mu Convent, a path veers east off the main route for about 1km to the **Sutra Stone Ravine**, where the text of the Buddhist Diamond Sutra has been carved on the rockface. This is one of the most prized of Tai Shan's many calligraphic works, and makes a worthwhile diversion as it's set in a charming, quiet spot.

Du's Teahouse
杜家茶馆, dùjiā cháguǎn • Daily 7am–sunset
One quirky sight, just off the main path, is **Du's Teahouse**, built on the spot where, more than a thousand years ago, General Cheng Yao Jin planted four pines, three of which are still alive. The teahouse, as well as everything in it, is quaintly built out of polished tree roots.

Around Zhongtianmen
Reached through a tunnel of cypress trees, the **Teapot Sky Pavilion** (壶天阁, hútiān gé) is so called because the peaks all around supposedly give the illusion of standing in a teapot, and here you will see a sheer cliff rising in front of you, called **Horse Turn Back Ridge** (回马岭, huímǎlǐng); this is where Emperor Zhen Zong had to dismount because his horse refused to go any farther.

  Not far above the ridge is **Halfway-to-Heaven Gate** (中天门, zhōngtiān mén), the midpoint of the climb. There are some good views here, though the **cable car** will be the most welcome sight if you're flagging.

Archway to Immortality
升仙房, shēngxiān fáng
The first landmark north of Zhongtianmen is **Cloud-Stepping Bridge** (云步桥, yúnbù qiáo). It's a tough climb from here to the **Archway to Immortality**; no matter, since according to mountain myth, those who have made it this far are assured their longevity. It was the view from this point which inspired Tang poet Li Bai to write: "In a long breath by the heavenly gate, the fresh wind comes from a thousand miles away"; though by this point most climbers are long past being able to appreciate poetry.

To the summit
On the way to the **summit**, the final section of the climb is the hardest, as the stone stairs are steep and narrow, and ascend almost vertically between two walls of rocks, often through thick white mist – by this point, almost everyone is unashamedly grasping the handrails as they haul themselves upwards. And then suddenly you're at the top on **Tian Jie** (Heaven Street), a tourist strip where you can buy "I climbed Tai Shan" T-shirts, slurp a pot noodle and get your picture taken dressed as an emperor. There are a couple of **restaurants** here, **hotels** and a few **shops**. This thriving little tourist village represents a triumph of the profit motive over the elements; it's often so misty you can hardly see from one souvenir stall to the next.

Bixia Temple
碧霞寺, bìxiá sì
On the southern slopes of the summit, **Bixia Temple** is the final destination for most genuine pilgrims, where offerings are made to a bronze statue of the princess in the main hall. It's a splendid building, the whole place tiled with iron to resist wind damage, and

all the decorations are metal, too. The bells hanging from the eaves, the mythological animals on the roof, and even the two steles outside are bronze. From 1759 until the fall of the Qing, the emperor would send an official here on the eighteenth day of the fourth lunar month each year to make an offering. Just below is a small **shrine to Confucius**, at the place where he was supposed to have commented, "the world is small".

Jade Emperor Temple

玉皇寺, yùhuáng sì

At the **Jade Emperor Temple**, you have truly arrived at the **highest point** of the mountain, and a rock with the characters for "supreme summit" and "1545m" carved on it stands within the courtyard. In Chinese popular religion, which mixes Taoism with much earlier beliefs, the Jade Emperor is the supreme ruler of heaven, depicted in an imperial hat with bead curtains hanging down his face. Outside the temple is the **Wordless Monument**, thought to have been erected by Emperor Wu more than two thousand years ago. The story goes that Wu wanted to have an inscription engraved that would do justice to his merits. None of the drafts he commissioned came up to scratch, however, so he left the stele blank, leaving everything to the imagination.

Sunrise Viewing Peak

Sunrise 4.45am in June, 7am in December

Southeast of the Jade Emperor Temple, the **Sunrise Viewing Peak** makes a fine point for watching the morning sun break free of the mountains and mist. It was here that the Song emperor performed the *feng* ceremony, building an altar and making sacrifices to heaven. On a clear day, you can see 200km to the coast, and at night you can see the lights of Ji'nan. There are numerous **trails** from here to fancifully named scenic spots; if the weather is good, and you've some energy left, it's a great place for aimless wandering.

ACCOMMODATION   **TAI SHAN**

In all **hotels**, hot water is generally only available in the evening; some may be closed in the winter, when it's imperative to phone ahead. There are plenty of **places to eat** along the eastern route to Zhongtianmen, but it's a good idea to take your own snacks as well; the food on offer past the midway point is unappealing and gets more expensive the higher you go.

Shenqi 神憩宾馆, shēnqì bīnguǎn. ☏0538 8223866. Within sprinting distance of Sunrise Peak, this is the fanciest place to stay on the mountain, with passably comfy rooms – when temperatures plummet on Tai Shan, you may discover a sudden appreciation for carpeted floors. **¥1200**

★Yunchao 云巢賓館, yúncháo bīnguǎn.

☏0538 8066666. Very close to Nantianmen, this is rather cheap, as far as Tai Shan goes, and surprisingly cheerful too – at least one of the staff will speak English, and the night shift are well versed at waking sunrise-seeking guests up at ungodly hours. At such times, calories from the ¥38 breakfast buffet may come in handy. Dorm beds **¥190**, doubles **¥480**

Qufu

曲阜, qǔfù

QUFU is, to put it bluntly, a strange little place. If you take an aimless walk around, it may appear to be little more than a small, dusty, slightly impoverished Shandong town – you'll spot men ambling around in Mao suits and hats, and ramshackle businesses secreted into crumbling alleyways, as if nothing at all had changed since the 1980s. Inside its old walled area, there's scarcely a convenience store to be seen, and (for now) just a single Western-style eatery. However, Qufu is of immense importance, and highly popular with Chinese tourists, for being the home town of **Confucius** (孔子, kǒngzǐ), a man who should, by rights, be an ever-present near the top of *Time* magazine's list of Most Influential People. Born around 551 BC, the sage spent a lifetime teaching his moral code (largely unappreciated by his contemporaries), and was buried just outside the town, in what became a sacred burial ground for his clan, the Kong. His teachings caught on after his death, however, and despite periodic purges, they have become firmly embedded in the Chinese psyche (see box, p.303 and p.942 for more on Confucianism in general). All around Qufu is architectural evidence of the esteem in which he was held by successive dynasties – most monumentally by the Ming, who were responsible for the two dominant sights, the **Confucius Temple** and the **Confucius Mansion**, whose scale seems more suited to Beijing.

Qufu has yet to truly come to terms with its popularity, and as such makes a particularly idiosyncratic place in which to spend a few days outside big-city China, with plenty to see concentrated in a small, walkable area, mostly within the confines of the town's flag-studded ancient walls. As a major tourist destination, expect the usual crowds and hustles – especially around the end of September, **on Confucius's birthdate** in the lunar calendar, when a **festival** is held here and reconstructions of many of the original rituals are performed. If it all gets too much, there are places to escape amid old buildings, trees and singing birds, such as the **Confucian Forest** to the north.

Confucius Temple

孔庙, kŏng miào • Daily 8am–5pm • ¥90 • Ticket office (unmarked in English) just to southeast of Star Gate • Audio-guides ¥20, plus ¥200 deposit

The **Confucius Temple** ranks among the greatest classical architectural complexes in China. It's certainly big: there are 466 rooms, and it's over 1km long, laid out in the design of an imperial palace, with nine courtyards on a north–south axis. It wasn't always so grand, first established as a three-room temple in 478 BC, containing a few of Confucius's lowly possessions: some hats, a zither and a carriage. In 539, Emperor Jing Di had the complex renovated, and from then on emperors keen to show their veneration for the sage – and ostentatiously to display their piety – renovated and expanded the complex for more than two thousand years. Most of the present structure is Ming and Qing.

Kui Wen Pavilion

The temple is accessed through its southern wall; from here a succession of gates leads into a courtyard holding the magnificent **Kui Wen Pavilion**, a wooden building constructed in 1018 with a unique triple-layered roof with curving eaves and four layers of crossbeams. It was renovated in 1504 and has since withstood an earthquake undamaged, an event recorded on a tablet on the terrace; recent years have, however, seen the pavilion transformed into a shop. The two adjacent pavilions are abstention lodges where visiting emperors would fast and bathe before taking part in sacrificial ceremonies. The **thirteen stele pavilions** in the courtyard beyond are worth checking out, containing 53 tablets presented by

QUFU COMBINATION TICKETS

If you plan to see the Confucius Temple, Mansion and Forest in a single day (quite possible, even if you start around midday), you'll save a little money by buying a **combination ticket** (¥150), sold at many hotels (usually for no extra charge), and outside the entrances to each site.

emperors to commemorate their visits, and gifts of land and funds for renovations made to the Kong family.

Five gates

Continuing north, you come to **five gates** leading off in different directions. The eastern ones lead to the hall where sacrifices were offered to Confucius's ancestors, the western to the halls where his parents were worshipped, while the central Gate of Great Achievements leads to a large pavilion, the **Apricot Altar**. Tradition has it that Confucius taught here after travelling the country in search of a ruler willing to implement his ideas. The cypress just inside the gate was supposed to have been planted by Confucius himself, and its state of health is supposed to reflect the fortunes of the Kong family.

The Hall of Great Achievements

大成殿, dàchéng diàn

The **Hall of Great Achievements**, behind the Apricot Altar, is the temple's grandest building, its most striking feature being 28 **stone pillars** carved with bas-relief dragons, dating from around 1500. Each pillar has nine gorgeous dragons, coiling around clouds and pearls towards the roof. There is nothing comparable in the Forbidden City in Beijing, and when emperors came to visit, the columns were covered with yellow silk to prevent imperial jealousy. Originally, the temple was solely dedicated to the worship of Confucius, but in 72 AD, Emperor Liu Zhuang offered sacrifices to his 72 disciples, too. Emperors of later dynasties (not wishing to be outdone) added more, and there are presently 172 "eminent worthies".

Hall to Qi Guan

Behind the Hall of Great Achievements is an inner hall for the worship of Confucius's wife, the **Hall to Qi Guan**, who also, it seems, merited deification through association (though Confucian values placed women way down the social hierarchy, with wives less important than their sons, and daughters-in-law less important than anybody). The phoenixes painted on its columns and ceiling are symbols of female power, in the same way as the dragon symbolizes masculinity.

The Hall of Poetry and Rites

诗社堂, shīshè táng

Next to the Hall of Great Achievements, the eastern axis of the temple is entered through the **Gate of the Succession of the Sage**. Here is the **Hall of Poetry and Rites** where Confucius was supposed to have taught his son, Kong Li, to learn poetry from the *Book of Odes* in order to express himself, and ritual from the *Book of Rites* in order to strengthen his character.

The Lu Wall

A solitary wall in the courtyard is the famous **Lu Wall**, where Kong Fu, a ninth-generation descendant of Confucius, hid the sage's **books** when Qin Shi Huang, the first emperor (see box, p.213), persecuted the followers of Confucius and burned all his books. Several decades later, Liu Yu, prince of Lu and son of the Emperor Jing Di, ordered Confucius's dwelling to be demolished in order to build an extension to his palace, whereupon the books were found, which led to a schism between those who followed the reconstructed version of his last books, and those who followed the teachings in the rediscovered originals.

Site of Confucius's home

In the east wall of the temple, near the Lu Wall, an unobtrusive gate leads to the legendary **site of Confucius's home**, sandwiched between the spectacular temple and the magnificent mansion, a tiny square of land just big enough to have held a couple of poky little rooms.

The western section

The temple's **western section** is entered through the Gate of He Who Heralds the Sage, by the Hall of Great Achievements. A paved path leads to a high brick terrace on which stands the five-bay, green-tiled **Hall of Silks and Metals** and the **Hall of He Who Heralds the Sage**, built to venerate Confucius's father, **Shu Lianghe**. He was originally a minor military official who attained posthumous nobility through his son. Behind is, predictably, the Hall of the Wife of He Who Heralds the Sage, dedicated to Confucius's mother.

Confucius Mansion

孔府, kǒng fǔ • Daily 8am–5pm • ¥60 • Entrance just northwest of the Drum Tower

The First Family Under Heaven – the descendants of Confucius – lived continuously at the **Confucius Mansion** for more than 2500 years, spanning 74 generations. The opulence and size of the mansion testifies to the power and wealth of the **Kong clan** and their head, the **Yansheng Duke**. Built on a north–south axis, the mansion is loosely divided into living quarters, an administrative area and a garden. In the east is a temple and ancestral hall, while the western wing includes the reception rooms for important guests and the rooms where the rites were learned. Intricate and convoluted, this complex of twisting alleyways and over 450 rooms (most of them sixteenth-century) has something decidedly eccentric about it. Unfortunately, one reason is that so many of these rooms have been converted into shops – you only have to head a few kilometres north of town to see whether Confucius really is rolling in his grave.

The Great Hall

In past the **old administrative departments** and through the **Gate of Double Glory**, the **Great Hall** was where the Yansheng Duke sat on a wooden chair covered with a tiger skin and proclaimed edicts. The flags and arrow tokens hanging on the walls are symbols of authority. Signs next to them reading "Make way!" were used to clear the roads of ordinary people when the duke left the mansion.

The residential apartments

The **residential apartments** of the mansion are to the north, accessible through gates that would once have been heavily guarded; no one could enter of their own accord under pain of death. Tiger-tail cudgels, goose-winged pitchforks and golden-headed jade clubs used to hang here to drive the message home. Even the water-carrier was not permitted,

---

CONFUCIANISM IN MODERN CHINA

When the Communists came to power they saw Confucianism as an archaic, feudal system and an **anti-Confucius campaign** was instigated, which came to a climax during the Cultural Revolution. Now, however, conservatives frightened by the growing generation gap and the new materialism of China are calling for a **return to Confucian values** of respect and selflessness, just as their nervous counterparts in the West preach a return to family values. Confucian social morality – obeying authority, regarding family as the seat of morality and emphasizing the mutual benefits of friendship – is sometimes hailed as one of the main reasons for the success of East Asian economies, just as Protestantism provided the ideological complement to the growth of the industrialized West. As one Chinese visitor commented, "Confucius is the one Chinese leader who never let the people down".

5

and emptied the water into a stone trough outside that runs through the apartment walls. A fire here during the twentieth century raged for three days as only twelve of the five hundred hereditary servants were allowed to go into the area to put it out.

The first halls

The first hall is the seven-bay **Reception Hall**, where relatives were received, banquets held and marriage and funeral ceremonies conducted. Today, the only remnants of its once-salubrious past are several golden throne chairs and ornate staffs. Directly opposite the Reception Hall, the **central eastern room** contains a set of furniture made from tree roots, presented to the mansion by Emperor Qianlong – an original imperial decree lies on the table.

Front Main Building

Past the outbuildings and through a small gate, you reach the **Front Main Building**, an impressive two-storey structure in which are displayed paintings and clothes. The eastern central room was the home of **Madame Tao**, wife of Kong Lingyi, the 76th duke. Their daughter, Kong Demao, lived in the far eastern room, while Kong Lingyi's concubine, Wang, originally one of Tao's handmaids, lived in the inner western room. It doesn't sound like an arrangement designed for domestic bliss; indeed, whenever the duke was away, Madame Tao used to beat Wang with a whip she kept for the purpose. When Wang produced a male heir, Tao poisoned her. A second concubine, Feng, was kept prisoner in her rooms by Tao until she died.

The rear building

The duke himself lived in the **rear building**, which has been left as it was when the last duke fled to Taiwan. Behind that is the garden where, every evening, flocks of **crows** come to roost noisily. Crows are usually thought to be inauspicious in China, but here they are welcome, and said to be the soldiers of Confucius, who protected him from danger on his travels. To the southeast of the inner east wing is a four-storey building called the **Tower of Refuge**, a planned retreat in the event of an uprising or invasion. The first floor was equipped with a moveable hanging ladder, and a trap could be set in the floor. Once inside, the refugees could live for weeks on dried food stores.

THE YANSHENG DUKE AND THE KONG FAMILY

The status of the **Yansheng Duke** – the title given to Confucius's direct male descendant – rose throughout imperial history as emperors granted him increasing **privileges and hereditary titles**; under the Qing dynasty, he was uniquely permitted to ride a horse inside the Forbidden City and walk along the Imperial Way inside the palace. Emperors presented the duke with large areas of sacrificial fields (so called because the income from the fields was used to pay for sacrificial ceremonies), as well as exempting him from taxes.

The Kongs remained a close-knit family, practising a severe interpretation of **Confucian ethics** – any young family member who offended an elder was fined two taels (about 70g) of silver and battered twenty times with a bamboo club. A female family member was expected to obey her father, her husband and her son. One elderly Kong general, after defeat on the battlefield, cut his throat for the sake of his dignity. When the news reached the mansion, his son hanged himself as an expression of filial piety; after discovering the body, his wife hanged herself out of female virtue. On hearing this, the emperor bestowed the family with a board, inscribed "A family of faithfulness and filiality".

The Kong family enjoyed the good life right up until the beginning of the twentieth century. **Decline** set in rapidly with the downfall of imperial rule, and in 1940, the last of the line, **Kong Decheng**, fled to Taiwan during the Japanese invasion, breaking the tradition of millennia. His sister, **Kong Demao**, penned *In the House of Confucius*, a fascinating account of life lived inside this strange family chained to the past. Half of Qufu now claims descent from the Kongs, and it's by far the most common family name in the city.

The temple

In the east of the complex you'll find the family temple, the Ancestral Hall and residential quarters for less important family members. The **temple** is dedicated to the memory of Yu, wife of the 72nd duke, and daughter of Emperor Qianlong. The princess had a mole on her face, which, it was predicted, would bring disaster unless she married into a more illustrious family. The Kongs were the only clan to fulfil the criteria, but the daughter of the Manchu emperor was not allowed to marry a Han Chinese. This inconvenience was got around by first having the daughter adopted by the family of the Grand Secretary Yu, and then marrying her to the duke as Yu's daughter. Her dowry included twenty villages and several thousand trunks of clothing.

Yan Miao

颜庙, yán miào • Daily 8am–5pm • ¥50 • Entrance on south side of complex

A little way northeast of the Confucius Mansion is the **Yan Miao**, a small temple dedicated to Yan Hui, who was regarded as Confucius's greatest disciple and sometimes called "The Sage Returned". A temple has been situated here since the Han dynasty, though the present structure is Ming. It's attractive, quieter than the Confucius Temple, and contains some impressive architectural details, such as the dragon pillars on the main hall, and a dragon head embedded in the roof. The eastern building now contains a display of locally excavated Neolithic and Zhou pottery.

Zhougong Miao

周公庙, zhōugōng miào • Daily 7.30am–4.30pm • ¥5

The temple of **Zhoughong Miao**, in the northeast of town, is dedicated to a Zhou-dynasty duke, a statue of whom stands in the main hall, together with his son Bo Qin and Bo Qin's servant. Legend has it that Bo Qin was a rasher man than his father, and the duke, worried that his son would not act sensibly in state matters, inscribed a pithy maxim from his own political experience on a slate and directed the servant to carry it on his back. Whenever Bo Qin was about to do something foolish, the ever-present servant would turn his back so Bo Qin would think again. The open terrace before the hall, where sacrifices were made to the duke, contains a striking stone incense burner carved with coiling dragons.

The Confucian Forest

孔林, kǒng lín • Daily 8am–5pm • ¥40 • Bus #1 via Gulou Nanjie and Gulou Beijie; taxi around ¥10

The **burial ground** of the Kongs, the large tract of the **Confucian Forest** lies 3km north of the town centre. The forest, like the temple, expanded over the centuries from something simple and austere to a grand complex, in this case centring around a single grave – **the tomb of Confucius**. Confucian disciples collected exotic trees to plant here, and there are now thousands of different varieties. It's an atmospheric place, sculptures half concealed in thick undergrowth, tombstones standing aslant in groves of ancient trees and wandering paths dappled with sunlight. A great place to spend an afternoon, it's one of the few famous scenic spots in China that it's possible to appreciate unaccompanied by crowds.

The Confucian cemetery

The imperial carriageway runs north, then west, from the forest's chunky main gate. Before long, you'll see a gateway and an arched stone bridge to your right; beyond this is the **Confucian cemetery** where Confucius and his son are buried. The **Hall of Deliberation**, just north of the bridge, was where visitors put on ritual dress before performing sacrifices.

An avenue leads to the **Hall of Sacrifices**, and behind that to a small grassy mound – the **grave**. Just to the west of the tomb, a hut, looking like a potting shed, was where Confucius's disciples each spent three years watching over the grave. Confucius's son is

5

buried just north of here. His unflattering epitaph reads: "He died before his father without making any noteworthy achievements".

According to legend, before his death Confucius told his disciples to bury him at this spot because the *feng shui* was good. His disciples objected, as there was no river nearby. Confucius told them that a river would be dug in the future. After the first Qin emperor, Qin Shi Huang, unified China, he launched an anti-Confucian campaign, burning books and scholars, and tried to sabotage the grave by ordering a river to be dug through the cemetery – thus inadvertently perfecting it.

ARRIVAL AND INFORMATION   QUFU

The #K01 bus (¥3) links the town centre, the bus terminal and both train stations; a taxi from the centre costs around ¥15 to the bus or main train stations, and ¥30–40 to the high-speed station.

By train Qufu's main station (曲阜站, qūfù zhàn), served by slow trains only, is inconveniently located 5km east of central Qufu. High-speed trains use the new Qufu East station (曲阜东站, qūfù dōngzhàn), an unnecessarily gigantic venue set a full 20km to the east. Tickets are easy to buy at either station, and there are several ticket offices in the town centre. Note that if you're going to Tai'an, it's easier to take the bus.
Main train station destinations Beijing (3 daily; 9–12hr); Ji'nan (5 daily; 2hr 20min–4hr); Nanjing (1 daily; 9hr 30min); Taishan (for Tai'an; 5 daily; 1hr 30min–2hr 30min).

Qufu East station destinations Beijing (1–2 hourly; 2hr 10min–2hr 40min); Ji'nan (2–4 hourly; 30–50min); Kaifeng (1 daily; 3hr 45min); Nanjing (1–4 hourly; 1hr 45min–2hr 30min); Qingdao (6 daily; 3hr 30min); Tai'an (21 daily; 20min).
By bus The bus station is 6km to the west of town on Jingxua Lu, though you'll only really need it to get to Tai'an, and possibly Ji'nan; buses on these routes dry up by 6pm. There's another bus station near the East train station, though this is of no use to travellers.
Destinations Ji'nan (2hr 30min); Tai'an (1hr).

GETTING AROUND

By bus Once in town, the only city bus you'll need is the #1, which runs via Gulou Nanjie and Gulou Beijie to the Confucian Forest.
By taxi Taxis to anywhere in the town centre cost about ¥5.
By bicycle Qufu is a great place to get around by bike; the youth hostel rents them out (¥8 for 4 hours; ¥100 deposit).

Local transport A cycle-rickshaw ride, where the passenger is slung low in the front, giving an uninterrupted dog's-eye view of the street, costs from ¥10. Horse-drawn carts aimed strictly at tourists are not cheap; start the bidding at ¥30 for a ride to the Forest.

ACCOMMODATION

Accommodation in Qufu is surprisingly patchy, given the city's popularity with domestic tourists, and higher-end places are few and far between.

Queli 阙里宾舍, quèlǐ bīnshè. 1 Queli Jie ☎0537 4866523, ⓦquelihotel.com. Located right next to the Confucius Temple and Mansion, this is the only real higher-end accommodation in town. Because of their trapped market, rooms are relatively poor value for money, but have satellite TV, 24hr hot water and English-speaking staff. Their on-site restaurant is the best place to eat in town. ¥568
Qufu International 曲阜国际饭店, qūfù guójì fàndiàn. 2 Hongdao Lu ☎0537 4418888. A typical Chinese tourist hotel, located just outside the city walls and

hence underpatronized – which means it's easier to bargain rates down. Their rooms are absolutely fine, though the a/c doesn't always cool them down enough in summer. ¥398
★**Qufu International Youth Hostel** 曲阜国际青年旅舍, qūfù guójì qīngnián lǚshè. Gulou Beijie ☎0537 4418989, ⓦyhachina.com. What a lovely place this is: a pleasant, well-run hostel with decent bedrooms and amiable staff. Their bar/restaurant is a good place to make new travel buddies, and worth a visit even if you're not staying here (see p.308). Dorm ¥45, twins ¥128

EATING

Qufu's local specialities are great in number, and include such **delicacies** as fragrant rice and boiled scorpions soaked in oil. The Kong family also developed its own cuisine, featuring dishes such as "Going to the Court with the Son" (pigeon served with duck) and "Gold and Silver Fish" (a white and a yellow fish together); unfortunately, fewer and fewer places are

5

serving these dishes. After dark, a small lane south of Wumaci Dajie becomes a night market as it fills up with **open-air food stalls**, offering tasty-looking hotpots, stews and skewers; the food's not bad and the atmosphere lively. Lastly, if you're on your way up to the Confucian Forest, keep your peepers peeled for ladies making **savoury pancakes**, known as *jian bing*, on highly photogenic rotating hotplates.

Kongfu Jiachang 孔府家常, kǒngfǔ jiācháng. West of the Drum Tower. Overpriced but good-quality Qufu cuisine, with nice evening views of the Drum Tower, which stands a stone's throw away. There's no English or picture menu; their *yipin doufu* (一品豆腐, yīpǐn dòufu; ¥48), a slab of tofu stuffed with snail and all sorts of other goodies, is probably the best option. Daily 9am–10.30pm.

★**Queli** 阙里宾舍, quèlǐ bīnshè. 1 Queli Jie. Good-value hotel restaurant, which whips up tasty local delicacies. Try the Qufu pancake, essentially a thin omelette smeared with shrimp paste and chicken mince (¥48), the *yipin* tofu (¥58), or spicy tofu soup (¥28). You could really

push the boat out with the Gold and Silver Fish (¥208), while on the budget side there are plenty of Chinese staples in the ¥20–40 range. Daily 11am–2pm & 5–8pm.
★**Qufu International Youth Hostel** 曲阜国际青年旅舍, qūfù guójì qīngnián lǚshè. Gulou Beijie ☎ 0537 4418989, ⓦ yhachina.com. This is as good as Western soul food gets in town, with a range of pizza, spaghetti and sandwiches, all backpacker friendly at ¥20–60. They also make superb shakes and good coffee, while at night it's a great place for a beer (from ¥8) over a game of pool. Restaurant daily 8am–11pm, bar sometimes open a little later.

SHOPPING

There are plenty of **stalls and shops** selling tourist gimmicks all through town, exploiting the Confucian connection to the hilt. Most appropriate perhaps are **books of translated Confucian sayings**, available at the *Queli* hotel. On Queli Jie, it's worth checking out the name-chops (which can be carved with your name in a few minutes from around ¥65), rubbings taken from steles in the temple, and locally crafted pistachio carvings.

Jiangsu

江苏, jiāngsū

Jiangsu is a long, narrow province hugging the coast south of Shandong. Low-lying, flat and wet, it is one of China's most fertile and long-inhabited areas. Today, much of it is industrial sprawl, but there are a few gems among all the new factory towns; provincial capital **Nanjing** is one of the country's great historical cities, while ancient **Suzhou** is famous throughout China for its gardens and silk production.

Visiting the region, you find yourself in a world of **water**. The whole area is intensively drained, canalized, irrigated and farmed, and the rivers, canals and lakes which web the plain give it much of its character. The traditional way to travel here was by **boat**, with the **Grand Canal** (see box opposite) once navigable all the way from Hangzhou in Zhejiang province to Beijing. The province's other great water highway – the **Yangzi River** – connects Nanjing with Shanghai, ensuring that trade from both east and west continues to bring wealth to the region.

Nanjing

南京, nánjīng

Formerly known in the West as Nanking, **NANJING** – the "Southern Capital" – stands as a direct foil to the "Northern Capital" of Beijing, and the city is still considered China's rightful hub by many Overseas Chinese, particularly those from Taiwan. Its current prosperity derives both from its proximity to Shanghai and from its gateway position on the **Yangzi River**, which stretches away west deep into China's interior. With leafy, shaded avenues and a laidback air, it's one of those cities that's perhaps better to live in than visit, though a wealth of historic sites means that it's well worth a few days of anyone's time. Most visitors hit charming **Xuanwu Lake** and its surrounding belt of parkland, while other highlights include the old **Presidential Palace**, and the truly gigantic **Nanjing Museum**.

Brief history

Occupying a strategic site on the south bank of the Yangzi River, Nanjing has had an important role from the earliest times, though not until 600 BC were there the beginnings of a walled city. By the time the Han empire broke up in 220 AD, Nanjing had been the capital of half a dozen local dynasties, and when the Sui reunited China in 589, the building of the Grand Canal began to considerably increase the city's economic importance. During the Tang and Song periods, the city rivalled nearby Hangzhou as the wealthiest in the country, and in 1368 the first emperor of the Ming dynasty decided to establish Nanjing as the **capital** of all China.

Turmoil and revolution

Although Nanjing's claims to be the capital would be usurped by the heavily northern-based Qing dynasty, subsequent anti-authoritarian movements associated themselves with efforts to restore the old capital. In the wake of the first Opium War – when the humiliating **Treaty of Nanking** was signed here – the **Taiping rebels** (see box, p.314) set up the capital of their Kingdom of Heavenly Peace at Nanjing. The siege and final recapture of the city by the foreign-backed Qing armies in 1864 was one of the saddest and most dramatic events in China's history. Following the overthrow of the Qing dynasty in 1911, however, the city flowered again, chosen as the national capital by both Sun Yatsen's Republican government, and the Nationalist administration under Chiang Kai-shek.

Modern times

In 1937, the name Nanjing became synonymous with one of the worst atrocities of World War II, after the **Rape of Nanking**, in which invading Japanese soldiers butchered an estimated 300,000 civilians (see box, p.312). Subsequently, Chiang Kai-shek's government escaped the Japanese advance by moving west to Chongqing, though after

THE GRAND CANAL

The **Grand Canal** (大运河, dàyùnhé) is, at 1800km, the longest canal on earth. The first sections were dug about 400 BC, probably for military purposes, but the historic task of linking the Yellow and the Yangzi rivers was not achieved until the early seventh century AD under the Sui emperor Yang Di, when as many as six million men may have been pressed into service for its construction.

The original function of the canal was specifically to join the fertile rice-producing areas of the Yangzi with the more heavily populated but barren lands of the north, and to alleviate the effects of regular crop failures and famine. Following its completion, however, the canal became a vital element in the expansion of **trade** under the Tang and Song, benefiting the south as much as the north. Slowly the centre of political power drifted south – by 800 AD the Yangzi basin was taking over from the Yellow River as the chief source of the empire's finances, a transformation cemented when the Song dynasty established its capital at **Hangzhou** and the Ming emperors subsequently based themselves in **Nanjing**. For centuries afterwards, the canal was constantly maintained and the banks regularly built up. A Western traveller, Robert Morrison, journeying in 1816 from Tianjin all the way down to the Yangzi, described the sophisticated and frequent locks and noted that in places the banks were so high and the country around so low that from the boat it was possible to look down on roofs and treetops.

Not until early in the twentieth century did the canal seriously start falling into **disuse**. Contributing factors included the frequent flooding of the Yellow River, the growth of coastal shipping and the coming of the rail lines. Unused, much of the canal rapidly silted up. But since the 1950s its value has once more been recognized, and renovation undertaken. The stretch **south of the Yangzi**, running from Zhenjiang through Changzhou, Wuxi and Suzhou, is now navigable year-round, at least by flat-bottomed barges, since passenger services have been killed off by new highways and high-speed trains. **North of the Yangzi**, the canal is seasonally navigable virtually up to Jiangsu's northern border with Shandong, and major works are going on to allow bulk carriers access to the coal-producing city of Xuzhou. Beyond here, towards the Yellow River, sadly the canal remains impassable.

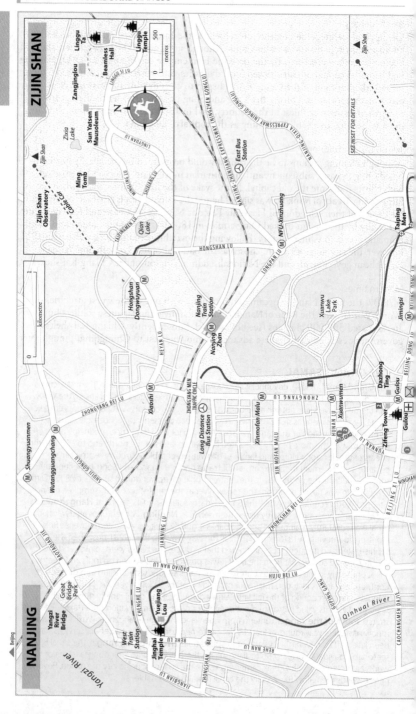

ZIJIN SHAN

NANJING

Linggu Ta
Linggu Temple
Beamless Hall
Zanglinglou
Linggu

Zijin Shan

Ming Tomb
Sun Yatsen Mausoleum
Zixia Lake

Zijin Shan Observatory
Qian Lake

0 metres 500

Cable Car

N

SEE INSET FOR DETAILS

Zijin Shan

LINGGU LU
SUILIANGE LU
MINGLING LU
SILIDANGMEN LU
LINGGU SI LU

Beijing

Yangzi River

NANJING ZHENHUAI EXPRESSWAY (NINGZHEN GONGLU)
NANJING-QIXIA EXPRESSWAY (NINGQI GONGLU)

East Bus Station

NFU-Xinzhuang

Taiping Men

HONGSHAN LU
LONGPAN LU

Hongshan Dongwuyuan

Nanjing Train Station
Nanjing Zhan

Xuanwu Lake Park

Jimingsi

BEIJING DONG LU

Xiaoshi

Zhongyang Men Traffic Circle

ZHONGYANG BEI LU
SHUILU GONGLU
HEYAN LU

Shuangyuanmen
Wutangguangchang

0 kilometre

Long Distance Bus Station

ZHONGYANG LU

Dazhong Ting
Gulou
Zifeng Tower
Xuanwumen

HUNAN LU
YUNNAN LU
BEIJING XI LU
NINGHAI LU

Xinmofan Malu
XIN MOFAN MALU
ZHONGSHAN BEI LU

JIANNING LU

HUJU BEI LU

DAQIAO NAN LU
CHENGHE LU

Yangzi River Bridge
Great Bridge Park

West Train Station

Jinghai Temple
Yuejiang Lou

REHE LU
REHE NAN LU
ZHONGSHAN LU
BEI LU

JIANGBIAN LU
BAOTAQIAO JIE

GUPING JIE
CAOCHANGMEN DAJIE

Qinhuai River

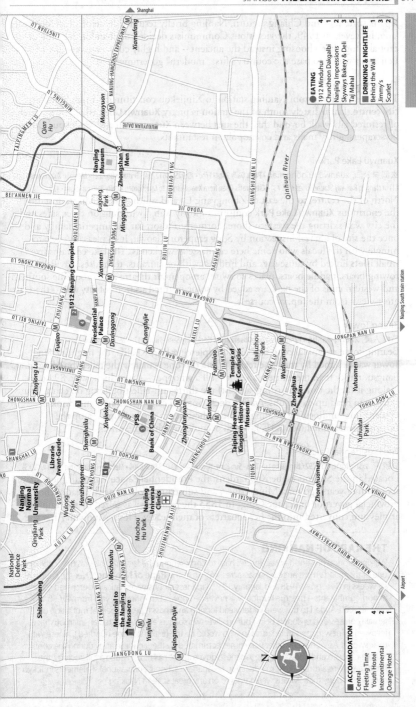

▲ Shanghai

● EATING	
1912 Minduhui	4
Chuncheon Dakgalbi	1
Nanjing Impressions	2
Skyways Bakery & Deli	3
Taj Mahal	5

● DRINKING & NIGHTLIFE	
Behind the Wall	1
Jimmy's	3
Scarlet	2

■ ACCOMMODATION	
Central	3
Fleeting Time Youth Hostel	4
Intercontinental	2
Orange Hotel	1

▶ Nanjing South train station

▶ Airport

5

Japan's surrender and Chiang's return, Nanjing briefly resumed its status. Just four years later, however, in 1949, the victorious Communists decided to abandon Nanjing as capital altogether, choosing instead the ancient – and highly conservative – city of Beijing in which to base the country's first "modern" government.

The city centre

The area stretching from Nanjing station to Xinjiekou constitutes Nanjing's modern **city centre**. Immediately south of the station is pretty **Xuanwu Lake**, edged by a stretch of restored city wall; beyond this, the area between **Xuanwumen** and **Xinjiekou** is full of skyscrapers, glitzy malls and cosmopolitan restaurants.

Xuanwu Lake Park

玄武湖公园, xuánwǔhú gōngyuán • **Park** Daily 24hr • Free • ☎ 025 83612204, ⓦ xuanwuhu.net • Metro to Xuanwumen (line #1) or Nanjing Railway Station (lines #1 & #3) • **City walls** Open from Xuanwumen to Taipingmen • Daily 8.30am–5pm • ¥30

North of the centre, to the east of Zhongyang Lu and south of the main train station, the enormous **Xuanwu Lake Park** comprises mostly water, with hills on three sides and the city wall skirting the western shore. Formerly a resort for the imperial family and once the site of a naval inspection by Song emperor Xiaowu, it's a pleasant place to mingle with the locals who come here en masse at weekends. The lake contains five small **islets** linked by causeways and bridges, with restaurants, teahouses, pavilions, rowing boats, paddle boats, places to swim, an open-air theatre and a zoo. The southern and western ends of the park are edged by some restored sections of **city wall** – there are great views from the top, of course.

Zifeng Tower

紫峰大厦, zǐfēng dàshà • 1 Zhongyang Lu • **Observation deck** Daily 8am–9pm • ¥120 • Metro to Gulou (line #1)

Bearing some resemblance to Dubai's cloudpiercing Burj Khalifa, the mighty **Zifeng Tower** was designed by the same team. While this one is merely the tallest building in Jiangsu, rather than the entire planet, it's still a whopper – 450m high, with 89 floors, making it (at the time of writing, at least) the thirteenth-tallest building on earth. You can pay to head up to the **observation deck**, but you can save money, and drink in opulent surroundings, by heading to the highest bar in the building – atop the *Intercontinental* hotel (see p.317), which occupies much of the tower.

The Presidential Palace

总统府, zǒngtǒng fǔ • 292 Changjiang Lu • Tues–Sun 8am–6pm • ¥40 • ☎ 025 84578700 • Metro to Daxinggong (lines #2 & #3)

Located in the Suzhou-esque Xu Gardens, the **Presidential Palace** was built more than six hundred years ago for a Ming prince, and subsequently became the seat of the provincial governor under the Qing. In 1853 the building was seized by the Taiping armies and converted into the headquarters of their leader, Hong Xiuquan. After the

---

THE RAPE OF NANKING

Walking around present-day Nanjing, it's hard to comprehend the fact that this was the scene of one of the world's most atrocious massacres, known as the **Rape of Nanking**. Over the course of six weeks in December 1938 and January 1939, Japanese troops systematically butchered scores of non-combatants – the true number will never be known, but estimates vary from 40,000 to over 300,000. Added to this were widespread looting and mass rape, the genital mutilation of female corpses, and prisoners being buried alive; two soldiers also conducted an infamous "race", followed by newspapers in Japan, as to who would be the first to slay one hundred Chinese with their swords. As with many other war crimes committed by the Japanese army during the conflict in Korea, Taiwan and elsewhere, the Japanese government has never issued a full apology, the subject remains airbrushed from education at Japanese schools, and nationalist elements in Tokyo continue to deny that civilians were targeted on any great scale in Nanking.

overthrow of the Qing, it became the Guomindang government's Presidential Palace. It was from here, in the early decades of the twentieth century, that first Sun Yatsen and later Chiang Kai-shek governed China. Visiting the palace today, you'll see exhibitions on the Taiping Uprising and the life and times of Sun and Chiang.

Around Zhonghuamen

South of the centre, the area around **Zhonghuamen**, Nanjing's old south gate, has enough for a full half-day of sightseeing. As well as the impressive gate itself, you'll find the spectacular Confucius Temple, and one of the city's most interesting museums – one pertaining to the Taiping Uprising (see box, p.314).

Temple of Confucius

夫子庙, fūzǐ miào • Daily 8am–9.30pm • Free • Electric boats ¥40/30min, paddle boats ¥20/30min • ☎ 025 52209788, Ⓦ njfzm.net • Metro to Sanshan Jie (line #1) or Fuzimiao (line #3)

The **Temple of Confucius** is set south of Jiankang Lu among a noisy welter of street vendors, boutiques, arcades and restaurants. The central **temple** resembles a theme park inside, complete with mannequins in period costume, and is hardly worth bothering about, but there is an attractive waterfront area along the canal here (where the Tang poet Liu Yuxi composed his most famous poem, *Wuyi Lane*), along which you can pick up **leisure boats** that trundle south to Zhonghua Men.

Taiping Heavenly Kingdom History Museum

太平天国历史博物馆, tàipíng tiānguó lìshǐ bówùguǎn • 128 ZhanYuan Lu • Daily 8.30am–5pm • ¥10 • ☎ 025 52201849 • Metro to Sanshan Jie (line #1) or Fuzimiao (line #3)

West of the Temple of Confucius is the absorbing **Taiping Heavenly Kingdom History Museum**, well worth a visit. The sad but fascinating story of the Taiping Uprising is told here in pictures and relics, with English captions. There are seals, coins and weapons aplenty, with clear maps showing the progress of the Taiping army from Guangdong. The building itself was the residence of Xu Da, a Ming prince, and became the home of one of the rebel generals during the uprising.

Zhonghuamen

中华门, zhōnghuámén • Daily 8.30am–8pm • ¥50 • ☎ 025 86625435 • Metro to Zhonghuamen (line #1)

In the far south of the centre, **Zhonghuamen** is now largely bereft of its wall and isolated in the middle of a traffic island, just inside the river moat near a metro station of the same name. This colossal gate actually comprises four gates, one inside another, and its seven enclosures were designed to hold three thousand men in case of enemy attack, making it one of the biggest of its kind in China. Today you can walk through the central archway and climb up two levels; up above, there's a tremendous view of the city spreading out beyond.

West of the centre

Few travellers make it out to the western reaches of central Nanjing, and access to the various sights here will remain complicated until the completion of the area's new metro lines. Still, it's worth persevering – those scaling **Shizi Shan** will have a spectacular view of the Yangzi River, while further south the **Memorial to the Nanjing Massacre** makes for a fascinating, if rather harrowing, visit.

Jinghai Temple

静海寺, jìnghǎi sì • 228 Jianning Lu, off Rehe Lu • Daily 8am–8pm • Free • ☎ 025 58802973 • Metro to Gulou (line #1) then bus #152

Jinghai Temple lies in the far northwest of town near the Yangzi River and the west train station. It was here that the British and Chinese negotiated the first of the many unequal treaties in the wake of the Opium War in 1842 (the treaty was later signed on a British naval ship in Nanjing harbour), and the temple buildings now house the

5

THE TAIPING UPRISING

One of the consequences of the weakness of the Qing dynasty in the nineteenth century was the extraordinary **Taiping Uprising**, an event that would lead to the slaughter of millions, and which has been described as the most colossal civil war in the history of the world. The Taipings were led by **Hong Xiuquan**, failed civil-service candidate and Christian evangelist, who, following a fever, declared himself to be the younger brother of Jesus Christ. In 1851, he assembled 20,000 armed followers at **Jintian village**, near Guiping in Guangxi province, and established the **Taiping Tianguo**, or Kingdom of Heavenly Peace. This militia routed the local Manchu forces, and by the following year was sweeping up through Hunan into central China. They **captured Nanjing** in 1853, but though the kingdom survived another eleven years, this was its last achievement. Poorly planned expeditions failed to take Beijing or win over western China, and Hong's leadership – originally based on the enfranchisement of the peasantry and the outlawing of opium, alcohol and sexual discrimination – devolved into paranoia and fanaticism. After a gigantic struggle, **Qing forces** finally managed to unseat the Taipings when Western governments sent in assistance, most notably in the person of Queen Victoria's personal favourite, Charles "Chinese" Gordon.

Despite the rebellion's ultimately disastrous failure and its overtly Christian message, the whole episode is seen as a precursor to the arrival of communism in China. Indeed, in its fanatical rejection of Confucianism and the incredible damage it wrought on buildings and sites of historic value, it finds curious echoes in Mao Zedong's Cultural Revolution.

Nanjing Treaty Museum. Unfortunately, the museum's detailed exposition of fractious Sino-British relations throughout the nineteenth and twentieth centuries is in Chinese only, but the temple is pleasant to stroll around nonetheless. It was originally built in the Ming dynasty by Emperor Chengzu to honour the Chinese Muslim naval hero **Zheng He**, who led the Chinese fleet on exploratory voyages to East Africa and the Persian Gulf; you'll see his name commemorated throughout the city.

Shizi Shan

狮子山, shīzi shān · Daily 7.30am–5.30pm · ¥40; elevator ¥10 · ☎ 025 58815369 · Metro to Gulou (line #1) then bus #152

Rising up behind the Jinghai Temple is **Shizi Shan**, a small mountain topped with an ornate, multistorey building, the **Yuejiang Lou** (阅江楼, yuèjiāng lóu). While the structure is of little historical importance, its 52m height alone makes it worth a look, and from the top level there's a tremendous view of the city on one side and the Yangzi on the other.

Memorial to the Nanjing Massacre

南京大屠杀纪念馆, nánjīng dàtúshā jìniànguǎn · 195 Chating Dong Jie · Tues–Sun 8.30am–4.30pm · Free · Metro to Yunjinlu (line #2)

Some way west of the river is the must-see **Memorial to the Nanjing Massacre**. This grim, gravelly garden includes a gruesome display of victims' skulls and bones, half-buried in the dirt, as well as a clearly labelled (in English) photographic account of the sufferings endured by the Chinese at the hands of the Japanese army during World War II.

Zijin Shan

紫金山, zǐjīn shān · Free · ☎ 025 84446111, ⓦ zschina.org.cn · Accessible from various points, including paths from Muxuyuan metro (line #2) · **Cable car** Daily 9am–5pm · One-way ¥35, return ¥60

Just east of the city, **Zijin Shan** (Purple Gold Mountain) is a cool and shady spot to escape the furnace heat of Nanjing's summer, with fragrant woods and stretches of long grass, but also here are the three most visited sites in Nanjing. Of these, the centrepiece, right in the middle of the hill, is **Zhongshan Ling**, the magnificent mausoleum of China's first president, Sun Yatsen. To the east of Zhongshan Ling is the **Linggu Temple** complex, and to the west are the **tombs** of the Ming emperors who ruled China from Nanjing. Visiting all three sites can easily take a full day, though each can be reached independently using public transport. Note that in some tourist literature and on maps it may be called Zhongshan Mountain Scenic Area.

NANJING'S CITY WALL

Though Nanjing was walled as many as 2500 years ago, the present **city wall** is basically the work of the first Ming emperor, who extended and strengthened the earlier walls in 1369–73. Built of brick and more than 32km long, it followed the contours of the country, skirting Xuanwu Lake in the north, fringing Xijin Shan in the east, and tracing the Qinhuai River (which doubled as a moat) to the west and south. The wall was mainly paid for by rich families resettled here by the emperor: one third of it was "donated" by a single native of Wuxiang in Zhejiang province. Its construction employed 200,000 conscripts, who ensured that the bricks were all the same size and specification, each one bearing the names of the workman and overseer. The bricks were held together, to an average height of 12m and a thickness of 7m, by a mortar of lime and glutinous rice paste.

Today you can walk around a restored section of wall, bordering Xuanwu Lake (see p.312), as well as a short section near Zhonghuamen (see p.313). The original structure, of red rock in places, is still plainly visible along a 300m section of the wall at the so-called **Shitoucheng**, in the west of the city between Caochangmen Dajie and Fenghuang Jie.

Nanjing Museum

南京博物馆, nánjīng bówùguǎn • 321 Zhongshan Dong Lu • Daily 9am–5pm, last entry 4pm • Free (take ID) • ☎ 025 84807923, ⓦ www.njmuseum.com • Metro to Minggugong (line #2)

East of the centre, and just west of the Zijin Shan slopes, the huge **Nanjing Museum** is one of the best provincial museums in China, especially in terms of clarity of explanations – nearly everything is labelled in English. The complex is gigantic, and exhibitions are spread across a dozen large halls, but highlights include some superb silk-embroidered sedan chairs and several heavy cast bronzes, dating from as early as the Western Zhou (1100–771 BC). The jade and lacquerwork sections, as well as the model Fujian trading ships, are also well worth seeing. Lastly, don't miss the "Scene of the Republican Period" gallery, which provides a cute little trip back in time to the days of Nanking.

Linggu Temple

灵谷寺, línggǔ sì • Daily 8am–5.30pm • ¥32 • Bus #202

On the eastern side of Zijin Shan, the highlight of **Linggu Temple** complex is the so-called **Beamless Hall**. Completed in 1381, and much restored since, it's unusual for its large size and particularly for its self-supporting brick arch construction, with five columns instead of a central beam. The hall was used to store Buddhist sutras before the Taiping rebels made it a fortress; now it's an exhibition hall. A couple of minutes' walk southeast from the Beamless Hall is Linggu Temple itself, a surprisingly small place attended by yellow-robed monks.

Linggu Ta

灵谷塔, línggǔ tǎ • Daily 6am–6.45pm • ¥70 • Bus #202

Leading northwest from the Linggu buildings and part of the same complex, a delightful footpath through beautiful cypresses and pines leads to **Linggu Ta**, an octagonal, nine-storey, 60m-high pagoda, built during the 1930s as a monument to the more than 30,000 Guomindang members killed in the fighting against insurgent Communists. It's well worth climbing up for the views over the surrounding countryside.

Sun Yatsen Mausoleum

中山陵, zhōngshān líng • Tues–Sun 8.30am–5pm • Free • ☎ 025 84446111 • Bus #201

Dr Sun Yatsen, the first president of post-imperial China, is the only hero revered by Chinese jointly on both sides of the Taiwan Straits. The **Sun Yatsen Mausoleum** is an imposing structure of white granite and blue tiles (the Nationalist colours) set off by the green pine trees. The mausoleum was completed in 1929, four years after Sun Yatsen's death. From the large bronze statue at the bottom, 392 marble steps lead up to

5

the Memorial Hall, dominated by a 5m-tall seated white marble figure of the great man himself. Beyond the figure is the burial chamber, with another marble effigy lying on the stone coffin; according to unsubstantiated rumours, the bones were removed from the coffin to Taiwan by fleeing Guomindang leaders in 1949. The Guomindang ideals – Nationalism, Democracy and People's Livelihood – are carved above the entrance to the burial chamber in gold on black marble.

The Ming Tomb

明孝陵, míngxiào líng • Daily 8.30am–5.30pm • ¥70 • ☎ 025 84446111 • Metro to Muxuyuan (line #2), or bus #20 from Gulou

About 2km west of the Sun Yatsen Mausoleum, the **Ming Tomb** marks the burial place of Zhu Yuanzhang, founder of the Ming dynasty and the only one of its fourteen emperors to be buried at Nanjing (his thirteen successors are all buried in Beijing; see p.124). So colossal was the task of moving earth and erecting the stone walls that it took two years and a hundred thousand soldiers and conscripts to complete the tomb in 1383. The site was originally far larger, but its halls and pavilions, and 22km-long enclosing vermilion wall, were mostly destroyed by the Taipings. Today what remains is a walled collection of trees, stone bridges and dilapidated gates leading to the lonely mound at the back containing the (as yet unexcavated) burial site of the emperor and his wife, as well as the fifty courtiers and maids of honour who were buried alive to keep them company.

The site comprises two parts, the tomb itself and the approach to the tomb, known as Shandao (Sacred Way) or, more commonly, **Shixiang Lu** (石像路, shíxiàng lù) – which leads to the tomb at an oblique angle as a means of deterring evil spirits, who can only travel in straight lines. It's a strange and magical place to walk through, the road lined with twelve charming pairs of stone animals – including lions, elephants and camels – and four pairs of officials. Most people visit the tomb first and the approach afterwards, simply because the road from Zhongshan Ling arrives immediately outside the tomb entrance. To reach the Sacred Way from the tomb entrance, follow the road right (with the tomb behind you) and then round to the left for about fifteen minutes.

ARRIVAL AND DEPARTURE   NANJING

BY AIR

Nanjing Lukou International Airport (南京禄口国际机场, nánjīng lùkǒu guójì jīchǎng) lies 42km southeast of the city. Express buses (every 15min; ¥20) run two routes into town, terminating at the two railway stations; there's also a metro connection to the South station on line S1. Lastly, a taxi costs ¥100–150, depending on your destination in the city.

Destinations Beijing (1hr 30min); Hong Kong (2hr 20min); Qingdao (1hr).

BY TRAIN

Although Nanjing has seventeen train stations, you're likely to arrive at either of the following.

Nanjing Station (南京站, nánjīng zhàn). A large and fairly chaotic station northeast of the city wall, connected by metro to the city centre. Departures go from the second and third floors; arrivals, the left luggage (6am–11pm; ¥1–5) and the metro entrance are on the first.

Destinations Beijing (9 daily; 9–18hr); Chengdu (3 daily; 24–34hr); Guangzhou (1 daily; 27hr); Hangzhou (24 daily; 3–8hr); Shanghai (every 10–20min; 1hr 40min–5hr); Suzhou (every 10–20min; 1hr 10min–4hr); Xi'an (16 daily; 8–23hr).

Nanjing South station (南京南火车站, nánjīng nán huǒchē zhàn). Enormous and brand-new station (claimed to be the largest in Asia) for high-speed trains to Beijing, Shanghai and other major destinations. Linked to the centre by metro line #1 in under 20min.

Destinations Beijing (every 10–20min; 3hr 45min–4hr 45min); Chengdu (7 daily; 12hr 30min); Guangzhou (7 daily; 7hr); Hangzhou (every 10–20min; 1hr 14min–2hr 30min); Shanghai (every 10–20min; 1hr 10min–2hr 40min); Suzhou (every 10–20min; 55min–2hr).

BY BUS

Nanjing long-distance bus station (南京长途汽车东站, nánjīng chángtú qìchē dōngzhàn). Part of the Nanjing train station complex, this is generally used by buses coming from and departing to points north and east of Nanjing (Shanghai and Yangzhou among them). You can only buy tickets for same- or next-day departure.

Nanjing South station (南京汽车南站, nánjīng qìchē nánzhàn). The South station is, likewise, part of the South train station complex, and serves many destinations in Anhui province.

Destinations Hangzhou (4hr); Hefei (6–7hr); Huang Shan (4hr); Qingdao (11hr); Shanghai (4–5hr); Suzhou (2hr 30min–3hr).

GETTING AROUND

By taxi Cabs are plentiful, though you're advised to take the metro during rush hour as the traffic can be terrible. Flag fall is ¥9 (plus ¥2 fuel surcharge).

By metro Nanjing had six lines running at the time of writing, with another three under construction. Line #1 connects the two main train stations, while the S1 spur-line runs to the airport from the South station. Trains run 5am–11pm; fares cost ¥2–4 depending upon distance travelled.

By bus Buses have a flat fare of ¥2 and give no change. There is no English information, and announcements are only in Chinese, so having an electronic map with GPS is handy.

INFORMATION

Tours Nearly all hotels have their own travel agencies, able to arrange half-day bus tours of the city's sights. A host of private operators cover Zijin Shan's various attractions from the train station square.

Websites For English-language listings, reviews and the latest on expat nightlife, check ⓦ hellonanjing.net.

ACCOMMODATION

Outside the summer months, you should be able to bargain a healthy discount on hotel rooms. There are plenty of hostels around, but unfortunately none is particularly good – cheap motels are an option.

Central 中心大酒店, zhōngxīn dàjiǔdiàn. 75 Zhongshan Lu ⓣ 025 83155888, ⓦ centralhotelnanjing .com. Adventurously designed from top to toe, this is one of the most luxurious places in town – in some cases, the en-suite facilities are almost as large as the rest of the room. Service can be a little scratchy, though. **¥700**

Fleeting Time Youth Hostel 流年青年客栈, liúnián qīngnián kèzhàn. 193 Shigu Lu ⓣ 025 85589069. The best hostel in town, despite the slightly out-of-the-way location – it's a short walk from the subway, though. This being a Chinese hostel, there's a bar in the lobby (of course), as well as a pool table (marginally less predictable), but the sleek design and well-kept rooms are a cut above the norm. Dorm beds **¥45**, doubles **¥140**

★**Intercontinental** 绿地洲际酒店, lǜdìzhōu jiǔdiàn. 1 Zhongyang Lu ⓣ 025 83538888, ⓦ ichotelsgroup .com/intercontinental. There are few more stunning hotels in all China than this behemoth, filling many floors of the Zifeng Tower (see p.312). Every single room is superbly stylish, and the same can be said of the many on-site bars and restaurants, which simply purr with quality. You'll get up to 40 percent off the rack rate by booking online. **¥1250**

★**Orange Hotel** 桔子水晶酒店, júzi shuǐjīng jiǔdiàn. 224 Zhongyang Lu ⓣ 025 86988971, ⓦ orangehotel.com.cn. Terrific lakeside cheapie whose rooms are stylish, comfortable and remarkable value for the price – doubles can go for as little as ¥200 at quiet times, and deluxe rooms are only a little more. **¥378**

EATING

Nanjing has a wide selection of local, regional **Chinese and foreign foods**; it's an especially great place to sample Jiangsu cuisine, the best areas for which are north of Gulou along **Zhongyang Lu** and northwest along **Zhongshan Bei Lu**. Xinjiekou and the Confucius Temple area are generally good districts to browse, but for just about every kind of Chinese cuisine – plus Indian, Japanese and Thai – head for pedestrianized **Shizi Qiao**, off Hunan Lu to the west of Xuanwu Lake Park.

1912 Minduhui 民都荟, 1912 míndūhuì. Block A-10, 1912 Nanjing complex ⓣ 025 86566877. Swanky-looking place in the 1912 complex – temple motifs on the walls and ceiling, and colonial trimmings quite in keeping with the area's history. Even the water pots, rice bowls and chopsticks are miniature works of art. For all this, it's not all that dear – try the crab tofu (¥28), or a round of dumplings (¥38). Daily 10.30pm–1.30am & 4.30pm–9.30pm.

Chuncheon Dakgalbi 春川一只鸡韩国料理, chūnchuān yīzhījī hánguó liàolǐ. 2 Shizi Qiao ⓣ 025 83241466. For something completely different, head to this earthy little place on Shizi Qiao. While not as fancy as

---

JIANGSU CUISINE

Jiangsu cuisine tends to be on the sweet side and is characterized by an emphasis on flavour rather than texture, and by the use of wine in cooking. That said, one of the best-known dishes, *yanshui ya* (brine duck), has none of these qualities. The duck is first pressed and salted, then steeped in brine and baked; the skin should be creamy-coloured and the flesh red and tender. Other Jiangsu dishes worth trying include *majiang yaopian* (pig's intestines), *jiwei xia* (a lake crustacean vaguely resembling a lobster, but much better tasting, locals affirm) and *paxiang jiao* (a type of vegetable that looks like banana leaves).

5

other Korean restaurants hereabouts, it's far cheaper and specializes in *dak galbi* – cuts of marinated chicken breast, broiled up at your table with veggies and spice. It's ¥58 for a portion, or ¥78 with cheese (highly recommended). Cheaper Korean noodle and broth dishes available too. Daily 10am–1pm & 3.30–9pm.

Nanjing Impressions 南京大牌档, nánjīng dàpái dàng. Shizi Qiao ☎400 1877177. The *Dapaidang* is a fabulous place to try Jiangsu grub in a great atmosphere, with classical Chinese decor and uniforms, and (sometimes) local Ping Tan singing performances while you eat. There's a picture menu, and it's always busy, so arrive early or expect to wait. Try the duck *shaomai* (¥12), or the steamed chicken (¥46). Daily 8am–11pm.

★**Skyways Bakery & Deli** 160 Shanghai Lu ☎025 83317103. Fantastic deli sandwiches on offer at this expat magnet: they bake their own baguettes, ciabatta and cookies, and have a case of handmade confections and cakes, as well as Illy coffee. A big, well-filled sandwich and a drink costs ¥28. Daily 8.30am–9pm.

Taj Mahal 泰姬玛哈印度料理, tàijīmǎhā yìndù liàolī. 117 Nanjing Lu ☎025 84214123, ⊛tajmahalrestaurant.com.cn. The kind of curry-house you'd love to have near your house, this place has chefs from the subcontinent, and serves authentic, reasonably priced North Indian fare in plain but clean surroundings. Mains go for ¥40–50 and the samosas are excellent. They will deliver free (min ¥100 order) within 3km, or you can pay the taxi-fare beyond that. Daily 10.30am–3pm & 5–10.30pm.

DRINKING AND NIGHTLIFE

Most foreign students and expats after Nanjing **nightlife** head for the boozy delights of Shanghai Lu, but for a more civilized time, the 1912 Nanjing complex, on Taiping Bei Lu, is the local answer to Shanghai's Xintiandi; a pedestrianized zone of restored buildings now housing upscale **bars** and restaurants.

Behind the Wall 答案吧, dá'àn ba. 150 Shanghai Lu ☎025 83915630. Head a few metres uphill along Nan Xiu Cun alley, and go up the nondescript staircase on the left, which leads to the patio entrance. Although the Mexican food is best avoided, the bar really comes alive in the evenings, with a good range of imported bottled beers (¥25), excellent cocktails (¥35), and even better sangria (¥20). Also has a nightly live flamenco guitarist (8.30–11.30pm) as well as occasional impromptu jam sessions. Daily 4.30pm–midnight.

Jimmy's 193 Shigu Lu ☎025 86792599. The best of the city's expat-oriented bars, drawing a good mix of foreigners and locals with excellent ale and generous happy hours. There's also tasty pizza (from ¥80) and good steaks, with the meat for the latter cured on site. Daily 4pm–1am.

Scarlet 盛世佳人, shèngshì jiārén. Block 8-1, 1912 Nanjing complex ☎025 86270999. Two-storey bar with the occasional Western DJs playing mostly Latin music, though dance sounds and rock come later. Not too dark and serves mid-price Western food, as well as some good cocktails for around ¥50. Also has outdoor seating. Daily 8.30pm–4am.

DIRECTORY

Books Be sure to head to the Librarie Avant-Garde, on Guangzhou Lu. While there are very few English-language books (though you may spot some Chinese-language Rough Guides), this former car-park has been morphed into a super-cool bookstore, and is the hangout venue of choice for many local hipsters.

Hospital The most central English-speaking medical care is the Global Doctor-run Nanjing Universal Clinics, at 6 Mochohu Donglu (☎025 86519991, ⊛www.globaldoctor.com.au).

Post office Nanjing's main post office (daily 8am–6.30pm) faces the Gulou traffic circle.

Suzhou

苏州, sūzhōu

With its centre riddled with **classic gardens** and picturesque **canals**, SUZHOU is justly one of eastern China's biggest tourist draws. Whereas most Chinese cities are busy building themselves up from the inside out, parts of central Suzhou remain remarkably quaint and calm – no mean feat in a city of around six million. As if greenery and waterways were not enough, Suzhou has also long been famed for its **silk** production, making it one of China's best places in which to shop for said commodity.

As it's just half an hour from Shanghai by high-speed train, many choose to visit Suzhou on a day-trip, though those who stay the night will see the soft light of innumerable **paper lanterns** dappling the canal sides, whose paved lanes make Suzhou one of those rare places that looks fantastic in the rain. The most popular lane with visitors is **Pingjiang Lu**, a canal-side street that has become a local version of Beijing's Nanluogu Xiang (see p.79), blending a traditional vibe with modern cafés and galleries. Additionally, beyond the industrial areas which surround the city are several smaller **canal towns**, and the majestic lake of **Tai Hu** (see p.325).

Brief history

He Lu, semi-mythical ruler of the Kingdom of Wu, is said to have founded Suzhou in 600 BC as his capital, but it was the arrival of the **Grand Canal** more than a thousand years later that marked the beginning of the city's prosperity. The **silk trade** too was established early here, reaching its zenith when the whole imperial court moved south under the Song. With the imperial capital close by at Hangzhou, Suzhou attracted an overspill of scholars, officials and merchants, bringing wealth and patronage with them. In the late thirteenth century, Marco Polo reported "six thousand bridges, clever merchants, cunning men of all crafts, very wise men called Sages and great natural physicians". These were the people responsible for carving out the intricate gardens that now represent Suzhou's primary attractions.

North Temple Pagoda

北寺塔, běisì tǎ · Renmin Lu · Daily 7.45am–5pm · ¥25

A short way south from the train station, the **North Temple Pagoda** looms up unmistakeably. On the site of the residence of the mother of Wu Kingdom king Sun Quan, the structure was first built in the third century AD, and rebuilt in 1582. The pagoda is, at 76m, the tallest Chinese pagoda south of the Yangzi, though it retains only nine of its original eleven storeys. Climbing it gives an excellent view over some of Suzhou's more conspicuous features, and there's also a very pleasant teahouse on site.

Silk Museum

丝绸博物馆, sīchóu bówùguǎn · 2001 Renmin Lu · Daily 9am–5pm · ¥15 · ☎ 0512 82112636, ⓦ szsilkmuseum.com

West of North Temple Pagoda and entered under a canopy of stylized silk threads, Suzhou's attractive and well-presented **Silk Museum** illustrates the development of the material's production from ancient times to the present day. There are looms, weaving machines and faded reproductions of early silk patterns, and although none of them is particularly exciting, the main reason to come here is to see a fascinating room full of silkworms munching mulberry leaves and spinning cocoons. There's also a shop on site (see p.325).

Suzhou Museum

苏州博物馆, sūzhōu bówùguǎn · 204 Dongbei Jie · Tues–Sun 9am–5pm · Free · ☎ 0512 67575666, ⓦ www.szmuseum.com · Limited numbers of visitors allowed at any time, meaning queues in peak season

Situated east of North Temple Pagoda and designed by the internationally renowned I.M. Pei, the **Suzhou Museum** is a successful attempt to update the city's characteristic white-wall-and-black-beam architectural style. The collection itself stands out for its quality (and detailed English captions): the first two galleries feature exquisitely delicate china and jade pieces – look out for the ugly toad carved out of jasper – but the museum's highlight is the craft gallery, which holds some fantastically elaborate carvings of Buddhist scenes in bamboo roots. The adjacent **Prince Zhong's Residence** (included in the same ticket) is a monument to the Taiping Rebellion, a collection of period maps, battle plans, paintings and artefacts housed in the nineteenth-century mansion of one of the uprising's leaders.

The Humble Administrator's Garden

拙政园, zhuózhèng yuán · Dongbei Jie · Daily 7.30am–5.30pm · ¥90, ¥70 Nov–March & June · ☎ 0512 67537002, ⓦ szzzy.cn · Free Mandarin-language tours every 10min include a short boat trip

Next door to Suzhou Museum lies the largest of the Suzhou gardens, covering forty thousand square metres, the **Humble Administrator's Garden**. It's based on water and set

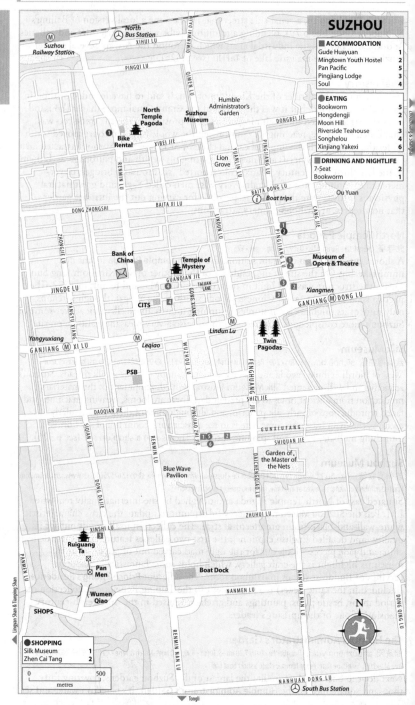

SUZHOU

ACCOMMODATION
Gude Huayuan	1
Mingtown Youth Hostel	2
Pan Pacific	5
Pingjiang Lodge	3
Soul	4

EATING
Bookworm	5
Hongdengji	2
Moon Hill	1
Riverside Teahouse	3
Songhelou	4
Xinjiang Yakexi	6

DRINKING AND NIGHTLIFE
7-Seat	2
Bookworm	1

SHOPPING
Silk Museum	1
Zhen Cai Tang	2

0   500
metres

out in three linked sections: the eastern part (just inside the entrance) consists of a small lotus pond and pavilions; the centre is largely water, with two small islands connected by zigzag bridges, while the western part has unusually open green spaces. Built during the Ming by Wang Xianchen, a retired imperial censor, the garden was named by its creator as an ironic lament on the fact that he could now administer nothing but gardening.

Lion Grove

狮子林, shīzi lín · 23 Yuanlin Lu; entrance to east of complex · Daily 7.30am–5pm · ¥40

South of the Suzhou Museum is another must-see garden, the **Lion Grove**. Tian Ru, the monk who laid this out in 1342, named it in honour of his teacher, Zhi Zheng, who lived on Lion Rock Mountain, and the rocks of which it largely consists are supposed to resemble the big cats. Once chosen, these strange water-worn rocks were submerged for decades in Tai Hu (see p.325) to be further eroded. Part of the rockery takes the form of a convoluted labyrinth, from the top of which you emerge occasionally to gaze down at the water reflecting the green trees and grey stone. The Qing emperors Qianlong and Kangxi were said to be so enamoured of these rockeries that they had the garden at the Yuanmingyuan Palace in Beijing (see p.97) modelled on them.

Temple of Mystery

玄妙观, xuánmiào guàn · Gong Chedao, just off Guanqian Jie · Daily 7.30am–4.45pm · ¥10

Right at the heart of the downtown area, the intriguingly named **Temple of Mystery** is rather incongruously located at the heart of the modern city's consumer zone. Founded during the third-century Jin dynasty, the temple has been destroyed, rebuilt, burned down and put back together many times, and for centuries was the heart of a great bazaar where travelling showmen entertained the crowds. Nowadays the complex, still an attractive, lively place, basically consists of a vast entrance court full of resting locals with, at its far end, a hall of Taoist deities and symbols; it's all encircled by a newly constructed park.

Museum of Opera and Theatre

戏曲博物馆, xìqǔ bówùguǎn · 14 Zhangjia Chedao · Daily 8.30am–4.30pm · Free · Opera performances Sun at 2pm (90min; ¥30; buy tickets 15min in advance on-site)

East from Guanqian Jie, the rooms of the unusual and memorable **Museum of Opera and Theatre** are filled with costumes, masks, musical instruments, and even a full-sized model orchestra, complete with cups of tea, though the building itself is the star, a Ming-dynasty theatre made of latticed wood. The Suzhou area is the historical home of the 500-year-old **Kunqu Opera** style, China's oldest operatic form – Beijing Opera has existed for a mere three hundred years. Along with the other local opera styles **Suqu** and **Pingtang**, Kunqu is distinguished by storytelling and ballad singing, performed in the Suzhou dialect.

Ou Yuan

耦园, ǒu yuán · 5–9 Xiaoxinqiao Chedao · Daily 8am–5pm · ¥20

Northeast of the opera museum, abutting the outer moat and along a canal, is the **Ou Yuan**, whose greatest asset is its comparative freedom from the loudhailer-toting tour groups that crowd the other gardens. Built by a husband and wife during the 1920s, it's also called The Couple's Garden Retreat. Here a series of hallways and corridors opens onto an intimate courtyard, with a pond in the middle surrounded by abstract rock formations and several relaxing teahouses. The surrounding area houses some of Suzhou's loveliest architecture, bridges and canals.

Twin Pagodas

双塔, shuāng tǎ · 22 Dinghuisi Chedao; entrance to south of complex · Daily 7am–4.30pm · ¥4

Several blocks east of Renmin Lu and immediately south of Ganjiang Dong Lu, the **Twin Pagodas** known as **Shuang Ta** are matching slender brick structures built during the Song dynasty by a group of students wishing to honour their teacher. Too flimsy to climb, the

5

SUZHOU'S GARDENS

Gardens, above all, are what Suzhou is all about. Some were founded during the Song dynasty, a thousand years ago, and in their Ming and Qing heyday it is said that the city had two hundred of them. Some half-dozen major gardens have now been restored, as well as a number of smaller ones, mostly in enclosed areas behind high compound walls.

Chinese gardens do not set out to improve upon a slice of nature or to look natural: they are a serious art form, the designer working with rock, water, buildings, trees and vegetation in subtly different combinations. As with painting and poetry, the aim is to produce for contemplation the **balance**, **harmony**, **proportion** and **variety** which the Chinese seek in life. The wealthy scholars and merchants who built Suzhou's gardens intended them to be enjoyed either in solitude or in the company of friends over a glass of wine and a poetry recital or literary discussion. Their designers used little pavilions and terraces to suggest a larger scale, undulating covered walkways and galleries to give a downward view, and intricate interlocking groups of rock and bamboo to hint at, and half conceal, what lies beyond. Glimpses through delicate lattices, tile-patterned openings or moon gates, and reflections in water created cunning perspectives which either suggested a whole landscape or borrowed outside features (such as external walls of neighbouring buildings), in order to create an illusion of distance.

Among the essential features of the Suzhou gardens are the white pine trees, the odd-shaped rocks from Tai Hu and the stone tablets over the entrances. The whole was completed by animals – there are still fish and turtles in some ponds today. **Differences in style** among the various gardens arise basically from the mix and balance of the ingredients; some are dominated by water, others are mazes of contorted rock, yet others are mainly inward-looking, featuring pavilions full of strange furniture. Almost everything you see has some symbolic significance – the pine tree and the crane for long life, mandarin ducks for married bliss, for example.

VISITING THE GARDENS

Among the Chinese, Suzhou is one of the most highly favoured tourist destinations in the country, and the city is packed with visitors from far and wide – meaning that you are rarely able to appreciate the gardens in the peace for which they were designed. The most famous ones attract a stream of visitors year-round, but many of the equally beautiful yet lesser-known gardens, notably Canglang Ting and Ou Yuan, are comparatively serene and crowd-free; the best strategy is to visit one or two of the popular gardens before 10am and spend the rest of the day in the smaller gardens. **Prices** for many of these sights are slightly lower in the off-season.

---

pink-and-lemon pagodas sprout from a delightful patch of garden. At the other end is a teahouse crowded in summer with old men fanning themselves against the heat.

Blue Wave Pavilion

沧浪亭, cānglàng tíng • 3 Canglangting Jie • Daily 7.30am–5.30pm • ¥20 • ☎ 0512 65293190

Just beyond Shiquan Jie and Renmin Lu towards the river, the under-visited but intriguing **Blue Wave Pavilion** is the oldest of the major surviving gardens, near the corner of Renmin Lu and Zhuhui Lu. Originally built in 1044 AD by the Song-dynasty scholar Su Zimei, it's approached through a grand stone bridge and ceremonial marble archway. The central mound inside is designed to look like a forested hill, making it very cool on hot days.

Garden of the Master of the Nets

网师园, wǎngshī yuán • 11 Touxiang Chedao; entrance to south of complex • Daily 7.30am–5.30pm • ¥40; ¥30 Jan–March, June & Nov–Dec • Night visits March–Nov 7–10pm, ¥100 • ☎ 051 265293190

In the south part of the moated area, the **Garden of the Master of the Nets** is a tiny, intimate place considered by many a connoisseur as the finest of Suzhou's gardens. Started in 1140, it received its curious name because the owner, a retired official, decided he wanted to become a fisherman. Nowadays, it boasts an attractive central lake, minuscule connecting halls, pavilions with pocket-handkerchief courtyards, delicate latticework and carved wooden doors – and rather more visitors than it can cope with. The garden is said to be best seen on moonlit nights, when the moon can be seen three times over from the Moon-watching

Pavilion – in the sky, in the water and in a mirror. Between March and November, the garden also plays host to nightly performances of traditional performing arts (see p.325).

Pan Men

盘门, pánmén • 1 Dong Dajie • Daily 7.30am–5.30pm April–Oct, 8am–5pm Nov–March • ¥40, plus ¥6 for tower

In the far southwestern corner of the moated area is one of the city's most pleasant districts, centred around **Pan Men** and a 300m stretch of the original city wall, built in 514 BC by King Helu of the Wu Kingdom; the gate is the only surviving one of eight that once surrounded Suzhou. There are two entrances, with the main and busiest on Dong Lu, but the best approach to this area is from the south, via **Wumen Qiao** (吴门桥, wúmén qiáo), a delightful high-arched bridge (the tallest in Suzhou) with steps built into it; it's a great vantage point for watching the canal traffic. Just inside Pan Men sits the dramatic **Ruiguang Ta** (瑞光塔, ruìguāng tǎ), a thousand-year-old pagoda now rebuilt from ruins, once housing a rare Buddhist pearl stupa (since moved to the Suzhou Museum).

ARRIVAL AND DEPARTURE   SUZHOU

BY AIR

There's no airport at Suzhou, though there are plenty of high-speed trains from Shanghai's Hongqiao airport.

BY TRAIN

Main train station (苏州站, sūzhōu zhàn). Suzhou's main station lies immediately north of town over a canal, servicing the main Shanghai–Nanjing rail line. Metro line #4 heads into the centre (it's also on line #2), or it's a short taxi ride.

Destinations Beijing (3 daily; 11–22hr); Hangzhou (every 10–20min; 1hr 20min–5hr); Nanjing (every 10–20min; 1hr–2hr 45min); Shanghai (every 10–20min; 25min–2hr); Shaoxing (10 daily; 2–4hr).

Suzhou North station (苏州北站, sūzhōu běi zhàn). The North station, on metro line #2, handles high-speed services only, and is the departure point for most services on the line to Beijing. There's a train ticket booking office (daily 8am–8pm) 50m south of Xuanmiao Guan on the west side of Gong Xiang.

Destinations Beijing (17 daily; 5hr–5hr 40min); Ji'nan (2–4 hourly; 3hr 20min–4hr).

BY BUS

Suzhou's rail connections are so good that you're unlikely to arrive by bus. The **North bus station** (苏州北汽车站, sūzhōu běi qìchē zhàn), near the train station, serves destinations to the north; the South station (苏州南汽车站, sūzhōu nán qìchē zhàn) sees arrivals from points south including Shanghai, Hangzhou and Nanjing.

Destinations Dongshan (1hr); Hangzhou (4hr); Nanjing (3hr); Shanghai (1–2hr).

GETTING AROUND

By bicycle Suzhou is made for cycling around, and many gift shops along Shiquan Jie rent bikes, as do many hotels and hostels. Expect ¥25–30/day, with a deposit of a few hundred yuan (or a passport).

By taxi Cabs are your best bet for getting around Suzhou's small centre. Fares start at ¥11 for the first 3km.

By metro The city's first two metro lines were in service at the time of writing, and lines #3 and #4 should have opened by the time you read this. Tickets cost ¥2–5.

By boat Canal boat tours of the city (¥120; 55min) depart daily at 6.20pm from the boat dock to the south of town, and booths just south of the Humble Administrator's Garden. Enterprising freelance boatmen may also offer you a ride, though prices are fixed near the intersection of Pingjiang Lu and Baita Donglu – it's ¥150 per boat for a 30min trip.

INFORMATION

Tourist information The best-located of the city's several tourist offices is near the intersection of Pingjiang Lu and Baita Donglu (daily 9am–5pm). They can issue maps and help with general travel queries.

Travel agents CITS (Mon–Sat 8.30am–5.30pm; ☏0512 65155207) is next to the *Lexiang Hotel* on Dajing Xiang, and can book tours, flights and train tickets. Nearly all hotels also have their own travel agencies.

Websites For general tourist information in English, try ⊛en.visitsz.com.

ACCOMMODATION

Suzhou has some excellent accommodation options for all budgets. The main **hotel area** is in the south of the city, around Shiquan Jie, though travellers are increasingly falling for the more rustic appeal of Pingjiang Lu, to the east. Prices tend to fall heavily out of season.

5

Gude Huayuan 古德花园, gǔdé huāyuán. 136 Pingjiang Lu ☎0512 67317199. Simple place on Pingjiang Lu, and as yet not bookable on accommodation websites – a bit annoying, but it helps to keep the rates low. The location is great, there's a bar downstairs, and rooms are certainly adequate for the price. **¥238**

★**Mingtown Youth Hostel** 明堂青年旅舍, míngtáng qīngnián lǚshè. 28 Pingjiang Lu ☎0512 65816869, ⓦyhachina.com. Filled with character, this friendly canal-side venue is hugely popular with budget travellers. Singles and doubles are remarkably stylish for the price, with wooden furniture and excellent en-suite facilities; dormitories can get a little stuffy, though. In the lobby you'll find a café-bar, and a pool table. Dorm beds **¥60**, doubles **¥180**

Pan Pacific 吴宫泛太平洋酒店, wúgōngfàn tàipíngyáng jiǔdiàn. 259 Xinshi Lu ☎0512 65103388, ⓦpanpacific.com. This top-end hotel was modelled on the old city gate, a design which strangely enough works well. Rooms are superb, the staff are sprightly and informative, and the outside gardens could function as a tourist draw in themselves. All in all, excellent value. **¥540**

Pingjiang Lodge 平江客栈, píngjiāng kèzhàn. 33 Pingjiang Lu ☎0512 65233888, ⓦthe-silk-road.com. Part of a small yet nationwide chain of "culture hotels", this appealingly rustic venue seeks to re-create the charm of old Suzhou. Its rooms have been traditionally styled, and prove particularly popular with Chinese families. **¥550**

★**Soul** 苏哥利酒店, sūgēlì jiǔdiàn. 27 Qiaosikong Xiang ☎0512 67770777, ⓦhotelsoul.com.cn. Squeezed into the busy town centre, this is a super find, with sharply designed rooms and common areas, and all manner of on-site amenities – a fitness centre, two restaurants, and a bar. They also run shuttle buses to the train station and the Humble Administrator's Garden. **¥398**

EATING

Suzhou cooking, with its emphasis on fish from the nearby lakes and rivers, is justly renowned; specialities include *yinyu* ("silver fish") and *kaobing* (grilled pancakes with sweet filling).

RESTAURANTS

Bookworm 老书虫, lǎo shūchóng. 77 Gunxiu Fang, round the back of Shiquan Jie ☎152 50074471, ⓦsuzhoubookworm.com. This expat-oriented venue has some tasty Western food on the menu, including burgers (¥50) and pizza (a little more), as well as drinks such as coffee and choco-banana shakes. Also a good place to visit in the evening (see opposite). Mon–Fri 11am–1am, Sat & Sun 10am–1am.

Hongdengji 洪灯记, hóngdēngjì. 62 Pingjiang Lu ☎0512 67211110. The most atmospheric restaurant in town, with tables set under a highly photogenic panoply of yellow lanterns. Unfortunately, the menu will be indecipherable to those unable to read Chinese – all the more excuse to have a look at what's going on in the open kitchens. The most popular menu item is the *maqiu* (麻球; ¥38), a hollow fried sphere served with dipping sauce. Daily 8am–8pm.

★**Songhelou** 松鹤楼菜馆, sōnghèlóu càiguǎn. Taijian Xiang ☎0512 67700688. The most famous restaurant in town – it claims to be old enough to have served Emperor Qianlong – is a giant place arrayed in umpteen rooms over several floors. The menu is elaborate and long on fish and seafood (crab, eel, squirrel fish and the like), though you'll find many simpler dishes for around ¥50. Daily 11am–1.30pm & 5–9pm.

Xinjiang Yakexi 新疆亚克西酒楼, xīnjiāng yǎkèxī jiǔlóu. 768 Shiquan Jie ☎0512 65291798. Xinjiang comfort food – pulled noodles with vegetables (*latiaozi*) and naan bread, among others – in a bright dining room bustling with local Uyghurs and tourists. Also sells lamb kebabs cooked on a grill outside for just ¥4, though most mains are ¥20–30. Daily 9am–midnight.

CAFÉS AND TEAHOUSES

Moon Hill 月山咖啡, yuèshān kāfēi. 78 Pingjiang Lu ☎0512 67283476. Something like an English tearoom set in a colonial-era Chinese building, this is quite the treat. If the mix of Oriental motifs and Western floral-print chairs don't get you, the coffee and desserts will. Daily 9.30am–10.30pm.

★**Riverside Teahouse** 水岸驿站, shuǐàn yìzhàn. 36 Pingjiang Lu ☎135 84847631. Traditional canal-side venue with tiny seats on the outside veranda, ideal for taking in the splendid views of local canal life over a herbal tea or green-tea latte (around ¥30); slightly fancier inside. At night the sight of soft light pouring through its latticed windows is rather magical. Daily 10am–10pm.

DRINKING AND NIGHTLIFE

Suzhou's nightlife is fairly well developed, with the oldest **bars** (as well as the oldest profession) along Shiquan Jie. However, the Ligong Di area (especially the 1912 Bar Street) on the southeastern corner of Jinji Lake is fast overtaking it as the nightlife centre of the city, especially with the expat community.

★**7-Seat** 座7, zuò 7. Gunxiu Fang. Tiny, atmospheric place redolent of bars in Tokyo's Golden Gai district – all of the chairs here (there are usually eight, despite the name) are clustered around a bar backed by myriad bottles of global ale, most of which cost ¥50 or so. It's almost impossible not to get chatting to someone here. Daily 5pm–1am.

Bookworm 老书虫, lǎo shūchóng. 77 Gunxiu Fang, corner and round the back of Shiquan Jie ☎ 152 50074471, ⊛ suzhoubookworm.com. Like sister operations in Beijing and Chengdu, this place is ground zero for local expats, and popular with locals too. You can take part in the many events such as pub quizzes, or just pop by for food (see opposite) or an evening drink. Mon–Fri 11am–1am, Sat & Sun 10am–1am.

ENTERTAINMENT

Garden of the Master of the Nets 11 Touxiang Chedao ☎ 0512 65293190. Between March and November, this classical Chinese garden hosts nightly performances of Chinese opera, folk dancing and storytelling. ¥100 includes admission to garden. Daily March–Nov 7.30–10pm.

SHOPPING

Suzhou offers numerous opportunities to shop for **silk**, although beware of outrageous prices – often ten times the going rate – especially in the boutiques along Shiquan Jie and Guanyin Jie, and the night market on Shi Lu pedestrian street (石路步行街, shí lù bùxíng jiē), over on the west side of the old town.

Silk Museum 丝绸博物馆, sīchóu bówùguǎn. 2001 Renmin Lu ☎ 0512 82112636, ⊛ szsilkmuseum.com. Slightly overpriced though it may be, the shop at this excellent museum is more likely to sell genuine items than most other silk shops in town – staff from many of said shops will try to nab you on your way in and out. Daily 9am–5pm.

Zhen Cai Tang 镇彩堂, zhèncǎitáng. 118 Pingjiang Lu ☎ 0512 66093747. By far the most interesting of the many shops along Pingjiang Lu, selling handmade silk scrolls, purses, chopstick holders and more. Staff will most likely be at the loom making stuff when you pop in. Daily 9am–9.30pm.

DIRECTORY

Hospital The best hospital in the city for foreigners is the Suzhou Kowloon Hospital (苏州九龙医院, sūzhōu jiǔlóng yīyuàn) at 118 Wangsheng Jie, way out east in the Suzhou Industrial Park Zone; it's about a ¥60 taxi-ride from the centre.

Post office Suzhou's main post office (daily 9am–6pm) is at the corner of Renmin Lu and Jingde Lu.

Visa extensions The PSB is at 201 Renmin Lu, at the junction with the small lane Dashitou Xiang.

Tai Hu

太湖, tàihú • Bus from Suzhou train station to Dongshan (1hr, ¥15)

Thirty-five kilometres west of Suzhou lies the enormous **Tai Hu**, one of the largest freshwater lakes in China. It's a popular focus for a day out, though there's not much to do but wander the wooded hills around the shore. Be warned that, in summer, algae blooms will make the lakeside slightly smelly.

Dongshan and the lake

Xishan island ferries ¥10 • Zijin An Nunnery Daily 7.30am–5pm • ¥30

Tai Hu's access point is rural **DONGSHAN** (东山, dōngshān), which sits at the end of a long promontory. Here, you can pop into the lovely **Zijin An Nunnery** (紫金庵, zǐjīn' ān), notable for its ancient statuary and location in a secluded wood surrounded by sweet-smelling orange groves. Then it's an easy hike up to Longtou Shan, or Dragon's Head Mountain. If the peak's not shrouded, there are stunning views of the surrounding tea plantations and the lake. Head back to Dongshan and walk northwest and you'll come to the pier for ferries (¥10) to the nearby island of **Xishan** (西山, xīshān). You'll find plenty of woods to wander through before returning to Dongshan for a bus back to Suzhou.

Zhejiang

浙江, zhèjiāng

ZHEJIANG, one of China's smallest provinces but also one of the wealthiest, is made up of two quite different areas. The northern part shares its climate, geography, history

5

and the Grand Canal with Jiangsu – the land here is highly cultivated, fertile and netted with waterways, hot in summer and cold in winter. The south, however, has much more in common with Fujian province, being mountainous and sparsely populated in the interior, thriving and semitropical on the coast.

Cities throughout the province tend to have an attractive, prosperous air. **Hangzhou**, the terminus of the Grand Canal, is one of the greenest and most visually appealing cities in China, with its famous lake a former resort of emperors; it's still a centre for silk, tea and paper-making. Nearby **Shaoxing**, a charming small town threaded by canals, offers the chance to tour its beautiful surroundings by boat. Off the coast, and accessible from Shanghai, **Putuo Shan** is a Buddhist island with more temples than cars; as fresh, green and tranquil as eastern China gets.

Hangzhou

杭州, hángzhōu

Few cities are as associated with a tourist draw as the Zhejiang capital of **HANGZHOU**, which has found fame for one simple reason – **Xi Hu**, a large lake right in the centre of the action. Encircled by gardens and a wreath of willow trees, crisscrossed with ancient walkways and bridges and punctuated by the odd temple or pagoda, the lake exudes an old-style air increasingly hard to find in modern China, and is a must-see if you're in this part of the land.

Hangzhou is particularly busy at weekends, when it's packed with trippers escaping from the concrete jungle of Shanghai, and in summer, when the whole country seems to be jostling for space around the lakeshore. This popularity has pushed up hotel prices, but it also brings advantages: there are plenty of restaurants, the natural environment is being protected and the bulk of the temples and gardens on the lakeside are in superb condition. Most of the places to see can be visited on foot or by bicycle, though those following the latter course of action should avoid evening rush hour – this is a city of almost nine million people, and the lake makes for something of a traffic obstacle.

Brief history

Hangzhou has little in the way of a legendary past or ancient history, for the simple reason that the present site was originally under water. Xi Hu itself started life as a wide **inlet** off the bay, and it is said that Emperor Qin Shihuang sailed in from the sea and moored his boats on what is now the northwestern shore of the lake. Only around the fourth century AD did river currents and tides begin to throw up a barrier of silt, which eventually resulted in the formation of the lake.

Development of the city

Hangzhou rapidly made up for its slow start. The first great impetus came from the building of the **Grand Canal** at the end of the sixth century (see box, p.309), and Hangzhou developed with spectacular speed as the centre for trade between north and south, the Yellow and Yangzi river basins. But the city really flourished from 1138, when the Song imperial family, chased south from Kaifeng by Mongol invasions, chose Hangzhou as the Chinese **capital**. There was an explosion in the silk and brocade industry, and indeed in all the trades that waited upon the court and their wealthy friends. Marco Polo, writing of Hangzhou towards the end of the thirteenth century, spoke of "the City of Heaven, the most beautiful and magnificent in the world". So glorious was the reputation of the city that it rapidly grew overcrowded: over a million people were crammed onto Hangzhou's sandbank, a population as large as that of Chang'an (Xi'an) under the Tang, but in a quarter of the space – tall wooden buildings up to five storeys high were crowded into narrow streets, creating a ghastly fire hazard.

Postimperial times

Hangzhou ceased to be a capital city after the Southern Song dynasty was finally overthrown by the Mongols in 1279, but it remained an important centre of commerce and a place of luxury, with **parks and gardens** outside the ramparts and hundreds of boats on the lake. Although the city was largely destroyed during the **Taiping Uprising** (see box, p.314), it recovered surprisingly quickly, and the **foreign concessions** established towards the end of the nineteenth century stimulated the growth of new industries alongside traditional silk.

Xi Hu

西湖, xīhú

A voyage on this lake offers more refreshment and pleasure than any other experience on earth...

Marco Polo

Xi Hu, the West Lake, forms a series of landscapes with rock, trees, grass and lakeside buildings all reflected in the water and backed by luxuriant wooded hills. The lake itself stretches just over 3km from north to south and just under 3km from east to west,

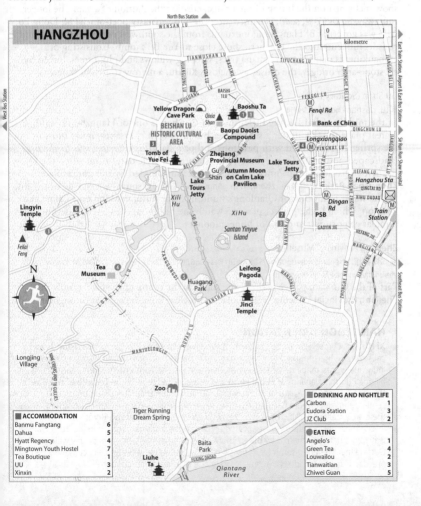

■ ACCOMMODATION	
Banmu Fangtang	6
Dahua	5
Hyatt Regency	4
Mingtown Youth Hostel	7
Tea Boutique	1
UU	3
Xinxin	2

■ DRINKING AND NIGHTLIFE	
Carbon	1
Eudora Station	3
JZ Club	2

● EATING	
Angelo's	1
Green Tea	4
Louwailou	2
Tianwaitian	3
Zhiwei Guan	5

5

though the surrounding parks and associated sights spread far beyond this. On a sunny day the colours are brilliant, but even with grey skies and choppy waters, the lake views are soothing and tranquil; for the Chinese they are also laden with literary and historic associations. Although the crowds and hawkers are sometimes distracting, the area is so large that you can find places to escape the hubbub.

As early as the Tang dynasty, work was taking place to control the waters of the lake with dykes and locks, and the two **causeways** that now cross sections of the lake originated in these ancient embankments. Mainly used by pedestrians and cyclists, the causeways offer instant escape from the noise and smog of the built-up area to the east. Strolling the causeways at any time, surrounded by clean, fresh water and flowering lilies, is a pleasure and a favourite pursuit of Chinese couples.

Bai Di (白堤, báidī) is the shorter and more popular of the causeways, about 1500m in length; starting in the northwest of the lake near the *Shangri-La* hotel, it runs along the outer edge of Gu Shan before crossing back to the northeastern shore, enclosing a small strip known as Beili Hu (North Inner Lake). The popular view-point of the low stone **Broken Bridge**, at the far eastern end of the causeway, gets its name because winter snow melts first on the hump of the bridge, creating the illusion of a gap. The longer causeway, **Su Di** (苏堤, sūdī), is named after the Song-dynasty poet-official Su Dong Po, who was governor of Hangzhou; it extends from the southwest corner of the lake and runs its full length to the northern shore close to Yue Fei's tomb. Consisting of embankments planted with banana trees, weeping willows and plum trees, linked by six stone-arch bridges, the causeway encloses **Xili Hu**, a narrow stretch of water.

Gu Shan (Solitary Hill)

孤山, gūshān • Tourist buggies ¥10

In the middle of Bai Di, the little island of **Gu Shan** is one of Hangzhou's highlights, a great place to relax under a shady tree. Bursting with chrysanthemum blossoms in the spring and sprinkled with pavilions and pagodas, this tiny area was originally landscaped under the Tang dynasty, but the present style dates from when the Qing Emperor Qianlong built himself a palace here, surrounded by the immaculate **Zhongshan Park** (中山公园, zhōngshān gōngyuán). On the southeastern side of the hill by the water is another of Qianlong's buildings, the **Autumn Moon on a Calm Lake Pavilion**, which is the perfect place to watch the full moon. It's a teahouse now, very popular after sunset and full of honeymooners.

Zhejiang Provincial Museum

浙江博物馆, zhèjiāng bówùguǎn • 25 Gushan Lu • Tues–Sun 8.30am–4.30pm • Free • ☎ 0571 87980281, ⓦ www .zhejiangmuseum.com • Tourist buggies ¥10

Part of the Gu Shan palace itself, facing south to the centre of the lake, is now the **Zhejiang Provincial Museum**, a huge place with clear English captions throughout and a

---

HANGZHOU ORIENTATION

Xi Hu is, of course, Hangzhou's focal point. Within the lake area itself are various **islands** and causeways, while the shores are home to endless **parks** holding Hangzhou's most famous individual sights, ranging from the extravagant and historic **Tomb of Yue Fei** to the ancient hillside Buddhist carvings of **Feilai Feng** and its associated temple, the **Temple of the Soul's Retreat**, one of China's largest and most renowned. Farther afield the terrain becomes semi-countryside, where beautiful tea plantations nestle around the village of **Longjing**, while there are excellent walking opportunities south down to the **Qiantang River**.

With most of Hangzhou's sights located on or near the lakeshore, you'll find that the ideal way to get between them is by **bike**; otherwise you can use local buses or simply walk. Outside the sweltering summer, it's possible to walk round the lake's entire circumference in one day, but you wouldn't have time to do justice to all the sights en route.

number of different wings. The main building in front of the entrance houses historical relics, including some superb bronzes from the eleventh to the eighth centuries BC. Another hall centres on coin collections and has specimens of the world's first banknotes, dating to the Northern Song. Modern galleries outside hold displays of painting and Tibetan Buddha statues.

Santan Yinyue

三潭印月, sāntán yìnyuè • ¥20; entrance fee included with most boat trips (see box, p.330)

East of the Su Di causeway and in the southern part of the lake is the largest of the islands here, **Xiaoying**, built up in 1607. It's better known as **Santan Yinyue**, meaning "Three Flags Reflecting the Moon", after the three "flags" – actually stone pagodas – said to control the evil spirits lurking in the deepest spots of the lake. Bridges link across from north to south and east to west so that the whole thing seems like a wheel with four spokes, plus a central hub just large enough for a pavilion, doubling as a shop and a restaurant. The admission fee to get onto the island is usually included if you take one of the tourist boat rides here.

Beishan Lu Historic Cultural Area

北山街历史文化节街区, běishān jiē lìshǐ wénhuàjié jiē qū • **Baopu Taoist Compound** Daily 7am–5pm • ¥5

The large **Beishan Lu Historic Cultural Area**, accessed from Beishan Lu, begins northeast of the lake with the seven-storey **Baoshu Ta** (保叔塔, bǎoshū tǎ), a 1933 reconstruction of a Song-dynasty pagoda. You can follow hillside tracks from here right up to **Lingering Rosy Cloud Mountain** (栖霞山, qīxiá shān) above the lake. About halfway along this path you'll see a yellow-walled monastery with black roofs lurking below to your left, the **Baopu Taoist Compound** (包朴道远, bāopū dàoyuàn). It's well worth a stop, especially in the late afternoon, if only because you might be able to discreetly watch one of the frequent ancestral worship ceremonies that are held here, with widows clutching long black necklaces to pay tribute to their husbands.

Above the monastery is **Sunrise Terrace**, traditionally the spot for watching the spring sun rise over the lake and Gu Shan. Further west, some steep stone stairs descend back down to the road, close to the Tomb of Yue Fei at the northwest end of the lake, next to the *Shangri-La* hotel.

Tomb of Yue Fei

岳飞墓, yuèfēi mù • 80 Beishan Lu, at the western end • Daily 7.30am–5.30pm • ¥25 • ☏ 0571 87986653

The **Tomb of Yue Fei** is one of Hangzhou's big draws, the twelfth-century Song general being considered a hero in modern China thanks to his unquestioning patriotism. Having emerged victorious from a war against barbarian invaders from the north, Yue Fei was falsely charged with treachery by a jealous prime minister, and executed at the age of 39. Twenty years later, the subsequent emperor annulled all charges against him and had him reburied here with full honours. Walk through the temple to reach the tomb itself – a tiny bridge over water, a small double row of stone men and animals, steles, a mound with old pine trees and four cast-iron statues of the villains, kneeling in shame with their hands behind their backs. The calligraphy on the front wall of the tomb reads, "Be loyal to your country".

Yellow Dragon Cave Park

黄龙洞公园, huánglóngdòng gōngyuán • Daily 7.30am–5.30pm • ¥15 • Bus #Y4

Immediately west of Yue Fei's tomb is a lane leading away from the lake and north into the hills behind. Thirty minutes' walk along here leads to the **Yellow Dragon Cave Park**, to the north of Qixia Shan, passing several small caves and temples on the way. For those of a less ambulatory nature, the park can also be approached from the north via an entrance at 69 Shuguang Lu. The main area of the park is charmingly secretive, sunk down between sharply rising hills with a pond, teahouses, a shrine to Yue Lao (the Chinese god of

5

BOAT TRIPS ON XI HU

One of the loveliest things to do in Hangzhou is take a boat trip on the lake. Tourist boats (¥55, including entrance fees for Santan Yinyue) launch from jetties around the lake, and head directly for the **islands**. Then there are the freelance boatmen in small canopied boats with four comfortable seats, who fish for tourists along major lakeside gathering points, especially the causeways, and charge around ¥100 per person for forty minutes. You can also take out a boat of your own – either electric putt-putters for four people (¥80/40min; ¥200 deposit), paddle boats (¥40/30min), or pedaloes (¥20/30min).

---

matchmaking), cherry blossoms in the early spring, and a pavilion where musicians perform traditional music. A nice touch is that all the staff wear Song-dynasty costumes.

Feilai Feng

飞来峰, fēilái fēng • Daily 7am–7pm • ¥45 • Bus #7 from Yue Fei tomb

Three kilometres west of the lake, Hangzhou's other famous sights are scattered around **Feilai Feng**, "The Hill that Flew Here". The hill's bizarre name derives from the tale of an Indian Buddhist devotee named Hui Li who, upon arrival in Hangzhou, thought he recognized the hill from one back home in India, and asked when it had flown here. Near the entrance is the **Ligong Pagoda**, constructed for him.

The main feature of Feilai Feng is the hundreds of **Buddhist sculptures** carved into its limestone rocks. These date from between the tenth and fourteenth centuries and are the most important examples of their type to be found south of the Yangzi. Today the little Buddhas and other figurines are dotted about everywhere, moss-covered and laughing among the foliage. It's possible to follow trails right up to the top of the hill to escape the tourist hubbub.

Lingyin Temple

灵隐寺, língyīn sì • Daily 7am–6pm • ¥75 • ☎ 0571 87968665 • Buses #Y2, #7 & #807

Deep inside the Feilai Feng tourist area you'll eventually arrive at the **Lingyin Temple**, or the **Temple of the Soul's Retreat**, one of the biggest temple complexes in China, and the oldest in Hangzhou. Founded in 326 AD by Hui Li, who is buried nearby, it once had three thousand monks, nine towers, eighteen pavilions and seventy-five halls and rooms. Today it is an attractive working temple with daily services, usually in the early morning or after 3pm.

In the 1940s the temple was so badly riddled with woodworm that the main crossbeams collapsed onto the statues; the 18m-high Tang statue of Sakyamuni is a replica, carved in 1956 from 24 pieces of camphorwood. Elsewhere in the temple, the old frequently brushes against the new – the **Hall of the Heavenly King** contains four large and highly painted Guardians of the Four Directions made in the 1930s, while the Guardian of the Buddhist Law and Order, who shields the Maitreya, was carved from a single piece of wood eight hundred years ago.

Southwest of the lake

Down in the **southwestern quarter of the lake**, in the direction of the village of Longjing, the dominant theme is **tea production**: gleaming green tea bushes sweep up and down the land, and old ladies pester tourists into buying fresh tea leaves. A fair few sights are scattered across the wide, fairly verdant area stretching down to the river – easily enough for a full day of exploration.

Tea Museum

茶博物馆, chá bówùguǎn • 88 Longjing Lu • Tues–Sun 8.30am–4.30pm • Free • ☎ 0571 87964221 • Bus #27 or #Y3 from Pinghai Lu in the town centre to the former Zhejiang Hotel, then follow a small lane, running parallel to the main road, southwest to the museum

Among the tea-fields west of the lake, you'll find the modest **Tea Museum**, a smart place with lots of captions in English, covering themes such as the history of tea and the etiquette of tea drinking.

Longjing

龙井, lóngjǐng · Bus #K27 from northwestern lakeshore, near Tomb of Yue Fei · Hikeable in under an hour from Nine Creeks and Eighteen Gullies

A couple of kilometres southwest of the Tea Museum, the village of **LONGJING**, with tea terraces rising on all sides behind the houses, is famous as the origin of **Longjing tea**, perhaps the finest variety produced in China. Depending on the season, a stroll around here affords glimpses of leaves in different stages of processing – being cut, sorted or dried. You'll be pestered to sit at an overpriced teahouse or to buy leaves when you get off the bus – have a good look around first, as there is a complex grading system and a huge range in quality and price. "Longjing" means **Dragon Well**, and the spring itself is at the end of the village, surrounded by a group of buildings done up in a rather touristy fashion.

Nine Creeks and Eighteen Gullies

九小溪和十八沟, jiǔ xiǎoxī hé shíbā gōu · Bus #K27 or #Y3 from northwest of lake

Between Longjing and the river, a delightful narrow lane known as **Nine Creeks and Eighteen Gullies** is great for a bike ride or a half-day stroll, following the banks of a stream and meandering through paddy fields and tea terraces with hills rising in swelling ranks on either side.

Tiger Running Dream Spring

虎跑梦泉, hǔpǎomèng quán · Daily 6am–6pm · ¥15 · Bus #504 from city centre, down eastern shore of lake

The area to the south and southwest of Xi Hu, down to the Qiantang River, was long a popular site for hermits to settle and is now a large forested area dotted with teahouses, shrines, waterfalls and pagodas. Of all the parks in this area, perhaps the nicest is the **Tiger Running Dream Spring**. The spring (originally found by a ninth-century Zen Buddhist monk with the help of two tigers, according to legend) is said to produce the purest water around, the only water that serious connoisseurs use for brewing the best Longjing teas – you can try a cuppa yourself for ¥20.

Liuhe Ta

六和塔, liùhé tǎ · Daily 7am–5.30pm · ¥20, plus ¥10 to ascend · ☎0571 86591364 · Bus routes include #318, #334, #K280 or #K291

South of the lake on Zhijiang Lu is the 1000-year-old **Liuhe Ta**, a pagoda occupying a spectacular site overlooking the Qiantang River, a short way west of the rail bridge. The story goes that a Dragon King used to control the tides of the river, wreaking havoc on farmers' harvests. Once a massive tide swept away the mother of a boy named Liuhe to the Dragon King's lair. Liuhe threw pebbles into the river, shaking the Dragon Palace violently, which forced the Dragon King to return his mother to him and to promise never again to manipulate the tides. In appreciation villagers built the pagoda, a huge structure of wood and brick, hung with 104 large iron bells on its upturned eaves. Today, ironically, the pagoda is a popular vantage point from which to view the dramatic **tidal bores** during the autumn equinox.

Baita Park

白塔公园, báitǎ gōngyuán · Daily 24hr · Free

Centred on a white pagoda, **Baita Park** is probably worth some of your time if you're near the river. Still under construction at the time of writing, it was turning into a sort of railway version of Beijing's 798 art zone (see p.98) – once the terminus of the Jiangshu rail line, it's now home to assorted galleries, cafés and the like, and a railway museum is on the way too.

BY PLANE
Hangzhou's airport (杭州萧山国际机场, hángzhōu xiāoshān guójì jīchǎng) is 27km east of town. The most useful airport bus into the city runs to and from Hangzhou train station (every 30min; around 1hr; ¥20).

Destinations Beijing (2hr); Hong Kong (2hr); Qingdao (1hr 30min).

BY TRAIN
Tickets for both stations can be bought at a booking office at 147 Huanshan Lu (daily 8am–8pm) just north of the junction with Jiefang Lu, with others scattered across the city.

Hangzhou Station (杭州火车站, hángzhōu huǒchē zhàn) is 2km east of the city centre; it handles some high-speed services. Reaching the lake from here on foot takes about 40min, while you can get bus #K7 direct to the lake or #K290 as far as Yan'an Lu. Otherwise, take metro line #1 to Ding'an Lu (for southeastern lake) or Longxiangqiao (for northeastern lake), but note that if returning to the train station by metro, you have to get off at Chengzhan station.

Destinations Beijing (3 daily; 14–20hr); Guangzhou (1 daily; 20hr); Nanjing (1–2 hourly; 1hr 50min–7hr); Shanghai (1–3 hourly; 1hr–2hr 30min); Shaoxing (9 daily; 1hr); Suzhou (10 daily; 2hr 30min–4hr).

Hangzhou East Station (杭州东站, hángzhōu dōng zhàn). Hangzhou's high-speed rail hub has services at almost alarmingly regular intervals. The easiest way to get to the northeastern lakefront is on metro line #1 or bus #K28.

Destinations Beijing (14 daily; 5hr–6hr 45min); Guangzhou (6 daily; 6hr–7hr 30min); Nanjing (every 10–20min; 1hr 20min–3hr 30min); Shanghai (every 5–10min; 45min–3hr); Shaoxing (every 10–20min; 20min); Suzhou (every 10–30min; 1hr 25min–2hr 15min).

BY BUS
The North, East, South and West bus stations serve the corresponding points of the compass. You're unlikely to need them.

Coach centre (客运中心, kèyùn zhōngxīn), also known as the East station, a large affair handling traffic to Shaoxing, Fuzhou and long-distance destinations. It's on metro line #1.

North bus station (汽车北站, qìchē běi zhàn), 9km out on Moganshan Lu, serves Shanghai and Jiangsu. Buses #K15, #K67 and #K290 run to the centre, with frequent private buses to the train station square.

West bus station (汽车西站, qìchē xī zhàn), 8km west on Tianmushan Lu, services Huang Shan (see p.404). Buses #K49, #K310 and #K502 travel to the centre.

South bus station (汽车南站, qìchē nán zhàn). South of the main train station on the corner of Dongbao Lu and Qiutao Lu. Useful for Wenzhou and Fujian province; it's a 2min walk north to Wujiang Lu station on metro line #1.

Destinations Huang Shan (3hr); Nanjing (4hr); Shanghai (2–3hr); Shaoxing (1hr 30min); Suzhou (2–3hr); Wenzhou (4hr–4hr 30min).

GETTING AROUND

By taxi Taxis are a convenient way to get around town, with the meter starting at ¥11 for the first 3km. It can be tough to find an empty one around the northern lakeshore.
By bus The useful tourist buses are marked with a "Y" plus their route number, and cost ¥3–5. Otherwise normal buses cost ¥1–1.5, and a/c buses ¥2.

By metro The metro system (daily 5.30am–11pm; ¥2–8) currently only has three lines, and there are plenty more on the way. Line #1 is the most useful for travellers, connecting both main train stations with the lake area.
By boat It would be a shame to leave Hangzhou without taking a boat ride on Xi Hu (see box, p.330).

INFORMATION

Tourist information There are offices at the airport and on Yan'an Lu, and several visitor information booths dotted around town.
CITS Nearly all Hangzhou hotels have their own travel agencies, and they're usually more helpful than the city's

CITS branches.
Websites For the expat view of town – including eating and nightlife listings – check out ⓦ morehangzhou.com. The official tourist website is ⓦ www.gotohz.gov.cn.

ACCOMMODATION

Hangzhou has some excellent **hotels** and a handful of **hostels** on and around the lakefront – there's not much point in staying anywhere else in this huge city unless you're pinching pennies. The one exception is the bucolic area west of the lake, which although a little far from the action, is quieter and perhaps more atmospheric – there are now plenty of guesthouses hereabouts.

Banmu Fangtang 半亩方塘客栈, bànmǔ fāngtáng kèzhàn. 272 Lingyingzhi Jie ⓣ 0571 87019723. A great

option in the lanes west of the lake, with tidy rooms (some with the dreaded see-through bathroom doors, and two with balcony), English-speaking staff, and environs which can make quite a pleasant change if you're becoming tired of urban China. **¥358**

Dahua 大华饭店, dàhuá fàndiàn. 171 Nanshan Lu, on the lakeside, several blocks south of Jiefang Lu ⓣ 0571 87181888, ⓦ dh-hotel.com. Spacious grounds with comfortable rooms and attentive service justify the prices – this hotel is actually better value than many of its competitors. Mao Zedong and Zhou Enlai stayed here whenever they were in town. Also has a good and reasonably priced restaurant overlooking the lake. **¥1380**

Hyatt Regency 凯悦酒店, kǎiyuè jiǔdiàn. 28 Hubin Lu ⓣ 0571 87121234, ⓦ hangzhou.regency.hyatt.com. Bill Clinton's abode of choice in Hangzhou, this hotel offers views of Xi Hu from its deluxe rooms (even from the bathtubs, if you're in a suite), which have been decorated with splashes of red and gold. There are excellent restaurants on site, as well as a swimming pool which makes you feel like you're paddling in the lake. ¥1000 extra for lake views. **¥2300**

Mingtown Youth Hostel 明堂国际青年旅舍, míngtáng guójì qīngnián lǚshè. 101 Nanshan Lu ⓣ 0571 87918948, ⓦ yhachina.com. A pleasant range of rooms, including a few with lake views and private bathroom. Has all the hostel facilities you'd expect, plus a decent restaurant-bar and a pleasant rooftop overlooking the lake. Dorm beds **¥70**, private rooms **¥170**

★**Tea Boutique** 天伦精品酒店, tiānlún jīngpǐn jiǔdiàn. 124 Shuguang Lu ⓣ 0571 87999888, ⓦ tea-boutique-hotel-hangzhou.com. Close to the Yellow Dragon Cave entrance, this is the city's best option at this price range – Oriental stylings in the rooms, Thai massage in the spa centre, Cantonese food in the on-site restaurant, and (here's where the name comes in) complimentary green tea, grown nearby and served in your room. **¥640**

★**UU** 旅行者漫步, lǚxíng zhěmànbù. 176 Shuguang Lu ⓣ 0571 87789096, ⓦ hzuuhotel.cn. Now this is a super little place. Set just a short walk from the lake, it's a rambling affair with quirkily decorated rooms, the loftier of which have rather lovely views of Qixia Shan to the east – do note, however, that there's no lift. Breakfasts, served in a second-floor café, are fantastic. **¥480**

Xinxin 新新饭店, xīnxīn fàndiàn. 58 Beishan Lu ⓣ 0571 87999090, ⓦ www.thenewhotel.com. Also called *The New Hotel*, this grand old building occupies one of the nicest locations in town, overlooking the northern shore of the lake; the ground-floor restaurant overlooks the waters and serves high-class local dishes. Rooms have been given an old-style makeover, with antique furniture and wood panelling. ¥200 extra for lake views. **¥1180**

EATING

As a busy tourist resort, Hangzhou has plenty of good places to **eat**. The wedge-shaped neighbourhood between Hubin Lu and Yan'an Lu is home to a number of **Chinese restaurants and fast-food joints**, while Hefang Jie is also a good spot for **Chinese restaurants and snacks**. Lastly, the area between Shuguang Lu and the park has its own little cultural microclimate – downmarket and sometimes downright seedy, but fascinating nonetheless. Many Chinese tourists make it a point to visit one of the famous **historical restaurants** in town: both *Louwailou* (Tower Beyond Tower) and *Tianwaitian* (Sky Beyond Sky) serve local specialities at reasonable prices, though a third, *Shanwaishan* (Mountain Beyond Mountain), has garnered a bad reputation over the years. All three were named after a line in Southern Song poet Lin Hejin's most famous poem: "Sky beyond sky, Mountain beyond mountain and tower beyond tower/Could song and dance by West Lake be ended anyhow?" For **tea**, there are umpteen places in the Xili Hu area, to the northwest of the lake.

Angelo's 6 Baoshishan, off Baochu Lu ⓣ 0571 85212100, ⓦ angelos-restaurant.com. Perhaps the best non-Chinese food in town, firing out delicious home-made pasta (from ¥88) and pizzas (from ¥66), as well as Italian surf-and-turf dishes. It's hidden away at the end of an atmospheric little alley – far from the tourist crowds, yet still very close to the lake. Daily 11am–2pm & 5.30pm–midnight.

HANGZHOU'S FREEDOM BIKE RENTAL NETWORK

Hangzhou's authorities have provided an astonishing 50,000 bicycles for the city's **Freedom Bike Rental Network** which, costing just ¥10 a day, is one of the best ways to get around Hangzhou's sights. You pay ¥300 for an electronic card which covers a ¥200 deposit, and they subtract the rental fee from the remaining ¥100. In fact the first hour is free, and young Chinese travellers have cottoned onto the fact that they don't have to pay at all if they simply change bikes every 55 minutes or so. You can change bikes at marked booths all over the city, but only a few of these issue cards and return deposits – there's one at Hangzhou train station.

5

Green Tea 绿茶餐厅, lǜchá cāntīng. 83 Longjing Lu ☎0571 87888022. Sitting amid tea plantations, and opposite the Tea Museum itself, this out-of-the-way yet very popular restaurant is quite a treat, a rickety pine structure sitting lakeside above the lily pads. Its collection of dishes is extensive (select from the picture menu near the entrance), but the green-tea pork (¥32) and black sesame dessert (¥10) deserve a special mention. Packed most evenings, so book ahead. Daily 11am–9.30pm.

Louwailou 楼外楼, lóuwài lóu. Gu Shan Island ☎0571 87969023. The best-known and seemingly most popular restaurant in Hangzhou – with visitors, at least (Lu Xun and Zhou Enlai, among others, have dined here), since locals tend to avoid it like the plague. Specialities include fish-shred soup (¥22), and beggar's chicken (a whole chicken cooked inside a ball of mud, which is broken and removed at your table; ¥180). Standard dishes cost surprisingly little, only around ¥45. Daily 11am–11pm.

Tianwaitian 天外天, tiānwài tiān. 2 Lingzhu Lu, at the gate to Feilai Feng and Lingyin Temple ☎0571 87960599. Chinese tourists flock here to sample the fresh seafood, supposedly caught from Xi Hu. Not as good as *Louwailou*, but a great location under some immense trees by the lake. Dishes are local cuisine and around ¥50 for mains – the West Lake Vinegar Carp is great, if you can afford it. Daily 7am–9pm.

★**Zhiwei Guan** 知味观, zhīwèi guān. 12 Yanggongdi ☎0571 87971913, ⓦ zhiweiguan.com.cn. In a very urbane atmosphere, with piped Western classical music, you can enjoy assorted *dianxin* by the plate, including *xiao long bao* (small, fine stuffed dumplings) and *mao erduo* (fried, crunchy stuffed dumplings). The *huntun tang* (wontun soup) and *jiu miao* (fried chives) are also good. It's possible to fill up for just ¥20 – add ¥6 more for a delicious mango cream dessert. Daily 10.30am–2pm & 4.30–8pm.

DRINKING AND NIGHTLIFE

For **nightlife**, Nanshan Lu and Shuguang Lu are the best bar strips in the Xi Hu area; the local hangouts are slightly outside the centre, especially in the area north of Shugang Lu. For good **information** about bars and restaurants, check ⓦ morehangzhou.com.

Carbon 北山十号, běishān shíhào. 10 Beishan Lu ☎0571 87968775. Strung about with fancy chandeliers, this loungey bar-restaurant gazes out at the Broken Bridge. The food is a little overpriced, but drinks can be surprisingly reasonable, with beers from ¥30, and rose mojitos at ¥55. A place to see and be seen. Daily 11am–11pm.

Eudora Station 以多瑞站, yǐduōruì zhàn. 101-7 Nanshan Lu ☎0571 87914670. Full to bursting point most nights, this is where many an expat comes to let their

hair down over a few bottles of cheap beer. There's sport on the telly, live music most nights, and decent pub grub. Daily 6pm–2am.

★**JZ Club** 黄楼, huáng lóu. 6 Liuying Lu ☎0571 87028298. One of the best jazz bars in the country, with artists hauled in from China and overseas for stints of a week or more. There's an extensive selection of single-malt scotch, and you might just be tempted to invest in a cigar. Daily 6pm–2am.

DIRECTORY

Hospital The Sir Run Run Shaw Hospital at 3 Qingchun Dong Lu (☎0571 86006613, ⓦ srrsh-english.com) is the best-equipped hospital in town, and has English-speaking staff. It's named after a Hong Kong movie tycoon.

Post office The most central post office is at 139 Qing

Chun Lu, just east of Zhonghe Bei Lu.

Visa extensions Enquire at the PSB in the centre of town, just south of Dingan Road metro stop at 35 Huaguang Lu (Mon–Fri 8.30am–noon & 2.30–5pm; ☎0571 87280114).

Moganshan

莫干山, mògān shān • ¥100 per day, ticket office daily 8am–6.30pm

The hill station of **MOGANSHAN**, 60km north of Hangzhou, was popular before World War II with the fast foreign set, and is currently reprising its former role as a resort to escape the stifling summer heat. The old European-style villas and po-faced communist-style sanatoriums here are being restored and turned into guesthouses, bars and cafés; there's little to do here but wander the incongruously European-looking village, hike in the bamboo forest with its many pagodas to rest in, and enjoy the views. The centre of the village is overly busy at weekends and in the summer, but a thirty-minute walk in any direction will take you into peace and quiet.

By train Moganshan transport terminates at the foot of the mountain at the hamlet of Deqing (德清, déqīng), 20min–1hr from Hangzhou by train.

Local transport From the station, a taxi or minivan the rest of the way up the mountain costs around ¥80–100;

avoid using the three-wheeler rickshaws for the same journey – they're slow and often cheat tourists.

Banks There are no ATMs in town, so arrive with enough money to last your stay.

ACCOMMODATION AND EATING

Moganshan has a surfeit of faded, Chinese-style two-star **accommodation** from ¥200, though better rooms in old lodges are preferable. For **food**, main street Yinshan Jie (you can walk the whole thing within a minute) is lined with restaurants offering local specialities such as wild game.

Moganshan Lodge 莫干山旅馆, mògànshān lǚguǎn. In a wing of the Songliang Shanzhuang (松梁山庄, sōngliáng shānzhuāng) at the southern end of the main street ☎05728033011, ⊛moganshanlodge .com. Foreign-owned bar-cum-café-cum-restaurant in an

old lodge with fantastic coffee and even better views from the patio. Also serves pukka British breakfasts, light lunches, and set dinners (¥125–145). The helpful owners can also help arrange good accommodation at various forest venues from ¥380.

Shaoxing

绍兴, shàoxīng

Located south of Hangzhou Bay in the midst of a flat plain crisscrossed by waterways and surrounded by low hills, **SHAOXING** is one of the oldest cities in Zhejiang, having established itself as a regional centre in the fifth century BC. During the intervening centuries – especially while the Song court was based in neighbouring Hangzhou – haoxing remained a flourishing city, though the lack of direct access to the sea has always kept it out of the front line of events. Even so, some of the nation's more colourful characters came from here, including the mythical tamer of floods Yu the Great, the wife-murdering Ming painter Xu Wei, the female revolutionary hero Qiu Jin and the great twentieth-century writer Lu Xun, all of whom have left their mark on the city.

For the visitor, Shaoxing is a quieter and more intimate version of Suzhou. Although the centre has its fair share of standard shopping streets, poke around and you'll find running streams, black-tiled whitewashed houses, narrow lanes divided by water, alleys paved with stone slabs and back porches housing tiny kitchens perched precariously over canals. The nicest area in which to get started is **Cang Qiao Heritage Street** (仓桥直街, cāngqiáo zhíjiē), a charming alleyway where the smell of street vendors' *chou dofu* – "stinky tofu" – is all-pervasive. You'll also find plenty of shops here selling the wines for which Shaoxing has achieved national renown (see box, p.337).

Qingteng Library

青藤书屋, qīngténg shūwū • Houguan Xiang, an alley west off Jiefang Lu • Daily 8am–5pm • ¥5

The Jiefang Lu area houses the former residences of a number of famous people. The tranquillity of the **Qingteng Library**, a perfect little sixteenth-century black-roofed building, belies the fact that it was once the home of eccentric Ming painter Xu Wei (1521–93), whose expressive, free-handed brush style proved incredibly influential to later generations of artists, but who is also notorious for attempting to commit suicide on multiple occasions, and for having murdered his wife.

Yingtian Pagoda

应天塔, yìngtiān tǎ • Entrance near crest of hill, on southeast corner of compound • Daily 8am–5pm • ¥2

Rising up above Jiefang Lu, the 38m **Yingtian Pagoda** crowns a low hill, Tu Shan. Part of a temple founded by the Song, burnt down by the Taiping rebels and subsequently rebuilt, the pagoda repays the stiff climb with splendid views over the town's canals and black-tiled roofs.

5

Qiu Jin's former residence

秋瑾故居, qiūjǐn gùjū • 100m off Jiefang Lu at 35 Hechangtang • Daily 8am–5pm • ¥10

A block to the south of the hill featuring Yingtian Pagoda, situated on a small lane, is the former residence of the radical woman activist **Qiu Jin**. Born here in 1875, Qiu Jin studied in Japan before returning to China and joining Sun Yatsen's clandestine revolutionary party. After editing several revolutionary papers in Shanghai and taking part in a series of abortive coups, she was captured and executed in Hangzhou in 1907 by Qing forces.

Lu Xun's former residence

鲁迅故居, lǔxùn gùjū • Luxun Lu • Daily 8.30am to 5pm • Free (bring ID) • ☎ 0575 85129163

Several sights associated with the writer **Lu Xun** (see p.968), whose childhood and early youth were spent in Shaoxing, are clustered together on Luxun Lu. The most interesting is **Lu Xun's former residence**, now converted into a **Folk Museum**. If you've seen the high, secretive outer walls so many compounds have, you'll find it a refreshing change to get to look at the spacious interior and numerous rooms inside a traditional house; drop in here for a wander through the writer's old rooms and for a stroll in his garden.

Sanwei Shuwu

三味书屋, sānwèi shūwū • Luxun Lu • Daily 8.30am to 5pm • Free (bring ID)

Immediately across the road from Lu Xun's former residence is the **Sanwei Shuwu**, the small school where he was taught as a young boy. In the one room open to visitors, there's a small desk on which you'll find a smooth stone and a bowl of water, in former times the only available tools for calligraphy students too poor to buy ink and paper. Visitors traditionally write their names in water on the stone for luck.

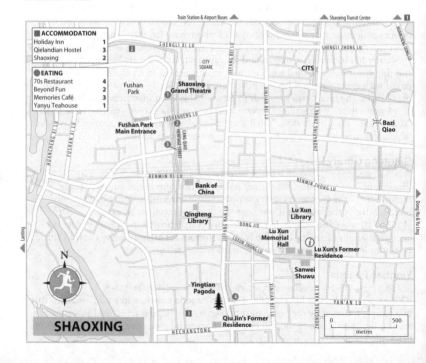

SHAOXING WINE

Near Shaoxing is **Jian Hu**, a lake whose unusual clarity has made the city known throughout China for its alcohol. Most famous is the city's sweet **yellow rice wine** (黄酒, huáng jiǔ), made from locally grown glutinous rice and available in Chinese supermarkets around the globe; a 500ml bottle will set you back anything from ¥5–20 in a regular shop, though the best are available for more like ¥40–400 at specialist outlets along Cang Qiao Heritage Street. Here you'll also find ruby-coloured **nu'er hong wine** (女儿红酒, nǚér hóngjiǔ), traditionally the tipple brides sipped to toast their new husbands – it was bought when the bride was born, and buried in the back yard to age.

Bazi Qiao

八子桥, bāzǐ qiáo • Baziqiao Zhi Jie, a small alley off Zhongxing Zhong Lu • 24hr • Free

In the east of the town and in the heart of one of Shaoxing's most picturesque and traditional neighbourhoods is the most famous of all the town's old bridges, **Bazi Qiao**. This thirteenth-century piece of engineering, which acquired its name because it looks like the Chinese character for the number eight, is still very much in use. Just to the west is a whacking great rose-coloured church – also worth a gander.

Dong Hu

东湖, dōnghú • Daily 7am–5.30pm • ¥40 • 20min boat rental for up to 3 people ¥85 • ☎ 0575 8601841 • Bus #1 or #28 from town

Easily accessible from Shaoxing, the photogenic **Dong Hu** is a 6km, twenty-minute bus ride to the east. Despite appearances, the lake is not a natural one – in the seventh century the Sui rulers quarried the hard green rock east of Shaoxing for building, and when the hill streams were dammed, the quarry became a lake to which, for picturesque effect, a causeway was added during the Qing dynasty. The cliff face and lake are now surrounded by a maze of streams, winding paths, pagodas and stepping-stone bridges. Once inside the site, you can rent a little boat to take you around the various caves, nooks and crannies in the cliff face. On the opposite shore, a flight of steps leads up to a path running to the clifftop, offering superb views over the surrounding paddy fields.

Yu Ling

禹陵, yǔlíng • Daily 8am–5pm • ¥50 • Bus #2 from city square

Yu Ling – Yu's Mausoleum – is a heaped-up chaos of temple buildings in a beautiful setting of trees, mossy rocks and mountains some 6km southeast of central Shaoxing. Yu, who founded the Xia dynasty around 2000 BC, earned his title "Tamer of Floods" by tossing great rocks around and dealing with the underwater dragons who caused so many disasters. It took him eight years to control a great flood in the Lower Yangzi. The original temple here was probably built around the sixth century AD, while Yu's tomb may be Han dynasty. Restored in the 1930s, the temple complex contains a large painted figure of Yu and scores of inscribed tablets. Outside, Yu's tall, roughly shaped **tombstone** is sheltered by an elegant open pavilion. The vigorous worshipping you'll see inside the temple shows what a revered figure Yu still is in flood-stricken eastern China.

ARRIVAL AND DEPARTURE   **SHAOXING**

BY PLANE

Shaoxing has no airport, but regular buses (hourly 6am–7.30pm; ¥25) run direct to Hangzhou airport (see p.332) from a stop opposite the train station.

BY TRAIN

Main train station (绍兴站, shàoxīng zhàn). Shaoxing station is north of the centre, on a spur line

between Hangzhou and the port of Ningbo; bus #2 runs from here along Jiefang Lu to the southern end of the city centre, though taxis will be very cheap too.

Destinations Hangzhou (13 daily; 1hr); Nanjing (2 daily; 7hr 30min); Shanghai (2 daily; 3hr); Suzhou (2 daily; 4hr 40min).

Shaoxing North station (绍兴北站, shàoxīng běi zhàn). The new north station, a whopping 25km from the centre, handles all high-speed services – free shuttle buses run to and from the city's main square.

Destinations Hangzhou (1–4 hourly; 20min); Nanjing (1–3 hourly; 1hr 40min–3hr 40min); Shanghai (2–4 hourly; 1–2hr); Suzhou (13 daily; 2hr–2hr 30min).

BY BUS

Shaoxing's **transit centre** (绍兴市公路客运中心,

shàoxīng shì gōnglù kèyùn zhōngxīn), in the far northeast of town, is where you'll most likely arrive by bus. Buses #8, #88 and #312 run to the city centre; taxis should only cost ¥15, but queues are quite bad and the touts (who will charge ¥30) annoying, so it's usually best to hit the main road and flag down a passing cab.

Destinations Hangzhou (every 30min; 1hr 30min); Shenjiamen (for Putuo Shan; hourly; 3hr).

GETTING AROUND

By taxi Taxis start at ¥7, and the meter will rarely tick beyond ¥20 unless you're heading to one of the more distant sights.

By canal boat There are few more pleasurable activities

in Shaoxing than taking a slow ride down the canals – the best place to pick one up is from the east bank, just opposite the *Yanyu Teahouse* (see below). A 25min ride will cost ¥120 for up to three people.

INFORMATION

Tourist office There is a fairly useful tourist office at Lu Xun's Former Residence (daily 8.30am–5pm; ☎0575 85129163). They speak some English, and can book city tours (including canal boats).

CITS at 288 Zhongxing Zhong Lu (☎0575 85200055) can arrange English-speaking guides for the surrounding area (¥500/day for the vehicle). They're quite informative and helpful, and speak good English.

ACCOMMODATION

Holiday Inn 世茂假日酒店, shìmào jiàrì jiǔdiàn. 89 Fanli Lu ☎0575 89108888, ⊛ihg.com. Pleasantly located by a canal just northeast of the centre, this is highly popular with international visitors, and rightly so – luxurious accoutrements such as plush-carpeted rooms, good restaurants and a gym, and all at three-star prices. **¥290**

★**Qielandian Youth Hostel** 伽蓝殿青年旅舍, qiélándiàn qīngnián lǚshè. 63 Hechangtang ☎0575 88326605. Overlooked by the Yingtian Pagoda, this is a spanking-new hostel option with a large, attractive,

café-cum-bar-cum-lobby area, good service standards, and rooms which are perfectly adequate – especially for the super-low prices. Dorm beds **¥50**, private rooms **¥100**

Shaoxing 绍兴饭店, shàoxīng fàndiàn. 9 Huanshan Lu ☎0575 85155888. The most upmarket hotel in town is this charming Ming-style complex, set in grounds so large that you can travel around them by boat. Rooms are modern and comfortable and it has all the facilities expected of a four-star, including good restaurants. You'll likely find discounts online. **¥660**

EATING

While walking around town you might be struck by the huge number of **stalls** selling that malodorous staple of Chinese street life, *chou dofu* (smelly tofu). Now assaulting nasal cavities across the nation, its original recipe was allegedly created by a Shaoxing woman who, tired of her limited cooking prowess, decided to experiment by throwing a variety of spices into a wok with some tofu. **Dried freshwater fish** is a great speciality in Shaoxing, as is the yellow **rice wine** that's these days more commonly used for cooking than drinking – *shaoxing ji* (Shaoxing chicken) is a classic dish prepared with it.

★**70s Restaurant** 70后饭吧, 70 hòufàn bā. Yanan Lu ☎0575 85225877. By far the most interesting-looking restaurant in Shaoxing – sadly no disco balls or goldfish-encasing platform shoes, rather an elegant and surprisingly mellow place to eat. They're proudest of their beef with mashed potato, served on a sizzle-platter in a curry-like sauce (¥40), though there are all sorts of interesting dishes on the magazine-menu. Wash it all down with some good fruit juice. Daily 9am–2pm & 5–9pm.

Beyond Fun 寻宝记半俸菜, xúnbǎojì bànfèng cài. 114 Cangqiaozhi Jie ☎0575 85223317. Wacky name, slightly wacky place serving cheap-and-cheerful local dishes, including Shaoxing chicken, as well as a roster of

more regular Chinese mains. Daily 10am–1.30pm & 4.30–8pm.

Memories Café 猞光咖啡, shēguāng kāfēi. 202 Cangqiaozhi Jie ☎0575 88881010. Dangling over a canal just off Cangqiao Heritage Street, this attractively decorated little venue is your best bet for coffee or tea, or even a Belgian beer in the evening. Daily 10am–10.30pm.

Yanyu Teahouse 雁雨茶艺馆, yànyǔ cháyìguǎn. 177 Pianmenzhi Jie ☎0575 85111877. Gazing out over a tranquil canal, this temple-style tearoom is Shaoxing in a nutshell – the good bits, at least. Teas cost ¥55 per person, and come with free fruit and snack food. Daily 9am–midnight.

ENTERTAINMENT

Shaoxing Grand Theatre 绍兴大剧院, shàoxīng dàjùyuàn. Cangqiao Heritage Street Ⓦ sxdjy.com. Built to resemble the Sydney Opera House, and almost the same size, this distinctive building is disliked by locals, and has become something of a white elephant. However, it's a great place in which to experience the local Yue opera style, which is considerably softer and more melodious than Beijing opera – check the website for details. Tickets ¥50–380. Performances at least once a week.

Putuo Shan

普陀山, pǔtuó shān

The Buddhist island of **Putuo Shan** is undoubtedly one of the most charming places in eastern China. A combination of religious reverence and relative inaccessibility means that it has no honking cars or department stores, only endless vistas of blue sea, sandy beaches and lush green hills dotted with ancient monasteries. As such, it's an ideal place to escape the noise, traffic and dirt of the big cities, but only midweek – Putuo Shan is just twelve square kilometres in area, and can get swamped with tourists on weekends. Indeed, the best times to come are April, May, September and October, when the weather is warm and the island not especially busy. Bring walking shoes, too; you'll get much more out of the place if you walk, rather than bus, between the attractions. If it's crowded, remember that there are over eighty temples here, and the vast majority of tourists will only be at the big ones – grab a map and just walk off, and you'll soon be on your own. Be warned, thanks to the "Buddhist Buck" and the fact that everything has to be shipped in, prices are relatively high here for both food and accommodation.

Brief history

Over the years more than a hundred monasteries and shrines were built at Putuo Shan, with magnificent halls and gardens to match. At one time there were four thousand monks squeezed onto the island, and even as late as 1949 the religious community numbered around two thousand. Indeed, until that date secular structures were not permitted on the island, and nobody lived here who was not a monk. Although there was a great deal of destruction on Putuo Shan during the Cultural Revolution, many treasures survived, some of which are in the Zhejiang Provincial Museum in Hangzhou (see p.328). Restoration continues steadily, and the number of monks has grown from only 29 in the late 1960s to several hundred. Three principal monasteries survive – **Puji**, the oldest and most central; **Fayu**, on the southern slopes; and **Huiji**, at the summit.

Puji Temple

普济寺, pǔjì sì • Daily 6am–9pm • ¥5

The three main monasteries on the island are in extremely good condition, recently renovated, with yellow-ochre walls offsetting the deep green of the mature trees in their forecourts. This is particularly true of **Puji Temple**, right in the centre of the island, built in 1080 and enlarged by successive dynasties. Standing among magnificent camphor trees, it boasts a bridge lined with statues and an elegantly tall pagoda with an enormous iron bell.

South of the temple and just to the east of the square ponds is the five-storey **Duobao Pagoda** (多宝塔, duōbǎo tǎ). Built in 1334 using stones brought over from Tai Hu in Jiangsu province, it has Buddhist inscriptions on all four sides.

Zizhu Temple

紫竹寺, zǐzhú sì • Daily 6am–6pm • ¥5, including admission to Chaoyin Dong

Down on the southeastern corner of the island, **Zizhu Temple** is slightly less touristed than most and, for that reason alone, makes a good spot in which to observe the monks' daily rituals. Just down from the temple is a cave, **Chaoyin Dong** (潮音洞,

5

cháoyīn dòng); the din of crashing waves here can be remarkable, and is thought to resemble the call of Buddha (hence this was a popular spot for monks to commit suicide in earlier days).

Guanyin Leap

观音跳, guānyīn tiào • Daily 6am–6pm • ¥6

On the island's southern tip is Putuo's most prominent sight, the **Guanyin Leap**, a headland from which rises a spectacular 33m-high bronze-plated statue of the Bodhisattva, visible from much of the island. In her left hand, Guanyin holds a steering wheel, symbolically protecting fishermen from violent sea storms. The pavilion at the base of the statue holds a small exhibit of wooden murals recounting how Guanyin

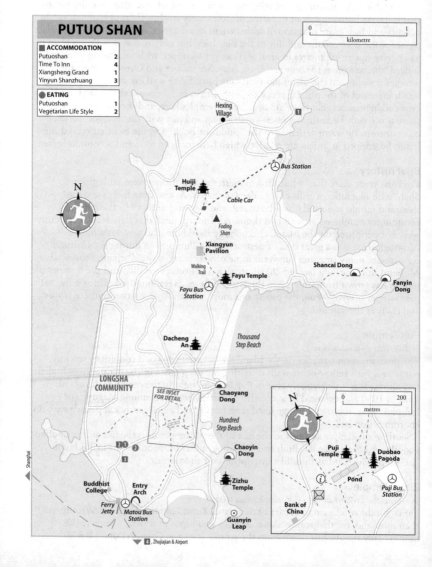

PUTUO SHAN

■ ACCOMMODATION
Putuoshan	2
Time To Inn	4
Xiangsheng Grand	1
Yinyun Shanzhuang	3

● EATING
Putuoshan	1
Vegetarian Life Style	2

Hexing Village

Bus Station

Huiji Temple

Cable Car

Foding Shan

Xiangyun Pavilion

Walking Trail

Fayu Temple

Shancai Dong

Fanyin Dong

Fayu Bus Station

Dacheng An

Thousand Step Beach

LONGSHA COMMUNITY

SEE INSET FOR DETAIL

Chaoyang Dong

Hundred Step Beach

Chaoyin Dong

Zizhu Temple

Buddhist College

Entry Arch

Ferry Jetty

Matou Bus Station

Guanyin Leap

Shanghai

▼ 4 Zhujiajian & Airport

Puji Temple

Duobao Pagoda

Pond

Puji Bus Station

Bank of China

aided Putuo villagers and fishermen over the years, while in a small room directly underneath the statue sit four hundred more statues representing the various spiritual incarnations of Guanyin. The view from the statue's base over the surrounding islands and fishing boats is sublime, especially on a clear day.

The northern temples

The two temples in the **northern half of the island**, Huiji and Fayu, make for a pleasant day-trip from town and tend to be less busy than those in the south. A paved marked path, called the Xiangyun Road, connects them, the whole walk taking under an hour. About halfway along is the **Xiangyun Pavilion**, where you can rest and drink tea with the friendly monks, who have sofas outside.

Huiji Temple

慧济寺, huìjì sì • **Temple** Daily 6am–9pm • ¥5 • **Cable car** Daily 7am–5pm • ¥50 return, ¥30 one-way

Huiji Temple stands near the top of **Foding Shan** (佛顶山, fódǐng shān), whose summit provides spectacular views of the sea and the surrounding islands. You can hike up or use the **cable car** from the minibus stand. The temple itself, built mainly between 1793 and 1851, occupies a beautiful site just to the northwest of the summit, surrounded by green tea plantations. The halls stand in a flattened area between hoary trees and bamboo groves, the greens, reds, blues and gold of their enamelled tiles gleaming magnificently in the sunshine. There's also a vegetarian restaurant.

Fayu Temple

法雨寺, fǎyǔ sì • Daily 6am–9pm • ¥5

Approaching **Fayu Temple**, listen out for cheesy Buddhist muzak wafting in from the forest – see if you can spot the speakers disguised as rocks. The temple itself forms a superb collection of more than two hundred halls amid huge green trees, built up in levels against the slope. With the mountain behind and the sea just in front, it's a delightful place to sit in peaceful contemplation. The Daxiong Hall has been brilliantly restored, and the Dayuan Hall has a unique beamless arched roof and a dome, around

THE CULT OF GUANYIN

Putuo Shan has been attracting Buddhist pilgrims from all over northeast Asia for at least a thousand years, and there are many tales accounting for the island's status as the centre of the **cult of Guanyin** (观音; guānyīn), the Bodhisattva of Compassion. According to one, the goddess attained enlightenment here; another tells how a Japanese monk named Hui'e, travelling home with an image of the goddess, took shelter here from a storm and was so enchanted by the island's beauty that he stayed, building a shrine on the spot. With the old beliefs on the rise again, many people come specifically to ask Guanyin for favours, often to do with producing children or grandchildren. Many Chinese tourists carry identical yellow cotton bags, which are stamped with symbols of the goddess at each temple, sometimes in exchange for donations.

5

PUTUO'S BEACHES

You'll appreciate Putuo's beauty much more by making the trip to Huiji Temple and Fayu Temple **on foot** via the two **beaches** that line the eastern shore: the windswept and empty Qianbu Sha (Thousand Step Beach) and more civilized Baibu Sha (Hundred Step Beach), separated by a small headland hiding the cave of **Chaoyang Dong**. Swimming is only permitted on Hundred Step Beach, where there are overly-keen lifeguards with whistles, and also showers (¥10). Be careful where you swim and when, though, as the waters can be extremely dangerous – also something to bear in mind if you're taking a banana-boat ride.

---

the inside of which squirm nine carved wooden dragons. This hall is said to have been moved here from Nanjing by Emperor Kangxi in 1689. Its statue of **Guanyin**, flanked by monks and nuns, is the focal point of the goddess's birthday celebrations in early April, when thousands of pilgrims and sightseers crowd onto the island for chanting and ceremonies that last all evening.

Fanyin Dong

梵音洞, fányīn dòng · Daily 8am–4.30pm · ¥5

Occasional minibuses head out along the promontory immediately east of Fayu Temple to **Fanyin Dong**, a cave whose name derives from the resemblance of the sound of crashing waves to Buddhist chants. The cave is set in the rocky cliff, with a small shrine actually straddling a ravine. Walking around on the promontory is a pleasure given the absence of crowds, and the difficulty of getting lost.

ARRIVAL AND INFORMATION   PUTUO SHAN

Note that Putuo Shan can only be reached by ferry – those arriving by plane or bus will have to put in some extra yards to get onto the island itself, though this mainly involves getting to Wugongshi Wharf (吴宫市码头, wúgōngshì mǎtóu), from where regular ferries (outbound 6.20am–5.25pm, last return 9.50pm; 15min; ¥25) zip over to Putuo Shan.

By air Zhoushan Putuoshan Airport (舟山普陀山机场, zhōushān pǔtuóshān jīchǎng) is, despite the nomenclature, actually on the neighbouring island of Zhujiajian (朱家尖, zhūjiājiān). On arrival, catch a bus (every 30min, 5.45am–8pm; ¥7) to Zhujiajian's Wugongshi Wharf, or hop in a cab (¥25, after haggling).
By ferry The ferry jetty is in the far south of Putuo Shan proper. You can buy tickets for outbound boats from any of the island's hotels or at the jetty office (daily 6am–6pm). There are two classes of ferries to Shanghai's Luchao Wharf (芦潮港码头, lúcháo gǎng mǎtóu): the fast ferry

(1 daily; 4hr; ¥250–349); and the overnight slow boat (Tues, Thurs & Sun; 13hr; ¥200). The slow boat back to Shanghai chugs into the city around sunrise time, providing a memorable view of the awakening metropolis.
By bus The area's main bus station is in Zhoushan (舟山普陀汽车站, zhōushān pǔtuó qìchē zhàn), a short ride from Wugongshi Wharf on bus #27 (25min; ¥3). It's only really useful for the runs to Ningbo (every 30min; 2hr 30min) and Shaoxing (hourly; 3hr).
Post office The post office (8am–4.30pm) is just past the Bank of China, up a small lane to the right.

GETTING AROUND

Upon arrival on the island itself, you can reach Putuo Shan's main "town", near Puji Temple, by following either the road heading west or the one east from the jetty, or by picking up a bus from the car park just east of the arrival gate. The westerly route is slightly shorter and takes you past most of the modern buildings and facilities on the island, including the banks.

By minibus Putuo Shan's three minibus routes connect the ferry port with Puji Temple and other sights farther north; they run 6am–6pm in summer and autumn, and 6.30am–5.30pm in the winter and spring (¥5–10). Each

major attraction has its own minibus station, with the destinations (and price) written in English at the stops – which is just as well, as routes aren't numbered.

ACCOMMODATION

Much of the island's **accommodation** is spread between the ferry terminal and Putuo Shan's main "town". Options include a number of **converted monasteries**, but be warned that during the weekend stampede out of Shanghai, rooms are scarce and expensive; prices given here represent weekend rates, outside of which (even in summer) they fall sharply. Another option is to stay in a **private house**; though technically illegal for foreigners, it's not hard to find people with rooms to let – they congregate at the jetty pier, and you should be able to bargain them down to around ¥150 per room.

Putuoshan 普陀山大酒店, pǔtuóshān dàjiǔdiàn. 93 Meicen Lu ☎ 0580 6092828. Very easy to spot, thanks to its spacious grounds and opulent design, this is the best hotel in the south of the island, with cheaper prices than some less-salubrious competitors. Traditional Chinese furniture in the classier rooms, and an on-site vegetarian restaurant (see below). **¥1700**

★Time To Inn 时光小驻客栈, shíguāng xiǎozhù kèzhàn. Off Zhujiajian Lu ☎ 159 90723533. Budget travellers rejoice – there's now a super little cheapo option on the airport island, within a short drive of the ferry wharf. The English-speaking couple who own the place love to host foreign guests, and you can expect free pick-ups and drop-offs from the airport and ferry terminal, or even local restaurants (for there's precious little in the surrounding residential area). Almost impossible to find by yourself – just let them know when and where you'll be arriving. **¥168**

Xiangsheng Grand 祥生大酒店, xiángshēng dàjiǔdiàn ☎ 0580 6696666. Perched up on a headland overlooking the sea by Fuding Shan in the north, this new five-star has big, comfortable rooms and most have balconies with fantastic views. Staff are friendly, the service is good and there are three restaurants serving seafood, Cantonese and Southeast Asian cuisine. Has all the facilities you'd expect, and runs a private minibus fleet for getting around the island. **¥1880**

Yinyun Shanzhuang 银云山庄, yínyún shānzhuāng. 66 Meicen Lu ☎ 0580 6094222. One of the cheapest certified places on the island, this is a surprisingly fancy affair, whose smallest rooms occasionally drop under the magical ¥400 barrier. Service is also slightly better than at most other such places you'll find on the island. **¥1080**

EATING

Most **food** must be brought in from the mainland, which would make it expensive even without the captive tourist market. All of the main temples have simple **vegetarian restaurants** which serve lunch (10.30–11.30am) and supper (4.30–5.30pm) for just ¥5–10 a person.

Putuoshan 普陀山大酒店, pǔtuóshān dàjiǔdiàn. 93 Meicen Lu ☎ 0580 6092828. The restaurant at this hotel (see above) is a safe bet, with a mainly vegetarian menu and good views onto the surrounding hills. Daily 6.30am–9.30am, 11am–2pm & 5–9pm.

★Vegetarian Life Style 枣子树, zǎozǐ shù. 84 Meicen Lu ☎ 0580 6091869. By far the best and most attractive place to eat on the island, hidden away in a small mall opposite the *Putuoshan* hotel. The picture menu is full of interesting veggie meals (from around ¥40), with white-costumed staff floating around with umpteen takes on tofu, eggplant, leaves, roots or shoots. Best of all, it's totally unsuitable for groups – you'll be able to eat in relative peace. Daily 10.30am–9.30pm.

Shanghai
and around

上海

NIGHT VIEW OVER SHANGHAI TOWER AND
JINMAO TOWER

Shanghai and around

上海, shànghǎi

6

The great metropolis of Shanghai is undergoing one of the fastest economic expansions the world has ever seen. As the city begins to recapture its position as East Asia's leading business city, a status it last held before World War II, the skyline is filling with high-rises – there are well over a thousand now. Gleaming shopping malls, luxurious hotels and prestigious arts centres are rising alongside, while underneath everything snakes the world's longest metro system. Shanghai's 24 million residents enjoy the highest incomes on the mainland, and there's plenty for them to splash out on; witness the rash of celebrity restaurants and designer flagship stores. In short, it's a city with a swagger, bursting with nouveau-riche exuberance and élan. And yet, for all the modernization, Shanghai is still known in the West for its infamous role as the base of European imperialism in mainland China during the 1930s.

Whichever side you were on, life in Shanghai then was rarely one of moderation. China's most prosperous city, in large part European- and American-financed, Shanghai introduced Asia to electric light, boasted more cars than the rest of the country put together, and created for its rich citizens a world of European-style mansions, tree-lined boulevards, chic café society, horse racing and exclusive gentlemen's clubs. Alongside, and as much part of the legend, lay a city of singsong girls, warring gangsters and millions living in absolute poverty.

Then came the **Japanese invasion**, civil war and the Communist victory. With their egalitarian, anti-Western stance, China's new rulers despised everything that prewar Shanghai had stood for and deliberately ran the city down, siphoning off its surplus to other parts of the country. Shanghai came to resemble a living museum, housing the largest array of **Art Deco architecture** in the world. Yet the Shanghainese never lost their ability to make waves for themselves. The present boom dates back to 1990, with the opening of the "New Bund" – the Special Economic Zone across the river in Pudong. Ever since, the city has enjoyed double digit growth, and if present plans for a new economic free trade zone come to pass, it will likely one day rival Hong Kong as Asia's financial centre.

Yet **old Shanghai** has not disappeared. Most of the urban area was partitioned between foreign powers until 1949, and their former embassies, banks and official residences still give large sections of the city an early twentieth-century European flavour. It's still possible to make out the boundaries of what used to be the **foreign concessions**, with the bewildering tangle of alleyways of the **old Chinese city** at its heart. Only along the **Huangpu waterfront**, amid the stolid grandeur of the **Bund**, is there some sense of space – and here you feel the past more strongly than ever. It's ironic that the relics of hated foreign imperialism are now protected as city monuments.

Shanghai does not brim with obvious **attractions**. Besides the Shanghai Museum, the Huangpu River cruises and a clutch of new art galleries, there are few tourist

Huangpu River cruises p.353
Nanjing Dong Lu: iconic shops p.357

Moganshan's galleries p.371
Made to measure p.386

HUANGPU RIVER CRUISE

Highlights

❶ The Bund Soak up Shanghai's colonial architecture along this historic thoroughfare. **See p.352**

❷ Huangpu River cruises Get out on the river for a sense of the maritime industry that's at the heart of the city's success. **See p.353**

❸ Shanghai Museum A candidate for the best museum in the country, with a wide range of exhibits housed in a building shaped like an ancient Chinese pottery vessel. **See p.358**

❹ Tianzifang Intriguing, fun shopping district with boutiques and cafés occupying traditional Shanghai houses. **See p.363**

❺ Shanghai Tower The view from the world's highest observation platform is simply awesome. **See p.366**

❻ West Bund A civilized riverside promenade with a glitzy array of art museums, all brand new. **See p.372**

❼ Cocktail bars Dress up and enjoy a drink with the smart set: Shanghai has the most sophisticated nightlife on the mainland. **See p.383**

HIGHLIGHTS ARE MARKED ON THE MAPS ON PP.350–351 & PP.354–355

sights with broad appeal. But the place absolutely excels in materialistic pleasures, so be sure to sample the fantastic **restaurants** and **nightlife**, and budget some time for serious shopping. Perhaps the greatest fascination is in simply absorbing the splendour of a city so extravagantly on the up. Shanghai is also one of the few Chinese cities that rewards aimless **wandering**; it's fascinating to stroll the Bund, explore the pockets of colonial architecture in the former French Concession, or get lost in the old city's alleys.

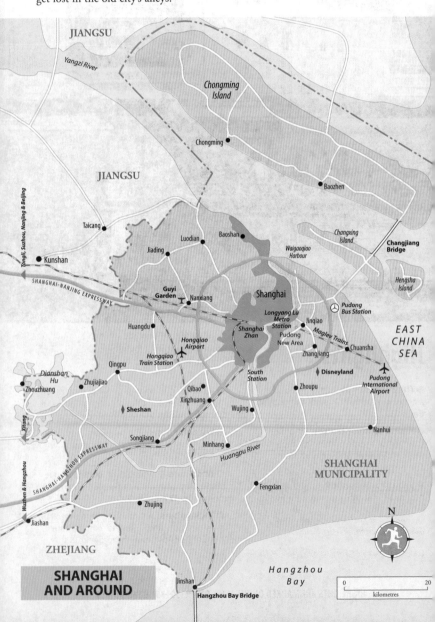

JIANGSU

Yangzi River

Chongming Island

Chongming

JIANGSU

Baozhen

Taicang

Kunshan

Changxing Island

Luodian

Baoshan

Changjiang Bridge

Jiading

Waigaoqiao Harbour

SHANGHAI-NANJING EXPRESSWAY

Hengsha Island

Guyi Garden

Nanxiang

Shanghai

Tongli, Suzhou, Nanjing & Beijing

Huangdu

Longyang Lu Metro Station

Pudong Bus Station

Jinqiao

EAST CHINA SEA

Shanghai Zhan

Pudong New Area

Hongqiao Airport

Maglev Trains

Chuansha

Hongqiao Train Station

Qingpu

Zhangjiang

Dianshan Hu

Zhujiajiao

◆ **Disneyland**

Pudong International Airport

Zhouzhuang

South Station

Qibao

Zhoupu

Xinzhuang

Wujing

◆ **Sheshan**

Nanhui

Xitang

Songjiang

Minhang

Huangpu River

SHANGHAI MUNICIPALITY

SHANGHAI-HANGZHOU EXPRESSWAY

Wuzhen & Hangzhou

Zhujing

Fengxian

Jiashan

N

ZHEJIANG

Hangzhou Bay

SHANGHAI AND AROUND

Jinshan

Hangzhou Bay Bridge

0   20
kilometres

Brief history

Located at the confluence of the Yangzi River, the Grand Canal and the Pacific Ocean, Shanghai was a major commercial port from the Song dynasty onwards, channelling the region's extensive cotton crop to Beijing, the hinterland and Japan. By the time of the Qing dynasty, vast **mercantile guilds** had established economic and, to some extent, political control of the city. In the words of East India Company representative Hugh Lindsay, "the city had become the principal emporium of Eastern Asia" by the 1840s.

The concession era

Following the **Opium Wars**, the British moved in under the Treaty of Nanking in 1842, to be rapidly followed by the French in 1847. These two powers set up the first **foreign concessions** in the city – the British along the Bund and the area to the north of the Chinese city, the French in an area to the southwest, on the site of a cathedral a French missionary had founded two centuries earlier. Later the Americans (in 1863) and the Japanese (in 1895) came to tack their own areas onto the British Concession, which expanded into the so-called International Settlement. Traders were allowed to live under their own national laws, policed by their own armed forces, in a series of privileged enclaves that were leased indefinitely. By 1900, the city's favourable position, close to the main trade route to the major silk- and tea-producing regions, had allowed it to develop into a sizeable port and manufacturing centre.

Shanghai's cheap workforce was swollen during the Taiping Uprising (see box, p.314) by those who took shelter from the slaughter in the foreign settlements, and by peasants attracted to the city's apparent prosperity. Here China's first urban proletariat emerged, and the squalid living conditions, outbreaks of unemployment and glaring abuses of Chinese labour by foreign investors made Shanghai a natural breeding ground for **revolutionary politics**. The Chinese Communist Party was founded in the city in 1921, only to be driven underground by the notorious massacre of hundreds of strikers in 1927.

The Communist era

Inevitably, after the **Communist takeover** in 1949, the bright lights dimmed. The new regime was determined that Shanghai should play its role in the radical reconstruction of China. The slums were knocked down to be replaced by apartments, the gangsters and prostitutes were taken away for "re-education", and foreign capital was ruthlessly taxed if not confiscated outright. For 35 years, Western influences were forcibly suppressed.

Even after 1949, the city remained a centre of radicalism – Mao, stifled by Beijing bureaucracy, launched his **Cultural Revolution** here in 1966. Certain Red Guards even proclaimed a Shanghai Commune, before the whole affair descended into wanton destruction and petty vindictiveness. After Mao's death, Shanghai was the last stronghold of the Gang of Four in their struggle for the succession, though their planned coup never materialized.

Modern Shanghai

Shanghai's fortunes rebounded during China's opening up in the post-Mao era: many key modernizing officials in the central government came from the Shanghai area, and Jiang Zemin and Zhu Rongji were both former mayors of the city. As well as a power base for the ruling party, Shanghai has always been the most **outward-looking** city in China, its people the most highly skilled labour force in the country, and renowned for their quick wit and entrepreneurial skills. Many Shanghainese fled to Hong Kong after 1949 and oversaw the colony's economic explosion, while a high proportion of Chinese successful in business elsewhere in the world emigrated from this area. Despite the incomprehensibility of the local Shanghainese dialect to other Chinese, it has always been easier for visitors to communicate with the locals here than anywhere else in the country, because of the excellent level of English spoken and the familiarity with foreigners and foreignness.

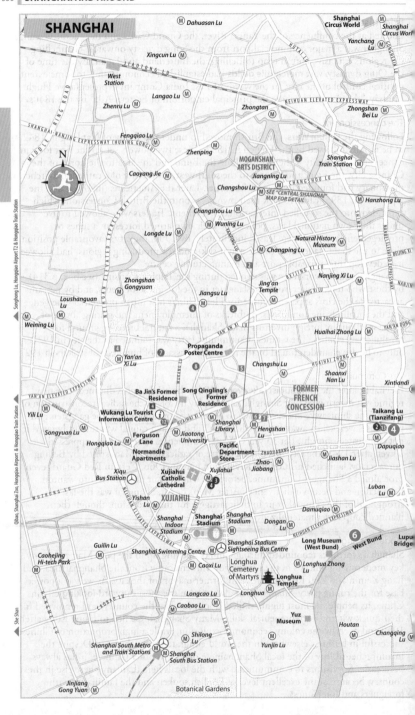

SHANGHAI

Dahuasan Lu Ⓜ

Shanghai Circus World

Ⓜ Shanghai Circus Worl

Yanchang Lu Ⓜ

Xingcun Lu Ⓜ

West Station

JIAOTONG LU

Langao Lu Ⓜ

Zhenru Lu Ⓜ

Zhongshan Bei Lu

NEIHUAN ELEVATED EXPRESSWAY

Zhongtan

Fengqiao Lu Ⓜ

SHANGHAI-NANJING EXPRESSWAY (HUNING GONGLU)

Zhenping

MOGANSHAN ARTS DISTRICT

❷

Shanghai Train Station Ⓜ

MIDDLE RING ROAD

Caoyang Jie Ⓜ

Jiangning Lu

CHANGSHOU LU

N

Changshou Lu Ⓜ

SEE "CENTRAL SHANGHAI MAP FOR DETAIL

Ⓜ Hanzhong Lu

Changshou Lu Ⓜ

Ⓜ Wuning Lu

Changping Lu Ⓜ

Natural History Museum Ⓜ

Longde Lu Ⓜ

❸

Nanjing Xi Lu

BEIJING XI LU

❷

Zhongshan Gongyuan

Jiangsu Lu Ⓜ

Jing'an Temple

NANJING XI LU

NANJING

Loushanguan Lu

❹

❺

YAN'AN XI LU

Huaihai Zhong Lu Ⓜ

YAN'AN DONG

Weining Lu Ⓜ

Ⓜ

Yan'an Xi Lu Ⓜ

❹

❼

Propaganda Poster Centre

❽

Changshu Lu

HUAIHAI ZHONG LU

FORMER FRENCH CONCESSION

Shaanxi Nan Lu

Xintiandi

Yili Lu Ⓜ

YAN'AN ELEVATED EXPRESSWAY

❺

Ba Jin's Former Residence

Song Qingling's Former Residence

⓫

Shanghai Library

Taikang Lu (Tianzifang)

Songyuan Lu Ⓜ

Wukang Lu Tourist Information Centre ⓘ

⓬

❻ ❼

Hengshan Lu Ⓜ

❷⓭ ❹

Hongqiao Lu Ⓜ

Ferguson Lane

⓮

Jiaotong University

Dapuqiao Ⓜ

Normandie Apartments

Pacific Department Store

ZHAOJIABANG LU

Zhao-Jiabang

Ⓜ Jiashan Lu

Xiqu Bus Station

Xujiahui Catholic Cathedral

Xujiahui Ⓜ

WUZHONG LU

Yishan Lu Ⓜ

Ⓜ ❸

❹

XUJIAHUI

Luban Lu Ⓜ

Shanghai Indoor Stadium

Shanghai Stadium

Shanghai Stadium

Dongan Ⓜ

Damuqiao Lu

NEIHUAN ELEVATED EXPRESSWAY

Guilin Lu

Shanghai Swimming Centre

Shanghai Stadium Sightseeing Bus Centre

Long Museum (West Bund)

❻

West Bund

Lupu Bridge

Caohejing Hi-tech Park

Caoxi Lu Ⓜ

Longhua Cemetery of Martyrs

Longhua Temple

Ⓜ Longhua Zhong Lu

Yuz Museum

Longcao Lu

Longhua

CAOBAO LU

Caobao Lu Ⓜ

Shilong Lu Ⓜ

Yunjin Lu Ⓜ

Houtan

Changqing Lu Ⓜ

Shanghai South Metro and Train Stations Ⓜ

Shanghai South Bus Station

Jinjiang Gong Yuan Ⓜ

Botanical Gardens

Songhong Lu, Hongqiao Airport T2 & Hongqiao Train Station

Qibao, Shanghai Zoo, Hongqiao Airport & Hongqiao Train Station

She Shan

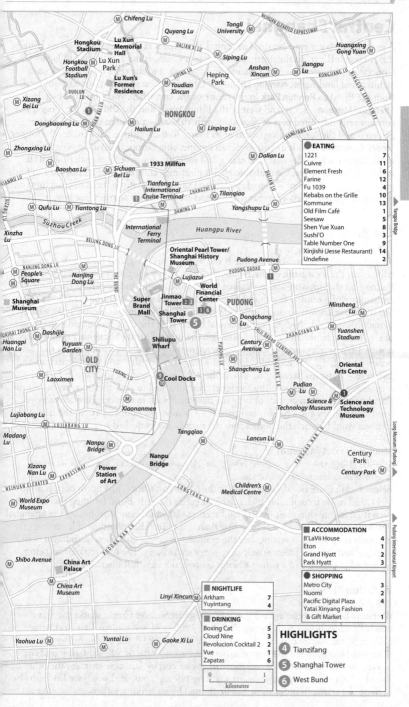

EATING

1221	7
Cuivre	11
Element Fresh	6
Farine	12
Fu 1039	4
Kebabs on the Grille	10
Kommune	13
Old Film Café	1
Seesaw	5
Shen Yue Xuan	8
Sushi'O	3
Table Number One	9
Xinjishi (Jesse Restaurant)	14
Undefine	2

ACCOMMODATION

B'LaVii House	4
Eton	1
Grand Hyatt	2
Park Hyatt	3

SHOPPING

Metro City	3
Nuomi	2
Pacific Digital Plaza	4
Yatai Xinyang Fashion & Gift Market	1

NIGHTLIFE

Arkham	7
Yuyintang	4

DRINKING

Boxing Cat	5
Cloud Nine	3
Revolucion Cocktail 2	2
Vue	1
Zapatas	6

HIGHLIGHTS

4 Tianzifang
5 Shanghai Tower
6 West Bund

0 _____ 1
kilometre

Central Shanghai

A good place to get your bearings in central Shanghai is at the **Bund**, on the west bank of the Huangpu River. To the north, across Suzhou Creek, is the area of the old Japanese Concession; while east over the Huangpu is Pudong, and the city's most conspicuous architectural landmarks. **Nanjing Lu**, one of China's busiest shopping streets, runs west from the Bund to **Renmin Park** in the centre of the city, where you'll find the excellent **Shanghai Museum**. South and west of the Bund, you'll find the **Old City**, the longest continuously inhabited part of Shanghai, with **Yu Yuan** – a restored classical Chinese garden – and the surrounding bazaar at its heart. To the southwest of here lies the **former French Concession**, with its cosmopolitan cuisine, chic European-style housing and revolutionary relics. The energetic eating and nightlife centre of Shanghai, **Huaihai Lu**, is the area's main artery. Central Shanghai is pleasingly compact, and it's not hard to find your way around on foot – though you'll need to use the **metro** or taxis to cross from one quarter to the next. Be aware that tourist areas are rife with **scammers** (see box, p.52).

The Bund

外滩, wàitān • Ⓜ Nanjing Dong Lu

Shanghai's original signature skyline is the **Bund**, a strip of grand Neoclassical colonial edifices on the west bank of the Huangpu River, facing the flashy skyscrapers of Pudong on the opposite shore. Named after an old Anglo-Indian term, "bunding" (the embanking of a muddy foreshore), the Bund's official name is **Zhongshan Dong Yi Lu** but it's better known among locals as Wai Tan (literally "Outside Beach"). By whatever name, this was old Shanghai's commercial heart, with the river on one side, the offices of the leading banks and trading houses on the other. During Shanghai's riotous heyday it was also a hectic working harbour, where anything from tiny sailing junks to ocean-going freighters unloaded under the watch of British – and later American and Japanese – warships. Everything arrived here, from silk and tea to heavy industrial machinery. Amid it all, wealthy foreigners disembarked to pick their way to one of the grand hotels through crowds of beggars, hawkers, black marketeers, shoeshine boys, overladen coolies and even funeral parties – Chinese too poor to pay for the burial of relatives would launch the bodies into the river in boxes decked in paper flowers.

Shanghai Post Museum

上海邮政博物馆, shànghǎi yóuzhèng bówùguǎn • 276 Suzhou Bei Lu • Wed, Thurs, Sat & Sun 9am–4pm • Free • ☎ 021 63936666, ⓦ shpost.com.cn • Ⓜ Tiantong Lu

Before tackling the Bund, have a look at the Main Post Office, just north of it, built in 1931, and easily recognizable by its clocktower. It's the only Bund building that has never been used for anything but its original function. The third floor now houses the **Shanghai Post Museum**, which is more interesting than it sounds. The collection of letters and stamps is only mildly diverting, but the examples of postal transport, including a train carriage, and the old, rather stately post-boxes are striking. The roof terrace was being renovated at the time of writing; when it is open, the view from here is superb.

Waibaidu Bridge

外白渡桥, wàibáidù qiáo

Waibaidu Bridge, whose arched metal frame spans Suzhou Creek, marks the Bund's northern edge. It was built by the British in 1908, and was China's first steel truss bridge. At the outbreak of the Sino-Japanese War in 1937, the bridge formed a no-man's-land between the Japanese-occupied areas north of Suzhou Creek and the **International Settlement** – it was guarded at one end by Japanese sentries, the other by British. Today it's a popular spot for wedding photographs, and you'll see brides-to-be braving the traffic in order to be briefly framed by its striking girders.

6

HUANGPU RIVER CRUISES

One highlight of a visit to Shanghai – and a great way to view the buildings of the Bund – is to take a **Huangpu River cruise** (黄浦江旅游, huángpǔjiāng lǚyóu). You'll get to see the paraphernalia of the shipping industry, from sampans and rusty old Panamanian-registered freighters to sparkling Chinese navy vessels, and to observe the colossal construction that is taking place on the eastern shore. Evening cruises offer spectacular views, with the city lit up like a pinball machine at night.

Cruises (1–3hr; ¥100–150; 2hr evening buffet cruise ¥200) leave from Shiliupu Wharf (十六浦码头, shí liù pǔ mǎtóu) opposite Jinling Dong Lu, at the south end of the Bund. You can buy tickets at the wharf or at the **Bund Tourist Information Centre** on the riverbank beside the entrance to the Bund Tourist Tunnel. Departure times vary depending on season and weather.

It is also possible to take cruises from **Pudong** from the Pearl Dock (明珠码头, míngzhū mǎtóu; 10am–1.30pm every 30min; 30min; ¥100).

The first building south of the bridge was one of the cornerstones of British interests in old Shanghai, the former **British Consulate**, once guarded by magnificently dressed Sikh soldiers. The blue building just to the northeast of here across the Suzhou Creek still retains its original function as the **Russian Consulate**.

Huangpu Park

黄浦公园, huángpǔ gōngyuán • Zhongshan Dong Yi Lu • Free

Right on the corner of the Huangpu and Suzhou Creek, **Huangpu Park** was a British creation – the British Public Gardens – established on a patch of land formed when silt gathered around a wrecked ship. Though it's established in the Chinese popular imagination as a symbol of Western racism, there's no evidence that there ever was a sign here reading "No Dogs or Chinese Allowed" – it is true, however, that troops banned Chinese people from entering unless they were servants accompanying their employer. After protests, the regulations were relaxed to admit "well-dressed" Chinese, who had to apply for a special entry permit. These days, the park contains a stone monument to the "Heroes of the People", and is also a popular spot for citizens practicing *tai ji* early in the morning, but it's best simply for the promenade that commands the junction of the two rivers.

Rockbund Art Museum

外滩美术馆, wàitān měishùguǎn • 20 Huqiu Lu • Tues–Sun 10am–6pm • ¥30 • ☎ 021 33109985, ⓦ rockbundartmusem.org

The narrow streets leading back from the Bund hold some fine Art Deco buildings; the **Rockbund Art Museum**, a strikingly tall and angular hulk tucked behind the *Peninsula* hotel, is one of the best. Dating back to the 1930s, when it was the headquarters of the Royal Asiatic Society, it has been restored and converted into an achingly cool four-storey gallery of contemporary art, hosting shows that usually mix China's biggest hitters with international artists. There's no permanent exhibition, so check the website for what's on and for the programme of events and lectures.

Fairmont Peace Hotel

和平饭店, hépíng fàndiàn • 20 Nanjing Dong Lu, by the Bund • Tours 10.30am & 2.30pm; 1hr; ¥100 • ☎ 021 63216888, ⓦ fairmont.com/peacehotel

Straddling the eastern end of Nanjing Lu is one of the most famous hotels in China, the **Fairmont Peace Hotel**, formerly the Cathay. The place to be seen in prewar Shanghai, it offered guests a private plumbing system fed by a spring on the outskirts of town, marble baths with silver taps, and vitreous china lavatories imported from Britain. The sensitively restored *Peace* is well worth a visit today, if only to walk around the Art Deco lobby and corridors. On the first floor, a little **museum** of the hotel's history (daily 10am–7pm; ☎ 021 63216888 ext 6751) displays relics such as room keys

6

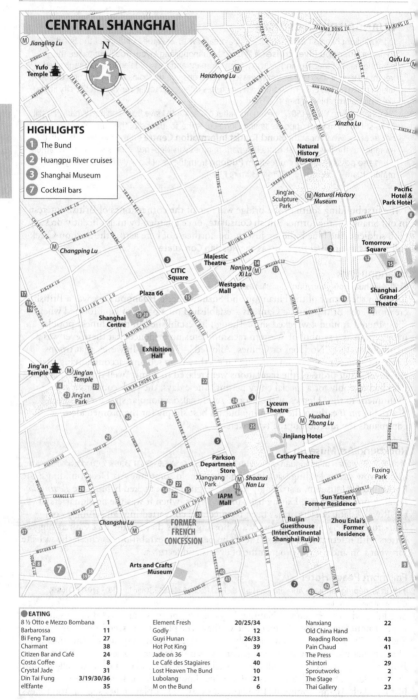

CENTRAL SHANGHAI

HIGHLIGHTS
1 The Bund
2 Huangpu River cruises
3 Shanghai Museum
7 Cocktail bars

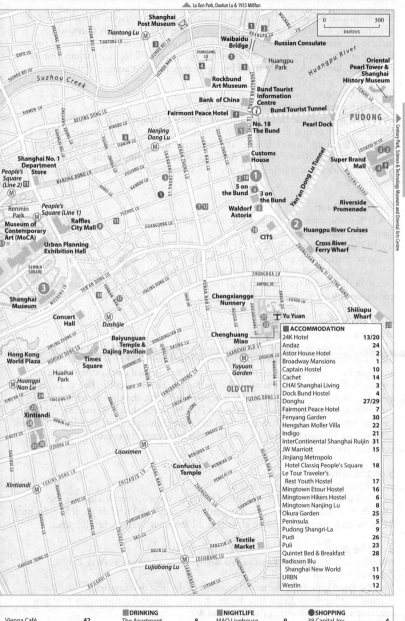

Lu Xun Park, Duolun Lu & 1933 Millfun

Century Park, Science & Technology Museum and Oriental Arts Centre

ACCOMMODATION	
24K Hotel	13/20
Andaz	24
Astor House Hotel	2
Broadway Mansions	1
Captain Hostel	10
Cachet	14
CHAI Shanghai Living	3
Dock Bund Hostel	4
Donghu	27/29
Fairmont Peace Hotel	7
Fenyang Garden	30
Hengshan Moller Villa	22
Indigo	21
InterContinental Shanghai Ruijin	31
JW Marriott	15
Jinjiang Metropolo Hotel Classiq People's Square	18
Le Tour Traveler's Rest Youth Hostel	17
Mingtown Etour Hostel	16
Mingtown Hikers Hostel	6
Mingtown Nanjing Lu	8
Okura Garden	25
Peninsula	5
Pudong Shangri-La	9
Pudi	26
Puli	23
Quintet Bed & Breakfast	28
Radisson Blu Shanghai New World	11
URBN	19
Westin	12

		DRINKING		NIGHTLIFE		SHOPPING	
Vienna Café	42	The Apartment	8	MAO Livehouse	9	38 Capital Joy	4
Wagas	13/14/15/18/32/37	Bar Rouge	1	Myst	6	Foreign Language Bookstore	1
Wang Baohe	9	Captain Bar	2			Garden Books	5
Xiao Shaoxing	17	Long Bar	3			Han City	2
Ye Shanghai	28	People 7	5			Nuomi	6
Yi Café	4	Senator	7			Triple-Major	7
Yuxin Sichuan Dish	16	Windows Too	4			Xinlelu	3

and lampshades from the Thirties, and plenty of old photographs, including one of Mao meeting Monty. Contact the museum to join one of the daily **tours**, which include the grander guest rooms, if they're not booked. There's a good **view** of the Bund from the balcony of the seventh-floor bar – staff will tolerate curious visitors popping in for a look, or you could buy an orange juice for around ¥50.

Bank of China

中国银行, zhōngguó yínháng • 23 Zhongshan Dong Yi Lu

Next door to the *Peace Hotel*, the **Bank of China** was designed in the 1920s by Shanghai architectural firm Palmer & Turner, who brought in a Chinese architect to make the building "more Chinese" after construction was complete. The architect placed a pagoda-like roof onto the Art Deco edifice, creating a delightful juxtaposition of styles, an idea that is being endlessly (and often less successfully) copied across the nation today.

No. 18 The Bund

外滩18号, wàitān shíbā hào • 18 Zhongshan Dong Yi Lu • **Art gallery** Tues–Sun 11am–9pm • ☎ 021 63238099, ⓦ www .bund18.com/art-culture/18gallery

No. 18 The Bund, originally the Chartered Bank of India and Australia, today is home to the city's ritziest shops, given gravitas by the building's Italian marble columns. As well as top-end retail outlets such as Cartier, the building houses swanky *Bar Rouge* (see p.383), which has a fantastic roof terrace with views of Pudong. There's also a **contemporary art gallery** that's worth a look.

Customs House

海关楼, hǎiguān lóu • 13 Zhongshan Dong Yi Lu

The **Customs House** is one of the few Bund buildings to have retained its original function, though its distinctive clocktower was adapted to chime *The East is Red* at 6am and 6pm daily during the Cultural Revolution (the original clockwork has since been restored). The clocktower was modelled on the one that houses Big Ben in London, and after its completion in 1927, local legend had it that the chimes, which struck each fifteen minutes, confused the God of Fire: believing the chimes were a fire bell, the god felt Shanghai was suffering from too many conflagrations, and decided not to send any more. Step into the downstairs lobby for a peek at the ceiling mosaics and their maritime motifs.

5 on the Bund

外滩5号, wài tān wǔ hào • 5 Zhongshan Dong Yi Lu

The section of the Bund south of Fuzhou Lu boasts some very posh addresses. No. 5, officially known as **5 on the Bund**, is entered on Guangdong Lu. Here you'll find the ritzy *M on the Bund* (see p.381) which kicked off the area's renaissance when it opened in 1999.

3 on the Bund

外滩3号, wài tān sān hào • 3 Zhongshan Dong Yi Lu • **Gallery of Art** Daily 11am–9pm • Free • ☎ 021 63215757, ⓦ shanghaigalleryofart.com

3 on the Bund is perhaps the most luxurious of the new developments: there's an Armani flagship store, Evian spa, five swish restaurants and continuingly changing contemporary exhibitions at the **Gallery of Art**.

Waldorf Astoria

华尔道夫酒店, huá'ěr dàofū jiǔdiàn • 2 Zhongshan Dong Yi Lu • ☎ 021 63229988, ⓦ waldorfastoriashanghai.com

Opened in 1910 as a private members' club for well-heeled Brits, this building closed its doors with the arrival of the Communists, then languished, semi-derelict, for decades. Happily, it has been restored to its full glory as the **Waldorf Astoria**. As with the other heritage hotels in the area, rooms are expensive, but it's worth a visit to check out the stylish interior – in this case, Neoclassical opulence. Don't miss the **Long Bar** (see p.384), a fine evocation of 1930s Shanghai, reconstructed from photos after the original was torn out in the 1980s. The eastern end of the original 12m-long bar commanded a view of the Huangpu, and only the club's elite members were allowed to sit there.

Nanjing Lu

南京路, nánjīng lù

Stretching west from the Bund through the heart of Shanghai lie the main commercial streets of the city, among them one of the two premier shopping streets, **Nanjing Lu**, with its two major parallel arteries, **Fuzhou Lu** (福州路, fúzhōu lù) and **Yan'an Lu** (延安路, yán'ān lù). In the days of the foreign concessions, expatriates described Nanjing Lu as a cross between Broadway and Oxford Street; along with Fuzhou Lu, it was lined with numerous teahouses that functioned as the city's most exclusive brothels.

Nanjing Dong Lu

南京东路, nánjīng dōng lù · Ⓜ Nanjing Dong Lu

The garish neon lights and window displays of **Nanjing Dong Lu** are iconic; come here in the evening to appreciate the lightshow in its full tacky splendour. The spectacle is more diverting than the **shopping** (see box below) – which is generally cheap rather than chic – and be aware that foreign men will be pestered by pimps.

Renmin Square

人民广场, rénmín guǎngchǎng · Ⓜ People's Square

Its perimeters defined by the city's main arteries – Xizang, Nanjing and Yan'an roads – **Renmin Square** (**People's Square** in English, and often labelled as such on maps) is the modern heart of Shanghai, though it started life as the city's racecourse, built by the British in 1862. The races became so popular among Shanghai's population – both foreign and Chinese – that most businesses closed for the ten-day periods of the twice-yearly meets, and by the 1920s the Shanghai Race Club was the third-wealthiest foreign corporation in China. It was converted into a sports arena in 1941 by Chiang Kai-shek, who thought gambling immoral. During World War II the stadium served as a holding camp for prisoners and as a temporary mortuary; afterwards, most of it was levelled, and while the north part was landscaped to create **Renmin Park**, the rest was paved to form a parade ground for political rallies. Only the racecourse's **clubhouse** survives, presently being converted into a private club.

NANJING DONG LU: ICONIC SHOPS

No. 635 Nanjing Dong Lu was once the glorious **Wing On** emporium, and diagonally opposite was the **Sincere**. These were not just stores: inside, there were restaurants, rooftop gardens, cabarets and hotels. The **Shanghai Department Store** near Guizhou Lu at no. 800, once the largest in China, is still going, a place of pilgrimage for out-of-towners. Off the circular overhead walkway at the junction between Nanjing Dong Lu and Xizang Zhong Lu, just northeast of Renmin Park, is the grandest of the district's department stores, the venerable **Shanghai No. 1 Store**. If you're after cheap clothes, you'll be spoilt for choice, but for something distinctly Chinese you'll have to look a bit harder. Your best bet for curiosities is to head to the **Shanghai First Food Store** at the west end of the street, at no. 720. Chinese people often buy food as a souvenir, and this busy store sells all kinds of locally made gift-wrapped sweets, cakes and preserves, as well as tea and pastries.

6

Shanghai Museum

上海博物馆, shànghǎi bówùguǎn • 201 Renmin Dadao • Daily 9am–5pm, last entry 4pm • Free; audio-guide ¥40 plus ¥400 deposit • ☎ 021 63723500, ⓦ shanghaimuseum.net/en • ⓜ People's Square

The unmistakeable pot-shaped **Shanghai Museum** is one of the city's highlights, with a fantastic, well-presented collection. On the ground floor, the gallery of ancient **bronzes** holds cooking vessels, containers and weapons, many covered with intricate geometrical designs that reference animal shapes – check out the cowrie container from the Western Han dynasty, with handles shaped like stalking tigers. Most of the exhibits in the sculpture gallery next door are of religious figures – boggle-eyed temple guardians, serene Buddhas and the like, including a row of huge, fearsome Tang-dynasty heads. Tang-dynasty figurines again steal the show in the first-floor ceramics gallery, in the form of multicoloured ferocious-looking beasties placed to guard tombs.

On the second floor, skip the calligraphy and carved seals unless you have a special interest and investigate the **painting** gallery, which shows some amazingly naturalistic Ming-dynasty images of animals. The colourful top-floor exhibition dedicated to Chinese **minority peoples** is the museum highlight. One wall is lined with spooky lacquered masks from Tibet and Guizhou, while nearby are colourfully decorated boats from the Taiwanese minority, the Gaoshan. The silver ceremonial headdresses of southwest China's Miao people are breathtaking for their intricacy, if rather impractical to wear. Elaborate abstract designs turn the Dai lacquered tableware into art. In the section on traditional costumes, look out for the fish-skin suit made by the Hezhen people of Dongbei, in the far north.

Urban Planning Exhibition Hall

城市规划展示馆, chéngshì guīhuà zhǎnshìguǎn • 100 Renmin Dadao • Tues–Sun 9am–5pm, last entry 4pm • ¥30 • ☎ 021 63722077, ⓦ supec.org • ⓜ People's Square

It's revealing of the Shanghai mindset that one of the city's grandest museums is dedicated not to the past but the future: the **Urban Planning Exhibition Hall** is interesting for its insight into the vision of the city planners, though if you're not keen on slick propaganda presentations it can be safely skipped. Most noteworthy is the tennis-court-sized model of the city on the second floor, showing what it will (hopefully) look like when the current round of modernization is finished in 2020. There's no room in this brave new world for shabby little alleyways; it's a parade ground of skyscrapers and apartment blocks.

Renmin Park

人民公园, rénmín gōngyuán • Daily 24hr (but only the north gate is open after 7pm) • Free • ⓜ People's Square

Renmin Park is surprisingly quiet, with rocky paths winding between shady groves and alongside ponds – the only sign that you are in the heart of a modern city is the view of skyscrapers looming above the treetops. At weekends the north section of the park serves as an informal marriage market, and is rammed with busybody parents setting up dates for their unmarried adult children.

Museum of Contemporary Art (MoCA)

上海当代艺术馆, shànghǎi dāngdài yìshùguǎn • Daily 10am–6pm • ¥50 • ☎ 021 63279000, ⓦ mocashanghai.org

The attractive little two-storey **Museum of Contemporary Art** (**MoCA**) nestles in a bamboo grove beside a lotus pond. There is no permanent collection but its themed shows are imaginatively curated, and there are regular talks and tours; check the website for details.

Nanjing Xi Lu

南京西路, nánjīng xīlù • ⓜ People's Sqaure, ⓜ Nanjing Xi Lu and ⓜ Jing'an Temple; bus #20 runs the length of the road

The western end of **Nanjing Xi Lu** was known to "**Shanghailanders**" (the Europeans who made their homes here) as Bubbling Well Road, after a spring that used to gush at the far end of the street. Then, as today, it was one of the smartest addresses in the city, leading into tree-lined streets where Westerners' mock-Tudor mansions sheltered behind high walls. Now it's also home to a number of malls and luxury hotels, including the **Shanghai Centre** (上海商城, shànghǎi shāngchéng) at 1376 Nanjing Xi Lu.

Jing'an Temple

静安寺, jìng'ān sì • 1686 Nanjing Xi Lu • Daily 7.30am–5pm • ¥50 • ⑩ Jing'an Temple or bus #20 from Renmin Square

The **Jing'an Temple** may be hemmed in by skyscrapers, but it refuses to be outdone; this recently rebuilt complex is religious architecture Shanghai style – lavish and shiny, designed to impress, and expensive to visit. Building work first began on the temple during the Three Kingdoms period, and its apparent obscurity belies its past as the richest Buddhist foundation in the city, headed by legendary abbot Khi Vehdu, who combined his abbotly duties with a gangster lifestyle. The abbot and his seven concubines were shadowed by White Russian bodyguards, each carrying a leather briefcase lined with bulletproof steel, to be used as a shield in case of attack.

Today, the temple is the primary place of **ancestral worship** in Shanghai, although an equal number of people come to pray for more material reasons – worshippers eagerly throw coins into incense burners in the hope that the gods will bestow financial success. The **central hall** is constructed of Burmese teak and features flying eaves and sturdy *dougongs*. Inside, an 8.8m-high, 15-tonne silver Buddha glimmers in the gloom. A side hall holds an elegant, slim Guanyin, made from a thousand-year-old camphor tree.

Head round the back, to the cloisters and meeting rooms, and you'll see that no expense has been spared in the new fittings; even the lift doors have been engraved with guardian Bodhisattvas.

Natural History Museum

上海自然博物馆, shànghǎi zìrán bówùguǎn • 399 Shanghaiguan Lu, near Datian Lu • Tues–Sun 9am–5.15pm, last admission 4.30pm • ¥30; cinema shows ¥40 • ☎ 021 68622000, ⓦ www.snhm.org.cn • ⑩ Shanghai Natural History Museum

A short walk north of Nanjing Xi Lu you'll find the charming **Jing'an Sculpture Park**, with the attractive new **Natural History Museum** at its centre. The museum's spiralling structure is designed to echo a nautilus shell, and the external walls emulate natural elements – including a northern stone wall inspired by tectonic plates, and most strikingly, a vertical garden on the east wall. Inside you'll find a quite overwhelming volume of animals: stuffed, plasticated or mechanical. Exhibition spaces are intelligently themed – Big Bang, evolution, early civilization, and so on – with educational captions in English.

As ever, the **dinosaurs** steal the show: there's an enormous skeleton of a Mamenchisaurus, and a pretty scary animatronic Tyrannosaurus. There's also a lifelike re-creation of the African savanna, cutesy dioramas of early Chinese villages and some gory Damien Hirst-style cross-sections – most strikingly, of an ocean sunfish. It would take several hours to do the place justice, more if you take in one of the documentary screenings in the **4D cinema**.

The Old City

老城, lǎochéng

Shanghai's **Old City** is an oval circumscribed by two roads, Renmin Lu and Zhonghua Lu, which follow the old path of the city walls. The Old City never formed part of the International Settlement and was somewhat contemptuously known by resident foreigners as the **Chinese City**. Based on the original **walled city** of Shanghai, which dated back to the eleventh century, the area was reserved in the nineteenth and early twentieth centuries as a ghetto for vast numbers of Chinese who lived in appalling squalor, while the foreigners carved out their living space around them.

Ring roads had already replaced the original walls and moats as early as 1912, and sanitation has obviously improved vastly since, but to cross the boundaries into the

6

Old City is still to glimpse a different world. The twisting alleyways are a haven of free enterprise, bursting with makeshift markets selling fish, vegetables, cheap trinkets, clothing and food. Ironically, for a tourist, the feeling is like entering a Chinatown in a Western city. The centre of activity today is an area known locally as **Chenghuang Miao** (after a local temple), where one of the main draws for Chinese tourists, the **Yu Yuan**, or Yu Garden, sits at the centre of a busy tourist bazaar.

Yu Yuan

豫园, yùyuán • Daily 8.30am–5.30pm, last entry at 5pm • April–Oct ¥40; Nov–March ¥30 • ☎ 021 63260830 • Ⓜ Yuyuan Garden

A classical Chinese garden featuring pools, walkways, bridges and rockeries, **Yu Yuan** (**Yu Garden** in English) was created in the sixteenth century by a high official in the imperial court in honour of his father. It may be less impressive than the gardens of nearby Suzhou (see p.322), but given that it predates the relics of the International Settlement by some three hundred years, the Shanghainese are understandably proud of it. Despite fluctuating fortunes, Yu Yuan has surprisingly survived the passage of the centuries. It was spared from its greatest crisis – the Cultural Revolution – apparently because the anti-imperialist "Little Sword Society" had used it as their headquarters in 1853 during the Taiping Uprising.

Undulating **dragon walls** – shaped like dragons, with scales, heads and all – divide the five-acre site into six areas, each of which is designed as a pocket landscape to be viewed from a well-placed hall or pavilion. Particularly impressive is the rockery outside the **Sansui Hall**, a miniature mountain range of peaks, grottoes and caves. At the centre of the garden, next to the Yuhua Hall, stands the craggy "Exquisite Jade Rock" – a five-tonne boulder riddled with holes, which was much admired as a wonder of nature in its day. Tour guides burn a joss stick under it, and the smoke emerges through a dozen holes at once.

The garden is at its brightest during the **Lantern Festival** on the fifteenth day of the traditional New Year, when it is decorated with thousands of lanterns.

Huxin Ting teahouse

湖心亭茶馆, húxīntíng cháguǎn • 257 Yuyuan Lu • Daily 8am–9pm • ☎ 021 63736950 • Ⓜ Yuyuan Garden

After visiting the garden, check out **Huxin Ting**, a two-storey teahouse on an island at the centre of an ornamental lake, reached by a zigzagging bridge. The Queen of England and Bill Clinton, among other illustrious guests, have dropped in for tea. It's cute but decidedly pricey – at least ¥60 for a cup, though it will be refilled as often as you like. Rely on the waiter's recommendation and you'll be given the most expensive option, so insist on seeing the menu.

Chenxiangge Nunnery

沉香阁, chénxiāng gé • 29 Chenxiangge Lu • Daily 8am–4pm • ¥10 • Ⓜ Yuyuan Garden

The **Chenxiangge Nunnery** is one of the more active of Shanghai's temples. This tranquil complex is enlivened by the presence of a few dozen resident nuns, who gather twice daily to pray and chant in the Daxiongbao Hall, under the gaze of the Sakyamuni Buddha. His gilded statue is flanked by images of 384 disciples, all supposedly the work of a single recent, still living, craftsman.

Baiyunguan Temple

白云观, báiyún guàn • 239 Dajing Lu • Daily 9am–5pm • ¥5 • ☎ 021 63287236 • Ⓜ Dashijie

At the end of Dajing Lu is the pretty Taoist **Baiyunguan Temple**. Worshippers light incense and burn "silver ingots" made of paper in the central courtyard – some burn paper cars and houses too – while Taoist priests wander round in yellow robes with their long hair tied in a bun. In the main hall there's a huge effigy of the Jade Emperor looking judgemental. Taoism is the most esoteric of China's three big religions, and there are some striking figures of Taoist Immortals on display at the side of the hall – look for the fellow with arms coming out of his eyes.

Dajing Pavilion

大镜阁, dàjìng gé • 237 Dajing Lu • Daily 9am–4pm • ¥5 • Ⓜ Dashijie

Next door to the Baiyunguan Temple, the **Dajing Pavilion** is a new structure built over the last surviving slice of a Ming-dynasty wall. Brick markings on the wall bear the names of the two emperors, Tongzhi and Xianfeng, who commissioned it as protection against Japanese pirates. The pavilion today contains a small exhibition on the history of the Old City.

Confucius Temple

文庙, wén miào • Wenmiao Lu • Daily 9am–5pm • ¥10 • Ⓜ Laoximen

Sunk deep into the southwestern corner of the Old City is the **Confucius Temple**. Shanghai has had a temple dedicated to Confucius since the Yuan dynasty but most of the present buildings date back to 1855, when the Small Swords Society (see opposite) made the temple a base. The only original Yuan building left is the elegant three-storey **Kuixing Pavilion**, near the entrance, which is dedicated to the god of artistic and intellectual endeavour. An appealing atmosphere of scholarly introspection infuses the complex – students wishing for good exam results tie red ribbons to the branches of the pine trees, and there's a statue of Confucius himself looking professorial.

6

Cool Docks

老码头, lǎo mǎ tóu • 479 Zhongshan Nan Lu • Ⓜ Xiaonanmen

Keep going east from the Old City till you hit the river, head south, past the ferry to Pudong, and suddenly things get startlingly salubrious: you've hit the **Cool Docks**, a strip of renovated warehouses just off the waterfront, now filling up with fancy restaurants. Clearly this is envisioned as the new Xintiandi (see p.362), though you have to wonder if the lack of transport connections is going to stymie the plan – and of course anything that has to name itself "cool", by definition, isn't. Still, it's a pleasant place for a meal if you sit outside by the artificial pond – check out *Kebabs on the Grille* or *Table Number One* (see p.381). In summer, an **artificial beach** sets up at the northern edge of the area, by the river (10am–10pm; admission varies, around ¥50). There's little more here than deckchairs and a shallow strip of sand, but there are regular events – check online – and you can bring your own food and drink.

Power Station of Art

上海当代艺术博物馆, shànghǎi dāngdài yìshù bówùguǎn • 200 Huayuangang Lu, near Miaojiang Lu • Daily 9am–5pm • Free • ☎ 021 31108550, ⓦ powerstationofart.com • Ⓜ Xizang Nan Lu, then a 15min walk

A couple of kilometres south of the Old City, on the site of the 2010 Expo, the huge **Power Station of Art** is a state-run contemporary art museum in a repurposed power station. Perhaps an attempt by the city fathers – aware that nothing confers prestige like a bright new gallery – to replicate the success of London's Tate Modern, the building, with its sturdy industrial fixtures and vast halls, is certainly striking. There's no permanent display, but generally three or four shows are on the go at a time, including international touring exhibitions; it's also home to the **Shanghai Biennale** (see p.385). Check out the rooftop café for great views, and the shop for artsy trinkets.

The former French Concession

法租界, fǎzūjiè

Established in the mid-nineteenth century, the **former French Concession** lay to the south and west of the International Settlement, abutting the Chinese City. Despite its name, it was never particularly French: before 1949, in fact, it was a low-rent district mainly inhabited by Chinese and White Russians. Other Westerners looked down on the latter as they were obliged to take jobs that, it was felt, should have been left to the Chinese.

6

Huaihai Zhong Lu is the main street running through the heart of the area. Not as crowded as Nanjing Lu, it is considerably more upmarket, particularly in the area around **Maoming Nan Lu** and **Shanxi Lu**, congested with fashion boutiques and department stores. West of Changshu Lu metro station you get a good taste of the former French Concession, with attractive streets lined with plane trees and villas. The largest villas have been converted to embassy properties, upmarket eating places and a fair few beauty salons but, oddly, not that many shops. The apex of sophistication, with a smartly international feel, is further west, around **Fuxing Xi Lu**, **Wukang Lu** and **Anfu Lu**. It's more a place to soak up the atmosphere on a sunny day than to take in specific sights, and a bicycle is the best way to explore.

Brief history

The French Concession was notorious for its **lawlessness** and the ease with which police and French officials could be bribed, in contrast to the well-governed areas dominated by the British. This made it ideal territory for gangsters, including the king of all Shanghai mobsters, **Du Yuesheng**, the right-hand man of Huang Jinrong. For similar reasons, political activists also operated in this sector – the first meeting of the Chinese Communist Party took place here in 1921, and both **Zhou Enlai** and **Sun Yatsen**, the first provisional president of the Republic of China after the overthrow of the Qing dynasty, lived here. The preserved former homes of these two in particular (see opposite) are worth visiting simply because, better than anywhere else in modern Shanghai, they give a sense of how the Westerners, and the Westernized, used to live.

Xintiandi

新天地, xīntiāndì • Ⓜ Xintiandi or Ⓜ Huangpi Nan Lu

The **Xintiandi** development, which comprises two blocks of renovated and rebuilt *shikumen* converted into a genteel open-air mall, was the first of its kind in China. It has met with such success that now town planners all over the country are studying its winning formula. Paved and pedestrianized, with narrow lanes (*longtang*) opening out onto a central plaza, Xintiandi is a great place to wind down or linger over a coffee, with upscale restaurants (see p.382) and shops, and plenty of outside seating.

Shikumen Open House Museum

石库门民居陈列馆, shíkùmén mínjū chénlièguǎn • 25 Xintiandi North Block • Daily 10am–10pm • ¥20 • ☏ 021 33070337

The **Shikumen Open House Museum**, at the south end of Xintiandi North Block, does an excellent job of evoking early twentieth-century Chinese gentility. This reconstruction of a typical *shikumen* is filled with everyday objects – typewriters, toys, a four-poster bed and the like – so it doesn't look as bare as the "Former Residences" elsewhere in the city. A top-floor display details how Xintiandi came about, admitting that most of it was built from scratch. A quote on the wall is perhaps more revealing than was intended: "Foreigners find it Chinese and Chinese find it foreign".

Site of the First National Congress of the Chinese Communist Party

中国一大会址纪念馆, zhōngguó yīdàhuìzhǐ jìniànguǎn • 76 Xingye Lu, at junction with Huangpi Nan Lu • Daily 9am–5pm, last admission 4pm • Free (bring ID)

On the east side of the complex you'll find, rather incongruously, one of the shrines of Maoist China, the **Site of the First National Congress of the Chinese Communist Party**. The official story is that on July 23, 1921, thirteen representatives of the Communist cells that had developed all over China – including its most famous junior participant, **Mao Zedong** – met here to discuss the formation of a national party. The meeting was discovered (it was illegal to hold political meetings in the French Concession) and, on July 30, the delegates fled north to nearby Zhejiang province, where they resumed their talks in a boat. Quite how much of this really happened is unclear, but it seems probable that there were in fact more delegates than recorded – the missing names would have been expunged according to subsequent political circumstances. There's a little **exhibition hall** downstairs, where the period relics – such as maps, money and a British policeman's uniform and truncheon – are more interesting than the outdated propaganda rants. The last room has a waxwork diorama of Mao and his fellow delegates.

Fuxing Park

复兴公园, fùxīng gōngyuán • 105 Fuxing Zhong Lu • Daily 6am–6pm • Free • Ⓜ Xintiandi

Attractive **Fuxing Park** was laid out by the French in 1909, and remains rather European in feel, which makes the statue of Marx and Engels in the northwest corner seem incongruous. Come in the morning or at dusk and you'll see middle-aged locals performing *tai ji*, ballroom dancing and opera singing.

Sun Yatsen's Former Residence

孙中山故居, sūnzhōngshān gùjū • 7 Xiangshan Lu • Daily 9am–4.30pm • ¥20 • ☏ 021 64372954 • Ⓜ Xintiandi

From Xintiandi it's a short walk to **Sun Yatsen's Former Residence**, which was home to the first president of the Chinese Republic and his wife, Song Qingling. The first building contains a dry exhibition of the man's books and artefacts, and can be safely skipped, but the elegantly furnished period house beside it is worth a look.

Zhou Enlai's Former Residence

周恩来故居, zhōu'ēnlái gùjū • 73 Sinan Lu • Daily 9am–4pm • Free • ☏ 021 64730420 • Ⓜ Xintiandi

The southern end of Sinan Lu constitutes a smart neighbourhood of old houses, among them, **Zhou Enlai's Former Residence**. Zhou was Mao's right-hand man, but he has always been looked upon with rather more affection than the Chairman. When he lived here he was head of the Shanghai Communist Party, and as such was kept under surveillance from a secret outpost over the road. There's not, in truth, a great deal to see, beyond a lot of hard beds on a nice wooden floor. The house has a terrace at the back with rattan chairs and polished wooden floors, and its garden, with hedges and ivy-covered walls, could easily be a part of 1930s suburban London.

Tianzifang

田子坊, tiánzifāng • Main entrance 210 Taikang Lu • ☏ 021 54657531 • Ⓜ Dapuqiao

Heading south from the former residences down Sinan Lu, the area begins to feel earthier; but turning right from the end of the road onto **Taikang Lu** (泰康路, tàikāng lù) will bring you to the latest fashionably artsy shopping and lunching quarter, **Tianzifang**. The unassuming entrance, an arch over alley 210 on the north side of the road, leads onto **Taikang Art Street** (泰康路田子坊, tàikānglù tiánzifāng), a narrow north–south alleyway off which you'll find an expanding web of alleys filling up with souvenir shops, cool boutiques, bars, galleries and restaurants, all housed in converted *shikumen* houses. At its northern end, Tianzifang exits onto Sinan Lu, but don't even try to come in from there – the entrance is tough to find.

Inevitably, Tianzifang gets compared with Xintiandi (see opposite); but whereas the architecture there is modern pastiche, this is a set of real, warts-and-all *longtangs*, with the result that it's quainter, shabbier, more charming. If you're looking for an artsy knick-knack or accessory, quirky souvenir, tasteful homeware or a designer original, this is the place to come, though it's all pretty expensive. Try to visit on a weekday; the narrow lanes get crowded at weekends. For a coffee stop, central *Kommune* (see p.380) is a local institution.

Ruijin Guesthouse (InterContinental Shanghai Ruijin)

瑞金宾馆, ruìjīn bīnguǎn • 118 Ruijin Er Lu, just south of Fuxing Zhong Lu • ☏ 021 64725222, ⊚ ruijinhotelsh.com • Ⓜ Shaanxi Nan Lu

The south section of **Ruijin Er Lu** (瑞金二路, ruìjīn èr lù) is busy and cramped, but there's a wonderful escape in the form of the stately **Ruijin Guesthouse**. This Tudor-style country manor was home in the early twentieth century to the Morris family, owners of the *North China Daily News*; Mr Morris raised greyhounds for the Shanghai Race Club and the former Canidrome dog track across the street. The house, having miraculously escaped damage during the Cultural Revolution because certain high-ranking officials used it as their private residence, is now the exclusive **InterContinental Shanghai Ruijin** hotel (see p.378). Even if you're not a guest, you can walk around the spacious, quiet grounds, where it's hard to believe you're in the middle of one of the world's most hectic cities.

Arts and Crafts Museum

工艺美术博物馆, gōngyì měishù bówùguǎn • 79 Fenyang Lu • Daily 9am–4pm • ¥8 • ☎ 021 64314074 • Ⓜ Changshu Lu

A grand French mansion from 1905 has been converted into Shanghai's **Arts and Crafts Museum**. Visitors are first confronted with a gamut of overpriced craft shops; ignore these and head upstairs to find an intriguing collection of jade, ivory, wood and embroidery, as well as craftspeople practising their trades. A lot of the works are very well made but seem chintzy – the most striking exhibits are the ivories, carved in the 1960s, that depict communist subjects such as political meetings. They're brilliantly executed but look very kitsch now.

Propaganda Poster Centre

宣传画年画艺术中心, xuānchuánhuà niánhuà yìshù zhōngxīn • Building 4, 868 Huashan Lu; the security guard at the entrance will give you a name card with a map on the back showing you the way • Daily 9.30am–4.30pm • ¥25 • ☎ 021 62111845, Ⓦ shanghaipropagandaart.com • Ⓜ Changshu Lu

The **Propaganda Poster Centre** provides a fascinating glimpse into communist China – you will not come across a more vivid evocation of the bad old days of Marx and Mao. The walls are covered with Chinese **Socialist Realist posters**, with more than three thousand examples arranged chronologically from the 1950s to the 1970s; there are, fortunately, English captions. Slogans like "the Soviet Union is the stronghold of world peace" and "hail the over-fulfillment of steel production by ten million tons", and images of sturdy, lantern-jawed peasants and soldiers defeating big-nosed, green-skinned imperialists or riding tractors into a glorious future, offer a dramatic portrayal of the communist dream.

The style of this dry communist art owes much to images with a very different message – **popular prewar calendar posters** – and the exhibition concludes with a room of these. These images, once disseminated all over China, show fetching Chinese girls in fashionable dress and make-up, and once served to introduce the Chinese to the delights of consumer culture, such as cigarettes and hair curlers.

Song Qingling's Former Residence

宋庆龄故居, sòngqìnglíng gù jū • 1843 Huaihai Xi Lu • Daily 9–11am & 1–4.30pm • ¥20 • ☎ 021 64747183 • Ⓜ Jiaotong University

As the wife of Sun Yatsen, Song Qingling was part of a bizarre family coterie – her sister Song Meiling was married to Chiang Kai-shek and her brother, known as T.V. Soong, was finance minister to Chiang. She lived in Shanghai between 1948 and 1981; today **Song Qingling's Former Residence** offers a charming step back into a residential Shanghai of the recent past. The trappings on display – including lovely wood panelling and lacquerwork, and her enormous limousines – are largely post-1949.

Wukang Lu

武康路, wǔkāng lù • Ⓜ Jiaotong University

As Rue Ferguson, **Wukang Lu** was one of the chic-est strips of real estate in old Shanghai, and today this quiet tree-lined strip of mansions seems quintessentially French Concession. Heading north from Huaihai Xi Lu, you'll pass one of Shanghai's most distinctive Art Deco buildings, László Hudec's **Normandie Apartments**, built in 1926. Though its battleship shape echoes New York's Flatiron building, it's built in

French Renaissance style, with elegant cantilevered balconies. A few minutes' walk north brings you to *Farine* (see p.380), where you can join well-heeled locals for a cappuccino before exploring the boutiques and galleries of Ferguson Lane. The **Wukang Lu Tourist Information Centre** (武康路 旅游资讯中心, wǔ kāng lù lǚ yóu zī xùn zhōng xīn; 393 Wukang Lu; daily 9am–5pm), a couple of minutes east, hosts a slick new display of scale models of the former French Concession's standout historical buildings, including many that are a short walk from here.

Ba Jin's Former Residence

巴金故居-千景旅游网, bā jīn gù jū - qiān jǐng lǚ yóu wǎng • 113 Wukang Lu • Tues–Sat 10am–4pm • Free (bring ID)

Heading east of the Wukang Lu Tourst Information Centre, past renovated mansions, you'll come to **Ba Jin's Former Residence**. Ba Jin was one of China's greatest novelists, who did his best work before the war in Shanghai. After being hounded during the Cultural Revolution he was rehabilitated when it was over, and lived the rest of his days in this rather twee mansion. His house is cosy, full of displays of his manuscripts and books, and has a lovely garden.

Pudong

浦东, pǔdōng

Historically, **Pudong** – the district opposite the Bund on the east bank of the river – was known as the "wrong side of the Huangpu"; before 1949, the area was characterized by unemployed migrants, prostitution, murders and the city's most appalling living conditions. It was here that bankrupt gamblers would "*tiao huangpu*", commit suicide by drowning themselves in the river. Shanghai's top gangster, **Du Yuesheng**, more commonly known as "Big-eared Du", learned his trade growing up in this rough section of town. In 1990, however, fifteen years after China's economic reforms started, it was finally decided to grant the status of Special Economic Zone (SEZ) to this large tract of mainly agricultural land, a decision which, more than any other, is now fuelling Shanghai's rocket-like economic advance. The area has since been completely transformed from a collection of rice paddies into a maze of skyscrapers.

| ARRIVAL AND DEPARTURE | PUDONG |

By metro Metro line #2 runs from the People's Square station to Lujiazui in less than 5min, and all the way to the Science and Technology Museum in 10min; lines #4, #6 and #9 also have stops in Pudong.

By ferry Ferries (every 15min daily 7am–10pm; ¥2) run from Jinling Wharf at the end of Jinling Dong Lu to the south end of Binjiang Dadao, a 5min walk to the Super Brand Mall. There's another ferry from just north of the Cool Docks, at the end of Fuxing Dong Lu, which takes you to the far southern end of Binjiang Dadao.

By Bund Tourist Tunnel The Bund Tourist Tunnel (外滩 观光隧道, wàitān guānguāng suìdào; ¥50 one-way, ¥70 return; entrance in the metro opposite Beijing Dong Lu), in which you're driven in a train past a light show, crosses under the river to emerge near the Oriental Pearl Tower.

Lujiazui

陆家嘴, lùjiāzuǐ • Ⓜ Lujiazui

Lujiazui is, above all, an area of commerce, with few activities of interest to the visitor besides giving your neck a good workout as you gaze upwards at the skyline. Here you'll find the bulbous **Oriental Pearl Tower**, the sturdy **World Financial Centre**, the elegant **Jinmao Tower** and the **Shanghai Tower**, the world's second-tallest building. Several attractions have been plonked here, to take advantage of the huge crowds of Chinese tourists who flock to the area; with the exception of the fascinating **Shanghai History Museum** these can be safely ignored.

6

Oriental Pearl Tower

东方明珠广播电视塔, dōngfāng míngzhū guǎngbō diànshìtǎ · 1 Century Ave · Daily 8am–9.30pm · ¥150 for access to highest level · ☎ 021 58791888, ⓦ orientalpearltower.com

The 457m-high **Oriental Pearl Tower** is a symbol of the city and a visit is mandatory for most Chinese visitors to Shanghai – but to be honest, it's best avoided, with its high entrance fee, long queues and tatty interior. You are better off visiting one of its taller and classier neighbours.

Shanghai History Museum

上海城市历史发展馆, shànghǎi chéngshìlìshǐ fāzhǎnguǎn · Daily 8am–9.30pm · ¥35

The **Shanghai History Museum**, at the base of the Oriental Pearl Tower, is surprisingly decent; the majority of exhibits, which focus on the nineteenth century onwards, do a good job of evoking the glory days, with convincing waxwork figures in dioramas of pharmacies, teahouses and the like. One of the old bronze lions from outside the HSBC building (see p.550) is on display, as well as a boundary stone from the International Settlement, and there's a detailed model of the Bund as it would have looked in the 1930s.

Jinmao Tower

金茂大厦, jīnmào dàshà · 88 Century Ave, enter on the north side · Observation deck daily 8.30am–10pm · ¥120 · ☎ 021 50475101, ⓦ www.jinmao88.com

The beautiful **Jinmao Tower**, an elegantly tapering postmodern take on Art Deco, has an **observation deck** on the 88th floor. An ear-popping lift whisks you up 340m to the top in a matter of seconds. The spectacle of the city spread out before you is of course sublime, but turn round for a giddying view down the building's glorious galleried atrium. You can also enjoy decent views for free by using the tower's front entrance (on the east side) and heading up to the *Grand Hyatt*'s lobby on the 54th floor, which has comfy, window-side chairs. For grand night-time views, visit the hotel bar *Cloud Nine*, on the 87th floor (see p.384).

Shanghai Tower

上海中心大厦, shànghǎi zhōngxīn dàshà · 501 Yincheng Zhong Lu · Observation deck daily 9am–9pm · ¥160 · ☎ 021 33831088, ⓦ shanghaitower.com

The **Shanghai Tower**, 632m high and with 121 storeys, is the second-tallest building in the world. This is a skyscraper with a twist, literally; the building corkscrews 120 degrees as it rises. In fact, that elegant curl is an outer layer of glass; by 2017 the space between the inner and outer layers will hold atriums that are open to the public. Plans are underway for the tower to host the world's highest hotel, which should open in 2018. The top-floor **observation deck** is not cheap, but it's the best in the area – and, at 561m, the highest in the world. Enter through the west side, and check out the time-lapse film of Pudong from 1840 to the present day as you queue for your ticket. There follows an impressive multimedia exhibition about skyscrapers with some fascinating designs and models, before good-looking if slightly robotic staff (said to be trainee models) usher you into the world's fastest lift. They'll tell you when you hit the top speed of 64km per hour – but your popping ears will already be giving you the news. The 360-degree viewing platform is pleasingly free of commerce, with full-length glass windows for maximum vertigo; it's pretty stunning to be able to look down on the world's third-tallest building, the World Financial Centre, just next door (see below).

World Financial Centre

环球金融中心, huánqiú jīnróng zhōngxīn · 100 Century Ave · Observation decks daily 8am–11pm, last admission 10pm · Little deck (423m) ¥120, larger deck (439m) ¥150, top deck (474m) ¥180 · ☎ 021 4001100555, ⓦ swfc-observatory.com

The lines at the **World Financial Centre** are strikingly simple: a tapering slab whose most distinctive feature is the hole in the top, it's called by locals "the bottle

6

opener". That hole was originally meant to be circular, but was redesigned as an oblong when the mayor complained that it would look like a Japanese flag hovering over the city.

For the **observation decks**, the entrance and ticket office is in the southwest side. The top level – the top bar of the bottle opener – features hardened glass tiles in the floor that allow you to look right down between your feet. Landmarks are detailed in the booklet that comes with your ticket, and you can get a photo printed for ¥50. The view is at least as impressive at night.

Century Avenue

世纪大道, shìjì dàdào

Century Avenue (Shiji Dadao) runs arrow-straight for 4km southeast from the river to **Century Park**. The simplest way to travel along its length is by metro; the Shanghai Science and Technology Museum station plays host, incongruously, to a huge **fake market** (see p.387). It's a ten-minute walk from there to the park, and you'll see plenty of skateboarders and kite flyers on the way; this is where Shanghai residents go for a sense of space.

Science and Technology Museum

上海科技馆, shànghǎi kējìguǎn • 2000 Century Ave • Tues–Sun 9am–5pm • ¥60; space theatre screenings (every 40min) ¥40; IMAX (hourly 10.30am–4.30pm) ¥30/¥40; IWERKS (every 40min) ¥30 • Ⓦ www.sstm.org.cn • Ⓜ Science and Technology Museum

The **Science and Technology Museum** is huge; rather too big perhaps, as the cavernous halls make some of the twelve exhibitions look threadbare – there isn't much English explanation or quite enough interactivity. The section on space exploration is good – a hot topic in China right now, with the nation fully intending to get to the moon as soon as possible – with real spacesuits and plenty of model spacecraft, and in the section on robots you can take on a robotic arm at archery and play a computer at Go. Of most interest, however, are the **cinemas**: the space theatre shows films on astronomy; the two IMAX domes in the basement show cartoons; and the IWERKS dome on the first floor is an attempt to take the concept of immersive realism even further – as well as surround sound and images there are moving seats, and water and wind effects.

Century Park

世纪公园, shìjì gōngyuán • Daily 7am–6pm • ¥10; tandem rental ¥50/hr, pedalo rental ¥60/hr • Ⓜ Century Park

Century Park is spacious and clean, and it's possible to feel that you have escaped the city. You can rent a tandem bike – sadly you're not allowed to ride your own bicycle – and pedaloes are available to rent on the central lake.

China Art Palace

中华艺术宫, zhōnghuá yìshù gōng • 161 Shangnan Lu, near Guozhen Lu • Tues–Sun 9am–5pm • Free; audio-guide ¥20, ¥200 deposit • Ⓣ 021 63272425, Ⓦ sh-artmuseum.org.cn • Ⓜ China Art Museum

The **2010 World Expo** was held on both banks of the Huangpu, either side of Nanpu Bridge. The majority of weird and wonderful national pavilions were dismantled after the show, but a couple of buildings have been left on the Pudong site as a legacy – the eighteen thousand-seat Mercedes Benz Arena (1200 Expo Avenue; Ⓦ mercedes-benzarena.com) and the **China Art Palace**, which, right on the metro, is worth the long trip.

The enormous red crown-like building, home of the China pavilion at the 2010 Expo site, is meant to look like a *dougong*, or roof bracket, with four legs like a *ding* pot. There are five floors; the lift starts you at the top and you work your way down. First you'll find an exhibition of early Chinese twentieth-century art, which shows Chinese artists who returned from abroad grappling with exciting foreign ideas such as Impressionism. The intricate animation based on the classic scroll painting, **Along the River During Qingming Festival**, which was the most popular exhibit at the Expo, is displayed here, though you have to pay ¥60 to see it.

The fourth floor is dedicated to the **Shanghai Film Animation Studio**, which churned out children's stories from the 50s to the 80s. There are plenty of cells and cut-outs; it might make you want to dig up more about this unjustly underappreciated art. The third and second floor hold temporary shows, usually big names from abroad, while the ground floor focuses on dull, academic works and Socialist Realist celebrations of such achievements as the Chinese conquering Mount Everest and the opening of the Mag-Lev – interesting only to show how bad Chinese official art remains.

Long Museum (Pudong)

龙美术馆, lóngměi shùguǎn • 2255 Luoshan Lu • Daily 9.30am–5pm • ¥50 • ☏ 021 68778787, ⓦ thelongmuseum.org/en • Ⓜ Huamu Lu, then a 15min walk

The rather forbidding-looking **Long Museum (Pudong)** – a minimalist brick with tiny windows – holds treasures from the collection of billionaires Wang Wei and Liu Yiqian. This is a permanent exhibition – their second, more popular and accessible museum at West Bund (see p.372) holds temporary shows. But though this place is a long way out (45 minutes on the metro from the centre of town, then a fifteen-minute walk) it's well worth the trip, a tremendously ambitious attempt to introduce the entire span of Chinese art, with all exhibits well captioned and displayed.

Exhibits are arranged chronologically across three floors; the earliest art is on the top floor. Avoid the calligraphy in the painting gallery and seek out the lively animal and bird studies, most from the Ming dynasty, and the lovely wooden screens in the furniture gallery. The gallery on revolutionary art is full of Soviet-influenced Socialist Realist paintings – images of Mao inspecting factories and the like. The ground-floor collection of twentieth-century and contemporary art is a mixed bag, but there's usually something to respond to – perhaps the gaudy satires of postmodernists Fang Lijun or Zhou Chunya.

Hongkou

North across the Waibaidu Bridge from the Bund, you come to **Hongkou** (虹口, hóng kǒu), an area that, before World War II, was the Japanese quarter of the International Settlement. The area immediately north of the bridge is tipped for a big renovation – you'll see some flashy new buildings, such as the bulbous International Cruise Terminal, and many more are planned. For the moment, the obvious interest lies further north, in the **Lu Xun Park** area (also known as **Hongkou Park**) and its monuments to the political novelist Lu Xun, although the whole district is lively and architecturally interesting.

1933 Millfun

一九三三老场坊, yījiǔsānsān lǎochángfāng • Ⓜ Hailun Lu, then a 10min walk

1933 Millfun, the brooding hulk squatting by the river, was built in 1933 by British architect Balfours as an abbatoir, the largest in East Asia. With six storeys, no roof, and made entirely of concrete, it has 26 freestanding "air bridges" radiating from a central atrium and connecting kinking walkways. Oddly angled ramps, staircases and struts create the impression of an Escher drawing: the livestock must have sensed something was up long before they saw the knives. Today the complex is home to a clutch of businesses – gyms, cafés and the like – serving the local hipsters.

Duolun Lu

多伦文化名人街, duōlún wénhuà míngrénjiē · Ⓜ Dongbaoxing Lu then a 5min walk, or bus #21 from Sichuan Zhong Lu

Duolun Lu is a heritage street of antique and bric-a-brac shops housed in elegant imitation Qing buildings, and plenty of public statuary. Here you'll find the *Old Film Café* (see p.380), charmingly decorated with film posters, and, at 27 Duolun Lu, the four-storey **Duolun Museum of Modern Art** (多伦现代美术馆, duōlún xiàndài měishùguǎn; Tues–Sun 10am–6pm; ¥10; ☏ 021 65872530, ⓦ duolunmoma.org), which puts on temporary shows of modern Chinese and international artists.

Lu Xun Park

鲁迅公园, lǔxùn gōngyuán · Daily 6am–7pm · Free · Ⓜ Hongkou Football Stadium

Lu Xun Park is one of the best places for observing Shanghainese at their most leisured. Couples frolic on paddle boats in the park lagoon and old men teach their grandkids how to fly kites. The park is also home to the pompous **Tomb of Lu Xun**, complete with a seated statue and an inscription in Mao's calligraphy, which was erected here in 1956 to commemorate the fact that Lu Xun had spent the last ten years of his life in this part of Shanghai. The tomb went against Lu Xun's own wishes to be buried simply in a small grave in a western Shanghai cemetery.

Lu Xun Memorial Hall

鲁迅纪念馆, lǔxùn jìniànguǎn · Daily 9–11am & 1.30–4pm · Free

The novelist is further commemorated in the **Lu Xun Memorial Hall**, also in the park, to the right of the main entrance. Exhibits include period photographs of the city, portraits of Lu Xun and original correspondence, among them letters and photographs from George Bernard Shaw.

Lu Xun's Former Residence

鲁迅故居, lǔxùn gùjū · Shanyin Lu, Lane 132, House 9 · Daily 9am–4pm · ¥8 · ☏ 021 56662608 · Ⓜ Hongkou Football Stadium

A block southeast of Lu Xun Park, **Lu Xun's Former Residence** is worth a look if you are in the area. The sparsely furnished house where Lu Xun and his wife and son lived from 1933 until his death in 1936 offers a fascinating glimpse into typical Japanese housing of the period – a good deal smaller than their European counterparts, but still surprisingly comfortable.

Western Shanghai

Due west from the city centre there is less to see, with a sprinkling of scattered sights too far apart to walk between. In the north, the **Moganshan Arts District** is worth a visit to experience the commercial side of China's modern art movements, while the nearby **Yufo Temple** – along with the **Longhua Temple** in the south – is among Shanghai's most important surviving religious sites. Just west of here, the riverside **West Bund** strip, once dedicated to heavy engineering, has been remodelled as an appealing arts district.

Yufo Temple

玉佛寺, yùfó sì · 170 Anyuan Lu · Daily 8am–5pm · ¥20 · ☏ 021 62663668, ⓦ yufotemple.com · Ⓜ Changshou Lu

Around 2.5km northwest of Renmin Square, the **Yufo Temple** is a more lively complex than the Jing'an Temple. The pretty buildings have flying eaves, complicated brackets and intricate roof and ceiling decorations. It's a busy place of worship, with gusts of incense billowing from the central burner while worshippers kowtow before effigies and tie red ribbons to the branches of trees, decorative bells and the stone lions on the railings.

The star attractions here, though, are the relics. Two **jade Buddhas** were brought here from Myanmar (Burma) in 1882 and the temple was built to house them. The larger, at nearly 2m tall, sits upstairs in a separate building at the back of the temple (follow the signs). You will be expected to join the devotees in paying ¥15 for a bottle of oil that is used to keep the lanterns by the statue burning. Carved from a single block of milky white jade, it is encrusted with agate and emerald. The second statue, in the western hall, is a little smaller, around 1m long. It shows a recumbent Buddha at the point of dying (or rather entering nirvana), with a languid expression like a man dropping off for a nap.

The central **Great Treasure Hall** holds three huge figures of the past, present and future Buddhas, as well as the temple drum and bell. The gods of the twenty heavens, decorated with gold leaf, line the hall like guests at a celestial cocktail party, and a curvaceous copper Guanyin stands at the back.

Moganshan Arts District

莫干山路50号, mògānshānlù wǔshíhào • 50 Moganshan Lu • Most galleries, though not all, are closed Mon • Ⓜ Shanghai Train Station is a 20min walk away; it's best to take a taxi

A kilometre northeast of the Yufo Temple, in a former industrial zone beside Suzhou Creek, the **Moganshan Arts District** (M50) is a complex of studios and galleries. In the early 1990s, attracted by cheap rents, artists began to take over the abandoned warehouse buildings here and use them as studios. Then the art spaces moved in, and now the design studios and cafés and more commercial galleries are arriving. What makes the area interesting is the way it is both shabby and sophisticated, jumbling together paint-spattered artists, slick dealers and pretentious fashionistas, and terrible kitsch with pretty decent work. Most of the smaller **galleries** double as studios and there's something for all tastes, from cutting-edge video installations to chintzy souvenirs (see box below). It's a good place to dip your toe into the thriving Shanghai art scene, but it's not comprehensive – nothing like Beijing's 798 (see p.98).

Entrance is through a gate signed **50 Moganshan Lu** (there's a map on the wall near here). When you've had your fill of art, flop onto a beanbag at the *Undefine* café (see p.380) at the back of the complex.

Xujiahui Catholic Cathedral

圣依纳爵主教座堂, shèngyīnàjué zhǔjiào zuòtáng • 158 Puxi Lu • Mon–Sat services 6.30am, Sun services 8am • Ⓜ Xujiahui

Xujiahui Catholic Cathedral (also called St Ignatius Cathedral) was built in 1910, on the grave of Paul Xu Guangqi, the first Jesuit convert, and was lauded as the finest church in the Far East. Vandalized during the Cultural Revolution, it was then used as a granary, but has now been well restored to its former glory, with some pretty stained-glass windows. The cathedral's library, with 200,000 volumes, as well as the

---

MOGANSHAN'S GALLERIES

There are dozens of galleries in the **Moganshan Arts District**, most of them small concerns selling work that can occasionally be rather derivative. The following are all worth a look.

Art Scene Warehouse 艺术景仓库, yìshùjǐng cāngkù. Building 4, 1F ☎021 62774940, ⓦ artscenewarehouse.com. A representative selection of contemporary paintings, in a minimalist white space. Tues–Sun 10.30am–6.30pm.

Island 6 Art Centre 六岛艺术中心, liùdǎo yìshù zhōngxīn. Building 6, 1F ☎021 62277856, ⓦ island6.org. This nonprofit arts collective prides itself on its technological nous, and puts together varied multimedia and cross-cultural shows. Daily 10am–7pm.

Shun 熏依社画廊, xūn yīshè huàláng. Building 3, 103/208 ☎021 52527198, ⓦ shunartdesign.com. Internationally curated group and solo shows from young Chinese artists. Tues–Sun 10am–5pm.

meteorological centre (built at the same time as the cathedral and now housing the Shanghai Municipal Meteorology Department), survive on the grounds.

Longhua Cemetery of Martyrs

龙华烈士陵园, lónghuá lièshì língyuán • 180 Longhua Xi Lu • Daily 6.30am–4pm • ¥1, exhibition hall ¥5 • Ⓜ Longhua

Southeast of the Xujiahui Cathedral, **Longhua Cemetery of Martyrs** is a park commemorating those who died fighting for the cause of Chinese communism in the decades leading up to the final victory of 1949. In particular, it remembers those workers, activists and students massacred in Shanghai by Chiang Kai-shek in the 1920s – the site of the cemetery is said to have been the main execution ground. In the centre is a glass-windowed, pyramid-shaped **exhibition hall** with a bombastic memorial to 250 Communist martyrs who fought Chiang's forces. With fountains and well-tended lawns, it's a pleasant place for a stroll.

Longhua Temple

龙华寺, lónghuá sì • 2853 Longhua Lu • Daily 5.30am–4pm • ¥10 • ☎ 021 64566085 • Ⓜ Longhua

Just south of the Cemetery of Martyrs is one of Shanghai's main religious sites, the **Longhua Temple**. Though there has been a temple on the site since the Han dynasty, the halls are only around a century old. It's the most active Buddhist site in the city, and a centre for training monks. On the right as you enter is a bell tower: on Chinese New Year, a monk bangs the bell 108 times, supposedly to ease the 108 "mundane worries" of Buddhist thought. You can whack it yourself, any time, for ¥10; three hits is considered auspicious.

The temple's associated tenth-century **pagoda** is an octagonal structure about 40m high (until the feverish construction of bank buildings along the Bund in the 1910s, the pagoda was the tallest edifice in Shanghai), its seven brick storeys embellished with wooden balconies and red-lacquer pillars. After a long period of neglect (Red Guards saw it as a convenient structure to plaster with banners), an ambitious rezoning project has spruced up the pagoda and created the tea gardens, greenery and shop stalls that now huddle around it.

West Bund

西岸, xī'àn

The riverside strip stretching from Lupu Bridge to Longyao Lu, once a site for airline manufacture, has been imaginatively remodelled as the **West Bund**, a leafy, 2km-long promenade and arts district. With a climbing wall, a jogging trail and a skate park, this is one of the few public places in Shanghai where you can find open space and some quiet, with plenty of spots to sit and watch tankers glide past on the Huangpu and herons fishing in the shallows.

The strip is book-ended by two contemporary galleries, the **Long Museum** to the north and the **Yuz Museum** to the south. There's also the **West Bund Art Centre** towards the southern end at 2555 Longteng Dadao, with the highly rated **ShanghART** gallery next door (ⓦwww.shanghartgallery.com). If you only have time or inclination for one gallery, pick the Long Museum – it's better and cheaper than the others. Note that it's only a ten minute walk upriver from the north end of the West Bund to Lupu Bridge (see opposite).

Long Museum (West Bund)

龙美术馆西岸, lóng měishùguǎn xī'àn • 3398 Longteng Dadao, near Ruining Lu • Tues–Sun 10am–5.30pm, last admission 4.30pm • ¥50 • ☎ 021 64227636, ⓦ thelongmuseum.org • Ⓜ Longhu Zhong Lu, then a 10min walk

Rather more successful than its older sister in Pudong (see p.369), the **Long Museum (West Bund)**, a pristine, concrete space with a repeated arch motif, designed by local firm Atelier

Deshaus, is one of the most striking museums in Asia. This riverside site was once used to unload coal, and the museum has been built around the old coal hopper – a massive udderlike hulk – and an angular unloader; stripped of function, they look as sculpturally distinctive as anything inside. With no permanent collection, it has three storeys displaying contemporary art, a basement for shows of older art, and a pleasant **café**.

Yuz Museum

余德耀美术馆, yú dé yào měishùguǎn • 35 Fenggu Lu, near Longteng Dadao • Prices vary; around ¥100 • ☎ 021 62105207, ⓦ www.yuzmshanghai.org • Ⓜ Yunjin Lu, then a 10min walk

The **Yuz Museum** is another huge private gallery designed to show off a billionaire's collection. The building, an old aircraft hanger remodelled by Japanese architect Sou Fujimoto, is truly vast, and the shows that work best are similarly grandiose – such as the entwined airplanes of Adel Abdessemed, displayed here in 2016.

Lupu Bridge

卢浦大桥, lúpǔdàqiáo • 909 Luban Lu • Viewing platform daily 9am–4pm (closed during high winds) • ¥80 • Ⓜ Luban Lu

Just past the far northern end of the West Bund riverside area you'll find massive **Lupu Bridge**, the world's second-longest steel-arch bridge. Head to the west side and you can buy a ticket to climb up to the open-air viewing platform at the apex of the bridge's arch, about 100m above the river. There are more than three hundred steps, so it's bracing exercise, and when you're at the top it's a great place to watch the passing boats.

Botanical Gardens

上海植物园, shànghǎi zhíwùyuán • 111 Longwu Lu • Daily 7am–4pm • ¥40 • ☎ 021 54363369, ⓦ shbg.org • Ⓜ Shilong Lu then a 20min walk; or bus #56 south down Longwu Lu

More than nine thousand plants are on show in these large and rather sprawling **Botanical Gardens**, including two pomegranate trees that are said to date from the reign of Emperor Qianlong in the eighteenth century; despite their antiquity, they still bear fruit. Look out, too, for the orchid chamber, where more than a hundred different varieties are on show, and the bonsai garden.

ARRIVAL AND DEPARTURE	**SHANGHAI**

Shanghai enjoys the best infrastructure on the mainland. All main arrival points are integrated with the metro system.

BY PLANE

PUDONG INTERNATIONAL AIRPORT

Pudong International Airport (浦东国际机场, pǔdōng guójì jīchǎng; PVG; ☎ 021 68341000, ⓦ shairport.com), 40km east of the city near the mouth of the Yangzi River, handles most international flights. There are two terminals, with a third due to open in 2019.

Destinations Beijing (2hr 20min); Chengdu (3hr 30min); Chongqing (3hr); Harbin (3hr); Hong Kong (2hr 45min); Kunming (3hr 30min); Nanning (3hr 15min); Shenzhen (2hr 45min); Ürümqi (5hr 25min); Wuhan (2hr 25min); Xi'an (2hr 45min).

By Maglev train (磁悬浮列车, cíxuánfú lièchē; daily 7am–9pm; every 20min; ¥50 one-way, ¥80 return). The train, suspended above the track and propelled by magnetism, whizzes from the airport to Longyang Lu metro station – which is a long way from the centre of town, in the eastern suburbs – in 8min, at 300km/hr.

By metro Pudong airport is on metro line #2, which will take you to the centre in around 90min (¥7). You have to change train at Guanglan Lu, where there will be a wait of up to 20min.

By airport bus Follow the signs to the stops. There are eight routes (around 90min; ¥20–30), with departures every 15min until the last plane lands. Bus #2 is generally the most useful as it goes to the Jing'an Temple metro station in the centre. Bus #1 goes to Hongqiao airport; bus #3 to Xujiahui; #4 to Hongkou Football Stadium, in the north; #5 to Shanghai Railway Station; #6 to Zhonghsan Park; and #7 to Shanghai South Railway Station, in the southern suburbs. The only bus that drops off in Pudong is #5 (Dongfang Hospital).

By taxi A taxi to Pudong or the Bund should cost around ¥180, to Nanjing Xi Lu around ¥150. Avoid touts and head for the rank.

6

HONGQIAO AIRPORT

Hongqiao airport (虹桥机场, hóngqiáo jīchǎng; SHA; ☎ 021 62688899, ⊛ en.shairport.com/hongqiaoair), 15km west of the city, handles domestic flights. It's well integrated with Hongqiao high-speed railway station (see opposite) and the metro.

Destinations Beijing (2hr 15min); Chengdu (3hr 25min); Chongqing (3hr); Guangzhou (2hr 30min); Harbin (3hr); Hong Kong (2hr 40min); Shenzhen (2hr 35min); Ürümqi (5hr 30min); Wuhan (2hr 5min); Xi'an (2hr 40min).

By bus Buses leave from the parking lot: bus #1 goes to Pudong airport; the airport shuttle goes to Jing'an Temple metro station in the city centre; bus #925 goes to Renmin Square; and #941 goes to the Shanghai Railway Station. Journeys can take up to an hour depending on traffic.

By metro Lines #2 or #10 will get you into the centre of town in less than an hour.

By taxi A taxi to Nanjing Xi Lu costs about ¥50, and to the Bund about ¥60. At busy times, such as Fri nights, you can wait more than an hour at the rank – walk to departures and pick up one that's just dropped someone off, or catch a bus for a couple of stops and then hail one from there.

BY TRAIN

There are handy booking offices (all open daily 8am–5pm) at 77 Wanhangdu Lu (near Jing'an Temple); 2 Jinling Dong Lu; 627 Nanjing Xi Lu; 124 Guizhou Lu; 296 Taixing Lu, close to Beijing Xi Lu; and, in Pudong, 10721 Zhangyang Lu.

Shanghai Railway Station (上海火车站, shànghǎi huǒchēzhàn). North of Suzhou Creek, this station offers services to most Chinese cities, with some high-speed trains. It's not well served by buses but is convenient for the metro; it's on lines #1, #3 and #4. Tickets are sold on the western side of the central plaza.

CRH destinations Changzhou (every 30min; 1hr); Nanjing (every 20min; 2hr); Suzhou (every 20min; 30min); Wuxi (every 20min; 40min); Xi'an (1 daily; 11hr); Zhengzhou (1 daily; 8hr); Zhenjiang (every 30min; 1hr 30min).

Other destinations Beijing (2 daily; 12–15hr); Changzhou (hourly; 2hr); Chengdu (3 daily; 27–42hr); Guangzhou (2 daily; 16hr); Harbin (1 daily; 24hr); Hefei (13 daily; 3hr); Hong Kong (every other day; 19hr); Huangshan (2 daily; 11hr); Lanzhou (7 daily; 24hr); Nanjing (frequent; 4hr); Shenyang (3 daily; 19–29hr); Suzhou (frequent; 1hr); Ürümqi (2 daily; 43hr); Wuxi (frequent; 1hr 30min); Xi'an (10 daily; 15–21hr); Zhengzhou (frequent; 10–15hr); Zhenjiang (frequent; 2hr).

Hongqiao station (上海虹桥站, shànghǎi hóngqiáo zhàn). Shanghai's new high-speed terminus – all D- and G-class fast trains – is taking more and more train traffic. It's beside the domestic airport, on metro lines #2 and #10.

CRH destinations Beijing (every 30min; 5hr); Changzhou (every 15min; 1hr); Chengdu (3 daily; 15hr); Guangzhou (7 daily; 7–12hr); Hangzhou (every 20min; 1hr); Harbin (1 daily; 12hr); Hefei (every 40min; 2hr–3hr 30min); Huangshan (1 daily; 5hr); Nanjing (every 15min; 1hr 20min); Shenyang (6 daily; 10hr); Suzhou (every 10min; 30min); Wuxi (every 20min; 1hr); Xi'an (9 daily; 7hr); Zhengzhou (every 30min; 5hr); Zhenjiang (every 30min; 1–2hr).

Shanghai South station (上海南站, shànghǎi nánzhàn). For cities south of Shanghai; it's on metro lines #1 and #3. No high-speed trains.

Destinations Changsha (3 daily; 10–16hr); Chongqing (2 daily; 20–28hr); Fuzhou (1 daily; 15hr); Guilin (4 daily; 20hr); Hangzhou (frequent; 2–3hr); Kunming (3 daily; 40hr); Nanchang (5 daily; 10hr); Nanning (3 daily; 28hr); Ningbo (frequent; 3hr).

BY BUS

For a few destinations, for example Suzhou (see p.318) and Hangzhou (see p.326), buses might offer a convenient way to leave the city: they're slightly cheaper than trains, and it's easy to get a seat.

Shanghai South bus station (上海南站, shànghǎi nán zhàn; 666 Shiliong Lu; ☎ 021 54362835) is, despite the huge crowds, comparatively easy to reach and get around. It's underneath Shanghai South train station, on metro lines #1 and #3.

Destinations Hangzhou (every 30min; 2hr); Nanjing (4 daily; 4hr); Suzhou (every 20min; 1hr 30min); Wuzhen (5 daily; 2hr); Xitang (6 daily; 1hr 30min); Zhouzhuang (hourly; 1hr).

Shanghai long-distance bus station (上海长途客运总站, shànghǎi chángtú kèyùn zǒngzhàn, 1662 Zhongxing Lu ☎ 021 56720594). This huge old station, the city's biggest, is behind Shanghai Railway Station; it's a long and circuitous walk from the metro station.

Destinations Hangzhou (frequent; 2hr); Nanjing (2 daily; 4hr); Suzhou (frequent; 1hr 30min).

Pudong bus station Some long-distance buses leave from the international airport, opposite exit 18; tickets cost around ¥80–100.

Destinations Hangzhou (hourly; 2hr); Nanjing (hourly; 4hr); Suzhou (hourly; 2hr).

GETTING AROUND

By metro The Shanghai metro (上海地铁, shànghǎi dìtiě; daily 5.30am–11pm) has fourteen lines, but not all are particularly useful for visitors. Line #1 runs north–south, with handy stations at Shanghai Railway Station, People's Square, Changshu Lu (for the former French Concession), Xujiahui and Shanghai Stadium. Line #2 runs east–west with stations at Jing'an Temple, Henan Lu and, in Pudong, Lujiazui and the Science and Technology Museum. The lines intersect at the enormous People's Square station (take careful note of the wall maps here for which exit to use). Line #8 is north–south, with useful stations at Hongkou Football Stadium, Qufu Lu and Laoximen (for the Old City); line #10 is useful,

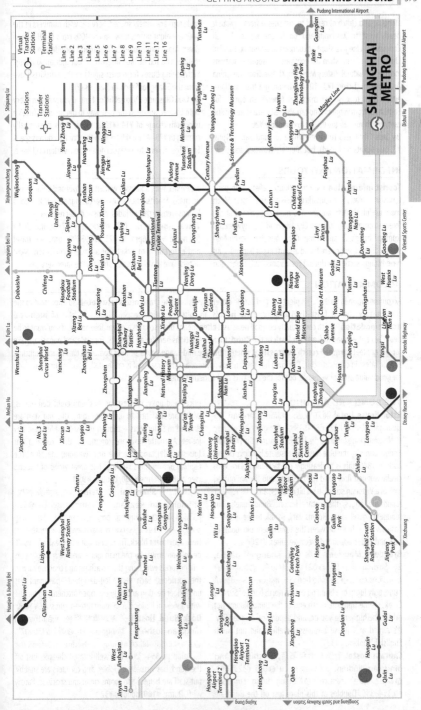

6

stopping at a clutch of central tourist sites – from Yuyuan it heads west to Xintiandi and on to the former French Concession. Line #12 stops at Longhua and Shaanxi Nan Lu. Line #13 is useful when it's going north–south – stations include the Natural History Museum, Xintiandi and the China Art Museum. Tickets (¥3–10) can be bought from stations, either from touchscreen machines (there's an option for English) or from vendors who can also sell you a stored-value card, which you can top up, for a refundable ¥20.

By bus City buses run everywhere (around 5am–11pm; ¥2; buy tickets on board), but they are crowded and slow,

and stops are widely spaced. Services with numbers in the 300s are night buses; those in the 400s cross the Huangpu River. Most large fold-out city maps include the routes, usually as a red or blue line with a dot indicating a stop. Sightseeing buses for tourist sights in the outskirts leave from the Shanghai Stadium (see p.387).

By taxi Cabs are easy to get hold of and, if you're not on a very tight budget, are often the best way to get around. There's a minimum charge of ¥14 (¥18 at night), with fares usually coming to ¥20–40 for rides within the city. Few drivers speak English, so it helps to have your destination written in Chinese.

INFORMATION AND TOURS

Tourist information You can pick up leaflets, with basic tourist information, at upmarket hotels and the airport. Much more useful, though, are the free magazines aimed at the foreign community, such as *City Weekend* (w cityweekend .com.cn/shanghai) and *Time Out Shanghai* (w timeout shanghai.com), which are found at most expat hangouts. All have listings sections including restaurants, club nights and

art events, with addresses written in *pinyin* and Chinese, but no maps. Smartshanghai (w smartshanghai.com) is a good listings website that includes maps and user reviews.

Travel agents The CITS office at 1277 Beijing Xi Lu (Mon–Fri 9am–6pm; ☎ 021 62898899) provides travel and entertainment tickets for a small commission. Most hotels have travel agencies offering the same services.

ACCOMMODATION

Accommodation in Shanghai is plentiful, and can be extremely stylish. The grand **old-world hotels** so important to the city's history cost at least US$150/night; **new hotels** are often a little cheaper. There is a glut of **high-end accommodation**, which can actually be good news as it often means big discounts are available online. If you want to be near the centre, head to **Renmin Park** or the **Bund**; there are options here for all budgets. For style and panache, make for the genteel **former French Concession**, where attractive mid-range hotels sit near upmarket dining and nightlife. For the latest in corporate chic, **Pudong** has the fanciest options, but the area itself is rather dull. If you're simply looking for good value and convenience, opt for the outskirts near a metro station.

THE BUND AND AROUND

Astor House Hotel 浦江饭店, pǔjiāng fàndiàn. 15 Huangpu Lu ☎ 021 63246388, w pujianghotel.com; m Nanjing Dong Lu; map pp.354–355. Across the Waibaidu Bridge, opposite the blue Russian Consulate building. Dating back to 1846, this is a pleasingly old-fashioned place with creaky wooden floors and high ceilings, and the antiquated look of a Victorian school. It's a bit cheaper, and a bit rougher round the edges, than other historic Bund hotels, but represents good value. Rooms vary, so ask to see a few – basically it's a choice between the atmospheric old rooms or new and better-appointed executive suites. **¥1200**

Broadway Mansions 上海大厦, shànghǎi dàshà. 20 Suzhou Bei Lu ☎ 021 63246260, w broadway mansions.com; m Nanjing Dong Lu; map pp.354–355. A huge, ugly lump of a building on the north bank of Suzhou Creek, visible from the north end of the Bund. Rooms get pricier the higher up you go, and depending on the view. It's aimed at Chinese business travellers and not much English is spoken. **¥1337**

Captain Hostel 老船长青年酒店, lǎochuánzhǎng qīngnián jiǔdiàn. 37 Fuzhou Lu ☎ 021 63235053, w captainhostel.com.cn; m Nanjing Dong Lu; map pp.354–355. Doubles at this place just off the Bund are

pricey and poky; it's best for its cheap eight-bed dorms, which are designed to look like cabins. Oh, and staff are dressed in sailor suits – though it hasn't made them any jollier. All bathrooms are communal. Bike rental ¥2/hr (guests only), and free use of a washing machine. The *Captain Bar* on the sixth floor has great views of Pudong (see p.384). Dorms **¥100**, doubles **¥950**

★**CHAI Shanghai Living** 上海灿客栈, shànghǎicàn kèzhàn. 400 Suzhou Bei Lu ☎ 021 63561812, w chailiving.com; m Tiantong Lu; map pp.354–355. Luxury serviced apartments in a genteel Art Deco apartment block. There's no lobby to speak of – you'll be met on arrival by the manager – and your neighbours will be locals who hang their washing and practise *tai ji* in the corridors. Each very well-designed apartment has underfloor heating and fully equipped kitchens; go for one with a view of Pudong. Minimum three-night stay. **¥1650**

Dock Bund Hostel 外滩源青年旅舍, wàitānyuán qīngnián lǚshè. 55 Xianggang Lu ☎ 021 53500077, w www.bmhotel.com/en/gyls-dock.html; m Tiantong Lu; map pp.354–355. This well-located cheapie, just off the Bund, has virtually no lobby, and corridors are shabby, but staff are helpful and rooms clean and spacious. Patchy wi-fi. Dorms **¥100**, doubles **¥320**

★Fairmont Peace Hotel 和平饭店, hépíng fàndiàn. 20 Nanjing Dong Lu, by the Bund ☎021 63216888, ⓦfairmont.com/peacehotel; ⓜNanjing Dong Lu; map pp.354–355. Occupying both sides of the road, this was formerly the Cathay, the most famous hotel in Shanghai, with a long list of illustrious former guests including Charlie Chaplin and Noël Coward. It's still well worth a visit to admire the Art Deco interior (see p.353) and visit the *Jazz Bar*. A low-rise extension at the rear contains modern luxuries such as a spa and sky-lit swimming pool. **¥2730**

Indigo 外滩英迪格酒店, wàitān yīngdígé jiǔdiàn. 585 Zhongshan Dong Er Lu ☎021 33029999, ⓦshanghai.hotelindigo.com; ⓜYuyuan Garden; map pp.354–355. This funky luxury hotel, at the far south end of the Bund, is right on the river, so the best rooms have fantastic views. The design stands out, with quirky detailing everywhere – in the lobby a pod for relaxing sits next to a fire-engine-red rickshaw, and in the bathrooms you'll find Japanese-style electric toilets and rubber ducks. Rooms are big and comfortable and the service is attentive. **¥2725**

★Mingtown Hikers Hostel 明堂上海旅行者国际青年旅馆, míngtáng shànghǎi Lǚxíngzhě guójì qīngnián lǚguǎn. 450 Jiangxi Zhong Lu ☎021 63297889; ⓜNanjing Dong Lu; map pp.354–355. Very well located just northwest of the Bund, this cheap and cheerful, friendly hostel offers four- and six-bed dorms and doubles, some of which are en suite (¥320). There's also a lively bar with a pool table. Dorms **¥100**, doubles **¥320**

Mingtown Nanjing Lu 南京路青年旅舍, nánjīng lù qīngnián lǚshè. 258 Tianjin Lu, near Shanxi Nan Lu ☎021 63220939; ⓜNanjing Dong Lu; map pp.354–355. This old apartment building, with brass fittings and tiled and wood floors, has been sympathetically converted; offering eight-bed dorms and en-suite doubles, it's clean, friendly and well located. Ask for a high floor for quiet and the view, a lower one if you don't fancy trudging up and down the steep stairs. Wi-fi is patchy, but the lobby and bar (where it works) are pleasant, so hanging out there is no hardship. There's a kitchen too, and a pool table. Dorms **¥140**, doubles **¥390**

Peninsula 上海半岛酒店, shànghǎi bàndǎo jiǔdiàn. 32 Zhongshan Dong Yi Lu ☎021 23272888, ⓦpeninsula.com/shanghai; ⓜNanjing Dong Lu; map pp.354–355. A sleek incarnation of the exclusive Hong Kong luxury brand. In keeping with the area, it's gone for a traditional, Art Deco look; black marble corridors lead to the white columned lobby, where a quartet plays and the local elite drink afternoon tea. **¥3948**

AROUND RENMIN SQUARE

24K Hotel 24K国际连锁酒店, 24K guójì liánsuǒ jiǔdiàn. 155 Weihai Lu ☎021 51181222, ⓜNanjing Lu, map pp.354–355; 555 Fuzhou Lu ☎021 5150358, ⓜPeople's Square, map pp.354–355; ⓦ24khotels .com. This no-frills business hotel chain scores for chirpy

design and good value. Not much English is spoken. Both branches are on busy roads near Renmin Square, and walkable from the metro. **¥288**

★Jinjiang MetroPolo Hotel Classiq Shanghai People's Square 锦江都城上海青年会经典酒店, jǐnjiāng dūchéng shànghǎi qīngnián huì jīng diǎn jiǔdiàn. 123 Xizang Nan Lu ☎021 63261040; ⓜDashijie; map pp.354–355. Clean, good-value business hotel. Rooms can be small and the Chinese breakfast is so-so, but the location – right on Renmin Square – puts you at the centre of the action. **¥780**

JW Marriott 明天广场JW万怡酒店, míngtiān guǎngchǎng JW wànyí jiǔdiàn. Tomorrow Square, 399 Nanjing Xi Lu ☎021 53594969, ⓦmarriott.com; ⓜPeople's Square; map pp.354–355. Occupying the top floors of Tomorrow Square, one of Shanghai's most uncompromising landmarks (something like an upraised claw), this swanky venue is well located and has magnificent views, making it one of the finest top-end destinations. **¥1640**

★Mingtown Etour Hostel 上海明堂新易途国际青年旅馆, shànghǎi míngtáng xīnyìtú guójì qīngnián lǚguǎn. 55 Jiangyin Lu ☎021 63277766; ⓜPeople's Square; map pp.354–355. The best of the cheapies, being very well located – in the alleyway behind Tomorrow Square, beside Renmin Park – yet quiet and surprisingly affordable. Everything centres on a relaxing courtyard bar with fish pond and pool table. Rooms vary, so ask to see a few – one or two have balconies. All bathrooms are shared between two or three rooms, doubles included. Dorms **¥120**, doubles **¥280**

Radisson Blu Shanghai New World 新世界丽笙大酒店, xīnshìjiè lìshēng dàjiǔdiàn. 88 Nanjing Xi Lu ☎021 63599999, ⓦradisson.com; ⓜPeople's Square; map pp.354–355. A convenient location right at the corner of bustling Nanjing Lu, and, in general, a slick upscale experience. That UFO on the roof is actually a revolving restaurant, though the view is more interesting than the food. **¥1221**

Westin 威斯汀大酒店, wèisītīng dàfàndiàn. 88 Henan Zhong Lu ☎021 63351888, ⓦwestin.com /shanghai; ⓜNanjing Dong Lu; map pp.354–355. Chinese luxury hotels usually try to impress with either a water feature or palm trees in the lobby; the over-the-top *Westin* goes for both, and then, as if that weren't enough to declare its intentions, the building has a crown on top. Rooms aren't so flashy, which is a good thing; ask for one with a view. Good on-site restaurants and spa. **¥1584**

JING'AN

★Cachet 凯世精品酒店, kǎi shì jīng pǐn jiǔ diàn. 931 Nanjing Xi Lu ☎021 33024990, ⓦcachethotels .com; ⓜNanjing Xi Lu; map pp.354–355. Smart, small, friendly and fashionable. Service is good, and rooms are big for this area, though you won't find a pool or much of a gym.

6

Ask to be put on a high floor, as lower rooms can be noisy – it's worth investigating the larger, pricier suites, as they have balconies. Breakfast is in an annexe off the lobby that doesn't feel very private. **¥1866**

★ **Le Tour Traveler's Rest Youth Hostel** 乐途国际青年旅舍, lètú guójì qīngnián lǚshè. Lane 36, 319 Jiaozhou Lu ☎021 62671912, w letourshanghai.com; m Jing'an Temple; map pp.354–355. This huge hostel was once a factory, and though it's been livened up, concrete floors give it an industrial feel. Rooms are small, but this place boasts the most facilities of any hostel in Shanghai; as well as a kitchen, rooftop bar, good wi-fi and bike rental there's a DVD room, a mini-gym and a ping-pong table. In a narrow alley just off busy Bai Lan Lu, a 10min walk north from the metro, it can be hard to find. Look out for the big green building; if you reach Wuding Lu you've gone too far. Dorms **¥120**, doubles **¥390**

Puli 璞丽酒店, púlì jiǔdiàn. 1 Changde Lu ☎021 32039999, w thepuli.com; m Jing'an Temple; map pp.354–355. This attractive new hotel is coolly minimal, with a handsome library and spa. Rooms have wooden floors, grey slate walls and striking if rather impractical sinks. Ask for a view of Jing'an Park. **¥2600**

URBN 雅悦酒店, yǎyuè jiǔdiàn. 183 Jiaozhou Lu ☎021 51534600, w urbnhotels.com; m Jing'an Temple; map pp.354–355. Though it doesn't quite live up to its hype, this hip little hotel is still pretty good value for this price range. The typical Shanghai idea of chic – low lighting and rough grey brick – is leavened with quirky touches, such as porthole-like doors and a wall made of leather suitcases behind reception. Breakfast is not included, and is rather pricey, so pop to the *Wagas* café down the road (see p.380) instead. **¥1600**

THE FORMER FRENCH CONCESSION

★ **Andaz** 新天地安达仕酒店, xīntiāndì āndáshì jiǔdiàn. 88 Songshan Lu ☎021 23101234, w shanghai .andaz.hyatt.com; m Xintiandi; map pp.354–355. This *Hyatt*-run property is, supposedly, "design led": lots of carved wooden screens, statement lighting and quirky art. Plus some fancy touches: loos are Japanese style, with heated seats and bidet attachments, and you can control the lights, a/c and TV from the in-room iPad. It's in a great location, at the edge of the Xintiandi complex, so there are plenty of restaurants on your doorstep. **¥2000**

B'LaVii House 宝丽会馆, bǎolì huìguǎn. 285 Hunan Lu ☎021 64677171; m Huangpi Nan Lu; map pp.350–351. This elegant, well-appointed mansion has rooms arranged around a courtyard, all individually decorated, though a common theme is dark wood furniture and red lacquer. The area is quiet and civilized, and there are plenty of dining options nearby. Booking is essential. **¥1757**

Donghu 东湖宾馆, dōnghú bīnguǎn. 70 Donghu Lu, a block north of Huaihai Zhong Lu ☎021 64158158,

w donghuhotel.com; m Changshu Lu; map pp.354–355. Of the seven buildings that make up the *Donghu*, the villas on the south side are the most interesting, with a chequered past; they served as an opium warehouse and the centre of gangland operations in the 1920s and 1930s. Make sure you get a room in here (Building One), and not the dull new annexe over the road (¥750). The location and the pleasant gardens make this a solid choice. **¥1733**

Fenyang Garden 汾阳花园酒店官方网站, fényáng huāyuán jiǔdiàn guānfāng wǎngzhàn. 45 Fenyang Lu ☎021 54569888, w fenyang gardenhotel.com; m Changhsu Lu; map pp.354–355. This elegant and discreet converted villa is set back from the road in well-maintained grounds. It's grand, featuring a fine clutch of chandeliers, and rooms are spacious and refined, though perhaps the place is not as slick as it could be – there's no business centre, service is only OK, wi-fi is patchy and breakfast is a little too Chinese for most foreign tastes. Still, overall it's a good, civilized option. **¥1107**

Hengshan Moller Villa 衡山马勒别墅饭店, héngshān mǎlèbiéshù fàndiàn. 30 Shaanxi Nan Lu ☎021 62478881, w mollervilla.com; m Shaanxi Nan Lu; map pp.354–355. Describing itself as a boutique heritage hotel, the main building is a gorgeous Scandinavian-Gothic fantasy built in the 1930s. You can stay in the well-appointed rooms here, with their balconies and fireplaces, but they're expensive (¥3250); most rooms are in a three-storey block just behind. Service is a little creaky. **¥1580**

InterContinental Shanghai Ruijin 瑞金宾馆, ruìjīn bīnguǎn. 118 Ruijin Er Lu (main entrance on Fuxing Lu) ☎021 64725222, w ruijinhotelsh.com; m Shaanxi Nan Lu; map pp.354–355. Cosy and exclusive Tudor-style villas in manicured gardens. Service can be lacklustre, but things are certain to improve with the InterContinental group at the helm. Ask for Building One, where Mao used to stay. **¥2400**

Okura Garden 花园饭店, huāyuán fàndiàn. 58 Maoming Nan Lu ☎021 64151111, w gardenhotel shanghai.com; m Shaanxi Nan Lu; map pp.354–355. The grounds are lovely at this Japanese-run mansion, and the lobby, which used to be the Cercle Sportif French Club, has some great Art Deco detailing; the rooms, however, in a giant monolith looming at the back, are nondescript. **¥1224**

Pudi 璞邸精品酒店, púdǐ jīngpǐn jiǔdiàn. 99 Yandang Lu ☎021 51585888, w boutiquehotel.cc; m Huangpi Nan Lu; map pp.354–355. A small boutique hotel, well located next to Fuxing Park, with stylish and unusual touches such as aquariums in the lobby and copper sinks, kitchenettes and big desks in the rooms. Don't bother with the restaurant or the breakfast. **¥1579**

Quintet Bed & Breakfast 五重奏旅店, wǔchóngzòu lǚdiàn. 808 Changle Lu, near Changshu Lu ☎021 62499088, w quintet-shanghai.com; m Changshu Lu; map pp.354–355. This courtyard house has been smartly converted into an exclusive guesthouse, with each room designed around a theme. Staff are knowledgable, and the whole place is non-smoking. Not many business facilities, but ideal for tourists looking for something a little different. Reservations essential. **¥1200**

PUDONG

Eton 裕景大饭店, yùjǐng dàfàndiàn. 69 Dongfang Lu ☎021 38789888, ⓦtheetonhotel.com; Ⓜ Pudong Avenue; map pp.350–351. This luxury Singaporean venue is stylish (think corporate boutique chic) and offers lavish facilities – flatscreen TVs in the bathroom – at cheaper rates than its competitors. Ask for a room with a view of the Huangpu. **¥1820**

Grand Hyatt 上海金茂凯悦大酒店, shànghǎi jīnmào kǎiyuè dàjiǔdiàn. Jinmao Tower, 88 Century Ave ☎021 50491234, ⓦshanghai.hyatt.com; Ⓜ Lujiazui; map pp.350–351. Occupying the top floors of the magnificent Jinmao Tower, this place is undeniably

fantastic – awesome views, great design, lots of lucky numbers (555 rooms, 88 storeys). The *Cloud Nine* bar (see p.384) is on the 87th floor. **¥2064**

★Park Hyatt 柏悦酒店, bóyuè jiǔdiàn. World Financial Centre, 100 Century Ave ☎021 68881234, ⓦshanghai.park.hyatt.com; Ⓜ Lujiazui; map pp.350–351. This ultramodern business hotel, on floor 79 in the World Financial Centre, has stolen the "highest hotel in the world" crown from its sister in the Jinmao Tower. The large rooms have great views, and on-site facilities include an infinity pool and a spa. **¥3215**

Pudong Shangri-La 浦东香格里拉大酒店, pǔdōng xiānggélǐlā dàjiǔdiàn. 33 Fucheng Lu ☎021 68828888, ⓦshangri-la.com/shanghai; Ⓜ Lujiazui; map pp.354–355. One of Pudong's monster hotels, with almost a thousand rooms. Popular with upscale business travellers for comfort, convenience and, of course, the views through the huge windows. **¥3115**

EATING

Food in Shanghai is fantastic; though there is fairly little in the way of street food, most types of **international** and **Chinese** cuisine are widely available and there are plenty of classy restaurants. Compared to, for example, Sichuan or Cantonese, **Shanghai cuisine** – lots of ginger, sugar and Shaoxing wine, but without heavy spicing – is not particularly well known or popular among foreigners. There are some interesting dishes, though, especially if you enjoy exotic **seafood**. Fish and shrimp are considered basic to any respectable meal, and eels and crab may appear as well; in season (Oct–Dec), you may get the chance to try *dazha* crab, the most expensive and, supposedly, the most delicious. Inexpensive **snack food** is easily available at any time of night or day – try *xiao long bao*, a local dumpling speciality.

BREAKFAST, CAFÉS AND FAST FOOD

Global fast-food chains are everywhere; but rather better (and certainly healthier) are Asian chains such as *Yoshinoya*, *KungFu* and *Ajisen* (for noodles and rice dishes). Every mall and shopping centre has a cluster of restaurants and fast-food joints, and often a food court too: try Raffles City Mall on Fuzhou Lu, the Super Brand Mall in Pudong or the flashy new IAPM Mall on Huaihai Zhong Lu. Shanghai also does cafés very well. For a good Western breakfast, head to a *Wagas* or *Element Fresh*. All the cafés listed below have free wi-fi.

Barbarossa 芭芭露莎, bābālùshā. 231 Nanjing Xi Lu, inside Remnin Park ☎021 63180220; Ⓜ People's Square; map pp.354–355. This mellow, onion-domed Arabian fantasy, beautifully situated by the lotus pond in Renmin Park, is a good pit stop. It's also a restaurant, but the food is overpriced. There's a bar upstairs too; happy hour daily 5–8pm. Daily 11am–late.

★Citizen Bar and Café 天台餐厅, tiāntái cāntīng. 222 Jinxian Lu, near Shanxi Nan Lu ☎021 62581620, ⓦcitizenshanghai.com; Ⓜ Shaanxi Nan Lu; map pp.354–355. A great Continental-style café tucked away in a gentrified neighbourhood. It's good for brunch, with a wide choice of bar snacks, and a very civilized venue for a predinner cocktail or a slice of apple pie. Daily 11am–1am.

Costa Coffee 科斯塔咖啡, kēsītā kāfēi. 388 Nanjing Xi Lu and elsewhere ☎021 63346035, ⓦcosta.net.cn /costa-mendian-en/shanghai; Ⓜ People's Square; map pp.354–355. The latest coffee colonizers are from the UK, and they're spreading fast, with eighty branches in Shanghai. It's hard to get excited about, but this branch is handy as there aren't too many cafés in the area. Daily 9am–10pm.

Element Fresh 新元素, xīnyuánsù. Shanghai Centre (east side), 1376 Nanjing Xi Lu ☎021 62798682, Ⓜ Jing'an Temple, map pp.354–355; 4F, K. Wah Centre, 1028 Huaihai Zhong Lu ☎021 54038865, Ⓜ Shaanxi Nan Lu, map pp.354–355; 2F, World Financial Centre, 100 Century Ave ☎021 68774001, Ⓜ Lujiazui, map pp.350–351; 2 Xintiandi North Block, 181 Taicang Lu, Xintiandi ☎021 63260950, Ⓜ Xintiandi, map pp.354–355; ⓦelement fresh.com. These airy, informal bistros are the best places in town for a Western breakfast (¥80 including limitless coffee) – there are plenty of options both hearty and healthy. It's also well liked for its deli-style sandwiches, smoothies and health drinks. The branch at the World Financial Centre is particularly useful, as affordable options are few and far between in Pudong; the Xintiandi branch, called *Element Fresh Vintage*, is more upmarket. Free delivery. Shanghai Centre daily 7am–11pm; K. Wah Centre Mon–Thurs & Sun 8am–11pm, Fri & Sat 8am–midnight; World Financial Centre daily 10am–10pm; Xintiandi daily 8am–2am.

6

6

★**Farine** Ferguson Lane, 378 Wukang Lu ☎021 64335798, ⓦfarine-bakery.com; ⓜShanghai Library; map pp.350–351. Artisanal bread and pastries, all baked on the premises. Excellent coffee too (though pricey at ¥38), and the outside seating is good for watching the smart set. Tues–Sun 7am–8pm.

Kommune 公社酒吧, gōngshè jiǔbā. Building 7, Lane 210, Taikang Lu ☎021 64662416, ⓦkommune .me; ⓜDapuqiao; map pp.350–351. Hip café at the heart of Tianzifang – head north up the easternmost of the north–south alleys, take the first left and it's just there. It's not cheap – nothing round here is – but it's popular thanks to the courtyard seating. Deli sandwiches from ¥38, smoothies from ¥48. Daily 9am–midnight.

Le Café des Stagiaires 54–56 Yongkang Lu, near Xiangyang Lu ☎021 34250210, ⓦcafedesstagiaires .com; ⓜShaanxi Nan Lu; map pp.354–355. This artsy café and bar on buzzing Yongkang Lu has plenty of panache. It's attractively decorated with European memorabilia, and the loos are papered with CVs – the name is French for "intern". As well as coffee, there's a good wine list and simple French food and pizza. Daily 9am–1am.

Old China Hand Reading Room 汉源书屋, hànyuán shūwū. 27 Shaoxing Lu, near Shanxi Nan Lu ☎021 64732526, ⓦhan-yuan.com; ⓜDapuqiao; map pp.354–355. Bookish but not fusty, this is the place to come for leisured reflection. There's a huge collection of tomes to peruse or buy, many printed by the café's own press, which specializes in coffee-table books about French Concession architecture. Afternoon coffee with a scoop of ice cream and biscuits is ¥45. Daily 10am–midnight.

Old Film Café 老电影咖啡吧, lǎo diànyǐng kāfēi bā. 123 Duolun Lu ☎021 56964763; ⓜDongbaoxing Lu; map pp.350–351. If you're in the area, this charming old house full of period detail is great for refreshments, though a coffee will set you back a steep ¥35. They screen black-and-white films upstairs at 7pm nightly. Daily 10am–1am.

Pain Chaud 34 Yongkang Lu ☎021 34250210; ⓜShaanxi Nan Lu; map pp.354–355. Freshly baked breads and pastries at this smart, French-style upmarket bakery, which also does tasty sandwiches (¥60) in crusty bread and excellent baguettes. It's not cheap, but the ¥30 deal for coffee and a croissant makes it a good bet for breakfast if you're staying nearby. Daily 8am–10pm.

The Press Shun Pao Plaza, 309 Hankou Lu ☎021 51690777; ⓜNanjing Dong Lu; map pp.354–355. This smart venue is worth checking out for the building alone – constructed in 1872, the vast, high-ceilinged space has some lovely plasterwork and huge windows. The food is so-so but it's a great coffee-and-cheesecake pitstop, which will set you back ¥60 or so. Daily 10.30am–9pm.

★**Seesaw** 433 Yuyuan Lu, inside the Jing'an Design Centre ☎021 52047828; ⓜJing'an Temple; map pp.350–351. Go through the arch and the hipsterish café is on the right, in the atrium of a renovated house. This may be the best coffee in town – there's a huge range of beans, including some from their own plantation in Yunnan, and they are roasted in house. A good selection of desserts, too. Daily 8.30am–10pm.

Undefine Room 105, Building 6, M50, 50 Moganshan Lu ☎021 62266020, ⓦundefine.com.cn; ⓜJiangning Lu; map pp.350–351. This Moganshan Arts District gem is a warehouse space turned café that displays art. The coffee is excellent (from ¥25), and goes well with the home-made brownies (¥30). Head up the quirky if impractical staircases to find cosy spaces with beanbags and study tables. Daily 10.30am–6pm.

Vienna Café 维也纳咖啡馆, wéiyěnà kāfēiguǎn. 25 Shaoxing Lu, near Ruijin Er Lu ☎021 6445213; ⓜShaanxi Nan Lu; map pp.354–355. Popular and charming Austrian-style French Concession café, almost managing that fin-de-siécle vibe. You can't fault their strudel or *Kaiserschmarrn* – pancake with apple sauce. Daily 8am–9pm.

Wagas 沃歌斯, wògēsī. 7 Donghu Lu, near Xinle Lu ☎021 54661488, ⓜChangshu Lu, map pp.354–355; 277 Huangpi Bei Lu, near Weihai Lu ☎021 53752758, ⓜPeople's Square, map pp.354–355; LGF, 11A, CITIC Square, 1168 Nanjing Xi Lu ☎021 52925228, ⓜJing'an Temple, map pp.354–355; 195 Anfu Lu ☎021 54042733, ⓜChangshu Lu, map pp.354–355; 265 Jiaozhou Lu ☎021 62720353, ⓜJing'an Temple, map pp.354–355; 169 Wujiang Lu ☎021 62670339, ⓜChangshu Lu, map pp.354–355; ⓦwagas.com.cn. Though this bright and breezy New York-style deli brand is relatively new, it's suddenly everywhere. Order the breakfast sandwich before 11am on a weekday and it's half-price – just ¥29. Wraps, sandwiches, pasta dishes and a Thai curry all offer good value at around ¥60. A nice range of juices and smoothies too, though these are comparatively pricey at around ¥40. All branches daily 7.30am–10pm.

RESTAURANTS

Restaurants are more expensive in Shanghai than elsewhere in China, although prices remain reasonable by international standards, and even the most upmarket Western restaurants have affordable lunch specials. Note that the Chinese are early diners, so many Chinese restaurants stop serving at 9pm; expat-oriented places will open much later.

THE BUND, NANJING DONG LU, RENMIN PARK AND AROUND

8½ Otto e Mezzo Bombana Rockbund, 169 Yuanmingyuan Lu, near Beijing Dong Lu ☎021 60872890, ⓦottoemezzobombana.com/shanghai; ⓜNanjing Dong Lu; map pp.354–355. The best of the fine-dining venues in the area. Chef Umberto Bombana has created a menu of northern Italian cuisine: home-made pastas, raviolis and ragout, all wonderfully done. Geat views of the Pearl Tower too. ¥600/person. Daily 4pm–late.

Godly 功德林素食馆, gōngdélín sùshíguǎn. 445 Nanjing Xi Lu ☎021 63270218; ⓜPeople's Square; map pp.354–355. A vegetarian restaurant specializing in fake meat dishes. It's all rather hit-and-miss; try the meatballs, roast duck, crab and ham, but avoid anything meant to taste like fish or pork, and be wary of ordering just vegetables, as they'll turn up too oily. Around ¥80/head. Daily 11am–2pm & 5–10pm.

★**Lost Heaven The Bund** 花马天堂, huāmǎ tiāntáng. 17 Yan'an Dong Lu, near Sichuan Nan Lu ☎021 63300967, ⓦlostheaven.com.cn; ⓜNanjing Dong Lu; map pp.354–355. This expat favourite specializes in the cuisine of Yunnan province. The decor is as seductive and exotic as the food, though the lighting is on the dark side. The chicken with coriander and the lamb ribs are excellent. About ¥250/person; reservations advised. Daily noon–2pm & 5.30–10.30pm.

M on the Bund 米氏西餐厅, mǐshì xīcāntīng. 7F, 5 on the Bund, entrance at Guang Dong Lu ☎021 63509988, ⓦm-restaurantgroup.com/mbund; ⓜNanjing Dong Lu; map pp.354–355. It's worth eating at the oldest of the luxury Bund restaurants if only for the extraordinary view. Chef Hamish Pollitt's menu mixes European and North African dishes, and sticks to the classics; lunch won't break the bank at ¥198 for two courses. There's a civilized afternoon tea at weekends, too (3–5pm; ¥150). Daily 11.30am–2.30pm & 6–10.30pm.

The Stage 威斯汀舞台餐厅, wēisītīng wǔtái cāntīng. Level 1, The Westin Bund Center, 88 Henan Zhong Lu, near Guangdong Lu ☎021 63350577, ⓦwestinshanghai.com/dining-the-stage-buffet-restaurant; ⓜNanjing Dong Lu; map pp.354–355. Upscale all-day buffet, and the "in" place for a Sunday brunch (11.30am–2.30pm) – ¥588 (plus fifteen percent service charge) for as much as you can eat and drink, including champagne and caviar, and acrobats to entertain you. Come hungry and not too hungover. Reservations required. Daily 6am–midnight.

Wang Baohe 王宝和酒家, wángbǎohé jiǔjiā. 603 Fuzhou Lu ☎021 63223673; ⓜNanjing Dong Lu; map pp.354–355. *Wang Baohe*, which has been around for more than two hundred years, bills itself as the "king of crabs and ancestor of wine". Crab set meals start at ¥350/person. It gets very busy in hairy crab season (Nov & Dec). Daily 11am–2pm & 5–9pm.

★**Yuxin Sichuan Dish** 渝信川菜, yúxìn chuāncài. 3F, 333 Chengdu Bei Lu ☎021 52980438; ⓜNanjing Xi Lu; map pp.354–355. This huge no-nonsense dining hall serves probably the best Sichuan food in Shanghai. It's very

popular with families and the white-collar crowd, so reservations are recommended. Go for the *koushui ji* ("mouthwatering chicken") and *shaguo yu* (fish hotpot) and work on developing a face as red as the peppers. It's cheap at ¥100/person. Little English is spoken, but there's a picture menu. Daily 11am–2pm & 5–9.30pm.

YU YUAN AREA AND AROUND

The Yu Yuan area has traditionally been an excellent place for snacks eaten in unpretentious surroundings. Although quality is generally good and prices low, there is a drawback in the long queues that form at peak hours (from 11.30am to 1.30pm in particular). For quick bites, check out the satay, noodle and corn-on-the-cob stands lining the street bordering the western side of Yu Yuan bazaar, and for a fine dining experience, head east to the Cool Docks.

Kebabs on the Grille 克比印度料理, kèbǐ yìndù liàolǐ. Cool Docks, 505 Zhongshan Nan Lu, near Maojiayuan Lu ☎021 61526567, ⓦkebabsonthegrille.com; ⓜXiaonanmen; map pp.350–351. One of the few places in Shanghai where you can get a good curry; the view of the Cool Docks plaza is a bonus. Try the Kashmiri chicken and garlic *naan* and leave room for the eponymous meaty skewers. There's an all-you-can-eat Sun brunch (¥150). Daily 11am–10.30pm.

Lubolang 绿波廊, lǜbōláng. 115–131 Yuyuan Lu ☎021 63280602; ⓜYuyuan Garden; map pp.354–355. Cantonese-style *dim sum* and Shanghai dishes. A good place for dumplings and noodles, though don't neglect classic local staples such as crab meat and cabbage. Daily 11am–2pm & 5–8.30pm.

Nanxiang 南翔馒头店, nánxiáng mántóudiàn. 85 Yuyuan Lu ☎021 63554206; ⓜYuyuan Garden; map pp.354–355. A famous dumpling place that's on the "must-do" list for Chinese tourists. The ground floor is for proles; the higher you go, the fancier it becomes, and the pricier the dumplings – though the staff don't get any less surly. Most customers are here for takeaway – eat in and there's a minimum spend of ¥60/person which will get you a decent selection of dumplings, whichever floor you pick. Daily 7.30am–9pm.

★**Table Number One** Waterhouse hotel, Cool Docks, 1–3 Maojiayuan Lu, near Zhongshan Nan Lu ☎021 60802918, ⓦtableno-1.com; ⓜXiaonanmen; map pp.350–351. Fine dining in a casual atmosphere from London chef Jason Atherton. The dining hall is simple to the point of being plain, but the food is lavishly presented on breadboards, in pots and the like. There are lots of small, tapas-like seafood dishes to share – the white crab with avocado sorbet (¥58) is especially good – while the suckling pork with apricot mustard is a solid main (¥258). Expect to pay about ¥400/person, which is good value: comparable Bund restaurants cost a lot more. Daily noon–10.30pm.

6

6

THE FORMER FRENCH CONCESSION AND WESTERN SHANGHAI

Most expats eat in the fomer French Concession, where prices approach international levels. The compensation, for travellers tired of Chinese food, is that the area brims with global cuisine: menus are bilingual, English is spoken and lots of thought goes into ambience.

1221 一二二一酒家, yī èr èr yī jiǔjiā. 1221 Yan'an Xi Lu, by Pan Yu Lu ☎021 62136585; ⓜYan'an Xi Lu; map pp.350–351. A little out of the way, a 10min walk east of the metro (though bus #71 stops right outside), this is foreigner-friendly Shanghai cuisine; it's a good place to sample local staples such as drunken chicken, fragrant crispy duck and lion's head meatballs. The teaboys' long-spouted teapots, and the deftness with which they are wielded, will give you something to talk about. Daily 11.30am–11pm.

Bi Feng Tang 避风塘, bìfēngtáng. 175 Changle Lu ☎021 64670628, ⓦbifengtang.com.cn; ⓜChangshu Lu; map pp.354–355. This cheap and tasty Cantonese fast-food chain diner makes a great final stop on a night out (though beware the merciless lighting). There's a picture menu, and you can't go too wrong with their *dim sum* and dumpling options. Finish off with custard tarts. Mon–Fri 10am–5am, Sat & Sun 8am–5am.

Charmant 小城故事, xiǎochéng gùshì. 1414 Huaihai Zhong Lu ☎021 64318107; ⓜChangshu Lu; map pp.354–355. Great Taiwanese place – convenient, cheap, as much a café as a restaurant – that's a handy stop after a night of drinking in the former French Concession. Go for Taiwanese-style pork and tofu dishes, and finish with a peanut butter smoothie. Daily 11.30am–2am.

★**Crystal Jade** 翡翠酒家, fěicuì jiǔjiā. Unit 12A-B, 2F, Building 7, Xintiandi South Block ☎021 63858752; ⓜXintiandi; map pp.354–355. Great Hong Kong food, sophisticated looks and down-to-earth prices make this *the* place to eat in Xintiandi, and one of the best places in town for *dim sum*. Try the barbecued pork – and leave room for mango pudding. Cheaper than it looks, at around ¥120/head. Daily 11am–3pm & 5–11.30pm.

Cuivre 1502 Huaihai Zhong Lu ☎021 64374219, ⓦcuivre.cn; ⓜChangshu Lu; map pp.350–351. This glamorous, upscale French restaurant is a great place for a date. It's hip – menus are on iPads – but not pretentious; the food is reliably good and there's an extensive wine list. The lobster risotto is recommended. Around ¥350/person, or ¥198 for three courses during their popular Sun brunch. Reservations essential. Wed–Fri 6–10.30pm, Sat & Sun noon–2pm & 6–10.30pm.

★**Din Tai Fung** 鼎泰丰, dǐngtàifēng. 11A, 2F, Building 6, Xintiandi South Block, 123 Xingye Lu ☎021 63858378, ⓜXintiandi, map pp.354–355; Shanghai Center, 1F, 1376 Nanjing Xi Lu, near Xikang Lu ☎021 62899182, ⓜJing'an Temple, map pp.354–355; 3F, Super Brand Mall, 168 Lujiazui Xi Lu ☎021 50478883,

ⓜLujiazui, map pp.354–355; 3F, IAPM Mall, 999 Huaihai Zhong Lu ☎021 54668191, ⓜShaanxi Nan Lu, map pp.354–355; ⓦdintaifung.com.tw. The winning formula at this Taiwanese chain is to offer Shanghai street food in upscale surroundings, with chefs behind a glass wall. The pork dumplings are excellent, but don't neglect the other varieties, particularly shrimp and crab roe. Eating here is a lot more expensive than eating in the street, of course, at around ¥100/person. All branches daily 11am–3pm & 5–11pm.

elEFANTE 20 Donghu Lu ☎021 54048085, ⓦel-efante .com; ⓜChangshu Lu; map pp.354–355. Upmarket venue offering Mediterranean food from chef Willy Trullas; the long menu includes good tapas and seafood dishes. When it's sunny, ask for a table on the patio. ¥400/person. Tues–Sun 11am–3pm & 6–10.30pm.

Fu 1039 福 1039, fú yīlíngsānjiǔ. 1039 Yu Yuan Lu, near Jiangsu Lu ☎021 52371878; ⓜJiangsu Lu; map pp.350–351. The best place in Shanghai for Chinese-style fine dining: great Shanghai food in an elegant colonial villa. Indulge in local classics such as smoked Mandarin fish and red-glazed pork and enjoy the view of the garden. Staff don't speak much English but there's a picture menu. Expect to pay around ¥400/person. Note that finding the entrance is tricky; it's down a narrow, unmarked alley off the main road. Daily 11am–2pm & 5–11pm.

★**Guyi Hunan** 古意湘味浓, gǔyì xiāngwèinóng. 89 Fumin Lu, near Julu Lu ☎021 62495628, ⓜChangshu Lu, map pp.354–355; IAPM Mall, 999 Huaihai Zhong Lu ☎021 54668537, ⓜShaanxi Nan Lu, map pp.354–355. These lively, popular places are the best in the city to sample Hunan cuisine – known for being hot and spicy and for its liberal use of garlic, shallots and smoked meat. Go for the chilli-sprinkled spareribs, fish with beans and scallions, the tangerine-jpeel beef – which tastes better than you might expect – or the chef's speciality, open-face fish. About ¥140/head. Both branches daily 11am–2pm & 5.30–10.30pm.

Hot Pot King 来福楼, láifúlóu. 2F, 146 Huaihai Zhong Lu, by Fuxing Xi Lu ☎021 64736380; ⓜChangshu Lu; map pp.354–355. English menus and understanding staff make this an accessible place to sample a local favourite. Order lamb, glass noodles, mushrooms and tofu (at the least) and chuck them into the simmering stock. Perfect for winter evenings. ¥90/person. Daily 11am–4am.

Shen Yue Xuan 申粤轩饭店, shēnyuèxuān fàn diàn. 849 Huashan Lu ☎021 62511166; ⓜShanghai Library; map pp.350–351. The best Cantonese place in Shanghai, with scrumptious *dim sum* at lunchtime and pleasant, if cavernous, decor. In warm weather, you can dine alfresco in the garden, a rarity for a Cantonese restaurant. Dinner for two is around ¥120/head. Daily 11am–11pm.

Shintori 新都里无二店, xīndūlǐ wú'érdiàn. 803 Julu Lu, three blocks south of Hengshan Lu ☎021 54045252;

6

Changshu Lu; map pp.354–355. Push open an unmarked door, then head down the bamboo-lined path – ideally with someone you want to impress. Entertaining presentation (such as plates made of ice) will give you something to talk about, though you'd better order a lot or you'll be bitching about the small portions. Finish with green tea tiramisu (¥60). Around ¥700/person. Mon–Fri 5.30–10.30pm, Sat & Sun 11.30am–10.30pm.

Sushi'O 155 Yanping Lu ✆ 021 62362619, ✉ sushi-o.cn; Ⓜ Changping Lu; map pp.350–351. This casual venue specializes in California-style sushi rolls, with a few rice and *tonkatsu* dishes. They also offer free delivery, and a happy hour on drinks daily 5–8pm. Daily 11am–10pm.

Thai Gallery 189 Huashan Lu, inside Jing'an Park, near Yan'an Zhong Lu ✆ 021 62179717, ✉ thaigallery.cn; Ⓜ Jing'an Temple; map pp.354–355. A popular Thai restaurant; the food is just OK, but the park location makes for a lovely ambience on a sunny day. Lots of outdoor seating. Daily 11.30am–2.30pm & 5.30–11.30pm.

★**Xiao Shaoxing** 小绍兴饭店, xiǎoshàoxīng fàndiàn. 118 Yunnan Nan Lu (east side), immediately north of Jinling Dong Lu ✆ 021 68662270; Ⓜ Dashijie; map pp.354–355. This big, bright restaurant won't win any prizes for its looks, but it's famous in Shanghai for its *bai qie ji* (chicken simmered in wine). Adventurous diners might also sample the blood soup or chicken feet. It has three storeys: prices and comfort rise the higher you go. No English menu. Daily 11am–2pm & 5–8.30pm.

Xinjishi (Jesse Restaurant) 新吉士餐厅, xīnjíshì cāntīng. 41 Tianping Lu ✆ 021 62829260, ✉ www .xinjishi.com; Ⓜ Jiaotong university; map pp.350–351. The decor is a bit tatty at the tiny, original branch of this restaurant chain, but there's nothing wrong with the tasty home-style cooking, with dishes from all over the country. Go for the red-cooked pork, braised fish head and other local faves. The other branches look better, but the food is not as good. Book ahead. Daily 11am–4pm & 5.30pm–midnight.

Ye Shanghai 夜上海, yè shànghǎi. House 6,

Xintiandi North Block, 338 Huangpi Nan Lu ✆ 021 63112323, ✉ elite-concepts.com/yes; Ⓜ Xintiandi; map pp.354–355. Shanghai cuisine in a quiet and classy venue with a European ambience. A good introduction to local tastes – particularly recommended are the drunken chicken, prawns with chilli sauce and the many crab dishes. Around ¥200/person. Daily 11.30am–2.30pm & 6.30–10pm.

PUDONG

Jade on 36 翡翠36餐厅, feīcuì sānshíliù cāntīng. 36F, Tower 2, Pudong Shangri-La, 33 Fucheng Lu ✆ 021 68828888, ✉ jadeon36.com; Ⓜ Lujiazui; map pp.354–355. A fashionable fine-dining experience with a diverse menu of quirky fusion dishes, such as foie gras lollipops or salmon poached in lemongrass. Expect to pay at least ¥600/head; the lavish Sunday brunch, including free-flowing champagne, is a reasonable ¥758. Views are sublime, and the attached bar is very swish. Mon–Sat 6–10.30pm, Sun 11.30am–2pm.

Sproutworks Basement 2, Super Brand Mall, 168 Lujiazui Xi Lu ✆ 021 68905966, ✉ sproutworks.com.cn; Ⓜ Lujiazui; map pp.354–355. This casual health-food restaurant features flavourful and healthy salads and sides. ¥45 gets you four portions: favourites include cranberries and breadcrumbs, kale with almonds and spicy butternut squash. Panini, soups and desserts are also available, and there are plenty of smoothies, too. Daily 10am–10pm.

Yi Café 一 咖啡, yī kāfēi. 2F, Tower 2, Pudong Shangri-La, 33 Fucheng Lu ✆ 021 68828888, ✉ shangri-la.com/shanghai/pudongshangrila/dining /restaurants/yi-cafe; Ⓜ Lujiazui; map pp.354–355. Ten open kitchens offer an enormous range of international cuisines at this all-day buffet. It's appealingly theatrical: servers whizz around on rollerblades and the dessert trolley is manned by a clown. Weekday lunch is ¥238, the very popular weekend brunch is ¥298, and dinner is ¥308 (all plus fifteen percent service charge). Daily 6am–10.30am & 11am–11pm.

DRINKING

Bars are found mostly in the **former French Concession** area. Nearly all serve food, and some have room for dancing. The full range of drinks is available, though beer is usually bottled rather than draught and prices are high; reckon on at least ¥30/drink in most places. Note that the *Café de Stagiaires* (see p.380), *Barbarossa* (see p.379) and *Citizen* (see p.379) cafés become decent bars after dark.

★**The Apartment** 47 Yongfu Lu, near Fuxing Xi Lu ✆ 021 4379478, ✉ theapartment-shanghai.com; Ⓜ Shanghai Library; map pp.354–355. A New York-style loft bar that's become an expat favourite. There's a big bare-brick bar area, a quieter dining room, and an airy patio upstairs. On weekend nights there's a ¥100 cover, which gets you two free drinks. Mon–Thurs & Sun 11am–2am, Fri & Sat 11am–4am.

Bar Rouge 7F, No. 18 The Bund, Zhongshan Dong Yi Lu ✆ 021 63391199, ✉ bar-rouge-shanghai.com; Ⓜ Nanjing Dong Lu; map pp.354–355. One of the oldest Bund bars, and the best known. Staff are snobbish, clientele are pretentious, but the terrace has unrivalled views over the Bund. There's a ¥100 cover at the weekend – and you won't get much change from a red bill for a drink, either. Happy hour daily 6–9pm; on Thurs women

6

get free cocktails and a complimentary manicure from 9.30 to 11.30pm. Dress up. Daily 6pm–3am.

Boxing Cat 拳击猫, quánjī māo. 82 Fuxing Lu ☏021 64312091, ⏅boxingcatbrewery.com; ⓜChangshu Lu; map pp.350–351. American pub grub and excellent beers from the on-site microbrewery, with barbecues on the patio in summer. Mon–Fri 5pm–2am, Sat & Sun 11am–3am.

Captain Bar 船长酒吧, chuánzhǎng jiǔbā. 6F, Captain Hostel, 37 Fuzhou Lu, by Sichuan Zhong Lu ☏021 63235053, ⏅captainhostel.com.cn; ⓜNanjing Dong Lu; map pp.354–355. This relaxed venue scores for its terrace with a great view of Pudong. It sits atop a backpacker hotel (see p.376) and is accessible from the grotty lift. Most hotel guests are put off by the prices – draught beer ¥50 – though that's still cheaper than anywhere else in the area. Happy hour daily till 8pm. Daily 5pm–late.

Cloud Nine 九重天酒吧, jiǔchóngtiān jiǔbā. 87F, Grand Hyatt, Jinmao Tower, 88 Century Ave ☏021 50491234, ⏅shanghai.grand.hyatt.com/en/hotel/dining /Cloud9.html; ⓜLujiazui; map pp.350–351. Inside, it's all rather dark and metallic, but the view is great. Pick a cloudless day, and arrive soon after opening time to bag one of the coveted windowside tables facing Puxi. ¥120 minimum spend/person, which gets you one cocktail. Mon–Fri 5pm–1am, Sat & Sun 2pm–1am.

Long Bar Waldorf Astoria, 2 Zhongshan Dong Yi Lu, near Guangdong Lu ☏021 63229988, ⏅waldorfastoriashanghai.com/english/dine_in_style /Long_Bar; ⓜNanjing Dong Lu; map pp.354–355. A sophisticated and upmarket lounge with an Art Deco look and a very long bar – modelled on the original that once graced this address (see p.357). The drinks menu is also huge, with some great whiskies, and there's live jazz from 10pm. Mon–Sat 4pm–1am, Sun 2pm–1am.

People 7 人间银七, rénjiānyínqī. 805 Julu Lu, close to Fumin Lu ☏021 54040707; ⓜShaanxi Nan Lu; map pp.354–355. This hip bar trades on its exclusivity. Not only is there no sign, there's also a rigmarole to get in, involving putting your hands into lighted holes outside (you'll have to ring for the code). A door slides back revealing a two-storey lounge bar, where the quirky elements – glasses with curved bottoms so they keep rolling round, baffling toilet doors with fake handles – will either delight or annoy. Daily 6pm–midnight.

Revolucion Cocktail 2 98 Yanping Lu, near Xinzha

Lu ☏021 62667969, ⏅revolucion-cocktail.com; ⓜChangping Lu; map pp.350–351. This casual and friendly Cuban cocktail bar keeps it colourful with parrot paintings on the walls. It gets very dancey at weekends, when they play plenty of latin sounds, plus the usual hip-hop. Their signature cocktails are rum based, but they have a good selection of bottled beers, too. If it's not to your liking, take a stroll – a lot of new bars are springing up around here. Daily 6pm–2am.

★Senator 98 Wuyuan Lu, near Wulumuqi Zhong Lu ☏021 54231330, ⏅senatorsaloon.com; ⓜShanghai Library; map pp.354–355. A sophisticated speakeasy from the people behind *Citizen* (see p.379). It's intimate and cosy and the staff really know their cocktails; tell them your mood and tastes and they'll suggest a drink to fit. They have a vast range of bourbons and most of the recipes date back to the prohibition era. Daily 5pm–1am.

Vue 32–33F, Hyatt on the Bund, 199 Huangpu Lu, north of Suzhou Creek ☏021 63931234, ⏅shanghaithebund .hyatt.com/en/hotel/dining/VueBar; ⓜTiantong Lu; map pp.350–351. A Shanghai must, this sleek designer bar has fantastic views of the Bund, and there's a jacuzzi on the outdoor terrace. The ¥100 cover for non-guests includes one free drink from a limited menu; cocktails start at ¥120, and windowside seating costs extra. Drinks offers Mon–Fri 5.30–7pm. Mon–Thurs & Sun 6pm–1am, Fri & Sat 6pm–2am.

Windows Too 蕴德诗酒吧, yùndéshī jiǔbā. I2F, City Plaza, 1618 Nanjing Xi Lu, by Huashan Lu ☏021 62889007, ⏅windowsbar.com; ⓜJing'an Temple; map pp.354–355. Cheap beer at ¥15 a bottle, noisy hip-hop, no class and no pretensions. It's packed nightly with those at the bottom of the Shanghai foreigner food-chain – students, teachers and backpackers – and those who'll deign to talk to them. ¥50 cover Fri and Sat, when it's very clubby. Daily 10am–late.

Zapatas 萨帕塔, sà pà tǎ. 5 Hengshan Lu, near Dongping Lu ☏021 64334104, ⏅zapatas-shanghai .com; ⓜHengshan Lu; map pp.350–351. No Mexican anarchist would be seen dead in the company of the lascivious frat-house crowd here who, come the revolution, will be first against the wall. It's a heaving party on Mon and Wed nights, when women are offered free margaritas before midnight, and tequila gets poured into the mouths of anyone dancing on the bar. Enter through the garden of *Sasha's*, the nearby restaurant. Happy hour daily 5–9pm. Daily 5pm–late.

NIGHTLIFE

Shanghai has perhaps the best **clubbing scene** in China. You won't hear much in the way of local sounds – but door prices are low (never more than ¥100), though you may have to pay to sit at a table. Most places have international DJs, and plenty of famous faces have popped in for a spin of the decks. Note that there are also dancefloors in *Zapatas* (see above), *Bar Rouge* (see p.383) and *Windows* (see above). The indie **music scene** is not as good as Beijing's, but it does exist, and is well worth dipping a toe into.

Arkham 1 Wulumuqi Lu, near Hengshan Lu ☎021 62580355, ⓦ arkhamshanghai.com; ⓜ Hengshan Lu; map pp.350–351. It's all about the dancing in these three dark caverns, haunt of impassioned promoters and punters, where sets are mostly techno with shows by international DJs and rappers. Drinks are pretty cheap at around ¥40. Occasional shows on weeknights; check the website. Fri & Sat 10pm till late.

★**MAO Livehouse** 光芒, guāng máng. 308 Chongqing Lu, near Jianguo Zhong Lu ☎021 64450086, ⓦ mao-music.com; ⓜ Madang Lu; map pp.354–355. A decent-sized, central venue for local and international rock and indie bands. The sound system passes muster and drinks are cheap, at around ¥25 a beer. Variable cover charge, usually around ¥50. Open during events only.

Myst 相关团购, xiāng guān tuán gòu. 1123 Yan'an Zhong Lu, near Fumin Lu ☎021 64379999, ⓦ mystshanghai.com; ⓜ Jing'an Temple; map pp.354–355. The ground floor of this multistorey cavern is loungey, the floor above is dancey and the top floor is for the VIPs to look down on the bopping proles. There are too many tables for a properly unrestrained dancefloor, but the shows are fun – a stage rises out of the floor, and skimpily dressed dancers show the locals how it is done. Don't expect much sophistication or any elbow room and you'll have a good time. There's usually no cover, and drinks aren't expensive. Daily 9pm–late.

★**Yuyintang** 育音堂, yùyīntáng. 851 Kaixuan Lu ☎021 52378662, ⓦ wyytlive.com; ⓜ Yan'an Xi Lu; map pp.350–351. Ground zero for the Converse-and-black-nail-varnish set. Rock/punk and electro gigs every weekend with a varying cover of around ¥40. With concrete floors and graffitied walls, it's pretty rough and ready, but the sound system is good, and bottles of beer just ¥15. Daily 9.30pm–late.

ENTERTAINMENT AND ART

Most visitors take in an **acrobatics** show, but Shanghai's flourishing contemporary art and music scenes are equally noteworthy, especially during the **Shanghai Arts Festival** (mid-Oct to mid-Nov; ⓦ www.artsbird.com), when the city receives a lot of visiting shows, or during the **Shanghai Biennale** (even-numbered years; ⓦ shanghaibiennale.com), held at the Power Station of Art (see p.361). You can check out the contemporary art scene year-round at the Moganshan Arts District (see p.371) or along the West Bund (see p.372). For art and entertainment listings consult an up-to-date expat magazine such as *cityweekend* or check ⓦ smartshanghai.com or *Time Out Shanghai* (see p.376). While it can be easiest to get tickets from the box office in advance, you can also buy **tickets online** from SmartShanghai (ⓦ smartshanghai.com /smartticket) – you pay cash upon delivery of the tickets to your hotel.

ACROBATICS

Shanghai Centre Theatre 上海商城剧院, shànghǎi shāngchéng jùyuàn. 1376 Nanjing Xi Lu, by Xikang Lu ☎021 62798948, ⓦ shanghaicentre.com; ⓜ Jing'an Temple. Light on the glitz but slick and full of breathtaking feats. Performances daily 7.30pm; tickets ¥100–280.

Shanghai Circus World 上海马戏城 shànghǎi mǎxìchéng. 2266 Gonghe Xi Lu ☎021 66522395, ⓦ era-shanghai.com; ⓜ Shanghai Circus World. Good old-fashioned spectaculars, the city's best, with audiovisual trickery enhancing the awe-inspiring acrobatic cavortings. Performances daily 7.30pm; tickets ¥120–600 (the pricier seats don't have much advantage over the cheaper ones).

CINEMA

Despite a glut of fantastically talented filmmakers, the Chinese film scene is stifled by government interference, and most cinemas are restricted to showing crowd-pleasers or propaganda pics. There's more interesting stuff on offer during the Shanghai International Film Festival (mid-June; ⓦ siff.com). The following cinemas show foreign blockbusters in their original languages and the latest Chinese releases in Mandarin Chinese only.

Broadband International Cineplex 万裕国际影城, wànyù guójì yīngchéng. 6F, Times Square, 99 Huaihai Lu ☎021 63910363, ⓦ swy99.com; ⓜ Huangpi Nan Lu. Tickets ¥80–100, half-price on Tues and Wed.

Palace IMAX 6F, IAPM Mall, 999 Huaihai Zhong Lu ☎021 51093988, ⓦ www.b-cinema.cn/w14313.jsp; ⓜ Shaanxi Nan Lu. The newest and probably the best of the city's cinemas, with six screens, not all of them IMAX. Tickets ¥100–180; half-price (not including IMAX films) all day Mon and Tues.

UME International Cineplex 新天地国际影城, xīntiāndì guójì yīngchéng. 5F, Xintiandi South Block ☎021 63733333, ⓦ ume.com.cn; ⓜ Xintiandi. An English schedule follows the Chinese when you call. Tickets start at ¥100, half-price before 7pm on Tues.

CLASSICAL MUSIC AND MUSICALS

Majestic Theatre 美琪大剧院, měiqí dàjùyuàn. 66 Jiangning Lu, near Nanjing Xi Lu ☎021 62174409; ⓜ Nanjing Xi Lu. When built in 1941 this was one of Asia's best theatres. It usually shows musicals, with some English-language drama, dance competitions and Chinese opera.

Oriental Arts Centre 上海东方艺术中心, shànghǎi dōngfāng yìshù zhōngxīn. 425 Dingxiang Lu, near Century Ave ☎021 68541234, ⓦ shoac.com.cn; ⓜ Science and Technology Museum. A fantastic, 40,000-square-metre behemoth, shaped like an opening

6

flower. Hosts a little bit of everything, but comes into its own as a concert venue, as the acoustics are superb.

Shanghai Concert Hall 上海音乐厅, shànghǎi yīnyuètīng. 523 Yan'an Dong Lu, near Xizang Zhong Lu ☎021 63862836, ⊛shanghaiconcerthall .org; ⓜDashijie. This beautiful old building was moved 60m east in 2003, at tremendous cost, to get it away from the din of Yan'an Lu. Today, it's the premier venue for classical music. Tickets from ¥80.

Shanghai Grand Theatre 上海大剧院, shànghǎi dàjùyuàn. 300 Renmin Dadao ☎021 63273094, ⊛shgtheatre.com; ⓜPeople's Square. Lovely building putting on popular contemporary dramas, operas and classical ballets, and hosting most of the visiting musicals. Regular performances by the in-house Shanghai Symphony Orchestra.

SHOPPING

The Shanghainese love **luxury goods**, but all those glitzy brand names that give the streets such a lot of their shine are not good value; high-end goods and international brands are generally twenty percent more expensive than they would be in the West. Ignore them, and instead plunge into the fascinating world of the backstreet boutiques and markets.

BOOKS

Foreign Language Bookstore 上海外文书店, shànghǎi wàiwén shūdiàn. 390 Fuzhou Lu ☎021 23204994, ⊛sbt.com.cn; ⓜNanjing Dong Lu; map pp.354–355. A useful resource, with plenty of English-language guides, coffee-table tomes and the like; the out-of-copyright English-language novels, published by Chinese publishers, are cheap. Daily 9.30am–7pm.

★**Garden Books** 韬奋西文书店, tāofèn xīwén shūdiàn. 325 Changle Lu, near Shanxi Nan Lu ☎021 54048728, ⊛gardenbooks.cn; ⓜShaanxi Nan Lu; map pp.354–355. The best selection of foreign-language books in the city and a charming café, known for its tasty ice cream, where you can read them. Daily 10am–10pm.

CLOTHES

Sartorial elegance is something of a local obsession, so you're spoilt for choice if you're looking for clothes. The choicest shopping is in the former French Concession; central Huaihai Zhong Lu itself is full of familiar brands, but the streets off it – such as Nanchang, Shanxi Nan Lu and Maoming Lu – are studded with fascinating little boutiques. For interesting local designers, head to Tianzifang (see p.363).

38 Capital Joy 158 Jinxian Lu, near Maoming Nan Lu ☎021 62560134; ⓜShaanxi Nan Lu; map pp.354–355. Elegant and affordable smart clothes for men, from Hong Kong designers. Off-the-peg suits start at ¥900, shirts at ¥400. Daily 10am–6pm.

★**Nuomi** 糯米, nuòmǐ. 196 Xinle Lu, near Donghu Lu ☎021 54034199, ⓜChangshu Lu, map pp.354–355; No. 12, Lane 274, Taikang Lu, Tianzifang ☎021 64663952, ⊛brownricedesigns.com; ⓜDapuqiao; map pp.350–351. Eco-conscious women's fashion created from recycled materials; look out for the purses made from old billboard paper and elegant cotton evening dresses. Both branches daily 10am–9.30pm.

Triple-Major Lane 25, Shaoxing Lu ☎021 54247308, ⊛triple-major.com; ⓜShaanxi Nan Lu; map pp.354–355. A diverse range of men's and women's clothes from local and international designers. Tues–Sun 1–8pm.

Xinlelu 414 Shanxi Bei Lu, Beijing Xi Lu ☎021 52133301, ⊛xinlelu.com; ⓜNanjing Xi Lu; map pp.354–355. Classic womenswear, some from local designers, and the store hosts regular launch parties and events; check the website. Daily noon–8pm.

ELECTRONICS

Obscure-brand laptops, MP3 players, memory sticks, RAM and low-end accessories such as headphones can be very cheap. Shop around, as many of the stalls sell the same things, and haggle (though this isn't the fake market; you'll get at most twenty percent off the asking price). Test everything thoroughly, and remember that for the majority of this stuff the warranty is not valid internationally.

Metro City 美罗城, měiluó chéng. 111 Zhaojiabang Lu, by Caoxi Bei Lu; ⓜXujiahui; map pp.350–351. This

---

MADE TO MEASURE

Tailoring is recommended in Shanghai; it's cheap, and the artisans are quick and skilled (provided you're clear about exactly what you want). At the **textile market** in the Old City, near Liushui Lu at 399 Lujiabang Lu (南外滩轻纺面料市场, nánwàitān qīngfǎng miànliào shìchǎng; daily 10am–7pm), on-site tailors will make you a suit for around ¥500, including material (you'll have to haggle a bit), which will take a couple of days; a shirt should be around ¥150. Rita at 129, Jennifer at 237 and the brothers at 309 are all a good bet.

For a more sedate experience, or a tailored *qipao*, try one of the dozen or so specialist tailors on **Maoming Nan Lu**, just south of Huaihai Lu. Three shirts in one of these stores should come to around ¥800; a suit will be around twice that.

mall, shaped like a giant bubble, is full of electronics stores. Daily 10am–7pm.

Pacific Digital Plaza 太平洋数码广场, tàipíngyáng shùmǎ guǎngchǎng. 117 Zhaojiabang Lu ☎021 54905900; Ⓜ Xujiahui; map pp.350–351. Great for low-end tech products and computer components. Daily 10am–8pm.

FAKE MARKETS

There are several fake markets catering largely to foreigners. As well as clothes, stalls have trainers, sunglasses, bags and watches on sale, and plenty of souvenirs.

Han City 假货市场, jiǎhuò shìchǎng. 580 Nanjing Xi Lu; Ⓜ People's Square; map pp.354–355. The most convenient fake market, on three floors of a mall. Bargain hard, as the persistent salespeople consistently start at ten times the real price. Daily 10am–8pm.

Yatai Xinyang Fashion & Gift Market 亚太新阳服饰礼品市场, yàtài xīnyáng fúshì lǐpǐn shìchǎng. Ⓜ Science and Technology Museum; map pp.350–351. Inside the Science and Technology Museum metro station, with the entrance close to the ticket machines, this is the biggest of the fake markets; as well as the usual shoes, bags and clothes there are plenty of tailors, and a whole zone for jewellery. Daily 10am–9pm.

DIRECTORY

Banks The head office of the Bank of China is at 23 Zhongshan Dong Yi Lu (the Bund), next to the *Peace Hotel* (Mon–Fri 9am–noon & 1.30–4.30pm, Sat 9am–noon). Next door is a Citibank ATM machine with 24hr access.

Consulates Australia, 22F, CITIC Square, 1168 Nanjing Xi Lu (☎021 22155200, ⓦ shanghai.china.embassy.gov .au); Canada, 8F, ECO City Building, 1788 Nanjing Xi Lu (☎021 32792800, ⓦ china.gc.ca); New Zealand, 2801-2802A and 2806B-2810, Corporate Ave 5, 150 Hubin Lu (☎021 54075858, ⓦ nzembassy.com/china); Republic of Ireland, 700a Shanghai Centre, 1376 Nanjing Xi Lu (☎021 62798729, ⓦ embassyofireland.cn); South Africa, 222 Yanan Dong Lu (☎021 53594977); UK, The British Centre, 17F, Garden Square, Beijing Xi Lu (☎021 62797651, ⓦ ukinchina.fco.gov.uk); US, 1469 Huaihai Zhong Lu (☎021 62797662, ⓦ shanghai.usembassy -china.org.cn).

Football Shanghai has two major teams: Shenhua (ⓦ shenhuafc.com.cn) play every other Sun at 3.30pm at the impressive 35,000-seat Hongkou Football Stadium, 444 Dongjianwan Lu, in the north of town. SIPG play at the Shanghai Stadium in the south of the city (on metro line #4), and are generally regarded as flashy upstarts. Tickets start at ¥80 and can be bought at the ground on the day, from the ticket office or from scalpers, or in advance from ⓦ mypiao.com. For more on Shanghai's football scene, check out English-language fanblog

ⓦ wildeastfootball.net.

Hospitals Hospitals with special clinics for foreigners include the Huadong Hospital at 221 Yan'an Xi Lu (☎021 62483180) and the Hua Shan Hospital at 12 Wulumuqi Lu (8F; daily 8am–10pm; ☎021 62483986, ⓦ huashan.org .cn). You'll find decent medical care at Parkway Medical and Dental Centres (24hr hotline ☎021 64455999, ⓦ parkwayhealth.cn), which has seven clinics. The most central are at the Shanghai Centre, 2F, 1376 Nanjing Xi Lu and 2258 Hongqiao Lu (both Mon–Fri 9am–7pm, Sat & Sun 9am–5pm). A consultation will cost around ¥1000. Parkway also manages a hospital, the East International Medical Centre (150 Jimo Lu, near Pudong Dadao; 24hr hotline ☎021 58799999, ⓦ seimc.com.cn).

Post offices The main post office is at 276 Suzhou Bei Lu, just north of and overlooking Suzhou Creek (daily 7am–10pm; ☎021 63936666). It offers a very efficient parcel service; the express option can get packages to Britain or the US within two days. Branch post offices are dotted around the city, with convenient locations on Nanjing Dong Lu, on Huaihai Zhong Lu, in the Portman Centre and near the Huangpu River ferry jetties at the corner of Jinling Dong Lu and Sichuan Bei Lu.

Visa extensions The PSB is at 210 Hankou Lu, near the corner of Henan Zhong Lu, with a visa extension office in Pudong at F3, 1500 Minsheng Lu, near Yinchun Lu (Mon–Fri 9am–11.30am & 1.30–4.30pm; Ⓜ Science and Technology Museum).

Around Shanghai

A few attractions **around Shanghai** make for ideal day-trips – and as they are all accessible by metro, they can be easily combined. Highlights include the lovely **Guyi Garden** in Nanxiang; the new **Disneyland**; **Qibao**, a historical theme park; and **She Shan**, the biggest hill in the area at 100m high.

Further afield, accessible by bus or on a tour, are the attractive **water towns** of **Zhujiajiao**, **Zhouzhuang**, **Xitang**, **Tongli** and **Wuzhen**, all of which are firmly on the tourist circuit.

6

Guyi Garden

古猗园, gǔyī yuán • 218 Huyi Gong Lu, near Guyi Yuan Lu, Nanxiang • Daily 7am–6pm • ¥12 • Ⓜ Nanxiang, then a cab (¥15)

It may not have the historical pedigree of Shanghai's Yu Yuan or anything in Suzhou (see box, p.322), but the huge classical **Guyi Garden** is in many ways more interesting than either. Guyi performs a Chinese garden's function – of being a tranquil, contemplative space – far better than its rivals by virtue of being beautiful, big enough to get lost in and pretty empty. It's a bit of a trek – nearly an hour on the metro – but that does mean there are no tour groups, only locals playing cards or practising *tai ji* among the pavilions, roofed corridors, kinking walkways, flowerbeds and groves of osmanthus and bamboo. There is also plenty of birdlife, including mallard and Mandarin ducks and tame black swans. The garden was created by Magistrate Min Shiji, who came to a sticky end: a plaque marks the spot where he was killed by his own servants. The garden was adapted and expanded during the Qing dynasty, until in 1789 it was bought by local merchants who turned it into a public park, and put up a temple to the City God. You can walk around it in a couple of hours; there are signs in English as well as Chinese, and a map by the entrance. Highlights include the raised **Tranquil Pavilion**, which gives an overview of the site; the **Fragrance Veranda**, constructed for the sniffing of nearby plum trees, orchids and chrysanthemums; and the **Nine Zigzag Bridge**, from which you can feed the carp.

Take the north exit of the Guyi Garden, cross the road and you will see the entrance to **Nanxiang Old Town**, a zone of narrow alleys crisscrossed with canals and lined with rickety wooden buildings. Many sell the famous local dumplings, grilled kebabs, radish cakes, alfafa pancakes and the like.

Disneyland

上海迪士尼乐园, shàng hǎi dí shì ní lè yuán • 360 Shendi Xi Lu, Chuansha • Daily 9am–9pm • One-day ticket ¥500, children ¥375; buy tickets online • Ⓦ shanghaidisneyresort.com • Ⓜ Shanghai Disney

Love it or loathe it, **Disneyland** is here – and it's huge. It feels a bit different, though, with no shows in English, and none of that "Main Street USA" shtick – this Disneyland is designed to be "distinctly Chinese", and the majority shareholder is not Disney but the Chinese government.

It's centred around Disney's largest ever theme-park **castle**, at the end of Mickey Avenue; crowd favourites include the Pirates of the Caribbean boat ride, the Tarzan live show and the very fast TRON rollercoaster.

You will need to plan if you don't want to get caught up in the queues. The best advice is buy your ticket online in advance, download the Shanghai Disney app to check on waiting times, and get there early – it's an hour on the metro. When the rope drops, hurry to get a fast pass (free) for the popular rides; you can ride the less busy attractions while waiting for your allotted slot.

Qibao

七宝, qībǎo • Daily 8.30am–4.30pm; Shadow-puppet Museum shows 1pm & 3pm • ¥30 all-inclusive ticket, or ¥10 at each attraction • Ⓜ Qibao; take exit two, turn right, then follow the brown signs

Qibao is a historical theme park in the western suburbs – essentially alleyways and a canal, lined with renovated buildings now given over to olde-worlde souvenir shops, snack stalls and museums. It's worth a look if you aren't visiting one of the larger water towns (see opposite), you like the idea of getting out of the city centre without any transport hassles (it's just an hour by metro), or you're hoping to get all your souvenir shopping done at once. The all-in ticket gives you access to nine tourist sights (all of them historical buildings with small exhibitions), or you can pay to see them individually. The most rewarding are the cute old **Bell Tower** (钟楼, zhōnglóu) and the **Shadow-puppet Museum** (皮影艺术馆, píyǐng yìshùguǎn). There are plenty of stalls and little eateries, with the biggest concentration along Nan Dajie (南大街, nándàjiē) – local specialities include smoked toad (熏癞蛤蟆, xūn làiháma) and red-braised pork (红烧肉, hóng shāo ròu). A thirty-minute **boat trip** from the wharf (游船码头, yóuchuán mǎtóu) costs just ¥20.

She Shan

余山, shéshān • Ⓜ She Shan

Such is the flatness of the surrounding land some 30km southwest of Shanghai that **She Shan**, a low range which only rises about 100m, is visible for many kilometres around. The park is divided in two; the East Hill has a forest park, while the more attractive West Hill has the historical attractions.

West Hill

西山, xīshān • Daily 8.30am–4.30pm • Free • **Observatory** Daily 8am–5pm • ¥12 • Free shuttle bus from Ⓜ She Shan (9am–3pm every 20min); the cable car costs ¥10

It's a pleasant walk up **West Hill** at any time of year, or a **cable-car ride** if you prefer, past bamboo groves and the occasional ancient pagoda. The peak here is crowned by an impressive **basilica**, a legacy of nineteenth-century European missionary work (She Shan has been owned by a Catholic community since the 1850s), though the present church was not built until 1925. Also on the hill are a **meteorological station** and an old **observatory**, the latter with an astronomical exhibition displaying an ingenious earthquake-measuring device – dragon heads, with balls in their mouths, ring a pendulum; when the pendulum swings due to an earthquake, it knocks a ball out, thus indicating the earthquake's direction.

East Hill

东山, dōngshān • Daily 8am–6pm • ¥45; sculpture park ¥120; rowing boats ¥60/hr • Ⓜ She Shan then 10min walk

East Hill has been redeveloped as a woodland park, including the artificial Moon Lake. A ten-minute walk west from the entrance brings you first to a **sculpture park**; the road curves south to get around the hill itself. There's nothing particularly distinguished about the thirty or so works of art, but they make diverting way-stations on a nice walk. With a long artificial **beach** around a **lake**, manicured lawns and plenty of playgrounds, this makes a good retreat to take the kids, and is busy with families at the weekend. Rowing boats can be rented, or if you want to escape the crowds, just head uphill into the woods.

The water towns

The extensive canal system surrounding Shanghai was once part of a network that transported goods all around imperial China, and the attractive **water towns** that grew up around them present some of eastern China's most distinctive urban environments. Whitewashed Ming and Qing timber buildings back onto the narrow waterways, which are crossed by charming humpback stone bridges; travel is by foot or punt as the alleys are too narrow for cars.

Today, these sleepy towns are a popular escape from the city, each one a nostalgia theme-park for the urban sophisticate. They're fine as day-trips but don't expect much authenticity – there are far more souvenir shops than dwellings – and avoid the weekends, when they're overrun. You'll usually be charged an **entrance fee**, which gets you into the historical buildings – mostly the grand old houses of wealthy merchants – although in some places the attractions may also be ticketed individually.

The water towns are attractively illuminated, and quieter, at night; if you are contemplating **staying over**, Wuzhen is the best choice (see p.391).

6

Zhujiajiao

朱家角, Zhūjiājiǎo • 30km west of Shanghai • **Attractions** Daily 8am–4pm • ¥10–30; combination ticket for all nine attractions ¥80 • **Boat trips** ¥60 for a six-person boat up the main canal; longer trips ¥120 • Buses from the Shanghai Stadium Sightseeing Bus Station (see opposite), plus pink tour buses from Pu'an Lu bus stop (普安路, pǔ'ān lù), just south of Renmin Square (6am–10pm every 20min; 1hr; ¥12); you could also catch a cab (¥50) from Ⓜ Xujing, at the end of line #2, or from the centre of town (around ¥200)

ZHUJIAJIAO is the most accessible of the water towns. The cluster of rickety old residences, stone alleys and humped bridges can easily be explored in a couple of hours, and there are nine ticketed **attractions** – old houses or small exhibition spaces. The best-preserved street is Bei Dajie, which has some elegant Qing-dynasty buildings as well as a plethora of snack vendors. In the peaceful **Kezhi Garden** (课植园, kè zhí yuán) at its northern end, you'll find a well-proportioned five-storey pavilion built in 1912. The standout sight is five-arched **Fangsheng Bridge** (放生桥, fàng shēng qiáo), the largest stone bridge in Shanghai, built in 1812.

Zhouzhuang

周庄, zhōuzhuāng • 60km west of Shanghai • **Attractions** Various hours • Combination ticket ¥100 • **Boat trips** ¥100 • Regular buses from Shanghai South bus station (1hr 30min), plus tour buses (see opposite)

Lying astride the large Jinghang Canal connecting Suzhou and Shanghai, ZHOUZHUANG grew prosperous from the area's brisk grain, silk and pottery trade during the Ming dynasty. Many rich government officials, scholars and artisans moved here and built beautiful villas, investing money into developing the stately stone bridges and tree-lined canals that now provide the city's main attractions. Zhouzhuang's most highly rated views are of the pretty sixteenth-century twin **stone bridges** in the northeast of town. Also firmly on the itinerary is **lunch** – there is no shortage of restaurants offering the local specialities of pig's thigh, meatballs and clams as a set meal (around ¥60/head).

Shen House

沈厅, shēntīng • South side of Fuan Bridge • Daily 8.30am–4.30pm

Zhouzhuang's biggest mansion is the **Shen House** in the east of town, built in 1742. More than a hundred rooms (not all open) are connected by covered colonnades, with grand public halls at the front and the more intimate family chambers at the back. Period furnishings help evoke a lost age of opulence, though it is all rather dark; the neat gardens offer a pleasant contrast.

Xitang

西塘, xītáng • 60km southwest of Shanghai • **Attractions** Daily 9am–5pm • ¥50; free on Fri morning & Sun afternoon • Regular buses from Shanghai South bus station (2hr), plus tour buses (see opposite)

XITANG is short on specific sights, although the lanes, canals and bridges are undeniably picturesque. And if it rains, at least you'll be dry: the locals, tired of the wet climate, built roofs over the main alleyways, the biggest of which is over 1km long. It runs alongside the central canal, and is lined with restaurants and stalls housed in half-timbered buildings. There are plenty of riverside restaurants serving local specialities such as pork with sweet potatoes.

Tongli

同里, tónglǐ • 80km southwest of Shanghai • **Attractions** Daily, various hours • ¥100, includes all attractions except the Sex Museum • Regular buses from Shanghai South bus station (1hr 30min), plus tour buses (see opposite)

Of all the water towns, TONGLI has the best sights, and with more than forty humpback bridges (some over a thousand years old) and fifteen canals it offers plenty of photo ops.

Tuisi Garden

退思园, tuìsī yuán • Beitu Lu • Daily 8am–6pm

Tongli's highlight is the UNESCO World Heritage Site **Tuisi Garden**, built by disillusioned retired official Ren Lansheng in 1886 as a place to retreat and meditate – though you'll have to come in the early morning, before the tour groups arrive, to appreciate the peacefulness of the place. With its harmonious arrangements of rockeries, pavilions and bridges, zigzagging over carp-filled ponds, it is comparable to anything in Suzhou.

Sex Museum

中华性文化博物馆, zhōnghuá xìngwénhuà bówùguǎn • Daily 9am–5.30pm • ¥20

Housed in a former girls' school, the **Sex Museum** has plenty of striking exhibits – figurines of Tang-dynasty prostitutes, special coins for use in brothels and a wide range of occasionally eye-watering dildos, for example.

6

Wuzhen

乌镇, wūzhèn • 120km southwest of Shanghai • **Attractions** Daily, various hours • West side ¥150 (¥80 after 6pm); east side ¥80 • Regular buses from Shanghai South bus station (2hr), plus tour buses (see below)

Further out than other water towns, sedate **WUZHEN** is less busy; if you're headed out on the weekend, this is the one to pick. Staying overnight within the old town is also a good bet – the entrance fee is waived and you'll get to see the place lit up by hundreds of red lanterns.

The prime draw is the little **Xiuzhen Taoist Temple** and its collection of folk art, including intricate wood carving and leather shadow puppets; you can watch the latter in action at the nearby **playhouse** (hourly shows 10am–5pm). Several of Wuzhen's houses are used to demonstrate local crafts such as silk painting or printing using dyes made from tea leaves, or as museums; check out the intricately carved pieces of the **Bed Museum** (江南 百床馆, jiāngnán bǎichuángguǎn). The **Fanglu Pavilion** (访卢阁, fǎnglú gé), near the centre of town, a teahouse with picturesque views over the canal, makes a good place for a rest, though as ever in these places, it isn't cheap (¥48 a pot).

| ARRIVAL AND DEPARTURE | THE WATER TOWNS |

By tour bus The cheapest option (¥130–150, including town entrance fees) is to take a day-trip bus from the Shanghai Stadium Sightseeing Bus Station (上海体育馆旅游集散中心, shànghǎi tǐyùguǎn lǚyóu jísàn zhōngxīn; ☎021 24095555) at 666 Tianyaoqiao Lu, on the south side of the Shanghai Stadium in the southwest of the city, a 10min walk from the Shanghai Stadium metro station. Services run from 7am till around 10am, with a couple of buses afterwards till noon; they all return in the afternoon. Often a (non-English-speaking) guide is provided, though you're free to wander off on your own. You can order tickets up to three days in advance on the phone and they'll deliver them to your hotel for a fee (¥10–30).

By bus There are public buses to the water towns from the Shanghai South bus station.

By taxi A day-trip will cost in the region of ¥500, or about half that for Zhujiajiao.

ACCOMMODATION

ZHOUZHUANG

International Youth Hostel 周庄国际青年旅馆, zhōuzhuāng guójì qīngnián lǚguǎn. 86 Beishi Jie ☎0512 57204566, ⓦwww.yhachina.com. Cosy establishment with spacious rooms – even the dorms. Staff are helpful and there's a café. Rates rise by fifty percent or more at weekends. Dorms ~~¥55~~, doubles ~~¥150~~

XITANG

Jinshui Lou Ge 近水楼阁客栈, jìnshuǐ lóugé kèzhàn. 10 Chaonan Dai ☎133 75731700. Simple place with whitewashed walls and exposed wooden beams. The small rooms are attractively decorated with reproduction Ming-dynasty furniture, including four-poster beds. ~~¥180~~

Xitang Youth Hostel 西塘忆水阑庭国际青年旅舍, xītáng yìshuǐ lántíng guójì qīngnián lǚshè. 6 Tangjia Lane, off Xi Xia Jie on the west side of town ☎0512 65218885, ⓦwww.yhachina.com. Traditional white walls and black tiles on the outside; inside there's a pleasant courtyard with bamboos overlooked by balconies, a small café and simple, clean rooms, some with wooden floors. Dorms ~~¥55~~, doubles ~~¥130~~

WUZHEN

Wuzhen Guesthouse 乌镇民宿, wūzhèn mínsù. 137 Xizha Jie ☎0573 88731230, ⓦwuzhen.com.cn. Not a single guesthouse, but a cooperative of quaint B&B-style properties all over town, run by local families who will cook your meals for you. It's worth paying extra for a riverside view; rates can reach ¥600. ~~¥100~~

The Yangzi basin

安徽 / 湖北 /
湖南 / 江西

GOLDEN MONKEYS, SHENNONGJIA

The Yangzi basin

Having raced out of Sichuan through the narrow Three Gorges, the Yangzi (here known as the Chang Jiang – "long river") widens, slows down and loops through its flat, low-lying middle reaches, swelled by lesser streams and rivers that drain off the highlands surrounding the four provinces of the Yangzi basin: Anhui, Hubei, Hunan and Jiangxi. As well as watering one of China's key rice- and tea-growing areas, this stretch of the Yangzi has long supported trade and transport; back in the thirteenth century, Marco Polo was awed by the "innumerable cities and towns along its banks, and the amount of shipping it carries, and the bulk of merchandise that merchants transport by it". Rural fringes away from the river – including much of landlocked Anhui and Jiangxi provinces – remain less developed than their coastal neighbours. But the situation is changing now the hydroelectric output of the mighty Three Gorges Dam, on the border between Hubei and Chongqing, is fuelling a local industrial economy with lower costs than at the glitzy seaboard.

The river basin itself is best characterized by China's two largest freshwater lakes: **Dongting**, which separates Hunan and Hubei, and **Poyang**, in northern Jiangxi, famed for porcelain produced at nearby **Jingdezhen**. While all four provincial capitals are located near water, only **Wuhan**, in Hubei, is actually on the Yangzi, a position that has turned the city into central China's liveliest urban conglomeration. Long settlement of the capitals has, however, left a good deal of history in its wake, from well-preserved Han-dynasty tombs to whole villages of Ming-dynasty houses, and a smattering of sites from the Three Kingdoms (see box, p.396). Many cities also remain studded with hefty European buildings, a hangover from their being forcibly opened up to foreign traders as **Treaty Ports** in the 1860s, following the Second Opium War. Perhaps partly due to these unwanted intrusions, the Yangzi basin can further claim to be the **cradle of modern China**: Mao Zedong was born in Hunan; Changsha, Wuhan and Nanchang are all closely associated with Communist Party history; and the mountainous border between Hunan and Jiangxi was both a Red refuge during right-wing purges in the late 1920s and the starting point for the subsequent Long March to Shaanxi.

Away from the river, wild mountain landscapes make for excellent hiking, the prime spot being Anhui's **Huang Shan**, followed by **Zhangjiajie National Forest Reserve** in

anachronistic mansion hides a series of tastefully decorated courtyards and halls embellished with opulently carved wooden furniture. Li was heralded a hero for his role in quelling the Taiping Rebellion, but later fell from favour after signing a number of unequal treaties with foreign powers. Knighted by Queen Victoria, by the end of his life Li was as reviled in China as he was respected in the West, despite spending much of his career attempting to reform dynastic China.

Lord Bao Memorial Hall

包公祠, bāogōng cí · Daily 8am–6pm · ¥50

Down at the southeastern side of town, **Baohe Park** (包河公园, bāohé gōngyuán) is an agreeable strip of lakeside willows and arched bridges off Wuhu Lu, where the **Lord Bao Memorial Hall** identifies Hefei as the birthplace of Bao, the famous Song-dynasty administrator (see p.272). Lord Bao's ability to uncover the truth in complex court cases, and his proverbially unbiased rulings, are the subject of endless tales – he also often appears as a judge in paintings of Chinese Hell. Along with gilded statues, some waxworks bring a couple of well-known stories to life: look for Lord Bao's dark face, improbably "winged" hat and the three guillotines – shaped as a dragon, tiger and dog, according to the status of the condemned – he had made for summary executions.

Provincial Museum

省博物馆, shěng bówùguǎn · Huaining Lu · Tues–Sun 9am–5pm · Free · ① 0551 63736677 · Bus #162 or #166 from Shifu Guangchang

Hefei's **Provincial Museum** provides sound evidence of Anhui's contributions to Chinese culture, all displayed in state-of-the-art fashion 10km southwest of the centre. The museum traces the passage of time in the region, starting with the dinosaurs and moving through the arrival of man – the *Homo erectus* cranium from Taodian in the south of the province is one of the museum's most treasured exhibits. Comparatively recent history emerges in a few Stone Age items and an exceptional Shang bronze urn decorated with tiger and dragon motifs. Elsewhere, there's an exhibit of the "Four Scholastic Treasures" for which the province is famed: high-quality ink sticks, heavy carved inkstones, weasel-hair writing brushes and multicoloured papers.

ARRIVAL AND DEPARTURE

HEFEI

BY PLANE

The new Xinqiao International Airport (合肥新桥国际机场, héféi xīnqiáo guójì jīchǎng) is located about 32km northwest of the city centre in Gaoliu, Fexi County, and reachable by taxi (¥120) or airport shuttle bus (¥25) from: Hefei bus station (合肥汽车站, héféi qìchēzhàn); Hefei Main bus station (汽车客运总站, qìchē kèyùn zǒngzhàn); South Gate Transfer Centre (南门换乘中心, nánmén huànchéng zhōngxīn); and City Air Terminal (城市航站楼, chéngshì hángzhàn lóu).

Destinations Beijing (16 daily; 1hr 45min); Guangzhou (15 daily; 1hr 55min); Nha Trang (1 daily; 3hr); Shenzhen (10 daily; 2hr); Tunxi (2 daily; 50min); Xi'an (9 daily; 1hr 35min); Xiamen (10 daily; 1hr 20min).

BY TRAIN

Hefei has three train stations. Hefei train station (合肥火车站, héféi huǒchē zhàn) is 3km northeast of the centre at the end of Shengli Lu; bus #119 runs down Shengli Lu and into town along Changjiang Lu. The new South train station (合肥南站, héféi nánzhàn) is on the Beijing–Fuzhou CRH line, and West train station (合肥西站, héféi xī zhàn) primarily deals with trains bound to other cities in Anhui.

Destinations Beijing (19 daily; 4–14hr); Huang Shan (25 daily; 2–7hr); Jiujiang (9 daily; 4hr 30min–6hr); Nanchang (7 daily; 6–8hr); Nanjing (82 daily; 1–4hr); Shanghai (56 daily; 3–7hr); Xi'an (11 daily; 14hr 30min–17hr).

BY BUS AND MINIBUS

Hefei's confusing array of bus stations often offer overlapping services, so try the closest one first. Most are in the east and northeast of the city. Below are three of the most useful ones.

Main bus station (客运总站, kèyùn zǒngzhàn), oppsite the train station. Best for destinations within

Anhui, including Tunxi.

Hefei long-distance bus station (合肥长途汽车站, héféi chángtú qìchēzhàn), Mingguan Lu. The city's largest bus station connects Hefei with major cities such as Beijing, Xi'an, Tianjin and Zhengzhou.

Anhui Provincial Tourist bus station (安徽省旅游汽车站, ānhuī sheng lǚyóu qìchē zhàn), Zhan Qian Lu, 600m northwest of the train station. The best bet for Jiuhua Shan, although there are also services from the motley collection of minibus stands on Shengli Lu.

Destinations Beijing (13hr); Jiuhua Shan (4hr); Jiujiang (5hr); Nanchang (6hr); Nanjing (3hr); Tunxi (4hr); Wuhan (6hr); Xi'an (14hr); Zhengzhou (8hr).

GETTING AROUND

Hefei's countless underpasses and traffic lights make large parts of the city troublesome to negotiate on foot. Fortunately taxis are both readily available and inexpensive.

By bus Buses cost ¥1–2 and operate daily 6am–8pm (or later).

By taxi Flag fall is ¥8 for the first 2.5km, then ¥1.4 per km.

By metro At the time of writing, Hefei's metro line #1 was scheduled to open in 2017. A total of 15 lines are planned in total, so check what's what before you arrive.

ACCOMMODATION

7 Days Inn 7天连锁酒店, qītiān liánsuǒ jiǔdiàn. 299 Changjiang Zhong Lu ☎0551 62248177. Right in the centre of town, this characterless but scrupulously clean chain hotel is undeniably great value. ¥134

Hefei Valent International Youth Hostel 合肥万能国际青年旅舍, héféi wànnéng guójí qīng nián lǚshè. Off Tunxi Lu, North Shuguang Lu ☎0551 63822066, ⓦyhachina.com. Situated in the Zhongyinyushi area, this YHA youth hostel is a colourful, clean little place and one of few budget options in the city. Dorms ¥50, doubles ¥150

Hilton 希尔顿酒店, xī'ěrdùn jiǔdiàn. 198 Shengli Lu ☎0551 62808888, ⓦhilton.com. This grand hotel has a huge, opulent lobby, quality rooms and all the other services you would expect at a *Hilton* including business centre and fitness rooms. ¥560

Holiday Inn 古井假日酒店, gǔjǐng jiàrì jiǔdiàn. 1104 Changjiang Lu ☎0551 62206666, ⓦholiday-inn .com.cn. *Holiday Inn* offers the usual range of facilities, along with a surprisingly good and inexpensive 24hr noodle bar. There's also a coffee shop alongside the fifth-floor reception and an indoor heated pool. ¥323

★**Jinjiang Inn** 锦江之星, jīnjiāng zhīxīng. 123 Lujiang Lu ☎0551 62641559, ⓦwww.jinjianginns .com. Hefei's downtown *Jinjiang* offers a great location on a leafy street just a few minutes back from Changjiang Lu. Inside you'll find the usual generic but clean and comfortable rooms. ¥189

EATING AND DRINKING

Off the Huaihe Lu pedestrian street, you'll find dozens of stalls and **canteens** in a warren of alleys where you can fill up on stir-fries, noodle soups and river food; there's also a night market there in the evenings.

★**Dongmen Kaoya Dian** 东门烤鸭店, dōngmén kǎoyā diàn. Changjiang Lu ☎0551 64299869. This is a fantastic, hugely popular example of a dying breed of basic Chinese canteen – no frills, but the open kitchen turns out delicious roast duck with a host of tasty accompanying dishes including *xiaolong* buns, dumplings and other northern delicacies. Expect to pay ¥20–60 per person for a meal, though snacks are as little as ¥3. Daily 6am–9.30pm.

Happy Grassland 欢乐牧场火锅, huānlè mùchǎng huǒguō. Basement next door to Mingjiao Temple, Huaihe Lu ☎0551 62679177. A basic *yuanyang* hotpot (a divided pot with one spicy-broth half and one clear-broth half) costs ¥42 in this cavernous basement restaurant. Friendly staff will help you pick out the best ingredients from the vast placemat menu. Daily 9am–2am.

Qingsong Coffee 青松咖啡店, qīngsōng kāfēidiàn. Lujiang Lu ☎0551 62639118. Warm, cosy, and a little bit smoky, this coffee shop does a good line in steak meals (¥26–130), albeit with some unusual side dishes including fruit salad with mayonnaise. Daily 9am–2am.

Qingzhen Lanzhou Lamian 清真兰州拉面 qīngzhēn lánzhōu lāmiàn. North of Changjiang Lu. This tiny little canteen bustles with diners who come for just one thing – a hearty bowl of Lanzhou stretched noodles with beef and coriander for just ¥14. Daily 8am–10pm.

Tongqing Lou 同庆楼, tóngqìng lóu. Maanshan Lu, at the intersections of Shengli Lu and Fengyang Lu ☎0551 62887799. One of the most popular and recognizable restaurant chains in the city, *Tongqing Lou* dishes up fine Anhui dishes to the white-collar crowd. Menus are bilingual and service is impressive for provincial China, but it's not cheap. At least ¥200 per head. 11am–11pm.

DRINKING

Old Captain Pub Hongding Xintiandi, south of Changjiang Lu ⓦ bit.ly/OldCaptainPub. Housed in Hongding Xintiandi, a low-grade version of Shanghai's gentrified shopping, dining and drinking zone, this pub offers a fair approximation of a Western bar. Daily 6pm–late.

DIRECTORY

Hospital There's one with English-speaking doctors on Lu Jiang Lu, just north of the Lord Bao Memorial Hall.
Visa extensions The PSB office is open Mon–Fri 9am–5pm and centrally located at 6 Huoqiu Lu, at the junction with Lu'an Lu (ⓣ 0551 2624550).

Jiuhua Shan

九华山, jiǔhuá shān • March–Nov ¥190, Dec–Feb ¥140 • Temple hours daily approximately 6.30am–9pm

Some 60km south of the Yangzi lies **Jiuhua Shan**, a sacred Buddhist mountain ever since the Korean monk **Jin Qiaojue** (believed to be the reincarnation of the Bodhisattva Dizang, whose doctrines he preached) died here in a secluded cave in 794 AD. Today, there are more than seventy temples – some founded back in the ninth century – containing a broad collection of sculptures, religious texts and early calligraphy. However, intense tourism and some outsized building projects threaten to overwhelm Jiuhua Shan's otherwise human scale. Fortunately, most of these developments, including a 99m-tall golden Buddha, are focused around the enormous new **tourist**

7

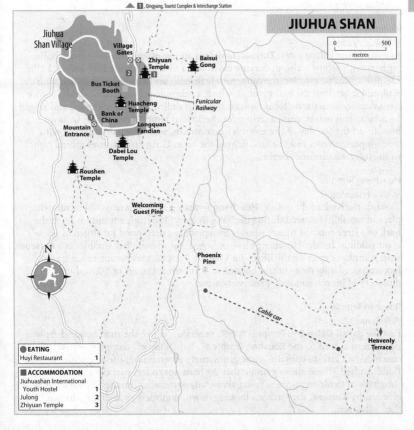

JIUHUA SHAN

▲ 1, Qingyang, Tourist Complex & Interchange Station

Jiuhua Shan Village

Village Gates
Zhiyuan Temple
Baisui Gong
Bus Ticket Booth
Huacheng Temple
Funicular Railway
Bank of China
Longquan Fandian
Mountain Entrance
Dabei Lou Temple
Roushen Temple
Welcoming Guest Pine
Phoenix Pine
Cable car
Heavenly Terrace

N

0 — 500 metres

● EATING
Huyi Restaurant 1

■ ACCOMMODATION
Jiuhuashan International Youth Hostel 1
Julong 2
Zhiyuan Temple 3

JIUHUA SHAN PRACTICALITIES

The mountain's official "**entrance**" is marked by a huge ornamental **gateway and temple** at the back of Jiuhua Shan village, though well-concealed, smaller flagstoned paths ascend from behind Zhiyuan Temple and at the corners of the main road in the village itself. Using these access points, you can do a good, easy **circuit walk** on the lower ridges in about an hour, or extend this to a full day's hike up around Jiuhua's higher peaks. If you'd rather save time and your legs, use the park **buses** and **cable car**. **Market stalls** along the village road sell postcards, trinkets, and waterproof maps and umbrellas for the frequently sodden weather. It's fine to take **photographs** in the temples, but ask permission before photographing any monks.

---

complex at the base of the mountain; higher up the slopes, you'll find an atmosphere of genuine devotion in the austere halls of **Jiuhua Shan village**'s temples.

7 Jiuhua Shan village

九华山, jiǔhuá shān

As it climbs the lower slopes, the twisting Jiuhua Shan road passes villages scattered amid the moist green bamboo stands, with some inspiring views of bald, spiky peaks above and valleys below. The road ends at picturesque **Jiuhua Shan village**, where the mountain's accommodation and the most famous temples huddle around a couple of cobbled streets and squares, all hemmed in by encircling hills.

Zhiyuan Temple

执园寺, zhíyuán sì

Just inside the village gates, **Zhiyuan Temple** is an imposing Qing monastery built with smooth yellow walls, upcurving eaves and a tiled roof nestled up against a cliff. Despite a sizeable exterior, the numerous little halls are cramped and stuffed with sculptures; head for the main hall, in which a magnificently gilded Buddhist trinity sits solemnly on separate lotus flowers, blue hair dulled by incense smoke, and ringed by *arhats*. This makes quite a setting for the annual **temple fair**, held in Dizang's honour on the last day of the seventh lunar month, when the hall is packed with worshippers, monks and tourists. Behind the altar, Guanyin statuettes ascend right to the lofty wooden roof beams.

Huacheng Temple

化城寺, huàchéng sì

Towards the back of the village, **Huacheng Temple** is the mountain's oldest surviving place of worship, founded during the Tang dynasty. The stone entrance is set at the back of a large cobbled square whose centrepiece is a deep pond inhabited by some giant goldfish. Inside, Huacheng's low-ceilinged, broad main hall doubles as a **museum**, with paintings depicting the life of Jin Qiaojue from his sea crossing to China (accompanied only by a faithful hound) to his death at the age of 90, and the discovery of his miraculously preserved corpse.

Roushen Temple

肉身寺, ròushēn sì

Past the garish **Dabei Lou Temple** (大悲楼, dàbēi lóu), where the road bends sharply right, steps ascend to the **Roushen Temple** ("Flesh Temple") complex, whose entrance-hall atrium contains some gruesomely entertaining, life-size sculptures of Buddhist hell. These are so graphic that it's hard not to feel that the artists enjoyed their task of depicting sinners being skewered, pummelled, strangled, boiled and bisected by demons, the virtuous looking down, doubtless exceedingly thankful for their salvation.

Baisui Gong

百岁宫, bǎisuì gōng • Funicular railway (缆车站, lǎnchē zhàn) from the main street (daily 8am–5.30pm; ¥75 one-way, ¥140 return)

The path up the mountain diverges at **Welcoming Guest Pine** (迎客松, yíngkè sōng). Bear left and it's a couple of kilometres past several pavilions and minor temples to **Baisui Gong**, a plain, atmospheric monastery whose interior is far from weatherproof, with clouds drifting in and out of the main hall. A rear room contains the mummy of the Ming priest Wu Xia, best known for compiling the Huayan sutras in gold dust mixed with his own blood; his tiny body is displayed seated in prayer, grotesquely covered in a thick, smooth skin of gold leaf. Steps descend to Zhiyuan Temple, or you can take the funicular railway down to the main street.

The upper peaks

Cable car (索道站, suǒdào zhàn) between Phoenix Pine and Heavenly Terrace: Daily 8am–5.30pm • March–Nov ¥85 one-way, ¥160 return; Dec–Feb ¥65 one-way, ¥120 return

To reach the **upper peaks** on foot, turn right at Yingke Song, and it's a two-hour climb to the uppermost ridges via **Phoenix Pine** (凤凰松, fènghuáng sōng), more temples, wind-scoured rocks, and superb scenery surrounding the **Heavenly Terrace** (天台正顶, tiāntái zhèngdǐng) summit area. You can also get here from the village by a combination of minibus and cable car.

ARRIVAL AND GETTING AROUND
JIUHUA SHAN

By bus The enormous Jiuhua Shan Tourist Interchange Station is part of the tourist complex at the base of the mountain. There's also a left luggage office here if you don't want to lug your pack around the mountain. On arrival at the Interchange Station, you'll need to buy a three-day bus pass (¥50), which covers transport to and from Jiuhua Shan village, plus limited journeys within the scenic area.

Destinations Hefei (4hr); Nanjing (4hr); Shanghai (8hr); Tangkou (4hr); Tunxi (2hr).

ACCOMMODATION

Aside from the following places in Jiuhua Shan village, there are also places to stay down at the tourist complex, but these are only worth considering if you arrive too late to ascend the mountain.

★**Jiuhuashan International Youth Hostel** 九华山国际青年旅舍, jiǔ huá shān guó jì qīng nián lǚ shè. 9 Jiuhuaxin Jie, Ke Cun ☎18815775678. North of the village, a few minutes' drive from the bus interchange, this hostel has some of the only dorm rooms in the area. With more of a low-budget hotel vibe than a backpacker haunt, it's modern and clean, and there are Western-style toilets. Dorms ¥47, doubles ¥171

Julong 聚笼大酒店, jùlóng dàjiǔdiàn. To the right of the village gates behind an illuminated fountain ☎0566 2831368, ⊛jiuhuashan.cc. Julong has some of the best rooms on the mountain, with flat-screen TVs and good bathrooms, though they are very overpriced. The restaurant serves equally expensive mountain fare, and there's also a wine bar. ¥732

Zhiyuan Temple 执园寺, zhíyuán sì. By far the cheapest option on the mountain, the pilgrims' dormitory offers hard beds in a barebones room, but the sound of

HUIZHOU HOUSES

One of the highlights of a visit to southern Anhui is the chance to see **Huizhou houses**, whose plan of two floors of galleried rooms based around a courtyard became the template for urban domestic architecture in eastern China. Tunxi's best two examples are hidden in the eastern backstreets, both threatened by ever-encroaching modern buildings. The more easterly house is that of the mathematician **Cheng Dawei** (程大位居, chéngdàwèi jū; ¥30; daily 8am–5pm); the other, closer to the old town, is known as the **Cheng Family House** (程氏三宅, chéngshì sānzhái; ¥30; daily 8am–5pm). Further examples can be found at the new riverside park development of **Hubian Gucun** (湖边古村, húbiān gǔcūn), where some forty original Huizhou houses and two *paifang* memorial arches have been relocated, and you'll find plenty more at Shexian (see p.406) or Yixian (see p.407).

monks chanting in the background might add character to an otherwise austere night. Foreigners are sometimes refused entry to temple accommodation these days, but it's still worth trying your luck. ¥20

EATING

There's no shortage of places to eat in Jiuhua Shan. It's worth trying some of the excellent **vegetarian food** on offer.

Huyi Restaurant 徽宜饭店, huī yí fàn diàn. 2nd Floor, Jinfeng Huangbin, in the village ☎ 156 05668995. Serves highly rated traditional Anhui food including choice soups and fish dishes. Around ¥78 per head. Daily 10.30am–10pm.

Huang Shan Shi (Tunxi) and around

屯溪, túnxī

The city of **Tunxi** has been renamed **Huang Shan Shi** (Yellow Mountain City), though the old town centre is now called Tunxi District, and most people still refer to it as simply Tunxi. The city is the core transport hub for connections to the Huang Shan mountain range, 50km off to the northwest (see p.408); it has the closest airport and train station to the mountain, and many long-distance buses pass through as well. Income from tourists has brought with it a certain superficiality to the city, with the addition of several new shiny malls, but has also meant more money fed into infrastructure, such as freshly laid tarmac roads. However, if you've even the slightest interest in **Chinese architecture**, then Tunxi and its environs are worth checking out in their own right, with a liberal sprinkling of seventeenth-century monuments and classical homes nearby at **Shexian** and **Yixian**.

An old trading centre, Tunxi is set around the junction of two rivers, with the original part of town along the north bank of the Xin'an Jiang at the intersection of Huang Shan Lu and Xin'an Lu, and a newer quarter focused around the train station 1km or so to the northeast.

● EATING & DRINKING	
Lao Jie Tong Ju Lou Dajiudian	3
Lao Jie Yi Lou	2
Mr Dai's Countryside Kitchen	1
Old Street Coffee Bar	4

■ ACCOMMODATION	
Ancient Town Youth Hostel	4
Huaisheng Home Youth Hostel	3
Huangshan Bed and Breakfast	1
Koala International Youth Hostel	2

Lao Jie

老街, lǎojiē

Tunxi's historic, flagstoned **Lao Jie** (Old Street) forms a long stretch of elderly, restored **shops** selling local teas, medicinal herbs and all manner of artistic materials and "antiques" – inkstones, brushes, Mao badges, decadent advertising posters from the 1930s and carved wooden panels prised off old buildings. Some, particularly around Zhong Ma Lu, have rebranded themselves as coffee shops, bars and restaurants, and make great perches to watch the world wander by beneath the characteristic **horse-head gables** which rise up above the roof lines in steps. These originated as fire baffles between adjoining houses; they stopped the spread of flames from building to building, but also served to discourage thieves, becoming increasingly decorative over time.

ARRIVAL AND DEPARTURE · HUANG SHAN SHI (TUNXI)

By plane Huang Shan Tunxi International Airport (黄山屯溪国际机场, huángshān túnxī guójì jīchǎng) is 5km from the downtown area. A taxi should cost ¥30–40 on the meter; city buses #18 and #19 go to the airport.
Destinations Beijing (2–4hr); Fuzhou (1h 15min); Guangzhou (1hr 45min); Hefei (50min); Shanghai (1hr).
By train Huang Shan Station (黄山火车站, huángshān huǒchē zhàn), at the end of Qianyuan Bei Lu, at the northern city limits, deals with both slow and mid-speed trains. From the train station, bus #6 takes a back road into town, while #12 follows Huang Shan Xi Lu southwest from the bus station – either route is a 20min walk. Huangshan North station (黄山北站, huángshān běizhàn), 18km north of Tunxi, is at the crossover of the Huangshan–Shanghai and Beijing–Hefei–Fuzhou CRH lines.
Huang Shan Station destinations Beijing (2 daily; 20hr);

Hefei (3 daily; 6hr–6hr 30min); Jingdezhen (5 daily; 2hr 40min–3hr 24min); Nanjing (6 daily; 5hr 30min–7hr 15min); Shanghai (2 daily; 12hr).
North station destinations Beijing South (8 daily; 6hr 30min); Hefei South (25 daily; 1hr 50min); Nanchang West (2 daily; 2hr–30min); Shanghai Hongqiao (1 daily; 4hr).
By bus Tunxi's main bus station (黄山汽车站, huángshān qìchē zhàn), serving both long-distance and local destinations, is located at Huangshan Dong Lu.
Destinations Beijing (17hr); Hefei (4hr); Jiuhua Shan (4hr); Nanjing (6hr); Qingyang (2hr); Shanghai (7hr); Shexian (1hr); Tangkou (1hr); Yixian (2hr).
By minibus Minibuses to Tangkou (¥15–20), the gateway for Huang Shan (see p.408), prowl the train station forecourt, leaving only when full. Some vehicles take the old route, which is slightly slower and cheaper than taking the expressway.

GETTING AROUND

Tunxi's centre is small enough to walk around, though you might need transport for arrival points.

By bus City buses cost ¥1–2. There is also an electric bus service which runs from the riverside park (Hubian Gu Cun) to Lao Jie for ¥2.
By taxi Flag fall is ¥5 for the first 3km, plus a ¥2 fuel surcharge, though drivers don't like using the meter. Hiring

a cab for trips to Shexian, Yixian or Huangshan should cost around ¥250–300 per full day.
By cycle rickshaw These anachronistic vehicles will try to draw your business – just make sure that you agree the *total* price before starting the journey.

ACCOMMODATION

As the gateway to Huang Shan, Tunxi has a decent range of accommodation choices, mainly concentrated around the train station and on the other side of town near Lao Jie and the river.

★**Ancient Town Youth Hostel** 小镇国际青年旅舍, xiǎozhèn guójì qīngnián lǚ shè. 10 San Ma Lu ☎0559 2522088. House in a faux-traditional Anhui house, this centrally located youth hostel has a large common area including a bar, teahouse and small gallery. Great for meeting fellow backpackers. Dorms **¥35**, doubles **¥120**
Huangshan Bed & Breakfast 黄山市屯溪湖边农家乐客栈, huángshānshì túnxī húbiān nóngjiālè kèzhàn. Hubian Cun ☎0559 2585268. East of the train station and north of Guojing Gong Lu, this isolated,

family-run B&B suffers from some train noise, but is hospitable and great value. Rooms are fitted to high specifications given the price, and downstairs there's free wi-fi, an enormous flat-screen TV and great food. The owner, Steven, used to be a local guide and is also a great source of information on the region. It's difficult to find by yourself, so call in advance to arrange free pickup. **¥140**
Huangshan Home Youth Hostel 黄山之家短租公寓, huángshān zhījiā duǎnzū gōngyù. A5 Huangshan Huayuan, 149 Beihai Lu ☎0559 5203109.

Tucked away down a small street in the middle of Tunxi, this well-located, homely if humble hostel is not a bad city budget option. Rooms could do with sprucing up but have all mod cons including a/c, TVs and bathrooms. Dorms ¥50, doubles ¥138
Koala International Youth Hostel 考拉旅舍, kǎolā lǚshè. 58-4 Beihai Lu ☎0559 2328000,

@ yhahuangshan@126.com. In a decent location, 200m from the train station, *Koala*'s comfortable and well-priced rooms and dorms, combined with the opportunity to meet other travellers, make it popular with international backpackers. The ground-floor café has a pool table and a choice of Western and Chinese meals. Dorms ¥50, doubles ¥240

EATING AND DRINKING

Tunxi has plenty of good **restaurants** serving regional cuisine. Anhui food is considered one of the "eight culinary traditions" of China, and originated in Huangshan. Local *huicai* dishes are often braised or stewed, with ample use of wild herbs. As well as the listings below there are numerous small restaurants around the Xin'an Nan Lu/Lao Jie intersection. Near the train station, cheap eats can be found at the string of **canteens** off Qianyuan Lu on Hehuachi Zaochi Yitiao Jie (荷花池早吃一条街, héhuāchí zǎochī yìtiáojiē).

Lao Jie Tong Julou Dajiudian 老街同聚楼大酒店, lǎojiē tóngjùlóu dàjiǔdiàn. Lao Jie ☎0559 2572777. The basic English menu at this lively restaurant offers dishes including spicy Mandarin fish (¥58) and local speciality, "furry" bean tofu (¥18). Two people can get a selection of dishes for ¥77. In the summer you can dine outdoors. Daily 9.30am–2am.

Lao Jie Yi Lou 老街一楼食业 lǎojiē yīlóu shíyè. Lao Jie ☎0559 2539797. Lao Jie's most famous restaurant is spread over several dining areas, all replete with ornate stone carving, Qing-style furnishings and traditionally dressed staff. Always busy, the restaurant's cuisine lives up to the decor, and choosing is made easier by the second-floor *huicai* buffet spread of every dish on the menu. "Fortunate chicken" costs ¥82, braised bean

curd and fish is ¥68. Daily 11am–1.30pm & 5–9pm.

Mr Dai's Countryside Kitchen 戴记土菜馆 dàijì tǔcàiguǎn. 62 Beihai Lu ☎0559 2120988. Handy for a meal before a train journey (or if you're staying at *Koala Hostel*, next door), Mr Dai and family turn out delicious local specialities including Huangshan fried chicken with sweet nuts (¥48) in their simple restaurant. Daily 8am–10pm.

Old Street Coffee Bar 老街咖啡吧, lǎojiē kāfēibā. 26 Zhong Ma Lu, off Lao Jie ☎0559 25311298. One of the first trendy cafés to open its doors on atmospheric Zhong Ma Lu, this cosy place does good coffee and a mix of Chinese and Western dishes (from ¥35). On summer evenings the outdoor seats offer perfect people-watching prospects, to the backdrop of the picture-pretty Huizhou houses. Daily 1–11pm.

Shexian

歙县, shèxiàn • The bus station is out on the highway, across from Ancient Huizhou Town, and has regular services to Tunxi (45min)

Anhui owes a good deal to **SHEXIAN**, an easy forty-minute bus ride 25km northeast of Tunxi up the Xin'an River, and once the regional capital – the name "Anhui" is a telescoping of Anqing (a Yangzi town in the southwest) and Huizhou, Shexian's former name. The region blossomed in the seventeenth century after local salt merchants started raising elaborate townhouses and intricately carved stone archways, some of which survive today, in a showy display of their wealth. The province's opera styles were formalized here, and the town became famous for *hui* inkstones and fine-grained *she* ink sticks, the latter still considered China's best. One of Shexian's charms is that most buildings remain in everyday use, and there's a genuine old-world ambience to soak up.

Ancient Huizhou Town

安徽古城景区, ānhuī gǔchéng jǐngqū • ¥100 • ☎0559 2156121, @ guhuizhouta.com

Over the river, just off **Jiefang Jie**, what constituted the ancient city of Shexian has been turned into a touristic scenic spot, branded **Ancient Huizhou Town**, complete with gate-ticket, tour guides, tourist centre and overenthusiastically refurbished buildings. Highlights include the restored **Nan Lou** (南楼, nánlóu) and **Yanghe Men** (阳和门, yánghé mén) gate towers; the highly decorative **Xuguo archway** (许国石坊, xǔguó shífāng), one of the finest in the region; and **Doushan Jie** (斗山街, dǒushān jiē), a street full of well-preserved Huizhou-style homes. There's also the **Xu Family Hall** (许家厅, xǔjiā tīng), **Hui Office Building** (徽州府衙, huīzhōu fǔyá), **Taoxingzhi Memorial Museum** (陶行知经念馆, táoxíngzhī jǐngniànguǎn) and **Toad Well** (蛤蟆井, háma jǐng) to check out. By far and away

> ## PAIFANG
>
> Any exploration of Shexian will reveal traditional Ming and Qing architectural features, most notably the **paifang** or ornamental archways – there are over eighty of these in She County alone. Wood or stone, *paifang* can be over 10m in height, and are finely carved, painted or tiled, the central beam often bearing a moral inscription.
>
> They were constructed for a variety of reasons, foremost among which, cynics would argue, was the ostentatious display of wealth. This aside, the gateways were built to celebrate or reward virtuous behaviour, family success, important historical events or figures, and to reflect prevailing values such as filial piety; as such, they provide a valuable insight into the mores of the time.

the best approach is to get lost in the labyrinth backstreets where locals, who still live in authentic Ming and Qing houses, snack on local delicacy "pressed buns" while gossiping on street corners.

Tangyue arches

堂越牌坊, tángyuè páifāng • ¥130 • Taxi from Shexian ¥30, from Tunxi ¥60

The **Tangyue arches** form a strange spectacle of seven ornamental gates standing isolated in a row, in a field about 5km west of Shexian. Given that there are plenty of other *paifang* to be seen in the region (see box above), the steep entry fee deters many would-be visitors, but these really are the best-preserved examples of Ming- and Qing-dynasty memorial arches anywhere in China. A sentimental story lies behind the construction of each archway: a father and son's fight to save the other in the face of execution was rewarded with the sparing of both of their lives, and the "Filial Piety Archway" was built in their honour.

Yixian

黟县, yīxiàn

YIXIAN, a county town 60km due west of Tunxi, is not of interest in itself and should only be seen as a stepping stone to the surrounding picturesque villages, two of which have been recognized as UNESCO World Heritage sites.

Xidi

西递, xīdì • Daily 7.30am–6pm • ¥104 • Regular buses from Yixian long-distance bus station (15min), and tourist buses hourly from Tunxi (1hr)

XIDI is the pick of the local villages and hence the most visited – it's a particularly attractive place comprising some 120 eighteenth-century houses set along a riverbank. There are endless examples of carved and gilded wooden screens and panels inside the houses, as well as thin line paintings on front walls showing pairs of animals or "double happiness" characters. Mirrors placed above the three-tiered door lintels reflect bad luck or reveal a person's true character – a useful tool for judging the nature of strangers.

Hongcun and Nanping villages

Hongcun ¥104, Nanping ¥40 • Regular buses from Yixian long-distance bus station (15–20min) and tourist buses hourly from Tunxi (1hr 30min)

Along with Mukeng, **HONGCUN** (宏村, hóngcūn) was used to film scenes from Ang Lee's Oscar-winning 2000 epic *Crouching Tiger, Hidden Dragon*. However, the village tourist bureau makes a lot more noise about the rather stunning collection of antique buildings than its place in cinematic history. The village street plan is said to resemble (with some imagination) the body of a buffalo, complete with horns, body and legs. A highlight is the **Shuren Hall** (树人堂, shù rén táng), a two-storey, heptagonal Qing-dynasty house containing ornate wooden carvings and the must-have Hongcun photo of Nanhu – a crescent-shaped lake traversed by bridges and flanked by trees and whitewashed village homes. Nearby **Nanping village** (南屏村, nánpíng cūn) of similar vintage, was used as a set in Zhang Yimou's disturbing film *Judou*.

Mukeng

木坑竹海, mùkēng zhúhǎi • ¥30; zipline ¥40 • Taxi or motorbike from Hongcun ¥20–30 return

The magical bamboo forests at **Mukeng**, 5km from Hongcun, is where the gravity-defying fight scene between Chow Yun Fat and Zhang Ziyi's characters was filmed in *Crouching Tiger, Hidden Dragon*. Despite its popularity, you can lose the crowds along a two-hour trail, which gradually climbs above an enchanting pond and then loops around the hillside giving spellbinding views before descending back to the entrance. If you want to try and relive some of the movie's astounding wirework, there's a zipline which speeds you from the highest point of the path nearly down to the bottom in an astoundingly fast thirty seconds.

ARRIVAL AND DEPARTURE
YIXIAN

By bus Tourist buses from Tunxi bus station run daily 8am–4pm direct to Xidi (1hr; ¥12.50) and Hongcun (1hr 30min; ¥14.50), while more regular buses serve Yixian town itself (¥1hr; 13), from where there are minibus shuttles to the villages every 30min (¥2–3), taking 15–20min.

By taxi A cab from Yixian should cost around ¥200 for the day, or ¥300 from Tunxi, but you'll need to haggle.

ACCOMMODATION

XIDI

Xidi Travel Lodge 西递行馆, xīdì xíng guǎn. ☎ 0559 2317070. This beautifully atmospheric guesthouse is built in the traditional style, with grey-tiled roof, whitewashed walls and simple modern rooms with a/c and featuring attractive wooden window screens. **¥120**

HONGCUN

Hongcun Old House Youth Hostel 老房子青年旅舍, lǎo fángzi qīngnián lǚ shè. Shangshuiquan Jie ☎ 0559 5545888. There's something of a boutique feel to this hostel, set in a stunning old building and with helpful, English-speaking staff. Dorms **¥60**, doubles **¥188**

Qingheyue International Youth Hostel 清河月, qīng hé yuè. 28–29, Hou Jie ☎ 0559 2171731. With a small garden, delightful terrace bar, including stage and guitar (which guests can use) and an old Huizhou house across the street where (for an additional ¥20) you can join staff for dinner, *Qingheyue* has a great feel to it. Owner Zhuang Qingfeng is a real character and likes to take guests to remote areas of the surrounding countryside to visit "the real" Huangshan. Dorms **¥60**, doubles **¥280**

Huang Shan

黄山, huángshān • Daily 6.30am–5pm • March–Nov ¥230, Dec–Feb ¥150

Rearing over southern Anhui, **Huang Shan** – the Yellow Mountains – are staggeringly scenic, with pinnacles emerging from thick bamboo forests, above which rock faces dotted with ancient, contorted pine trees disappear into the swirling mists. This magical landscape has left an indelible impression on Chinese art; painters are a common sight on mountain paths, huddled in padded jackets and sheltering their work from the drizzle beneath umbrellas. Indeed, so great is Huang Shan's influence on the national psyche – it's said that once you've ascended these peaks you will never need to climb another mountain – that it's the ambition of every Chinese to conquer it at least once in their lifetime. Consequently, don't expect to climb alone: noisy multitudes swarm along the neatly paved paths, or crowd out the cable-car connections to the top. All this can make the experience depressingly like visiting an amusement park, but then you'll turn a corner and come face to face with a huge, smooth monolith topped by a single tree, or be confronted with views of a remote square of forest growing isolated on a rocky platform. Nature is never far away from reasserting herself here.

Huang Shan barely rises above 1870m, but as you **hike** up either of the staircases on the trails it can begin to feel very high indeed. You'll need between two and eight hours to walk up, depending on whether you follow the easier eastern route or the lengthy and demanding western trail. There are three **cable cars** that take upwards of twenty minutes to ascend, though queues can be horrendous (there's usually less of a wait to go down), and services are suspended during windy weather. Once at the top, there's a half-day of relatively easy hiking around the peaks.

Ideally, plan to spend two or three days on the mountain to allow for a steady ascent and circuit, though it's quite feasible to see a substantial part of Huang Shan in a single full day. Accommodation in Tangkou and Wenquan will store surplus **gear**: just bring a day-pack, suitable footwear and something warm and weatherproof for the top – rain is likely year-round, and there's often snow during winter.

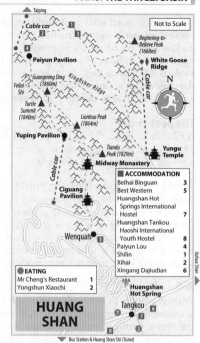

The eastern route

Cable car (索道, suǒdào): daily 8am–4.30pm • March–Nov ¥85 each way, Dec–Feb ¥65 each way • Bus from Tangkou service centre to Yungu Temple ¥19

The **eastern route** is by far the easier of the two trails: the road from Wenquan (see p.410) ends at **Yungu Temple** (云谷寺, yúngǔ sì), where a cable car can whisk you to the summit area at **White Goose Ridge** (白鹅峰, bái'é fēng) in twenty minutes – once you've queued two hours or so for your turn. Alternatively, you can climb the steps to the ridge in under three hours, though the forest canopy tends to block views and the path is thick with **porters** ferrying laundry, rubbish and building materials up and down the slopes.

The western route

Cable car (索道, suǒdào) daily 8am–4.30pm • March–Nov ¥85 each way, Dec–Feb ¥65 each way • Bus from Tangkou service centre to Ciguang Pavilion ¥19

The exceptional landscapes on the 15km **western route** are accompanied by up to eight hours of exhausting legwork – though you can shorten things by catching another **cable car** halfway up the mountain from the trailhead at Ciguang Pavilion.

Ciguang Pavilion to Kingfish Ridge

There are around two thousand steps from the **Ciguang Pavilion** (慈光阁, cíguāng gé) to the misleadingly named **Midway Monastery** (半山寺, bànshān sì), after which things start to get interesting as you continue up an increasingly steep and narrow gorge. The rocks are huge, their weirdly contorted figures lending some credence to the usual gamut of names hailing from ancient times, and the broken hillside is riddled with caves. A steep, hour-long detour from Banshan – not a climb for those nervous of heights – follows steps cut into the cliffs up to 1829m-high **Tiandu Peak** (天都峰, tiāndū fēng), where **Kingfish Ridge** (鲫鱼背, jìyú bèi), a narrow path extending over a precipice, provides Huang Shan's most spectacular views.

Yuping Pavilion to the top

On the main track, at the top of the Ciguang Pavilion cable car, the beautifully positioned **Yuping Pavilion** (玉屏楼, yùpíng lóu) is the true halfway house, at around three hours into the journey. The vegetation thins out here, exchanged for bare rocks with only the occasional wind-contorted tree, one of which, **Welcoming Guest Pine** (迎客松, yíngkèsōng), has been immortalized in countless scroll paintings, photographs, cigarette packets and beer labels. The steps wind on up to a pass where more strange rocks jut out of the mist; bear right for the climb to Huang Shan's 1864m-high apex at **Lianhua Peak** (莲花峰, liánhuā fēng). From here, it's just a short climb to where you finally reach the peak circuit at **Guangming Ding** (光明顶, guāngmíng dǐng), with a TV tower and weather station off to the right, and **Feilai Shi** (飞来石, fēilái shí) ahead.

The peak circuit

It takes around three hours to make the beautiful but often busy **circuit around the peaks**. If you're staying on the mountain, early morning or late afternoon typically gives the least crowds and best light.

White Goose Ridge and Beginning to Believe Peak

North (anticlockwise) from the eastern steps and **White Goose Ridge** (白鹅峰, bái é fēng) cable-car terminus, the first stop is where a track leads out to **Beginning to Believe Peak** (始信峰, shǐxìn fēng). This cluster of rocky spires makes a wonderful perch to gaze down to lowland woods and rivers, with white-rumped swifts and pine and rock silhouettes moving in and out of shifting silver clouds. Tour groups concentrate on the higher levels, so the lower stairs are more peaceful.

Beihai

From Beginning to Believe Peak, the path continues round to the first of a few accommodation options at **Beihai** (北海, běihǎi). Crowds congregate each morning on the terrace nearby to watch the sunrise over the "northern sea" of clouds, one of the most stirring sights on the mountain. The views are good even without the dawn, and the area tends to be busy all day. Another twenty minutes on the main path brings you to the well-placed *Xihai Fandian* restaurant, a good place from which to watch the sunset over the "western cloud sea".

Three ways down the mountain

A short way from Xihai the track splits: ahead is the Taiping **cable-car station** down to Songgu town on the mountain's northern foothills. Stay on the main track for **Paiyun Pavilion** (排云亭, páiyún tíng); on a clear day you'll see a steep gorge squeezed between jagged crags below, all covered in pine trees and magnolias. Farther round, the lonely tower of **Feilai Shi**, the "Far-flying Rock" (飞来石, fēilái shí), looks across at cascades that are especially evident after rain. Beyond here, the path undulates along the cliff edge to where the western steps descend on the right (below the TV tower and weather station), and then winds back to the White Goose Ridge cable car.

Tangkou

汤口, tāngkǒu • Bus to/from Huang Shan ¥19

The area's main gateway and with plenty of places to stay and eat, **TANGKOU**, anchored around merging routes from Tunxi and Jiuhua Shan, lies around 50km northwest of Tunxi on Huang Shan's southern foothills. Buses drop you at the tourist service centre at the entrance to the **new town** where there's a *KFC* and a *7 Days Inn*, but no sights or particular charm. If you've arrived early enough to move on, do so, at least as far as the **old town**, right at the base of the mountain, where a hint of character still exists between the cranes, and there are lovely if daunting views up to the peak.

Wenquan

温泉, wēnquán • Bus to/from Tangkou service centre ¥11

Around 3km uphill from Tangkou, where the mountain's two main ascent routes diverge, **WENQUAN** ("Hot Springs") is an altogether more pleasant prospect than

Tangkou, surrounded by pine and bamboo forest and perched above the clear blue Taoyuan Stream and a noisy waterfall. The first thing you'll see here is the arched bridge over the gully, where the road heads on 8km to the eastern route's trailhead; follow the footpath upstream and it's about half an hour to **Ciguang Pavilion**, at the start of the western route. Wenquan is named for its 42.3°C **thermal pools**, which are accessible at **Huangshan Hot Spring** (黄山温泉, huángshān wēnquán; daily 10am–10pm; ¥298) – great for a soak after hiking, though expensive.

ARRIVAL AND INFORMATION   HUANG SHAN

Transport pours into the Huang Shan region from all over eastern China. There are direct long-distance **buses** to Huang Shan's main access-town, **Tangkou**, from Shanghai, Hangzhou and Nanjing, as well as Jiuhua Shan, Hefei and other places within Anhui. Much of this, and all rail and air traffic, passes through **Tunxi** (aka Huang Shan Shi; see p.404), with regular **shuttle buses** connecting the train and bus stations at Tunxi with Tangkou. Some bus timetables might refer to Tangkou as "Huang Shan" on their timetables.

By bus Tangkou's long-distance bus station is in the tourist service centre on the edge of the new town, connected to the old town by tourist buses, local minibuses, or a 30min walk. Buying outbound tickets at the station is straightforward. Destinations from Tangkou Hangzhou (3hr 45min); Hefei (4hr); Jiuhua Shan (3–4hr); Nanjing (5hr); Shanghai

(6hr 30min); Tunxi (1hr).
Banks and ATMs There are branches of the Bank of China in Tangkou and on the mountaintop at the *Beihai* hotel.
Mountain essentials You can pick up umbrellas, walking sticks, warm clothes and mountain maps from hawkers and stalls around Tangkou.

GETTING AROUND

By bus An efficient local bus service connects Tangkou service centre with the old town and the trailheads.
By minibus and taxi Private minibuses and cars at

Tangkou tout for business and can be bargained down to prices that work out lower than the bus per head, if there are enough people.

ACCOMMODATION

There are no accommodation bargains anywhere at Huang Shan, but spending extra to stay overnight on the **mountaintop** will allow you to see it without the crowds at dawn and dusk, and is highly recommended. Local **agencies** might get you discounted rates, but during the week you can usually haggle a similar deal yourself at even the most expensive places. Note that in winter, hotels either drop their prices or close until spring.

TANGKOU
Huangshan Hot Springs International Hostel 黄山温泉国际青年旅舍, huángshān wēnquán guójì qīngnián lǚshè. Just off the main road by the bridge ☎0559 5562478, ⓦyhhuangshan.com. Not much in the way of character or comfort, but cheap, friendly and in a decent location on the road down to the river. The downstairs café serves Chinese meals. Dorms **¥50**, doubles **¥100**
Huangshan Tankou Haoshi International Youth Hostel 汤泉大酒店, tāngquán dàjiǔdiàn. 1, C1 Tangquan Lu ☎0559 5568586. While it's not going to win any awards for its decor, this affordable option is in a great spot, just 10min from Tunxi bus station and 30min to Huangshan south gate by taxi. Dorms **¥50**, doubles **¥110**
Xingang Dajiudian 黄山新港大酒店, huángshān xīngǎng dàjiǔdiàn. ☎0559 5561088. On the main road up the hill from the bridge, this ageing property has rooms overlooking a pleasant central courtyard. Carpets and furniture are a little shabby, but more expensive rooms have updated fittings including flat-screen TVs and computers. **¥200**

WENQUAN
Plans to convert Wenquan into a five-star villa and hotel complex have left most of the small hotels in this pretty valley closed for the time being.
★**Best Western** 黄山温泉度假酒店, huángshān wēnquán dùjià jiǔdiàn. ☎0559 5582222, ⓦbestwestern.com. It might not be on the mountaintop, but this hotel's simply styled, clean and comfortable rooms in an incredible setting make it one of the best choices in the area. **¥450**

PEAKS
Beihai Binguan 北海宾馆, běihǎi bīnguǎn. ☎0559 5582555. Even in this elevated position, the four-star *Beihai Binguan* boasts a Bank of China ATM. The rooms are lacklustre for the money though, despite a standard thirty-percent discount on off-peak weekdays. **¥1130**
Paiyun Lou 排云楼宾馆, páiyúnlóu bīnguǎn. ☎0559 5581558, ⓦwww.pylhotel.com. *Paiyun Lou* is in a quiet location and has been attractively remodelled from its former slovenly state, but there are no views from the

rooms. That said, you don't need to go far to find one. Dorms **¥120**, doubles **¥1200**

Shilin 石林大酒店, shílín dàjiǔdiàn. ☎0559 5584040, ⓦshilin.com. A good range of comfortable and functional rooms, with views from the better ones. Dorms are comfortable but, as ever on the mountain, wildly overpriced. Dorms **¥200**, doubles **¥1030**

Xihai 西海饭店, xīhǎi fàndiàn. ☎0559 5588888, ⓦwww.hsxihaihotel.cn. In a great location, with well-kept rooms at a range of prices, *Xihai* is the best choice at the top of the mountain. They even had the forethought to provide bright-blue down jackets for snowy sunrise mornings. Dorms **¥200**, doubles **¥1190**

EATING

As Tangkou expands, there are increasingly more dining choices **in town**, but up **on the peak** it's mostly plain Chinese food at inflated prices, only occasionally justified by delicious mountain produce. The main road through Tangkou, and the path along the river, are lined with small canteens and restaurants; some have bilingual menus offering arresting delights such as squirrel hotpot and scrambled mountain frog. If there's no price on the menu, agree the cost in advance to avoid being ripped off.

Mr Cheng's Restaurant 程先生餐馆, chéngxiānshēng cānguǎn. Opposite the post office, Old Tangkou ☎130 85592603. Small café run by friendly and helpful Simon Cheng. The kitchen rustles up a host of reasonably priced Chinese classics (¥25–40), plus traveller favourites including pancakes and Western breakfasts. Simon can also assist with travel arrangements and mountaintop hotel bookings; he also offers luggage storage. Daily 7am–10pm.

Yongshun Xiaochi 永顺小吃, yǒngshùn xiǎochī. Down by the river, Old Tangkou. A hole-in-the-wall canteen, typical of many in this part of town, turning out fresh and tasty noodles with veg and pork for ¥12 per bowl. Daily 6am–9pm.

Hubei

湖北, húběi

Hubei is Han China's well-watered agricultural and geographic centre. Until 280 BC, this was the independent state of **Chu**, whose sophisticated bronze-working skills continue to astound archeologists, but for the last half-millennium the province's eastern bulk, spliced by waterways draining into the Yangzi and Han rivers, has become an intensely cultivated maze of rice fields. According to some, the region alone could supply the national need, though floods in 2016 exposed the three-pronged problem of land exploitation, climate change and inadequate water management systems. Hubei's central location and mass of transport links into neighbouring regions saw the province

---

QU YUAN AND THE DRAGON BOAT FESTIVAL

The former state of **Chu**, which encompassed northern Hunan, was under siege in 278 BC from the first stirrings of the ambitious Qin armies, who later brought all of China under their control. At the time, the lakeside town of **Yueyang** was the haunt of the exiled poet-governor **Qu Yuan**, a victim of palace politics but nonetheless a great patriot of Chu. Hearing of the imminent invasion, Qu picked up a heavy stone and drowned himself in the nearby Miluo River rather than see his beloved state conquered. Distraught locals raced to save him in their boats, but were too late. They returned later to scatter *zongzi* (packets of meat and sticky rice wrapped up in reeds and lotus leaves) into the river as an offering to Qu Yuan's spirit.

The **Dragon Boat Festival**, held throughout China on the fifth day of the fifth lunar month (June or July), commemorates the rowers' hopeless rush – though many historians trace the tradition of food offerings and annual boat races to long before Qu's time. At any rate, it's a festive rather than mournful occasion; people consume huge quantities of steamed *zongzi*, and local dragon-boat teams compete to the steady boom of a pacing drum. You need to be up early to get the most from the festivities – the race only lasts only a few minutes.

become the first in the interior to be heavily industrialized. The colossal **Three Gorges hydroelectric dam** upstream from Yichang, car manufacturing – up and running with the help of foreign investment – and long-established iron and steel plants provide a huge source of income for central China.

As the "Gateway to Nine Provinces", skirted by mountains and midway along the Yangzi between Shanghai and Chongqing, Hubei has always been of great strategic importance. The central river regions feature prominently in the historical sixteenth-century novel *Romance of the Three Kingdoms* (see p.969), while the capital, **Wuhan**, thrives on industry and played a key role in China's early twentieth-century revolutions. In the west, the ranges that border Sichuan contain the holy peak of **Wudang Shan**, alive with Taoist temples and martial-arts lore, and the remote **Shennongjia Forest Reserve**, said to be inhabited by China's yeti.

Wuhan

武汉, wǔhàn

One way or another, almost anyone travelling through central China has to pass through **WUHAN**, Hubei's vast capital. The name is a portmanteau label for three original settlements, separated by the Han and Yangzi rivers but connected by bridges, tunnels and ferries. On the west bank of the Yangzi, **Hankou** is the city's trade and business centre and boasts the best services and accommodation. South across the Han River is lightly industrial **Hanyang**, while **Wuchang** recedes southeast of the Yangzi into semirural parkland.

Wuhan's sheer size lends atmosphere and significance, even if the metropolis is not a traditional tourist centre. Hankou's former role as a foreign concession has left plenty of colonial European heritage in its wake, while Wuchang's **Provincial Museum** is one of China's best. There are also a couple of temples and historical monuments to explore, some connected to the **1911 revolution** that ended two thousand years of imperial rule (see p.932). On the downside, Wuhan's continued growth and development and the ongoing metro construction mean that the city currently feels like an enormous building site, and can make it a challenge even to cross the road. Furthermore, the city has a well-deserved reputation – along with Chongqing and Nanjing – as one of China's three summer "furnaces": between May and September you'll find the streets melting and the gasping population surviving on a diet of watermelon and iced treats.

Brief history

Wuhan first boomed during the nineteenth-century Taiping Rebellion, when trade was deflected away from the rebel capital, downstream at Nanjing. During the 1880s, the provincial viceroy **Zhang Zhidong** founded the country's first modern steelworks here, and the city became known as "the Chicago of China". But the twentieth century was not kind to Wuhan: on October 10, 1911, a **bomb** exploded prematurely at the Hankou headquarters of a revolutionary group dedicated to replacing imperial rule with a democratic government. Imperial troops executed the ringleaders, sparking a citywide uprising against the Manchus (Qing rulers), which levelled Hankou and soon spread across China, forcing the last emperor, Pu Yi, to abdicate. Hankou's foreign concession area was rebuilt, but anti-Western riots broke out in 1925 and again in 1927, prompting their return to Chinese administration. A few months later, the Guomindang stormed through on their Northern Expedition, returning briefly in 1937 to establish a national government in town before being forced farther west by the Japanese. Thirty years later, Wuhan saw more fighting, this time between the PLA and various Red Guard factions, who had been slugging it out over differing interpretations of Mao's Cultural Revolution.

Hankou

汉口, hànkŏu

The largest of Wuhan's districts, **Hankou** was a simple fishing harbour until it opened as a treaty port in 1861 – a move greatly resented by the Chinese, who took to stoning any foreigners bold enough to walk the streets. Consequently, the Chinese were barred from the riverside concession area, which over the following decades was developed as a smaller version of Shanghai, complete with a racetrack and a **Bund** (flood-preventing

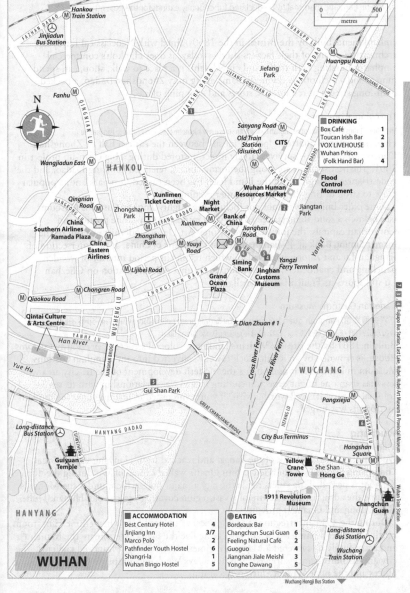

Airport & Wuhan Train Station

DRINKING	
Box Café	1
Toucan Irish Bar	2
VOX LIVEHOUSE	3
Wuhan Prison (Folk Hand Bar)	4

7

WUHAN

ACCOMMODATION	
Best Century Hotel	4
Jinjiang Inn	3/7
Marco Polo	2
Pathfinder Youth Hostel	6
Shangri-la	1
Wuhan Bingo Hostel	5

EATING	
Bordeaux Bar	1
Changchun Sucai Guan	6
Feeling Natural Café	2
Guoguo	4
Jiangnan Jiale Meishi	3
Yonghe Dawang	5

Wuchang Hongji Bus Station

7

THE DEMISE OF THE YANGZI RIVER DOLPHIN

The **baiji**, or **Yangzi river dolphin** (白鱀豚, báijì tún), was once a common sight along the middle Yangzi, and one of only four freshwater dolphin species worldwide. The animals – 2.5m long, with a long thin snout and a stubby dorsal fin – were seen as a good omen by fishermen, lending their name to Anhui's Baiji beer, which had their Latin name, *Lipotes vexillifer*, stamped on the bottle cap. But as China's population expanded, new forms of fishing, industrial pollution, river traffic and dam projects quickly decimated the numbers of sonar-guided baiji. A six-week, 3200km survey in 2006 failed to find a single dolphin, and they have since become the first aquatic mammal to be declared functionally extinct for the past fifty years.

embankments built by the British in the 1860s) lined with Neoclassical European architecture. Many of their facades survive today, as does Hankou's commercial emphasis: bursting with traffic and crowds, this is a place to walk, shop, eat, spend money and watch others doing the same along busy **Zhongshan Dadao**, a packed, 3km-long stretch of restaurants, stores and shopping plazas.

The colonial quarter

Metro line #1 runs overground above Jinghan Dadao with stops every kilometre or so; line #2 runs to Jianghan Lu

Hankou's **colonial quarter** – located mostly between the eastern half of Zhongshan Dadao and the river – survives largely intact, restored during a big clean-up project in 2001. The best sections are along the former Bund, renamed Yanjiang Dadao, and the pedestrianized Jianghan Lu; the Bund itself has been turned into parkland, a popular place to stroll during the stifling summer evenings.

Some older buildings to look for include the mighty **Jinghan Customs Museum** (see below), a solid Renaissance edifice with imposing grey-stone portico and Corinthian capitals; the unusual seven-storey Art Deco/Modernist exterior of the former **Siming Bank** at 45 Jianghan Lu; and the **Bank of China**, at the intersection of Jianghan Lu and Zhongshan Dadao, which retains its period interior of wooden panelling and chandeliers; while Hankou's defunct **old train station** on Chezhan Lu still sports its French Gothic shell.

Jianghan Customs Museum

江汉关博物馆, jiānghàn guān bówùguǎn • Cnr Yanjiang Lu and Yanjiang Dadao • Daily 9am–5pm • Free • ☏ 027 86794127 • Bus #7, #9, #30, #68, #212, #248 to Yanjiang Dadao Wuhan Guan

Built in 1861 by the British, Wuhan's landmark colonial structure, previously **Customs House**, is crowned by an iconic clock tower. Converted into the **Jianghan Customs Museum** in late 2015, it documents the modern development of the tri-city area with less bias than one might expect, including its awkward relationship with its semi-colonial history. It's well worth a visit, if you're interested in learning how the modern metropolis was forged.

Wuchang

武昌, wǔchāng

Wuchang, on the east bank of the Yangzi and reached from Hanyang via the **Great Changjiang Bridge**, was founded as Sun Quan's walled capital of Wu during the Three Kingdoms period. Tang rulers made the city a major port, which, under the Mongols, became the administrative centre of a vast region covering present-day Hunan, Hubei, Guangdong and Guangxi provinces.

During the 1911 insurrection, appalling scenes erupted here when ethnic Han troops mutinied under a banner proclaiming "Long live the Han, Exterminate the Manchu" and accordingly slaughtered a Manchu regiment and over eight hundred civilians. The city and its bureaucracy survived, and nowadays Wuchang comprises government offices and the huge Wuhan University campus.

Yellow Crane Tower

黄鹤楼, huánghè lóu • Daily 7am–6pm • ¥80 • Metro to Pangxiejia, or bus #10, #401 or #402

Overlooking the river from the low ridge of She Shan (蛇山, shé shān), the 50m-high **Yellow Crane Tower** is a riot of bright tiles and red columns. Legend has it that She Shan was once home to a Taoist Immortal who settled his tab at a nearby inn by drawing a picture of a crane on the wall, which would fly down at intervals and entertain the guests. A few years later the Immortal flew off on his creation, and the landlord, who doubtless could afford it by then, built the tower in his honour. The current structure is no less magnificent for being an entirely modern Qing-style reproduction, sited 1km from where an earlier version burned down in 1884; climb (or take the lift) to the top to see Wuhan and the Yangzi at their best.

Hong Ge and the 1911 Revolution Museum

红阁, hónggé /武汉辛亥革命博物馆, wǔhàn xīnhài gémìng bówùguǎn • Both: Yuemachang Pengliuchang Lu (near Snake Hill) • Tues–Sun 9am–5pm • Free with ID • Metro to Pangxiejia, or bus #401 or #402

At the southern foot of She Shan, **Hong Ge** is an imposing colonial-style red-brick mansion that housed the Hubei Military Government during the 1911 uprising. A bronze Sun Yatsen stands in front, although at the time he was abroad raising funds. A little further south, the striking V-shaped **1911 Revolution Museum** was opened in 2011 to commemorate a hundred years since the revolution, although its bold red exterior is more memorable than the exhibits inside.

Changchun Guan

长春观, chángchūn guān • Wuluo Lu • Daily 9am–5pm • ¥10 • Bus #15, #18 or #25

Around 1km east of Hong Ge, the russet-walled Taoist complex of **Changchun Guan** made its name through the Yuan-dynasty luminary Qiu Chuzi, who preached here and later founded his own sect. The halls are simply furnished with statues of the Three Purities, the Jade Emperor and other Taoist deities. Next door, Changchun's **vegetarian restaurant** is well worth a visit (see p.420).

Hubei Provincial Museum

湖北省博物馆, húběi shěng bówùguǎn • Donghu Lu • Tues–Sun 9am–5pm, last admission 3.30pm • Free • Bus #14, #401 or #402

The **Hubei Provincial Museum** features a display of items unearthed from the Warring States Period's tomb of the Marquis Yi. The marquis died in 433 BC and was buried in a huge, multilayered, wooden lacquered coffin in nearby Suizhou, then a major city of the state of Zeng. His corpse was accompanied by fifteen thousand bronze and wooden artefacts, 21 women and a dog. The museum has comprehensive English explanations of contemporary history and photos of the 1978 excavation.

Hubei Art Museum

湖北美术馆, húběi měishùguǎn • Donghu Lu, opposite the provincial museum • Tues–Sun 9am–5pm • Free • ☎ 027 82768112

The sizeable **Hubei Art Museum**, comprising 25,000 square metres of floor space over five floors, is an impressive nod to Wuhan's artistic legacy; the city is home to the prestigious Hubei Institute of Fine Arts and has produced many notable artists over

---

BELLS OF BRONZE

The Hubei Provincial Museum's impressive orchestra of 64 **bronze bells**, ranging in weight from a couple of kilos to a quarter of a tonne, were found in the marquis's waterlogged tomb along with the wooden frame from which they once hung in rows. Played with hand-held rods, each bell can produce two notes depending on where it is struck; the knowledge of metals and casting required to achieve this initially boggled modern researchers, who took five years to make duplicates. Brief performances (¥15) can be enjoyed in the museum's auditorium at 10.30am, 11.30am, 2.30pm and 3.30pm.

the years. The exhibitions vary greatly, from traditional to contemporary, but there's plenty to see from here and all over China.

East Lake

东湖, dōnghú • Bus #114, #401 or #402

The shores of Hankou's vast **East Lake** not only host the high-speed rail station, the provincial museum and the university, but also have designated **scenic areas** in their own right. It is a lovely spot, and locals will proudly tell you how it's five times the size of Hangzhou's West Lake (see p.327). **Moshan** (磨山风景区, móshān fēngjǐng qū), the pick of the lake' scenic locations, is known for its springtime plum and cherry blossoms, on view at Wuhan's **Botanical Gardens** (磨山植物园, móshān zhíwùyuán; daily 8am–5.30pm; ¥60).

ARRIVAL AND DEPARTURE WUHAN

More than 10km across, Wuhan has an extensive choice of transit points – there are four train stations and at least three main long-distance bus stations. Train and bus timetables usually spell out the district where services arrive, though the new CRH terminal is simply written on tickets as "Wuhan Station".

BY PLANE

Tianhe International Airport (天河飞机场, tiānhé fēijīchǎng) sits 30km to the north of Wuhan, with bus links (every 30min; ¥17–32) running to the long-distance bus stations and the China Southern airline office on Hangkong Lu in Hankou. There's also a direct hourly bus to the CRH station. A taxi into town will cost at least ¥80.

Destinations Beijing (1hr 40min); Guangzhou (1hr 35min); Hong Kong (1hr 50min); Shanghai (1hr 25min); Xiamen (1hr 30min).

BY TRAIN

Wuhan is central China's railway hub. Hankou and Wuchang are historic stations while the far newer Wuhan train station deals mainly with CRH. Check your ticket to be sure of where you arrive / depart from.

Hankou train station (汉口火车站, hànkǒu huǒchēzhàn) is an enormous "European style" construction on Fazhan Dadao. It mostly handles services from the north, along with express trains from Yichang. The station is well equipped with left luggage (¥10/24hr), and plenty of fast-food outlets and shops. Buses #9, #38, #519, #533, #561, #610 and metro line #2 will get you down to Hankou's waterfront.

Wuchang train station (武昌火车站, wǔchāng huǒchēzhàn) is southeast of the Yellow Crane Tower on Zhongshan Lu. Trains from southern China tend to stop here. Buses #10, #59, #66, #74, #507, #511, #518, #538, #561, #564, #577 will take you over the river to the station.

Pangjiaxia metro station is 1km away; exit the station and turn right.

Wuhan train station (武汉火车站, wǔhàn huǒchēzhàn). High-speed trains from across the country arrive at this station in northeast Wuchang. The station is connected to the city via metro line #4, but buses #610 (¥2) and #725 (¥1) also run into Hankou. A taxi to the town centre will cost around ¥50.

Destinations Beijing (many daily; 4hr 30min–18hr); Changsha (many daily; 1hr 30min–6hr); Chengdu (many daily; 9–10hr); Guangzhou (many daily; 3hr 30min–15hr); Nanchang (many daily; 2hr 45min–9hr 30min); Shanghai (many daily; 5–15hr); Shiyan (many daily; 4hr–9hr 30min); Wudang Shan (14 daily; 5–8hr); Xi'an (many daily; 5–15hr); Yueyang (many daily; 1–4hr); Yichang (many daily; 1hr 45min–5hr).

BY BUS

Fujiapo (付家坡车站, fùjiāpō chēzhàn), 358 Wuluo Lu, Wuchang. Wuchang's main station has services all over the country, including Shanghai, Yichang and Zhangjiajie. Bus #15, #18 or #25 run into town.

Jinjiadun (武昌 金家墩汽车站, wǔchāng jīnjiādūn qìchē zhàn), 170 Fazhan Dadao, Hankou. Opposite the train station, this major depot is connected to the city by metro line #2 and bus #38 to Yanjiang Dadao.

Wuchang Hongji (宏基汽车站, hóngjī qìchē zhàn), 519 Zhongshan Lu, Wuchang. Not far from Fujiapo,

WUHAN TOURIST BUS ROUTES

A convenient way to see the sprawling tri-city is to take the special **tourist buses** – all those beginning with the number four – that follow routes designed to cover the key sites (daily 7am–10pm, every ten minutes; all-day ticket ¥5). Lines #401 and #402 cover some of the most famous attractions including the Guiyuan Buddhist Temple, Yellow Crane Tower, East Lake and Provincial Museum. Bus #401 runs from Wuhan Passenger Port to East Lake, and #402 runs to the lake from Wuchang Railway Station.

Hongji has yet more services for the same destinations. Take bus #402 or #503 from Hankou.

Destinations Changsha (4hr); Hefei (6hr); Jingzhou (3hr 30min); Jiujiang (4hr); Nanchang (6hr); Shanghai (12hr); Yichang (4hr); Yueyang (4hr); Zhangjiajie (12hr).

INFORMATION

Tours CITS, 909 Zhongshan Dadao, Hankou (☏027 82822120), are a well-informed, English-, German- and French-speaking agency, which can organize Three Gorges cruises and trips to Shennongjia and Wudang Shan. The tourist information centres near stations and notable tourist sites (daily 8.30am–midnight) have little to offer foreign visitors, least of all any spoken English.

The best information sources are the five-star hotels, most of which have a good selection of free maps and government-issued tourist brochures and leaflets on things to do in the city.

Maps Maps (¥8) of Wuhan showing transport routes can be picked up at kiosks and hotels around town, though English is currently lacking.

GETTING AROUND

By bus The main city-bus terminals are just opposite Hankou and Wuchang train stations. Services are regular and cheap – it only costs ¥2 between Wuchang and Hankou stations – and crawl out to almost every corner of the city between around 6am and 10pm.

By metro Metro line #1 is an elevated rail roughly following the curve of the river along Jinghan Dadao, while line #2 starts at Hankou Train Station and heads south across the river. Line #3 crosses the river, and line #4 connects Huangjinkou in the west of the city with Wuhan train station. At the time of writing, six more lines were under construction. Tickets are reasonable, ranging from ¥2 to ¥5.

By taxi Cabs are ubiquitous and run at ¥10 for the first 3km.

By ferry During daylight hours, there are passenger ferries across the Yangzi between the southern end of Hankou's Yanjiang Dadao and Wuchang's city-bus terminus, below and just north of the Changjiang Bridge; trips cost ¥1.5 and take about 15min.

By bike Wuhan's bike rental service is free; to use one, you'll need to get a rental card, available for a ¥300 deposit outside most metro stations.

ACCOMMODATION

Wuhan's hotels are fairly upmarket, but there are some cheaper options, and mid-range places can be good value. All of the following are located in **Hankou**.

Best Century Hotel 好百年饭店, hǎobǎinián fàndiàn. 131 Yanjiang Dadao ☏027 82777798. This is one of the few options to stay in a bona fide colonial-era building, though the facade is more impressive than the interior. The modern styling of the rooms is fading fast, and the cheaper rooms come in all shapes and sizes, some of which only have interior windows, so ask to see a few. River views are more expensive, but also noisier. Still, it's comfortable enough and is in a great location. **¥230**

Jinjiang Inn 锦江之星, jǐnjiāng zhīxīng. 5 Nanjing Lu ☏027 59353666 & 62 Hongshan Lu ☏027 87810088, ⓦjinjianginns.com. Two of Wuhan's *Jinjiang Inns* offer great locations for travellers, the one on Nanjing Lu very central, the other opposite East Lake Park. Of the two, the Nanjing Lu branch is slightly nicer, but both have the same clean and comfortable rooms. **¥113**

Marco Polo 马哥孛罗酒店, mǎgē bóluó jiǔdiàn. 159 Yanjiang Dadao ☏027 82778888, ⓦmarco polohotels.com. Located on the waterfront, this international hotel is the lap of luxury, but good discounts during quiet times mean it can be a comparative bargain. Rooms are super sleek in blond wood, and standalone tubs overlook the river in the better rooms. **¥780**

Pathfinder Youth Hostel 深路者国际青年旅舍, shēnlùzhě guójì qīngnián lǚshè. 368 Zhongshan Lu, near Hubei Art Gallery ☏027 88844092. What was once a funky budget haunt with graffiti on the walls is looking a tad dilapidated these days; the damp has set in, and *Pathfinder* is well overdue for a new lick of paint and some staff training. That said, this YHA hostel remains popular with students and backpackers, and operates a great café-bar with occasional live music. Dorms **¥45**, doubles **¥160**

Shangri-La 香格里拉大酒店, xiānggélǐlā dàjiǔdiàn. 700 Jianshe Dadao ☏027 85806868, ⓦshangri-la.com. Wuhan's first international five-star may have been superseded in some ways by the *Marco Polo*, but the prize for the city's comfiest bed is still safe with the *Shangri-La*, and visiting celebs choose to stay here. Several restaurants and all the usual five-star amenities make for a smooth stay. **¥658**

Wuhan Bingo Hostel 武汉汉阳造国际青年旅舍, wǔhàn hànyáng zào guójì qīngnián lǚshè. 9–7 Hangyangzao Culture Zone ☏027 84770648. This solid budget option is in a great spot, inside a converted old factory area that has become an art-district-cum-youth-zone. Rooms are as colourful as the neighbourhood, and there's a great roof terrace. Dorms **¥55**, doubles **¥175**

EATING

Wuhan's **food** reflects its position midway between Shanghai and Chongqing, and **restaurants** offer a good balance of eastern-style steamed and braised dishes – particularly **fish and shellfish** – along with some seriously spicy flavours. There's also a strong snacking tradition in town, with many places specializing in **dumplings**: various types of *shaomai*; *tangbao*, soup buns stuffed with jellied stock which burst messily as you bite them, much to the amusement of other diners; and *doupi*, sticky rice packets stuffed with meat and rolled up in a bean-paste skin.

HANKOU

Bordeaux Bar 波尔图酒吧, bō'ěrtú jiǔbā. Yanjiang Dadao ☎027 82778779. One of many such café-bars in the area, replete with pavement tables and dimmed lighting. The Western-style pasta and steak dishes, along with Chinese dishes, are expensive; expect at least ¥120/head. Daily 10.30am–1.30am.

Feeling Natural Café 西餐酒吧, xīcān jiǔbā. Jianghan 1 Lu ☎027 82825919. This big, open, airy and friendly café-bar just off Jianghan Lu serves a good range of Western meals including breakfasts (from ¥25), burgers (from ¥20), pastas and salads. Special deals every night make this place a popular drinking spot, and you can also partake in shisha-smoking (¥50). Daily 10am–3am.

★**Guoguo** 锅锅, guōguō. Jiaotong Lu. Ridiculously popular canteen serving excellent, inexpensive breaded dumplings dripping in chilli oil. Order at the counter, then wait in line. Daily 11am–8pm.

Jiangnan Jiale Meishi 江南家乐美食, jiāngnán jiālèměishí. Jiaotong Lu. Two doors up from *Guoguo*, this busy canteen serves up the whole range of local delicacies at just a fraction of the cost of the more proper restaurants. Daily 11am–8pm.

Yonghe Dawang 永和大王, yǒnghé dàwáng. Jianghan Lu, and elsewhere. Open around the clock, this restaurant chain's logo looks suspiciously like *KFC's*, but the food is very different: big bowls of *doujiang* (beef noodle soup), steamed buns and fried rice. ¥25 will see you well fed. Daily 24hr.

WUCHANG

Changchun Sucai Guan 长春素菜馆, chángchūn sùcàiguǎn. Wulou Lu, just east of the Changchun temple. Vegetarian restaurant with Ming decor and a resolutely Chinese menu. The "beef" and "chicken" are made from bean-curd sheets, "prawns" from bean starch, and so on. Portions are good, liberally laced with chillies and aniseed, and very tasty. Mains from ¥30 or so. Daily 8.30am–8.30pm.

DRINKING

Box Café 盒子咖啡, hézǐ kāfēi. Yanjiang Dadao end of Chezhan Lu. Cosy and friendly little coffee shop opposite the former US embassy. Coffees from ¥20, beers from ¥15. Daily 11am–11pm.

Toucan Irish Bar 88 Ximachang Jie, inside the Holiday Inn Riverside ☎027 84716688. Pasties, pies and of course stout served in a prosaic Celtic pub setting. Not the most authentic expat haunt, but if you're looking to recharge and relax you could do worse. Expect to pay at least ¥100 per person for food and a drink. Daily 11am–midnight.

VOX LIVEHOUSE Guoguan Dasha, 118 Lumo Lu ☎13437 251621, ⊕facebook.com/voxlivehouse. Credited by the *Guardian* as the venue that "transformed Wuhan's music scene", this punk rock stalwart, out by East Lake, is popular with both Wuhan's lively student population and resident expats looking for something beyond karaoke. Door tickets vary for gigs, from free to ¥200. Daily 7.30pm–2am.

Wuhan Prison (Folk Hand Bar) 123 Lumo Lu ☎13545 116266. Excellent if poky place, down the road from *VOX LIVEHOUSE*. There's a strong selection of imported lager (¥25) and cocktails on offer, as well as occasional gigs. Daily 7pm–late.

SHOPPING

For **"antique" souvenirs**, try the shops at the Hubei Provincial Museum, Wuchang (see p.417). Like most Chinese cities, Hankou is a very good place to buy **clothes** – hit the new Grand Ocean Plaza or numerous smaller shops on Zhongshan Dadao.

DIRECTORY

Hospitals The Tongji, east of the Jiefang Dadao/Qingnian Lu crossroads in Hankou, is considered Wuhan's best.

Left luggage There are booths charging ¥5–10 a bag at the bus (daily 8am–8pm) and train stations (24hr).

Pharmacies In addition to smaller places elsewhere, Hankou's Hangkong Lu has a string of pharmacies stocking traditional and modern medicines, the biggest of which is the Grand Pharmacy, or, according to the English sign, the "Ark of Health". The most modern pharmaceutical chain in town is Professional Phuan Pharm, and they have branches at the northern end of Jianghan Lu and on Jiefang Dadao near the junction with Qingnian Lu.

Visa extensions The Foreign Affairs Department of the PSB (Mon–Fri 8am–noon & 2.30–5.30pm; ☎027 85395370) is contained within the ecofriendly but somehow daunting Wuhan Citizens Home, set just off Jinqiao Dadao, a 30min bus ride northeast of Hankou (bus #229 and #248). In spite of the sheer size of the building and the number of staff, expect long queues and strict requirements.

Jingzhou

荆州市, jīngzhōu shì

Around 240km west of Wuhan lies **JINGZHOU**, a historic walled city that had significant impact on the region during the Warring States and Three Kingdoms periods. The city is on the north bank of the Yangzi, where the Wuhan–Yichang expressway joins the highway up to Xiangfan in northern Hubei. The city divides into two districts: easterly **Shashi** is an uninteresting modern port, while **Jingzhou** itself, 10km west, is ringed by around 8km of moats and well-maintained, 7m-high battlements built by the Three Kingdoms hero Guan Yu. There are several notable temples and monuments to take in, including the Ming-era **Longevity Pagoda** (万寿宝塔, wànshòu bǎo tǎ) and the **Zhanghua Temple** (章华寺, zhāng huá sì) which hosts seasonal celebrations of the Taoist saint Guan Yu.

Jingzhou Museum

荆州博物馆, jīngzhōu bówùgǔan • Jingzhong Lu • Daily 8.30am–5.30pm • Free • City bus #1 from Shashi's long-distance bus station

The **Jingzhou Museum** includes a fantastic collection of Western Han (221 BC–24 AD) funerary remains that were excavated from more than 180 tombs located to the north. The exhibition here focuses on the tomb of a court official named Sui; in many regards the items on display are similar to those in Wuhan's provincial museum (see p.417) – the house-like sarcophagi and copious lacquerwork, for example – but the bonus here is Sui's astoundingly well-preserved **corpse**, along with some comfortingly practical household items and wooden miniatures of his servants.

Xiongjia Tombs

熊家冢, xióngjiā zhǒng • Daily 9.30am–4.30pm • ¥30 • Buses from Jingzhou cost ¥8 (1hr), round-trip taxis ¥100–150

The site where Jingzhou Museum's artefacts were found is 40km north of the city in the small village of Zhangchang. Sometimes compared to the Terracotta Warriors, the **Xiongjia Tombs** (presumed to belong to one of the Chu emperors and his family) offers an eerie glimpse into a 2000-year-old burial chamber, full of legions of horse skeletons and painted wooden chariots ready to do battle in a giant burial pit. There are a hundred chambers, many of which have yet to be excavated, but archeologists have already discovered China's largest cache of jade.

ARRIVAL AND DEPARTURE   JINGZHOU

By train Jingzhou's train station is northeast of the centre on the bus #1 route. Tickets for high-speed trains can easily be secured at the station on the day of travel.
Destinations Wuhan (many daily; 1hr 30min–3hr);

Yichang (many daily; 30min–1hr).
By bus Buses arrive at Shashi's long-distance bus station on Taqiao Lu. Bus #101 connects the station with Jingzhou.
Destinations Wuhan (4hr); Yichang (2hr).

Yichang

宜昌, yíchāng

You may well end up spending a night at **YICHANG**, a transport terminus on the Yangzi 120km upstream from Jingzhou and virtually in the shadow of the **Three Gorges Dam**. Ringed by car showrooms (western Hubei has long been a car manufacturing centre), the town is where visitors land after riding ferries and hydrofoils down through the Three Gorges – or it can be used as a staging post for visiting the dam itself. To the north, wild **Shennongjia Forest Reserve** is just a bus ride away (see p.424).

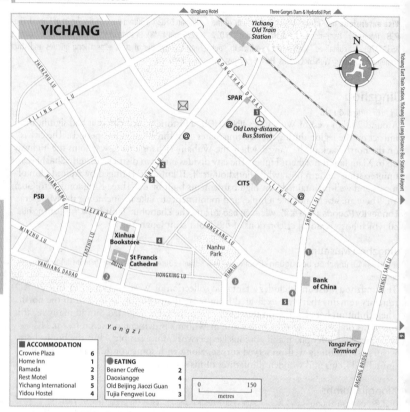

YICHANG

ACCOMMODATION

Crowne Plaza	6
Home Inn	1
Ramada	2
Rest Motel	3
Yichang International	5
Yidou Hostel	4

EATING

Beaner Coffee	2
Daoxiangge	4
Old Beijing Jiaozi Guan	1
Tujia Fengwei Lou	3

0 — 150 metres

The town

The town itself is of little interest, though remnants of Yichang's treaty port days provide a dash of character, such as the **St Francis Cathedral** (圣方济各堂, shèngfāngjǐ gè táng) on Zili Lu. In the face of the rapidly encroaching Japanese, Yichang also played a critical role in the 1938 evacuation of 30,000 people and nearly 100,000 tonnes of equipment west to Chongqing; a monument on Yanjiang Dadao commemorates this mammoth undertaking. Early evening is a good time to head down to the river and watch crowds flying kites, gorging themselves on shellfish at nearby street restaurants or cooling off with an ice cream.

ARRIVAL AND DEPARTURE
YICHANG

All plane, ferry, hydrofoil and train tickets are most easily booked through hotel tour desks (you don't have to be staying to use these). However, train tickets come with a fee, so you might want to buy them at the station or at one of the numerous train ticket offices around the city for a ¥5 service charge – much less than the hotels add on.

BY PLANE

By plane Yichang Sanxia airport (三峡机场, sānxiá jīchǎng) is 40km southeast of town, covered by an hourly shuttle bus (1hr; ¥20) to *Qingjiang Hotel* on Dongshan Lu in town, a ¥100–120 taxi fare.
Destinations Beijing (2hr–2hr 30min); Chongqing (1hr); Guangzhou (1hr 50min); Shanghai (1hr 35min).

BY TRAIN

Yichang Old train station (宜昌 火车站, yíchāng huǒchē zhàn). The Old train station is at the north side of town atop a broad flight of steps; this station is on the line north to Zhengzhou in Henan, or south to Zhangjiajie in Hunan.
Yichang East train station (宜昌 火车东站, yíchāng huǒchē dōng zhàn). High-speed trains for

Wuhan and beyond leave from the enormous East station which can be reached by bus #1 (¥1) or a ¥20 taxi ride. There's left luggage and an internet café here.

Destinations Beijing (8 daily; 7–18hr); Jingzhou (many daily; 30min–1hr); Shanghai (9 daily; 8–24hr); Wuhan (many daily; 1hr 45min–6hr); Xi'an (1 daily; 15hr 30min); Zhangjiajie (3 daily; 4hr 30min–5hr).

BY BUS

There are information desks and left-luggage offices at both terminals.

Yichang East long-distance bus station (宜昌东长汽车站, yíchāng dōng cháng qìchē zhàn; ☏0717 6445314) is next to Yichang East train station, and has services all over the province and the rest of the country.

Old long-distance bus station (长汽车客运站, chángqìchē kèyùnzhàn), 500m to the east of the train station on Dongshan Dadao. A few long-distance buses originate and terminate here, although as they all travel via the new East station, it's far better to buy tickets and start your journey there.

Destinations Changsha (6hr); Jingzhou (2hr); Jiujiang (8–10hr); Muyu Zhen (5hr); Wudang Shan (6hr); Wuhan (4hr); Xiangfan (5hr); Xing Shan (4hr);

BY BOAT

By hydrofoil For those without the time or money for a full Three Gorges cruise, taking the hydrofoil will give glimpses of the grandeur, albeit accompanied by a noisy engine. Hydrofoils run from Taiping Xi hydrofoil port (太平溪码头, tàipíngxī mǎtóu) above the Three Gorges Dam to Badong (for Shennong Stream), Wushan (for Lesser Three Gorges) and Fengjie; at the time of writing they continued to Fengjie, though Fengjie will be the terminus once regional highways are completed. The hydrofoil company lays on free transport between the port and their offices in town. There are five departures daily to Wanzhou (5hr; ¥300); when you buy your ticket, get the agent to write down the address of their office to show a cab driver, as this is where the bus to the port leaves from. Staff onboard the hydrofoil sell bus tickets from the terminus to Chongqing.

By ferry Public ferry tickets for the two-day journey upstream to Chongqing (see box, p.760) can be bought through your accommodation. Fares to Chongqing range from ¥152 for a berth in an open dorm to ¥1042 per person for a private cabin. Some boats also stop at Wushan, Fengjie, Wanxian, Shibaozhai and Fengdu.

GETTING AROUND AND TOURS

By bus City buses normally cost ¥2.

By taxi A cab costs a fixed ¥6 within the city centre and shouldn't go above ¥10 to reach the outskirts.

Boat tours and cruises A number of private cruise companies run Yangtze River tours, mostly catering to the luxury end of the market. Dragon Cruises (☏0717 8860467) operates five-star multiday cruises March–Nov, departing weekly from Yichang.

ACCOMMODATION

Crowne Plaza 宜昌万达皇冠假日酒店, yíchāng wàn huángguān jiàri jiǔdiàn. 169 Yanjiang Dadao ☏0717 6588888. Excellent indoor pool, banquet halls and all-mod-con rooms make this riverside luxury hotel popular among the executive class of Yangtze River cruisers. **¥508**

Home Inn 如家酒店, rújiā jiǔdiàn. 126 Dongshan Dadao ☏0717 6915818, ⓦhomeinns.com. This branch of the budget chain offers clean, comfortable rooms and a good location next to the long-distance bus station. Decent value for an overnight stay. **¥179**

Ramada 华美达酒店 huáměidá jiǔdiàn. 27 Yunji Lu ☏0717 6528888, ⓦramada.com. Rooms and bathrooms are a little small for the money, but this is still far and away Yichang's most comfortable hotel, with a great location and all of the amenities you'd expect from this international chain. **¥370**

Rest Motel 锐思特汽锁酒店, ruìsītè qìsuǒ jiǔdiàn. 31 Yunji Lu ☏0717 6236888, ⓦrestmotel.com.cn. A very central location, low prices and more character than the average budget business-chain motel make the *Rest Motel* a good option, although some rooms suffer from road noise. **¥130**

Yichang International 国际大酒店, guójìdà jiǔdiàn. 121 Yanjiang Dadao ☏0717 6222888. Once Yichang's long-standing top option, the *International* offers a good location, nice views and decent discounts, although some of the cheaper rooms come in unusual shapes and sizes – ask to see another room if you're not happy. **¥260**

Yidou Hostel 宜豆青年旅馆, yídòu qīngnián lǚguǎn. 40 Fusui Lu ☏0717 6225733. A solid budget option, this centrally located hostel has colourful rooms and offers bike rental. Dorms **¥50**, doubles **¥140**

EATING

You certainly won't go hungry in Yichang. **Canteens** and **street stalls** seem to line every back alley, and there's a good collection of local places on Yi Ma Lu. **Western fast food** can be found near the old long-distance bus station in the centre of town, and there are also a growing number of **coffee shops**.

7

Beaner Coffee 宾乐美式咖啡, bīnlè měishì kāfēi. Yunji Lu. Generic Western-style café serving expensive coffee and a reasonable imitation of Western food including sandwiches, pasta and steaks. The location just off Yanjiang Dadao makes it a good place to take a break after a riverside wander. Around ¥50–100 per person. Daily 11am–11pm.

Daoxiangge 稻香阁, dàoxiāng gé. 31 Shengli Si Lu ⓘ0717 6222107. Enduringly popular place specializing in fish, but whose menu also stretches to dumplings (¥20) and game meats. Expect to pay ¥50–100 per person. Daily 9am–2pm & 4.30–9pm.

Old Beijing Jiaozi Guan 老北京饺子馆, lǎoběijīng jiǎoziguǎn. 23 Shengli Si Lu ⓘ1517 1847227. A simple restaurant that serves up a variety of cheap and tasty northern-style dumplings; plain pork and cabbage are by far the best. Around ¥30 per person. Daily 11am–9pm.

Tujia Fengwei Lou 土家风味楼, tǔjiā fēngwèi lóu. 33 Yi Ma Lu ⓘ0717 6230577. Small, friendly and very popular place serving home-style dishes – the Tujia is a local ethnic group, scattered through the Yangzi gorges – including very spicy hotpots and tasty sweet-and-sour ribs (¥38). Daily 9.30am–9.30pm.

Three Gorges Dam

长江三峡大坝, chángjiāng sānxiá dàbà • ¥105; includes 1hr 30min tour of site in a perspex-roofed minibus

The largest construction in China since the Great Wall, the **Three Gorges Dam**, 35km west of Yichang at Sandouping, can be done in a day-trip. Completed in 2006, by 2010 the dam raised water levels upstream by up to 175m, by holding back a 660km-long lake. It is the world's largest producer of hydroelectric power, capable of generating 22,500 megawatts, or the equivalent of over fifteen nuclear power plants.

Part of the dam's stipulated purpose is also to control the disastrous summer **flooding** which has long afflicted the lower Yangzi. The dam received its first serious test in 2010, when torrential monsoonal rains upstream were just contained; this happened again in 2012. **Critics** of the dam, meanwhile, label it a vanity project that submerged countless archeological sites, required the relocation of millions of people, and which will become redundant through siltation within seventy years. Whatever your opinion on the dam, it's unquestionably an impressive sight.

ARRIVAL AND DEPARTURE   THE THREE GORGES DAM

By bus Take a northbound bus #4 from Yunji Lu in front of the train station to the Yemingzhu stop, then bus #8 (¥10) to Liuzhashou Reception Centre (六闸首游客接待中心, liùzháshǒu yóukè jiēdài zhōngxīn) – ask the driver where to get off (roughly 1hr 30min).

By bus tour Daily bus tours depart from the old ferry terminal on Yanjiang Dadao. Tours leave at 8am and return at 1pm, and cost ¥150 including entry ticket.

Shennongjia Forest Reserve

神农架林区, shénnóng línqū • Five-day combo ticket ¥269 in summer, ¥130 in winter (bring your passport); independent scenic spot tickets ¥60–140 • Daily 6.30am -5.30pm

Hidden away 200km northwest of Yichang in Hubei's far west, **Shennongjia Forest Reserve** encloses a rugged chain of mountains, culminating in the 3053m-high Shennongjia Peak, the tallest peak in central China. The area has been famed for its plant life ever since the legendary Xia king Shennong – credited with introducing mankind to farming, medicine and tea – scoured these heights for herbs. More recently, the plant-hunter Ernest Wilson found several new species here in the early twentieth century. And, more fancifully, Shennongjia has been the setting for numerous sightings of the Chinese **wild man** – even if he eludes you, there's a chance of seeing endangered **golden monkeys** here. The park was made into a UNESCO heritage site in 2016; it's divided into six scenic areas, best accessed from the tourist village of **Muyu**. However, note that some have limited access for foreigners – check the current situation on arrival.

The reserve

The reserve entrance takes you directly into the **Yazikou** (鸭子口, yāzikǒu) area, where you hand over the entrance fee and add your name and passport number to the list of the few foreigners who make it here each year.

Xialong Tan

小龙潭, xiǎolóng tán

From the gates, 6km of gravel track runs southwest up a valley to the couple of Forestry Department buildings that comprise **Xiaolong Tan**, where close-up views of **golden monkeys** (金丝猴, jīnsīhóu) are available at the "animal hospital". There's also a **Wild Man Museum**, where paintings, newspaper clippings, maps and casts of footprints document all known encounters with the gigantic, shaggy, red-haired **ye ren**, first seen in 1924. The creature was most recently spotted in June 2003 by a party of six, including a local reporter, who described the beast as being 1.65m tall, of greyish hue, with shoulder-length hair and a footprint measuring some 30cm.

Jinhou Ling

金猴岭, jīnhóu lǐng

There are some good walks around Xiaolong Tan. One route (much of it along a vehicle track) climbs south for around 2.5km to a forest of China firs on the slopes of **Jinhou Ling**, a prime spot to catch family groups of golden monkeys foraging first thing in the morning. Favouring green leaves, stems, flowers and fruit, the monkeys live through the winter on lichen and moss, which cover the trees here. The males especially are a tremendous sight, with reddish-gold fur, light blue faces and huge lips. A far rougher trail continues to the top of the mountain in four hours.

Dalong Tan

大龙潭, dàlóng tán

A relaxed, 3km stroll north of Xiaolong Tan is **Dalong Tan**, a cluster of run-down huts by a stream, from where there's an undemanding 8km walk up the valley to **Guanyin Cave** (观音洞, guānyīn dòng). Most of this is through open country, which gets plenty of wildflowers in the spring; birders can spot **golden pheasants** (红胸山鸡, hóngxiōng shānjī) and grouse-like **tragopans** (红胸角稚, hóngxiōng jiǎozhì).

The Banbi Yan road

The gravel **road** from Xiaolong Tan curves westwards up the valley, climbing almost continually along the ridges and, in clear weather, affording spectacular views. On the way, you'll cross **Da Shennongjia** (大神农架, dà shénnóngjià), though the rounded peak is barely noticeable above the already high road. Better are the cliffscapes about 10km along at **Fengjing Ya** (风景垭, fēngjǐng yà) and the "forest" of limestone spires where the road finally gives up the ghost 17km due west of Xiaolong Tan at **Banbi Yan** (板壁岩, bǎnbì yán).

Muyu Zhen

木鱼镇, mùyú zhèn

From Yichang, the road climbs through well-farmed, increasingly mountainous country overloaded with hydroelectric stations, passing tea fields and immense tower karst formations before following the narrow Shennong gorge to emerge at the rapidly expanding settlement of **MUYU ZHEN**, 17km south of the reserve. For the time being, the town manages to feel quite remote, with locals still using woven basket backpacks to haul produce up and down the mountain, and wild honey collectors selling their hard-earned wares on the main street. However, tourism is changing things: modern apartments are being built on the edge of town, and the **airport**, opened in 2014 – but so far with little commercial traffic – is expected to bring a surge in visitors. The highest in China outside the Tibetan Plateau, Shennongjia Hongping Airport sits at 2580m above sea level. Its construction caused significant damage to the surrounding environment, provoking much controversy. By 2020 the airport is expected to handle 250,000 passengers a year, so you might want to visit Shennongjia sooner rather than later.

ARRIVAL AND INFORMATION

By plane Newly opened Shennongjia Hongping Airport is 50km from Muyu Zhen.
Destination Wuhan (1 daily; 1hr).
By bus The bus station is located at the northern end of town, a short walk from the hotels and restaurants. You can buy tickets here, although it's worth getting them the day before if you plan on leaving early.
Destination Yichang (4hr).
Tourist office The Shennong Tourism Office (☏ 0719 3456018) on the main street doesn't seem to open very often, but theoretically can provide information.

GETTING AROUND

By minibus To reach the reserve gates at Yazikou from Muyu, flag down one of the plentiful early-morning Songbai-bound minivans on the main road (¥10). Hiring the whole minibus for the day costs ¥300–400.
By taxi Taxis to the reserve gates at Yazikou can be bargained to ¥20.

ACCOMMODATION

There's abundant **accommodation** at Muyu Zhen, though things can get busy at weekends and holidays. Most of the **cheaper places** are to be found on the main road through town, so it's quite easy to haggle over a few places before deciding. Aside from at the upscale hotels, it's always worth checking the **hot water** situation before you check in.

Laojin Shanzhuang 老金山庄, lǎojīn shānzhuāng. Above and behind Holiday Hotel ☏ 0719 3313555. This small and simple hotel has cheap, clean and spacious rooms with the odd glimpse of mountain. The rooms have 24hr hot water and flat-screen TVs; the owners are friendly but don't speak any English. ¥131
Shennong Holiday Hotel 假日酒店, jiǎrì jiǔdiàn. Set off the main road at the bottom of town ☏ 0719 3452600. An enormous property recently redeveloped by Shennong Tourism with clean and comfortable, if spartan, rooms but no views. The larger and better furnished deluxe rooms are worth the extra money. Doubles ¥98, deluxe ¥350
Teafield Farmstay 茶园农庄, cháyuán nóngzhuāng. Above Shennong Shanzhuang ☏ 158 97876848. Halfway up the hill, this farmstay has clean, simple rooms and delicious fresh food served in the small dining room by the welcoming owners. The rooftop terrace is a great place to enjoy a cuppa surrounded by tea fields. Get a Chinese-speaker to call ahead to arrange pickup from town. ¥140

EATING

The hills are alive with wonderful **medicinal herbs** and exotic **game**; Muyu's cuisine reflects this, but most places also serve a selection of favourites from around the country.

Luanchao Luanchi 乱炒乱吃, luànchǎo luànchī. Top end of the main street ☏ 138 86843410. Local specialities plus a good selection of Sichuan dishes including *yuxiang qiezi* (¥18) are best enjoyed in the upstairs open-sided dining room. Daily 8.30am–10pm.
Xiaolou Yushui Renjia 小楼渔水人家, xiǎolóu yúshuǐ rénjiā. Across the bridge south of the Shennong Tourism Office ☏ 0717 6222107. Delicious mountain dishes served in a lovely location, right on the river. Bamboo rice, mountain mushrooms, "wild" vegetables and spicy pork (¥48) all feature on the menu. If the weather is nice, ask if you can eat outside. Daily 9am–2pm & 4–9pm.

Wudang Shan

武当山, wǔdāng shān • ¥140 (¥119 during some hols); Zixiao Gong (Grand Purple Cloud Palace) ¥15; Jindian Gong (Golden Palace) ¥20; cable car ¥80 up, ¥70 down

Way up in northwestern Hubei, the 72 peaks of **Wudang Shan**, the Military Mountain, are steeped in legends surrounding its Taoist temples and fighting style. Wudang is associated with **Zhen Wu**, a martial deity whose portly statue graces many local temples, and whose birthday is celebrated on the third day of the third lunar month – a good time to visit the mountain. Wudang's martial arts would have come in handy considering the vast number of outlaws who've inhabited these mountains over the centuries, not least the rebel peasant **Li Zicheng**, who amassed his forces and eventually deposed the last Ming emperor from here.

Many temple buildings here date to an imperial building frenzy during the fifteenth century – the work took three hundred thousand labourers ten years to complete – and the mountain is currently enjoying a bloom of tourist-funded religious fervour. The Zixiao Gong is the best-preserved Taoist building on the mountain, and the Jindian Gong atop the main peak is splendid. The relatively easy ascent, coupled with the mountain's superb scenery and the availability of transport connections, makes this an appealing trip.

Wudang Shan town
武当山市镇, wǔdāngshān shìzhèn

The market town of **Wudang Shan**, base for ascents of the mountain, sits with the famed ranges rising immediately to its south. It's not a big place, stretching thinly for a few kilometres along the main road, **Taihe Lu** (太和路, tàihélù), with a few side streets branching off. South down Huangbang Lu is the new **Wudang Shan Museum** (武当山博物馆, wǔdāngshān bówùguǎn; free), which traces the history of martial arts here and has plenty of English signs.

On the mountain

It's possible to **hike** from Wudang Shan town to the summit in about eight hours; the footpath starts near the train station. Otherwise, a road ascends from the **mountain**

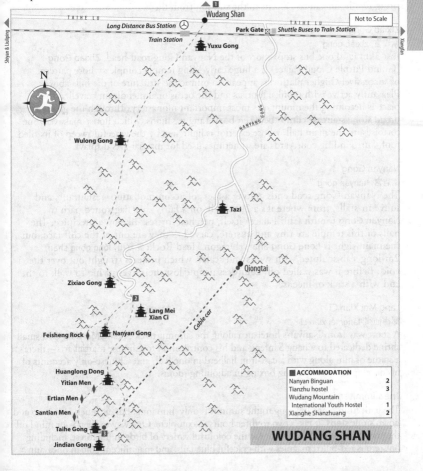

ACCOMMODATION	
Nanyan Binguan	2
Tianzhu hostel	3
Wudang Mountain	
International Youth Hostel	1
Xianghe Shanzhuang	2

WUDANG SHAN

WUDANG'S MARTIAL ARTS

Wudang is most famous for its **martial arts**, which command as much respect as those of Henan's Shaolin Monastery (see p.263). It's said that the Song-dynasty monk **Zhang Sanfeng** developed Wudang boxing – from which *tai ji* is derived – after watching a fight between a snake and a magpie, which revealed to him the essence of *neijia*, an internal force used (in typical Taoist manner) to control "action" with "non-action".

Those interested in learning some Wudang **wushu** can try several academies: good options are Wudang Daoist Traditional Internal Kungfu Academy (武当山传统武术馆, **wǔdāngshān chuántǒng wǔshùguǎn**; ☏ 1359786695, ⓦ wudanggongfu.com) and Wudang Daoist Martial Arts Academy (☏ 13593716770, ⓦ wudangmartialarts.com), where you should be able to negotiate a course from around ¥2000 per week.

gates some 2km from town, providing two options for reaching the top, both covered by buses. The easiest, and a popular option for those short of time or energy, is to catch the bus to the **cable-car station at Qiongtai** (琼台索道站, qióngtái suǒdào zhàn), from where gondolas ascend to the summit area. The other option is to bus it halfway up the mountain to the clutch of temples and hotels at Nanyan Gong, and then make the tiring two-hour staircase ascent to the summit from there.

Zixiao Gong

紫霄宫, zǐxiāo gōng

Just 3km (and one bus stop) short of the Nanyan Gong road-head, **Zixiao Gong** (Grand Purple Cloud Palace) is a huge early Ming temple complex whose pattern of successively higher platforms appears to mimic the structure of the hills above. Pleasantly active with monks, tourists and the occasional mendicant traveller, the place is becoming the mountain's most important monastery. Through the gates, a broad stone staircase climbs between boxy Tang pavilions, which house massive stone tortoises, to the main hall, whose exterior is lightened by the graceful sweep of its tiled roof. Surrounding courtyards are sometimes used for martial-arts displays.

Nanyan Gong

南岩宫, nányán gōng

The Nanyan Gong road ends among a mess of accommodation, restaurants and souvenir stalls, from where it's a 2km walk on a fairly easy flagstoned path to **Nanyan Gong** (South Cliff Palace) itself, perched fortress-like on a precipice. The halls of this temple are tiny and austere, carved as they are out of the cliff face, but the main sight is **Long Gong Shan** (Dragon Head Rock; 龙宫山, lóng gōng shān), a 2m-long slab sculpted with swirls and scales, which projects straight out over the void. Before it was walled off, countless people lost their lives trying to walk to the end with a stick of incense.

Lang Mei Xian Ci

郎梅仙祠, lángméi xiān cí

A short way from Nanyan's hotel area along the summit track is **Lang Mei Xian Ci**, a small shrine dedicated to Zhang Sanfeng and his contribution to Chinese martial arts – there's a statue of him along with a cast-iron halberd in one hall, and Chinese-only accounts of his development of Wudang boxing in adjoining rooms.

The summit staircase

The path from Nanyan Gong to the summit is only 4km long, but, as much of it is up and down stone **steps**, it takes two to three hours to complete. One way to keep your mind off the endless steps is to watch out for the colourful variety of **birds** in the forest, including boisterous red-billed magpies with graceful blue tails, and magnificent golden pheasants.

Halfway up to Tianzhu, the path divides at **Huanglong Dong** (黄龙洞, huánglóng dòng; Yellow Dragon Cave) to form an eventual circuit via the peak. Turn left for the longer but less steep "hundred-step-ladder" (a lie; it's considerably more), with superb views through the canopy of cloud-swept, apparently unscalable cliffs. Alternatively, bearing right puts you on the even steeper, dangerously uneven staircase to the summit area via **Santian Men** (三天门, sāntiān mén), the Three Sky Gates – a route perhaps best saved for the descent.

Tianzhu Peak

天主蜂, tiānzhǔ fēng

Whichever route you take, paths converge outside an encircling wall that has turned 1600m-high **Tianzhu Peak** and its temples into a well-defended citadel. Inside, the Ming-dynasty **Taihe Gong** (太和宫, tàihé gōng) is impressive for the atmosphere of grand decay enclosed by the thick green tiles and red walls of **Huangjing Hall** (皇经堂, huángjīng táng), where monks stand around the cramped stone courtyards or pray in the richly decorated, peeling rooms that are squeezed inside.

Jidiang Gong

金殿宫, jīndiàn gōng • ¥20

Above Taihe Gong, and accessed via yet another steep staircase, the mountain is literally crowned by **Jindian Gong** (Golden Palace Temple), a tiny shrine with a gilded bronze roof embellished with cranes and deer, whose interior is filled by a statue of armour-clad Zhen Wu sitting behind a desk in judgement. It's a magical place: **views** from the front terrace (clearest in the morning) look down from the top of the world, with sharp crags dropping away through wispy clouds into the forest below.

ARRIVAL AND DEPARTURE   WUDANG SHAN

By train Wudang town's train station on Chezhan Lu is served by trains from around the country, but sleeper tickets can be scarce, so it's worth booking your ticket as soon as you arrive.
Destinations Beijing (4 daily; 19–22hr); Chongqing (3 daily; 11hr); Shanghai (3 daily; 22–25hr); Wuhan (5 daily; 6hr–8hr).
By bus The town's long-distance bus station is at the junction of Taihe Lu and Chezhan Lu.
Destinations Wuhan (8–10hr); Yichang (6hr).

ACCOMMODATION

Accommodation in Wudang Shan town is plentiful along Taihe Lu and tends toward the cheap, no-frills end of the market, though en-suite rooms are the norm. Prices can climb unreasonably at peak times, however.

WUDANG SHAN TOWN

Wudang Mountain International Youth Hostel 武当山国际青年旅舍, wǔdāngshān guójì qīngnián lǚshè. 2 Gongyuan Lu ☎ 0719 5662333. Located right in the centre of town, this clean, international hostel is the best bet for budget and solo travellers with a clean lounge and bar area. Dorms ¥40, doubles ¥138

NANYAN

Places to stay line the road at Nanyan for the few hundred metres between the bus drop-off and the start of the hiking trails up the mountain. Advertised rates are outrageous, but only apply when demand outstrips supply – come on Sun or at the beginning of the week when it's quieter, and you can pretty much name your price. Quality of rooms is similar across the board – modern, prematurely aged and basically clean – but check when hot water is available.

Nanyan Binguan 南岩宾馆, nányán bīnguǎn. ☎ 0719 5689182. Slightly better-than-average choice of large doubles and twins with decent amenities, or smaller budget rooms with basic bathrooms. There's also a reasonable on-site restaurant. ¥120

Xianghe Shanzhuang 祥和山庄, xiánghé shānzhuāng. 23 Wudang Lu ☎ 0719 5689018. The first hotel after the bus stop, this place offers plain rooms at eminently bargainable prices; it's absolutely typical of Nanyan's offerings. ¥96

THE SUMMIT

Tianzhu hostel Next to the upper cable-car terminus, just outside the Tianzhu Feng temple complex. A good place to stay overnight, with a chance to catch the sunrise and experience the mountain without tourist hordes. ¥150

7

DIRECTORY

Banks There's a Bank of China with ATM on Taihe Lu in Wudang Shan town.
Left luggage There's a left luggage office at the park gates where you can drop off any luggage you don't want to haul up the mountain (¥10/item/day).

Hunan

湖南, húnán

In many ways, **HUNAN** is a pastiche of the tourist image of rural China – a view of endless muddy tracts or paddy fields rolling past the train window, coloured green or gold depending on the season. But the bland countryside, or rather the peasants farming it, has greatly affected the country's recent history. Hunan's most famous peasant son, **Mao Zedong**, saw the crushing poverty inflicted on local farmers by landlords and a corrupt government, and the brutality with which any protests were suppressed. Though Mao is no longer accorded his former god-like status, monuments to him litter the landscape around the provincial capital **Changsha**, which is a convenient base for exploring the areas where he spent his youth.

Both Hunan and Hubei – literally "south of the lake" and "north of the lake" respectively – take their names from **Dongting Hu**, China's second-largest lake, which also provided the origins of dragon-boat racing. South of Changsha, **Heng Shan** houses a pleasant assortment of mountain temples, while **Zhangjiajie Scenic Reserve** in the far west boasts inspiringly rugged landscapes. A few hours south of here lies the picturesque town of **Fenghuang**, a well-preserved ancient town where you'll find remnants of the Southern Great Wall.

Changsha

长沙, chángshā

CHANGSHA, Hunan's high-rise-filled capital, had been an important river town for millennia before its demarcation as a treaty port in 1903. Europeans had hoped to exploit the city's trading position, upstream from Dongting Lake astride the Xiang River, but found that the Hunanese had a very short fuse (something other Chinese already knew): after the British raised the market price of rice during a famine in 1910, the foreign quarter was totally destroyed by rioting. Guomindang forces torched much of the rest of the city in 1938 as they fled the Japanese advance (see p.934), and recent modernizations have finished the job of demolishing the past. Today, away from the bustling shopping district and vibrant nightlife, sights linked to Chairman Mao account for the majority of Changsha's formal attractions. However, there are also

CHANGSHA AND THE CHAIRMAN

Primarily, Changsha is known for its links with **Mao Zedong**, who arrived here in 1911 at the age of 18, as nationwide power struggles erupted following the collapse of the Manchu dynasty. By 1918 there was a real movement for Hunan to become an independent state and, for a time, this found favour with local warlord **Zhao Hendi**, though he soon turned violently on his own supporters. Mao, back in his hometown of Shaoshan, heading a Communist Party branch, was singled out for persecution and in 1925 fled to Guangzhou, taking up a teaching post at the Peasant Movement Training Institute. Within three years he returned to Hunan, organizing the abortive **Autumn Harvest Uprising** and establishing guerrilla bases in rural Jiangxi.

Mao was by no means the only young Hunanese caught up in these events, and a number of his contemporaries surfaced in the Communist government, including **Liu Shaoqi**, Mao's deputy until he became a victim of the Cultural Revolution; and **Hua Guofeng**, Mao's lookalike and briefly empowered successor.

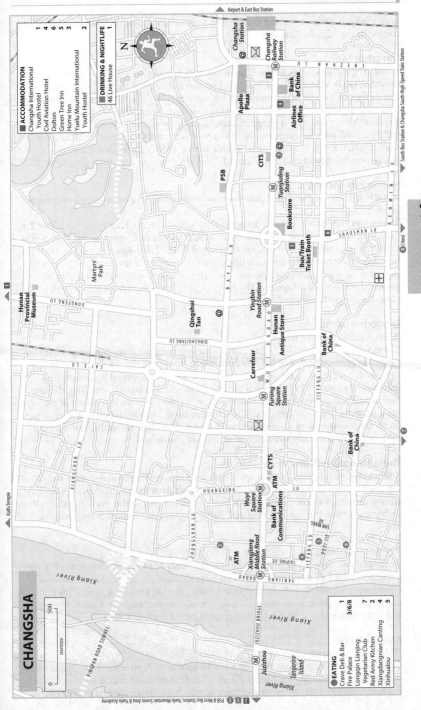

CHANGSHA

ACCOMMODATION
Changsha International Youth Hostel	1
Civil Aviation Hotel	4
Dolton	6
Green Tree Inn	5
Home Inn	3
Yuelu Mountain International Youth Hostel	2

DRINKING & NIGHTLIFE
46 Live House	1

EATING
Crave Deli & Bar	1
Fire Palace	3/6/8
Longqin Lianjing	7
Vegetarian Club	2
Red Army Kitchen	4
Xiangdangnian Canting	5

0 metres 500

some pleasant parks to wander around and some of the most pungent, spice-infused cuisine in the Middle Kingdom.

Qingshui Tan

清水潭, qīngshuǐ tán • Bayi Lu • Daily 8am–4.30pm • Free • Bus #113 stops outside

Qingshui Tan is Mao's former Changsha home and the site of the first local Communist Party offices. Outside, on Qingshuitan Lu, are a number of **antiques** stores, and at weekends an informal and jolly antiques market lines the pavement. A white marble statue of Mao greets you at the gate, and the garden walls are covered with stone tablets carved with his epigrams. Near the **pool** is a scruffy vegetable patch and the reconstructed room in which Mao and his second wife, Yang Kaihui (daughter of Mao's influential teacher, Yang Changji), lived after moving here from Beijing in 1921.

Hunan Provincial Museum

湖南省博物馆, húnán shěng bówùguǎn • Closed for refurbishment at the time of writing • Bus #113 or #126 from the train station

The **Hunan Provincial Museum**, dominated by relics from the Han-era tomb of **Xin Zui**, the Marquess of Dai who died around 160 BC, was one of Changsha's highlights. The subterranean tomb was one of three discovered in 1972 during construction work at Mawangdui, about 4km northeast (the others contained her husband and son). It has, alas, been closed for a major upgrade, but make sure you ask around to see if it's reopened – if the old museum is anything to go by, the spruced-up version will be correspondingly fascinating.

Tangerine Island

桔子岛, júzi dǎo • Subway line #2 to Juzi Zhou

Changsha's name – literally "Long Sand" – derives from a narrow midstream bar now called **Tangerine Island**. The lengthy **Juzizhou Bridge** spans the river above, affording a good opportunity to gaze down on the island, which was settled by Europeans following the riots of 1910. Several of their former homes are still standing, though they've suffered overenthusiastic renovation, while the northern two-thirds of the island has a pavilion and hotel complex. The southern tip is a neatly laid-out park, centring on an enormous bust of a young and wild-haired Mao Zedong, gazing out over the river, which he famously swam across on his 65th birthday.

Yuelu Mountain Scenic Area

岳麓山, yuèlù shān • Daily: May–Oct 7.30am–6pm; Nov–June 8am–5.30pm • Free (¥50 for the academy) • Bus #1, #112, #202, #302

On the west side of the river, **Yuelu Mountain Scenic Area** looms large over Changsha's vibrant university district. It's the most popular hiking spot in the city, a forested hillside with paths woven through the trees and plenty of pavilions, teahouses and temples.

Yuelu Academy

岳麓书院, yuèlù shūyuàn

By far and away the scenic area highlight is the **Yuelu Academy**. An institute of higher learning established during the Northern Song dynasty, it's one of the four notable Confucian academies of the last thousand years. The architecture and gardens are exquisite. From the central axis path, you can explore the teaching studios, libraries and lecture halls that cultivated many great minds of ancient China.

Kaifu Temple

开福寺, kāifú sì • Daily 9am–6pm • ¥10

The monk Baoning founded the Zen **Kaifu Temple** in 927, after the Tang dynasty had collapsed, when Hunan was part of the independent state of Chu. What survives today is a nineteenth-century renovated version, in which are sixteen points of interest.

Quaint in places, Kaifu remains an active temple and attracts the Changsha faithful to worship in an incense-infused sanctuary, away from the clamour of the city. Arrive at midday to sample some of the meat-free delicacies on offer.

ARRIVAL AND DEPARTURE

CHANGSHA

BY PLANE

Huanghua airport (黄花飞机场, huánghuā fēijīchǎng), 15km east of town, is connected to the city by taxi (¥150) or shuttle bus (¥16.50) to the airline office (daily 6.30am–8pm; ☎0731 84112222), which is in the same building as the *Civil Aviation Hotel* on Wuyi Dadao.

Destinations Beijing (2hr–2hr 30min); Chongqing (1hr–1hr 15min); Guangzhou (1hr 15min); Hong Kong (1hr 40min); Kunming (2hr 5min); Shanghai (1hr 30min–2hr); Shenzhen (1hr 15min); Tianjin (5 weekly; 2hr); Zhangjiajie (50min).

BY TRAIN

Ticket offices at both train stations are always crowded, so buy online.

Changsha train station (长沙火车站, chángshā huǒchēzhàn). Adorned by Mao Zedong's calligraphy and still broadcasting the *East is Red* every hour (the de facto anthem of the republic during the Cultural Revolution), this centrally located station at the eastern end of Wuyi Dadao deals with regular trains. Trains head north from Changsha to Zhangjiajie, Yueyang and Hubei province; west to Guizhou, Jishou and Zhangjiajie; east to Nanchang in Jiangxi; and south via Hengyang to Guangdong and Guangxi. There's also a special tourist train daily to Shaoshan.

Changsha South High Speed Rail Station (长沙南高铁站, chángshānán gāotiě zhàn). Changsha sits on the CRH line from Wuhan and Guangzhou. The huge,

airport-like station is several kilometres south of the city centre – around ¥30 in a taxi.

Destinations Beijing (34 daily; 5–20hr); Guangzhou (many daily; 2hr 40min–9hr); Guilin (19 daily; 7–11hr); Guiyang (6 daily; 12–13hr); Hengyang (many daily; 30min–2hr); Jishou (6 daily; 7–9hr); Nanchang (4 daily; 3hr 30min–5hr 30min); Shaoshan (many daily; 2hr 30min); Shenzhen (32 daily; 2hr 50min–12hr); Wuhan (many daily; 1hr 30min–5hr); Yueyang (many daily; 30min–2hr); Zhangjiajie (8 daily; 5–11hr).

BY BUS

Changsha's three main long-distance bus stations are all way out of town in the suburbs.

East bus station (汽车东站, qìchē dōngzhàn) lies 4km from the centre on Shiyuan Dayi Lu, reached by city bus #126, and serves easterly destinations.

Destinations Hefei (9hr); Nanchang (6hr).

West bus station (汽车西站, qìchē xīzhàn) is 8km out on Xiaoxiang Bei Lu, reached by city bus #302; it serves mostly provincial destinations within Hunan.

Destinations Anhua (3hr); Fenghuang (6hr); Heng Shan (3hr); Jiujiang (12hr); Nanyue (3hr); Wuhan (4hr); Yichang (6hr); Yueyang (3hr); Zhangjiajie (6hr).

South bus station (汽车南站, qìchē nánzhàn), on Shizhongyi Lu, 10km from the centre on the city bus #7 route, serves southern Hunan and down into Guangxi.

Destinations Guilin (7hr); Xiamen (13hr).

INFORMATION AND GETTING AROUND

Travel agents CITS are at 160 Wuyi Dadao (☎0731 84468904), and can organize Chinese-guided day-trips to Shaoshan (from ¥120) and Hengshan (¥390).

By bus Changsha's city buses run about 6am–9pm daily, and almost all travel via the train-station square. Regular buses cost ¥1 and a/c services are ¥2.

By metro Changsha's metro opened in 2014. Line #1 runs north–south, line #2 east–west, connecting the city with the South High Speed Rail Station. Three more lines are set to open in the next few years.

By taxi Flag fall is ¥8 for the first 2km, and each additional kilometre costs ¥2.

ACCOMMODATION

★**Changsha International Youth Hostel** 长沙国际青年旅舍, chángshā guójì qīngnián lǚshè. 61 Gongshang Lane, off Dongfeng Lu, north of the Provincial Museum ☎0731 82990202, ⓦyhachina .com. A friendly hostel, with English-speaking staff, set in an attractive old building close to the provincial museum. A little out of the way, but the only place in town you're likely to bump into backpackers – give reception a call and they will guide you here. Dorms ¥40, doubles ¥108
Civil Aviation Hotel 民航大酒店, mínháng dàjiǔdiàn. 47 Wuyi Dadao ☎0731 829125888. A

well-run, tidy and slightly worn airlines-owned operation inside an ugly block of a building, featuring the standard mid-range amenities. It can get busy with tour groups. ¥288
Dolton 通程国际大酒店, tōngchéng guójì dàjiǔdiàn. 159 Shaoshan Lu ☎0731 84168888, ⓦdoltonhotel.com. Once the best hotel in Changsha, the *Dolton* is an opulent sprawl of marble and chandeliers, with five-star service, although rooms are starting to look dated. There's also a swimming pool and an ATM in the lobby. ¥689
Green Tree Inn 格林豪泰酒店, gélín háotài jiǔdiàn. 98 Shaoshan Lu ☎0731 88186998, ⓦ998.com. Chain

7

hotel offering decent, good-value rooms with a/c, showers and moderately soft beds, though some are better kept than others – don't be shy about asking to see several options. **¥130**

Home Inn 如家酒店, rújiājiǔdiàn. 34 Wuyi Dadao ☎0731 8221777. Very close to the train station, with the usual stripped-down but comfortable en-suite rooms. Those facing the main road are noisy. **¥150**

Yuelu Mountain International Youth Hostel 长沙岳麓山国际青年旅舍, chángshā yuèlùshān guójì qīngnián lǚshè. Villa No. 1, Lushan Huaqiaocun, 50 Xinmin Lu ☎0731 85368418. If you don't mind being a bit out of town, with good access to hiking and the Yuelu Academy, this well-priced, YHA-affiliated hostel is a sure-fire bet. Dorms **¥30**, doubles **¥138**

EATING

Strong flavours and copious chillies are the signatures of **Hunanese food** – Mao himself claimed that it was the fiery food that made locals so (politically) red. Pungent regional specialities include air-cured and chilli-smoked meat; *dong'an ji*, chicken seasoned with a vinegar-soy dressing; *gualiang fen*, a gelatinous mass of cold rice noodles covered in spicy sauce; and *chou doufu* (literally "stinky tofu"), deep-fried fermented bean curd. Head to **San Wang Jie** (三王街, sānwángjiē) and **Pozi Jie** (坡子街, pōzijiē) for a plethora of hot and spicy restaurants to choose from.

★**Crave Deli & Bar** 梦寐以求西餐吧, mèngmèi yǐqiú xīcānbā. C31 Xijie, Wanda Guangchang, Kaifu Qu ☎153 88034382, ⓦcravedelibar.com. In a new location, this American–Canadian-operated café/bar is a great place to meet English-fluent locals and Changsha-based foreigners. There's a range of deli sandwiches, including paninis and bagels. Flatbread pizza costs ¥28–58; imported bottled beers ¥15–40. Daily 10am till late.

Fire Palace 火宫殿, huǒgōng diàn. 507 Shaoshan Bei Lu; Wuyi Dadao; and the western end of Jiefang Lu ☎0731 85814228. A busier, noisier and more enjoyable place to wolf down Hunanese food would be hard to imagine. Get an order card from the waiting staff, request some beer, and stop trolleys loaded with small plates of goodies as they pass. Around ¥50–100 per person. There are three branches in town. Daily 11am–2pm & 5–10pm.

Longqin Lianjing Vegetarian Club 龙钦莲境素食禅茶会所, lóngqīn liánjìng sùshí chánchá huì suǒ. 178 Baisha Lu, Furong Qu, opposite the ancient Baisha well ☎0731 85232968. This really is a fabulous place. The interior is classically designed with a modern twist; stock up on Hunan brews upstairs at the teahouse, or head downstairs for the to-die-for vegan restaurant. If you've had enough of oil, spice and beer, this is the antidote

you seek. Set menu ¥80. Daily 11am–2pm & 5–9pm.

Red Army Kitchen 红军灶, hóng jūn zào. C dong, 101 Hao, Xicheng Gongyu, Leifeng Dadao ☎159 74281617. No trip to Changsha would be complete without a visit to a revolution-themed restaurant, northwest of the centre. If you're prepared to overlook the inherent contradiction in this Communist-kitsch approach, dining here will cast you back in time, as staff in CCP military garb serve delicious spice-infused dishes to the soundtrack of The East is Red. Around ¥100 per head. Daily 11am–10pm.

Xiangdangnian Canting 湘当年餐厅, xiāngdāngnián cāntīng. Off Taiping Jie ☎0731 84863798. A filmreel banner of old Changsha photographs leads the way from Taiping Jie to this atmospheric Hunan restaurant. Specialities include Hunan taro (¥49) and Mao Zedong braised pork (¥31). Daily 9am–2pm & 4.30–9.30pm.

Xinhualou 新华楼, xīnhuálóu. 35 Wuyi Dadao ☎0731 84152057. This multi-award-winning restaurant is now something of a hot-spot for spice fiends. Trolleys of smoked tofu and meats, crisp-cold vegetables dressed in sesame oil, black-skinned chicken soup and host of noodle dishes means *Xinhualou* is packed no matter the time of day. Around ¥30 per person. Daily 6.30pm–1.30am.

DRINKING AND NIGHTLIFE

Around the sympathetically reconstructed old street of **Taiping Jie** (太平街, tàipíng jiē) are several Western-style bars. For something a little more club-like, head around the corner to **Jiefang Xi Lu**, Changsha's nightlife hub, where a few mega-clubs contend for your twilight hours. Check out ⓦwnichangsha.com for current listings.

46 Live House. Basement, 52 Xiangcai Dasha, Xinmin Lu ☎13307312298, ⓦsite.douban.com/changsha4698. Opened in 2006, this stalwart of the Changsha rock scene is still

going strong. Located near the university district, and popular with students, this is the place to come if you want to avoid the KTV / disco crowd and rock out, Hunan-style. Daily 6pm–late.

SHOPPING

Changsha has long had a reputation for **silk embroidery**, which you can buy at various stores along Wuyi Dadao. Taiping Jie has a smattering of shops selling **pottery** and other souvenirs, and there are **antique stores** along Qingshuitang Lu.

DIRECTORY

Banks and exchange There are plenty of Bank of China branches in the city centre (generally Mon–Sat 8am–noon & 2.30–5pm).

Hospital Global Doctor Clinic, 4F Hunan Brain Hospital, 427 Furong Zhong Lu, Section 3 (☎0731 85230250).

Left luggage Both the train and bus stations have left-luggage offices.

Visa extensions The Foreign Affairs Department of the PSB (Mon–Fri 8am–noon & 2.30–5.30pm; ☎0731 84590788) is in the Hexi Jiaojing Building, west of the river on the north side of Wuyi Dadao.

Shaoshan

韶山, sháoshān · Tourist Area entry ¥52–80

Mao Zedong's birthplace, the hamlet of **SHAOSHAN**, lies 90km southwest of Changsha. Established as a pilgrimage site for idolatrous Red Guards during the Cultural Revolution, Shaoshan now seethes with Chinese tourists, who flock back to visit the Great Helmsman's hometown and don't seem to mind that it's become something of a theme park. Golf buggies whiz tourists from luxury hotels to Red-themed restaurants. It's all very surreal, but perhaps an accurate reflection of the peculiar consumer-communism that's now endemic across the country.

The **Shaoshan Tourist Area**, containing the village and the surrounding area – excluding the new town, 5km away – divides into three scenic areas, which aren't up to much. A hop-on, hop-off visit to the village, with a free peek into Mao's Family Home and exhibition hall, will suffice.

Mao's Family Home

毛泽东故居, máozédōng gùjū · Daily 8am–5pm · Free

Just before the village proper is **Mao's Family Home**, a compound of bare adobe buildings next to a lotus-filled pond, where Mao was born on December 26, 1893. The home is neatly preserved, with a few pieces of period furniture, the odd photograph, and wonderfully turgid English explanations completing the spartan furnishings. Here he led a thoroughly normal childhood, one of four children in a relatively wealthy peasant household that comfortably survived the terrible famines in Hunan during the first decade of the twentieth century. Though a rebellious youth, he did not become politicized until he moved to Changsha in his late teens.

Mao Zedong Exhibition Hall

毛泽东纪念馆, máozédōng jìniànguǎn · Daily 8am–5pm · ¥10

Just off the huge village square, next to a bronze statue of an elderly Mao and a swarm of souvenir stalls, stands the **Mao Zedong Exhibition Hall**, in which photos and knick-knacks chart Mao's career. Today there's a great distinction between Mao the heroic revolutionary, and the Mao who inflicted the disastrous Great Leap Forward (see p.935) and Cultural Revolution (see p.936) on his country. The exhibition reflects this: noticeable omissions include the Little Red Book and just about any mention of the years between 1957 and his funeral in 1976.

ARRIVAL AND GETTING AROUND   SHAOSHAN

Minibuses regularly shuttle passengers between Shaoshan bus station and the village (¥2.50 single), and between the sights (¥10), though you might prefer to walk.

By train The new high-speed line has made Shaoshan far more accessible than it used to be. The station is by the bus terminal.
Destinations Changsha (12 daily; 25min); Guiyang (9 daily; 3hr 15min); Huaihua (17 daily; 1hr 15min).
By bus The bus station is in the new town, 5km from the

tourist village.
Destinations Changsha (every 30min; 1hr 30min).
On a tour Tour buses leave from the square outside Changsha train station ticket office at 7am (guided day-tour in Chinese from ¥120).

Heng Shan

衡山, héngshān

Some 120km south of Changsha lies one of China's holiest sites. Spread over 80km
or so, the **Heng Shan** range forms seventy-two low peaks dressed in woodland with a
smattering of **Buddhist and Taoist temples**, some of which were established more than
1300 years ago. It's somewhere to relax and admire the scenery (frosted in winter,
golden in autumn and misty year-round), either tackling the easy walks between
shrines on foot, or resorting to local transport and cable cars to ascend the heights.
The principal mountain is known as **Nanyue** ("Southern Peak"), as is the access village.

Nanyue village

南岳, nányuè

Banners strung across the highway welcome visitors to the **NANYUE** village, home
to the two largest and most architecturally impressive temple complexes in the area,
Nanyue and **Zhusheng**. The Changsha–Hengyang highway runs along the eastern side
of the village; midway along, an ornamental stone archway forms the "entrance" to the
village proper and leads through to the main street, Dongshan Lu.

Nanyue Temple

南岳大庙, nányuè dàmiào • Daily 8am–6pm • Summer ¥60, winter ¥40

Off Dongshan Lu, streets lead through the old village centre to **Nanyue Temple**. The
site has served as a place of worship since at least 725 AD, but the older buildings
succumbed to fire long ago and were replaced in the nineteenth century by a smaller
version of Beijing's Forbidden City. It's a lively place, echoing with bells and thick with
smoke from incense and detonating firecrackers – there are furnaces in the courtyards
to accommodate the huge quantities offered up by the crowds. Seventy-two pillars,
representing Heng Shan's peaks, support the massive wooden crossbeams of the main
hall's double-staged roof, and gilt phoenixes loom above the scores of kneeling
worshippers paying homage to Taoist and Buddhist deities.

Zhusheng Temple

祝圣寺, zhùshèng sì • Daily 8am–6pm • ¥10

Far quieter than Nanyue Temple, with more monks and fewer tourists, is **Zhusheng
Temple**. A purely Buddhist site, the entire monastery – whose name translates as
"Imperial Blessings" – was reconstructed for the anticipated visit of **Emperor Kangxi** in
1705, but he never showed up. The smaller scale and lack of pretence here contrast
with Nanyue's extravagances, though there's a series of five hundred engravings of
Buddhist *arhats* set into the wall of the rear hall, and a fine multifaced and many-
handed likeness of Guanyin to seek out among the charming courtyards.

In the hills

Daily 9am – 5pm • Entry to all temples and a bilingual map of the mountain is ¥120 in summer, ¥80 in winter; cable car single ¥45, return
¥80 • Minibuses (¥10) run between Nanyue village and Shangfeng Temple, below the summit, in under an hour

There's a good day's walking to be had between Nanyue and Zhurong Gong, at Heng
Shan's apex, 15km from town. The main road through Nanyue leads to the park gates
behind Nanyue Temple; from here there's the choice of hiking, catching a minibus or
taking the cable car to the halfway point. Even major temples along the way are small
and unassuming, requiring little time to explore, and tracks are easy; allow around
eight hours for a return hike along the most direct route.

Nanyue to Banshan Ting

On foot, the first two hours are spent passing occasional groups of descending tourists
and black-clad Taoists, as the road weaves past rivers and patches of farmland before
reaching the temple-like Martyrs' Memorial Hall, built to commemorate those killed

during the 1911 revolution. Entering pine forests shortly thereafter, you'll arrive at the cable-car terminus at **Banshan Ting**, (literally "halfway pavilion"; 半山亭, bànshān tíng).

Xuandu Temple
玄都寺, xuándū sì

Not far from Banshan Ting, **Xuandu Temple** is Hunan's Taoist centre, founded around 700 AD. Even so, an occasional Buddhist saint graces side shrines, but the best feature is the unusually domed ceiling in the second hall, watched over by a statue of Lao Zi holding a pill of immortality.

To the summit

From the cable-car station, the rest of the ascent passes a handful of functioning, day-to-day temples with monks and nuns wandering around the gardens – **Danxia Temple** (丹霞寺, dānxiá sì) and **Zushi Gong** (祖师宫, zǔshī gōng) are larger than most – before arriving outside **Shangfeng Temple**'s red timber halls, which mark the minibus terminus. Overpriced hotels here cater to those hoping to catch the dawn from the sunrise-watching terrace, a short walk away below a radio tower. On a cloudy day, it's better to push on for a further twenty minutes to the 1290m **summit**, where **Zhurong Gong** (祝融宫, zhùróng gōng), a tiny temple built almost entirely of heavy stone blocks and blackened inside from incense smoke, looks very atmospheric as it emerges from the mist.

ARRIVAL AND DEPARTURE   HENG SHAN

BY TRAIN
Three train stations are connected to Nanyue village, the Heng Shan trailhead, by direct buses.
Hengshan Station (衡山火车站, héngshān huǒchēzhàn). 20km east of Nanyue at Xintang town, with minibuses making the run in 30min.
Destinations Changsha (5 daily; 1hr 45min); Guangzhou (5 daily; 6hr 30min–7hr 30min); Shanghai (2 daily; 16–21hr); Wuchang (3 daily; 6–7hr).
Hengshan West (衡山西, héngshān xī). The closest station to the mountain is 5km west of Nanyue, a 15min minibus transfer away.
Destinations Changsha (14 daily; 35min); Guangzhou South (22 daily; 2hr 15min); Shanghai Hongqiao (1 daily; 6hr); Wuhan (6 daily; 2hr).
Hengyang East (衡阳东, héngyáng dōng). Located 25km south of Nanyue at Hengyang town, this station is on the Changsha South–Guangzhou CRH line. Buses to

Nanyue can take over an hour.
Destinations Changsha (49 daily; 42min–2hr); Shanghai (3 daily; 6–7hr); Shenzhen North (28 daily; 4hr 45min).

BY BUS
Nanyue bus station At the southern end of the village, just off the highway. Map sellers, rickshaw drivers and hotel touts descend on new arrivals at the bus station. If you can't find direct buses to your destination here, head first for Hengyang (衡阳, héngyáng), where there are more options.
Destinations Changsha (3hr); Guilin (6hr); Hengyang (1hr–1hr 30min).

ON A TOUR
Tour agents Changsha CITS runs daily Chinese-only tours to Nanyue from ¥120 (see p.433).

ACCOMMODATION AND EATING

Heng Shan is also fairly easily visited as a day-trip from Changsha (see p.430), but there's accommodation both in Nanyue village and up on the mountain itself. The mountain **peasant guesthouses** (农家乐, nóng jiā lè) are usually converted farmhouses without websites or phone numbers; owners will accost you. Rustic but homely and cheap – ¥100 a night or so – these are well worth considering, but insist on seeing the property before committing. In Nanyue village, you'll find a mass of restaurants on Dongshan Lu; up on the mountain, food stalls lurk at strategic points, so there's no need to carry much.

NANYUE
Guofeng Hotel 国峰宾馆, guófēng bīnguǎn. Opposite the bus station ☎0734 5678526. This place has clean, modern rooms, if a little plain, with LCD TVs. More

expensive rooms have computers. ¥128
OP Youth Hostel 南岳衡山国际青年旅舍, nányuè héngshān guójì qīngnián lǚshè. 47 Jinpen Xiaoqu, Jinshan Lu ☎0734 5678567. This colourful YHA hostel is

popular with the local crowd, as it's one of the few budget options in the area (if you don't bag a room on the hillside). In a good spot, but a little hard to find. Take free bus #1 to the Tourist Centre; the hostel is a hundred metres away down a small lane between two hotels. Dorms ¥40, doubles ¥88

Zhangjiajie (Wulingyuan Scenic Reserve)

张家界, zhāngjiājiè / 武陵源风景区, wǔlíngyuán fēngjǐngqū • Daily 7am–6pm • Tickets valid for four days: high season ¥245, low season ¥136; glass bridge ¥138

Hidden away in the northwestern extremities of Hunan, **Zhangjiajie**, otherwise known as **Wulingyuan Scenic Reserve**, protects a mystical landscape of sandstone shelves and fragmented limestone towers splintering away from a high plateau, often misted in low clouds and scored by countless streams, with practically every horizontal surface hidden under a primeval, subtropical green mantle. Among the 550-odd tree species – twice Europe's total – within its 370 square kilometres are rare **dove trees**, **ginkgos** and **dawn redwoods**. The redwoods are identified by their stringy bark and feathery leaves; now popular as an ornamental tree, they were believed extinct until 1948. The region is also home to several million ethnic **Tujia**, said by some to be the last descendants of western China's mysterious prehistoric Ba kingdom.

On the downside, Zhangjiajie is beginning to suffer from its popularity, with more accessible parts of the reserve often almost invisible under hordes of litter-hurling tour groups. The peak Heavenly Pillar received such fame after featuring in the blockbuster film *Avatar*, that it was renamed Avatar Hallelujah Mountain. The world's highest (300m) and longest (430m) **glass bridge**, which lies perilously over the Zhangjiajie Grand Canyon, has brought the park further attention since opening in 2016, particularly since it was briefly closed 13 days after opening for "urgent repairs" due to the volume of visitors.

Fortunately, the reserve is big enough that even on the main circuit, it's easy to lose the crowds, and the majesty of the scenery comfortably overrides manmade intrusions. The area is best explored over two or three days, and you'll need comfortable walking shoes and the right seasonal dress – it's humid in summer, cold from late autumn, and the ground is often covered in light snow early in the year.

ZHANGJIAJIE DAY-TRIPS

It's worth spending several days in the region, but if your time is limited you can still get to grips with Zhangjiajie's astounding natural beauty in as little as half a day: walk from the village (or take the very short bus ride) to the **cable-car station** (索道站, suǒdào zhàn; ¥65 one-way, ¥118 return) then ride up to **Huangshi village** (黄石寨, huángshí zhài), where the cable car terminates. From here hike the two-hour circuit anticlockwise (most tour groups go the other way) around this minor, island-like plateau, surrounded by breathtaking views of the sea of pinnacles. Towards the end of the circuit, bearing left at the police post before Star Picking Tower will put you on the 45-minute trail back down to the park entrance.

For more of a hike, the left path from the park entrance follows a valley up to Huangshi, a trail which takes around two or three hours. Once at the top, you can pick up the plateau circuit and walk or take the cable car back down. Alternatively, bearing right at the park entrance offers several more hiking loops, the shortest of which (around 4hr) runs along **Golden Whip Stream** (金鞭流, jīnbiānliú) branching off to the right and returning to base through a particularly dense stand of crags below two facing outcrops known as the **Yearning Couple** (engraved tablets along the path identify many other formations). Alternatively, bearing right at a couple of kilometres – consult a map – takes you past **Bewitching Terrace** (迷魂台, míhún tái) into the Shadao valley. From here, basic trails continue through magnificent scenery around the western edge of the plateau to **Black Dragon village** (黑龙寨, hēilóng zhài), then circuit back to the park gates. This is a lengthy day's walk, and you won't see many other tourists along the way.

Zhangjiajie village

森林公园, sēnlín gōngyuán • Buses every 15min (daily 6am–5.30pm; 1hr; ¥12) from Zhangjiajie city bus station

Having exited the train or long-distance bus stations at **Zhangjiajie city** (see below), 33km from the reserve entrance, most visitors catch transport directly to the southern boundaries of the reserve at **Zhangjiajie village**. Despite the name, what was once a couple of streets in the valley, the "village" is now a thronging, rapidly commercializing tourist town, through which a road leads downhill to the park entrance.

Suoxi Valley Nature Reserve

索溪峪镇, suǒxīyù zhèn • Daily 6.30am-6.30pm • March–Nov ¥245; Dec–Feb ¥136 • Regular shuttle buses from Zhangjiajie village

With many of the same facilities as Zhangjiajie village, **Suoxi Valley Nature Reserve** makes a good base for exploring the east and north of the reserve. Set in the Suoxi Valley, it's 10km as the crow flies from Zhangjiajie village, but the better part of a day away on foot. Attractions here include groups of **rhesus monkeys** and relatively open **river gorges**, where it's possible to cruise – or even go whitewater rafting – between the peaks (see opposite).

Suoxi valley

Around the 2km-long **Baofeng Hu** (宝峰湖, bǎofēng hú), a lake accessed by a ladder-like staircase from the **Suoxi valley** floor, there's a chance of encountering golden pheasants, the grouse-like tragopans and, if you're very lucky, **giant salamanders** – secretive, red-blotched monsters which reach 2m in length. Once considered a great delicacy, the endangered salamanders are now protected, and wild populations are being supplemented by captive-bred animals. There's also **Huanglong Dong** (黄龙洞, huánglóng dòng; Yellow Dragon Cave), a few kilometres east of Suoxi, a mass of garishly lit limestone caverns linked by a subterranean river, and **Hundred Battle Valley** (百战谷, bǎizhàngǔ) where the Song-dynasty Tujia king, Xiang, fought imperial forces.

Tianmen Shan

天门山, tiānmén shān • Daily 8am–6pm • Cable car (天门山索道, tiānménshān suǒdào) ¥258 return including park entrance; Bailong Elevator ¥56 each way

The **Tianmen Shan** region roughly covers the north of the park, and is named after an isolated 1250m-high peak which is now readily accessible from Zhangjiajie city by a 7km-long mountain **cable car**, the longest on earth. The 11km road which covers the route incorporates 99 hairpin bends and is an equally impressive feat of engineering. At the top, steps lead to a giant natural **rock arch**, which has attracted high-wire walkers, jet fly-throughs and even French free climber "Spiderman" Alain Robert. You can also access the area from Suoxi village – set off along the **Ten-li Corridor** (十里画廊, shílǐ huàláng), from where there's a 30km circuit.

High points include the mass of lookouts surrounding **Shentangwan** (神堂湾, shéntáng wān), a valley thick with needle-like rocks; **Immortals' Bridge** (仙人桥, xiānrén qiáo), a narrow strip of rock bridging a deep valley; and the astounding, 330m-high glass **Bailong Elevator** (袁家界百龙电梯, yuánjiājiè bǎilóng diàntī;) at Yuanjiajie – yet another record-breaker, it's the world's tallest outdoor lift.

ARRIVAL AND DEPARTURE   ZHANGJIAJIE (WULINGYUAN SCENIC RESERVE)

Zhangjiajie city (张家界市, zhāngjiājiè shì) is the regional hub, 33km south of the reserve gates, and accessible by planes, trains and buses from all over China.

By plane Zhangjiajie airport is 10km west of Zhangjiajie city. An airport bus connects with the city for ¥5; taxis cost ¥15.

Destinations Beijing (2hr–2hr 30min); Changsha (50min);

Chengdu (1hr 30min); Guangzhou (1hr 45min); Nanjing (1hr 45min); Shanghai (1hr 45min).

By train Zhangjiajie city's train station is south of the centre. Outside the station there are buses to the reserve, as well as taxis and local buses. Train tickets are in short supply, especially at weekends, so book your outbound ticket on arrival. Direct services head east to Changsha, north to

Yichang in Hubei, and south to Jishou and Liuzhou in Guangxi. For Guizhou and points west you'll have to change trains at the junction town of Huaihua, 4hr southwest – sleeper tickets out of Huaihua are hard to come by at the station, but you may be able to upgrade on board.

Destinations Changsha (8 daily; 5–11hr); Huaihua (for connections to Guiyang or Changsha; 13 daily; 3hr 20min–7hr 15min); Jishou (for Fenghuang; 12 daily; 2–4hr); Yichang (2 daily; 5hr).

By bus The city bus station is just across from the train station and shares the same park transport links. Leaving, there are regular buses covering the journey to Changsha and down to Fenghuang (or Jishou if you don't want to wait for a direct bus). Buses depart every 15min (daily 6am–5.30pm; 1hr; ¥12) for Zhangjiajie village, a 15min walk to the Wulingyuan entrance.

Destinations Changsha (6hr); Fenghuang (4hr); Jishou (for Fenghuang; 2hr); Wuhan (12hr).

GETTING AROUND

By minibus Minibuses prowl the train station square for the hour-long journey to the reserve at either Zhangjiajie village (¥15) or Suoxi (¥20). Minibuses also run from Zhangjiajie village to Suoxi (¥15).

By taxi Taxis from transit points charge around ¥80 for the journey to Zhangjiajie village, or ¥110 for Suoxi.

On a tour If you're on a Chinese package tour to Zhangjiajie, they may try to sting you for ¥50–100 based on a supposedly higher foreigners' entrance fee to the reserve; this is nonsense, and if the tour staff won't back down, tell them you'll pay the surcharge yourself at the gates.

INFORMATION

Guides and tour agents English-speaking freelance guides congregate inside the entrance at Zhangjiajie village and charge ¥100 per day. The travel service at the

Xiangdian International Hotel offers general hiking advice and arranges whitewater rafting day-tours in the Suoxi valley (¥250 per person).

ACCOMMODATION AND EATING

There's **accommodation and food** available at Zhangjiajie's villages, but you should take water and snacks on long journeys. Accommodation prices double at weekends and holidays, when it's busiest. Ask around about basic hotels within the reserve, which are recommended for getting away from it all – local guides can take you there.

ZHANGJIAJIE CITY
It's only worth staying here if you arrive too late to get the last bus to the park (around 7pm).

Home Inn 如家酒店, rújiājiǔdiàn. Jiefang Lu ☎ 0744 8209222. In a handy location just off central Renmin Square, *Home Inn* offers the usual comfortable, sterile rooms that are typical of this nationwide chain. **¥209**

ZHANGJIAJIE VILLAGE
19 Youth Hostel 十九号青年客栈, shíjiǔhào qīngnián kèzhàn. Jundi Lu, Wujiayu ☎ 0744 5621619. Locally run guesthouse with an emphasis on friendship and camaraderie, this well-located hostel, 200m or so from the entrance gate, is a good place to meet hikers. **¥150**

Hollyear Inn 和一宾馆, héyī bīnguǎn. Halfway down the main street on the right ☎ 0744 5718989. Shabby rooms set around nice quiet gardens, though the silence is broken by an incredible frog chorus on summer evenings. **¥168**

Xiangdian International Hotel 香殿山庄, xiāngdiàn shānzhuāng. Top of the village towards the park gate ☎ 0744 5712999, ⊛ xiangdianhotel.com .cn. Easily the best accommodation in the village, with comfortable, if small, traditionally styled rooms with all mod cons, set around a series of attractive courtyard gardens, complete with koi carp ponds, and the mighty peaks looming high on the skyline. There's also billiards, a bowling alley, and a helpful travel service. **¥468**

Fenghuang and around
凤凰, fènghuáng

Tucked away close to the border with Guizhou, 160km south of Zhangjiajie, Jishou (see p.444) and Huaihua are the traditional jumping-off points for the charming town of **FENGHUANG**, with its stilted houses, flagstoned streets and communities of Miao and Tujia peoples. Fenghuang is a great place to unwind for a couple of days, although its popularity with domestic tourists means it is no longer a peaceful retreat. Almost every house has been converted into some sort of commercial enterprise, and in the evenings bars and clubs blare out music over the water until the early hours. On the plus side, Fenghuang's development gives great accommodation and dining choices, while the myriad narrow backstreets still offer plenty of genuine local life and a sense of the town's twelve-hundred-year history. Fenghuang is also a good base to explore smaller outlying settlements and the renovated **Southern Great Wall**.

Xiong Xiling's former residence

熊希龄故居, xióngxīlíng gùjū • Wenxing Jie • Daily: summer 7.30am–6pm; winter 8am–5.30pm • Admission with through-ticket

Fenghuang is the hometown of several important Chinese, including **Xiong Xiling**, an ethnic Miao who became premier of China's first republican government. Near the North Gate, you can visit his **former home**, a simple affair preserved as it was and holding a few photos, including those of his three wives, with some English captions.

Sheng Congwen's former residence

沈从文故居, shěncóngwén gùjū • Just off Dongzheng Jie • Daily: summer 7.30am–6pm; winter 8am–5.30pm • Admission with through-ticket

Shen Congwen (1902–88), one of China's greatest writers who was of mixed Miao–Tujia heritage, was from Fenghuang, and many of his stories centre on the Miao people and the local landscapes (*Recollections of West Hunan* and *Border Town* are available in English). After the 1949 revolution, Shen's writing was banned in both mainland China and Taiwan after he failed to align with either, effectively ending his career, but his works have enjoyed a revival since the 1980s. His **former residence**, a pleasantly proportioned, traditional grey-brick courtyard building, evokes a soulful ambience, though there's little to see beyond some period wooden furniture.

Shen Congwen's tomb (沈从文墓地, shěncóngwén mùdì) is 1km east of here, in a wooded memorial **park** along the river's south bank. The epitaph on the gravestone translates as "Thinking in my way you can understand me. And thinking in my way you can understand others".

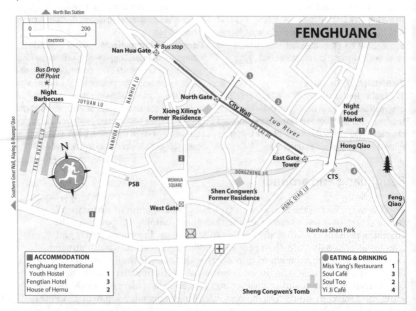

FENGHUANG ORIENTATION

Fenghuang is a small, easily navigable place largely south of the **Tuo River**, which runs roughly west to east. The old town is bounded on its north side by the river, with a restored section of the city's **Ming walls** running along the river bank, punctuated from west to east by the splendid Nanhua, North and East **gates**. The main thoroughfare, **Dongzheng Jie**, is a pedestrianized alley squeezing its way through from Wenhua Square, in the centre, to the East gate and **Hong Qiao**, a 300-year-old covered bridge. To the west and south, Nanhua Lu and Hong Qiao Lu define the old town, the latter curling north from the southeast corner of town to end up at Hong Qiao.

Southern Great Wall

南方长城, nánfāng chángchéng • ¥45 • Bus from the roundabout at the western end of Jianshe Lu (30min) • Admission with three-day through-ticket

The pretty countryside near Fenghuang has some worthwhile and easily accessible sights, the nearest being the **Southern Great Wall**, which, astonishingly, wasn't recognized for what it was until 2000. Originally constructed in 1554 as a defence against the Miao, the wall ran from Xiqueying in western Hunan to Zhenyuan Guizhou. There are several hundred metres of intact, newly renovated wall at a site 13km west from Fenghuang which, while not as rugged as its northern counterpart, is nevertheless impressive and significantly less visited; if you come in winter you'll probably have the place to yourself.

Alaying

阿拉营, ālāyíng • Buses from the western end of Jianshe Lu in Fenghuang (¥7; 1hr)

Alaying, a Miao village 7km west of the Southern Great Wall, makes a useful transit point for visiting Huangsi Qiao (see below), though it's also worth a visit in itself on **market days** (on dates ending with a 2 or 7), when you can buy Miao handicrafts and mingle with villagers from the outlying hills.

Huangsi Qiao

黄丝桥, huángsīqiáo • Bus from Alaying (15min; ¥2)

Just a few kilometres from Alaying, **Huangsi Qiao** (Huang's Silk Bridge), another ancient settlement, prospered after a **silk merchant** called Huang decided to build a bridge to attract people to the town. A smaller version of Fenghuang, with attractive stilted houses, the town is only half a kilometre across and has gate towers to·the north, east and west.

ARRIVAL AND DEPARTURE   FENGHUANG

BY PLANE

The nearest airports to Fenghuang are at Tongren (铜仁市, tóngrénshì) in Guizhou province, 40km away, and Huaihua (怀化市, huáihuà shì), 56km away.

Fenghuang destinations Beijing (3hr); Guangzhou (1hr 30min).

Huaihua destinations Kunming (1hr 35min); Shanghai (3hr).

BY TRAIN

CRH Huaihua South is 80km from Fenghuang, on the Shanghai-to-Kunming CRH line. There are deluxe shuttle buses from the station to Fenghuang for ¥50.

Destinations Changsha (45 daily; 1hr 30min); Shanghai (7 daily; 7hr).

Other services Fenghuang's nearest train station is 45km away at Jishou (see p.444), on the line to Guiyang, Zhangjiajie

and Changsha. From Jishou station, a bus or a taxi over the bridge takes you to the bus station on Wuling Lu. From here, hop one of the regular shuttle buses to Fenghuang (1hr 10min; ¥25). If you arrive too late to travel on to Fenghuang, try the *7 Days Inn* opposite Jishou's station (see p.445). In Fenghuang, onward bus tickets can be purchased from the CTS by the southern entrance to Hong Qiao.

Destinations Changsha (6 daily; 7–9hr); Guiyang (3 daily; 8–12hr); Zhangjiajie (12 daily; 2–4hr).

BY BUS

Fenghuang's North station (北站, běizhàn) is a kilometre or so out of town up Fenghuang Lu, though on arrival buses will either drop you at Nanhua Lu bridge or halfway down Fenghuang Lu.

Destinations Changsha (5hr); Jishou (1hr); Tongren (1hr); Zhangjiajie (4hr).

7

GETTING AROUND

By taxi Old Fenghuang is small enough to walk around, but outside of the maze of narrow lanes it's easy to find taxis which should cost ¥6 for anywhere in town. A taxi to the outlying sights can be negotiated for ¥250–300 per day.

On a tour Chinese-language day-trips covering Alaying, Huangsi Qiao and Daxiagu (a nearby gorge and waterfall) can be arranged through CTS for around ¥100 per person, including lunch.

INFORMATION

Through-tickets Combined "through-tickets" (通票, tōngpiào) are sold for accessing the old town sights, plus a 30min boat ride down the river, valid from one to three days (¥98–168).

Travel agent There's a friendly and helpful English-speaking

CTS (7am–11pm; ☎0743 3221360) on the south side of the Hong Qiao bridge. They can arrange local tours, as well as bus, train and plane tickets and car and driver hire for around ¥250–300 per day.

ACCOMMODATION

Fenghuang is overloaded with **hotels** and **hostels**; outside of summer weekends and Chinese national holidays, it's easy to find a room. Unless you really need your home comforts, there's little point staying in the new town, although it has more luxury options; the character, charm and history of the **old town** is best enjoyed from the riverside balcony of your room. Fenghuang has developed a raucous nightlife scene centred on the north bank of the river near Nanhua Bridge; avoid the area if you like peace and quiet.

Fenghuang International Youth Hostel 凤凰中天青年旅馆, fènghuáng zhōngtiān qīngnián lǚguǎn. 11 Shawan, near Hong Qiao ☎0743 3260546, ⓦyhachina .com. This YHA hostel with a beautiful old facade is usually staffed by students, whose lack of experience is tempered by their eagerness to help. Low prices and an excellent location make this a good bet. Dorms **¥45**, doubles **¥120**

Fengtian Hotel 凤天宾馆, fèngtiān bīnguǎn. 8 Nanhua Lu ☎0743 3501000. This four-star affair is

tastefully furnished, with 24hr hot water and heating to boot. A nice way to treat yourself in winter, if you've been enduring unheated guesthouses, although it feels a tad removed from the old city. **¥400**

House of Hemu 禾沐园, hémùyuán. 1 Zhaoyang Lu ☎18974350887. Centrally located down a small lane in the ancient city and centred around a courtyard, this boutique guesthouse blends old Fenghuang with modern styles. Dorms **¥74**, doubles **¥248**

EATING

One of the major pleasures in Fenghuang – taken between alley wanderings – is eating, especially if you're on the adventurous side. At **restaurants** by the East Gate Tower and along Hong Qiao Lu, cages and tubs of live ducks, pheasants, rabbits, bamboo rats (looking like a cross between a giant sewer rat and a guinea pig), frogs, snakes, newts and catfish line the doorways – not to mention dead stuff resembling road kill; they all await their turn in the pot. In the evenings, the streets come alive with **barbecues**, particularly around Hong Qiao and along Nanhua Lu, where you can stuff your face for a few yuan. Fenghuang also has a decent selection of Western **cafés** and **pubs**, most of which have English menus.

Miss Yang's Restaurant 杨小姐餐厅, yáng xiǎo jie cān tīng. 48 Yao Ling Shao ☎15200795629. If you're in the market for the local delicacy of duck-blood cakes, look no further. This establishment specializes in Miao and Tujia cuisine, with dishes such as rice noodles with cured pork. Expect to jostle for space at peak times. Mains ¥30–70. Daily 11am–9pm.

Soul Café / Soul Too 素咖啡馆, sù kāfēiguǎn. 17 Hui Long Ge ☎0743 3229927; 18 Lao Ying Shao ☎0743 3260396, ⓦbit.ly/SoulFenghuang. Two branches of the same outfit, these cafés offer some Western comfort food

including home-made yoghurt, Italian-style ice cream, cheesecake, and tasty pizza (¥59–65), pasta (¥35–38) and sandwiches as well as imported wines and hookahs. Daily 8am–midnight.

Yi Ji Café 艺技咖啡, yìjì kā fēi. Hui Long Ge, on the north bank of the river near the pagoda ☎158 12246861. Run by friendly Mr Xiao from Hubei province who worked in the coffee industry in Yunnan, this hole-in-the-wall place is the only place to get an artisan coffee in town (¥14–145). Daily 8am–11pm.

Jishou

吉首, jíshǒu

Though settled for over two thousand years, **Jishou** today is quite an unremarkable third-tier city, mainly used as a **transport hub** for getting between Jiangjiajie (280km) and Fenghuang (45km). Though it's the capital of **Xiangxi Miao-Tujia Autonomous County**, the city remains a largely ramshackle place, with few distractions for tourists beyond offering easy access to Dehang National Park. Should you get waylaid in town, a walk along the Dong River will reveal some colourful sights – people from local ethnic groups still descend the hills to sell their wares in traditional clothing. The Ancient City of Qianzhou is worth a look, too.

Ancient City of Qianzhou

乾州古城, qiánzhōu gǔchéng · Just south of the city centre, on the banks of the Wangrong River · Daily 8am–5.30pm · ¥65

Reconstructed city walls and towering battlements allude to the **Ancient City of Qianzhou**'s past status as an administrative centre and base camp for soldiers stationed on the Southern Great Wall during the Ming and Qing dynasties. Despite claiming to be "a celebration of ethnic customs", Qianzhou is very much a Han settlement, its temples developed during the imperial efforts to placate the restive Miao and Tujia peoples. Around the **Hu Family Lake** (胡家湖, hújiā hú) are some lovely teahouses and a workshop which provides space for local artisans to sell their handicrafts.

Dehang National Park

德夯, déhang · Daily, daylight hours · ¥100 · Minibuses from Jishou train station leave every 50min (¥10)

The scenic **Dehang National Park**, 25km from Jishou, a bucolic ravine flanked by shafts of karst limestone peaks, is home to the **Miao** minority people. At the entrance gate in the hamlet of **Dehang Miaozhai** (德夯苗寨, déhang miáo zhài) are several crass touristic attractions, including a song-and-dance show and innumerable tat stalls. But beyond this, much of the settlement remains unruffled by tourism, and you can enjoy a day or two away from it all, staying in one of the traditional wood-and-stone guesthouses.

Beyond the arched **Jielong Bridge** (接龙桥, jiē lóng qiáo), where locals congregate to hawk bamboo handicrafts, visitors enter a mini Jiangjiajie – a world of towering stone pillars, buffalo-tilled rice paddies and riverside hikes that ascend through a 164-square-kilometre geopark. Follow the path through the **Nine Dragon Steam Scenic Area** (九龙溪, jiǔ lóng xī) to see the **Liusha Waterfall** (流沙瀑布, liúshā pùbù) which, at 216m, is one of the region's tallest.

ACCOMMODATION JISHOU

Jishou is home to the usual business chains, while in and around the hamlet at the foot of Dehand National Park are some locally run guesthouses.

7 Days Inn 7天吉首火车站店, qītiān jíshǒu huǒchē zhàn diàn. Jishou Railway Station, 1 Renminbei Lu ☎ 0743 2113777. A typical chain business hotel with reasonably helpful staff and in a solid location, just a stone's throw from the train station – useful if arriving late or leaving early. **¥150**

Fengyuqiao Guesthouse 风雨桥客栈, fēngyǔ qiáo kèzhàn. Across the bridge from the square, at the beginning of the Yuquanxi Scenic Area trail ☎ 135 74309026. This rustic riverside guesthouse has plenty of atmosphere but, alas, no a/c. Still, if you're looking for the real experience, look no further. Prices vary according to the season and demand. **¥50**

Hongjiang Ancient Commercial City

洪江古商城, hóngjiāng gǔshāngchéng · Daily 9am–5pm · ¥117 including guided tour in Chinese (1hr) · Bus from Huaihua South or Huaihua West bus stations (1hr 10min; ¥18), then walk to the area between Yuanjiang Lu and Xiongxi Lu; taxi from Huaihua ¥200–300

Superficially, **Hongjiang Ancient Commercial City** looks like the town China forgot – a riverside market town dominated by crumbling Mao-era dwellings and reform-era bathroom-tile buildings. But its scruffy facade hides a marvellously preserved **ancient commercial quarter**, which was once the mercantile centre of the region, as the plethora of ancient guildhalls, banks, auction houses, official mansions, opium dens and brothels testifies.

7

Strategically located at the confluence of the Yuan and Wushui rivers, Hongjiang attracted merchants from all over China, making it uniquely cosmopolitan – as well as a major opium-trafficking point. Walking the labyrinth of cobblestone alleys and admiring the stone-and-wood architecture can take the best part of a day. Whether or not you speak Chinese, it might be worth joining one of the **guided tours** that sets out from the entrance gate, at least so that you see the main historic sights (and get to watch costumed performers re-enact ancient stories). Or you might prefer to head to Qianyang (see below) instead, which is less touristy than Hongjiang.

EATING

Local cuisine incorporates some influences from neighbouring Guizhou province, adding a sour edge and some fresh colours to standard Hunan dishes.

She Quan She Mei 食全食美, shíquán shíměi. Cnr of Xinfu Xi Lu and Xin Min Lu ☎0745 7628818. This traditionally decorated restaurant is about as authentic as it gets. Popular with cheek-reddened locals, tofu, river fish and locally grown greens are the order of the day. Around ¥60 per head. Daily 11am–2pm & 5–10pm.

Qianyang Ancient Town

黔阳古城, qiányáng gǔchéng • General entry free, ¥48 for some sites • Buses from Huaihua South and Huaihua West bus stations (50min; ¥15)

With Fenghuang established as the key regional military stronghold and Hongjiang the business centre, **Qianyang** emerged as an administrative hub during the Song dynasty. The superb **ancient town** has better hotels and cafés, and is an all-round more pleasant place to stay, than Hongjiang, just a half-hour drive away.

A quintessential western Hunan settlement, Qianyang comprises thirty streets and lanes, over twenty ancestral halls, ten courtyard houses, a number of temples and some remnants of the city walls. Sites such as the gorgeous riverside **Lotus Tower** express the cultural richness and sophistication of the town's past. As tourism is a relatively new phenomenon here, locals remain curious and friendly.

ACCOMMODATION

Qianyang already has far better accommodation options than Hongjiang. Several locals have converted their family homes into guesthouses, while in the new town there's a handful of business hotels.

North Alley Hostel 巷北客站, xiàng běi kè zhàn. Off Beizheng Jie ☎0745 7738636. A clean and cheerful boutique hostel located in the heart of the old town, this is one of the few places veering towards international standards in terms of comfort and design, though service remains resolutely casual. **¥180**

Jiangxi

江西, jiāngxī

Caught between the Yangzi in the north and a mountainous border with Guangdong in the south, **Jiangxi** is generally considered a bit of a backwater, but to dismiss it out of hand is to ignore some significant attractions – namely, some major revolutionary history and a town that has been producing the highest-quality ceramics for almost six and a half centuries.

A network of rivers covering the province drains into Poyang Hu, China's largest freshwater lake. When the construction of the Grand Canal created a route through Yangzhou and the lower Yangzi in the seventh century, Jiangxi's capital, **Nanchang**, became a key point on the great north–south link of inland waterways. The region enjoyed a long period of quiet prosperity until coastal shipping and the opening up of treaty ports took business away in the 1840s. The twentieth century saw the province's fortunes nosedive: the population halved as millions fled competing warlords and, during the 1920s and 30s, fighting between the Guomindang and Communist forces raged in the southern **Jinggang Shan** ranges. This conflict eventually led to an evicted Red Army starting on their Long March across China.

Things picked up after the Communist takeover, and a badly battered Nanchang licked its wounds and reinvented itself as a centre of heavy industry. Transport links provided by the Poyang and Yangzi tributaries have also benefited the east of the province, where **Jingdezhen** retains its title as China's porcelain capital. North of the lake the mountain area of **Lu Shan** is easily visited from Nanchang and offers a pleasant reminder of Jiangxi's past, when it served as a summer retreat for Chinese literati and colonial servants.

Nanchang

南昌, nánchāng

Hemmed in by hills, **NANCHANG** sits on Jiangxi's major river, the Gan Jiang, some 70km south of where it flows into Poyang Hu. Built on trade, Nanchang has served as a **transport hub** for central-southern China and established itself as a handy base for car and plane manufacturers. More recently, the city has exchanged its reliance on heavy industry – which gave the city a sullen, Soviet atmosphere – for consumerism, tossing up office blocks and shopping malls with abandon.

The city centre

Nanchang sprawls eastward from the Gan Jiang River, but the centre is a compact couple of square kilometres between the river and Bayi Dadao. The Cold War-era **museum** and revolutionary **Bayi Monument** (八一纪念塔, bāyī jìniàntǎ) are overshadowed

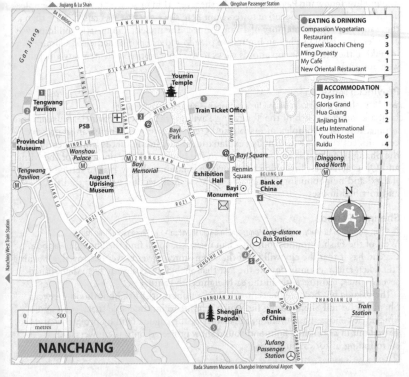

by their modern neighbours, skyscrapers and shopping malls, which surround **Renmin Square** (人民广场, rénmín guǎngchǎng). Popular with locals, the square is a great place for an early-evening wander, when you'll see fan dancing, *tai ji* and kite-flying. Running west of the square, Zhongshan Lu takes you to the heart of Nanchang's bustling shopping district, past the water and greenery of **Bayi Park** (八一公园, bāyī gōngyuán) to the north.

August 1 Uprising Museum

八一纪念馆, bāyī jìniànguǎn · Daily 9am–5pm, last entry 3.30pm · Free; show your passport · ☎ 0791 8661 3806

The Nationalist army occupied Nanchang in December 1926, but when Chiang Kai-shek broke with the Communists the following year, Zhou Enlai and Zhu De, two Communist officers, mutinied and took control of the city with thirty thousand troops. They were soon forced to flee into Jiangxi's mountainous south, but the anniversary of the uprising – August 1, 1927 – is still celebrated as the birth of the People's Liberation Army and the PLA flag remains emblazoned with the Chinese characters "8" and "1" (八一, bāyī) for the month and day.

Formerly a hotel, the imposing grey edifice of the **August 1 Uprising Museum** was occupied by the embryonic PLA as their 1927 headquarters and is mostly of interest as an example of Nanchang's colonial architecture. Inside, the meeting room has been preserved as it was, and there is the usual collection of military memorabilia including guns, medals and uniforms, with some English descriptions.

Tengwang Pavilion

滕王阁, téngwáng gé · Yanjiang Lu · Daily: summer 7.30am–6.30pm; winter 8am–5pm · ¥50, ¥80 with a guide · Metro line #1 to Tengwang Station or take bus #2, #7, #8, #26 or #302

The mighty **Tengwang Pavilion** overlooks the river, 1km or so west of Youmin Temple. There have been 26 consecutive towers built here since the first was raised more than a thousand years ago in memory of a Tang prince. The present "Song-style" building was completed in 1989 but has an impressive pseudo-old exterior nonetheless. Climbing (or taking the lift) to the top affords views to the skyscrapers of the new city emerging west across the river.

Provincial Museum

省博物馆, shěng bówùguǎn · Xinzhou Lu · Tues–Sun 9am–4.30pm · Free · ⊕ jxmuseum.cn

Half a kilometre south of the Tengwang Pavilion, the surreal **Provincial Museum** is a huge, futuristic complex of marble and green glass towers. There's an impressive ceramics collection (with English explanations), including pieces from as early as the Shang dynasty, all the way through to the blue and white porcelain of the Ming and Qing dynasties, for which the province is famous. Many Hakka settled in Jiangxi and neighbouring Fujian, and there's a small section on their traditions and fortified houses.

Shengjin Pagoda

绳金塔, shéngjīn tǎ · Daily: pagoda 7am–6pm; sound-and-light show 8pm · Free · Bus #5 from Xiangshan Lu

West of the Fushan roundabout off Zhan Qian Lu, you'll find the **Shengjin Pagoda**. Legend has it that the city will fall if the seven-storey tower is ever destroyed, a warning still taken fairly seriously despite the fact that Shengjin has already been demolished several times, most recently in the early eighteenth century.

The pagoda has become the centrepiece of a mini tourist neighbourhood, between Shenjinta Jie and Shenjindong Jie, which is home to innumerable snack stalls and knickknack shops. Each evening, the history of the pagoda (and by proxy the city) is played out in a stunning **light-and-sound show** projected onto the towers and surrounding historical buildings.

Bada Shanren Museum

八大山人纪念馆, bādàshānrén jìniànguǎn • Tues–Sun 9am–4.30pm • ¥20 • Bus #20 from Yanjiang Lu

For a reprieve from the city, head 5km south to the **Bada Shanren Museum**. This whitewashed Ming-era compound set in parkland was the studio of the painter Zhu Da, also known as Bada Shanren, a wandering Buddhist monk of imperial descent who came to live in this former temple in 1661 and was later buried here. He is said to have painted in a drunken frenzy; his pictures certainly show great spontaneity. There are a number of originals displayed inside and some good reproductions on sale.

ARRIVAL AND DEPARTURE
NANCHANG

BY PLANE

Changbei International Airport (昌北国际机场, chāngběi guójì jīchǎng) is 23km north of the centre; the airport bus (¥15) terminates at the *Civil Aviation Hotel* (民航大酒店, mínháng dàjiǔdiàn) on Hongcheng Lu. Alternatively, taxis can whisk you into town for ¥70.

Destinations Beijing (2hr); Chengdu (2hr); Guangzhou (1hr 30min); Hefei (1hr 15min); Kunming (2hr 15min); Shanghai (1hr 15min); Shenzhen (1hr 45min).

BY TRAIN

Nanchang train station (南昌火车站, nánchāng huǒchē zhàn) is 700m east of the Fushan roundabout at the end of Zhan Qian Lu; it handles regular trains. Nanchang lies on the Kowloon–Beijing train line and just off the Shanghai–Kunming line, with connections through easterly Yingtan down into Fujian province.

Destinations Beijing (7 daily; 12–22hr); Changsha (4 daily; 6hr); Fuzhou (6 daily; 3hr 30min–15hr 30min); Guangzhou (2 daily; 12–14hr); Hefei (2 daily; 6hr 40min); Jingdezhen (2 daily; 5hr 18min); Jinggang Shan (2 daily; 4hr); Jiujiang (28 daily; 1–2hr); Shenzhen (2 daily; 12hr 50min); Yingtan (11 daily; 1hr–2hr 30min).

Nanchang West station (南昌西站, nánchāng xī zhàn), 20km southwest of the main station, deals with the city's high-speed trains.

Destinations Beijing (8 daily; 9–12hr); Changsha Nan (55 daily; 1hr 40min); Fuzhou (12 daily; 3–5hr); Guangzhou (14 daily; 4–12hr); Hangzhou East (42 daily; 2hr 15min–3hr); Hefei Nan (2 daily; 4hr 12min); Huangshan Bei (2 daily; 2hr 26min); Jinggang Shan (1 daily; 3hr); Jiujiang (20 daily; 1–2hr); Shanghai (3hr–14hr 20min); Shenzhen (8 daily; 5–10hr); Yingtan (40 daily; 30–40min).

BY BUS

Nanchang has four main bus stations, of which the following three are most useful to travellers.

Long-distance Bus Station (长途汽车站, chángtú qìchēzhàn). Nanchang's biggest station is conveniently located just south of the centre on Bayi Dadao, and can be reached by bus #1. The station is huge and often crowded, but ticket offices are user-friendly and there's usually no problem getting seats. Good for services to all over the country, except for Jingdezhen and Lu Shan.

Qingshan Passenger Station (青山客运站, qīngshān kèyùnzhàn) well north of the centre on Qingshan Nan Lu and reached by bus #123. This is the only station with direct buses to Lu Shan (9.30am & 3.40pm; ¥62); alternatively, catch one of the regular services to Jiujiang and change there.

Xufang Passenger Station (徐坊客运站 xúfāng kèyùnzhàn) on Jinggang Shan Dadao in the south of town; reached on bus #1. Services to Jingdezhen, Changsha, Hefei, Jiujiang (for Lu Shan), Shanghai and Wuhan. Chaotic and crowded, but tickets are readily available outside of peak holidays.

Destinations Changsha (5hr); Ciping (8hr); Hefei (6hr); Jingdezhen (3hr); Jinggang Shan (6hr); Jiujiang (2hr); Lu Shan (4hr); Shanghai (12hr); Wuhan (5hr); Yingtan (2hr 30min).

7

GETTING AROUND

Get a Hongcheng Yikatong card for use on buses and the new metro.

By bus City buses #5, #18, #219, #221, #305 run from the train station along Bayi Dadao into town.
By metro At the time of writing only line #1, Shuanggang–Yaohu Lake West, was in operation, though

more are in the pipeline.
By taxi Cabs cruise downtown arrival points, with a ¥6 standing charge.

ACCOMMODATION

There's plenty of accommodation in town, although good budget choices are a little thin on the ground.

7 Days Inn 7天连锁酒店, qītiān liánsuǒ jiǔdiàn. 142 Bayi Dadao ☎0791 88857688. In an excellent

location across from the main long-distance bus station, this reliable chain-hotel has clean, modern rooms and attentive staff. **¥218**

Gloria Grand 凯莱大酒店，kǎilái dàjiǔdiàn. 88 Yanjiang Bei Lu ☎0791 86738855, ⓦnanchang-grand .gloriahotels.com/. This modern, international-style joint-venture hotel is the most foreigner-friendly in Nanchang, with a smart café serving Western food, a Chinese restaurant and a French-Japanese fusion restaurant. **¥608**

Hua Guang 华光宾馆，huáguāng bīnguǎn. 58 Xiangshan Bei Lu ☎0791 86777222. Shabby hotel with plain, faded (if clean) rooms, hard beds and brusque staff, but about the cheapest deal you'll find in the heart of town. **¥148**

Jinjiang Inn 锦江之星，jǐnjiāng zhīxīng. 255 Minde Xi Lu ☎0791 86788111, ⓦwww.jinjianginns.com. In a central location, with smart, bright rooms and modern amenities, all at a good rate, this place is hard to fault. There's a fair-value restaurant here too. **¥170**

★**Letu International Youth Hostel** 乐途青年旅舍，lètu qīngnián lǚshè. 253 Shengjin Ta Meishi Jie, Xihu Qu ☎0791 8523919, ⓦyhachina.com. Friendly YHA youth hostel by the pagoda and near plenty of snack shops. The affiliated bar has nightly live music, and the staff are helpful and speak some English. Dorms **¥50**, doubles **¥119**

Ruidu 瑞都大酒店，ruìdū dàjiǔdiàn. 399 Guangchang Lu ☎0791 86201888. An upmarket place, nicely located on the southeast corner of Renmin Square. Rooms are attractive and well kept, but don't have fridges or bathtubs, which you might expect at this price. **¥340**

EATING AND DRINKING

Nanchang's gastronomy covers everything from **dumpling houses** and spicy **Hunanese restaurants** to the regional **Gan cooking** – lightly sauced fresh fish, crayfish, snails and frogs. **Soups** are a Jiangxi favourite – egg and pork soup is a typical breakfast – often served in huge pots as communal affairs. Restaurants are spread all over the city, though the streets around **Bayi Park** have the highest concentration, and **Yongshu Lu** is lined with eateries, from holes in the wall to fancy banquet dining halls.

★**Compassion Vegetarian Restaurant** 慈心素食馆，cíxīn sùshí guǎn. Shengjin Meishi Jie ☎0791 86450025. As the prayer flags suggest, this is a Buddhist, meat-free restaurant, well located near the Shengjin Pagoda. Dishes average at ¥38, and portions are quite big – the place is geared for group diners. A refreshing break from heavy oils and spices. Daily 11am–2pm & 5–9pm.

Fengwei Xiaochi Cheng 风味小吃城，fēngwèi xiǎochīchéng. 54 Zhongshan Lu. The name translates as Regional Flavour Snack City, and there's certainly plenty on offer at this no-frills crowded canteen where you can fill up for less than ¥20. Ordering is easy (the food's on display), and regular dishes include eggs with tomato, sweet-and-sour pork and delicious pickled cucumbers. Daily 10am–9pm.

Ming Dynasty 明朝铜鼎煨汤府，míngcháo tóngdǐng wèitāngfǔ. 144 Bayi Dadao ☎0791 6293683. The big bronze cauldron outside marks this as a Jiangxi-style soup restaurant. The soup is traditionally a breakfast favourite with locals, but portions here are enough to make a good lunch or dinner. A variety of flavours is on offer, including black chicken and young pigeon; individual pots start at ¥18, while three- to four-person pots cost from ¥30. Daily 7am–2pm & 5–9pm.

My Café 湖南王贩卖灵魂深处的品味，húnánwáng fànmài línghúnshēnchùde pǐnwèi. Minde Lu, near Supu Lu ☎015377520521. High ceilings, comfy sofas and laidback staff make this a cosy and relaxing place to spend a couple of hours reading and sipping Earl Grey tea (¥30). Daily 9am–midnight.

New Oriental Restaurant 新东方大酒店，xīndōngfāng dàjiǔdiàn. 18 Yanjiang Zhong Lu ☎0791 86700777. This vast, opulent and gaudy Gan-style restaurant looks straight onto the river and the Tengwang Pavilion, and also serves Cantonese dishes. Around ¥50–100 per person. Daily 11am–2pm & 4.30–10pm.

DIRECTORY

Hospital First City Hospital, Xiangshan Lu ☎0791 88862261.

Left luggage Offices at train and bus stations open roughly daily 6am–7pm.

Post office The main post office (daily 8am–6pm) is at the corner of Bayi Dadao and Ruzi Lu.

Visa extensions On Shengli Lu, just north of Minde Lu (daily 8am–noon & 2.30–5.30pm; ☎0791 88892000).

Lu Shan

庐山，lúshān • Daily 6am–6pm • National park: summer ¥180, winter ¥135

Lu Shan mountain and the forested range around it rise abruptly from the level shores of Poyang Hu to a dizzying 1474m, the cool heights bringing welcome relief from the summer cauldron of the Yangzi basin. The town of **LU SHAN**, developed in the late nineteenth century by Methodist minister-turned-property-speculator **Edward Little** as a hill-station-style resort for European expats, became popular with the Chinese elite soon after foreigners lost their grip on the region. Chiang Kai-shek built a summer residence and training school for officials here in the 1930s, and, twenty years later, Lu Shan hosted one of the key meetings of the Maoist era. Today, proletarian holidaymakers pack out its restaurants and tramp its paths, and the mansions have been converted into hotels. Crowds reach intense proportions between spring and autumn, so winter – though very cold – can be the best season to visit, and a weekend's walking is enough for a good sample of the scenery.

Guling

牯岭, gǔlǐng

Some 30km uphill from the lowlands on a sharply twisting road, **GULING** township comprises a handful of quaintly cobbled streets, European stone villas and bungalows in Lu Shan's northeastern corner. There are some sights here, though these are generally only of interest to those making revolutionary pilgrimages: a bigger attraction for most foreign visitors is the combination of stunning scenery and cool mountain air.

7

Revolutionary sights

All daily 8am–6pm • Meilu Villa and Zhou Enlai's Residence combined ticket ¥25; People's Hall ¥50

The **Meilu Villa** (美庐别墅, měilú biéshù) is a former home of both Chiang Kai-shek – it's named after his wife, Song Meiling – and Mao Zedong. Not far away are **Zhou Enlai's Residence** (周恩来故居, zhōu'ēnlái gùjū) and the **People's Hall** (人民剧院, rénmín jùyuàn), the latter venue of many a historic meeting – including one in 1959 when Marshal Peng Dehui openly criticized the Great Leap Forward, and was subsequently denounced as a "Rightist" by Mao, triggering the Cultural Revolution.

Into the hills

Covering some 500 square kilometres, Lu Shan's highlands form an elliptical platform tilted over to the southwest, comprising a central region of lakes surrounded by pine-clad hills, with superb rocks, waterfalls and views along the vertical edges of the plateau. **Hiking** is undoubtedly one of the area's greatest pleasures, and there are a number of trails laid out within the park – maps of varying detail are widely available. Although it can be tempting to try to walk everywhere, some of the paths lie quite a distance from Guling and it's well worth taking advantage of park transport to save your energy for the trails proper.

The Floral Path

For an easy walk out from town (3hr round-trip), follow the road downhill to the southwest from Guling Lu and the Jiexin Garden to the far end of **Ruqin Lake** (如琴湖, rúqín hú), where you pick up the Floral Path. This affords impressive views of the Jinxui valley as it winds along Lu Shan's western cliff edge past the **Immortal's Cave** (仙人洞, xiānrén dòng), once inhabited by an ephemeral Taoist monk and still an active shrine, complete with a slowly dripping spring.

Southern Lu Shan

The most spectacular scenery can be found on Lu Shan's **southern fringes**. Proper exploration requires a full day's hike, and this is one even hardened walkers should hop on a bus for. **Lulin Hu** (芦林湖, lúlín hú) is a nice lakeside area with the attractive Dragon Pools and elderly Three Treasure trees over to the west. Due east of here – about 5km by road but less along walking tracks – is one of China's few subalpine **botanical gardens** (植物园, zhíwù yuán), the finest spot in Lu Shan to watch the sunrise, though the peaks are famously often obscured by mist, and clear days are a rarity; even the local brew is suitably known as "Cloud Fog Tea".

ARRIVAL AND DEPARTURE
LU SHAN

Lu Shan is most easily reached direct from Nanchang or via Jiujiang (九江, jiǔjiāng) a Yangzi port near the foot of the mountain, where the closest airport, train and long-distance bus stations are located.

BY PLANE
Jiujiang airport lies 40km south of Jiujiang city. A taxi from the airport to Lu Shan costs ¥100–150; or you can take one of the regular buses to Jiujiang bus station, and then transfer to a Lu Shan service.
Destinations Beijing (2hr 15min); Guangzhou (1hr 30min).

BY TRAIN
Jiujiang train station is 3km southeast of the city centre. There is now a tourism bus that connects the station with Lu Shan (¥15).
Destinations Ganzhou (22 daily; 6–9hr); Hefei (7 daily; 4hr 30min–7hr); Nanchang (50 daily; 1–2hr); Shanghai (3 daily; 12–15hr).

BY BUS
Lu Shan is served by few direct long-distance services, so go first to Jiujiang for Wuhan and points east, and to Nanchang for southern or westerly destinations.
Lu Shan bus station Buses from Nanchang stop on He Dong Lu, while minibuses from Jiujiang (¥15) might drop passengers anywhere.
Destinations Jiujiang (1hr); Nanchang (2hr).
Jiujiang bus station Jiujiang's long-distance bus station is on Xunyang Lu, from where there are regular buses to Lu Shan until 5pm, earlier in winter.
Destinations Changsha (8hr); Hefei (5hr); Wuhan (4hr); Yichang (8–10hr).

GETTING AROUND
By bus A bus network extends throughout the scenic area; week-long bus passes are available for ¥80.
By cable car Numerous cable cars and ropeways offer easy access to some of Lu Shan's most scenic spots including: Three Cascades (¥80 return); Hanpo Pass (¥50 return); and Xiufeng Peak (¥80 return).

ACCOMMODATION AND EATING

Lu Shan gets very busy in **summer** – arrive early on the day to ensure a **room** – and expensive, as hotel-owners raise rates and refuse to bargain. The summer prices listed below tumble during **winter**, when it gets cold enough to snow, so check the availability of heating and hot water. There are plenty of **restaurants** in Guling, mostly good value, and some post their menus and prices outside. For local flavours – mountain fungus and fish – try the stalls and open restaurants around the market.

Guling Dajiudian 牯岭大酒店, gǔlǐng dàjiǔdiàn. 7 He Xi Lu ☎0792 8282435. Handy for the buses, this remodelled three-star has comfortable rooms, a swimming pool and a gym, plus friendly staff. **¥360**
Lu Shan Binguan 庐山宾馆, lúshān bīnguǎn. 70 He Xi Lu ☎0792 8282060. This is a heavy stone mansion set among parkland on the edge of the woods, with pleasant, comfortable rooms, good-value suites and a fine restaurant. **¥400**
Lu Shan Dasha 庐山大厦, lúshān dàshà. 506 He Xi Lu ☎0792 8282178. A regimental exterior betrays this hotel as the former Guomindang Officers' Training Centre; rooms are suitably well furnished and comfortable. **¥320**
Lu Shan International Nature Youth Hostel 大自然国际青年旅舍, dà zì rán gúojì qīngnián lǚshè. 1 Hubei Lu ☎0792 8288989, ⓦhihostels.com. Set below Five Old Man Peak, Lu Shan's HI-affiliated hostel offers friendly travel advice and cheap, comfortable accommodation nestled into the pine forest. Dorms **¥50**, doubles **¥150**

DIRECTORY

Bank and exchange The Bank of China on Hemian Jie has an ATM.
Hiking equipment Stores selling maps, raincoats and provisions can be found on Guling Jie.
Post office The post office (9am–5pm) is on Guling Jie.

Jingdezhen
景德镇, jǐngdézhèn

Across Poyang Hu from Nanchang and not far from the border with Anhui province, **JINGDEZHEN** has been producing **ceramics** for at least two thousand years. Lying in a river valley not only rich in clay but also the vital feldspar needed to make porcelain, the city's defining moment came in the fourteenth century: China's capital was at

KAOLIN AND SHIPWRECKS

The popularity of **Jingdezhen pottery** brought revenues and expertise which provided a platform for innovation. Workshops experimented with new glazes and a classic range of decorative styles emerged: *qinghua*, blue and white; *jihong*, rainbow; *doucai*, a blue-and-white overglaze; and *fencai*, multicoloured famille rose. The first examples reached Europe in the seventeenth century and became so popular that the English word for China clay – *kaolin* – derives from its source nearby at Gaoling. Factories began to specialize in **export ware** designed for Europe and Chinese colonies throughout Southeast Asia, which reached the outside world via the booming Canton markets: the famous **Nanking Cargo**, comprising 150,000 pieces salvaged from the 1752 wreck of the Dutch vessel *Geldermalsen* and auctioned for US$15 million in 1986, was one such shipment. Foreign sales petered out after European production technologies improved at the end of the eighteenth century, but Jingdezhen survived by sacrificing innovation for cheaper manufacturing processes, and more recently has reinvented itself as a centre of ceramic study and research.

7

Nanjing, and Jingdezhen was considered conveniently close to produce porcelain for the Ming court. An imperial kiln was built in 1369, and its wares became so highly regarded – "as white as jade, as thin as paper, as bright as a mirror, as tuneful as a bell" – that Jingdezhen retained official favour even after the Ming court moved to Beijing fifty years later.

Today, in spite of attempts to smarten up the place with ceramic lampposts and public bins, Jingdezhen remains a scruffy city, mostly as a result of the scores of smoky kilns that still employ some fifty thousand people. Nonetheless, Jingdezhen is worth a visit if you're in the market for some **pottery**, or even getting your hands dirty at the Pottery Workshop (see box, p.454).

The markets

There are plenty of shops aimed at tourists, but it's more fun to head to the **markets**. On Jiefang Lu, south of the central square, the pavements are clogged with stacks of everything that has ever been made in porcelain: metre-high vases, life-sized dogs, Western- and Chinese-style crockery, antique reproductions including yellow- and green-glazed Tang camels, ugly statuettes and simple porcelain pandas. Haggling can be fun, but it's just as entertaining to watch other people and wonder how they are going to get their new acquisitions home – and where on earth they'll put them once they do.

Jingdezhen China Ceramics Museum

中国陶瓷博物馆, zhōngguó táocí bówùguǎn • Out of town • Daily 8am–5pm • Free • ⓦ jdztcg.com

Opened in 2015 in a multistorey exhibition hall on the edge of town, the impressive **Jingdezhen China Ceramics Museum** provides a comprehensive overview of Jingdezhen and its fabled chinaware with an enormous collection of 30,000 fine ceramics. Visitors learn how the art form evolved from the Han dynasty through the ages, as Jingdezhen developed an international reputation for the highest quality craftsmanship (see box above). Also on display are Mao-era ceramics, adorned with socialist iconography, and a few contemporary pieces of the post-reform era.

Ancient Kiln Folk Customs Museum

景德镇古窑民俗博览区, jǐngdézhèn gǔyáo mínsú bólǎnqū • On the town fringes on the west side of the river, about 3km from the bus station • Daily 8am–5pm • ¥95; English-speaking guides ¥100 • ⓦ chinaguyao.com • Bus #1, #16 or #17 to Cidu Dadao, then cross the road and head toward the ornamental arch

To experience the manufacturing side of Jingdezhen's pottery world, visit the **Ancient Kiln Folk Customs Museum**. From the main road, a fifteen-minute forested walk leads to a surprising collection of antique buildings divided into two sections. A Ming mansion houses the museum itself, and its ornate crossbeams, walled gardens and gilt eave

GET YOUR HANDS DIRTY

Jingdezhen is busy rekindling its world status as a ceramics centre. You can join in the fun at the **Pottery Workshop** (W potteryworkshop.com.cn), where introductory sessions are on offer, as well as more advanced courses. Not a bad way to get up close and personal with the art and industry that defines the town.

screens are a great backdrop to the **ceramics display** which covers everything from thousand-year-old kiln fragments through to the Ming's classic simplicity and overwrought, multicoloured extravagances of the late nineteenth century. The museum also puts on hourly **musical performances** in its Waterside Pavilion – all of the performers play ceramic instruments.

Ancient Porcelain Workshop

Next door to the museum building, another walled garden conceals the **Ancient Porcelain Workshop**, complete with a Confucian temple and working pottery, where the entire process of throwing, moulding and glazing takes place.

National Park of the Royal Kiln Site

御窑国家考古遗址公园, yùyáo guójiā kǎogǔ yízhǐ gōngyuán • 187 Zhushan Zhong Lu • Daily 8am–5pm • ¥60 • ☏ 0798 8201378

The **National Park of the Royal Kiln Site**, in the centre of town, is a commemorative park celebrating Jingdezhen's status as the producer of porcelain for the emperor and his imperial entourage, from the Ming dynasty until the demise of imperial China. The site uses a mixture of overenthusiastically restored old buildings and exhibition halls to tell of its royal relationship, culminating in the **Longzhu Ge**, an iconic Tang-dynasty tower, revamped in 2013 to house five floors of exhibition halls.

ARRIVAL AND DEPARTURE
JINGDEZHEN

By train Jingdezhen's train station is 1.5km southeast of the town centre, on Tongzhan Lu; it's served by bus #28. Destinations Hefei (2 daily; 11hr); Nanchang (2 daily; 5hr); Shanghai (1 daily; 17hr); Tunxi (10 daily; 2hr 30min–4hr 30min).

By bus The long-distance bus station is 3km west across the river; take bus #28 into town. Destinations Changsha (8hr); Ganzhou (9hr); Hangzhou (6hr); Jiujiang (2hr); Nanchang (3hr); Shanghai (9hr); Tunxi (3hr 30min); Wuhan (5hr); Yingtan (3hr).

GETTING AROUND

By bus Jingdezhen has a basic bus network with regular and a/c services that cost ¥1–2.
By taxi Many taxi drivers refuse to use their meters, and are eager to show you the long way round, but you should be able to negotiate a fare of ¥6–12 for anywhere in town.
By motorbike taxi At ¥5 for anywhere in town, motorbike taxis are the quickest and cheapest – if not the safest – way to get around for solo travellers.

ACCOMMODATION AND EATING

Food stalls offering hotpots and stir-fries can be found east of Guangchang along Tongzhan Lu, while more Western fast-food choices are near the bridge on Zhushan Lu. If you're looking to pass the time before a train journey, try one of the Western-style coffee shops on Zhejiang Lu.

Jingdezhen International Youth Hostel 景德镇国际青年旅舍, jǐngdézhèn guójì qīngnián lǚshè. 139 Xinchangdong Lu ☏ 0798 8448886. This smart, modern YHA hostel is located right next to the Pottery Workshop where artisans sell their wares in open markets and host workshops. There's a reasonable café downstairs and plenty in the neighbourhood. Dorms ¥45, doubles ¥150

Jingdezhen Xiaolu International Youth Hostel 景德镇晓庐国际青年旅舍, jǐngdézhèn xiǎolú guójì qīngnián lǚshè. 18 Zhushan Zhong Lu ☏ 0793 7217766. Welcoming, good-value YHA hostel located in the heart of town with one of the few bars that sells imported beers. Dorms ¥45, doubles ¥105

Jinggang Shan

井冈山, jǐnggāng shān • Daily 9am–5pm • ¥260, tickets valid for three days and include admission to all sights • Buses within the park ¥70

When mutinying officers Zhou Enlai and Zhu De were driven out of Nanchang after their abortive uprising, they fled to the **Jinggang Shan** ranges, 300km southwest along the mountainous border with Hunan. Here they met up with Mao, whose Autumn Harvest Uprising in Hunan had also failed, and the remnants of the two armies joined to form the first real PLA divisions. Their initial base was near the country town of **Ciping**, and, though they declared a Chinese Soviet Republic in 1931 at the Fujian border town of Ruijin, Ciping was where the Communists stayed until forced out by the Guomindang in 1934.

Today, Jinggang Shan doesn't attract huge numbers of tourists, making the picture-perfect **forest scenery** and meandering **hiking trails** an attractive proposition.

THE LONG MARCH

In 1927, **Chiang Kai-shek**, leader of the Nationalist Guomindang (GMD) government, began an obsessive war against the Chinese Communist Party. Driven underground, the Communists set up remote rural bases, or soviets, across central China. The main **Jiangxi soviet** in the Jinggang Mountains was led by **Mao Zedong** and **Zhu De**, the Communist commander-in-chief. Ignoring Japanese incursions into Manchuria, Chiang blockaded the mountains with a steadily tightening ring of bunkers and barbed wire, systematically clearing areas of guerrillas with artillery bombardments. Hemmed in and facing eventual defeat, the First Front army, comprising some eighty thousand Red soldiers, broke through the blockade in October 1934 and retreated west to team up with the Hunan soviet – marking the beginning of the **Long March**.

Covering a punishing 30km a day, the Communists moved after dark whenever possible, but still faced daily skirmishes. After incurring severe losses during a battle at the Xiang River near Guilin in Guangxi, the marchers found their progress north impeded by massive GMD forces, and were obliged to continue west to Guizhou, where they took the town of Zunyi in January 1935, and an emergency meeting of the Communist Party hierarchy was called – the **Zunyi Conference**. Mao emerged as the undisputed leader of the Party, with a mandate to "go north to fight the Japanese" by linking up with **Zhang Guotao** in Sichuan. In one of the most celebrated and heroic episodes of the march, they took the Luding Bridge across the Dadu River, only to negotiate the Great Snowy Mountains, where hundreds died from exposure before the survivors met up on the far side with the Fourth Front army.

The meeting between these two branches of the Red Army was tense. Mao wanted to start resistance against the Japanese, but Zhang Guotao favoured founding a Communist state in Sichuan's far west. Zhang eventually capitulated, and he and Mao took control of separate columns to cross the last natural barrier they faced, the Aba grasslands in northern Sichuan. Here, while Mao was bogged down by swamps, hostile nomads and dwindling food reserves, Zhang's column suddenly retreated to Ganzi, where Zhang set up an independent government. Mao struggled through southern Gansu, finally arriving in Communist-held Yan'an, Shaanxi province, in October 1935. While the mountains here were to become a Communist stronghold, only a quarter of those who started from Jiangxi twelve months before had completed the 9500km journey.

Immediately after the Long March, Mao admitted that in terms of losses and the Red Army's failure to hold their original positions, the Nationalists had won. Yet in a more lasting sense, the march was an incredible success, uniting the Party under Mao and defining the Communists' aims, while cementing their popular image as a determined and patriotic movement. After Zunyi, Mao turned the march into a deliberate **propaganda mission** to spread the Communist faith among the peasantry and minority groups. As Mao said, "Without the Long March, how could the broad masses have learned so quickly about the existence of the great truth which the Red Army embodies?"

7

Ciping

茨坪, cípíng

Once site of the Communist guerrillas' headquarters, **CIPING** is little more than a village, the main streets forming a 2km elliptical circuit, the lower half of which is taken up with a lake surrounded by well-tended gardens. Completely destroyed by artillery bombardments during the 1930s, it was rebuilt after the Communist takeover and has recently been remodelled to take better advantage of tourism.

Revolutionary Museum

井岗山博物馆, jǐnggāngshān bówùguǎn • Daily 8am–4pm

Opposite watery Yicuihu Park on Hongjun Lu lies the almost comically overbearing **Revolutionary Museum**, built in the monumental style so beloved of totalitarian regimes. Steps lead up behind to a vast statue commemorating the Communist struggle, from where there would be a great view across the valley – if the museum were not blotting it out. Exhibitions mainly consist of maps and dioramas showing battlefields and troop movements up until 1930, after which the Communists suffered some heavy defeats. There are also busts of prominent revolutionaries, paintings of a smiling Mao preaching to his peasant armies and cases of the spears, flintlocks and mortars that initially comprised the Communist arsenal.

Former Revolutionary Headquarters

革命旧居群, gémìng jiùjūqún • Daily 8am–4pm

On the east side of Yicuihu Park, a group of mud-brick rooms forms a reconstruction of the **Former Revolutionary Headquarters**. As the site marking where Mao and Zhu De coordinated their guerrilla activities and the start of the Long March, it is the town's biggest attraction as far as visiting cadres are concerned.

Into the hills

Having waded through the terribly serious displays in town, it's nice to escape into Jinggang Shan's surprisingly wild **countryside**. Some of the peaks provide glorious views of the **sunrise** – or frequent mists – and there are colourful plants, natural groves of pine and bamboo, deep-green temperate cloud forests, and hosts of butterflies and birds.

Wulong Tan

五龙潭, wǔlóng tán

One of the nicest areas to explore is **Wulong Tan** (Five Dragon Pools), about 8km north along the road from the Martyrs' Tomb. A footpath from the roadhead leads past some poetically pretty waterfalls dropping into the pools (of which there are actually eight) between a score of pine-covered peaks.

Wuzhi Peak

五指峰, wǔzhǐ fēng

Less than 10km south of town is Jinggang Shan itself, also known as **Wuzhi Feng**, apex of the mountains at 1586m. The more well-trodden trails are obvious and well signposted in English, though they can become slippery in the wet. As the trees and waterfalls below slide in and out of the clouds, the peace and beauty make it hard to imagine it as the cradle of guerrilla warfare for the Communists back in the 1920s and 30s.

ARRIVAL AND INFORMATION JINGGANG SHAN

There's a bus station at Ciping, and an airport and train station at newly built Jinggang Shan city (井岗山市, jǐnggāng shān shì), which is a good 40min from Ciping by bus (¥10) or taxi (¥60–70).

By plane Jinggang Shan airport (井冈山机场, jīnggǎng shān jīchǎng) is served by an expensive daily flight from Beijing and another from Guangzhou. There is no direct transport to Ciping, so you'll need to transfer to Jinggang Shan city bus station and then change to a Ciping service.

Destinations Beijing (2hr 30min); Guangzhou (1hr).

By train Jinggang Shan's train station is on the Nanchang–Shenzhen line. In Ciping there's a booking office on Hongjun Lu.

Destinations Ganzhou (1 daily; 4hr); Nanchang (3 daily; 4hr); Shenzhen (1 daily; 11hr).

By bus Ciping's bus station is on the northeastern side of the village's circuit, served by buses from Nanchang and elsewhere across the region. Heading south, you'll need to change at Ganzhou (赣州, gànzhōu), down towards the Guangdong border.

Destinations Ganzhou (5hr); Hengyang (8hr); Nanchang (8hr).

ACCOMMODATION

JINGGANG SHAN CITY

Cuihu Hotel 翠湖宾馆, cuìhú bīnguǎn. 2 Hongjun Nan Lu ☎0796 6557666. One of Ciping's more affordable hotels, though with a rather institutional atmosphere, the *Cuihu* has standard-issue Chinese rooms complete with hard beds and dated furnishings. ¥240

Jinggang Shan Binguan 井冈山宾馆, jīnggǎngshān bīnguǎn. 16 Hongjun Bei Lu ☎0796 6552272. Housed in a clearly Soviet-inspired building, this was a former favourite with Party cadres. Despite a recent makeover, the rooms are plain and the prices a little too high. ¥338

Nanhu Binguan 南湖宾馆, nánhú bīnguǎn. 19 Hongjun Nan Lu ☎0796 6556666. This conference-sized effort has a palatial, marble-clad lobby and surprisingly spacious rooms. There's a wood-decked terrace too, with splendid mountain views, and – of all things – a pool table. ¥400

7

Fujian, Guangdong and Hainan Island

福建 / 广东 / 海南岛

HAKKA ROUNDHOUSE, YONGDING

Fujian, Guangdong and Hainan Island

There's something very self-contained about the provinces of Fujian, Guangdong and Hainan Island, which occupy 1200km or so of China's convoluted southern seaboard. Though occasionally taking centre stage in the country's history, the provinces share a sense of general isolation from mainstream events by the mountain ranges surrounding Fujian and Guangdong, physically cutting them off from the rest of the empire. Forced to look seawards, the coastal regions have a long history of contact with the outside world: this is where Islam entered China, and porcelain and tea left it along the Maritime Silk Road; where the mid-nineteenth-century theatricals of the Opium Wars, colonialism, the Taiping Uprising and the mass overseas exodus of southern Chinese were played out; and where today you'll find some of China's most Westernized cities. Conversely, the interior mountains enclose some of the country's wildest, most remote corners, parts of which were virtually in the Stone Age at the turn of the twentieth century.

8

Possibly because its attractions are thinly spread, the region receives scant attention from foreign visitors, except those transiting between the mainland and Hong Kong or Macau. And a superficial skim through the region – especially the enormous industrial sprawl surrounding the Guangdong capital, **Guangzhou** – can leave a gloomy impression of uncontrolled development and its attendant ills. Yet below the surface, even Guangzhou has some antique architecture and a strangely compelling, lively atmosphere, while smaller cities – including the Fujian port of **Quanzhou**, and **Chaozhou** in eastern Guangdong – seem partially frozen in time, staunchly preserving their traditions in the face of the modern world. Scenically, the **Wuyi Shan** range in northeastern Fujian contains the region's lushest, most picturesque mountain forests; while way down south on **Hainan Island** lie the country's best and busiest **beaches** where you can also **surf**, **sail** and **scuba dive**.

As one of the longest-developed areas of the mainland, getting around the region is seldom problematic, with high-speed rail now connecting all but remote areas. The **weather** is nicest in spring and autumn, as summer storms from June to August bring sweltering heat and humidity, thunder, downpours and floods. By contrast, the mountainous reaches of Guangdong and Fujian can get very cold in winter.

CANTONESE STIR-FRY

Highlights

❶ Wuyi Shan Scenic Area Dramatic gorges and great hiking trails among some of the finest scenery in southern China. **See p.466**

❷ Quanzhou Old port town with an iconic temple and mosque, plus an excellent maritime museum. **See p.470**

❸ Gulangyu Islet Uniquely relaxing island sporting vehicle-free streets, European-style colonial mansions and sea views. **See p.475**

❹ Hakka mansions These circular mud-brick homes, sometimes housing upwards of four

hundred people, are China's most distinctive traditional architecture. **See p.482**

❺ Cantonese food Sample China's finest cuisine, from *dim sum* to roast goose, in one of Guangzhou's restaurants. **See p.499**

❻ Diaolou Magnificent watchtowers scattered throughout the countryside of Kaiping, fusing the architectural styles of East and West. **See p.505**

❼ Hainan Island Soak up the sun while swimming, diving or surfing at the country's best beaches. **See p.525**

HIGHLIGHTS ARE MARKED ON THE MAP ON P.462

Fujian

福建, fújiàn

Fujian, on China's southeastern coast, is well off the beaten track for most Western travellers, which is a pity because the province possesses not only a wild mountainous interior, but also a string of old ports, including **Xiamen**, one of China's more relaxed big cities.

Contact between the coastal area and the outside world has been flourishing for centuries. In the Tang dynasty, the port of **Quanzhou** was considered on a par with Alexandria, and teemed with Middle Eastern traders, some of whose descendants still live in the area today. Fujian's interior, however, remains largely unvisited, with the exception of the scenic **Wuyi Shan** area in the northwest of the province, and the **Hakka regions** around southwesterly **Yongding**.

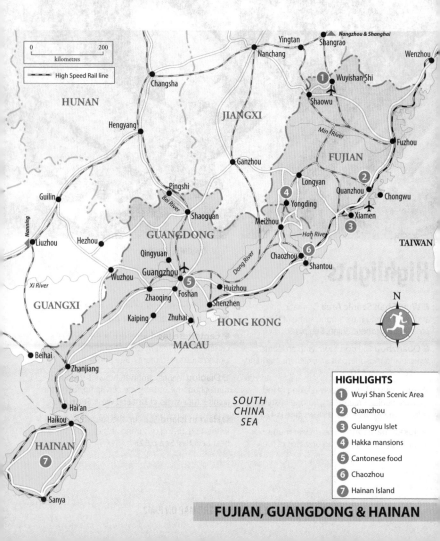

HIGHLIGHTS

1. Wuyi Shan Scenic Area
2. Quanzhou
3. Gulangyu Islet
4. Hakka mansions
5. Cantonese food
6. Chaozhou
7. Hainan Island

FUJIAN, GUANGDONG & HAINAN

Fuzhou

福州, fúzhōu

The capital of Fujian province is modern **FUZHOU**, with gilded skyscrapers looming over the main roads. The city is centred on **Wuyi Square** (五一广场, wǔyī guǎngchǎng), an open expanse dominated by a gleaming-white **statue of Mao Zedong** commemorating the Ninth Congress of the CCP in 1969. However, long before the revolution, Fuzhou was an important trading centre. During the fifteenth century, Fuzhou's shipbuilders earned themselves the distinction of building the world's largest ocean-going vessel, the *Baochuan*, sailed by the famous Chinese navigator **Zheng He**, who used it to travel all around Asia and Africa. Marco Polo visited too, noting the high-profile presence of Mongol armies to suppress any potential uprisings; the city is no less well defended today, forming the heart of Fujian's military opposition to Taiwan. Fuzhou's mercantile maritime heritage informs its few lowly tourist sites – worth taking if you layover here on the way to Wuyi Shan (see p.466) or the historic port town of Quanzhou (see p.470).

Three Lanes and Seven Alleys

三坊七巷, sānfāng qīxiàng • Daily, daylight hours • Residences are typically ¥15 or ¥20 to enter or buy a two-day combo ticket for ¥120 • Buses #5, #18, #22 and #55 to Shaungpaoqiao

To get a taste of Old Fuzhou, head to the area just off Nanhou Jie, where you'll find a gentrified "ancient" neighbourhood poetically branded the **Three Lanes and Seven Alleys**. Though extensively renovated in 2007, the old quarter is still an atmospheric place where 65 of the 268 Tang and Song classical residences, temples and gardens are open to visitors. The main street, Nanhou Jie, is lined with a spattering of galleries and snack stalls, and tourist shops selling local handicrafts such as buffalo-bone combs.

Lin Zexu Memorial Hall

林则徐纪念馆, línzéxú jìniànguǎn • Cnr Daoshan Lu & Nanhou Jie • Daily 8.30am–5pm • Free • Buses #8 & #101 stop nearby, outside the mosque on Bayiqi Bei Lu

A kilometre west of Wuyi Square is the **Lin Zexu Memorial Hall**, which comprises a quiet, attractive couple of halls and courtyards with funereal statues of animals. Lin Zexu (1785–1850) is fondly remembered as the patriotic Qing-dynasty official who fought against the importation of opium by foreigners – even writing a letter to Queen Victoria on the subject. His destruction of thousands of chests of the drug in 1840 sparked the first Opium War and, rather unfairly, he was exiled to Xinjiang.

Fujian Provincial Museum

福建省博物馆, fújiànshěng bówùguǎn • Tues–Sun 9am–5pm • Free • ☎ 0591 83757627

Located within the scenic grounds of **Xihu Park** (West Lake Park), the **Fujian Provincial Museum** is well worth a visit if you're interested in local culture and history. The museum houses thousands of pieces of porcelain and examples of primitive iron tools including a 3500-year-old coffin-boat removed from a Wuyi Shan cave. However, the real highlight for children and adults has to be the **dinosaur collection** in the Natural History building. Regular art exhibitions are also hosted in the museum's ground-floor gallery.

Gu Shan

鼓山, gǔshān • Daily 8am–4pm • ¥40; cable car to summit ¥80 (10min) • Gu Shan special line bus from Wuyi Square (¥10), or take buses #7, #29, #36, #40, #58, #69, #70, #73, #97, #108, #112 or #115 to Gu Shan Xiayuan

Fuzhou's most-touted tourist attraction is **Gu Shan** (Drum Hill), about 8km east of the city, packed with scenic spots and pavilions, and offering some pleasant woodland walks and a vegetarian restaurant. The highlight is the heavily restored **Yongquan Temple** (永泉寺, yǒngquán sì), which boasts two 7m-high pottery pagodas covered with over a thousand images of the Buddha, and a collection of classics written by monks in their own blood.

8

The park complex gets phenomenally busy at weekends; one way to escape the crowds is to climb the 2500 stone steps behind the temple to Gu Shan's wooded **summit** – allow at least an hour including rest-stops at the seven pavilions along the way. Alternatively, you could take the **cable car** up in ten minutes.

ARRIVAL AND DEPARTURE   FUZHOU

BY PLANE
Fuzhou Changle International Airport (福州长乐
国际机场, fúzhōu chánglè guójì jīchǎng) is 50km

southeast of the city, from where airport buses run to either the *Apollo Hotel*, north of the South bus station on Wuyi Zhong Lu (daily 5.30am–8.30pm; every 25min; ¥20), or

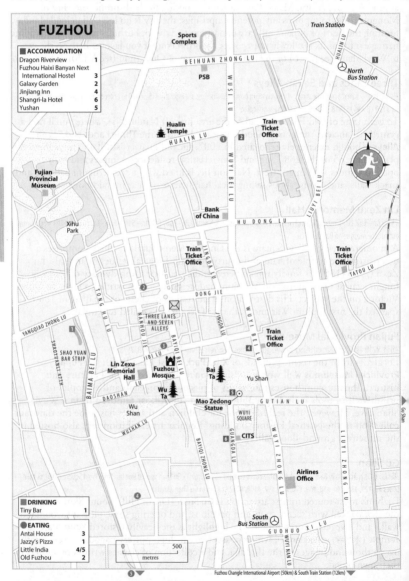

FUZHOU

ACCOMMODATION
Dragon Riverview	1
Fuzhou Haixi Banyan Next International Hostel	3
Galaxy Garden	2
Jinjiang Inn	4
Shangri-la Hotel	6
Yushan	5

DRINKING
Tiny Bar	1

EATING
Antai House	3
Jazzy's Pizza	1
Little India	4/5
Old Fuzhou	2

Fuzhou Changle International Airport (50km) & South Train Station (12km)

the *Minjiang Hotel* (daily 5.50am–4.50pm; hourly; ¥20); both take around an hour. A taxi to the centre takes slightly less time, costs around ¥100 with hard bargaining, or ¥25 per person sharing – touts will find you.

Destinations Beijing (2hr 25min); Guangzhou (1hr 30min); Haikou (6 weekly; 2hr); Hong Kong (1hr 30min); Shanghai Pudong (1hr 10min); Shenzhen (1hr 50min).

BY TRAIN

Fuzhou is Fujian's rail hub, and the terminus for lines northwest to Wuyi Shan and the rest of China. Both Fuzhou's stations serve high-speed rail; the majority goes to the South station. Check your ticket to see if your train departs Fuzhou or Fuzhou South; some stop at both.

Fuzhou Station (福州火车站, fúzhōu huǒchē zhàn) is in the far northeast of town, from where bus #51 runs straight down Wusi and Wuyi roads to the South bus station and the Min River, while buses #K2 and #2 cover the same places but along a circuitous route. Allow plenty of time to get to the station, as gates close 10min before departure.

Fuzhou South (福州南火车站, fúzhōu nán huǒchē zhàn) is inconveniently located about 12km south from the centre, with the #K2 bus connecting it with Fuzhou train station; a taxi costs about ¥50.

CRH destinations Beijing Nan (7 daily; 7hr 43min–10hr 48min); Changsha Nan (3 daily; 4hr 46min–5hr 54min); Guiyang Bei (1 daily; 9hr); Longyan (17 daily; 2hr 40min–3hr 20min); Nanchang (16 daily; 3hr 34min); Shanghai Hongqiao (18 daily; 6hr 20min); Shenzhen North (18 daily; 5hr 20min); Tianjin (5 daily; 7–12hr); Wuyi Shan (38 daily; 1hr 30min).

Other destinations Beijing (2 daily; 20hr–35hr); Chongqing (2 daily; 36hr); Guiyang (2 daily; 28–35hr); Nanchang (16 daily; 3hr – 9.52hr).

BY BUS

Both North and South bus stations handle traffic to just about everywhere outside the city including overnight sleeper-buses to Hong Kong, Shenzhen and Guangzhou.

North station (北站, běizhàn) is a few minutes" walk south of the train station, at the junction of Hualin Lu and Beihuan Zhong Lu. Bus #51 runs straight down Wusi and Wuyi roads to the South bus station and Min River, while buses #K2 and #2 do the same run but round the houses. Note that Longyan and Nanchang buses leave only from here.

South station (南站, nánzhàn) is at the junction of Guohuo Lu and Wuyi Lu. Overnight sleeper buses to Hong Kong run from here.

Destinations Guangzhou (12hr); Hong Kong (14hr); Longyan (7hr); Nanchang (9hr); Quanzhou (2hr 30min); Shenzhen (12hr); Wuyi Shan (7hr); Xiamen (4hr).

GETTING AROUND

By bus Buses (¥1) run all over town till 10pm, but can get very crowded.

By taxi Fares start at ¥8, plus a fuel surcharge of ¥2. If you can't flag one down, try to stand by one of the blue taxi-signs.

ACCOMMODATION

Most of Fuzhou's accommodation is upmarket, though touts for budget options approach arrivals at the train and North bus stations – despite many of those places not being able to take foreigners.

Dragon Riverview 龙城豪景, lóngchéng háojǐng. Apt 1118, Kowloon City Plaza, Wusi Lu ☎0591 87598335. Great budget choice and much more pleasant than all the other cheapies around the train station, this place rents clean, airy and largish mini-apartments with balconies. A little tricky to find, it's in an apartment building down the end of a small street of restaurants, immediately north of the North bus station – the entrance is left and left again, just past the underground garage. No English spoken. ¥128

Fuzhou Haixi Banyan Next International Hostel 福州海西榕树下国际青年旅社, fúzhōu hǎixī róngshù xià guójì lǚshè. 39 Meixian Jie, Taotou Lu. ☎0591 83644944. In a decent location within the city, this is one of the few budget offerings in town, with a pleasant terrace and garden and clean a/c dorms. However, it has become rather popular with visiting businessmen, who can be quite noisy at night. Some English spoken. Dorms ¥55

Galaxy Garden 银河花园大饭店, yínhéhuāyuán dàfàndiàn. 243 Wusi Lu, cnr with Hualin Lu ☎0591 87831888, ✉galaxy88@126.com. Close to the train and North bus stations, this business-oriented hotel has large rooms, crisp bedding, smart furnishings and attentive, helpful staff, although their English is limited. Usually charges under half the advertised rate. ¥800

Jinjiang Inn 锦江之星, jǐnjiāng zhīxīng. Wuyi Bei Lu ☎0591 83799898. Popular business chain hotel with clean, comfortable, en-suite rooms. Just a 10min walk north of Wuyi Sqaure. Good value for money. ¥218

Shangri-La Hotel 福州香格里拉大酒店, fúzhōu xiāng gé lǐ lā dà jiǔdiàn. 9 Xinquan Nan Lu ☎0591 87988888, ✉shangri-la.com. High-rise, international-standard hotel with smart, luxurious rooms, located right in the centre of town near the Three Lanes and Seven Alleys. The health club has gym equipment and an indoor pool. ¥816

Yushan 于山宾馆, yúshān bīnguǎn. 10 Yushan Lu, off Gutian Lu ☎0591 83351668. Well located just below Yu Shan and next to an old pagoda, *Yushan* has large, wooden-floored rooms in an attractive, traditional-style buiding. Rooms are comfortable enough, if a little spartan, though the staff are helpful. ¥548

EATING

The highest concentration of places to eat (and with plenty of unremarkable joints) is along downtown **Dong Jie**. The junction of **Gutian Lu and Baiqi Lu** hosts several swanky Chinese and foreign restaurants where you're looking at over ¥100 a head. For **snacks**, hole-in-the-wall operations surround transit points, while street vendors peddle small, bagel-like "cut buns" (刮包, guābāo), stuffed with vegetables or a slice of spiced, steamed pork.

Antai House 安泰楼酒家, āntàilóu jiǔjiā. 39 Jibi Lu ☎0591 87550890. A Fuzhou institution, this three-floor place serves up relatively inexpensive local Min cuisine, much of it flavoured with taro. The soups are very good, and their seafood dishes are recommended. Under ¥50 per person. Daily 11.30am–10pm.

Jazzy's Pizza 圣杰士比萨餐厅, shèngjiéshì bǐsà cāntīng. 258 Wusi Lu, by the junction with Haulin Lu ☎0591 87855877. Chinese reboot of *Pizza Hut*, with crispy American-style pizzas, as well as passable pastas, salads and steak. Pizzas start at ¥49, and you shouldn't exect to spend more than around ¥100 a head, whatever you order. Mon–Fri 11am–10pm, Sat & Sun 10.30am–10.30pm.

Little India 印度尼泊尔餐厅, yìndù níbóěr cāntīng. 161, Building 2, Neijin Jie, Wanda Plaza, Taijiang District; 5 Guanglu Fang, Gulou District ☎0591 83616335. These two lovely Nepalese-owned restaurants are some of the few quality, foreign-run establishments in the city. The interior decor is (as you'd imagine) inspired by the Himalayas, and such treats as a *masala dosa* (¥40) or *aloo pala* (¥45) won't break the bank. Service is generally friendly, especially if the boss is in town. Daily 11am–midnight.

Old Fuzhou 老福州大酒楼, lǎo fúzhōu dà jiǔ lóu. 83 Shenfu Lu, near the Three Lanes and Seven Alleys ☎0591 87629577. This is where to sample local cusine at its most authentic. Service is sloppy, but the delicious Min food and rowdy atmosphere more than make up for it. Specialities include fish balls in soup; expect ¥50–100 per person. Daily 10am–10pm.

DRINKING

Currently, the most popular after-dark area with foreigners is the new **Shao Yuan bar strip** (芍园一号, sháoyuán yīhào), located on the river between Baima Bei Lu and Shaoyuanyi 47th. By law, all nightlife in Fuzhou must cease at 2am – the kind of place that opens later is usually less than reputable.

Tiny Bar 小酒吧, xiǎo jiǔbā. Shao Yuan bar strip, on right-hand side of entrance. This intimate bar is partly (and convivially) Irish-owned and very popular with expats and Chinese alike. Serves imported beers and very tasty cocktails, though the quality of the drinks comes with a high price tag. Also shows foreign sports on TV. Daily 3pm–2am.

Wuyi Shan Scenic Area

武夷山风景区, wǔyíshān fēngjǐng qū • Daily 8am–5pm • One-day pass ¥210, two-day pass ¥235, three-day pass ¥255; buy at the offices at North or south entrances

Away in Fujian's northeast, 370km from Fuzhou and close to the Jiangxi border, the sixty-square-kilometre **Wuyi Shan Scenic Area** contains some of southern China's most fabled scenery. Since its recognition as a UNESCO World Heritage Site in 1999, it has grown from obscurity to become a tourist site par excellence with crowds, cable cars, and all that commercialization entails in China. The park consists of two main areas accessed via the North and South entrance points, themselves divided up into five principal tourist sites: **Wuyi Palace, Da Hong Pao, Shuilian Cave, Huxiang Stone** and **Yixian Tian.**

A highlight of a visit is rafting (see box, p.468) on the **Jiuqu River**, which meanders at the feet of the mountains and offers spectacular views of the most notable mounds, called the **Thirty-Six Peaks** – of which **Great King Peak** is the most impressive. The scenery is classic Chinese scroll-painting material, and the area offers walks through lush green vegetation, deep red sandstone mountains and soaring cliff faces. However, Wuyi Shan has become a victim of its own fame in recent years – you won't find much traditional life inside the park, as villagers have largely moved out. While the resort

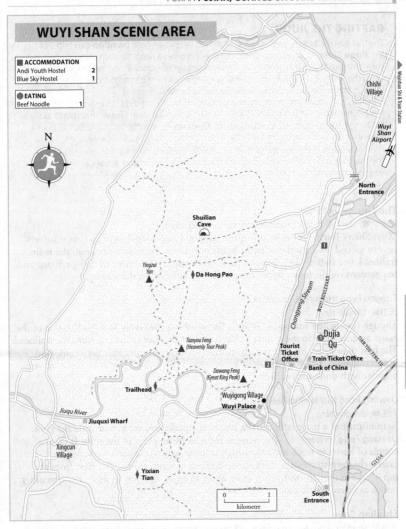

WUYI SHAN SCENIC AREA

■ ACCOMMODATION
Andi Youth Hostel   2
Blue Sky Hostel   1

● EATING
Beef Noodle   1

N

Chishi Village

Wuyishan Shi & Train Station

Wuyi Shan Airport

North Entrance

Shuilian Cave

Chongyang Stream

Yingzui Yan

Da Hong Pao

WUYI BOULEVARD

Dujia Qu

Tianyou Feng (Heavenly Tour Peak)

Tourist Ticket Office

Train Ticket Office
Bank of China

TIAN YOU FENG LU

Dawang Feng (Great King Peak)

Trailhead

Jiuqu River

Wuyigong Village
Wuyi Palace

Jiuquxi Wharf

Xingcun Village

G1914

Yixian Tian

0   1
kilometre

South Entrance

8

district east of the river, **Dujia Qu**, remains the natural centre of orientation outside of the scenic area, the newly laid **Wuyi Boulevard** connects row upon row of Da Hong Pao teashops (see p.469), hotels and restaurants with major transport depots such as Wuiyishan Dong high-speed railway station.

Orientation

Around 10km south of the main long-distance arrival point, Wuyishan Shi (town), **DUJIA QU** (度假区, dùjià qū) sits on the east bank of the Chongyang Stream, providing a functional blob of amenities and services. It's worth pushing on over the river for 1km to **WUYIGONG** (武夷宫, wǔyí gōng), set in the cleft between the confluence of the Jiuqu and Chongyang, where there are further facilities and the **Wuyi Palace**, a Song-dynasty complex after which the village is named. The main **trailhead** area is about 4km west of Wuyigong, on the road to **Xingcun**.

RAFTING THE JIUQU

The traditional way to appreciate Wuyi Shan is to take a two-hour **bamboo-raft trip** along the **Jiuqu River** (¥130). At busy times, the river becomes a noisy bamboo conveyor belt, but there's stupendous gorge scenery all the way from the first crook in the meandering river right up to the ninth, and it's well worth the ticket. Watch out for the strange, boat-shaped **coffins** in caves above the fourth crook, which are said to be 4000 years old.

During the busy summer months or at weekends and holidays, it's essential to book tickets in advance at the tourist ticket office in Wuyi Shan. Rafts leave year-round (daily 6.40am–4.30pm) from the small village of **Xingcun**, accessible on public bus #6 from Wuyishan Shi and Wuyigong (daily 8am–9pm; every 15min; ¥2.5). The wharves themselves are in the hamlet of Jiuquxi (九曲溪, jiǔqǔ xī), down a side lane just off the main road 1km before town, so tell the bus driver when you get on, and it'll save you the trek from the station.

The Thirty-Six Peaks

三十六峰, sānshíliùfēng • Trailhead area about 4km west of Wuyigong

Wuyi Shan's **Thirty-Six Peaks** look quite large and imposing, but in fact are relatively easy to ascend, and a series of paths heads north into the mountains from the main trailhead area (where there is also a park ticket office). A number of tiny pavilions and **tea gardens** on the lower slopes can provide sustenance on the way up.

Tianyou Feng (Heavenly Tour Peak)

天游峰, tiānyóu fēng

Though the highest summit (2180m), **Tianyou Feng (Heavenly Tour Peak)** is one of the easier ascents – it's no more than a thirty-minute clamber to the top from the trailhead. The best time to get up here is early morning, when you can catch the sunrise and watch the mists clear to reveal the nine crooks in the Jiuqu River. It is, however, very popular with domestic tourists.

Dawang Feng (Great King Peak)

大王峰, dàwáng fēng

Reminiscant of a stone column, the first of the peaks you see as you enter the park, **Dawang Feng**, is north of Wuyigong at the easternmost end of the river. It takes a couple of hours to reach the 580m-high summit, where the cliffs are scaled by extremely steep stone steps – it's almost a climb at some points. The view from the top is superb though, and you're more likely to enjoy the view in peace than on other peaks, as fewer people make it up here.

Shuilian Cave

水帘洞, shuǐlián dòng • Accessible on foot or by bike via easy trails; park minibuses come here from the Tianyou Feng area or Wuyigong

Ensure you set aside time for **Shuilian Cave**, about 6km north of the river. The cave – more of an overhang, really – is at the bottom of a red sandstone cliff inscribed with Chinese characters, down which a large waterfall cascades in the summer months (at other times it's more of a trickle). Behind the water curtain is the wooden **Hall of the Three Sages** (三圣大厅, sānshèng dàtīng), an antique-style complex. One enterprising local has also domesticated the pigeons that live in the cliffs; for ¥3 he'll supply you with corn and command his birds to peck it from your hands. He sells cold drinks too.

ARRIVAL AND DEPARTURE   WUYI SHAN SCENIC AREA

Most long-distance transport arrives 15km north of the park at Wuyishan Shi (武夷山市, wǔyíshān shì), the regional town.

By plane Wuyishan airport (武夷山机场, wǔyíshān jīchǎng) is at the village of Chishi (赤石, chìshí), a few kilometres to the northeast of the scenic area and to the south of Wuyishan Shi. Frequent minibuses connect it with Dujia Qu and Wuyishan Shi.

Destinations Beijing (6 weekly; 2hr 15min); Guangzhou (1hr 20min); Shanghai (1hr); X'ian (2hr); Xiamen (45min).

By train Wuyishan train station (武夷山火车站, wǔyíshān huǒchē zhàn) is the oldest railway depot and deals primarily with slower trains. It's about 5km from Wuyishan Town, and connected by frequent minibuses with Dujia Qu, the main hotel zone opposite the scenic area. Wuyishan East and Wuyishan North stations now handle the bulk of the CRH services. Check your ticket to see which station you depart from.

Destinations Beijing South (5 daily; 8hr); Fuzhou (36 daily; 1hr 20min–4hr 56min); Hangzhou East (14 daily; 2hr 30min); Huangshan North (13 daily; 1hr 30min); Shanghai (12 daily; 3hr 30min–10hr); Xiamen North (16 daily; 3hr).

By bus The main bus station (武夷山汽车站, wǔyíshān qìchē zhàn) is in the north of Wuyishan Shi on Wujiu Lu, connected to the scenic area by minibuses (40min).

Destinations Fuzhou (7hr); Shangrao (3hr); Xiamen (8hr).

On a tour Plenty of tour agencies offer trips from Fuzhou.

GETTING AROUND

By bus Regular bus #6 runs until early evening between the scenic area, Wuyishan Town and Xingcun (¥2–4). Stand by the road to flag them down anywhere.

By tourist bus Minibuses travel around all the scenic area sights until 6pm, though you can only use them with the two-day entrance ticket. The main terminal is at Wuyigong Palace.

By bike Cycling is a pleasant way to get around the park, though you'll need to be fit for the hills. Rent bikes from *Andi Youth Hostel* (¥25 per day, plus ¥300 deposit; see below). Beware tourist buses on the road: they are badly driven, and drivers seem tipsy by the end of the day.

ACCOMMODATION

8

Dujia Qu holds a plethora of identikit **hotels**, although, apart from the ease of access to amenities and restaurants, either Wuyigong or even Xingcun (which is far less touristy) are more mellow spots to stay. **Prices** at the more expensive places are generally flexible outside of summer and weekends, and hard bargaining should secure a hotel room for as little as ¥150.

Andi Youth Hostel 安邸青年旅舍, āndǐ qīngnián lǚshè. 16 Lantang Village, Wuyigong ❶0599 5231369, ❸ad513@sina.cn. Very Chinese-feeling youth hostel, with dorms and doubles in a converted house decorated with classic Chinese calligraphy and pictures. Serves good tea, basic food at mealtimes, and has a small bar. Also has wi-fi and rents bikes too, but no English spoken. Doubles ¥158, dorms ¥50

Blue Sky Hostel 蓝色天空青年旅舍, lánsè tiānkōng qīngnián lǚshè. Jiulongwan, Dujia Qu ❶189 50663809. Located near several restaurants in Dujia Qu, this hostel is a decent choice. What owner Mr Zheng lacks in English, he makes up for in kindness; he's a well of information on the local area. Dorms ¥40, doubles ¥100

EATING

Foodwise, it's the local Shilin bullfrogs that make **Wuyi cuisine** special; along with other popular items such as bamboo shoots and fungus, they're served almost everywhere. Rabbit, venison and pheasant or other game, as well as what is claimed to be bear, are also popular. Most places have ingredients on show outside to make ordering easy by pointing, but be warned that tourists are often seriously **overcharged** – always check the price of everything when ordering.

WUYI ROCK TEA

The renowned *terroir* (水土, shuǐtǔ) of Wuyi Shan has produced fine tea since the Song dynasty. However, the world-famous **Da Hong Pao** (大红袍, dà hóng páo), also known as **Wuyi rock tea**, only emerged in the sixteenth century, after Ming-dynasty monks from Anhui developed a new means of cultivation to create a heavily oxidized variant. As a result, the slopes of Wuyi saw some of the world's first **black and oolong teas**. Today, Wuyi's tea crop is expensive and much sought after. The tea bushes can be seen throughout the region, but are concentrated in picturesque Da Hong Pao, an Arcadian valley in the scenic area – a great spot for a leisurely walk.

Beef Noodle 牛肉面馆, niúròu miànguǎn. Mantuoyuan Lu, Dujia Qu ✆0591 83301668. It's the red restaurant along this small road of inexpensive canteens, and there are no prizes for guessing the house speciality.

A hearty bowl of outstanding noodles in soup will set you back ¥15–20, which is ¥5 more than the local competition, but worth it. Daily 8am–8.30pm.

Quanzhou

泉州, quánzhōu

QUANZHOU, a small, prosperous and sympathetically preserved town 150km southwest of Fuzhou on the coastal highway to Xiamen, was for centuries a great port. Sitting astride trade routes that reached southeast to Indonesian Maluku, and west to Africa and Europe, the city became uniquely cosmopolitan, with tens of thousands of Arabs and Persians settling here, some of them to make colossal fortunes – the Arabs of Quanzhou are also believed responsible for introducing to the West the Chinese inventions of the compass, gunpowder and printing.

The Song dynasty saw the peak of Quanzhou's fortunes, when the old Silk Road through northwestern China into Central Asia was falling prey to banditry and war, deflecting trade seawards along the **Maritime Silk Road**. Marco Polo visited Quanzhou around this time; the Italian **Andrew Perugia**, Quanzhou's third Catholic bishop, died here in 1332, having supervised the building of a cathedral; and fourteen years later the great Moroccan traveller **Ibn Battuta** saw the port bustling with large junks. But by the Qing era, the city was suffering from overcrowding and a decaying harbour, and an enormous **exodus** began, with people seeking new homes across Southeast Asia.

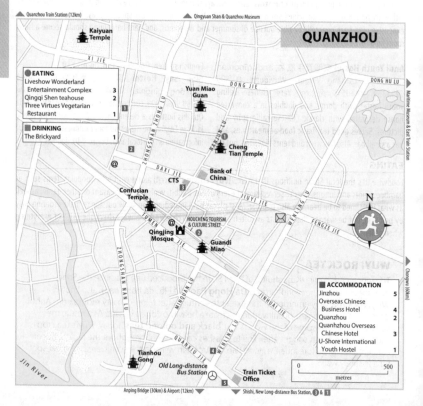

Guandi Miao

关帝庙, guāndì miào • Junction of Tumen Jie & Mingquan Lu • Daily 6am–6pm • Free

Guandi Miao, a splendid and busy temple, is dedicated to the Three Kingdoms' hero-turned-god-of-war-and-healing, **Guan Yu** (see box, p.396). The temple's roofline is typically florid and curly, and the atmospheric interior – guarded by life-sized statues of soldiers on horseback – features low-ceilinged halls, smoke-grimed statues and wall engravings showing scenes from Guan Yu's life.

Qingjing Mosque

清净寺, qīngjìng sì • Tumen Jie • Daily 8am–5.30pm • ¥3 • ☎ 0595 22982505

The granite **Qingjing Mosque** provides proof of just how established the Arabs became in medieval Quanzhou. Founded by Arab settlers in 1009, Qingjing ranks as one of the oldest mosques in China and is highly unusual in being Middle Eastern in design, though only parts of the original buildings survive. The gate tower is said to be an exact copy of a Damascus original, its leaf-shaped archway embellished with Arabic calligraphy and designs, while parts of the walls and supporting pillars of the original prayer hall stand alongside. A side room has a detailed account of the Arab presence in Quanzhou; the small, tiled building next door is the modern prayer hall. Behind the mosque, the "**Houcheng Tourism and Culture Street**" (后成街, hòuchéng jiē) is not as mawkish as it sounds, containing some original buildings, most of which now hold souvenir shops and teahouses.

Confucian Temple

府文庙, fǔwén miào • Daily 8am–5.30pm; concerts daily 8pm • Free • ☎ 0595 22281076

Between the Qingjing Mosque and Zhongshan Lu, an ornamental gateway leads north past a motorbike park to a broad paved square, at the back of which is the **Confucian Temple**, the largest such complex in southern China. The building is unexceptional, but there's a reasonable exhibition of Confucian texts. What sets this temple apart are the nightly performances of traditional **Nanyin music**. Nanyin is the umbrella term of variety of operatic and folk styles that evolved in Quanzhou. The free shows are held in the temple's affiliated teahouse (in the same building) each evening; get there early to grab a seat.

Yuan Miao Guan

元妙观, yuánmiào guān • Zhuangyuan Jie • Daily 5am–6pm • Free

The renovated **Yuan Miao Guan**, a colourful Taoist temple shoehorned between modern buildings, is small but perfectly formed – the quality of the workmanship, especially the carved pillars, is probably the best in the city. Little visited by tourists, it's highly recommended if you want to experience an authentic, functioning temple.

Kaiyuan Temple

开元寺, kāiyuán sì • Xi Jie • Daily 7.30am–5.30pm • ¥10 • ☎ 0595 22394182 • Bus #2 from the old long-distance bus station

Quanzhou's most impressive historical remains are at the huge **Kaiyuan Temple**, a restful complex dotted with magnificent trees. Founded in 686, Kaiyuan was built, legend has it, after the owner of a mulberry grove dreamed a Buddhist monk asked him to erect a place of worship on his land. "Only if my mulberry trees bear lotus flowers," replied the owner dismissively – whereupon the lotus flowers duly appeared. The temple is highly regarded architecturally, not least for its details, which include one hundred stone columns supporting the roof of the main hall, most of which are carved with delicate musicians holding instruments or sacrificial objects.

The pagodas and exhibition hall

Having survived everything from earthquakes to the Red Guards, the temple's two unimaginably solid **stone pagodas** were added in the thirteenth century and are carved on each of their eight sides with two images of the Buddha; inside, one of them has forty Buddhist stories inscribed on its walls. The temple grounds also hold a special **exhibition hall** housing the hull of a twelfth- or thirteenth-century wooden sailing vessel found in 1974 (a series of photos details the stages of the excavation), still with the herbs and spices it had been carrying preserved in its hold.

Maritime Museum

海外交通史博物馆, hǎiwàijiāotōngshǐ bówùguǎn • Dong Hu Lu, just past its junction with Tian'an Bei Lu • Tues–Sun 8.30am–5.30pm • Free • ☏ 0595 22100561 • Bus #19 or #23 from near the old long-distance bus station on Quanxiu Jie

Over on the northeast side of town, the **Maritime Museum** shows how advanced medieval Chinese shipbuilders were, compared to their European contemporaries. At the museum's heart is its collection of hundreds of lovingly made **wooden models**. These illustrate everything from small, coastal junks to Zheng He's mighty *Baochuan* – possibly the largest wooden vessel ever made – and ornate pleasure boats used by the wealthy for touring China's famous lakes and rivers. Don't miss the first-floor collection of tombstones dating back to Quanzhou's heyday, which belong to a great mixture of people, including Italians and Spaniards, Nestorian Christians from Syria and the fourteenth-century Bishop, Andrew Perugia. Next door and part of the same complex, a newly opened **Quanzhou Islamic Culture Exhibit** documents the early Arab-Persian influence on the city, displaying more gravestones unearthed from the region.

Quanzhou Museum

泉州博物馆, quánzhōu bówùguǎn • Bei Qing Dong Hu Lu, north of West Lake Park, at the edge of the old town • Tues–Sun 8.30am–5.30pm • Free • ☏ 0595 22757518 • Bus #6 or #15 from the old long-distance bus station

In a larger, gaudier building than the Maritime Museum lies the **Quanzhou Museum**, regrettably not quite as rich in artefacts. However, if you'd like to learn more about Quanzhou than just its maritime and mercantile heritage, this isn't a bad place to start. Exhibitions include a retrospective look at the music of Nanyin, as well as a more general display on the culture of Southern Fujian. The museum is located at the foot of **Qingyuan Shan** – well worth hiking in, before or after your culture fix (see below).

Qingyuan Shan

清源山, qīngyuán shān • Daily 5.30am–4pm • ¥40 • Bus #3 from Tumen Jie, via Zhongshan Zhong Lu

The **Qingyuan Shan** scenic area is 3km to the north of Quanzhou, with good views over the town from small crags and pavilions, though most people come out here for the huge, Song-dynasty **sculpture of Laozi** (老君岩, lǎojūnyán) which is said to aid longevity if you climb onto its back and rub noses. There's also a lovely teahouse near the top of the park where you can get a set tea for around ¥55.

DAY-TRIPS FROM QUANZHOU

About 60km east of Quanzhou, **Chongwu** (崇武古城, chóngwǔ gǔchéng) is an old walled city built entirely of stone, now restored as a huge museum piece. The adjacent new town has one of southern China's largest fishing fleets, with just about every man employed in this industry – the women work in local stone quarries, carting huge rocks around on carrypoles and wearing characteristic blue jackets and wide-brimmed straw hats.

Slightly closer to the southeast is the town of **Shishi** (石狮, shíshì), from where you can pick up a ride for the 5km to the beautiful **Sisters-in-law Tower** (姑嫂塔, gūsǎo tǎ), another Song-dynasty monument, overlooking the coast. Finally, 30km south, just off the expressway to Xiamen and outside the town of Anhai, is the spectacular 2km-long, 800-year-old **Anping Bridge** (安平桥, ānpíng qiáo), which crosses an estuary.

ARRIVAL AND DEPARTURE

BY PLANE

Quanzhou Jinjiang Airport (泉州晋江机场, quánzhōu jìnjiāng jīchǎng) is about 12km south of the city centre; a taxi costs ¥50, or the slower #16 bus costs ¥1.

Destinations Beijing (1hr 15min); Changsha (1hr 20min); Chengdu (2hr 10min); Chongqing (1hr 50min); Guangzhou (1hr 15min); Hangzhou (1hr 10min); Hong Kong (1hr 20min); Ji'nan (3hr 35min); Kunming (4hr); Macau (1hr 15min); Nanchang (1hr); Nanjing (1hr 30min); Nanning (2hr); Shanghai (1hr 35min); Shenzhen (1hr 15min); Wuhan (1hr 35min); Zhengzhou (3hr 35min).

BY TRAIN

Tickets can be bought in town at the train ticket office (泉秀路火车售票处, quánxiù lù huǒchē shòupiào chù) on Quanxiu Lu, next to the Agricultural Bank of China and opposite the old bus station. The South and East stations handle very few trains, and no CRH services.

Quanzhou Station (泉州火车站, quánzhōu huǒchē zhàn) is a new station located about 12km north of the centre, and handles most inter-city trains. Bus #3 connects the station to the centre of town; taxis cost about ¥50.

Destinations Fuzhou (75 daily; 1hr–1hr 30min); Hangzhou (25 daily; 5–6hr); Longyan (17 daily; 1hr 40min); Shanghai (17 daily; 6–8hr); Wuyi Shan (17 daily; 2hr 30min).

BY BUS

There are frequent daytime buses from both the new and old long-distance bus stations to Xiamen and Fuzhou, and to practically anywhere between Ningbo and Shenzhen; both deal with more or less the same routes. There's no reason to depart from the new bus station, but you may get dropped there.

Old long-distance bus station (泉州汽车站, quánzhōu qìchē zhàn). Just on the edge of the centre, it's within walking distance, or ¥10 by taxi, to all accommodation and sights.

New long-distance bus station (客运中心站, kèyùn zhōngxīnzhàn). Located 3km southeast of town down Quanxiu Jie, bus #15 from outside will take you northwest up to Wenling Lu and the old bus station (get off when you see the giant stone column on a roundabout). A taxi, motorcycle or rickshaw will cost under ¥10.

Destinations Fuzhou (2hr 30min); Guangzhou (10hr); Hangzhou (11hr); Shenzhen (10hr); Xiamen (1hr 30min).

ACCOMMODATION

Jinzhou 金州大酒店, jīnzhōu dàjiǔdiàn. 615 Quanxiu Lu ☎0595 22586788. Next to the old long-distance bus station, this reasonably smart place has very agreeable, comfortable rooms that are actually better than the *Quanzhou*, but without the Disneyland exterior or facilities. There are plenty of eating options nearby. ¥458

Overseas Chinese Business Hotel 华侨之家宾馆, huáqiáo zhījiā bīnguǎn. 159 Wenling Lu ☎0595 22175395. This is the least expensive option in town where they will register you with the police. Rooms are large and clean enough, if slightly tatty, though it looks set for renovation in the near future. ¥80

Quanzhou 泉州酒店, quánzhōu jiǔdiàn. 22 Zhuangfu Xiang ☎0595 22289958, ⌨quanzhouhotel.com. A fantastically Baroque white-and-gold monstrosity, right in the centre of town. Rooms are of an international standard but – though comfortable enough – disappointingly, they don't quite live up to the kitschy grandeur of the hotel's exterior. ¥592

Quanzhou Overseas Chinese Hotel 泉州华侨大厦, quánzhōu huáqiáo dàshà. Baiyuan Lu ☎0595 22282192, ⌨overseaschinesehotel.com. Smart four-star business hotel right in the centre of town; rooms come with all mod cons. It's a little bland, but well run. ¥625

U-Shore International Youth Hostel 泉州巷里国际青年旅社, quánzhōu xiànglǐ guójì qīngnián lǚshè. 107 Zhuangfu Alley, Licheng District ☎0595 22870566. This lovely hostel, set in an old house, is tucked away down a lane near the centre of town. Staff are friendly and some English is spoken, though management can be a tad neglectful. Still, for the money, there are few budget offerings that can rival *U-Shore* for its cleanliness and location. Dorms ¥45

EATING

Northern Zhongshan Lu, the area around the Kaiyuan Temple and the backstreets off Tumen Jie, are all thick with cheap noodle stalls and canteens.

Liveshow Wonderland Entertainment Complex 领秀天地, lǐngxiù tiāndì. Just south of Quanxiu Jie ☎0595 28855777, ⌨1showing.com. This complex, between the long-distance bus stations, houses inexpensive food outlets serving imitation Western fodder and Chinese snacks. Regular performances by touring bands and entertainers attract a drinking crowd, too (see p.474). Daily 11am–midnight.

8

Qingqi Shen teahouse 请其神茶店, qīngqíshén chádiàn. 22 Houcheng Lu ☎ 0595 28275777. Housed in an old brick home in the lane over the bridge at the back of the Houcheng Tourism and Culture Street, this serves traditional teas, juices and dry snacks in a most atmospheric and serene environment. Tea for two will set you back upwards of ¥48. Daily 9am–midnight.

Three Virtues Vegetarian Restaurant 三德素食馆, sāndé sùshíguǎn. Upstairs at 124 Nanjun Lu ☎ 0595 22276705. Good veggie food is available in a tranquil ambience with an ample picture menu and mains in the ¥20–60 range. Particularly good are the pineapple stuffed with fragrantly spiced fried rice, and the fake-meat kebabs. Daily 9am–10pm.

DRINKING

The Brickyard Unit 101, Building 6, Liveshow Wonderland ☎ 0595 22779179, ⊕ facebook.com /thebrickyardchina. Friendly, partly Canadian-owned bar in a vibrant nightlife complex, this place is the most foreigner-friendly in town, with imported booze and a

comfortable brick interior with guitars on the walls. Also serves pretty good Western food including craft beer and burgers. A little expensive, but then everywhere in Wonderland is. Daily 2pm–2am.

Xiamen

厦门, xiàmén

Joined to the mainland by a 5km-long causeway, **XIAMEN**, an island city formerly known to the West as **Amoy**, is more focused, clean and prosperous than the provincial capital, Fuzhou. It also has more to see: the old streets and buildings, shopping arcades and a bustling seafront all contrast with the city centre's twenty-first-century skyscrapers. A ten-minute ferry ride to the southwest of town, little **Gulangyu Islet** was once the preserve of colonial Europeans and Japanese, whose mansions still line the island's traffic-free streets – staying here is highly recommended, though weekends and holidays see the whole city overcrowded.

Brief history

Xiamen's strategic value as a port, midway between Guangzhou and Shanghai – and just a short hop across the straits to Taiwan – was noticed by the **British**, who took root on Gulangyu Islet after the city was opened up to foreign trade in 1842. By the start of the twentieth century, Xiamen's prosperity was supported by a steady turnover in trade and the trickling back of wealth from the city's emigrants, who had used its status as an international port to find work overseas.

The **arrival of the Communists** in 1949 saw total chaos around Xiamen, with thousands of Nationalists streaming across the straits to Taiwan to escape Red forces. Today, although the small islands of **Jinmen** and **Mazu** – visible offshore – are still Taiwanese territory, the threat of conflict has receded as the mutual economic gains brought by closer cooperation have increased. Today, Xiamen's pleasant climate, healthy economy and relatively sympathetic urban development mean it is recognized as having among the best standards of living of any city in China.

Overseas Chinese Museum

华侨博物馆, huáqiáo bówùguǎn • 493 Siming Nan Lu • Tues–Sun 9.30am–4pm • Free • ☎ 0592 2085345, ⊕ www.hqbwy.org.cn • Bus #96 from Xiahe Lu or Zhong Shan Lu/Siming Bei Lu

The **Overseas Chinese Museum** traces the history of the huge Fujianese diaspora around the world. The museum features three floors of pottery, bronzes, lots of photos and some amazing model boats, though there's little English on the displays. Especially interesting is the exhibit describing the hardships faced by the Chinese labourers building the transcontinental railway in North America in the nineteenth century – more than a quarter of them died out there.

Nanputuo Temple

南普陀寺, nánpǔtuó sì • 515 Siming Nan Lu • Daily 4am–6pm • ¥3 • ☎ 0592 2088554, ⓦ nanputuo.com • Buses #1, #87 & #96 all run to the temple via Xiahe Lu and Zhong Shan Lu/Siming Bei Lu

The **Nanputuo Temple** is one of China's most organized, modern-looking Buddhist temples, its roofs a gaudy jumble of flying dragons, human figures and multicoloured flowers. Among its collection of treasures is a set of tablets carved by resistance fighters at the time of the early Qing, recording Manchu atrocities. Inside the main hall, behind the Maitreya Buddha, is a statue of **Wei Tuo**, the deity responsible for Buddhist doctrine, who holds a stick pointing to the ground – signifying that the monastery is wealthy and can provide board and lodging for itinerants. Today the temple is a huge draw for tour groups; if you need to escape the crowds, you can always take a stroll uphill from Nanputuo to the top of forested **Wulao Shan** (五老山, wǔlǎo shān), which affords some lovely views.

Xiamen Botanical Gardens

厦门植物馆, xiàmén zhíwùguǎn • Wanshi Lu • Daily: May–Sept 5.30am–6.30pm; Oct–April 6.30am–6pm • ¥40 • ☎ 0592 2024785, ⓦ xiamenbg.com • Four stops on bus #87 from the Xiahe Lu / Bailuzhou Lu intersection

The **Xiamen Botanical Gardens** are home to 5300 varieties of plant life, including a redwood tree brought here by President Nixon in the 1970s. Southeast of the gardens' north (main) gate, you can climb up the hillside to **Tiger Stream Rock** (虎溪岩, hǔxī yán), a great little temple nestling amid a pile of huge boulders and crammed with gilded stone statues; slip through the cave to one side and climb the rock-hewn steps to the top. A second small temple right at the summit, **Bailu Dong** (白鹿洞, báilù dòng), commands spectacular views over the town and the sea.

Huli Shan Gun Emplacement

胡里山炮台, húlǐ shān pàotái • Nan Huandao Lu • Daily 9am–6pm • ¥25 • ☎ 0592 2084184 • Buses #86 & #96 from Xiahe Lu or ZhongShan Lu/Siming Bei Lu

On the southwest corner of the island is the hulking **Huli Shan Gun Emplacement**, a late nineteenth-century hunk of German heavy artillery that had a range of 16km and was used during the Qing dynasty to fend off foreign imperialists. One of the highlights here is the sea view, and you can also rent a telescope to look across to the Taiwanese islet of **Jinmen**, which lies less than 20km to the west.

Gulangyu Islet

鼓浪屿, gǔláng yǔ • Joint ticket for attractions ¥100; golf buggies ¥50/day

Gulangyu Islet was once Xiamen's foreign concession. Opened to foreign trade after the first Opium War, it was home to representatives from several nations until World War II; the architectural relics of that period are mostly still intact. The narrow tangle of lanes can be confusing, but the island's size (it's less than two square kilometres) means you can't go very far wrong. A stroll through the streets will uncover plenty of attractions, especially along **Fuzhou Lu** (福州路, fúzhōu lù) and **Guxin Lu** (鼓新路, gǔxīn lù), overhung with flowers and blossom throughout the year. Crowds tend to gravitate to the main sights in the south of the island; on busy days you'll find the northwest far quieter, with a surprising number of lovely colonial buildings, along with three wooded hills and a small, near-deserted beach. Note that the only **vehicles** allowed on Gulangyu are battery-powered golf buggies.

SPYING ON TAIWAN

Several kiosks along the Xiamen waterfront and on Gulangyu itself sell tickets for boat trips offering circuits of **Gulangyu** (30min; ¥15) or, more adventurously, out towards neighbouring **Jinmen** Islet (1hr 40min; ¥136) – you don't get too close, so bring binoculars for good views of Taiwan's front line.

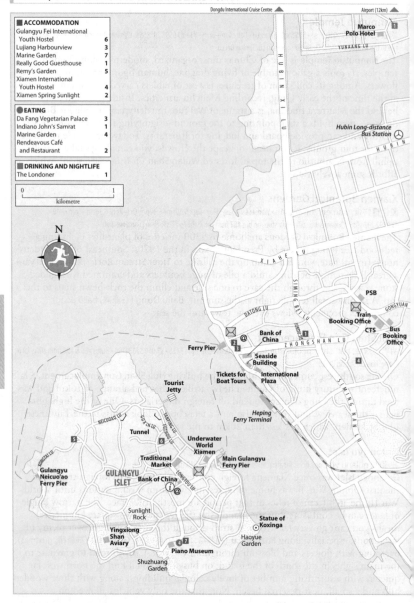

ACCOMMODATION

Gulangyu Fei International Youth Hostel	6
Lujiang Harbourview	3
Marine Garden	7
Really Good Guesthouse	1
Remy's Garden	5
Xiamen International Youth Hostel	4
Xiamen Spring Sunlight	2

EATING

Da Fang Vegetarian Palace	3
Indiano John's Samrat	1
Marine Garden	4
Rendeavous Café and Restaurant	2

DRINKING AND NIGHTLIFE

| The Londoner | 1 |

ARRIVAL AND DEPARTURE

By ferry The main ferry (every 10–15min, 5.45am–midnight; ¥8 return) runs from the pier across from the *Lujiang* to the main Gulangyu ferry dock; keep your ticket for the return. Travelling on the upper deck costs ¥1 extra, which is collected by an inspector. This ferry is horrendously packed at weekends and during holidays, when it's better to get the far less busy ferry from the same place to Gulangyu Neicuo'ao ferry pier (鼓浪屿内厝, gǔlàngyǔ nèicuò) on the west of the island, which runs every 30min from 8.35am–6pm (¥8 return).

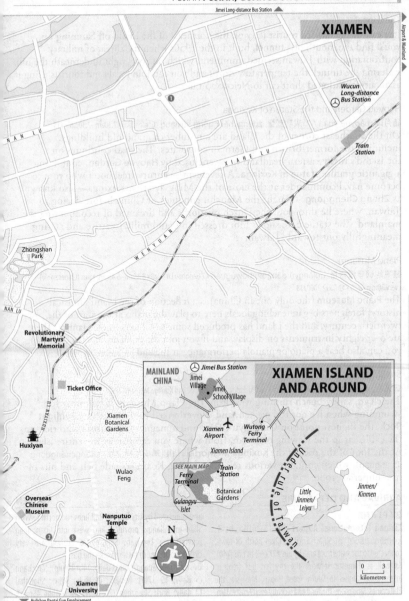

Underwater World Xiamen

海底世界, hǎidǐ shìjiè • Daily 9.30am–6.30pm • ¥90, children and students ¥50 • ☎ 0592 2067668

From the main ferry pier disembarkation point, a splendid bronze sculpture of a giant octopus diagonally to your right marks the entrance to **Underwater World Xiamen**, with walk-through aquariums, seal displays, penguins, turtles and a massive whale skeleton.

The tunnel

Just east of the disused tourist jetty on the northeast of the island off Sanming Lu, you'll find the mouth of a **tunnel**, built in the 1950s when the threat of military confrontation with Taiwan seemed imminent, which burrows right underneath the hill. Entering the tunnel, the temperature drops and you can join locals and tourists using it as an air-conditioned short cut to Neicuo'ao Lu.

Haoyue Garden and the Statue of Koxinga

皓月园, hàoyuè yuán / 郑成功塑像, zhèngchénggōng sùxiàng • Garden: daily 7.30am–7.30pm • ¥15

On the southeast corner of the island are a number of grand old buildings, including the former British and German consulates. The road continues on to the island's rocky eastern headland, now enclosed by **Haoyue Garden**, containing a gigantic granite **statue of Koxinga**. A seventeenth-century freebooter who rose to become naval commander at the close of the Ming dynasty, Koxinga – also known as **Zheng Chenggong** – fought the Manchu conquest of China before fleeing to Taiwan, where he threw out the Dutch overlords and dreamed of reconquering the mainland. The statue here shows him dressed in grand military attire and staring meaningfully out towards Taiwan.

Piano Museum

鼓浪屿钢琴博物馆, gǔlàngyǔ gāngqín bówùguǎn • 7 Ganghou Lu • Daily 8.15am–5.45pm; tours (Chinese only) every 30min • ¥30 • ☎ 0592 2060238

The **Piano Museum** (the only one in China) is a reflection of the island's musical history; foreigners began teaching locals here to play the piano at the start of the twentieth century, and the island has produced some of China's finest pianists. There are over eighty instruments on display, and if you join the guided tours (in Chinese), you can also hear a piano or pianola performance at the end.

Sunlight Rock

日光岩, rìguāng yán • Daily 6am–8pm • ¥60, including cable-car ride and Koxinga Memorial Hall

The clean, sandy **beach** running west from the Piano Museum is tempting for swimming when it's not too packed, and is overlooked to the north by **Sunlight Rock**, the highest point on Gulangyu (93m) and a magnet for tourists who ride up the cable car to the viewing platform, from where you can survey the entire island. At the foot of the rock is the **Koxinga Memorial Hall** (郑成功纪念馆, zhèngchénggōng jìniànguǎn), which contains various relics, including Koxinga's jade belt and bits of his "imperial" robe.

ARRIVAL AND DEPARTURE   XIAMEN

BY PLANE

Xiamen International Airport (厦门高崎国际机场, xiàmén gāoqí guójìjīchǎng) is 12km north of town, connected to the waterfront area by bus #27 (¥6) or taxi (¥40). As well as domestic services, the city has less frequent international flights to South Korea, Japan, Malaysia, the Philippines, Singapore, Thailand and recently even Amsterdam. Destinations Beijing (2hr 40min); Guangzhou (1hr 5min); Hefei (1hr 20min); Hong Kong (1hr 15min); Macau (1hr 20min); Shanghai (1hr 30min); Shenzhen (1hr); Wuyi Shan (46min).

BY TRAIN

Xiamen train station 厦门火车站, xiàmén huǒchē zhàn) is on Xiahe Lu, about 4km east from the seafront

and connected by city bus #1. Rail lines run north to Wuyi Shan and Jiangxi province, and west into Guangdong province via Longyan. Services to Fuzhou are very circuitous; it's much faster to take the bus.
Destinations Guangzhou (3 daily; 14hr 30min); Nanchang (5 daily; 15–17hr); Nanjing (1 daily; 30hr); Shanghai (2 daily; 8hr); Shenzhen (20 daily; 14hr–16hr 45min); Wuyi Shan (1 daily; 13hr 30min); Xi'an (1 daily; 37hr).

BY BUS

Most long-distance services leave before 10am, so organizing beforehand is a good idea. It's best to book through your hotel or at a travel agent, as finding the best bus station is horrendously complex; otherwise, the three options below have the most departures to the destinations listed underneath. There's a bus booking office opposite the *Huaqiao* hotel, on Xinhua Lu.

Hubin (湖滨汽车站, húbīn qìchēzhàn), 2km northeast of the centre on Hubin Nan Lu; exit the station, turn right and it's 100m to the stop for city bus #23 to the seafront. Probably your best bet for most destinations regional and national.

Jimei bus station (集美汽车站, jíměi qìchēzhàn) 159 Yinjiang Lu, on the mainland just north of Xiamen. From 400m east of the station on Jiyuan Lu, catch bus #903 or #981 to Jimei Dadao, then change to get the #1 to seafront Xiahe Lu.

Wucun (捂村汽车站, wǔcūn qìchēzhàn), about 200m north of the train station, is useful only for its frequent connections to Quanzhou (every 15min; 6.20am–9.30pm). Transport into town is as for the train station.

Destinations Chaozhou (4hr); Fuzhou (4hr); Guangzhou (9hr); Longyan (5hr); Quanzhou (1hr 30min); Shenzhen (14 daily; 9hr); Yongding (3–4hr).

BY FERRY

Daily ferries (hourly 8.30am–5.30pm; ¥170/NT$700) operate between Xiamen's two international ports and Jinmen/Kinmen, in the Republic of China (Taiwan). You'll need a valid Taiwanese visa to buy a ticket.

Dongdu International Cruise Centre (东渡厦门国际邮轮中心, dōngdù xiàmén guójì yóulún zhōngxīn) at the northern end of Hubin Xi Lu, from where the ferry takes about an hour to Jinmen.

Wutong ferry terminal (五通客运码头, wǔtōng kèyùn mǎtóu), is in the northeast of the city close to the airport; it's less convenient to get to than Dongdu, but less hectic, and the ferry is 30min faster.

INFORMATION AND GETTING AROUND

Tourist office The only useful place is the Visitor's Center on Gulangyu, at 100 Longtou Lu (daily 9am–5.15pm; ☏0599 2060777, ⍈glyylq.com), where the staff speak English and are very helpful – it's also well air-conditioned and has seating. For general information, try the city-wide website ⍈visitxm.com.

Maps Vendors sell city maps with bus routes marked (¥6) near the Gulangyu ferry terminal and outside the stations.

Travel agents CS, at the *Huaqiao* hotel, Xinhua Lu (☏0592 2660888; daily 9am–5.30pm). They can book

domestic and international flights, private long-distance buses, and Chinese-language one-day tours to the Hakka homelands (see p.482; ¥150–210 including lunch).

By taxi Cabs are plentiful, but in high demand and cost minimum ¥8, plus a ¥3 fuel surcharge and a twenty-percent night surcharge (11pm–5am). There are also private cars which may approach you in the street; these are slightly more expensive and actually illegal, though commonly used.

8

ACCOMMODATION

Finding low-end accommodation can be hard, especially during the summer; the majority is near the train station. Some of Xiamen's best places to stay are on Gulangyu – note that you'll have to carry your own luggage as there are no buses or taxis on the island. At weekends, and especially in the summer months, booking ahead is absolutely essential.

DOWNTOWN XIAMEN

Lujiang Harbourview 鹭江宾馆, lùjiāng bīnguǎn. 54 Lujiang Lu ☏0592 2022922, ⍈lujiang-hotel.com.In a well-maintained colonial building in a prime site on the seafront, this excellent hotel has comfortable rooms and is the ideal place to stay for views over Gulangyu Islet, especially from the rooftop terrace. **¥940**

Really Good Guesthouse 好实在家庭旅馆, hǎoshízài jiātíng lǚguǎn. 18 Jukou Jie ☏0592 2121097. No English sign, but this tiny guesthouse down an alley probably has the some of the cheapest rooms in the centre. Although the rooms are on the small side and have hard beds, they're quite clean and good enough for a couple of days. **¥118**

Xiamen International Youth Hostel 厦门国际青年旅社, xiàmén guójì qīngnián lǚshshè. 41 Nanhua Lu, Siming District, near Xiamen University ☏0592 2082345. Claiming to be the oldest youth hostel in town, this

recently refurbished backpacker haunt is one of the few budget options on Xiamen Island. There's a lovely courtyard to hang out in and meet other guests, and some of the doubles even have balconies. It's clean and friendly, though staff don't offer information easily. Dorms **¥60**, doubles **¥238**

Xiamen Spring Sunlight 厦门春光酒店, xiàmén chūnguāng jiǔdiàn. 36 Haihou Lu ☏0592 2665558. Useful location opposite the Gulangyu ferry terminal. Behind its colonial-style facade the rooms are modern and spotless, if a little bland, though it's much cheaper than other places on the seafront. Worth paying the ¥50 extra for a seaview. **¥399**

GULANGYU ISLET

★**Gulangyu Lu Fei International Youth Hostel** 鼓浪屿鹭飞国际青年旅舍, gǔlàngyǔ lù fēi guójì qīngnián lǚshè. 20 Guxin Lu ☏0592 2082678, ⍈www.yhalf.cn. Located in a charming three-storey

Mediterranean-style villa on a hill about 400m from the main ferry terminal towards the middle of the island, this hostel is by far the best of Gulangyu's three hostels, being prettiest and in the quietest spot – follow the signs for the Organ Museum and it's about 50m away. Clean, light and airy dorms and rooms, plus all the amenities you'd expect, and a peaceful patio, with an inexpensive Chinese restaurant next door. Dorms **¥55**, doubles **¥218**

Marine Garden 海上花园酒店, hǎishàng huāyuán jiǔdiàn. 27 Tianwei Lu ☎0592 2062688. Just above Shuzhuang Garden, this plush, mildly garish faux-colonial place has quality rooms, a pool, tennis court and good views over the beach. Probably the best accommodation on the island, and a thoroughly pleasant oasis of calm, with an excellent Chinese restaurant (see below). Doubles **¥840**

Remy's Garden 雷米的酒店, léimǐde jiǔdiàn. 65 Kang Tai Lu ☎0592 2196957. A very romantic option, this small, German-owned hotel housed in an old colonial building has just eight rooms (shared bath and en suite), all of which are uniquely and beautifully decorated. Also serves a range of reasonably priced European wines and excellent coffees, which you can drink in the courtyard garden. Doubles **¥288**

EATING

Xiamen has plenty of places to eat **fresh fish and seafood**, particularly oysters, crabs and prawns. Head for the restaurants around Gulangyu's market area, or the backstreets behind the *Lujiang Harbourview*, and establish a price in advance: seafood is generally sold by weight (see box, p.43). Otherwise, the vibrant and cramped market street down Renhe Lu (just off Lujiang Lu, past the *Xiamen Spring Sunlight*) contains an abundance of inexpensive snack-stalls, tiny restaurants and barbecue seafood places – you can get half a lobster here for ¥30–50.

Da Fang Vegetarian Palace 大方素食馆, dàfāng sùshíguǎn. 3 Siming Nan Lu ☎0592 2093236. Just 2min up the road from Nanputuo Temple and far better value than the restaurant there, this great vegetarian place serves fine food in a sophisticated ambience. The fake meat and fish dishes are fantastic, especially the black-pepper steak. Also recommended are the rice noodles (mains ¥20–30). Daily 9.30am–10pm.

Indiano John's Samrat 印度风, yìn dù fēng. 2nd Floor, 69 Jiangtou Bei Lu ☎0592 5557699, ⓦfacebook .com/IndianoJohnsSamrat. This well-established Indian restaurant may have an eccentric Hollywood-meets-Bollywood theme, but the food is authentic. A vegetable curry at ¥48 is very reasonable. For those who like it spicy, prawn vindaloo (¥78) comes highly recommended. Beers are sold in three glass sizes: the Good, the Bad and the Ugly. Daily 11.30am–1.30am.

Marine Garden 海上花园酒店, hǎishàng huāyuán jiǔdiàn. 27 Tianwei Lu ☎0592 2062688. This lovely hotel (see above) has a great Chinese restaurant which will allow you to enjoy an after-meal stroll in the hotel's uncrowded gardens. The chefs specialize in Fujianese and Cantonese cuisine, and prices are reasonable (mains ¥40–200). Particularly good is the whelk and leek wrapped in lettuce leaf, as is the Hainan coconut porridge. Daily 11am–2pm & 5.30–9.30pm.

Rendeavous Café and Restaurant 朗地咖啡, lǎngdì kāfēi. 35 Minzu Lu ☎0592 2196199. Best of a clutch of arty cafés along this road, this bohemian place is in a slightly shabby but beautiful colonial house, its nooks and crannies furnished with the original tile floors, sofas and bookcases. Also has an outdoor terrace, and serves great coffee and decent Western food (mains ¥38–68), though service is slow. Daily 1pm–11.30pm.

DRINKING AND NIGHTLIFE

For nightlife, the area just north of Yundang Lu is awash with new bars, clubs and restaurants. Check out ⓦwhatsonxiamen .com for English-language reviews and listings.

The Londoner 5–8, Guanren Lu, behind the Marco Polo Hotel ☎0592 5089783, ⓦthelondonerxiamen.com. A veteran of the expat scene, this has everything Brits abroad miss – warm ale, half-cooked pies and a cheery atmosphere to compensate. For ¥50, you'll get passable fish and chips. The place is a firm favourite with the sporting crowd, airing live fixtures, and thus the ideal place to get to know the vibrant Xiamen expat community. Daily 11am–2am.

DIRECTORY

Consulates Philippines, near the geographic centre of Xiamen at 2 Lianhua Bei Lu ☎0592 5130355.

Post offices Xiamen's main post office (daily 8am–6.30pm) is on the seafront, just north of the *Xiamen Spring Sunlight*; there's another large branch on Xinhua Lu, south of the junction with Siming Dong Lu, and one on Gulangyu Islet.

Visa extensions The PSB office is across from the post office on Gongyuan Nan Lu ☎0592 2262203.

The Hakka homelands

Fujian's hilly southwestern border with Guangdong is an area central to the **Hakka**, a Han subgroup known to locals as *kejia* (客家, kèjiā; guest families) and to nineteenth-century Europeans as "China's gypsies". Originating on the Northern Plains during the third century and dislodged ever southward by war and revolution, the Hakka today form large communities in Guangdong, Fujian and Southeast Asia. They managed to retain their original languages and customs by remaining aloof from their neighbours in the lands in which they settled, a habit that caused resentment and forced them to build strong defences. Traditional villages and hamlets sport fortress-like **mansions** (*tulou*, literally "mud building"), of which there are more than thirty thousand across the countryside. The largest are four or five storeys high, circular, and house entire clans.

Entry to the area is at **YONGDING** (永定, yŏngdìng), a heavily built-up city around 120km west and inland from Xiamen, from where local transport heads out to the sights.

Hongkeng

洪坑村, hóngkēngcūn · Daily 8am–7pm · ¥90

An hour's bus ride east of Yongding, **Hongkeng village** – where you can stay overnight (see opposite) – features a collection of traditional Hakka buildings, many still lived in, laid out along a small stream. Those worth investigating include a 1920s schoolhouse; **Fuyu Lou**, the old courthouse building; **Rushen Lou**, one of the smallest multistorey roundhouses; and **Kuijiu Lou**, a splendid, 165-year-old square-sided Hakka mansion, its interior like a temple squeezed into a box.

Zhencheng Lou

振城楼, zhènchéng lóu

Hongkeng's well-maintained centrepiece is the century-old **Zhencheng Lou**, considered to be the most perfect Hakka roundhouse. Plain and forbidding on the outside, the huge outer wall encloses three storeys of galleried rooms looking inwards to a central courtyard where guests were entertained, and which contained the clan shrine. The galleries are vertically divided into eight segments by thick fire walls, a plan that intentionally turns the building into a giant *bagua*, Taoism's octagonal symbol. This powerful design occurs everywhere in the region, along with demon-repelling mirrors and other Taoist motifs.

Other villages

From Hongkeng it's easy to organize trips to surrounding *tulou*, including **Chengqi Lou** (承启楼, chéngqǐ lóu), the largest roundhouse of them all, built in 1709, with more than three hundred rooms housing more than four hundred people; **Tianluo Keng** (田螺坑, tiánluó kēng), a remote grouping of five large houses – including three roundhouses, one square walled house and one oval – that date back three centuries and still house around six hundred people; and **Yuchang Lou** (裕昌楼, yùchàng lóu), the oldest and tallest of the roundhouses – Yuchang's five storeys have stood since 1309, despite a drunken, 15-degree lean to its 21m-tall uprights.

ARRIVAL AND DEPARTURE   THE HAKKA HOMELANDS

All long-distance transport terminates at Yongding.

By train Yongding Station (永定火车站, yŏngdìng huŏchē zhàn) is 3km north of the town with relatively infrequent connections to the rest of Fujian and eastern Guangdong. A taxi to most places in town costs under ¥10.

Destinations Fuzou (2 daily; 10hr 45min); Guangzhou (2 daily; 7hr 30min); Shanghai (1 daily; 23hr); Shenzhen (5 daily; 7hr 20min); Xiamen (8 daily; 4hr 50min).
By bus Yongding's main bus station (永定汽车站, yŏngdìng qìchēzhàn) is on the large roundabout just

east of the river, about 2km south of the train station. Seven daily direct buses head between Yongding and Xiamen's Hubin bus station, and two connect with

Quanzhou's new bus station.

Destinations Longyan (1hr); Quanzhou (5hr); Xiamen (4hr 30min); Zhiling (1hr).

GETTING AROUND

By bus Direct services (1hr; ¥16) depart Yongding's bus station and drop you at Hongkeng outside a row of guesthouses, close to Zhencheng Lou itself.

By minibus Minibuses in the region are plentiful but seem to run fairly randomly, so be prepared to stand by the road and flag down whatever comes along. Services dry up by mid-afternoon.

By taxi and motorbike taxi In Yongding or Hongkeng it's easy to organize taxis, and your accommodation can usually help – reckon on around ¥200 for a full day, which would mean around four or five sites, but be prepared to haggle. If you're on your own, a motorcyle taxi will cost about ¥120 for the day.

ACCOMMODATION AND EATING

Places to eat surround Yongding's bus station and main streets; you'll find all sorts of rice noodles, snacks and *kourou* (口肉, kǒuròu), a Hakka dish made from slices of soya-braised pork belly on a bed of bitter kale.

YONGDING

Dongfu 东府酒店, dōngfǔ jiǔdiàn. 1–2 Wenquan Lu ☎ 0597 5830668. Large, white, fancy-looking and good-value business hotel which has clean, pleasant rooms and helpful staff. Located on the large roundabout, close to the bus station and a couple of kilometres south of the train station, it's also handy for the restaurants on Dong Jie, though the rooms at the front are noisy. **¥148**

HONGKENG

★**Fuyulou Changdi Inn** 福裕楼常棣客栈, fúyùlóu chángdì kèzhàn. Hongkeng village ☎ 0597 5535900, ⓦ fuyulou.net. Friendly, twenty-room guesthouse by the river, inside a large *tulou* next to Kuijulou, near Zhencheng Lou. Built in 1880, it has clean but basic rooms (some en suite) and also serves well-priced local food. English is spoken. **¥100**

8

Guangdong

广东, guǎngdōng

Halfway along **Guangdong**'s 800km coastline, rivers from all over the province and beyond disgorge themselves into the South China Sea through the tropically fertile **Pearl River Delta**, one of China's most densely cultivated and developed areas. Perched right at the delta's northern apex and adjacent to Hong Kong and Macau, the sprawling provincial capital, **Guangzhou**, is the centrepiece of an emerging industrial megacity, but its famous **food** merits a stop, as does an assortment of museums, parks, monuments and pretty colonial quarters. Outlying delta towns have some interesting history to pick up in passing, but in truth the area is emphatically focused on industry and commerce – as demonstrated by the border city of **Shenzhen** (深圳, shēnzhèn) where China's "economic miracle" took its first baby steps.

Further afield, the rest of the province is more picturesque. Over in the east near Fujian, the ancient town of **Chaozhou** (潮州, cháozhōu) has well-preserved Ming architecture peppered among a warren of narrow streets, though the regional highlight lies to the east in the form of the fantastical towers around the town of **Kaiping** (开平, kāipíng).

Guangzhou

广州, guǎngzhōu

GUANGZHOU, once known to the Western world as **Canton**, was for centuries where China met the rest of the world – commercially, militarily and otherwise. Increased competition from elsewhere in China may have diminished Guangzhou's role as a centre of international commerce, but with the money continuing to roll in from the industrial and manufacturing complexes which cover the surrounding Pearl River Delta, there is little suggestion that the city is a fading power.

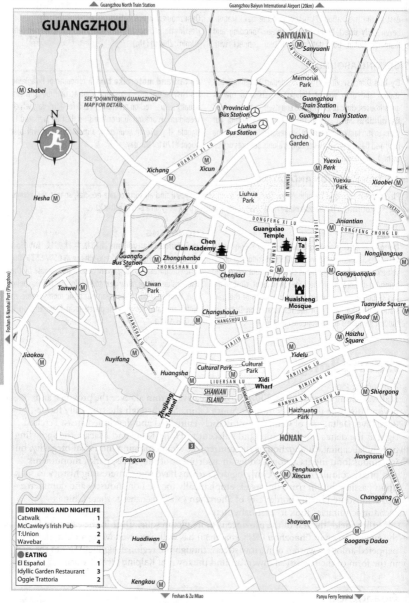

For visitors, however, Guangzhou's attractions are limited and mainly business-oriented, as the biannual Canton Trade Fair attests. The city is vast, untidy and unbelievably crowded, and actual tourist sights are relatively trivial, though a peek at the European colonial enclave of **Shamian Island** and the fascinating 2000-year-old **tomb of the Nanyue King** prove the city's lengthy and varied cultural heritage. Often the pervading impression is of endless anonymous

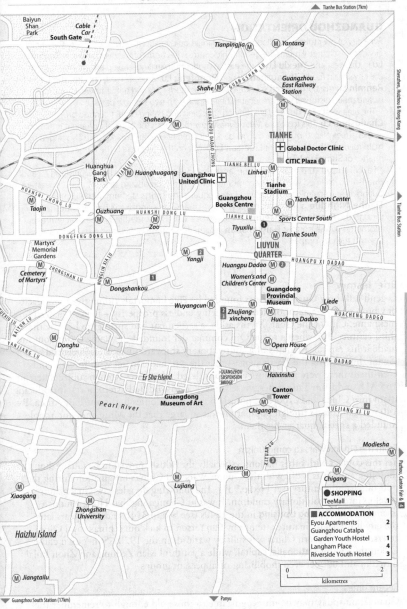

Tianhe Bus Station (7km)

Baiyun Shan Park

Cable Car
South Gate

Tianpingjia (M) (M) Yantang

GUANGSHAN LU

Shahe

Guangzhou East Railway Station

Shaheding

Shenzhen, Huizhou & Hong Kong

TIANHE

GUANGZHOU DADAO ZHONG

TIANHE BEI LU

Linhexi

+ **Global Doctor Clinic**

CITIC Plaza 1

Huanghua Gang Park

TIANLE LU

Huanghuagang (M)

Guangzhou United Clinic +

Tianhe Stadium

HUANSHI ZHONG LU (M) Taojin

Guangzhou Books Centre

Tianhe Sports Center

Ouzhuang (M) HUANSHI DONG LU

Zoo

TIANHE LU

Sports Center South

Tiyuxilu

DONGFENG DONG LU

Tianhe South

Tianhe Bus Station

Martyrs' Memorial Gardens

ZHONGSHAN LU

LIUYUN QUARTER

NONGJIN XIALU

Yangji (M)

Huangpu Dadao (M) 2

HUANGPU XI DADAO

Cemetery of Martyrs'

Women's and Children's Center

Dongshankou

Guangdong Provincial Museum

Liede (M)

Wuyangcun (M)

HUACHENG DADGO

WUTIU LU

Zhujiang-xincheng

Huacheng Dadao

BAIYUN LU

YANJIANG LU

Donghu (M)

Opera House

LINJIANG DADAO

Er Sha Island

GUANGZHOU SUSPENSION BRIDGE

Haixinsha

Pearl River

Guangdong Museum of Art

Canton Tower

Chigangta

YUEJIANG XI LU 4

Modiesha

Pazhou, Canton Fair & 4

Kecun

Chigang (M)

LIUYAN

Lujiang (M)

● **SHOPPING**
TeeMall 1

Xiaogang (M)

Zhongshan University

■ **ACCOMMODATION**
Eyou Apartments 2
Guangzhou Catalpa
Garden Youth Hostel 1
Langham Place 4
Riverside Youth Hostel 3

Haizhu Island

Jiangtailu (M)

0 ————————— 2
kilometres

Guangzhou South Station (17km)

Panyu

8

blocks of chrome and concrete blurring together as you zip over the multiple elevated expressways in a taxi. Yet there's something about this chaotic caricature of Hong Kong that somehow manages to be enjoyable. The Cantonese are compulsively garrulous, turning Guangzhou's two famous obsessions – eating and business – into social occasions, and filling streets, restaurants and buildings with the sounds of yueyu, the Cantonese language.

GUANGZHOU ORIENTATION

For a city of over thirteen million people, Guangzhou is relatively easy to navigate. The original city core – still pretty much the geographic centre – lies north of the river between **Renmin Lu** in the west and **Yuexiu Lu** in the east. A modern urban landscape predominates, cut by the city's main roads: **Zhongshan Lu** and **Dongfeng Lu** run east–west, and **Jiefang Lu** and **Renmin Lu** run north–south. It's not all relentless modernity and traffic, however: most of Guangzhou's historical sites are located here, along with two sizeable parks.

The area west of Renmin Lu is a thriving shopping and eating district centred on **Changshou Lu**. This formed a Ming-dynasty overflow from the original city, and it retains its former street plan, though the narrow back lanes, old houses and markets are also ringed by main roads, such as waterfront **Liuersan Lu**. Right on the river here is the former foreigners' quarter of **Shamian Island**.

East of Yuexiu Lu the city opens up, as the main roads – Zhongshan Lu, Dongfeng Lu and Huanshi Lu, all lined with glassy corporate offices – run broad and straight through eastern Guangzhou to culminate in the vast, open square and sports stadium at the centre of **Tianhe**. **Nightlife** is the east's biggest draw – many of Guangzhou's bars are out this way, though the **Provincial Museum** is well worth a visit. For something more peaceful, a few kilometres to the north is **Baiyun Shan**, a formalized string of hills and parkland just beyond the city proper.

Brief history

Legend tells how Guangzhou was founded by **Five Immortals** riding five rams, each of whom planted a sheaf of rice symbolizing endless prosperity – hence Guangzhou's nickname, City of the Goat. Myths aside, a settlement had sprung up here by the third century BC, when a rogue Qin commander founded the **Nanyue Kingdom** and made it his capital. Remains of a contemporary shipyard uncovered in central Guangzhou during the 1970s suggest that the city had contact with foreign lands even then: there were merchants who considered themselves Roman subjects here in 165 AD, and from Tang times, vessels travelled to Middle Eastern ports, introducing **Islam** into China and exporting porcelain to Arab colonies in distant East Africa. By 1405, Guangzhou's foreign population was so large that the Ming emperor Yongle founded a special quarter for them.

From the Opium Wars to communism

Yet this contact with other nations, especially the **British**, proved to be Guangzhou's undoing, ending as it did with the Opium Wars and China's humiliation during the mid-nineteenth century (see box, p.931). The following decades saw Guangzhou develop into a revolutionary cauldron. It was in Guangdong that Hong Xiuquan formulated his **Taiping Uprising** in the 1840s (see box, p.314), and sixty years later the city hosted a premature attempt by **Sun Yatsen** to kick out China's royal Qing rulers. When northern China was split by warlords in the 1920s, Sun Yatsen chose Guangzhou as his **Nationalist capital**, while a youthful Mao Zedong and Zhou Enlai flitted in and out between mobilizing rural peasant groups.

Recent times

Guangzhou today may be unrecognizable to those old enough to remember the years before the economic boom that has transformed the cityscape, yet the city retains a sense of character and pride which manifested itself angrily in **protests** against limitations on the Cantonese language in 2010. Beijing reversed the proposals, but Guangzhou folk remain suspicious of all things "northern", often identifying more with their linguistic cousins in Hong Kong and Macau than the rest of China. Local pride has been enhanced by the influx of **migrants** from the provinces over recent decades. The city enjoys real wealth; its level of development makes it the de facto **capital** of China's deep south. As such, it remains a popular destination for many seeking work or looking to study at a reputable university. Hankering back to its mercantile past, Guangzhou has also become one of China's most cosmopolitan cities and is home to large communities from Africa, the Middle East, India and elsewhere.

Guangdong Museum of Art

广东美术馆, guǎngdōng měishùguǎn • 38 Yanyu Lu • Tues–Sun 9am–5pm • ¥15 • ☏ 020 87351468, ⓦ gdmoa.org • Metro to Wuyangcun or Haixinsha; bus #89, #131 or #194

At the eastern end of Yanjiang Lu, bridges cross to **Er Sha Island** (二沙岛, èrshādǎo), the focus of much upmarket housing development and home to the **Guangdong Museum of Art**. The museum holds one of China's largest collections of contemporary art with over 13,000 pieces in their archives; it also hosts regular special exhibitions, some of which have been quite controversial in China.

Sacred Heart Cathedral

石室圣心大教堂, shíshì shèngxīn dàjiàotáng • Yuzi Hutong • Mon–Fri 8.30–11.30am & 2.30–5.30pm, Sat & Sun 8.30am–5pm • Sun Masses in English 3.30pm • Free • ☏ 020 83392860 • Metro to Haizhu Square (exit B1), or Yide Lu; bus #8, #9, #61, #82, #40, #58 or #194

North from the river and running west from Haizhu Square, **Yide Lu** is stuffed with small shops selling toys and dried marine produce – jellyfish, shark's fin, fish maw and whole salted mackerel – along with sacks of nuts and candied fruit. Set north off the road, the Catholic **Sacred Heart Cathedral** – also known as the Stone House – is a Gothic-style cathedral completed in 1888, impressive for its size and unexpected presence as well as being a working church.

Five Immortals' Temple

五仙观, wǔxiān guān • Junction of Huifu Xi Lu and Liurong Lu • Daily 9am–noon & 1.30–5pm • ¥10 • ☏ 020 83336853 • Metro to Haizu Square or Gongyuan Qian; bus #3, #5, #6, #8, #33, #39, #66, # 72, #82, #106, #110, #124 or #206

Despite dating to 1377, the **Five Immortals' Temple** building itself isn't of much interest, though there are some obviously ancient statues around the place: weathered guardian lions flank the way in, and some stylized Ming sculptures at the back look like giant chess pieces. The Five Immortals – three men and two women – are depicted too, riding their goatly steeds as they descend through the clouds to found Guangzhou. More impressive is a fourteenth-century **bell tower** behind the temple, in which hangs a 3m-high, five-tonne bronze bell, silent since being blamed for a plague which broke out shortly after its installation in 1378 – it has been called the "Forbidden Bell" ever since.

Huaisheng Mosque

怀圣清真寺, huáishèng qīngzhēnsì • 56 Guangta Lu • Daily 8.30am–5pm • Free • Metro to Ximenkou, exit B; bus #56

Huaisheng Mosque and its grey, conical tower, **Guangta**, loom over a surrounding wall that bars entry to non-Muslims. Looking like a lighthouse, Guangta is possibly the world's oldest minaret outside Mecca and something of a stylistic fossil, said by some to have been built by the seventh-century Islamic missionary Abu Waqas. During the fifteenth century, Huaisheng's environs were known as Fanfang, the foreigners' quarter; today there's a smattering of halal canteens and restaurants in the vicinity, including the famous **Huimin Fandian** (see p.499).

Temple of the Six Banyan Trees

六榕寺, liùróng sì • 87 Liurong Lu • Daily 9am–5pm • ¥5, plus ¥10 extra to climb the pagoda • Gongyuan Qian metro exit B, then a 500m walk

Temple of the Six Banyan Trees lies north of the Huaisheng Mosque and is associated with the poet-governor **Su Dongpo**, who named the temple on a visit in 1100 and drew

8

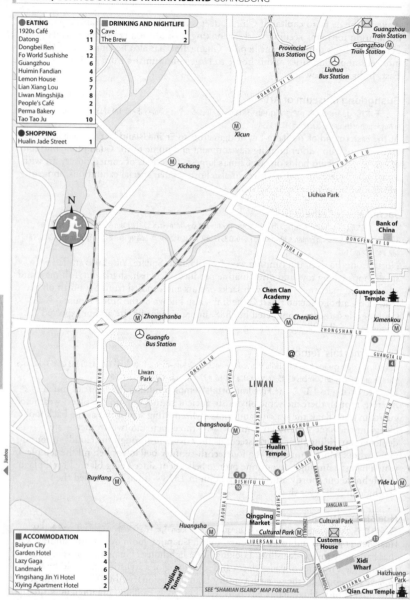

EATING
1920s Café	9
Datong	11
Dongbei Ren	3
Fo World Sushishe	12
Guangzhou	6
Huimin Fandian	4
Lemon House	5
Lian Xiang Lou	7
Liwan Mingshijia	8
People's Café	2
Perma Bakery	1
Tao Tao Ju	10

SHOPPING
Hualin Jade Street	1

DRINKING AND NIGHTLIFE
Cave	1
The Brew	2

ACCOMMODATION
Baiyun City	1
Garden Hotel	3
Lazy Gaga	4
Landmark	6
Yingshang Jin Yi Hotel	5
Xiying Apartment Hotel	2

the characters for "Liu Rong" (Six Banyan Trees) on the two stone steles just inside the gates. Very little of the temple itself survives, and the site is better known for the 57m-high, seventeen-storey **Hua Ta** (花塔, huātǎ), a contemporary pagoda enshrining relics brought from India by Emperor Wu's uncle. Carvings of lions, insects and birds adorn the pagoda's wooden eaves. At the top is a gigantic bronze pillar covered with over a thousand reliefs of meditating figures rising up through the roof, solid enough to support the five-tonne begging bowl and pearl that you can see from ground level.

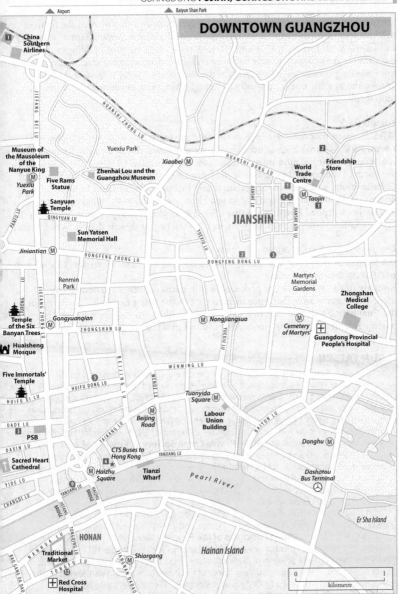

DOWNTOWN GUANGZHOU

(Map labels:)

▲ Airport   ▲ Baiyun Shan Park

China Southern Airlines

JIEFANG BEI LU

HUANSHI ZHONG LU

Museum of the Mausoleum of the Nanyue King

Yuexiu Park

Yuexiu Park

Five Rams Statue

Zhenhai Lou and the Guangzhou Museum

Xiaobei Ⓜ

HUANSHI DONG LU

World Trade Centre

Friendship Store

JIANSHE LU

JIANSHE 6TH LU

Taojin Ⓜ

JIANSHIN

Sanyuan Temple

QINGYUAN LU

Sun Yatsen Memorial Hall

Jiniantian Ⓜ

DONGFENG ZHONG LU

YUEXIU LU

DONGFENG DONG LU

JIEFANG ZHONG LU

PANFU LU

Renmin Park

Martyrs' Memorial Gardens

Zhongshan Medical College

Temple of the Six Banyan Trees

Gongyuanqian

ZHONGSHAN LU

Nongjiangsua Ⓜ

Cemetery of Martyrs' Ⓜ

Guangdong Provincial People's Hospital

Huaisheng Mosque

BEIJING LU

YUEXIU LU

WENMING LU

Five Immortals' Temple

HUIFU DONG LU

WENDE LU

Tuanyida Square Ⓜ

Labour Union Building

BAIYUN LU

HUIFU XI LU

TAIKANG LU

DADE LU

Beijing Road Ⓜ

DAXIN LU

PSB

Donghu Ⓜ

Sacred Heart Cathedral

CTS Buses to Hong Kong

YANJIANG LU

Haizhu Square Ⓜ

Tianzi Wharf

Dashatou Bus Terminal

Pearl River

TIDE LU

CHANGDI LU

JIEFANG BRIDGE

HAIZHU BRIDGE

Er Sha Island

NANHUA LU

TONGGONG LU

HONAN

JIANGNAN DADAO

Shiorgong Ⓜ

Hainan Island

BAO GANG DA DAO

Traditional Market

TONGFU LU

Red Cross Hospital

0   1
kilometre

8

Guangxiao Temple

光孝寺, guāngxiào sì • 109 Jinghui Lu • Daily 5am–5.30pm • ¥5 • ☎ 020 81077170 • Ximenkou metro exit B and turn right up Guangxiao Lu

The spacious and peaceful **Guangxiao Temple** is the oldest of Guangzhou's Buddhist complexes. In 113 BC this was the residence of **Zhao Jiande**, last of the Nanyue kings (see p.491), becoming a place of worship only after the 85-year-old Kashmiri monk Tanmo Yeshe built the first hall in 401 AD. The temple was later visited by Buddhist luminaries such as the sixth-century monk Zhiyao Sanzang, who planted the fig trees still here today; the Indian founder of Chan (Zen) Buddhism, **Bodhidharma** (see p.263); and Chan's Sixth Patriarch, Huineng. Though none of the original buildings survives, the grounds are well ordered and enclose pavilions concealing wells and engraved tablets from various periods, while three halls at the back contain some imposing Buddha images; the westerly one is unusually reclining, while a more ordinary trinity fills the central hall.

Yuexiu Park

越秀公园, yuèxiù gōngyuán • 988 Jiefang Bei Lu • Daily 6am–10pm • Free • ☎ 020 86662357 • Metro to Yuexi Park, exit B1

Yuexiu Park is China's biggest urban park, encompassing almost a square kilometre of sports courts, historic monuments, teahouses, three artificial lakes and shady groves. To the north of the porcelain dragons at the front gate are **Beixiu Lake** and the **Garden of Chinese Idiom**, where many strange stone and bronze sculptures lurk in the undergrowth, illustrating popular sayings. Head south, and you'll wind up at the much-photographed **Five Rams Statue** (五羊石像, wǔyáng shíxiàng), commemorating the myth of Guangzhou's foundation – though at least one of these is definitely not a ram.

Zhenhai Lou and the Guangzhou Museum

镇海楼, zhènhǎi lóu / 广州博物馆, guǎnzhōu bówùguǎn • Daily 9am–5.30pm • ¥10, free middle Wed of each month • ☎ 020 83545253, ⓦ guangzhoumuseum.cn

Roughly in the middle of the park atop a hill, paths converge at **Zhenhai Lou**, a three-storey gate tower that once formed part of the Ming city walls. Today it houses the **Guangzhou Museum**, full of locally found exhibits ranging from Stone Age pottery fragments and ivory from Africa found in a Han-dynasty tomb, to

8

SUN YATSEN

Born in 1866, **Sun Yatsen** grew up during a period when China laboured under the humiliation of colonial occupation, a situation widely blamed on the increasingly feeble Qing court. Having spent three years in Hawaii during the 1880s, Sun studied medicine in Guangzhou and Hong Kong, where he became inspired by that other famous Guangdong revolutionary, Hong Xiuquan (see box, p.314), and began to involve himself in covert anti-Qing activities. Back in Hawaii in 1894, he abandoned his previous notions of reforming the imperial system and founded the **Revive China Society** to "Expel the Manchus, restore China to the people and create a federal government". The following year he incited an uprising in Guangzhou under **Lu Haodong**, notable for being the first time that the green Nationalist flag, painted with a white, twelve-pointed sun (which still appears on the Taiwanese flag), was flown. But the uprising was quashed, Lu Haodong was captured and executed, and Sun fled overseas.

Orbiting between Hong Kong, Japan, Europe and the US, Sun spent the next fifteen years raising money to fund revolts in southern China, and in 1907 his new Alliance Society announced its famous **Three Principles of the People** – Nationalism, Democracy and Livelihood. He was in Colorado when the Manchus finally fell in October 1911; on returning to China he was made provisional president of the Republic of China on January 1, 1912, but was forced to resign in February in favour of the powerful warlord **Yuan Shikai**. Yuan established a Republican Party, while Sun's supporters rallied to the Nationalist People's Party – **Guomindang** – led by **Song Jiaoren**. Song was assassinated by Yuan's henchmen following Guomindang successes in the 1913 parliamentary elections, and Sun again fled to Japan. Annulling parliament, Yuan tried to set himself up as emperor, but couldn't even control military factions within his own party, which plunged the north into civil war on his death in 1916. Sun, meanwhile, returned to his native Guangdong and established an independent Guomindang government. By the time of his death in 1925, he was greatly respected by both the Guomindang and the four-year-old Communist Party for his lifelong efforts to unite the country.

fifth-century coins from Persia, a copy of *Good Words for Exhorting the World* (the Christian tract which inspired the Taiping leader, Hong Xiuquan), and nineteenth-century cannons tumbled about in the courtyard (two made by the German company, Krupp). A statue of Lin Zexu and letters from him to the Qing emperor documenting his disposal of the British opium stocks always draws big crowds of tongue-clicking Chinese.

Sun Yatsen Memorial Hall

中山纪念堂, zhōngshān jìniàn táng • 259 Dongfeng Zhong Lu • Daily 8am–6pm • ¥10 • ☎ 020 83561631, ⓦ www.zs-hall .com • Metro to Sun Yatsen Memorial Hall, exit C

Directly to the south of Yuexiu Park, the most visible building is the large rotunda and blue-tiled roof of the **Sun Yatsen Memorial Hall**, built on the spot where the man, regarded by Nationalists and Communists alike as the father of modern China, took the presidential oath in 1912. Inside is a plain auditorium with seating for two thousand people; it's occasionally used as a concert hall.

Sanyuan Temple

三元宫, sānyuán gōng • 11 Yinguan Lu • Daily 8am–5pm • ¥1 • ☎ 020 83551548 • Metro to Sun Yatsen Memorial Hall, exit C

Just north of the Sun Yatsen Memorial Hall, **Sanyuan Temple** can be found by simply heading for the gaggle of hawkers touting brightly wrapped packs of ghost money and incense. This is actually the largest Taoist temple in Guangzhou, and the oldest, too – it was first consecrated in 319 – though the current arrangement of spartan halls occupied by statues of Taoist deities is Qing. A busy place of worship, the temple is splashed in red- and gold-painted bats, cranes and other Taoist motifs; the dark wooden benches present an opportunity to sit in a serene spot.

Museum of the Mausoleum of the Nanyue King

西汉南越王墓, xīhàn nányuèwángmù • 867 Jiefang Bei Lu • ☎ 020 36182920 • Daily 9am–5.30pm, last admission 4.45pm • ¥12 • Yuexiu Gongyuan/Park metro

Over the road from the west side of Yuexiu Park looms the red sandstone facade of the **Museum of the Mausoleum of the Nanyue King**. Discovered in 1983 during foundation-digging for a residential estate, it houses the 2000-year-old site of the tomb of **Zhao Mo**, grandson of the Nanyue Kingdom's founder Zhao Tuo, and really deserves an hour of your time. An English-language video provides background to the mass of exhibits. The museum's building itself has won several awards for combining modern and traditional Chinese style, although the actual tomb is quite drab.

The exhibition

Zhao Mo made a better job of his tomb than running his kingdom, which disintegrated shortly after his death: excavators found the mausoleum stacked with gold and priceless trinkets. They're on view in the museum, including a **burial suit** made from more than a thousand tiny jade tiles (jade was thought to prevent decay), and the ash-like remains of slaves and concubines immured with him. Several artefacts show Central Asian influence in their designs, illustrating how even at this early stage in Guangzhou's history there was contact with non-Chinese peoples.

Chen Clan Academy

陈家祠, chénjiā cí • Daily 8.30am–5.30pm, last admission 5pm • ¥10 • ☎ 020 81814559 • Chen Clan Academy metro, exit D

Just north off Zhongshan Lu's western arm, a pedestrian walkway leads to the **Chen Clan Academy**. The complex was founded after subscriptions were invited from anyone named **Chen** (one of the most common Chinese surnames) and the result – part ancestor temple, part school – is a maze of rooms and courtyards, all decorated with the most garish tiles and gorgeously carved screens and stonework that money could buy in the 1890s. Have a look at the extraordinary brick reliefs under the eaves, both inside and out. One of the first, on the right as you enter, features an opera being performed for what looks like a drunken horse, which lies squirming on the floor with mirth. Other cameos feature stories from China's "noble bandit" saga, *Outlaws of the Marsh*, and some of the sights around Guangzhou.

Liwan

荔湾区, lìwān qū

Below the western end of Zhongshan Lu lies **Liwan** district, where the ring of part of the old city walls can be traced along **Longjin Lu** in the north, and **Dishifu Lu** and others to the south. Though a couple of wide, modern main roads barge through, most of this district, with east–west **Changshou Lu** at its core, retains its Ming-dynasty street plan and a splash of early twentieth-century architecture, making for excellent random walks. In addition to some of Guangzhou's biggest shopping plazas and a crowd of markets spreading into each other south from Changshou Lu right down to the river, several famous **restaurants** are located here, and the area is particularly busy at night.

Hualin Temple

华林寺, huálín sì • Wenchang Nan Lu • Daily 8am–5.30pm • ¥8 • Changshou Lu metro, exit A

Shops and markets selling jade run all the way from the pedestrian square on Xiajiu Lu right up to Changshou Lu, culminating in two multistorey jade shopping malls built on either side of the Buddhist **Hualin Temple**, which was founded as a modest nunnery by the Brahman prince Bodhidharma in 527. After his Chan teachings caught on in the seventeenth century, the main hall was enlarged to house five hundred *arhat* sculptures ranged along the cross-shaped aisles, and Hualin remains the most lively temple in the city – during **festivals** you'll be crushed, deafened and blinded by the crowds, firecrackers and incense smoke.

Dishifu Lu and Xiajiu Lu

The area south of Hualin Temple is a great place to throw away your map and roam through the maze of alleys and Qing-era homes (some of which are protected historic relics), and just enjoy the atmosphere of a bustling and living city. In the middle of this are two streets, lined with restored 1920s facades and pedestrianized at the weekends: **Dishifu Lu** to the west, and **Xiajiu Lu** to the east. Countless places to shop and eat line these streets; the pavements are always crammed to capacity.

Qingping Market

清平市场, qīngpíng shìchǎng • Daily around 9am–6pm • Huangsha metro, exit D, then follow Liversan Lu east

Between Xiajiu Lu and the river, **Qingping Market** was once one of China's most challenging – not to say gory – markets, full of large-scale streetside butchering in the interests of local culinary demands. Scaled back considerably in recent years, it remains a lively and busy affair, amply illustrating the Cantonese interest in fresh and unusual food, with each intersecting east–west lane forming dividing lines for the sale of different goods: dried medicines, spices and herbs, fresh vegetables, livestock, birds and fish – a great place to experience real Cantonese life.

Shamian Island

沙面岛, shāmiàn dǎo • Huangsha metro exit D, then cross the bridge

South of Liuersan Lu across a muddy canal, **Shamian Island** is a tear-shaped sandbank about 1km long and 500m wide which was leased to European powers as an Opium War trophy, the French getting the eastern end and the British the rest. Here the colonials re-created their own backyards, planting the now massive **trees** and throwing up solid, Victorian-style **villas**, banks, embassies, churches and tennis courts –

practically all of which are still standing. Shamian today serves as a quiet bolt-hole for many long-term travellers in the city, and as a picturesque backdrop for wedding photographers. There's restricted traffic flow, and the well-tended architecture, greenery and relative peace make it a refreshing place to visit, if only to sample the restaurants (see p.500).

The main thoroughfare is east–west **Shamian Dajie**, with five numbered streets running south across the island. Though sharing such a tiny area, the British and French seemingly kept themselves to themselves, building separate bridges, churches and customs houses. Wandering around, you'll find facades have largely been restored to their original appearance – most were built between the 1860s and early twentieth century – with plaques sketching their history.

Shamian Park

沙面公园, shāmiàn gōngyuán

Next to the atypically, and looming, modern *White Swan* hotel on the **Shamian Nan Jie** esplanade, a focus of sorts is provided by **Shamian Park**, where two **cannons**, cast in nearby Foshan during the Opium Wars, face out across the river. You might catch Cantonese opera rehearsals here on Saturday afternoons.

Tianhe

天河, tiānhé • Metro to Linhexi/Linhe West

Guangzhou's new business district, **Tianhe** coalesced around a sports stadium built in 1986 as a showcase for the National Games, and is where to get a taste of the city's modern side. The district is worth at least a day, sporting some of China's tallest buildings and the marvellous **Guandong Provincial Museum** in the **Zhujiang New Town** area, whose many bars, clubs and restaurants all cater to Western expatriate tastes. Tianhe also has a few nooks and crannies hiding Guangzhou's artistic side (though the **Guangzhou Opera House** here is possibly the ugliest building dedicated to the arts in the world), alongside small designer boutiques dotted through **Liuyun** Quarter's leafy streets.

8

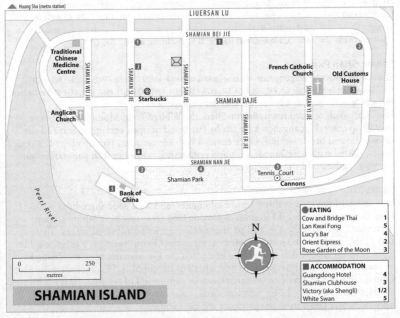

● EATING	
Cow and Bridge Thai	1
Lan Kwai Fong	5
Lucy's Bar	4
Orient Express	2
Rose Garden of the Moon	3

■ ACCOMMODATION	
Guangdong Hotel	4
Shamian Clubhouse	3
Victory (aka Shengli)	1/2
White Swan	5

SHAMIAN ISLAND

Guangdong Provincial Museum

省博物馆, shěng bówùguǎn • 2 Zhujiang Dong Lu • Daily 9am–5pm • Free; you must show your passport • ☎ 020 38046886, Ⓦ www.gdmuseum.com • APM subway line to Opera House station exit B, or Zhujiang New Town metro, exit B1

In Zhujiang New Town, the multimillion-dollar **Guangdong Provincial Museum** is, according to its promotional material, shaped "like a moonlight treasure box". It boasts some of the best natural history exhibitions in the country, including dinosaurs and whales, as well as its top-notch exhibits of Duanzhou inkstones, and Chaozhou woodcarving and porcelain. Don't miss the History of Guangdong section on the fourth floor – despite its slightly nationalistic tone – which includes a real dragon boat. As well as being free, it's also one of the best air-conditioned museums in the city, making it extra appealing in summer.

Liuyun Quarter

六运季度, liùyùn jìdù • Tiyu Xilu metro, exit H

Just across the road from the enormous TeeMall, the **Liuyun Quarter** is one of the most pleasant and little-known areas of the city to wander about in. With a faintly European feel, it's a maze of leafy avenues and backstreets, low-rise apartment buildings, and tiny boutiques featuring the work of local designers. You can while away an afternoon here shopping for clothes, or just people-watching from one of the many pavement cafés – you'll probably spot more than one outrageously dressed wannabe fashion designer.

Canton Tower

广州塔, guǎngzhōu tǎ • Daily 9am–11pm • 30th Floor ¥50, 107th Floor ¥150, Top Observation Deck ¥488 • ☎ 020 89338222, Ⓦ cantontower.com • Chigang Pagoda metro, exit A

Designed as a "feminine" skyscraper by its Dutch architects, this 600m tower is twisted, which led to its local nickname of "young girl with a tight waist". The tallest structure in the city, it dominates the eastern part of the city, especially at night when coloured lights play across its sinewy curves. It's possible to ascend the tower, from where the cityscapes are truly awesome, though the privilege doesn't come cheap; in addition to the entry fee, you can fork out more for some very expensive revolving restaurants, as well as vertigo-inducing "adventure" activities. You can experience similar views for much less cost from the *Four Seasons Hotel* in the IFC building across the river.

Baiyun Shan Park

白云山公园, báiyún shān gōngyuán • ¥5; cable car ¥45 (round trip) • ☎ 020 37222222 • South Gate: bus #63 or #245 to Yuntai Garden; West Gate: bus #18B, #36, #38, #66, #76A, #76, #127, #223, #245, #265, #424, #529, #660, #664, #734, #805 or #864 to Baiyunshan Ximen; Metro line #3 to Meihuayuan, then walk 1.2km to the park's West Gate

Just 7km north of downtown, **Baiyun Shan**, the White Cloud Mountains, are close enough to central Guangzhou to reach by city bus, but open enough to leave all the city's noise and bustle behind. Once covered with monasteries, Baiyun's heavily wooded slopes, dotted with refreshment stalls and restaurants, now offer lush panoramas out over Guangzhou and the delta region.

Routes to the top

The park encloses almost thirty square kilometres, and it's a good three-hour walk from the west entrance off Luhu Lu to **Moxing Ling** (Star-touching Summit), past strategically placed teahouses and pavilions offering views and refreshments. There's also a **cable car** from the south entrance as far as the **Cheng Precipice**, a ledge roughly halfway to the top, which earned its name when the Qin-dynasty minister **Cheng Ki** was ordered here by his emperor to find a herb of immortality. Having found the plant, Cheng nibbled a leaf only to see the remainder vanish; full of remorse, he flung himself off the mountain but – being now immortal – was caught by a stork and taken to heaven. Sunset views from the precipice are spectacular.

ARRIVAL AND DEPARTURE | GUANGZHOU

Guangzhou has multiple transit points spread all over the city, making it a daunting place to arrive at or depart from. Leaving, you'll generally need a few days to arrange tickets or at least check out the options, especially for the train.

BY PLANE

The regional airline, China Southern (daily 9am–6pm; ☎020 86120330), has its headquarters just east of Guangzhou train station at 181 Huanshi Xi Lu, with its well-organized ticket office upstairs.

Guangzhou Baiyun International Airport (白云国际飞机场, báiyún guójì fēijīchǎng; ☎020 36066999, ⓦ www.gbiac.net/en) lies 20km north of the city centre. The second-busiest in China, it deliberately rivals Hong Kong's, but has considerably cheaper fares, and is well connected to cities across China, Southeast Asia and worldwide. It has few distractions or decent restaurants, however. The easiest way to get into town is on metro line #1 from the Airport South station, which takes just 30min (daily 6.10am–11pm; ¥12–13). Taxis into town should cost ¥100–150 on the meter. Airport bus line #1 (5am–11pm, every 10–15min; ¥13–16) connects with the China Southern office at Guangzhou train station, although other routes run to various places in the city including CITIC Plaza in Tianhe.

Destinations Beijing (2hr 40min–3hr 40min); Changsha (1hr 15min); Chengdu (2hr 15min); Chongqing (1hr 40min); Dalian (4hr); Fuzhou (1hr 30min); Guilin (1hr 10min); Guiyang (1hr 40min); Haikou (1hr 10min); Hangzhou (2hr); Harbin (4hr); Hefei (1hr 55min); Hohhot (3hr 20min); Hong Kong (1hr 10min); Kunming (2hr 30min); Lanzhou (3hr–4hr 40min); Nanchang (1hr 25min); Nanjing (2hr); Nanning (1hr 20min); Qingdao (3–4hr); Sanya (1hr 25min); Shanghai (2hr 15min); Tianjin (3hr); Ürümqi (3hr 30min); Wuhan (1hr 45min); Xiamen (1hr 10min); Xi'an (2hr 30min); Yichang (1hr 55min); Zhengzhou (2hr 15min).

BY TRAIN

Demand for train tickets out of Guangzhou is very high. There are several advance-ticket offices around town, where there's no commission and the queues are usually shorter than at the stations: the most convenient are in the Liwan Plaza (Changshou Lu metro, exit A); and at 305 Huanshi Zhong Lu (Haizu Square metro, exit B1). Trains to the same destination can leave from any one of the following, so make sure you double-check the departure point on your ticket. CRH trains stop at Guangzhou South & North, and some at Guangzhou Station. Only fast trains to Shenzhen and Hong Kong run from Guangzhou East.

Guangzhou Station (广州火车站, guǎngzhōu huǒchēzhàn), just north of the city centre, is pretty confrontational, the vast square outside perpetually seething with passengers, hawkers and hustlers. Mainline services from most central, northern and western destinations terminate here. The ticket hall is at the eastern end of the station; crowds are horrendous at peak times, when entry is through guarded gateways that are closed off when the interior becomes too chaotic. New arrivals exit on the west side of the square, convenient for the metro, which is just to the right of the bus station, but not easily visible or signposted.

Guangzhou East (广州东火车站, guǎngzhōu dōng huǒchēzhàn) is 5km east of the centre at Tianhe and is handily located on metro line #1. The high-speed Hong Kong Express trains all terminate here, as well as many services from Shenzhen – although it's busy, it's by far the most convenient and comfortable station to use in the city.

Guangzhou South (广州南站, guǎngzhōu nánzhàn) is in the city's Panyu district, around 17km south of the centre and a 30min ride on metro line #1. It's most useful for trains heading through the western delta via Shunde and Zhongshan to the Macau border at Zhuhai. The ticket office is just outside the main station as you come out of the metro, to the right, though there is also a small ticket office upstairs on level 3.

Guangzhou North (广州北站, guǎngzhōu běizhàn). Located in distant Huadu district, this station around 30km from town, deals with high-speed trains on the Wuhan-Guangzhou CRH line as well as some older trains on the Jingguan railway line. Huadu Coach Terminal is just 100m away with buses to and from various locales in the city.

Destinations Beijing (10 daily; 10–29hr); Changsha (many daily; 2hr 25min–8hr 44min); Chaozhou (3 daily; 6hr 55min–8hr); Chengdu (8 daily; 13hr 25min–40hr 55min); Foshan (24–41min); Guilin (37 daily; 2hr 44min–11hr 9min); Guiyang (28 daily; 5hr 30min–21hr 57min); Haikou (5 daily; 11hr 18min–15hr 44min); Kowloon, Hong Kong (13 daily; 2hr); Kunming (5 daily; 16hr 22min–28hr 44min); Nanchang (17 daily; 4hr 52min–12hr 28min); Nanning (45 daily; 3hr 20min–13hr 57min); Shanghai (8 daily; 6–22hr); Shenzhen (many daily; 36min–2hr 19min); Wuhan (many daily; 3hr 37min–20hr); Xiamen (2 daily; 13hr); Xi'an (15 daily; 7hr 36min–28hr 30min); Zhaoqing (many daily; 1hr 40min–2hr 40min); Zhuhai (many daily 1hr–1hr 19min); Beihai (5 daily; 5hr 50min).

BY BUS

Guangzhou has over seventeen bus stations. Although most of them are busy, especially at rush hour, buying tickets is often far easier than for any train services. Below are the main central bus stations with almost all major

8

THE YANGCHENG TRAVEL PASS

If you don't like queuing for tickets, invest in a **Yangcheng Pass** (羊城通, yángchéng tōng) stored-value card, which can be used on the metro, buses, some taxis, and even at convenience stores. These can be bought at metro station ticket offices but can only be charged at branches of 7-Eleven and other convenience stores inside stations (look for a freestanding sign and queue outside the shop). The standard card costs ¥80 with a ¥30 deposit.

destinations served by multiple departure points – check which is best at ⓦ chinabusguide.com.

The provincial bus station (省汽车客运站, shěng qìchē kèyùnzhàn), west of Guangzhou train station at 145 Huanshi Xi Lu, handles arrivals from almost the entire country. It's always full to bursting, but tickets are easy to get – the ticket office is on the first floor – and there are at least daily departures to everywhere in Guangdong.

Liuhua station (流花车客运站, liúhuāchē kèyùnzhàn) is at 158 Huanshi Xi Lu, across the road from the provincial bus station. This is a clutch of depots handling destinations within 100km or so of Guangzhou – including all delta towns and Qingyuan.

Tianhe bus station (天河客运站, tiānhé kèyùnzhàn), at 633 Yanling Lu, is 7km out towards the eastern suburbs, and handles traffic from eastern Guangdong and central China. It's easily accessible by metro and is the terminus for a branch of the orange line #1. You can buy tickets for departures from here at the provincial bus station – they'll stamp your ticket on the back for a free shuttle bus to the Tianhe station, which takes around 30min.

Dashatou bus terminal (大沙头巴士总站, dàshātóu bāshì zǒngzhàn) 466 Yanjiang Dong Lu, by the Dashatou ferry pier. Dedicated station for direct, non-stop buses to Tsim Sha Tsui in Hong Kong (8 daily; 2–3hr; ¥85) and Macau (6 daily; 2–3hr; ¥75). About 1.5km south

of Dongshankou metro station; buses #7 and #89 can get you to either Tianhe or Guangzhou railway station.

Express buses to Hong Kong are also run by CTS (ⓣ 020 83374810, ⓦ ctsbus.hkcts.com), take 3–4hr and depart from various hotels between 5.15am and 7.35pm – several go from *Landmark* (see p.498); buy tickets at the departure points. Remember, during rush hours it may be a good idea to get the MTR from the border at Shenzen Bay Port (around 3hr; ¥65) which will save you time and money.

Destinations Beihai (13hr); Changsha (20hr); Chaozhou (6hr); Foshan (30min); Fuzhou (13hr); Guilin (6hr); Haikou (10hr); Hangzhou (10hr); Kowloon (2hr); Nanjing (22hr); Nanning (10hr); Panyu (1hr); Qingyuan (1hr); Sanya (14hr 30min; Shenzhen (1hr 30min); Xiamen (10hr); Zhaoqing (1hr 30min); Zhuhai (1hr 30min).

BY FERRY

Guangzhou has two major ferry terminals, Lianhuashan, 38km from town and near Lianhua Shan mountain (莲花山客运港 liánhuāshān kèyùngǎng; ⓦ cksp.com.hk) in Panyu district, and Nansha (南沙客运港, nánshā kèyùn gǎng, ⓣ 020 84688963, ⓦ nskyg.com), around 70km southeast from the centre. Both operate around four services a day to Hong Kong International Airport and China Ferry Terminal / China HK City in Kowloon (both around 1hr 20min). Check their websites for the latest sailing schedule.

INFORMATION

Tourist information Offices (daily 9am–5.30pm) are located around the city, including at the airport, but they speak no English and are of little use apart from getting a free map – which most hotels can supply you with anyway. For a useful website with expat-related and tourist

information, try ⓦ cityweekend.com.cn/guangzhou. Guangzhou has an English-speaking travellers' information and emergency line (ⓣ 020 86666666), which can be of use if you get into a jam.

GETTING AROUND

By metro Guangzhou's extensive metro system has nine lines in service, with three more scheduled by 2020 as well as proposed extensions on existing lines. Metro stations can be hard to locate at street level, but are signposted from nearby roads; keep an eye out for the red posts with yellow bands, and the metro logo at the top – something like a split "Y". Fares are ¥2–19, according to the number of stops from your starting point, and trains run every 2–3min approximately 6am–11pm. Carriages have

bilingual route maps, and each stop is announced in Mandarin, Cantonese and English. Avoid rush hour, as carriages and stations are crammed to bursting, and metal crowd-control barriers go up – which is why the carrying of balloons is strictly forbidden on the system (in case you were wondering). The Guangfo line connects with the neighbouring city of Foshan.

By bus Guangzhou's cheap and slow bus network covers most of the city from ¥2 a ride (no change given). Finding

8

PEARL RIVER CRUISES

Second only to the Yangzi in importance as an industrial channel, the undulating brown **Pearl River** (珠江, zhūjiāng) originates in eastern Yunnan province and forms one of China's busiest waterways, continually active with ferries and barges loaded down with coal and stone. Its name derives from a legend about a monk who lost a glowing pearl in its waters, and although it shone on the riverbed night after night, nobody was ever able to recover it.

Evening cruises depart daily between 6pm and 11pm from **Xidi Wharf** (西堤码头, xīdī mǎtóu), roughly opposite the Customs House on Yanjiang Lu, or 1km east at the more popular **Tianzi Wharf** (天字码头, tiānzì mǎtóu), which has more luxurious and expensive boats – ticket offices line the waterfront. Prices range from ¥48, or ¥98; some include dinner (cruises last 1hr 15min–1hr 30min). You can sit back and watch the lights of the city slip slowly past your table, with fine views of Guangzhou's busy waterfront, flanked by ever-higher buildings and dominated by coloured lights from the Canton Tower, Guangzhou's tallest structure (see p.494). The route also takes you past the *White Swan* on Shamian Island, back under Renmin Bridge, past Haizhu Bridge and then down to the grand Guangzhou suspension bridge at the far end of Er Sha Island.

which bus to get on, however, is tricky if you don't read Chinese, though many buses now announce stops in both Mandarin and English.

By taxi Taxis are plentiful except at rush hour (when they often take longer than the metro anyway). Fares start at ¥10 for the first 2.5km, and ¥2.6 for each succeeding kilometre; larger vehicles charge more. All cabs are metered and drivers rarely try any scams, though the city's complex traffic flows can sometimes

make it seem that you're heading in the wrong direction.
By motorbike taxi Outside many stations you may be accosted by a variety of motorcycle taxis, from beat-up regular motorcycles to three-wheelers that carry two people. These should cost about two-thirds the price of regular taxis for short journeys, though be warned that drivers generally disregard not only the rules of the road, but seemingly the laws of physics too.

ACCOMMODATION

Guangzhou's business emphasis means that budget accommodation is limited, though some new cheaper options have emerged in recent years. Prices rise during the fortnight-long trade fairs (see box, p.500), when beds will be in short supply. **Shamian Island** or along the **Pearl River** are the best places for travellers to stay. Otherwise, there are several relatively inexpensive hotels in central Guangzhou, mostly near the riverfront, and upmarket accommodation in the city's northern and eastern quarters, where you will also find a few budget options near Guangzhou train station.

SHAMIAN ISLAND

Guangdong Hotel 广东鹅潭宾馆, guǎngdōng étán bīnguǎn. 2 Shamian Si Jie ☎ 020 81218298; map p.493. Across from the lavish *White Swan*, this used to be one of Shamian's cheaper options, but a recent revamp has turned this old backpacker haunt into a mid-range hotel. Still, its location is hard to match. ¥450

Shamian Clubhouse 沙面会馆, shāmiàn huìguǎn. 6 Shamian Dajie ☎ 020 81102388; map p.493. By far the most atmospheric hotel on the island, and housed in an old red-brick French customs house, this place has opulent, high-ceilinged rooms with period furniture and fittings, and even a wrought-iron lift. Utterly charming, though few of the staff speak any English. If you like character and luxury, this is the place to stay. Doubles ¥450

Victory (aka Shengli) 胜利宾馆, shènglì bīnguǎn. Shamian Lu and Shamian Si Jie ☎ 020 81216688, ⓦ vhotel.com; map p.493. Formerly the Victoria in

colonial days, this upmarket choice covers two separate buildings; the newly renovated annexe (on Si Jie) is both more luxurious and more expensive. ¥500

White Swan 白天鹅宾馆, báitiān'é bīnguǎn. Shamian Nan Jie ☎ 020 81886968, ⓦ whiteswanhotel .com; map p.493. A monolithic eyesore looming over Shamian, and a Chinese Disneyland of new-money opulence inside, this was once Guangzhou's most upmarket place to stay. It's probably still the city's most famous, and was recently expanded to be even bigger and more garish than before. It's a favourite with Americans in town to adopt Chinese orphans. ¥1050

CENTRAL GUANGZHOU

Guangzhou Catalpa Garden Youth Hostel 广州东 山梓园青年旅舍, guǎngzhōu dōngshān zǐyuán qīngnián lǚshè. 12 Gonghe Lu ☎ 020 87654343; map pp.484–485. A YHA-affiliated hostel, 100m from Yangji

8

metro, this is a great budget option if you plan to explore the downtown area. There's a decent café and handy laundry facilities. Dorms ¥85, doubles ¥190

Landmark 华厦大酒店, huáxià dàjiǔdiàn. 8 Qiaoguang Lu ☏020 83355988, ⊕hotel-landmark .com.cn; map pp.488–489. Towering four-star business hotel with a great location between Haizu Square and the river, this place has all the facilities you might need, and is also the starting point for most of the CTS buses to Hong Kong. ¥630

Lazy Gaga 广州春天青年旅舍, guǎngzhōu chūntiān qīngnián lǚshè. 215 Haizhu Zhong Lu ☏020 81923232, ⊕gagahostel.com; map pp.488–489. Centrally located and just a 3min walk from the Ximenkou metro station, this trendy hostel is popular with the party crowd. There are video games, table football and a communal kitchen. Just don't expect to get to sleep too early. Dorms ¥60, doubles ¥180

Yingshang Jin Yi Hotel 迎商金艺宾馆, yíngshāng jīnyì bīnguǎn. 318 Dade Lu ☏020 83391188; map pp.488–489. Comfortable and conveniently located hotel just 600m from Haizu Square and the river. Even though it doesn't look so great from the lobby, the rooms are large and clean, with good bathrooms, and it's altogether excellent value. The beds are supremely comfortable. ¥162

NORTHERN GUANGZHOU

Baiyun City 白云城市酒店, báiyún chéngshì jiǔdiàn. 179 Huanshi Xi Lu ☏020 86666889, ⊕baiyuncityhotel.com; map pp.488–489. Right next to the China Southern office and the east side of the Guangzhou train station plaza, it's reasonably priced and very handy for early departures from or late arrrivals to the station. Rooms are comfy, if a little on the small side. ¥330

Garden Hotel 花园酒店, huāyuán jiǔdiàn. 368 Huanshi Dong Lu ☏020 83338989, ⊕gardenhotel .com; map pp.488–489. The city's most opulent accommodation, this offers a stunning marble-floored lobby decorated with gold-inlay wood panelling and piano

bar. It also features a restaurant in its formal gardens that boasts its own waterfall. ¥1193

Xiying Apartment Hotel 禧盈酒店, xīyíng jiǔdiàn. 65 Taojin Keng, just off Taojin Lu ☏020 83583988, ⊕xiyinghotel163.com; map pp.488–489. Just two metro stops east of Guangzhou station, this clean and affordable hotel tucked away off Taojin Lu offers apartment-style rooms, some with kitchens and washing machines. ¥238

EASTERN GUANGZHOU

★**Eyou Apartments** 亦友雅家短租公寓, yìyǒu yǎjiā duǎnzū gōngyù. 1318, Block A, International Apartment, 16 Huacheng Dadao ☏020 38017199; map pp.484–485. One of the best options in Tianhe, it's literally just round the corner from *McCawley's Irish Pub* and rents out mini-apartments which have small kitchens and laundry facilities. A little hard to find: catch the metro to Wuyangcun, take exit B, cross the road, then turn right at the ABC bank, and it's on the left after a bakery. ¥258

Langham Place 广州朗豪酒店, guǎngzhōu lǎngháo jiǔdiàn. 638, Xingang Dong Lu ☏020 89163388, ⊕langhamhotels.com/en; map pp.484–485. This luxury hotel occupies a great position near the Canton Fair exhibition halls. It has a great pool and spa, plush rooms, attentive staff and all mod cons, including walk-in wardrobes and electric curtains. Also offers wonderful views of the city from the *Sky Bar*, and Cantonese fusion food to die for in the *Ming Court* restaurant. ¥1020

SOUTH OF THE RIVER

Riverside Youth Hostel 广州江畔国际青年旅舍, guǎngzhōu jiāngpàn guójì qīngnián lǚshě. 15 Changdi Jie, Luju Lu ☏020 2239 2500, ⊕yhachina.com; see map, pp.484–485. Just across the water from Shamian Island, in a vibrant part of Liwan, this is Guangzhou's only genuine IYHF hostel. Very clean and efficient, but a little hard to reach; catch the metro line #1 to Fangcun, take exit B2, then follow Luju Lu to Changdi Jie, turn right and walk 200m. Dorms ¥65, doubles ¥185

EATING

Eating out is the main recreation in Guangzhou, something the city is famous for and caters to admirably, and it would be a real shame to leave town without having eaten in one of the more elaborate or famous **restaurants**. Once it was hard to find anything but Cantonese food, though now you can also track down a good variety of Asian, European and even Indian – not to mention regional Chinese. Restaurants aside, the city's numerous **food stalls** are never far away (streets off Beijing Lu have the best selection). Here you can pick up a few slices of roast duck or pork on rice, meat and chicken dumplings, or noodle soups, usually for less than ¥10 a plate. Be sure to try a selection of **cakes** and the fresh **tropical fruits** too; local lychees are so good that the emperors once had them shipped direct to Beijing.

CENTRAL GUANGZHOU

1920s Café 一九二零餐厅, yījiǔèrlíng cāntīng. 183 Yanjiang Lu ☏020 83336156, ⊕1920cn.com;

map pp.488–489. This refined German restaurant, with mains (¥50–130) including bratwürst, schnitzel, German noodles and sauerkraut, also has a pleasant,

CANTONESE COOKING

Cantonese cooking is one of China's four major regional styles and is unmatched in the clarity of its flavours and its appealing presentation. Spoiled by good soil and a year-round growing season, the Cantonese demand absolutely fresh ingredients, kept alive and kicking in cages, tanks or buckets at the front of the restaurant for diners to select themselves. Westerners can be repulsed by this collection of wildlife – even other Chinese have been known to say that the Cantonese will eat anything with legs that isn't a piece of furniture, and anything with wings that isn't an aeroplane. The cooking itself is designed to keep textures distinct and flavours as close to the original as possible, using a minimum amount of mild and complementary seasoning to prevent dishes from being bland.

No full meal is really complete without a simple plate of rich green and bitter **choi sam** (*cai xin* in Mandarin), Chinese broccoli, blanched and dressed with oyster sauce. Also famous is **fish and seafood**, often simply steamed with ginger and spring onions; and nobody cooks **fowl** better than the Cantonese, always juicy and full of flavour, whether served crisp-skinned and roasted or fragrantly casseroled. Guangzhou's citizens are also compulsive snackers, and outside canteens you'll see **roast meats**, such as whole goose or strips of barbecued pork, waiting to be cut up and served with rice for a light lunch, or burners stacked with **sandpots**, a one-person dish of steamed rice served in the cooking vessel with vegetables and slices of sweet *lap cheung* sausage. **Cake shops** selling heavy Chinese pastries and filled buns are found everywhere across the region – make sure you try roast-pork buns and flaky-skinned **mooncakes** stuffed with sweet lotus seed paste.

DIM SUM

Perhaps it's this delight in little delicacies that led the tradition of **dim sum** (*dian xin* in Mandarin) to blossom in Guangdong, where it's become an elaborate form of breakfast most popular on Sundays, when entire households pack out restaurants. Also known in Cantonese as **yum cha** – literally, "drink tea" – *dim sum* involves little dishes of fried, boiled and steamed snacks being stuffed inside bamboo steamers or displayed on plates, then wheeled around the restaurant on trolleys, which you stop for inspection as they pass your table. On being seated, you're given a pot of tea, which is constantly topped up, and a card, which is marked for each dish you select and which is later surrendered to the cashier. Try *juk* (rice porridge), spring rolls, buns, cakes and plates of thinly sliced roast meats, and small servings of restaurant dishes like spareribs, stuffed capsicum, or squid with black beans. Save most room, however, for the myriad types of little fried and steamed **dumplings** which are the hallmark of a *dim sum* meal, such as *har gau*, juicy minced prawns wrapped in transparent rice-flour skins, and *siu mai*, a generic name for a host of delicately flavoured, open-topped packets.

8

almost-riverside outdoor patio – perfect if you fancy knocking back a beer or two. Haizu Square metro, exit D. Daily 11am–1am.

Datong 大同大酒家, dàtóng dàjiǔjiā. 63 Yanjiang Xi Lu ☎ 020 81888988; map pp.488–489. If you're after an authentically noisy, crowded *dim sum* session with river views, head upstairs to floors five or six between 7am and noon. *Datong* chefs pride themselves on their roast suckling pig. Window seats are in high demand, so arrive early. Daily 7am–11pm.

Huimin Fandian 回民饭店, huímín fàndiàn. 325 Zhongshan Liu Lu ☎ 020 81303991; map pp.488–489. At the crossroads with Renmin Lu, the city's biggest and most popular Muslim restaurant serves lamb hotpots, roast duck, lemon chicken, spicy beef and a few vegetarian options at reasonable prices. Just head up the stairs past the live seafood. Daily 7am–10pm.

Lemon House 越茗苑, yuèmíng yuàn. 507 Huifu Dong Lu ☎ 020 83189715; map pp.488–489. Serving up succulent, spicy Southeast Asian dishes, *Lemon House* is locked in competition with the much busier and harder-to-get-into *Tiger Prawn* across the street for the mantle of best Vietnamese in town. Few people realize, however, that it's more or less the same food, and owned by the same people. Mains ¥30–50. Daily 10am–11pm.

NORTHERN AND EASTERN GUANGZHOU

Dongbei Ren 东北人, dōngběi rén. 668 Renmin Bei Lu ☎ 020 81361466 and at 1 Taojin Bei Lu ☎ 020 83576277; map pp.488–489. Hugely popular nationwide chain serving Manchurian food. The sautéed corn kernels with pine nuts, steamed chicken with mushrooms, or eggs and black fungus are all good, and there are plenty of vegetarian options. No English spoken,

THE CANTON FAIR

The **China Import and Export Fair** (to give it its official name) is a bi-annual event held in Guangzhou since 1957. It is the largest of its kind in China, with 15,800 stands available at its gargantuan purpose-built halls in Pazhou, southeast of the city. The spring session runs from April 14 to May 5 and the autumn session from October 15 to November 4, both in three phases for different categories of products. During these times, accommodation prices in the city double or triple, and metro lines and buses to Pazhou become unbelievably busy. For more details see ⓦcantonfair.org.cn/en or phone ⓣ020 28888999.

but they have a photo menu. Around ¥20–50 per person, more if you go for seafood. Daily 10am–11pm.

Oggie Trattoria No. 1, Tiyudong Lu ⓣ020 87575628, ⓦoggirestaurant.co; map pp.484–485. There are five *Oggie* branches in Guangzhou these days, though this one in Zhujiang New Town, near the Grand View Mall, remains pizzeria *numero uno*. Once an expat haunt, this diner is now popular with cosmopolitan Canton hipsters. Italian staples are on offer, with pizzas around ¥90 and pasta dishes ¥50. Well worth the visit if you're missing the taste of home. Daily 11.45am–11pm.

People's Café 35 Jianshe Wu Ma Lu & 106–107 Xinsheng Lu, near W Hotel, Zhujiang New Town ⓣ020 83766677; map pp.488–489. This Korean-run operation offers a menu as eclectic as the variety of foreigners and locals who frequent it. From pizza to fried rice, *People's* has it all. It's open throughout the day and night, making it a popular haunt for the cool crowd. Try the Full Breakfast for ¥58. 24hr.

Perma Bakery 38 Jianshe Wu Ma Lu ⓣ020 83807050, ⓦfacebook/PermaGZ; map pp.488–489. A hole-in-the-wall place near Taojin metro station, in an eclectic and atmospheric neighbourhood, this French-operated bakery and café serves up some of the best breads available in south China. Ideal if you're pining for a continental breakfast; croissants are ¥14 and fresh brewed coffee ¥22. Daily 8am–8.30pm.

WESTERN GUANGZHOU

Guangzhou 广州酒家, guǎngzhōu jiǔjiā. 2 Wen Chang Nan Lu, on the corner with Xiajiu Lu ⓣ020 8138 0388, ⓦgzr.com.cn; map pp.488–489. The oldest, busiest and most famous restaurant in the city, with entrance calligraphy by the Qing emperor Kangxi and a rooftop neon sign flashing "Eating in Guangzhou". The menu is massive, and you won't find better crisp-skinned chicken or pork anywhere – bank on at least ¥80 a person for a decent feed. Daily 7.30am–3pm & 5.30–10pm.

Lian Xiang Lou 莲香楼, liánxiāng lóu. 67 Dishifu Lu ⓣ020 81811638; map pp.488–489. Established in 1889, *Lian Xiang Lou* is famous for its mooncakes (baked dough confections stuffed with sweet lotus paste), which you can buy from the downstairs shop. The upstairs restaurant does commendable roast suckling

pig, brown-sauced pigeon, and "Lotus 8" fried duck with lotus flowers (¥138); other mains are about ¥35–80. Daily 7am–10pm.

Liwan Mingshijia 荔湾名食家, lìwān míngshíjiā. 99 Dishifu Lu ⓣ020 81391405; map pp.488–489. Ming-style canteen and teahouse decked in heavy marble furniture, crammed with diners wolfing down *dim sum*-style snacks. Some of the finest *sheung fan* (stuffed rice rolls), *zongzi* (steamed packets of rice and meat) and *tangyuan* (glutinous riceballs filled with chopped nuts in a sweet soup) you'll find. The English menu-card is without prices, though most dishes are only around ¥10. Daily 7am–11.30pm.

Tao Tao Ju 陶陶居, táotáo jū. 20 Dishifu Rd ⓣ020 81396111, ⓦtaotaoju.co.uk; map pp.488–489. Looks upmarket, with huge chandeliers, wooden shutters and coloured leadlight windows, but prices are very good value. Roast goose is the house speciality, and they also do cracking seafood – plain boiled prawns or fried bean-noodle crab are both excellent – along with crisp-skinned chicken, lily-bud and beef sandpots, and a host of Cantonese favourites. Comprehensive English menu, with mains ¥18–120. Daily 7am–4pm & 5.30–11pm.

SHAMIAN ISLAND

★**Cow and Bridge Thai** 牛桥泰菜, niú qiáo tài cài. 54 Shamian Bei Lu ⓣ020 81219988; map p.493. Great place to dine on what is unquestionably the finest Thai food in Guangzhou. The food is beautifully presented and the service impeccable. Main dishes are pricey, with curries starting at ¥50, but there are much cheaper weekday lunch sets starting at ¥35 (noon–2pm). There's another branch at 175 Tianhe Beilu. Daily 11am–11pm.

Lan Kwai Fong 兰桂坊, lánguìfāng. Shamian Nan Lu ⓣ020 81216523; map p.493. Taking its name from Hong Kong's central bar and restaurant district, this mid-price Guangdong restaurant's two outlets – one overlooking the tennis courts and one at the eastern end of the park – are extremely popular with locals, especially at the weekend. Mains from ¥35. Daily 11am–3pm & 5–9.30pm.

Lucy's Bar 露丝吧, lùsī bā. 3, Shamian Nan Lu ⓣ020 81366203, ⓦlucyscafe.cn; map p.493. Pleasant "American" restaurant to sit outside in the evening and eat reasonable Mexican-, Thai- and Indian-style dishes, along with burgers, pizza and grills. Mains ¥35–170; beer ¥33 a pint. Daily 11am–1am.

Orient Express 车站西餐酒廊, chēzhàn xīcān jiǔláng. 1 Shamian Bei Lu ☏020 81218882, ⓦorientexpress-restaurant.com; map p.493. Fancy French gastronomy is available at this Gallic-owned restaurant where meals are served either in the garden or aboard one of two luxury train carriages. The à la carte is quite pricey (from about ¥200 per head), but the two-course ¥78 set menu is a bargain. Daily 11am–11pm.

Rose Garden of the Moon 玫瑰园西餐厅, méiguìyuán xīcāntīng. 3 Shamian Nan Lu ☏020 81218008; map p.493. Romantic open-air restaurant set in the park with a reasonable Western-style menu from around ¥80 a head. The highlight is the

riverside views – tables and a barbecue are set up next to the water after 6pm. Daily 11am–2am.

SOUTH OF THE RIVER

Fo World Sushishe 佛世界素食社, fóshìjiè sùshíshè. 2–8 Niu Nai Chang Jie, south of Tongfu Lu ☏020 84243590; map pp.488–489. Down a small alley, this is hard to find: look for the sign reading "Fut Sai Kai". Huge portions of vegetarian food are on offer at this Buddhist restaurant, all made from bean curd: crispy chicken drumsticks in sweet-and-sour sauce, salt-fried prawns and chicken-ball casserole, with heaps of straightforward vegetable dishes too. Full English menu; most mains are under ¥30. Take the metro to 2nd Workers' Cultural Palace. Daily 7am–9pm.

DRINKING AND NIGHTLIFE

Guangzhou's **clubs** range from warehouse-sized discos to obscure, almost garage-like affairs. There are a few in the centre on Changdi Dama Lu (长堤大马路, chángdī dàmǎlù), just behind the waterfront, which is an up-and-coming clubbing area, and out in the east of the city is the very trendy Party Pier (琶醍珠江啤酒文化创意, páxīng zhūjiāng píjiǔ wénhuà chuàngyì), attractively located on Yuejiang Xi Lu, between the river and the Zhujiang beer factory. Some places have a **cover charge**, though most make their money from pricey drinks. Expats favour the **bars** located in Guangzhou's eastern reaches, where the booze is cheaper (¥20–35 a pint), pub-style meals can be had for ¥40, and the music is directed to Western tastes. Club hours are 8pm–2am; bars are open anytime from lunch to 2am, but don't expect much to be happening before 9pm. For the latest in an ever-changing scene, check ⓦgzstuff.com, ⓦcityweekend.com.cn/guangzhou or ⓦguangzhounightlife.com.

8

BARS

The Brew Bar & Bistro Unit 11–13, Yuhai Food St, 1 Jianshi Liu Ma Lu ☏020 83828299, ⓦthebrew-china.com; map pp.488–489. Four of these expat favourites are scattered across the Pearl River Delta, though *The Brew's* Jianshe branch in downtown Guangzhou is usually the liveliest. A 5min walk south of the *Garden Hotel*, this cosy venue hosts regular bands, DJs and open-mic nights, plus serves a mean hamburger (¥68) and pints on tap (Tiger ¥35). Tao Jin metro exit A. Daily 11.30am–2am.

McCawley's Irish Pub 麦考利酒吧西餐厅, màikǎolì jiǔbā xīcāntīng. 16 Huacheng Dadao ☏020 38017000, ⓦmccawleys.com; map pp.484–485. One of many foreign-style establishments in the area, this is an immensely popular two-floor faux Irish pub, with oak panelling and flock wallpaper. It's especially busy when they show international sports. Unlike the drinks, the average pub grub is overpriced unless you order the week-night food specials, though the Tex-Mex is good. Metro Zhujiang New Town, exit B1. Daily 10am–2am.

T:Union 凸凸空间与乐府, tūtū kōngjiān yú yuèfǔ. Ground Floor, Dongfang Huayuan, 361–365 Guangzhou Dadao Zhong ☏020 87992345; map pp.484–485. Unquestionably the hippest place in town to catch touring bands and live music, this is where the Canton cool congregate, drink Tsingtao and talk rock. It's a

tad hard to find, and business is slow when there's no show, but if you're interested in checking out something cultural while in Guangzhou, this is the place to be. Daily 7pm–2am or later.

CLUBS

Catwalk 163 Tianhe Bei Lu ☏020 62869999, ⓦbit.ly/CatwalkGuangzhou; map pp.484–485. Guangzhou's biggest "super-club", where you can expect to find international DJs and a wealthy clientele dressed to kill inside its glamorous, state-of-the-art interior. Get in early or you'll either not get in at all, or not get a spot at the bar – which means paying a minimum table charge of ¥1200 on Fri & Sat (for 4–5 people). Security is, unfortunately, fairly annoying; you won't get in if you've dressed down. Daily 9pm–3am.

Cave 墨西哥餐厅酒吧, mòxīgē cāntīng jiǔbā. 360 Huanshi Dong Lu ☏020 83863660; map pp.488–489. Located in a basement and perhaps best visited in a group, this place offers leather-sofa booths around a stage where nightly dance shows start at 10pm: Chinese-, Latin-, belly- and "sexy"-dance all precede DJ sets at the small UV-lit dancefloor. A very Chinese clubbing experience. Daily 9pm–4am.

Wavebar A16, Party Pier, Yue Jiang Xi Lu ☏020 34489898; map pp.484–485. Foreigners often complain about this bar (bad service and bad drinks), yet it remains one of the most popular with expats and visitors alike, mainly due to its funky interior and funkier music – a mix of house, hip-hop and techno. It has enough room to dance and is still one of the better offerings inside the Party Pier complex, which includes quieter bars where you can sit overlooking the river. Daily 7.30pm–3am.

SHOPPING

Wende Lu, running south from Zhongshan Lu, and various small shops in the streets between Dishifu Lu and Liuersan Lu, have varying selections of authenticated **antiques**, jade, lacquerwork, scrolls, chops and cloisonné artefacts. For **general clothes outlets**, head to Beijing Road Shopping District (北京路, běi jīng lù) where you'll find a plethora of local boutiques, knockoff fashion shops and snack stalls (see p.498). The streets running east off the southern end of Renmin Lu are good for very **Chinese items**: Yide Lu has several huge wholesale warehouses stocking dried foods and toys – action figures from Chinese legends, rockets and all things that rattle and buzz; other shops in the area deal in home decorations, such as colourful tiling or jigsawed decorative wooden dragons and phoenixes, and at New Year you can buy those red-and-gold good-luck posters that are put up outside businesses and homes. For out-and-out **tourist souvenirs**, such as batiks and clothing, carved wooden screens and jade monstrosities, try the streets of Shamian Island.

Hualin Jade Street Market 华林寺玉器一条街, huálín sì yùqì yī tiáo jiē; map pp.488–489. This labyrinthine market near Hualin Temple (see p.492) is worth a snoop if seeking some jade pendants or amulets. Metro Changshou Lu. Daily.

TeeMall 天河城, tiān hé chéng. 208 Tianhe Lu, Tianhe Qu. w www.teemall.com.cn; map pp.484–485.

If you're in the market for some high-end clothes, try TeeMall, in Tianhe – one of the largest, brashest emporiums in South China, with a host of luxury stores and fine restaurants. Of note, Fang Suo Commune (方所, fāngsuǒ), shop #388, is a delightful coffee shop and bookstore with plenty of English-language books on offer. Daily 10am–10pm.

DIRECTORY

Consulates Further information on consulates can be found on the Guangzhou local government's website (w english .gz.gov.cn). Visa sections of the various consulates are usually only open around 9–11.30am, and getting served isn't always easy. Australia, 12th Floor, Development Centre, No. 3 Linjiang Lu, Zhujiang New City t 020 38140111, visa office t 020 38140250, w guangzhou.china.embassy .gov.au; Canada, Suite 801, China Hotel Office Tower, Liu Hua Lu t 020 86660569; France, Room 801-3, *Guangdong International*, 339 Huanshi Dong Lu t 020 28292000; Germany, Floor 14, TeeMall, 208 Tianhe Lu t 020 83130000, w kanton.diplo.de; Italy, Room 1403, Heijing International Financial Plaza, 8 Huaxia Lu, Zhujiang New Town, Tianhe t 020 38396225; Japan, *Garden* hotel, 368 Huanshi Dong Lu t 020 83343009; Malaysia, Floor 19, CITIC Plaza, 233 Tianhe Bei Lu t 020 38770765; Netherlands, Floor 34, TeeMall, 208 Tianhe Lu t 020 38132200; Philippines, Room 709, *Guangdong International*, 339 Huanshi Dong Lu t 020 83311461; Thailand, Floor 2, *Garden* hotel, 368 Huanshi Dong Lu t 020 83804277; UK, Floor 2, *Guangdong Inter-national*, 339 Huanshi Dong Lu t 020 83143000; US, 43 Hua Jiu Lu, Zhujiang New Town t 020 38145775,

w guangzhou.usembassy-china.org.cn; Vietnam, Floor 2, Building B, *Hotel Landmark Canton*, 8 Qiaoguang Lu, Haizhu Square t 020 83305911.

Hospitals The Guangzhou United Family Clinic, PICC Building, 301 Guangzhou Dadao Zhong, Tianhe (daily 8.30am–5.30pm; t 020 87106000, 24hr emergency hotline t 020 87106060, w unitedfamilyhospitals.com), has overseas-qualified doctors. There are English-speaking dentists at AllSmile Dental Clinic, Room 603–604, 6/F Metro Plaza, 183 Tianhe Bei Lu (Mon–Sat 9am–6pm; t 020 87553380).

Left luggage There are offices at the train (daily 7am–11pm; ¥10/day) and bus (daily 8am–6pm; ¥10/day) stations.

Post offices There are major post offices with parcel post on the western side of the square outside Guangzhou train station (daily 8am–8pm), and across from the Cultural Park entrance on Liuersan Lu (daily 8am–6pm). Shamian Island's post counter is open Mon–Sat 9am–5pm for stamps, envelopes and deliveries.

Visa extensions The PSB office is on the 6th Floor, 155 Jiefang Nan Lu t 020 83111895 (Haizu Square metro, exit B2; Mon–Fri 9am–noon & 1–5pm).

The Pearl River Delta

At a glance, the **Pearl River Delta** seems entirely a product of the modern age, dominated by industrial complexes and the glossy, high-profile cities of **Shenzhen**, east on the crossing to Hong Kong, and westerly **Zhuhai**, on the Macau border. Back in the 1980s, these were marvels of Deng Xiaoping's reforms, rigidly contained

Special Economic Zones of officially sanctioned free-market activities, previously anathema to Communist ideologies. These exploded into manufacturing warrens, encapsulating sweatshop China. Nowadays, however, much of the grime has been glossed over; skyscraper-festooned downtowns are connected by a first-rate transport infastructure, and jingling tills are the backing-track of a consumer society. Yet within this urban sea, one of the world's most pre-eminent megacities, you'll still stumble upon the vestiges of history: don't miss **Foshan**'s splendid **Ancestral Temple**, or **Kaiping**'s bizarre antique architecture. Historians might also wish to visit **Humen**, where the destruction of British opium in 1839 ignited the first Opium War.

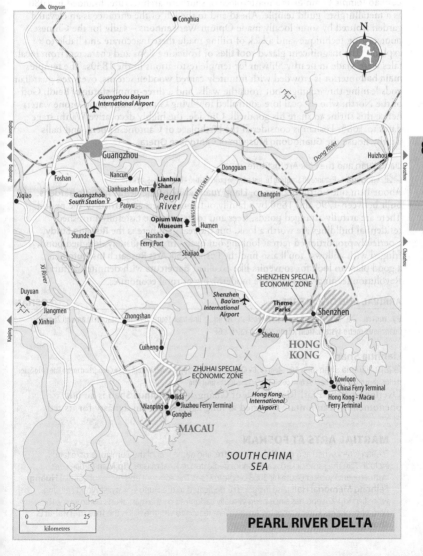

PEARL RIVER DELTA

Foshan

佛山, fóshān

Twenty-five kilometres southwest of Guangzhou and now connected to the capital by metro, the satellite of **FOSHAN** was once very much a town in its own right, with a history dating back to the seventh century. Along with neighbouring **Shiwan**, Foshan became famous for its ceramics and the splendour of its guildhall-temples, two of which survive on **Zumiao Lu**, a kilometre-long street shaded by office buildings and set in the heart of what was once the old town centre.

Zumiao Temple Complex

祖庙, zǔmiào • 21 Zumiao Lu • Daily 8.30am–6pm • ¥20 • From Guanzhou, take the metro to Zumiao

Zumiao Temple Complex is a masterpiece of southern architecture, founded in 1080 as a metallurgists' guild temple. Ahead and to the left of the entrance is an elevated garden fronted by some locally made Opium War **cannons** – sadly for the Chinese, poor casting techniques and a lack of rifling made these inaccurate and liable to explode. The magnificent glazed **roof tiles** of frolicking lions and characters from local tales were made in nearby Shiwan for temple restorations in the 1830s. The temple's **main hall** interior is crowded with minutely carved wooden screens, oversized guardian gods leaning threateningly out from the walls, and a three-tonne **statue of Beidi**, God of the North, who in local lore controlled low-lying Guangdong's flood-prone waters – hence this shrine to snare his goodwill. Outside, the highly decorative Wanfu stage dates to 1685; Foshan is considered the birthplace of Cantonese opera, and halls nearby house the **Guangdong Museum of Cantonese Opera**.

8

Liang Yuan and the Folk Art Institute

梁园, liángyuán • Entrance off Songfeng Lu, just past the police station • Daily 9am–5pm • ¥10

About 1km due north of Zumiao, **Liang Yuan** is one of the delta's historic **gardens**, built between 1796 and 1850 by a family of famous poets and artists of the period. There are artfully arranged ponds, trees and rocks, and the tastefully furnished residential buildings are worth a look, but the real gem here is the **Risheng Study**, a perfectly proportioned retreat looking out over a tiny, exquisitely designed pond, fringed with willows. You'll also find the **Foshan Folk Arts Research Institute** here, a good place to look for souvenirs like excellent **papercuts** with definite Cultural Revolution leanings, showing the modernizing of rural economies.

ARRIVAL AND DEPARTURE — FOSHAN

By metro The easiest way to reach Foshan is on Guanzhou's metro system: from Xilang station, catch a GF line train south to Zumiao station in around 25min.

Lianhua Shan

莲花山, liánhuā shān • Daily 8am–4pm • ¥50 • ⓣ 020 84861298, ⓦ pylianhuashan.com • Take Guangzhou metro line #4 to Shiqi station, then taxi (¥15) or bus #92 from outside the station for the final 3km

Overlooking the Pearl River south of Guangzhou, **Lianhua Shan** is an odd phenomenon, a mountain quarried as long ago as the Han dynasty for its red

MARTIAL ARTS AT FOSHAN

Foshan is renowned as a **martial-arts centre**, and at the rear of the Zumiao Temple (and included on the same ticket) is a museum dedicated to local master **Yip Man** (Bruce Lee's instructor and subject of the hit 2008 biopic *Ip Man*). The adjacent and more substantial **Huang Feihong Memorial Hall** (also included) is dedicated to the Hung Gar stylist Wong Feihung, who died in 1924 and has since been virtually canonized by the martial-arts community, the hero of countless kung fu movies. An excellent reason to visit the hall is the **free martial-arts shows**, held at 10.30am and 3pm daily.

stone, used in the tomb of the Nanyue king, Zhao Mo. After mining it in such a way as to leave a deliberate arrangement of crags, pillars and caves, Ming officials planted the whole thing with trees and turned it into a pleasure garden laid with lotus pools, stone paths and pavilions. A 50m-high pagoda was built in 1612, and the Qing emperor Kangxi added a fortress to defend the river. Still a popular excursion from Guangzhou, it's an interesting spot to while away a few hours, though frequently crowded.

Kaiping

开平, kāipíng • Daily 8.30am–5.30pm • Each village ¥30–100, multiple-entry ¥180; additional ¥20 to climb Ruishi Lou • Ⓦ www.kptour.com • Kaiping's Yici Station (义祠站, yìcízhàn) handles traffic to Guangzhou's Fangcun bus station (daily 6am–7.10pm; every 20min; 3hr; ¥57), Shenzhen, Zuhai and Hong Kong

Though more than 100km west of Guangzhou, the delta's excellent road network makes **KAIPING** an excellent day-trip. The town itself has no particular charm – its secret attractions lie dotted around the countryside beyond in the form of more than a thousand towers known as **diaolou** (碉楼, diāolóu). A fusion of European, Chinese and fantastical architectural styles, the towers were built in the late nineteenth and early twentieth centuries as protection against bandits and paid for with the proceeds of villagers who had found success overseas in that period.

Many of the *diaolou* are in clusters, the main sites being the villages of **Zili** (自力村, zìlì cūn), **Majianglong** (马降龙村, mǎjiàngóng cūn), **Sanmenli** (三门里村, sānménlǐ cūn) and **Jingjiangli** (锦江里村, jǐnjiāngǐ cūn), where you will find **Ruishi Lou** (瑞石楼, rùishílóu; Sat & Sun only), arguably the most majestic of the lot.

GETTING AROUND

By bus Buses crisscross between Kaiping's Yici bus station and the sites, and it is perfectly possible – if slow – to make it round by hopping on and off these.

By taxi or minibus You can hire one of the many waiting taxis or minibuses for a day-tour of Kaiping's sights for around ¥400–500, but be prepared to negotiate.

Humen

虎门, hǔmén

The routine industrial face of **HUMEN** ensures most visitors pass without a second look, but it also belies a colourful history. In 1839, after enduring a six-week siege of their warehouses in Guangzhou, the British were finally forced to hand over 1200 tonnes of **opium** to the Chinese authorities. The cargo was brought to Humen, mixed with quicklime, and dumped in two 45m pits on the beach at **Shajiao** (沙角, shājiǎo), later to be flushed out to sea. Incensed, the British massacred the Chinese garrisons at Humen, and attacked Guangzhou in what became the First Opium War. The Guangdong governor, Lin Zexu, was blamed and replaced by an ineffectual nephew of the emperor, **Qishan**, who infuriated his uncle at the end of the war by unilaterally agreeing to hand over Hong Kong to Britain as compensation for the lost opium.

Opium War sites

Humen's bloody associations are recounted at the **Lin Zexu Park Opium War Museum** (林则徐公园 鸦片战争博物馆, lín zéxú gōngyuán yāpiàn zhànzhēng bówùguǎn; ☎0769 85512065; daily 8.30am–5pm; free) on Jiefang Lu, a twenty-minute walk between the skyscrapers northwest of Humen's bus station. If you can take another battering of justifiable moral outrage after this, follow this up with a visit to the diorama-rich **Sea Battle Museum** (海战博物馆, hǎizhàn bówùguǎn; daily 8.30am–5pm; free) on Weiyuan Island – reached at the end of the #9 bus route. Nearby, **Weiyuan Fort** (威远炮台, wēiyuǎn pàotái; daily 8.30am–6pm, ¥8), almost underneath Humen Bridge, provides a pleasant break from the city and a chance to see an actual historical site in the flesh – though most is covered by trees, the thick outer walls still look impregnable.

8

SHENZHEN ORIENTATION

Shenzhen is shaped like a snake crawling along the Hong Kong border, and has no natural centre. **Luohu** (in Hong Kong you'll see the Cantonese rendering: Lo Wu) was long considered downtown and remains a good introduction to the city. Around **Lao Jie**, the tangle of narrow lanes that formed the old town of **Bao'an** is now a pedestrianized warren of shops selling cheap shoes, bags and DVDs. Here you'll also find a potent symbol of capitalism's entry into China: the country's first *McDonald's*. Westwards, you'll find the flash, if slightly crass **Central Business District** in **Futian**, home to Ping'an IFC, currently the city's tallest building, and Futian Railway Station, Asia's largest underground station. Further west, sprawling **Nanshan** district is home to the OCT Loft, a flourishing hub of design and culture. Nanshan's western side encompasses **Shekou**, a port area where China's first foreign factory was built in 1979. Now a large commercial hub, Shekou has a thriving expat community and plenty of boisterous bars.

Shenzhen

深圳, shēnzhèn

Some Westerners may be familiar with **SHENZHEN** as a global high-tech centre, but the city's reputation as China's economic ground zero ensures that it's well known to all its countrymen: it was in this one-time fishing village that China's modern "economic miracle" was born first through manufacturing, now through innovation. Today, the migrant city's gleaming skyscrapers – and ongoing construction – are testament to a continued success, as is the daily flow of thousands of commuters across the border, not just from Shenzhen to Hong Kong, but increasingly in the opposite direction. This doesn't necessarily mean there's anything of great interest to the casual visitor: however, if you've just travelled around the Chinese interior, you might want to explore the blossoming nightlife and dining scene, or indulge in some retail therapy in a city busy casting off its seedy border-town reputation and striding into the future.

Brief history

Thanks to its proximity to then-British-colony Hong Kong, Shenzhen – then a tiny hamlet called Bao'an – was chosen in 1979 as the country's first "Special Economic Zone", a free-market experiment that provided both the model for the subsequent move away from a controlled economy and the spark for meteoric growth. By 1990, the city had four harbours, its manufacturing industries were turning over $2 billion a year, and a new nuclear power station was needed to cope with the energy demand. Delegations from all over China poured in to learn how to remodel their own businesses, cities and provinces.

Shenzhen may not have been the cause of capitalism in the People's Republic, but it has provided invaluable propaganda to those who promoted its virtues. It is no coincidence that in 1992, Deng Xiaoping chose Shenzhen as the place to make his memorable statement, "Poverty is not Socialism: to get rich is glorious", voicing the Party's shift away from Communist dogma – and opening the gate for China's financial explosion.

Shenzhen Museum

深圳博物馆, shēnzhèn bówùguǎn • 6 Tongxin Lu, Luohu • Tues–Sun 10am–5.30pm • Free • ⓦ shenzhenmuseum.com.cn • Da Ju Yuan metro

Lizhi Park (荔枝公园, lìzhī gōngyuán; Shennan Zhong Lu; free) is a surprisingly refreshing open space with a fun boating lake. South of the park, on Shennan Zhong Lu, the **Shenzhen Museum** holds thousands of relics dug up during the construction of the city, paintings and works of calligraphy, as well as many historical items on loan from museums around China.

Lianhua Shan Park

莲花山公园, liánhuāshān gōngyuán • Hongli Xi Lu, Futian • Daily 6am–7pm • Free • ☎ 0775 83067950 • Metro to
Lianhuacun, Children's Palace or Lianhua West

Lianhua Shan Park, about 3km north of the border and train station, has some beautiful
gardens and is one of the main public spaces where local people hang out. After
enjoying the day-glo marvels flying at Kite Square (if you're there in the autumn),
head up the hill for a great view of the city where a giant bronze Deng Xiaoping gazes
happily across the skyline – a sight for which he is largely responsible – toward Hong
Kong. Otherwise, just enjoy the genial atmosphere of people relaxing and enjoying
their precious free time.

Theme parks

Daily 9am–10pm • ¥120–140 each • Shennan Daddao, Nanshan • Window on the World metro station, Hua Qiao Cheng metro station
(for Splendid China) and Shi Jie Zhi Chuang metro station (for the Folk Culture Village)

For Shenzhen's biggest guilty pleasure, head thirty minutes west to the city's three
biggest **theme parks**, situated next to each other on the Guangshen Expressway – look
for a miniaturized Golden Gate Bridge spanning the road.

By far the best of these, **Window on the World** (世界之窗, shìjiè zhīchuāng) is a collection
of scale models of famous monuments such as the Eiffel Tower and Mount Rushmore,
while **Splendid China** (锦绣中华, jǐnxiù zhōnghuá) offers the same for China's sights. The
latter's ticket also includes admission to the **Folk Culture Village** (民俗文化村, mínsú
wénhuàcūn), an enjoyably touristy introduction to the nation's ethnic groups – there are
yurts, pavilions, huts, archways, rock paintings and mechanical goats, and colourful
troupes performing different national dances.

Happy Valley

欢乐谷, huāngǔ • Mon–Fri 9.30am–9pm, Sat & Sun 9am–10pm • Adults ¥180, children 1.2–1.5m ¥90, smaller children free •
☎ 0755 26949184, ⌂ sz.happyvalley.cn • Window on the World metro station, exit A

Just north of the theme parks is **Happy Valley**, Shenzhen's bigger answer to Hong
Kong's Disneyland – and, many would say, considerably better. It's best avoided at
weekends and national holidays when queues can be interminable, but there are some
genuinely exciting rides here.

Nantou Ancient Town

南头古城, nántóu gǔchéng • Nantou Tianqiao Bei, Nanshan • Free • Metro to Shenzhen University or Taoyuan,
than a ¥10 taxi

Tucked away in a chaotic neighbourhood of hurriedly erected apartment blocks in
Nanshan district, **Nantou Ancient Town** is evidence that Shenzhen isn't quite the
30-year-old place it pertains to be. Founded in 331 as an administrative centre of
the Dongguan Prefecture, Nantou was an important Pearl River city in its heyday.
Nantou was walled in 1394, and it was here that Hong Kong was ceded to the
British after the first Opium War. What remains are the ancient gates, ancestral
halls, shrines and notable residences, worthy of exploring if you're tired of
Shenzhen's prolific modernity.

Wutong Mountain

梧桐山, wútóng shān • 18km east of Luohu • Free • Buji metro, then a ¥30 taxi; bus #211 from Luohu/Dongmen

A protected national park, the rivers of which feed Luohu Resevoir (and ultimately
Hong Kong), **Wutong Mountain** is the city's principle hiking spot – there are several
clearly marked forest tracks to follow. The verdant scenery, bisected by streams and
waterfalls, feels a world away from the concrete jungle of downtown Luohu. Equally
noteworthy is **Wutong Art Town** (梧桐艺术小镇, wú tóng yì shù xiǎo zhèn) at the mouth
of the park, a colourful village festooned with vegan eateries and shops selling local
handicrafts, as well as a few hippy cafés.

8

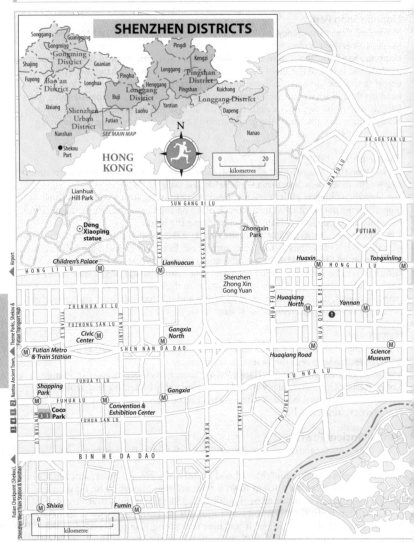

Dapeng peninsula

大鹏半岛, dàpéng bàndǎo • 40km east of Luohu • Bus #H92 from Futian Transport Hub or #E11 from Yinghu

Way out on Shenzhen's eastern periphery is Dapeng, a forest-coated headland poking into the South China Sea that is named after the Great Roc, a mythical bird. Beaches here rival Hainan, including **Xichong** and **Dongchong**, popular with local surfers, and **Jinshuiwan**, a cove with on-shore winds that is great for windsurfing.

Dapeng Ancient Fortress

大鹏所城, dàpéng suǒchéng • Entry daily 9am–6pm; you're free to remain inside after 6pm • ¥20 • Local bus #756 from Dapeng

The real highlight of this peninsula is the **Dapeng Ancient Fortress**, a well-preserved Ming-era walled town, built to defend locals from Japanese pirates. The warren of

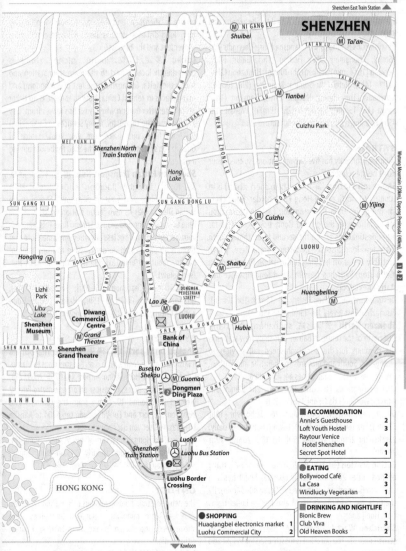

SHENZHEN

ACCOMMODATION

Annie's Guesthouse	2
Loft Youth Hostel	3
Raytour Venice Hotel Shenzhen	4
Secret Spot Hotel	1

EATING

Bollywood Café	2
La Casa	3
Windlucky Vegetarian	1

DRINKING AND NIGHTLIFE

Bionic Brew	1
Club Viva	3
Old Heaven Books	2

SHOPPING

Huaqiangbei electronics market	1
Luohu Commercial City	2

stone backstreets remains home to several elderly Hakka, though many have changed their occupation from fishing to selling tourist knick-knacks. Despite some commercialization, it remains mostly authentic and offers a fascinating glimpse into the side of South China that's fast fading from view.

ARRIVAL AND DEPARTURE   SHENZHEN

BY PLANE

Shenzhen Bao'an International Airport (深圳宝安国际机场, shēnzhèn bǎo'ān guójì jīchǎng; w eng.szairport.com) is 32km northwest of town. It's one of China's busiest airports – far cheaper to fly out of

here than Hong Kong, it's swamped with travellers from south of the border. The airport is at the end of the green Luobao metro line to Shenzhen (¥9; 40min to downtown); there are also buses to Kowloon (¥100) and Hong Kong Airport (¥180) for which you buy tickets from a booth in the arrival terminal. A taxi to Shenzhen costs ¥100–150.

Destinations Beijing (3hr); Changsha (1hr); Chengdu (2hr 15min); Chongqing (2hr); Fuzhou (1hr); Guilin (1hr); Guiyang (1hr 45min); Haikou (1hr 10min); Hangzhou (2hr); Harbin (4hr); Hefei (1hr 50min); Kunming (2hr 10min); Nanchang (1hr 30min); Nanjing (2hr); Nanning (1hr); Sanya (1hr 15min); Shanghai (2hr 10min); Wuhan (1hr 45min); Xiamen (1hr); Xi'an (2hr 40min).

BY TRAIN

Shenzhen currently has five railway stations, so check your ticket before you set off.

Shenzhen Station (深圳站, shēnzhèn zhàn) is in Luohu, just north of the Hong Kong border. Buy tickets for the bullet train to Guangzhou East and Guanzhou main stations on the ground floor; ticket counters for other destinations are on the second floor, though with fairly few long-distance departures from here, you're probably better off heading to Guanzhou first. There's a metro stop, local bus terminus and long-distance bus station next door.

Destinations Guangzhou (every 10–15min; 1hr 30min); Guangzhou East (every 10–15min; 1hr 15min).

Shenzen North (深圳北站, shēnzhèn běi zhàn). Just north of the centre in Bao'an, this shiny new station is the terminus for the ultra-high-speed rail services to Guangzhou South and onwards to Changsha and Wuhan. Easy to reach, it's on metro lines #4, #5 and #6.

CRH destinations Changsha (25 daily; 2hr 52min–3hr 44min); Wuhan (1 daily; 4hr 15min–5hr).

Other destinations Changsha (26 daily; 9hr–10hr 50min); Fuzhou (1 daily; 18hr); Guangzhou (many daily; 29min–2hr 20min); Wuhan (5 daily; 18hr 20min–19hr 20min).

Futian Station (福田火车站, fútián huǒchē zhàn) opened in Dec 2015 and mainly operates bullet trains to and from Guangzhou South (every 35min; 40–54min). By the time you read this, it might also handle bullet trains from Hong Kong.

Shenzhen West (深圳西, shēnzhèn xī) is a small station near Shekou port that is mostly used for freight and slow trains.

Destinations Chengdu (1 daily; 37hr 45min); Hefei (1 daily; 19hr 37min); Lanzhou (1 daily; 43hr).

Shenzhen East (深圳东, shēnzhèn dōng), in Buji, is an old train station that's been spruced up to deal with CRH as well as some middle- and lower-speed trains.

Destinations Chengdu East (1 daily; 39hr 54min); Hefei daily (19hr 21min); Nanchang (3 daily; 11hr).

BY BUS

Due to the Pearl River Delta's popularity with migrant workers, almost every village across the country has a bus service to Shenzhen, and there are rumoured to be over forty long-distance stations here. Below are the most convenient and the biggest.

Luohu (罗湖汽车站, luōhú qìchē zhàn) is conveniently located next to the main train station and serves the delta, Guangzhou, the rest of Guangdong and many places in central China. Note that there is no ticket office here; after finding where your bus leaves from, buy a ticket from the conductor. Many services to Guangzhou go from here, but make sure you know which of Guangzhou's bus stations you're headed for before buying a ticket.

Shenzhen Futian Transport Hub (福田综合交通枢纽, fútián zōnghé jiāotōng shūniǔ) is at 8001 Shennan Dadao, 8km west of downtown Shenzhen, in Futian District. Has its own metro station which is on the blue Longgang line and orange Shekou line. This station is your best bet for more or less anywhere in China. Note that there is an under-used border crossing to Hong Kong at Futian, about a 10min taxi ride from the Transport Hub (see below).

Destinations Chaozhou (5–6hr); Fuzhou (13hr); Guangzhou (3hr); Guilin (9–15hr); Haikou (14hr); Hong Kong (1–2hr); Nanning (8–10hr); Yangshuo (8–10hr).

BY FERRY

Shekou ferry port (蛇口码头, shékǒu mǎtóu) lies 15km west of the centre, with direct connections to Macau, Hong Kong and Hong Kong Airport (☏ 0755 26691213, ⊕ cksp.com.hk). Access is easiest on orange metro line #2 which takes around 30–40min from the centre; buses between the port and Lo Wu include the #204 to Jianshe Lu; a taxi will set you back around ¥80.

Destinations Hong Kong (every 30min, 7.30am–9pm; 1hr; ¥110); Hong Kong Airport (hourly, 7.45am–9pm; 30min; ¥260); Macau (6 daily, 7.45am–7.30pm; 1hr; ¥180).

ON FOOT

The two pedestrian border crossings to Hong Kong are open daily 6.30am–midnight. Border formalities are streamlined, and shouldn't take more than an hour at either option.

Luohu (罗湖口岸, luóhú kǒu'àn). Crossing from Shenzhen, there's a lack of directional signs; you need to get onto the overpass from upstairs at the train station and then head south past souvenir stalls, roasted-meat vendors and pet shops. The Hong Kong side, known here as Lo Wu, is on the MTR East Rail Line into town.

Futian Checkpoint (福田口岸, fútián kǒu'àn). An option if you've just arrived at the huge Futian Transport Hub nearby, this crossing is slightly less hectic than Luohu and easily accessed on metro line #4. It's called Lok Ma Chau on the Hong Kong side, and it's on the MTR East Rail Line into Kowloon.

INFORMATION

Useful websites The handy website ⓦshenzhenstuff .com has the city's latest entertainment and practical info.

There's also a government website (ⓦenglish.sz.gov.cn), although it doesn't seem to be regularly updated.

GETTING AROUND

If you're spending any length of time in the city, consider buying a Shenzhen Pass (深圳通, shēnzhèn tōng), a stored-value card for use on Shenzhen buses and the metro, which can be bought and recharged at metro stations.

By metro Shenzhen's efficient metro system has grown exponentially in recent years. There are currently five operational lines with six more under construction. The metro already connects to the airport, all the train stations, most of the bus stations and the ferry terminals (¥2–9; daily, every 3min or so, 6.30am–11pm; ⓦszmc.net).

By bus The city has almost five hundred bus lines which operate from 7am–11pm, with "N" night buses running

on busier routes. Most buses are a/c and announce stops in Mandarin and English. Tickets are ¥1–10; night buses from ¥2.

By taxi Taxis are plentiful; flag fall starts at ¥10, with burgundy and silver non-electric taxis adding a ¥3 fuel surcharge – the less plentiful sky-blue electric taxis are bigger, have "E-taxi" on the side, and don't have a surcharge. Few drivers speak English, so it's best to have your destination written down in Chinese.

ACCOMMODATION

Shenzhen has a glut of **business-oriented hotels**, including the international standbys *Marco Polo*, *Shangri-La*, *Sheraton* and *Holiday Inn*. Chinese **budget chains** such as *7 Days Inn* and *Home Inn* are dotted around the city, while an emerging **hostelling culture** has seen budget and mid-range options emerge in hip places such as the OCT Loft, Wutong Mountain and the Dapeng Peninsula.

8

Annie's Guesthouse 安妮文艺生活驿站, ānnī wényì shēnghuó yìzhàn. 81 Kengbei Cun, Wutong Mountain ⓣ0755 25225403. This lovely boutique hotel in Wutong Art Township at the mouth of Wutong Mountain National Park is the best option for hikers heading to the hills. Staff are enthusiastic, and the eccentrically decorated rooms are all en suite and clean. An ideal mountain retreat, if a tad hard to find. ¥200

★**Loft Youth Hostel** 侨城旅友国际青年旅舍, qiáochéng lǚyǒu guójì qīngnián lǚshè. 7 Xiangshan Dong Jie, Nanshan ⓣ0755 86095773, ⓦyhachina.com. IYHF hostel backing onto the achingly cool "Loft Creative Area", a former factory now housing art galleries, cafés, bars and trendy offices. Clean and modern dorms, doubles, twins and triples, some en suite. Take the Luobao metro line to Qiaochengdong and leave by exit A; turn right when you leave the station, right again at the petrol station and you'll find the hostel on the corner of Enping and Xiangshan East St. A bit out of the centre, but

far cleaner, newer and more comfortable than options elsewhere. Dorms ¥60, doubles ¥180

Raytour Venice Hotel Shenzhen 深圳威尼斯睿途酒店, shēnzhèn wēinísī ruìtú jiǔdiàn. Overseas Chinese Town, Nanshan ⓣ4008 306 808, ⓦen .szvenicehotel.com. Venetian-themed luxury hotel located between the Window of the World and Happy Valley theme parks, complete with fancy outdoor pool which occasionally hosts expat pool parties. There's also a popular in-house club – *V Bar* – and an Italian restaurant. ¥987

Secret Spot Hotel 秘点冲浪客栈, mìdiǎn chōnglàng kèzhàn. No. 3 Gate, Shalanzhai, Xichong ⓣ13823619335. Now surrounded by copycat guesthouses, this surfer-friendly forerunner at Xichong, on the Dapeng Peninsula, is a fantastic, American–Chinese-run bed and breakfast. There's an affliated bar on the beach serving Western food and beer in an environment more akin to Thailand than China. ¥300

EATING

No longer just a place of migrant and Cantonese canteens, Shenzhen's **dining scene** could almost give Hong Kong a run for its money. There are great Indian restaurants near the Luohu border, artsy cafés in the OCT Loft, and Western restaurants are now found in parts of the city other than the expat mainstays of Futian and Shekou.

Bollywood Café 宝莱坞印度菜原味馆, bǎo lái wù yìn dù cài yuán wèi guǎn. 3rd Floor, 1038 Jianshe Lu, Luohu ⓣ0775 8222 0370. This Indian restaurant just opposite Guomao metro station (Exit A) is a stalwart of the Indian community in Shenzhen. Clean, well-managed and

serving up mouthwatering South Asian food to the soundtrack of Bollywood hits, this place is hard to beat. If you're tired of local cuisine, *Bollywood Café* may just be up your street. Daily 11am–11.30pm.

La Casa 悦方, yuè fāng. No. 139 Coco Park, Fuhua

Lu, Futian ☎ 0755 8290 3279. An orginal foreigner haunt in Futian, with open-mic and quiz nights, *La Casa* has been a tad superseded by some of its bigger, brasher neighbours. However, this Canadian-run diner and bar is still a great place for newcomers to meet old hands over freshly baked pizza and a pint of imported lager. Daily 11am–2pm.

Windlucky Vegetarian 云来居, yúnláijū. 4th Floor, Dongmen Ding Plaza, Guangchang ☎ 0755 25908588. This vegan Buddhist chain is clean, quiet and offers green healthy food ordered via an iPad menu. It's the perfect place to watch the commercial hubbub of the Dongmen area play out over a plate of faux Peking duck. Around ¥60 a head. Daily 11.30am–2pm & 6–9pm.

DRINKING AND NIGHTLIFE

The main foreigner-friendly **nightlife** areas are the **Shekou port** area (Sea World metro station on the orange Shekou line), and closer to the centre at **Coco Park** in Futian (Shopping Park metro station on the blue Longgang and green Luobao lines). For something less commercial, try the **OCT Loft** near Qiaochengdong metro, or **Baishizhou**, where some craft-brew bars have sprung up. Upmarket bars can be found in the **OCT Bay**, Nanshan. For up-to-date info on Shenzhen's nightlife, check out ⊕ shenzhenparty.com.

NANSHAN

Bionic Brew Shangye Buxingjie, off Shanhe Jie in Baishizhou ⊕ bionicbrew.com. Located in an atmospheric if slightly chaotic old neighbourhood, Shenzhen's first craft brewery has some excellent beers, New York-style pizza and a relaxed vibe. Daily 5pm–1am.
Club Viva No. 140 Coco Park, Fuhua Lu, Futian / Above Starbucks, F3, Seaworld ☎ 0755 2531 3765. With two locations on two very boozy bar strips, this is Shenzhen's original crass-and-brash nightclub. There's open-air

seating, resident/guest DJs and discounted shots. Not for those seeking a quiet pint. Daily 5pm–3am.
Old Heaven Books 旧天堂书店, jiù tiān táng shūdiàn. Building 120, A5, OCT Loft, Wenchang Jie ☎ 0755 8614 8090. Along with sister live house *B10*, this café, record shop and bookstore is the centre of all things cultural in Shenzhen. Expect talks and live music by night. By day, it's simply the coolest place to drink tea and nose through a good book. Daily 10.30am–1am.

SHOPPING

With the growing strength of the yuan – not to mention the internet – Shenzhen isn't the shopper's paradise it used to be, and most things are cheaper in Hong Kong or almost anywhere else in China. Even so, with a bit of haggling, you can get some reasonable prices, though remember **counterfeit goods** are rife here.

Huaqiangbei electronics market 华强北, huá qiáng běi. Futian. A tangled web of malls, shops and stalls have collectively become one of the world's largest electronics markets. If you are shopping for a rare component or some obscure software, you'll almost certainly find it here. Just beware of touts and dodgy products. Usually daily 10am–10pm.

Luohu Commercial City 罗湖商业城, luóhú shāngyè chéng. Luo Hu border. Immediately to your right as you clear customs at the Luo Hu border is a chaotic mall with five floors of shops selling big-brand knockoffs, including bags, watches, clothes, DVDs and all manner of electronics of questionable lineage.

DIRECTORY

Left luggage There's an office at the northeastern corner of the train station square (daily 7am–10pm; ¥5–40 per day, depending on size).
Post offices The main downtown branch is at 3040 Jianshe Lu (Mon–Sat 8am–8pm), with a smaller office

(same hours) just inside Luo Hu bus station.
Visa extensions For visa extensions go to the PSB office at 4016 Jiefang Lu in Luo Hu (☎ 0755 84465490, ⊕ sz3e.com; Mon–Fri 9.30am–noon & 2–4pm).

Qingyuan

清远, qīngyuǎn

Sitting on the banks of the **Bei River**, about 80km northwest of Guangzhou, **QINGYUAN** is an industrial jumble solely of interest as a jumping-off point for river trips 20km upstream to the poetically isolated, elderly temple complexes at Feilai and Feixia – and the fact that the resort at the **Sankeng Hot Spring** (三坑温矿泉, sān kēng wēn kuàng quán),

just north of the town, is favoured by some of China's best professional football teams. The city centre lies to the north of the river, and if you find yourself at a loose end, a walk down on the promenade along Yanjiang Lu is a pleasant way to spend an evening.

Feilai Temple

飞来古寺, fēilái gǔsì · Daily 8am–5.30pm · ¥15

Taking the boat from Qingyuan's Wuyi dock, it's a placid, hour-long journey upstream past a few brick pagodas, bamboo-screened villages and wallowing water buffalo being herded by children. Hills rise up on the right, then the river bends sharply east into a gorge and past the steps outside the ancient gates of **Feilai Temple**, a romantically sited Buddhist monastery whose ancestry can be traced back 1400 years. You'll need about forty minutes to have a look at the ornate ridge tiles and climb up through the thin pine forest to where a modern pavilion offers pretty views of the gorge scenery. If you have time to spare before your boat heads on, the temple gates are a good place to sit and watch the tame cormorants sunbathing on the prows of their owners' tiny sampans in the early morning and evening.

Feixia Temple

飞霞古寺, fēixiá gǔsì · Daily 8am–5.30pm · ¥35 · ☎ 0763 3780168

Some 3km further upstream from Feilai Temple at the far end of the gorge, **Feixia Temple** is both far more recent and much more extensive. The complex comprises two entirely self-sufficient Taoist monasteries, founded in 1863 and expanded fifty years later, which were built up in the hills in the Feixia and Cangxia grottoes, with hermitages, pavilions and academies adorning the 8km of interlinking, flagstoned paths in between. A couple of hours is plenty of time to have a look around.

The temple buildings

A broad and not very demanding set of steps runs up from Feixia's riverfront through a pleasant woodland where, after twenty minutes or so, you pass the minute Jinxia and Ligong temples, cross an ornamental bridge, and encounter Feixia itself. Hefty surrounding walls and passages connecting halls and courtyards, all built of stone, lend Feixia the atmosphere of a medieval European castle. There's nothing monumental to see – one of the rooms has been turned into a **museum** of holy relics, and you might catch a weekend performance of **traditional temple music** played on bells, gongs and zithers – but the gloom, low ceilings and staircases running off in all directions make it an interesting place to explore.

Changtian Pagoda

If you walk up through the monastery and take any of the tracks heading uphill, in another ten minutes or so you'll come to the short **Changtian Pagoda** perched right on the top of the ridges, decorated with mouldings picked out in pastel colours, with views down over Feixia and the treetops.

ARRIVAL AND DEPARTURE   **QINGYUAN**

By train The train station (清远站, qīngyuǎn zhàn) lies 14km east of Qingyuan, with high-speed connections to | Guangzhou South train station. Taxis and motorcycle-taxis can take you into town for about ¥30, as there's no bus.

FEILAI AND FEIXIA FERRIES

Qingyuan's **Wuyi Dock** (五一马头, wǔyī mǎtóu) lies about 1km north of the train station, or 14km east of the town centre (about ¥30 in a taxi). Charter boats seating up to ten people for a return trip to Feilai and Feixia cost ¥400–500, depending on your bargaining skills. On your own, try heading here at the weekend, when you may find other small groups with whom to split the cost of a single boat-hire; it's sometimes possible to join a package group if you're lucky.

Destinations Beijing (2 daily; 13hr); Guangzhou (15 daily; 30min).

By bus Qingyuan has two bus stations, both south of the river and a couple of kilometres apart: New Town bus station (新城汽车客运站, xīnchéng qìchē kèyùn zhàn) and Zhongguan bus station (中冠汽车客运站, zhōngguàn qìchē kèyùn zhàn) with regular connections to Guangzhou (Liuhua station), Foshan and Shenzhen until around 8pm.

Destinations Foshan (2hr); Guangzhou (1hr 30min); Shenzhen (2hr 30min); Zhaoqing (5hr).

ACCOMMODATION

7 Days Inn 7天清远新城汽车站连江路店, qī tiān qīng yuán xīn chéng qì chē zhàn lián jiāng lù diàn. 16 Zuo, Lianjiang Lu, Bahao Qu ☎0763 3368268. The New Town bus station branch of this business chain won't win any awards for style, but it's well located, a stone's throw from the Bei River, and has clean en-suite rooms with TV and a/c. ¥180

Sheraton Qingyuan Lion Lake Resort 清远狮子湖 喜来登度假酒店, qīngyuán shīzǐhú xǐlái dēng dùjià jiǔdiàn. Shizihu Ave, 1 Henghe Jie ☎0763 8888888. Located about 10km southwest of the bus stations and 20km from the train station, this international-standard resort boasts a golf course, hot springs and, unexpectedly, Arabian architecture. It's a bit tacky, but has the most comfortable rooms in town. ¥888

EATING, DRINKING AND NIGHTLIFE

Yanjiang Lu and Shanglang Lu are the best bet for **eating** and **nightlife**, with both streets strung with various restaurants, canteens, KTVs, bars, music-pubs and even a swish new club. The promenade along the river is also popular with locals playing music, dancing, or singing karaoke (badly) in the open air.

Huizhou

惠州, huìzhōu

Straddling the **Dong River**, about 69km northeast of Shenzhen, lies the predominantly Hakka city **HUIZHOU**, its relaxed pace belying the fact that it's one of the oldest settlements in the Pearl River Delta. In the not-so-distant past, Huizhou administered Shenzhen and Dongguan; these newer cities have surpassed Huizhou economically, but **Goose Town**, as it's commonly known, affords visitors a history-imbued respite from the clamour of big-city life, particularly around beautiful West Lake.

West Lake Park

西湖公园, xīhú gōngyuán • Free • Intercity Rail from Changpin, a town in Dongguan Prefecture, to Xihu East, next to the lake (45min)

The centrepiece of the city is the picture-postcard **Sizhou Pagoda**, located on a mound in the mountain-flanked **West Lake Park**. The man-made **Su Embankment** that crosses the lake is lined by stone sculptures bearing the immortal words of Northern Song-dynasty scribe Su Dongpo (see p.527) who spent three years in exile in Huizhou, mostly enthusing about the delicious fruit and pretty local maidens. **Su Dongpo Memorial Hall** has a scant exhibition recalling his life and times in Huizhou.

Cross the lake via **Nine Bends Bridge**, from where you can watch peddle-boaters while passing through tree-enshrouded islands. On the lake's north shore, the **Yuanmiao Temple** is a Taoist shrine of Tang origin, rebuilt in 1990 after being damaged in the Cultural Revolution.

ARRIVAL AND DEPARTURE | HUIZHOU

By bus Huizhou's chaotic bus station (惠州汽车站, huìzhōu qìchē zhàn) is walking distance from West Lake Park and runs services to most major destinations in the province.

Destinations Guangzhou (2hr 30min); Shenzhen (1hr 20min).

By train The CRH train station Huizhou South (惠州南站, huìzhōu nánzhàn) lies on the Xiamen–Shenzhen line but is a 40min bus ride from the city district. Huizhou Station (惠州火车站, huìzhōu huǒchēzhàn) is located north of the river and deals with slower trains. The new Dongguan–Huizhou Intercity Rail, also known as Guanhui, connects the West Lake (Xihu East) with Changpin. At the time of writing, more stations were under construction on the Guanhui line as it becomes part of a

8

grander transport scheme to better connect the Pearl River Delta (the Dongguan–Huizhou Intercity Railway). **Huizhou Station** destinations Beijing (2 daily; 28hr);

Nanchang (14 daily; 9hr).
Huizhou South destinations Xiamen (33 daily; 3hr); Shenzhen (44 daily; 30min).

ACCOMMODATION

Jinjiang Inn 锦江之星, jǐnjiāng zhīxīng. 2 Xiapu Lu, Huicheng Qu ☏0752 2077888. Right in the middle of Xiapu, this generic business chain is clean, comfortable and well priced, and there are plenty of eating options within walking distance. **¥150**

Kande International Hotel Huizhou 惠州康帝国际酒店, huìzhōu kāngdì guójì jiǔdiàn. 18 Huaicheng

Xi Lu, Huicheng district ☏0752 2688888, ⓦkandehotel.com/en. This Guangdong-based luxury hotel chain doesn't quite deliver international service standards, but the location – opposite the West Lake – is unrivalled, and the cocktail lounge and buffet restaurant offer opulence hard to find elsewhere in the city. **¥500**

EATING AND DRINKING

Hakka cuisine is the mainstay of the locals and you can find *kejia cai* (客家菜) on most streets. Some of the best **eating** and **drinking** can be found along Binjiang Lu, overlooking Binjiang Park and the Dong River – there are several open-air riverside bars to explore here.

American Retro 非诚往事酒吧, fēichéng wǎngshì jiǔbā. 11 Huisha Tiyi Lu ☏0752 2111836. Opened by two former Huizhou English teachers from the US and UK, this is where the city's expats generally congregate to rub shoulders with the dice-tumbling locals over hot dogs and other Western fast-food snacks. The bar has a classic Americana theme, with pictures of Marilyn Monroe and Elvis, as well as frequent gigs from Hong Kong-, Shenzhen- and Guangzhou-based bands. A

pint of lager is around ¥25. Daily 6pm–3am.
Dengpin Vegetarian Restaurant 登品素食府, dēngpǐn sùshífǔ. 3 Huisha Tiyi Lu ☏0752 2201399. Next to the Xinhua Bookstore and overlooking the East River, this fabulous vegetarian restaurant serves daily buffet meals including faux meat dishes, vegan versions of Hakka delicacies, a salad bar and soft drinks. Meals are a steal at ¥26 per person. Arrive early if you don't want to dine on scraps. Daily 11.30am–2pm and 5.30–8pm.

Zhuhai

珠海, zhūhǎi

Frequently overlooked as simply the gateway to Macau or Shenzhen's little economic sister, the coastal city of **ZHUHAI**, around 150km southwest of Guangzhou, was one of the five original **special economic zones** (SEZs) established to experiment with capitalism in 1978. Though it hasn't quite managed Shenzhen's level of growth, it too has transformed from an obscure southern fishing settlement into a thoroughly modern city. However, a large Cantonese-speaking population and a gentler pace of life give "Pearl Sea", as the name translates, a more localized feel than its big brother across the river. Abounding with green spaces and devoid of the heavy industry that corrupts many manufacturing hubs in the Pearl River Delta, Zhuhai is comparatively unpolluted, its location at the mouth of the river ensuring a welcome, fresh sea breeze. Attractions remain limited, but when the construction of the much-delayed **Hong Kong-Zhuhai–Macau Bridge** is completed (though nobody knows when that will be), the city is likely to see a lot more tourist traffic.

The coastline, which has boldly been termed the **Chinese Riviera**, defines the character of the city. The palm-shaded **Lovers Road** (情侣路, qínglǚ lù) replete with cycle lane, waterfront promenade and coconut vendors, is the principal coastal strip from where most visitors orientate themselves. The forest-coated offshore island **Yeli Dao** (野狸岛, yě lí dǎo), connected to the city by a viaduct, is popular with hikers, while south along the stretch, the **Fisher Girl** (渔夫女孩, yúfū nǚhái) statue is the must-get Zhuhai snap. Just past **Seaside Park** (海滨公园, hǎibīn gōngyuán), **Golden Beach** (金海滩, jīn hǎitān) is a popular, if grubby, commercial bay shadowed by some mid- to high-end hotels. For better sands, many use Zhuhai as a base to explore the **Wanshan Archipelago** (万山群岛, wàn shān qúndǎo).

Beishan

北山, běishān • Beishan Cun, Nanping Town • ⓦ beishan.org.cn/en, ☎ 186 66983616

Located in Nanping Town, about three kilometres northwest of the Macau border, **Beishan**, a restored Qing-dynasty village, is one of the few historical sites in the city. Managed by local artist Xue Wen, who promotes the **Beishan World Music Festival** each spring and the **Bieshan Jazz Festival** each autumn, the village has become the unofficial Zhuhai culture hub, and is regularly used to host touring bands.

The complex is centred on the **Yang Family Ancestral Hall** (杨氏大宗祠, yáng shì dà zōngcí) – now used as a social space – containing wood and jade sculptures and an ancestral shrine. Opposite, the **Kang Zhenjun Temple** (康真君庙, kāngzhēnjūn miào) houses a contemporary art space. Next door, the **Xue Yihan Memorial Hall** (薛翙汉纪念堂, xuēyìhàn jìniàn táng) is dedicated to the memory and artwork of Xue Wen's father, a notable sculptor and printmaker. A Mao-era **theatre** has been restored to its former socialist glory, complete with a red star above the stage.

Jintai Buddhist Temple

金台寺, jīntái sì • Huangyang Shan, Doumen district • ☎ 0756 3342111 • Bus #K4 or #609 from Xiangzhou bus station

Lodged into the forested hillside of Huanyang Mountain (583m) and overlooking a turquoise lake in the predominantly rural district of Doumen, around 40km from Gongbei, **Jintai Buddhist Temple** is a picturesque site. The temple remains a living place of worship, populated by chanting monks and saturated with incense smoke. Rebuilt twenty years ago on the site of a renowned Song-dynasty monastery damaged during Chairman Mao's reign, the faux-Ming architecture doesn't retain much historical value. Nonetheless, the 3000-square-metre complex is worthy of a visit for the enjoyable hike from the foot of the hill and the stunning vistas you can enjoy from the temple.

Wanshan Archipelago

万山群岛, wànshānqúndǎo • Bus or taxi to Xiangzhou Port bus station, then ferry to islands

The **Wanshan Archipelago** comprises **Wailingding** (外伶仃, wài língdīng), **Dong'ao** (东澳, dōng ào), **Hebao** (荷包, hébāo) and **Guishan** (桂山, guìshān). The islands vary greatly in degrees of development – each promotes its own distinctive character. Wailingding is the most developed for tourism, its port cluttered with guesthouses and seafood restaurants, and its hilly interior crisscrossed by hiking paths. The beach is popular with boaters and scuba divers. By contrast, picturesque Guishan retains an unspoilt fishing-village charm – ideal for those wishing to escape the humdrum of modern Zhuhai.

ARRIVAL AND DEPARTURE	**ZHUHAI**

By bus Gongbei bus station (拱北汽车站, gōngběi qìchēzhàn) is next to the border with Macau and runs coaches to all major regional destinations. If heading to Guangzhou, remember to identify which bus station you want (see box below).

Destinations Guangzhou (2–4hr); Shenzhen (3hr).

THE ZHUHAI–MACAU BORDER

The mainland **border with Macau** is at Zhuhai. The crossing point itself is in the Gongbei district (拱北口岸, gōngběi kǒu' àn), located a couple of hundred metres east of Gongbei bus station and Zhuhai train station. The **border crossing** (daily 7am–midnight) is pretty straightforward in either direction, and takes about thirty minutes to an hour depending on how busy it is. Be very careful of your possessions either end, as pickpocketing is rife.

Zhuhai is well connected to Guangzhou via the Guangzhou Intercity Railway to Guangzhou South station (daily 7am–10.35pm, every 10–40min; 50min–1hr 25min; ¥70). Buses between Gongbei bus station and Guangzhou take between two to four hours (daily 6.10am–9.15pm, every 20min; ¥70–80). Six daily **nonstop bus** departures run direct between Macau and the Dashatou bus terminus, right in the centre of Guangzhou (3hr; ¥75).

8

By train The MRT (Guangzhou Intercity Mass Transit) light railway connects Guangzhou South with Zhuhai Station, located near the Macau border in Gongbei district. Some long-distance services also leave from here.

Destinations Guangzhou South (every 10–40min; 50min–1hr 25min); Guilin (1 daily; 3hr 58min); Zhongshan (34 daily; 30min).

By ferry There are regular sailings to and from Zhuhai's Jiuzhou ferry terminal (九州港, jiǔzhōu gǎng) with Shekou in Shenzhen, Hong Kong International Airport, HK-Macau ferry terminal, and China ferry terminal in Kowloon.

On foot You can walk into Zhuhai via the Macau border in Gongbei district (see box, p.517).

ACCOMMODATION

For a long time, accommodation in Zhuhai was geared to hosting **gamblers** on their way to and from Macau, so accommodation mostly consisted of rather tawdry business and luxury hotels. The city is now starting to open up and options are increasing, but it's best to book somewhere before you arrive to guarantee finding somewhere decent.

Jinjiang Inn 锦江之星, jǐnjiāng zhīxīng. 6 Shihua Sanxiang, Jida district ☎0756 3298800. Popular business chain hotel with a few properties throughout the city. The hotel is nondescript but inexpensive and comfortable, plus it's centrally located with easy access to most points of interest. ¥150

Zobon Art Hotel Zhuhai 中邦艺术酒店, zhōngbāng yìshù jiǔdiàn. 33 Qinglu Zhong Lu, Xiangzhou Qu ☎0756 3220333, ⓦzobornarthotel .com/en-us. Above *Starbucks* and overlooking the Pearl River estuary, this locally managed luxury hotel has a boutique feel. It doesn't quite match international brands for service, but is well located and has all you'd expect of a quality hotel including gym and buffet-restaurant. ¥500

EATING AND DRINKING

The raucous bar street Jiuba Jie (酒吧街, jiǔ bā jiē) in Gongbei district is a glut of boozy **karaoke bars** and tacky **theme-restaurants**; several expat bars have begun to redefine the nightscape elsewhere in the city. Zhuhai's principal culinary draw remains its much-celebrated seafood.

De Yue Fang 得月坊, déyuèfāng. Yeli Dao, Mingting Gongyuan, Qinglu Lu ☎0756 2173283. Moored off Yeli Island, this iconic five-storey restaurant inside a classical Chinese ship is a great, if somewhat tacky, place to try out fine Cantonese cuisine. Book ahead and expect to pay ¥100 per head for congee, *dim sum* and fresh seafood, kept in bubbling fish tanks.

London Lounge 伦敦廊, lúndūn láng. Ground Floor, Longzhouwan Gardens, Jida district ☎0756 33236781, ⓦlondonlounge.bar. As the name suggests, this British-style pub dishes out imported ales and warm pies to homesick expats. British staples such as cheesy beans on toast (¥40) dominate the menu, though there are a few Continental alternatives. Major sports tournaments are on

the big screen, and the bar sometimes plays host to local and foreign bands. Though hardly a culture-soaked space, it's a great place to seek out expats and English-speaking Zhuhaiers for some travel tips.

Wanzai Seafood Street 湾仔海鲜街, wānzǎi hǎixiān jiē. Xiangzhou district. Zhuhai's most famous culinary attraction, at this street-long market you can sift through mountains of live crabs, lobsters, prawns and fish, as well as seaweed and any other water-born plant, animal or mineral. After selecting your creature of choice, grab a table at one of a number of indistinguishable restaurants opposite, from where you can order beer and vegetables; your fresh ocean delicacies will be cooked and brought to you. Around ¥80 per person. Taxi ¥15 from downtown. Daily 11am–9pm.

SHOPPING

Gongbei Underground Shopping Plaza 拱北地下广场, gǒngběi dìxià guǎngchǎng. Right below the Macau border crossing. Shenzhen's faux-DVD and knockoff-designer stores might be in decline, but this emporium of all things made-in-China will keep you busy

for hours. There are hundreds of shoebox stores selling everything from electronics to handbags and jade jewellery to handicrafts. There are also some kitschy snack stalls to check out. Daily; hours vary.

Chaozhou

潮州, cháozhōu

In the far east of Guangdong, on the banks of the Han River, **CHAOZHOU** is one of the province's most culturally significant towns, and a splendid place to visit. In addition to some of the most active and manageable street life in southern China, there are some fine historic **monuments**, excellent shopping for local **handicrafts**, and a nostalgically dated small-town ambience to soak up. Chinese-speakers will find that Chaozhou's Teochew **language** is related to Fujian's minnan dialect, different from either Mandarin or Cantonese, though both of these are widely understood.

Brief history
By the time of the Ming dynasty, Chaozhou had reached its zenith as a place of culture and refinement; the origins of many of the town's monuments date back to this time. A spate of tragedies followed, however. After an **anti-Manchu uprising** in 1656, only Chaozhou's monks and their temples were spared the imperial wrath – it's said that the ashes of the 100,000 slaughtered citizens formed several fair-sized hills. The town managed to recover somehow, but was brought down again in the nineteenth century by **famine** and the **Opium Wars**. Half a million desperately impoverished locals fled Chaozhou and eastern Guangdong through the port of Shantou, 40km south, many of them **emigrating** to Southeast Asia, where their descendants comprise a large proportion of Chinese communities in Thailand, Malaysia, Singapore and Indonesia.

The old quarter
Chaozhou's **old quarter** may be past its heyday, but it remains a functioning part of town. The biggest menace here is overenthusiastic pedestrianization and reconstruction along main **Shang Dongping shopping street**; and a boom in souvenir stalls, which has started to displace the original traders. But turn down one of the anonymous alleys running towards Huangcheng Lu and you'll find an engaging warren of narrow streets packed with ageing but well-maintained traditional buildings. Look for old wells, Ming-dynasty stone archways and antique family mansions, protected from the outside world by thick walls and heavy wooden doors, and guarded by mouldings of gods and good-luck symbols. Down in the south of town, **Jiadi Xiang**, a lane west off Taiping Lu, is an immaculate Qing period piece, its flagstones, ornamental porticoes and murals (including a life-sized rendition of a lion-like *qilin* opposite no. 16) restored for the benefit of residents, not tourists.

8

Kaiyuan Temple
开元寺, kāiyuán sì • Eastern end of Kaiyuan Lu • Daily 6am–6pm • ¥5

If you bother with only one sight in Chaozhou, make it the lively **Kaiyuan Temple**, founded in 738 AD and still a magnet for Buddhist pilgrims – though these days they are outnumbered by tourists. Three sets of solid wooden doors open onto courtyards planted with figs and red-flowered phoenix trees, where a pair of Tang-era **stone pillars**, topped with lotus buds, symbolically support the sky. The various halls are pleasantly proportioned, with brightly coloured lions, fish and dragons along the sweeping, low-tiled roof ridges. Off to the west side is a **Guanyin pavilion** with a dozen or more statues of this popular Bodhisattva in all her forms. Another room on the east side is full of bearded Taoist saints holding a *yin–yang* wheel, while the interior of the **main hall** boasts a very intricate, vaulted wooden ceiling and huge brocade banners almost obscuring a golden Buddhist trinity.

Xu Fuma Fu
许驸马府, xǔ fùmǎ fǔ • 4 Dongfucheng • Daily 8.30am–5.30pm • ¥20 • ☎ 0768 2250021

Less touristy than Kaiyuan Temple, **Xu Fuma Fu** is a well-preserved family mansion on an alley running parallel just behind Zhongshan Lu, 100m west of the junction with Wenxing Lu. Dating in part to the Song dynasty, its peaceful wooden interior, darkened by age, is festooned with red lanterns, some rooms containing period furniture (and a couple of waxworks). There's also a small courtyard garden.

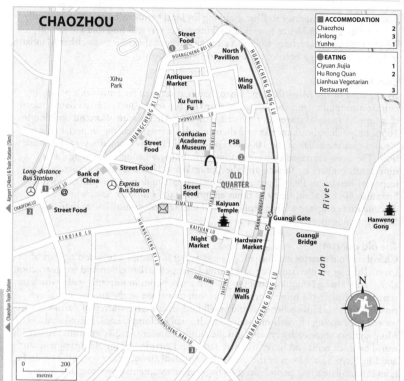

Fenghuang Pagoda

Confucian academy and museum

海阳县儒学宫, hǎiyángxiàn rúxuégōng • Daily 8am–5pm • ¥10 • ☏ 0768 2236199

Wander south down Wenxing Lu and you'll come to both a Ming-style memorial archway and a former **Confucian academy** – now a newly renovated **museum**, full of prewar photos of town. Tall trees offer cool shade in the gardens, good for a stroll and to appreciate the architecture and simple tranquillity of the site.

The town walls

Daily 8.30am–5.30pm • ¥20

Running north to south by the west bank of the Han River, the **old town walls** are seven metres high and almost as thick. These were only ever breached twice in Chaozhou's history, and more than 1500m still stand in good condition. The walls run from the **North Pavilion** (北亭, běitíng), first constructed during the Song dynasty, down as far as Huangcheng Nan Lu. There are access steps at several points along the wall, including above the main **Guangji Gate** (广济门, guǎngjì mén), where there's also a guard tower which houses an **exhibition** on the history of the adjacent Guangji Bridge.

Guangji Bridge

广济桥, guǎng jì qiáo • Daily 9am–5pm • ¥50

Piles for the **Guangji Bridge** (also known as Xiangzi Bridge), a 500m-long span over the Han River, were sunk during the Southern Song dynasty in the twelfth century, and the wooden floating section of pontoons in the middle (which can be removed to allow the passage of large vessels) was an innovation in bridge-building. Restored in 2009

SHOPPING IN CHAOZHOU

Chaozhou is a great place to buy traditional **arts and crafts**. For something a bit unusual, the **hardware market**, just inside the Guangji Gate along Shangdong Ping Lu, has razor-sharp cleavers, kitchenware and old-style brass door rings. **Temple trinkets**, from banners to brass bells, ceramic statues – made at the nearby hamlet of Fengxi – and massive iron incense-burners, are sold at numerous stores in the vicinity of Kaiyuan Temple. It's also a good area to find silk embroideries and ceramic tea sets – in fact Chaozhou considers itself the **ceramics** capital of China, and prices here are low.

For those who enjoy haggling, an impromptu **antiques market** springs up most mornings along the pavement of Huangcheng Lu outside Xihu Park, and in the evenings a mostly clothing **night market** competes with motorcyclists and cars for road space along Kaiyuan Lu.

after years of work, it is an impressive sight, with small pavilions built over each stone pier so that it resembles a street, the line of eighteen boat pontoons floating in the middle, and an iron statue of a cow on the other side to ward off floods. It looks so splendid that it has become a symbol for the city, and is now rated as one of China's four most famous ancient bridges.

ARRIVAL AND DEPARTURE
CHAOZHOU

BY PLANE

Jieyang Chaoshan Airport (揭阳潮汕机场, jiēyáng cháoshàn jīchǎng) is 24km from the centre of town and has services to most major Chinese cities as well as Bangkok, Seoul, Hong Kong and Singapore. An airport bus (¥12) runs to the *Chaozhou Hotel* and long-distance bus station every hour from 6am till an hour before the last flight. A taxi costs about ¥80 on the meter but you may be charged a stiff surcharge for the driver returning empty.

Destinations Beijing (3hr); Chengdu (2hr 40min); Guangzhou (1hr).

BY TRAIN

CRH High-speed trains stop at Chaoshan station (潮汕站, cháoshàn zhàn), shared between Chaozhou and neighbouring Shantou. Located 15km from Chaozhou and 30km from Shantou, it's connected by a fast bus service that leaves from just outside the station to both the city centres.

Destinations Shenzhen (64 daily; 2hr 15min); Xiamen

(31 daily; 1hr 30min).

Other services Chaozhou Station (潮州火车站, cháozhōu huǒchē zhàn) is about 5km northwest; on exiting, walk straight ahead out of the station and, taking your life in your hands, cross the main road to catch city buses #1 or #13 (daily 6.30am–8.30pm; ¥2), which run down to Huangcheng Lu. A taxi costs around ¥15. The station ticket office opens daily 6–11.30am & 1.30–5.30pm, or try the travel agency in the lobby of the *Yunhe Dajiudian*.

Destinations Guangzhou (3 daily; 6hr 30min); Meizhou (2 daily; 2hr).

BY BUS

Long-distance buses stop just west of the centre on Chaofeng Lu, with traffic to Guangzhou, Shenzhen and Fujian. Express coaches east and west along the coastal road use a private station on Huangcheng Xi Lu.

Destinations Guangzhou (6hr); Shenzhen (5hr); Xiamen (5hr 30min).

GETTING AROUND

By rickshaw Everything in the old town is within walking distance, though motor- and cycle-rickshaws – the only vehicles able to negotiate the older backstreets – are

abundant. Agree a price before you get on; ¥7–10 should cover most old-town journeys.

ACCOMMODATION

Cheaper places to stay are clustered around the bus station, but few good budget options are willing to take foreigners.

Chaozhou 潮州宾馆, cháozhōu bīnguǎn. Opposite the long-distance bus station ☎0768 2333333, ⓦchaozhouhotel.com. The smartest hotel in town, a four-star with an impressive marble-floored lobby and many English-speaking staff. Large, tastefully decorated

and clean rooms with bathrooms. Has a good restaurant, plus a classical teahouse. **¥368**

Jinlong 金龙宾馆, jīnlóng bīnguǎn. Huangcheng Nan Lu ☎0768 2383888, ⓦwww.jinlong-hotel.com. Smart business option at the bottom of the old town, not

8

quite as swanky as the *Chaozhou* hotel, but makes a good effort. Clean, comfortable and handily placed for reaching the town centre. Its lobby has a bar. **¥318**

Yunhe 云和大酒店, yúnhé dàjiǔdiàn. 26 Xihe Lu ☎0768 2136128. Don't be fooled by the Doric columns outside the marble lobby with its low-slung and dazzling chandelier: the rooms here are far from five-star, but are comfortable and very good value nonetheless, with a certain kitsch charm. **¥160**

EATING

Chaozhou's cooking style focuses on light and sweet flavours, with an emphasis on the freshness of ingredients. **Seafood** is a major feature, while local steamed and roast **goose**, flavoured here with sour plum, rivals a good Peking duck. Less traditionally, many dishes receive a garnish of fried **garlic chips**, an idea sparked from migrants returning from Southeast Asia. There's a good string of restaurants on Huangcheng Xi Lu, overlooking Xihu Park; but wherever you are, and at pretty much any time of the day or night, you will never be far from street stalls doling out hotpots and noodles for just a few yuan.

★**Ciyuan Jiujia** 瓷苑酒家, cíyuàn jiǔjiā. Huangcheng Xi Lu ☎0768 2253990. Very popular, unpretentious restaurant with superb goose (¥100–200 for a whole bird, or ¥60 for a portion with vinegar and garlic dip), crispy-fried squid, steamed crab, fish ball soup, fried spinach and a selection of *dim sum*. No English menu, so take a dictionary. Daily 9am–2pm & 4–8pm.

★**Hu Rong Quan** 胡荣泉, húróng quán. 140 Taiping Lu ☎131 92132573. This bakery, specializing in mooncakes, makes the best spring rolls you'll ever eat, stuffed with spring onions, yellow beans, mushrooms and a little meat. They also have some tables outside where you can enjoy their wonderful ¥10 wonton soups. Daily 8.30am–11pm.

Lianhua Vegetarian Restaurant 莲华素食府, liánhuá sùshífǔ. At the back of the square opposite Kaiyuan Temple ☎0768 2238033. Meat-free restaurant, where a delicious, enormous six-dish set meal, including sweet-and-sour "ribs" and "kebabs", will set you back about ¥60 for two. Beggars hang around the entrance, but they're good-natured and not persistent. Daily 11am–2pm & 5–8.30pm.

Zhaoqing

肇庆, zhàoqìng

Road, rail and river converge 110km west of Guangzhou at **ZHAOQING**, a smart, modern city founded as a Qin garrison town to plug a gap in the line of a low mountain range. The first Europeans settled here as early as the sixteenth century, when the Jesuit priest **Matteo Ricci** spent six years in Zhaoqing using Taoist and Buddhist parallels to make his Christian teachings palatable. Emperor Wanli eventually invited Ricci to Beijing, where he died in 1610, having published numerous religious tracts. Since the tenth century, however, the Chinese have known Zhaoqing for the limestone hills comprising the adjacent **Seven Stars Park**. Swathed in mists and surrounded by lakes, the mounds lack the scale of Guilin's peaks, but make for an enjoyable wander, as do the surprisingly thick forests at **Dinghu Shan**, just a short local bus ride away from town.

Chongxi Ta and Matteo Ricci Museum

崇禧塔, chóngxǐ tǎ • Eastern end of Jiangbin Lu • Wed–Sun 8.30am–4.30pm • ¥20 • ☎0758 2262644

Overlooking the river, **Chongxi Ta** is a Ming pagoda which, at 57.5m, is the tallest in the province. The views from the top – which is a lot higher than it looks from the ground – take in cargo boats and the red cliffs across the river surmounted by two more pagodas of similar vintage. Also part of the complex, the **Matteo Ricci Museum** is an example of one of those Chinese museums that have absolutely no genuine artefacts at all, but it is quite informative about the Italian cleric's journey nonetheless, and worth a wander round.

The city walls

Zhaoqing's most interesting quarter surrounds solid sections of the ancient **city walls** on Jianshe Lu, which you can climb and follow around to Chengzong Lu; head north from here along Kangle Zhong Lu and enter a tight knot of early twentieth-century lanes, shops and homes – all typically busy and noisy – along with a brightly tiled **mosque** (清真寺, qīngzhēn sì); there's also a row of plant and bonsai stalls west of the mosque on Jianshe Lu.

Plum Monastery

梅庵, méi'ān • Mei'an Lu • Daily 8.30am–4pm • Free; you must show your passport

West of the walls and on the edge of town, the small **Plum Monastery** was established in 996 AD and has close associations with Huineng, the sixth patriarch of Chan Buddhism. It was Huineng who planted a plum tree here, giving the temple its name, and he is remembered in various paintings and sculptures around the complex. As you get deeper inside, the rumble of the road recedes and you can enjoy its pleasant interior or goggle at the "long-lived tortoise" enclosure.

Seven Stars Park

七星岩公园, qīxīngyán gōngyuán • Daily 7.30am–5.30pm • ¥60 • Bus #19 from opposite the bus station (¥1)

Arranged in the shape of the Big Dipper and said to be fallen stars, the seven isolated limestone pinnacles that make up **Seven Stars Park** rise 2km north of town on the far side of **Star Lake** (星湖, xīnghú). The crags are quite modest, named after objects they resemble – Chanchu (Toad), Tianzhu (Heavenly Pillar), Shizhang (Stone Hand) and so on. An interlocking network of arched bridges, pathways, graffiti-embellished caves and willows makes for a pleasantly romantic two-hour stroll.

Dinghu Shan

鼎湖山, dīnghú shān • Daily 7am–6.30pm • Entry ¥60; Butterfly Valley ¥30; minibus to Boarding Park ¥20 • ☏ 07958 2621332, ⓦ dinghushan.net • Bus #21 (¥2) every 30min from the stop between HSBC and the main bus station; last bus back to Zhaoqing at 10pm

Twenty kilometres east of Zhaoqing, the thickly forested mountains at **Dinghu Shan** were declared China's first national park way back in 1956. With well-formed paths giving access to a waterfall, temples and plenty of trees, the small area open to the public gets particularly crowded at the weekends, but at other times Dinghu Shan makes an excellent half-day out – particularly in summer, when the mountain is cooler than Zhaoqing. Don't bother with accommodation here though, as rooms are ridiculously expensive.

8

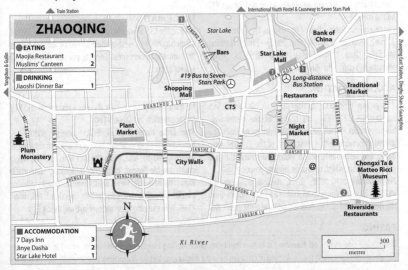

ZHAOQING'S INKSTONES

Produced for more than a thousand years, Zhaoqing's Duanzhou **inkstones** are some of the finest in China – you can buy them at stationery and art stores around town, or at the souvenir shops at the Duanzhou Lu/Tianning Lu intersection.

Around the park

It's best to make an anticlockwise circuit of the park: from the gate, either walk or take an open minibus up to the top at **Baoding Park** which overlooks a very pretty lake. After admiring the lake from above, follow the road down to the right where traditional boats can take you across the water to **Butterfly Valley** which, unsurprisingly, is full of butterflies.

The road descends from the lake to the large **Qingyun Temple** (清云寺, qīngyún sì), traditionally one of the four most famous in southern China, which has several vegetarian restaurants. Walking down through the temple complex, you emerge onto a forest path which winds upwards at a stream, which you can follow up to a 30m-high **waterfall**. The plunge pool here has been excavated and turned into a swimming area. Following the stream down, there's a very atmospheric **cave temple** (¥1 donation expected), and then eventually the path ends up back at the gates. It's a couple of hours' walk in total, but if you're not planning to stay the night, be careful not to linger too long.

ARRIVAL AND INFORMATION   ZHAOQING

BY TRAIN

Buy train tickets in town at the CTS office (see below) and save yourself a journey out to the stations.

Zhaoqing East (肇庆东站, zhàoqìng dōngzhàn), east of the centre, is a new station handling CRH to Guangzhou, Guilin and Nanning.

Destinations Guangzhou South (41 daily; 35–45min); Guilin (21 daily; 2hr 15min); Nanning (24 daily; 3hr).

Zhaoqing Station (肇庆火车站, zhàoqìng huǒchē zhàn), 4km northwest of town, handles both CRH and slower trains. Bus #1 runs into town; a taxi costs about ¥17 on the meter.

Destinations Guangzhou (79 daily; 1hr 30min–2hr 30min); Haikou (5 daily; 9hr 30min–11hr); Nanning (4 daily; 10hr–10hr 40min); Sanya (2 daily; 14hr); Shenzhen (5 daily; 4hr–5hr 30min).

BY BUS

Zaoqing Yueyun bus station (肇庆粤运汽车客站, zhàoqìng yuèyùn qìchē kèzhàn, ⓦzhqyy.com) is at 17 Duanzhou Si Lu, close to Star Lake Mall, with long-distance connections to just about everywhere between Guilin and Guangzhou – check which of Guangzhou's bus stations you're headed for when you buy a ticket.

Destinations Guangzhou (2hr); Guilin (10hr); Haikou (12hr); Qingyuan (5hr); Yangshuo (8hr 30min).

INFORMATION

Staff at the CTS office (daily 8am–9pm; ☏0758 222 9908, ⓦzqcts.com), just west of the *Huaqiao Dasha*, are helpful and some members speak English; you can also buy train tickets here.

ACCOMMODATION

7 Days Inn 七天酒店, qī tiān jiǔ diàn. 40 Jianshe San Lu ☏0758 2271777. This branch of the nationwide business chain, notwithstanding the lime green walls, is a decent affordable option. Just north of the Xi River, with banks and restaurants within walking distance, this is a great base from which to explore the city proper. ¥160

Jinye Dasha 金叶大厦, jīnyè dàshà. 6 Jianshe Lu ☏0758 222133. Fairly comfortable and just a block from the river, so many of the upper rooms have great views. Not

far from the night market, it also has a restaurant and KTV. Discounts often available. ¥180

Star Lake Hotel 湖星级酒店, húxīngjí jiǔdiàn. 37 Duanzhou Si Lu ☏0758 2211888, ⓦstarlakehotel-zq.com. Towering over the lake, this is the best hotel in town, with a stylish marble-floored lobby and sumptuous, comfortable rooms that have great views. Boasts three restaurants including a buffet-style Western one on the 29th floor (lunch ¥88, dinner ¥168), with stunning views out over lake and river. ¥538

EATING

Head down side streets off **Jianshe Lu** to find numerous places selling *zongzi*, sandpots (stews served in earthenware pots) and light Cantonese meals. A string of canteens near the **night market** on **Wenming Lu** (文明路, wénmíng lù) bustles every evening, but for something more refined check out the cluster of Cantonese fish restaurants with river views at the end of **Gongnong Lu**.

Maojia Restaurant 毛家饭店, máojiā fàndiàn. 4th Floor, Star Lake Mall, Duanzhou Si Lu ☎0758 2213998, ⓦmaojiahotel.com. Part of a popular restaurant chain dedicated to Chairman Mao; the hero's smiling face adorns the walls of this surprisingly stylish, modern branch. The chefs specialize in spicy Hunanese dishes, though the Cantonese food is very good too, especially the barbecued pork. It's good value, with mains from ¥30. Daily 10am–1pm.

Muslims' Canteen 清真饭店, qīngzhēn fàndiàn. 2 Jiangbin Lu ☎0758 2557298. For something different, try this spacious, airy canteen next to the river, which serves up typical Hui food – lamb skewers (羊肉串, yángròu chuàn), beef noodles (牛肉面, niúròu miàn), flat bread (扁平面包, biǎnpíng miànbāo) et al – at around ¥50 a head. The only English in here is on the Coca-Cola signs. Daily 8am–8.30pm.

DRINKING

Zhaoqing's scant nightlife revolves around the few bars on **Xinghu Xi Lu** and riverfront **Jiangbin Lu**.

Jiaoshi Dinner Bar 教士餐吧, jiàoshì cānbā. 19 Xinghu Xi Lu ☎0758 2806666. One of a few bars along this road, serving up a German ambience and beer. Pretty

laidback, the owner speaks a little English, it has the obligatory KTV in the back, and a nice view over the lake. Daily 7.30pm–2am.

Hainan Island

海南岛, hǎinán dǎo

Rising out of the South China Sea between Guangdong and Vietnam, **Hainan Island** marks the southernmost undisputed limit of Chinese authority. A 300km-broad spread of beaches and mountain scenery, the island, alas, reveals the effects of exploitation of its natural environment.

Haikou, Hainan's capital, is of importance only as a transit point; the most obvious reason to visit the island is to flop down on the sandy **beaches** near the southern city of **Sanya**, warm year-round, where you can sip on the fresh coconuts that have earned Hainan its much overused "Coconut Island" moniker. Frankly, there's not a whole lot more to the place, though anyone hooked on marine adventure sports can explore Hainan's emerging **scuba diving and surfing** potential.

Hainan's extremely hot and humid **wet season** lasts from June to October. It's better to visit between February and April, when the climate is generally dry and tropically moderate, and prices reduce considerably.

Brief history

Today a province in its own right, Hainan was historically the "Tail of the Dragon", an enigmatic full stop to the Han empire. Chinese settlements were established around the coast in 200 AD, but for millennia the island was seen as being inhabited by unspeakably backward races, only fit to be a place of exile. So complete was Hainan's isolation that, as recently as the 1930s, ethnic **Li**, who first settled here over two thousand years ago, still lived a hunter-gatherer existence in the interior highlands.

Modern Hainan is no primitive paradise, however. The Japanese occupied the island in 1939, and by the end of the war had executed a full third of Hainan's male population in retaliation for raids on their forces by Chinese guerrillas. Ecological decline began in the 1950s during the Great Leap Forward, and escalated through the 1960s with the **clearing of Hainan's forests** to plant cash crops.

With very little industry to speak of, outside of agriculture, tourism is the principal source of income for most islanders these days, especially since the island has been promoted as China's tropical holiday destination.

8

Haikou

海口, hǎikǒu

Business centre, main port and first stop for newly arrived holidaymakers, **HAIKOU** has all the atmosphere of a typical Southeast Asian city. There's a smattering of colonial architecture, a few parks and monuments, modern skyscrapers and broad streets choked with traffic and pedestrians. An indication of the ethos driving Haikou is that you meet few locals: officials, businessmen and tourists are all from the mainland, while Li, Miao and Hakka flock from southern Hainan to hawk trinkets, as do the Hui women selling betel nuts – all drawn by the opportunities that the city represents. More than anything, Haikou is a truly tropical city: humid, laidback, pleasantly shabby and complete with palm-lined streets, something particularly striking if you've just emerged from a miserable northern Chinese winter. It doesn't have a great deal to offer in sights, but you might end up having to stay overnight in transit.

The Old Quarter

Haikou's **old quarter**, boxed in by Bo'ai Bei Lu, Datong Lu and pedestrianized Deshengsha Lu, is the best area to stroll through, with its grid of restored Nationalist-era architecture housing stores and businesses. **Jiefang Lu** and pedestrianized **Zhongshan Lu** are the main streets here, especially lively in the evening when they're well lit and bursting with people out shopping, eating and

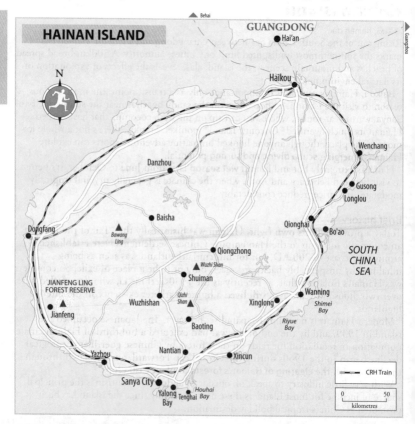

socializing; there's also a busy **market** west of Xinhua Lu. Otherwise, **Haikou Park** (海口公园, hǎikǒu gōngyuán) and its lake are small but quite pleasant, particularly in the early morning when the park comes to life with martial-art sessions, dancing and games of badminton.

Five Officials' Temple

五公祠, wǔgōng cí • Daily 8am–6pm • ¥20 • ☎ 0898 65353047 • Bus #1, #11, #202

A few kilometres southeast of the centre, **Five Officials' Temple** is a brightly decorated complex built in 1889 to honour Li Deyu, Li Gang, Li Guang, Hu Chuan and Zhao Ding, Tang men of letters who were banished here after criticizing their government. Another hall in the grounds commemorates Hainan's most famous exile, the Sichuanese governor-poet **Su Dongpo**, who lived in the island's northwest between 1097 and 1100 and died on his way back to the imperial court the following year.

Hainan Provincial Museum

海南省博物馆, hǎinánshěng bówùguǎn • 68 Guoxing Lu • Tues–Sun 9am–5pm • Free; you must show your passport • ☎ 0898 65238880 • Buses #29, #33, #34, #43 or #45

Despite a large, modern and imposing exterior, **Hainan Provincial Museum** manages to be much smaller on the inside than it appears from without. Still, it's free and there are three very interesting and informative exhibitions on the second floor about the history and culture of Hainan, as well as one about the tribal minorities, that are well worth an hour's browsing.

8

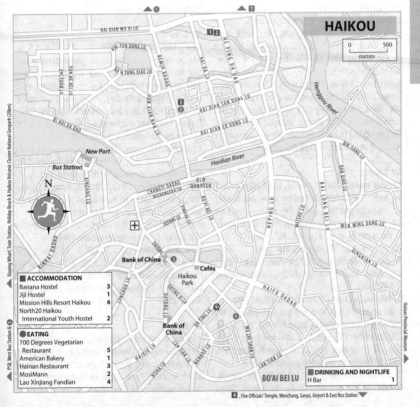

HAIKOU

■ ACCOMMODATION	
Banana Hostel	3
Jiji Hostel	1
Mission Hills Resort Haikou	4
North20 Haikou International Youth Hostel	2

● EATING	
700 Degrees Vegetarian Restaurant	5
American Bakery	1
Hainan Restaurant	3
MosiMann	2
Lao Xinjiang Fandian	4

■ DRINKING AND NIGHTLIFE	
H Bar	1

Holiday Beach

假日海滩, jiàrì hǎitān • Bus #37 heading west from the clock tower on Changti Dadao, near Renmin Dadao Bridge; also served by buses #24 or #40; a taxi is around ¥50

If touring Haikou's spattering of historical sites seems a bit too serious, Haikou boasts its own stretch of golden sand in the form of 6km-long **Holiday Beach** to the west of the city. While a good place to laze, the beach also has plenty of activities with windsurfers, kayaks and jet skis all for hire. It can get a bit crowded close to town, but keep heading west and the crowds thin out.

Haikou Volcanic Cluster National Geopark

海口石山火山群国家地质公园, hǎikǒu shíshān huǒshān qún guó jiā dìzhì gōngyuán • 142 Xian Dao, Xiuying Qu • Daily 8.30am–5.30pm • ¥60

Around 20km southwest of Haikou, the verdant **Haikou Volcanic Cluster National Geopark** offers an easy retreat from the concrete jungle Haikou is fast becoming. The park comprises forty dormant **volcanoes** dating from the Holocene period some ten thousand years ago, as well as around thirty **caves**. Most visitors come here for a gentle **hike** concluding with a walk around the rim of the park's largest volcano, rather than to see the caves, which contain snack kiosks and some paltry Chinese-language exhibitions on the local geology.

ARRIVAL AND DEPARTURE	HAIKOU

Aside from flying in, you can buy tickets for ferry-bus-train combinations between Haikou and various cities on the mainland.

8

BY PLANE

Haikou airport (海口美兰国际机场, hǎikǒu měilán guójì jīchǎng) is 25km southeast of town; shuttle buses (every 30min; 5.30am–9pm; ¥15) run between here and the *Civil Aviation* hotel on Haixiu Dong Lu. A taxi takes around 30min to the town centre (¥50–60 on the meter).
Destinations Beijing (3hr 35min); Changsha (2hr); Chengdu (2hr 25min); Guangzhou (1hr 15min); Guilin (1hr 30min); Hong Kong (1hr 35min); Kunming (1hr 55min); Nanjing (2hr 50min); Shanghai (2hr 45min); Shenzhen (1hr 15min); Wuhan (2hr 20min); Xiamen (1hr 50min); Xi'an (2hr 50min); Zhuhai (55min).

BY TRAIN

Regular trains Haikou Station lies about 20km west of the centre, not far from the western shore, and handles services to the mainland – when they put the entire train onto a boat – as well as some high-speed rail. It's connected to the centre by buses #28, #35, #37, #40 or #57 (¥3; 50min), while taxis (¥60–80) are a little faster.
Destinations Beijing (1 daily; 32hr); Guangzhou (3 daily; 10hr 30min–12hr); Sanya (6 daily; 2hr 30min); Shanghai (1 daily; 34hr).
CRH Haikou East train station, which lies about 14km east of the city centre, is Haikou's principal high-speed railway station. It can be reached by buses #12, #38, #49, #53 or #56. The island's CRH lines are divided into the older East Ring and newer West Ring, which connects Haikou with Sanya by forming an entire loop around the island.
Destinations Dongfang City (18 daily; 1hr 20min); Qionghai/Bo'ao (28 daily; 45min–1hr 16min); Sanya (22 daily; 1hr 24min–2hr).

BY BUS

New bus station (海口汽车总站新港汽车站, hǎikǒu qìchē zǒng zhàn xīngǎng qìchē zhàn) near the harbour handles the bulk of mainland traffic – you'll find standard and luxury buses to destinations as far afield as Chongqing, Nanning, Shenzhen and Guangzhou, and tickets include ferry costs – as well as buses to Sanya, Tongshi, Wuzhishan and Wenchang. The station is a ¥20 taxi ride from the centre, or take bus #20.
Destinations Chongqing (28hr); Guangzhou (12hr); Guilin (12hr); Sanya (3–5hr); Shenzhen (15hr); Tongshi (2hr); Wenchang (1hr); Wuzhishan (3hr); Zhanjiang (5hr).
East bus station (海口汽车东站, hǎikǒu qìchē dōngzhàn), 2km down Haifu Dadao (bus #11 or #44), serves smaller destinations on the east coast.
Destinations Dongpo (2hr); Lingshui (2hr 30min; Qionghai (2hr 30min); Sanya (3–5hr); Wenchang (1hr).
West bus station (海口汽车西站, hǎikǒu qìchē xīzhàn), 5km out on Haixiu Xi Lu (bus #17 or #30), serves smaller destinations on the west coast.
Destinations Dongcheng (2hr 30min); Haitou (2hr); Haiwei (2hr).

BY FERRY

Most hotels and travel agencies in town can make ferry bookings, with a day's warning. Using them is a good idea, since services change frequently and both ports are a way out of the centre. There's usually no trouble getting a seat, though rough seas can suspend services.

The New Port (新港, xīngǎng; ☎ 0898 66210596) is north of Changti Dadao on Xingang Lu; the ticket office opens daily 9am–4pm and bus #6 runs to the centre. The terminal for ordinary and fast ferries (¥30/90) to Hai'an at Guangdong's southernmost tip, is where you catch a bus for the 150km run to Zhanjiang city (湛江, zhànjiāng), whose long-distance bus and train stations cover southern China.

Destinations Hai'an (9 daily); 1hr–1hr 30min).

Xiuying Wharf (秀英港, xiùyīng gǎng;

☎ 0898 66210596; Binhai Dadao, 5km west of the city on the #7 bus route to the centre). Its ticket office has unpredictable opening hours, so it's best to talk to a travel agent. Ferries from here service Guangzhou (berth ¥160–360) and Beihai in Guangxi province (seat ¥140, berth ¥160–500), from where there are buses and trains to Nanning, the provincial capital.

Destinations Beihai (2 daily; 12hr); Guangzhou (3 weekly; 24hr).

INFORMATION AND GETTING AROUND

Tourist information There's a general lack of tourist information in Haikou, with most agencies only geared to getting you to Sanya as fast as possible. Online you can try ⓦ en.visithainan.gov.cn, or call the multilingual, toll-free Hainan tourism hotline (☎ 8008 88686).

Maps Detailed maps of the island, including even minor sights marked in English, are sold by hawkers and

kiosks (¥7–10).

By taxi Taxis are so absurdly plentiful that you have only to pause on the street for one to pull up instantly. The safest bet is to insist on the meter, which starts at ¥10 for a ride; it's also possible to negotiate fares in advance, however, and, if done well, you may pay only two-thirds of the meter rate (check with your hotel how much trips should cost).

ACCOMMODATION

There's plenty of central accommodation in Haikou. Many of the budget hotels are located on Haidian Island. Room rates are always flexible; in summer, ensure that a/c is part of the bargain.

★**Banana Hostel** 巴那那青年旅舍, bānànà qīngnián lǚshè. On east side of Renmin Ave, just north of the junction with Sandong Lu, in the north of town ☎ 0898 66286780, ⓦ haikouhostel.com. This IYHF establishment is one of only a few places in town geared towards budget travellers. Spacious, clean rooms are supplemented with a small bar serving cold beer and fantastic pizzas. Though staff are decidedly listless, the British owner is a well of information. Hidden down an alley, by a black-and-red restaurant, it's slightly hard to find – call them if you get lost. Dorms ¥50, doubles ¥138

Jiji Hostel 骑迹, jìjì. 7 Fuhai Huayuan, Fuhai Lu, Haidian Island ☎ 0898 32695676. Clean and simple Northern Chinese-operated hostel focusing heavily on cyclists and cycling. Mountain bikes for hire and cross-island tours run regularly to their sister hostel in Sanya. Dorm ¥50, doubles ¥150

Mission Hills Resort Haikou 海口观澜湖旅游度假区, hǎikǒu guānlán hú lǚyóu dùjià qū. 1 Mission

Hills Blvd ☎ 0898 6868 3888, ⓦ missionhillschina.com /en-US/haikou. This lavish hotel, about 20km east of the Volcanic Cluster National Geopark, has an affiliated golf club and targets A-list clientele with luxury suites. There's a business centre and kids club as well as a spa and boutique. If it's out of your budget, you can still visit to relax in volcanic mineral hot springs, of which there are over two hundred. It's a worthy day-trip: one "zone" of five springs costs ¥98. Doubles ¥899

North 20 Haikou International Youth Hostel 北纬 海口国际青年旅舍, běiwěi hǎikǒu guójì qīngnián lǚshè. Building 18, Fuhai Villa, Fuhai Rd ☎ 0898 66184115. Deriving its name from Haikou's location 20 degrees north of the equator, this youth hostel, overlooking the slightly foul-smelling Baisha River, is more oriented to the local backpacking crowd than foreigners. However, if other hostels are sold out it's an adequate budget option, clean-ish and a good place to meet Chinese travellers. Dorms ¥50, doubles ¥100

EATING

Perhaps because Haikou has many migrants from the mainland, food here is not as exotic as you might have hoped. But do try to check out a **Laoba Cha** (老爸茶, qí lóu xiǎo chī jiē) joint, where the Hainaese take tea and snacks in what amounts to an island version of Cantonese *dim sum*. The highest concentration of restaurants is in the old quarter along Jiefang Lu, but if you just want to pick and mix, make your way to the Qilou Snack St (骑楼小吃街, qí lóu xiǎo chī jiē).

700 Degrees Vegetarian Restaurant 700度純素生活馆, qībǎi dù chún sù shēng huó guǎn. 25 Jinyu dong Lu, in Longhua district ☎ 400 9968 700. With a contemporary old-meets-new design, this meat-free

restaurant has more to offer than the standard temple-affiliated fake-meat restaurants. Propagating a healthy (as well as a spiritual) life, the cuisine here is gutter oil and MSG free and there's no smoking or alcohol, so it's ideal not

8

just for veggies and Buddhists but anyone who feels like a detox. Great soups at ¥17; main dishes average around ¥40. Daily 11am–8pm.

American Bakery First Floor, outside Jiangnan Xiaoqu, Heping Dadao, Haidian Island ☏ 0898 62270150. In the grand tradition of expats turning their hobbies into vocations, this place combines home-baked bread with Brazilian jujitsu classes. It's a little odd, but you'd be hard pressed to find better bread or more authentic coffee (¥17 to ¥25) in the city. Mon–Sat 11am–midnight.

Hainan Restaurant 琼菜坊, qióngcàifāng. 17 Datong Lu, close to the Hainan Overseas Chinese Hotel ☏ 0898 66522933. As implied by the name, there are lots of Hainan speciality foods on offer here, and the menu is heavy on the seafood. There's no English menu, but plenty of pictures to point at. Mains will set you back ¥30–50. Daily 11.30am–10.30pm.

MosiMann 莫西曼美食吧, mòxīmànměishíbā. 17-5 Jinghai Garden, Renmin Ave, Haidian Island ☏ 0898 66276798. This local effort at steak, sports and all things Americana is not bad. Stodgy staples like potato wedges for ¥25 and beef steak sandwiches at ¥40, in addition to a pool table and draft beer, has made the place popular with local expats. Daily 10.30am–midnight.

Lao Xinjiang Fandian 老新疆饭店, lǎoxīnjiāng fàndiàn. 23 Wuzhishan Lu ☏ 0898 65375027. Muslim restaurant selling hearty Uyghur fare – beef noodles, mutton and heavily seasoned lamb, as well as chicken kebabs, all of which you can pick from a photo menu. Mains from ¥35. Daily 9am–9pm.

DRINKING AND NIGHTLIFE

Your best bet for nightlife is the Western-style Binjiang Hai'an Bar St (滨江海岸酒吧街, bīnjiāng hǎi'àn jiǔbā jiē), just north of the river and easiest reached by taxi.

H Bar 诃吧, hēbā. 3F Binjiang Haian Bar St ☏ 0898 66253415. Probably the most foreigner-friendly place in the complex, with Western residents often frequenting at the weekend, and every Wed when they have a ladies' night. Live guitar music most days, and BBQ snacks served. Daily 7.30pm–2am.

SHOPPING

Like all major Chinese cities, Haikou has undergone a consumer revolution in recent years, and **shopping malls** housing brand-name stores are now plentiful. However, if you're after **local produce**, try the streets around **Zhongshan Lu**, where shops sell numerous coconut-flavoured items (including coffee, wafers and tea), palm sugar and betel nut; **clothing sections** also stock Hainan shirts, which differ from their Hawaiian counterparts in their use of dragons instead of palm trees on bright backgrounds. Whole shark skins – like sandpaper, dried jellyfish and other maritime curiosities in the shops along **Jiefang Lu** are also worth a look.

DIRECTORY

Hospital Hainan People's Hospital, Yangzao Lu, just west off Longhua Lu ☏ 0898 6226666.

Post office The main post office, with parcel post service, is on Jiefang Lu (Mon–Sat 8am–6pm).

Visa extensions The Foreign Affairs Department (Mon–Sat 9am–noon & 3–5.30pm; ☏ 0898 68530977) is at the beginning of Jinlong Lu, the continuation of the southern end of Longhua Lu; catch bus #21 from Renmin Dadao. Be warned that they can be ridiculously heavy-handed to those applying for visa extensions – go elsewhere unless it's an emergency.

The east coast

If you can resist heading straight to Sanya, it's worthwhile spending a couple of days hopping down along Hainan's **east coast** – home to some of the few surfable beaches in China, plus some relatively uncrowded sand, at **Qishuiwan** and **Shimei Bay**. This stretch of coast is easily accessible from the main towns, all of which are served by express buses and have stops on the **high-speed rail-line** to Sanya – minibuses or taxis can get you between the stations and the coast. Be warned that unless a resort is maintaining the local beach, it will be none too clean, so finding your own undiscovered strip of tropical paradise is unlikely.

Wenchang

文昌, wénchāng • CRH from Haikou (30min; ¥19) and Sanya (1hr 20min; ¥64)

The pleasant, if unremarkable small town of **Wenchang**, connected to Sanya and Haikou by the East Coast CRH line, is generally used as a jumping-off point by those heading to beaches like Gusong. In many ways it's just a mini Haikou, predominantly populated by Han Chinese.

Old town

Wenchang's mercantile ancestors began to settle the island's eastern periphery during the Tang dynasty and continued to come over several waves of migration through the following centuries. Testament to this lineage is Wenchang's well-preserved **old town** located near the river. This eclectic neighbourhood is centred on **Lao Jie** (老街, lǎo jiē), an old shopping street replete with renovated Nationalist-era arcades, a spattering of temples, ancestral halls and Laoba tea canteens. It may not be a key destination, but old Wenchang is worthy of a visit, especially if you're transitioning to or from the coast.

Wenchang Confucius Temple

文昌孔庙, wénchāng kǒngmiào • No. 77 Wenchang Dong Lu • ¥15

In the middle of a cluttered neighbourhood where a number of Nationalist-era villas survive, including the marvellous **Li Family Ancestral Shrine** dating back to 1936, lies the old town's centrepiece, the **Wenchang Confucius Temple**. Originally built during the Northern Song dynasty and relocated to its present site during the Ming dynasty, this lovely mustard-coloured homage to China's favourite sage is the oldest of its kind on the island. As such, it's regarded as "the birthplace of modern civilization" – at least according to the tourist blurb.

The superbly laid out **complex** comprises classical gardens, a Dragon Gate and Chongsheng Memorial Hall, where sacrifices were once made to Confucius in the hope that filial sons might pass the imperial examination. But the real highlight is the exquisite fusion of Chinese **traditional** with the colourful **flora** of subtropical Hainan, including two sacred banyan trees.

Old Street

老街, lǎojiē

A five-minute walk from the Confucius Temple lies Wenchang's main commercial drag, **Old Street**, also known as 文南街, wénnán jiē. The strip exhibits some of the region's fine **arcades** (骑楼, qí lóu), constructed around the turn of the century for southern shoppers to take shelter from the hot, wet weather. It's a great place to stroll and imagine what life was like before the establishment of the People's Republic. The street is also home to some great little places to grab a bite to eat, including several atmospheric Laoba tea canteens.

Gusong

古松村, gǔsōng cūn • High-speed trains to Wenchang leave every hour from Haikou East (30min); take bus #9 from Wenchang to Longlou (45min; ¥7), then taxi to Gusong ¥40

Usually accessed via **Wenchang** (文昌, wénchāng), **Longlou** (龙楼, lónglóu) is a small market town of no real significance except that it makes a handy base for visiting nearby beaches. There's decent sand at **Qishuiwan** (淇水湾泳滩, qíshuǐwān yǒngtān), but the highlight is the eyewateringly picturesque **GUSONG** fishing village, well worth a visit to snap a few photos of the lighthouse on the rocks, and maybe dine in one of the relatively inexpensive and basic seafood restaurants here. Only time will tell if Gusong will survive the ecological damage being inflicted upon it by the emerging tourist industry here including a few unfinished hotels and, rather ironically, the construction of a tourist ecological park nearby.

Bo'ao

博鳌, bó'ao • City bus #2 from Qionghai town (¥7; 45min), then taxi from Qionghai's bus or train station ¥40–45, or ¥10 sharing

BO'AO, about 50km south of Wenchang near Qionghai town (琼海, qiónghǎi), is famous for the Bo'ao Business Forum for Asia held here every spring, so its beaches and water are clean, it has a good tourist infrastructure, and hassles are at a minimum. The beach can be reached on foot and is safe for swimming – just avoid the currents around the mouths of three rivers that arrive into the sea, which can be dangerous. The beach behind the Confucian temple is pretty and quiet.

Shimei Bay

石梅湾, shíměi wān • Only accessible by taxi (¥60–80 from Wanning), so it's advisable to get your driver's number and arrange for them to pick you up, or ask one of the resorts to book one for you

Shimei Bay, accessed via **Wanning** town (万宁, wànníng), has to rate as one of the best beaches on Hainan, maintained as it is by two huge and exclusive resorts. The best section of the beach is accessed through the *Le Méridien* hotel, and they even have a bar slap-bang on the sand, serving ice-cold, imported bottled beers for just ¥30.

Riyue Bay

日月湾, rìyuè wān • Local buses between Wanning (around 1hr) and Sanya (around 1hr 45min) might stop on the highway outside Riyue if requested – ask when you get on; taxi from Wanning or Lingshui ¥100

About 20km south of Wanning and some 6km east of Shimei, **Riyue Bay** is popular with Hainan's embryonic **surfing** community (see box opposite), due to its exposure to Pacific swells. Even if you're not catching waves, this is an idyllic spot where new hotels are only just getting a foothold, and you can almost imagine you're on the hippy trail.

ACCOMMODATION

Djombo 琼博旅馆 qióngbó lǚguǎn. Wenhua Jie, Bo'ao ☏ 0898 62778082. This reasonable cheapie is on a recently gentrified street in the centre of Bo'ao. Rooms are basic, but clean enough, and there are another couple of similar places on the same street. No English spoken; make sure they register you with the police. **¥100**

Longlou Jiudian 龙楼酒店, lónglóu jiǔdiàn. Just uphill from the bus station, Longlou ☏ 0898 63586888. Longlou's sole accommodation, with a rack rate that can be knocked down to less than half. Rooms are decent for the price; get one overlooking the coconut grove behind the hotel, rather than on the road. **¥150**

Riyue Bay Surfing Club 日月湾冲浪俱乐部, rìyuèwān chōnglàng jùlèbù. Riyue Bay ☏ 0898 62254626. Very basic on-site dorm rooms, along with a restaurant where you can eat local Chinese food for under ¥40. They also arrange good rates on private rooms at nearby hotels. Dorms **¥60**, doubles **¥188**

Sanya

三亚, sānyà

Some 320km across the island from Haikou, on Hainan's southern coast, **SANYA** is, sooner or later, the destination of every visitor to the island. **Sanya City** itself is a rather pleasant, once-scruffy fishing port, surrounded by concrete high-rise holiday resorts, that has twice hosted the Miss World contest; but what pulls in the crowds – a large number of whom are Russian – are the surrounding beaches at **Dadonghai**, **Sanya Bay** and **Yalong Bay**. Chinese tourists also flock to overcrowded and overpriced scenic spots such as **Tianya Haijiao**, all of which are of little interest to foreigners.

Note that though the beaches here are good, a trip to Sanya can involve a few irritations, especially for those on a budget: at peak times – from October to February and especially Chinese New Year – room rates soar and the usual tourist hassles intensify. Off season, however, beaches are uncrowded and the atmosphere is pretty mellow.

Sanya City

Despite its resort image, **Sanya City** doesn't have anything particular to see: recent investment has given the downtown area the appearance of any other mildly prosperous Chinese city, and its proximity to the beaches is only betrayed by the

---

SURFING AT HAINAN

Hainan has some of the best **surfing beaches** in China, and there are two easily accessible surf resorts on the east coast with foreign co-owners. **Riyue Bay** (see opposite) is home to the **Jalenboo Surfing Club** (board rental ¥100/day; 2hr lesson in English ¥400; ⓦsurfinghainan .com). Closer to Sanya, and with warmer water, is **Houhai Bay**, where the **Karma Surf Hostel and School** (similar rates) surf from a number of different beaches depending on the season (ⓦfacebook/surfhostelkarma.com, or call Francesco on ☎136 97559284).

Northeastern and eastern swells bring waves of around 1–2m most of the year, though during typhoon season (June–Sept), waves will be more like 3–5m and sometimes up to 6m. Riyue Bay is a northeast open bay and probably better during the winter months, when it gets up to 5m waves, and is hence the setting for several surf competitions. For those who know their surfing, Houhai is comparable to Huntington Beach, while Riyue is more like the Hawaiian North Shore.

---

presence of matching-short-and-shirt-wearing holidaymakers. Sanya's real charm, however, is its laidback atmosphere: the **No. 1 Market** (第一市场, dìyī shìchǎng) – though earmarked for gentrification – is a mass of small backstreets centred around Xinjian Jie and an interesting place to wander aimlessly, as is the **Fishing Village** (渔村, yúcūn), located between the harbour and Luhuitou.

Dadonghai beach
大东海, dàdōnghǎi • Bus #2 or #8 from Sanya bus station to the Summer Mall

Some four kilometres south of the centre, often crowded and seasonally blistering hot, 3km-long **Dadonghai beach** has pretty well everything you could ask for in a tropical shore: beachside bars and kiosks renting out beach umbrellas, jet skis, catamarans and rubber rings complete the scene. It's hugely popular with holidaying Russians – almost every shop along the strip has both Chinese and Cyrillic script.

Sanya Bay
三亚湾, sānyàwān • Bus #206 from the town centre

Opposite man-made Phoenix Island, 23km-long **Sanya Bay** is a stretch of sand mostly frequented by locals. With few facilities, the beach is more suited to an evening stroll than a day on the sand. However, a few restaurants and hotels are popping up along the strip, and it is far more accessible from town than any other beaches.

Yalong Bay
亚龙湾, yàlóng wān • Bus #15 from Dadonghai (30min) to the giant stone totem pole, from where you can walk through to the beach; taxi ¥60 on the meter from the town centre

Lying 22km east of Sanya by road, the beach at **Yalong Bay** is more pleasant than Dadonghai's – it's better maintained and the water is cleaner and clearer. The golden sands are overlooked by a backdrop of expensive hotels and resorts.

Houhai Bay
后海湾, hòu hǎiwān • From Dadonghai, take bus #28 or #29 to the end of the line (40min), then follow the signs to the Wuzhizhou Island ferry, and Houhai Bay is just to the south of the pier

Houhai Bay, 32km east of Sanya, is stunningly pretty and without a resort in sight, with surfer-friendly hotels instead lining the beachfront. The settlement here, **Tenghai** (滕海村, ténghǎi cūn), once a fishing village, is home to a spattering of backpacker hostels and locally managed restaurants. The sands aren't exactly golden, but there's a relaxed ambience, some great surfing (see box above), and it's one of the least exploited spots in Hainan. A perfect place to lose a few days.

8

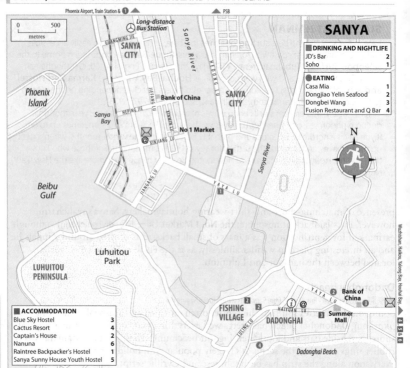

SANYA

Luhuitou Peninsula

鹿回头, lù huí tóu • Bus #2 & #4 from Sanya • ¥60

Overlooking Sanya Bay, around 5km south of downtown, en route to the ultra commercial **Xiaodong Hai** (小东海, xiǎo dōng hǎi) tourist resort, **Luhuitou Peninsula** is home to a spattering of mediocre attractions. The big selling point, however, is the park's soaring view of the city and coast from its summit 280 metres above the water. Luhuitou is home to a troop of macaque monkeys, who often steal tourists' food.

ARRIVAL AND DEPARTURE
SANYA

By plane Sanya Phoenix International Airport (三亚凤凰 国际机场, sānyà fènghuáng guójì jīchǎng; ☏0898 88289390, ⊛www.sanyaairport.com) is about 15km to the northwest, from where you'll need to catch a taxi for ¥50–60, or bus #8 (¥5) into the city. Most hotels have airline agents on hand, or either of the helpful visitor information offices can book domestic flights.

Destinations Beijing (3hr 50min); Guangzhou (1hr 20min); Hong Kong (1hr 45min); Shanghai (3hr 5min); Shenzhen (1hr 35min).

By bus Sanya's main long-distance bus station (三亚汽车站, sānyà qìchēzhàn) is in the city at the northern end of Jiefang Lu, and handles normal and luxury buses to Haikou, and services to just about everywhere else on the island. For mainland destinations, change at Haikou.

Destinations Dongfang (3hr); Haikou (3–5hr); Lingshui (2hr); Qionghai (4hr 30min); Tongshi (2hr); Wanning (3hr); Wenchang (4hr); Yazhou (1hr).

By train The train station, which handles CRH and regular trains, lies just north of the bus station and is accessible to the centre with bus #4 or around ¥25 in a taxi.

Destinations Beijing West (1 daily; 36hr); Haikou East (20 daily; 2hr); Guangzhou (1 daily; 14hr 20min).

INFORMATION

Visitor information centres Sanya is blessed with two useful, English-speaking information centres (daily 9am–9pm; ☏0898 38812301, ⊛english.sanya.gov.cn) one at the airport, and the other opposite the *Seascape*

Garden Hotel near the crossroads of Luling Lu and Yuya Lu. Both are mines of information, and are useful for booking tours. They also have free computers with internet access.

Tour agents Any of the hotels or hostels, even those without their own travel desks, will arrange scuba diving, climbing, coral island or fishing trips and, if not able to actually book air tickets themselves, will be more than happy to point you in the direction of one of the many agencies in the town that can.

Websites Useful websites include ⓦ whatsonsanya.com, ⓦ sanyaweb.com and ⓦ english.sanya.gov.cn.

GETTING AROUND

By bus Public buses #2 and #8 run regularly between the bus station in Sanya City and Dadonghai; bus #15 runs every 15min from Sanya to Yalong Bay, via the Summer Mall at Dadonghai, as do buses #28 or #29 to Houhai Bay.

By taxi There's the usual overload of taxi cabs. Flag fall is ¥8, with every extra kilometre ¥2, and many drivers insist on a minium ¥10 fare.

By bike Sanya is a great place to cycle around and experience the laidback atmosphere in the backstreets away from the beach; hostels rent them for around ¥30/day.

ACCOMMODATION

Sanya's accommodation is constantly developing, with increasing options across the board. The city itself can be an interesting place to stay, but most folk head towards mostly cheap and cheerful **Dadonghai**, backpacker-friendly **Houhai** or more exclusive and expensive **Yalong Bay**.

SANYA CITY

Raintree Backpacker's Hostel 雨树背包客旅舍, yǔshù bēibāokè lǚshě. 4F Shan Shui Yun Tian Building, 46 Hedong Lu ⓣ0898 38898877, ⓔpg82happy@163.com. If the beaches are a bit hectic, this quiet, family-run hostel is a good escape option, just 10min by bike from Dadonghai. It has seen better days, but remains a rare budget option in town. Rustic rooms, some with balconies overlooking the river, bikes for rent, and what the family lack in English ability, they make up for in helpfulness. Dorms **¥50**, doubles **¥180**

DADONGHAI

Blue Sky Hostel 蓝天国际青年旅舍, lántiān guójì qīngnián lǚshè. Lanhai Xiang, Haiyun Lu ⓣ1387 6791920, ⓦyhachina.com. This quirky spot is backpacker central: free wi-fi, plus laundry facilities and English-speaking staff who can arrange anything from dive trips to hiking in the rainforest. Dorms **¥50**, doubles **¥200**

Captain's House 船长餐厅, chuánzhǎng cāntīng. Opposite Luying Lu's Sanya Royal Garden Resort on Yu Cun Lu ⓣ0898 88983778. This maritime-themed hostel is popular with the Russian set. What puts it apart is its location at the mouth of Fishing Village Rd, which affords guest access to an eclectic, not-yet-redeveloped local neighbourhood. Dorms **¥40**, doubles **¥120**

YALONG BAY

Cactus Resort 仙人掌度假酒店, xiānrénzhǎng dùjià jiǔdiàn. Longtang Lu ⓣ0898 88568866, ⓦsanya-resort-cactus.gloriahotels.com. Set back from the beach and almost in the jungle, this is more peaceful than most of the big hotels in Yalong and is just a 5min stroll from the sea. Lovely swimming pool, all expected five-star facilities, and nonguests can also enjoy the "fish massage" at the spa here for just ¥68. **¥1188**

HOUHAI BAY

Nanuna 冲凉度假酒店, chōng liáng dù jià jiǔ diàn. 88 Lanhai Shequ, Haitang Wan ⓣ0898 88751498, ⓦnanunahotel.com/en. With a palm-tree-flanked infinity pool, sea views and architecture that wouldn't look out of place along the Costa del Sol, *Nanuna* is a far trendier hotel than most in Sanya. Ideal if you're looking to get away from it all. **¥380**

Sanya Sunny House Youth Hostel 三亚天晴小屋国际青年旅舍, sānyà tiānqíng xiǎowū guójì qīngnián lǚshè. Haitang Wan, Tenghai ⓣ133 37641170. Located just behind all the cool surf schools and boutique hotels a street back from the good surfing beach (see box, p.533), is Houhai's unrivalled budget option. Basic but comfortable private rooms and dorms are on offer, and the young staff members are keen to serve, dine or even party with guests. Dorms **¥30**, doubles **¥100**

EATING

Like accommodation, **eating** here can be an expensive business (though the excellent seafood is reasonably priced): don't eat anywhere – especially cheaper spots – without getting solid confirmation of **prices** before ordering, or you could end up being asked to pay vastly over the odds. The stretch of **Haiyuan Lu** between the turnoff to the *Blue Sky* hostel and the junction with Haiyuan Lu is home to Dadonghai's best-value and most varied selection of food, including Japanese, Italian and generic Western restaurants, plus a string of small Chinese seafood canteens which spill out onto the street at night.

SCUBA DIVING FROM SANYA

Low visibility and only moderate maximum depths don't make Hainan the most exciting location for scuba diving, but it can be good fun – and there's always the simple novelty of diving in China. Don't bother with Dadonghai; the best areas near Sanya are just east at **Yalong Bay** (clear water and best for its coral growth, and a variety of fish); **Tianya Haijiao**, over to the far west of Sanya Bay (good for molluscs); and – best of all – **Wuzhizhou Island**, in Lingshui Bay around 30km east of Sanya (coral, fish, molluscs and crystal-clear water). Bookings can be made through virtually any hotel (the hostels are the best), but touts, who are more amenable to bargaining, often patrol the beachfront at Dadonghai and Yalong Bay.

Yalong Bay is the least expensive, and boat dives around the west of the bay for certified divers run at ¥580–680 for one tank, with additional tanks ¥200. Without certification, you can do a controlled thirty-minute "resort" dive for ¥300–400. Snorkelling trips cost around ¥200 for a couple of hours.

Trips to Tianya Haijiao (diving around West Island) and Wuzhizhou Island are both about fifty percent more expensive than Yalong Bay, and require you to pay an "island landing fee" of ¥148 on top of diving costs. You can dive at Wuzhizhou for considerably less, however, by booking in nearby Houhai Bay (see p.535), whose operators dive on the same sites but don't "land".

For the cheapest eats, head to the area around the **No.1 Market** in Sanya City, where it's easy to get a good feed for under ¥10 – the best-value seafood restaurants are also here, around the **fish market**. Imported alcohol and various foodstuffs are available at *Corner's Deli* on the 5th floor of Summer Mall.

SANYA CITY
Fusion Restaurant & Q Bar 福生餐厅, fúshēng cāntīng. 15 Luling Lu ☏ 0898 88210007. A good date-spot and one of the few fine-dining options in town, this swanky place isn't quite a fusion restaurant, despite the name. The menu is something of a mixture: customers can choose from Italian, Spanish or classic Asian dishes, while the affiliated bar serves cocktails, whiskies and imported beers. Main courses average around ¥50. Daily 11.30am–midnight.

DADONGHAI
Dongbei Wang 东北王, dōngběi wáng. 2F, 135 Yuya Lu ☏ 0898 88212585. Lively, enjoyable Manchurian restaurant, with an illustrated Russian menu. Portions are huge (one is enough for two people) and the service good. The fried whole fish with pine nuts is a treat, as is cold shredded beef with aniseed. Two can fill up for ¥60. Daily 11am–11pm.

Dongjiao Yelin Seafood 东郊椰林海鲜城, dōngjiāoyēlín hǎixiānchéng. 109 Yayu Lu ☏ 0898 88210999. A warehouse of a restaurant, offering a glut of seafood and Hainanese dishes in an opulent setting. Seafood is seasonally priced and about ¥400 per platter, though the other mains are ¥46–220. Daily 11am–11pm.

SANYA BAY
Casa Mia 卡萨米亚意大利餐厅, kǎ sà mǐ yà yì dà lì cān tīng. 2F, Lanse Hai Haian, Sanya Wan Lu ☏ 0898 88889828. This Italian-run restaurant is one of the best expat restaurants in town. Chic decor, solid service, and imported wine make *Casa Mia* well worth seeking out. Pizzas ¥78–88. Daily 11.30am–10pm.

DRINKING AND NIGHTLIFE

As far as Sanya's nightlife is concerned, KTVs and Chinese-style nightclubs abound, although there are a few smaller, more authentic Western bars around too.

JD's Bar Luling Rd, next to Danjiu Seafood Restaurant, between Sanya City and Dadonghai ☏ 186 89807430, ⓦ facebook.com/sanyajds. Not far from Dadonghai, this newly opened Sino-British joint venture is popular with Sanya's expat crowd. Specializing in Mexican food (burritos ¥35) and imported beers (Tiger draught ¥17) this is a great place to get some insider advice, make some English-speaking friends and take in a live music show. Daily 6pm–2am.

Soho 苏荷酒吧, sūhé jiǔbā. Yuya Lu, Sanya City ☏ 0898 88706677, ⓦ www.sohobar.com.cn. Shanghai-style dance bar which is busy all year round, with Shanghai prices, chandeliers, and showy Chinese singers performing before foreign DJs round off the night. Popular with both locals and foreigners – it gets pretty crowded. Daily 9pm–2am.

SHOPPING

Sanya is a good place to pick up **pearls**: white, pink, yellow or black. The best buys are from local hawkers on Dadonghai beach, who sell strings of "rejects" for ¥40 or less with hard bargaining. Most of these pearls are perfectly genuine, just not of good enough colour, shape or size for commercial jewellery. If in doubt, scratch the surface – flaking indicates a thinly coated plastic bead.

DIRECTORY

Post offices There are post offices on Xinjiang Lu, Sanya City, and on Yula Lu in Dadonghai (daily 7.30am–6pm).
Visa extensions For visa issues, head to the Foreign Affairs Department in the north of the city, just over the bridge on

Fenghuang Lu (Mon–Sat 9am–noon & 3–5.30pm; ☎898 88869015). If extending your visa, make sure you have registered with the police every day of your stay, as they are real sticklers for the rules here, and quite unsympathetic.

Jianfeng Ling Forest Reserve

尖峰岭森林自然保护区, jiānfēnglǐng sēnlín zìrán bǎohùqū • Daily 8.30am–6.30pm • ¥50 • ☎010 84238625

Jianfeng Ling Forest Reserve encloses a tiny pocket of mountain rainforest 115km northwest of Sanya, left untouched following a logging ban in 1992, when a UNESCO survey found 400 types of butterfly and 1700 plant species up here. It's a very peaceful spot, and much cooler than the coast, making it a great relief from frying on the beach.

From the main-road township of **JIANFENG** (尖峰, jiānfēng), it's 18km uphill to the park gates at **Tianchi** (天池, tiānchí), where the road reaches the forest's edge at a couple of tranquil lakes – both have upmarket resorts. From here a boardwalk leads off uphill for an hour-long circuit walk taking in some massive trees, vines, orchids, ferns, birds, butterflies and beautiful views from the 1056m ridge. There are also boardwalks around both lakes, which make for a most congenial sunset stroll.

ARRIVAL AND DEPARTURE JIANFENG LING FOREST RESERVE

By bus and rickshaw There's no direct bus from Sanya bus station, but ask around and you'll be told which bus to take. Make sure to tell your driver that you're going to Jianfeng Ling, and you'll be dropped at a small main-road

bus depot, where you catch a motor-rickshaw for the few kilometres to Jianfeng township. From here, hire another rickshaw for the last 18km up to Tianchi (¥60).

ACCOMMODATION

In addition to the hotel below, there's a slightly down-at-the-heels resort in the park up by the forest boardwalk, which you can book at the park entrance.

Hainan Tianchi Blossom Hotel 海南天池桃花园酒店, hǎinán tiānchí táohuāyuán jiǔdiàn. Tianchi ☎0898 31856888. Right next to the biggest lake, this

resort has some lovely rooms in the main building, but the deluxe ones are worth the extra as they are in chalets (with patios), actually on the water. **¥680**

Wuzhishan town

五指山市, wǔzhǐshān shì • The bus station is north of the river on Huayu Bei Lu, from where you can head to Haikou, Sanya and Wuzhi Shan Nature Reserve

Lacking heavy traffic or industry, **Wuzhishan town** – also known as **Tongshi** (通什, tōngshí) – is a pleasantly unpolluted spot two hours north of Sanya, surrounded by pretty countryside. Set at the base of low hills, the centre sits on the southern bank of a horseshoe bend of the Nansheng River and mostly consists of the handful of streets around its market area where there's a chance to see Hainan's dark-dressed **minorities** – Miao, and the occasional older Li women with tattoos. It's all pretty relaxed, and wander out of town (especially north; take the first right over the bridge down Shangzhuang Lu) and you'll soon find yourself in vivid green fields and increasingly poor villages, ultimately built of mud and straw and surrounded by split bamboo pickets to keep livestock in.

8

THE SOUTH CHINA SEA ISLANDS

Chinese maps of China always show a looped extension of the southern borders reaching 1500km down through the South China Sea to within spitting distance of Borneo, enclosing a host of reefs and minute islands. These sit over what might be major **oil and gas reserves**, and are consequently claimed by every nation in the region – China, Malaysia, the Philippines, Taiwan and Vietnam have all put in their bids, based on historical or geographic associations.

Occupied by Japan during the 1940s but unclaimed after World War II, the **Spratly and Paracel islands** are perhaps the most contentious groups. Vietnam and China both declared ownership of the Paracels in the 1970s, and seventy Vietnamese soldiers were killed when the Chinese seized the islands in 1974, coming to blows again in 1988 when the Chinese navy sank two Vietnamese gunboats. Then, in 1995, the Philippines stepped in, destroying Chinese territorial markers erected over the most westerly reefs in the Spratly group and capturing a nearby Chinese trawler. Ongoing minor brawls encouraged the nations of the region – including China – to hammer out a landmark agreement in November 2002, which basically allows access for all, while territorial disputes are settled one by one. However, neither China nor Vietnam has kept to the letter of the agreement, and indeed in July of the same year, China established Sansha City on the Paracels to oversee its territory in the South China Sea.

In 2013, reports showed China had begun reclaiming land around three sites in the Spratlys and in 2015 images confirmed China was building an airfield at Firey Cross Reef. In early 2016, China landed two commercial flights on its artificial islands, sparking outrage in Vietnam and the Philippines. Whether Beijing is flexing its imperial muscles or simply securing precious resources, the ongoing South China Sea dispute remains contentious.

Nationality Museum

民族博物馆, mínzú bówùguǎn • Daily 9am–5.30pm • Free; you must show your passport

The newly refurbished **Nationality Museum**, 250m from the university, has historical exhibits which include prehistoric stone tools and a bronze drum decorated with sun and frog motifs, similar to those associated with Guangxi's Zhuang; Ming manuscripts about island life; Qing wine vessels with octopus and frog mouldings; and details of the various modern conflicts culminating in the last pocket of Guomindang resistance being overcome in 1950. Artefacts and photos illustrate Hainan's cultural heritage, too – Li looms and textiles, traditional weapons and housing, speckled pottery from Dongfang and pictures of major festivals.

ACCOMMODATION

There are a few basic places opposite the bus station asking under ¥100 for a double, and a few mid-range and swankier places along the river.

Wuzhi Shan Nature Reserve

五指山国家级自然保护区, wǔzhǐshān guójiājí zìrán bǎohùqū • 25km east of Quzhishan town • Closed to tourists at time of writing, but usually daily 9am–6pm • ¥50 • ☎ 0898 86550075 • An irregular bus (40min; ¥9) leaves from opposite the bus station in Wuzhishan town to Shuiman village (水满乡, shuǐmǎn xiāng); from here, walk or catch a motor-rickshaw (¥10) the final 4km to the gates – last bus back to Wuzhishan town departs Shuiman at 6pm

At the time of writing, **Wuzhi Shan Nature Reserve** was closed to foreigners, due to an incident involving a stray American hiker. This may change, so check ahead with the tourist office in Sanya (see p.534). The nature reserve has a very luxurious resort 1km or so inside the gate, from where a paved path leads off into the rainforest. At the first junction, the left path will lead you on a gentle thirty-minute stroll up a stream to a very lovely **waterfall**, while the right path eventually gets to the **peak** of Whuzi Shan itself: it's an 11km **hike**, quite tough, and takes around three hours going up (two coming down), so take plenty of water and wear appropriate footwear. Although it's often clouded over, the summit offers contorted pines, begonias and, if you're lucky, absolutely stunning views.

ACCOMMODATION
WUZHI SHAN NATURE RESERVE

Shuiman Yuan 水满园, shuǐmǎn yuán. Shuiman village ☎ 0898 86550333. Just 4km from the Wuzhi Shan Nature Reserve and close to the bus stop for Wuzhishan town, this lovely little resort has spacious, quiet rooms overlooking either the jungle or Wuzishan mountain itself. It's the best option if you can't afford the five-star *Wuzhishan Yatai Rainforest Resort* actually inside the park. ¥258

LI AND MIAO

Hainan's million-strong **Li** population take their name from the big topknot (*li*) which men once wore. They probably arrived on Hainan from Guangxi about 200 BC, when they occupied the coast and displaced the aboriginal inhabitants before themselves being driven into the highlands by later Chinese migrations. The Li built villages with distinctive tunnel-shaped houses, evolved their own shamanistic religion, and used poisoned arrows to bring down game. Li women were known for their **weaving** skills, and the fact that, until very recently, many got their faces heavily **tattooed** with geometric patterns – apparently to make them undesirable to raiding parties of slavers from the coast, or rival **clans**. The latter have never coexisted very well, quarrelling to this day over territorial boundaries, and only united in their dislike of the Han Chinese – there were fourteen major rebellions against their presence on the island during the Qing era alone.

Though traditional life has all but vanished over the last half-century, there are still a few special events to look out for. Best is the **San Yue San festival** (held on the third day of the third lunar month), the most auspicious time of the year in which to choose a partner; while in more remote corners of the highlands, **funerals** are traditionally celebrated with gunfire and three days of hard drinking by male participants.

Touted as Hainan's second "native minority" by the tourist literature, the **Miao** are comparatively recent arrivals, forcibly recruited from Guizhou province as mercenaries to put down a Li uprising during the Ming dynasty. When the money ran out, the Miao stopped fighting and settled in the western highlands, where they formed a fifty-thousand-strong community in the remotest of valleys.

8

Hong Kong and Macau

香港 / 澳门

EVENING VIEW FROM THE PEAK, HONG KONG

9

Hong Kong and Macau

The handover of Asia's last two European colonies, Hong Kong in 1997 and Macau in 1999, opened new eras for both. Despite a visible colonial heritage, the dominant Chinese character underlying these two SARs, or "Special Administrative Regions of China" is obvious: after all, Hong Kong and Macau's population is 97 percent Chinese, the main language is Cantonese, and there have always been close ties – if tinged with distrust – with their cousins north of the border. It is hard to overstate the importance that the handovers had for the Chinese government, in sealing the end of centuries of colonial intrusion with the return of the last pieces of foreign-occupied soil to the motherland. The ensuing "One Country, Two Systems" policy has seen both cities enjoy considerable economic benefits from closer ties with the mainland, as high-spending visitors flocked to Hong Kong to shop and Macau to gamble. However, as the limits to China's appetite for political reform become apparent, the regime has slowly begun to chafe.

First under colonial and now mainland Chinese rule, Hong Kong and Macau's citizens have never had a say in their futures, so they have concentrated their efforts on other things – notably, **making money**. With its emphasis on economics and consumerism, **Hong Kong** offers huge variety and concentrations of **shops**, alongside a colossal range of **cuisines** and futuristic cityscapes sandwiched between the South China Sea and ranks of verdant mountains. The excellent **infrastructure**, including the efficient public transit system, the helpful tourist offices and all the other facilities of a genuinely international city make this an extremely soft entry into the Chinese world.

Macau has leapt ahead in recent years as a haven for **gambling**, its thirty-odd casinos making the enclave a veritable Las Vegas of the East. The gaming boom has transformed much of the city, but evidence of its colonial past persists in its extensive quarters of antique, Mediterranean-style architecture, along with Portuguese wine and Macanese cooking, a fusion of colonial and Chinese styles.

TEMPLE STREET NIGHT MARKET

Highlights

① Star Ferry The crossing from Tsim Sha Tsui to Hong Kong Island is the cheapest harbour tour on earth – and one of the most spectacular. **See p.549**

② Harbour view from the Peak At dusk, watch the city's dazzling lights brighten across Hong Kong, Victoria Harbour and Kowloon. **See p.554**

③ Markets in Central and Kowloon Join local shoppers in the city's bustling street markets, from Hong Kong Island's backstreet vegetable stalls (p.553) to Mong Kok's goldfish vendors (p.563).

④ Sai Kung Peninsula Get away from the crowds and concrete amid beautiful seascapes,

beaches and wild countryside in this often overlooked corner of Hong Kong. **See p.566**

⑤ Dim sum Tuck into an authentic *dim sum* lunch alongside enthusiastic families – try the *har gau* (prawn dumplings) and barbecue pork buns. **See p.581**

⑥ Old Macau Seek out forts, beautiful Portuguese churches and restored Chinese mansions among Macau's narrow alleyways and cobbled civic squares. **See p.590**

⑦ Coffee, tarts and port Thanks to Macau's Portuguese heritage, many cafés serve ink-black coffee, delicious custard tarts and port wine alongside delicious Macanese dishes. **See p.601**

HIGHLIGHTS ARE MARKED ON THE MAP ON P.544

9

THE HONG KONG DOLLAR

Hong Kong has its own currency, the **Hong Kong dollar**, which is pegged at just under eight to the US dollar. Chinese yuan cannot officially be used in Hong Kong, though in practice more and more stores are accepting the mainland's currency. In this chapter, the symbol "$" refers to Hong Kong dollars throughout, unless stated.

Thanks to sky-high rates for accommodation, visitors will spend more **money** in Hong Kong and Macau than elsewhere in China, though public transport and local food are good value. Travellers on a tight **budget** who stay in dormitories can just about get by on $500 a day, though at the other end of the market in hotels, restaurants and shops, prices quickly rise to international levels.

Hong Kong

香港, xiāng gǎng

HONG KONG – fully known as the Hong Kong SAR – wears a lot of hats. The city is one of the world's largest financial hubs, though its modern face hides a surprisingly traditional culture. Known for some of the most densely populated urban areas on earth, swaths of the territory are in reality covered by surprisingly undeveloped countryside; and while the city owes its most recent prosperity to flocks of newly minted shoppers from the mainland, relations with Beijing have never been more strained, thanks to 2014's democratic protests (see p.940). While Hong Kong's famous addiction to money and brand names tends to mask the fact that most people work long hours and live in tiny apartments, the city is bursting with energy and the population of seven million is sophisticated and well informed compared to their mainland cousins, the result of a relatively free press.

Orientation

Hong Kong comprises 1100 square kilometres of the south China coastline and a number of islands east of the Pearl River Delta. The principal urban area is spread

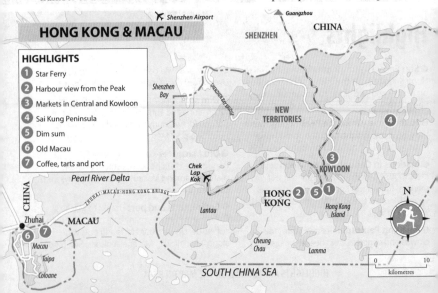

HONG KONG & MACAU

HIGHLIGHTS
1. Star Ferry
2. Harbour view from the Peak
3. Markets in Central and Kowloon
4. Sai Kung Peninsula
5. Dim sum
6. Old Macau
7. Coffee, tarts and port

along the north shore of **Hong Kong Island**, which offers traces of the **old colony** – from English place names to anachronistic double-decker trams trundling along what was once the shoreline – and superb **modern cityscapes** of towering buildings teetering up impossible slopes, along with whole districts dedicated to selling dried seafood and herbs for Traditional Chinese Medicine. The south of the island offers several popular **beaches**, a huge **amusement park**, and even decent **hiking** opportunities.

Immediately north of Hong Kong Island, across Victoria Harbour, the **Kowloon Peninsula** – and especially its tip, **Tsim Sha Tsui** – is Hong Kong's principal tourist trap, boasting a glut of accommodation, shops and markets offering an incredible variety of goods. North of Tsim Sha Tsui, Kowloon merges with the **New Territories**, a varied area of **New Towns** and older villages, secluded beaches and undeveloped country parks. In addition, the **Outlying Islands** – particularly **Lamma** and **Lantau** – are worth a visit for their seafood restaurants and relatively laidback pace of life.

Brief history

While the Chinese justifiably argue that Hong Kong was always Chinese territory, its development only began with the **arrival of the British** in 1842, following the first **Opium War** (see p.931). Further gunboat diplomacy eighteen years later secured Britain the Kowloon Peninsula too, and in 1898 Britain obtained a 99-year lease on an additional one thousand square kilometres of land north of Kowloon, the New Territories. Until World War II, the territory prospered as turmoil in mainland China drove money and **refugees** south into the apparently safe confines of the British colony. This confidence proved misplaced in 1941 when **Japanese forces** seized Hong Kong along with the rest of eastern China, though after Japan's defeat in 1945, Britain swiftly reclaimed the colony. As the mainland fell to the Communists in 1949, a new wave of refugees swelled Hong Kong's population threefold to 2.5 million, causing a housing crisis that set in motion themes still current in the SAR: **land reclamation**, the need for efficient infrastructure, and a tendency to save space by building upwards.

Approaching the handover

In the last twenty years of British rule, the spectre of 1997, when Britain's lease on the New Territories expired, loomed large. Negotiations on the future of the colony led in 1984 to the **Sino-British Joint Declaration**, paving the way for Britain to hand back sovereignty of the entire territory in return for Hong Kong maintaining its capitalist system for fifty years. However, fears grew that repression and the erosion of freedoms would follow the handover. The constitutional framework provided by the **Basic Law** of 1988, in theory, answered some of those fears, illustrating how the "One Country, Two Systems" policy would work. But the following year's **crackdown in Tian'anmen Square** only seemed to confirm the most pessimistic views of what might happen following the handover, especially to members of Hong Kong's embryonic **democracy movement**. When **Chris Patten** arrived in 1992 to become the last governor, he accelerated the pace of democratic reform, infuriating Beijing and ensuring that the road to the handover would be a rough ride.

Post-1997

After the histrionics of the build-up, however, the **handover** was an anticlimax. The British sailed away, Beijing undid Patten's reforms, and Tung Chee-hwa, a shipping

---

HONG KONG PHONE NUMBERS

Hong Kong phone numbers have no area codes; local calls only require the eight digits shown in our listings. From outside the territory, dial the normal international access code + ☎852 (the "country" code) + the number. However, **from Macau** you need to dial ☎01 + the number. To call Hong Kong from mainland China, dial ☎00 + 852 + the number.

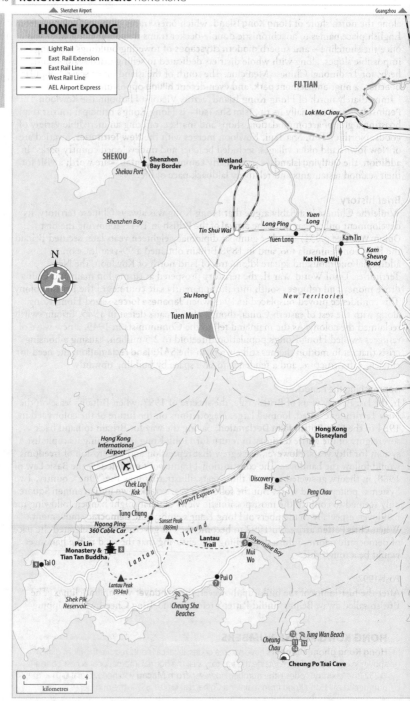

Shenzhen Airport

Guangzhou

HONG KONG

	Light Rail
	East Rail Extension
	East Rail Line
	West Rail Line
	AEL Airport Express

FU TIAN

Lok Ma Chau

SHEKOU

Shenzhen Bay Border

Shekou Port

Wetland Park

Shenzhen Bay

Tin Shui Wai

Long Ping

Yuen Long

Yuen Long

Kam Tin

Kam Sheung Road

Kat Hing Wai

N

Siu Hong

New Territories

Tuen Mun

Hong Kong Disneyland

Hong Kong International Airport

Chek Lap Kok

Airport Express

Discovery Bay

Peng Chau

Tung Chung

Ngong Ping 360 Cable Car

Po Lin Monastery & Tian Tan Buddha

Tai O

Lantau Peak (934m)

Sunset Peak (869m)

Lantau Island

Lantau Trail

Silvermine Bay

Mui Wo

Shek Pik Reservoir

Cheung Sha Beaches

Pui O

Tung Wan Beach

Cheung Chau

Cheung Po Tsai Cave

0   4
kilometres

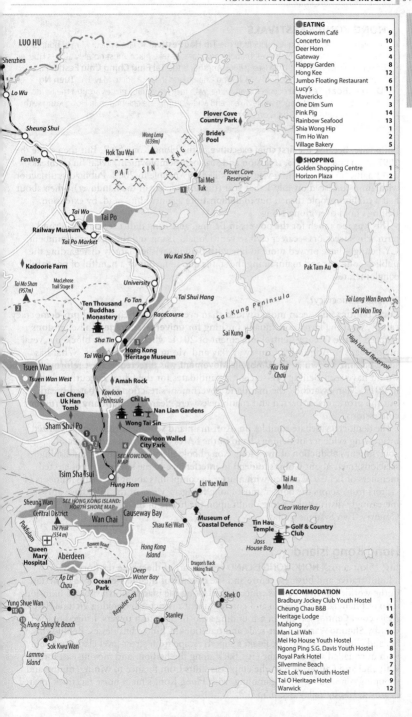

Map labels:

LUO HU
Shenzhen
Lo Wu
Sheung Shui
Fanling
Hok Tau Wai
Wong Leng (639m)
Plover Cove Country Park
Bride's Pool
PAT SIN LENG
Tai Mei Tuk
Plover Cove Reservoir
Tai Wo
Tai Po
Railway Museum
Tai Po Market
Kadoorie Farm
Wu Kai Sha
Pak Tam Au
Tai Mo Shan (957m)
MacLehose Trail Stage 8
University
Fo Tan
Ten Thousand Buddhas Monastery
Tai Shui Hang
Racecourse
Sai Kung Peninsula
Sai Kung
High Island Reservoir
Tai Long Wan Beach
Sai Wan Ting
Sha Tin
Hong Kong Heritage Museum
Tai Wai
Kiu Tsui Chau
Tsuen Wan
Tsuen Wan West
Lei Cheng Uk Han Tomb
Amah Rock
Kowloon Peninsula
Chi Lin
Nan Lian Gardens
Wong Tai Sin
Sham Shui Po
Kowloon Walled City Park
SEE KOWLOON MAP
Tsim Sha Tsui
Hung Hom
Lei Yue Mun
Tai Au Mun
Sheung Wan
SEE HONG KONG ISLAND: NORTH SHORE MAP
Sai Wan Ho
Central District
Wan Chai
Causeway Bay
Clear Water Bay
The Peak (554m)
Shau Kei Wan
Museum of Coastal Defence
Tin Hau Temple
Golf & Country Club
Pokfulam
Bowen Road
Hong Kong Island
Joss House Bay
Queen Mary Hospital
Aberdeen
Deep Water Bay
Dragon's Back Hiking Trail
Ap Lei Chau
Ocean Park
Repulse Bay
Shek O
Yung Shue Wan
Stanley
Hung Shing Ye Beach
Sok Kwu Wan
Lamma Island

9

HONG KONG'S FESTIVALS

Festivals specific to Hong Kong include the **Tin Hau Festival**, in late April or May, in honour of the Goddess of the Sea. Noisy celebrations and parades take place, most notably at Joss House Bay on the Sai Kung Peninsula (see p.566). Another is the **Tai Ping Ching Chiu Festival** (also known as the Bun Festival), held on Cheung Chau Island in late April to May. The **Tuen Ng (Dragon Boat) Festival** occurs in early June, with races in various places around the territory. Other Chinese festivals, such as New Year and Mid-Autumn, are celebrated in Hong Kong with as much, if not more, gusto as on the mainland.

billionaire, became the **first chief executive** of the Hong Kong SAR. But then came the **1997 Asian financial crisis**, recession and soaring unemployment, avian flu outbreaks and finally, SARS, a baffling virus that killed 299 people in 2003. Public dissatisfaction with Tung coalesced on July 1 that year (the anniversary of the handover), when about half a million people turned out to **demonstrate** against him – and, by extension, Beijing's hold over Hong Kong.

This was too much for the powers in Beijing, and Tung didn't see out his second term. His successors – career civil servant Donald Tsang and the current incumbent, CY Leung – have proved more in line with Beijing's wishes, largely disregarding the public's concerns and maintaining the status quo in favour of a handful of powerful conglomerates.

Towards democracy?

Local politics now seem more divided than ever into pro-Beijing and pro-democracy camps, with the latter continually pushing for **universal suffrage**. These tensions erupted in the **Occupy Central** movement of 2014, when protesters blocked several major roads in Admiralty, Causeway Bay and Mong Kok for 79 days. What has since became known as the **Umbrella Movement** was directed against reforms that would have seen Beijing pre-screening candidates for the Chief Executive election in 2017. Many watched the mainland government's reaction with bated breath, but the protesters dispersed and roadblocks were cleared without any government concessions.

The democracy debate rumbles on. Anti-mainland sentiment has been galvanized by growing evidence of Beijing's hand in the SAR's affairs, from the mainland government's **abduction** of five Hong Kong booksellers (ostensibly for publishing salacious tracts about China's leaders) to interference in the swearing-in of elected members of LegCo. Coupled with a surge in complaints about the rising numbers of visitors from across the border, most Hong Kongers' views of the PRC have grown increasingly distrustful, casting doubt upon the future of the much-vaunted "One Country, Two Systems" policy.

Hong Kong Island

Just 15km across, **HONG KONG ISLAND** is the heart of the whole territory, the administrative and business centre and site of some of the most expensive real estate in the world. Development is concentrated along the island's north shore, a 6km-long strip of financial, commercial and entertainment districts overlooking **Victoria Harbour**. At its core, **Central** sprouts an astounding array of high-tech towers, fringed to the west by **Sheung Wan**'s smaller-scale and traditional Chinese businesses. Behind this, t he land climbs steeply to **The Peak**, a superb escape from street-level claustrophobia with unequalled views over the city. Back along the harbour and moving east through **Wan Chai** and **Causeway Bay**, the emphasis shifts from finance to wining, dining and shopping – not to mention gambling, with Hong Kong's main horse racetrack located nearby at **Happy Valley** (see p.557).

The south side of Hong Kong Island dips into the sea in a series of dangling peninsulas and inlets. The attractions here are separate towns such as **Aberdeen** and **Stanley** and also beaches, the best of which fronts the little outpost of **Shek O**. If you're travelling with children, **Ocean Park**, a huge adventure theme park, has enough to keep them occupied for a day (see p.558).

Central

CENTRAL takes in the densely crowded heart of Hong Kong's financial district, and extends for a few hundred metres in all directions from Central MTR Station. The waterfront area here was in redevelopment limbo at the time of writing, with the **Hong Kong Observation Wheel** (daily 10am–11pm; $100; ⊚ hkow.hk) standing amid construction works, but the **Star Ferry Terminal** remains one of Hong Kong Island's major arrival points. Central's main west–east roads are Connaught Road, Des Voeux Road (with its tramlines) and Queen's Road Central, with a mesh of smaller streets heading south and uphill.

Hong Kong Maritime Museum

Pier 8, next to Central's Star Ferry Terminal • Mon–Fri 9.30am–5.30pm, Sat & Sun 10am–7pm • $30 • ☎ 3713 2500, ⊚ hkmaritimemuseum.org • MTR Hong Kong, Exit A2

Hong Kong's **Maritime Museum** exhibits an engrossing, well-planned collection of historical seafaring relics, from shipwreck porcelain to cannons and original scroll paintings depicting the nineteenth-century war against piracy. There are also scores of carefully made wooden models of ships and, on the upstairs "decks", superlative harbour views and the fantastic KM Koo Ship Bridge Simulator, where you can try your hand at captaining a container ship or the Star Ferry. The simulator is included in your ticket price, but operating hours are limited to four 30-minute sessions on Saturdays and Sundays.

The International Finance Centre (IFC)

Corner of Connaught Rd and Finance St • ☎ 2295 3308, ⊚ ifc.com.hk • MTR Central, Exit A

At the core of Central's web of elevated walkways, the **International Finance Centre** (**IFC**) houses a **mall** and the Airport Express terminus, while above it rears the 88-storey, 420m-high **IFC2** tower, once Hong Kong's tallest building. This is so beautifully proportioned that it's not until you see the top brushing the clouds that you realize the tower stands half as high again as anything else in the area – though, sadly, you can't ride the lift up to see the view.

Exchange Square

8 Connaught Place • MTR Central, Exit A

Inland from the IFC, **Exchange Square** is surrounded by three pastel-pink marble and glass towers housing Hong Kong's Stock Exchange. The square itself, full of sandwich-guzzling office staff at lunchtime, is decorated with bronze statuary by Elisabeth Frink and Henry Moore, and holds **The Forum**, a five-storey glass-clad cube containing a branch of Standard Chartered. The square's street-level **bus station** is useful for reaching many of the island's outlying sights.

THE STAR FERRY

One of the most enjoyable things to do in Hong Kong is to spend ten minutes riding the humble **Star Ferry** between Tsim Sha Tsui in Kowloon and the pier in front of the IFC2 Tower on Hong Kong Island (daily 6.30am–11.30pm; upper deck $2.50, lower deck $2; ☎ 2367 7065, ⊚ starferry.com.hk). The views of the island are superb, particularly at dusk when the lights begin to twinkle through the humidity and the spray. You'll also get a feel for the frenetic pace of life on Hong Kong's waterways, with ferries, junks, hydrofoils and larger ships looming up from all directions.

9

The Hong Kong and Shanghai Bank (HSBC)

1 Queen's Road Central • MTR Central, Exit K

The **Hong Kong and Shanghai Bank (HSBC)** dates from 1985; designed by Sir Norman Foster, it reputedly cost over US$1 billion. The whole building is supported off the ground so that it's possible to walk right underneath – a necessity stipulated by the *feng shui* belief that the island's centre of power, Government House, which lies directly to the north, should be accessible in a straight line from the main point of arrival on the island, the Star Ferry. The two bronze **lions** out the front, named Stephen and Stitt after former HSBC directors, date from the 1930s and bear shrapnel scars from World War II.

Statue Square

MTR Central, Exit K

Immediately north of the HSBC building, **Statue Square** is an oddly empty space. Its main point of interest is the **Court of Final Appeal** on its eastern side, a hefty Neoclassical granite structure with a domed roof dating to 1912 – it's one of Central's few historic buildings. Until 2011 the building housed Hong Kong's Legislative

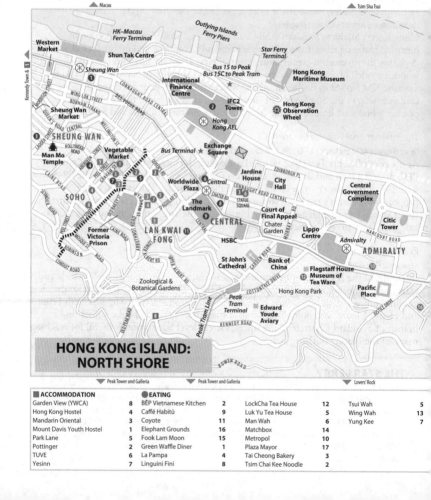

HONG KONG ISLAND: NORTH SHORE

Council or LegCo, the city's equivalent of a parliament – this has since relocated to Admiralty's Central Government Offices.

Lan Kwai Fong

MTR Central, Exit D2

South of Queen's Road Central, the land slopes sharply upwards. **Lan Kwai Fong**, with its focus around an L-shaped lane of the same name, forms a lively mass of bars and restaurants and spreads south over Wyndham Street/Hollywood Road and west to Pottinger Street. The southern end of Lan Kwai Fong itself is taken up with the 27-storey California Tower, but most of the fun still happens at street level. On weekend evenings the area is closed to traffic and the party spills into the road.

Soho and Hollywood Road

MTR Central, Exit D2

Soho – the district between Hollywood and Caine roads – is an extension of Lan Kwai Fong, though the emphasis here is towards eating rather than drinking.

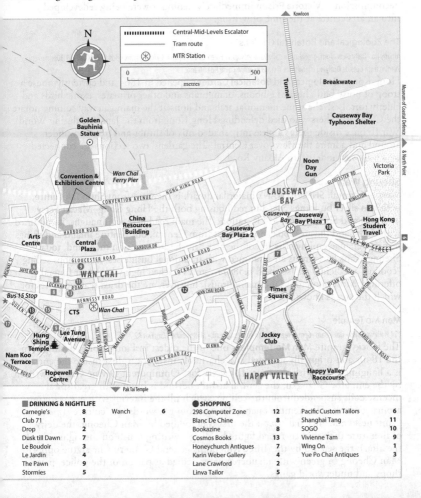

◼ DRINKING & NIGHTLIFE			● SHOPPING				
Carnegie's	8	Wanch	6	298 Computer Zone	12	Pacific Custom Tailors	6
Club 71	1			Blanc De Chine	8	Shanghai Tang	11
Drop	2			Bookazine	8	SOGO	10
Dusk till Dawn	7			Cosmos Books	13	Vivienne Tam	9
Le Boudoir	3			Honeychurch Antiques	7	Wing On	1
Le Jardin	4			Karin Weber Gallery	4	Yue Po Chai Antiques	3
The Pawn	9			Lane Crawford	2		
Stormies	5			Linva Tailor	5		

9

THE MID-LEVELS ESCALATOR

Head east along Queen's Road from the Central MTR – or follow the walkways from IFC – and you'll reach the covered **Mid-Levels Escalator**, which rises in sections 800m up the hill as far as Conduit Road and the Mid-Levels residential area. During the morning (6–10am), when people are setting out to work, the escalators run downwards only; from 10.20am to midnight they run up. Places to get off and explore include the restaurant district between Wellington Street and Lyndhurst Terrace; the narrow lanes west of the escalator between Queen's Road and Hollywood Road, full of crowded produce markets and fancy greengrocers; Hollywood Road itself, lined with antique shops (see p.585); and the restaurant, bar and café district of Soho, along Elgin and Staunton streets.

Hollywood Road itself is of interest for the slew of antique shops and fine art galleries that run the length of it, with goods and prices ranging from the touristy to the serious-collectors-only. Within sight of the Mid-Levels Escalator, the Art Deco frontage of the former **Central Police Station** at 10 Hollywood Road and the decommissioned **Victoria Prison** immediately behind it were being redeveloped into an arts centre at the time of writing.

The Zoological and Botanical Gardens

Albany Rd · Daily 6am–7pm; greenhouse daily 9am–4.30pm · Free · ☎ 2530 0154, ⓦ lcsd.gov.hk · Bus #12 (10am–11.30pm; every 20min) from outside Outlying Islands Pier 6 stops near the Caine Rd entrance

Hong Kong's **Zoological and Botanical Gardens** opened in 1864 and currently house a troop of noisy buff-cheeked gibbons, orangutans and other primates, exotic birds and elderly tortoises. The stone memorial arch and lions at the main gateway commemorate the Chinese soldiers who died defending Hong Kong from the Japanese during World War II; once inside there's a pleasantly shaded mix of shrubs and trees to wander around and admire the views over Central. The gardens' two sections are connected by a walkway underneath Albany Road.

Sheung Wan

West of Central, **SHEUNG WAN**'s major landmark is the waterfront **Shun Tak Centre**, with two silver buildings edged in red housing both the Hong Kong–Macau Ferry Terminal and Sheung Wan MTR station. The main road here, Connaught, is crammed with traffic and the area looks no different from Central, but venture inland and things begin to change rapidly. The site of the first British settlement on the island, today Sheung Wan's backstreets are crammed with traditional businesses, from shops selling "cooling" medicinal tea (see box, p.581) to stores stacked high with paper funeral offerings. Most numerous (and malodorous), however, are the dried seafood stores for which the area is known.

Man Mo Temple

124 Hollywood Rd · Daily 8am–6pm · Free · ⓦ man-mo-temple.hk · MTR Sheung Wan, Exit A2

The blocky granite **Man Mo Temple** is one of the oldest in Hong Kong, dating from the 1840s and originally founded as a charitable institution. Just inside the entrance is a hanging board with the four characters for "Omnipotent Divine Grace", written by the emperor Guangxu; the central atrium beyond is hung with great spiral incense coils suspended from the ceiling, which fill the interior with eye-watering, aromatic smoke. The temple's name derives from the words for "culture" (*man* in Cantonese) and "martial" (*mo*): the first is embodied by Man Cheong, the deity of literature (he's the red-robed figure holding a writing brush on the right side of the altar); the second by the Three Kingdoms general Guan Yu (the statue opposite Man Cheong in green with a halberd), later deified as patron of the police, pawn shops and underworld gangs.

Ladder Street

MTR Sheung Wan, Exit A2

Running steeply downhill from Hollywood Road to Queen's Road Central, **Ladder Street** is a set of broad, worn stone steps. This is one of many such stairways scattered between here and Central, a relic of the nineteenth-century sedan-chair carriers who used them to get their loads up and down the hillsides. Just a short way down from Hollywood Road on the left is **Upper Lascar Row**, commonly known as **Cat Street**, a wall-to-wall stretch of curio stalls loaded with coins, ornaments and Chairman Mao badges.

Sheung Wan Market and Western Market

Sheung Wan Market 345 Queen's Rd • Daily 6am–8pm • **Western Market** 323 Des Voeux Rd • Daily 10am–7pm • MTR Sheung Wan, Exit B

A few minutes' walk west along Queen's Road Central brings you to **Sheung Wan Market**, a multistorey maze full of Chinese shoppers after fresh vegetables, fish and meat, with an inexpensive **cooked food** area up top. For a complete contrast, head north along Morrison Street to **Western Market**, a distinctive, Edwardian brick building, featuring a ground floor of stalls selling tourist tack and an upstairs gallery of cramped fabric shops selling beautiful, but pricey, lengths of silk brocade.

Dried goods shops

MTR Sheung Wan, Exit B

West of Morrison Street, you enter a web of lanes centred around **Bonham Strand West**, **Queen's Road West** and **Wing Lok Street**, whose shops specialize in dried foods and Traditional Chinese Medicine products such as birds' nests, ginseng, deer antlers, edible fungus, assorted dried marine creatures and shark fins. There's a fine line between food and medicine in China, but the best way of telling the difference here is seeing what is displayed in tiny red and gold gift packages (rare medicines), and what is shifted by the sackful (usually food).

Hong Kong Park

Main entrances off Cotton Tree Drive and Supreme Court Rd • Daily 6am–11pm; Edward Youde Aviary daily 9am–5pm • Free • ⓦ lcsd.gov.hk • MTR Admiralty, Exit C1

Hong Kong Park is a beautiful spot, landscaped in tiers up a steep hillside and full of greenery, ponds and waterfalls; it's a favourite location for **wedding photographs** and there's even a registry office here. The highlight of the park is the **Edward Youde Aviary**, where raised walkways lead you through a re-created rainforest canopy inside a giant meshed enclosure, with rare and colourful birds swooping about, nesting and breeding; a separate enclosure houses various endangered species of hornbill – fantastic black-and-white-banded birds with oversized curved beaks.

Flagstaff House Museum of Tea Ware

Hong Kong Park • Mon & Wed–Sun 10am–6pm • Free • MTR Admiralty, Exit C1

The **Flagstaff House Museum of Tea Ware** is another worthwhile sight, based near the park's Supreme Court Road entrance. Housed in an elegant colonial structure built in

---

HONG KONG FOR FREE

Hong Kong might be an expensive place compared with the Chinese mainland, but there are a number of **free things** to take advantage of while you're here. These include entry to all downtown and country parks, plus the Zoological and Botanical Gardens (see p.552); the Edward Youde Aviary and the Flagstaff House Museum of Tea Ware in Hong Kong Park (see p.553); some government-run museums; martial-arts performances in Kowloon Park on Sunday afternoons (see p.562); the ferry ride through Aberdeen Harbour to the *Jumbo* floating restaurant (see p.558); Mong Kok's bird garden and goldfish market (see p.563); harbour views from Tsim Sha Tsui waterfront (see p.561); and the Central Plaza Viewing Deck (see p.556).

9

the 1840s, the museum holds three thousand Chinese artefacts related to tea making. You can try some good samples – and buy good-value tea and reproduction antique teaware – next door at the pleasant *LockCha Tea House* (daily 10am–8pm; ⓦlockcha .com), which also serves excellent vegetarian *dim sum*.

The Peak

Victoria Peak rises 552m over Central and the harbour, providing those wealthy enough to own property up here with fantastic views and a more temperate climate than at sea level. While the summit itself is closed to the public, the surrounding parks and exclusive streets are known collectively as **The Peak**. Reasons to come up here include not just the superb vistas and forest walks, but also the unnerving ascent – either leaning back at an extreme angle on the **Peak Tram**, or careering around corners at the top of a double-decker bus (see box below).

The Peak Tower and Galleria

Mon–Fri 10am–11pm, Sat & Sun 8am–11pm • Sky Terrace 428 $48 • ☎ 2522 0922, ⓦ thepeak.com.hk

All transport up the Peak terminates around 390m above sea level at the ugly, wok-shaped **Peak Tower**, which features cafés and a branch of Madame Tussauds (daily 10am–10pm; $255), with wax models ranging from Marilyn Monroe to K-Pop superstars. The whole affair is topped by the Sky Terrace 428 observation deck, where you pay to see the view, though very similar – and free – ones can be had from a small stone terrace 100m to the east of the tower, and from the roof of the adjacent shopping complex, the **Peak Galleria**. Wherever your standpoint, the vistas are stupendous down over the island's intensely crowded north shore (incredibly, you're still lower than the tops of the IFC2 and ICC towers here), across the busy harbour to a lower-rise, unspectacular Kowloon and the green peaks of the New Territories – a cityscape which is no less spectacular when lit up at night.

The Peak Circle Walk

While it's not worth ascending to the very top of the Peak – capped, as it is, by security fencing and radio masts – it is worth strolling around the level, partially forested **Peak Circle Walk** via Lugard and Harlech roads, an easy hour-long return stroll from the Peak Tower with 360-degree views of the western end of the island. This is the first stage of the **Hong Kong Trail**, which winds for 50km between the island's hills before dropping back down to sea level at the end of the **Dragon's Back hike** (see box, p.559).

ASCENDING AND DESCENDING THE PEAK

The most popular way to arrive at or depart from the Peak is aboard the **Peak Tram** (daily 7am–midnight; $32 one-way, $45 return; ⓦthepeak.com.hk), actually a funicular railway whose incredibly steep track climbs the 386m to the Peak Tower in about eight minutes. The tram's lower terminus is on Garden Road, reached aboard bus #15C from outside the Outlying Islands Ferry Piers (daily 10am–11.40pm; every 20min).

For an equally fun ride, sit upstairs at the front of bus #15 (daily 10am–midnight; every 20min) as it tackles low branches and hairpin bends on the half-hour ascent from the Outlying Islands Ferry Piers. You can also pick it up at Exchange Square bus station or along Queen's Road East.

An excellent way to descend the Peak – or, if you're a hardened jogger, to ascend it – is on foot via the **Old Peak Road**, a concrete track whose unsigned beginning is a little hard to find around the side of the Peak Tower. The extremely steep, twenty-minute descent lands you among high-rise residences southwest of the Zoological and Botanical Gardens, which you can reach by continuing down the road for a further fifteen minutes.

FROM TOP *DIM SUM* SELECTION (P.581); NANLIAN GARDENS (P.564) >

9

Wan Chai

Both Wan Chai MTR station on Hennessy Rd and tram-lined Johnston Rd are within walking distance of the sights; there's also a Star Ferry service (see p.549) between the Tsim Sha Tsui ferry terminal and the Wan Chai ferry pier, just east of the Convention and Exhibition Centre

East of Central, **WAN CHAI** is a nondescript district of broad, busy main roads and more towers, though these mainly house commercial, rather than financial, institutions. Back in the 1950s, Wan Chai was a thriving red-light district, famed as the setting for Richard Mason's novel *The World of Suzy Wong*, and there's still a vaguely sleazy feel to its core of **bars and clubs**. The main arteries here are parallel **Hennessy Road**, **Lockhart Road** – both lined with shops and restaurants – and the waterfront expressway **Gloucester Road**.

The Convention and Exhibition Centre

Convention Avenue • ☎ 2582 8888, ⓦ hkcec.com • MTR Wan Chai, Exit A1

Wan Chai's most striking building is the **Hong Kong Convention and Exhibition Centre**, whose curved roof juts out into the harbour and ostensibly resembles a manta ray. This is where the British formally handed Hong Kong back to the Chinese in June 1997, and as such is a draw for mainland tourists who pose beside the seafront **Forever Blooming Bauhinia statue**. Adjacent flagpoles fly the red- and gold-spangled banner of the People's Republic, and the five-petalled bauhinia emblem of the Hong Kong SAR.

Central Plaza

Gloucester Rd • Public viewing area Mon–Fri 8am–8pm • Free • MTR Wan Chai, Exit A1

Immediately south of the Convention and Exhibition Centre soars the 78-storey **Central Plaza**. With a triangular cross section and topped by a tall spire, it has been dubbed "The Big Syringe" by locals; the tower's glowing cladding changes colour every fifteen minutes from 6pm to 6am. For splendid **360-degree views** over the city, catch the lift to the public viewing area on the 46th floor.

Queen's Road East

MTR Admiralty, Exit J, or MTR Wan Chai, Exit A3

Up against the Peak's foothills, **Queen's Road East** features a mix of tiny boutiques and furniture stores, and many of the latter deal in traditional Chinese designs. Partway along and built into a roadside grotto, the tiny **Hung Shing Temple** is dedicated to a deified Tang-dynasty official skilled in foretelling the weather; hip restaurants line the lower reaches of nearby Ship Street before it dead-ends at **Nam Koo Terrace**, a decaying old mansion that is reputedly the most haunted spot in Hong Kong. Between Queen's Road East and Johnston Road a slew of backstreet **markets** jam the narrow lanes, making the newly developed **Lee Tung Avenue** – full of luxury brands and high-end pastry shops – feel decidedly out of place.

Pak Tai Temple

Stone Nullah Lane • Daily 8am–5pm • Free • MTR Wan Chai, Exit A3

A short walk from the eastern end of Queen's Road East, the **Pak Tai Temple** is a solid, granite-block building with a roof decorated with a procession of glazed pottery figurines depicting lively scenes from Chinese legends. The temple is fairly plain inside, with a mighty bronze statue of Pak Tai, the flood-quelling deity of the north, stamping down on the evil forms of a turtle and a snake.

Bowen Road and Lovers' Rock

Bus #15 (10am–12.15am every 15min) to the Peak from Outer Islands Ferry Piers via Exchange Square and Queen's Rd East, or a steep walk up Wan Chai Gap Rd from behind Pak Tai Temple

Up on the steep, forested slope above Queen's Road East is **Bowen Road**, a pedestrian track popular with joggers. As well as providing a surprisingly shaded, rural walk, with the sounds of the city drifting up from below, Bowen Road gives access to **Lovers' Rock**, a huge stone boulder pointing skywards through the canopy, draped in festive red ribbons. The rock becomes a pilgrimage site during the annual Seven Sisters' Festival during the seventh lunar month (usually in August).

Causeway Bay

Causeway Bay's MTR station is on Hennessy Rd, which, along with its extension, Yee Wo St, is also covered by trams

East of the Aberdeen expressway, **Causeway Bay** forms a knot of lively, seething streets packed with restaurants, accommodation and shopping plazas. You might also visit midweek for the horse races in nearby Happy Valley, or for relief from urban claustrophobia in Victoria Park.

The Noon Day Gun

Take the tunnel underneath Gloucester Rd from the car park next to the *Excelsior Hotel*; MTR Causeway Bay, Exit D1

Causeway Bay's sole tourist sight is the waterfront **Noon Day Gun** – immortalized in Noël Coward's song *Mad Dogs and Englishmen*. This small naval cannon is fired off with a loud report every day at noon, a tradition dating back to the early days of the colony (though the exact reasons for the practice remain obscure); at other times, the gun is covered up and there's nothing to see.

Victoria Park

Open 24hr • MTR Causeway Bay, Exit E

The eastern end of Causeway Bay is dominated by **Victoria Park**, which has shady paths, swimming pools and other sports facilities. The park has become the location for the annual candlelit vigil held on June 4 to commemorate the victims of Tian'anmen Square, and the hardtop football pitches regularly host big events – the city's largest Chinese New Year fair and the Hong Kong Flower Show (mid-March) are the most popular. Visit on a Sunday and you'll join the throngs of Indonesian maids who enjoy their day off in the park.

Happy Valley Racecourse

Races Sept–June Wed 7–11pm • $10 • ☎ 2895 1523, ⓦ hkjc.com • Tram to Happy Valley or MTR Causeway Bay, Exit A

Occupying a former malarial swamp, **Happy Valley Racecourse** provides Hong Kong with one of the city's few legal outlets for gambling, and as such is indescribably popular during racing season. Standing trackside in the public enclosure you can mix with the beer-fuelled expat crowd and chat to staff to make sense of the intricate accumulator bets that Hong Kong specializes in; alternatively, join the hard-bitten Chinese punters up in the stands for all the cigarette smoke and Cantonese cursing you can handle.

The Museum of Coastal Defence

175 Tung Hei Rd • Mon–Wed & Fri–Sun 10am–5pm • Free • ☎ 2569 1500, ⓦ hk.coastaldefence.museum • Island Line MTR to Shau Kei Wan; take Exit B1 and follow the signs for 10min via Shau Kei Wan St East and Tung Hei Rd

Around 6km east of Causeway Bay, the splendid **Museum of Coastal Defence** is located inside the 1887 Lei Yue Mun Fort, which itself is built into a hill overlooking the narrow eastern end of the harbour. There are great views from the seawards-facing gun emplacements, while the former barracks and ammunition rooms are filled with an exhaustive collection of artefacts, mannequins and photographs covering the history of Hong Kong's naval militias from the Ming dynasty to the handover.

To get across the harbour to **Lei Yue Mun** village and its excellent seafood restaurants, take the MTR one stop west to Sai Wan Ho, where a ferry runs to Sam Ka Tsuen Pier every thirty minutes.

Aberdeen

Bus #70 (every 15–20min) from Exchange Square in Central; bus #73 (every 30min) from Repulse Bay, Deep Water Bay and Stanley; bus #48 (every 15min) from Ocean Park

Down on the south coast, **ABERDEEN** is the largest separate town on Hong Kong Island, with a population of more than sixty thousand living in garishly coloured tower blocks

9

ABERDEEN HARBOUR CRUISES

Approach Aberdeen Harbour and you'll be grabbed by locals touting for **boat tours** in traditional flat-bottomed sampans (around $50/person for a 30min ride). The trips offer photogenic views of houseboats complete with dogs, drying laundry and outdoor kitchens, as well as luxury yachts, boat yards and **floating restaurants**, which are especially spectacular when lit up at night.

Cheapskates can, in fact, enjoy a ten-minute **free harbour trip** by catching a ferry to the garishly decorated *Jumbo* restaurant (see p.583) from a signed dock with a red gateway near the fish market; there's no pressure to actually have a meal here if you just want to look around. You'll also pass through the harbour if you use one of Aberdeen's **ferries to the Outlying Islands** (see p.567).

around the sheltered **harbour**. Aberdeen is a **fishing port** – its fleet of family-run trawlers once provided around a third of Hong Kong's seafood catch – and despite the industry's gradual decline, there's still a busy fish market at the harbour early each morning. The harbour is also an important venue for the annual Dragon Boat Festival, held on the fifth day of the fifth lunar month (usually in June).

Ocean Park

Hours vary, see website for details • $385; children aged 3–11 $193; children under 3 free • ☎ 3923 2323, ⓦ oceanpark.com.hk • South Island Line MTR to Ocean Park; bus #629 from Central Star Ferry pier (9.45am–3.45pm; hourly) and Admiralty (9am–5pm; every 15min); bus #48 (every 15min) from Aberdeen to the western entrance; bus #73 (every 30min) from Stanley to the highway outside

Ocean Park, a gigantic theme and adventure park, covers an entire peninsula to the east of Aberdeen. Once you're inside, all rides and shows are free and you could easily spend the best part of a day here. The park is popular with tour groups and you may find yourself frustrated by queues at the biggest attractions, so make sure you arrive early in order to enjoy yourself at a relaxed pace. Pick of the sights include three **giant pandas**, with two kept in their own 2000-square-metre complex; scary rides such as the Dragon roller coaster and Abyss turbo drop; plus the **Grand Aquarium**, a huge coral-reef aquarium that contains more than five thousand fish.

Stanley

Bus #6, #6A or #260 from Central (every 10–20min); bus #73 (every 30min) from Aberdeen or Repulse Bay; green minibus #40 (every 10min) from Times Square in Causeway Bay

Straddling the neck of Hong Kong's most southerly peninsula, **STANLEY** was already settled by fishermen and pirates when the British took Hong Kong Island in 1842. Today, this small residential town feels uncomfortably overcrowded with expats and tourists, the former filling the seafront restaurants at weekend lunchtimes, the latter gravitating towards **Stanley Market**, a couple of covered lanes selling a mishmash of souvenirs including clothes, embroideries, paintings and trinkets. Stanley also hosts Hong Kong's liveliest **dragon boat races**, held on the fifth day of the fifth lunar month, usually falling in June.

Murray House and Blake Pier

Just back from the shore, **Stanley Plaza** faces one of Hong Kong's oldest colonial buildings, two-storey **Murray House**, which was dismantled and removed from its original 1840 site in Central to make way for the Bank of China. Today, its elegant stone colonnades house a handful of bars and restaurants; opposite, the reconstructed **Blake Pier**, its iron pillars and corrugated roof dating to 1900, extends Stanley's heritage architecture right to the seafront.

Tin Hau Temple

Across the square from Murray House is a **Tin Hau Temple**, built in 1767. Tin Hau is the southern Chinese protective deity of fishermen, and her temples can be found throughout Southeast Asia. This temple, besides generously devoting a good deal of space to statues of other gods, is worth a look for the blackened and barely recognizable

tiger skin spread-eagled on one wall, the remains of an animal killed near here in 1942 – the last ever shot in Hong Kong.

Shek O
Bus #9 (every 15min) from Shau Kei Wan MTR

In the far southeast of the island, **SHEK O** is Hong Kong Island's most remote settlement, with an almost Mediterranean flavour in its stone houses, narrow lanes and seafront location. There's strong surf beating the wide, white **beach**, which has a shady area of vine trellises at one end for barbecues and, during the week, is more or less deserted. Come for sunbathing and lunch at one of the cheap local restaurants. The surrounding headlands are also popular for **hiking**, especially the fearsome-sounding but straightforward two-hour-long **Dragon's Back** trail (see box below).

You can't miss the beach – it's just 50m from the bus stop, beyond a small roundabout. Nearby shops such as the Tung Lok Beachside Store sell beachwear, inflatable floats, plastic buckets and so on, and also have storage lockers. Most of the other businesses in the village are fairly inexpensive restaurants.

Kowloon

A 4km-long strip of the mainland ceded to Britain in perpetuity in 1860 to add to their offshore island, **KOWLOON** was accordingly developed with gusto and confidence. The skyline here has never matched Hong Kong Island's, thanks to Kowloon being in the flight path of the old airport at Kai Tak, though things could be changing: 2010 saw the completion of Hong Kong's tallest building, the 484m-high **International Commerce Centre** (ICC), atop Elements Mall and the Airport Express terminal in West Kowloon. With rocketing rents and dwindling space along Hong Kong Island's north shore, it could be that the ICC marks a shift in venue for the SAR's next wave of cutting-edge, harbourside architecture.

Initially, it's hard to see how such an intensely commercial and crowded place as Kowloon could possibly appeal to travellers. One reason is the staggering **view** across the harbour to Hong Kong Island's skyscrapers; another is the sheer density of **shopping** opportunities here – from high-end jewellery to cutting-edge electronic goods and outright tourist tat – especially in the couple of square kilometres at the tip of the peninsula that make up **Tsim Sha Tsui**. To the north, **Yau Ma Tei** and **Mong Kok** are less touristy – though even more crowded – districts teeming with soaring tenements and local **markets**, some of which sell modern daily necessities, others with a distinctly traditional Chinese twist.

These days, it's not so clear-cut where Kowloon really ends. The original "border" with the New Territories to the north was **Boundary Street**, though now the Kowloon district runs on for a further 3km or so, as the commercial emphasis shifts towards towering **residential estates** clustered around shopping plazas, parks and other amenities. A scattering of sights here includes one of Hong Kong's busiest temples, **Wong Tai Sin Temple**, and its prettiest, the **Chi Lin Nunnery** with its Tang-style architecture and beautiful attached garden.

HIKING THE DRAGON'S BACK

One of the easiest coastal hikes in Hong Kong, the **Dragon's Back** takes just a couple of hours to complete, and at weekends you'll find plenty of other people along the trail.

Catch **bus #9** from Shau Kei Wan MTR station and get off at **To Tei Wan**, where there's a roadside parking bay and a billboard showing a map of the route, then follow the track up onto the ridgetop Dragon's Back itself. The trail runs north, passing views of Stanley and beautiful seascapes, before eventually descending to **Big Wave Bay**, where there are beaches and snack stalls, and a final 2km walk along the road south to Shek O.

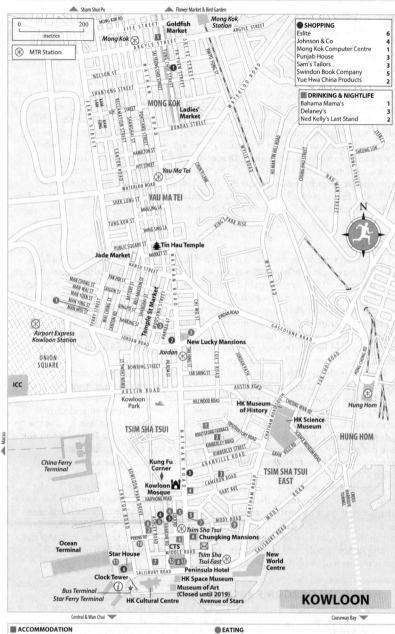

SHOPPING

Eslite	6
Johnson & Co	4
Mong Kok Computer Centre	1
Punjab House	3
Sam's Tailors	3
Swindon Book Company	5
Yue Hwa China Products	2

DRINKING & NIGHTLIFE

Bahama Mama's	1
Delaney's	3
Ned Kelly's Last Stand	2

KOWLOON

Tsim Sha Tsui

The tourist heart of Hong Kong, **TSIM SHA TSUI** is an easy place to find your way around. The prime arrival point, the **Star Ferry Terminal**, is right on the southwestern tip of the peninsula. East from here are outstanding views of Hong Kong Island and a number of harbourside museums and galleries, one of which – the city's **Museum of Art** – is currently closed for major renovation work, and is expected to reopen in 2019.

The first street built in Kowloon, **Nathan Road**, bisects Tsim Sha Tsui from north to south, with the lanes on either side busy around the clock with shoppers. In among all this brash commercial activity, **Kowloon Park** offers a bit of space to rest, surrounded by ornamental paving and shrubberies.

Hong Kong Cultural Centre

Salisbury Rd, 50m east of the Star Ferry Terminal • Box office daily 9am–9pm • Free • ☎ 2734 2009, ⓦ hkculturalcentre.gov.hk • MTR Tsim Sha Tsui and East Tsim Sha Tsui, Exit L6

A drab, brown-tiled building, the **Hong Kong Cultural Centre** is notable for its astonishing lack of windows over one of the most picturesque urban landscapes in the world; inside are concert halls, theatres and galleries. Adjacent is the **Clock Tower**, the only remaining piece of the Kowloon Railway Station, from where you could once take a train all the way back to Europe, via Mongolia and Russia.

Hong Kong Space Museum

10 Salisbury Rd • Mon & Wed–Fri 1–9pm, Sat & Sun 10am–9pm • $10; planetarium shows $24–32 • ☎ 2721 0226, ⓦ hk.space.museum • MTR Tsim Sha Tsui and East Tsim Sha Tsui, Exit J4

The Chinese have a genuinely long history of astronomical observations – they were the first to record Halley's Comet in 240 BC, and the later emperors set up accurate observatories with the help of Jesuit priests. Hong Kong's **Space Museum**, undergoing a revamp at the time of writing but expected to reopen in early 2017, promises to trace the entire history with hands-on displays and interactive exhibits. There's also a Space Theatre planetarium here, which presents Omnimax shows for an additional fee.

Avenue of Stars

MTR Tsim Sha Tsui and East Tsim Sha Tsui, Exit J3

For **harbour views**, head down to the promenade that runs for around 500m east from the Clock Tower; it's especially good at night, when Central's skyscrapers flash and pulse to a synthesized beat during the **Symphony of Lights** (daily 8pm; free). The eastern end of the promenade – closed for renovation until late 2018 – becomes the **Avenue of Stars**, a tribute to Hong Kong's film industry (once the third largest in the world).

The Peninsula Hotel

Salisbury Rd • ☎ 2920 2888, ⓦ peninsula.com • MTR Tsim Sha Tsui, Exit E

The **Peninsula Hotel** is one of the SAR's great surviving pieces of colonial architecture. Built in the 1920s facing the now-demolished Kowloon Railway Station, the hotel offered a spot of elegance to Hong Kong's weary new arrivals. Even if you don't stay here – it's one of the most expensive hotels – echoes of former splendour linger in the elegant lobby, where **afternoon tea** (2–6pm; $358 per person) is still served daily to the sounds of a string quartet performing on the balcony above.

Nathan Road

MTR Tsim Sha Tsui, Exit A1–E

Running north through the heart of Kowloon, **Nathan Road** is by no means a beautiful street, but nonetheless houses a concentrated collection of electronics shops, tailors, jewellery stores and fashion boutiques, and is somewhere to experience the commercial spirit that really drives Hong Kong. Actually shopping here is not always such a good idea – for more details, see "Shopping", p.585.

9

There's a multicultural flavour provided by the hulking, dubious block of **Chungking Mansions**, the centre of Hong Kong's budget accommodation (see p.579), and the lower floors form an atmospheric shopping arcade where immigrants from the Indian subcontinent rub elbows with Western tourists, businessmen from central and southeastern Asia, and African entrepreneurs.

Kowloon Park

Main entrance at the corner of Haiphong Rd and Nathan Rd • Daily 5am–midnight • Free • MTR Tsim Sha Tsui, Exit A1

West of Nathan Road, half of Tsim Sha Tsui is occupied by **Kowloon Park**, which is invisible from Nathan Road but marked at its southeastern corner by the white-domed **Kowloon Mosque**, which caters to the area's substantial Muslim population. The park itself provides a welcome, green respite from the rest of Tsim Sha Tsui, with a swimming pool, aviary and bird ponds (featuring colourful flamingos), a sculpture walk and the **Kung Fu Corner** (up behind the mosque), where experts in various martial arts demonstrate every Sunday between 2.30 and 4.30pm.

Hong Kong Museum of History

100 Chatham Rd South • Mon & Wed–Fri 10am–6pm, Sat & Sun 10am–7pm • Free • ☎ 2724 9042, ⓦ hk.history.museum • MTR Tsim Sha Tsui, Exit B2

The **Hong Kong Museum of History** features "The Hong Kong Story", a permanent exhibition that walks visitors through the SAR's history through eight different galleries. While the museum was set for renovation at the time of writing, for now the pick of the exhibits is a poignant diorama of Stone Age foragers on an as-yet-undeveloped seashore; a reconstructed old-style Tanka junk, complete with fishing nets; and an entire street, including shops and temple buildings, which you can explore.

Hong Kong Science Museum

2 Science Museum Rd • Mon–Wed & Fri 10am–7pm, Sat & Sun 10am–9pm • $20 • ☎ 2732 3232, ⓦ hk.science.museum • MTR Tsim Sha Tsui, Exit B2

Adjacent to the Museum of History, the **Hong Kong Science Museum** comprises four floors full of things to prod, poke and pull apart, and is a handy place to bring children for a couple of hours on a rainy day. By far the best feature is the huge "Energy Machine", which features wooden balls racing around the entire museum on a complex giant maze of tracks, buckets, pulleys, drums and gongs – ask at the front desk for performance times.

International Commerce Centre (ICC)

1 Austin Rd West • Sky100 observation deck Mon–Thurs & Sun 10am–9pm, Fri 10am–10pm, Sat 10am–11.30pm • $168 • ☎ 2613 3888, ⓦ shkp-icc.com • MTR Kowloon, Exit C

At 484m, the **International Commerce Centre** is Hong Kong's tallest building. While most of the floors are occupied by investment banks, the very highest are accessible to the public via the pricey **Sky100 observation deck**, a floor of restaurants on the 101st storey, or – at the very top – the *Ritz-Carlton*'s swanky bar, *Ozone* (the world's highest; ⓦ ritzcarlton.com), all of which offer astounding views across the city from the massive Kwai Tsing container terminal below to the green hills that encircle Hong Kong's urban core. Even if you don't make it out here, it's worth checking the tower out after dark when the building is transformed by a light show depicting carp swimming up its glassy flanks.

Temple Street Night Market

Temple St • Daily dusk–11pm • ⓦ temple-street-night-market.hk • MTR Jordan, Exit A, or MTR Yau Ma Tei, Exit C

Every evening, **Temple Street Night Market** becomes one of Hong Kong's biggest tourist draws, and it's crammed with stalls selling souvenir T-shirts, leatherwear, games and assorted trinkets. The most established section sits between Nanking Street and Kansu Street, but push on north past a square housing the local **Tin Hau Temple** and you'll find yet more stalls selling everything from antiques to sex toys. Just before the temple is a crowd of fortune-tellers (some of whom, mysteriously, use live budgerigars in their routines), and a couple of outdoor karaoke tents where locals compete in screaming out Cantopop classics.

9

Jade Market

Kansu St • Daily 9am–6pm • MTR Yau Ma Tei, Exit C

Set right underneath a busy overpass, the **Jade Market** features several hundred stalls under a canvas awning – it looks temporary, but has actually been here for decades. Being so hard, jade is believed to prevent decay and many southern Chinese people wear pendants or bangles made from the stone as protection against old age. The finest dark green variety comes from Myanmar (Burma); other varieties include white jade from Hetian (Khotan) in Xinjiang province (see p.858). You'd have to really know your precious stones to find a bargain, but the market is still a fun place to browse.

The Ladies' and Goldfish markets

Tung Choi St • Daily 10am till late • MTR Mong Kok, Exit D2

East of Nathan Road as it cuts through the frenetically crowded heart of **Mong Kok** district, the lower end of Tung Choi Street hosts the **Ladies' Market**, which flogs piles of cheap clothes, jewellery, toys and bags. Parallel streets are thick with shops specializing in computers, cameras and mobile phones, and are more reliable than Tsim Sha Tsui. Push on north over Argyle Street and Tung Choi Street transforms into a **Goldfish Market**, lined with shops stocking aquaria, corals, exotic fish and even some dubiously exotic breeds of snakes, lizards and turtles.

The Flower Market and Bird Garden

Flower Market Flower Market Rd • Daily 7am–7pm • ⓦ flower-market.hk • **Bird Garden** Yuen Po St • Daily 7am–8pm • ⓦ bird -garden.hk • MTR Prince Edward, Exit B1

North of Mong Kok, over Prince Edward Road, it's a short walk east to the **Flower Market**. This is best on Sundays and in the run-up to Chinese New Year, when people come to buy narcissi, orange trees and plum blossom to decorate their apartments to bring good luck. Running at an angle from here up to Boundary Street, the **Bird Garden** displays hundreds of birds for sale, along with intricately designed bamboo cages.

North of Boundary Street

The 3km-deep area between Boundary Street and the steep Kowloon Hills – beyond which lie the New Territories – offers a mix of temples, more bargain shopping, some surprisingly ancient history and two unusual parks. With the exception of Kowloon Walled City Park, for which you may need a bus, all are within twenty minutes of downtown Kowloon by MTR.

Sham Shui Po

MTR Sham Shui Po

SHAM SHUI PO lies just 1km northwest of the Boundary Street and Nathan Road intersection. The district is jammed with **wholesale garment outlets**, which line central Cheung Sha Wan Road for a couple of blocks either side of the MTR station. While you shouldn't expect the height of fashion, there are some very good deals to be had if you're prepared to dig around. Parallel **Ap Liu Street** is lined with cheap electronics shops, though these are mostly obscured by the stalls of the **flea market** held here every day from about noon until 9pm; don't expect to find anything remotely valuable, but it's a fun, untouristy place to browse.

Lei Cheng Uk Han Tomb Museum

41 Tonkin St • Mon–Wed & Fri–Sun 10am–6pm • Free • MTR Cheung Sha Wan, Exit A3, and follow signs along Tonkin St

One MTR stop on from Sham Shui Po, **Lei Cheng Uk Han Tomb Museum** is constructed over a 2000-year-old Han-dynasty tomb, which looks like a large brick oven and was

9

uncovered in 1955. The tomb yielded a few bronzes and bits of pottery, but no evidence that it was ever used for a burial; its value lies in the fact that it proves a long Han Chinese presence in the area. There's an informative display and you can peer through a glass window into the chamber itself.

Kowloon Walled City Park

Tung Tsing Rd • Daily 6.30am–11pm; exhibition rooms 10am–6pm • Free • MTR Lok Fu, Exit B and walk 1km south along Junction Rd; bus #1 (every 10min) from the Tsim Sha Tsui Star Ferry Terminal or Nathan Road

Kowloon Walled City Park is the site of a Qing-dynasty fortified garrison post whose soldiers refused to cede sovereignty to Britain when it took over the New Territories in 1898. For nearly a century it remained a self-governing enclave of criminals and vagrants, off-limits to the authorities until they negotiated its closure and demolition in 1994. It's now an attractive spread of lawns, trees and traditional buildings, which include the "city's" reconstructed *yamen* (courthouse building).

Wong Tai Sin Temple

Lung Cheung Rd, Wong Tai Sin • Daily 7am–5pm • Free • MTR Wong Tai Sin, Exit B2

The **Wong Tai Sin Temple** is a thriving complex – pulling in more worshippers than any other temple in Hong Kong – and dedicated to the mythical Immortal Huang, a fourth-century Taoist hermit believed to have had healing powers. Big, bright and colourful, it provides a good insight into popular Chinese religion: expect vigorous kneeling, incense burning and the noisy rattling of fortune sticks in canisters, as well as the presentation of food and drink to the deities. Large numbers of **fortune-tellers**, some of whom speak English, have stands to the right of the entrance and charge around $50 for palm-reading, and about half that for fortune stick interpretation (though these can also be looked up online).

Chi Lin Nunnery

5 Chi Lin Drive, Diamond Hill • Daily 9am–4.30pm • Free • ☎ 2354 1888, ⓦ chilin.org • MTR Diamond Hill, Exit C2, and follow the signs

Modern **Chi Lin Nunnery** is an elegant, dark wooden temple built without nails in Tang-dynasty style. Two large courtyards are open to visitors: the first is filled with lotus ponds, while the second holds the **Hall of Celestial Kings**, where 28 thick cedar columns support the heavy tiled roof over a Buddha statue and his gilded entourage.

Nan Lian Gardens

60 Fung Tak Rd, Diamond Hill • Daily 7am–9pm • Free • ☎ 3658 9366, ⓦ nanliangarden.org • MTR Diamond Hill, Exit C2, and follow the signs

Opposite Chi Lin Nunnery and connected by a walkway, the tranquil and beautiful **Nan Lian Gardens** continue the Tang theme in an exquisite reconstruction of a contemporary garden; there are contorted pine trees, artfully shaped hillocks, ornamental ponds populated by fat koi carp, and brightly painted bridges and pavilions.

The New Territories

Many people visit Hong Kong without ever leaving the built-up downtown areas, though the **NEW TERRITORIES**, a 30km-deep swath between Kowloon and the Guangdong border, comes complete with beautiful coastlines, antique villages and craggy mountains. A whole series of designated **country parks** includes the unspoilt **Sai Kung Peninsula** to the east, which offers excellent walking trails and secluded beaches, and there are also less demanding nature fixes available at the **Hong Kong Wetland Park** and **Kadoorie Farm**. Elsewhere, there's architectural and cultural heritage to soak up around the otherwise modern **New Towns**, which are satellite settlements built from scratch in the last forty years to absorb the overflow from Hong Kong's burgeoning population.

9

Travelling around the New Territories is straightforward, with the MTR extending right to the Chinese border, and frequent buses and minibuses are available where needed.

Tai Mo Shan

MTR Tsuen Wan West, Exit D, then turn left and walk 150m to the station where bus #51 departs (hourly, 6.20am–11.20pm); tell the driver where you're going

Hong Kong's 957m apex, **Tai Mo Shan**, is nearly twice the height of the Peak on Hong Kong Island; people come up here on winter mornings hoping to see frost. The two-hour walk up the west face from the roadside **Tai Mo Shan Visitor Centre** at the base of the mountain to the summit is steep but not difficult, and follows a sealed road past the turnoff to the *Sze Lok Yuen Youth Hostel* (see p.580). Views from the top encompass Hong Kong Island, the Sai Kung Peninsula and Shenzhen's wall of skyscrapers, which is magnificent on a clear day. It's very exposed, however – bring a hat, plenty of water, sunscreen and a map, as there are multiple trails down to the roads on the mountain's eastern flank.

Kam Tin and Kat Hing Wai

$3 donation • MTR Kam Sheung Road, Exit B, and follow signposts; bus #64K (every 15min) from Tai Po Market MTR via Kadoorie Farm

Northwest of Tai Mo Shan, **KAM TIN** is the site of **Kat Hing Wai**, one of Hong Kong's last inhabited **walled settlements**. Dating back to the late sixteenth century when a clan named Tang settled here, the village is still surrounded by thick, 6m-high walls and corner towers. Take note of the gates, too – confiscated by the British in the late nineteenth century, they were eventually tracked down in Ireland in the 1920s and returned. Inside the walls, there's a wide lane running down the middle of the village, with tiny alleys leading off it. Old ladies in traditional hats pester visitors with cameras for donations, and most of the buildings are modern, but the atmosphere is as different from downtown Hong Kong as you could imagine.

Hong Kong Wetland Park

Wetland Park Rd, Tin Shui Wai • Mon & Wed–Sun 10am–5pm • $30 • ☎ 3152 2666, ⊛ wetlandpark.gov.hk • MTR Tin Shui Wai, Exit E1 to the Light Rail platform, then train #705 to Wetland Park; bus #967 (every 20min) from Admiralty

Hong Kong Wetland Park covers 150 acres of saltwater marsh up along the Chinese border, and is part of a larger system of lagoons that draws wintering wildfowl between November and February, and migrating birds from August to October. The park is carefully landscaped with paths, bridges and hides, has an excellent visitor centre, and makes a great half-day out. Highlights include the mangrove boardwalk, where you can watch mudskippers and fiddler crabs scooting across the mud; the huge lotus ponds (look out for the occasional swimming snake); and Pui Pui, a saltwater crocodile thought to be an abandoned pet, who was captured in Hong Kong's Shan Pui River after evading a crack team of hunters for months. There's a branch of *Café de Coral* here, which serves inexpensive lunches and drinks.

Sha Tin

MTR Sha Tin

The booming New Town of **SHA TIN**, which spreads along either side of the Shing Mun River, is best known to Hong Kongers as the site of the territory's second **racecourse**. It's probably the most pleasant of the New Towns, with water out front and towering green mountains to the east, though it's a rather anonymous experience wandering the vast maze of air-conditioned shopping malls that fill the centre.

Hong Kong Heritage Museum

1 Man Lam Rd • Mon & Wed–Fri 10am–6pm, Sat & Sun 10am–7pm • Free • ☎ 2180 8188, ⊛ www.heritagemuseum.gov.hk • MTR Che Kung Temple and follow signposts

Exhibits at the **Hong Kong Heritage Museum** are similar to those at the Hong Kong Museum of History (see p.562), and if you've seen those there may seem little need to

9

come here. That said, the Cantonese Opera Heritage Hall has a fun mock-up of a bamboo opera stage and plenty of flamboyant costumes; the Gallery of Chinese Art features some excellent ceramics and jade; and there's a great temporary exhibit about **Bruce Lee** running until July 2018 that includes his hand-drawn action sequences from *Enter the Dragon*, movie costumes and plenty of well-worn training equipment.

Ten Thousand Buddhas Monastery

221 Pai Tau Village • Daily 9am–5pm • Free • MTR Sha Tin; exit station down ramp, follow the road around to the left and take the first road right, past the government offices to the end, where you'll find a sign and footpath for the monastery

Sha Tin's **Ten Thousand Buddhas Monastery** dates only to the 1960s, but is one of the most interesting temples in the New Territories. The steep stairway from town is flanked by five hundred life-sized statues of Buddhist saints, and leads you to a courtyard filled by garish concrete sculptures. The main hall, after which the monastery is named, houses some 13,000 miniature statues of Buddha arranged on shelves, while the embalmed and gilded body of the temple's founder sits in the lotus position in front of the main altar. Check out the outlying waterfall too, with its placid statue of Guanyin and statues of warrior monks arranged on the hillside as if planning a raid on Sha Tin. Lunch is available at a basic **vegetarian restaurant**.

Tai Po

MTR Tai Po Market

TAI PO is one of the New Territories' most established towns, with a historic centre surrounded by new housing and industrial estates. Follow signs for fifteen minutes to the attractive **Man Mo Yi Tai Temple** on Fu Shin Street, and then head for the action in the busy market packing out the surrounding lanes. Uphill from here at the end of Shung Tak Street, the **Hong Kong Railway Museum** (Mon & Wed–Sun 10am–6pm; free) occupies Tai Po's old Chinese-style station, which was built in 1913; model trains and photographs cover the construction of the original Kowloon-to-Canton Railway, and there are some old coaches and engines displayed out back.

Kadoorie Farm

Lam Kam Rd • Daily 9.30am–5pm; closed holidays • $30 • ☎ 2483 7200, ⓦ kfbg.org.hk • Bus #64K (every 15min) from Tai Po Market MTR

Out on the road between Tai Po and Kam Tin (see p.565), **Kadoorie Farm** is an organic farm and wildlife sanctuary, located up the steep rear slopes of Tai Mo Shan. It's a good place for children and zoologists, offering walks, guided tours and close views of orphaned birds, wild boar, leopard cats and muntjac deer – this is probably your only chance to see some of Hong Kong's most elusive creatures.

Plover Cove Country Park and Tai Mei Tuk

ⓦ afcd.gov.hk • MTR Tai Po Market, then bus #75K (every 20min) to Tai Mei Tuk

The coastline northeast of Tai Po fringes **Plover Cove Country Park**, which surrounds the massive Plover Cove Reservoir. Easy access means it gets very busy at weekends and holidays. The bus from Tai Po Market MTR station terminates at the western edge of the reservoir, just outside the county park in the small village and service centre of **TAI MEI TUK**. There are a few low-key restaurants here, as well as the *Bradbury Jockey Club Youth Hostel* (see p.580). Tai Mei Tuk is also the starting point for the 15km-long, exposed but straightforward day-hike around the **Plover Cove Reservoir Trail**, and it's about an hour's walk along the road, past barbecue sites overlooking the reservoir, from **Bride's Pool**, an attractively wooded picnic and camping site beside a shallow stream and waterfalls.

The Sai Kung Peninsula

Hong Kong's easternmost projection, the rugged **Sai Kung Peninsula** is a mass of jagged headlands, spiky peaks, vivid blue seascapes and tiny offshore islands. Most of the area is enclosed within **country parks**, with a range of picnic spots and walking trails around the coast leading to Hong Kong's finest beaches.

Sai Kung

MTR Choi Hung, then green minibus #1A (every 5min) to terminus

The peninsula's access point is busy **SAI KUNG**. Moderately developed and with a large expat population, it has a bustling fishing port and a promenade packed with pricey seafood restaurants and fishermen flogging their wares. Shops sell swimming gear, sunscreen and bright inflatables, and there's a market and supermarket if you fancy putting your own lunch together. The harbour is full of cruisers, small fishing boats and sampans, whose owners will offer rides out to various islands; the nearest and most popular is **Kiu Tsui Chau** or Sharp Island, which boasts several beaches. Hap Mun beach, at the island's southern tip, is the prettiest.

Tai Long Wan beach

MTR Choi Hung, then green minibus #1A (every 5min) to Sai Kung Town, then minibus #29R to Sai Wan Ting (Mon–Sat 8.30am, 9.15am, 11.30am & 3.30pm; Sun 11 services 8.30am–4.30pm) from outside *McDonald's* on Chan Man St; a taxi from Sai Kung Town to Sai Wan Ting is about $100

If you're after a fantastic beach, head 10km northeast of Sai Kung Town to **Sai Wan Ting**, a pavilion at the end of a road. From here it's a ninety-minute walk to **Tai Long Wan**, a 3km-wide bay lined with a chain of **golden beaches** – the largest, Tai Wan, is considered the most beautiful. Take great care in the water, as there can be strong rip currents – though they do little to deter surfers when the waves come rolling in. There are beachside restaurants and surfboard rental shacks at Sai Wan and Ham Tin Wan villages.

To catch bus #94 (daily 6.30am–9.35pm; every 30–35min) back to Sai Kung Town, follow the trail 7km inland again from Ham Tin Wan, passing a couple more villages and the track up Sharp Peak, to the main road at **Pak Tam Au**.

Clear Water Bay

MTR Diamond Hill, then bus #91 (every 20min)

Down on the New Territories' southeastern extremity, **Clear Water Bay** is a rural area with a couple of popular **beaches** and an important temple. For the beaches, get off the bus at either the Tai Au Mun stop or the Clear Water Bay terminus; you'll need to bring everything you'll need for a day out, as there are no nearby shops or facilities.

Joss House Bay

MTR Diamond Hill, then bus #91 (every 20min) to the Clear Water Bay terminus and take the green minibus #16 (6.30am–8.30pm; every 15–30min) to the end of the road outside the members-only Clear Water Bay Golf and Country Club; from the car park, follow signposts and steps for 500m down to the Tin Hau temple

From the Clear Water Bay bus terminus it's 2.5km south to **Joss House Bay** and the wonderfully located **Tin Hau Temple**. As land reclamation has changed coastlines across Hong Kong, this temple has become a rarity – a Tin Hau temple that still looks out over the sea. As such, it's of immense significance: on the 23rd day of the third lunar month each year (Tin Hau's birthday) a colossal celebration takes place in the bay. A nearby **stone inscription**, dated to the Song dynasty and recording a visit by a government official, is the oldest such carving in Hong Kong.

The Outlying Islands

Hong Kong's 260-odd **Outlying Islands** offer a mix of stunning seascapes, low-key fishing villages and rural tranquillity, with very little in the way of high-density development. The islands of **Lamma** and **Cheung Chau** are fairly small and easy to explore in a day, while **Lantau** has a far greater range of sights and might even merit a couple of visits. You could also make use of local **accommodation** (see p.580) to base

9

yourself on any one of the three, or just hop over whenever you please for an evening out at one of the many **seafood restaurants**. The main point of departure is the **Outlying Islands Ferry Piers** in Central; Lamma and Cheung Chau can also be reached by ferry from Aberdeen, while the **MTR** extends along Lantau's north coast.

Lamma Island

Lying just to the southwest of Aberdeen, Y-shaped **Lamma Island** is the third-largest in the SAR – though at only around 7km in length, it's still pleasantly compact. Most of the 6000-strong population live in west-coast **Yung Shue Wan**, and the rest of the island is covered in open, hilly country, with an easy hour-long trail out past a couple of beaches to **Sok Kwu Wan**, a tiny knot of seafood restaurants on the east coast – walk from one to the other, enjoy a meal, and then catch a ferry back to Hong Kong Island.

Yung Shue Wan

YUNG SHUE WAN is a pretty tree-shaded village where the boats from Central and Aberdeen dock, with a large expat population, some low-key modern buildings, and very little to do other than seek out either accommodation or somewhere to eat (see p.580 & p.584). For the **trail to Sok Kwu Wan**, follow the easy-to-find cement path that branches away from the shore past the apartment buildings on the outskirts of the village.

Hung Shing Ye Beach

About fifteen minutes along the path from Yung Shue Wan, you'll find **Hung Shing Ye Beach**, a nice place if you stick to the northern half; stray a few metres to the south, though, and you'll find your horizon rapidly being filled by Lamma's all-too-obvious **power station**. There are beachside showers, and the *Concerto Inn* (see p.584) is a decent place to dine.

Sok Kwu Wan

Some forty minutes along the path from Hung Shing Ye, **SOK KWU WAN** comprises a row of **seafood restaurants** built out over the water – though there are plans to build a major housing development just to the north of the existing village. For now, though, the food and the atmosphere are good, and the restaurants are often full of large parties enjoying lavish and noisy meals; some places operate **private boat services** for customers. Make sure you don't miss the last scheduled ferry back to Central, because there's nowhere to stay here – your only option at this point would be to hire a sampan to Aberdeen (around $200–250).

Cheung Chau Island

Hourglass-shaped **Cheung Chau Island** covers just 2.5 square kilometres, but is the most crowded of all the outlying islands with a population of around 25,000. Historically, Cheung Chau was notorious as an eighteenth-century base for **pirates**, who enjoyed waylaying the ships that plied the Guangdong coast. Today, it still gives the impression of being an economically independent little unit, its main streets busy with shops, snack stalls and seafood restaurants. Ferries dock on the west side of the island, where a harbourside promenade overlooks a typhoon shelter crammed with boats.

If you can, visit during the extraordinary **Tai Ping Ching Chiu (Bun) Festival** in May, when festivities – including Chinese opera performances, Taoist rituals and frantic bun-steaming – build over the course of a week. On the final day, the small town's narrow streets fill to critical mass to watch a procession of raucous lion dances and ornate carnival floats. The evening is rounded off with a race to climb up a vast tower of buns.

OPPOSITE TAI LONG WAN BEACH, SAI KUNG PENINSULA (P.567) >

ISLAND FERRIES

The following is a selection of the most useful island ferry services – full timetables can be picked up at the Outlying Islands Ferry Piers in Central. Prices quoted below rise by a third on Sundays and public holidays.

TO YUNG SHUE WAN, LAMMA ISLAND

From Outlying Islands Ferry Pier 4 At least hourly departures 6.30am–12.30am (40min; $17.10). Operated by HKKF ⓦ hkkf.com.hk.

From Aberdeen Pier (on the waterfront near the fish market). Eleven departures daily 6.40am–10.50pm (35min; $12). Operated by Chuen Kee Ferry ⓦ ferry.com.hk.

TO SOK KWU WAN, LAMMA ISLAND

From Outlying Islands Ferry Pier 4 11–16 departures daily 7.20am–11.30pm (35min; $21). Operated by HKKF ⓦ hkkf.com.hk.

TO CHEUNG CHAU ISLAND

From Outlying Islands Ferry Pier 5 24hr departures, every 30min 6.10am–11.45pm, then three services 11.45pm–6.10am (ordinary ferry 1hr, $13.20; fast ferry 35min, $25.80). Operated by First Ferry ⓦ www.nwff.com.hk.

From Aberdeen Pier (on the waterfront near the fish market). Seven departures Mon–Fri 7.10am–10.45pm, 12 departures Sat & Sun 7.10am–10.30pm (55min; $32). Operated by Maris Ferry ⓦ marisferry.com.hk.

TO MUI WO (SILVERMINE BAY), LANTAU ISLAND

From Outlying Islands Ferry Pier 6 At least hourly departures 6.10am–11.30pm, then at 12.30am and 3am (ordinary ferry 1hr, $15.20; fast ferry 40min, $29.90). Operated by First Ferry ⓦ www.nwff.com.hk.

Pak Tai Temple

Pak She St • Daily 7am–5pm • Free • ☎ 2981 0663

The 200-year-old **Pak Tai Temple** is the island's main sight; Pak Tai, "Emperor of the Northern Heaven", protects against natural disasters, and is something of a patron deity for the island's fishermen. Though the building is the standard heavy granite affair, the roofline is embellished with a pair of brightly coloured ceramic dragons, and the temple also owns an iron sword said to date from the Song dynasty, reputedly fished out of the sea.

Beaches

Through the town and across the island's narrow waist, crowded **Tung Wan Beach** is a 700m-long strip of sand, with various places to rent beach gear or have a snack. At the south end of the beach is *Warwick Hotel*, the island's largest (see p.580); continue on around the headland and you'll come to the far more scenic – and far less crowded – **Kwun Yam Wan Beach**, named after the tiny temple tucked on the hillside behind the relaxed beach bar.

The south of the island

Turn right from the ferry and it's a half-hour walk to Cheung Chau's **southern headland**. You can circumnavigate this with a bit of scrabbling up and down rocks and across bays; there's also a nice picnic pavilion with sea views, and the **Cheung Po Tsai Cave**, which is named after Cheung Chau's most famous pirate, who used to hide here early in the nineteenth century. The cave – tightly set into the base of some large granite boulders – has been attracting increasing numbers of visitors after featuring in a local television series, but you'll still need to bring your own torch.

Lantau Island

9

Mountainous **Lantau Island** is twice as large as Hong Kong Island but far less developed, despite the proximity of the International Airport just off the north coast. More than half of the island is a designated **country park**, with trails linking monasteries, old fishing villages and secluded beaches. There are some major sights here, notably **Hong Kong Disneyland** on the northeastern coast; the western fishing village of **Tai O**; and **Po Lin Monastery**, with its mighty Big Buddha and the **Ngong Ping 360** cable-car ride. Roads and buses (⑩ newlantaobus.com) link everything – and the MTR extends along Lantau's north coast – so getting around isn't difficult.

Mui Wo

Ferry from Central; bus #1 from Tai O, bus #2 from Po Lin Monastery

MUI WO has a clutch of restaurants and residential buildings grouped around the **ferry pier**, in front of which is a **bus stop** with departures to the rest of the island – though as most only run every hour or so, don't count on getting anywhere in a hurry. There's also a nice **beach** and a sprinkling of low-key hotels 500m to the north (see p.580), set in an attractive, curved, sandy bay.

The south coast

Bus #1 or #2 from Mui Wo, bus #1 from Tai O, bus #2 from Po Lin Monastery

The road west from Mui Wo passes through the village of **PUI O** on its way to the southern shore, which is where Lantau's best beaches are located. **Cheung Sha Upper and Lower beaches** are the nicest: expect long, empty stretches of sand fringed with trees, with a couple of café-restaurants near the bus stops. Beyond here, the road heads inland past the **Shek Pik Reservoir** – look north here and you'll glimpse the Big Buddha sitting up on the ridge.

Tai O

Bus #1 from Mui Wo, bus #11 from Tung Chung, bus #21 from Po Lin

Right at Lantau's far northwestern corner, the fishing village of **TAI O** is home to two thousand people. It's an interesting place for a wander, with old lanes, shrines, historic temples and a quarter full of tin-roofed **stilt houses** built over the mudflats. The main street is lined with stalls selling dried and live seafood – the smell here is from locally made fermented prawn paste, which features on menus all over, including the plush *Tai O Heritage Hotel* (see p.580).

Tung Chung

MTR Tung Chung; bus #3 from Mui Wo, bus #23 from Po Lin Monastery, bus #S1 from the airport

TUNG CHUNG is a burgeoning New Town near the airport. There's a Qing-dynasty stone fort about 2km west along the coast, but the real reason to come here is for transport as it's all tightly grouped together: there's the MTR; the Ngong Ping 360 Cable Car to Po Lin Monastery (see box, p.572); and a host of **buses**.

Po Lin Monastery

Ngong Ping Village • Daily 8am–6pm • Free • ☎ 2985 5248, ⑩ www.plm.org.hk • Bus #2 from Mui Wo, bus #21 from Tai O, bus #23 from Tung Chung; Ngong Ping 360 Cable Car from Tung Chung (see box, p.572)

Located high up on the Ngong Ping Plateau, the **Po Lin Monastery** is one of the largest temples in Hong Kong. The complex is overshadowed by the adjacent bronze **Tian Tan Buddha** (daily 10am–5.30pm), a 34m-high sculpture that depicts the Buddha sitting cross-legged in a lotus flower – climb the steps to his feet for views over the temple and surrounding countryside. Po Lin's **vegetarian restaurant** serves set meals (daily 11.30am–4.30pm; meal tickets from $60), and there's an attached canteen that's cheaper.

NGONG PING 360 CABLE CAR

The 5.7km ride between Po Lin Monastery and Tung Chung aboard the **Ngong Ping 360 Cable Car** (Mon–Fri 10am–6pm, Sat & Sun 9am–6.30pm; 25min; $130 one-way, $185 return; ⓦnp360.com.hk) provides fantastic panoramas of Lantau's steep north coast. Airport buses run from Tung Chung, so Lantau is the perfect place to spend a last afternoon in Hong Kong before catching an evening flight out. Just make sure to leave enough time before you fly; the cable car's popularity means long queues (regularly 1hr plus) in both directions. Buying your ticket in person rather than through a travel agent will help you to skip at least part of the line, and the earlier in the day you visit, the shorter the queuing time.

Lantau Peak and Sunset Peak

Rearing over Po Lin, 934m-high **Lantau Peak** – properly known as Fung Wong Shan – is a popular place to watch the sunrise (you can stay the night before at the nearby *S.G. Davis Youth Hostel*; see p.580). The steep, 2km-long trail from Po Lin Monastery to the summit takes about an hour to complete, and on a clear day views reach as far as Macau. You can pick up a trail here and continue 5km (2hr 30min) east to the slightly lower Tai Tung Shan, or **Sunset Peak**, for a full day out.

Hong Kong Disneyland

Fantasy Rd • Hours vary, see website for details • $539; children aged 3–11 $385; children under 3 free • ☎ 3550 3388, ⓦ hongkongdisneyland.com • MTR Disneyland Resort

Up on Lantau's northeastern side, **Hong Kong Disneyland** is a tame place compared with Disney's other parks, but still makes a fun day out for children. It's split into seven zones: **Main Street USA**, a re-created early twentieth-century American shopping street; **Adventureland**, home to Tarzan's treehouse and a jungle river cruise; **Tomorrowland**, where excellent rides include a *Star Wars*-inspired roller coaster; **Fantasyland**, with gentle rides modelled on classic Disney films; Wild West-themed **Grizzly Gulch**; **Toy Story Land**, which features characters from the eponymous animated films; and **Mystic Point**, with a sinister forest and haunted mansion.

ARRIVAL AND DEPARTURE   HONG KONG

BY PLANE

HONG KONG INTERNATIONAL AIRPORT

The airport (ⓦ hongkongairport.com) is at Chek Lap Kok, off the north coast of Lantau Island. Hong Kong is a major international gateway for flights both within Asia and beyond, and you can also fly to every provincial capital and many big cities on the mainland. That said, you can save money (and not lose much time) by picking up a flight over the border in Shenzhen – see box opposite.

Airport tourist office Buffer Halls A and B, Arrivals Level, Terminal 1 (daily 8am–9pm).

Destinations Beijing (3hr 20min); Chengdu (2hr 45min); Chongqing (2hr 35min); Guilin (1hr 30min); Kunming (2hr 40min); Shanghai (2hr 30min); Wuhan (2hr); Xi'an (2hr 55min).

TRANSPORT INTO TOWN

Airport Express The fastest way into town from Hong Kong International Airport is from inside the terminal aboard the Airport Express rail service; trains depart every 10min between 5.50am–12.45am to Kowloon (22min; $90 single) and Central on Hong Kong Island (24min;

$100). If you're travelling in a group, note that multiple ticket purchases save a lot of money: two singles between the airport and Hong Kong cost $170, while four singles are $280. At Kowloon and Hong Kong stations, you'll find taxi ranks and free hotel shuttle buses (coloured blue and marked with a "K" or "H" respectively), which, even if you're not staying at one of the hotels they serve, can deliver you within a short walk of most accommodation.

Tung Chung MTR station A more complicated but cheaper rail option is to catch bus #S1 from the airport to Tung Chung MTR station ($3.50), and then take the Tung Chung line into town along a parallel route to the Airport Express (around $25). It's slower – with more stops – but cheaper, and you can change trains at Lai King and get on the Tsuen Wan line via Mong Kok, Jordan and Tsim Sha Tsui to reach Kowloon's accommodation.

Airbuses An even slower and cheaper option (expect an hour or more to reach Tsim Sha Tsui) is to take one of the dozen Airbus routes into town from outside the ground floor of the terminal. The airport customer service counters can tell you where to catch them and sell you tickets ($15–48; you'll need exact change on the buses). Routes have round-the-clock

FLYING FROM SHENZHEN

Though you can fly from Hong Kong to all major Chinese cities, flights are much more frequent (and prices occasionally lower) if you're **flying from Shenzhen airport**, which is easily reached by bus in just two hours from downtown Hong Kong – any travel agent can book you a ticket ($130). Buses drop you at the Shenzhen Bay border, and then you walk 500m to the other side via Hong Kong and Chinese customs and pick up another bus to the airport. Buses run every fifteen minutes, so don't worry if you get stuck in a passport queue along the way.

services, and there's plenty of room for luggage.

Taxis Taxis into the city are metered and reliable (see p.575 for more). You might want to get the arrival hall tourist office to write down the name of your destination in Chinese characters for the driver, though they should know the names of the big hotels in English. It costs roughly $300 to get to Tsim Sha Tsui and about $350 for Hong Kong Island. There may be extra charges for luggage and for tunnel tolls – on some tunnel trips the passenger pays the return charge, too. Rush-hour traffic can slow down journey times considerably, particularly if you're using one of the cross-harbour tunnels to Hong Kong Island.

IN-TOWN CHECK-IN

Leaving by air Many international airlines allow you to check-in for your flight from Hong Kong airport up to 24hr in advance downtown at the Hong Kong and Kowloon Airport Express stations, including checking through your in-hold luggage. This is useful if you have a late flight and don't want to drag your luggage around for the rest of the day after leaving your hotel, and also means you won't have to join the often lengthy check-in queues at the airport. However, you must purchase an Airport Express ticket in order to access the stations' check-in areas, which ties you to using the train rather than travelling to the airport by other means.

BY TRAIN

HUNG HOM RAILWAY STATION

This train station (ⓦmtr.com.hk) in eastern Tsim Sha Tsui handles Express trains from China, plus the East Rail MTR line to the pedestrian border crossings between Shenzhen and Lo Wu or Lok Ma Chau.

Transport into town At Hung Hom, signposted walkways lead to a city bus terminal and taxi rank; there's also the MTR from here to Tsim Sha Tsui East station, which exits into Middle Road (see map, p.560).

Tickets Express tickets are available from Hung Hom station or the tourist information booth in Admiralty MTR station. Online booking (ⓦwww.it3.mtr.com.hk/b2c) is available for services within Guangdong only, and you'll have to collect the tickets in Hong Kong.

Destinations Beijing West (1 on alternate days; 24hr; hard/soft sleeper $600/935); Guangzhou East (12 daily; 2hr; $210); Shanghai (1 on alternate days; 20hr; hard/soft sleeper $550/825).

BY BUS

There's no long-distance bus station in Hong Kong, but CTS (138 Hennessy Rd, Wan Chai; ☎2832 3888, ⓦctsbus.hkcts .com), and other companies run direct services from downtown Hong Kong to Guangzhou (3hr 30min; $110) and Shenzhen or Shenzhen airport (1hr 40min; $130).

BY FERRY

Hong Kong has two main ferry terminals handling traffic to Macau and the Pearl River Delta (see p.503). The hydrofoils get very busy at the weekends and on holidays, when you'll need to buy tickets in advance; note that you need a passport, but not a special visa, to travel to Macau. The fares given here are weekday daytime fares – expect to pay a small premium for weekend/holiday fares and for night sailings (6pm–6.30am).

HONG KONG–MACAU FERRY TERMINAL

Located inside the Shun Tak Centre in Sheung Wan, Hong Kong Island (MTR Sheung Wan, Exit D), this terminal handles departures to Macau's main Outer Harbour Ferry Terminal and the Taipa Ferry Terminal, with the two routes operated by Turbojet ($164; ⓦturbojet.com.hk) and Cotai Water Jet ($165; ⓦcotaiwaterjet.com) respectively.

TRAVEL AGENTS

Hong Kong is full of budget travel agents, who are all able to organize international flights as well as train tickets, tours, flights and visas for mainland China. CTS (ⓦctshk.com) at 138 Hennessy Rd, Wan Chai (☎2832 3888), and Floor 1, Alpha House, 27–33 Nathan Rd, Tsim Sha Tsui (entrance on Peking Rd; ☎2315 7171), is especially good for China visas and direct buses to Shenzhen airport. Alternatives include Hong Kong Student Travel (608 Hang Lung Centre, 2 Paterson St, Causeway Bay; ☎2833 9909, ⓦen.hkst.com) and Shoestring Travel (Flat A, 4F, Alpha House, 27–33 Nathan Rd, Tsim Sha Shui; ☎2723 2306, ⓦshoestringtravel.com.hk).

9

Destinations Macau Outer Harbour (every 15min 7am–midnight and then approximately hourly; 55min); Taipa (approximately every 30min 7am–11.30pm; 55min).

Destinations Macau Outer Harbour (approximately every hour 7.30am–10.30pm; 55min); Taipa (5 daily; 55min).

ON FOOT

There are two pedestrian crossings between Hong Kong and Shenzhen: Lok Ma Chau/Huanggang (24hr) and more popular Lo Wu/Luohu (6.30am–midnight), both on the East Rail MTR line to Hung Hom. It's possible to walk across the border at Lo Wu, but at Lok Ma Chau shuttle buses ($10) run across the bridge between the Mainland and Hong Kong border posts.

CHINA FERRY TERMINAL

Located on Canton Road in Tsim Sha Tsui, Kowloon (MTR Tsim Sha Tsui, Exit A1), this terminal operates ferries to Macau's Outer Harbour Ferry Terminal ($164; ⓦ turbojet .com.hk), the Taipa Ferry Terminal ($165; ⓦ cotaiwaterjet .com) and destinations around the Pearl River Delta (ⓦ cksp.com.hk).

GETTING AROUND

Transport around the island is easy, with the MTR, buses and trams covering the north shore. A new MTR line linking Admiralty with the south coast opened in 2016, but buses are plentiful too, and nowhere is more than an hour from Central. Hong Kong's public transport system is efficient, extensive and inexpensive – though best avoided during the weekday rush hours (7–9am and 5–7pm). All signs are written in English and Chinese, although the English signs are sometimes so discreet that they're practically invisible.

BY MTR

Hong Kong's trains are all operated by MTR (ⓦ mtr.com .hk), whose interconnected network covers Hong Kong Island's north shore and Kowloon; the Airport Express; the Tung Chung line between Central and Lantau; and two routes extending through the New Territories to the Shenzhen border. Lines on Hong Kong Island have recently been extended south across the island to Aberdeen. The LRT (Light Rail Transit) traverses the northwestern New Territories, though tourists rarely use it except to reach the Hong Kong Wetland Park (see p.565). Services run between about 6am and 1am, and you can buy single-journey tickets ($4.50–30) from easy-to-use dispensing machines at the stations, or use an Octopus Card (see box opposite). A clear, colour-coded map can be found on p.576, at all stations and on tourist maps handed out by the HKTB.

BY BUS

Hong Kong's double-decker buses are comfortable and air-conditioned, and are essential for reaching the south of Hong Kong Island and parts of the New Territories. Swipe your Octopus Card or pay as you board (exact change is required); the fare is posted up on the timetables at bus stops, and ranges from $3.50 to $45, though the majority of fares are less than $10. Most buses run from early morning until late evening every day; unusual operating hours are specified. Useful bus terminals include Exchange Square in Central; outside the Ferry Terminal in Central; and outside the Star Ferry Terminal in Tsim Sha Tsui, Kowloon – though there is talk of shifting this one elsewhere. Check routes on Hong Kong Island at ⓦ www.nwstbus.com.hk and in Kowloon at ⓦ kmb.hk.

HONG KONG AND CHINA VISAS

Currently, nationals of the US, Canada, Australia and New Zealand receive a 90-day tourist **visa** on arrival in Hong Kong; South African passport holders can stay for 30 days, and British nationals can stay for 180 days. For present information, contact your local HKTB office or check ⓦ www.immd.gov.hk.

BUYING CHINESE VISAS IN HONG KONG

To enter China you need a **visa**. If you haven't picked one up from a Chinese consulate or embassy at home, it's quickest to obtain one through a **travel agency** (see box, p.573). Agents can also arrange hotel accommodation and onward journeys into China, which you may need evidence of to support your visa application. **Fees** vary from $500 to $1700 or more, according to factors like your nationality, whether you want a single-entry or double-entry visa, if you want to stay for up to one month or three months, and whether you want next-day processing or can wait three to four days. **Beware**: visas issued in Hong Kong are only extendable once on the mainland, and some multi-entry visas require you to leave China every thirty days even if valid for several months. It's also possible that you will be refused a further visa in Hong Kong if you've been in China recently.

OCTOPUS CARD

If you plan to travel around a good deal, get hold of an **Octopus Card** (⊛octopus.com.hk), a rechargeable stored-value ticket that can be used for travel on all MTR services, most buses and most ferries. The card itself costs $50 and you add value to it with the machines in the MTR. Over-65s can register for a special card and enjoy a $2 flat fare for most journeys on public transport. The fare is electronically deducted each time you use the card by swiping it over the yellow sensor pads at station turnstiles or, on a bus, beside the driver. Octopus cards can also be used in many retail outlets, including Park'n'Shop supermarkets, *Maxim's* restaurants and 7-Eleven stores.

BY MINIBUS

Green-topped minibuses have set stops and routes, but can also be hailed (though not on double yellow lines). They cost a few dollars more than regular buses, and you pay the driver the exact amount or swipe your Octopus Card as you enter. Red-topped minibuses are owner-operated and neither routes or fares are fixed; on these you need to pay in cash as you get off. Both types of minibus only take sixteen seated passengers, and won't stop, or will refuse you entry, if full. Drivers are unlikely to speak English; when you reach your stop, call out "Yau lok, m'goi!" ("I want to get off, please!") and the driver should pull over and let you off.

BY TAXI

Hong Kong's taxis come in three colours: red on Hong Kong Island and Kowloon (with a fixed fare of $22 for the first 2km), green in the New Territories ($18.50) and blue on Lantau ($17). They're usually easy to find and can be hailed in the street, though if they're scarce – likely during rainstorms, rush hours and between 3–4pm when drivers change shifts – look for them outside hotels. Note that there is a toll to be paid on any trips through the tunnels between Kowloon and Hong Kong (from $10 for the Cross Harbour Tunnel to a whopping $55 for the Western Harbour Crossing), and drivers often add $10–15 on top of this – as they are allowed to do – for the return journey. Few taxi

drivers speak English, so be prepared to show the name of your destination written down in Chinese. It is obligatory for passengers to wear seat belts.

BY TRAM

Trams (⊛hktramways.com) have been rattling along Hong Kong Island's north shore since 1904 and remain as popular as ever with locals and tourists alike, especially for the view from the upstairs deck. The trams run between Kennedy Town in the west and Shau Kei Wan in the east, via Central, Wan Chai and Causeway Bay (some terminating at Happy Valley; check the front of the tram). You board the tram at the back, and swipe your Octopus Card or drop the money into the driver's box ($2.30; no change given) when you get off.

BY FERRY

Star Ferry The Star Ferry (⊛starferry.com.hk) runs between Tsim Sha Tsui in Kowloon and Pier 7 in front of the IFC2 Tower on Hong Kong Island (daily 6.30am–11.30pm; upper deck $2.50, lower deck $2); there's a separate service between Tsim Sha Tsui and the Convention and Exhibition Centre in Wan Chai (daily 7.20am–10.50pm; $2.50).

Other ferries A large array of boats run between Hong Kong and the Outlying Islands, most of which use the Outlying Islands Ferry Piers in front of the IFC; details are given in the box on p.570.

INFORMATION

Listings magazines To find out what's on, try the weekly *HK Magazine* (free; ⊛hk-magazine.com), available in hotels, cafés and restaurants, or *Time Out Hong Kong* ($18; ⊛timeout.com.hk), offering much the same mix of information along with more weighty reviews.

Maps The free HKTB maps, and the maps in this guide, should be enough for most purposes, though hikers may want to invest in the *Countryside Maps* – a series of five separate sheets ($63 each) focusing on footpaths across the SAR. The paperback *Hong Kong Guide* ($110) is also a useful general-purpose street atlas. Both can be bought from bookshops (see p.586).

Newspapers Hong Kong's two English-language daily papers are the *South China Morning Post* (⊛scmp.com), whose bland coverage of regional news does its best to toe

the party line, and the *Standard* (⊛thestandard.com.hk), a business-oriented freebie which can be outspoken about politicians' failings. Other papers, such as *The New York Times International Edition* and journals such as *Time* and *Newsweek*, are widely available.

Tourist offices The Hong Kong Tourism Board or HKTB (☎2508 1234, ⊛discoverhongkong.com) issues leaflets, pamphlets, brochures and maps covering everything you can do in Hong Kong. Their two downtown offices are in the Star Ferry Terminal in Tsim Sha Tsui (daily 8am–8pm), and in an old railway carriage outside the Peak Mall, on the Peak (daily 11am–8pm). There are also two offices (8am–9pm) at Hong Kong Airport, in the "buffer halls" just after you pass customs. English-speaking staff provide useful advice on accommodation, shopping, restaurants, bus routes and hiking trails.

MTR SYSTEM

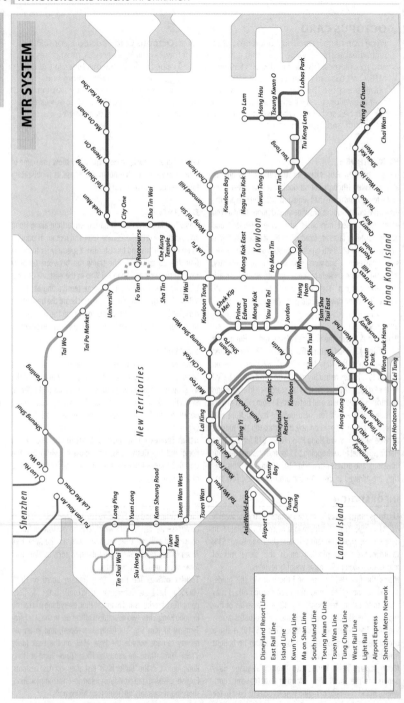

Legend:
- Disneyland Resort Line
- East Rail Line
- Island Line
- Kwun Tong Line
- Ma on Shan Line
- South Island Line
- Tseung Kwan O Line
- Tsuen Wan Line
- Tung Chung Line
- West Rail Line
- Light Rail
- Airport Express
- Shenzhen Metro Network

ACTIVITIES

Martial arts For excellent tuition in many styles of martial arts, contact CS Tang (w cstang.www3.50megs.com).

Rugby Each year on the last weekend in March, Hong Kong plays host to an international Rugby Sevens tournament (for more information, visit w hkrugby.com).

Running The Hong Kong Marathon takes place in February each year (w hkmarathon.com).

Tennis For tennis courts, contact the Hong Kong Tennis Association (w www.tennishk.org), whose website lists clubs, facilities and events.

Windsurfing For windsurfing rentals and instruction, try the Windsurfing Centre (w ccwindc.com.hk) on Cheung Chau Island.

ACCOMMODATION

Hong Kong boasts a colossal range of accommodation, though **booking ahead** is essential to secure better rates at higher-end places and because budget accommodation fills up quickly. At the upper end of the market are some of the best **hotels** in the world, sometimes costing upwards of $4000 a night, as well as mid-range options starting at around $1200. Many of these hotels add on a 10% service charge – check whether this is included or not. At the cheaper end, you'll be lucky to find a double for less than $350, although shared dormitories can come in as low as $150 a night for a bed. It's wise to check whether these rooms have a window, and whether you have to pay extra for the use of air-conditioning.

HONG KONG ISLAND

Accommodation on the island is mostly upmarket, though there's a small budget enclave in Causeway Bay and the secluded *Mount Davis Youth Hostel* (see p.578).

Garden View (YWCA) 1 MacDonnell Rd, Mid-Levels ☎ 2877 3737, w yhk.com.hk; map pp.550–551. This comfortable YWCA-run hotel is off Garden Rd, a sweaty walk uphill from the Zoological and Botanical Gardens;

TOURS

The HKTB website (w discoverhongkong.com) provides a handy overview of some popular **tours** provided by private operators, including harbour cruises aboard a decked-out Star Ferry (from $95; w www.starferry.com.hk); coach tours across the SAR with Gray Line (from $480; w www.grayline.com.hk); and boat trips out to see the renowned **pink dolphins** with Hong Kong Dolphinwatch ($420; w hkdolphinwatch.com). Some great options that don't make the official list include a sunset cruise on the traditional red-sailed junk *Aqualuna* (from $130; w aqualuna.com.hk); sea-kayaking in the Sai Kung Geopark with Kayak and Hike ($800; w kayak-and-hike.com) and around Lamma with Sea Kayak Hong Kong ($650; w seakayakhongkong.com); and **culinary tours** that see you snacking your way around interesting neighbourhoods with Hong Kong Foodie Tasting Tours (from $720; w www.hongkongfoodietours.com).

WALKING TOURS

Whether you want to explore city streets or hike rugged country trails, Hong Kong is an excellent place to explore on foot. Of course, there's nothing to stop you going it alone – try the easy Peak Circle Trail (see p.554) or the more challenging Dragon's Back (see box, p.559) – but there are also some excellent outfits that operate walking tours.

Big Foot Tour ☎ 6075 2727, w bigfoottour.com. Fun walking tours around different city neighbourhoods, led by excellent guides with plenty of humour thrown in. All tours are four hours long, and start from $700 per person.

HK Free Walk ☎ 6171 0366, w hkfreewalk.com. One of the few tours out there for those travelling on a budget – guides work for tips on their 2–3hr walks through Tsim Sha Tsui.

Walk Hong Kong ☎ 9187 8641, w walkhongkong.com. Informative guided walks with interesting themes; tour the city's World War II battlefields, or learn about *feng shui* and Taoism as you trip around the

city's temples. From $450 per person.

★**Walk In Hong Kong** ☎ 5511 4839, w walkin.hk. This outfit organizes a wide range of walks, mostly urban, that delve into the different aspects of life in the city – take a look at traditional businesses in Sheung Wan or visit a home in Sham Shui Po. From $650 for a three-hour evening tour including dinner.

Wild Hong Kong ☎ 6087 1439, w wildhongkong.com. Adventurous hikes in Hong Kong's country parks, taking in well-known trails as well as lesser-known spots like Lantau's Yellow Dragon Gorge. $400–600 per person depending on group size.

9

minibus #1A from outside City Hall runs past. Rooms are nothing special, but it's a good option should you wish to escape from the crush of the city. $1200

Hong Kong Hostel 3F, Block A, 47 Paterson St, Causeway Bay ☎ 2392 6868, ⓦ hostel.hk; map pp.550–551. The lack of a sign makes this tricky to find, but the friendly staff and great location make it worth the effort – that said, note that rooms are spread between two blocks, with limited space for socializing. Dorms $150, doubles $350

Mandarin Oriental 5 Connaught Rd, Central ☎ 2522 0111, ⓦ mandarinoriental.com; map pp.550–551. Unassumingly set in a plain concrete box, this is one of the best hotels in the world with unmatched service, plus a selection of first-class dining and drinking options (the lobby in particular is a great place to people-watch, as anyone who's anyone in Hong Kong seems to pass through). While rooms are beautifully appointed, they're on the small side compared to the competition. $4500

Mount Davis Youth Hostel 123 Mount Davis Path ☎ 2817 5715, ⓦ yha.org.hk; map pp.550–551. Perched on the top of a mountain above Kennedy Town, this self-catering retreat has superb, peaceful views over the harbour. Extra-friendly staff and spotless rooms go a good way towards compensating for the slightly grotty bathroom facilities. Getting here can be a major expedition, unless you catch the infrequent shuttle bus from the ground floor of the Shun Tak Centre – phone the hostel for times. Dorms $160, doubles $330

Park Lane 310 Gloucester Rd, Causeway Bay ☎ 2293 8888, ⓦ parklane.com.hk; map pp.550–551. With a great location near Victoria Park, this plush hotel is conveniently sited for Causeway Bay and the MTR. The rooms are slowly being upgraded after a change in ownership, and it's worth checking whether you're booking one of the fancy new ones (from $2180) or an older "classic" room. $1900

★**Pottinger** 21 Stanley St, Central ☎ 2308 3188, ⓦ thepottinger.com; map pp.550–551. Perched above Queen's Road Central, this discreet and stylish hotel offers a great location and considerate service; rooms are on the small side, but decorated with appealing touches of

chinoiserie. There is no gym or pool, but guests have the run of facilities at a nearby martial arts club. $3000

★**TUVE** 16 Tsing Fung St, Tin Hau ☎ 3995 8899, ⓦ tuve.hk; map pp.550–551. This boutique hotel takes itself a bit seriously, but stands out from its competitors for the attention to detail that has gone into the uber-minimalist rooms; the beds are excellent, complimentary minibars well-stocked and staff helpful. Located in an untouristy neighbourhood, one MTR stop from Causeway Bay. No breakfast available. $1400

★**Yesinn** 2F, Nan Yip Bldg, 472 Hennessy Rd, Causeway Bay ☎ 2213 4567, ⓦ yesinn.com; map pp.550–551. With a friendly vibe, some great common spaces (including two roof terraces) and plenty of activities, this hostel is an excellent place for meeting other travellers. Nine-bed and 21-bed dorms available. Dorms $150, doubles $500

KOWLOON

Most of the following accommodation is located in **Tsim Sha Tsui**, though this area's long-standing monopoly on budget accommodation is slowly easing; a growing number of excellent, modern hostels are located in less touristy neighbourhoods elsewhere in Kowloon.

Benito 7–7B Cameron Rd, Tsim Sha Tsui ☎ 3653 0388, ⓦ hotelbenito.com; map p.560. Bright, clean and modern hotel close to everything that matters in Tsim Sha Tsui. Cheaper rooms are only fractionally larger than in a guesthouse, however. $880

Dragon Hostel 7F, Sincere House, 83 Argyle St, Mong Kok ☎ 2395 0577, ⓦ dragonhostel.com; map p.560. Hard to find – the street entrance is a bland doorway just around the corner in Fa Yuen Street – but helpful management and clean, if extremely plain, single, double and triple rooms (most with their own bathroom) make this place stand out. Dorms $115, en-suite doubles $350

Heritage Lodge 800 Castle Peak Rd, Mei Foo ☎ 2100 2888, ⓦ heritagelodgehk.com; map pp.546–547. On a hilltop ten minutes' walk from Mei Foo MTR station (shuttle service available), this unusual hotel is housed in the grounds of a former hospital, and is now run as a social enterprise. Rooms and suites are well appointed

---

YOUTH HOSTELS AND CAMPING

The **Hong Kong Youth Hostels Association** (ⓦ yha.org.hk) operates seven self-catering hostels – mostly a long way from the centre – offering dormitory accommodation for International Youth Hostel Federation members from $110. They've also been rolling out a "Hassle-Free Camping" scheme (from $130 per person), where they'll set up a tent and bedding for you outside a hostel, and you have free run of the hostel's kitchen and bathrooms.

You can also **camp for free** at the forty campsites run by the Agriculture, Fisheries and Conservation Department (ⓦ afcd.gov.hk; click on "Country and Marine Parks"), all in relatively remote sites. Facilities are basic – pit latrines and tank water that must be boiled – and you'll need to be self-sufficient. Pitches are available on a first-come, first-served basis, so get in early on weekends and holidays.

and good value, and the organic restaurant on site is run by a local organization that provides employment for older people. **$750**

Luxe Manor 39 Kimberley Rd, Tsim Sha Tsui ☎3763 8888, ⊛theluxemanor.com; map p.560. Another boutique option, with stylish rooms and strikingly decorated themed suites that will either appeal or appal. The hotel restaurant, Scandinavian *FINDS*, and surreal *Dada Bar* are worth a look for their over-the-top decor too. **$1400**

★**Mahjong** 1F, Pak Tai Mansion, 2A–2B Ma Hang Chung, To Kwa Wan ☎2705 1869, ⊛themahjonghk .com; map pp.546–547. One of Hong Kong's newer generation of backpacker hostels, which offers only dorm accommodation with bags of charm and hotel-grade mattresses. The staff's enthusiasm about their neighbourhood makes the out-of-the-way location seem like an advantage, and there are female-only ($220) and potentially awkward, but apparently popular double-bed dorms ($399) available too. Dorms **$180**

Mei Ho House Youth Hostel Block 41, 70 Berwick St, Sham Shui Po ☎3728 3500, ⊛yha.org.hk; map pp.546–547. Housed in a historic 1950s estate, within easy walking distance of Sham Shui Po MTR, this hostel compensates for its relatively high prices with spotless en-suite rooms and spacious common areas, which give it a decidedly upmarket feel. Dorms **$250**, doubles **$780**

★**The Peninsula** Salisbury Rd, Tsim Sha Tsui ☎2920 2888, ⊛peninsula.com; map p.560. One of the classiest hotels in the world, *The Peninsula* has been overlooking the harbour and Hong Kong Island for eighty years. Rooms are housed in the original building or a newer high-rise block with better views, and most have been recently renovated. **$3880**

★**Salisbury (YMCA)** 41 Salisbury Rd, Tsim Sha Tsui ☎2268 7000, ⊛ymcahk.org.hk; map p.560. Superb location next door to *The Peninsula* and with views over the harbour and Hong Kong Island; facilities include indoor pools, a fitness centre and squash court. For the price, the doubles are unbeatable value; relatively expensive four-bed dorms with attached showers are also available. Dorms **$400**, doubles **$1540**

Sealand House Block D, 8F, Majestic House, 80 Nathan Rd, Tsim Sha Tsui ☎2368 9522, ⊛sealandhouse.com .hk; map p.560. Located inside a residential block across from Kowloon Mosque, this is the cleanest, roomiest and friendliest of the upper-price-range guesthouses, with a choice of shared or en-suite facilities. **$500**

CHUNGKING MANSIONS

Set at the southern end of Nathan Road, Chungking Mansions is an ugly monster of a building, its lower three floors forming a warren of tiny shops and restaurants, the upper sixteen storeys crammed with budget guesthouses. While the Mansions has a reputation for sleaze and poor maintenance, recent attention from the health and safety departments have wrought great changes: the guesthouses are generally well run, if cramped and sometimes windowless. The building is divided into five blocks, lettered A to E, each served by two tiny lifts that are subject to long queues.

Asia Inn Block C, 16F ☎9515 7520; map p.560. Quite possibly the cleanest corner of Chungking Mansions, with gleaming tiled rooms, most with private bathrooms. Excellent security, keen staff and fast internet, although some rooms – particularly the singles – are ridiculously tiny. **$400**

Chungking House Block A, 4F and 5F ☎2739 1600, ⊛chungkinghouse.com; map p.560. Long-running place with clean, decent-sized rooms spread over two floors; cheaper ones are not such a good deal and none are nonsmoking. **$350**

★**Dhillon Hostel** Block D, 10F ☎3104 1651; map p.560. A real gem of a place that's clean and friendly; they've taken the trouble to make the admittedly small, windowless rooms as welcoming and bright as possible. The owner runs most of the hostels in Block D. **$300**

Dragon Inn Block B, 3F ☎2367 7071, ⊛www .dragoninn.info; map p.560. The no-nonsense but efficient manager and bright rooms (within the Mansions' limits, at any rate) make this a good choice – they also offer a discount on stays of a week or more. **$360**

MIRADOR MANSIONS

This is another block at 54–64 Nathan Rd, on the east side between Carnarvon Rd and Mody Rd, next to the Tsim Sha Tsui MTR station. With a mix of residential apartments and guesthouses, Mirador Mansions is cleaner and brighter than Chungking Mansions, and queues for the lifts are smaller.

★**Garden Hostel** Flat F4, 3F ☎2311 1183, ⊛gardenhostel.com.hk; map p.560. A friendly travellers' hangout with washing machines, lockers and a patio garden. A *wing chun* martial arts school is also based here, and you can arrange lessons with them. Beds in the four- and six-bed dorms get cheaper if you pay by the week. Beware other hostels using the same name – this is the real one. Dorms **$100**, doubles **$250**

Mei Lam Guesthouse Flat D1, 5F ☎2721 5278, ⊛meilamgh.com; map p.560. Helpful, English-speaking owner and very presentable singles and doubles, all spick-and-span, with full facilities – although the cheapest rooms do lack windows. Worth the higher-than-usual prices. **$350**

THE NEW TERRITORIES

The most appealing areas of the New Territories are surprisingly poorly served by hotels and guesthouses. If you're planning to stay in areas like Sai Kung or Clear Water Bay, the best accommodation options are the private houses and apartments listed on Airbnb (⊛airbnb.com).

9

Bradbury Jockey Club Youth Hostel 66 Tai Mei Tuk Rd, Tai Po ☎ 2662 5123, ⓦyha.org.hk; map pp.546–547. Rooms are spartan and the facilities are aged, and you're liable to feel like the first visitor in a while, but lots of boating, walking and cycling opportunities await outside. To get here from Tai Po, take bus #75K to Tai Mei Tuk, then walk towards the Plover Cove Reservoir from the bus stop, and the hostel is on the left. Dorms $110, twin rooms $380

Royal Park Hotel 8 Pak Hok Ting St, Sha Tin ☎ 2601 2111, ⓦroyalpark.com.hk; map pp.546–547. One of the New Territories' better hotels – though there's not a lot of competition – right in the centre of Sha Tin. Rooms are excellent value and vast compared to what the same money would buy downtown, and there's an appealing indoor/outdoor pool. $950

Sze Lok Yuen Youth Hostel Tai Mo Shan, Tsuen Wan ☎ 2488 8188, ⓦyha.org.hk; map pp.546–547. Facilities here are basic, with hard beds and concrete barbecue pits, but it's a good spot should you wish to watch sunrise or sunset from Tai Mo Shan. Take bus #51 from Tsuen Wan to Tai Mo Shan (tell the driver where you're going), and then walk for 40 minutes uphill – the hostel is just off the main track up Tai Mo Shan. Dorms $115

OUTLYING ISLANDS
LAMMA
Man Lai Wah Yung Shue Wan, Lamma ☎ 2982 0220, ⓔmanlaiwahhotel@yahoo.com; map pp.546–547. Right ahead of the ferry pier on the left, this great low-key place has small, double-bed flats with balconies and harbour views, even if the furnishings aren't brand new. $650

CHEUNG CHAU
★**Cheung Chau B&B** Tung Wan Rd, Cheung Chau ☎ 2986 9990, ⓦbbcheungchau.com.hk; map pp.546–547. Set just back from the beach, this small, modern hotel has 28 rooms across three buildings; those in the older

block are spotless and pleasant (though the cheapest are windowless), while the newest rooms come with fun decorative flourishes and more space. $650

Warwick Tung Wan Beach, Cheung Chau ☎ 2981 0081, ⓦwww.warwickhotel.com.hk; map pp.546–547. Based in a multistorey block overlooking the beach, this is the most expensive of the island's accommodation, with a tiny swimming pool and restaurant. Most rooms have balconies and great views, but the dolphin-themed decor is ageing badly and some rooms smell of damp. $788

LANTAU
★**Ngong Ping S.G. Davis Youth Hostel** Ngong Ping, Lantau ☎ 2985 5610, ⓦyha.org.hk; map pp.546–547. From the Ngong Ping bus terminal (see p.572) follow the paved footpath and signposts south, away from the Tian Tan Buddha and past the public toilets; it's a 10min walk. Basic dorms and tent pitches at the base of Lantau Peak, and you can eat at the nearby Po Lin Monastery. It's cold on winter nights, though – bring a sleeping bag. Dorms $180, camping $65

Silvermine Beach 648 Silvermine Bay, Mui Wo, Lantau ☎ 6810 0111, ⓦsilvermineresort.com; map pp.546–547. Located right on the beachfront, a few minutes' walk from the Mui Wo Ferry Pier. The rooms are comfortable and quiet, with excellent-value long-term packages and online discounts available. The restaurant spilling out onto the terraces offers popular barbecues and Thai grub. $1400

★**Tai O Heritage Hotel** Shek Tsai Po St, Tai O, Lantau ☎ 2985 8383, ⓦwww.taioheritagehotel.com; map pp.546–547. Converted from a colonial-era police station, this pretty hotel sits on a headland looking over the South China Sea from the most remote end of Lantau. Tastefully decorated rooms come with marble bathrooms and the hotel restaurant is good too. Where else in Hong Kong can you sleep in a former armory? $1140

EATING

Thanks to its cosmopolitan heritage and the importance attached to food in Chinese culture, Hong Kong boasts a superb range of **restaurants**. The most prominent cooking style is local **Cantonese**, though you can also find places specializing in Chaozhou, Hakka, Beijing, Sichuanese and Shanghainese food. International options include **fast-food chains**, curry houses, sushi bars, pizzerias and restaurants offering Southeast Asian, South American and vegetarian cuisine. The restaurants listed below are a fraction of the total and are on the less expensive end of the market; Chinese characters are given where there is no English sign. For up-to-date reviews, pick up copies of the free weekly *HK Magazine* (ⓦhk-magazine.com), or check ⓦwomguide.com and ⓦopenrice.com.

WESTERN BREAKFASTS AND SNACKS
Caffé Habitū 77–79 Gloucester Rd, Wan Chai, Hong Kong Island ⓦcaffehabitu.com; map pp.550–551. Small local chain with a handful of downtown outlets serving good coffee ($28 for a double espresso), hot breakfasts and cake. Mon–Sat 8am–9pm, Sun 10am–7pm.

Elephant Grounds 8 Wing Fung St, Wan Chai, Hong Kong Island ⓦelephantgrounds.com; map pp.550–551. This small, hip chain blends and roasts its own coffee beans, which are then brewed and served any way you like, from a single espresso ($30) to the whacky-sounding but delicious smoked *affogato* ($60). Food is less reliable than the beverages, but there's an enticing ice-cream menu. Mon–Fri 11am–late, Sat & Sun 10am–late.

Green Waffle Diner Ka Ho Building, 35–39 Graham St, Central, Hong Kong Island ⓦbit.ly/2aKyDHc; map pp.550–551. Hong Kong's take on diner-style food, with cooked breakfasts, brunch skillets, chocolate chip pancakes and the eponymous green waffles (flavoured with pandan leaves; $31) on the menu. Mains from $80. Tues–Fri 11am–11pm, Sat 9am–11pm, Sun 9am–6pm.

Tai Cheong Bakery 35 Lyndhurst Terrace, Central, Hong Kong Island; map pp.550–551. A favourite with Chris Patten, Britain's last governor of Hong Kong, this establishment has been going since 1954 and is famous for its Hong Kong-style egg tarts (not grilled like Macau's version; $8) and flaky *char siu* pastries ($11). Mon–Sat 7.30am–9pm, Sun 9.30am–9pm.

DIM SUM

Dim sum (also known as *yum cha*) is the classic Cantonese way to start the day – a selection of little dumplings and dishes eaten with tea. Many restaurants serve *dim sum* from early in the morning until mid-afternoon, when they switch over to more extensive menus, but the following places are particularly well known for their *dim sum*. Make sure to get in early at the weekends, as whole families fill up the restaurants.

Dim Dim Sum 28 Man Fai St, Jordan ⓣ2771 7766, ⓦdimdimsum.hk; map p.560. Part of a small chain serving *dim sum* all day, with all the standards plus a few more unusual dishes such as *cheung fun*, which is stuffed with Yunnanese mushrooms, and salty egg yolk custard buns shaped like pigs' faces. Under $100 per person. Daily 10am–1am.

★**LockCha Tea House** K.S. Lo Gallery, Hong Kong Park, Hong Kong Island ⓣ2801 7177, ⓦlockcha.com; map pp.550–551. Vegetarian *dim sum* served in an elegant teahouse full of wooden screens. Atmospheric but expensive: from $40 per person for the tea, $20 per *dim sum* serving. Bookings advised, especially at weekends. Daily 10am–8pm, Sat 10am–9pm.

Luk Yu Tea House 24–26 Stanley St, just west of D'Aguilar St, Hong Kong Island ⓣ2523 5464; map pp.550–551. A snapshot of the 1930s, with old wooden furniture and ceiling fans, this self-consciously traditional *dim sum* restaurant is perhaps best visited for the surroundings, rather than the food or service, which barely justify the tourist-inflated prices. Upwards of $200/person. Daily 7am–10pm.

Metropol 4F, United Centre, 95 Queensway, Hong Kong Island ⓣ2865 1988; map pp.550–551. Huge place that still uses trolleys to wheel the *dim sum* selection around – a dying sight in Hong Kong. Try the flaky *char siu* pastries and crunchy *har gau* prawn dumplings, and expect to pay around $120 per person. Daily 8am–10.45pm.

★**One Dim Sum** 15 Playing Field Rd, Prince Edward ⓣ2789 2280; map pp.546–547. Prepare to queue at this straightforward *dim sum* joint; diners come to eat their crispy sweet-and-sour won ton, *siu mai* and the particularly delicious mango custard rolls, among other things. English menu available. Mon–Fri 11am–midnight, Sat & Sun 10am–midnight.

Tim Ho Wan 9–11 Fuk Wing St, Sham Shui Po ⓣ2788 1226; map pp.546–547. Now with branches across the city, this restaurant draws crowds that queue around the block for cheap, Michelin-star-rated lotus-leaf steamed rice, *char siu* pastries and *fun guo* dumplings. No bookings. Around $50/person. Mon–Fri 10am–10pm, Sat & Sun 9am–10pm.

RESTAURANTS

Downtown Hong Kong is thick with places to eat, and nowhere is a meal more than a few paces away. Cantonese places are ubiquitous, with the highest concentration of foreign cuisines in Central, Soho, Wan Chai and Tsim Sha Tsui; the scene is, however, notoriously fickle, with places continually opening and withering away. Outside the centre, there are several popular Western-oriented restaurants along Hong Kong Island's south coast, while the Outlying Islands are famous for their seafood. Restaurant opening hours are from around 11am to 3pm, and 6pm to late, though cheaper Chinese places open all day, winding down around 9pm. Service is traditionally bad in Hong Kong, with staff typically offhand to the point of rudeness, but this has more to do with their insane workload than personal animosity. Don't worry too much about tipping: expensive restaurants add on a ten-percent service charge anyway, while in cheaper places it's customary just to leave the small change.

CENTRAL

★**BÊP Vietnamese Kitchen** 88–90 Wellington St ⓣ2581 9992, ⓦbep.hk; map pp.550–551. Part of a small, locally run Vietnamese chain, whose crisp, clean and

MEDICINAL TEA

All through downtown Hong Kong you'll see open-fronted shops with large brass urns set out on a counter, offering cups or bowls full of dark brown **medicinal tea** at around $5 a drink. The Cantonese name for this is *leung cha* or "cool tea", because in Traditional Chinese Medicine tea is considered "cooling" to the body. The teas are made from various ingredients and claim various health benefits – ones to try include sweet *ng fa cha* (five-flower tea) and the extremely bitter *ya sei mei* (twenty-four-flavour tea).

9

sharp flavours make a nice break from Chinese fare. The *bánh mì* sandwiches ($58), rice-skin rolls ($78) and poached chicken salad ($78) are excellent, and two can eat very well for $300. No reservations; expect to queue at lunchtime. Daily noon–4.30pm & 6–11pm.

Man Wah 25F, Mandarin Oriental, 5 Connaught Rd ☎ 2825 4003, ⓦ mandarinoriental.com; map pp.550–551. Expect subtle and accomplished southern-Chinese food at connoisseurs' high prices (well upwards of $1000 per person). It's perhaps worth it if you want one definitively excellent Cantonese meal – though the view east towards Admiralty and Wan Chai sometimes outperforms the menu. Daily noon–2.30pm & 6.30–10.30pm.

★**Tsim Chai Kee Noodle** 98 Wellington St ☎ 2850 6471; map pp.550–551. This restaurant is easily located by the small Chinese sign and lunchtime queue tailing downhill; what makes it worth the wait, and worth being jammed into the packed interior, are the *wuntun* – jokingly known here as "ping-pong *wuntun*" because of their huge size – served in soup for $28. Daily 11am–9.30pm.

Yung Kee 32–40 Wellington St ☎ 2522 1624 ⓦ yungkee.com.hk; map pp.550–551. An enormous place with bright lights, scurrying staff and ample seating, this is one of Hong Kong's institutions. Their roast goose and pigeon are superb, and the *dim sum* is also good. Moderately expensive – expect $350 a head – but highly recommended. Daily 11am–11.30pm.

SOHO

La Pampa 32 Staunton St ☎ 2868 6959, ⓦ www .lapampa.com.hk; map pp.550–551. Argentinian restaurant that does what it does – mainly barbecued steak – exceedingly well. You order by weight, your meal is grilled just how you want it, and served with nominal quantities of vegetables. Count on at least $400 per person.

Mon–Fri noon–2.30pm & 6–11pm, Sat & Sun noon–5pm & 6–11pm.

★**Linguini Fini** 49 Elgin St ☎ 2387 6338, ⓦ linguinifini.com; map pp.550–551. This trendy restaurant serves classic Italian dishes with a New York spin, using fresh local ingredients wherever possible. Try the Brooklyn Special pizza ($279) with fried aubergine and roasted garlic, or linguini with clams and tomato broth ($159) – the cocktails are worth a look too. Reservations recommended. Daily 8am–10.30pm.

WAN CHAI AND CAUSEWAY BAY

Coyote 114–120 Lockhart Rd, Wan Chai ☎ 2861 2221, ⓦ coyote.com.hk; map pp.550–551. Lively Tex-Mex bar and grill that's full of tequila-quaffing patrons digging into plates of barbecued ribs, nachos and spicy pizzas. The lunch buffet is a very reasonable $108 per person; at other times, expect to pay around $200 each. Daily 11am–2am.

Fook Lam Moon 35–45 Johnston Rd, Wan Chai ☎ 2866 0663, ⓦ fooklammoon-grp.com; map pp.550–551. Very Cantonese institution with astounding roast suckling pig, crispy-skinned chicken, abalone and bird's nest soup. Service is not good, however – unless you're famous in Hong Kong. Around $1000 a head. Daily 11.30am–3pm & 6–11pm.

Matchbox 2 Sun Wui Rd, Causeway Bay ☎ 2881 0616; map pp.550–551. Come to this retro *cha chaan teng* for good-quality Hong Kong standards such as baked pork-chop rice or their glorious deep-fried French toast. A meal and drink will come to under $100, and their "nostalgic" afternoon tea set is great value at $46 for noodles, tea and eggs on toast. Daily 7am–11pm.

★**Plaza Mayor** 9 Moon St, Wan Chai ☎ 2866 6644, ⓦ plazamayor.hk; map pp.550–551. Top-notch Spanish tapas – the garlic shrimps and "broken egg" dishes are both

CHA CHAAN TENGS

Hong Kong's cheapest meals are found at **cha chaan tengs** – literally "tea canteens", which serve simple breakfasts and lunches. The cooked-food sections of most indoor produce markets also offer great value for money, with a single-plate meal – *wuntun* noodle soup, or rice with roast pork – costing around $40. City-wide versions of these places include *Café de Coral*, *Fairwood* and the above-average *Tsui Wah*.

Café de Coral Basement, Star House, 3 Salisbury Rd, Tsim Sha Tsui ☎ 2736 4900. Serves up *cha chaan teng* standards throughout the day, but meals here can have a slightly factory-assembled feel to them. That said, their roast meats on rice (from $25) are the pick of the bunch. Daily 6.30am–10pm.

Fairwood 7 Ashley Rd, Tsim Sha Tsui ☎ 2856 8628, ⓦ www.fairwood.com.hk. Though best known for its curries, this chain serves a solid menu of Hong Kong favourites including noodle soup topped with luncheon

meat and a fried egg ($32) for breakfast, baked pork-chop rice ($39) for lunch and deep-fried French toast ($24) for afternoon tea. Daily 7am–10pm.

★**Tsui Wah** 15–19 Wellington St, Central ☎ 2525 6338, ⓦ tsuiwah.com. With a menu that runs the gamut from sizzling king prawns to jumbo hot dogs, this impressive operation serves up great Hainan chicken (cooked in stock and served with rice; $56) and delicious crispy buns with condensed milk ($19) – best washed down with a cup of extra-strong milk tea. 24hr.

CURRY HOUSES IN CHUNGKING MANSIONS

It's an ugly building, but Chungking Mansions on Nathan Road, Tsim Sha Tsui, is where you'll find some of Hong Kong's best-value curry houses. A filling meal will cost around $100 per head.

Delhi Club 3F, Block C ☎ 2368 1682. A curry house *par excellence*, once you ignore the spartan surroundings and slap-down service. Daily noon–3.30pm & 6–11.30pm.

★**Khyber Pass Mess Club** 7F, Block E ☎ 2721 2786. Consistently good Indian, Pakistani, Bangladeshi and Malay dishes, all halal and one of the best in Chungking Mansions. Daily noon–3pm & 6–11.30pm.

Sher-I-Punjab 3F, Block B ☎ 2312 0366. Offers friendly service in clean surroundings, if slightly more expensive than some of its neighbours. Daily noon–3pm & 6–11.30pm.

Taj Mahal Club 3F, Block B ☎ 2722 5454. Excellent North Indian food, and good value if you avoid the relatively expensive drinks. Daily noon–3.30pm & 6–11.30pm.

---

excellent – best washed down with a bottle of *tempranillo* from their extensive wine cellar. Good service too, attentive but not overwhelming. Booking essential; expect $250 a head. Mon–Sat 11am–midnight, Sun 6pm–midnight.

Wing Wah 89 Hennessy Rd at Luard Rd, Wan Chai ☎ 2527 7476; map pp.550–551. Known for its *wuntun* noodles ($42), this locally famous noodle house also serves mostly inexpensive one-bowl meals, with a couple of unusual specials (from $65) and Cantonese desserts – try the mango sago with coconut milk ($50). Mon–Sat noon–2am.

SOUTH COAST HONG KONG

Happy Garden 786 Shek O Village ☎ 2809 4165; map pp.546–547. One of several laidback places with outdoor tables between the main bus stop and the seafront, with luridly coloured drinks and excellent Thai food – try the papaya salad or huge fish cakes. Mains around $80. Daily noon–10pm.

Jumbo Floating Restaurant Aberdeen Harbour ☎ 2553 9111, ⊛ jumbokingdom.com; map pp.546–547. A Hong Kong institution, with several restaurants spread across three garishly decorated floors. While touristy and expensive – the set meals start at around $600 per head – as a one-off trip it can also be a lot of fun. Mon–Sat 11am–11.30pm, Sun 9am–11.30pm.

Lucy's 64 Main St, Stanley ☎ 2813 9055, ⊛ lucys.hk; map pp.546–547. A cosy restaurant, tucked away down a backstreet in Stanley Market, where the menu changes regularly – expect the likes of spinach and feta souffle, and salmon fishcakes with fennel and French bean salad. Mains around $120, and reservations recommended. They also run a sandwich shop at Stanley Waterfront Market. Mon–Sat noon–3pm & 6–10pm, Sun 10am–3pm & 6–9pm.

TSIM SHA TSUI

Aqua 29F & Penthouse, 1 Peking Rd ☎ 3427 2288; map p.560. Dark wooden floors and superlative harbour views set the scene for an unexpectedly successful blend of Italian and Japanese dishes. The atmosphere is informal, and the prices around $500 per head; a cheaper option is to

head to the upstairs bar for a drink (prices start at $108 for a glass of wine). Reservations essential. Daily noon–2.30pm & 6–11pm.

Chee Kei 52 Lock Rd ☎ 2368 2528, ⊛ cheekeiwonton .com; map p.560. Bright Chinese diner serving unpretentious, good-quality *wuntun* and noodle soups, fried pork steak, crispy prawn rolls and fishballs. About $40 per dish. Daily 11am–11pm.

Felix 28F, Peninsula Hotel ☎ 2696 6778; map p.560. The incredible views of Hong Kong Island (not least from the gents' glass-walled urinals) warrant a visit to this Philippe Starck-designed restaurant. The Eurasian menu averages over $650 per person, but you can just come for one of their famous Martinis at the bar – a great perch for watching a summer storm or the 8pm "Symphony of Lights" across the harbour. Restaurant daily 6–10.30pm; bar daily 5.30pm–1.30am.

Ka Ka Lok Corner of Ashley Rd and Ichang St ☎ 2376 1198; map p.560. A fast-food counter with the sole distinction of serving the cheapest fried noodles, rice and fish 'n' chips in Hong Kong – nothing costs more than $35 or so. No seats, but Kowloon Park is 100m away. Daily 8am–3am.

★**Peninsula Hotel Lobby** The Peninsula ☎ 2696 6772; map p.560. The set tea, served in the lobby and accompanied by a string quartet, comes to around $358 per person – pricey, but a good way to get a glimpse of a more elegant, civilized and relaxed Hong Kong. Dress is smart-casual; no plastic or nylon footwear, sportswear or sleeveless shirts for men. Daily 2–6pm.

Spring Deer 1F, 42 Mody Rd ☎ 2366 4012; map p.560. Faded restaurant that must have been grand when they last redecorated in the 1960s. The food – especially the steamed lamb and Peking duck – is worth it, though; expect to pay around $300 per person. Daily noon–3pm & 6–11pm.

Sweet Dynasty Pacific Centre, 28 Hankow Rd ☎ 2199 7799; map p.560. While this restaurant offers tasty but expensive noodles and rice dishes, it's best to stick to the Southeast Asian-style desserts, featuring sago, tofu, mango, lotus seeds and red beans – the pomelo pudding in coconut milk is exceptional. Mon–Fri 8am–midnight, Sat & Sun 7.30am–midnight.

9

JORDAN, MONG KOK AND SHAM SHUI PO

Light Vegetarian 13 Jordan Rd ☎2384 2833; map p.560. Comprehensive Chinese vegetarian menu, including bean starch "sharks fin" soup, stir-fried broccoli, vegetarian sweet and sour pork and a big *dim sum* selection. Dishes from $45. Daily 11am–1pm.

★**Mak Man Kee** 51 Parkes St, Jordan ☎2736 5561, ⓦmmk.com.hk; map p.560. You'd never guess from the anonymous white tiles and cramped interior, but this famous, long-running family business is held by many to serve the best *wuntun* noodles in town, a bowlful of which costs just $32. Daily noon–12.30am.

Shia Wong Hip 170 Ap Liu St, Sham Shui Po ☎2728 5600; map pp.546–547. Hidden behind the market stalls that line Ap Liu St, this old-school Cantonese diner has been dishing up snake soup ($42 per bowl) in Sham Shui Po for fifty years. The soup is made to a secret recipe and contains five different types of snake; these are housed in the wooden drawers at the rear of the shop. Less adventurous diners can opt for the delicious sticky rice with Cantonese sausage. Daily 11am–11.30pm.

LEI YUE MUN

Gateway Lei Yue Mun, 750m from Yau Tong MTR (Exit A1), 3km east of Tsim Sha Tsui ☎2727 4628, ⓦgatewaycuisine.com; map pp.546–547. If you want to blow some money on an excellent Cantonese seafood meal with atmospheric harbour views, you won't get better than this: try the sautéed tiger prawns, steamed scallops, razor shells with black beans and steamed grouper. A seven-dish meal costs around $350 per person in a group. Daily 11am–11pm.

OUTLYING ISLANDS

CHEUNG CHAU

Hong Kee Turn left off the ferry and it's part of the row of restaurants 300m along ☎2981 9916; map pp.546–547. No-frills alfresco seafood place, on the harbourside promenade, serving a range of stir-fries and fresh seafood. Order a plate of prawns and a beer, and watch the sun go down. Around $75 per person. Daily 5–11pm.

★**Pink Pig** Turn right from the pier, follow the shore and it's 350m past a row of seafood restaurants ☎5180 0692, ⓦfacebook.com/thepinkpig.cc; map pp.546–547. Casual bar and café with great views of Lantau and occasional live music, serving locally brewed beer (from $38), cocktails in plastic glasses and tasty snacks including

truffle mayo fries and pulled-pork nachos for around $30 a pop. Tues–Sun afternoons–early evenings.

LAMMA

Bookworm Café 79 Main St, Yung Shue Wan ☎2982 4838; map pp.546–547. This long-running vegetarian Western restaurant is slightly too worthy, but their bean burgers, fresh juices and cheesecake are excellent and there's a secondhand-book exchange, too. Mains from $75. Mon–Wed & Fri–Sun 10am–9pm.

Concerto Inn Hung Shing Ye beach, just uphill off the main path ☎2982 1668, ⓦconcertoinn.com.hk; map pp.546–547. The food here – an Asian-European fusion with a heavy emphasis on seafood – is hit-and-miss in quality, but the outdoor terrace is a lovely place to sit and have an ice-cold sundowner after a few hours on the beach. Mon, Tues & Thurs–Sun 9am–9pm, Wed 9am–5pm.

Rainbow Seafood 23–24 First St, Sok Kwu Wan ☎2982 8100, ⓦlammarainbow.com; map pp.546–547. Built on stilts right over the water, this huge open-plan restaurant seats eight hundred people and serves consistently good fish, crab, scallop and prawn dishes (beware the small portions of lobster, though). Book ahead unless you want a half-hour wait; those with reservations can use the restaurant's free ferry service between Central/Tsim Sha Tsui and Lamma. Daily 10am–11pm.

LANTAU

Deer Horn Mui Wo Centre, 3 Ngan Wan Rd, Mui Wo ☎3484 3095; map pp.546–547. Run by a Nepalese couple and serves a mix of decent Italian dishes and better Nepali food, including chicken *momos* ($65) and delicious yak cheese fritters ($68). Mon & Wed–Sun noon–late.

Mavericks Pui O Beach ☎2984 1328, ⓦmavericks.hk; map pp.546–547. There are few reasons to get off the bus in Pui O, but this beach bar and restaurant is one of them. The hip menu runs from grilled fish ($128) to a vast double-decker burger ($138), and there are also some imaginative veggie options, though portions are on the small side and service can be slow. DJs play on the weekend, so this is a fun spot to round off a day on Lantau. Fri 5–10pm, Sat & Sun 11am–11pm.

Village Bakery 16 Mui Wo Ferry Pier Rd, Mui Wo ☎2980 3344, ⓦvillagebakerylantau.blogspot.co.uk; map pp.546–547. Set yourself up for a picnic at this bakery and café where the bread and cakes are cooked fresh each morning – the strawberry jam doughnuts ($12) are particularly good. Eat-in also available. Mon–Sat 7am–7pm, Sun 8am–7pm.

DRINKING AND NIGHTLIFE

The most concentrated collection of bars is in the **Lan Kwai Fong/Wyndham Street** area on Hong Kong Island, which is perennially popular for late-night carousing with drinkers spilling out onto the streets. Other locations include the long-established, slightly sleazy expat scene around **Wan Chai**, and a scattering of options in **Tsim Sha Tsui**. Some venues charge a $50–500 entrance fee on certain nights (generally Fri & Sat), though almost everywhere also offers daily happy hours at some point between 3pm and 9pm – worth catching, as drinks are otherwise pricey. For event details, consult free *HK Magazine* (ⓦhk-magazine.com), ⓦhkclubbing.com or *Time Out Kong Kong* (ⓦtimeout.com.hk) – the latter also contains listings for the city's **gay scene**.

CENTRAL

Club 71 67 Hollywood Rd, Central ☎2858 7071; map pp.550–551. Away from Lan Kwai Fong's rowdy mess of bars, this tiny bohemian place still gets busy, but happy hour prices are reasonable and there's a front-of-house terrace. It's hard to find – look for 69 Hollywood Rd and take the small lane around to the back. Mon–Sat 3pm–2am, Sun 6pm–1am.

Drop Basement, 39–43 Hollywood Rd, Central; entrance on Cochrane St ☎2543 8856, ⓦfacebook.com /dropbarhk; map pp.550–551. One of Hong Kong's off-beat nightclubs, this late-night venue doesn't really get going until 1am, though it can be tough to get in after 11pm at weekends. Local and overseas DJs play thumping dance music, and Martinis fuel the chic-but-fun crowd. Mon–Sat 9pm–6am.

★**Le Boudoir** Basement, 65 Wyndham St, Central ☎2530 3870, ⓦfacebook.com/leboudoirhk; map pp.550–551. Down a long flight of stairs from street-level, this lounge bar is decked out with velvet couches, chandeliers and other *belle époque* finery, serving delicious, grown-up cocktails – there's not a jelly shot in sight. Daily 6pm–3am.

Le Jardin Wing Wah Lane ☎2526 2717; map pp.550–551. Almost impossible to find unless you already know it's there – go right to the end of Wing Wah Lane and take the steps up to the hidden entrance. This comfortable bar has a covered terrace and is usually quieter than alternatives in nearby Lan Kwai Fong. Mon–Fri 4.30pm–late, Sat 5pm–late.

Stormies 46 D'Aguilar St, Lan Kwai Fong ☎2845 5533, ⓦfacebook.com/stormiescdg; map pp.550–551. With a great location at the top of D'Aguilar Street, this long-running bar makes a lively spot for people-watching over a beer. Free shots whenever a typhoon signal goes up. Daily noon–2am.

WAN CHAI

Carnegie's 53–55 Lockhart Rd ☎2866 6289; map pp.550–551. The noise level here means conversation is only possible by flash cards and, once it's full, hordes of punters, keen to party the night away, fight for dancing

space on the bar. Regular live music. Mon–Thurs 11am–late, Sat noon–late, Sun 4pm–late.

★**Dusk till Dawn** 76 Jaffe Rd ☎2528 4689; map pp.550–551. Another long-running Wan Chai institution that pulls in partygoers with their fantastic Filipino bands, who play covers of everything from Guns N' Roses to Taylor Swift. Sun–Thurs noon–6am, Fri & Sat 3pm–7am.

The Pawn 62 Johnston Rd ☎2866 3444, ⓦthepawn .com.hk; map pp.550–551. Smart bar in a restored pawnbroker's building dating from 1888, with the facade and some old wooden fixtures still in place. There's also a balcony overlooking the busy road, plus a well-regarded restaurant on the second floor. The bar offers sophisticated cocktails (from $90), plus an extensive list of imported spirits and pricey bar snacks (from $60). Daily noon–1am.

Wanch 54 Jaffe Rd ☎2861 1621, ⓦthewanch.hk; map pp.550–551. A Hong Kong institution, this tiny bar has live music – usually folk and rock – every night. It also serves sandwiches ($35) and free snacks 6–7.30pm. Mon–Sat 11am–2am, Sun noon–2am.

TSIM SHA TSUI

Bahama Mama's 4–5 Knutsford Terrace, just north of Kimberly Rd ☎2368 2121; map p.560. A good atmosphere, with a vibrant mix of nationalities, and plenty of space for pavement drinking. There's a beach-bar theme and outdoor terrace that prompts party-crowd antics. On club nights, there's a great range of mixed music. Mon–Thurs 4pm–3am, Fri & Sat 4pm–4am, Sun 4pm–2am.

Delaney's Basement, Mary Building, 71–77 Peking Rd ☎2301 3980; map p.560. Friendly and comfortably familiar Irish pub with draught beers, including Guinness ($80); features Irish folk music most nights. Huge servings of pub food available too (mains from $142). Daily 8am–2am.

Ned Kelly's Last Stand 11A Ashley Rd ☎2376 0562; map p.560. Popular, long-running Australia-themed venue, featuring a nightly performance from an excellent ragtime jazz band. Daily noon–1.45am.

SHOPPING

Many visitors come to Hong Kong to go **shopping**, drawn by the incredible range of goods packed into such a small area. While some things are good value for money – particularly **silk**, **jewellery**, **Chinese arts and crafts**, and some **computer accessories** – it's essential to research online prices for identical goods before buying, and to shop around. The farther you are from touristy Tsim Sha Tsui, the better-value shopping becomes, and the less likely that you'll be ripped off by some **scam**.

ANTIQUES, ARTS AND CRAFTS

Chinese collectors value their heritage, which means that Hong Kong is one of the most expensive places in the world to buy antiques – there are also huge numbers of fakes floating around. But if you know your stuff, the range and quality are excellent. Hollywood Road (see

9

p.552) is at the centre of the trade, and Upper Lascar Row is a fun place to browse for lower-end reproductions and souvenirs. Hong Kong is also a reasonable place to pick up modern arts and crafts, with a couple of big chain stores dealing in Chinese products – prices are cheaper on the mainland, however.

★**Honeychurch Antiques** 29 Hollywood Rd, Central ☎ 2543 2433, ⓦ honeychurch.com; map pp.550–551. Long-running, intimate and foreign-owned gallery with a range of genuine Chinese, Japanese and Tibetan curios and antiques; prices are relatively low for Hong Kong and the shop is well worth a browse. Mon–Sat 10am–6pm.

Karin Weber Gallery 20 Aberdeen St, Central ☎ 2544 5004, ⓦ karinwebergallery.com; map pp.550–551. Specializes in contemporary paintings from the mainland and Southeast Asia, as well as antique Chinese furniture. Tues–Sat 11am–7pm.

Yue Hwa China Products 301–309 Nathan Rd, Jordan, ☎ 3511 2222, ⓦ yuehwa.com; map p.560. Chinese medicines, clothing, tea, books, spirits and every conceivable knick-knack produced on the mainland, all in one place and with prices that are often subject to negotiation. Daily 10am–10pm.

Yue Po Chai Antiques 132–136 Hollywood Rd, on the corner of Ladder St and Hollywood Rd, Central ☎ 2540 4374; map pp.550–551. Across from Man Mo Temple, this place is crowded with dusty glass cabinets stuffed with porcelain – both real and reproduction (though this isn't necessarily made clear). They'll haggle a little over prices. Mon–Sat 10.30am–6pm.

BOOKSHOPS

Bookazine 3F, Prince's Building, Chater Rd, Central ☎ 2522 1785, ⓦ bookazine.com.hk; map pp.550–551. Excellent English-language bookshop with a good range of popular fiction and local interest; it also hosts regular literary events and book signings. Mon–Sat 9.30am–7.30pm, Sun 10am–7pm.

Cosmos Books 30 Johnston Rd, Wan Chai ☎ 2866 1677, ⓦ www.cosmosbooks.com.hk; map pp.550–551. Offers an excellent range of both English- and Chinese-language books on all topics, from cookbooks to guides, novels, martial art manuals and bestsellers. Daily 10am–8pm.

Eslite 2–3F, Star House, 3 Salisbury Rd, Tsim Sha Tsui ☎ 3419 1088, ⓦ esliteliving.com; map p.560. Browse Hong Kong's two branches of this Taiwanese chain for a huge selection of English and Chinese books and magazines, fun gadgets and hip stationery. Daily 10am–10pm.

Swindon Book Company 13–15 Lock Rd, Tsim Sha Tsui ☎ 2366 8001, ⓦ swindonbooks.com; map p.560. Hong Kong's oldest English-language bookshop, with a solid range of works on Hong Kong and China including academic and out-of-print titles that you won't see elsewhere. Mon–Sat 10am–8pm, Sun 12.30–6.30pm.

CLOTHES

Clothes are good value in Hong Kong, particularly local casual-wear brand names such as Giordano and Baleno, which have branches across the city. **Designer clothes** are often more expensive than elsewhere because of the cachet attached to

---

A NICE SUIT, SIR?

Tailor-made clothes are a speciality of the Hong Kong tourist trade, and wherever you go in Tsim Sha Tsui you'll be accosted by Indian tailors offering this service. Sales pitches are hardcore and prices are relatively low, but not rock bottom; a man's suit, with a couple of shirts and ties, will cost upwards of $1500, more likely twice this. Don't commit yourself without knowing exactly what's included. Expect at least two or three fittings over several days if you want a good result. You'll need to pay about fifty percent of the price as a deposit.

Johnson & Co 44 Hankow Rd, Kowloon ☎ 2366 7172, ⓦ www.johnsonco.com.hk; map p.560. This long-established business has been clothing military and naval customers for over sixty years. Excellent jewellers, too. Mon–Sat 10am–7pm.

Linva Tailor 38 Cochrane St, Central; ☎ 2544 2456; map pp.550–551. Well-established ladies' tailor, popular with locals who want *cheongsams* for parties. It can take up to three months to make an elaborately embroidered piece – fortunately, they also arrange shipping. Mon–Sat 10am–6pm.

Pacific Custom Tailors 19 Des Voeux Rd, Central ☎ 2845 5377, ⓦ pacifictailor.com.hk; map pp.550–551. Upmarket, elegantly tailored suits with prices to

match. The entrance is on Pedder Street. Mon–Sat 10am–7.30pm.

Punjab House Shops G–H, Burlington Arcade, 90 Nathan Rd, Tsim Sha Tsui ☎ 2366 6612, ⓦ punjabhouse.com.hk; map p.560. Former favourite of the British Forces and Fire Fighters, offering good-quality male and female formal wear. Mon–Sat 9am–9pm, Sun 10am–7pm.

Sam's Tailors Shops K–L, Burlington Arcade, 90 Nathan Rd, Tsim Sha Tsui ⓦ samstailor.com; map p.560. Probably the best-known tailor in Hong Kong, Sam is famous as much for his talent for self-publicity as for his clothes. Mon–Sat 9.40am–7pm, Sun 10am–noon.

upmarket foreign brands, but sales and **discount outlets** are worth checking out. If you just want to browse, head to Granville Road in Tsim Sha Tsui or Soho on Hong Kong Island.

Blanc De Chine 123 Prince's Building, Central ☏ 2104 7934, ⓦ www.blancdechine.com; map pp.550–551. Offers elegant designs that are loosely based on traditional Chinese clothes, mostly in silk or cashmere, at high prices. Also sells stylish jewellery to match. Mon–Sat 10.30am–7.30pm, Sun noon–6pm.

Horizon Plaza Lee Nam Rd, Ap Lei Chau Island, Aberdeen (entrance around side on Li Wing St); bus #95 from Aberdeen or #671 from Causeway Road, near Victoria Park; map pp.546–547. Twenty-eight floors of discount outlets – including Joyce, Lane Crawford and Armani – where designer boutiques send last season's (or last month's) stuff that didn't sell, with savings of up to eighty percent. The lobby has a comprehensive directory, and there's a café or two on site. Opening hours vary.

Shanghai Tang 1 Duddell St, Central ☏ 2525 7333, ⓦ shanghaitang.com; map pp.550–551. A must-visit store, which specializes in trendy new versions of traditional Chinese styles like the *cheongsam* split-sided dress, often in vibrant colours. Expensive, even during sales. Daily 10.30am–8pm.

Vivienne Tam 309 The Landmark, 15 Queen's Rd, Central ☏ 2868 2826, ⓦ viviennetam.com; map pp.550–551. Funky shirts and dresses in David-Hockney-meets-Vivienne-Westwood style, often featuring Chinese motifs. Daily 10.30am–7.30pm.

ELECTRONIC GOODS

With the advent of **internet shopping**, prices in Hong Kong for electronic goods such as cameras, mobile phones and computers are no longer the bargain they once were – and it's still difficult to get a warranty and possible to get ripped off. If you do decide to buy, make sure you know exactly what you want, and the price you'd pay for it at home and online. **Chain stores** such as Fortress (ⓦ fortress.com.hk/en) are reliable places to get a base price, though hard bargainers will do better at the three computer centres listed below. For secondhand mobile phones and household appliances, and gadgetry of all kinds, try Ap Liu Street in Sham Shui Po, Kowloon (exit A2 from Sham Shui Po MTR).

298 Computer Zone 298 Hennessy Rd, Wan Chai; map pp.550–551. A disconcerting maze of shops crammed into three levels, with a well-concealed entrance despite the huge sign. Discounted computers and accessories, plus a vast collection of novelty USB drives. Daily 11am–9pm.

Golden Shopping Centre 156 Fuk Wa St, Sham Shui Po, Kowloon; Sham Shui Po MTR, exit D2; map pp.546–547. Another claustrophobic warren of tiny stalls selling all sorts of cheap computer components and accessories. Daily 10am–10pm.

Mong Kok Computer Centre Corner of Nelson St and Fa Yuen St, Mong Kok; map p.560. Yet more discounted electronics, mostly mobile phone-oriented. Daily 10am–10pm.

JEWELLERY

Hong Kongers love jewellery, and the city houses literally thousands of jewellers. Some offer pieces that look remarkably like famous international jewellery houses' designs, but at much lower prices. The **Hong Kong Tourist Board** (see p.575) can point you in the direction of reputable stores, but retailers with outlets city-wide include Chow Tai Fook (ⓦ chowtaifook.com) and Chow Sang Sang (ⓦ chowsangsang.com).

MALLS AND DEPARTMENT STORES

In summer, the air-conditioning in Hong Kong's numerous, glossy shopping malls makes as good a reason as any to visit, and most have nice cafés to boot. Some of the best include Times Square (Causeway Bay MTR), IFC Mall (inside the IFC; Central MTR), Pacific Place (Admiralty MTR) and Langham Place (Mongkok MTR). Department store chains include:

Lane Crawford IFC Mall, Central; map pp.550–551. Hong Kong's oldest Western-style department store, selling upmarket labels and classy homewares. Daily 10am–9pm.

SOGO East Point Centre, 555 Hennessy Rd, Causeway Bay; map pp.550–551. This labyrinthine store is a Japanese import stocking a vast range of immaculately presented goods inside one of the largest (and busiest) department stores in Hong Kong. Mon–Thurs & Sun 10am–10pm, Fri & Sat 10am–10.30pm.

Wing On 26 Des Voeux Rd, Central; map pp.550–551. A long-established store, with branches throughout Hong Kong SAR. Standard, day-to-day goods rather than luxuries. Daily 10am–7.30pm.

DIRECTORY

Banks and exchange Banks are generally open Mon–Fri 9am–4.30pm, Sat 9am–12.30pm; almost all have ATMs capable of accepting foreign cards. Licensed moneychangers, who open all hours including Sun, don't charge commission but usually give poor rates, so shop around and always establish the exact amount you will receive before handing any money over.

Emergencies For emergency services, call ☏ 999.

Hospitals Government hospitals have 24hr casualty wards, where fees range from $990 for basic treatment in casualty to $23,000 for a day in intensive care. Major hospitals include the Princess Margaret Hospital, Lai King Hill Rd, Lai Chi Kok, Kowloon ☏ 2990 1111; and the Queen Mary Hospital, 102 Pok Fu Lam Rd, Hong Kong Island ☏ 2255 3838. For an ambulance, dial ☏ 999.

Internet Most accommodation and café chains offer free

9

wi-fi for their customers. Hong Kong Central Library, opposite Victoria Park in Causeway Bay, Hong Kong Island (Mon, Tues & Thurs–Sun 10am–9pm, Wed 1–9pm), has free internet, though you have to wait for a terminal to become available, as well as free wi-fi.

Laundry There are many laundries in Hong Kong where you pay by dry weight of clothes ($10–20/kilo) and then pick them up an hour or two later; ask at your accommodation for the nearest one.

Left luggage There's an office on Level 3 of Terminal 2 at Hong Kong airport (daily 5.30am–1.30am), and at the Central and Kowloon stations for the Airport Express. There are also coin-operated lockers in the China Ferry Terminal in Tsim Sha Tsui. It costs $20–80 depending on size of locker and time used. You can also negotiate to leave luggage at your guesthouse or hotel, but ensure you're happy with general security first. If you're flying out late from Hong Kong and need to get rid of your bags for the day, consider using the in-town check-in (see p.573).

Police Crime hotline and taxi complaints ☎ 2527 7177. For general police enquiries, call ☎ 2860 2000.

Post offices Hong Kong's general post office is at 2 Connaught Place, Central (Mon–Sat 8am–6pm, Sun 9am–5pm). The Kowloon main post office is at 10 Middle Rd, Tsim Sha Tsui.

Macau

澳门, àomén

Sixty kilometres west across the Pearl River Delta from Hong Kong lies the former Portuguese enclave of **MACAU**, which occupies a peninsula and a couple of islands. Its atmosphere has been unmistakeably shaped by a **colonial past** – predating Hong Kong's by nearly three hundred years – which has left old fortresses, Baroque churches, faded mansions, cobbled public squares, unusual food and Portuguese place names in its wake.

Until very recently, Macau's **casinos** were the main draw for millions of big-spending tourists from the mainland and Hong Kong; in 2013, the territory's gaming revenue hit a record of US$45 billion (more than six times that of Las Vegas over the same period) and the city's **construction boom** for themed resorts and upscale hotels peaked. Since then, however, gambling revenue and visitor numbers have tumbled as the mainland's anticorruption drive and economic slowdown hit home; but while the high rollers may have deserted Macau, the quieter streets and hotels make it a far more pleasant place to visit than ever before.

Macau comprises several distinct areas. The largest and most densely settled one is the **peninsula**, bordering the Chinese mainland to the north, where the original Portuguese colony was located and where most of the historic sights and facilities remain. Off to the southeast and linked to the peninsula by bridges are **Taipa** and **Coloane**, once separate islands but now joined by a low-lying area of reclaimed land known as **Cotai**, which has been developed as an entertainment strip. It's all very compact, so it's possible to get around much of the peninsula on foot; that said, public transport and taxis are available for longer stretches. A day-trip from Hong Kong is possible (tens of thousands do it every weekend), though you really need to spend a couple of nights here to do the place justice.

Brief history

For more than a thousand years, all **trade** between China and the West was indirectly carried out overland along the Silk Road through Central Asia. But from the fifteenth

---

MACAU CURRENCY

The Macau currency is the **pataca** (abbreviated to "MOP$" in this book; also written as "M$" and "ptca"), which is worth fractionally less than the HK dollar. HK dollars are freely accepted as currency in Macau, and a lot of visitors from Hong Kong don't bother changing money at all. Chinese yuan are widely accepted too, though the 1:1 exchange rate used by most businesses means you're better off changing your money to patacas for all but the smallest transactions.

century onwards, seafaring European nations started making exploratory voyages around the globe, establishing garrisoned ports along the way and so creating new maritime trade routes over which they had direct control. In 1557 – having already gained footholds in India (Goa) and the Malay Peninsula (Malacca) – the **Portuguese** persuaded Chinese officials to rent them a strategically well-placed peninsula at the mouth of the Pearl River Delta, known as **Macao**. With their trade links with Japan, India and Malaya, the Portuguese found themselves in the profitable position of being

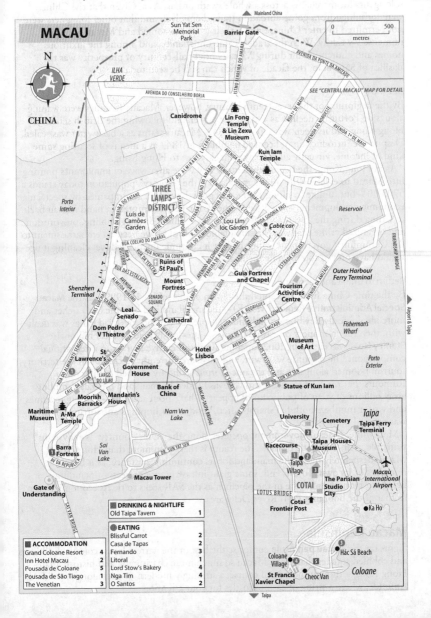

MACAU

N

CHINA

Mainland China

Sun Yat Sen Memorial Park

Barrier Gate

AVENIDA DA PONTE DA AMIZADE

ILHA VERDE

AVENIDA DO CONSELHEIRO BORJA

SEE "CENTRAL MACAU" MAP FOR DETAIL

0   500
metres

Canidrome

Lin Fong Temple & Lin Zexu Museum

Kun Iam Temple

AVENIDA DO CORONEL MESQUITA

AVENIDA DE OUVIDOR ARRIAGA

AVE DO ALMIRANTE LACERDA

RUA 1º DE MAIO

AVENIDA DO NORDESTE

AVENIDA 1º DE MAIO

Porto Interior

THREE LAMPS DISTRICT

Luís de Camões Garden

RUA DA RIBEIRA DO PATANE

RUA DA PATANE

RUA ENTRE CAMPOS

ESTRADA DO REPOUSO

AVENIDA DE COELHO DO AMARAL

R. DE FRANCISCO XAVIER PEREIRA

AVENIDA DO OURO DE OURIQUE COSTA

Lou Lim Ioc Gárden

AVENIDA SIDONIO PAIS

Cable car

Reservoir

FRIENDSHIP BRIDGE

RUA COELHO DO AMARAL

RUA DE OUTOBRO

RUA HORTA DA CONPANHIA

RUA DA TERCEIRA

Ruins of St Paul's

Mount Fortress

RUA DAS ESTALAGENS

AVENIDA DE ALMEIDA RIBEIRO

SENADO SQUARE

RUA DO CAMPO

Guia Fortress and Chapel

AVENIDA DA VITÓRIA

ESTRADA CALCIMAS

Tourism Activities Centre

AVENIDA DA AMIZADE

Outer Harbour Ferry Terminal

Shenzhen Terminal

Leal Senado

Dom Pedro V Theatre

RUA CENTRAL

Cathedral

AV DO INFANTE D. HENRIQUE

AVENIDA DO DR R. RODRIGUES

GONZAGA GOMES

RUA DE LUÍS DA AMIZADE

ALAMEDA DE CARLOS D'ASSUMPÇÃO

Fisherman's Wharf

St Lawrence's

RUA PADRE ANTONIO

AV DA PRAIA GRANDE

AV DOUTOR MARIO SOARES

Hotel Lisboa

Museum of Art

Porto Exterior

Government House

Bank of China

MACAU-TAIPA BRIDGE

AV. DR. SUN YAT SEN

RUA DO ALMIRANTE SERGIO

Moorish Barracks

Mandarin's House

LARGO DO LILAU

Nam Van Lake

CALC. DA BARRA

Maritime Museum

A-Ma Temple

Statue of Kun Iam

AV. DR. SUN YAT SEN

Barra Fortress

AV DA REPUBLICA

Sai Van Lake

AV. DR. SUN YAT SEN

Macau Tower

SAI VAN BRIDGE

Gate of Understanding

Taipa

University

Cemetery

Taipa Ferry Terminal

Racecourse

Taipa Houses Museum

Taipa Village

The Parisian

Macáu International Airport

COTAI

Studio City

Ka Ho

LOTUS BRIDGE

Cotai Frontier Post

Coloane Village

St Francis Xavier Chapel

Cheoc Van

Hác Sá Beach

Coloane

Taipa

Airport & Taipa

■ **DRINKING & NIGHTLIFE**
Old Taipa Tavern   1

● **EATING**
Blissful Carrot	2
Casa de Tapas	2
Fernando	3
Litoral	1
Lord Stow's Bakery	4
Nga Tim	4
O Santos	2

■ **ACCOMMODATION**
Grand Coloane Resort	4
Inn Hotel Macau	2
Pousada de Coloane	5
Pousada de São Tiago	1
The Venetian	3

9

sole agents for merchants across a whole swath of East Asia. Given that the Chinese were forbidden from going abroad to trade themselves, and that other foreigners were not permitted to enter Chinese ports, their trade blossomed and Macau grew immensely wealthy. With the traders came **Christianity**, and among the luxurious homes and churches built during Macau's brief half-century of prosperity was the Basilica of **São Paulo**, the facade of which can still be seen today.

Decline

By the beginning of the seventeenth century, however, Macau's fortunes were waning alongside Portugal's decline as a maritime power, and following the British seizure of Hong Kong and its deep-water port in 1842, Macau's status as a backwater was sealed. Despite the introduction of **licensed gambling** in 1847 as a means of securing some kind of income, virtually all trade was quickly lost to Hong Kong.

As in Hong Kong, the twentieth century saw wave after wave of **immigrants** pouring into Macau to escape strife on the mainland – the territory's population today stands at 570,000 – but, unlike in Hong Kong, this growth was not accompanied by spectacular economic development. Indeed, when the Portuguese attempted to hand Macau back to China during the 1960s and 1970s, they were rebuffed: the gambling, prostitution and organized crime that was Macau's lifeblood would have been an embarrassment to the Communist government if they had let it continue unchecked, yet cleaning it up would have proved too big a financial drain.

Return to China and recovery

By the time China finally accepted the return of the colony in 1999 – as the **Macau Special Administrative Region** (MSAR) – the mainland had become both richer and more ideologically flexible. A pre-handover spree of violence by Triad gangs was dealt with, then the monopoly on casino licences – previously held by local billionaire **Stanley Ho** – was ended in 2002, opening up this lucrative market to international competition. The response was swift, and there are currently **33 casinos** in the territory; tourism boomed alongside and the once torpid economy reached boiling point. Rumours that the SAR's soaring growth was funded by mainland officials gambling away billions of yuan of public funds appear to have been accurate – gaming revenues and visitor numbers both fell sharply after President Xi Jinping's anticorruption drive was ramped up in 2013.

Meanwhile, Macau's **government** operates along the "One Country, Two Systems" principle, with very little dissent. The reality is that, even more than Hong Kong, Macau desperately needs the mainland for its continuing existence, as it has no resources of its own. To this end, some giant infrastructure projects – including a bridge to Hong Kong – are in the pipeline, as the SAR seeks to tie its economy closer to that of the booming Pearl River Delta area.

Macau Peninsula

Sights on the **Macau peninsula** comprise the best of the narrow lanes, colonial buildings and cobbled squares that make Macau so much more charismatic and historic than Hong Kong – though there is, of course, a strikingly modern district along Avenida da Amizade, where a string of casinos jostles for your attention.

Senado Square

Macau's older core centres around **Senado Square** (Largo do Senado), a cobbled, pedestrianized square east of Avenida de Almeida Ribeiro and surrounded by unmistakeably European-influenced buildings, with their stucco mouldings, colonnades and shuttered windows. There's an excellent **market** (daily 10am–7pm) in the lanes immediately west of the square, which is good for cheap clothes.

Leal Senado

Senado Square • Tues–Sun 9am–9pm; public library Mon–Sat 1–7pm • Free

At Senado Square's southern side – across Avenida de Almeida Ribeiro – stands the **Leal Senado**, which is generally considered the finest Portuguese building in the city. The interior courtyard is decorated with wonderful blue-and-white Portuguese tiles, while up the staircase from the courtyard is the richly decorated **senate chamber**, which is still used by Macau's municipal government. The senate's title *leal* (loyal) was earned after Macau refused to recognize the Spanish king's rule over Portugal in the sixteenth century. Adjacent to the chamber is the wood-carved **public library**, which includes a vast collection of China-themed books, some in English, which date back to the colony's foundation.

Cathedral

Largo da Sé • Daily 7.30am–6.30pm • Free

East off Senado Square, two small lanes slope uphill to a cobbled square and the uninspiring concrete facade of Macau's sixteenth-century **Cathedral** (Sé), which has an interior that impresses in scale, rather than ornamentation. One of the most active churches in Macau, there are daily Masses read here in Cantonese and Portuguese.

Lou Kau Mansion

Travessa da Sé • Tues–Sun 10am–6pm • Free

Just east off Senado Square, the **Lou Kau Mansion** (Casa de Lou Kau) is the house of the wealthy nineteenth-century merchant who sponsored the Lou Lim Ieoc Garden (Jardim Lou Lim Ieoc; see p.594). The building, a two-storey grey-brick structure with internal galleries around a central atrium, has been perfectly restored and has an open roof that lets in light and air but keeps out the heat. The house regularly hosts demonstrations of folk art and traditional music.

St Dominic's Church

Senado Square • Daily 10am–6pm • Free

At Senado Square's northern end, the honey-and-cream-coloured, seventeenth-century Baroque church **St Dominic's** (São Domingos) is adjoined by Macau's **Religious Museum** (daily 10am–6pm), which contains a treasury of sacred art under a timbered roof. On May 13 the church is the starting point for a major procession in honour of Our Lady of Fatima.

Ruins of St Paul's

Rua de São Paulo

North from Senado Square, you'll find the streets flanked by *pastellarias* (biscuit shops) and stores selling reproduction antique furniture. At the top of Rua de São Paulo, a broad stone staircase rises to the **Ruins of St Paul's** (Ruínas de São Paulo) built in 1602 and hailed as the greatest Christian monument in East Asia before being destroyed by fire in 1835. Only the massive stone **facade** has survived, standing at the head of the stairs like a theatre backdrop and lavishly carved in a riot of Christian iconography – there are doves, symbols of the Crucifixion, angels, statues of Jesuit saints – and political motifs such as peonies (representing China) and chrysanthemums (Japan). Immediately west of St Paul's stands **Na Tcha Temple** (daily 8am–5pm), a diminutive

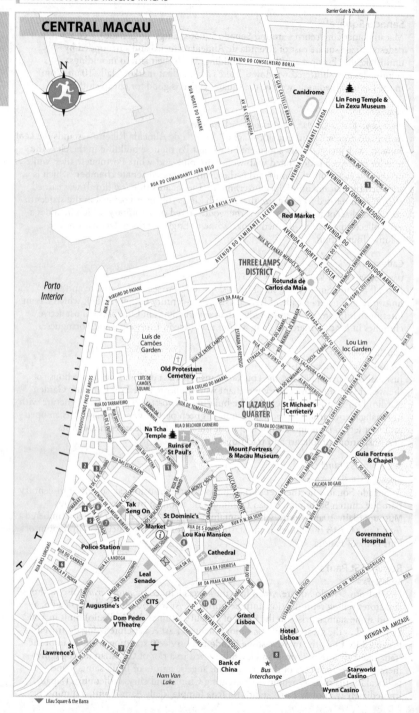

Barrier Gate & Zhuhai

CENTRAL MACAU

N

AVENIDO DO CONSELHEIRO BORJA

Canidrome

Lin Fong Temple &
Lin Zexu Museum

RUA NORTE DO PATANE

AV DA CONCORDA

RUA DO COMANDANTE JOÃO BELO

RUA DA BACIA SUL

AVENIDA DO ALMIRANTE LACERDA

RAMPA DO FORTE DE MONG HA

AVENIDA DO CORONEL MESQUITA

1

Red Market

1

Porto
Interior

RUA DA RIBEIRO DO PATANE

AVENIDA DO ALMIRANTE LACERDA

RUA DE FERNÃO MENDES PINTO

AVENIDA DE HORTA E. COSTA

AVENIDA DO

ANTONIO BOTE

RUA DE FRANCISCO XAVIER PEREIRA

OUVIDOR ARRIAGA

THREE LAMPS
DISTRICT

Rotunda de
Carlos da Maia

RUA DA BARCA

RUA DU PEDRO COUTINHO

Luís de
Camões
Garden

RUA DE ENTRE CAMPOS

ESTRADA DO REPOUSO

ESTRADA DE ADOLFO LOUREIRO

Lou Lim
Ioc Garden

Old Protestant
Cemetery

LUÍS DE
CAMÕES
SQUARE

RUA COELHO DO AMARAL

RUA DO COELHO DO AMARAL

RUA MANUEL DE ARRIAGA

RUA DA SÉ CADORA CABRAL

RUA DO ALMIRANTE ALBUQUERQUE

RUA DO CONSELHEIRO FERREIRA DE ALMEIDA

RUADOVISCONDE-PAÇO DE ARCOS

RUA DO TARRAFEIRO

RUA DE S. OUTUBRO

LARGO DA
COMUNHÃNA

RUA DE TOMAS VEIRA

ST LAZARUS
QUARTER

St Michael's
Cemetery

ESTRADA DA VITTORIA

RUA DOS FAITOES

RUA D BELCHIOR CARNEIRO

ESTRADA DO CEMETERIO

3

Na Tcha
Temple

Ruins of
St Paul's

Mount Fortress
& Macau Museum

Guia Fortress
& Chapel

CALC. DO PAIOL

2

RUA DAS ESTALAGENS

RUA DE ANTONIO

RUA DE

RUA DE S. OUTUBRO

GUIMARÃES

RUA DE PESANHA

RUA PALHA

RUA MONTE OBSCURE

CALÇADA DO MONTE

RUA DO CAMPO

ABRIO NUNES

5

CALCADA DO GAIO

RUA NOVA À SUA

A AVENIDA DE ALMEIDA RIBEIRO

4

6

5

7

Tak
Seng On

RUA DOS MERCADORES

St Dominic's
Market

RUA DE S DOMINGOS

RUA P. N. DA SILVA

Government
Hospital

Police Station

RUA DO CAMBOA

RUA A S ANDEGA

SANTA CROZE

Lou Kau Mansion

6

i

Cathedral

RUA DA FORMOSA

RUA DO CAMPO

6

PRAÇA P. F. HORTA

LARGO DE STO AGOSTINHO

RUA DA SÉ

AV. DA PRAIA GRANDE

ESTRADA DE S. FRANCISCO

AVENIDA DO DR. RODRIGO RODRIGUES

Leal
Senado

RUA DO SEMINARIO

St
Augustine's

RUA CENTRAL

CITS

9

AV. INFANTE D. HENRIQUE

Dom Pedro
V Theatre

RUA DO P. J ORO

AV. DOM JOÃO IV

10

Grand
Lisboa

Hotel
Lisboa

AVENIDA DA AMIZADE

St
Lawrence's

TRA V P A VIA

RUA DE S LOURENÇO

AV DA PRAIA GRANDE

AV DR MARIO SOARES

Bank of
China

Bus
Interchange

8

Starworld
Casino

Nam Van
Lake

Wynn Casino

Lilau Square & the Barra

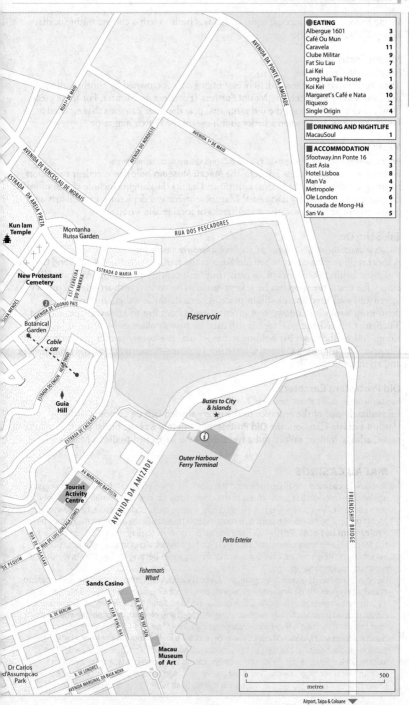

Airport, Taipa & Coloane ▼

9

shrine festooned with incense coils, which was built to halt a cholera outbreak that ravaged Macau in 1888.

Mount Fortress

Fortaleza do Monte • Open 24hr • Free

The tree-covered slope immediately east of St Paul's is crowned by another colonial relic, the seventeenth-century **Mount Fortress** (Fortaleza do Monte). For some great views, take a stroll around the old ramparts, past the huge cannons that repelled a Dutch attack in 1622 when a lucky shot blew up the Dutch magazine.

Macau Museum

Fortaleza do Monte • Tues–Sun 10am–6pm • MOP$15 • ☎ 2872 3656, ⓦ www.macaumuseum.gov.mo

Housed within the Mount Fortress, the **Macau Museum** holds an excellent collection focusing on the SAR's traditions, culture and habits. Highlights include videos of folk customs, a mock-up of a traditional Macanese street and depictions of local arts and crafts, complete with evocative soundtracks of local sellers' cries.

Tak Seng On

396 Avda de Almeida Ribeiro • Daily 10.30am–7pm; closed the first Monday each month • Free

A short walk northwest from Senado Square, the restored premises of **Tak Seng On** offer a glimpse behind the scenes of an early twentieth-century pawnshop. After standing empty for years, the shop has been kept much as it was left, with its original privacy screen and well-used abacus still in place. A separate thick-walled, multistorey depository with slit windows kept inventory safe from fire and thieves. The shape of Tak Seng On's red and gold sign is still used by **pawnbrokers** in Macau and Hong Kong, and symbolizes a bat holding a coin – "bat" is a homonym for good fortune in Chinese. The adjoining **Cultural Club** (daily 10.30am–8pm; free) houses a small gallery and an upstairs tearoom.

Old Protestant Cemetery

Praça Luís de Camões • Daily 8.30am–5.30pm • Free

Immediately east of the entrance to the nicely shaded **Luís de Camões Garden** (Jardim Luís de Camões), the **Old Protestant Cemetery** was the burial place for all the non-Catholic traders, sailors and adventurers who happened to die in Macau. The

---

MACAU CASINOS

Macau's 33 **casinos** are all open around the clock. To enter, you must be at least 18 years of age and go through a security check at the door; many casinos also require you to show your passport. Photography is not allowed and – while dress codes aren't strict – wearing shorts or flip-flops is frowned upon in most establishments. Once inside, many games have a **minimum bet** of MOP$10–100. For information on how to play the various games, ask the Macau Government Tourism Office (MGTO) for a leaflet; signs in tiny print at casino entrances politely suggest that punters should engage in betting for fun only, and not as a means of making money.

Each casino has its own atmosphere and (almost exclusively Chinese) clientele, and a **casino crawl** along Avenida da Amizade will provide ample opportunities for people-watching, even if you're not interested in gambling. The gold-windowed *Sands* has a Las Vegas slickness and colossal, open interior; the *Wynn* offers a sophisticated and elegant atmosphere; while the road between the two is lined with smaller casinos: lively *Starworld Casino* is the best of the bunch with its lobby dance shows. Save time, too, for a look around the old *Hotel Lisboa*, the orange- and white-tiled building at the junction of Avenida da Amizade and Avenida do Infante D. Henrique, as the darkly atmospheric casino is still one of Macau's best-known despite being upstaged by the *Grand Lisboa* over the road, whose soaring, gold-topped tower proves that casino mogul Stanley Ho has no rivals when it comes to ostentation.

gravestones have been restored and are legible, recording the last testaments to these mainly British, American and German individuals who died far from home in the early part of the nineteenth century. Famous residents include the artist **George Chinnery**, who spent decades painting scenes of colonial life in India, Hong Kong and Macau; and the Protestant missionary **Robert Morrison**, who produced an early English–Chinese dictionary.

Lou Lim Ieoc Garden

Estrada de Adolfo Loureiro • Daily 6am–9pm • Free

A few hundred metres northeast of the Mount Fortress, the scenic and calming **Lou Lim Ieoc Garden** (Jardim Lou Lim Ieoc) comprises a formal Chinese garden crowded with bamboos, pavilions, rocks and ancient trees arranged around a large pond. Financed during the nineteenth century by the wealthy Chinese merchant Lou Kau, it was modelled on Suzhou's classical gardens (see box, p.322) and typically manages to appear much more extensive than it really is. The garden is a popular spot for early morning exercise, and the southeast corner is occupied by the **Macau Tea Culture House** (Tues–Sun 9am–7pm) with tea-themed exhibits arranged on two floors of a mustard-coloured mansion.

Guia Hill

Main entrance on Avda de Sidónio Pais • Daily 8am–6pm • Free; cable car to summit MOP$2

Guia Hill is Macau's highest and steepest natural vantage point, despite rising only a few hundred metres above sea level. From the main entrance, the path winds through a small botanical garden as you ascend; the entire hilltop is one breezy park, planted with trees and shrubs and offering outstanding views of the SAR and neighbouring parts of China.

At the summit stands the seventeenth-century **Guia Fortress** (Fortaleza da Guia), the dominant feature of which is a whitewashed lighthouse that was added in 1865 and is reputed to be the oldest on the Chinese coast. Also inside the fort stands the **Guia Chapel** (daily 10am–6pm), which contains Christian frescoes featuring Chinese characters and dragons that were uncovered during routine conservation work in 1998.

Avenida da Amizade

East of Guia Hill, the main thoroughfare is **Avenida da Amizade**, which runs southwest from the Outer Harbour Ferry Terminal through a burgeoning **casino district**. Casinos aside, the most obvious attraction is the **Tourism Activities Centre** (Mon & Wed–Sun 10am–6pm), set back slightly on Rua de Luís Gonzaga Gomes, which houses the entertaining **Wine Museum** (free) and the **Grand Prix Museum** (free) – the latter features a scale mock-up of Macau's race circuit, plus a handful of Formula 1 cars.

Macau Museum of Art

Avda Xian Xing Hai • Tues–Sun 10am–7pm • MOP$5 • ☎ 8791 9814, ⓦ www.mam.gov.mo

The waterfront **Macau Museum of Art** houses collections of nineteenth-century China trade paintings, lively Shiwan ceramic figurines and modern Macanese works. Behind the museum, a 20m-high **bronze statue of Kun Iam** (see below) stands in front of views of the **Taipa Bridge** and **Friendship Bridge**, both crossing to Taipa.

Kun Iam Temple

Avda do Coronel Mesquita • Daily 7am–6pm • Free • Bus #12 from the *Hotel Lisboa*

Macau's major **Kun Iam Temple** is a centuries-old complex dedicated to the Goddess of Mercy. Though a popular and busy sight, there's something a little decrepit about the temple's grubby granite halls and peeling frescoes. Historically, the temple marks the site of the first **Sino-American treaty**, signed in a rear courtyard in 1844, at which the Americans (in exchange for substantial trade rights similar to those recently forced by

9

Britain) agreed to stop importing opium into China – a trade the British continued for another seventy years.

The Red Market and Three Lamps District

The **Red Market** (daily 7.30am–7.30pm), an Art Deco affair designed in 1936 by local architect Jio Alberto Basto, lies near the intersection of Avenida de Horta e Costa and Avenida do Almirante Lacerda. Arranged over three levels, the market is a very down-to-earth venue for buying slabs of meat and fresh vegetables for the dinner table, along with live chickens, fish and shellfish.

Just south across Avenida de Horta e Costa, a warren of lanes chock-full of market stalls, cheap clothing stores and noodle shops leads down to the cobbled Rotunda de Carlos da Maia, a roundabout marking the centre of the **Three Lamps District** or Sam Jan Dang. The whole area is a great place to browse and watch people bargaining for daily necessities.

To the border

Bus #3 or #10 from Avda de Almeida Ribeiro or *Hotel Lisboa*

North of the Red Market, Avenida do Almirante Lacerda passes Macau's **Canidrome** – Southeast Asia's only greyhound track, with races every Monday, Thursday, Saturday and Sunday from 8pm – and the **Lin Fong Temple** (daily 7am–5pm; free), whose main point of interest is the accompanying **Lin Zexu Museum** (Tues–Sun 9am–5pm; MOP$5), a monument to the man who destroyed British opium stocks in Guangzhou and so precipitated the first Opium War (see p.931). Another 700m north is the Portas do Cerco, or **Barrier Gate**, the nineteenth-century stuccoed archway marking the border with China. These days the old gate itself is redundant – people use the modern customs and immigration complex (daily 6am–1am) to one side.

The Barra

The small but hilly tongue of land south of Senado Square is known as **the Barra** – a tight web of lanes with colonial mansions and their gardens. The best way to begin an exploration is to walk south along **Rua Central** past the peppermint-coloured **Dom Pedro V Theatre** (Teatro Dom Pedro V). Built in 1860, the refurbished theatre (◍wh .mo/theatre/en) still hosts regular music recitals in its small auditorium. Opposite is the church of **St Augustine**, which started life late in the sixteenth century as a palm-thatched hut – the thatch fronds account for the church's Chinese name, Long Song Miu or "Long-whiskered Dragon Temple". Further down on Rua de São Lourenço, the square-towered **St Lawrence's** is a wonderfully tropical nineteenth-century church, its mildewed exterior framed by palms and fig trees.

Lilau Square

At the Barra's heart, **Lilau Square** (Largo do Lilau) is a tiny, pretty square with a fig tree and **spring**, whose waters are said to impart longevity. This is the site of Macau's original residential area, and almost all the buildings here are over a century old. The showcase sight is **Mandarin's House**, just off to one side at 10 Travessa de Antonio da Silva (Mon, Tues & Thurs–Sun 10am–6pm; free), a heavy-walled traditional Chinese mansion built in 1869. The sixty-room complex has been carefully restored, though it's still a little bare inside.

Moorish Barracks

South of Lilau Square, Rua Central morphs into Calçada da Barra, which runs down to the A-Ma Temple (see p.598). Pick of the historic buildings here is the strikingly crenellated, yellow-and-white **Moorish Barracks**, built in 1874 to house a Goan regiment and home to the Harbour Authority since 1905; you can enter during office

hours (Mon–Fri 9am–noon & 2pm–5pm; free) to admire the startling array of antique weaponry in the small lobby.

The A-Ma Temple

Rua do Almirante Sérgio • Daily 7am–6pm • Free

Founded in the fifteenth century, the **A-Ma Temple** is dedicated to a girl whose spirit is said to appear to sailors in distress and guide them to land. When the Portuguese arrived during the 1550s, they unintentionally named the entire territory after her, as "Macau" is a corruption of *a ma gok*, the name of the headland where the temple is set. The complex comprises a series of small halls and pavilions set among granite boulders, some of which are carved with nautical motifs and symbols relating to the A-Ma story. The busiest time to visit is during the **A-Ma Festival**, held on the twenty-third day of the third moon (April or May).

The Maritime Museum

Rua do Almirante Sérgio • Mon & Wed–Sun 10am–6pm • MOP$10

Macau's **Maritime Museum**, directly opposite the A-Ma Temple, is excellently presented, and covers old explorers, seafaring techniques, equipment, models and boats. The whole collection is made accessible by abundant explanatory notes and video displays in English.

Avenida da Republica

The peninsula's southwestern extremity is accessed along tree-lined **Avenida da Republica**, the old seafront promenade. Today, its views take in **Sai Van Lake** and the 338m-high **Macau Tower** (Mon–Fri 10am–9pm, Sat & Sun 9am–9pm; up to MOP$135, depending on the level of observation deck; ⓦmacautower.com.mo). At night, the waterfront promenade also offers Macau's version of Hong Kong's multicoloured harbourside skyline – except, of course, that here the financial institutions are casinos instead of banks.

Taipa, Cotai and Coloane

Originally two separate islands, **Taipa** and **Coloane** were once home to a few small fishing villages; now, joined by the rapidly developing strip of reclaimed land known as **Cotai**, they have become one of the main draws for visitors to Macau. Despite the development, both retain peaceful pockets of colonial architecture that are reminiscent of European villages, and Coloane also has a pair of decent beaches (see opposite).

Taipa

Taipa, the site of Macau's international airport, racecourse, sports stadium, university and high-rise residential suburbs, at first seems too workaday to warrant a special stop. However, tiny **Taipa Village**, with its covered market square and quiet backstreets, makes a pleasant place for an extended lunch (see p.603). The village is also home to an interesting small museum; with five restored mint-green 1920s villas, the lakeside **Taipa Houses Museum** (Tues–Sun 10am–6pm; MOP$5) offers a glimpse of life in Macau a century ago.

Cotai

Formerly a spread of mudflats, reeds and sea between Taipa and Coloane islands, **Cotai** has now been landfilled and built upon to accommodate a burgeoning entertainment district. Foremost of the developments is the extraordinary **Venetian**, a full-scale reproduction of Venice's St Mark's Square housing Macau's largest casino floor, with 800 gaming tables, 3500 slot machines, and a 15,000-seat arena. More recent additions include **Macau Studio City** with the Golden Reel – the world's first figure-eight ferris wheel – and **The Parisian**, which has a half-scale Eiffel Tower out front.

Coloane

9

Coloane, Macau's southern extremity, comprises eight square kilometres of hills, further colonial fragments and some decent **beaches**, making it a pleasant place to spend a few hours. In the northeast of Coloane, Seac Pai Van Park (daily 8am–6pm; free) is well worth a stop to visit the **Giant Panda Pavilion** (Tues–Sun 10am–1pm & 2–5pm; MOP$10; ⓦwww.macaupanda.org.mo), where the two resident pandas laze about in air-conditioned comfort.

Coloane Village

All Coloane buses stop at quiet **Coloane Village**, which overlooks mainland China just across the water; here, *Lord Stow's Bakery* (see p.602) is one of the main draws, with four outlets selling irresistible Portuguese egg tarts known as **natas**. The village's old-style architecture is concentrated along Rua dos Negociantes, which runs south from the village roundabout one block back from the shore. The street culminates in an attractive square, presided over by the yellow-and-white **St Francis Xavier Chapel**, where a relic of the saint's arm bone is venerated.

Coloane's beaches

Tree-lined **Hác Sá Beach** is the largest in Macau, with a strip of black sand and some fine restaurants and cafés nearby (see p.603), as well as showers, toilets and a **sports and swimming pool complex** (May–Oct Mon 1–9pm, Tues–Sun 8am–noon & 1–9pm; MOP$15), which gets pretty crowded at weekends. Otherwise, try smaller **Cheoc Van** – if the sea doesn't tempt you, there's a nice public pool here too (same hours; MOP$15).

ARRIVAL AND DEPARTURE **MACAU**

BY PLANE

Macau International Airport Macau's airport juts into the sea off Taipa. Buses #MT1 and #MT2 both run circular routes between the airport and the bus terminus outside *Hotel Lisboa*, with #MT2 stopping at the Taipa Ferry Terminal before heading into town.

Destinations Beijing (3hr 15min); Chengdu (2hr 40min); Shanghai (2hr 20min); Wuhan (1hr 35min); Xiamen (1hr 20min).

Hong Kong–Macau helicopter Sky Shuttle runs a helicopter service to Macau (MOP$4450; ⓦskyshuttlehk .com) from the Hong Kong–Macau Ferry Terminal in Sheung Wan (every 30min 10am–11pm; 15min).

BY FERRY

Macau has two ferry ports – one on the peninsula and one on Taipa. During the week you seldom need to book tickets in advance, though weekend and holiday traffic can become very busy. Allow at least half an hour to clear customs before departure; you need a passport, but no special visa, to travel between Macau and Hong Kong.

Outer Harbour Ferry Terminal The main terminal sits at the northern end of Avenida da Amizade. Turbojet ferries

(MOP$153; ⓦturbojet.com.hk) run to Hong Kong's two jetfoil terminals around the clock. Tickets can be bought on the second floor of the terminal or from discount booths on the ground floor. Exit the terminal and there's a taxi rank and bus stop immediately outside; buses #3, #3A and #10A will get you into town.

Destinations China Ferry Terminal, Canton Road, Tsim Sha Tsui (hourly 7am–10.30pm; 55min); Shun Tak Centre, Sheung Wan, Hong Kong Island (every 15min 7am–midnight, and then approximately hourly; 55min).

Taipa Ferry Terminal Not far from Macau's airport, the Taipa Ferry Terminal is served by regular jetfoils (MOP$154; ⓦcotaiwaterjet.com) from Hong Kong and Kowloon, and a handful of services to Shenzhen's Port, Shekou (MOP$245; ⓦxunlongferry.com, Chinese-only). Note that the proximity of the Cotai Strip's hotels and the small size of this temporary terminal (construction of its permanent replacement is already running seven years behind schedule) can mean long queues during busy periods. Taxis and buses into town depart from a stop outside (#MT1 or #MT2 across the bridge to the *Grand Lisboa*), and the terminal is served by masses of free casino buses heading to the Cotai Strip.

TAIPA AND COLOANE BUSES

From Avenida de Almeida Ribeiro on the peninsula, buses #11 and #33 stop at Rua de Cunha in Taipa Village. Buses #25 and #26A stop outside the *Hotel Lisboa* before going on to Taipa and Coloane.

MACAU ENTRY REGULATIONS

Visa regulations currently state that citizens of Britain can stay for six months, while travellers from Ireland and most European countries can stay 90 days on arrival; citizens of Australia, New Zealand, Canada, South Africa, the US and several others can stay 30 days on arrival – check Ⓦen.macaotourism.gov.mo for the latest.

Destinations China Ferry Terminal, Canton Road, Tsim Sha Tsui (5 daily; 55min); Shun Tak Centre, Sheung Wan, Hong Kong Island (every 30min 7am–midnight; 55min); Shekou (9 daily 9.15am–9pm; 1hr).

BY BUS

Macau has no long-distance bus station, but CTS, based at the Outer Harbour Ferry Terminal (☎2832 2950, Ⓦctshk .com), run daily services between Macau and Hong Kong, Guangzhou and Shenzhen for between MOP$100–170.

ON FOOT

There are two land borders between Macau and Zhuhai. It's possible to walk across the Portas do Cerco/Gongbei crossing (daily 6am–1am) near the old Barrier Gate (see p.596), and buses #3A and #5 go via Avenida de Almeida Ribeiro, while #AP1 runs via both ferry terminals and the airport. Macau's newer Lotus Flower Bridge border crossing (open 24hr) links Cotai with Hengqin in Zhuhai. A shuttle bus (¥3, exact change required) runs across the bridge itself, and bus #25 will get you to Avenida Amizade on the peninsula.

GETTING AROUND

BY BUS

Macau's comprehensive public bus network is operated by TCM (Sociedade de Transportes Colectivos de Macau; Ⓦtcm.com.mo). Buses run along most routes from 7am to 11pm daily. Fares are a flat MOP$3.20 on the peninsula, MOP$4.20 to Taipa, and MOP$5 to Coloane, except Hác Sá beach, which is MOP$6.40; you need the exact fare, as change is not given. If you're planning to use buses frequently, consider getting a Macau Pass (Ⓦmacaupass .com), which confers small discounts on the city's buses. Important interchanges include the Outer Harbour Ferry Terminal, outside the *Hotel Lisboa*, Avenida de Almeida Ribeiro, Barra (near the A-Ma Temple), and the Portas do Cerco Barrier Gate. It's also worth noting that most of the

major casinos operate free shuttle buses to and from the ferry terminals.

BY TAXI

Taxis have a fixed fee of MOP$17, with surcharges levied for trips from the peninsula to Taipa (MOP$2) and Coloane (MOP$5), as well as for hailing a cab at the airport (MOP$5). The one-way fare from downtown to Coloane's Hác Sá beach (the longest trip you can possibly make) costs about MOP$110. Note that unrequested detours and inflated surcharges are common; if in doubt, ask for a receipt and check with the transport affairs hotline (☎8866 6363). It is useful to have your destination written down in Chinese, as few drivers speak English.

INFORMATION

Tourist offices The Macau Government Tourist Office, or MGTO (☎2833 3000, Ⓦen.macaotourism.gov.mo) provides helpful leaflets on Macau's fortresses, museums, parks, churches, self-guided walks and outlying islands, as well as a good city map. The main office (daily 9am–6pm) is at Senado Square 9, with additional counters (all same hours) at the airport, the ferry terminals and the Zhuhai border crossing at Portas do Cerco. In Hong Kong, the Macau Government Tourist Office is at the Macau Ferry Terminal, Shun Tak Centre,

Sheung Wan, Hong Kong Island (☎2857 2287).
Travel agents Beng Seng Travel (310–312 Shun Tak Centre, 200 Connaught Rd, Hong Kong; daily 8.30am–1am; ☎2540 3838, Ⓦbengsengtravel.com – Chinese only) can organize discounted ferry tickets and accommodation in Macau; CTS (Outer Harbour Ferry Terminal, Avenida da Amizade, Macau; daily 9am–8pm; ☎2832 2950, Ⓦctshk .com), can book all flights, buses and accommodation, as well as visas for mainland China.

ACCOMMODATION

Accommodation is **good value** in Macau – the money that would get you a dingy box in Hong Kong provides a clean room with a private shower and a window here. Still, there are fewer real budget options, and on weekends, holidays and during the Macau Grand Prix (third weekend in November) **prices** can more than double from those given here. Online deals and agents in Hong Kong such as CTS (Ⓦctshk.com) offer good-value transport and accommodation packages. The densest concentration and widest variety of hotels is found on the peninsula – especially in the vicinity of Avenida de Almeida Ribeiro – though Taipa, Cotai and Coloane also host numerous upmarket resorts. Note that **addresses** in Macau are written with the number after the name of the street.

MACAU PENINSULA

★ **5footway.inn Ponte 16** Rua de Constantino Brito 8 ☎ 2892 3118; map pp.592–593. This Singaporean-run budget hotel has 20 bright, spotless rooms a few minutes' walk from the *Ponte 16* resort; communal spaces are nicely designed and staff are helpful. Note that the hotel has no elevator. MOP$600

East Asia Rua da Madeira 1 ☎ 2892 2433, ⓦ eastasiahotelmacau.com; map pp.592–593. One of Macau's oldest hotels. It's a little shabby and basic, but comfortable enough, with friendly staff and good views from some of the upstairs rooms. MOP$550

Hotel Lisboa Ave de Lisboa 2–4 ☎ 2888 3888, ⓦ hotelisboa.com; map pp.592–593. Once the most ostentatious building in Macau, the *Lisboa's* retro orange and white exterior hides a thoroughly modern interior, from the glitz of the lobby to the comfortable rooms, each with spa-bath. Nonsmokers will want to avoid the older East Wing rooms, and families may wish to steer clear of the sleazy hotel mall. MOP$920

Man Va Rua da Caldeira 30 ☎ 2838 8655, ⓦ manvahotelmacau.com; map pp.592–593. Rooms here are decent and clean, if a little drab, but helpful management and a great location make them good value. MOP$500

Metropole Ave da Praia Grande 493–501 ☎ 2838 8166, ⓦ metropolehotelmacau.com; map pp.592–593. A few hundred metres west of the *Lisboa* is this well-located, smart hotel. You should find good deals for rooms here on most discount booking websites. MOP$900

Ole London Praça de Ponte e Horta 4–6 ☎ 2893 7761, ⓦ olelondonhotel.com; map pp.592–593. Smart little boutique hotel with spotless, modern rooms; the cheapest are windowless, so it's best to pay a little extra for one looking out onto the square outside. MOP$750

★ **Pousada de Mong-Há** Colina de Mong-Há, off Avda do Coronel Mesquita ☎ 2851 5222, ⓦ bit.ly/1Dh5f2D; map pp.592–593. Operated by Macau's nearby tourism school, this hotel offers huge rooms at very reasonable rates, and the students who run the hotel provide very considerate service. It's on a hillside slightly out of the centre, but there's an irregular shuttle service downtown. MOP$800

★ **Pousada de São Tiago** Fortaleza de São Tiago da Barra, Avda da República ☎ 2837 8111, ⓦ saotiago .com.mo; map p.589. This hotel was constructed from a seventeenth-century fortress on the southern tip of the peninsula, with walled stairways lined by gushing streams, huge stone archways and twelve luxurious suites. There's nothing else like this in all of China. Breakfast not included. MOP$3600

San Va Rua da Felicidade 67 ☎ 8210 0193, ⓦ sanvahotel.com; map pp.592–593. An unusual budget option, with clean, no-frills rooms in an atmospheric early-1900s building, which features wooden shutters and balconies over Rua da Felicidade. No a/c or en-suite bathrooms available. MOP$360

TAIPA, COTAI AND COLOANE

Grand Coloane Resort Estrada de Hác Sá, Coloane ☎ 2887 1111, ⓦ grandcoloane.com; map p.589. At the far end of Hác Sá's fine beach, this resort is good for a quiet day or two, midweek, although it fills up with Hong Kong families at the weekend, drawn by its restaurants and excellent sports facilities, including two pools and a spa. Rooms are getting a little worn, but with one of their frequent online deals it's still good value for money. MOP$1088

Inn Hotel Macau Estrada Governador Nobre Carvalho 822, Taipa ☎ 2882 1666, ⓦ macau.innhotel.com; map p.589. Decorated in shades of brown, rooms here are comfortable, if a little bland – check that you're getting one of their newly renovated ones. Handily within five minutes' walk of Taipa Village, facilities include several restaurants, a pool and an in-house florist. MOP$828

★ **Pousada de Coloane** Praia de Cheoc Van, Coloane ☎ 2888 2143, ⓦ hotelpcoloane.com.mo; map p.589. Offers great scenery in a somewhat remote location by Cheoc Van beach, on Coloane's far south shore. All rooms have balconies overlooking the beach, and there's a swimming pool and Portuguese restaurant. If you want a relaxing holiday experience, this is the place for it. MOP$900

The Venetian Estrada do Istmo, Cotai ☎ 2882 8877, ⓦ venetianmacao.com; map p.589. A 3000-room resort, convention centre and casino complex, all packed into a full-scale replica of St Mark's Square in Venice (including canals with gondolas). The convention space here alone is greater than the total available in Hong Kong. Palatial rooms are well serviced, modern and huge, if lacking character. MOP$2500

EATING

Places specializing in Macanese and Portuguese food are plentiful, as are **Cantonese restaurants**. Prices for the typically generous portions are low compared to Hong Kong, with bills even in smart venues rarely exceeding MOP$250 per person – that said, watch out for little extras such as water, bread and so forth, which can really add to the cost of a meal. A bottle of house red will set you back around MOP$120 in a restaurant. For the latest openings, check ⓦ yummymacau.com.

CAFÉS & BAKERIES

Caravela Patio Comandante Mata e Oliveira 7, off Avda Dom João IV ☎ 2871 2080; map pp.592–593. Down an alley near the *Grand Lisboa*, this smart place serves top coffee, *natas* and light meals (mains from $90) through the day, and has a host of Portuguese expat regulars, who can

9

get snotty about visitors taking "their" chairs. Daily 8am–8pm.

Koi Kei Rua da Felicidade 70–72 ☎ 2893 8102, ⓦ koikei.com; map pp.592–593. This popular *pastellaria* has branches all over town, selling powdery almond biscuits, honey-sweet sheets of dried pork and crisp egg rolls. Prices start around $35. Daily noon–7pm.

Lai Kei Avda do Conselheiro Ferreira de Almeida 12 ☎ 2837 5781, ⓦ facebook.com/laikeiicecream; map pp.592–593. With a dining room straight out of the 1960s, this family-run café has been serving up ice cream sandwiches (MOP$17) for almost 70 years; all their ice cream is made in-store and without preservatives. Daily noon–7pm.

★**Lord Stow's Bakery** Rua do Tassara 1, Coloane Village Square ☎ 2888 2534, ⓦ lordstow.com; map p.589. Offers the best baked custard tarts ($10) in Macau, made to a secret recipe without animal fat. Buy takeaways from the bakery, or sit down for coffee and a light meal at one of their two cafés in Coloane. Bakery daily 7am–10pm; cafés daily from 9am.

Margaret's Café e Nata Rua Comandante Mata e Oliveira ☎ 2871 0032; map pp.592–593. Surrounded by gloomy apartment blocks, this is an excellent café with outdoor benches and first-rate sandwiches and baked custard tarts (MOP$10) – the latter attracts queues of hungry visitors. Mon & Tues 8.30am–6pm, Thurs–Sun 8.30am–6pm.

★**Single Origin** Rua de Abreu Nunes 19, off Avda do Conselheiro Ferreira de Almeida ☎ 6698 7475; map pp.592–593. A great speciality coffee shop in an interesting neighbourhood. Quality beans are expertly brewed in a variety of different ways and served along with light meals (from $40) in a small but airy café. Daily noon–8pm.

RESTAURANTS
MACAU PENINSULA
★**Albergue 1601** Calçada da Igreja de São Lazaro 8 ☎ 2836 1601, ⓦ albergue1601.com; map pp.592–593. This picture-perfect restaurant – housed in a striking colonial building on a tree-shaded square at the edge of the St Lazarus district – serves good Portuguese standards, such as clams with white wine and garlic (MOP$148). Book ahead and budget at least MOP$400 a head. Daily noon–3pm & 6–10pm.

★**Café Ou Mun** Travessa do São Domingos 12, off Senado Square ☎ 2837 2207, ⓦ oumuncafe.com; map pp.592–593. Serves fantastic coffee and consistently excellent Portuguese meals; the *feijoada de bacalhau* (stewed salt cod and white beans; MOP$128) comes highly recommended. Very popular at lunchtime. Daily 10am–9pm.

Clube Militar Avda da Praia Grande 975 ☎ 2871 4004; map pp.592–593. Smart, old-world dining room with ceiling fans and silver service inside a private club, though the restaurant is open to the public. Stay off the à la carte menu and opt for the set-price lunchtime buffet, which is fantastic value at MOP$150. No shorts, trainers or sandals, and reservations recommended for evenings and weekends. Daily noon–2.30pm & 7–10.30pm.

Fat Siu Lau Rua da Felicidade 64 ☎ 2857 3580, ⓦ fatsiulau.com.mo; map pp.592–593. A very popular traditional restaurant whose speciality is marinated roast pigeon, though they also do a great crab curry. Around MOP$200/head. Daily 12.30–10.30pm.

Litoral Rua da Almirante Sérgio 261-A ☎ 2896 7878; map pp.592–593. Reputedly the best place for Macanese food in Macau, with excellent charcoal-grilled African chicken, *feijoada* and stewed chicken rice. Their *serradura* is the business, too. Portions are huge and two could easily share one main and a salad. Around $350 a head with wine. Daily noon–3pm & 5.30–10.30pm.

Long Hua Tea House Rua Norte de Mercado Almirante Lacerda 3, 1/F ☎ 2857 4456; map pp.592–593. Just north of the Red Market, this *cha chaan teng* serves up a small range of *dim sum* (MOP$25/plate) and tasty rice- and noodle-based standards (from MOP$68) in an airy dining room with oodles of retro charm. No English menu. Daily 7am–2pm.

Riquexo Avenida de Sidónio Pais 69-B ☎ 2856 5655; map pp.592–593. Pronounced "rickshaw", this Portuguese canteen has no frills at all, though the food is hearty and nearby office workers flock here for lunch. The menu changes daily but is likely to include *minchi* (minced pork and potato, topped with a fried egg) and some form of *bacalhau* at MOP$65–115 a serving. Mon–Fri 11am–6pm.

MACANESE FOOD

Macanese cuisine marries Chinese with Portuguese elements, which are further overlaid with tastes from Portugal's Indian and African colonies. You'll find an array of dishes ranging from *caldo verde* (vegetable soup) to *bacalhau* (dried salted cod). Macau's most interesting Portuguese colonial dish is probably **African chicken**, a concoction of Goan and East African influences, comprising grilled chicken covered with a mildly spiced peanut and coconut sauce. Other things worth trying include Portuguese baked custard tarts (*natas*), which are served in many cafés; almond biscuits, formed in a wooden mould and baked in a charcoal oven, which can be bought by weight in many *pastellarias*, such as *Koi Kei* (see above), around São Paulo and Rua da Felicidade; and sheets of pressed roast meat, also sold in *pastellarias*.

TAIPA

Blissful Carrot Rua Direita Carlos Eurgenio 79A, Taipa Village ☎6298 8433, ⓦfacebook.com/blissfulcarrot; map p.589. For a change from huge Macanese meals, pop into this cute vegetarian café, a short walk east of Rua do Cunha. Fresh juices, rice bowls and sandwiches fill the pan-Asian menu (a meal will cost MOP$100–150), and their vegan brownies (MOP$32) are the business. Thurs–Tues 10am–8pm.

★Casa de Tapas Rua dos Clérigos, Taipa Village ☎2857 6626, ⓦcasadetapasmacau.com; map p.589. Serves gently modernized and very delicious versions of classic Spanish tapas; lamb skewers come with sweet onion confit, garlic prawns with white wine jelly. Hearty mains (from MOP$158) available, if you manage to leave space for them, and it's all served up in a pretty candy-pink shophouse with a roof terrace. Mon–Thurs & Sun noon–midnight, Fri & Sat noon–1am.

O Santos Rua da Cunha 20, Taipa Village ☎2882 5594, ⓦosantoscomidaportuguesa.com; map p.589. Friendly place serving huge helpings of pork and bean stew, rabbit, roast suckling pig and other Portuguese mainstays; they're famous for their rice with shredded duck. Mains around MOP$160. Mon & Wed–Sun noon–3pm & 6–10pm.

COLOANE

Fernando Hác Sá beach, not far from the bus stop ☎2888 2531, ⓦfernando-restaurant.com; map p.589. A casual, cheerful atmosphere and great Portuguese food make this place a favourite with expats. You might need a taxi to get home, though, as buses back to town fill up quickly. Advance booking recommended, and a necessity at weekends. About MOP$250/head, cash only. Daily except May 1, noon–9.30pm.

Nga Tim Next to the St Francis Xavier Chapel, Coloane Village ☎2888 2086; map p.589. A friendly Chinese place with outdoor tables under a colonnade, ideal for lunch or an evening drink; the best dishes on the menu are crab or pork knuckle. Mains around MOP$70. Daily noon–1am.

DRINKING AND NIGHTLIFE

Macau's **nightlife** is surprisingly flat, if you don't count the casinos – though these more than make up for a lack of action elsewhere, with huge pool parties and big-name visiting DJs (check ⓦhkclubbing.com for upcoming events).

MacauSoul Rua de São Paulo 31A, Macau ☎2836 5182, ⓦmacausoul.com; map p.589. An intimate wine bar near the ruins of São Paulo, with an extensive and exclusively Portuguese wine list (from $50/glass) that the owners are happy to help you navigate, and an eclectic selection of music playing in the background. Reservations recommended, cash only. Wed & Thurs 3pm–10pm, Fri–Sun 3pm–midnight.

Old Taipa Tavern Rua dos Negociantes 21, Taipa Village ☎2882 5221; map p.589. Despite being known as "OTT", this pub makes a pleasant, low-key spot for a drink (from MOP$45), with outside seating set on a quiet square in Taipa Village. Food served. Daily noon–1am.

DIRECTORY

Banks and exchange Most banks have branches around the junction of Avenida de Almeida Ribeiro and Avenida Praia Grande, where you'll also find plenty of ATMs. Banks generally open Mon–Fri from 9am until 4pm or 4.30pm, but close by lunchtime on Sat. There are also licensed moneychangers that open seven days a week, including a 24hr one in the basement of the *Hotel Lisboa*, and one near the bottom of the steps leading up to São Paulo.

Festivals The usual Chinese holidays are celebrated in Macau, along some local specialities such as the Feast of Na Tcha (eighteenth day of fifth lunar month, usually falling in June). Catholic festivals include the annual Procession of the Passion of Our Lord, the God Jesus between St Augustine's Church and the Cathedral (Feb 13–14), and the Procession of Our Lady of Fatima from St Dominic's church (May 13). For a full list, see ⓦwww.macaotourism.gov.mo.

Hospital There's a 24hr emergency department at the Centro Hospitalar Conde de São Januário, Calçada Visconde São Januário (☎2831 3731); English is spoken.

Police The main police station is at 823 Avenida da Amizade (☎2855 7777). For emergencies, call ☎999.

Post offices Macau's main post office is on the east side of Senado Square (Mon–Fri 9am–6pm, Sat 9am–1pm). Small red booths all over the territory also dispense stamps.

Guangxi and Guizhou
广西 / 贵州

610 Guangxi
636 Guizhou

Guangxi and Guizhou

The subtropical southwestern provinces of Guangxi and Guizhou are defined by limestone: local rivers are coloured a vivid blue-green by it; weathered karst hills worn into poetic collections of sharp peaks scatter the landscape; and a network of caverns, some flooded, others large enough to fit a cathedral, extends underground. Though now something of a tourist phenomenon, historically this rugged topography has proved an immense barrier to communications. The porous rock created some of China's least arable land, with agriculture often confined to the small alluvial plains in between peaks. Too poor to be worth invading, for a long time the region was ignored by mainstream China, and evolved into a stronghold for ethnic groups.

10

A period of social stability during the early Qing dynasty caused a population explosion in eastern China and the Han expanded westwards into Guangxi and Guizhou. Some ethnic minorities kept their nominal identity but more or less integrated with the Chinese, while others resisted assimilation by occupying isolated highlands. However the new settlers put pressure on resources, creating a hotbed of resentment against the government. This finally exploded in central Guangxi's **Taiping Uprising** of 1850 (see box, p.314), and the **Miao Uprising** of 1854–73 in Guizhou, marking the start of a century of devastating civil conflict. Even today, and despite recent massive central-government investment, local economies remain relatively underdeveloped and few of the cities – including **Nanning** and **Guiyang**, the provincial capitals – have much to offer except transport to more interesting locations.

Despite its bleak history, the region offers a huge range of diversions. The landscape is epitomized by the tall karst towers surrounding the city of **Guilin** in northeastern Guangxi, familiar to Chinese and Westerners alike through centuries of eulogistic art. Equally impressive are cave systems at **Dragon Palace Scenic Area** and **Zhijin** near Anshun in western Guizhou. There's also the chance of close contact with ethnic groups, particularly the **Miao**, **Dong** and **Zhuang**, whose wooden villages, exuberant festivals, and traces of a prehistoric past are all worth indulging in. It's also one of the few places in the country where you can be fairly sure of encountering rare wildlife, notably cranes at **Caohai** in Guizhou's far west.

The new high-speed train service from Guangdong to Guiyang and a network of new highways that punch through the mountains mean that **travel** across the region is fairly straightforward – though navigating rural roads still means slow and often uncomfortable journeys on infrequent minibuses, while local dialects are sometimes incomprehensible. **Weather** is fairly localized, though you should expect hot, wet summers and surprisingly cold winters, especially up in the hills. The period between March and June often sees periods of heavy rain, which can put a dampener on river trips, for example.

CORMORANT FISHING ON THE LI RIVER

Highlights

❶ **Li River** Cruise between Guilin and Yangshuo through a forest of tall, weirdly contorted karst peaks. **See p.615**

❷ **Dong villages** Communities of wooden houses, bridges and drum towers pepper remote rural highlands along the Guangxi–Guizhou border. **See p.626**

❸ **Detian Waterfall** Straddling the China–Vietnam border, this is one of the loveliest waterfalls in China, and little visited as it's off the main tourist routes. **See p.632**

❹ **Fanjing Shan** Remote Buddhist holy mountain, its peak dotted with temples, offering fantastic views and a mystic atmosphere. **See p.650**

❺ **Zhijin Caves** The largest, most spectacular of China's subterranean limestone caverns, full of creatively named rock formations. **See p.654**

❻ **Caohai** Spend a day punting around this beautiful lake, a haven for ducks and rare black-necked cranes. **See p.655**

HIGHLIGHTS ARE MARKED ON THE MAP ON PP.608–609

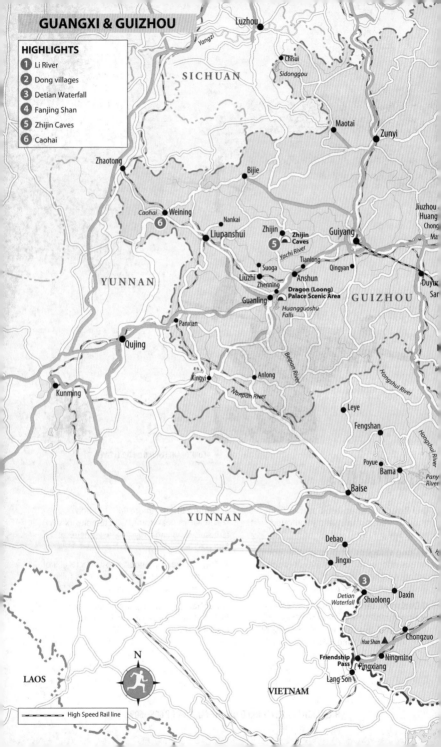

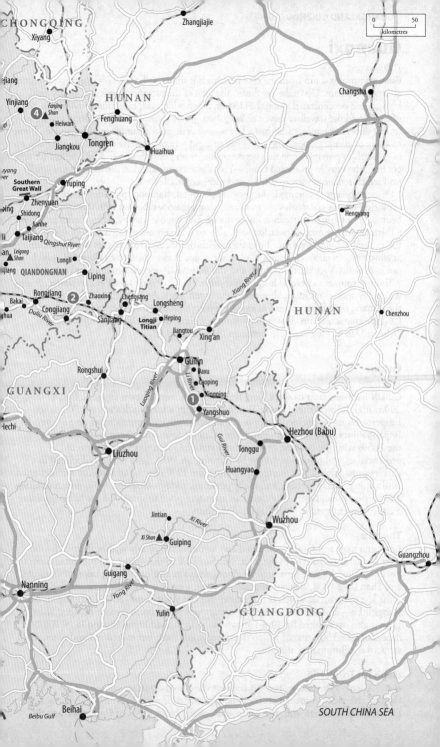

10

Guangxi

广西, guǎngxī

Guangxi unfolds south from the cool highlands it shares with Guizhou to a tropical border abutting Vietnam. Up in the northeast, the pick of the province's peak-and-paddy-field landscape is concentrated along the **Li River**, down which you can cruise between the city of **Guilin** and the travellers' haven of **Yangshuo**. Easily accessible, this has become a massive tourist draw, but remoter hills just a few hours north around **Longji** and **Sanjiang** are home to a mix of ethnic groups, whose architecture and way of life make for a fascinating trip up into Guizhou province, hopping between villages on public buses. Indeed, the further you get from the heavily promoted Guilin–Yangshuo tourist corridor, the more places you'll find which remain underexploited – and more enjoyable for it.

Diagonally across Guangxi, the provincial capital, **Nanning**, provides a base for exploring Guangxi's southwestern corner along the **open border with Vietnam**, heartland of China's thirteen-million-strong Zhuang nationality. They constitute about a third of the regional population and, although largely assimilated into Chinese life today, archeological evidence links them with Bronze Age **rock friezes** west of Nanning at **Ningming**. Nearby are a couple of other major draws: the **Detian Waterfall**, which pours over the Vietnamese border, and the massive limestone sinkholes at **Leye**.

Though subject to fiercely hot, humid summers, Guangxi's **weather** can be deceptive – it actually snows in Guilin about once every ten years. Another thing of note is that the **Zhuang language**, instead of using *pinyin*, follows its own method of rendering Chinese characters into Roman text, so you'll see some unusual spelling on signs – "Minzu Dadao", for example, becomes "Minzcuzdadau".

Guilin

桂林, guilín

GUILIN has been famous since Tang times for its scenic location among a host of craggy, 200m-high hills on the **Li River**. The city rose from a rural backwater in 1372 when Emperor Hongwu decided to appoint a minor relative to govern from here as the **Jinjiang Prince**, and this quasi-royal line ruled for fourteen generations, dying out in the 1650s with the collapse of the Ming dynasty. Guilin was later resurrected as provincial capital until supplanted by Nanning in 1914, after which it declined to a shabby provincial shell. Smartened up since the 1990s by the addition of well-designed landscaping, shady avenues and rocky parkland, today – despite tourist-driven inflation and hard-sell irritations – the city is an attractive place to spend a day while organizing a cruise downstream to the village of Yangshuo.

The lakes

Look at a map and Guilin's medieval city layout is still clearly visible, defined by the river to the east, Gui Hu to the west, Nanhuan Lu to the south, and protected from the north by Diecai Shan. Separated by Zhongshan Lu, tree-lined **Rong Lake** (榕湖, rónghú) and **Shan Lake** (衫湖, shānhú) originally formed a moat surrounding the inner city walls – the last remnant of which is the tunnel-like **Old South Gate** (古南门, gǔ nánmén) on Ronghu Lu – and are now crossed by attractively hunchbacked stone bridges. Shan Lake is also overlooked by 40m-tall twin pagodas named **Riyue Shuang Ta** (日月双塔, rìyuè shuāngtǎ; ¥30), one of which is painted gold, the other muted red and green, both attractively illuminated at night.

Elephant Trunk Hill

象鼻山, xiàngbí shān · Daily 7am–10pm · ¥75; bamboo raft ¥50/person · ☎ 0773 2803000

Guilin's riverside promenade is Binjiang Lu, shaded from the summer sun by fig trees. Down at the southern end, these also strategically block views of **Elephant Trunk Hill**, said to be the fossilized body of a sick imperial baggage elephant who was cared for by locals. For once the name is not poetically obscure; the jutting cliff with an arched hole at the base really does resemble an elephant taking a drink from the river. The top tourist attraction in town, it's suitably overpriced (and crowded), but there's an easy walk over a wooden bridge from the entrance and up to a podgy pagoda on top, and, at river level, you can have your photo taken holding a parasol while you sit next to a cormorant on a brightly coloured bamboo raft; rafts are also available for short river-trips, though the Guilin–Yangshuo route is much better.

Fubo Shan

伏波山, fúbō shān • Daily 7am–7pm • ¥60 • ☎ 0773 2803000

Two kilometres upstream from Elephant Trunk Hill, at the north end of Binjiang Lu, **Fubo Shan** is a complementary peak, whose grottoes are carved with worn Tang- and

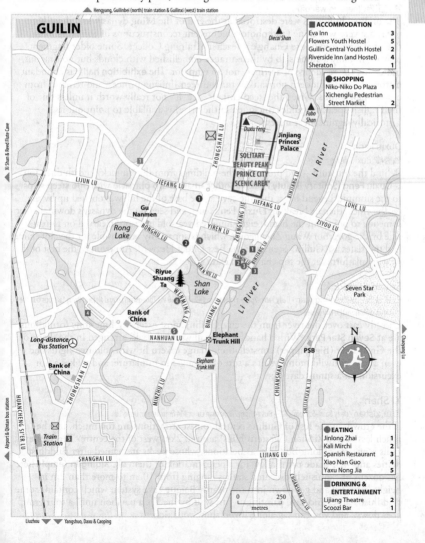

10

Song-dynasty Buddha images. At the base is the "Sword-testing Stone", a stalactite hanging within 10cm of the ground, which indeed appears to have been hacked through. Steps to Fubo's summit (200m) provide smog-free views of Guilin's low rooftops.

Jinjiang Princes' Palace

独秀峰王城, dú xiùfēng wángchéng • Daily 7.30am–6pm, summer till 6.30pm • ¥130 • ☎ 0773 2803149, ⓦ glwangcheng.com

North off Jiefang Lu, the **Jinjiang Princes' Palace** is where Guilin's Ming rulers lived between 1372 and 1650. Resembling a miniature Forbidden City in plan (and predating Beijing's by 34 years), it is still surrounded by 5m-high stone walls (no charge to visit) and is situated next to a small limestone outcrop from where there are decent views.

Jinjiang Princes' Palace
靖江王府, jìngjiāng wángfǔ

The original buildings were destroyed at the end of the Ming dynasty and those here today are very well done (and photogenic) recent reconstructions of buildings from the late Qing, and house Guangxi's Teachers Training College. Some older fragments remain, notably a **stone slab** by the entrance embellished with clouds but no dragons, indicating the residence of a prince, not an emperor. The **exhibition hall** has abundant historical curios, modern portraits of the fourteen Jinjiang princes, and remains from one of their **tombs**. Given the steep entrance fee, it's not really worth it unless one of the English-speaking guides (included in the price) is available to point out its historically significant features.

Duxiu Feng
独秀峰, dúxiù fēng

Behind the museum – and protecting the buildings from the "unlucky" north direction – is **Duxiu Feng (Solitary Beauty Peak)**, another small, sharp pinnacle with 306 steep steps to the summit. Legend has it that the **cave** at the base of the hill was opened up by the tenth prince, thereby breaking Duxiu Feng's luck and seeding the dynasty's downfall. Get someone to point out the bland, eight-hundred-year-old **inscription** carved on Duxiu's side by the governor Wang Zhenggong, which is apparently responsible for the city's fame and translates as "Guilin's Scenery is the Best Under Heaven". Annoyingly, the best of the viewing platforms at the top charges an extra ¥30.

Seven Star Park

七星公园, qīxīng gōngyuán • Daily 7am–7pm • ¥70, cavern ¥40 • Bus #10 via Zhongshan Lu and Jiefang Dong Lu stops outside or 20min walk from the city centre

Directly east over the river from the city, Guilin's most extensive limestone formations are at **Seven Star Park**. With a handful of small wooded peaks arranged in the shape of the Great Bear (Big Dipper) constellation, a large cavern lit with coloured lights and even a few semiwild monkeys, it's a sort of Guangxi in miniature, and makes a fun excursion on a sunny day.

Xi Shan

西山, xīshān • Daily 8am–5.30pm • ¥75 • Bus #4 from Zhongshan Lu, or #14 from Jiefang Dong Lu

If the crowds at the rest of Guilin's central tourist attractions are too much, try the much less visited **Xi Shan** (Western Hills) around 2km west of the centre. The Western Hills is an area of long Buddhist associations, whose peaks are named after Buddhist deities and well-made paths allow for a peregrination of them all. **Xiqinglin Temple** here has dozens of exquisitely executed statues ranging from 10cm to more than 2m in height. Also try and get down into the nearby **Baique** cave system which contains some Buddhist statues and cave paintings – just wait by the Yixia pavilion until a tour group goes down, and you can tag along if you show your ticket.

Reed Flute Cave

芦笛岩, lúdí yán · Daily 8am–5.30pm · ¥120 · Bus #3 from Zhongshan Lu

Some 6km north of Xi Shan, **Reed Flute Cave** is a huge warren eaten into the south side of Guangming Shan, which once provided a refuge from banditry and Japanese bombs. The caverns are not huge, but there are some interesting formations and a small underground lake, which makes for some nice reflections. You're meant to follow one of the tours (some in English) that run every twenty minutes, but you can always linger inside and pick up a later group if you want to spend more time.

10

ARRIVAL AND DEPARTURE   GUILIN

There are several options for Li River cruises to Yangshuo, mainly arranged through accommodation (see box, p.616).

BY PLANE
Liangjiang International Airport (桂林两江国际机场, guìlín liǎngjiāng guójì jīchǎng) is 30km west of the city, connected by an airport bus (every 30min 6.30am–9pm; ¥20) which terminates near the train station on the corner of Shanghai Lu and Minzhu Lu. A taxi to downtown costs around ¥100. Guilin is linked to almost forty cities across the mainland, as well as to Hong Kong, Seoul, Osaka and Kuala Lumpur.

Destinations Beijing (2hr 50min); Chengdu (1hr 50min); Guangzhou (6 weekly; 1hr); Hong Kong (1hr 25min); Kunming (1hr 35min); Shanghai (2hr 20min); Shenzhen (6 weekly; 1hr 20min); Xi'an (1hr 50min).

BY TRAIN
CRH The new Guilinbei (north) train station (桂林火车北站, guìlín huǒchē běi zhàn) is around 8km north of the centre and handles most high-speed services. Bus #100 heads to the centre of town stopping all along Zhongshan Lu, while a taxi should cost no more than ¥30–40. However, some services use Guilin station (see above) while others use Guilinxi (west) train station (桂林西火车站, Guìlín xī huǒchē zhàn) which is a whopping 25km out of town, northwest of the Gulinbei station, so check which one you'll be using when you book. Bus #22 (40–50min) heads to the centre from the latter, or a taxi should cost ¥50–60.

Destinations Beijing (2 daily; 10hr 40min); Changsha (12 daily; 3hr 40min); Guangzhou (39 daily; 2hr 30min–5hr 37min); Guiyang (27 daily; 2hr 21min–3hr 10min); Nanning (26 daily; 2hr 22min–2hr 53min); Shanghai (1 daily; 9hr 31min); Shenzhen (3 daily; 3hr 5min).

Other services Centrally located Guilin train station (桂林火车站, guìlín huǒchē zhàn) is set at the back of a large square off Zhongshan Lu, and handles most of the regular trains as well as a handful of high-speed services. Confusingly, some slow services also use Guilinbei station. Queues are not too bad at the station ticket office (daily 7.30–11.30am, 12.30–2.30pm, 3–7pm, & 7.30–9.30pm), though you can usually book through your accommodation for a fee.

Destinations Beijing (4 daily; 19hr 30min–27hr); Changsha (8 daily; 5hr 11min–7hr 27min); Guangzhou (1 daily; 10hr 30min); Kunming (1 daily; 20hr 22min); Nanning (12 daily; 4hr 5min–8hr 9min); Shanghai (5 daily; 17hr 35min–26hr 21min); Shenzhen (1 daily; 13hr 30min).

BY BUS
Guilin long-distance bus station (桂林汽车客运枢纽, guìlín qìchē kèyùn shūniǔ) is 200m north of the Guilin train station 100m back from Zhongshan Nan Lu. Bear in mind you're likely to get a much better seat here than if picking through-services up at Yangshuo.

Destinations Guangzhou (20 daily; 8hr); Hengyang (4 daily; 2hr 30min–3hr 40min); Nanning (16 daily; 5hr 40min); Sanjiang (6 daily, last at 1.50pm; 3hr); Yangshuo (every 10–20min; 1hr).

Yangshuo buses Express buses to Yangshuo (1hr 30min; ¥25) arrive and depart from the long-distance bus station every few minutes through the day, though touts will usher you onto services from anywhere along Zhongshan Nan Lu.

Rice terrace buses Express buses to the rice terrace ticket office in Heping (hourly; 1hr 30min) or Longsheng (every 30min; 2hr) leave from the new Qintan bus station (琴潭汽车客运站, qín tán qìchē kèyùn zhàn), 1km west of the long-distance bus station off Heishan Lu (buses #26, #85, #88 or #89 from the centre). From Longsheng, minibuses run to Dazhai or Ping An via the ticket office. There is one 8.30am departure from Guilin's train station square, going all the way to Dazhai (3hr; ¥50). Check with your accommodation in Guilin or Dazhai/Ping An about direct private minibuses.

INFORMATION

Tour agents The best option for booking tours is from one of the hostels, though all the hotels organize tours too (though at a price commensurate to the price of your room). There are many tour companies on Binjiang Lu, though almost none speak any English and the prices are the same as the mid-range hotels.

Maps The useful *Tour and Communication Map of Guilin* (¥10) is sold at some hotels, though most give out their own maps for free; the hostel ones are usually very good.

10

GETTING AROUND

By bus Buses can get you most places you need to go, but you're probably better off walking if your destination is within the centre.

By taxi Be careful when getting taxis in Guilin as being a major tourist destination, some of them will try and rip you off – insist on the meter and make sure they don't take you round the houses when they do (having a map open on your phone will help).

ACCOMMODATION

Guilin's hotels are mostly mid-range and upmarket, with a choice of hostels if you're after a budget bed. In addition, the *Scoozi Bar* (see opposite) has a few very popular dorm rooms attached to its premises. Competition is pretty stiff and year-round discounted rates of fifty percent are not unusual. The nicest location is along the river, with lakeside options the next best thing. Everywhere has a booking desk for cruises and local tours, and tours booked from the hostels generally work out being great value as you'll get a ¥10 discount on many of the entrance tickets.

Eva Inn 四季春天酒店, sìjì chūntiān jiǔdiàn. 66 Binjiang Lu, close to the Sheraton ☎ 0773 2830666, ⓦ evainn.com. Pleasant boutique-style place with smart, modern rooms and decent service despite the pokiness of the lobby. Most notable for being the least expensive of the riverside hotels with a water view, especially from its stylish rooftop café. **¥278**

Flowers Youth Hostel 花满国际青年旅馆, huāmǎnguójì qīngnián lǚguǎn. 6 Shangzhi Gang, Block 2, Zhongshan Nan Lu ☎ 0773 6919838, ⓔ yhaguilin@yahoo.com.cn. Hidden away behind the bright yellow *Home Inn* directly opposite the train station: walk through a dreary alley to the back of the hotel from where it's signposted up a flight of stairs. Recently redecorated in bright colours, it's a clean and friendly place, with a bar, café, internet, dorms and slightly scruffy doubles, as well as good-value tours. It's aimed at Chinese backpackers, so they may not speak English well but they do have the cheapest beds in town. Dorms **¥25**, doubles **¥80**

★**Guilin Central Youth Hostel** 木犀旅舍, mùxī lǚguǎn. 3 Renmin Lu, near the Sheraton ☎ 0773 2819936, ⓦ guilinhostel.com. Excellent location in the centre of the action downtown and close to the river, with a health-conscious café/bistro, modern dorms and plain, comfortable doubles and triples. Really well run by staff who speak very good English, it's a great place to get information or book tours. Dorms **¥45**, doubles **¥145**

★**Riverside Inn (and Hostel)** 桂林九龙别墅酒店, guìlín jiǔlóng biéshù jiǔdiàn. 5 Zhu Mu Xiang, Nanmen Qiao ☎ 0773 2580215, ⓦ guilin-hostel.com. Hidden down a quiet lane right in the town centre and set up like a European B&B, it also has a riverside restaurant next door and a hostel the other side. Very friendly and organized (so usually full), rooms at both locations are clean and comfortable, and many have balconies with water views, as do the communal seating areas. Dorms **¥40**, doubles **¥139**

Sheraton 大宇大饭店, dàyǔ dàfàndiàn. 15 Binjiang Lu ☎ 0773 2825588, ⓦ sheraton.com/guilin. One of the nicest hotels in town, with the best rooms overlooking the river and across to Seven Star Park, though you pay about fifty percent extra for the privilege. Also has a nice coffee shop serving a ¥130 buffet breakfast. **¥3400**

EATING

Guilin's restaurants are famous for serving rare game meats, and many places display live caged pheasants, cane rats, turtles, fish and snakes outside. Less confrontational options include Western, Italian and Thai restaurants on pedestrianized Zhengyang Jie, with standard Chinese food available along Nanhuan Lu, Wenming Lu and Yiren Lu. For cheap stir-fries and one-dish meals, try the canteens around the long-distance bus station.

Jinlong Zhai 金龙寨, jīnlóng zhài. 4F, corner of Zhongshan Lu and the adjacent plaza ☎ 0773 2825533, ⓦ jinlongzhai.com. Famous Guangxi chain specializing in local country dishes, such as roast fowl and fatty pork slices with taro (both ¥58) – the roast duck (¥42) is especially recommended. They also do Sichuanese staples, and kebabs barbecued at your table. Daily 9am–2.30am.

Kali Mirchi Shangshui pedestrian street, almost opposite the Guilin Central Youth Hostel ☎ 137 37396451. Probably the best Indian food in town, this understated pink concrete bunker of an eatery doesn't have a massive menu, but their curries, cooked by Indian chefs, are authentic and tasty. The lamb rogan josh (¥48) is excellent as are the veggie options such as dal fry (¥38). Daily 11.30am–10.30pm.

Spanish Restaurant 66 Bingjian Lu ☎ 0773 2888255. The Chinese manager here lived for more than eleven years in Argentina and speaks excellent Spanish. Great tapas (¥12–48), including a very nice tortilla Española (¥39), and good paella (¥45), with friendly service in a Spanish ambience. Also serves decent pizza (from ¥35) and a small, but very good, selection of wines from ¥40/glass. Located next to the *Guilin Central Youth Hostel*. Daily 11am–midnight.

★**Xiao Nan Guo** 小南国菜馆, xiǎonánguó càiguǎn. 3 Wenming Lu (and another eight branches around town) ☏ 0773 2855518. Big, bright, cheerful and very popular local-style restaurant, without your menu choices languishing in sight. There's no English menu, but it does have mouthwatering pictures on the menu, which look as good as the dishes actually taste. The *chashao* (roast pork) is excellent (meat dishes from ¥39), as are the freshwater fish

dishes (from ¥29). Daily 9.30am–2pm & 5–10.30pm.

Yaxu Nong Jia 雅叙农家菜馆, yǎxù nóngjiā càiguǎn. 21-2 Nanhuan Lu ☏ 0773 2835028. One of several smart, "country-style" restaurants along this street, with staff dressed in peasant garb and live fish outside awaiting your delectation. Good and earthy, with local beer fish around ¥80 and other fish dishes from ¥15–58 per *jin* (500g). Daily 9am–2am.

10

DRINKING AND ENTERTAINMENT

There's a knot of tourist-oriented, characterless and pricey pubs along Renmin Lu and pedestrianized Zhengyang Jie, and a couple of expensive clubs nearby, which play very loud music – okay places to go with a crowd. For the local scene, try along Chaoyang Lu (朝阳路, chāoyáng lù) in the Guanxi Normal University area.

Lijiang Theatre 漓江剧院, líjiāng jùyuàn. 38 Binjiang Lu ☏ 0773 282 2303. Nightly performances at 8pm of *Fantastic Guilin*, a contemporary take on local ethnic dances, incorporating ballet, acrobatics and amazing visuals for your enjoyment. Seats ¥150–220 depending on where you sit. Bring warm clothing in winter.
Scoozi Bar Down the steps by the bridge on the corner

of Jiefang Lu and Linjiang Lu ☏ 181 78358886. This new laidback riverside bar-cum-hostel run by the helpful Cookie has quickly become a favourite with both expats and tourists, with a pool table, Kirin on tap (¥20), a range of cocktails (¥15–55) and imported bottled beers (¥20–30) as well as their very popular pizza (¥29, plus ¥5 per topping). Daily 7am–2am (or later).

SHOPPING

Zhongshan Lu is lined with modern shops as well as department stores, the best of which is the Niko-Niko Do Plaza on the corner with Jiefang Lu. For local flavour, try osmanthus tea (*guicha*) or osmanthus wine (*guijiu*), both of which can be pleasant. For souvenirs – mostly outright tack and ethnic textiles – try your bargaining skills at the shops and stalls on Binjiang Lu and Zhengyang Jie, though more or less all the tourist tat in Guilin is pretty overpriced.

Xichenglu Pedestrian Street Market 西城路步行街, xīchéng lù bùxíngjiē. Just north of Shanhu Bridge, west off Zhongshan Lu. The red tent-stalls at this night market are somewhat better value for souvenirs (and

a range of other goods) than most places, and there's certainly more wiggle room on prices, though again, you'll have to haggle hard. Daily 8pm–midnight.

DIRECTORY

Visa extensions The visa extension department is at 16 Shijiayuan Lu (Mon–Fri 9.30am–noon & 3–6pm; ☏ 0773 5829930).

The Li River

漓江, lí jiāng

The **Li River** meanders south for 85km from Guilin through the finest scenery that this part of the country can provide, the shallow green water flanked by a procession of jutting karst peaks shaped by the elements into a host of bizarre forms, every one of them with a name and associated legend. In between are pretty rural scenes of grazing water buffalo, farmers working their fields in conical hats, locals poling themselves along on half-submerged bamboo rafts, and a couple of small villages with a scattering of old architecture; the densest concentration of peaks is grouped around the middle reaches between the villages of **Caoping** and **Xingping**.

A **cruise** through all this is, for some, the highlight of their trip to China. The scenery is at its best between May and September, when the landscape is at its lushest and the river runs deepest – a serious consideration, as the water can be so shallow in winter that vessels can't complete their journey. At the far end, the village of **Yangshuo** sits surrounded by more exquisite countryside, making it an attractive place to kick back for a couple of days, though subject to severe tourist overload during the peak summer season.

10

Daxu to Wangfu Shi

Aside from a few minor peaks, the first place of interest on the Li is around 25km along at the ancient (but newly spruced-up) west-bank town of **DAXU** (大圩, dàxū), which features a long, cobbled street, a few old wooden buildings, and a Ming-dynasty arched bridge. After this it's all rather flat until a grouping of peaks around **Wangfu Shi** (望夫石, wàngfū shí), an east-bank outcrop said to be a wife who turned to stone while waiting for her travelling husband to return home.

Yangdi to Yellow Cloth Shoal

South of Caoping is the east-bank settlement of **Yangdi** (杨堤, yángdī) and then you're into the best of the scenery, the hills suddenly tightly packed around the river. Pick of the peaks are **Eight Immortals Crossing the River** (八仙过江, bāxiān guòjiāng), and **Nine Horses Fresco Hill** (九马画山, jiǔmǎ huàshān), a 100m-high cliff on whose weathered face you can pick out some horsey patterns – first identified by ex-premier Jiang Zemin. Look into the water past here for **Yellow Cloth Shoal** (黄布滩, huángbù tān), a flat, submerged rock at one of the shallowest spots on the river.

Xingping

兴坪, xīngpíng

XINGPING, 70km downstream from Guilin and around 15km from Yangshuo, is a small market town hemmed in by mountains on the west bank of the river. Xingping is somewhere you can enjoy doing very little, either hanging out along **Lao Jie** (老街, lǎojiē), an old lane back from the dock, or watching locals buying everything from fruit to carry poles, medicinal herbs and bamboo chairs at the **market**, held on calendar dates ending in a 3, 6 or 9. Tourism is fast developing here, with a **high-speed train station** just 6km away. For the present, though, it's still a nicer and quieter version of Yangshuo –– if you are willing to forego any nightlife, it's a much better place to experience the Li River landscape.

CRUISING THE LI RIVER

The most popular Li River cruises take about four hours, cover the best stretches of scenery between Yangdi and Xingping and can be organized through the CITS or accommodation in Guilin (see p.614). The cheapest fares – around ¥290 – are on **Chinese cruise boats** from Daxu wharf (大圩码头, dàxū mǎtóu) and get you transport to the wharf, a filling meal, return bus from Yangshuo, and a shouty Chinese guide. **Foreign cruise boats** (¥440–800 depending on where you book) depart further downstream at Zhujiang wharf (竹江码头, zhújiāng mǎtóu) and are pretty much the same except they shout at you in English. The cruise boats are air-conditioned and have comfortable seating inside, but the upper observation-decks are usually open.

However, the best way to experience the river and feel part of the landscape is on a covered **bamboo raft** (¥205) through the pick of the scenery between **Yangdi wharf** (杨堤码头, yángdī mǎtóu) and Xingping. You get a bus to the wharf and the cruise, but have to feed yourself – bring a packed lunch or they usually stop at a riverside restaurant where a meal costs around ¥30. The same bus then meets you at Xingping, after a short detour to see the **¥20 Scenery** (20元背景图, èrshí yuán bēijǐngtú), and will then take you on a two-hour tour of a few sights around Yangshuo, before returning to Guilin. There's no room on the raft for luggage, but you can leave it on the bus so you can get off the bus anywhere from Xingping to Yangshuo. Operators in Yangshuo also offer a similar version of this trip, but it's more expensive.

Pickups for both kinds of trip are from hotels in town. Cruises pick up at 8–9am and bamboo rafts between 7–8.30am and 9.30–11am; they get you back to Guilin at about 6–8pm with around three to four hours on the river. During peak season (July–Oct) the river gets crowded, but be aware that in winter the river often runs too low for the cruise vessels to make it down as far as Xingping, let alone Yangshuo, though you get charged the same amount and won't be told this beforehand.

XINGPING HIKES

For a fairly stiff hike from Xingping, ask for directions to the ninety-minute trail over the hills to the tiny, photogenic riverside village of **Yucun** (鱼村, yúcūn), though a far easier path (though sometimes closed) leads upstream from the docks for the twenty-minute walk to the **¥20 Scenery** (20元背景图, èrshí yuán bēijǐngtú) – the landscape on the back of a twenty yuan note. For panoramic views that are slightly easier to get to, you can take a thirty-minute hike up the well-marked path from near the dock up to the pavilion on top of Laowozai Hill (老挝崽山, lǎowōzǎi shān). You'll have to haul yourself up the last stretch using ladders, but the views up and down the Li River are worth it.

10

ARRIVAL AND DEPARTURE

XINGPING

By train Yangshuo's CRH train station (see p.619) is just 6km away and so much closer to Xingping than its namesake, with five daily shuttle buses (10min; ¥10) coinciding with arrivals/departures, or a taxi is around ¥30.

By bus and minibus Xingping's bus station is 200m east of the river, with shuttle buses to and from Yangshuo's South bus station throughout the day (every 15min; 45min; ¥10), with the last bus back at 7.20pm. More

expensive minibuses are available, leaving when full, or costing ¥150. Buses to Guilin leave at 3am and 3pm (2hr 30min; ¥35).

By boat Relatively expensive six-person bamboo rafts are available by the dock for trips downstream to Yangshuo (¥260/person), or upstream to Nine Horses Fresco Hill (¥98/person) and the Yangdi (¥216/person), while there's a cheaper big boat heading down to Yucun too (¥68/person).

ACCOMMODATION AND EATING

All the following places have good food, as do many cafés along Lao Jie. For more regular and cheaper Chinese food, try the many restaurants and canteens along Rongtan Lu towards the bus station.

Kelly's Guesthouse 凯利客栈, kǎilì bīnguǎn. 12 Lao Jie ☏ 187 78305445, ✉ dasu126@msn.com. The most interesting rooms in town, with rooms with futons on stripped-pine floors and enormous windows and great views – no rooftop terrace unfortunately. Patrons also enjoy free use of bikes, and the restaurant serves decent Western and Chinese options. **¥120**

This Old Place YHA 兴坪老地方国际青年旅舍, xīngpíng lǎodì fāng guójì qīngnián lǔshè. 50m from the dock at 5 Rongtan Lu ☏ 0773 8702887, ⓦ topxingping.com. Well-run hostel with clean, modern rooms and dorms, with a comfortable and sociable rooftop terrace from which you can watch the sunset over the river. They can also arrange tours, activities and bike rental (¥30),

and staff speak excellent English. There are two restaurants; the one in the lobby does great pizzas from a wood-fire oven. A YHA card will get you roughly ten percent off rack rates. Dorms **¥35**, doubles **¥100**

Xingping Our Inn 宝熊庄, bǎoxióng zhuāng. Dahebei village, ¥2 ferry ride across the river from Xingping ☏ 135 97302073, ⓦ ourinnxp.com. Fairly idyllic location situated on a small peninsula across the river, with very large, very comfortable rooms, stunning views and a pretty garden. Tourism is fast growing here though, and there are other guesthouses popping up, as well as a newly constructed walking path along the river. They also serve locally sourced regional food in their restaurant. **¥168**

Yangshuo

阳朔, yángshuò

Nestled 70km south of Guilin in the thick of China's most spectacular karst scenery, **YANGSHUO** rose to prominence during the mid-1980s, when tourists on Li River cruises realized that the village made a great place to settle down and get on intimate terms with the river and its peaks. Yangshuo has grown considerably since then and, despite retaining an outdated reputation as a mellow haven among Western travellers, has become a rowdy draw for domestic tourists, with the majority of its bars, restaurants and shops catering to their tastes. It remains, however, an easy place to spend a few days: hills surround everything, village lanes swarm with activity, and there are restaurants and accommodation everywhere. You can rent a bike and spend a day zipping between hamlets, hike around or go **rock climbing** on nearby peaks, or study **cooking** or **martial arts** (see box, p.622). Just note that during Yangshuo's **peak-season**

10

CORMORANT FISHING

When you've had enough scenery for one day, do something unusual and spend an evening watching **cormorant fishing** (book through your hotel; ¥70–90/person for 90min including transport). This involves heading out on a bamboo raft or small boat just after dusk, in a small flotilla of tourist craft, closely following a tiny wooden fishing boat from which a group of cormorants fish for their owner. Despite being turned into a tourist activity at Yangshuo, people still make their living from this age-old practice across the region, raising young birds to dive into the water and swim back to the boat with full beaks. The birds are prevented from swallowing by ties around their necks, but it's usual practice for the fisherman to slacken these off and let them eat every seventh fish – apparently, the cormorants refuse to work otherwise.

tourism (July–October) accommodation is scarce and many attractions will be overcrowded, meaning Xingping (see p.616) just upriver, and Bama (see p.635) are far mellower and better alternatives, especially during busy periods.

Green Lotus Peak and Pantao Shan

Squeezed between the highway and the river, **Green Lotus Peak** (碧莲峰, bìlián fēng) is the largest in the immediate area – there's a track to the top off the highway east of the post office, but it involves some scrambling. An easier path (leading to better views) ascends **Pantao Shan** (蟠桃山, pántáo shān) from behind the market.

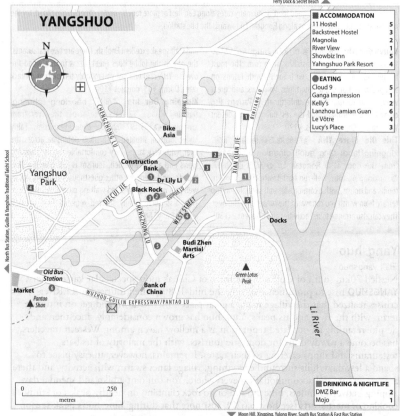

YANGSHUO

Ferry Dock & Secret Beach

■ ACCOMMODATION
11 Hostel	5
Backstreet Hostel	3
Magnolia	2
River View	1
Showbiz Inn	5
Yahngshuo Park Resort	4

● EATING
Cloud 9	5
Ganga Impression	1
Kelly's	2
Lanzhou Lamian Guan	6
Le Vôtre	4
Lucy's Place	3

■ DRINKING & NIGHTLIFE
| DMZ Bar | 2 |
| Mojo | 1 |

North Bus Station, Guilin & Yangshuo Traditional Taichi School

Yangshuo Park

Bike Asia

Construction Bank

Dr Lily Li

Black Rock

Docks

Budi Zhen Martial Arts

Green Lotus Peak

Li River

Old Bus Station

Market

Pantao Shan

Bank of China

WUZHOU-GUILIN EXPRESSWAY/PANTAO LU

0 — 250 metres

▼ Moon Hill, Xingping, Yulong River, South Bus Station & East Bus Station

Produce market

农贸市场, nóngmào shìchǎng

Yangshuo's **produce market**, just across the road and west from the bus station on Pantao Lu, is an interesting place to hang out, especially on market days (held on dates ending in a 3, 6 or 9). There's a good selection of game, fruit, nuts and mushrooms displayed on the stalls as well as the street outside – look out for rats and pheasants, fresh straw and needle mushrooms, and spiky water caltrops. The back of the market, where the fowl are dispatched, is not for the squeamish.

10

Xi Jie (West Street)

西街, xījiē

Flagstoned, vehicle-free **Xi Jie (West Street)** is Yangshuo's main tourist drag, stretching down to the water past restaurants, bars, accommodation and shops selling a vast array of souvenirs and named after the Westerners who used to frequent it rather than its geographical location. Trends change here continually, with the current emphasis towards ethnic textiles, traditional paintings, fans, and a few "new antiques". There's very little that you can't purchase elsewhere in the country for far less, even after bargaining; if you do decide to buy, check everything carefully before parting with your cash. In summer, shops stay open late and at night the street is uncomfortably clogged with crowds as they shop and orbit between the many restaurants and thumping dance-bars.

ARRIVAL AND DEPARTURE
YANGSHUO

Agents at accommodation and all around town can book long-distance bus tickets along with flights, taxis to Guilin airport (¥240, or a shared vehicle at ¥80/person) and train tickets from Yangshuo CRH station.

By train The misleadingly named Yangshuo Station (阳朔 火车站, yángshuò huǒchē zhàn) is actually 32km away near Xingping and shuttle buses run between it and the East bus station in Yangshuo, 3km southeast from the centre on Shina Lu to coincide with trains (30min; ¥20) or a taxi runs to about ¥60.
Destinations Guangzhou (7 daily; 2hr 25min); Guiyang (6 daily; 2hr 56min–3hr 22min).
By bus Yangshuo's new North bus station (阳朔汽车站, yángshuò qìchē zhàn), 2km northwest of the centre just off the highway, has buses up the expressway to

Guilin's long-distance bus station (¥25) every 20min or so until 10pm; make sure you get an express bus as the stopping services take much longer. There's also a new shuttle bus service from here to Guilin airport (8am–8.30pm; ¥50). Local services to Xingping (¥10) and other villages depart from the South bus station (阳朔汽 车南站, yángshuò qìchē nán zhàn), which is about 3km south of the centre on Kangzhan Nan Lu.
Destinations Guangzhou (3 daily, 3 nightly; 5–7hr); Guilin (every 10–20min; 1hr–1hr 30min); Guilin airport (8 daily; 1hr 20min); Nanning (11.30am daily; 6hr).

INFORMATION

Tourist information All accommodation have tour desks, or you can find information at foreigner-oriented cafés, most of which are located around central Guihua Lu. In addition, touts are everywhere, though they're relatively low-pressure

and easy enough to brush off if you're not interested.
Maps *The Yangshuo Fairy Guide* map of the town, river and surrounding area is available at most hotels and many shops (¥10) and shows bus and cycling routes.

ACCOMMODATION

Yangshuo's accommodation ranges from basic dorm beds to comfy doubles, with nice touches like balconies, folksy furnishings and wooden floors, though locations within a couple of hundred metres of West Street's nightclubs may not be. During peak season (including the first two weeks of October), and even weekends, prices rise astronomically and it's hard

PETTY CRIME IN YANGSHUO

Be warned that **petty crime** is on the rise in Yangshuo. Be wary of your possessions while swimming, and of your wallet and bags when getting on or off buses. Increasingly, bags are snatched from tourists' bicycles by motorcycling thieves, so don't keep your stuff loose in the basket.

10

to find anywhere in the centre for under ¥300. Conversely, stiff competition means rates can halve during the winter, when you'll want to check the availability of heating and hot water; in summer a/c is a must.

★**11 Hostel** 阳朔11青年客栈, yángshuò shíyī qīngnián kèzhàn. 11 Lianfeng Xiang ☎0773 6912228, ✉yangshuo11hostel@QQ.com. Clean, recently renovated and comfortable hostel tucked down an alley just metres from the river which is well managed and also excellent for information about and booking of tours, transportation, and activities. The rooftop terrace (with free washing machines) is relatively peaceful as there's no bar. Dorms ¥40, women-only dorms ¥50, doubles ¥130

Backstreet Hostel 桂花街国际青年旅馆, guìhuājiē guójì qīngnián lǚguǎn. 60 Guihua Xiang ☎0773 8814077, ✉947927871@qq.com. Down a quiet lane, with good dorms and doubles, it's a little worn round the edges but the least expensive hostel in the centre of town. No rooftop, bar or views, and as it's aimed at Chinese backpackers, there's not much English spoken here. Dorms ¥35, women-only dorms ¥40, doubles ¥100

Magnolia 白玉兰酒店, báiyùlán jiǔdiàn. 1 Diecui Lu ☎0773 8819813, ✉magnoliahotel@hotmail.com. Smart, good-value, mid-range place close to the downtown action, but far enough away to give you some sleep, with arty minimalist decor set off by pleasing pot plants. Rooms are large, very clean, and some have balconies for ¥100 more. ¥300

★**River View** 望江楼酒店, wàngjiānglóu jiǔdiàn. 11–15 Binjiang Lu ☎0773 8822688, ⊚riverview.com.cn. Nice, quiet hotel boasting comfortable rooms and a great location with the pricier rooms (¥458) having balconies that overlook the river across the road. Also has a good café/restaurant with tables in the street. ¥248

Showbiz Inn 秀界国际青年旅舍, xiùjiè guójì qīngnián lǚshè. 7 Lianfeng Xiang ☎0773 8883123. Pretty similar to the *11 Hostel* next door, though slightly cheaper and slightly less well run. Great views from their rooftop bar and the whole place has a nice lived-in feeling with lots of travellers having left graffiti. Dorms ¥40, doubles ¥120

Yahngshuo Park Resort 阳朔公园度假酒店, yángshuò gōngyuán dùjià jiǔdiàn. Northern end of Yangshuo Park, a 10min walk west of Xi Jie ☎0773 6919888, ⊚park.yangshuoresorthotel.com. This characterless mid-range option is quiet, has good facilities and the rooms are comfortable, clean and with nice bathrooms. Perhaps the only place in central Yangshuo where you're sure of a peaceful night's sleep. ¥268

EATING

Yangshuo's numerous restaurants and cafés are split between those by the canals between Xi Jie and Guihua Lu, which mainly cater to Chinese tourists seeking exotic foreign food (Indian, German, Spanish, and even British pub grub), and those along Chengzhong Lu and Guihua Lu, which serve backpacker staples and Chinese and Western food to a foreign crowd. Everywhere opens early for Western breakfasts, and keeps going well into the night. For inexpensive Chinese canteens and food stalls, try the area around the old bus station.

★**Cloud 9** Upstairs, corner of Chengzhong Lu and Xi Jie ☎0773 8813686. More recommended by guidebooks than locals these days, but the seasonal country-style food is still flavourful and it's worth trying one of their slow-simmered medicinal soups (¥16–20), rural specialities such as braised and steamed pork with taro (¥45), or Sichuanese classics like crispy-skinned chicken (¥50). Daily 9am–11pm.

Ganga Impression 恒河, hénghé. Block B, Yangguang 100 (just north of Guihua Lu) ☎0773 8811456. Not so fancy looking, but probably the most authentic-tasting north Indian food in the region. Very tasty curries and tandoor breads, with real basmati rice as well as *lassi* and Indian desserts, it's reasonably priced and

has good service. Chicken tikka masala or lamb rogan josh with rice will cost you ¥45, though vegetarian dishes like *palak paneer* are slightly less. Daily 11am–11pm.

Kelly's 43 Guihua Lu ☎0773 8813233. Friendly foreigners' café/restaurant, with Western food alongside good home-style Sichuan cooking – try their fiery hot boiled beef slices (¥38) or famous apple pie (¥28). A nice, bright environment, with art on the walls and a non-smoking, a/c room upstairs. Also good are the breakfasts for ¥30–38 (ask for English-style eggs), and Kelly speaks great English. Daily 7.30am–1am.

Lanzhou Lamian Guan 兰州拉面馆, lánzhōu lāmiàn guǎn. 61 Pantao Lu, opposite the old

---

BEER FISH

Several mid-price Chinese restaurants at the southern end of Xie Lu, as well as on the north end of Guihua Lu (the best are up the alley, after it crosses Diecui Lu) serve the spicy local speciality **beer fish** (啤酒鱼, píjiǔ yú), which costs ¥35–80 per 500g – the most expensive and having the least bones being the *maogu* fish (毛骨鱼, máogǔ yú).

THE LIU SAN JIE SHOW

Yangshuo's most spectacular after-dark event is **Liu San Jie** (刘三姐; ⓦyxlsj.com), an open-air song, dance and light spectacular put together by renowned film director Zhang Yimou. Featuring a cast of 600 local cormorant fishermen, minority women, singing children and the like, the whole affair starts at 7.40pm or 8.50pm (8pm only in winter), lasts an hour, and should cost ¥230 or ¥320 – note that the more expensive seats are usually booked up by tour groups, and you won't see much from the cheaper seats (¥190). It takes place about 2km downstream from town and the transfer is included in the price – book through your accommodation.

long-distance bus station ⓣ136 47865006. This Muslim-run joint does hearty bowls of *lanzhou* noodle soup (spiced to your desired heat), and you can watch the noodles being made by the chap twirling the dough around at the front of the shop. No English menu, but plenty of pictures to point at on the wall – it also has a few rice and dry noodle dishes, all for ¥10–25, and fancier beef dishes for up to ¥100. Daily 8am–midnight.
Le Vôtre 乐德法式餐厅, lèdé fǎshì cāntīng. 81 Xi Jie ⓣ0773 8828040. Yangshuo's fanciest dining, inside a Ming-era building complete with period furnishings or in the courtyard outside. Food is French for Chinese tastes

– snails (¥50), pâté (¥35), steak *au poivre* (¥95) – plus pizza (¥35–55) or Chinese seafood (¥80–160/person). Also, excellent coffee and baguettes (¥12) for breakfast. Daily 11am–1am.
★**Lucy's Place** 露茜餐吧, lùxī cānbā. 30 Guihua Lu ⓣ139 77351663. Foreigner-friendly establishment, similar to others nearby, with the usual mix of Chinese and Western meals, plus Lucy is a good source of tourist information. Has a slightly grungy, rustic feel with farm implements and tourist graffiti covering the walls. Sandwiches and burgers ¥25–45, with other Chinese and Western mains at ¥35–50. They also construct tailor-made breakfasts. Daily 7am–11pm.

DRINKING AND NIGHTLIFE

For drinking, almost all the backpacker-style restaurants along Guihua Lu have bars and there are also a load of fairly similar loud bars along Xian Qian Lu, though the best places to hang out are the places listed below, or the rooftop bars at the hostels near the river, such as the *Showbiz Inn* or the nearby and more raucous *Monkey Janes*. West Street is strung with almost identical clubs and bars, all of which play similar generic pounding techno or have a man with guitar for the Chinese crowds. It's hard to recommend any really, and they generally stay open till around 2am during high season.

DMZ Bar 41 Guihua Lu ⓣ186 11791884, ⓦthedmzbar .com. Foreigner-run, and the smallest bar in Yangshou, this friendly and slightly grungy place is a regular hangout for both tourists and old China hands. It's more or less just opposite Dr Lily Li's clinic, on the other side of the small canal. It may look like it has closed down during the day, but that's just its style. They serve the coldest Beer Lao in

town (¥20). Daily noon–3am.
Mojo 莫祚, mòzuò. 6F, rooftop of the Alshan Hotel, 18 Xie Lu ⓣ151 078837601. This rooftop place is funky and a little beat-up, but popular with local and foreign residents. It also has an open-air dancefloor that overlooks the river, which gets going at weekends with mostly hip-hop (occasionally live), as well as dance tunes. Daily 7pm–3am or later.

DIRECTORY

Bank There's a Bank of China on the west end of Xi Jie with a 24hr automated foreign-bill exchanger and ATMs, with many other ATMs around town.
Books Many cafés and hostels offer book exchanges, and the *DMZ Bar* sells English-language comics and books.
Laundry Most hostels have washing machines, either for free or ¥10, or there are several laundries around town including a super-fast 1hr-service at *Speed Queen* by the Jin

Long Supermarket on Chengzhong Lu (¥20/kg).
Medical For acupuncture or Chinese massage, contact English-speaking Dr Lily Li at 2F, 46 Guihua Lu (ⓣ130 77632299, ⓦdr-lily-li.com). Therapeutic massages cost ¥108/hr, and – if pain is any indication of quality – might be the best you'll ever have. Relaxation massage (¥90–288/hr) or foot massages (¥88–98/hr) are also available.

Around Yangshuo

Since Yangshuo is such a tourist scrum these days, you're better off getting out into the countryside to enjoy the scenery, the best of which is west along the **Yulong River**. Markets, which rotate through the villages on specific dates, make good excuses to drop into otherwise torpid communities; the one at Xingping (see p.616) is particularly

10

TOURS AND ACTIVITIES AT YANGSHUO

Yangshuo has well-established guides for any number of organized activities that take advantage of its spectacular natural location. **Freelance guides** work Yangshuo's streets and cafés; all claim to have unique, untouristed places to take you for lunch with a farming family and offer insights into village life. Some have been doing this for years, including the English-speaking, cheery and helpful "Wendy" Li Yunzhao (☎1319 7638186, ✉liyunzhaowendy@sina.cn). Expect to pay about ¥50 per person per day depending on the size of the group – one or two people costs ¥150.

COOKERY

The **Yangshuo Cooking School** (☎137 88437286, ✇yangshuocookingschool.com) in nearby Chao Long runs one-day to one-week courses (¥180/day for 4hr), including hotel pickup and a market visit, and they can cater for vegetarians.

BICYCLE RENTAL AND TOURS

Accommodation or operators at the western end of Yangshuo's West Street **rent bicycles** for ¥20–50 a day, depending on whether you want an ordinary rattletrap or an off-roader with decent springs: ¥500 or your ID may be asked for as a deposit. The excellent **Bike Asia** in town at 5 Furong Lu (March–Dec; ☎0773 8826521, ✇bikeasia.com), rent out the best bikes for ¥70 a day including maps, helmets and repair kits; high-end mountain bikes cost ¥100. They also run guided 40km bike-tours in English around Yangshuo, which cost ¥240 and leave daily at 9am; two to five-day trips are also available.

ALONG THE LI AND YULONG RIVERS

Accommodation can arrange **bamboo raft trips** between Xingping and Yangdi (2hr; ¥250–300 depending on season). It's probably better, however, to take a similarly priced raft along the less-crowded yet equally pretty Yulong tributary, the best stretch being from Fuli Bridge to Jiuxian docks. Kayaking is also available along both rivers for slightly less. The now badly named **Secret Beach**, 2km upstream from town, down a small track, is the nicest place for a swim.

MARTIAL ARTS

Yangshuo has become a martial arts hangout, with the long-established **Budi Zhen school** founded by the incredible, and sadly late Master Gao and now run by his twin sons. Visit their training hall (步地真功夫馆, bùdì zhēngōngfu guǎn) off West Street (☎1397 7350377, ✉budizhen.info@gmail.com), to study a whole range of martial disciplines at around ¥100/hr lesson. For **tai ji** try the **Yangshuo Traditional Taichi School** (阳朔传统太极学校, yángshuò chuántǒng tàijí xuéxiào), housed in a Qing-dynasty farmhouse at Jima village close to the Yulong River (☎152 9592 0102, ✇traditionaltaichischool.com). Master Kim teaches courses up to instructor-level with all classes costing ¥1490 (part-time) or ¥2040 (full-time) per week including food and accommodation, though for long-term students prices go down considerably. Introductory classes cost just ¥100, and include lunch.

ROCK CLIMBING, CAVING, ABSEILING AND ZIP-LINING

Yangshuo has many opportunities for the adventurous and is a popular **rock-climbing centre** with over four hundred mostly short but very tough graded climbs on local peaks ranging from 5.6 to 5.13. New climbs are being pioneered all the time and the *Yangshuo Rock Climbs* available from climb-shops will show you most of them, along with detailed climbing information. **Black Rock**, 12 Guihua Lu (☎0773 8819656, ✇blackrockclimbing.net), are one of the most established operators and have a range of climbing courses from 1hr samples (¥120) and full-day multi-pitch tours (¥500). They also do full-day **caving** (¥600), and half-day **abseiling** (¥450) or **zip-lining** (¥450) tours. For climbers, *The Rusty Bolt* on Guihua Lu (very close to *Black Rock*) is the spot to go to socialize and get the latest information.

good. All can be reached from Yangshuo on local transport, cycling or hiking, either on your own or with guides. There is also a handful of self-contained, quiet places to stay in the area. **Moon Hill** offers great views, but is firmly on the main tourist itineraries.

The Yulong River

玉龙河, yùlóng hé

Paralleling the highway to Guilin west of Yangshuo, the **Yulong River** offers a 12km walk or cycle between small hamlets, with a couple of old stone bridges and at least two older-style villages with antique buildings. The road from Yangshuo leaves the highway near the bus station – you might have to ask for directions to **Chaoyang** (朝阳, cháoyáng), the first large settlement along the way – and follows the east side of the Yulong via **Xia Tangzhai** (下堂寨, xiàtáng zhài), the old villages of **Huang Tu** (黄土, huángtǔ) and **Gu Cheng** (古城, gǔchéng), before rejoining the highway at **Baisha** (白沙, báishā), whose market runs on dates ending in a 1, 4 or 7 and from where you can either cycle or catch a bus back to Yangshuo.

Moon Hill

月亮山, yuèliàng shān • Daily 8am–7pm • ¥15 • Minibus from Yangshuo South bus station to Gaotian (高田, gāotián), and ask the driver to put you off at the right spot, return by flagging down passing traffic; or taxi for ¥50 after bargaining

Moon Hill lies on the highway 8km from town, named after a large crescent-shaped hole that pierces the peak. It takes an easy thirty minutes to ascend the eight hundred stone steps through bamboo to the summit where fairy-tale views take in the whole of the Li River valley, fields cut into uneven chequers by rice and vegetable plots, and Tolkienesque peaks framed through the hole. In summer, be sure to take water, or you'll have to pay through the nose to the little old ladies who stalk the area with drinks.

ACCOMMODATION AND EATING   AROUND YANGSHUO

For transport information to these places, contact the hotels directly.

Giggling Tree Guesthouse 咯咯树宾馆, gēgē shù bīnguǎn. Aishanmen village, about 5km south of Yangshuo along the Yulong River ☏ 136 67866154, ⓦ gigglingtree.com. Converted stone farmhouse buildings now forming an attractive Dutch-owned hotel and restaurant, with courtyard, tiled roofs and a beautiful mountain backdrop. Rooms are very large, beautifully furnished and have lovely wooden floors and ceilings. Dorms **¥100**, doubles **¥290**

★**Snow Lion** 雪狮岭度假饭店, xuěshīlǐng dùjià fàndiàn. Mushan village, about 2.5km south of Yangshuo ☏0773 8826689, ⓦsnowlionresort.com. Fantastic food and scenery coupled with comfortable and airy rooms make this a great place for a break, and all rooms have their own balconies. Located 150m from the village and owned by the same people who own *Cloud 9* in town. **¥288**

Longji Titian

龙脊梯田, lóngjǐ tītián • ¥100 • ☏ 0773 7583088, ⓦ txljw.com (Chinese only)

Around 90km north of Guilin, **Longji Titian** – literally "Dragon's Spine Terraces" – is a range of steep-sided and closely packed hills, whose slopes have been carved out over centuries of farming to resemble the literal form of a contour map. Most of the people up here are **Zhuang**, but there are also communities of **Yao**, some of whom still hunt for a living. The Yao women also have a custom to never cut their hair, and you will see them with it piled up on top of their heads like turbans, though if you want a photo, it'll cost you ¥10. Tourism is well established, with the wooden villages of **Ping An** and **Dazhai** acting as comfortable bases for viewing the terraces or hiking around the hilltops. Day-trips are offered by agents in Guilin (see p.613), but you'll get more by staying for a couple of nights, and it's easy to get here on local buses.

Ping An

平安, píng'ān

PING AN is a small Zhuang village of wooden homes and cobbled paths squeezed into a steep fold between the terraces, whose seven hundred or so inhabitants all share the

10

PING AN TO DAZHAI HIKE

Though there is no direct vehicle road, it's possible to **hike** between Ping An and Dazhai in around four hours, via the attractive village of **Zhongliu** (中六, zhōngliù), where there is very basic food but no accommodation. Yao women along the way will offer their services as guides (around ¥50), though with basic maps from accommodation, they're not really necessary.

---

surname Liao. You get dropped off in a car park and walk up 500m of stone steps to the village, where you're faced with a glut of **accommodation**, all offering cosy rooms with or without en suite in "traditional-style" three-storey houses – look for something with a view. Ping An is the focus of Chinese package tours, though these visitors tend not to wander very far from the village centre and generally all leave by 3pm. Walks around Ping An include short climbs to lookouts at **Seven Stars** (七星, qīxīng) and **Nine Dragons and Five Tigers** (九龙五虎, jiǔlóng wǔhǔ), either of which give superlative views of the rice terraces.

Dazhai

大寨, dàzhài • Cable car daily 8.30am–7pm • ¥70 one-way, ¥120 return

DAZHAI is a larger but slightly less touristy version of Ping An, reached along a separate road. The relatively few package tourists who visit are funnelled off up the cable car to the viewing point at **Jinfo Ding** (金佛顶, jīnfó dǐng), and the village is consequently more peaceful than Ping An. Further up the hillside are hamlets such as **Tiantou** (田头, tiántóu), just over 1km and twenty minutes' walk up steps – quite a hike with a heavy pack, though the tough old ladies at Dazhai will offer their services as porters for ¥30–50. Up on the ridge-tops, there are further walks to fabulous views at **Xi Shan** (西山, xīshān), or over to Ping An via Zhongliu village (see box above).

ARRIVAL AND DEPARTURE   LONGJI TITIAN

By bus Longji Titian is accessed from the hamlet of Heping (和平, hépíng), on the Guilin–Sanjiang highway. At Heping, you purchase your entrance ticket and find minibuses uphill to Ping An or Dazhai which depart when full (¥10; 30min). Leaving, if you can't find direct transport to Guilin or Sanjiang, first catch a minibus 12km north to the town of Longsheng (龙胜, lóngshèng), which has better connections, including to Guilin (see p.610).

By minibus Minibuses can be organized through your accommodation here or in Guilin. Shared they should cost ¥50/person, with a whole minibus costing around ¥500.

On a tour Day-tours from Guilin cost around ¥300–350/person and include return transport, entry and an English-speaking guide, with around 5hr on site.

ACCOMMODATION AND EATING

All accommodation serves food – Western staples and some good Chinese meals, including rice or chicken grilled in bamboo tubes (竹筒鸡, zhútǒng jī). Do try the local rice-wine too, which is sweet, fizzy, has rice floating in it and about the same alcohol content as a strong beer.

PING AN

Longji International Youth Hostel 龙脊国际青年旅舍, lóngjí guójì qīngnián lǔshě. ☎ 0773 7583265, ⓦ www.yhachina.com. The only hostel in the centre of the village (and not as busy as those in Dazhai), with clean rooms (though firm beds) in a nice wooden building with all the normal hostel facilities such as wi-fi and laundry. Serves good Western (though better Chinese) food in its restaurant. Dorms ¥30, doubles ¥128

Ping An Jiudian 平安酒店, píngān jiǔdiàn. ☎ 0773 7583198. A 15min walk up the hill from the village, it has two buildings, with the more expensive one having really nice, comfortable VIP rooms with views (¥400), though the economical ones aren't bad either. ¥160

DAZHAI

Dayao Zhai Tavern 大姚县翟酒店, dàyáoxiàn zhái jiǔdiàn. ☎ 0773 7585699. At the north of the village and to the right of the stream, this is typical of the accommodation here, but is quieter, being on the edge. Comfortable, clean a/c rooms, in a traditional building, and for ¥20 extra you get a computer in the room. Very good restaurant downstairs. ¥128

Dragon's Den Hostel 龙穴青年旅舍, lóngxué qīngnián lǔshě. Tiantou hamlet ☎ 0773 7585780, ⓦ dragonsdenhostel.com. Above Dazhai at Tiantou, this traditional wooden building has clean rooms and dorms, and fantastic views of the best of the scenery. Rooms have a/c and wi-fi; ¥30 extra for a room with a view; ¥5 cheaper/person with YHA membership. Dorms ¥40, doubles ¥90

Sanjiang

三江, sānjiāng

Some 80km west of Longsheng near the Guizhou border, **SANJIANG** is a small, dishevelled service town on the Rongshui River. Most of the people here are **Dong**, renowned for their wooden houses, towers and bridges that dot the countryside hereabouts, most notably at **Chengyang** village to the north. Sanjiang's own unmissable **drum tower** rises 47m over the river; this one is modern, but similar towers were traditionally used as lookout posts in times of war, or social areas in times of peace. While there is no real reason to stop at Sanjiang except in transit to **Zhaoxing** (see p.626), you might get stuck here between connections – though Chengyang is a better place to stay the night.

10

Chengyang

程阳, chéngyáng • ¥80 • Traditional music and dance show daily at 10.30am & 3.30pm; ¥30

CHENGYANG, 18km north of Sanjiang on the Linxi River, is an attractive Dong village reached over a covered **wind-and-rain bridge**, an all-wooden affair built in 1916. The village forms a collection of renovated two- and three-storey traditional wooden houses surrounding a square-sided drum tower, and makes a pleasantly rural place to spend a day. You can walk out to smaller hamlets with similar congregations of dark wood and cobbles, many with their own, less elaborate bridges and towers. Look for creaky black **water wheels** made from plaited bamboo, somehow managing to supply irrigation canals despite dribbling out most of their water in the process. For views over the whole region, return to Chengyang's main-road entrance and make the short climb to two pavilions on the ridge above, offering vistas of dark, gloomy villages nestled among vivid green fields.

ARRIVAL AND DEPARTURE

SANJIANG

BY TRAIN

CRH Sanjiang South train station (三江火车站, sān jiāngnán huǒchē zhàn) is 10km south of the town and connected by regular buses (¥2) to Sanjiang west bus station, or a taxi costs ¥20–30.

Destinations Guilin (21 daily; 30min–1hr); Guiyang (17 daily; 1hr 51min–2hr 20min).

Other services Sanjiang County train station (三江县 火车站, sānjiāng xiàn huǒchē zhàn) is about 10km northwest of town on the Huaihua–Liuzhou rail line, with services to Mayang in Hunan, for Fenghuang (see p.441). Minibuses (¥5) meet arrivals and land them in central Sanjiang, from where you can catch a bus to Chengyang.

Destinations Chongqing (7.28pm; 13hr 21min); Liuzhou (9 daily; 2–3hr 47min); Mayang (12.16am; 5hr).

BY BUS

Sanjiang Hedong bus station (河东汽车站, hédōng qìchē zhàn) lies east of the river in the newer part of Sanjiang, with connections south as far as Guilin and north to Zhaoxing and Congjiang.

Destinations Guilin (6 daily, last at 2pm; 3hr 30min); Longsheng (3 daily; 2hr); Zhaoxing (2–3 daily; 2–3hr).

Sanjiang Hexi (west) bus station (河西汽车站, héxī qìchē zhàn), in the older part of Sanjiang, serves local destinations, including Chengyang.

Destination Chengyang (4 daily, mornings only; 40min).

Chengyang There are morning-only buses to Chenyang (¥5) from Sanjiang's Hexi bus station, and you will be dropped at the village ticket office. Returning, stand on the main road and flag down traffic; the last bus to Sanjiang passes by around 5pm. There are also very crowded and badly driven minibuses (¥8) plying the route, which leave from outside the Hexi bus station (and run slightly later).

ACCOMMODATION AND EATING

SANJIANG

There are plenty of cheap, basic places to stay near both bus stations, but none takes foreigners. The same is true for Chengyang, where hotel building seems incessant, though most Chinese tour groups head to Sanjiang at sunset. Noodle and hotpot stalls surround the Hedong bus station in Sanjiang, while the *Sanjiang Hotel* has a sit-down restaurant, and makes a good place to wait for buses.

Sanjiang Hotel 三江酒店, sānjiāng jiǔdiàn. 2 Chinhua Lu ☎ 0772 8626888. Fairly nice mid-range hotel around a 5min walk from the long-distance bus station – turn right, then left after 150m up the main road and it's just on the left. Rooms are clean and well equipped, and rooms often heavily discounted. **¥368**

10

CHENGYANG

Dong Village Hotel 董村酒店, dǒngcūn jiǔdiàn. 50m left as you cross the larger of the two bridges ☎0772 8582421. Best (and priciest) of Chengyang's many family-run, folksy guesthouses – most others charge ¥80. The clean and rustic rooms have a/c (vital in the summer), and there's a communal balcony with rocking chairs to admire the view from. The kitchen serves home-cooked food – certainly better than the appalling Western dishes available at Chengyang's restaurants – though it closes after dark. **¥180**

Into Guizhou: Sanjiang to Kaili

The road west of Sanjiang enters Guizhou and cuts through Dong territory and up to the Miao stronghold of **Kaili**, a 300km-long run of traditional villages, steeply terraced hillsides, vivid blue rivers and winding roads. Daily buses run from Sanjiang to **Zhaoxing** – itself a highlight – from where you can town-hop on to Kaili. Two days is a likely minimum for the trip, and it's not one that you'll get much out of by rushing in any case – no high-speed trains stop at either.

Zhaoxing

肇兴, zhàoxīng • ¥100 • Free traditional music and dance show daily at 10.30am and 3.30pm

ZHAOXING, around four hours by bus from Sanjiang, is an extremely attractive single-street Dong town set in a small valley, with a generous smattering of old wooden buildings including five square-based **drum towers**, each differently styled and built by separate clans. Accompanying wind-and-rain bridges and theatre stages are decorated with fragments of mirrors and mouldings of actors and animals. The whole village has just been given a makeover, and although it's become much easier to visit, it may lose some of its charm as a result – it's better to head for one of the other villages.

Tang An and Shage

The countryside of rice terraces and muddy tracks that surround Zhaoxing provides fine country walks, the best of which is 7km uphill through paddy fields to **Tang An** (堂安, táng'ān), a photogenic collection of wooden buildings. To escape any last trappings of government-sponsored gentrification, carry on up through Tang An a further 2km to the smaller hamlet of **Shage** (傻哥, shǎgē), which is more authentic and also has lovely views.

ARRIVAL AND DEPARTURE   **ZHAOXING**

By bus There's no bus station at Zhaoxing; buses running between Sanjiang and Congjiang or Liping drop off and collect along the main street. As no services originate at Zhaoxing, and buses are often already full by the time they pass through, you might need to ask at your accommodation about how to use minibuses to get to your next port of call.

There is, however, a fairly erratic minibus service between Zhaoxing and Congiang train station (¥20) which leaves when full, or your accommodation can arrange a private car for the same journey for ¥50/person.

Destinations Congjiang (2 daily; 1hr 30min); Heping (9 daily; 1hr 30min); Sanjiang (2–3 daily ; 2–3hr).

SANJIANG TO RONGJIANG

INFORMATION

Tourist office Zhaoxing's tourist office is opposite the main-street meat market (daily 8.30am–5.30pm; ☎0855 6130800), supplying hand-drawn maps of the local area (¥10), which also describe Dong culture and traditions.

ACCOMMODATION AND EATING

There is plenty of inexpensive accommodation in Zhaoxing, though better views and a more peaceful environment – if extremely basic rooms – are available up at Tang An for under ¥50. For food, the main road is lined by open-fronted stir-fry restaurants, but given the amount of dust stirred up by passing traffic you might opt for an indoor venue.

10

Dong Village 侗乡涉外旅馆, dòngxiāng shèwài lǚguǎn. On the street parallel to Zhaoxing's main street ☎0855 6130188. Nice wooden building and typical of the guesthouses in the village, with clean and comfortable, if slightly basic rooms. Also serves inexpensive local-style rice food – the owner is quite a good cook. **¥80**
Zhaoxing Binguan 肇兴宾馆, zhàoxīng bīnguǎn.

Just uphill from Zhaoxing's tourist office ☎0855 6130899. Costlier than the in-town hotels but much more scenic, with staff in local costume, and very comfortable, clean, recently renovated rooms in a large wooden building. Also has a good Chinese restaurant and a balcony overlooking the rooftops of the village. **¥200**

Congjiang and Basha

CONGJIANG (从江, cóngjiāng) is a not too unattractive logging town on the Duliu River some two hours west from Zhaoxing. The reason to stop here in transit to Kaili is to make a side-trip to **BASHA** (岜沙, bāshā), a Miao hill village 8km southwest whose inhabitants grow a long topknot and wear traditional clothes and heavy metal jewellery as a matter of course, not just for festivals. Unusually, the men also carry home-made flint-lock guns, with even the children carrying toy ones. Basha is really a loose grouping of five separate wooden villages on a forested ridge, with cobbled lanes and paths off across the fields to explore; there are several places to stay here too.

ARRIVAL AND DEPARTURE

CONGJIANG AND BASHA

By train Congjiang high-speed train station (从江火车站, cóng jiāng huǒchē zhàn) is 10km from the town and connected by regular buses (¥2), or a taxi costs ¥20–30.
Destinations Guilin (21 daily; 30min–1hr); Guiyang (17 daily; 1hr 51min–2hr 20min).

By bus Congjiang's bus station is on main street Jiangdong Nan Lu, with only two direct buses to Zhaoxing daily, and more frequent departures to Rongjiang and Kaili.
Destinations Guiyang (7am & 10.40am; 4hr); Kaili (2 daily; 4hr 30min); Rongjiang (10 daily; 2hr); Zhaoxing (2 daily 7.30am & 1pm; 1hr 30min).

GETTING AROUND

Minibus and motorbike Turn left out of Congjiang's bus station, walk 100m to the bridge, cross it and you'll find freelance minibuses and motorbikes to Basha (¥10 on either) hanging around on the left-hand corner.

ACCOMMODATION AND EATING

CONGJIANG

There's plenty of poor-value accommodation near Congjiang's bus station, though the nearby stir-fry places serve excellent inexpensive meals, including the very tasty local version of sour fish soup (酸汤鱼, suāntāngyú), where they fry the fish first.
Kaitai Holiday Hotel 开泰假日酒店, kāitài jiàrì jiǔdiàn. Directly across the bridge on Xincheng Lu ☎0855 6929999. By far the best option in town: the carpets might be a little threadbare but the rooms are comfortable and clean, and half of them have river

views. It also boasts a small bar in the lobby with imported liquors. **¥188**

BASHA

Gufeng Zhai Qingnian Luguan 古风寨青年旅馆, gǔfēngzhài qīngnián lǚguǎn. ☎0855 6925035. The pick of Basha's accommodation, this is a lovely, quiet and clean wooden hostel with outstanding views from the lounge, and a small terraced garden. Beds are comfortable, bathrooms are clean, and there's even wi-fi, though no a/c. Serves basic meals for ¥30. **¥100**

10

Rongjiang and Zengchong

RONGJIANG (榕江, róngjiāng) is a comparatively large, modern town two hours northwest of Congjiang across the mountains, and has a frenetic Sunday **market** where you can watch villagers bargaining the last Mao out of a deal. As at Congjiang, you're in Rongjiang to get out – this time 30km east to the isolated Dong village of ZENGCHONG (增冲, zēngchōng), which sports a four-hundred-year-old drum tower. Zengchong makes no concessions to the few tourists who drop in – it's a poor, muddy, rickety place with a couple of tiny stores, where Chinese-speakers might negotiate a homestay for the night for around ¥20–30.

ARRIVAL AND DEPARTURE   RONGJIANG AND ZENGCHONG

By train Rongjiang's high-speed train station is 5km from the town and connected by buses (¥2; 10min) which coincide with the trains; a taxi should cost around ¥10–15, or ¥5 in a shared taxi.
Destinations Guangzhou (6 daily; 4hr); Guilin (9 daily; 1hr 10min); Guiyang (10 daily; 1hr 20min); Sanjiang (4 daily; 37min).

By bus Rongjiang's bus station is on the east side of town, with services to both Congjiang (10 daily; 2hr) and Kaili (8 daily; 3hr).
Getting to Zengchong Reaching Zengchong takes two steps; first catch one of the hourly buses to Wangdong (往洞, wǎngdòng) – the last bus leaves Rongjiang at 5.20pm – and then walk or hitch for the final 6km.

ACCOMMODATION

There are plenty of decent, inexpensive places to stay near Rongjiang's bus station, but none is currently authorized to take foreigners.

Dongxiangmi Grand Hotel 东香蜜湖大酒店, dōng xiāng mì hú dà jiǔdiàn. 33 Huancheng Xi Lu ☎0855 6653669. Located near to the bus station, this three-star is the best hotel in the county (though the *Ritz* it ain't) and

the only obvious option for foreign tourists. It's fairly modern, has large, clean rooms, a restaurant with a handful of western options (like breakfast) and is well run, if pricey. ¥298

Nanning

南宁, nánníng

Way down in southern Guangxi, fairly close to China's open border with Vietnam, NANNING was just a medium-sized market town when European traders opened a river route from neighbouring Guangdong in the early twentieth century, starting a period of rapid growth that saw the city supplanting Guilin as the provincial capital. The city has capitalized on recent trade agreements with Vietnam, and today Nanning is a fairly nondescript boom town with a mix of leafy boulevards, high-rise modern architecture and a handful of narrow, colonial-era streets. There's good shopping, decent food, a **museum** strong on regional archeology, and both international and domestic transport connections, which are the main reason to come here.

The Provincial Museum

省博物馆, shěng bówùguǎn • Gucheng Lu • Tues–Sun 9am–5pm • Free • ☎0771 2847055, ⓦ www.gxmuseum.com • Bus #6, #34 or #79 from Chaoyang Lu

Nanning's well-presented **Provincial Museum** provides an insight into the **Baiyue culture**, which flourished in southern Guangxi from prehistoric times until the early Han dynasty. The pick of the exhibits are **bronze storage drums** embossed with stylized images of rowers and birds which, according to a Ming historian, became a symbol of power: "Those who possess bronze drums are chieftains, and the masses obey them; those who have two or three drums can style themselves king". Drums were cast locally right up until the late Qing dynasty; their ceremonial use survives among several ethnic groups in China, Southeast Asia and Indonesia.

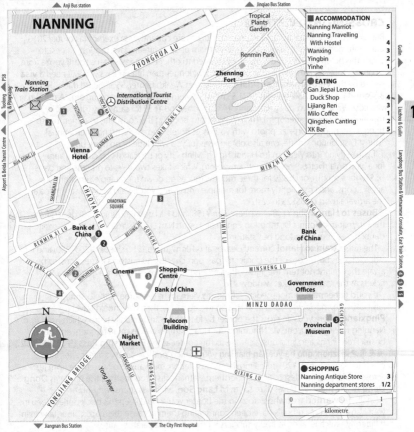

ARRIVAL AND DEPARTURE

NANNING

The easiest way of organizing onward travel from Nanning is to go to the Nanning International Tourist Distribution Centre (南宁国际旅游集散中心, nánníng guójì lǚyóu jísàn zhōngxīn), just 5min walk from the train station at 5 You'an Nan Lu (daily 9am–6pm; ☎ 0771 2102456, ☜ yunde.net). They can book buses to Vietnam and destinations served by the Langdong bus station, train tickets (excluding Hanoi), as well as tours and car rental. The government website (☜ english .nanning.gov.cn) carries timetables, as well as other transport information, though check if it's been updated recently.

BY PLANE

Nanning airport (南宁吴圩机场, nánníng wúxū jīchǎng) is 32km southwest of Nanning, with flights across China, and also to Vietnam, Laos, Myanmar and Thailand. Airport bus #1 (hourly; 45min; ¥15) runs to outside the *Weiyena* (Vienna) hotel near the train station on Chaoyang Lu; or the more frequent #301 bus (every 15–20min) will take you to the centre for just ¥3. Taxis run exactly the same route for around ¥100, or ¥25 per person shared.

Destinations Bangkok (2hr); Beijing (3hr 10min); Chengdu (2hr); Chongqing (1hr 35min); Guangzhou (1hr 15min); Guilin (55min); Guiyang (1hr); Hanoi (2 weekly; 50min); Ho

Chi Minh City (3 weekly; 2hr); Hong Kong (1hr 40min); Kunming (1hr 25min); Shanghai (2hr 40min); Shenzhen (1hr 25min); Vientiane (3 weekly; 1hr 35min); Xi'an (2hr 15min); Yangon (1 weekly; 2hr 40min).

BY TRAIN

Nanning Station (南宁火车站, nánníng huǒchē zhàn) sits at the top of Chaoyang Lu, and is used by the majority of regular trains, some CRH services, as well as those to Vietnam. For buying tickets you're advised to use the less crowded International Tourist Distribution Centre ticket office.

CRH destinations Beihai (3 daily; 1hr 45min); Beijing

10

CROSSING INTO VIETNAM

British, French, German, Italian and Spanish citizens are currently visa exempt (as of July 2016, but confirmed only for a year) for visits to Vietnam of up to fifteen days, though it's best to check this before you go, and it may be extended to other countries' citizens too. If you're from a country that requires a visa, or you're visiting for longer than fifteen days you will need a **visa** issued by the **Vietnamese Consulate**, 27F Yahang Wealth Center, 55 Jinhu Rd (Mon–Fri 8.30am–11.30am & 2.30–6pm; ☎0771 5510561, ⓦvietnamconsulate-nanning.org). A thirty-day visa costs ¥380 for two-day processing, ¥480 for one, and ¥650 for same day (drop off in morning and collect after 5pm). There is no photo-booth at the consulate so remember to bring a recent passport-size photo with you. Most hotels, and the Nanning International Tourist Distribution Centre, can also obtain visas for you with little or no mark-up.

If you're flying into Vietnam (to Hanoi, Ho Chi Minh City or Da Nang) you can also apply for a "visa on arrival" online at ⓦvietnamvisa.org, which takes two days to process and costs US$16 for a month, or US$29 for three months (prices go down for multiple simultaneous applications, and cost slightly more for multiple entry), and you'll need to pay a stamp fee at the arrival airport of US$25 in cash.

Buses to Hanoi (8hr; ¥148), Haiphon (8hr; ¥158) and Ha Long Bay (8hr; ¥168) depart from the International Tourist Distribution Centre on You'an Nan Lu (see p.629); you can also catch Hanoi buses from Langdong bus station.

The direct **train to Hanoi** currently leaves at 6.10pm (up to 12hr; sleeper ¥200–350) and it stops for ages both sides of the border for passport checks and customs inspections, so be aware they might not turn the lights off till around 1am – eye shades are a good idea. Buy tickets at the station at ticket window #16.

If you'd rather make a more sedate journey to Vietnam to see some of the beautiful landscape down this way, such as at Hua Shan (see p.634), then you should travel to **Pingxiang** where you can cross the border by foot. There are five daily trains which head from Nanning to Pingxiang, one via Ningming (for Hua Shan), as well as more frequent and faster buses. From Pingxiang, minibuses shuttle to the border at the **Friendship Pass** (中国和越南边境友谊之路, zhōngguó hé yuènán biānjìng yǒuyì zhīlù), or there are two direct afternoon buses to Hanoi (5–6hr; ¥70) from Pingxiang's bus station; minivans also head there from just across the border. For destinations to northern Vietnam, first stop south of the border is **Dong Dang** where there are buses 5km south to **Lang Son**, which is a transport hub.

Finally, be **warned** that when crossing the border you should keep this book buried deep in your bags – customs officials have been confiscating them because the maps colour Taiwan in differently, which is taken to imply support for the island's separatist cause.

(daily 9.13am; 13hr 42min); Guangzhou (5 daily; 4hr 21min); Guilin (13 daily; 2hr 30min–2hr 53min).

Other destinations Beijing (2 daily; 22hr 53min–30hr); Chengdu (1 daily; 27hr 30min); Chongqing (1 daily; 22hr 20min); Guangzhou (5 daily; 12hr–15hr); Guilin (12 daily; 3–7hr); Hanoi (1 daily 6.10pm; 12hr); Kunming (7 daily; 12hr 35min–15hr 27min); Pingxiang (2 daily; 4hr–5hr 15min); Shanghai (4 daily; 24hr 13min–32hr 30min); Tuolong/Ningming (1 daily; 4hr 7min).

Nanning East (南宁火车东站, nánníng huǒchē dōng zhàn) is the largest in Guangxi, about 11km east of the main station and used by high-speed trains, most notably those heading to Guangzhou and the new Kunming service which starts in 2017. It is served by buses #7, #28, #29, #37, #82, #83, #94 and #209.

CRH destinations Beihai (16 daily; 1hr 35min); Beijing (daily 8am; 13hr 9min); Guangzhou (36 daily; 3hr 19min–4hr 21min); Guilin (16 daily; 2hr 22min–2hr 44min); Kunming (TBA); Shanghai (1 daily; 12hr 10min).

BY BUS

Beida Transit Centre (北大客运中心, běidà kèyùn zhōngxīn), 1km from the train station at 26 Beida Bei Lu, is of most use for traffic to Daxin (for Detian Waterfall), and Kunming.

Jiangnan bus station (江南汽车站, jiāngnán qìchēzhàn) is 7km south of Chaoyang Lu at 236 Xingguangon Dadao and served by the #41 bus (allow 40min), or a taxi costs around ¥20. Destinations cover the southwestern border area such as Ningming and Pingxiang, as well as Guilin, and inter-provincial buses to Haikou and Guangzhou.

Destinations Bama (4 daily; 4hr); Beihai (hourly until 3.40pm; 3hr); Daxin (every 30min; 3hr); Guangzhou (8 night buses daily 5.30–9.30pm; 14hr); Haikou (4.40pm, 5.40pm & 6.40pm; 6hr); Ningming (3 daily; 4hr); Pingxiang (4 daily; 5hr).

Langdong bus station (琅东客运站, lángdōng kèyùn zhàn), 10km east of the centre on Minzu Dadao

– a #6 bus will get you to Chaoyang Lu within 50min. Nanning's biggest bus station, with departures for Vietnam, as well as cities all across China including frequent services to Guilin and Guiyang. Buy tickets at the International Tourist Distribution Centre, or the *Vienna* hotel from where the airport bus also runs; they also have timetables in English.

Destinations Guilin (every 15min; 5hr); Guiyang (hourly; 16hr); Ha Long Bay (8.20am & 9am; 8hr); Hanoi (6 daily, 7.30–9.40am; 8hr); Yangshuo (every 15min; 4hr).

Anji station (安吉汽车站, ānjí qìchē zhàn). On Anji Dadao 9km north of Nanning train station, reached via bus #276.

Destinations Bama (3 daily; 4hr); Fengshan (6 daily; 5hr).

GETTING AROUND

By bus Bus maps, which are pretty good for navigation too, are available from the otherwise useless tourist office next to the train station or from the main bus stations. Bus #6 is very useful, running as it does from the main train station, down Chaoyang Lu, and then along Minzu Dadao.

By taxi In the city itself, a taxi costs ¥9 to hire for the first couple of kilometres, with a ¥1 fuel surcharge added to all trips.

By three-wheeler rickshaw These cost about the same as a taxi, but are far more adept at slipping through the traffic, quite often via the pavement.

ACCOMMODATION

There's abundant good-value, central accommodation in Nanning for all budgets. Unusually for China, the train station area is by no means seedy or unpleasant.

Nanning Marriot 南宁鑫伟万豪酒店, nánníng xīn wěi wànháo jiǔdiàn. 131 Minzu Dado ⚐0771 5366688, ⓦmarriott.com. Pretty much the only international standard hotel in town, the rooms are large and well equipped, as you'd expect from *Marriot*, as are the spa, gym and pool. One of its three restaurants serves Western food, including breakfasts (¥128). **¥539**

Nanning Travelling With Hostel 南宁瓦舍旅行酒店, nánníng wǎ shè lǚxíng jiǔdiàn. 3 Jiefang Lu ⚐0771 2813977. Centrally located hostel just 2km from the train station, with good, clean dorms as well as doubles and triples. Also has a stylish communal area with a café serving international food. They speak English and can help with information and Vietnam visas. Wi-fi throughout. Dorms **¥40**, doubles **¥130**

★**Wanxing** 万兴酒店, wànxīng jiǔdiàn. 47 Minzhu Lu ⚐0771 2381000, ⓦnnwxhotel.com. Behemothic, budget business hotel not far from Nanning train station

with two buildings, a block apart. The newer and far better wing is at this address, and you can't miss it. Bright doubles with large comfortable beds, and usually discounted by almost half if booked online. **¥438**

Yingbin 迎宾饭店, yíngbīn fàndiàn. 71 Chaoyang Lu ⚐0771 2116288, ⓔyingbin.hotel@yahoo.com. Unpretentious budget option more or less opposite Nanning train station, taking up almost a whole block above fast-food canteens. Clean throughout, but some rooms are basic with hard beds – have a look at a few. **¥135**

Yinhe 银河宾馆, yínhé bīnguǎn. 84–86 Chaoyang Lu ⚐0771 2116688. Two buildings 50m apart; the northernmost budget wing, though slightly institutional, has spick-and-span doubles (¥160), while the main hotel has more comfortable rooms with computers (as does the budget wing for ¥30 more), though the carpets are showing wear. **¥380**

EATING

The best place for inexpensive buns, dumplings, noodles, grilled chicken wings, steamed packets of lotus leaf-wrapped *zongzi* and basic stir-fries are along the eastern end of Hua Dong Lu or at the night market on Zhongshan Lu – though be careful of pickpockets with long tweezers. Western fast-food chains are grouped in the modern plaza development north of the corner of Chaoyang Lu and Minzu Dadao.

Gan Jiepai Lemon Duck Shop 甘界牌柠檬鸭店, gānjièpái níngméngyā diàn. 12–2 Yuanhu Nan Lu ⚐0771 5855585. Popular place specializing in local cuisine and featuring the zingy lemon duck (whole bird ¥148) of its name. Well-presented dishes, good portions and a comfortable environment make this an enjoyable place to eat. This branch is just off Minzu Dado, with another further south at 16-2 Qingshan Lu. Around ¥40–50 per person If ordering other dishes off the photo menu.

Daily 11am–11pm.

Lijiang Ren 漓江人, líjiāng rén. 2F Gelan Yuntian Plaza, Chaoyang Lu ⚐0771 2843805. Yunnanese chain situated up the wooden stairs on the southwest corner of the building offering chilli-rich stews and stir-fries in comfortable period surroundings. Mains come in at around ¥25–80 for large portions. Daily 9.30am–10pm.

Milo Coffee 米罗咖啡, mǐluó kāfēi. 7 You Ai Lu ⚐0771 2428908. Situated a few minutes' walk from

TRAVELLING TO HAINAN ISLAND

As an alternative route to **Hainan Island** (see p.525), there are ferries running from Guangxi's sole seaport at Beihai (北海, běihǎi), some 200km southeast of Nanning, connected by frequent high-speed trains, and buses (every 30min from Jiangnan station). There are two daily sailings to Haikou in Hainan from the Beihai International Port (北海国际客运港, běihǎi guójì kèyùngǎng), departing at 6pm and 6.30pm (☎0779 3904011; 12hr; seats ¥140, basic private cabins ¥280/person). Note that toilets are shared, and hot water urns and a snack shop are the only sources of refreshment.

the train station, this place isn't especially cheap, but good if you're hankering after coffee (¥18–48) and light Western-style meals (¥20–38). In addition, its very comfortable sofas and good a/c make it an ideal place to nurse a drink if you've got to wait for a train. Daily 10am–1.30am.

Qingzhen Canting 清真餐厅, qīngzhēn cāntīng. 25 Xinhua Lu ☎135 58483838. Inexpensive Muslim restaurant on the first two floors of the pale green mosque. Spicy noodle soups are served for under ¥8 on the ground floor with more sophisticated dishes such as lemon duck or

a pretty good South Asian-style mutton curry upstairs for ¥30–80. Daily 6.30am–8pm; second floor till 10pm.

XK Bar 中西吧, zhōngxī bā. 13-8 Yuanhu Road Xiyili ☎135 57118234. Intimate Sino-British-owned bar tucked down a backstreet off Minzu Dado about 1km east of the museum. Has a nice mix of local and expat clientele and serves inexpensive sausage (or pie) and mash, fish and chips (¥30–35) and some German beers. The English owner can point you in the direction of the rest of the expat scene, including the *Queen's Head English Style Pub*, though it's way out of the centre. Daily 7.30pm–after 2am.

SHOPPING

Nanning is a great place to shop for clothes, either at the Nanning department stores full of good-quality, low-price attire along Chaoyang Lu (including a Wal-Mart) or at the brand-label stores along Xingning Lu, such as Giordano, Baleno Meters/Bonwe and Yishion.

Nanning Antique Store 南宁古董店, nánníng gǔdǒng diàn. 19-2 Gucheng Lu. Along with a string of similar shops on the same street next to the Provincial

Museum, this has a touristy and expensive selection of teapots, chopsticks, paintings and jade, set across two floors. Daily 9am–6pm.

DIRECTORY

Banks The main Bank of China (foreign exchange Mon–Fri 8–11.30am & 2.30–5.30pm) is on Gucheng Lu.
Hospital The City First Hospital (市第一医院, shì dìyī yīyuàn) is southeast of the centre at 89 Qi Xing Lu and is probably the best in the region.

Visa extensions The visa department (Mon–Thurs 9am–4.30pm, Fri 9am–noon; ☎0771 2891264) is 1.5km north of the train station, at 4 Xiuling Lu. Catch bus #14, #31, #71, #72, #84 or #85 and get off after the hospital – it's about 100m south of the East Gate of Guangxi University.

Detian Waterfall

德天瀑布, détiān pùbù • Daily 6am–6.30pm • ¥80 • ☎0771 5595608

Perched right on the Vietnamese border 150km west of Nanning, **Detian Waterfall** is worth the trip not just for the falls – best in full flood during the summer rains – but also because it draws you into the Zhuang heartlands: a world of dark karst hills, grubby towns, water buffalo wallowing in green paddy fields, and farmers in broad-sleeved pyjamas and conical hats.

The **village** down the hill from the park entrance is more or less just a bus stand surrounded by hotels, gift shops and restaurants, but the falls themselves form a delightful set of cataracts broader than their 30m height and framed by limestone peaks and fields. Paths lead down to the base past a series of pools and bamboo groves; at the bottom you can hire a **bamboo raft** and be punted over to straddle the mid-river borderline. The best part, however, is to follow the road along the top to its end in a field, where you'll find a **stone post** (known as Stone 53) proclaiming the Sino-Vietnamese frontier in French and

10

Chinese, along with a bizarre **border market** – a clutch of trestle tables laden with Vietnamese sweets, cigarettes and stamps in the middle of nowhere – haggle hard and check anything you buy carefully as they're used to ripping off tourists, and few customers are likely to return.

ARRIVAL AND DEPARTURE	DETIAN WATERFALL

By bus During the summer at least, there's one direct bus daily to Detian from Nanning's Langdong bus station at 8.30am (3hr; ¥75). Otherwise, catch a bus from the Beida Transit Centre to Daxin (大新, dàxīn; every 30min; 3hr; ¥45–55), from where there are hourly minibuses direct to Detian (2hr; ¥40).

ACCOMMODATION AND EATING

There are fairly cheap places to eat in the main square of the village where you can fill up for under ¥30, or the *Detian Shanzhuang* has more formal (and expensive) dining.

Detian Binguan 德天宾馆, détiān bīnguǎn. ☎0771 5595608. This place offers clean, comfortable rooms just off and above the main square and bus station with many other less expensive options opposite. You can use the receipt to get your ticket to the falls validated for an extra day at the entrance. **¥178**

Detian Shanzhuang 德天山莊大酒店, détiān shānzhuāng dàjiǔdiàn. ☎0771 3773570. Perched on a slope above the falls, so some rooms (for ¥210 extra) offer stunning views of the cascade and across the river into Vietnam. Rooms are a bit shabby, but then you're paying for the location. Also has a mid-price restaurant, but few other facilities. **¥158**

Hua Shan

花山, huāshān • ¥80

If you fancy seeing more of the countryside between Nanning and Vietnam, **Hua Shan** is well worth the slight effort. Set in a beautifully isolated spot where tall karst peaks flank the **Zuo River**, waterfront cliffs at Hua Shan are daubed with **rock art** associated with prehistoric local culture. You can only get here by boat, and it's a placid journey up the Zuo, with buffalo wallowing in the shallows, people fishing from bamboo rafts and tending family plots, and the banks thick with spindly-branched, red-flowering kapok trees. The boat docks by the paintings, where steps lead to viewing platforms to see them close up. Nobody has worked out a definitive interpretation of the 1900 figures, but they include drummers and dancers, dogs and cattle, a dragon-boat race, men with arms bent upwards, a "king" with a sword, and just two women, long-haired and pregnant. Interesting as the paintings are, as with many of the best travels, the journey there is more rewarding than the destination. The site is currently being considered for UNESCO World Heritage status, which if successful will inevitably lead to development, which will make it more accessible, though no doubt more crowded.

ARRIVAL AND GETTING AROUND	HUA SHAN

The access point for Hua Shan is Ningming (宁明, níngmíng). From Ningming you need to get to the site entrance and ticket office at Hua Shan village, 10km downstream from the rock art itself.

By train Ningming station (宁明站, níngmíng zhàn) is right on the river, with one daily departure each to Nanning (2.54pm; 4hr 36min) and the Vietnam border at Pingxiang (12.05pm; 1hr).

By bus Ningming's bus station is 5km distant from the train station and river in the town itself. Regular buses run to Nanning until 7.50pm (2hr) and to Pingxiang until 6.20pm (1hr).

By rickshaw and boat You can take a rickshaw (¥50; 30min) along a very bumpy 9km road from Ningming to Hua Shan village, where you can get to the rock paintings by hiring a private boat (up to 6 people) for ¥300–400 (plus entry ticket ¥80/person), though if you hang around the dock you can often tag along for free with package groups – the trip from the Hua Shan village takes two hours there and back, with 30min at the site.

ACCOMMODATION AND EATING

NINGMING

Ningming is a cheaply built-up concrete town. Good street food is available along Dehua Lu where, as probably the only foreigner in town, you'll be the focus of good-natured attention. **Jin Yuan Hotel** 金圆旅馆, jīnyuán lǚdiàn. Near the bridge on Jiangbin Nan Lu, about 3km south of the train station, and 3km east of the bus station – ¥10 in a rickshaw from either ☎0771 8622189. Good rooms for the price, which are clean and very homey – and some even overlook the river. **¥108**

HUA SHAN VILLAGE

Hua Shan Resort 华山度假村, huáshān dùjiàcūn. ☎137 68596977. Huge, clean rooms with balconies looking out upon jungles and cliffs on the edge of the village make this a great place to stay, and only slightly more expensive than the cheapest hotels in Ningming. Has an overpriced but decent restaurant opposite, and very flexible room rates. **¥180**

10

Bama and around

巴马, bā mǎ

Some 250km north of Nanning, **BAMA** autonomous county is a little-known destination, and well worth getting off the beaten trail to visit. There's nothing much to the town of Bama itself but the surrounding countryside is filled with some wonderful **karst scenery** cut through by the winding Panyang River, over sixty (largely unexplored) **limestone caves** and many relatively unspoilt villages – comparisons can be made to Yangshuo before it became such a boom town. Tourism here is in its infancy, and most of the elderly Chinese tourists are here for its famous "longevity villages", where more than eighty centenarians reside. This is put down to the clean air and water, as well as the locals' consumption of many hemp products; they cook with hemp oil and eat hemp seed. One of several such villages you can visit is **Pingan** (40min from Bama).

However, the region's obvious attractions have been spotted by the tourist board, and change will probably happen quickly, with a few of the larger caves already being developed for tourism, and package tours are set to be introduced – although given the sheer number of caves, you can easily head off yourself to explore deserted ones. It's not exactly set up for foreign tourists, though with the opening of *The Farmhouse Retreat* (see below) between Poyue and Fengshan it's become easier. Attractions include the undeveloped **Xing Shan waterfall** (on the Poyue–Fengshan road), the 80m high **Baimo Cave** (5km from Poyue), the even bigger three caverns at **Fairy Cave** (25km from Poyue) and **San Min Hai**, "the three gates sea", an underground river so big it has tides, and can be navigated by boat. The last three are all being developed and will likely charge fairly hefty entrance fees when facilities are completed (¥100–150).

ARRIVAL AND DEPARTURE   BAMA

By bus Bama (and Poyue) are both only accessible by bus, most easily from Nanning and there are numerous buses to Bama from all of Nanning's bus stations (4hr), with one daily bus at 8.30am from Guilin's long-distance bus station (9hr) and another from Baise (which has an airport) at 9.30am (3hr 40min). From Bama, minibuses run to Poyue regularly when full (40min), while there are buses from Nanning's Anji bus station (9km north of Nanning train station on Anji Dadao) to Fengshan (6 daily; 5hr), which pass by *The Farmhouse Retreat* above Poyue (see below).

GETTING AROUND

Buses and minibuses run out to all of the sights (ask for details at your accommodation), or an easier option would be to hire a minivan for the day (6–8 people; 8hr; ¥450–500) or a motorbike from *The Farmhouse Retreat*.

ACCOMMODATION

The Farmhouse Retreat Poyue ☎188 77845663, ⓦthefarmhouseretreatbama.com. Although there are numerous hotels in Bama itself (¥70–300), none are really set up for non-Chinese-speaking visitors, and this place run by English-speaking outsiders is by far your best bet. Situated on a hill by the road to Fengshan, it commands sublime views over Poyue village, and along the Panyang River and surrounding karst scenery. Rooms are fairly basic, but clean and comfortable, and the price includes breakfast and dinner (for two people), made with organic ingredients grown in their garden. **¥130**

Guizhou

贵州, guìzhōu

A traditional saying describes **Guizhou** as a land where there are "no three days without rain, no three fields without a mountain, and no three coins in any pocket". This is sadly accurate: Guizhou records the highest rainfall in China and has a poverty ensured by more than eighty percent of its land being covered in untillable mountains or leached limestone soils.

Still, ethnic identity and romantic landscapes have become marketable commodities in China, and Guizhou is beginning to capitalize on its two major assets. The province's most visible minority groups are the many branches of **Miao**, concentrated in the southeast around **Kaili**; and the **Bouyei**, who are based around the provincial capital, **Guiyang**, and the westerly town of **Anshun**. The Miao in particular indulge in a huge number of festivals, some of which attract tens of thousands of participants and are worth any effort to experience. As for **scenery**, there are spectacular **limestone caverns** at **Dragon (Loong) Palace Scenic Area** and Zhijin, both accessed from Anshun; impressive **waterfalls** at **Huangguoshu** – again near Anshun; and everywhere terraced hills, dotted with small villages. Naturalists will want to clock up rare **black-necked cranes**, which winter along the northwestern border with Yunnan at **Caohai Lake**; and at least have a stab at seeing the reclusive **golden monkey**, which lives in the cloud forests atop Guizhou's single holy mountain, northeasterly **Fanjing Shan**.

While Guizhou's often shambolic towns are definitely not a high point of a trip to the region, the one place worth a visit in its own right is **Zhenyuan**, over on the eastern side of the province, which features some antique buildings and temples squeezed along a beautiful stretch of river.

Brief history

Chinese influence was established here around 100 BC, but it wasn't until the government began settling Han migrants in the province during the seventeenth century that the local **ethnic groups** began to fight back, resistance culminating in the **Miao Uprising** of 1854–73, which rivalled the contemporary Taiping insurrection in terms of chaos and bloodshed. Sixty years later the region still hadn't recovered: Red Army soldiers passing through Guizhou in the 1930s found people working naked in the fields and an economy based on opium, and it's only in the last decades that Guizhou's population has exceeded numbers prior to the uprising. Today it's mining – coal and limestone – and tourism that keep Guizhou's economy afloat.

Guiyang

贵阳, guìyáng

GUIYANG lies in a valley basin, encircled by a range of hills that hems in the city and concentrates its traffic pollution. Established as a capital during the Ming dynasty, modern Guiyang is a patchwork of elderly apartment blocks rubbing shoulders with glossy new high-rises and department stores, all intercut by a web of wide roads and flyovers. The effect may be downmarket and provincial, but Guiyang is a friendly place, whose unexpected few antique buildings and surprisingly wild parks lend a bit of character. With a spare half-day, it's worth making an easy side-trip to the old garrison town of **Qingyan**, whose cobbled lanes and merchants' guildhalls provide a relief from Guiyang's crowded streets.

Along the river

The start of a 500m-long paved riverside promenade begins at the rather bland **Qianming Temple** (黔明寺, qiánmíng sì) and runs east to an arched stone bridge across the river to **Jiaxiu Lou** (甲秀楼, jiǎxiù lóu; ¥10), a 29m-high, three-storey pavilion. This dates back to 1598, built to inspire students taking imperial examinations; it now holds a teahouse and photos from the 1930s. Continue on across the bridge to the far bank, and you're outside **Cuiwei Yuan** (粹惟园, cuìwéi yuán; ¥5), a Qing-dynasty ornamental garden whose buildings have served a variety of purposes over the years, and currently house tearooms and souvenir shops.

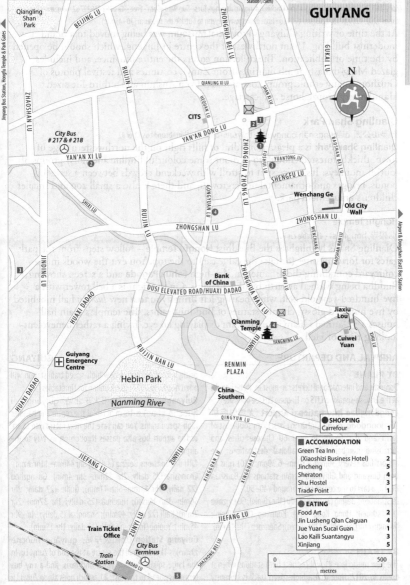

GUIYANG

10

SHOPPING
Carrefour 1

ACCOMMODATION
Green Tea Inn
 (Xiaoshizi Business Hotel) ... 2
Jincheng 5
Sheraton 4
Shu Hostel 3
Trade Point 1

EATING
Food Art 2
Jin Lusheng Qian Caiguan ... 4
Jue Yuan Sucai Guan 1
Lao Kaili Suantangyu 3
Xinjiang 5

Wenchang Ge

文昌阁, wénchāng gé

About 750m northeast of the centre up Wenchang Nan Lu, you'll find a restored fragment of Guiyang's old city wall, the 7m-high battlements capped by **Wenchang Ge**, a gate tower with flared eaves and wooden halls, built in 1596 and nowadays converted to yet another breezy teahouse.

The Provincial Museum

10

省博物馆, shěng bówùguǎn • Linchengdong Lu, Jinyang • Tues–Sun 9am–5pm • Free • ☎ 0851 86822762, ⓦ gzmuseum.com • Buses #208, #209,#218, #263 and #281 run from downtown Guiyang to outside the museum (30–45min)

At the time of writing Guiyang's **Provincial Museum** was being moved to a brand-new modernist building, 15km northwest of the centre in Jinyang, which should be opened by the time of publication. The collection covers the entire province, and includes glazed Ming-dynasty tomb figurines from Zunyi, costumes and festival photos of Guizhou's many ethnic groups, opera masks from Anshun and a third-life-sized Han-dynasty bronze horse and carriage.

Qianling Shan Park

黔灵山公园, qiánlíngshān gōngyuán • Daily 6am–6pm • ¥5 • Northbound bus #1 or #2

Qianling Shan Park is a pleasant handful of hills right on the northwestern edge of town, thickly forested enough to harbour some colourful birdlife and noisy groups of loutish monkeys. It's a nice spot to stroll with weekend crowds between a series of ponds, bridges and ornamental undergrowth, and there is also a small **zoo** and smaller children's **amusement park**.

Hongfu Temple

弘福寺, hóngfú sì • ¥5; cable car ¥12

Qianling Shan's highlight is the Buddhist **Hongfu Temple** – follow steps from the park gates for forty minutes (or take the cable car) to the top. You exit the woods into a courtyard containing the ornamental, 4m-high **Fahua Pagoda** and a screen showing Buddha being washed at birth by nine dragons. On the right is a bell tower with a five-hundred-year-old bell, while bearing left brings you to a new *luohan* hall inhabited by five hundred glossy, chunky statues of Buddhist saints. The temple's main hall houses a 32-armed Guanyin, each palm displaying an eye, facing a rather benevolent-looking King of Hell.

ARRIVAL AND DEPARTURE

GUIYANG

BY PLANE

Domestic and international tickets can most easily be bought at the English-speaking CITS on Hequan Lu (see opposite).

Longdongbao International Airport (龙洞国际机场, lóngdòng guójì jīchǎng) lies 15km southeast of town and has flights to over 60 Chinese cities and increasing numbers of international destinations; the airport bus (every 30min 8.30am–6.30pm; ¥10) runs to both Guiyang and Guiyangbei train stations via Baoshan Bei Lu; a taxi to the centre costs around ¥40–50.

Destinations Beijing (3hr); Chengdu (1hr 20min); Guangzhou (1hr 40min); Hong Kong (2hr); Kunming (1hr 10min); Nanning (1hr); Shanghai (2hr 30min); Shenzhen (1hr 40min).

BY TRAIN

The new metro line #1 will connect both stations when it opens in 2017. Note that a high-speed track is currently

being built to Anshun. A new high-speed train station will open nearby in 2017; check online for timetables.

Guiyangbei (North) (贵阳火车北站, guìyáng běi huǒchē zhàn) is 16km north of the centre and handles high-speed trains. You can take the new metro into town, or the airport bus also passes through on its way to the airport.

CRH destinations Beijing (3 daily; 8hr 44min–11hr 9min); Changsha (25 daily; 2hr 22min–3hr 4min); Guangzhou (22 daily; 4hr 11min–5hr 41min); Guilin (27 daily; 2hr 56min–3hr 44min); Huaihua (25 daily; 1hr 32min–2hr 7min); Kaili (22 daily; 40min); Shanghai (5 daily; 9hr–9hr 45min); Yuping/Tongren South (17 daily; 1hr 15min).

Guiyang Station (贵阳火车站, guìyáng huǒchē zhàn) is 1km south of the centre at the end of Zunyi Lu. In the large square outside you'll find taxis, and a city bus terminus ahead to the east: #1, which goes along Zunyi Lu and Zhonghua Lu, turning west along Beijing Lu and back to the train station down Ruijin Lu; and bus #2, which does the same route in reverse, are the two best routes for getting you close to the hotels.

Destinations Anshun (27 daily; 1hr 10min); Beijing (7 daily; 26hr 42min–41hr 30min); Changsha (8 daily; 12–15hr); Chengdu (6 daily; 13hr 33min–24hr 44min); Chongqing (7 daily; 8hr 32min–13hr); Guangzhou (5 daily; 20hr 27min–23hr 53min); Huaihua (30 daily; 6hr–7hr 47min); Kaili (26 daily; 2hr 20min–3hr); Kunming (18 daily; 7–11hr); Liupanshui/Shuicheng (26 daily; 3hr 16min–5hr 49min); Shanghai (6 daily; 26hr 10min–30hr); Yuping/Tongren South (23 daily; 4hr 25min–7hr 44min); Zhenyuan (11 daily; 3hr 43min–5hr 31min); Zunyi (5 daily; 3hr–4hr 43min).

BY BUS

Coming from either long-distance bus station, touts will pick up passengers for share-taxis going to the centre for around ¥10, saving you time and stress. For up-to-date bus information you can translate the Guizhou Provincial Transport Department website ⓦ www.qjt.gov.cn.

Jinyang bus station (金阳客车站, jīnyáng kèchēzhàn) is a colossal depot about 15km west of the city, handling departures to more or less everywhere; from here, catch bus #8, #209 or #266 to Guiyangbei train station, #219 or #224 to Guiyang train station, #28 or #29 (among many others) to Yan'an Lu and the centre of town, which takes about 1hr. Taxis charge about ¥50–60.

Destinations Anshun (7am–7pm every 30min; 1hr 30min); Chongqing (every 40min; 6hr 30min); Guangzhou (3 daily; 16hr); Huangguoshu (8 daily, last bus 10am; 3hr); Kunming (6 daily; 7hr); Nanning (6 daily; 9hr); Zhijin (7 daily; 1hr 30min); Zunyi (7am–7pm every 30min; 2hr 30min).

Dongzhan (East) bus station (龙洞公共汽车站, lóngdòng gōnggòng qìchē zhàn) is a bus station near the airport in Longdongbao that handles some provincial buses heading east and north of Guiyang (including Kaili). From here take a #240 bus to the train station; a taxi is again about ¥50–60, and takes 40min to an hour to the centre.

Destinations Anshun (8am–6pm every 40min; 1hr 30min); Kaili (every 20min; 2–3hr); Rongjiang (4 daily; 5hr); Zunyi (8am–6.20pm; every 40min; 2hr 30min).

GETTING AROUND

Getting around Guiyang can be a pain due to the horrendous traffic, some of the worst in China. Walking is usually quicker for shorter journeys, especially at rush hour.

By bus The bus system is straightforward, although buses are usually pretty crowded and slow, so are best avoided.

By taxi Taxis are in short supply, and if you can find a free one they start at ¥9 on the meter with a ¥1 fuel surcharge added to all journeys. Since there aren't enough taxis in the city, you can usually stop one which already has people in it and see if they're going your way (usually ¥10 within the centre), or you can use an illegal unmarked taxi, which will stop if you are standing by the road and usually charge double the normal fare.

By motorbike taxi The best way to hop round the centre is by motorbike taxi and you'll see them lining up at various roads within the city and on corners, usually wearing cheap red or yellow helmets. E-bikes cost ¥10 for up to 3–4km, and proper motorbikes usually charge ¥15 – they don't generally go on trips over 10km.

By metro The new Guiyang metro should open in 2017, with the first line running from Changbacun in the south to Xiamai West passing through Guiyang train station, Baoshan Bei Lu, Yan'an Lu, Beijing Lu, Jinyang and Guiyangbei train station.

INFORMATION

Travel agents CITS are at 7F, Longquan Dasha, 1 Hequan Lu, near the corner with Yan'an Dong Lu ☎ 0851 86901575 (Mon–Fri 9am–5pm; phone line 24hr). The 25-storey yellow tower is easy to find, but the entrance is not, especially as there is no CITS sign outside – you have to cut down the first alley on the left north of the junction, then turn left at the police post to a lift lobby at the back. The helpful staff speak English, French and German, and are a mine of information about the province, as well as being the easiest place to book flights, hotels and tours.

ACCOMMODATION

Guiyang's accommodation is mostly mid-range, and the few budget options for under ¥100, along Dadao Lu by the train station, are a bit grotty and usually fill quickly.

Green Tea Inn (Xiaoshizi Business Hotel) 格林豪泰 贵阳小十字商务酒店, gélín háo tài guìyáng xiǎo shízì shāngwù jiǔdiàn. Yan'An Lu/Zhonghua Lu intersection ☎0851 85223555, ⓦwww.998.com /HotelList. The best located of the chain hotels, it's right opposite the main post office, just west of the *Trade Point*. Some rooms might be a tad small and the corridors can smell of smoke, but they keep it very clean, the bathrooms are nice, and the beds are really comfortable. **¥158**

Jincheng 金城酒店, jīnchéng jiǔdiàn. 3 Dadao Lu

10

⊕0851 5764111. Almost opposite the *Home Inn* sign east of the train station, this mid-range place is one of the nicest near the train station for the price. Its cosy, slightly shabby rooms have comfortable beds, computers and very flexible prices. ¥336

Sheraton 喜来登贵航酒店, xǐláidēng guìháng jiǔdiàn. 49 Zhonghua Nan Lu ⊕0851 8588 8888, ⊚sheraton.com/hengg. Amazing marble construction featuring a bar on the 37th floor and an Italian restaurant on the 38th that offer great views at a price. Rooms are as luxurious and comfortable as you'd expect, and it also has a gym, pavement café outside, and an indoor swimming pool. ¥1105

Shu Hostel 贵阳墅国际青年驿栈, guìyáng shù guójì qīngnián yì zhàn. 86 Wujin Lu (near junction of Zhongshan Nan Lu and Junding Lu) ⊕181 9828 7383. Best of the hostel options in Guiyang, the location isn't ideal, situated by a busy road, but the dorms are good enough (if a little stuffy) and the rooms are quite comfortable and have enormous windows. However, the owner is Singaporean, speaks excellent English, and is a font of knowledge about off-the-beaten-trail locations in the region. Dorms ¥40, doubles ¥168

★**Trade Point** 柏顿宾馆, bódùn bīnguǎn. 18 Yan'an Dong Lu ⊕0851 5827888, ⊚www.trade-pointhotel.com. Sharp, four-star option in a central location with local, Cantonese and Western restaurants (the latter does buffets for breakfast 7–10.30am at ¥50/person for guests, ¥82 nonguests) and all executive trimmings, as well as a good coffee shop on the second floor. ¥528

EATING

With its predilection for chillies and sour soups (as well as dog meat), Guizhou's cuisine comes under the umbrella of western Chinese cooking, though there's a wide variety of food available in town. Snack stalls are scattered through the centre; the block on Fushui Lu north of Zhongshan Lu has several long-established, inexpensive duck canteens, serving it crisp-fried in the local style (ask them to hold the pepper if you don't want a numb mouth). One local speciality is thin crêpes – called "silk dolls" (丝娃娃, sīwáwa) – which you fill from a selection of pickled and fresh vegetables to resemble an uncooked spring roll. The best places to try them lie just outside Qianling Shan Park. Hotpots are a Guizhou institution, with tables centred round a bubbling pot of slightly sour, spicy stock, in which you cook your own food – the best are along Qingyun Lu and serve freshwater fish, fried in a hotpot at your table. The main drag for nightlife is along Xingguan Lu, which is dotted with Chinese-style drinking venues.

Food Art B1 Huijin Xing Licheng Mall, 66 Yan'an Xi Lu ⊕0851 88554530. Modern-looking restaurant in the basement of a shopping mall and your best bet for well-presented and tasty Italian food in Guiyang. The chef is Italian and it serves good pizza (¥48–98), excellent pastas and lasagne (¥38–68) as well as meat and fish dishes such as grilled lamb chops with Greek salad (¥78). And they make their own *gelato* (¥18–29). Daily 11am–10pm.

Jin Lusheng Qian Caiguan 金芦笙黔菜馆, jīn lúshēng qián càiguǎn. 18 Gongyuan Lu ⊕0851 5821388. Another ethnic theme restaurant, this time Miao. Downstairs is an inexpensive canteen with mostly noodle soups; head upstairs for more formal settings and a proper picture-menu with pricey mains around ¥45, with what looks like a pyramid of pig particularly popular. Daily 8am–9pm.

★**Jue Yuan Sucai Guan** 觉园素菜馆, juéyuán sùcàiguǎn. 49 Fushui Bei Lu ⊕0851 85841957. Vegetarian restaurant near a small Buddhist temple with a colourful upstairs dining area. Along with fairly inexpensive stir-fries, they also do Eight Treasure "Duck" (stuffed with sweet bean paste and sticky rice; ¥68), spicy hotpot (¥58) and curry tofu balls (¥30); all are made from meat substitutes. Photo menu and large portions. Daily 8am–8pm.

Lao Kaili Suantangyu 老凯里酸汤鱼, lǎo kǎi lǐ suān tāng yú. Fu Shui Bei Lu on the corner of Yuantong Ji ⊕0851 88111222. Popular place to try Kaili's famous spicy and tangy *suantangyu* (sour fish soup), one of the region's best known specialities. It has red lanterns (and seating) outside, as well as staff dressed in full Miao dress. Choose your fish from the tanks which costs ¥48–98 per *jin*, with one *jin* easily enough per person. Daily 11am–9.30pm.

Xinjiang 新疆维吾尔天山餐厅, xīnjiāng weíwú'ěr tiānshān hengg. Zunyi Lu, set back off the street north of Jiefang Lu ⊕138 85196882. Lively, rough and ready place offering various grilled meats, stews and noodles, from just a few yuan up to around ¥35. Best are the inexpensive lamb kebabs and fresh bread, cooked at the outside bread oven and barbecue. Daily 11am–10pm.

DIRECTORY

Banks The main Bank of China (Mon–Fri 9–11.30am & 1.30–5pm) with a foreign exchange is just west of Zhonghua Lu on Huaxi Dadao.

Visa extension The visa department is 16km northeast of the city on Lincheng Xi Lu in Jinyang (Mon–Fri 9am–noon & 1.30–5pm; ⊕0851 7987284), about 5min walk from the Wal-Mart. Bus #48 from downtown Guiyang stops almost outside. A relatively efficient and friendly branch.

CANINE CUISINE

Dog meat is somewhat appreciated not only in southwestern China, but also in culturally connected countries across Southeast Asia, with the meat considered to be warming in cold weather and an aid to male virility. For some Westerners, eating dog can be akin to cannibalism; others are discouraged by the way restaurants display bisected hindquarters in the window, or soaking in a bucket of water on the floor. If you're worried about being served dog by accident, 我不吃狗肉, **wǒ bùchī gǒuròu**, means "I don't eat dog". That being said, the practice is on the decline since so many people keep pet dogs these days, and most of the customers in city dog restaurants are from outside the region wanting to try the "local" foods. It's now mostly prevalent in rural areas.

Qingyan

青岩, qīngyán • Daily 8.30am–6.30pm • ¥10 for the streets (and the walls), ¥80 ticket for all the old buildings too

The remains of a Ming-dynasty fortified town 36km south of Guiyang at **QINGYAN** makes for an interesting few hours' excursion. On arrival, don't despair at the shabby bus station area, but turn left and left again then cross the road to the ticket office and entrance to the **old town** (古镇, gǔzhèn), which was founded in 1373 as a military outpost during the first major Han incursions into the region. The best area is at the southern end, where a flagstoned street lined with low wooden shops – most of them now given over to tourism concerns – leads to the **Baisui memorial arch** (百岁坊, bǎisuì hen), decorated with crouching lions, and out through the town wall into the fields via the solid stone south gate. Taking a stroll around the city walls is also recommended.

ARRIVAL AND DEPARTURE
QINGYAN

By bus Bus #203 from Guiyang train station runs to Qingyan (1hr 30min–2hr; ¥2) via Huaxi (花溪, huāxī), where most of Guizhou's universities are, so the traffic is quite bad and rush hour is best avoided. Transport back to

Guiyang runs until late afternoon.
By taxi It's much easier to take a cab which should cost around ¥70 and takes an hour.

ACCOMMODATION AND EATING

There are plenty of places to snack as you wander Qingyan's lanes – deep-fried balls of tofu are a local speciality – and even some accommodation.

Guzhen Kezhan 古镇客栈, gǔzhèn kèzhàn. 38 Dong Jie Lu ☎0851 83200031. An atmospheric hotel housed in an old guildhall next to the market, which can get noisy, so the rooms at the back are better. Still, it's clean and pleasant, with high ceilings and all mod cons, such as wi-fi. **¥168**

Zunyi

遵义, zūnyì

Some 170km north of Guiyang, **ZUNYI** is surrounded by heavy industry, but the city centre contains a pleasant older quarter and hilly parkland. It was here that the Communist army arrived on their **Long March** in January 1935 (see box, p.455), in disarray after months on the run and having suffered two defeats in their attempts to join up with sympathetic forces in Hunan. Having captured the city by surprise, the leadership convened the **Zunyi Conference**, at which Mao Zedong supplanted Russian Comintern advisers as political head of the Communist Party. The Russians had modelled their strategies on urban-based uprisings, but Mao felt that China's revolution could only succeed by mobilizing the peasantry, and that the Communist forces should base themselves in the countryside to do this. His opinions carried the day, marking the Communists' first step towards Beijing.

Zunyi is awkwardly laid out around triangular **Fenghuang Shan** (凤凰山, fènghuáng shān), with the old town and revolutionary sites 3km from arrival points on Fenghuang Shan's southwestern slopes.

The Zunyi Conference Site

遵义会议址, zūnyì huìyìzhǐ • Daily 8.30am–5.30pm • Free, passport required • Bus #1 or #3 from the train station via Beijing Lu

The **Zunyi Conference Site** occupies a block of the **old town** and adjacent lanes, with several restored 1930s grey-brick buildings restored and turned into museums. These include the grand **Zunyi Conference Museum** (遵义会议博物馆, zūnyì huìyì bówùguǎn) on Ziyin Lu, stocked with old photos, maps, heroic sculptures and a few period weapons captioned in Chinese; and the **Site of the Red Army Political Department** (红军总政治部 旧址, hóngjūn zǒng zhèngzhìbù jiùzhǐ) in the grounds of a French Catholic church behind, built in 1866 in an interesting compromise between Chinese and European Gothic styles. Strangely, the original Conference Hall is not even signposted – it's the locked, two-storey brick building on the right as you enter the Zunyi Conference Museum grounds. Just up the lane from here, 500m-long **Red Army Street** (红军街, hóngjūn jiē) has, ironically, been turned into the inevitable pedestrianized "old street", full of souvenirs and local snack stalls.

ARRIVAL AND DEPARTURE   ZUNYI

By train Zunyi's bus and train stations are within 100m of each other at the grimy eastern side of town. The train station sits off the eastern end of Beijing Lu, with services through the day to Guiyang and Chongqing. Destinations Chongqing (2 daily; 6hr 24min–8hr);

Guiyang (5 daily; 3hr–4hr 43min).
By bus The bus station is 100m from the train station. There are buses to Guiyang between 7am and 7pm (hourly; 2hr 30min) and three morning buses to Chishui (6hr).

ACCOMMODATION AND EATING

Frankly, Zunyi isn't a great place to stay, and frequent transport onwards means that you might not have to. Inexpensive accommodation surrounds the stations, where hostel staff pounce on passing foreigners. The area also has abundant places to get a bowl of noodles or plate of dumplings.

7 Days Inn 7天连锁酒店, qītiān liánsuǒ jiǔdiàn. 36 Beijing Lu, 250m west of the station area ☎ 0851 18702888, ⊕ www.7daysinn.com. Not quite up to the chain's usual standards – it looks as if it was built in a hurry and on a tight budget – but much more pleasant than anything else in the neighbourhood. **¥185**

Keyunzhan Binguan 客运站宾馆, kèyùnzhàn bīnguǎn. Right beside the bus station ☎ 0851 28460000. Basic, echoing concrete building offering bare comforts, but good enough if you get stuck in town for the night – though rooms at the front collect traffic noise wafting up from the street. **¥88**

Chishui

赤水, chìshuǐ

CHISHUI is a fairly large riverside town on the Sichuanese border, among a forested spread of red sandstone formations: *chishui* means "red water", and during the summer rains the river runs a vivid ochre colour. A substantial fragment of the old city walls stands down by the river, but the town is basically just a stepping-stone out to bamboos and waterfalls at Sidong Gou.

Sidong Gou

四洞沟, sìdòng gōu • Daily 8am–5pm • ¥85 • Minibus from the tourist bus station on Hebinxi Lu to the park gates ¥120, including entrance ticket

Some 15km from town, **Sidong Gou** comprises verdant pockets of bamboos, 3m-high *spinulosa* tree ferns, gingers, orchids and moss-covered rocks flanking a narrow gully. Six kilometres of flagstoned paths follow either side of a small, bright-red river, up through thick bamboo forests past four big **waterfalls** – including one split by a large boulder – and several water curtains to walk behind, to the trail's end at 30m-high **Bailong Falls** (白龙瀑布, báilóng pùbù).

ARRIVAL AND DEPARTURE CHISHUI

By bus Chishui's Keyun bus station (客运汽车站, kèyùn qìchēzhàn) is uphill from the river on Renmin Lu. From Guiyang, you'll need to change buses in Zunyi, which is pretty straightforward. To head into Sichuan, cross the river to tiny Jiuzhi (九支, jiǔzhī) and pick up one of the frequent minibuses to Luzhou (3hr), for connections to Yibin (see p.758).

10

ACCOMMODATION AND EATING

Stalls and cheap diners down along the river wall are the best places to eat, and there are also a few places to stay, though most suffer from damp.

Chishui Dajiudian 赤水大酒店, chìshuǐ dàjiǔdiàn. 106 Renmin Xi Lu ☏ 0851 22821334. Situated right next to the bridge that crosses the river into Sichuan, this place has some reasonable, fairly clean rooms which were renovated not too long ago. The deluxe rooms are worth paying ¥20 more for. **¥120**

Southeastern Guizhou

Southeastern Guizhou forms a landscape of high hills cut by rivers and dotted with dark wooden houses with buffaloes plodding around rice terraces. Women working in the fields have babies strapped to their backs under brightly quilted pads, and their long braided hair is coiled into buns secured by silver hairpins and fluorescent plastic combs. They are **Miao**, and their villages around the district capital, **Kaili**, are noted for their exuberant festivals, which though increasingly touristed have managed to retain their cultural integrity. Beyond Kaili, there's a scenic route southeast to the mountainous border with Guangxi province, where **Dong** hamlets sport their unique drum towers and bridges (see p.626). Kaili is connected by good road and rail links to Guiyang and neighbouring Hunan, with buses and minibuses providing regular services elsewhere. The new high-speed train line from Guangzhou to Guiyang passes though the region, and has brought with it an ethnic tourism boom.

Kaili

凯里, kǎilǐ

KAILI, 170km east of Guiyang, is a moderately industrialized, easy-going focus for China's 9.4 million Miao ethnic minority, though there's little to see in town. The most interesting **market area** is along the eastern end of Ximen Jie, a narrow street packed with village-like stalls selling vegetables, trinkets, meat and even some minority clothing. Dage Xiang heads uphill from here to **Dage Park** (大阁公园, dàgé gōngyuán), a paved area with a granite **pagoda** where old men gather to smoke and decorate the trees with their caged songbirds. The whole area at the top of Dage Xiang comes alive at night, when barbecue stalls with tables are set up, creating a very convivial atmosphere.

Minority Culture Museum

贵州省凯里博物馆, guìzhōu shěng kǎilǐ bówùguǎn · Zhaoshan Lu · Daily 9am–5pm · Free with passport

The town's only other diversion is the excellent **Minority Culture Museum** at the south end of Zhaoshan Lu, with three floors of bright festival garments and silver jewellery, a philately collection, photographs of many of the more famous festivals, and a potted history of the region – most displays have captions in English. Although a great little museum, it's not that visited, so remember to visit the galleries on each floor in an anticlockwise direction, or the automatic lights won't come on.

10

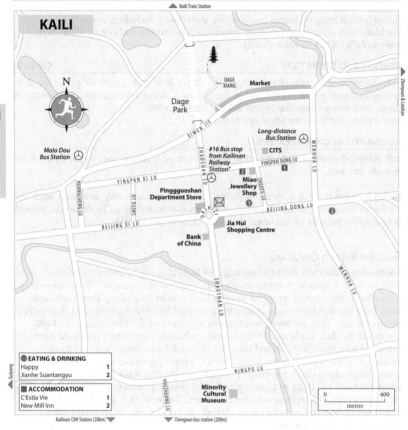

KAILI

Kaili Train Station

DAGE XIANG

Market

Dage Park

Long-distance Bus Station

XIMEN JIE

CITS

Maio Dou Bus Station

ZHAOSHAN LU

#16 Bus stop from Kailinan Railway Station"

YINGPAN DONG LU

YINGPAN XI LU

DASHI LU

ZHOUXI LU

WENHUA LU

HUANGCHENG LU

Pingguoshan Department Store

Miao Jewellery Shop

BEIJING DONG LU

BEIJING XI LU

Jia Hui Shopping Centre

Bank of China

SHAOSHAN LU

WENHUA LU

NINGPO LU

YOUZHUANG LU

Minority Cultural Museum

0   400
metres

Guiyang

Zhenyuan & Leishan

● EATING & DRINKING
Happy 1
Jianhe Suantangyu 2

■ ACCOMMODATION
C'Estla Vie 1
New Mill Inn 2

Kailinan CRH Station (20km) ▼   ▼ Chengnan bus station (200m)

ARRIVAL AND DEPARTURE

KAILI

BY PLANE

Kaili Huangping airport (凯利黄平机场, kǎilì huángpíng jīchǎng) must rate as being one of the furthest from the city it serves, a whopping 54km north in Huangping (see p.646). The tiny airport has flights to Guangzhou, Beijing, Kunming, Shanghai, Hangzhou, Chengdu and Guiyang, though lacks an airport bus; a taxi to Kaili should cost around ¥200, while one to Hunagping 14km away (from where hourly buses to Kaili run until 6pm) costs ¥20–25.

BY TRAIN

CRH The new Kailinan (South) train station (凯里南火车站, kǎilǐ nán huǒchē zhàn) is around 20km southwest of the centre and handles all high-speed services. Bus #16 (every 30min; 40min) heads straight to the centre; a taxi costs ¥50–60, and easily available share-taxis charge only ¥10 per person.

Destinations Beijing (1 daily; 10hr 17min); Changsha (5 daily; 2hr 36min–3hr 30min); Guangzhou (39 daily; 2hr 30min–5hr 37min); Guiyang (22 daily; 40min); Huaihua (20 daily; 1hr–1hr 27min); Shanghai (5 daily; 8hr 30min); Yuping (15 daily; 35min) ; Zhenyuan (11 daily; 1hr 14min–2hr 15min).

Other services The more centrally located Kaili train station (凯里火车站, kǎi lǐ huǒchē zhàn) is in the north of town, on the Hunan–Guiyang line. Catch buses #1 or #2 to the centre; a taxi or motorbike costs ¥10–15.

Destinations Beijing (3 daily; 24hr 20min–32hr 30min); Changsha (10 daily; 10hr 13min–15hr 30min); Guangzhou (1 daily; 19hr); Guiyang (26 daily; 2hr 20min–3hr); Huaihua (25 daily; 3hr 42min–4hr 51min); Shanghai (5 daily; 23hr 41min–27hr 11min); Yuping (22 daily; 2hr 10min).

BY BUS

Chengnan bus station (城南客车, chéngnán kèchē) Kaili's main bus station is a couple of kilometres south of the centre on Youzhuang Lu and connected to it via bus #16, which also heads to the CRH station. Bus #11 will get you to the Miao Dou bus station, or a taxi there (or the centre) should be ¥10.

Destinations Guilin (hourly; 4–5hr); Guiyang (every 30min till 4.40pm; 1hr 20min); Rongjiang (14 daily; 3hr); Tongren (hourly; 3hr); Zhenyuan (hourly; 2hr 30min).

Miao Dou bus station (苗都客运站, miáo dōu kèyùn zhàn), just west of the centre on Shiyu Lu, serves buses heading northeast to Matang, Chong An, Huangping,

Jiuzhou and Longcheng, in that order.

Destinations Chong An (hourly; 45min); Huangping (6 daily; 1hr 15min); Jiuzhou (4 daily, 2hr); Longcheng (2 daily, last at 2.20pm; 3hr); Matang (leave when full; 20min).

Long-distance Chengnan bus station (长途客运站, chángtú kèyùnzhàn) is just on the edge of the town centre on Wenhua Bei Lu, and is now quite badly named as most long-distance services leave from the Chengnan bus station. It does, however, have a handful of erratic local services for Xijiang, Leishan and Shidong.

INFORMATION AND TOURS

Travel agents Kaili's CITS is just left inside the gates at the old *Yingpanpo* hotel (Mon–Sat 8.30am–6pm; ☏ 0855 8222506, ⊛ guizhoucits.com). They have information about village festivals and market days, useful bilingual maps of Kaili and its environs (¥10), and guiding services in English starting at ¥500 per day. Ask for Wu Zeng Ou who is very knowledgeable about the region – especially the

Dong areas – and speaks excellent English. They can also arrange cars from ¥4/km.

Private guides For an extremely helpful and reliable Miao guide, contact Li Maoqing (8 Shaoshan Lu; ☏ 013 985298315, ✉ leemqing@hotmail.com, ⊛ tribaltours .net); he charges similar rates to the CITS and also speaks good English.

ACCOMMODATION

The old bus and train stations both sit among basic lodgings charging ¥100 or even less, though not all are foreigner-friendly and all have hard beds.

C'Estla Vie 营盘坡民族宾馆, yíngpánpō mínzú bīnguǎn. 44 Yingpan Dong Lu ☏ 0855 823 9111. This is probably the top mid-range in the centre of town, providing spotlessly clean rooms, soft beds and modern bathrooms. Also has an attached restaurant, and although staff speak no English, they're very friendly. **¥288**

New Mill Inn 新磨坊连锁酒店, xīnmòfāng liánsuǒ jiǔdiàn. 26 Yingpan Dong Lu ☏ 0855 2100188. Hidden down an alley off Yingpan Dong Lu, this is the nicest of Kaili's less expensive options. Rooms are very clean with surprisingly comfortable beds, and wooden floors. Staff don't speak any English but do their best to help you out. **¥138**

EATING

Bun and noodle stalls surround the old long-distance bus station on Wenhua Lu, though the best munching can be done at night either along the night-food street running west off Dage Xiang or around the pagoda in the old town, where you can eat various inexpensive barbecued foods on sticks at plastic outside tables.

Happy 开心, kāixīn. North off Beijing Dong Lu ☏ 189 08552949. Hidden behind barbecue stalls, this is a popular Taiwanese-style café selling bubble tea and light meals, including *siwawa* (¥15; "silk doll" thin crêpes) as well as various fairly inexpensive and tasty fried-rice dishes (¥18). Has an English menu and friendly service. Daily 11am–11.30pm.
Jianhe Suantangyu 剑河酸汤鱼, jiànhé

suāntāngyú. 83 Beijing Dong Lu ☏ 136 6855 8222. Best place in town to try the local speciality sour soup fish (酸汤鱼, suān tāng yú). Choose your fish, sit down and they'll kill it and bring it to you to cook on the table in a wonderfully pungent and tangy hotpot. Prices are ¥65–70/jin (500g), and a jin per person is more than sufficient to fill you up. Daily 11.30am–11pm.

DIRECTORY

Banks The main Bank of China and ATM is on Zhaoshan Lu (foreign exchange Mon–Fri 8.30–11am & 2–5pm) – the

last branch with foreign exchange until you reach Guilin in Guangxi province.

Northwest of Kaili

Some interesting places northwest of Kaili can be tied together into a long day-trip, or used as a stage in a roundabout journey to Zhenyuan (see p.649). The new valley road and elevated highway from Kaili to Jiuzhou, have made access to the area far easier, and has brought considerable and well-needed economic development, although at a cost to natural beauty – for rural idylls you just need to get a few kilometres off the main road, or head up further northwest to Longchang or Pingxi (both of which have accommodation).

Matang

麻塘, mátáng

MATANG, a village about 20km west of Kaili, is inhabited by **Geyi**, a group who, despite similarities with the Miao, insist on their individuality. Buses heading to Huangping or Longchang drop you off by a pink gateway on the main road, from where it's a twenty-minute walk to the village, an attractive place with many wooden buildings, although it hasn't had much maintenance in recent years and is looking a bit dog-eared. Big groups get a welcome dance and the main attraction is shopping for embroideries and **batik**, a Geyi speciality.

Chong An

重安, chóng'ān

Past Matang and about 35km from Kaili, **CHONG AN** is a rapidly developing riverside town with a few old wood-and-stone buildings at its core; but the main reason to visit is the superb **market** held every fifth day, where you'll be battered by diminutive Miao grandmothers as they shop or bring in clothes (everything from traditional pleated skirts to jeans) for dyeing in boiling vats of indigo. There's also a **suspension bridge** here, with chains smelted from locally mined iron, built in 1874 on the orders of Zhou Dawu, a Qing general who had been fighting the Miao. If it's not a market day, you're better off hiking 45 minutes into the mountains to the much more charming and little-visited Miao village of **Miao Do**.

Jiuzhou

旧洲, jiùzhōu

Some 20km north of Chong An, **HUANGPING** (黄平, huángpíng) is an anonymous small town, from where minibuses run high up into the hills to **JIUZHOU**. Jiuzhou is

---

VISITING MIAO VILLAGES

Miao villages around Kaili are best visited on market days or during one of the many annual festivals. Many have been heavily renovated as promoted tourist destinations, and although they are quite easy to get to now, they have lost something in authenticity, although often you need walk just a few kilometres to nearby villages to find more genuine places. **Markets** operate on a five-day cycle, with the busiest at Chong An and Shidong; most festivals take place in early spring, early summer or late autumn and attract thousands of people for buffalo fights, dances, performances of *lusheng* (a long-piped bamboo instrument) and horse or boat races; you should book transport and accommodation well in advance. The biggest event of the year is the springtime **Sisters' Meal**, the traditional time for girls to choose a partner: don't miss it if you're in the region. Just note that Chinese information sometimes confuses lunar and Gregorian dates – "9 February", for instance, might mean "the ninth day of the second lunar month".

If there's nothing special going on, head south of Kaili to the picturesque villages of Langde Shang and Xijiang, though easy access means plenty of other visitors. Kaili's CITS can suggest less touristic alternatives, where it's possible to end up sharing lunch at a farmer's home (usually sour fish or chicken hotpot) and being given impromptu festival performances by young women in their best silver and embroidered jackets – you'll have to pay, of course, but it's worth the price. Beware the hospitable Miao custom of encouraging guests to indulge in their very drinkable but potent **sticky rice wine**.

Most villages are connected by at least daily bus services from Kaili, and also make possible stopovers on the way out of the region. Return transport can leave quite early, however, so be prepared to stay the night or hitch back if you leave things too late. There are no banks in many of the villages.

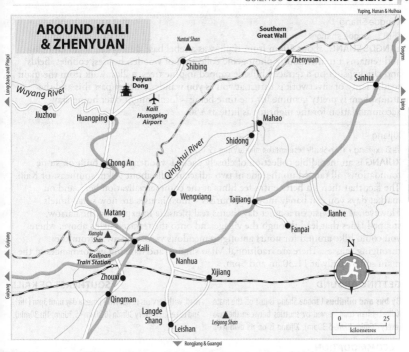

AROUND KAILI & ZHENYUAN

a surprise: a substantial market town whose main street is lined with old buildings, some dating back three hundred years, and most of which have been recently restored. Also recently tarted-up are the southern-style **Tianhou Temple** (天后宫, tiānhòu gōng), the merchants' **guildhall**, and a European **Catholic church**, which is just up the hill from the newly constructed ancient gates and section of wall, built in anticipation of a flood of tourists coming up the new highway from Kaili.

GETTING AROUND

By bus and minibus Buses and minibuses shuttle along the main road between Kaili and Huangping all through the day, taking about an hour and a quarter and stopping at both Matang and Chong An, with fewer services making it up to

NORTHWEST OF KAILI

Jiuzhou (45min) and beyond to little-visited Longchang and Pingxi. There are also buses between Huangping and Shibing (施秉, shībǐng), 30km to the northeast, which itself has services to Zhenyuan until late afternoon.

ACCOMMODATION AND EATING

CHONG AN

Wangjiang Lou 望江楼, wàngjiāng lóu. ☎137 65525658. Right in the middle of the village, this has clean, neat rooms with a/c, though only squat toilets. A step up from the other more basic accommodation nearby and there's also a reasonable restaurant on the second floor. **¥78**

JIUZHOU

Sheraton Gold 喜来登黄金宾馆, xǐláidēng huángjīn bīnguǎn. 8 Majia Hutong ☎0855 2461666. Best option in the centre of town, and there's not much else so be sure to make a reservation before you turn up. The rooms are basic but bearable (they have slightly nicer rooms for ¥108) and there are several eating options nearby on the main road. **¥68**

Southeast of Kaili

Southeast of Kaili, the road runs down to **Leishan** (雷山, léishān), staging post for buses heading south over twisting mountain roads to Rongjiang and Guangxi province through the Dong regions (see p.626). On the way to Leishan, either Langde Shang or Xijiang villages offer picturesque places to get off the bus and explore.

10

Langde Shang

郎德上, lángdé shàng

LANGDE SHANG, about 40km from Kaili, was a rebel base during the Miao Uprising and remains a tremendously photogenic collection of wooden houses, cobbles, fields and chickens set on a terraced hillside capped in pine trees, a 2km walk from the main road. Plenty of silverwork is thrust at you as you wander, but get past this and the atmosphere is pretty genuine for the time being – locals might offer home-stay accommodation for the night for as little as ¥50.

Xijiang

西江, xījiāng • ¥120 • Shuttle bus from ticket office to village ¥5

XIJIANG is an incredible collection of closely packed wooden houses built on stone foundations, all ranged up the side of two adjacent hills about 90km southeast of Kaili. The fact that there's a hefty entry fee hints at the commercialization here, and on market days you can barely move for tourists – most houses are now small hotels. However, if you visit on a quiet day there's real pleasure in exploring the narrow, stepped lanes that lead through the village and onto the terraced fields above, where you could hike around for hours among tremendous views and away from the thronging masses. There are traditional Miao singing and dancing performances in the main square daily at 11.30am and 5pm.

GETTING AROUND   SOUTHEAST OF KAILI

By bus and minibus Langde Shang is just off the main Kaili–Leishan road, served by shuttles between the two (every 30min, 8am–5.30pm). Xijiang is on its own loop road, with services to Kaili five times a day until 3pm (1hr), and to Leishan every 30min (6.30am–5.30pm; 1hr 30min).

ACCOMMODATION

Xijiang Yue Hotel 西江月酒店, xijiāngyuè jiǔdiàn. Xijiang village ☎ 0855 3348678. Located on the main square by the river (look for four red lanterns outside), this hotel's neat, clean rooms are well equipped. Their restaurant has a lovely outdoor terrace, most pleasant in the evenings when you can see the lanterns twinkling across the village. **¥288**

Shidong

施洞, shīdòng

SHIDONG is a single-street town on the banks of the **Qingshui River**, 60km northeast from Kaili. There's a great market here, one of the best in the region, held on the riverside

THE MIAO

The **Miao** – or Hmong, as they are better known outside of China – are spread through Guizhou, Yunnan, Sichuan, Vietnam, Laos and Myanmar. Forced off their lands by the Qing-dynasty government, rebels in Guizhou such as **Zhang Xiumei** took a lesson from the Taipings in adjacent Guangxi and seeded their own **uprising** in 1854, which was only put down in late 1873 after a huge slaughter involving whole towns being obliterated: out of a provincial population of seven million, over half died during the revolt.

Miao women are famous for their **embroideries**: girls traditionally spent years stitching their wedding jackets, though most are made by machine nowadays. Patterns are sometimes abstract, or incorporate plant designs, butterflies (the bringer of spring and indicating hoped-for change), dragons, fish – a China-wide good luck symbol – and buffalo motifs. Each region produces its own styles, such as the sequined, curly green and red patterns from the southerly Leishan district, Chong'an's dark geometric work, and the bright, fiery lions of Shidong.

Many of the design themes recur in Miao **silverwork**, the most elaborate pieces again being made for wedding assemblages. Women appear at some festivals weighed down with coil necklaces, spiral earrings and huge headpieces, all of which are embossed or shaped into flowers, bells and beasts.

shingle, where jostling farmers sort through the selection of livestock, clothing, foodstuffs and modern silverwork and textiles. Shidong also hosts the second and third days of the Miao Sisters' Meal festival, featuring bullfights (head-to-head combat between rival buffaloes), dragon-boat races, communal dancing and mass consumption of rice wine. The colourful dragon boats can be viewed in a boathouse next to the main road.

ARRIVAL AND DEPARTURE SHIDONG

By bus Buses leave from Kaili's main bus station direct to Shidong every hour and a half until 5pm, and take 3hr.

ACCOMMODATION

Yingbin Zhaodaisuo 迎宾招待所, yíngbīn zhāodàisuǒ. ☏ 0855 5359174. Right next to the post office on the main street, this place offers extremely basic accommodation with shared bathrooms and no a/c. There's another similar place, *Luoping Zhaodaisuo*, on the other side of the post office. Note that rates increase tenfold during festivals. ¥50

10

Zhenyuan
镇远, zhènyuǎn

ZHENYUAN town – occupying a straight, constricted valley 100km northeast of Kaili on the **Wuyang River** – sprang up in the Ming dynasty to guard the trade route through to central China. Quite aside from a couple of genuinely old structures to check out, Zhenyuan is probably the only town in the whole province that could be described as attractive: the aquamarine river runs westwards, with tall, antique-style houses piled together along both banks, all lit at night by lanterns.

The old town
古城, gǔchéng

Zhenyuan's old town sits north of the river along Xinzhong Jie, comprising a kilometre of wood and stone buildings, built in the Qing style and backed up against stony cliffs. Partway along, the town museum (镇远博物馆, zhènyuǎn bówùguǎn; daily 7.30am–5pm; ¥10) is more interesting perhaps as an unrestored example of Qing architecture than for the exhibition of old photos. Past here, the road turns north with the river and you'll reach a multiple-arch, solid stone **Ming-dynasty bridge** (祝圣桥, zhùshèng qiáo) over the river to sixteenth-century **Qinglong Dong** (青龙洞, qīnglóng dòng; daily 7.30am–6pm; ¥60), whose separate Taoist, Buddhist and Confucian halls appear to grow out of a cliff face, all dripping wet and hung with vines.

The Southern Great Wall
南长城, nán chángchéng • Daily 7am–6pm • ¥30

By the western end of the old bridge you'll find a small set of steps (and ticket office), which lead through back lanes, via forest and a small temple, to a fragment of the thirteenth-century **Southern Great Wall**. The wall, which runs eastwards to Fenghuang in Hunan (see p.441), is almost totally demolished, standing only 3m at its highest point, but there are superb views northeast into Hunan from the ridge – especially beautiful at night when the lights from towns and villages across the landscape seem to reflect the stars.

ARRIVAL AND DEPARTURE ZHENYUAN

By train The train station is about 3km west of town on the south side of the river – a taxi to the old town is ¥10. Zhenyuan Station (镇远站, zhènyuǎn zhàn) is on the Hunan–Kaili–Guiyang line. There's no train booking office in town, so best book tickets when you arrive, as the ticket office at the station isn't very big.

Destinations Guiyang (15 daily; 3hr 43min–6hr 37min);

Huaihua (11 daily; 2hr 40min–3hr 30min); Kaili (11 daily; 1hr 14min–2hr 15min); Yuping (11 daily; 1hr).

By bus The bus station is next to the train station. There are half a dozen buses daily southwest via Shidong to Kaili, and also east to Yuping (for Fanjing Shan) and Tongren (铜仁, tóngrén) for connections to Fenghuang in Hunan.

10

ACCOMMODATION AND EATING

The old town is lined with accommodation and attractive restaurants, though food isn't memorable; in summer, it's more fun to head over the new bridge to the opposite bank and enjoy simple hotpots at alfresco tables with the rest of town.

One Meter Sunshine Inn 一米阳光客栈, yīmǐ yángguāng kèzhàn. Next to the river by the Ming-dynasty bridge ☎0855 5723996. One of the few places that has an English sign, this small inn is fantastically placed and its inexpensive rooms are clean enough (if a little basic), with balconies looking over the river at its most picturesque point. **¥158**

Yongfurong Kezhan 永福荣客栈, yǒngfúróng kèzhàn. 200m down Xinzhong Jie from the bridge ☎0855 5730888. This well-run place has comfortable and very chic ethnic-style rooms which are clean and have modern bathrooms and river views; you can also enjoy the vista from their lounge. Their larger more luxurious rooms cost ¥100 more. **¥188**

Fanjing Shan

梵净山, fánjìng shān • ¥110 (¥90 in winter) • Minibus from Heiwan to cable-car station ¥20; cable car ¥90 one-way, ¥180 return

Hidden away in Guizhou's remote northeastern corner, not far from the Hunan border, **Fanjing Shan** is an ancient religious site, the name translating as "Mountain of the Pure Buddhist Land". With its upper reaches covered in wild cloud forests, it's also home to endangered **golden monkeys** (金丝猴, jīnsī hóu), though with the entire population numbering only four hundred adults, you'll be lucky to see them. Tourist development has tamed the formerly epic ascent, especially if you use the modern cable car, but despite an influx of tourists, Fanjing Shan remains one of Guizhou's highlights – though visit on a weekday if you can, when there are fewer people about.

Heiwan

Fanjing Shan's park gates are at **HEIWAN** (黑湾, hēiwān), a couple of streets that funnel visitors from the grubby bus station past restaurants and stalls of overpriced tourist tat to a large square. Here there are the park gates, a ticket office, a car park and a drinks stand – a good place to stock up on liquids as prices inside the park are expensive. Take something warm for the top – it snows in winter – but don't bring up more than a day-pack.

To the summit

From Heiwan, minibuses cover the twenty-minute, 9km run to the foot of Fanjing Shan. Here, you can catch a **cable car** to just below the summit area in 25 minutes, though this still leaves a good forty-minute walk to Fanjing Shan's 2572m-high summit.

There are more than eight thousand **steps** up the mountain – so climbing them is only for the fit and healthy to attempt – which follow steep ridges with no regard for gradient. Allow three to four hours to ascend and at least two to come down. Steps are numbered with red paint and carved inscriptions, and refreshment shacks provide sustenance until step 4500 and then there's nothing until the top. The forest – hung with vines and old man's beard and with a dwarf bamboo understorey – is vibrantly green and stiflingly humid in summer.

The summit area

Give yourself as much time as you can to explore along the stone and boardwalked **paths**, which lead through woodland and rhododendron thickets until you reach the summit area itself at **Zhenguo Temple** (镇国寺, zhènguó sì), a largish place surrounded by three enormous slate stacks which offer some of the most epic sights in the region. Each stack has small temples crowning them as well as others perched on spurs or hidden in crevices.

The tallest stack, **Golden Summit** (金顶, jīndǐng), is especially mystic-looking, often wreathed in mist, and the steep climb up to the temple at the top takes you up narrow steps carved into fissures in the rock, with chains on the side to help haul yourself up. The views from the top are truly stupendous, and worth every bit of effort.

ARRIVAL AND DEPARTURE   FANJING SHAN

By train and bus Fanjing Shan is best reached via Yuping (玉屏, yùpíng), a stop on the Kaili–Zhenyuan–Hunan train line, where you'll find buses through the day to Jiangkou (江口, jiāngkǒu; 2hr). Here you change again for further frequent departures (1hr) to the park gates at Heiwan. There are also direct buses to Heiwan from the city of Tongren (铜仁, tóngrén; 1hr 30min), which is quicker if you're coming from Hunan.

ACCOMMODATION AND EATING

At Heiwan, the road leading from the bus station to the gates is lined with many hotel-cum-restaurants which all charge the same rate for identical clean, neat rooms for around ¥168. There is no accommodation in the park itself, although there are a couple of basic but pricey canteens serving instant noodles near the summit.

Western Guizhou

Extending for 350km between Guiyang and the border with Yunnan province, **western Guizhou** is a desperately poor region of beautiful mountainous country and depressingly functional mining towns. **Anshun** is a transit hub for visiting **Bouyei villages**, the tourist magnets of **Dragon (Loong) Palace Scenic Area** and **Huangguoshu Falls** and the remoter, more spectacular **Zhijin Caves**.

All routes west from Anshun ultimately lead to Yunnan's capital, Kunming (see p.663), whether you travel by bus along one of the three highways or – more comfortably – take the train. The landscape here forms a tumultuous barrier of jagged peaks and deep valleys, rising to a high plateau where wintering birdlife can be spied on at **Caohai** – being poled around this shallow lake on a sunny day is one of Guizhou's highlights.

Anshun

安顺, ānshùn

Some 100km west of Guiyang, **ANSHUN** was established as a garrisoned outpost in Ming times to keep an eye on the empire's unruly fringes. Today it's a small city, whose rough-around-the-edges feeling has virtually disappeared in just the past few years. Massive amounts of central government funding has meant that mud streets on the fringes have been replaced by shopping malls, stadia, a new ten-lane motorway to Pingba, and soon a high-speed rail link from Guangzhou via Guiyang. There's not a great deal to see or do here, but it remains the most convenient base for exploring the many natural and cultural attractions in the region.

The town centre

Anshun's central crossroads is overlooked to the northwest by a hillock topped by a short Ming-dynasty **pagoda** (白塔, báitǎ), with a park around

AROUND ANSHUN

10

THE BOUYEI

The limestone countryside around Anshun is homeland to China's 2.9 million **Bouyei**, whose villages are built of split stone and roofed in large, irregularly laid slate tiles. Bouyei specialities include blue-and-white **batik work** and **ground opera** (地戏, dìxì), a traditional form of Ming opera, in which performers wear brightly painted wooden masks. Though native to the region and overlaid with animistic rituals, the current forms are said to have been imported along with Han troops in the Ming dynasty, and are based on Chinese tales such as *The Three Kingdoms*. The Spring Festival period is a good time to see a performance, held in many villages around Anshun, including Shitou Zhai and Tianlong.

---

the base containing some representative, restored antique buildings, including a long stone **church** with a Chinese-style bell tower. The other point of interest is the **Confucian temple** (文化庙, wénhuà miào; ¥10), built in 1394, hidden away in the northeastern backstreets (just north of the river on Ruilin Lu) which, while somewhat neglected, has some superbly carved dragon pillars, rivalling those at Qufu's Confucius Mansion (see p.303). There is also a traditional arts centre opposite the gates, selling local crafts.

ARRIVAL AND DEPARTURE   ANSHUN

BY TRAIN

Anshun Station (安顺火车站, ānshùn huǒchē zhàn), on the Guiyang–Kunming line, is 1km south of town at the end of Zhonghua Nan Lu; catch bus #5 between here and the East bus station, or a taxi costs about ¥25–30.

Destinations Guiyang (26 daily; 1hr 9min–2hr 15min); Kunming (15 daily; 5hr 50min–9hr 41min); Liupanshui/ Shuicheng (24 daily; 2hr 9min–4hr 8min).

BY BUS

East bus station (东汽车站, dōng qìchē zhàn). Anshun's new main bus station is about 10km east of the centre and handles the majority of traffic to all destinations, with bus #5 running from here to the centre and train station.

Destinations Dragon (Loong) Palace Scenic Area (every 25min; 1hr); Guiyang (every 20min; 1hr 30min); Huangguoshu (every 20min; 1hr); Liupanshui (hourly; 2hr 30min).

Beimen bus station (北门客车站, běimén kèchēzhàn) is 1km north of the centre on Zhonghua Bei Lu, and has buses to Zhijin every 30min (4hr).

ACCOMMODATION

Zhonghua Nan Lu north of the train station, is awash with inexpensive hotels where small, noisy rooms are available for under ¥100. There are also three *7 Days Inns*, one of which is also near the train station on Gui Huangguoshu Jie near the *Magical Fuyun Hotel*.

Magical Fuyun Hotel 参芪富蕴酒店, cānqí fùyùn jiǔdiàn. 18 Gui Huangguoshu Jie ☎0853 3290000. Best value of the mid-range places near the train station and refurbished not long ago, the rooms are modern, comfy and clean. Also has a travel agent and a decent restaurant. **¥208**

Tielu Jiudian 铁路酒店, tiělù jiǔdiàn. West side of the train station square ☎0853 3290555. Immediately left out of the train station, this place has pretty comfortable, tidy carpeted rooms for the price, although only has wi-fi in the lobby. Set back from the road, it's also quiet. **¥168**

EATING

There are some excellent and inexpensive noodle stands in front of the train station where you can eat for under ¥10. Locals, however, say the best option is the crossroads by the night market at Dong Jie, and Guofu Jie and its surrounding streets, which become crammed after dark with stalls and tents selling noodles and lamb kebabs.

Magical Fuyun Restaurant 参芪富蕴餐厅, cānqí fùyùn cāntīng. 18 Gui Huangguoshu Jie ☎0853 3290000. Western food and comfy sofas and done out with wrought-iron chandeliers and flowing drapes, it serves a range of steaks, pizzas and pasta from around ¥45, as well as overpriced coffee and reasonably priced cocktails. Daily 9.30am–11.30pm.

Tianlong

天龙屯, tiānlóng tún • Daily 8.30am–6pm • ¥35

Some 30km east of Anshun off the Guiyang highway, **TIANLONG** is an old but renovated stone settlement founded as a garrison town in the Ming dynasty whose inhabitants, though dressing in embroidered coloured smocks like the **Bouyei**, insist they are in fact descendants of the original Han settlers. Tour groups come for the free hourly opera shows at the **Dixi Performance Hall** (地戏堂, dìxì táng); otherwise a couple of twisting stone alleys and a nineteenth-century **church-school** built by French priests will keep you busy for an hour or so.

10

Wulong Temple

伍龙寺, wǔlóng sì • Daily 8am–6pm • ¥20

Some 3km east of Tianlong, sheer-sided **Tiantai Shan** (天台山, tiāntái shān) is crowned by fortress-like **Wulong Temple**, founded by the traitorous Ming general **Wu Sangui**, who defected to the Manchu cause in 1644 and was rewarded by being made overlord of all Guizhou. The top hall contains a rather fine, carved wooden Buddha.

ARRIVAL AND DEPARTURE   TIANLONG

By minibus Tianlong doesn't have its own bus station, but minibuses run from Pingba (every 10min; 10min) and Anshun East (every 20min; 1hr) to the new tourist reception centre (with ATM and canteen). Heading on, go east to Pingba (平坝, píngbà) for connecting traffic to Guiyang.

Shitou Zhai

石头寨, shítóu zhài • Museum daily 9.30am–5.30pm • Free

Six-hundred-year-old **SHITOU ZHAI** lies 30km southwest of Anshun off the Huangguoshu road. The village – whose name translates as "Stone Head Stockade" – comprises forty or so stone houses grouped around a rocky hillock, all surrounded by vegetable plots and disguised modern houses. At the gates, **Bouyei** women, wearing traditional dark-blue embroidered dresses, act as guides. You will be offered batik jackets for sale, and might witness the whole process, from drawing the designs in wax, to dyeing in indigo and boiling the wax away to leave a white pattern. There's a fixed-price shop in the village's tiny **museum**. You can easily walk out to similar, more tranquil surrounding villages, which aren't quite as swamped with visitors.

ARRIVAL AND DEPARTURE   SHITOU ZHAI

By bus There's no direct traffic to Shitou Zhai, which lies off the old Anshun–Huangguoshu highway; tell the driver, and buses will drop you at the junction, leaving a 2km walk along a quiet road to the village gates. To move on, return to the main road and flag down passing traffic.

Dragon (Loong) Palace Scenic Area

龙宫风景区, lónggōng fēngjǐng qū • Daily 9am–6pm • ¥120 • ☏ 0853 5864898

This extensive scenic area features not only waterfalls, over ninety caves, temples, traditional villages and a vertigo-inducing ropeway across mountain peaks but also the partially flooded cavern complex comprising **Longgong Caves**. It lies 28km from Anshun and you can be dropped at one of two entrances, which are about 5km apart. From the nearer, **Loong Palace gate**, you begin by being ferried down a river between willows and bamboo to a small knot of houses; walk through the arch, bear left, and it's 250m up some steps to **Kuanyin Dong** (观音洞, guānyīn dòng), a broad cave filled with Buddhist statues. A seemingly minor path continues around the entrance but this is the one you want: it leads through a short cavern lit by coloured lights, then out around a hillside to **Jiujiu Tun** – site of an old guard post – and then across a rope-bridge to **Yulong Dong** (玉龙洞, yùlóng dòng), a large and spectacular cave system through which a guide will lead you (for free). Out the other side, a small river enters **Long Gong** (Dragon's Palace) itself, a two-stage boat ride through tall, flooded caverns picked out with florid lighting, exiting the caves into a broad pool at Longgong's eastern entrance. You could easily spend a day or two here wandering all the mountain paths, many of which are relatively uncrowded and offer lovely views over the forested peaks. If you are short of time, enter through the further eastern **Longtan entrance** which is much closer to Long Gong, and it's possible to get in and out in a couple of hours.

10

ARRIVAL AND DEPARTURE — DRAGON (LOONG) PALACE SCENIC AREA

By minibus Minibuses run through the day between Longgong's two entrances and Anshun's east bus station (every 25min; 30–40min; ¥10); and there are regular minibuses from Longgong to Huangguoshu (10am–4pm; 1hr; ¥30). The last bus from the caves departs around 6pm.

Huangguoshu Falls

黄果树瀑布, huángguǒshù pùbù • ¥180

Clogged with sightseers during holidays and weekends, and safely skipped if you've ever seen a large waterfall before, **Huangguoshu Falls** lie 64km from Anshun along the Anshun–Yunnan highway. You get dropped off at the bustling Huangguoshu township and walk down 3km to the entrance (unless you buy the minibus ticket); at 67m this may not quite rank as China's highest cataract, but in full flood the thunder rolls way off into the distance. A staircase descends past plagues of souvenir stalls to the blue-green river below the falls; the most imposing view of Huangguoshu is off to the left where the full weight of its 81m span drops into the **Rhino Pool** – prepare yourself for a good soaking from the spray. Be sure not to miss the **Water Curtain Cave** either, whose six windows allow you to view the water from behind the falls; the angle of light produces vivid rainbows. If the queues are too much, enter through the upper water entrance and then walk down the right-hand side of the river. Eventually, you'll come to a viewing platform above the falls (which also features wooden loungers) as well as, fairly incongruously, a **French Catholic church**, although it's not in a good state of repair and you can't currently enter.

ARRIVAL AND DEPARTURE — HUANGGUOSHU FALLS

By bus Minibuses connect Huangguoshu with the Dragon (Loong) Palace Scenic Area and Anshun (both daily 7am–7pm; 1hr) and Guiyang (daily 10am–5pm; 2hr). If you're Yunnan-bound, first catch a minibus 7km west to the small town of Guanling (关岭, guānlǐng) and look for connections there.

Zhijin Caves

织金洞, zhījīn dòng • Daily: April–Sept 8.30am–5.30pm; Oct–March 9am–5pm • ¥140

About 100km from Anshun or 150km from Guiyang – there's direct traffic from either – the dismal country town of **ZHIJIN** (织金, zhījīn) sits among some gorgeous limestone pinnacles, beneath which are the astounding **Zhijin Caves**, some 25km northeast. Minibuses from Zhijin to the caves leave you at the **visitors' centre** where you have to hook up with one of the guided tours that run whenever they have ten people. The caves are immensely impressive and absolutely worth the money; tours with Chinese commentary last up to two hours and wind through untold numbers of caverns, the largest of which is 240m long, 170m wide and 60m high.

ARRIVAL AND DEPARTURE — ZHIJIN CAVES

By bus Zhijin town's bus station (织金汽车站, zhījīn qìchē zhàn) handles traffic to Anshun and Guiyang. It's just about possible to get here, tour the caves and get out without staying the night, but you'll need to arrive early on, with the first bus leaving Anshun at 7am and the last bus departing Zhijin at 5.30pm.

Destinations Anshun (every 30min; 4hr); Guiyang (hourly; 6hr).

GETTING AROUND

By minibus From Zhijin's bus station, catch a taxi (¥10) to the Yuping local bus station (玉屏汽车站, yùpíng qìchē zhàn), from where minibuses to the caves (40min) depart when full until mid-afternoon.

By taxi If minibuses to the caves don't fill, you'll need a taxi (around ¥250, including waiting time).

ACCOMMODATION

Hongzhou International Hotel 宏洲国际大酒店, hóngzhōu guójì dàjiǔdiàn. 151 Jinbei Dadao, about 4km north from the bus station ☎ 0857 7758888. Best bet if you don't fancy any of the three cheap options around the main bus station, this place has very nice clean, modern rooms with a nice atmosphere. You'll need a cab from the station. ¥308

Caohai and Weining

WEINING (威宁, wēiníng) – a small, run-down shell of a place populated by a friendly mix of Hui, Yi and Dahua Miao – sits above the clouds on a 2000m-high plateau in Guizhou's far northwestern corner. Immediately south of the town, 5km-wide **Caohai** (草海, cǎohǎi), the "Grass Lake", forms the core of a regional nature reserve. Caohai is a twitcher's paradise: wintering wildfowl shelter here in huge numbers, with over 170 different species spotted annually – including four hundred rare **black-necked cranes** (黑颈鹤, hēijǐng hè).

On the lake

Boats ¥120 per hour for 2–3 people • Rickshaw from town ¥10, or it's a 30min walk

At the lakeshore you'll be approached by touts wanting to take you out on a **boat trip** to find the birds; prices are posted, so don't pay more. Chinese tourists head first for a meal at the hamlet of **Longjia** (龙家, lóngjiā) on the far shore, famed for its food. On a sunny day, Caohai's overall tranquillity is a complete break with daily life in China; wintering cranes often hang out in the shallows near the shore and are not too hard to catch on camera. Be sure to bring your boots as it gets quite muddy.

ARRIVAL AND DEPARTURE — WEINING AND CAOHAI

By train Caohai Station (草海火车站, cǎo hǎi huǒchē zhàn) is a few kilometres (¥10 by taxi) outside Weining town. It's a minor branch with only four services a day to the nearest main station, 100km south of Weining at Liupanshui (六盘水, liùpánshuǐ) on the direct Guiyang–Anshun–Kunming line.

Destinations from Liupanshui Anshun (22 daily; 2–3hr 28min); Guiyang (27 daily; 3hr–5hr 53min); Kunming (17 daily; 3hr 35min–10hr 35min); Weining (4 daily; 1hr 11min–2hr).

By bus The bus station is right in the centre of Weining, with services to Anshun, Guiyang, Liupanshui and into Yunnan. Buses are the most convenient way to get to and from Liupanshui.

Destinations Anshun (hourly; 4hr); Guiyang (6 daily; 7hr); Liupanshui (every 30–40min; 3hr).

ACCOMMODATION AND EATING

The *Xichen International Hotel* is the only proper hotel in Weining that takes foreigners, though many of the cheaper hostels around the bus station are happy to take you. The restaurants outside the bus station do inexpensive stir-fries and hotpots, and street-stalls selling chilli-dusted potato kebabs are everywhere in winter.

Xichen International Hotel 洗尘国际大酒店, xǐchén guójì dà jiǔdiàn. 4-1 Kaihang Lu, about 2.5km west of the bus station and 1km northwest of the lake ☎ 0857 6555555. Weining's only high-class hotel for foreigners, this new hotel has comfortable international-standard rooms, with shiny marble bathrooms and deep mattresses on the beds, though sadly no views of the lake. ¥398

10

Yunnan
云南

PLOUGHING RICE TERRACES, YUANYANG

Yunnan

云南, yúnnán

Yunnan has always stood apart from the rest of China, set high on the empire's barbarous southwestern frontiers, and shielded from the rest of the nation by the unruly, mountainous neighbours of Sichuan and Guizhou. This remote and diverse province of border markets, mountains, jungles, lakes, temples, modern political intrigue and the remains of vanished kingdoms is also home to over 28 recognized ethnic groups, the greatest number of any province in China. Providing almost half the population and a prime reason to visit Yunnan, the indigenous list includes Dai and Bai, Wa, Lahu, Hani, Jingpo, Nu, Naxi and Lisu plus a host shared with other provinces, such as the Yi (see p.755), or adjoining countries. Each minority has its own spoken language, cuisine, distinctive form of dress for women, festivals and belief system, and with enough time you should be able to flesh out the superficial image of these groups laid on for the tourist industry.

In recent years tourism has boomed out of all proportion to Yunnan's remote image, bringing battalions of tour buses, souvenir stalls and loudspeaker-toting guides from far and near; the upside is improved resources geared to their needs, including backpacker cafés and companies offering cycling and trekking trips, ensuring that Yunnan is one of the easiest regions to explore in China.

The northeast of the province is home to the attractive capital, **Kunming**, whose mild climate earned Yunnan its name, meaning literally "south of the clouds". A scattering of local sights – including the brilliant green, near-vertically terraced valleys at **Yuanyang** – extends southeast from the city towards the border with **Vietnam**. Northwest of Kunming, the Yunnan plateau rises to serrated, snowbound peaks, extending to **Tibet** and surrounding the popular ancient historic towns of **Dali** and **Lijiang**; there's one of China's great hikes here too, through **Tiger Leaping Gorge**. The **far west**, laid out along the ghost of old trade routes, has less of specific interest but allows gentle probing along the **Myanmar (Burma) border**, especially up the rugged **Nu Jiang valley**. Yunnan's deep south comprises a further isolated stretch of the same frontier, which reaches down to the tropical forests and paddy fields of **Xishuangbanna**, a botanical, zoological and ethnic cornucopia abutting Myanmar and **Laos** – about as far from Han China as it's possible to be.

SAN TA PAGODAS, DALI

Highlights

❶ Kunming's bars Check out the laidback nightlife in one of China's most relaxed cities. **See p.670**

❷ Yuanyang Base yourself in this attractive town and visit nearby minority villages set in a landscape spectacularly sliced up by rice terraces. **See p.675**

❸ Dali An old town with nearby mountain trekking, a kung fu monastery, and lush scenery. **See p.679**

❹ Lugu Lake Tranquil and relatively little-visited lakeside resort with matriarchal villages, situated on a back-road route into Sichuan. **See p.694**

❺ Tiger Leaping Gorge Relax for a few days on the ridge of this dramatic gorge, and trek between farmstead guesthouses. **See p.695**

❻ Meili Xue Shan Dramatic jagged scenery along the northwestern border with Tibet. **See p.703**

❼ Nu Jiang valley One of the remotest corners of China, this culturally diverse, narrow valley has a wild feel and allows for some interesting treks through unspoilt country. **See p.706**

❽ Jungle trekking, Xishuangbanna Explore a region populated by many different ethnic groups, each with their own distinctive dress and customs. **See p.714**

HIGHLIGHTS ARE MARKED ON THE MAP ON PP.660–661

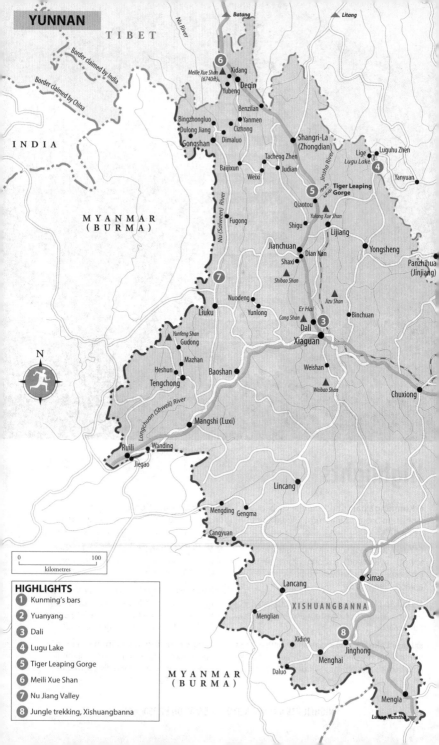

YUNNAN

TIBET

Batang

Litang

Nu River

Border claimed by India

Border claimed by China

INDIA

Meilie Xue Shan (6740m)
Xidang
Deqin
Yubeng

Benzilan
Bingzhongluo
Yanmen
Dulong Jiang
Cizhong
Gongshan
Dimaluo

Shangri-La
(Zhongdian)

Lige
Luguhu Zhen
Lugu Lake

Tacheng Zhen
Baijixun
Judian
Weixi

Yanyuan

**MYANMAR
(BURMA)**

Nu (Salween) River

Fugong

Qiaotou

Yulong Xue Shan

**Tiger Leaping
Gorge**

Jinsha River

Shigu

Lijiang

Jianchuan
Dian Nan
Shaxi

Yongsheng

Panzhihua
(Jinjiang)

Shibao Shan

Jizu Shan

Nuodeng
Er Hai
Yunlong
Cang Shan
Dali

Binchuan

Liuku

Xiaguan

Yunfeng Shan
Gudong
Mazhan

Weishan

Chuxiong

Heshun
Tengchong

Baoshan

Weibao Shan

Longchuan (Shweli) River

Mangshi (Luxi)

Ruili
Wanding
Jiegao

Lincang

Mengding
Gengma

Cangyuan

0   100

kilometres

Lancang

Simao

XISHUANGBANNA

Menglian

Xiding

Menghai
Jinghong

Daluo

Mengla

**MYANMAR
(BURMA)**

Luang Namtha

HIGHLIGHTS

1 Kunming's bars
2 Yuanyang
3 Dali
4 Lugu Lake
5 Tiger Leaping Gorge
6 Meili Xue Shan
7 Nu Jiang Valley
8 Jungle trekking, Xishuangbanna

N

Getting around can be time-consuming, thanks to Yunnan's sheer scale, but the state of country **buses and roads** is often surprisingly good; new expressways are springing up at a regular rate and it's an undeniable achievement that some of the lesser routes exist at all. Yunnan's fairly limited **rail network** has been somewhat expanded too, with services to Dali and Lijiang making these popular destinations more accessible than ever, and a new high-speed service to Kunming set to make connections with the rest of China much easier too.

The **weather** is generally moderate throughout the year, though northern Yunnan has cold winters and heavy snow up around the Tibetan border, while the south is always warm, with a torrential wet season in summer.

Brief history

According to the Han historian Sima Qian, the Chinese warrior prince Zhuang Qiao founded the pastoral **Dian Kingdom** in eastern Yunnan during the third century BC. The Dian were a slave society, who vividly recorded their daily life and ceremonies involving human sacrifice in sometimes gruesome **bronze models**, which have been unearthed from their tombs. In 109 AD the kingdom was acknowledged by China: the Emperor Wu, hoping to control the Southern Silk Road through to India, sent its ruler military aid and a golden seal. However, the collapse of the Han Empire in 204 AD was followed by the dissolution of Dian into private statelets.

The Dali and Nanzhao kingdoms

In the eighth century, an aspiring Yunnanese prince named **Piluoge**, favouring Dali for its location near trade routes between central and southeastern Asia, invited all his rivals to dinner in the town, then set fire to the tent with them inside. Subsequently he established the **Nanzhao Kingdom** in Dali, which later expanded to include much of modern Myanmar, Thailand and Vietnam. In 937, the Bai warlord **Duan Siping** toppled the Nanzhao and set up a smaller **Dali Kingdom**, which survived until **Kublai Khan** and his Mongol hordes descended in 1252.

YUNNANESE FOOD

Yunnanese food splits broadly into three cooking styles. In the **north**, the cold, pastoral lifestyle produces dried meats and – very unusually for China – **dairy products**, fused with a Muslim cuisine, a vestige of the thirteenth-century Mongolian invasion. Typical dishes include wind-cured ham (火腿, huǒtuǐ), sweetened, steamed and served with slices of bread; dried cheese or yoghurt wafers (乳扇, rǔshàn or 乳饼, rǔbǐng); the local version of crisp-skinned duck (烧鸭, shāoyā), flavoured with Sichuan peppercorns – you'll see drum-shaped duck ovens outside many restaurants; and a tasty fish claypot (沙锅鱼, shāguō yú).

Eastern Yunnan produces the most recognizably "Chinese" food. From here comes chicken flavoured with medicinal herbs and steamed inside a specially shaped earthenware steamer (气锅鸡, qìguōjī), and perhaps the province's most celebrated dish, **crossing-the-bridge noodles** (过桥米线, guòqiáo mǐxiàn), a sort of individualized hotpot eaten as a cheap snack: you pay by the size of the bowl. The curious name comes from a tale of a Qing scholar who retired every day to a lakeside pavilion to compose poetry. His wife, an understanding soul, used to cook him lunch, but the food always cooled as she carried it from their home over the bridge to where he studied – until she hit on the idea of keeping the heat in with a layer of oil on top of his soup.

Not surprisingly, Yunnan's **south** is strongly influenced by Burmese, Lao and Thai cooking methods, particularly in the use of such un-Chinese ingredients as lime juice, coconut, palm sugar, cloves and turmeric. Here you'll find a vast range of soups and stews, roughly recognizable as **curries**, displayed in aluminium pots outside fast-turnover restaurants, and oddities such as purple rice-flour pancakes sold at street markets. The south is also famous in China for producing good **coffee** and red pu'er, Yunnan's best **tea**.

The Muslim Uprising

Directly controlled by China for the first time, Yunnan served for a while as a remote dumping ground for political troublemakers, and escaped the population explosions, wars and migrations that plagued central China. However, the Mongol invasion had introduced a large Muslim population to the province, who, angered by their deteriorating status under the Chinese, staged the **Muslim Uprising** in 1856. Under the warlord **Du Wenxiu**, the rebellion laid waste to Kunming and founded an Islamic state in Dali before the Qing armies ended it with the wholesale massacre of Yunnan's Muslims in 1873, leaving a wasted Yunnan to local bandits and private armies for the following half-century.

Modern times

Strangely, it was the **Japanese invasion** of China during the 1930s that sparked a resurgence of Yunnan's fortunes. Blockaded into southwestern China, the **Guomindang government** initiated great programmes of rail-and-road building through the region, though it's only recently that Yunnan has finally benefited from its forced association with the rest of the country. Never agriculturally rich – only a tenth of the land is considered arable – the province looks to mineral resources, tourism and its potential as a future conduit between China and the much discussed, but as yet unformed, trading bloc of **Vietnam**, **Laos**, **Thailand** and **Myanmar**. Should these countries ever form an unrestricted economic alliance, the amount of trade passing through Yunnan would be immense, and highways, rail and air services have already been planned for the day trade runs freely across these borders.

11

Kunming

昆明, kūnmíng

Basking 2000m above sea level in the fertile heart of the Yunnan plateau, **KUNMING** does its best to live up to its traditional nickname, the City of Eternal Spring. Until recently it was considered a savage frontier settlement; the authorities only began to realize the city's promise when people exiled here during the Cultural Revolution refused offers to return home to eastern China, preferring Kunming's climate and more relaxed life. Today, its citizens remain mellow enough to mix typically Chinese garrulousness with introspective pleasures, such as quietly greeting the day with a stiff hit of Yunnanese tobacco from fat, brass-bound bamboo pipes.

The city's potential as a hub for both domestic tourism and cross-border trade has seen Kunming develop rapidly in recent years. With its sprouting malls and streets bustling with shoppers from every corner of the country – not to mention some interesting markets and an excellent museum – Kunming is no longer the sleepy outpost of old, and its modern infrastructure, together with a student and expat-fuelled nightlife, ensures the city is an enjoyable stopoff. Which is just as well, as virtually every traveller coming through Yunnan will end up here at some point.

Brief history

Historically the domain of Yunnan's earliest inhabitants, Kunming long profited from its position on the caravan roads through to Myanmar, India and Asia. It was visited in the thirteenth century by Marco Polo, who found the locals of **Yachi Fu** (Duck Pond Town) using cowries for cash and enjoying their meat raw. The city suffered widespread destruction as a result of the 1856 Muslim rebellion and events of forty years later, when an uprising against working conditions on the **Kunming–Haiphong rail line** saw 300,000 labourers executed after France shipped in weapons to suppress the revolt.

In the 1930s, **war with Japan** brought a flock of wealthy east-coast refugees to the city, whose money helped establish Kunming as an industrial and manufacturing base for the wartime government in Chongqing. The Allies provided essential support for this,

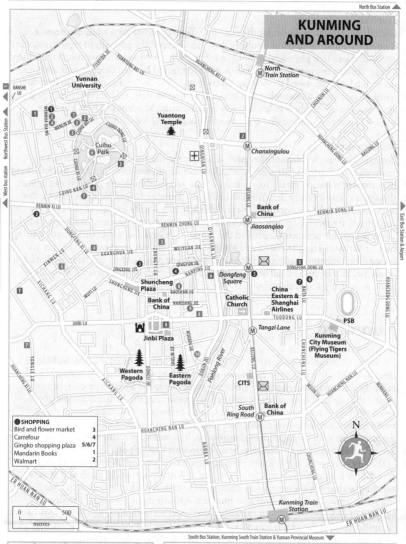

KUNMING AND AROUND

North Train Station

Yunnan University

Yuantong Temple

Chanxingulou

Cuihu Park

Bank of China

Jiaosanqiao

Renmin Dong Lu

Dongfeng Square

Shuncheng Plaza

Bank of China

Catholic Church

China Eastern & Shanghai Airlines

PSB

Jinbi Plaza

Tangzi Lane

Kunming City Museum (Flying Tigers Museum)

Western Pagoda

Eastern Pagoda

Ponhong River

CITS

South Ring Road

Bank of China

Kunming Train Station

N

● SHOPPING
Bird and flower market	3
Carrefour	4
Gingko shopping plaza	5/6/7
Mandarin Books	1
Walmart	2

Qiongzhu Temple

Jin Dian

Kunming

Gaoyao

Huating Temple

Tiahua Temple

WESTERN HILLS

Dian Chi

Kunyang

■ **ACCOMMODATION**
Cloudland		Home Inn	1	The Hump Hostel	8
International Hostel	7	Horizon (Zhong Wei)	6	Kunming	5
Cuihu (Green				Lost Garden	
Lake Hotel)	3			Guesthouse	4
Fairyland	2				

● **EATING**
1910 Gare du Sud	10	Jian Xin Yuan	8	Shiping Huiguan	7
French Café	4	The Park Bar and Grill	6	SnB	9
Heavenly Manna	2	Prague Café	3	Yingjiang Dai	5
Hongdou Yuan	1	Salvadors	2		

■ **DRINKING AND NIGHTLIFE**
Camel Bar	6	Humdinger	3	Mask	5
Chapter One	2	Kundu Night		Nordica	7
Fu Bar	1	Market	5	Yunnan Arts Theatre	4

importing materials along the Burma Road from British-held Burma (Myanmar) and, when that was lost to the Japanese, with the help of the US-piloted **Flying Tigers**, who escorted supply planes over the Himalayas from British bases in India. The city consolidated its position as a supply depot during the Vietnam War and subsequent border clashes and today is profiting from snowballing tourism and foreign investment. Neighbouring nations such as Thailand trace their ancestries back to Yunnan and have proved particularly willing to channel funds into the city, which has become ever more accessible as a result.

Bird and flower market

花鸟市场, huāniǎo shìchǎng · Daily 6am–11pm

Running west off central Zhengyi Jie, Jingxing Jie leads into one of the more offbeat corners of the city. Once a huge **bird and flower market**, the area has now been rebranded as "Old Street" (老街, lǎojiē) and features rather less in the way of birds and flowers and rather more in the way of standard cheap tat. That said, some birds – as well as lizards, pigs, snakes and cute bunny rabbits – remain, and look beyond the "jade" bangles, blindingly powerful torches and overly embroidered handbags on display and you'll see that this is one of the few areas where Kunming's original wooden buildings remain standing. Their increasing decrepitude suggests they won't be here for much longer, but for the moment cutting down the back alleys here can give a real glimpse back in time, just metres from the city's most modern shopping streets.

Cuihu Park (Green Lake Park)

翠湖公园, cuìhú gōngyuán · Daily dawn–10pm · Free

Cuihu Park is predominantly lake, and is a good place to join thousands of others exercising, singing, feeding wintering flocks of black-headed gulls, or just milling between the plum and magnolia gardens and over the maze of bridges. Main **entrances** are at the south, north and east of the park. There are outdoor barbecue places and bars within the park itself, and the road encircling Cuihu Lu is lined with restaurants and bars, which spill into adjacent **Wenlin Jie**, the best place in the city to look for a drink and food (see p.670). Immediately north of the park, the **Yunnan University** campus offers a glimpse of old Kunming, its partially overgrown 1920s exterior reached via a wide flight of stone steps.

Yuantong Temple

圆通寺, yuántōng sì · Yuantong Jie · Daily 9am–5.30pm · ¥6

East from Cuihu Park, the Qing-vintage **Yuantong Temple** has undergone major renovations to emerge as Kunming's brightest Buddhist temple. A bridge over the central pond crosses through an octagonal pavilion dedicated to a multiarmed Guanyin and white marble Sakyamuni, to the threshold of the main hall, where two huge central pillars wrapped in colourful, manga-esque **dragons** support the ornate wooden ceiling. Faded frescoes on the back wall were painted in the thirteenth century, while the rear annexe houses a graceful, gilded bronze Buddha flanked by peacocks, donated by the Thai government. Nice vegetarian food is served here (11–11.30am; ¥7).

Kunming City Museum (and Flying Tigers Museum)

昆明市博物馆, kūnmíngshì bówùguǎn · Daily 9.30am–5pm · Free

Besides more bronze drums and some dinosaur skeletons, the highlight of the **Kunming City Museum**, east of Beijing Lu along Tuodong Lu, is the **Dali Sutra Pillar**. In its own room on the ground floor, it's a 6.5m-high, pagoda-like Song-dynasty sculpture, in pink sandstone; an octagonal base supports seven tiers covered in Buddha images, statues of fierce guardian gods standing on subjugated demons, and a mix of Tibetan and Chinese script, part of which is the Dharani Mantra. On the second floor the **Flying Tigers Museum** displays a series of well-labelled (in English too) photos and a handful of items of original military equipment which illustrate the history of this little-known yet important US air unit, whose efforts to help resupply Chinese forces over the Himalayas ("the Hump") during World War II from British Burma played an integral part in defeating the Japanese forces in Asia.

Two pagodas

Two large Tang-dynasty pagodas, each a solid thirteen storeys of whitewashed brick crowned with four jolly iron cockerels, rise a short walk south of the city centre. The **Eastern Pagoda** (东寺塔, dōngsì tǎ) on Shulin Jie sits in a little ornamental garden, while the **Western Pagoda** (西寺塔, xīsì tǎ) is a few minutes' walk away at the back of a flagstoned square on Dongsi Jie. You can't enter either, but the sight of these 1300-year-old towers surrounded by modern office blocks is striking.

Yunnan Provincial Museum

云南省博物馆, yúnnánshěng bówùguǎn • 6393 Guangfu Lu • Tues–Sun 9am–4.30pm • Free with passport except special exhibitions • Buses #K15, #165, #169, #174, #253, #255, #A12 & #D7 stop at Guandu Old Town from where it's a 500m walk; a taxi will take around 40min

Out of the centre in an impressive, new three-storey copper-coloured modernist block, the **Yunnan Provincial Museum** gives an insight into Yunnan's history from prehistoric time until the present, and also includes halls focused on porcelain, pottery, paintings and items made of gold. Best are the **bronzes**, dating back more than two thousand years to the Warring States Period and excavated from tombs south of Kunming. The largest pieces include an ornamental plate of a tiger attacking an ox and a coffin in the shape of a bamboo house; but lids from storage drums used to hold cowries are the most impressive, decorated with dioramas of figurines fighting, sacrificing oxen and men and, rather more peacefully, posing with their families and farmyard animals outside their homes. One advantage of it being so far out of town is that it's usually pretty empty.

ARRIVAL AND DEPARTURE
KUNMING

BY PLANE
Kunming Changshui International Airport (昆明长水国际机场, kūnmíng chángshuǐ guójì jīchǎng), known locally as New Kunming Airport (昆明新机场, kūnmíng xīnjīchǎng), lies 25km northeast of the city centre. As well as domestic services, there are international flights to Bangkok, Chiang Mai, Hong Kong, Da Nang, Dhaka, Dubai, Ho Chi Minh City, Kathmandu, Kolkata, Kuala Lumpur, Mandalay, New Delhi, Paris, Phnom Penh, Singapore, Seoul, Taipei, Vientiane and Yangon. Outside the airport, shuttle buses (¥25) head into town every 20–30min: #1 terminates at the *Xiyi Hotel* on Dongfeng Xi Lu, just west of Cuihu Park; while #2 services the southeast of the centre, calling at the *Telecom International Hotel* near the junction of Huancheng Nan Lu and Chungcheng Lu, and Kunming train station. A taxi into town can take up to an hour and costs around ¥100–120. Metro line #6 (every 25min; ¥5) runs from the airport, but at time of writing only as far as the East bus station, still 10km from the city centre, though line #3 will provide a link to the centre when it opens (scheduled for 2017).

Destinations Baoshan (1hr); Beijing (3hr 30min); Changsha (2hr); Chengdu (1hr 35min); Chongqing (daily; 1hr 35min); Dali (50min); Guangzhou (2hr 10min); Guilin (6 weekly; 1hr 25min); Guiyang (1hr 15min); Hong Kong (2hr 25min); Jinghong (55min); Lhasa (3hr); Lijiang (1hr); Mangshi (1hr); Nanning (1hr); Shanghai (3hr 10min); Shenzhen (2hr 10min); Xi'an (2hr 10min).

BY TRAIN
CRH By the time of publication, the new high-speed rail link to Nanning via Baise may have opened; another to Changsha via Guiyang is also scheduled. Both are slated to connect to Shanghai in as little as ten hours. They will be served by the new, gargantuan Kunming South train station (昆明南火车站, kūnmíng nán huǒchē zhàn), situated a whopping 28km south of the centre, though served by metro lines #1 and #4. Check online for more details on services when it has opened.

Other services Kunming Station (昆明火车站, kūnmíng huǒchē zhàn) is at the southern end of

Beijing Lu and handles the regular train services; the building is two-tiered, with the ticket windows downstairs (daily 5am–midnight) and departures upstairs. It has a metro station; useful buses from here include #23 up Beijing Lu and #59, which heads up Qingnian Lu to within striking distance of Yuantong Temple and Cuihu Park. If you're immediately heading onwards, bus #C71 to the South bus station is useful (though it's also connected by metro) and buses #C72 or #80 run to the Western bus station. Note that trains to Xiaguan (for Dali) and Lijiang are slower than making the same journey by bus.

Destinations Beijing (4 daily; 33–48hr); Chengdu (6 daily; 17hr 19min–22hr 37min); Chongqing (1 daily; 24hr); Guangzhou (4 daily; 16hr 35min–28hr); Guilin (1 daily; 19hr); Guiyang (20 daily; 6hr 28min–11hr); Lijiang (5 daily; 7hr–10hr 25min); Nanning (7 daily; 12–15hr); Shanghai (3 daily; 34–40hr); Shenzhen (1 daily; 29hr); Xiaguan (11 daily; 5hr 11min–11hr); Xi'an (2 daily; 34–35hr); Xichang (4 daily; 7hr 50min–8hr 30min).

BY BUS

Kunming's four main bus stations are scattered around the city perimeter, generally at the point of the compass relevant to the destination. They are all a long way out: allow plenty of transit time, even in a cab, especially during rush hours (about 7–9am & 5–7pm). Agents in town (including most accommodation) can buy tickets for you for a fee to save you schlepping out yourself.

West bus station (西部汽车客运站, xībù qìchē kèyùnzhàn), also known as Majie bus station (马街客运站, mǎjiē kèyùn zhàn), is 10km out towards the Western Hills. On arrival, catch bus #82 to the western end of Nanping Jie or bus #18 to Kunming train station; a taxi is ¥30–40.

Destinations Deqin (daily at 7pm; 15hr); Lijiang (hourly 8am–2.40pm; 8–9hr); Liuku (8 daily; 11hr); Ruili (hourly 8.30–11am, then sleeper bus hourly 5–9pm; 12–13hr); Shangri-La (6 daily; 9hr 30min); Tengchong (7daily; 10hr); Xiaguan/Dali (every 15min; 4hr).

South bus station (南部汽车客运站, nánbù qìchē kèyùnzhàn) is 15km southeast of the centre; take the metro or bus #C71 to Kunming train station, or a taxi for ¥45.

Destinations Baoshan (19 daily; 7hr 40min); Fugong (daily 6.30pm & 7.30pm; 10hr 30min); Jianshui (hourly till 7.10pm, sleeper bus at 8.30pm; 3–4hr); Jinghong (hourly; 9–10hr); Luang Prabang (daily 6.30pm; 26hr); Weishan (daily 2 morning & 2 night buses; 6hr 30min); Yuanyang (hourly 12.30–7pm; 5hr).

East bus station (东部汽车客运站, dōngbù qìchē kèyùnzhàn), 10km out. It is for services to Shilin and points east, plus the Vietnam border. Bus #60 runs to Kunming train station via Bailong Lu; a taxi costs ¥30. Metro line #6 runs northeast from the station to the airport

11

LEAVING CHINA

Kunming is a springboard for travel into Thailand, Laos, Vietnam and Myanmar, all of which maintain consulates in town.

For **Thailand**, there are flights to Bangkok from Kunming and depending on the security situation, it may also be possible to catch a ferry (or tag along with a cargo ship) from Jinghong in Xishuangbanna (see p.715). Many nationalities can stay visa-free in Thailand for 30 days if arriving at an airport, or 15 days arriving by land; if you need longer, head to Kunming's consulate for a visa.

You can fly to **Laos**, and there's also a direct bus from Kunming's South bus station to Luang Prabang (daily 6.30pm; 26hr; ¥398). Laos visas might again be available at the border depending on your nationality. For **Vietnam** either fly, or catch a bus to Hekou (see p.676) and cross the border on foot.

For **Myanmar**, arrange both visas and currently obligatory tour package in Kunming before either flying direct to Yangon or crossing the border on foot near Ruili (see p.711).

KUNMING'S CONSULATES

The Guandu Consular District (外国领馆区, wàiguó lǐngguǎnqū), home to an increasing number of consulates, is around 15km southeast of the city centre and can be reached by taxi for around ¥30–40. Most only process visas on weekday mornings.

Cambodia Royal Consulate General, 14F Guan Fang Plaza, 258 Baiyun Lu ☏0871 63317320, ✉camcg.kmg @mfa.gov.kh.

Laos Consulate General, 6800 Caiyun Bei Lu, Foreign Consular Zone, Guandu District (next to the *Empark Hotel*) ☏0871 67334522, ✉cglaokun@yahoo.com.

Myanmar (Burma). Consulate General, 99 Yingbin Lu, Foreign Consular Zone, Guandu District

☏0871 68162804, ⊛mcgkunming.org.

Thailand Royal Consulate General, South Building, *Kunming Hotel*, 145 Dongfeng Dong Lu ☏0871 63168916, ⊛www.thaiembassy.org/uanis.

Vietnam Consulate General, Suite 507, Hongda Mansion, 155 Beijing Lu ☏0871 63522669, ⊛vietnamconsulate-kunming.org.

though there are plans to connect it to the metro.

Destinations Hekou (hourly till 3pm, then sleeper bus at 7pm & 7.30pm; 7–8hr); Shilin (hourly 8am–6.40pm; 2–3hr).

North bus station (北部汽车客运站, běibù qìchē kèyùnzhàn). Unless arriving from Panzhihua in Sichuan, you're unlikely to find yourself here; the metro runs from here through town via both train stations, as does bus #23.

Destinations Panzhihua (6 daily; 4hr 30min).

GETTING AROUND

By bus You might resort to city buses (¥1–2) to reach some of the further-flung sights, but they're slow and not that useful around the centre.

By metro Limited sections of the still-under-construction metro are operational but at time of writing only cover areas well outside the city centre. The comprehensive six-line network is due for completion in 2018, though there have been considerable delays.

By taxi Taxis ply all the main streets in central Kunming, charging a minimum ¥8 for the first 3km and ¥1.60 for each additional km during the day. At night a minimum ¥9.80 charge applies.

By bicycle Bicycles can be rented through *The Hump* or *Cloudland* hostels for ¥30–40/day.

INFORMATION

Travel agents Travel agents abound in Kunming, with virtually every hotel able to organize visas and private tours around the city, and to Shilin, Dali, Lijiang and Xishuangbanna, and to obtain tickets for onwards travel. Expect to pay commissions of at least ¥20 for bus or train ticket reservations, though plane tickets shouldn't attract a mark-up. The best bet for travel and tourist advice without the hard sell is at one of the city's youth hostels; staff at *The Hump* and (to a lesser extent) *Cloudland* are generally helpful and informative.

ACCOMMODATION

Cloudland International Hostel 大脚氏国际青年旅舍, dàjiǎoshì guójì qīngnián lǚshè. 23 Zhuantang Lu ☎0871 64103777. Although a little hard to find, in a street at right-angles to Xichang Lu, northwest of its junction with Xinwen Lu, *Cloudland* has rooms in tiers around a flower-filled courtyard, and a good café. Not as well-organized as *The Hump*, and doesn't have as good travel information, but it's certainly in a more peaceful location. En-suite doubles cost ¥150. Dorms ¥35, doubles ¥138

★**Cuihu (Green Lake Hotel)** 翠湖宾馆, cuìhú bīnguǎn. 6 Cuihu Nan Lu ☎0871 65158888, ⓦgreenlakehotelkunming.com. *The* place to stay in Kunming. Long-established, luxurious, and good value in pleasant surroundings by Cuihu Park, with a fancy lobby (with bar and café), impeccably polite staff, a pool, gym, spa, and three excellent restaurants. Airport transfers can be arranged; all major credit cards are accepted. ¥1106

Fairyland 四季酒店鼓楼店, sìjì jiǔdiàn gǔlóu diàn. 716 Beijing Lu ☎0871 6285777. One of half a dozen branches of this budget business hotel in Kunming, this one has the advantages of not only being right next door to Chanxianglou metro station (line #2), but also not far from Yuantong Temple and Cuihu Park. Cheaper rooms are a tad small, but pay ¥20 more and you get a spacious, comfortable place to stay. ¥184

Home Inn 如家酒店, rújiā jiǔdiàn. 492 Dongfeng Xi Lu ☎0871 65387888, ⓦhomeinns.com. Handily, if noisily, located not far from the university area and Cuihu Park, what this chain hotel lacks in charm it mostly makes up for in cleanliness. Decent wi-fi and en-suite rooms throughout. ¥229

Horizon (Zhong Wei) 天恒大酒店, tiānhéng dàjiǔdiàn. 432 Qingnian Lu ☎0871 63186666, ⓦwww.horizonhotel.net. An overblown, multi-starred place in a great location with a mountain of marble in the lobby and an overflow of cafés and restaurants; rooms are a little dated and drab at the moment but are now undergoing extensive renovation. ¥800

★**The Hump Hostel** 驼峰客栈, tuófēng kèzhàn. Jinbi Lu ☎0871 63640359, ⓦthehumphostel.com. Clean, well-organized and secure hostel that features a comfy lounge-bar-restaurant – its walls adorned with dozens of photos documenting the Flying Tigers Squadron who flew over the "Hump" (see p.666) – and rooftop terrace. They provide good travel information and have a bus/train/tour booking service. The only downside is noise from surrounding nightclubs, but they'll give you earplugs if you ask. The basic rooms are windowless cells but the standard (¥165), triple (¥195) and family rooms (¥225) are much nicer, and have en-suite bathrooms and windows. Dorms ¥35, doubles ¥90

Kunming 昆明饭店, kūnmíng fàndiàn. 52 Dongfeng Dong Lu ☎0871 63162063. Another big, upmarket hotel with an ageing, gaudy lobby, reasonable service, decent rooms, a range of sports and fitness facitities, a bar and restaurants specializing in Cantonese, Korean and Western food. ¥780

Lost Garden Guesthouse 一丘田七号客栈, yī qiū tián qī hào kèzhàn. 7 Yiqiutian, off Huanggong Dong Jie ☎0871 65111127, ⓦlostgardenguesthouse.com. Tucked down an alley near Cuihu Lake, the location is great and it's run by friendly, English-speaking staff who can help with transportation and tour info. Also has a very pleasant rooftop terrace where they serve Western food and coffee.

A little bit more expensive than other hostels, but the dorms are very good, and although the rooms are a bit bare for the price, they're clean, bright and comfortable enough. Dorms ¥55, doubles ¥180

EATING

Kunming is stacked with good places to eat, from street stalls and Western cafés to smart restaurants offering local cuisine. Back lanes off Jinbi Lu hold some great cheap places where you can battle with the locals over grilled cheese, hotpots, fried snacks rolled in chilli powder, loaves of excellent meat-stuffed soda bread, and rich duck and chicken casseroles. There's a string of varied restaurants along the newly built street of wooden houses along Nanqiang Jie (just north of and running parallel to Tuo Dong Lu) where Indian, Chinese, Korean, Japanese, Thai and Western food can all be found, as can a decent cup of coffee.

★**1910 Gare du Sud** 火车南站, 1910 huǒchē nánzhàn. 8 Houxin Jie, accessed from Chongshan Lu, near its junction with Xunjin Lu ☎0871 63169486. Traditional Yunnan fare served in a former French colonial train station and famous for its grilled *rubing*, a typical local cheese. There's a large balcony and courtyard and photos of colonial Kunming throughout. A popular place with trendy middle-class locals but nowhere near as expensive as you'd think, and two can eat very well for ¥100–150. Daily 11am–9pm.

French Café 兰白红咖啡, lánbáihóng kāfēi. 70 Wenlin Jie ☎0871 65382391. Arguably making the best European breads and pastries around, this café attracts Kunming's fairly substantial French expat crowd, with the filled baguettes and paninis (¥20–30) or crêpes (¥15–30) highly recommended (though the other dishes not so much). Also serves good-value set breakfasts till 1pm (¥25–30). Daily 9am–midnight.

Heavenly Manna 吗哪, mana. 74 Wenhua Xiang ☎0871 65369399. Home-style Yunnanese dishes: inexpensive, varied, interesting and very spicy indeed, with most dishes on the bilingual menu ¥15–40. The setting is no-frills low wooden tables and chairs; watch out for the low ceiling with protruding pipes upstairs. Daily 11am–9.30pm.

Hongdou Yuan 红豆园餐厅, hóngdòuyuán cāntīng. 142 Wenlin Jie ☎0871 5392020. Branch of popular Sichuanese–Yunnanese chain, with an easy-to-follow photo menu. Not everything is spicy; they do excellent crisp-skinned duck with cut buns, cold-sliced pork, stewed spareribs and rice-coated pork slices. The sweet and sour fish is good too. Look at around ¥40–50 per head for two. Daily 11am–2pm & 5–9pm.

Jian Xin Yuan 建新园, jiànxīn yuán. 196 Baoshan Jie ☎0871 3186320. Original location (from 1906) of this popular Kunming-wide chain serving local-style spicy noodle soups. Excellent cold noodles are downstairs, though most foreigners opt for the hot noodles (¥18–40) served upstairs, which usually has more space. No English sign, but it's always the busiest place on the street and expect to wait around mealtimes. Daily 24hr.

The Park Bar and Grill Cuihu Park ☎153 68171162. One of many open-air places to eat in the middle of the park, this one serves up pretty good Western dishes (¥20–87) such as burgers, salads or steaks, though best of all are the barbecued meats. They also have a popular all-you-can-eat meat and salad special on Sat and Sun after 5pm. They do great cocktails and have a surprisingly good whisky selection. Daily 9.30am–late.

Prague Café 布拉格咖啡馆, bùlāgē kāfēi guǎn. 40 Wenlin Jie ☎0871 65332764. This offshoot of a successful Lijiang enterprise offers a wide range of very strong coffees (¥15–30) and a decent breakfast, as well as a book exchange. One of the better cafés in this locality, it's a good place to while away an afternoon. Also serves a range of Japanese and Western dishes which are mostly around ¥35–40. Daily 9am–midnight.

Salvadors 沙尔瓦多咖啡馆, shā'ěrwǎduō kāfēiguǎn. 76 Wenhua Xiang ☎0871 65363525, 🌐salvadors.cn. Expat-run and -populated and somewhere to get information and conversation from jaded, in-the-know foreign residents. Well-stocked bar plus coffee and pub-style menu with hummus, feta cheese and avocado featuring, and also the best Mexican food in town, with most mains ¥35–50. Daily 9am–10pm.

Shiping Huiguan 石屏会馆, shípíng huìguǎn. 24 Zhonghe Xiang, Cuihu Nan Lu ☎0871 63627444. Tucked back off the street behind an ornamental archway and heavy stone wall, this elegantly restored courtyard restaurant is a great place to sample Yunnanese cuisine. It tends to get booked out by tour groups and wedding parties, so reservations are essential. Ranges from ¥20 for fried greens and ¥38 for the house speciality of stinky tofu up to ¥100 for steaming plates of meat. Daily 11am–10pm.

SnB 15 Nanqiang Jie ☎138 88999508. When you see the plastic food in the window at this Korean–Japanese joint, you know exactly what your plate will look like when it's served to you in the slightly minimalist stripped-pine interior. The sushi (¥15–30) is served by the plate, but everything else is as a set, from the rice *bibimbap* (¥30) to the rather good fried pork *donkasu* (¥35), and curry (¥25). Daily 10am–9.30pm.

Yingjiang Dai 盈江傣味园, yíngjiāng dǎiwèiyuán. 66 Cuihu Bei Lu ☎0871 65337889. Somewhat modified for the mainstream Chinese clientele, though Dai favourites like sweet pineapple rice (¥22), grilled fish (¥58), sour bamboo shoots and *laab* (spicy mince salad; ¥38) are all pretty delicious, and if you're lucky you can snag an outside table from where you can see the lake. Daily 11am–10pm.

11

DRINKING, NIGHTLIFE AND ENTERTAINMENT

Kunming is a great place to go out, with plenty of friendly, reasonably priced bars and clubs patronized by a good mix of locals and foreigners; the most Western-friendly are in the Wenlin Jie area, though rapidly rising rents here means there's also a new crop of grungier bars springing up just north of here along Jianshe Lu. Check *Go Kunming* (w gokunming.com) for the latest venues, entertainment and cultural events.

Camel Bar 骆驼酒吧, luòtuó jiǔbā. 2F, 310 Jinbi Lu ☏ 0871 63195841, w camelbarkm.com. Not far from *The Hump*, this place is a bit more polished than most in the city, appealing to middle-class Chinese rather than just students. There's a pricier menu to match, with drinks from ¥18 and main dishes, including pizza and burgers, starting at ¥35. It gets lively with dancing at weekends, but during the day is a good place to relax over a coffee. Daily 9am–1am.

Chapter One 联系, liánxì. 146 Wenlin Jie ☏ 0871 6365635, w chapteronekunming.com. Good pub atmosphere, cheap happy-hour drinks (9.30am–7.30pm) and a decent range of inexpensive, mostly Western food served all day, such as burgers and breakfasts (¥20–40), as well as unlimited-refill coffee (¥20). Daily 9.30am–midnight.

★**Fu Bar** 139 Jianshe Lu ☏ 180 87105596. One of the liveliest and fun places at the moment, this Dai-run joint, where the owner speaks English (her husband is foreign) is located just north of the university. A great atmosphere with friendly staff and mixed clientele, live music (Wed–Sat), Western-style bar food (or there are some great earthy Dai restaurants opposite) and a selection of ice-cold local and imported beers which can also be enjoyed on the terrace out front. Daily 6pm–late.

Humdinger 玩啤西餐吧, wán pí xīcān bā. 111 Zhengyi Lu ☏ 0871 63601611. This high-end, chic microbrew-pub may not have the best party atmosphere, but it's a great place to start the night with a jar of one of their range of craft beers (¥38–45) and their excellent wood-fired pizzas (¥58–88). The other Western dishes, such as smoked pork ribs or burgers (both ¥58), are also good. Very busy (with mostly locals) at weekends, when they have live music at 9.45pm. Daily 5.30pm–late.

Kundu Night Market 昆都夜市, kūndū yèshì. Off Xinwen Lu. If you can't live without cheesy techno and flashing lights, head to this clutch of bars and clubs with late-night restaurants, and tattoo parlours in between. Everywhere is free to get in, but drinks cost at least ¥30. Might be of interest to see how the Chinese party. Daily 6pm–late.

Mask 脸谱酒吧, liǎnpǔ jiǔbā. 131 Kundu Night Market ☏ 0871 66438358. Popular Chinese hipster spot on the square in the heart of the Kundu. Considerably less cheesy than its neighbours, it also attracts a smattering of expats for its regular weekend live bands, which are usually followed by DJ sets that carry on till very late. Daily 8pm–late.

Nordica 诺地卡, nuòdìkǎ. 101 Xiba Lu ☏ 0871 64114692, w tcgnordica.com. In the Kunming "Loft" arts this area, this small Scandinavian-run converted factory complex of galleries, a café and studio spaces holds exhibitions, concerts, dance performances, and other artistic endeavours on a fairly ad hoc basis – check their website to see what's going on. Or just drop by and hang with the friendly artistic community. Mon–Sat 11am–9pm.

Yunnan Arts Theatre 云南艺术剧院, yúnnán yìshù jùyuàn. 132 Dongfeng Xi Lu ☏ 183 13884842. Large-scale, energetic dance shows, based (loosely) on authentic ethnic folk culture, play out every night. Tickets at ¥180–480 can be bought during the day from the box office outside the theatre, or from any travel agency in town.

SHOPPING

Nanping Jie and Zhengyi Lu are full of ordinary clothing and shoe stores; the bird market area is where to find jolly souvenirs. Yunnan's famous *pu'er* tea, usually compressed into attractive "bricks" stamped with good-luck symbols, is sold almost everywhere.

Gingko shopping plaza Kunming's most upmarket department stores – three strung across Beijing Lu and Baita Lu, crammed with luxury brands.

Mandarin Books 52 Wenhua Xiang. Kunming's best English-language bookshop is near the university. It has many imported novels, obscure academic texts, guidebooks and much that is published in English in China, all of it fairly pricey. Daily 10am–9pm.

Supermarkets Carrefour supermarket on Nanping Jie, or the similarly enormous Walmart, south off Renmin Xi Lu, just west of the junction with Dongfeng Xi Lu, have imported Western food, plus Yunnan ham sold in slices, chunks and entire hocks.

DIRECTORY

Cinema The best in town, showing some films in English, is the Beijing-run Broadway Cinema, inside the Shuncheng Plaza between Shuncheng Jie and Jinbi Lu. There's an IMAX screen here too.

Hospital English-speaking, Western-trained medics can be found at the Kunming International Clinic (昆明福华国际门诊, kūnmíng fúhuá guójì ménzhěn; ☏ 0871 64119100) at 429 Guangfu Lu, on the second floor of

Yunnan Kidney Hospital.

Massage There are several genuine massage studios staffed by blind masseurs around town, charging around ¥50/hr, including a string of shops at the end of Yuantong Jie near Cuihu Park.

Visa extensions "Public Security Bureau Visas and Permits Office" – the visa extension office, in other words – is opposite Kunming City Museum at 118 Tuodong Lu (Mon–Fri 9–11.30am & 1–5pm; ☎ 0871 63357157). They speak good English but are slow with visa extensions; expect five days.

Around Kunming

There are many popular sights around Kunming that have been pulling in visitors for centuries. Don't miss the extraordinary sculptures at westerly **Qiongzhu Temple**, or the view over Dian Chi lake from the Dragon Gate, high up in the **Western Hills**. Further afield, the spectacular **Stone Forest** makes an enjoyable day-trip if you can accept the fairground atmosphere and the crowds dutifully tagging behind their tour guides.

Jin Dian Park

金殿公园, jīndiàn gōngyuán • Daily 8am–7pm • ¥20 • Bus #71 from Beijing Lu, north of Dongfeng Guangchang

Around 10km northeast of the city, steps at **Jin Dian Park**, also known as the Golden Temple, head up through woodland to a cluster of pleasantly worn Qing-dynasty halls housing weapons used in 1671 by the rebel Ming general Wu Sangui – the man who deliberately let the Manchu armies through the Great Wall, and then later revolted against China's new overlords. Behind the halls is Jin Dian itself, a **gilded bronze temple** built as a replica of the one atop Wudang Shan in Hubei (see p.426). The woods here are full of fragrant camellias and weekend picnickers, and a tower on the hilltop encloses a large Ming bell from Kunming's demolished southern gates.

Avoid taking the cable car from the back of the park to the **1999 Horticultural Expo Site** – a monster scam at over ¥100 for a walk through vast, drab squares of low-maintenance flowerbeds. The Chinese do excellent gardens, but this isn't one of them.

Qiongzhu Temple

筇竹寺, qióngzhú sì • Daily 8am–5pm • ¥10 • Taxi around ¥100 return including waiting time; bus #82 from the western end of Nanping Jie or bus #C72 from Kunming train station to the West bus station, and then bus #C61 (7am–7pm) to the temple – check with the driver because not all #C61 buses come here

Up in the hills 10km west of Kunming and tedious to reach on public transport, tranquil **Qiongzhu Temple** features a fantastic array of over-the-top Buddhist sculptures. Late in the nineteenth century, the eminent Sichuanese sculptor **Li Guangxiu** and his five assistants were engaged to embellish Qiongzhu's main halls with five hundred clay statues of *arhats*, which they accomplished with inspired gusto, spending ten years creating the comical and grotesquely distorted crew of monks, goblins, scribes, emperors and beggars that crowd the interior; some sit rapt with holy contemplation, others smirk, roar with hysterical mirth or snarl grimly as they ride a foaming sea alive with sea monsters. Unfortunately it all proved too absurd for Li's conservative contemporaries and this was his final commission. There's also a good, if pricey, **vegetarian restaurant** here, which is open at lunchtime.

The Western Hills

西山, xīshān • Daily 8.30am–6pm • Park entry ¥20, Long Men area ¥30 • Bus #33 or #66 from Jinbi Square

The well-wooded **Western Hills**, 16km outside Kunming, are an easy place to spend a day out of doors with cable cars and pleasant walking trails ascending a 2500m-high ridge for superb vistas over **Dian Chi**, the broad lake southwest of town.

From the park gates at Gaoyao (高峣, gāoyáo) it's over an hour's walk to the main sights, but take time to visit the atmospheric **Huating Temple** (华亭寺, huátíng sì) and **Taihua Temple** (太华寺, tàihuá sì), the latter reached along a warped, flagstoned path through old-growth forest. Past here you come to two **cable-car stations**: one crosses back towards town (¥40), the other climbs to the Dragon Gate area (¥25). You can walk up too: just carry straight on along the road and it's about twenty minutes to the Dragon Gate ticket office. Then it's up narrow flights of stone steps, past a group of minor temples, and into a series of chambers and narrow tunnels which exit at **Dragon Gate** (龙门, lóngmén) itself, a narrow balcony and ornamented grotto on a sheer cliff overlooking the lake. It took the eighteenth-century monk **Wu Laiqing** and his successors more than seventy years to excavate the tunnels, which continue up to where another flight of steps climbs to further lookouts.

The Stone Forest

石林景区, shílín jǐngqū • Daily 8.30am–6pm • ¥175; cable car ¥25 • Day-trips are run by every tour desk in Kunming; public buses from the East bus station (¥35) – make sure you get one to the scenic area and not to Shilin town

Yunnan's renowned **Stone Forest** comprises an exposed bed of limestone spires weathered and split into intriguing clusters, 90km east of Kunming. It takes about an hour to cover the main circuit through the pinnacles to **Sword Peak Pond**, an ornamental pool surrounded by particularly sharp ridges; you can climb along a narrow track leading right up across the top of the forest. This is the most frequented part of the park, with large red characters incised into famous rocks, and ethnic **Sani**, a Yi subgroup, in unnaturally clean dresses strategically placed for photographers. This area can be intimidatingly crammed with Chinese tour groups, but the paths that head out towards the perimeter are much quieter, leading to smaller, separate stone groupings in the fields beyond where you could spend the whole day without seeing another visitor. There are several cable cars that run from the visitors centre to the park entrance, and then to all the main sights.

Southeastern Yunnan

The region southeast of Kunming is a nicely unpackaged corner of the province, and there are good reasons, besides the **Vietnamese border crossing** at Hekou, to head down this way. Amiable, old-fashioned **Jianshui** boasts a complement of Qing architecture, and an unusual attraction in nearby caves, while **Yuanyang** is the base for exploring the cultures and impressive terraced landscapes of the Hong He valley. Jianshui and Yuanyang can be tied together in a trip to the border, or each are directly accessible by bus from Kunming.

Jianshui

建水, jiànshuǐ

JIANSHUI, a country town 200km south of Kunming, has been an administrative centre for over a thousand years. There's a good feel to the place, buoyed by plenty of **old architecture** and a very casual approach to tourism, making for a pleasant overnight stop. While you're here, visit **Yanzi Dong**, an impressive limestone cavern out in the countryside nearby.

The old town

On arrival, head straight for Jianshui's scruffy **old town**, a web of lanes entered through the huge red gateway of **Chaoyang Lou** (朝阳楼, cháoyáng lóu), the Ming-dynasty eastern gate tower. Past here, cobbled Lin'an Lu runs through the old town, lined with wooden-fronted shops, but cutting down and along parallel Guilin Jie leads into a completely unrestored quarter, past blocks of mud-brick mansions and a stack of ancient **wells**, many of which are clearly still used by locals.

Zhu Family Gardens

朱家花园, zhūjiā huāyuán • Hanlin Jie • Daily 8am–10pm • ¥50

Right in the centre of the old town, the traditionally arranged **Zhu Family Gardens** are a Chinese box of interlocking halls and courtyards, brightly painted and in good condition. The gardens were laid out in the 1880s, when the Zhus were at their height of wealth; they later fell from grace and the gardens only escaped complete destruction during the 1960s because the family had fought both the Manchus in 1911 and the Nationalist armies twenty years later. Pick of the small pavilions is the open-sided **Hua Ting**, an elegant timber and stone hall facing a small pond.

Confucian Academy

文庙, wénmiào • Lin'an Lu • Daily 8am–10pm • ¥60

West along Lin'an Lu is the main entrance to Jianshui's venerable **Confucian Academy**. Past the large lily pond out front, there are ornamental stone gateways and halls containing statues of the Great Sage and his more gifted followers, with worried parents bringing their offspring here to kowtow to this patron of learning before school exams in the summer. Although what survives here is in good condition, it's clear the academy has suffered very badly over the years.

Yanzi Dong

燕子洞, yànzi dòng • ¥133 • Buses leave Jianshui bus station when full, approximately every 30min 7am–3pm (30min; ¥10–15); last bus back 6pm; minibus or taxi from Jianshui about ¥300 return, including waiting time

Yanzi Dong, the Swallows' Caves, lie about 30km from Jianshui in the forested Lu River valley. For the last few centuries people have come to see the tens of thousands of **swiftlets** who nest here – the noise of wheeling birds is deafening during the early summer – but even without the birds the caves are an enjoyable Chinese-style tourist attraction, featuring a dragon-boat ride, a few coloured lights, some spectacular rock formations, and an **underground restaurant** selling bird's-nest cakes (an expensive delicacy for the Chinese). If you can, catch the **Bird Nest Festival** on August 8, the only day of the year that collecting the then-vacant nests is allowed – a very profitable and dangerous task for local Yi men, who scale the 60m-high cliffs as crowds look on.

ARRIVAL AND DEPARTURE   JIANSHUI

By bus Jianshui's bus station is on Yinghui Lu in the bland modern town, 1km northeast of the old town; catch bus #1, #12 or #13 to the Chaoyang Lou, or a taxi (¥8–10) to Lin'an Lu Hanlin Jie intersection in the old town. There are regular departures to Kunming and Yuanyang – the latter a long trip on a direct, scenic but rough road south – though less frequent services to Hekou.

Destinations Hekou (4 daily, last at 11am; 4hr); Jinghong (11am daily; 10hr); Kunming (every 30min in the morning; hourly in the afternoon; 4hr); Yuanyang (every 20–30min; 2–3hr).

ACCOMMODATION

Guilin Inn Jianshui 建水桂林客栈, jiàn shuǐ guìlín kèzhàn. Corner of Hanlin Jie and Lin'an Lu ☎0873 3188619. Best of the centrally located cheapies, the rooms at this place aren't the best (with hard beds and the cheapest rooms without a/c) but the price is great, the public areas surprisingly pleasant, and the staff friendly and helpful. ¥88

★**Lin'an Inn** 临安客栈, lín'ān kèzhàn. 32 Hanlin Jie ☎0873 7655866. Just north of the Zhu Gardens, this friendly courtyard-style hotel has large, clean, airy rooms which are excellent value, and some enormous beds. Although very friendly and welcoming, neither the owners (nor their dogs) speak English. ¥228

Zhu Family Gardens 朱家花园, zhūjiā huāyuán. 16 Hanlin Jie ☎0873 7667109. This has to be the pick of Jianshui's places to stay, at least for atmosphere, with its rooms full of imitation Qing furniture and a genuine sense of history. Unsurprisingly expensive. ¥480

EATING

★**Xiangman Lou** 香满楼, xiāngmǎn lóu. 65 Hanlin Jie ☎0873 7655655. This wooden building in the heart of the old town is the best place to eat in Jianshui. There's an extensive menu including the local speciality *qiguo*, a casserole whose inverted funnel design simultaneously poaches meat and creates a soup, as well as regional mushroom dishes and a decent selection for vegetarians.

Expect to pay around ¥42 per person for a full meal. Daily 11.30am–9pm.

The Hong He valley

Hong He (红河, hónghé), the Red River, starts life near Xiaguan in Yunnan's northwest and runs southeast across the province, entering Vietnam at Hekou and flowing through Hanoi before emptying its russet-coloured waters, laden with volcanic soil, into the Gulf of Tonkin. For much of its journey the river is straight, channelled by high mountain ranges into a series of fertile, steep-sided valleys. These have been **terraced** by resident **Hani**, whose mushroom-shaped adobe-and-thatch houses pepper the hills around **Yuanyang**. In spring and autumn thick mists blanket the area, muting the violent contrast between red soil and brilliant green paddy fields. Though the best time to see them is between March and May, when the paddies are full of water, they are spectacular at any time.

11

Yuanyang

元阳, yuányáng

The access point for viewing the rice terraces is **Yuanyang**, a district 80km south of Jianshui and 300km from Kunming. The name covers two settlements: the riverside township of **Nansha** (元阳南沙, yuányáng nánshā), terminus for Jianshui buses; and, where you actually want to base yourself, **XINJIE** (元阳新街镇, yuányáng xīnjiēzhèn), 30km uphill at the top of a high ridge. Xinjie is a small, untidy brick-and-concrete town which becomes a hive of activity on **market days** (every five days), when brightly dresssed Hani, Miao, Yi and Yao women pour in from surrounding villages.

Around Xinjie

Xinjie sits surrounded by pretty villages and deeply terraced hillsides, some within walking distance or a short drive on local transport. One easy walk is a loop, via various hamlets, to the Hani village of **Jinzhuzhai** and **Longshuba**, a Yi settlement, which nestle quietly amid trees, giant bamboo and paddy fields. Try and catch at least one village **market**, where fruit and veg, daily necessities, wild honey, buffaloes and chickens are sold, and watch men discreetly gambling in the background. Markets run between villages on a rota, and activity peaks around noon.

Rice terraces

Daily just before sunrise–just after sunset • All viewing platforms ¥100 combination tickets

There are several places from where you can view the famous **terraces**, though you'll need to buy a fairly pricey ticket to use them. A roadside viewing platform 18km northwest of town at **Mengping** (勐平, měngpíng) gives you the best view of **sunset** while the southwestern road will get you to more viewpoints at **Bada** (坝达, bàdá; 16km from Xinjie) and the renovated farm village of **Duoyishu** (多依树, duōyīshù; 27km), famed for its (unfortunately often cloudy) sunrises, and where there's a range of basic accommodation. Although the viewing platforms have the best spots, pretty similar views can be had from anywhere in the area, where you can enjoy the views without the crowds (often hundreds of Chinese amateur photographers at sunrise and sunset), the amazingly pushy locals selling postcards, and without paying.

ARRIVAL AND INFORMATION   HONG HE VALLEY

By bus Nansha bus station (南沙汽车站, nánshā qìchē zhàn) in Yuanyang is the main long-distance bus station for the region and is at river level, right at the junction of the road up to Xinjie.
Destinations Hekou (daily 9am & 11am; 3hr); Jianshui

(every 30min; 2hr); Kunming (4 daily; 7hr).
Services There's an Agricultural Bank ATM along Xinjie's pedestrianized shopping street off the square which claims to take foreign cards, but don't count on it.

GETTING AROUND

By minibus Minibuses shuttle between Nansha and Xinjie bus stations throughout the day (¥10; 1hr). Private minibuses ply popular routes from village to village for a few yuan per person (they display their destinations in their front windows). If you're pushed for time you'll probably need to hire a minibus at Xinjie; around ¥400 for the vehicle should cover a day's (8hr) exploration and get you around most of the sights.

ACCOMMODATION AND EATING

Accommodation in Xinjie is plentiful though fairly dire on the whole; there are also several better, but basic guesthouses among the terraces at Duoyishu village.

XINJIE

Yunti 云梯大酒店, yúntī dàjiǔdiàn. Across the road from the main square ☏ 0873 5624858. Of the two *Yunti* hotels in Xinjie, this three-star has the better rooms but lesser views. With large, very clean and well-equipped (though poorly maintained) rooms, this is the most comfortable place in town (though that's not saying much). It also has a restaurant that serves Chinese and international food. **¥198**

Yunti Sunshine 云梯顺捷酒店, yúntī shùnjié jiǔdiàn. In the main square ☏ 0873 5621588. Boasting wonderful views, the rooms here have an unfinished quality to them, but are perfectly acceptable for a night (if you don't mind hard beds). You also have a grandstand spot for morning aerobics in the square – which kicks off at 7am sharp, accompanied by blasting techno. Bring earplugs. **¥138**

DUOYISHU

Sunny Guesthouse 阳光客栈, yángguāng kèzhàn. ☏ 1598 7371311. Down at the bottom of the village, the friendly *Sunny* is hard to find but run by fluent English-speakers, so give them a call before you arrive and they'll come and find you. Somewhere between a guesthouse and a hostel, rooms are basic but have fantastic views down the valley. Dorms **¥55**, doubles **¥150**

Yuanyang International Youth Hostel 元阳国际青年旅舍, yuányáng guójì qīngnián lǚshè. ☏ 136 9498158, ⓦ yhachina.com. At the top of the village, down a flight of steps from the main road, the modern building is functional but hardly pretty, much like this hostel's rooms. There's an excellent terrace for watching the sunrise though, and the bar downstairs also turns out a good selection of evening meals. Book well ahead, and note that solo travellers may have to share double rooms. Dorms **¥55**, doubles **¥110**

Hekou and the border

河口, hékǒu

HEKOU, 360km southeast of Kunming, is only worth a visit if you're in transit between China and Vietnam – the border post is a few minutes' walk from the bus station. On the other side, **Lao Cai** has a huge game market, a few despondent hotels, and a train station 3km south that offers two services daily for the ten-hour run to Hanoi. Most travellers take a bus or motorbike-taxi (US$5) to the hill resort town of **Sa Pa**.

ARRIVAL AND INFORMATION

HEKOU

By bus Arriving from Vietnam, head 50m up the main road and the bus station is on the left. Here you can catch fast buses to Kunming's East bus station or ordinary buses to Yuanyang and Jianshui.

Destinations Jianshui (4 daily; 4hr); Kunming (4 morning and 4 sleeper buses daily; 7–8hr); Yuanyang (2 daily; 3hr).

Services To change money, walk up the main street from the border, turn right after 200m, and you'll arrive at the Bank of China (daily 8am–5.30pm; foreign exchange closed Sun).

Northwestern Yunnan

Vigorously uplifted during the last fifty million years as the Indian subcontinent buckled up against China, **northwestern Yunnan** is a geologically unsettled region of subtropical forests, thin pasture, alpine lakes and shattered peaks painted crisply in blue, white and grey. **Xiaguan** is the regional hub, springboard for the route north via a string of old towns, once staging posts on the *chama dao*, the "Tea-Horse Road" **trade routes** between China and Tibet, along which goods were transported on horseback. The lakeshore town of **Dali** is the first, home to the Bai nationality and backed by a long mountain range; but **Lijiang**, a few hours up the road at the base of Yulong Xue Shan, pulls in the biggest crowds as the former capital of the **Naxi** kingdom (though now best avoided). Hikers can organize themselves here for a two-day trek through **Tiger Leaping Gorge**, where a youthful Yangzi River cuts through the deepest chasm on Earth. Nearby is **Lugu Lake**, lakeside home to the matrilineal **Mosuo**, while north again is the Tibetan monastery town of **Shangri-La**. By now you're barely in Yunnan, and a day's further travel will carry you up to **Deqin**, where a spectacular string of peaks marks the Tibetan borderlands.

If possible, it's probably best to head up this way in autumn: winters are extremely cold, and while early spring is often sunny, summers – though fairly mild – can also be very wet, leading to landslides. Also be aware that some border regions might be **closed off** during March, historically a time of political unrest in Tibet (see p.871).

Xiaguan

下关, xiàguān

Some 380km west of Kunming underneath a string of mountaintop wind turbines, **XIAGUAN** – also confusingly known as **Dali City** (大理市, dàlǐ shì) – is a sprawling transport hub on the southern shore of Er Hai Lake. With Dali so close – less than an hour's ride up the lakeshore – you won't need to spend the night here, but you'll almost certainly pass through Xiaguan at some stage, if only to top up your **China visa** at the local, highly amenable, visa extension (PSB) office. Both the holy mountain of **Jizu Shan** and **Weishan**, a small, largely unspoiled market town to the south, are just about manageable as day-trips from the town's bus stations.

ARRIVAL AND DEPARTURE   XIAGUAN

Xiaguan is where most long-distance "Dali" transport actually terminates; Dali Old Town itself (大理古城, dàlǐ gǔchéng) is less than an hour from the city on frequent public transport – Xiaguan is often now referred to as Dali. Though it's possible to get tickets at the respective train and bus stations in Xiaguan, booking in Dali at a small mark-up (¥20) saves a lot of hassle, and for buses often includes a complementary shuttle to the station. A taxi from bus or train stations in Xiaguan to Dali takes around 40min and costs ¥50–60.

BY PLANE
Dali airport (大理机场, dàlǐ jīchǎng) is 15km east of Xiaguan, for which you'll need a taxi (around ¥120–130 to Dali Old Town).
Destinations Beijing (3hr 20min); Chengdu (1hr 25min); Chongqing (1hr 30min); Jinghong (1hr); Kunming (55min); Shanghai (3hr 25min); Wuhan (3 weekly; 2hr 25min); Xi'an (4 weekly; 2hr 30min).

BY TRAIN
Xiaguan train station (下关火车站, xiàguān huǒchēzhàn) is in the east of town on Weishan Lu; city

bus #8 (every 30min; 30min) to Dali Old Town stops right outside. Buy tickets on the first floor.
Destinations Kunming (9 daily; 5hr–7hr 49min); Lijiang (8 daily; 1hr 41min–3hr).

BY BUS
Dali bus station (大理汽车客运站, dàlǐ qìchē kèyùn zhàn). Just 500m east from the train station on Weishan Lu, catch city bus #8 from outside the train station to Dali Old Town.
Destinations Fugong (daily 11.30am; 9–10hr); Jinghong (2 daily 8.20am & 9.40am; 14hr); Jizu Shan (every 30min;

ROUTES THROUGH THE NORTHWEST
Xiaguan, just a stone's throw from Dali, is just five hours from Kunming by bus, and from here there are at least regular, if not always speedy, services through the rest of the region. **Trains** link Kunming to Xiaguan and Lijiang, with talk of an extension to Shangri-La; and you can also **fly** to Lijiang and Shangri-La. There are overland routes **into Sichuan** from Lijiang and Shangri-La too; but at the time of writing the **Tibet road** from Deqin, which follows the dramatic upper reaches of the Lancang River to Markam, then turns west towards Lhasa, was closed to foreigners. Ask agencies in Dali, Lijiang and Shangri-La about the latest situation.

1hr 30min); Kunming (hourly; 4–5hr); Liuku (every 40min until 2.40pm; 5hr).

North bus station (客运北站, kèyùn běizhàn), 3km north of the centre on the Dali highway (Yuhua Lu) – the #8 bus also stops right outside.

Destinations Deqin (sleeper bus daily 4.30pm; 12–15hr); Jianchuan, for Shaxi (every 45min; 1hr); Lijiang (every 20–30min; 3–4hr); Shangri-La (every 30min until noon; 8–9hr).

South bus station (客运南站, kèyùn nánzhàn) Nanjian Lu. Only useful for buses to Weishan (every 10–15min; 1hr 30min). It's at the terminus of the #2 bus

route from the North bus station.

Xingcheng express bus station (兴盛高快客运站, xīngshèng gāokuài kèyùnzhàn), around 2.5km west of the train station, on Nanjian Lu (south off Weishan Lu). For Dali Old Town, turn right out of the bus station, then right again along Weishan Lu and the #8 bus stop is by the train station.

Destinations Baoshan (every 30min–1hr; 3hr); Kunming (every 30–40min; 4–5hr); Lijiang (5 daily; 3hr 30min); Mangshi (3 daily; 6hr); Ruili (2 daily 8.30am & 8pm; 10–12hr); Shangri-La (hourly; 7hr); Tengchong (3 daily; 7hr).

GETTING AROUND

By bus Xiaguan has a good city bus network, several of which run from arrival points, through town and north to Dali. Fare in town is ¥2, with most buses running 7am–8pm.

By taxi A taxi is the easiest option for crossing Xiaguan between bus stations and should cost no more than ¥15–30.

DIRECTORY

Visa extensions Xiaguan's helpful PSB (Mon–Fri 9–11.30am & 2–5pm; ☎0872 2142149) is located north of town on the Xiaguan–Dali highway, on the bus #8 route:

get off at the Century Middle School stop (世纪中学, shìjì zhōngxué), and the PSB is the building in front of you with a radio tower on the roof.

Jizu Shan

鸡足山, jīzú shān • ¥80 • Shuttlebus from ticket office to mountain ¥20

The holy mountain of **Jizu Shan** lies about 90km northeast of Xiaguan, and is associated with Buddhism's Chan (Zen) sect; Tibetans also consider it a place of pilgrimage. There are a handful of temples here, but perhaps the best thing about a visit is the scenery, especially views from the mountain's summit. On the trek up, you can ponder various unlikely explanations for Jizu Shan's odd name – it means "Chickenfoot Mountain". A more likely explanation, however, is that it's named after a mountain near Bodhgaya in India, where the Buddha gained enlightenment.

On the mountain

The vehicle road ends halfway up the mountain, in woodland between the simple **Shizhong Temple** (石钟寺, shízhōng sì) and larger **Wanshou Nunnery** (万寿庵, wànshòu ān). There's a knot of cheap restaurants off to one side here, whose owners also offer beds. Follow the road up to a sharp kink, then take the unsigned path alongside the horse pen up the mountain. It's 3.5km on foot from here to the top, following steps through the forest and onto heathland; 1km along, there's also a **cable car** (¥75 one-way) to just below the summit. Walking, give yourself at least two hours to complete the ascent, which ends where the ninth-century **Lengyan Pagoda** (楞严塔, lèngyán tǎ) and accompanying **Jinding Temple** (金顶寺, jīndǐng sì) – identical to Kunming's Jin Dian (see p.671) – rise splendidly against the skyline.

ARRIVAL AND DEPARTURE   JIZU SHAN

By bus To reach Jizu Shan, catch one of the frequent buses (1hr 30min) from Xiaguan's Dali bus station on Xingshen Lu.

ACCOMMODATION

Jizu Shan Hotel 鸡足山宾馆, jīzúshān bīnguǎn. On the main mountain road, 300m below Zhusheng Temple ☎0872 7350478. Basic hostel-style accommodation, but better than those at the temple and

good enough for a single night. You may want to bring your own sleeping bag for dorms – it can be cold and damp. Dorms ¥50, doubles ¥280

Weishan

巍山, wēishān

WEISHAN, a charismatic old town 50km south of Xiaguan, is now largely forgotten, but as the cradle of the Nanzhao kingdom and a prosperous former stop on the tea-horse trade routes, it has a distinguished past. Today it's a supply town for the local Bai, Muslim and – especially – **Yi** population, but its history, still evident in some impressive ancient buildings, makes it worth a visit.

The old town

Head east from Weishan's bus station, and you'll soon be walking the cobbled lanes of the **old town**; there are few street signs, but the only thing you need to find anyway is **Gongchen Lou** (拱辰楼, gǒngchén lóu), a huge old gate tower marking the centre of town. Climb it (¥10) and you'll see Weishan's pedestrianized main street, lined with old wooden shops, running 500m south to smaller **Xinggong Lou** (星拱楼, xīnggǒng lóu), once a bell tower. Weishan's back lanes are full of markets and wobbly adobe houses, but the town's biggest appeal is the fact that nothing is geared to tourism, and people are just getting on with their lives – the barber shop on the east side of the square around Gongchen Lou, and seemingly unchanged for the last hundred years, is a particular treat.

ARRIVAL AND DEPARTURE   WEISHAN

By bus Weishan's bus station is at the western edge of town, with departures to Xiaguan's South bus station every 10–15min until 5.30pm.

Destinations Kunming (3 daily; 5hr); Xiaguan/Dali (every 10–15min; 1hr 30min).

ACCOMMODATION AND EATING

For food, head to Xiaochi Jie (小吃街, xiǎochī jiē) or "Snack Street", the first lane running east, south of Gongchen Lou, which is lined with inexpensive restaurants.

Mengshe Stagehouse 蒙舍驿站, mēngshě yìzhàn. 9 Nan Jie, 50m past Xinggong Lou ⊕ 0872 6123338. This reconstructed old inn has a lovely wooden facade, Bai-style wall murals, with smallish but colourfully decorated rooms. The young owner also serves a decent breakfast which can be eaten in the small garden at the back. ¥80

Weishan Xiongzhao Hotel 巍山雄詔大酒店, wēi shān xióng zhào dà jiǔdiàn. Guanwei Dong Lu ⊕ 0872 8816666. A 10min walk from the old town and the best hotel in the area, this marble-embellished establishment has comfortable international-quality rooms which are pretty good value – make sure you get a garden-facing one as the road can be noisy. Also features Chinese and Western restaurants, fitness centre and bar. ¥428

Dali Old Town

大理古城, dàlǐ gǔchéng

A thirty-minute bus ride north of Xiaguan, **DALI OLD TOWN** draws swarms of holidaying middle-class urban Chinese seeking an "old China" experience, while a trickle of foreign backpackers still pass though what used to be one of the main stops of the Asian hippy-trail. Despite the tourist overkill along the main streets, Dali is pretty, interesting and relaxed, full of old houses and an indigenous **Bai** population rubbing shoulders with local Yi and Muslims. To the east lies the great lake, **Er Hai**, while the invitingly green valleys and clouded peaks of the **Cang Shan range** rear up behind town, the perfect setting for a few days' walking or relaxation. It's no longer the foreigner hippy enclave it once was, though, and most of the Western businesses and the drugs-fueled party scene have disappeared. However, its bohemian reputation lingers on, and it still attracts a few soul-searching Chinese hipsters who tend to be pretty cool (and often speak English). Much of this transformation is down to the appointment of the former mayor of Lijiang, who made the town the monstrosity it is today, being sent to Dali to work his magic, so it might not be what you expect when you arrive.

DALI'S FESTIVALS

If you can, visit Dali during the **Spring Fair**, held from the fifteenth day of the third lunar month (April or May). The event spans five hectic days of horse trading, wrestling, racing, dancing and singing, attracting thousands of people from all over the region to camp at the fairground just west of town. You'll probably have to follow suit, as beds in Dali will be in short supply. In addition, an impressive but frankly scary **Yi torch festival** is held on the 24th day of the sixth lunar month – flaming torches are paraded at night, and people even throw gunpowder at each other.

Brief history

There's much more to Dali than its modern profile. Between the eighth and thirteenth centuries, the town was at the centre of the Nanzhao and Dali kingdoms, which at one point expanded into Myanmar, Sichuan and Thailand; while in the mid-nineteenth century it briefly became capital of the Islamic state declared by **Du Wenxiu**, who led a Muslim rebellion against Chinese rule. But the revolt failed and the Yunnan governor, Cen Yuying, unleashed a merciless slaughter of Dali's unarmed civilian population; the town was utterly devastated, never to recover its former political position.

The South Gate

南门, nánmén • Daily 8am–6pm • ¥20

Get your bearings on top of Dali's old **South Gate**, where you can study Xiaguan, the lake, town and mountains from the comfort of a teahouse. Dali's antique **pagodas** stand as landmarks above the roof lines, solitary Yi Ta due west, and the trinity of San Ta a few kilometres north. From here the town's original, grid-like street plan, and the line of its old walls, are still apparent, despite encroachment from highways and Xiaguan's ever-spreading suburbs.

The central streets

Fuxing Lu, choked with tour groups and souvenir stalls selling ethnic silverware and embroideries, runs north through the town: about 150m along, the heavy stone **Wuhua Gate** (五华楼, wǔhuá lóu) is a modern construction, similar in style to the South Gate. Past here, Fuxing Lu is crossed by **Renmin Lu** and **Yangren Jie** (the now badly named "Foreigners Street") which – along with parallel **Bo'ai Lu** – are where to find most of Dali's bars, cafés, masseurs, tour agents, and trinket and clothing stalls. Escape the hustle by detouring east down Renmin Lu to the splendid blue, multitiered Bai-style **Catholic church** (天主教堂, tiānzhǔ jiàotáng) in an alley off to the south.

Dali Museum

大理博物馆, dàlǐ bówùguǎn • Daily 8.30am–5pm • Free

Down on Fuxing Lu near the South Gate, **Dali Museum** takes the form of a small Chinese palace with guardian stone lions and cannon in the courtyard. It was built for the Qing governor and appropriated as Du Wenxiu's "Forbidden City" during the Muslim insurrection. Historic relics include a strange bronze model of two circling dragons, jaws clenched around what might be a tree; a few Buddhist figurines from the Nanzhao period; and some lively statues of an orchestra and serving maids from a Ming noblewoman's tomb – a nice addition to the usual cases of snarling gods and warrior busts. It is, however, usually very crowded.

The north of town

Dali's north end is far less touristy than the south, and it's worth just wandering the cobbled residential back lanes. **Yu'er Park** (玉洱公园, yù'ěr gōngyuán; daily 6am–8pm; free) is a pleasant, if small, patch of trees; and Dali's northwesterly **produce market** is worth a look too, especially when crowds of hawkers, farmers and shoppers descend for the weekly market. Finally, the **North Gate** (北门, běimén) can again be climbed for views; Zhonghe Lu to the east is lined with little **marble factories**, turning out the grey-streaked sculptures for which Dali is famous.

San Ta

三塔, sāntǎ • Daily 8am–7pm • ¥121, or ¥190 including Chongsheng Temple • bus #19 from outside the South Gate on Wenxian Lu

The ostentatious Three Pagodas, or **San Ta**, were built around 850: the 69m-tall, square-based **Qianxun tower** is a century older than the two smaller octagonal pagodas behind. As the structures are sealed, the stiff entrance fee gives access only to souvenir stalls around their base, so you're probably just as well looking at them from outside the gate – though if you have bought the full ticket you can visit the huge and completely forgettable **Chongsheng Temple** (崇圣寺, chóngshèng sì) behind, built from scratch in 2005.

ARRIVAL AND DEPARTURE   DALI OLD TOWN

By bus Dali Old Town doesn't have its own bus station: arriving from the north will see you dropped off on the highway outside the East Gate, from where you can either walk into town or catch bus #2 up Yu'er Lu. From the south, your bus will terminate at Xiaguan and you'll need to catch

city bus #8, or grab a cab (¥50–60) into Dali Old Town. Leaving, book long-distance bus tickets through agents in town – who will also tell you where to pick buses up – or head down to the relevant stations in Xiaguan and sort things out yourself.

11

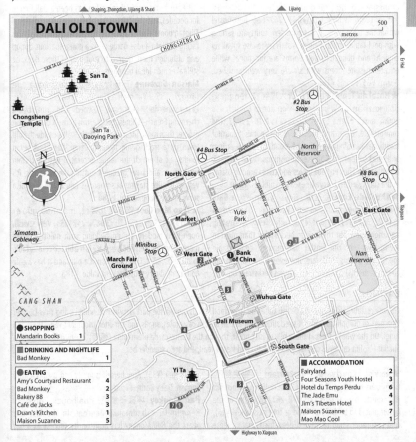

DALI OLD TOWN

▲ Shaping, Zhongdian, Lijiang & Shaxi   ▲ Lijiang

0   500
metres

San Ta

Chongsheng Temple

San Ta Daoying Park

#2 Bus Stop

#4 Bus Stop

North Reservoir

North Gate

#8 Bus Stop

Market

Yu'er Park

East Gate

Ximatan Cableway

Minibus Stop

West Gate

Bank of China

Nan Reservoir

March Fair Ground

CANG SHAN

Wuhua Gate

Dali Museum

South Gate

Yi Ta

● **SHOPPING**
Mandarin Books   1

■ **DRINKING AND NIGHTLIFE**
Bad Monkey   1

● **EATING**
Amy's Courtyard Restaurant   4
Bad Monkey   2
Bakery 88   3
Café de Jacks   3
Duan's Kitchen   1
Maison Suzanne   5

■ **ACCOMMODATION**
Fairyland   2
Four Seasons Youth Hostel   3
Hotel du Temps Perdu   6
The Jade Emu   4
Jim's Tibetan Hotel   5
Maison Suzanne   7
Mao Mao Cool   1

▼ Highway to Xiaguan

INFORMATION AND GETTING AROUND

Travel agents For booking English-speaking tours, your best bet is to book through your accommodation, with *The Jade Emu* seeming to offer the best service and prices.

Tour operators There are a number of specialist tour operators based in Dali. These include Climb Dali (☎0872 2501920, ⓦclimbdali.com), with offices at 20 Renmin Lu; and Amiwa (☎135 7788 7173, ⓦamiwa-trek.com), a

trekking company with Bai guides. Agents in Dali can also organize train tickets for a fee.

By taxi Taxis endlessly ply the streets of Dali, so finding one is no problem – basic charges will be ¥50–60 into Xiaguan and ¥100 for the airport. Nowhere within Dali itself should cost more than ¥10 but they'll ask for ¥20 or ¥30 and many won't negotiate.

ACCOMMODATION

Dali has plenty of places to stay, both inside and outside the old city walls, though rates can double during festivals. If you're really looking to avoid the tourist hordes, consider the more remote accommodation towards the Cang Shan range and at Xizhou (see p.685).

Fairyland 连锁酒店, liánsuǒ jiǔdiàn. 31 Yangren Jie, west off Bo'ai Lu ☎189 87080802. Probably the smartest place in town for the price, though not especially cheap, with modern hotel rooms inside an attractive, restored old Bai courtyard house. **¥268**

Four Seasons Youth Hostel 春夏秋冬青年旅舍, chūnxiàqiūdōng qīngnián lǚshè. 46 Bo'ai Lu (entrance on Renmin Lu) ☎0872 2671668. Best hostel within the town walls, it has a modern courtyard setting with pool table, amiably clueless staff (who also speak no English) and obligatory bar. Dorms are functional while private en-suite rooms with a/c are very well furnished. Dorms **¥65**, rooms **¥160**

★ **Hotel du Temps Perdu** 风清大理客栈, fēngqīng dàlǐ kèzhàn. 81 Wenxian Lu, sign not in English, it's 200m south of the South Gate ☎157 18729055. The comfortable, clean and modern rooms in this beautiful traditional building are arranged around a central atrium and decked out in Chinese furnishings, with helpful, friendly staff. They put out tables and chairs among plants in the courtyard and serve free tea and nibbles. **¥220**

★ **The Jade Emu** 金玉缘, jīnyù yuán. West Gate Village, across the western highway from town ☎0872 2677311, ⓦjade-emu.com. Newly renovated, and more aimed at the foreign backpacker than most in town, this well-run hostel has modern comfortable rooms and dorms (beds are, however, a bit hard in the cheapest dorms) and located in a quiet backstreet outside

town. The exterior is nicely done out with Bai-style decorations, there's good Western and Chinese food, English-speaking staff, and they have excellent travel information. Dorms **¥20**, doubles **¥98**

Jim's Tibetan Hotel 吉姆藏式酒店, jímǔ zāngshì jiǔdiàn. 4 Luyuan Xiang ☎0872 2677824, ⓦjims-tibetan-hotel.com. Likeable Jim has been a Dali fixture for decades, and this colourful modern take on a traditional Tibetan home – with a rooftop terrace and multiple floors facing out into a rose garden – is a quiet, spacious option and although more geared to tour groups these days, he still takes individual travellers. **¥300**

Maison Suzanne 苏珊娜的房子, sūshānnà de fángzi. 35 Nanmen Xincun ☎0872 2475489, ⓔsuzanne-dali@gmx.com. Owned and run by a charming French–Chinese couple, this homely place is a bit quieter than most, located a 5–10min walk outside the old town up a track going towards Cang Shan. Just seven rooms, all of which are large, decorated with a certain rustic elan, and have greenery outside the windows. It's very much like staying at someone's house and they also serve food (see opposite). **¥280**

★ **Mao Mao Cool** 猫猫果儿客栈, māomāo guǒ'ér kèzhàn. 419 Renmin Lu ☎0872 2474653. Very stylish, open-plan modern atrium building with goldfish pond; rooms have wooden floors and are just a bit too comfortable to be minimalist. Quiet location is a plus and it has a café and small library too; excellent value. **¥188**

EATING

Chinese restaurants outside the South Gate and streetfood stands around the park between Renmin Lu and Yu'er Lu offer steamers of dumplings and Bai specialities such as fish or tofu casseroles, snails and stir-fried mountain vegetables and fungi. On the whole, food at these places isn't great, though the home-made plum wine (梅酒, méijiǔ) is worth a try. Similar Muslim canteens display grilled kebabs and fresh bread, and are a sounder bet.

★ **Amy's Courtyard Restaurant** 庭院餐厅, tíngyuàn cāntīng. 2 Bo'ai Lu. No English sign but it's just south of the gate ☎00872 2672385. One of the better places to try Bai fish-head or tofu casseroles (¥16), cold cucumber salad (¥18) and deep-fried goat's cheese

with sugar (¥35). Amy herself is lovely and speaks a little English. Daily 8am–11pm.

Bad Monkey 坏猴子酒吧, huàihóuzi jiǔbā. 59 Renmin Lu ⓦbadmonkeybar.com. In the last few years the *Bad Monkey* has built on its success as a bar (see below) and upgraded its food with a foreign chef and a diverse menu of international foods including vegetarian options. As well as the British fish and chips, and full English, they also have daily food specials (¥60 including a beer) of Mexican (Mon), pizza (Tues), Canadian ribs (Wed), Indian (Fri) and a Sunday roast. Daily 8.30am–11pm.

Bakery 88 88号西点店, bāshíbā hào xīdiàndiàn. 52 Yangren Jie Zhong Xin, Bo'ai Lu ☎0872 2679129. German-owned (but not-managed) café with superb European cakes and breads to eat in or takeaway. The breakfast bagels (¥24) and baba ganoush (¥25) can make a nice change from the usual Chinese/Western options – sandwiches from ¥20–40. Daily 8.30am–10pm.

Café de Jacks 樱花园西餐厅, yīnghuāyuán xīcāntīng. 82 Bo'ai Lu ☎0872 2671572. Comfortable place to spend an afternoon over a coffee (¥12–25) and banana cake (¥20), or dig into their selection of curries, burgers and pizzas – from ¥32 – and Bai dishes (¥22–42).

The open fire makes it cosy on winter evenings. Daily 9.30am–midnight.

Duan's Kitchen 段的厨房, duàn de chúfáng. 12 Renmin Lu ☎153 31689560. Probably the best place to try the local food, it isn't cheap (as indicated by the posh-rustic decor and stemmed wine glasses) but this family-run restaurant delivers the goods with the braised fish in garlic (¥58), pork ribs infused with plum (¥48) and fried Dali cheese (¥36); all excellent, though the veggie dishes come in a bit cheaper at ¥18–28. Daily 11.30am–2pm & 5.30–9pm.

Maison Suzanne 苏珊娜的房子, sūshānnà de fángzi. 35 Nanmen Xincun ☎0872 2475489. As well as accommodation, this family-run guesthouse also does food, cooked by the French half of the couple, and served downstairs in a lounge/kitchen area. It features some great Gallic dishes such as Burgundy beef (¥58), walnut and blue cheese salad (¥30) and fabulous almond pie (¥20), though if you're not staying there, you should phone ahead and make a reservation. Open daily in the evenings.

DRINKING AND NIGHTLIFE

★**Bad Monkey** 坏猴子酒吧, huàihóuzi jiǔbā. 59 Renmin Lu ☎0872 2675460, ⊛badmonkeybar.com. More or less the last of the expat bars in town and run by a pair of English wide boys, Bad Monkey is the black hole around which the rest of Dali's foreigner nightlife has revolved for more than a dozen years. Hosting nightly live

music they serve their own range of microbrewed craft beers (¥25–35) as well as cocktails, wine and food, and it's packed out virtually every night, though they also have a slightly quieter location a few doors down which boasts the same menu. Daily 8.30am–late.

DIRECTORY

Banks The Bank of China (foreign exchange daily 8am–7pm) is on Fuxing Lu.

Bookshop Mandarin Books, 285 Fuxing Lu

(☎0872 2679014). Branch of Kunming's excellent English-language bookshop, with a wide range of special- and local-interest titles; not cheap, however.

Around Dali

Lying either side of Dali, **Er Hai Lake** and the **Cang Shan range** can keep you busy for a few days, though the lake itself is probably of less interest than the villages dotting its shore (which are set to be "developed" soon). Some of these also host **markets**, full of activity and characters, where you can watch all manner of goods being traded and pick up locally made tie-dyed cloth.

Cang Shan

苍山, cāngshān · ¥30 · ⊛dlcsdzgy.gov.cn

Cang Shan, the Green Mountains, are just that: a 50km-long range peaking between 2000m and 4000m, cloaked in thick forest, cloud and – often well into spring – snow. Ascending the heights is easy thanks to two **cableways**, linked by a pleasant walking trail, or the new two-stage cable car which heads almost to the top. Or you can take the route less travelled and hike.

The best option is to avoid the congested peak (which is often a disappointment – cold, shrouded in clouds and so with very little to see), and instead take the well-made, level, 13km-long **hiking track** that connects the two lower cableway stations at Gantong Temple and Zhonghe Temple, allowing an easy 4hr walk through thick forest between the two. Along the way are some fantastic lookouts and, in summer, plenty of squirrels, birds and butterflies. Whatever the conditions are when you start out, take along food,

11

11

water and weatherpoof gear, as the weather up the mountain is considerably colder than at the bottom, and can change in an instant.

ARRIVAL AND DEPARTURE — CANG SHAN

BY CABLE CAR

Gantong Temple Cableway (感通寺索道, gǎntōngsì suǒdào; ¥50 one-way, ¥80 return). Take bus #4 heading south down the highway for 5km to the Guanyin Tang temple complex (观音堂, guānyīn táng), from where you can catch a cab (¥10) uphill to the Gantong Temple terminus. The ascent from here in modern, enclosed gondolas offers a fantastic 25min journey over the treetops,

with unsurpassed views of the lake, town and peaks.

Zhonghe Temple Cableway (中和寺, zhōnghésì suǒdào; ¥35 one-way, ¥50 return). Cab from town to the lower terminus ¥10. This is more like a ski lift, ferrying you up the mountain in open-sided chairs; at the top is small Zhonghe Temple itself. It doesn't run on windy days, or if they don't think enough people are going to show – in which case, you can hike up from here in about two hours.

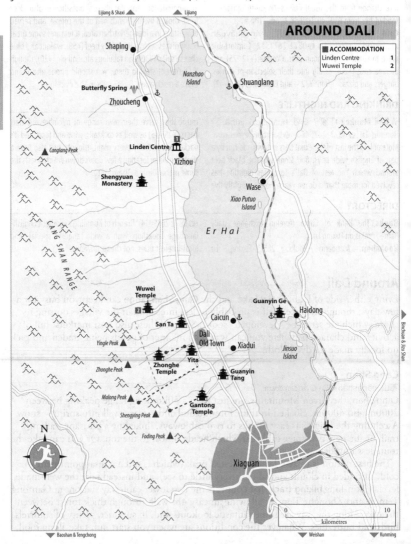

AROUND DALI

■ ACCOMMODATION	
Linden Centre	1
Wuwei Temple	2

Ximatan Cableway (洗马潭索道, xǐ mǎ tán suǒdào; ¥200 return to the peak or ¥100 return to the halfway point, shuttlebus from ticket office to cableway ¥20 return). Running from around 4km west of the south gate (the ticket office is about 2km before), this two-stage cableway runs all the way to the top of the mountain offering great views from the cabs until about the halfway point, and carries on to the unexciting peak.

ACCOMMODATION

Wuwei Temple 无为寺, wúwéi sì. In the hills 8km north of Dali; a cab to the gates costs ¥35–40. A wonderfully peaceful Buddhist temple whose monks teach *tai ji* and kung fu, although foreigners are usually taught by other English-speaking foreigners. This is not an ordinary hotel, but a working monastery with strict rules for students: no meat, smoking or alcohol; dorms for women and monk's cells for men; and five hours' training a day, six days a week (Fri is the rest day, and the best to arrive on). Note that there is no electricity here, and no way to phone, so just turn up – it'll be okay. Accommodation, food and training per week **¥500**

Er Hai and villages

洱海, ěrhǎi

Er Hai stretches 40km along the flat valley basin east of Dali, its shore fringed with Bai villages. At present, only tourist boats venture out on the lake; for a more authentic experience you'll want to head to the villages (although they too are becoming more tourist-focused), especially on market days – there's transport from both Dali and Xiaguan.

Xizhou

西洲镇, xīzhōu zhèn

Some 20km north from Dali, **XIZHOU** has a daily morning market and substantial numbers of Bai mansions in its backstreets, most in a run-down state; signs in English guide you to them. You can spend an enjoyable morning wandering around with a camera, before winding up at the **Linden Centre**, a 1940s mansion beautifully restored by an American art collector and now a cultural centre and very suave hotel, its rooms a mix of traditional and modern furnishings – drop in for a tour.

Zhoucheng

周城, zhōuchéng

At the top of Er Hai's western shore, **ZHOUCHENG** is a small strip along the highway with a low-key afternoon market, best known for its dark blue tie-dyed cloth. The adjacent **Butterfly Spring** (蝴蝶泉, húdié quán; ¥80) is an electric-blue pond haunted by clouds of butterflies when an overhanging acacia flowers in early summer. You can also catch a ferry across the lake to Shuanglang from here.

Shaping and the eastern lakeshore

Overlooking the very top of the lake around 30km from Dali, **SHAPING** (沙坪, shāpíng) is worth a visit for its **Monday market**, when what seems like the entire regional population crowds on to the small hill behind town to trade.

Public transport dries up beyond Shaping as the road cuts around to Er Hai's east shore; there's a great Tuesday market at **SHUANGLANG** (双廊, shuānglàng) and another on dates ending in 5 or 0 at **WASE** (挖色, wāsè), about 15km south. From Wase, there are buses through the day to Xiaguan's Dali bus station.

ARRIVAL AND DEPARTURE ER HAI AND VILLAGES

By bus Regular buses depart from outside Dali's west gate for Xizhou (30min), Zhoucheng (40min) and Shaping (50min), all along Er Hai's western side; moving on from these places, stand by the roadside and flag down passing traffic. There's also a regular bus service through the day between Xiaguan and Wase, on the east side of the lake.

By bicycle Agents in town rent out bikes, but be aware that roads on both sides of the lake are fairly narrow, considering the number of fast-moving trucks and buses on them at any one time.

By boat Cruises are available between four tourist ferry piers with a multitude of different cruises available. The main two are the dock at Cai Cun (才村, cáicūn), on the lakeshore around 4km east of Dali at the end of bus #C2 route from North Gate, though more depart from Zhoucheng's Taoyuan dock (桃源码头, táoyuán mǎtóu), a 20min taxi ride from the old town. Trips generally depart between 8 and 10am and 12.30 to 2pm, take around 4hr (¥220 upwards) and stop off at two or three islands on the way. It's best to ask your accommodation which one would be most suitable.

ACCOMMODATION

Linden Centre 喜林苑, xǐlín yuàn. Xizhou village ☎0872 2452988, ⓦlinden-centre.com. A meticulously and luxuriously renovated Bai mansion filled with antiques and fine art, which describes itself as a living museum. Whether or not the commendable concept of cultural exchange behind the centre appeals, this is an undeniably beautiful place to stay, and it's also child-friendly with a pool and games room. The rooms are stylish and comfortable enough, though lack some conveniences such as TVs. **¥1000**

Shaxi

沙系, shāxī • ¥30

SHAXI, 90km northwest of Dali, is a tiny rustic relic of the once busy **tea-horse trade route** between China and Tibet. Listed as an endangered site by the World Monuments Fund, much of the old town has been sympathetically restored and, although it now feels a little sterile, its architectural delights remain largely intact: **Xingjiao Temple** (兴教寺, xīngjiào sì) was founded in 1415 and overlooks cobbled **Sifang** (四方, sìfāng), the main square; and there are stacks of muddy alleyways, old bridges and wood and stone mansions to admire in Shaxi's handful of back lanes. It's all very small and quiet – the best time to come is for the **Friday market**, when Yi and Bai villagers descend from the remote hills roundabout.

Shibao Shan

石宝山, shíbǎo shān • ¥50 • Taxi from Shaxi ¥200–250 return, including waiting time

Shibao Shan forms a high, forested sandstone ridge scattered with small temples, a three-hour hike or a forty-minute taxi ride from Shaxi. The main sight here is the **Shizhong Temple** (石钟寺, shízhōng sì), a series of galleries of Tang-dynasty Buddhist figures carved into an overhang, with wooden awnings protecting the more exposed images. Some of the carvings depict Nanzhao kings, others show Buddha, Guanyin and other saints; many show a strong Indian influence. At the end is a carving of, as the sign tactfully phrases it, "female reproductive organs", and a further niche – generally closed off from view – decorated with graphically sexual frescoes.

ARRIVAL AND DEPARTURE   SHAXI

By bus and minibus Shaxi lies southwest of the Dali–Lijiang highway town of Jianchuan (剑川, jiànchuān), where any traffic heading between Dali and Lijiang can drop you off, or minibuses go there from Xiaguan North bus station. From Jianchuan, minibuses to Shaxi (45min) run when full. There's no bus station at Shaxi; minibuses congregate from about 8am onwards on the road above the old town and, again, leave when full.

ACCOMMODATION AND EATING

Despite its diminutive size, Shaxi has plenty of accommodation, all of it in converted old mansions. Being more than four hours from the nearest tourist centres of Dali and Lijiang, and with some pleasant walks in the surrounding countryside, it's worth staying at least one night. There are plenty of places to eat too, with stir-fry kitchens along the road in the new town and tourist cafés in the old.

★**Horse Pen 46** 马围客栈, mǎwéi kèzhàn. 46 Sifang Lu, the old town square ☎0872 4722299, ⓦhorsepen46.com. A great location, with English-speaking owners, good hiking information and a cosy bar/communal area. Rooms are perfunctory (and they call them "stalls") but comfortable, and the not-too-restored old building is very atmospheric. Dorms **¥40**, doubles **¥80**

★**Laomadian Lodge** 沙系老马店, shāxī lǎomǎdiàn. Sideng Jie ☎0872 4722666, ⓦyourantai.com. Located right on the main square in the old town, *Laomadian* is in a class of its own, beautifully restored, with genuinely luxurious en suites, good dorms and a restaurant, *Karma Café*, in the

OPPOSITE KUNMING BARS >

same building. Dorms ¥80, doubles ¥560
Old Theatre Inn 古茶马客栈, gŭchámă kèzhàn.
Duan Jia Deng Village ⊕0872 4722296, ⓦshaxichina
.com. Located a short bicycle-ride outside the town among
the fields (bikes are provided), this lovely converted old

schoolhouse has just five well-equipped and comfortable
rooms, as well as an antique temple stage where traditional
performances are sometimes held. Food is either Bai or
Western and can be served in the courtyard or on a terrace
overlooking the rice paddies. ¥480

Lijiang

丽江, lijiāng

LIJIANG, capital of the **Naxi Kingdom**, nestles 150km north of Dali at the foot of the
inspiringly spiky and ice-bound massif of **Yulong Xue Shan**, the Jade Dragon Snow
Mountain. It should be lovely, surrounded as it is by green fields and pine forests, the
town's winding cobbled lanes forming a centuries-old maze, flanked by clean streams,
weeping willows and rustic stone bridges. It is, however, China's biggest tourist black spot,
in many ways little more than a cultural theme park, and the template against which all
"old towns" in China are being remodelled – about eighty percent of the "old" town is in
fact new and many old buildings have been knocked down to build more photogenic
"old" buildings. Hordes of visitors pack out the streets, while the Naxi family homes that
line them have all been converted into rank after rank of identical guesthouses and
souvenir shops, mostly run by Han Chinese posing in inappropriate ethnic garb; do check
out **Sifang market** though (no fee), which is one of the last bastions of local culture. All in
all though, the "old" town lacks any kind of authentic atmosphere and most foreign
tourists are terribly disappointed by their visit, so it can safely be skipped – better to go to
the old town at nearby Baisha (see p.693). It can, however, be used as a base for some of
the genuine culture lurking around the town's fringes (and is the springboard for Tiger
Leaping Gorge and the north), and plenty of potential **excursions** into the countryside.

Dayan old town

大研古城, dàyán gŭchéng

It's not easy to navigate Dayan's crowded backstreets, and you will inevitably get lost,
but as there are few specific sights this hardly matters. Dong Dajie and adjacent lanes
follow streams south to **Sifang** (四方, sifāng), formerly the main marketplace, a broad
cobbled square sided with the inevitable souvenir shops selling silver jewellery, hand-
woven cloth, *pu'er* tea, bongos and bright baubles. It's fun at dusk, when Naxi women
gather for surprisingly authentic-feeling group dances, in which everyone is welcome to
join. Heading south again takes you right into Dayan's maze, and eventually you'll find
where Sifang's **market** (now called Zhong Yi market) has relocated, an acre of dried
goods, fresh herbs, vegetables and fruit, jerked meat, pickles and Lijiang's famous copper
and brass utensils. Clothing stalls towards the bottom of the market sell the handmade
fleece jackets worn by Naxi women, and there are inexpensive local canteens nearby.

Mu Palace and Lion Hill

South of Sifang, the **Mu Palace** (木府, mùfŭ; daily 8.30am–5.30pm; ¥60) was home of
the influential Mu family, the Qing-dynasty rulers of Lijiang, though they fell into

---

LIJIANG ORIENTATION

There are two parts to Lijiang: the **old town of Dayan** with all the quaint architecture,
markets and pedestrianized streets; and the **new town**, a bland place of wide roads and
low-rise boxes, which surrounds Dayan, mostly to the south and west. The old town's layout is
indescribable, but at its core is the central market square, **Sifang**, and **Dong Dajie**, the road
north from here to a wide, open area at the old town's border known as **Gucheng Kou** (古城
口, gŭchéng kŏu). Beyond lies the new town and the crossroads at **Fuhui Lu** and **Xin Dajie**,
the latter running 1km north to **Black Dragon Pool Park**.

decline during the nineteenth century. What was left of the mansion was destroyed during the terrible **earthquake** that flattened half the town in 1995, but the grounds – containing some ornamental pavilions and flower gardens – have been restored. You can walk through them and up onto pretty **Lion Hill** (狮子山, shīzi shān; ¥15), site of some ancient cypress trees and the **Wangu Tower** (万古楼, wàngǔ lóu), where you can look down over Dayan's sea of grey-tiled roofs.

Black Dragon Pool Park

黑龙潭公园, hēilóngtán gōngyuán • Daily 8am–9pm • Free with "Old Town Maintenance Fee" ticket

Up on Lijiang's northern outskirts, **Black Dragon Pool Park** is a beautiful place to stroll. The sizeable, pale green pool here is known as **Yuquan** (Jade Spring) and, with the peaks of Yulong Xue Shan rising behind, the elegant mid-pool **Deyue Pavilion** is outrageously photogenic. In the early afternoon, you can watch traditionally garbed musicians performing Naxi music in the lakeside halls.

A path runs around the shore between a spread of trees and buildings, passing the cluster of compounds that comprise the **Dongba Cultural Research Institute** (东巴文化研究室, dōngbā wénhuà yánjiūshì). The word *dongba* relates to the Naxi shamans, about thirty of whom are still alive and kept busy here translating twenty thousand rolls of the old Naxi scriptures – *dongba jing* – for posterity. Further around, almost at the top end of the pool, is a group of relocated halls which once formed part of the important **Fuguo Temple**. The finest of these is **Wufeng Lou** (五凤楼, wǔfèng lóu), a grand Ming-dynasty palace with a triple roof and interior walls embellished with reproductions of the murals at Baisha (see p.693).

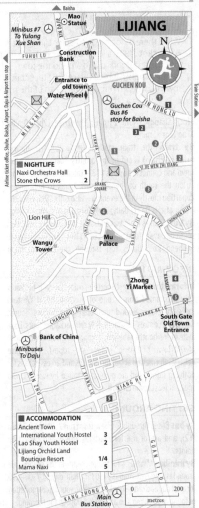

11

LIJIANG

■ NIGHTLIFE
Naxi Orchestra Hall — 1
Stone the Crows — 2

■ ACCOMMODATION
Ancient Town
  International Youth Hostel — 3
Lao Shay Youth Hostel — 2
Lijiang Orchid Land
  Boutique Resort — 1/4
Mama Naxi — 5

● EATING
Lamu's House of Tibet — 1   Prague Café — 3
N's Upstairs Kitchen — 2   Sakurakim Bar and Café — 4
Outdoor Barbecue — 5

ARRIVAL AND DEPARTURE

LIJIANG

Tickets for all onwards travel can be booked for a fee through accommodation – if not yours, then the *Mama Naxi* for instance – or tour agents around town.

By plane Lijiang's airport (丽江三义机场, lìjiāng sānyì jīchǎng) is 30km southwest along the highway. Airport buses (¥20, pay on board) deliver you to the *Blue Skies Hotel* (民航售票处, mínháng shòupiàochù), a 1.5km walk west of the old town just off Fushui Lu. Taxis to

or from the airport charge ¥100 (or ¥80 If prebooked through your accommodation).

Destinations Beijing (3hr 30min); Chengdu (1hr 25min); Chongqing (1hr 40min); Guangzhou (2hr 30min); Guiyang (1hr 30min); Jinghong (1hr 10min); Kunming

LIJIANG FEES

While there is no charge to enter Lijiang itself, you do have to buy an "Old Town Maintenance Fee" **ticket** (¥80; valid for a week, available from most hotels and tourist sites) before you can visit specific sights in and around the town – though you still have to pay additional entry fees for these sights, where they exist. Strict checks are prevalent along all entrances into the "old" town apart from through the north of the market.

(1hr); Shanghai (3hr 25min); Shenzhen (2hr 20min); Xi'an (2hr 15min).

By train The train station (丽江火车站, líjiāng huǒchēzhàn) is out in the country 10km southeast of town and connected by bus #18 – catch this to Chong Shui Lu on the south of the old town. Trains to Kunming – departing mostly in the evening – also call at Dali en route.

Destinations Dali (7 daily; 2hr); Kunming (6 daily; 7–10hr).

By bus Lijiang's main bus station is in the new town, 1km south of Dayan, from where bus #11 or #8 will get you to Gucheng Kou. Buses run through the day to major destinations in the province and beyond. Early-morning services depart for Baishui Tai, Tiger Leaping Gorge and Qiaotou; for other destinations see specific accounts.

Destinations Chengdu (daily 1pm; 20hr); Daju (daily 8am; 3hr); Dali/Xiaguan (hourly, some stop in Dali Old Town; 3hr); Deqin (2 daily; 8–9hr); Jianchuan (for Shaxi; hourly; 2hr); Kunming (9 daily; 9hr); Lugu Lake (4 daily, last at 8.30am; 6hr); Liuku (9am daily; 9hr); Panzhihua (8 daily; 6hr); Qiaotou (6 daily; 2hr); Shangri-La/Xiang Gelila (10 daily; 4hr); Shigu (leave when full; 2hr); Xishuangbanna (daily 7.30; 12hr 30min).

INFORMATION

Information Your best source of information is probably your accommodation or one of the handful of Western cafés; the places around town calling themselves "Tourist Reception Centres" or similar only sell packaged tours. Look instead for booths labelled "Comprehensive Service Kiosk of Old Town of Lijiang" (daily 9am–10pm), which give neutral information about local buses and access details for outlying sights, and are generally staffed by women who speak at least some English.

Maps Lijiang maps are sold everywhere and given out by accommodations, though the best bilingual map is called *Lijiang Old Town* (¥10), sold by the service kiosks above.

Travel agents For ambitious schedules – including long-distance trekking – contact The Yak Traveller, at 188 Minzhu Lu (☎0888 5102666, ✆theyaktraveller.com).

Visa extensions The PSB office is south of the old town on Taihe Lu (☎0888 5132310) – ask your accommodation for directions.

GETTING AROUND

By bus Buses through the new town run 7.30am–8.30pm (¥2), and are of use for reaching arrival and departure points.

By minibus Minibuses for touring sights in the countryside around Lijiang cost around ¥150 for a half-day, or ¥200–250 for a full day and can be booked through your accommodation or found at Gucheng Kou around Xin Dajie in the morning.

By taxi Plentiful on the streets around the old town, charging a fixed minimum ¥7 for the first 3km, and ¥1.60 for each additional km, plus a ¥1 fuel surcharge on top.

By bicycle Ask your accommodation to help you arrange this, and prices are around ¥30–50 per day, plus your passport or ¥500 as a deposit.

ACCOMMODATION

Lijiang's abundant accommodation is mostly in faux Naxi-style wooden houses with two or three storeys arranged around a small central courtyard. Avoid staying in the old town, which means not only having to pay the maintainance fee, but finding hotels from addresses is a nightmare. A map (see above) is good for rough locations, but you're best off ringing ahead and getting someone to meet you.

Ancient Town International Youth Hostel 古城国际青年旅舍, gǔchéng guójì qīngnián lǚshè. 44 Mishi Alley, Xinyi Jie ☎0888 5105403. One of two YHA-affiliated places in town, set inside another old courtyard home; rooms are bare but clean, and there's a large atrium area for socializing. Probably the nicest inside the old town, but be warned that no English is spoken here. Dorms ¥25, doubles ¥118

Lao Shay Youth Hostel 老谢车马店, lǎoxiè chēmǎdiàn. 71 Guangbi Xiang, Guangyi Jie ☎0888 5116118, ✆laoshay.com. Located at the heart of the old town, the rooms aren't bad – and it has a wide variety of choices – though levels of English and friendliness of staff can be variable. It's a little pricier than its competitors. Dorms ¥39, doubles ¥198

★**Lijiang Orchid Land Boutique Resort** 丽江兰花土地精品度假村, líjiāng lánhuā tǔdì jīngpǐn dùjiàcūn.

TO SICHUAN VIA PANZHIHUA

From Lijiang, the quickest route into Sichuan begins by catching a direct bus to Chengdu (1pm daily; 20hr) or possibly slightly quicker, take a bus 200km east to heavily industrialized **PANZHIHUA** (攀枝花, pānzhīhuā; 8 daily; 6hr), a stop on the Kunming–Chengdu **rail line**. Buses set down right outside the train station: try and prebook your onward train, as there isn't much in the way of decent accommodation near the stations, and town is a good 15km away. There are eight daily trains to Chengdu (12–14hr) via Xichang and Emei Shan (probably the only reason to come this way), with five daily trains (5–7hr) to Kunming the other way.

13 Baowu Xiang, Nanmen Jie & 80 Xingren Xiang, Qiyi Jie ☎0888 5112269. Both locations (the first is near the south gate so easier to find, and has the better management) have the old town regulation faux-antique exterior, but these chic boutique hotels mix modern style with a touch of local flavour on the inside. The rooms are most excellent: smart and modern, individually decorated and worth the slightly higher-than-average price. Outstanding service. **¥350**

★**Mama Naxi** 22 Jixiang Lu ☎0888 5107713 or ☎135 78399565. The town's most popular backpacker guesthouse, thanks largely to its welcoming management and cosy atmosphere. Situated about 10min walk from the old town in a residential area near the bus station, it's well away from the tourist scrum and offers a range of clean, modern rooms and dorms as well as having the best travel information around; they also rent bikes (¥40/day), and can book buses, trains, taxis, and tours. They offer communal dinners (6.30pm; ¥25) cooked by the garrulous owner. It's a little hard to locate so you will need to phone ahead for them to meet you on Jixiang Lu. Dorms **¥40**, doubles **¥120**

EATING

Local dishes include *baba*, a stodgy deep-fried flour patty stuffed with meat or cheese and honey; roast and steamed pork; Yunnan ham; chicken steamed in special *qiguo* casseroles; crossing-the-bridge noodle soup (过桥米线, guò qiáo mǐxiàn); chicken steamed with local herbs; grilled fish; and wild plants such as fern tips. Mongolian-style hotpots, cooked at the table in a distinctive copper funnel-pot, are a staple of Naxi home cooking. Keep an eye open in the markets for the best walnuts in Yunnan, and bright orange persimmons growing on big, leafless trees around town – these have to be eaten very ripe and are an acquired taste.

★**Lamu's House of Tibet** 西藏屋西餐厅, xīzàngwū xīcāntīng. 56 Xinyi Jie ☎0888 115776. Bright, colourful restaurant serving tasty Tibetan, Western and Chinese staples, including excellent veg or yak *momos* (¥20/25) and yak hotpot (¥108 for two), though the steaks (¥88) and breakfasts (¥48) are good too. Also has a lot of trekking information (in English) about Tiger Leaping Gorge. Daily 9am–10.30pm.

N's Upstairs Kitchen 二楼小厨, èrlóu xiǎochú. 17 Jishan Xiang ☎0888 5120060. Overlooking Maicao Chang (卖草场, màicǎo chǎng), this slightly scruffy, but very friendly family-run joint has some of the best (and biggest)

THE NAXI

The Naxi are descended from Tibetan nomads who settled the Lijiang region before the tenth century, bringing with them a shamanistic religion known as **Dongba**. A blend of Tibetan Bon, animism and Taoist tendencies, Dongba's scriptures are written in the only hieroglyphic writing system still in use, with 1400 pictograms. The Naxi deity **Sanduo** is a warrior god depicted dressed in white, riding a white horse and wielding a white spear. Murals depicting him and other deities still decorate temples around Lijiang, and are a good excuse to explore nearby villages.

Strong **matriarchal** influences permeate Naxi society, particularly in the language. For example, nouns become weightier when the word female is added, so a female stone is a boulder, a male stone a pebble. Inheritance passes through the female line to the eldest daughter. Women do most of the work, and own most of the businesses; accordingly, the Naxi women's costume of caps, shawls and aprons is sturdy and practical, while retaining its symbolic meaning; the upper blue segment of the shawl represents night, a lower sheepskin band represents daylight, and two circles around the shoulder depict the eyes of a frog deity. Naxi men often appear under-employed, though they have a reputation as good gardeners and musicians. You'll likely see a few falconers too. *Forgotten Kingdom*, by Peter Goullart, available at bookshops in town, is an entertaining account of Lijiang and the Naxi during the 1930s.

burgers around (¥58), great breakfasts (¥20–38), pizzas (from ¥45), and local coffee (¥15). Daily 8.30am–10pm.

★**Outdoor Barbecue** 烤肉区, kǎoròu qū. Junction of Guangyi Jie and Qiyi Jie. An area with dozens of barbecue stalls selling everything from chicken skewers to insect larva kebabs, which gets absolutely rammed around dinner time. Just point and choose, expect to pay ¥5 per skewer, or three for ¥10. Daily 11am–midnight and beyond.

Prague Café 布拉格咖啡馆, bùlāgē kāfēi guǎn. 80 Mishi Xiang, off Xinyi Jie ☎ 0888 5123757. Scores highly for its location, excellent coffee and light meals such as sandwiches and pasta from ¥35. Also a great range of cakes, including cheese and blueberry, from ¥20. Daily 8.30am–10pm.

Sakurakim Bar and Café 樱花屋金酒吧, yīnghuāwū jīnjiǔbā. On Sifang ☎ 1376 9006900, ⓦ sakura.yn.cn. A behemoth of the Lijiang nightlife scene, there are about five places here, all under the Sakura umbrella and all offering reasonably priced beers and coffees, and Japanese, Korean and local set meals from ¥38–45. It's fine for lunch but gets very, very noisy in the evening when the nightclub fires up. Daily 9am–1am.

NIGHTLIFE

Parallel and west of Dong Dajie, narrow Xinhua Jie and Jiuba Jie ("Bar Street") are lined with barn-sized nightclubs, all sporting identical heavy wooden furniture, smoke machines, green-and-blue spots and dancers in fake ethnic garb doing fake ethnic moves to high-decibel pop.

Stone the Crows 乌鸦酒吧, wūyā jiǔbā. 134 Wuyi Jie ☎ 0888 5106772. Lawai-central hereabouts, this place has been stoking the embers of Lijiang's sputtering foreign party crowd for years. Western music, acceptable Western food and drinks with overwhelmingly Western chat in an enjoyably (and increasingly) ramshackle setting. Drinks from ¥20 and there's a pool table. Daily 6pm–1am or later.

Around Lijiang

Rich pickings surround Lijiang, with a stock of pleasant countryside, temples and villages on the lower slopes of **Yulong Xue Shan**, which rises about 18km north. Several of the following sights are within **bicycle range**; there's also transport to all of them from Lijiang.

Lashi Hai

拉市海, lāshì hǎi • ¥30; boating and horseriding about ¥120, book through your accommodation • Shared taxis from outside Zhong Yi market ¥10/person each way

Lashi Hai is a seasonal wetlands area 10km west of Lijiang, with the pleasant, near-deserted Tibetan Buddhist **Zhiyun Temple** (指云寺, zhǐyún sì; ¥15) on the far shore. The lake is best visited in winter, when hosts of migratory wildfowl pour in. Horseriding here trammels part of the old tea-horse route (or so the locals say), and it's also a popular spot for people to come and take wedding pictures, so keep a watch out for radiant meringue-clad brides and their bashful, heavily made-up, husbands-to-be.

NAXI MUSIC AND DANCING

The **Naxi Orchestra** is an established part of Lijiang's tourist scene. Using antique instruments, the orchestra performs Song-dynasty tunes derived from Taoist scriptures, a tradition said to have arrived in Lijiang with Kublai Khan, who donated half his court orchestra to the town after the Naxi chieftain helped his army cross the Yangzi. The orchestra regrouped after the Cultural Revolution, though the deaths of many older musicians have reduced its repertoire. To counter this, the orchestra's scope has been broadened by including traditional folk singing in their performances.

The orchestra plays nightly in Lijiang in the well-marked **hall** on Dong Dajie (7–8.30pm; ¥120–160; some agents/hotels offer discounted tickets). The music is haunting, but introductory commentaries overlong; try to catch the orchestra practising in the afternoon in Black Dragon Pool Park, for free.

There are also free ethnic dance performances in Sifang Square (11.10am, 2.10pm & 6.10pm) in which participation is encouraged and you can join the lines of blue-clad (and mostly elderly) Naxi dancers.

Baisha

白沙, báishā • Bus #11 from Lijiang old town to the "Guchen Cou" stop (古晨塃, gǔ chén còu), then bus #6, or it's about a 1hr bike ride (though the road is usually quite busy)

BAISHA, a small village about 10km north of Lijiang, is known for two things: the **Dabaoji Gong** temple complex (大宝积宫, dàbǎojī gōng; Lijiang Maintenance Fee ticket) with some fifteenth-century **murals** – admittedly in sad condition; and **Doctor He**, a traditional Chinese physician whose knowledge of local medicinal herbs is second to none. Baisha comprises little more than a single main street and there's no trouble at all locating the sights (Doctor He's surgery is amply signed in several languages); the village is also a staging post on the way to Yuhu or Wenhai (see box, p.694).

ACCOMMODATION AND EATING · BAISHA

Baisha There International Youth Hostel 白沙那里 国际青旅, báishā nàlǐ guójì qīng lǚ. Baisha old town, just behind the temple complex ☎0888 5340550. Lovely little youth hostel in a quiet backstreet with surprisingly comfortable en-suite rooms surrounding an ornamental fish pond, and the more basic dorms facing a lawn. Also has a small café, two friendly dogs and rents bicycles (¥30/day). Dorms **¥35**, doubles **¥148**

Yulong

玉龙, yùlóng

YULONG, 3km north of Baisha, is worth a quick pause to look at the small, Tibetan **Yufeng Temple** (玉峰寺, yùfēng sì; ¥25, plus the Lijiang Maintenance Fee ticket), set among pine forest. It's not of great interest in itself, but the pair of ancient, intertwined **camellia trees** in the top terrace produce huge magenta flowers in spring, when the courtyard with its mosaic floor is a nice spot for peaceful contemplation. Wait for any tour buses to depart before entering.

Yuhu

玉湖村, yùhú cūn

Four kilometres beyond Yulong, the tiny Naxi settlement of **YUHU** is where the eccentric Austrian-American botanist-anthropologist **Joseph Rock** based himself from 1921 to 1949, and where he wrote articles on the Naxi that appeared in *National Geographic* magazine. His old wooden **house** (洛克故居, luòkè gùjū; ¥15), now a simple museum to his memory with a few period photos, is on the main street and is visited daily by busloads of foreigners. Yuhu is otherwise little disturbed by tourism and, set in grassland on the slopes of Yulong Xue Shan, is an attractive place to stop over and do some hiking – again, Wenhai (see box, p.694) makes a good target.

ACCOMMODATION AND EATING · YUHU

Nguluko Guest House 雪嵩客栈, xuěsōng kèzhàn. ☎0888 5131616 or ☎139 88838431, ✉lilyhe9@gmail .com. Provides six simple but clean rooms in a rustic, Naxi courtyard building, with meals served in their café in the north of the main square – otherwise set meals cost ¥15–25. The boss (the wife) can also help arrange hiking (¥500/day) and cut-price horseriding tours (¥300/4hr). Price is per person, half-board. **¥100**

Yulong Xue Shan (Jade Dragon Snow Mountain)

玉龙雪山, yùlóng xuěshān • ¥135 (plus Lijiang Old Town Maintenance Fee ticket and a ¥20 environmental protection ticket) • **Impression Lijiang show** Daily 9am, 11am, 12.30pm & 2pm; 1hr 15min • ¥248 (plus park entrance fee) • ☎0888 888 2111; book through ⓦ wondersofyunnan.com or via your accommodation (it's often booked up days ahead) • Minibus #7 (leaves when full, get there around 8–9am; ¥25–30; 1hr) from near the Chairman Mao statue in Red Sun Square in Lijiang to the entrance, then bus #7 to Dry Sea Meadow and the cable-car stations; from there minibuses (¥20) can shuttle you to the cable-car stations

With a summit at 5596m, **Yulong Xue Shan** can't be climbed without proper equipment, but you can take in alpine meadows, glaciers and the peaks via three separate **chairlifts**.

Yunsha Ping (云杉坪, yúnshān píng; chairlift ¥75 return) is a 3205m plateau with boardwalks leading out to grassland and fir trees, and views of the mountain's peaks rising above. Similar **Maoniu Ping** (牦牛坪, máoniú píng; ¥85 return) is higher at 3600m,

---

WENHAI

As an alternative to the cable cars for exploring Yulong Xue Shan, **WENHAI** (文海, wénhǎi) is a beautiful lakeside village in the mountain's foothills that's a 17km, five-hour trek on the road from Baisha; though if you hire a guide in Basha (¥100) they can reduce that to two hours as they know all the shortcuts. **Xintuo Ecotourism** (📞 139 88826672, 🌐 ecotourism.com.cn) charge around ¥1000 for a three-day, two-night return trek to Wenhai from Lijiang, including all transport, guides, accommodation and food. Contact them in advance about accommodation if you plan to visit independently; there are also plenty of homestays here for ¥30–50.

---

with a temple; while the cable car at **Glacier Park** (干海子, gānhǎizǐ; ¥180 return) is an impressive 3km long and climbs to 4506m, where a one-hour walk takes you to a windswept viewing point over the **Yulong Glacier**. **Ganhaizi** is by far the most spectacular spot, and despite the altitude can get very crowded. Another attraction on the mountain is the **Impression Lijiang** show, a spectacular song and dance show, with a cast of over five hundred from ten minorities (and over a hundred horses) and directed by the famous Chinese director Zhang Yimou, which is staged at Dry Sea Meadow and uses the mountains as a backdrop – remember it's outdoors and be prepared for the weather.

Shigu

石鼓, shígǔ • Minibuses to Shigu (2hr) run whenever full from Lijiang's bus station

Seventy kilometres west of Lijiang on the banks of the Yangzi River, **SHIGU** (Stone Drum) is a small place named after a tablet raised here in the sixteenth century by one of Lijiang's Mu clan to mark a particularly bloody victory over an invading army – whether a Tibetan or Chinese force depends on who is telling the story. The river makes its first major **bend** here, deflected sharply to the northeast towards Tiger Leaping Gorge, having flowed uninterrupted in a 1000km arc from its source away on the Tibet/Qinghai border; there are viewpoints along the waterfront.

Lugu Lake

泸沽湖, lúgū hú • ¥100

Some 200km north of Lijiang, **Lugu Lake** is shallow and attractive, surrounded by mountains and bisected by the Sichuan border. The people up here are **Mosuo**, who maintain matrilineal traditions such as *axia* marriage, where a woman takes several husbands. Women run the households and children are brought up by their mothers – men have no descendants or property rights. It's glibly marketed as a "Girl Kingdom" free-for-all to single Chinese men – who inevitably head back home disappointed – and tourism has become well established in recent years, but the lake remains a pleasant place to kick back and do nothing much for a couple of days, before making the tiring bus journey to Xichang in southern Sichuan.

At more than 2500m above sea level, and surrounded by forested mountains, Lugu Lake's 10km-long, hourglass-shaped surface is a wonderfully tranquil setting – particularly if you have just escaped the seething crowds of Lijiang. Arriving from the south you'll first reach settlements dotted along the shore leading up to, and past, the Sichuan border. There's not a vast amount to do here beyond strolling in the villages and surrounding hills, and taking the odd boat trip to one of the lake's five islands, but it is all wonderfully relaxing, calm and, above all, peaceful. Minibuses shuttle between villages, **wooden canoes** can be hired out for trips across the lake, and accommodation can provide just about everything you'll need.

The villages

The largest village, where buses from Lijiang drop tourists, is **LUOSHUI** (落水, luòshuǐ) on the west shore, with cobbled streets, a central square, some gift shops, guesthouses and a few basic facilities. It's quaint enough, but most people don't stay long, opting instead to head northwest to tiny **LIGE** (里格, lǐgé), set on an attractive bay. Lige mostly comprises guesthouses and restaurants these days, but remains a quiet and enjoyable place to rest up for a few nights. Venture further beyond Lige and you're into Sichuan, where **LUGU HU ZHEN** (泸沽湖镇, lúgūhú zhèn) is the main town and **Wuzhiluo** (五指落, wǔzhǐluò) – a nearby string of houses along the shore – the nicest spot to settle down.

ARRIVAL AND DEPARTURE
right-aligned: LUGU LAKE

By plane Ninglang Lugu Lake airport (泸沽湖机场, lúgūhú jīchǎng), about 2hr south of the lake at Ninglang, opened in 2015 and currently only has 4 weekly flights to Kunming (1hr) though a service to Guangzhou is on the cards.

By bus Lugu Lake is on a back road between Lijiang and Xichang in southern Sichuan province (see p.754), with daily connections to both as well as Kunming. Buses from Lijiang (4 daily, last at 8.30am; 5–6hr) stop at Luoshi and Lige on

the northwest side of the lake, though minibuses also ply the route and leave when full from Gucheng Kou around Xin Dajie in Lijiang. Once the new highway from Lijiang is finished journey times will be reduced to just 3–4hr. Buses to and from Xichang (2 daily; 6hr) terminate at Lugu Hu Zhen on the eastern shore. Leaving, you'll need to book your seat for all destinations through accommodation the day before, especially during busy periods.

ACCOMMODATION AND EATING

Village restaurants lay on evening barbecues of grilled lake fish and whole suckling pigs, while _Lao Shay_ and _Wind's_ hostels serve pretty decent Chinese and Western staples – though come prepared for laidback service.

LIGE

Husi Teahouse Hostel 湖思茶屋, húsī cháwū. ☏ 0888 5825071, ⊛ husihostel.com. Right on the lakeshore, the restaurant area has fantastic views across the water, as do some more expensive en-suite rooms (¥288) on the upper floors. En suites are a definite step up in quality from the dorms or those with shared bathrooms. Dorms **¥40**, doubles **¥88**

WUZHILUO

Wind's Guesthouse 湖畔青年旅舍, húpàn qīngnián lǚshè. ☏ 0888 5824284 or ☏ 138 08004749. Fulfils all the usual backpacker needs – dorms, café, laundry and bike rental – and is located on a rather under-visited side of the lake. Wind speaks fairly good English, is a mine of trekking information, and can book buses. Dorms **¥35**, doubles **¥128**

Tiger Leaping Gorge

虎跳峡, hǔtiào xiá · ¥65

Around 100km north of Lijiang, just east of the highway to Shangri-La, the Yangzi River channels violently through **Tiger Leaping Gorge**, the 3000m-deep rift between Haba Xue Shan to the north and Yulong Xue Shan to the south. The **hiking trail** through the gorge is one of the most accessible and satisfying in China, with dramatic scenery and – despite the 2500m-plus altitude – relatively straightforward walking.

Qiaotou to Walnut Garden

Buses from Lijiang stop on the main road at **QIAOTOU** (桥头, qiáotóu), also known as **Hutiaoxia Zhen** (虎跳峡镇, hǔtiàoxiá zhèn), a knot of cafés and shops at the western entrance to the gorge and where you'll need to buy your entrance ticket. Buses then head out of town towards _Tina's_ at Jiantang village in the gorge, and after a few kilometres cross a bridge before a school where hikers need to start heading uphill – you'll be followed by **horse teams** offering to carry you or your bags for a fee. From here the going is fairly easy until you reach the _Naxi Family Guesthouse_ after a couple of hours, and where most people stop for lunch. It's then around two more hours out of the village to a snack-stand (the last for about two hours) at the start of the steep, twisting and quite demanding **Twenty-eight Bends**. At the top of this you're about six to seven hours into the hike at 2670m, near the _Tea Horse Guesthouse_ and gifted with superb views. Most people stop overnight here or carry on another hour to the _Halfway Guesthouse_ at **Bendiwan village** (本地湾村, běndìwān cūn).

From here the track levels out a bit before a couple of hours' descent, via some waterfalls, to the vehicle road at _Tina's Guesthouse_, with a further thirty-minute level

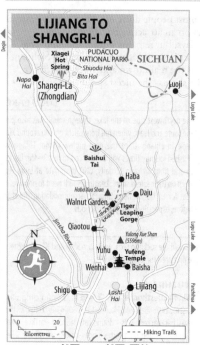

LIJIANG TO SHANGRI-LA

track to **WALNUT GARDEN** (核桃园, hétáo yuán) and more accommodation.

While at *Tina's*, take advantage of their free minibus to get to a trailhead a ten-minute drive away, which will take you on a two-hour round trip right down into the gorge, and across a rope bridge to **MIDDLE TIGER LEAPING STONE** in the centre of the violently frothing river where the force of the water causes the rock to vibrate. Note that these are privately maintained paths, and fairly steep in places, and you'll have to pay the locals to use them (¥20–30).

Walnut Garden to Daju

One option from Walnut Garden is simply to arrange a ride with minibuses (or order a taxi) **back to Qiaotou** along the vehicle road. Alternatively, it's a couple of hours eastwards, partly along the road, to the **New Ferry** over the Yangzi River. How much you'll pay depends on the whim of the ferryman, but don't expect to get off lightly – ¥40 or more per person (¥100–150 for the whole boat) is normal. From here, you've another hour's walk to the vehicle roadhead at **Xiahu Tiao** (下虎跳, xiàhŭ tiào), and then a final 7km to **DAJU** (大具, dàjù), where buses head south to Lijiang.

Walnut Garden to Baishui Tai

Accommodation at Walnut Garden can arrange a **guide** for the popular two-day trek, via an overnight stop in pretty **HABA village** (哈巴村, hābācūn), to **Baishui Tai**, which has charmless guesthouses and a bus on to Shangri-La (see opposite). You might prefer to tackle this trek southwards from Baishui Tai as an alternative route into Tiger Leaping Gorge – in this direction, it heads downhill much of the time.

ARRIVAL AND DEPARTURE

By bus Qiaotou, at the western end of Tiger Leaping Gorge, sits on the highway between Lijiang and Shangri-La and is served through the day by several buses from both – though coming from Lijiang, most people get the convenient private bus run by *Tina's* (see opposite). Daju, at the eastern end of the gorge, has a handful of daily services to Lijiang, the last of which is at 1.30pm. There is one daily bus between Lijiang and Shangri-La through the gorge, which

TIGER LEAPING GORGE

leaves early morning, and passes through Qiaotou, Tina's (at around 11am), Walnut Garden, Haba and Baishui Tai. Coming from Shangri-La to Lijiang, the bus leaves at around noon and stops at *Tina's* at around 3.30–4pm.

By taxi If you're pushed for time, you could hire a six-person taxi, which can reach most of the villages from *Tina's* often along very rough roads; accessible are Halfway (¥100), Qiaotou (¥150), Haba (¥200) and Baishui Tai (¥350).

ACCOMMODATION AND EATING

Halfway Guesthouse 中途客栈, zhōngtú kèzhàn. Bendiwan village ☎ 133 12526698 or ☎ 139 88700552. Housed in a lovely wooden building with rooms around a central courtyard (with more expensive and luxurious rooms in a new annexe with balconies overlooking the gorge; ¥200–300), this family-run place has been the main

accommodation in the area for the last quarter-century, and they've got it down to a tee. Also has a restaurant, and you can eat on a viewing terrace. Dorms **¥40**, doubles **¥120**

Naxi Family Guesthouse 纳西雅阁, nàxī yăgé. Changshen village ☎ 139 88736431. Pleasant rooms with great views around a traditional courtyard and friendly staff

HIKING TIGER LEAPING GORGE

To hike Tiger Leaping Gorge, you'll need to be fit, carrying full weatherproof gear, a torch and a first-aid pack, and a water bottle. Solid boots are a plus but, as long as your shoes have a firm grip, not essential. **Weather** can be warm enough in summer to hike in a T-shirt, but don't count on it; winters are cold. **Accommodation** along the way is in guesthouses, so you won't need a tent. **Two days** is the minimum time needed for a hike; give yourself an extra day to make the most of the scenery.

Originally there were two trails through the gorge, but the former **Lower Path** has been surfaced to handle tour buses, and isn't suitable for hiking any more – though it's useful if you're looking for a quick ride out at the end of your trek. The remaining **Upper Path** is the route described. End points are at westerly **Qiaotou**, on the Lijiang to Shangri-La road, and easterly **Daju**, a small township on a back route to Lijiang. Most people come from Lijiang and take the morning private bus (picks up from hotels in Lijiang 7–8am), which stops off in Qiaotou for you to buy tickets, and then drops you at the trailhead by the school. The bus can then take your luggage to *Tina's Guesthouse* (see below) from where you can pick it up after your trek – it's a good idea to only carry a light day-pack if possible, as the climb is quite demanding. Alternatively, you can continue on from Walnut Garden to Daju, or – with a guide – north to Baishui Tai (see p.702). Before you arrive, try to pick up the home-made **maps** that float around cafés in Lijiang and Shangri-La.

There seem to be almost continual roadworks going on in the gorge, connected with ongoing construction of the **hydro dam** across the river near Qiaotou and regular seasonal **landslides**, a potentially lethal hazard; do not hike in bad weather and take care during the June–September rainy season. There have been a couple of knifepoint **muggings** of solo travellers in past years (though not for a long time), so try not to walk alone. For current information, check ⓦtigerleapinggorge.com, maintained by *Sean's Guesthouse* in Walnut Garden.

make this an enjoyable stopoff if you're taking things at a relaxed pace. Even if you don't stay here, this will be your lunch stop if you've left in the morning. Dorms ¥35, doubles ¥70

Sean's Spring Guesthouse 山泉客栈, shānquán kèzhàn. Walnut Garden ☎0887 880682939 or ☎157 58456256, ⓦtigerleapinggorge.com. A pleasantly friendly place with a wide range of pretty comfortable rooms, good meals, beer, warm beds and the eponymous Tibetan owner, who speaks excellent English and organizes tours. The views are fantastic, though you'll need to pay US$30 for a room with en suite (or equivalent in RMB). US$11

Tea Horse Guesthouse 茶马客栈, chámǎ kèzhàn. Yongsheng village ☎1398 8717292. Aside from the

fantastic views shared by the few other places here, *Tea Horse* also offers decent food which you can eat on their viewing terrace. It's also a great place to rest after the gruelling Twenty-eight Bends. Dorms ¥40, doubles ¥150

Tina's Guesthouse 中峡国际青年旅舍, zhōngxiá guójì qīngnián lǚshě. Jiantang village ☎0887 8202258 or ☎139 88750111. Large and pretty ugly compared to most of the guesthouses along the gorge, *Tina's* is still a comfortable place to stay (if you don't mind frosty service), has excellent facilities, and the views from inside are as good as anywhere else. This is the main stop for buses in and out of the gorge, and, if you're coming from Lijiang, this is where your luggage will end up. Dorms ¥30, doubles ¥120

Shangri-La

香格里拉, xiānggélǐlā · 中甸, zhōngdiàn

SHANGRI-LA (often written as **Xiang Gelila**), and also known as **Zhongdian**, **Dukezong** and **Gyalthang** (in Tibetan) sits on a high plateau at the borderland between Yunnan, Sichuan and Tibet. When this former logging town was hit by a 1998 ban on deforestation, the provincial government renamed it Shangri-La after the Buddhist paradise of James Hilton's 1930s novel, *Lost Horizon*, to try to stimulate a tourist boom. They also spent a fortune turning the dismally poor Tibetan settlement here into a fairly convincing "old town", complete with obligatory traditional houses, cobbled streets, religious monuments, cafés, guesthouses and bars. Much of the old town was destroyed by a massive fire in 2014, but in typical Chinese fashion, all of it has already been rebuilt in the same style, though it has lost some of its former charm. There are also less contrived attractions in the **monastery** just north of town and excellent possibilities for local hiking and horseriding. Shangri-La's altitude is over 3000m, so take it easy if you've arrived from the lowlands, and be aware that it's very cold between October and March, and chilly at night even in the summer.

The old town

古城, gǔchéng

Down at the southern outskirts of Shangri-La, the old town is good for a couple of hours' wander, though there are no essential sights; streets are unsigned and weave off

1 2 Market, Bus Station, Deqin & Ganden Sumtseling Monastery ▲   ▲ Bita Hai & Baishui Tai

SHANGRI-LA (ZHONGDIAN)

● SHOPPING
Shangri-La Handicraft Centre ... 1

DONG WANG LU

HEPING LU

CHANGZHENG DADAO

XIANGBALA DADAO

JIANTANG DONG LU

NEW TOWN

SI GEI LUO XIANG

AN KANG XIANG

LONG TAN NAN LU

LONG TAN BEI LU

WENMING JIE

RONG BA LU

CHI CI KA JIE

GA MA XIANG

Longtan Reservoir

Khampa Caravan

TUANJIE LU

Airline Office

DAWA LU

BEIMIN JIE

BEIMIN LU

DA WA LU

ATM

Turtle Mountain

CUO LANG JIE

CANG FANG JIE

CANG FANG JIE

WU LING JIE

XIANGBALA DA DAO

Airport ◀

OLD TOWN

HONG XUE LANG

JIN LONG JIE

▲ Turtle Hill

JIN LONG JIE

LE DUO LANG

N

DIANCAXA

NA YANG LANG

■ ACCOMMODATION
Banyan Tree Ringha 1
Barley 4
Barley Villa 8
The Compass Lodge 7
Dragoncloud Guesthouse ... 5
Kersang's Relay Station 6
Kevin's Trekker Inn 3
Songtsam Retreat 2
Zinc Journey Arro Khampa ... 9

■ DRINKING
Bad Monkey 2
The Raven Café and Bar ... 1

● EATING
The Compass Café and Bakery ... 3
Flying Tigers Café 4
Helen's Pizza 1
Kailash 2
Karma Café 5

0   200
metres

in all directions, but as the whole place is only a few hundred metres across you can't get seriously lost. The alleyways are lined with sturdy two-storey wooden Tibetan homes, all rebuilt after the fire with a great deal of skill and care. The southern part down the hill feels a lot more authentic than the more heavily rebuilt north, and is marked by its original cobbled streets. Overlooking the old town, **Turtle Hill** is topped by a small temple and huge **golden prayer wheel**, apparently the largest in the world.

The new town

Despite a backdrop of scruffy concrete-and-tile buildings, there's also a bit of interest in the **new town**. Changzheng Dadao is lined with shops aimed at Tibetan customers, where you can buy everything from electric blenders for churning butter tea, to carpets, horse saddles, copperware and fur-lined jackets and boots. The **farmers' market** (建塘农市场, jiàntáng nóng shìchǎng), about a block north of the post office, has more of the same along with big blocks of yak butter and other foodstuffs.

Ganden Sumtseling Monastery

松赞林寺, sōngzànlín sì · ¥150 · Northbound bus #3 from Changzheng Dadao

Shangri-La's star attraction is the splendid **Ganden Sumtseling Monastery**, just north of the new town. Destroyed during the 1960s but later reactivated, it now houses four hundred Tibetan monks. Among butter sculptures and a forest of pillars, the freshly painted murals in the claustrophobic, windowless main hall are typically gruesome and colourful. Don't forget that, as in all Gelugpa-sect monasteries, you should walk clockwise around both the monastery and each hall.

ARRIVAL AND DEPARTURE

SHANGRI-LA

Shangri-La has regular bus connections to Lijiang, Deqin and Sichuan. Travelling on to Tibet requires permits and planning (see box, p.878). Incidentally, "Zhongdian" or "Xiang Gelila" are the names you'll see used most frequently on transport timetables; only the tourist industry favours "Shangri-La".

By plane Tiny Shangri-La airport (香格里拉机场, xiānggélǐlā jīchǎng), confusingly known as Deqing airport, is 7km south; a taxi costs ¥40, or, if there is one, catch bus #6 to the bus station, in the far north of town.
Destinations Chengdu (1hr 15min); Chongqing (1hr 45min); Guangzhou (2hr 30min); Kunming (1hr); Lhasa (2hr).
By bus The bus station is at the far north end of town at the intersection of Xiangbala Lu and Kangding Lu; from here, bus #1 runs south to the old town's outskirts.
Destinations Dali (6 daily; 7–10hr); Daocheng, Sichuan (daily 7.30am; 5hr); Deqin (6 daily, last at noon; 4–5hr); Kunming (6 daily; 9–12hr); Lijiang (every 30–40min until 5.40pm; 4hr); Lijiang Express (4 daily; 3hr); Xiaguan (every 30min until 12.30pm, plus 2 sleeper buses in the eve; 6hr).

GETTING AROUND

By bus Buses run 7am–6.30pm and charge ¥1, though Shangri-La is small enough not to warrant a bus journey in town.
By bicycle Some accommodation rents out bikes at around ¥20–40/day, plus passport as a deposit.
By taxi Taxis cost around ¥7–10 within the town limits, though this rises swiftly for trips to the surrounding countryside.

ACCOMMODATION

Banyan Tree Ringha 仁安悦榕庄, rén ān yuè róng zhuāng. Hong Po village ☎0887 8288822, ⓦbanyantree.com. Located in a secluded valley 4km north of the centre this place vies with the *Songtsam Retreat* to be the plushest place in town, offering large, well-equipped, two-storey reconstructed Tibetan farmhouses that all offer superb mountain vistas. Great service, a spa and three restaurants (one in a posh yurt), complete the package. **¥1633**
Barley 青稞客栈, qīngkē kèzhàn. 76 Beimen Jie ☎0887 8232100. Colourful, if slightly ramshackle, courtyard guesthouse with a warm terrace. It's run by a Tibetan family, who have taken some trouble to make the simple rooms attractive and comfortable. Untouched by the fire, it's far more atmospheric than the rebuilt places, and a portion of the profits go to the Dixi school for disadvantaged kids. Dorms **¥30**, doubles **¥120**
★Barley Villa 青稞别院, qīngkē biéyuàn. On the far side of the old town near Tancheng Square ☎0887 8290688. This beautifully refurbished Tibetan-style

farmhouse around a bright open courtyard (nothing to do with the hostel) is one of the nicest and atmospheric places to stay in town. The larger, more expensive, rooms upstairs (¥380) are bordering on luxurious, and well worth paying extra. Doubles ¥220

The Compass Lodge 舒灯库乐, shūdēng kùlè. 50 Shang Ye Jie, just outside the East Gate of the old town ☎ 0887 8223638, ⓦ thecompass.asia. This foreign-owned lodge, as well as having a Western-style café/bakery (see below) also has modern, comfortable international-standard en-suite rooms decorated with ethnic touches – a good option if you're after a complete escape from China. Price includes breakfast. ¥300

Dragoncloud Guesthouse 龙行客栈, lóng xíng kèzhàn. 94 Beimen Jie ☎ 0887 8289250. New, centrally located guesthouse in the old town and offering straightforward, snug wood-panelled, en-suite rooms, with very helpful English-speaking staff and a decent (though sometimes slow) restaurant serving local and international dishes. The larger, more expensive and quieter rooms upstairs cost ¥160. Dorms ¥50, doubles ¥100

Kersang's Relay Station 恪桑藏驿, késāng zàngyì. 1 Yamenlang, Jinlong Jie, behind the Arro Khampa restaurant ☎ 0887 8223118 or ☎ 136 18877910. Tibetan-run guesthouse decked in pine, rugs and colourful furnishings. The more expensive upper rooms (¥380) are large and really

quite nice; the cheaper ones can feel a little small and dark. It has a very nice rooftop terrace with views of the temple and town. Dorms ¥50, doubles ¥220

Kevin's Trekker Inn 龙门客栈, lóngmén kèzhàn. Just outside the old town, slightly hidden up an ally just north of Dawa Lu ☎ 0887 8228178, ⓦ kevintrekkerinn.com. Modern concrete buildings around a large courtyard; the big lounge area, cheerful rooms and the manager's trekking and touring information make this an excellent choice. Ask for one of the upper rooms which have great views. Dorms ¥35, doubles ¥120

Songtsam Retreat 松赞林卡酒店, sōngzànlínkǎ jiǔdiàn. ☎ 0887 8288889, ⓦ songtsam.com. The very upmarket wing of the Ganden Sumtseling Monastery's accommodation, and a tasteful, atmospheric – not to mention luxurious – place to stay. The more expensive deluxe rooms (¥1660) are bigger and all have views over the monastery building. ¥1380

★**Zinc Journey Arro Khampa** 阿若康巴南索达庄园, āruò kāngbā nánsuǒdá zhuāngyuán. 15 Jinlong Jie, Donglan Lu ☎ 0887 8881006. At the bottom end and quieter part of the old town, this is the most luxurious place to stay within Shangri-La itself. The seventeen beautifully decorated timber and stone rooms surround a courtyard restaurant area and have bags of character as well as international-class facilities. ¥980

EATING

For cheap eats, there are many Muslim places in the new town serving noodles and dumplings. As there's no street lighting, mind those cobbles on the way home.

The Compass Café and Bakery 舒灯库乐, shūdēng kùlè. 50 Shang Ye Jie, just outside the East Gate of the old town ☎ 0887 8223638. Unashamedly Western food served in very clean, diner-style surroundings – pizza (¥58–75), burgers (¥42), fish and chips (¥60), sandwiches (¥35–50) and even some decent curries (¥45–75) – cooked up by an Indian–Singaporean couple. The pastries, including cheesecake (¥28) and carrot cake (¥22), and coffee are also very good. Tues–Sun 8.30am–10pm.

★**Flying Tigers Café** 飞虎队咖啡厅, fēi hǔ duì kāfēi tīng. 91 Jinlong Jie ☎ 0877 8286661. This smart and friendly Gallic-owned and -run wine bar/bistro features a wide variety of foreign foods with a local twist, served in a pleasant wooden interior or at outside tables. Current favourites include yak burgers with Emmental or blue cheese (¥58, avocado ¥10 extra) and fresh ravioli with local mushrooms (¥40). They also have a selection of over thirty wines and great coffee. Mon–Sat 11am–11.30pm.

Helen's Pizza 比萨屋, bǐsàwū. Dawa Lu ☎ 0887 8224456. Helen whips up what are certainly the best pizzas and calzoni; in town – yours for only ¥40–55 – perhaps because her husband is Italian and they use imported olive oil, not yak butter. They also have local

Chinese food, other Italian dishes such as lasagne (meat or veg; ¥50), and even Korean dishes using home-made kimchi (from ¥28). Daily 9am–10pm.

★**Kailash** 凯拉什餐厅, kǎi lā shí cāntīng. By the small stupa on Beimin Lu ☎ 0887 8225505. This Tibetan joint serves up big portions of Tibetan, pseudo-Indian and Chinese dishes; all go well with their hot Tibetan bread (¥100). Recommended are the momos (¥25), various curries (meat ¥38–48/veg ¥18–28) and braised yak meat with mushrooms (¥68). With a colourful interior, the ambience is pleasant, attracting a mix of Chinese tourists, grizzly locals and foreigners. Daily 10am–10pm.

Karma Café 卡玛咖非, kǎmǎ kāfēi. 3 Lunhuolang, Jinlong Jie ☎ 0887 8224768 or ☎ 139 08887878. A little hard to find, and accessed via a narrow lane running up the east side of the Arro Khampa hotel, you could easily walk past this place without even realizing. It's worth the effort of tracking down, though; decrepit from the outside, inside it's a beautifully restored old house serving outstanding yak steak and mashed potatoes for ¥88 while a Tibetan set meal (¥100–160/person) will leave you bursting; ordering à la carte is a bit cheaper. Great place for quiet coffee too. March–Nov daily 10.30am–10pm.

DRINKING

Bad Monkey 乌鸦酒吧, wūyā jiǔbā. 19 Dianlaka ☎ 139 88742294. Dali's infamous *Bad Monkey* (see p.683) has its first franchise branch here and it shares its cyber-ethnic decor, and drinks menu, including the microbrewed craft beers. Not run by foreigners, but by some friendly English-speaking Tibetan hipsters. They don't have a big food menu, just snacks, but they do have nightly live music. Daily 4pm–late.

★**The Raven Café and Bar** 乌鸦酒吧咖啡厅, wūyā jiǔbā kāfēi tīng. 3 Building D8, Tancheng Wangjiao ☎ 182 13215600. Down a backstreet near the lake in the new town (and a wee bit hard to find) this is the *Raven* run by the original and legendary owner, a foreigner who's been here longer than most. With an excellent range of beers and liquors, they also serve good pizzas and other bar food. A great old-school (smoky) bar atmosphere and mostly patronized by local and foreign residents. Daily 11am–1.30am.

SHOPPING

Shangri-La Handicraft Centre 1 Jinlong Jie ☎ 0887 8227742, ⓦ ymhfshangrila.com. This cultural centre employs Tibetans to preserve local crafts, and supports the community. Tues–Sun 10am–6pm.

Around Shangri-La

11

There is limitless **trekking** around Shangri-La, and a number of specialist agents can help you out with routes and guides. If you're planning anything major though, contact them well before you're in town – they'll need time to organize things. Cafés and hotels also provide information and can book you on **trips out** from Shangri-La, including the popular three-day hike via Baishui to **Tiger Leaping Gorge** (see p.695).

Napa Lake

纳帕海, nàpà hǎi · ¥60 · A taxi from town costs ¥80–100 return

Shallow **Napa Lake**, 8km north of town, is a seasonal wetlands dotted with picturesque villages, which attracts rare black-necked cranes in winter. In summer it's more of a pasture for yaks, thick with grass and flowers; there's a **Botanic Garden** (¥30) and café just outside, where at certain times of the year you can see blue poppies and orchids. The best way to see it is by bicycle from Shangri-La, and a ride from the old town and around the entire lake by road and back, is about 40km.

Xiagei Hot Springs

下给温泉, xiàgěi wēnquán · ¥30 · A taxi from town costs ¥80–100 return

Ten kilometres east of town, the **Xiagei Hot Springs** are attractively situated beside a river and below a cave. Eschew the claustrophobic private rooms and swim in the small

---

REACHING SIGHTS AROUND SHANGRI-LA

You can cycle from Shangri-La to a couple of the closer sights, but anywhere further will require a **vehicle** – either rented through Turtle Mountain (see below), your accommodation, or by heading down to the little square on Tuanjie Lu, at the edge of the old town, where minibus drivers will approach you and offer their services. The likely rate is ¥250–350 per day, depending on destination and bargaining skills.

TOUR AGENTS

Haiwei Trails 19 Lu, Old Town ☎ 0887 8289245 or ☎ 139 88756540, ⓦ haiweitrails.com. Plenty of imaginative treks and mountain-biking across northwestern Yunnan.

★**Khampa Caravan** Dawa Lu ☎ 0887 8288648, ⓦ khampacaravan.com. Long-established agency that offers everything from easy day-hikes and sorting out Tibet logistics, to multiday treks to Lijiang or into Sichuan; one of their specialities is the demanding fourteen-day kora circuit around Meili Xue Shan (see p.703). All their guides are local Tibetans, fluent in English.

Turtle Mountain off Beimen Jie at 32 Gun Ma Lang ☎ 0877 8233308, ⓦ nizuroadhouse.com. An excellent option whose American owner, long resident in Shangri-La, has solid hiking and exploring information. They also stock a range of camping supplies and rent these as well as ski gear, snowboards, motorbikes (with breakdown support) and jeeps.

public pool; a shop on site sells swimming costumes and towels. There's also a walking trail, and rafting trips sometimes available on the river.

Pudacuo National Park

普达措国家公园, pǔdácuò guójiā gōngyuán • ¥258, including bus inside the park • Shuttlebus (¥30 return) from the bus station at 9.30am, which also stops after at Moonlight Square near the East Gate; a taxi costs ¥150 return

Pudacuo National Park covers a huge area some 25km east of Shangri-La past Xiagei, with **two alpine lakes** within day-trip range. The first, **Shuodu Lake** (属都海, shǔdūu hǎi), is a renowned beauty spot that attracts plenty of tour buses. However, day-trippers don't seem to get much further than the restaurant and the huge shop in the car park that sells traditional medicines such as ginseng and dried ants. Turn right and follow the lakeshore for a pleasant, easy walk through old forest. Horses can carry you all the way around the lake, which will take about two hours (¥150–200 but negotiable), or you can walk it in four.

Bita Lake

碧塔海, bìtǎ hǎi • Boats a negotiable ¥50/person

The less visited of Pudacuo's two sections, attractive **Bita Lake** is set at an altitude of 3500m and surrounded by lush meadows and unspoilt forest. The best way to explore the place is to ask to be dropped at either of its two entrances, south or west, and then be picked up at the other. Most visitors arrive at the south entrance, from where it's an easy walk down to the lake. Take a rowing boat across to the ferry quay, and you can then walk for around two hours along a well-marked trail to the west entrance.

Baishui Tai

白水台, báishuǐ tái • ¥30 • One morning and one afternoon bus from Shangri-La (3–4hr)

Around 60km southeast of Shangri-La on the north side of Haba Xue Shan from Tiger Leaping Gorge, **Baishui Tai** is a large, milky-white series of limestone terraces, built up over thousands of years as lime-rich water cascaded down a hillside. Plenty of less prosaic legends account for their formation too, and this is one of the holy sites of the Naxi. Wooden ladders allow in-depth exploration of the tiers, which glow orange at sunset. The village at the foot of the site, **Sanba** (三坝, sānbà), is busy transforming itself into a tourist town of guesthouses, all of which offer basic and fairly unattractive rooms.

Although it used to be quite remote, Baishui Tai is now on a back road from Qiaotou, at the mouth of Tiger Leaping Gorge (see p.695), which links it to Shangri-La; you can also **hike** from here to Walnut Garden in two days via Haba village (see p.696).

Deqin

德钦, déqīn

DEQIN lies around 120km north of Shangri-La across some permanently snowy ranges, only 80km from the Tibetan border at Yunnan's northwestern extremes. The town itself, a charmlessly ramshackle, tile-hung outpost, is no great shakes, but there are exciting opportunities for hiking around nearby **Meili Xue Shan**, whose thirteen peaks are of great religious significance to Tibetans.

Feilai Temple

飞来寺, fēilái sì • Observation platform ¥60 • Taxi from Deqin about ¥30 each way; buses from Lijiang or Shangri-La usually run everyone up there for an extra ¥5–10

Unless you miss all transport out, it's better to skip Deqin town altogether in favour of heading another 15km north to the Meili Xue Shan viewing point just beyond **Feilai Temple** – a name which now refers not only to the small temple complex itself but also to the growing cluster of hostels, guesthouses and restaurants along the main road below. There are sublime vistas of the mountain from here, but, in a demonstration of extreme greed, the local authorities have built a **wall**, trying to force tourists to pay to use an observation platform. Walk a hundred metres down the hill, though, and the wall runs out, or head into the five-star resort just above which doesn't seem to mind foreigners taking snaps of the views from their terrace.

ARRIVAL AND DEPARTURE   DEQIN

By bus Deqin's bus station (7am–7pm) is on the main street towards the north end of town.

Destinations Kunming (1 daily; 15hr); Lijiang (2 daily; 11hr); Shangri-La (6 daily, last at 2.40pm; 4–5hr).

GETTING AROUND

Minibus Minivans cruise Deqin's main street looking for passengers, and set off only once full. The trip to Feilai Temple is ¥10 per person.

Taxi You'll see a few, often informal, taxis along Deqin's main street and you're likely to be approached by drivers. The 10km run up to Feilai Temple should cost around ¥30.

ACCOMMODATION AND EATING

As a well-established tourist stop, there is no shortage of places to stay or eat at Feilai. In Dequin itself, if you miss the last bus south at 2.40pm, you can stop over at any one of a number of accommodation options near the bus station (mostly ¥150–200); all are pretty much of a muchness.

Feeling Village Youth Hostel 觉色真乡青年旅社, jué sè zhēn xiāng qīngnián lǚshè. Feilai Temple, down the hill from the viewpoint then follow the sign leading up to the right ☎0887 8416133. A pretty Tibetan-style building with decorations inside and out and basic but comfortable rooms and dorms, although the cheapest dorms can be a bit grubby. The staff speak English and it's an easy place to organize a minibus to Xidang.

Dorms ¥30, doubles ¥120
Meili Guesthouse 梅里客栈, méilī kèzhàn (no English sign). Feilai Temple, south side of the main road, just before the ninety-degree bend leading up to the temple ☎0887 8416998 or ☎139 88755717. As well as basic, comfortable rooms, this straightforward guesthouse has a restaurant and, best of all, hot water around the clock. Dorms ¥40, doubles ¥240

Meili Xue Shan

梅里雪山, méilī xuěshān • Three different tickets covering a number of sites (¥150–230)

Sacred to Tibetan Buddhists as home to the protective warrior god Kawagarpo, as well as attracting tourists drawn by its natural beauty, the **Meili Xue Shan** range is visited by tens of thousands of pilgrims each year. While the arduous two-week **kora circuit** of the mountain conducted by the faithful is not for everyone, there are also some less demanding hikes – still with spectacular views. The highest mountain of the range, at 6740m, is **Kawagarbo** (see box, p.704) at the head of the valley, whose glacier-streaked slopes and peak you'll see dramatically emerging from the clouds if you're lucky. It also remains unclimbed, and the last attempt in 1991 by a Sino-Japanese team ended with disaster and they all died.

Entry to the park area is from **Xidang**, while most visitors stay in **Yubang** as a base for hiking local trails. Any visit to the area should be taken seriously, despite the relatively well-worn paths: always carry food, water, a torch and first-aid kit. Full weatherproof gear and good hiking shoes are a necessity.

Xidang

西当, xīdāng

From the Feilai Temple viewing point, it's a ninety-minute drive to the Meili Xue Shan **reserve entrance** at pretty **XIDANG** village, which sits high above the Lancang Jiang (Mekong River). There's basic hostel accommodation here and a three-hour ascent on foot along a reasonable road to the **Mingyong glacier** (明永冰川, míngyǒng bīngchuān; ¥78), one of the world's lowest at 2700m, and advancing relatively quickly at 500m per year. You'll find a fair few souvenir shops and guesthouses at the glacier viewing point.

About 3km past Xidang village on the path to Yubeng, **Xidang Hot Springs** (温泉, wēnquán) sound better than they are – instead of invitingly steaming outdoor pools, the water is piped into people's houses where you pay to take a shower.

Yubeng

雨崩, yŭbēng • ¥85

From Xidang's hot springs, a wide and well-marked **trail** heads west up to the hamlet of **Yubeng**, with snack stands and food shacks dotting the way. The route kicks off with a gruelling four-hour and steep ascent to 3800m-high **Nazongla Pass**, where there are some teashops serving food, though if you can carry on for another ten minutes you're better off resting at the small viewing platform which has the best views up the valley. This is then followed by ninety minutes down a well-marked trail to **UPPER YUBENG** (雨崩上村, yŭbēng shàngcūn), a Tibetan settlement of considerable charm, though the lower part of it is now a solid corridor of guesthouses.

From here, a path leads up to a lovely alpine meadow, from where you can take a well-marked three-hour hike to the ill-fated **Base Camp**, from where it's another hour to an ice lake. In summer, very basic food and lodgings are available at *Base Camp*, though this should be confirmed with locals; otherwise, it's quite possible to do the return journey in eight to nine hours.

Lower Yubeng

雨崩下村, yŭbēng xiàcūn

Though plenty of visitors stay at the guesthouses in Upper Yubeng, it's worth persevering to the even prettier (and less busy) **LOWER YUBENG** – take the trail to the left as you come into Upper Yubeng and walk for thirty minutes, over a stream and then a bridge. The most popular trip from Lower Yubeng is the straightforward four-to-five-hour walk to the dramatic **Yubeng Shenpu** (雨崩神瀑, yŭbēng shénpù), a sacred waterfall, with bears, snow leopards and the highly endangered Yunnan golden monkey said to be lurking in the nearby forests. For the more adventurous, there's also a ten-hour hike to **Holy Lake** (神湖, shén hú) way up at 4500m, though this would need some organization in advance and is not for mountain novices.

Rather than go back to Deqin via Xidang again, it's far better to head down the **Ninong valley** (倪农谷, nínónggŭ) from Lower Yubeng along the right-hand side of the river, an amazing route which passes just metres from the frothing, roaring rapids in places, and takes around four to six hours. The mostly gentle path starts at the stupa in Lower Yubeng and is easy to follow (just keep going down), though note that for the last few kilometres the path rises sharply when it crosses the river as the valley drops, and is eventually hundreds of metres up. Although the path is fairly wide, there's no railing and an almost vertical drop so if you suffer from vertigo, just keep your eyes fixed on the path, don't look down, and don't stop till you reach the end. The path eventually emerges from the valley at the village of **Ninong** (倪农村, nínóng cūn) where minivan taxis congregate to take you back down to Deqin.

ARRIVAL AND DEPARTURE

MEILI XUE SHAN

By taxi, minibus or bus The run between Feilai Temple and the Meili Xue Shan entrance at Xidang costs about ¥150 for a cab or ¥15/person in a minibus, which depart once full. There's also an 8am bus. From Xidang at the bottom of the Ninong valley back to Deqin, minivans charge ¥25/person shared, or ¥200 for a whole vehicle.

THE KAWAGARBO

Meili Xue Shan's highest peak, unclimbed **Kawagarbo** (6740m), is holy to Tibetans, who trek around its base every year to complete the **Kawa Karpo kora**, or pilgrimage circuit, three circumnavigations of which are said to guarantee a beneficial reincarnation. The circuit takes fourteen days or so, beginning in Deqin and ending in the village of Meili. If you plan to attempt it, be aware that the route **crosses the Tibetan border** and you need permits, as the police keep an eye on this area; you also definitely need a **guide** – you're above 4000m most of the time and people have died attempting the trek solo. Travel agencies in Shangri-La can make all arrangements for you.

11

ACCOMMODATION

Since both Upper and Lower Yubeng have become fixtures on the Chinese tourist trail, prices have skyrocketed and are now highly seasonal. In the highest October season (when the area is at its most spectacular) prices can jump to over eight times the low-season price, so phone ahead to book if possible, to avoid any nasty financial shocks.

UPPER YUBENG

Time Interval Inn 神瀑客栈, shénpù kèzhàn. Upper Yubeng ☎ 0887 8411082. Not run by locals, but some bright young outsiders – which is not a bad thing as many locals seem sick of the tourists already. In a nice new wooden building, with snug but comfortable doubles, and dorms in a separate (older) building. Has a restaurant and a pleasant bar and balcony upstairs. Dorms ¥60, doubles ¥150

LOWER YUBENG

Aqinbu's Mystic Waterfall Lodge 神瀑客栈, shénpù kèzhàn. Lower Yubeng ☎ 0887 8411082. At the end of Lower Yubeng, this now extensive farmhouse-style hostel has more expensive en-suite rooms (¥200) in a new annexe, which have the best views of the brilliant green, cloud-swept mountains rearing up behind. It makes a handy base for further treks, on which the helpful owner can advise. Dorms ¥100, doubles ¥150

11

The far west

Southwest of Xiaguan, **Yunnan's far west** bumps up against the **Myanmar border**, an increasingly tropical area of mountain forests and broad valleys planted with rice and sugar cane, all cut by the deep watershed gorges of Southeast Asia's mighty **Mekong** and **Salween rivers** (in Chinese, the Lancang Jiang and Nu Jiang, respectively). Settlements have large populations of **ethnic minorities**, and mainstream China has never had a great presence in the region; indeed, at times it's still often unclear whether rules and regulations originate in Beijing or with the nearest officer in charge.

The far west's main artery, the underused G56 Expressway, roughly follows the route of the old **Burma Road**, built during World War II as a supply line between British-held Burma and Kunming, from where goods were shipped to China's wartime capital, Chongqing. Something of the road's original purpose survives today, with towns along the way, especially **Ruili**, right on the Burmese frontier, still clearly benefiting from the cross-border traffic. With the exception of geologically unsettled **Tengchong**, however, sights are few and – unless you're heading into Myanmar – the main point of visiting is simply to experience a fairly untouristed, if not actually remote, corner of the country, not least along the upper reaches of the **Nu Jiang valley**.

Transport through the far west is by bus, though you can also fly to Tengchong and the district capital Mangshi, just a couple of hours by road from Ruili. Some minor scuffles along the Myanmar border in the past, plus the area's perennial drug-trafficking problems, mean you'll encounter regular **police and military checkpoints** in the region, where you have to show passports and wait while vehicles and luggage are checked for contraband, which can take up to half an hour. The **weather** is subtropically humid, especially during the wet season between May and October, when landslides frequently cut smaller roads.

The Nu Jiang valley

Far over near China's border with Myanmar, the **Nu Jiang**, or **Salween River**, enters Yunnan from Tibet and flows south for over 500km through the province. To the east towers the Gaoligong mountain range, a huge rock wall that has kept this area an isolated backwater: the only connection with the rest of the province is the road from Xiaguan via **Liuku** to the head of the valley at **Bingzhongluo**, and nearby **Dimaluo** from where hardy trekkers can hike over the mountains to Deqin.

There are some fascinating attractions in this, Yunnan's last true wilderness and part of the UNESCO **Three Parallel Rivers** World Heritage Site. The Nu Jiang itself is narrow, fast, full of rapids and crisscrossed by precarious rope bridges, and the settlements clinging to the gorge's sides are highly picturesque. Most of the population are Tibetan, Lisu or Dulong, and there are a surprising number of Catholics, the result of French and Swiss Jesuit missionary work during the nineteenth century. There are 27 distinct ethnic groups represented in the valley, making it one of the most diverse regions in China.

The far north of the Nu valley connects to Tibet, but is effectively a dead end for tourists and is also relatively poor, and degrees of alcoholism can be seen among the local people. Though tourism promises to be a lucrative new source of income, as yet there are fairly few facilities and the long bus journey up the valley means it's well off the tour-bus trail. Certainly it is not a good idea to venture too far alone, and a local guide is always advised for any ambitious walk.

Liuku

六库, liùkù

Buses from Kunming, Tengchong, Xiaguan or Baoshan can get you to **LIUKU** – also known as **Lushui** (泸水县, lúshuǐ xiàn) – the capital of Nu Jiang prefecture. This rapidly expanding, modern town straddles both sides of the Nu Jiang, its streets lined with the usual clothing, shoe and mobile-phone emporiums; there's little to see aside from nightly dancing down by the river and an eight-storey pagoda on a ridge north of town, and most people only stop overnight on the way up to Bingzhongluo. Around December 20, however, the Lisu hold the **Kuoshijie festival**, at which, besides singing and dancing, you'll see local men showing off by climbing poles barefoot using swords as steps.

ARRIVAL AND DEPARTURE LIUKU

By bus Liuku's bus station (7am–7pm) is on the east side of the river, 2km south of the town centre. A taxi into town from the bus station is a flat ¥15. Buses that don't terminate here may drop you at the main crossroads outside town; a taxi is also ¥15. If you're heading to Bingzhongluo you best get the 8.20am direct bus, or you'll have to get the 9.40am to Gongshan and hope to catch the last bus north at 6pm. Destinations Baoshan (5 daily; 4hr); Bingzhongluo (daily 8.20am; 9hr); Fugong (every 40min until 1pm; 4hr); Gongshan (every 40min until 1pm; 8hr); Kunming (6–7 daily; 12hr); Tengchong (4–5 daily; 5hr); Xiaguan (every 30min until 3.30pm, then one sleeper bus at 7pm; 5hr).

ACCOMMODATION AND EATING

For food, try the covered night market area along the east bank of the river between Zhenxing Lu and the road bridge. As well as barbecues and Sichuan restaurants, there are also a couple of waterfront bars.

Jindou Binguan 金都宾馆, jīndū bīnguǎn. 282 Chuancheng Lu ☎0886 3629555. Useful sprawling budget option in the middle of town, whose serviceable tile-clad doubles are pretty large and come with a/c, en-suite showers and squat toilets. It can feel a bit institutional, and none of the staff speak English, but it's really great value. **¥50**

Shengshi Hongbang Hotel 晟世红邦大酒店, shèngshì hóngbāng dàjiǔdiàn. Cnr of Renmin Lu & Xiangyang Dong Lu ☎0886 8887888. One of just two more upmarket places in town, featuring clean en-suite rooms with sometimes noisy a/c and Western toilets. The really good rooms are about triple the price. **¥214**

Fugong

福贡, fúgòng

Heading north from Liuku, the river becomes increasingly hemmed in by a gorge and begins to reveal its fierce character, with scenic Lisu villages clinging to the steep hillsides. So it's a shame that **FUGONG**, a township of bleak concrete vistas 123km along, is such a dump, though things perk up with the **market** held every fifth day, well attended by local Lisu, Dulong and Nu villagers.

ARRIVAL AND DEPARTURE FUGONG

By bus Fugong's bus station is in the centre of town, just off the main street.
Destinations Bingzhongluo (1 daily; 5hr); Gongshan (every 40min until 3pm; 4hr); Kunming (1 daily; 16hr); Liuku (every 40min until 3pm; 4hr).

ACCOMMODATION

Fugong Binguan 福熙宾馆, fúxī bīnguǎn. Next door to the bus station ☎ 0886 3411442. You'd only really stop in Fugong if you arrived too late to leave again. Conveniently next to the bus station (there are many others clustered here), this place has clean-enough doubles with attached bathrooms for an overnight stay ahead of an early escape. **¥80**

Gongshan

贡山, gòngshān

The two-street town of **GONGSHAN** is around a four-hour bus ride north of Fugong. You'll likely see plenty of **Dulong** people here, the smallest ethnic minority in Yunnan with a current population of just six thousand. Until relatively recently you might have seen older women with tattooed faces, supposedly for beautification, though the practice seems to have started as a way to dissuade Tibetan slave-traders from kidnapping them. There is plenty of bustle and construction at Gongshan, though little to divert visitors longer than it takes to catch the next bus to Bingzhongluo or Dimaluo.

ARRIVAL AND DEPARTURE   GONGSHAN

By bus Gongshan's bus station is on the main street through town. Departures for Bingzhongluo leave until 6pm, after which you'll have to walk around 1km north to the crossroads to flag down one of the minibuses which run all day when full. This is also the best place to find a minibus direct to Dimaluo.

Destinations Bingzhongluo (hourly until 6pm; 1hr 30min); Fugong (every 40min until 1pm; 4hr); Liuku (every 40min until 1pm; 8hr).

ACCOMMODATION

Gongshan Tongbao 贡山通宝大酒店, gòngshān tōngbǎo dàjiǔdiàn. ☎ 0886 3513339. The Tongbao is directly across from the bus station, and is nothing extraordinary, though useful if you must stay in Gongshan; there are a string of other similar establishments on the road going north into town. **¥100**

Bingzhongluo

丙中洛, bǐngzhōngluò • ¥100

A bumpy ninety-minute ride north of Gongshan through dramatic gorge scenery brings you to **BINGZHONGLUO**, the last major village on the main road until you reach Tibet, though foreigners can only go as far as the border. It's a scruffy little place, but the setting is stunning, and it's a great base for hiking – there are a couple of hostels in town which can fix you up with basic maps, as well as guiding services for more taxing routes.

There are also several villages off the road to Tibet, such as Qiunatong, Wuli and Chugan, which are easy solo day-trips, accessible on foot and a great way to get some good vistas and experience the local culture, particularly if on a budget; you can pick up irregular minibuses along the main road if your feet get tired. There's also a church overlooking the village from high on a ridge to the north, an hour's walk away if you follow the path that leads off the end of the high street.

ARRIVAL AND DEPARTURE   BINGZHONGLUO

By bus Bingzhongluo doesn't have a bus station and services stop halfway down the village's main street outside the Jia Yuan Hotel (佳源宾馆, jiā yuán bīnguǎn) whose reception also acts as a ticket office. There is only one long-distance departure each day, but there are hourly shuttles to Gongshan where you can pick up connections for further afield.

Destinations Fugong (1 daily; 5hr); Gongshan (hourly; 1hr 30min); Liuku (daily 8am; 9–11hr).

TREKKING INFORMATION

Treks On foot or horseback, can be arranged through English-speaking Aluo at the International Youth Hostel (☎ 139 88672792, ✉ aluoluosang@hotmail.com) or if he's busy then through the Guodaofang Hostel (☎ 139 88672792). Both charge around ¥250 per person per day and it can be worth hiring a porter too, for another ¥300/day. A horse will cost you from ¥260/day. Check before you leave whether you need to bring your own food, or if it will be supplied en route, though you might want to take some of your own anyway as

they don't exactly serve haute cuisine. Prices will be more in winter or for very long treks.

ACCOMMODATION

Bingzhongluo International Youth Hostel 丙中洛国际青年旅舍, bǐngzhōngluò guójì qīngnián lǚshè. Take the first turning downhill off to the right on the main street after the bus stop ☎ 0886 3581168 or ☎ 189 08861299, ✉ aluoluosang@hotmail.com. Friendly place with English-speaking staff, clean rooms, hard beds, and shared bathrooms, though the rooms at the back have en suites for ¥20 more. The manager, Aluo, also runs a guesthouse in Dimaluo and can provide guiding services. Dorms ¥35, doubles ¥120

Gudaofang Hostel 古道坊客栈, gǔdàofāng

kèzhàn. On the main street, near the turning for the youth hostel ☎ 0886 3581181 or ☎ 139 88672792. Rooms are upstairs, and mattresses are a step up from the IYH's. There's also a pleasant café on the ground floor and an attached ethnic gift shop. Dorms ¥40, doubles ¥120

Yudong 玉洞宾馆, yùdòng bīnguǎn. Opposite the bus stop ☎ 0886 3581285 or ☎ 139 88689887. No surprises here at this Chinese-style effort, just standard, clean rooms with shared bathrooms, though the ones at the back (¥120) have amazing vistas and Western toilets. It could do with a lick of paint and some maintenance, however. ¥80

11

Dimaluo

迪麻洛, dímáluò

Around 34km south of Bingzhongluo, **DIMALUO** is a community of Catholic Tibetans set in a lovely valley and first stop on the trek across the mountains to Cizhong near Deqin (see p.702). Here, there's a rough-and-ready village with accommodation and an intriguing, recently refurbished **Catholic church** built in Tibetan style. There's also another older one, in fact the oldest in the region, a stiff two-and-a-half-hour walk away up at **Baihanlu** (白韩璐, báihánlù), which was built way back in the Qing dynasty. There's not a great deal more to do in the village apart from enjoy the peaceful surroundings.

ARRIVAL AND DEPARTURE   DIMALUO

By bus or minibus Minibuses head directly here from Gongshan (leave when full; 1hr), or board any bus or minibus heading south from Bingzhongluo (hourly or so; 1hr) and get off at the road bridge after 24km (there's a

signpost). Cross the river and walk south until you reach the next valley, then follow it upwards for another 9km (you'll pass a small dam) which takes about two hours.

ACCOMMODATION AND EATING

Aluo Inn 阿罗酒店, āluó jiǔdiàn. ☎ 1890 8861299, ✉ aluoluosang@hotmail.com. About 100m past the main square. Actually Aluo's home, this feels very much like a homestay, though rooms are extremely basic and dorms

are just mattresses on the floor. There are no restaurants in the village, but they cook up local food for ¥25–45 (remember to say grace) and he has quite a collection of local alcoholic drinks. Dorms ¥35, doubles ¥80

TREKKING FROM DIMALUO

From Dimaluo it's possible to trek to neighbouring valleys and avoid having to catch the bus all the way back down to Liuku. You'll need a guide, though: expect to pay around ¥250 per day per person, including very basic food and accommodation.

The most popular option begins with a stiff, three-day hike (8hr/day walking) across the Nushan range to **Cizhong** (茨中, cízhōng), a village with another stone church in the parallel Lancang River valley; the locals even make their own red wine for Communion, though Christianity has been laid on top of much older, animist beliefs. There is a fair-weather bus service (daily 8am; south from Cizhong to **Deqing** (德钦, déqīn; 8hr), from where you can catch a bus to Lijiang or Shangri-La (see p.697).

This is organized by Aluo (see opposite) and his partners in Cizhong, who have set up some rudimentary hostels along the way and also do an eight-day/seven-night "all-inclusive" package between Lijiang and Liuku via Deqing, Cizhong, Dimaluo and Bingzhongluo for ¥2500/person.

Tengchong

腾冲, téngchōng

Some 250km west of Xiaguan, **TENGCHONG** was once an important administrative post, though now isolated and well off the main highway. The town's scruffy old core is surrounded by modern main roads and apartments, though earthquakes have left Tengchong largely bereft of historic monuments or tall buildings. The old stone **gate tower** (文星楼, wénxīng lóu) survives at the eastern end of central Fengshan Lu; there's a big – though rather too organized – **jade market** (玉泉园, yùquán yuán) at the northern edge of town; and a museum at the **Anti-Japanese War Memorial Hall** (滇西抗日纪念馆, diānxī kàngrì jìniànguǎn), which includes copious photos and a memorial to the US-organized "Flying Tigers" (see p.764). None of it is really worth the effort of making a diversion here, but if you're flying through, then Heshun might pass an afternoon.

Laifeng Shan Park

来风山公园, láifēngshān gōngyuán • Free

Just west of the centre, Tengchong's main attraction is **Laifeng Shan Park**, several square kilometres of hilly green woodland. Paths ascend through the forest to Laifeng Temple, a monastery-turned-museum, and a resurrected, thirteen-storey pagoda – looking much like a lighthouse ringed in multiple balconies – which will guide you to the park from Tengchong.

Heshun

和顺, héshùn • ¥80 including all buildings • Bus #6 from town (¥1); taxi ¥20

Five kilometres west of Tengchong, **HESHUN** is an attractive old village with several hundred stone houses packed together in a narrow maze of streets. Once a quiet retreat for Overseas Chinese, this is now a fully fledged tourist attraction, including a barrage of new-built Qing-style shops and a couple of unremarkable **museums**. Head away from the busy main gate, however, and you could still spend half a day exploring Heshun with a camera.

ARRIVAL AND DEPARTURE
TENGCHONG

BY PLANE

Tengchong Tuofeng airport (腾冲驼峰机场, téngchōng tuófēng jīchǎng) is probably the main reason to come to Tenchong (as the bus travel in the region is very slow) and is located 12km south of the city; a taxi to the centre (or Heshun) costs around ¥60–80, or there's an airport bus that runs through the downtown (hourly; 30min).
Destinations Beijing (5hr 10min); Chengdu (4 weekly; 1hr 50min); Chongqing (1hr 30min); Jinghong (1hr); Kunming (50min); Shanghai (5hr); Shenzhen (2hr 20min).

BY BUS

Main bus station (旅游客运站, lǚyóu kèyùnzhàn), 1km south of the centre down Rehai Lu. Kunming and Xiaguan traffic, plus buses to Liuku in the Nu Jiang valley (see p.706).
Tengchong bus station (腾冲客运站, téngchōng kèyùnzhàn), east of the centre on Dongfang Lu, with frequent departures to Ruili.
Destinations Kunming (10 daily; 7–8hr); Liuku (hourly until 11am; 7hr); Ruili (7 daily, last at 12.30pm; 4hr); Xiaguan (10.30am, noon & 7.30pm; 5–6hr).

INFORMATION AND GETTING AROUND

Maps Large maps of Tengchong and Heshun are available free from most hotel receptions.

By taxi A taxi to anywhere within Tengchong's small centre costs ¥8–10 and to Heshun ¥15–20.

ACCOMMODATION AND EATING

While Tengchong itself sports dozens of ordinary hotels, Heshun is where to find guesthouses and hostels (and if you arrive after 5pm, you won't have to pay the town entrance fee). In Tenchong, evening stalls selling charcoal-grilled chicken and fish pop up along Guanghua Lu and Dong Jie, while there is a string of decent places to eat on Dongfang Lu, south of its junction with Feicui Lu.

TENGCHONG

Home Inn 如家酒店, rújiā jiǔdiàn. Dongfang Zhong Lu ☎0875 5144999, ⓦhomeinns.com. Unsurprising branch of this nationwide budget hotel chain, with all the usual bargain comforts including Western toilets and relatively comfortable beds. Rooms are tiny but spotless, and the staff are helpful even if they don't speak English. **¥139**

Yudu Dajiudian 玉都大酒店, yùdū dàjiǔdiàn. 15 Tengyue Lu, Binhe Xiaoqu ☎ 0875 513866. This modern affair, near the jade market, is one of Tenchong's plusher venues but pretty good value; rooms come with some elbow room, lovely soft beds, and modern glass-walled showers. **¥580**

HESHUN

Heshun Lao Shay Youth Hostel 和顺青年旅舍, héshùn qīngnián lǚshè. A good 1km walk over the bridge from the main gate, beside the big banyan tree ☎ 0875 5158398, ⓦ yhachina.com. Nice-looking courtyard compound with wooden buildings, though all rooms are a bit basic – beds are definitely on the hard side and doubles are poor value – but it does offer good travel information, a café and a washing machine. Dorms **¥30**, doubles **¥280**

Zongbingfu Kezhan 总兵府客栈, zǒngbīngfǔ kèzhàn. ☎ 0875 5150288. Smart place with some genuine character, whose period rooms – all with modern furnishings – are housed in an old courtyard building. Call ahead and get someone to meet you at the main gate and guide you there. **¥810**

Ruili

瑞丽, ruìlì

Once the capital of the Mengmao Dai kingdom, the frontier town of **RUILI** revels in the possibilities of its proximity to Myanmar, 5km south over the Shweli River: so porous is the border between Jiegao in China and **Mu Se** in Myanmar that locals quip, "Feed a chicken in China and you get an egg in Myanmar". Myanmar, Pakistani and Bangladeshi nationals wander around in sarongs and thongs, clocks are sometimes set to Rangoon time (90min behind Beijing), and markets display foreign goods. Many Chinese in town are tourists, attracted by the chance to pick up cut-price trinkets, though recent massive growth means thousands are now here for work. The town's **markets** are fascinating; many foreign traders speak good English and make interesting company. The surrounding countryside, studded with Dai villages and temples, is only a bike ride away, though they're fast being absorbed by the city. Drop in if you're on the way to Myanmar, but if you're looking for Dai culture, Jinghong is much more pleasant and not as hard to get to.

The jade and gem market

瑞丽珠宝街, ruìlì zhūbǎo jiē • Daily 9am–5pm

By day Ruili's broad pavements and drab construction pin it down as a typical Chinese town; fortunately, its **markets** and people are anything but typical. The **jade and gem market**, in the north of town along Bianmao Jie, has a "Disneyland Myanmar" look, but there is serious business being done. Dealers come to stock up on ruinously expensive wafers of deep green jade; unless you really know your stuff it's safer just to watch the huddles of pensive merchants, or negotiate souvenir prices for coloured pieces of sparkling Russian glass "jewels", chunks of polished substandard jade and heavy brass rings.

Huafeng market

华丰市场, huáfēng shìchǎng

Dai and Jingpo haunt Ruili's huge **Huafeng market** on Jiegang Lu. **Burmese shopkeepers** here can sell you everything from haberdashery and precious stones to birds, cigars, Mandalay rum and Western-brand toiletries. The ad-hoc stalls have gone and there's a huge Dai-themed shopping mall at the centre, but it has a well-stocked supermarket in the basement. It's also still something of a meeting place, and families and young people congregate here at sunset at the outdoor barbecue stalls near the main gate.

Farmers' market

综合农贸市场, zònghé nóngmào shìchǎng

For a rough-and-ready shopping experience, try the morning **farmers' market** at the western end of Maohan Lu, where you'll find not only meat (the live animal section, including dogs for consumption, is not for the faint-hearted), fish, fruit and vegetables, but also locally made wood and cane furniture as well as shoes, clothes and even roadside jewellers selling "gold" rings and bracelets. If you manage to keep your appetite, this is also a good place to pick up a bowl of spicy noodles from stalls in the heart of the market's covered area.

ARRIVAL AND DEPARTURE — RUILI

By plane The nearest airport is 100km northeast at Mangshi (芒市, mángshì), also known as Luxi (潞西, lùxī). Getting to and from Mangshi's airport costs ¥35 in a bus or ¥80/person in a taxi.

Destinations from Mangshi Beijing (3 weekly; 3hr 45min); Diqing, Tibet (1 weekly; 1hr); Guangzhou (2hr 35min); Kunming (1hr).

By bus The long-distance station is around 3km northwest of the town towards the highway and has at least daily services to everywhere along the highway between here and Kunming; there's also at least one departure daily for the lengthy ride down to Jinghong in Xishuangbanna. As there's no easy-to-get bus into town from here, the town's

avaricious taxi drivers will try to charge ¥20 to the centre which should be (at most) a ¥10 ride, though with a bit of arguing you might get it down to ¥15.

Destinations Jinghong (daily 10am; 24hr); Kunming (10 daily; 15hr); Liuku (8am daily; 7hr); Mangshi (leave when full; 2hr); Tengchong (hourly until 1.20pm; 4hr); Xiaguan (daily 9am & 11am; 6hr).

By minibus Minibuses to Mangshi depart from the minibus station opposite the north end of Jiegang Lu, while vans to closer sights go from Nanmao Jie – keep repeating the name of your destination and you'll be shepherded to the correct vehicle.

INFORMATION AND GETTING AROUND

Maps Ruili's centre is small enough to get around on foot; large double-sided maps of Ruili and attractions in the surrounding area can be bought from hotel receptions (¥10).

By bike Bikes can be rented from the Merida bicycle shop (美利达, měilìdá) on Biancheng Lu for ¥50/ day.

ACCOMMODATION

Ruili is littered with basic hotels and there's a good choice of rooms right in the town centre, though there are no real budget bargains. You need air-conditioning in summer.

Ba Shi 巴实宾馆, bā shí bīnguǎn. 5 Renmin Lu ☎ 0692 4129088. The rooms are inexpensive and decent enough, and the luxury rooms for ¥120 are really quite nice, although they could all be better maintained. It's the

atmosphere of the place that's most attractive though, with a little bit of greenery (and a supermarket entrance) in the car park out back and friendly (though non-English-speaking) staff. ¥100

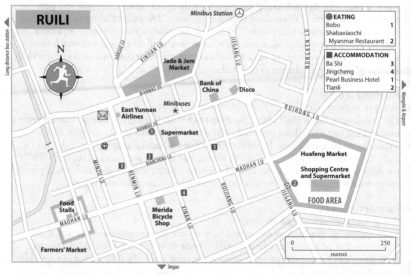

RUILI

EATING
Bobo	1
Shabaxiaochi	
Myanmar Restaurant	2

ACCOMMODATION
Ba Shi	3
Jingcheng	4
Pearl Business Hotel	1
Tianli	2

Minibus Station

Long distance bus station

Jade & Jem Market

Bank of China   Disco

East Yunnan Airlines

Minibuses

NANMAO JIE   Supermarket

RUIHONG LU

Huafeng Market

Shopping Centre and Supermarket

FOOD AREA

Food Stalls

Merida Bicycle Shop

Farmers' Market

Mangshi & Airport

0   250
metres

Jiegao

> ### RULI TO MYANMAR
>
> At present it is possible for foreigners to cross on foot from Ruili into **Myanmar** but you must have previously arranged to be met by an official tour guide at the border. You'll need to have set everything up – including visas – before leaving Kunming (see p.663). Check online for the latest information as the situation may change with the recent partial relaxing of tourism regulations.

Jingcheng 景成大酒店, jǐngchéng dàjiǔdiàn. Maohan Lu ☎0692 4159666. The kind of rooms every other business hotel in town tries to have, this starred pile is very clean and well-maintained, and has a restaurant and gym, all enclosed inside central Ruili's tallest building. ¥300

Pearl Business Hotel 明珠商务酒店, míngzhū shāngwù jiǔdiàn. Biancheng Lu ☎0692 6636222. Easy to find thanks to neon lights outside and a video games arcade on the ground floor. The lobby of this new, and currently smart, hotel is up the lift on the third floor. The rooms are marginally better-maintained than most in this price bracket. ¥196

Tianli 天丽宾馆, tiānlì bīnguǎn. 136 Biancheng Lu ☎0692 4155000. Yet another of Ruili's simple, clean options whose spacious tiled doubles with new furniture, clean bathrooms and a/c are good value, if absolutely ordinary and functional. ¥120

EATING AND DRINKING

As well as clear influence from Myanmar, the town's dining also features flavours from further afield including Thailand, as well as China's own cuisine. For conventional Chinese food, head to the string of buffet restaurants on Biancheng Lu near the corner with Renmin Lu, serving the local fast-food buffet-style rice meals for ¥10, or barbecue or noodles are available inside the main gate of Huafeng market.

Bobo 步步冷饮店, bùbù lěngyǐndiàn. Xinan Lu. Sited on a covered rooftop, this relaxed café boasts a vast array of fruit juices (¥10) and a shorter food list featuring many Burmese and Thai dishes such as Thai fried rice with sausage (¥20) and hot and sour fish (¥35). The menu is in English, though little is spoken. There's a second, ground-floor branch, not far away on Nanmao Jie. Daily 9am–9pm.

Shabaxiaochi Myanmar Restaurant 沙巴小店缅甸 餐厅, shābā xiǎo diàn miǎndiàn cāntīng. On the right as you enter Huafeng market by the main gate. With outdoor seating at the front of the market and excellent Burmese food, this restaurant has no English on the menu (or the sign) but there are photos and the rice dishes on the second page (¥12–20) are very tasty, especially the beef. Daily 8pm–11pm.

Around Ruili

Villages and Buddhist monuments dot the plains around Ruili, though most of the destinations below are only of mild interest in themselves, really just excuses to get out into the attractive countryside; though the town is spreading so fast most of them may soon be under the shadow of the tower blocks. For more about the Dai, see the Xishuangbanna section (see box, p.714).

Jiegao and the border

姐告, jiěgào • 6km from the centre of town; minibuses from Nanmao Jie or a taxi from town cost you an outrageous ¥50–80

The quickest trip is virtually inside town. Hail a shared red taxi and it's just ten to fifteen minutes to **Jiegao**, a huge bubble-shaped duty-free trading estate on Ruili's southern outskirts, surrounded on all sides by Myanmar. There are three official crossings – for people, cars and trucks – and multiple unofficial ones, set amid a vast grid of shops selling everything from pneumatic drills to washing-up bowls. Look out for the jade-encrusted bridge on the way there.

Jiele Jin Ta

姐勒金塔, jiělè jīntǎ • ¥5 • A taxi from town costs around ¥25–30

About 5km east of Ruili and on a dirt track just off the Wanding road is the two-hundred-year-old **Jiele Jin Ta**, a group of seventeen portly Dai pagodas painted gold and topped with silver bell-bearing crowns that tinkle melodically in the wind. It's

THE DAI

Although the **Dai** once spread as far north as the Yangzi valley, they were driven south by the Mongol expansion in the thirteenth century. They are found not only in southwest China but also throughout Thailand, Laos and Vietnam. Reputed to be skilful farmers, they have always flourished in fertile river basins, growing rice, sugar cane, rubber trees and bananas.

Accordingly, **Dai cuisine** is characterized by sweet flavours not found elsewhere in China – you'll encounter rice steamed inside bamboo or pineapple, for instance. Oddities such as fried moss and ant eggs appear on special occasions.

Dai women wear a *lunghi* (sarong) or long skirt, a bodice and a jacket, and keep their hair tied up and fixed with a comb, and often decorated with flowers. Married women wear silver wristbands. Dai men sport plenty of **tattoos**, usually across their chests and circling their wrists. Their homes are raised on stilts, with the livestock kept underneath. Some of the most distinctive and ornate Dai architecture is well decoration, as the Dai regard water as sacred. They're Buddhists, but like their compatriots in Southeast Asia follow the Thervada, or Lesser Wheel school, rather than the Mahayana school favoured throughout the rest of China. When visiting Dai temples, it's important to **remove your shoes**, as the Dai consider feet to be the most unclean part of the body.

become somewhat of a Dai cultural centre, and the Dai's flag flutters from several flagpoles around the site, many visitors wear *lunghis* (sarongs) and there are quite a few good and inexpensive Dai food stalls and restaurants outside. It is said to house several of Buddha's bones, though nobody seems entirely sure who said that, or where they are.

West to Jiexiang town

All sites can be reached via minibus #1 from Nanmao Jie

West of Ruili, it's 5km to a small bridge near the region's largest Buddhist monastery, the nicely decorated **Hansha Temple** (喊沙寺, hǎnshā sì). Ten kilometres further on, the town of **JIEXIANG** (姐相, jiěxiàng) boasts the splendid Tang-era **Leizhuang Nunnery** (雷奘相佛寺, léizàngxiàng fósì), whose complex is dominated by a huge central pagoda and four corner towers, all in white. Another fine temple with typical Dai touches, such as "fiery" wooden eave decorations, **Denghannong Temple** (等喊弄寺, děnghǎnnòng sì) is further west again. The current halls only date from the Qing dynasty, but Buddha is said to have stopped here once to preach.

Xishuangbanna

西双版纳, xīshuāngbǎnnà

A tropical spread of rainforests, plantations and paddy fields nestled 750km southwest of Kunming along the Myanmar and Laos borders, **Xishuangbanna** has little in common with the rest of provincial China. Foremost of the region's many ethnic groups are the **Dai**, northern cousins to the Thais, whose distinctive temples, bulbous pagodas and saffron-robed clergy are a common sight down on the plains, particularly around **Jinghong**, Xishuangbanna's increasingly touristed capital. The region's remaining 19,000 square kilometres of hills, farms and forest are split between the administrative townships of **Mengla** in the east and **Menghai** in the west, peppered with villages of Hani, Bulang, Jinuo, Wa and Lahu. Cultural tourism aside, there are plenty of hiking trails and China's **open border with Laos** to explore.

Xishuangbanna's emphatically tropical **weather** divides into a dry stretch between November and May, when warm days, cool nights and dense morning mists are the norm; and the June–October **wet season**, featuring high heat and torrential daily rains. The busiest time of the year here is mid-April, when thousands of tourists flood to Jinghong for the Dai **Water-splashing Festival**; hotels and flights will be booked solid for a week beforehand. **Getting around** Xishuangbanna is easy enough, with well-maintained roads connecting Jinghong to outlying districts.

Brief history

There was already a Dai state in Xishuangbanna two thousand years ago, important enough to send ambassadors to the Han court in 69 AD; it was subsequently incorporated into the Nanzhao and Dali kingdoms. A brief period of full independence ended with the Mongols' thirteenth-century conquest of Yunnan and the area's division into **twelve rice-growing districts** or *sipsawng pa na*, rendered as "Xishuangbanna" in Chinese. A fairly "hands-off" approach to Chinese rule ended in the 1950s, since when more contentious aspects of religion have been banned, extensive deforestation has occurred, and recent mass planting of **rubber** as a cash crop has drastically altered the landscape. Many minority people feel that the government would really like them to behave like Han Chinese, except in regards to dress – since colourful traditional clothing attracts tourists – and it's certainly true that Xishuangbanna is a rather anaemic version of what lies across the border in Laos.

Jinghong

景洪, jǐnghóng

JINGHONG, Xishuangbanna's fast-developing capital, sits on the southwestern bank of the **Lancang River** (澜沧江, láncāng jiāng), which later winds downstream through Laos and Thailand as the Mekong. Ever since the Dai warlord Bazhen drove the Bulang and Hani tribes off these fertile central flatlands, and founded the independent kingdom of Cheli in 1180, Jinghong has been maintained as an administrative centre. There was a moment of excitement in the late nineteenth century when a battalion of British soldiers marched in during a foray from Burma, but they soon decided that Jinghong was too remote to be worth defending.

Today the towering gaudiness of Jinghong's newly acquired high-rises and strip malls, bedecked with faux-ethnic fibreglass mouldings – not to mention parties of domestic

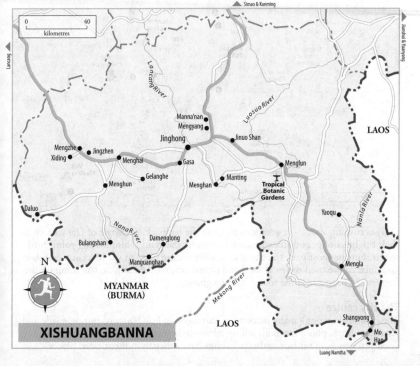

11

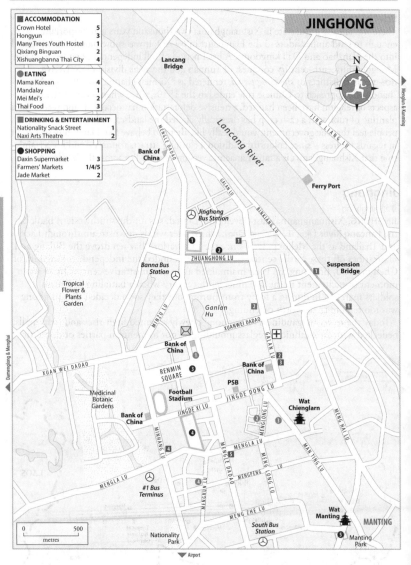

JINGHONG

ACCOMMODATION	
Crown Hotel	5
Hongyun	3
Many Trees Youth Hostel	1
Qixiang Binguan	2
Xishuangbanna Thai City	4

EATING	
Mama Korean	4
Mandalay	1
Mei Mei's	2
Thai Food	3

DRINKING & ENTERTAINMENT	
Nationality Snack Street	1
Naxi Arts Theatre	2

SHOPPING	
Daxin Supermarket	3
Farmers' Markets	1/4/5
Jade Market	2

tourists rushing about – is a stark contrast to the laidback, easy style of Dai women in their bright sarongs and straw hats who meander the gently shimmering, palm-lined streets. For the most part, the city is an undemanding place to spend a couple of days, and once you've tried the local food and poked around the temples, you jump on the frequent transport into the rest of Xishuangbanna.

The city centre

The pick of Jinghong's many **markets** is Zhuanghong Lu's 500m of Burmese jade and jewellery shops, plus a few stalls selling ethnic-style textiles and trinkets. It's quite a good place to shop for jade and many shops have officially authenticated pieces –

remember to bargain hard and aim to pay a third of the starting price. There are also big **farmers' markets** (农贸市场, nónghè shìchǎng), packed with Dai women picking over piles of tropical fruit and veg, almost next to the bus station on Mengle Dadao, west of the centre on Mengla Lu, and west of Manting Park on Menghai Lu.

Riverside **Binjiang Lu** is a great place to stroll in the evening, when the bars, snack stalls and night market lining the river fire up and where you can watch locals flying kites and bringing their cars, trucks and buses to the water's edge to give them a good clean.

Tropical Flower and Plants Garden

热带花卉园, rèdài huāhuìyuán • 99 Xi Lu • Daily 7.30am–6pm • ¥40

Jinghong's **Tropical Flower and Plants Garden**, 500m west of the centre down Xuanwei Dadao, holds over a thousand different types of palm, fruit tree and brightly flowering shrubs and vines, nicely arranged around a lake. The different sections – an aerial flower section, bougainvillea area, and so on – host afternoon performances of Dai dancing for tour groups.

Medicinal Botanic Gardens

药用植物园, yàoyòng zhíwùyuán • Daily 9am–6pm • ¥120

Across the road from the tropical flower garden, the **Medicinal Botanic Gardens** consist of quiet groves scattered among the shaded gloom of closely planted rainforest trees. They lead to a large **Traditional Medicine Clinic**, whose friendly staff may invite you in for a cup of tea and impromptu *qi gong* demonstration.

Manting

曼听, màntīng • Bus #3 from the centre

A kilometre southeast of the centre via Manting Lu, **Manting** was once a separate village, now absorbed into Jinghong's lazy spread. Near the end of the road, **Wat Manting** (曼听佛寺, màntīng fósì) is Jinghong's main Buddhist monastery and the largest in all Xishuangbanna. Check out the very Dai gold trim, the guardian creatures at the gates, the glossy *jinghua* murals adorning the temple walls and a giant ceremonial canoe in the monastery grounds. Traditionally, all Dai boys spend three years at temples like Wat Manting getting a grounding in Buddhism and learning to read and write.

Manting Park

曼听公园, màntīng gōngyuán • Daily 7.30am–5.30pm • ¥40, includes the elephant shows at 11am, 2.50pm & 4.10pm, and the peacock show at 1.30pm; evening show 6.50pm, ¥190–320

Next to Wat Manting is the more secular **Manting Park**, where the royal slaves were once kept. A giant gold statue of former premier Zhou Enlai welcomes visitors, tour groups are treated to water-splashing displays every afternoon, and there's also a large pen bursting with **peacocks**, which you can feed. Corners of the park are very pleasant, with paths crossing over one of the Lancang River's tiny tributaries to full-scale copies of Jingzhen's Bajiao Ting (see p.722) and a portly, Dai-style pagoda. The park also hosts evening shows featuring Dai dancing and mass water-splashings.

ARRIVAL AND DEPARTURE   JINGHONG

Remember to confirm visa requirements for Laos and Thailand before booking transport – the nearest consulates are in Kunming (see box, p.667).

BY PLANE

Daily flights link Jinghong with Kunming, Xiaguan/Dali, Lijiang and a few cities elsewhere in China as well as Luang Prabang in Laos.

Xishuangbanna airport (西双版纳嘎洒机场, xishuāngbǎnnà gāsā jīchǎng) lies about 10km southwest of the city; catch bus #1 to its terminus at the western extension of Mengla Lu, or it's a 10min, ¥30 taxi ride into the centre along an expressway.

Destinations Anshun (3 weekly; 1hr 15min); Chengdu

NEW YEAR FESTIVITIES

Dai New Year celebrations, once set by the unpredictable Dai calendar, are now held **April 13–16** annually. The first day sees a **dragon-boat race** on the river, held in honour of a good-natured dragon spirit who helped a local hero outwit an evil king. On the second day everybody in Jinghong gets a good soaking as **water-splashing** hysteria grips the town, and basinfuls are enthusiastically hurled over friends and strangers alike to wash away bad luck. Manting Park also hosts cockfighting and dancing all day. The finale includes **Diu Bao** (Throwing Pouches) games, where prospective couples fling small, triangular beanbags at each other to indicate their affection, and there's a mammoth **firework display**, when hundreds of bamboo tubes stuffed with gunpowder and good-luck gifts are rocketed out over the river. Nightly carousing and dancing – during which generous quantities of *lajiu*, the local firewater, are consumed – take place in the parks and public spaces. Look out for the **Peacock dance**, a fluid performance said to imitate the movements of the bird, bringer of good fortune in Dai lore, and the **Elephant-drum dance**, named after the instrument used to thump out the rhythm.

11

(2hr); Dali (55min); Guilin (4 weekly; 2hr); Kunming (55min); Lijiang (1hr 10min); Luang Prabang (3 weekly; 1hr); Tengchong (55min).

BY BUS

You can reach Jinghong direct from: Kunming's South bus station; Xiaguan; Tengchong; Ruili; and Luang Namtha in Laos (10.40am; 7hr). Coming from Yuanyang in southeast Yunnan, if you miss the one daily bus, aim first for Jianshui (see p.672) and change buses there. In Jinghong, buy bus tickets at the relevant stations – and watch out for pickpockets.

Banna bus station (版纳客运服务站, bǎnnà kèyùn fúwùzhàn), right in the centre on Minzu Lu, is where to find most traffic heading to outlying villages around Xishuangbanna.

Destinations Menghai (every 20min; 1hr 30min); Menghan/Ganlanba (every 50min; 1hr 20min); Menglun (every 20min; 1hr); Menyang (every 30min; 30min); Yuanyang (daily noon; 6–7hr).

Jinghong bus station (景洪客运站, jǐnghóng kèyùnzhàn), on the northern arm of Mengle Dadao, handles almost all long-distance traffic, including those from Luang Namtha in Laos.

Destinations Jianshui (9.30am & 10.30am; 13hr); Kunming (every 30min until 6.30pm, then 5 sleeper buses; 9hr); Ruili (daily 8am; 24hr); Xiaguan (daily 8.30am & 10.30am; 14hr).

South bus station (客运南站, kèyùn nánzhàn), 1km south of town, deals in traffic around Xishuangbanna, and a few Kunming services; catch bus #3 or a cab to the centre.

Destinations Damenglong (every 30min; 1hr 30min).

BY FERRY

Mekong ferries used to operate between Jinghong and Chiang Saen in northern Thailand, but were suspended in 2011 after the drug-related killing of thirteen Chinese sailors. If they haven't been reinstated, it is still possible, however, to get a lift down to Thailand on one of the cargo vessels that leave from just down the river at the Guanlae port, where you can negotiate with any captain for a rate for a lift – around ¥500–600.

Jinghong ferry port (景洪港, jǐnghóng kèyùnzhàn) is across the river via the main suspension bridge – bus #2 from the nearby main road will get you into the town centre. The port ticket office (daily 8am–5.30pm; ☎0691 2211899) is where to check on the latest situation regarding boats to Thailand.

INFORMATION AND ACTIVITIES

Cruises Nightly pleasure cruises, taking in the lights of Jinghong, depart on two-hour trips from the ferry port from 7pm (¥198). Most boats feature their own entertainment in the form of cabaret floor shows. Tickets are available from most travel agencies in town, or from the ferry port.

Trekking agents Guided treks offered by Jinghong's tourist cafés explore remoter villages, waterfalls and forest, with the chance of encountering wildlife. Most trips

include overnight stays with a local host family and cost around ¥450 per person per day all-inclusive (min. 2 people), though prices fall as the number of people in your group goes up. Enquire with the English-speaking Achun at *Mei Mei's Café* (☎0691 2161221, ✉zhanyanlan @hotmail.com) who is also a mine of information and will happily provide a map and instructions for you to head off on your own.

GETTING AROUND

By bus City buses operate 7am–7pm (¥2), though nowhere in Jinghong is more than a 20min walk away. Bus #5 runs east–west across the town centre and #4 north–south.

By bicycle *Many Trees* hostel rents bikes at ¥30 per day for exploring the town and Xishuangbanna's lowlands – though country roads are steep, twisting and long, and heavy traffic along the narrow roads, particularly south along the river toward Menghan, can make this a dangerous option.

By taxi Cabs charge ¥10 for anywhere in town.

ACCOMMODATION

All but the smallest lodgings have restaurants and even computers in the room for an extra ¥20 or so. You'll need air-conditioning in summer.

Crown Hotel 皇冠大酒店, huángguān dàjiǔdiàn. 70 Mengle Dadao ☎ 0691 2199888, ⓦ newtgh.com. One of a number of upmarket places grouped around the Mengle/Mengla roads intersection, all aimed at wealthy Chinese tourists. Unmemorable, but clean and comfortable, most of the rooms are located around the quiet garden in the back. The same company operates a five-star hotel out towards the airport. **¥300**

Hongyun 鸿云酒店, hóngyún jiǔdiàn. 12 Galan Nan Lu ☎ 0691 2165777. Older place, now showing its age, with carpeted, quite spacious en suites with a/c and squat toilets – not bad value. Upper rooms just about have views of the river. **¥120**

Many Trees Youth Hostel 曼丽翠国际青年旅舍, mànlìcuì guójì qīngnián lǚshè. 2F, 5 Manyun Xiang, down a lane opposite the gymnasium on Galan Lu, then up the stairs through the large restaurant ☎ 0691 2126210. Veteran and haphazardly brightened up Chinese hostel, but a/c rooms are a fair deal for the money, and they've got a rooftop washing machine (¥10). The restaurant downstairs is pretty good too. Dorms **¥40**, doubles **¥100**

Qixiang Binguan 气象宾馆, qìxiàng bīnguǎn. 10 Galan Nan Lu ☎ 0691 2130188. Run by the Weather Bureau, this place's small tiled rooms with a/c are a budget bargain, though there isn't a lift and there are only squat toilets throughout. They also have triples for ¥100. **¥80**

Xishuangbanna Thai City 西双版纳傣都大酒店, xīshuāngbǎnnà dǎidū dàjiǔdiàn. 26 Minghang Lu ☎ 0691 2137888. This three-star establishment was once as upmarket as Jinghong got, and it's still of a decent standard – and good value – full of clean, furnished rooms, though in need of some maintainance. **¥200**

EATING

Jinghong is the best place in Xishuangbanna to try authentic Dai cooking, either in restaurants or on the street. Formal menus often feature meat or fish courses flavoured with sour bamboo shoots or lemongrass, while oddities include fried moss, and pineapple rice for dessert – the fruit is hollowed out, stuffed with pineapple chunks and sweet glutinous rice, and steamed. Tourist cafés are comparatively expensive places to eat, but aside from their Western/Dai menus they also hand out local information, rent bikes and arrange tours. In the evening the night market along the river, south of the suspension bridge, is packed with open-air barbecues.

Mama Korean 韩国小吃店, hánguó xiǎochīdiàn. 13 Menghun Lu ☎ 1597 4955043. A bit of a treat for fans of real Korean food, this Korean-run place is much better than most in China and does authentic-tasting soups such as *kimchi jjigae* (¥25) and *dwenjang jjigae* (¥30) as well as other favourites such as the rice-based *kimchi bokimbap* and *bibimbap* (both ¥25) and *kimbap* rice and seaweed rolls (¥15). Daily 9am–9pm.

Mandalay 耶待纳美餐厅, yēdàinàměi cāntīng. Above Dico's on Renmin Square ☎ 0691 2141640. A vast canteen serving up cheap and plentiful Dai and Chinese dishes, and they also have a decent stab at pizza. It's best to stick to the Dai side of the menu though – the fish with lemongrass is fantastic (¥38). Otherwise expect to pay around ¥25 per person. Daily 11am–10pm.

★**Mei Mei's Café** 美美咖非, měiměi kāfēi. 107 Menglong Lu ☎ 0691 2161221, ⓦ meimei-cafe.com. One of a clutch of similar cafés along this newish development serving great breakfasts (¥30–38) and other Western staples such as burgers and sandwiches (¥25–32), pastas and pizzas (¥28–42), as well as a smattering of Chinese and Yunnanese specialities (¥20–30). Talk to the manager Achun who can give you information on, and help book, local treks. They also give away free city and regional maps in English and sell great coffee too. Daily 8am–11pm.

Thai Food 泰国风味, tàiguó fēngwèi. 193 Manting Lu, opposite Mei Mei's Café ☎ 0691 2161758. Terrific food, great value and always busy, this semi-outdoor eatery is a Jinghong institution. It's had a makeover and is a very nice place to eat, with a massive choice of spicy Thai favourites such as *pad thai* (¥12), shrimp fried rice (¥18) and *tom yum* soup (¥40). Daily 11am–9pm.

DRINKING AND ENTERTAINMENT

Nationality Snack Street 民族食尚街, mínzú shíshàng jiē. Binjiang Lu. A line of large, wooden restaurant-bars with loud – sometimes live – music on the promenade above the riverside, decked out in coloured fairy lights. It's a nice idea (and about the only bar area), but the establishments are all much the same and a drink costs at least ¥30. Daily from 5pm.

Naxi Arts Theatre 蒙巴拉纳西艺术宫, měngbālā

nàxī yìshùgōng. Galan Zhong Lu. Hugely popular with Chinese tour groups, during the high season they put on two shows a night here, but if you come early they usually do a half-hour warm-up in the square outside the theatre from about 7pm which you can watch for free. Tickets for the full performance cost ¥260 or ¥380, though you can get a substantial discount if you book your ticket through *Mei Mei's*.

SHOPPING

Markets For fresh fruit, including mangoes, coconuts, bananas, mangosteens and durian, head to either of the big produce markets on Mengle Dadao or Mengla Lu.
Supermarket Jinghong's best supermarket is the Daxin

Mart, underneath Renmin Square on Mengle Dadao; aside from daily necessities, you can buy cheese and small packets of Yunnan ham.

DIRECTORY

Hospital The Provincial Hospital is at the lower end of Galan Lu.
Laundry *Many Trees Youth Hostel* charges ¥10 a load, while some of the foreigner cafés also offer laundry services.
Massage Taiji Blind Massage (太极宣人按摩中心, tàijí xuānrén ànmó zhōngxīn) is 100m north of the Jingde

Dong Lu/Mengle Dadao intersection, on the east side of the road. Go through the arch marked "Blind Massage" then immediately turn left up the staircase to the second floor. Full body ¥60/hr, feet ¥70/hr. Daily 8am–midnight.
Visa extensions PSB at 13 Jingde Lu (Mon–Fri 8–11.30am & 3–5.30pm; ☎ 0691 2130366) – look for the yellow English sign.

Northern and eastern Xishuangbanna

Aside from ethnic villages to the north of Jinghong, heading east through Xishuangbanna allows access to the excellent **botanic gardens** at Menglun, beyond which lies the open **border with Laos**. All traffic out this way departs from Jinghong's Banna bus station.

Huayao villages

MENGYANG (勐养, měngyǎng), 30km north of Jinghong, is a market and transport stop surrounded by a host of **Huayao** villages. The **Huayao** ("Flower Belt") form one of three Dai subgroups, though they differ greatly from the lowland "Water Dai", who scorn them for their over-elaborate costumes – Huayao women wear turbans draped in thin silver chains – and the fact that they are not Buddhists. Though you'll see plenty of Huayao at Mengyang, the village considered most typical is about 10km further north along the main road at **MANNA'NAN** (曼那囡, mànnà'nān).

Jinuo Shan
基诺山, jīnuò shān

Some 18km east of Mengyang, **JINUO SHAN** is home to the independently minded **Jinuo**. Jinuo women wear a distinctive white-peaked hood, while both sexes pierce their ears and sport tattoos. The **Jinuo Folk Culture Village** (基诺山民族山寨, jīnuòshān mínzú shānzhài; ¥80) here is a bit touristy, but at any rate can give you a glimpse of Xishuangbanna's smallest ethnic group.

Menghan
勐罕, měnghǎn

MENGHAN, 30km southeast of Jinghong, is the main settlement of the fertile "Olive-shaped Flatland", as its alternative name, **Ganlanba** (橄榄坝, gǎnlǎnbà), translates. This is one of Xishuangbanna's three major agricultural areas, won by force of arms over the centuries and now vitally important to the Dai (the other two are west at Damenglong and Menghai). Immediately west of town, the **Xishuangbanna Dai Garden** (傣园, dǎiyuán; daily 8am–6pm; ¥100) offers a sanitized version of minority life and daily water-splashing festivals in Dai costume (¥40 extra) to visiting tour groups. You can stay here too, inside "Dai Family Homes" – or at any rate, a tourist industry vision of them – which also provide meals.

Menghan itself is pleasantly surrounded by paddy fields and low hills, with plenty of day-walks and cycle rides – accommodation will be able to help you rent a bike. One popular trip is to take a bike across the Mekong on the local ferry, and then head left for Dai villages.

Manting

曼听, màntīng

A couple of kilometres east of Menghan at **MANTING**, the excellent **Manting Buddhist Temple** (曼听佛寺, màntīng fósì) and **Dadu Pagoda** (大独塔, dàdú tǎ) are fine reconstructions of twelfth-century buildings destroyed during the 1960s. Paths lead further east from Manting along and across the river to more pagodas and villages, somewhere to spend a couple of days of easy exploration.

ACCOMMODATION   MENGHAN

Huaxin Binguan 华鑫宾馆, huáxīn bīnguǎn. 179 Xiandao, Menghan ☏ 0691 2411258. Up on the north side of the main road, but not far from the lake, this basic but clean place is a decent deal, and there's a tasty local restaurant directly across the street. **¥80**

Xishuangbanna Sha La Hotel 沙拉酒店, shālā jiǔdiàn. 68 Xiandao, Menghan ☏ 0691 2494168. Ugly, multistorey three-star affair up the road from the *Huaxin*. En-suite twins and doubles are modern, clean, comfortable and come equipped with the standard dark-wood furnishings, but lack any semblance of character. **¥341**

Menglun

勐仑, měnglún

MENGLUN, about 40km east of Menghan, comprises a dusty grid of streets overlooking the broad flow of the Luosuo River. Take the side street downhill through the all-day market, and within a couple of minutes you'll find yourself by a large pedestrian suspension bridge crossing to Menglun's superb **Tropical Botanic Gardens** (热带植物园, rèdài zhíwùyuán; daily 24hr; ¥80). These were carved out of the jungle in 1959, and are now divided up into shaded palm and bamboo groves, clusters of giant fig trees, lily ponds, vines and shrubs. There are plenty of birds and butterflies flitting about too – in all, an enjoyable mix of parkland and forgotten, overgrown corners. Look for Chinese visitors serenading the undistinguished-looking "Singing Plant", which is supposed to nod in time to music.

ARRIVAL AND DEPARTURE   MENGLUN

By bus There's no bus station at Menglun, so vehicles pull up wherever convenient on the main road, usually among the restaurants and stores on the eastern side of town. To catch onward transport, head to the main road and flag down passing traffic.

ACCOMMODATION

Tropical Plant Gardens Hotel 热带植物园宾馆, rèdài zhíwùyuán bīnguǎn. ☏ 0691 8716852. Within the park itself, this government-run guesthouse has a tremendous location but, partly because of this, suffers

---

INTO LAOS

Beyond Menglun, the main road runs southeast for 130km, via Mengla (勐腊, měnglà), to the **Lao border**, just beyond Mo Han township (边贸站, biānmào zhàn). Assuming you've already obtained a visa from the Laotian consulate in Kunming (see box, p.667), the border crossing itself should be uncomplicated, though note that it closes mid-afternoon. On the far side lies the Laotian village of **Ban Boten**, where yuan (and US$) are accepted, but there's nowhere to stay or change currency for Laotian kip. The nearest banks and beds are a ¥10 truck ride away at the town of **Luang Namtha**, from where you can hitch out to the early-morning markets at Muong Sing to see local people in full tribal regalia. There's transport from Luang Namtha to **Nung Kie** via Muong Tai, and thence by boat down the Mekong to **Luang Prabang** (though you can also come the whole way from the border by road).

from both damp and trespassing insects. If these don't scare you off, it's a fair place to stay and has a pool, though you'll want to scoop the bugs out before taking the plunge.

Prices almost halve in low season and there are also several budget options along the road outside the gates for ¥80–120. **¥480**

Western Xishuangbanna

Western Xishuangbanna, which butts up against the (closed) Myanmar border, is a little bit less explored than the east – many treks out of Jinghong's cafés come here – and has a couple of good markets. Most traffic out this way departs from Jinghong's Banna bus station, though Damenglong is reached from the South bus station.

Damenglong
大勐龙, dàměnglóng

DAMENGLONG – also known as **Menglong** – is a scruffy, busy crossroads town 55km southwest of Jinghong, with a big, all-day **Sunday market**. The disappointingly shoddy **Black Pagoda** (黑塔, hēitǎ) is just south of the central crossroads and shouldn't be confused with the **North Pagoda** (北塔, běitǎ; ¥5), 2km north of town above the village of **Manfeilong** (曼飞龙, mànfēilóng). A long flight of stairs ascends to the North Pagoda, which is adorned with fragments of evil-repelling mirrors and silver paint, and is worshipped for the two **footprints** left by Sakyamuni in an alcove at the base. It is also known as the Bamboo Shoot Pagoda (笋塔, sǔntǎ; ¥10), after its nine-spired design, which resembles an emerging cluster of bamboo tips.

ACCOMMODATION AND EATING   DAMENGLONG

Eating options are street stalls or the Sichuanese place east from the crossroads, heading towards the highway.

Jintai Binguan 金泰宾馆, jīntài bīnguǎn. ☎0691 2740334. There's not a huge amount of choice in Damenglong, but this friendly and clean, eggshell-blue

building down a backstreet towards the market is one of the better choices; no English spoken. **¥50**

Menghai
勐海, měnghǎi

Western Xishuangbanna's principal town, **MENGHAI** is centrally placed on the highland plains 55km from Jinghong. A relatively organized assemblage of 1km-long high street and back lanes, the town is little more than a stop on the way towards outlying Dai and Hani settlements, but has an important history. Menghai was once a **Hani** (Aini) settlement until, as elsewhere, the Hani were defeated in battle by the Dai and withdrew into the surrounding hills. They remain there today as Xishuangbanna's second-largest ethnic group and long-time cultivators of **pu'er tea**, the local red, slightly musty brew that's esteemed from Hong Kong to Tibet for its fat-reducing and generally invigorating properties.

ARRIVAL AND DEPARTURE   MENGHAI

By bus Menghai's bus station – with buses to Jinghong and other centres, and minibuses to outlying villages – is at the eastern end of town.

Destinations Jinghong (every 20min; 1hr 30min); Xiding (daily 10.40am & 3.30pm; 1hr).

The Mengzhe road

Minibuses heading west from Menghai can drop you 20km along at the bizarre **Jingzhen Octagonal Pavilion** (景真八角亭, jǐngzhēn bājiǎo tíng), built in 1701, according to one story to quell an angry horde of wasps, though more likely as a symbol of unity between Han and Dai Buddhists. This, and **Manlei Buddhist Temple** (曼磊佛寺, mànlěi fósì; ¥20), a further 10km on past **MENGZHE** (勐遮, měngzhē), are inferior copies of older buildings, but have recently been renovated so appear quite grand now (and attract more tourists), and hold important collections of Buddhist manuscripts written on fan-palm fibre.

Xiding

西定, xīdìng

From Mengzhe, it's worth heading 15km southwest to the Hani village of **XIDING**, whose busy **Thursday market** is one of the best in the region. You'll need to get here on Wednesday, and sleep over in one of Xiding's rudimentary guesthouses, as the market kicks off at dawn. There are also quite a few trekking oportunities from the village that lead through jungle and tea plantations, as well as a twenty-minute walk to the village of Nannoushan, which offers tea plantations and some impressive views, especially at dawn.

Menghun

勐混, měnghún

Some 25km southwest of Menghai is **MENGHUN**, whose excellent **Sunday market** starts at daybreak and continues until noon. Akha women arrive under their elaborate silver-beaded headdresses, Bulang wear heavy earrings and oversized black turbans, and remote hill-dwellers come in plain dress, carrying ancient rifles. Most common of all are the Dai, who buy rolls of home-made paper and sarongs. Take a look around Menghun itself, too, as there's a dilapidated nineteenth-century **monastery** with a pavilion built in the style of Jingzhen's octagonal effort, and a **pagoda** hidden in the bamboo groves on the hills behind town.

11

ACCOMMODATION

MENGHUN

Daijia Hotel 傣家宾馆, dǎijiā bīnguǎn. On the main road, just north of the village centre and signed in English from near the post office ☎ 0691 5511209. Though very basic, this clean establishment is almost certainly your best bet for a night in Menghun, though there are several other options to inspect nearby. ¥60

Daluo and the Myanmar border

At the end of the road 50km west of Menghun, and served by two daily buses from Menghai, **DALUO** (打洛镇, dǎluò zhèn) is set just in from the Myanmar border. Here there's a multi-trunked, giant **banyan tree** whose descending mass of aerial roots forms a "one tree forest", and a daily **border trade market**, timed for the arrival of Chinese package tours between 11am and 1pm. Chinese nationals can also get a two-hour visa for Myanmar, ostensibly to shop for jade; in fact, many are really going over to catch transvestite stage shows held for their benefit.

Sichuan and Chongqing

四川 / 重庆

CUBS AT THE PANDA BREEDING RESEARCH BASE, CHENGDU

Sichuan and Chongqing

Ringed by mountains that, according to the Tang poet Li Bai, made the journey here "harder than the road to heaven", Sichuan (四川, sìchuān) and Chongqing (重庆, chóngqìng) stretch for more than 1000km across China's southwest. Administratively divided in 1997, when Chongqing was carved off the eastern end of Sichuan province, the region has long played the renegade, differing from the rest of China in everything from food to politics and inaccessible enough both to ignore central authority and to provide sanctuary for those fleeing it. Recent divisions aside, Sichuan and Chongqing share a common history, and the area splits more convincingly into very different geographic halves. The more gentle of the two lies east, where peaks surround one of the country's most densely settled areas, the fertile Red Basin, whose subtropical climate and rich soil conspire to produce endless green fields turning out three harvests a year.

12

This bounty has created an air of easy affluence in **Chengdu**, Sichuan's relaxed capital, and the southern river towns such as **Zigong**. Elsewhere, visitors have the opportunity to join pilgrims on **Emei Shan** in a hike up the holy mountain's forested slopes, or to **cruise down the Yangzi** from Chongqing, industrial powerhouse and jumping-off point for one of the world's great river journeys. You'll also find that the influence of Buddhism has literally become part of the landscape, most notably at **Leshan**, where a giant Buddha sculpted into riverside cliffs provides one of the most evocative images of China; and farther east at **Dazu**, where wooded hillsides conceal a marvellous procession of stone carvings.

In contrast, **western Sichuan** is dominated by densely buckled ranges overflowing from the heights of Tibet: a wild, thinly populated land of snowcapped peaks, where yaks roam the tree line and roads negotiate hair-raising gradients as they cross ridges or follow deep river valleys. The west's appeal is its Tibetan heritage – clearly visible in the many important monasteries – and raw, rugged alpine scenery. Travelling north towards Gansu takes you through ethnic Hui and Qiang heartlands past the vivid blue lakes and medieval battlements at **Songpan** and **Jiuzhaigou**, with the tranquil village of **Langmusi** the most remote of targets, right on the provincial border. Due west of Chengdu, the real wilds begin beyond **Kangding**, with the monastery towns of **Dêgê** and **Litang** the pick of destinations – not forgetting an exciting back-road **route to Yunnan**.

Travelling around Sichuan is fairly straightforward, but those heading westwards need to prepare for unpredictably long and uncomfortable journeys. The most useful **rail**

RECLINING BUDDHA, DAZU

Highlights

❶ Teahouses A central feature of Sichuanese social life. **See p.734**

❷ Giant Panda Breeding Research Base, Chengdu One of the few zoos in China where the animals are clearly happy, healthy and well cared for. **See p.736**

❸ Huanglongxi Crowded but enjoyably touristy village of Qing-dynasty shops and temples. **See p.742**

❹ The Big Buddha, Leshan You will never forget the first time you see this gargantuan riverside statue looming above you. **See p.749**

❺ Emei Shan A tough climb is rewarded with gorgeous scenery and monasteries that make atmospheric places to stay. **See p.751**

❻ Dazu China's most exquisite collection of Buddhist rock art, illustrating religious parables and cartoon-like scenes from daily life. **See p.759**

❼ Chongqing hotpot Chongqing is the birthplace of one of China's most popular dishes, though be warned it's one of the spiciest things you can eat in Sichuan (or anywhere, for that matter). **See p.766**

❽ Cruising the Yangzi Relax as your boat glides past the magnificent scenery of the towering Three Gorges. **See p.769**

❾ Litang Tibetan monastery town in the heart of Sichuan's wild west, where monks and cowboys tear around on motorbikes. **See p.783**

HIGHLIGHTS ARE MARKED ON THE MAP ON PP.728–729

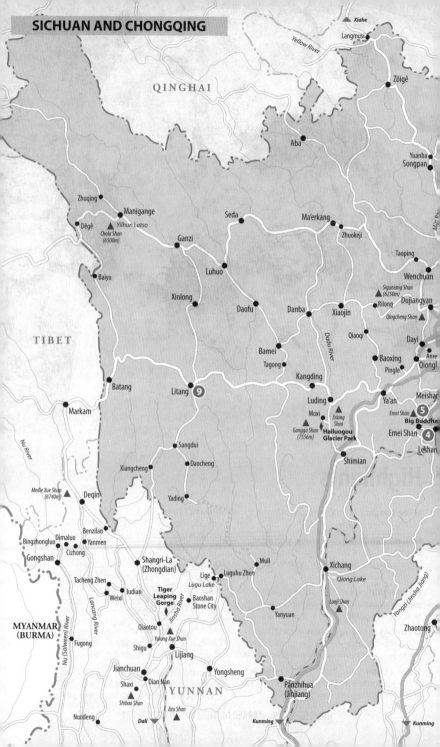

GANSU

SHAANXI

Tianshui

Baoji

Juzhaigou Kou
Juzhaigou Town
Juzhaigou

Huanglong

Xuebaoding
(5588m)

Pingwu

Doutuan
Shan

Hanzhong

Jianmenguan

Guangyuan

Puan

SHAANXI

Daning River

Maoxian

Jiangyou

Wulian

Zitong

Bazhong

Cheng Kou

Langzhong

Little
Three
Gorges

Wuxi

Ningchang

Dachang

Sanxingdui
Museum

Mianyang

Deyang

Guanghan

Kaixian

Daning River

Baidi Cheng

Wushan

Xindu

Luodai

Nanchong

Yunyang

Wanzhou

Fengjie

Wu
Gorge

Qutang
Gorge

Chengdu

Huanglongxi

3

Zhang Fei Temple

Xinglong

Shibaozhai

Yangzi

Jialing River

Zhongxian

HUBEI

SICHUAN

Laitan

CHONGQING

Hechuan

Ming Shan

Baoding
Shan

Neijiang

6

Dazu

7

Changshou

Fengdu

Fuling

Wulong

Wu River

Qianjiang

Rongxian

Youtingpou

Jiangjin

Nanchuan

Wulong

Zigong

Fushui

Yangzi

Jinfo Shan

Xiyang

HUNAN

Min River

Shunan
Bamboo
Sea

Zhongshan

Yibin

Luzhou

Chuqi River

Hejiang

Sinan
Shan

Chángníng

Chisui

Sidonggou

Dejiang

Jishou

Gongxian

Luobiao

Zunyi

YUNNAN

GUIZHOU

Huaihua

Weining

Liupanshui

N

Liuzhi

Yachi River

Guiyang

0   100

kilometres

Kunming

Kunming

SICHUANESE COOKING

Dominating the southwestern China cooking school, **Sichuanese cooking** is noted for its heavy use of **chilli**, which locals explain as a result of climate – according to Traditional Chinese Medicine, chillies dispel "wet" illnesses caused by Sichuan's seasonally damp or humid weather. But chillies don't simply blast the tastebuds, they stimulate them as well, and flavours here are far more complex than they might appear at the initial, eye-watering, mouthful.

Sichuan cuisine's defining taste is described as **mala** – "numb and hot" – created by the potent mix of chillies and **huajiao** (Sichuan pepper), with its soapy perfume and mouth-tingling after-buzz. One classic *mala* dish is *mapo doufu*, bean curd and minced pork; others include "strange-flavoured chicken" (dressed with sesame paste, soy sauce, sugar and green onions mixed in with the chillies and *huajiao*), and the innocently named "boiled beef slices", which actually packs more chillies per spoonful than almost any other Sichuanese dish.

Other more general dishes include **hot and sour soup**, flavoured with pepper and vinegar; **double-cooked pork**, where a piece of fatty meat is boiled, sliced thinly and then stir-fried with green chillies; **fish-flavoured pork** (whose "seafood" sauce is made from vinegar, soy sauce, sugar, ginger and sesame oil); **gongbao chicken**, the local version of stir-fried chicken and peanuts; and **smoked duck**, a chilli-free cold dish, aromatic and juicy. There's also a great number of Sichuanese **snacks** – *xiaochi* – which some restaurants specialize in: green beans with ginger, pork with puréed garlic, cucumber with chilli-oil and sesame seeds, *dandan mian* ("carry-pole" noodles, named for the way in which street vendors used to carry them around), tiger-skin peppers, scorched then fried with salt and dark vinegar, pork steamed in ground rice (served in the bamboo steamer), and a huge variety of sweet and savoury dumplings.

One Chongqing speciality now found all over China is **huoguo** (hotpot), a social dish eaten everywhere from streetside canteens to specialist restaurants. You get plates or skewers of meat, boiled eggs or vegetables, cooked – by you at the table – in a bubbling pot of stock liberally laced with chillies and cardamom pods. You then season the cooked food in oil spiced with MSG, salt and chilli powder. The effect is powerful, and during a cold winter you may well find that hotpots fast become your favourite food.

12

routes are the high-speed Chengdu–Chongqing link, and the Xi'an–Kunming line, which runs southwest from Chengdu via Emei Shan and Xichang. Expect hot, humid summers and cold winters, with the north and west frequently buried under snow for three months of the year.

Brief history

In prehistoric times, what is now eastern Sichuan and Chongqing was divided into the eastern **Ba** and western **Shu kingdoms**, slave societies with highly developed metalworking skills and bizarre aesthetics. Agricultural innovations at the end of the third century BC opened up eastern Sichuan to intensive farming, and when the Qin armies stormed through, they found an economic base that financed their unification of China in 221 BC – as did Genghis Khan's forces almost 1500 years later. In between, the area became the Three Kingdoms state of **Shu** – a name by which Sichuan is still sometimes known – and later twice provided refuge for deposed emperors.

Otherwise too distant to play a central role in China's history, the region leapt to prominence in 1911, when government interference in local rail industries sparked the nationwide rebellions that toppled the Qing empire. The next four decades saw rival warlords fighting for control, though some stability came when the **Nationalist government** made Chongqing their capital after the Japanese invaded China in 1937. The province suffered badly during the Cultural Revolution – Jung Chang's autobiography, *Wild Swans*, gives a first-hand account of the vicious arbitrariness of the times in Sichuan. It was the first province to reject Maoist ideals, when the Sichuan governor Zhao Ziyang allowed farmers to sell produce on the free market, spearheading the reforms of his fellow native Sichuanese **Deng Xiaoping**. So effective were these reforms that by the 1990s Sichuan was competing vigorously with the east-coast economy, a situation for which Chongqing – the already heavily industrialized gateway river port between Sichuan and eastern China – claimed a large part of the credit; Chongqing's economic weight secured separate administrative status for the city and its surrounds. Meanwhile, development continues across the region, bringing all the problems of runaway growth: appalling industrial pollution, ecological devastation and an unbelievable scale of urban reconstruction.

Chengdu

成都, chéngdū

Set on the western side of the Red Basin, **CHENGDU** is a determinedly modern city, full of construction sites, high-rise department stores and residential blocks. But it's also a cheerful place: seasonal floral displays and ubiquitous **ginkgo trees** lend colour to its many excellent parks, and the population is also nicely laidback, enjoying its **teahouse culture** at every opportunity and unfazed by this being interpreted as laziness by other Chinese.

Chengdu was styled Brocade City in Han times, when the urban elite were buried in elegantly decorated tombs, and its silk travelled west along the caravan routes as far as imperial Rome. A refuge for the eighth-century Tang emperor Xuan Zong after his army mutinied over his infatuation with the beautiful concubine Yang Guifei, the city later became a **printing** centre, producing the world's first paper money. Sacked by the Mongols in 1271, Chengdu recovered soon enough to impress Marco Polo with its busy artisans and handsome bridges, since when it has survived similar cycles of war and restoration to become a major industrial, educational and business centre. There are some **downsides** – the city's traffic congestion and pollution can be atrocious – but on the whole it's not hard to spend a couple of days here touring historical monuments, spiking your tastebuds on one of China's most outstanding cuisines, and getting close-up views of locally bred **pandas**.

12

Renmin Park

人民公园, rénmín gōngyuán • Free except during floral exhibitions (¥5–10) • Metro to People's Park

Just west of central **Tianfu Square** (天府广场, tiānfǔ guǎngchǎng), a huge space with dancing fountains, a subterranean metro stop and a white statue of Mao Zedong, **Renmin Park** comprises a few acres of trees, paved paths, ponds and ornamental gardens with seasonally varying displays. Near the north entrance there's an ever-busy **teahouse** shaded by wisteria (marked by a large bronze teapot at the gate) and the tall **Monument to the Martyrs**, an obelisk commemorating the 1911 rail disputes that marked the beginning of the end for the Qing empire – hence the unusual motifs of trains and spanners. Otherwise, the park is just a good place to stroll: look for vendors with little burners and a slab of marble along the paths who execute skilful designs of Chinese zodiac animals in **toffee**; there's also a **canteen** next to the teahouse serving Sichuanese snacks.

Kuan Xiangzi

宽巷子, kuān xiàngzi

After an uprising in 1789, a Manchu garrison was stationed in Chengdu and built themselves a miniature version of Beijing's *hutongs* in the area north of Renmin Park along **Kuan Xiangzi** and two adjacent lanes. The old streets and grey-brick houses here have been renovated and turned into an "antique" entertainment district, full of snack stalls, restaurants, and crowds orbiting between them – all especially busy at night, when competing coloured lights are added to the mix.

CHENGDU

0 — 250 metres

N

◄ Chaotianzi Bus Station

◄ Giant Panda Breeding Research Base & Zhaojue Temple Bus Station

Jinsha Museum ►

DRINKING, NIGHTLIFE AND ENTERTAINMENT	
Carol's By The River	4
Jah Bar	4
Jinjiang Theatre	2
Jin Li Theatre	3
Little Bar	7
Little Bar II	6
Poly Centre	9
Shamrock	8
Shufeng Yayun Theatre	1
Underground Bar	5

● SHOPPING	
Blue Sheep	5
Carrefour	1
Sanfo Outdoor	4
Sichuan Province Antique Store	3
Songxian Qiao curio market	2

Fu River

YIHUAN LU

HENGDE LU

HONGXING LU

YU SHA LU

TAI SHENG NAN LU

HONGZHAO LU

JIEFANG LU

ERHUAN LU

Beimen Bus Station

North Train Station

City Bus Terminus

North Train Station

Chengbei Bus Station

ER HUAN GAO JIA LU

YI HUAN LU BEI ER DUAN (1ST RING ROAD)

JIU LI DI BEI LU

XI TI LU

SHAWAN LU

YI HUAN LU BEI YI DUAN (1ST RING ROAD)

HUA PAI FANG JIE

YONGLING LU

Yong Ling

RENMIN BEI LU

North Renmin Road

Wenshu Monastery

Wenshu Temple

WENSHU FANG

RENMIN ZHONG LU

XINHUA DADAO

QINGYUN JIE

Luomashi (interchange)

XI YULONG JIE

DONGCHENGGEN LU

DE SHENG LU

JINSI LU

SHUNCHENG LU

South Taisheng Road

Main Bank of China

Renmin Stadium

YIHUAN LU (1ST RING ROAD)

YIHUAN LU (1ST RING ROAD)

HONGXING LU

SAN HUAI SHU LU

DEP'O KAIJIE

JIEFANGXIANG

JIANGHAN LU

YIHUAN LU

ZHONG DIAN

Wide and Narrow Alley

Chengdu University of CTM (interchange)

YING MEN KOU LU

JIN TANG JUAN DONG LU

SHI TA LIAO LU

FU NAN LU

CHA DIAN ZI LU

ER HUAN LU

East Shuhan Road

Baiguolin

QING JIANG DONG LU

Qingyang Gong

SHI'ERQIAO LU

YONGLING LU

NAN XIN JIE

XI NAN JIE

TONGHUIMEN

TONGHUIMEN LU

JINHE LU

TIAN LI MS2

XIA TONG REN LU

Cultural Park

Sichuan Museum

12

▲ Wuguiqiao Bus Station

Jin River

East Gate

Wangjiang Lou Park

Dongmen Bridge

Sichuan University

North Gate

South Gate

BAR STREET AREA

Niuwangmiao

ERHUAN LU

XINHUA DADAO

WUCHENG JIE

DONGFENG LU

RENMIN DONG LU

DAGI ST LU

BUTISHI JIE

ZIDONG LU

QINGLONG JIE (1ST RING ROAD)

Chunxi Road

Chunxi Road

SHANGDONG JIE

SHANGDONG DAJIE

Tianfu Sq. (interchange)

TIANFU SQUARE

SHAANXI JIE

RENMIN XILU

PSB

TIDU JIE

SHANDONG JIE

Xinnanmen Bus Station

Airport Bus Stop

Tourist Bus Terminus

KEHUA BEI LU

BINJIANG LU

LINJIANG LU

Sichuan Gymnasium

JINXIU LU

Global Doctor

JINXIANGUAN LU

US Consulate

Nijianqiao

YUEHE DONG LU

RENMIN NAN LU

RENMIN NAN LU

Jinjiang Hotel

Jinjiang Bridge

Huaxiba

NAN LU

People's Park

Rail Ticket Booth

Renmin Park

YIHUAN LU (1ST RING ROAD)

XIMIANQIAO JIE

ZHIMIN DONGDAJIE

ZHIMIN DAJIE

Wuhou Ci

JIN LI

JINLI LU

Baihuatan Park

YIHUAN LU (1ST RING ROAD)

YIHUAN LU (1ST RING ROAD)

LONGFENG LU

YIHUAN LU (2ND RING ROAD)

Roman Holiday Square

Shi Yang Chang Bus Terminal

Du Fu's Thatched Cottage

Shuangliu Airport & South Train Station

12

● **EATING**

Bookworm	10
Chen Mapo Doufu	2
Damiao Hot Po	3
Element Fresh	6
Langqin Pozhang	8
Long Chaoshou	5
Mi Xun Teahouse	7
Muslim Restaurants	4
Tandoor	9
Vegetarian Lifestyle	1

■ **ACCOMMODATION**

Chengdu Airport Express	9
Dragon Town	3
Hello Chengdu	1
Holiday Inn Express	4
Home Inn	2
Mix	8
Mrs Panda	7
Sofitel Wanda	6
Temple House	8
Traffic	8

12

TOURIST BUS ROUTES

Two useful **tourist buses** leave from outside the *Traffic* hotel on Linjiang Lu between about 8am and 6pm: **bus #901** (¥3) travels via Chunxi Lu, Wuhou Ci, Renmin Park, Qingyang Gong, Dufu Caotang and terminates at the Jinsha Museum; while **bus #902** (¥2) heads northeast to the Giant Panda Breeding Research Base.

Wenshu Temple

文殊院, wénshū yuàn • East off Renmin Zhong Lu • Daily 8am–6pm (5.30pm in winter) • ¥5 • Metro line #1 to Wenshu Monastery

Wenshu Temple, a bustling, atmospheric Chan (Zen) establishment dedicated to the Buddhist incarnation of Wisdom, sits 1.5km north of Tianfu Square. The elegant, single-storey halls are filled with motifs of **lions** – the symbol of Wenshu – such as the mural in the fourth hall, though this looks more like a shaggy, red-haired dog. If you bear east (right) immediately on entering the temple you'll encounter a narrow, eleven-storey **pagoda**. According to some, the gold-leafed object visible in the base includes the skull of **Xuanzang**, hero of *Journey to the West* (see box, p.844), though other temples in China also claim to own his mortal remains. It also features a pleasant open-air **teahouse** area, along with a fine and reasonably priced **vegetarian restaurant**.

Qingyang Gong

青羊宫, qīngyáng gōng • Daily 8am–5.30pm • ¥10 • Tourist bus #901, bus #G34 from anywhere on the ring road, or bus #58 from north side of Renmin Park; or metro line #2 to Chengdu University of TCM, then walk 500m south

Sited about 2km west of Renmin Park, **Qingyang Gong**, or the Green Ram Temple, is dedicated to Taoism's mythical proponent, Laozi. According to legend, Laozi lost interest in teaching and headed west into the sunset, first baffling posterity by saying that he could be found at the green ram market once his philosophy was understood – hence the temple's unusual name. Straight ahead from the entrance, the Bagua Pavilion is an eight-sided hall with supporting posts wreathed in golden dragons, which houses a statue of Laozi astride his buffalo. His tale is again reflected at the main **Three Purities Hall**, where two **bronze rams** have been worn smooth by the caresses of luck-seekers. The bizarre right-hand "ram" is actually the simultaneous incarnation of all twelve zodiacal animals.

Sichuan Museum

四川博物馆, sìchuān bówùguǎn • Qingyang Shang Jie • Tues–Sun 9am–5pm • Free with ID • Tourist bus #58 from north side of Renmin Park

The **Sichuan Museum**, about 700m west of Qingyang Gong, provides a thorough – if unimaginatively presented – look at the province's recorded history. Spread over

---

SICHUAN TEAHOUSES

Teahouses hold much the same place in Sichuanese life as a local bar or pub does in the West; some are formal establishments with illuminated signs; others are just a humble spread of bamboo or plastic chairs in the corner of a park, a temple or indeed any available public space. Whatever the establishment, just sit down to have a waiter come over and ask you what sort of tea you'd like – the standard jasmine-scented variety costs around ¥12 a cup, up to over ¥100 or more for a really fine brew. Most are served in the three-piece Sichuanese *gaiwancha*, a squat, handleless cup with lid and saucer. **Refills** are unlimited – either the waiter will give you a top-up on passing your table, or you'll be left with a flask of boiling water. In a country where it's usually difficult to find somewhere to relax in public, teahouses are very welcome: idlers can spend the whole day chatting, playing mahjong, reading or just staring into space, without anyone interrupting – except cruising masseurs and ear-wax removers.

three floors, there is Han-dynasty pottery, antique bronzeware, ethnic embroideries and artefacts (including a collection of what are politely termed "double-bodied" statuettes from Tibet), shadow puppets and even examples of Chengdu's once-famous silk brocade. It's easy to spend an hour here, but save time for the livelier **Songxian Qiao curio market** (送仙桥古玩艺术城, sòngxiānqiáo gǔwán yìshù chéng) across the road.

Du Fu's Thatched Cottage

杜甫草堂, dùfǔ cǎotáng • Daily 8am–6pm; winter till 5.30pm • ¥60 • Tourist bus #901, or #58 from north side of Renmin Park

Vehicles jamming the car park at **Du Fu's Thatched Cottage**, 500m west of Sichuan Museum, attest to the respect the Chinese hold for the Tang-dynasty poet. Du Fu's works record the upheavals of his sad and difficult life with compassion and humour, and are considered, along with the more romantic imagery of his contemporary Li Bai (see p.745), to represent the archetype for Chinese poetry.

Three centuries after his death in 770, a pleasant park was founded at the site of Du Fu's cottage, and around 1800 it was expanded to its current layout of artfully arranged gardens, bamboo groves, pools, bridges and whitewashed halls. Besides antique and modern statues of Du Fu – depicted as sadly emaciated – there's a small museum illustrating his life.

Wuhou Ci

武侯祠, wǔhóu cí • Wuhouci Dajie • Daily 8am–6pm • ¥60 • Tourist bus #901, or bus #1 from Renmin Nan Lu

Southwest of the centre, **Wuhou Ci** is a memorial hall nominally dedicated to **Zhuge Liang**, the strategist of Three Kingdoms fame. However, as his emperor **Liu Bei** is also buried here, the whole site is really a big shrine to the Three Kingdoms era (see box, p.396). To the left of the entrance, the **Three Kingdoms Culture Exhibition Hall** has contemporary sculptures, lacquered furniture, painted bricks showing daily life, and a few martial relics such as arrowheads and copper cavalry figurines. Elsewhere, halls and colonnaded galleries house brightly painted statues of the epic's heroes, notably a white-faced Liu Bei flanked by his oath-brothers Guan Yu and Zhang Fei; and Zhuge Liang (holding his feather fan) and his son and grandson. Over in the complex's northwestern corner, **Liu Bei's tomb** is a walled mound covered in trees and guarded by stone figures.

Jin Li

锦里, jǐn lǐ • Bus #1 from Renmin Nan Lu runs past, as does tourist bus #901

Immediately east of Wuhou Ci, **Jin Li** is yet another of Chengdu's newly built "old" streets: this one is more of an alley, about 300m long, and jammed with wooden-fronted shops selling souvenirs and snacks. The street winds up at an open-air **theatre**, where performances of Sichuanese opera are held nightly (see box, p.741).

The Tibetan quarter

Bus #1 from Renmin Nan Lu, or tourist bus #901 to Wuhou Ci

The district south of Wuhou Ci forms Chengdu's **Tibetan quarter**, full of shops stocked to their roofs with heavy clothes, boots, amber and turquoise jewellery, knives and prayer wheels, conches and other temple accessories – not to mention heavy-duty blenders capable of whipping up a gallon of butter tea in one go. Move beyond the periphery, and this is not just for the tourists: customers are Tibetan monks, cowboys, and Khampa women with braided hair, looking decidedly tall and robust next to the local Chinese.

12

> ## PANDAS
>
> Two animals share the name panda: the **giant panda**, black-eyed symbol of endangered species worldwide; and the unrelated, raccoon-like **red panda**, to which the Nepalese name "panda" was originally applied in the West. The Chinese call the giant panda *da xiongmao*, meaning "big bear-cat".
>
> News of giant pandas first reached Europe in the nineteenth century through the French zoologist and traveller **Père Armand David**, who came across a skin in China in 1869. They are decidedly odd creatures, bearlike, endowed with a carnivore's teeth and a digestive tract poorly adapted to their largely vegetarian diet. Though once widespread in southwestern China, they've probably never been very common, and today their endangered status is a result of human encroachment combined with the vagaries of their preferred food – **fountain bamboo** – which periodically flowers and dies off over huge areas, leaving the animals to make do with lesser shrubs and carrion, or starve. Half of Sichuan's panda habitat was lost to logging between 1974 and 1989, which, coupled with the results of a bamboo flowering during the 1980s, reduced the total wild population to just over a thousand animals, scattered through **reserves** in Sichuan, Yunnan and Guizhou.

Jinsha Museum

金沙遗址博物馆, jīnshā yízhǐ bówùguǎn • Daily 8am–5.30pm • ¥80 • Terminus of the #901 tourist bus route; or bus #5 from Renmin Park

Around 5km west from the centre, the **Jinsha Museum** sits over the remains of one of western China's major prehistoric settlements. The fascinating collection here, housed in two halls set among gardens, leaves plenty of questions unanswered. The Chengdu region was already settled as early as 2700 BC, though its first cultural flowering came a thousand years later at Sanxingdui (see p.742), which itself went into a decline as the settlement at Jinsha blossomed from 1200 to 600 BC.

Covering five square kilometres in total, Jinsha has yielded domestic remains, tools and artefacts of all descriptions, thousands of graves, and scores of sacrificial pits filled with ornaments and animal bones, all dating back to the Shang dynasty. The **first hall** is built right over these pits, which were dug a couple of metres deep into the grey soil in a regular grid pattern; the glass-sided building is well lit, and wooden boardwalks allow a close look. The **second hall** houses dioramas of the site, plus the pick of the finds, including some beautifully coloured, translucent jades, small statues of tigers and kneeling slaves with bound hands, and a thin, serrated gold disc interpreted as depicting *rishen*, the Sun God.

The Giant Panda Breeding Research Base

大熊猫繁育研究基地, dàxióngmāo fányù yánjiū jīdì • Daily 8am–6pm • ¥58 • Hostel minibus tours ¥108; tourist bus #902 can take 2hr through Chengdu's traffic; it's quicker to ride the metro to the North train station and then catch a cab (¥15; 15min); a cab from most places in the centre is ¥30–35

Some 8km northeast of central Chengdu, the excellent **Giant Panda Breeding Research Base** offers close-up views of both giant and arboreal red pandas. Perhaps uniquely for China, this zoo is a genuinely pleasant place to visit, well laid out with a decent amount of information in English, and even spacious enclosures for the animals, who are fed truckloads of fresh bamboo by concerned staff. Several hostels and travel agencies offer the chance to be a "volunteer keeper" for the day (¥700) – basically a worthy-sounding way of paying to hand-feed a few of the inhabitants. Try to get here early, as the pandas slump into a stupor around 10am after munching their way through piles of bamboo.

ARRIVAL AND DEPARTURE   CHENGDU

Most accommodation can make train, bus and plane bookings, though expect to pay a ¥20–40 booking fee per person for train tickets.

BY PLANE

The massive new all-singing-all-dancing Tianfu International Airport is currently being built around 50km to the southwest of the city, but will not be opened until 2020.

Shuangliu airport (双流机场, shuāngliú jīchǎng) is 16km southwest of town, connected by several airport buses (7am–8pm; approximately every 30min; ¥10), with #300 and #303 running to the centre of town. Heading back to the airport, #300 can be picked up along Renmin Nan Lu, just south of Tianfu Square, while the #303 departs every 20min from the Civil Aviation Office on Renmin Nan Lu, just north of the junction with Binjiang Lu. A taxi to anywhere in the centre should cost around ¥80–100. Chengdu has direct flights to over 130 cities in China and worldwide, including London, Paris, Amsterdam, San Francisco, Frankfurt, Seoul, Hanoi, Bangkok and Osaka.

BY TRAIN

Chengdu is halfway along the Xi'an–Kunming rail line, and also connected to routes into Guizhou and central China through easterly Chongqing. You can reach Chongqing in just 2hr aboard a D-class train, via the high-speed rail link. It's easiest to buy train tickets online, or through your accommodation, for a ¥20–40 fee. Bus #16 and the metro run the length of Renmin Lu between the two stations.

North train station (成都火车站, chéngdū huǒchēzhàn). Chengdu's main station is 4km north of the city centre and handles most regular, and a handful of high-speed services, though it's currently slated for an upgrade to allow for many more. A city bus terminus and metro station are just west off the station square, from where you should be able to find transport to within striking distance of your accommodation.

South train station (火车南站, huǒchē nánzhàn). This small station, 4km south of the centre, services all stops along the Chengdu–Kunming line, including Xichang and Panzhihua.

East train station (火车东站, huǒchē dōngzhàn). A new station around 10km east of the city and connected to the centre by metro line #4; used for several high-speed train services, predictably those heading east.

CRH destinations Beijing (1 daily; 14hr 28min); Chongqing (30 daily; 1hr 26min–2hr 25min); Emeishan (11 daily; 1hr–1hr 40min); Guangyuan (1 daily; 3hr 38min); Guangzhou (2 daily; 14hr); Jiangyou (13 daily; 1hr 10min–2hr 10min); Shanghai (3 daily; 15hr); Wuhan (16 daily; 8hr 44min–9hr 47min).

Other destinations Beijing (5 daily; 22hr 19min–32hr); Chongqing (6 daily; 2hr 9min–4hr 49min); Dujiangyan (21 daily; 19–39min); Emei (18 daily; 1–3hr); Guangyuan (20 daily; 4–6hr 22min); Guangzhou (6 daily; 25–43hr); Guiyang (7 daily; 12hr 25min–19hr 22min); Jiangyou (17 daily; 2hr 17min–3hr 10min); Kunming (6 daily; 17hr

35min–22hr 20min]; Lhasa (3–7 weekly; 43hr); Panzhihua (9 daily; 11hr 25min–15hr); Qingcheng Shan (9 daily; 45min); Shanghai (4 daily; 29–37hr); Wuhan (10 daily; 11hr 20min–16hr); Xi'an (14 daily; 10–18hr); Xichang (10 daily; 8hr 33min–11hr 23min).

BY BUS

Chengdu's many long-distance bus stations are mostly scattered around the city perimeter.

Beimen (北门汽车站, běimén qìchēzhàn, or North Gate) is 1km northeast of the centre on the first ring road and near the junction with Jeifang Lu. It can be reached via metro line #3 then bus #802 from the North train station.

Destinations Langzhong (18 daily; 4hr); Yibin (6 daily 1–6.40pm; 4hr); Zigong (every 30min till 1.30pm; 3hr).

Chadianzi (茶店子客运站, chádiànzi kèyùn zhàn), 8km northwest of the city centre on the third ring road; it's on metro line #2, or bus #82 goes from here to Wuhouci Dajie and Binjiang Lu. Chadianzi is the main station for western Sichuan; most services depart first thing in the morning, when you might need a taxi to get here in time (¥35–40).

Destinations Dujiangyan (every 20min; 40min); Huanglongxi (every 20min; 50min); Jiuzhaigou (daily 7.30am & 9am; 8hr 30min); Songpan (3 daily; 4hr 10min); Zöigé (daily 6.30am; 8–9hr).

Chengbei (North City) (城北汽车站, chéngběi qìchēzhàn). Just west of the North train station on Erhuan Lu, it has services in multiple directions.

Destinations Chongqing (daily 2.30pm; 4hr); Dazu (5 daily; 4hr); Dujiangyan (11 daily; 40min); Kangding (5 daily; 8hr 30min); Leshan (11 daily; 2hr 10min); Yibin (3 daily 2.40–4.10pm; 4hr).

East bus station (东汽车站, dōng qìchē zhàn). 10km east of the centre in the East Square of the East train station, it's mainly of use for getting to Xichang.

Destinations Dazu (5 daily; 4hr); Xichang (every 30min; 6hr).

Shiyangchang bus station (石羊场客运站, shí yáng chǎng kè yùn zhàn), 4km southwest of the centre, with buses to south and southwest Sichuan and Xichang; bus # 28 heads into the centre.

Destinations Leshan (9 daily 5–7pm; 2hr); Xichang (8 daily; 6hr); Ya'an (every 20min; 2hr).

Wuguiqiao (五桂桥中心站, wǔguìqiáo zhōngxīnzhàn), 3km east of the city centre, reachable on bus #81 from People's Park.

Destinations Chongqing (6 daily; 4hr); Dazu (5 daily; 4hr); Yibin (every 40min; 4hr); Zigong (8 daily, last at 5.50pm; 3hr).

Xinnanmen (新南门汽车站, xīnnánmén qìchēzhàn), centrally located next to the *Traffic* hotel and most easily reached from the *Jinjiang Hotel* metro stop.

Destinations Daocheng (daily 10am; 13hr 30min); Emei Shan (every 30min till 4pm; 2hr); Ganzi (daily 10am; 10hr); Huanglongxi (every 30min; 50min); Jiuzhaigou Scenic Spot (3 daily, am only; 8hr 30min); Kangding (9 daily; 4hr

12

TRAVELLING TO TIBET

While road routes **into Tibet** remain off-limits to foreigners at time of writing, rail and air links remain open and regular, and you'll find plenty of agencies here organizing tours. Flights to Lhasa cost about ¥2000 single and you'll need to book directly from the airline; train tickets are ¥754 hard sleeper, or ¥1196 soft sleeper, and can be hard to get hold of, so book at least a few days (or better still a week or two) in advance, and there are only three to seven trains a week. Before buying any tickets, you'll have to show a **permit for Tibet** (an extra ¥400). Most likely you'll have to secure the permit through a travel agent as, at the time of writing, it was not possible to visit Tibet independently; you had to be part of an organized tour (see box, p.878).

50min); Leshan (7 daily; 2hr); Ya'an (every 30min; 2hr).

Zhaojue Temple Station (照觉寺汽车站, zhàojuésì qìchēzhàn) 5km northeast of the centre;

bus #64 from the east side of Tianfu Square.

Destinations Guangyuan (every 20–40min; 4hr); Jiangyou (hourly; 2hr).

GETTING AROUND

Chengdu's roads are pretty bad at rush hours, so it's best to take the metro or cycle.

By metro Chengdu's metro line #1 runs north–south through the city, with line #2 running northwest–southeast. Lines #3 (running northeast–southwest) and #4 (east–west) have recently opened. Useful stops include the train stations, *Jianjiang Hotel*, Tianfu Square and Chunxi Lu. Trains run 7am–11.30pm and cost ¥2–8.

By bus Buses run from about 6am until after dark, and charge ¥2; there are also some useful tourist buses linking major sights, leaving from outside *Traffic* hotel (see opposite).

By taxi Cabs are everywhere and cost ¥8 to hire. It's often hard to find a free one, though unlicensed motorbike taxis (¥10–15 for hops around the centre) are much easier to get, congregating on street corners – they usually wear cheap red or yellow helmets.

By bike Motorbikes are illegal in the downtown area, so bicycles (and electric mopeds) remain popular, with cycle lanes and guarded parking throughout the city. Many hostels rent bikes for around ¥25–30/day, plus ¥500 (or your passport) as a deposit.

INFORMATION

Guides The best independent guide in Chengdu is Tray Lee (☎ 1390 8035353, ✉ leevisit@qq.com; inside Chengdu ¥150–200/day, outside ¥300–600/day plus transportation), who can often be found in Renmin Park. He speaks excellent English, has been guiding foreigners around the province for more than 25 years and can take you to off-the-beaten-track locations.

Information For local news, events and the latest bars and restaurants, check expat-run online magazine *Go Chengdoo* (Ⓦ gochengdoo.com) or its rival *More Chengdu* (Ⓦ morechengdu.com).

Travel agents and tours Hostels and other accommodation all offer part- and multi-day tour packages

of the city and surrounds – you don't have to be staying to make bookings. Tours include 2hr Sichuan opera trips (¥120); three hours at Chengdu's Giant Panda Breeding Research Base (¥108 including entry); a day-trip to Qingcheng Shan (¥150); four days at Jiuzhaigou and Huanglong (around ¥1000). Hostels also arrange five-seater minibuses with a driver for the day to tour local sights (plus Leshan or Emei Shan) at ¥500–800 depending on distance. A few can also book you on Yangzi ferry trips through the Three Gorges (see p.768), though this is probably better done in Chongqing. Tibet packages should come in from around ¥3000–3500 with flights, or ¥2000 with the train.

ACCOMMODATION

Chengdu has a great number of places to stay, with a choice for every budget; the following are all central, within the second ring road. Everywhere can make transport bookings, and hostels also offer bike rental, travellers' noticeboards and good-value tours (see above).

HOSTELS

Dragon Town 龙城宽巷子青年旅馆, lóngchéng kuānxiàngzǐ qīngnián lǚguǎn. 26 Kuan Xiangzi ☎ 028 86648408, Ⓦ dragontown.com.cn. This hostel is set in one of Chengdu's crowded old-style tourist streets

that's either quaint or a bit tacky, depending on your point of view. Despite the entrance being at the back of a busy restaurant, the hostel is quite pleasant, with an ornamental pond. The rooms and dorms are very clean, smart and comfortable. Dorms ¥60, doubles ¥320

★**Hello Chengdu (formerly Sim's Cozy)** 观华青年旅舍, guānhuá qīngnián lǚshè. North Section 4, 211 Yihuan Lu ☎028 83355322, ✉hellochengduhostel@hotmail.com. Top hostel choice in Chengdu, they do everything you want from a hostel: inexpensive but comfortable and clean rooms and dorms; friendly and helpful staff who speak very good English; bike rental (¥30/day); excellent free maps of the city; pleasant communal areas; and it serves quite decent, reasonably priced Western and Chinese food and drink. The travel information and trips on offer are second to none and they'll book train or bus tickets for you too. Dorms ¥55, doubles ¥120

Mix 驴友记国际青年旅舍, lǘyǒujì guójì qīngnián lǚshě. 23 Xinghui Xi Lu ☎028 83222271, ⊛mixhostel.com. Nasty tiled building on the outside but cosy place once you're through the door, just a 10min walk from the metro and in a fairly quiet residential district. Shared bathrooms only, hence the slightly lower price, but they have a sister hostel nearby with en suites. Dorms ¥30, doubles ¥108

Mrs Panda 交通饭店, jiāotōng fàndiàn. Behind the Traffic hotel at 6 Linjiang Lu, near Xinnanmen bus station ☎028 85450470. A decent central choice and handy for the bus station, the dorms here are inexpensive and clean, though the simple rooms are poor value compared with those in the *Traffic* next door. The *Mrs Panda Kitchen* serves tasty Western and Chinese staples. Dorms ¥45, doubles ¥138

HOTELS

Chengdu Airport Express 成都空港商务酒店, chéngdū kōnggǎng shāngwù jiǔdiàn. ☎028 85208899, ⊛airportexpresshotel.com. Just a few hundred metres from the terminals – call the hotel and they will send a free shuttle bus to pick you up – not only is this place hugely convenient, it's also smart, clean, quiet and the rooms are excellent value. ¥335

Holiday Inn Express 鼓楼快捷假日酒店, gǔlóu kuàijié jiàrì jiǔdiàn. 72 Daqiang Xi Jie (at the junction with Gulou Jie) ☎028 86785666, ⊛hiexpress.com.cn. Comfortable, modern and efficient – what you'd expect from this budget international chain. Well-maintained rooms offer excellent value, and the room price includes breakfast and dinner buffet meals at the hotel's Western/Chinese restaurant (¥58 for nonguests). ¥438

Home Inn 如家酒店, rújiā jiǔdiàn. 9 Shaocheng Lu ☎028 86253111. Across from the north entrance to Renmin Park, this branch offers the fairly bland and utilitarian rooms associated with this chain, plus a decent canteen on the ground floor – prices are a little on the high side but you're paying mostly for the park being just over the road. ¥250

Sofitel Wanda 索菲特万达大饭店, suǒfēitè wàndà dàfàndiàn. 15 Binjiang Zhong Lu ☎028 66669999, ⊛sofitel.com. It's hard not to be impressed by this gleaming tower and the acres of marble in the lobby. Restaurants, bars, a sauna, spa, gym and a swimming pool are part of the package. ¥612

★**Temple House** 春熙里酒店, chūnxīlǐ jiǔdiàn. 81 Bitieshi Jie ☎028 86663666, ⊛thetemplehousehotel.com. Mixing historic with modern right in the heart of downtown, this place has an elegant lobby housed in an old townhouse, but with ultramodern and stylish luxury rooms in an attached new building. Also offers a pool, range of spa treatments, several excellent (though pricey) restaurants, with attentive and helpful English-speaking staff. ¥1899

Traffic 交通饭店, jiāotōng fàndiàn. 77 Linjiang Lu, near Xinnanmen bus station ☎028 85451017. Well-maintained stand-by, and pretty good value considering the location. The rooms are large and come with TVs and shared or private bathroom (¥38 extra), with new fittings. ¥108

EATING

★**Bookworm** 老书虫, lǎo shūchóng. 2–7 Yujie Dong Lu, off Renmin Nan Lu ☎028 85520177, ⊛chengdubookworm.com. Comfy expat haunt decorated in a style that could be described as neo-Edwardian elegance and serving decent pizzas, sandwiches, burgers, salads, hummus and pasta (all ¥45–75) as well as desserts (¥35–45) such as crème brûlée. With a well-stocked library and bar (with a good selection of wines), it also hosts regular intellectual events as well as bands and recitals. Daily 9am–1am.

★**Chen Mapo Doufu** 陈麻婆豆腐, chén mápó dòufu. 197 Xi Yulong Jie ☎028 86743889. Founded in 1862, this is the home of Grandma Chen's bean curd, where at lunchtime ¥20 buys a large bowl of tofu glowing with minced meat, chilli oil and *huajiao* sauce. At dinner they add a small bowl (¥12) to your main order from a good range of mouth-numbingly spicy Sichuanese favourites on the photo menu for around ¥16–48. Daily 11am–3pm & 5–10pm.

Damiao Hot Pot 大妙火锅, dà miào huǒguō. 11 Zhai Xiangzi ☎028 86251111. If you want to try the classic Sichuanese hotpot, this smart, traditional-looking place is far more foreigner-friendly than most as it's very clean, they have an English menu, and offer a choice of spicy or non-spicy broth; it's a little pricey though, and costs around ¥250–300 for two. There's also a small stage in the middle and you can enjoy a traditional Sichuan opera show at dinnertime. Daily 10.30am–10.30pm.

Element Fresh 新元素, xīn yuánsù. 1301 1/F, Sino-Ocean Taikoo Li Chengdu, 8 Zhongshamao Jie ☎028 65953208. Located in a new restaurant and shopping development, this latest outlet of Shanghai's famous *Element Fresh* chain serves up the same healthy Western and Asian menu in clean, stylish surroundings. Especially popular are

12

the salads, such as the classic Cobb salad (¥95), their signature steaks (¥199), and yummy desserts (¥39–59). The Asian dishes such as the very good Malaysian *laksa* noodle soup (¥79) are slightly cheaper. Daily 10am–10pm.

Langqin Pozhang 朗钦颇丈, lǎngqīn pōzhàng. Floor 3, 246 Wuhouci Da Jie ☎028 85561027. Directly across from *Holly's Hostel*, signposted from the main road, this is the pick of several Tibetan eateries in the area. Though lacking the spit-and-sawdust atmosphere of some of its neighbours, the food is tasty, with spicy potato and yoghurt balls a particular treat. Around ¥40/person. Daily 10am–10pm.

Long Chaoshou 龙抄手饭店, lóng chāoshǒu fàndiàn. At the crossroads of pedestrian alleys, just east of Chunxi Lu and south of the Dico's. A big, busy dumpling house renowned for its *chaoshou* (¥28), Sichuanese *wuntun* noodle dishes (¥8–13) and other local snacks, a limited English menu gives just a fraction of what is on offer. Eat in the downstairs canteen; the upper floors have the same food and terrible table service at ten times the price. Daily 9am–9pm.

Mi Xun Teahouse 谧寻茶室, mì xún cháshì. Temple House hotel, 81 Bitieshi Jie ☎028 62974193. A good choice if you're going to try one of Sichuan's famous teahouses, this place is not only elegant and atmospheric (located in an ancient courtyard), but there's usually someone around who speaks English. As well as afternoon tea (¥40 upwards), they also do tasty and well-presented vegetarian and vegan food (around ¥80 for two). Daily: lunch 11am–2pm, tea 2–5.30pm, dinner 5.30–9.30pm.

Muslim restaurants 皇城寺大饭店, huángchéngsì dà fàndiàn. A line of similar earthy restaurants running north from the mosque catering to Chengdu's large Muslim population, they serve everything from *lamian* soup (¥14–20) to meat-and-potato stew (¥30) and other non-pork Sichuan dishes (¥12–44). Uyghurs stand outside grilling kebabs and bread, if you fancy a takeaway. There are more upmarket versions round the corner on Xiyu Jie. Daily 8.30am–11pm.

Tandoor 天都里印度餐厅, tiāndūlǐ yìndù cāntīng. Behind the Sunjoy Inn, opposite Bookworm on Yujie Dong Lu ☎028 85551958. Indian dining (and excellent service) for the well-heeled; comparatively expensive in the evening, but at lunch there are set-meal bargains available. All the non-veggie standards (¥55–75) such as butter chicken, and a decent spread of vegetarian options (¥40–55) like *palak paneer*. Daily 11am–2.30pm & 5.30–10.30pm.

Vegetarian Lifestyle 枣子树铂金店, zǎozishù bójīn diàn. 4F Bojincheng Building, 27 Qinglong Jie, just west of the main Bank of China ☎028 6282848. Local branch of *Jujube Tree* Shanghai chain, serving excellent, imaginative vegetarian Asian dishes, such as fruit sushi rolls (¥30), and fake meat dishes such as sweet-and-sour ribs (¥38) in a minimalist setting with plenty of window seats overlooking the street. Daily 11am–10pm.

DRINKING, NIGHTLIFE AND ENTERTAINMENT

Chengdu's nightlife venues open and close rapidly, so check the latest at ⓦ gochengdoo.com or ⓦ morechengdu.com. Don't overlook the *Bookworm*'s (see p.739) Friday-night jazz sessions (9pm–late) either. The liveliest bar and club district centres around the Jiuyan Bridge, just north of the Sichuan University campus, just east of the US consulate on Lingshiguan Lu.

Carol's By The River 卡罗西餐吧, kǎluó xīcānbā. Hongmen Jie-Linjiang Xi Lu ☎028 85585529. Open-fronted sports bar with a pool table, outside tables, draught beer from ¥20 and regular live music throughout the week. Daily 3pm–1am.

Jah Bar 家吧, jiābā. Next door to Carol's, Hongmen Jie/Linjiang Xi Lu ☎1368 9051773. Very relaxed reggae-centric spot with couches by the river and a lot more grungy and random than *Carol's* next door. If you're lucky you may catch one of their irregular live music events. Daily 5pm–late.

Little Bar 小酒吧玉林店, xiǎojiǔbā yùlín diàn. 55 Yulin Xi Lu ☎028 85568552. Small, vaguely bohemian place with a good range of inexpensive beers (from ¥15) and spirits. Previously famed for live music, which has now moved to its new sister venue, so it's now somewhere to chill out or hold a conversation rather than party. Daily 7pm–2am.

Little Bar II 小酒吧芳沁街, xiǎojiǔbā fāngqìnjiē. 87 Fangqin Lu ☎028 85158790. Bigger brother to the original, this is Chengdu's premier rock venue with live bands every Friday and Saturday evening, when there is a ¥30–100 cover charge. Be warned: punk is alive and well, and living in Chengdu (though so are folk and jazz on occasion). Daily 7pm–2am.

Poly Centre 吧成都保利中心, bā chéngdū bǎolì zhōng xīn. Just east of the US consulate on Lingshiguan Lu. The currently popular bars and clubs for the cool kids to hang out at (and dance to international hip-hop, techno and electronica) are on the 19th to 21st floors of this enormous tower block, with current favourites being *Here We Go* ("Chengdu's highest bar") on the 21st, and the hip-hop focused *NASA* on the 19th. Daily 5pm–2am, later on weekends.

Shamrock 三叶草西餐酒, sānyècǎo xīcān jiǔbā. 15, Section 4, Renmin Nan Lu ☎028 885236158, ⓦ shamrockinchengdu.com. This pub has been going forever and attracts a mature crowd, but is trying to move with the times, and now offers swing/salsa classes during the week, and the tried-and-tested DJ and drinks offer on Fridays and Saturdays. The food is surprisingly tasty, too, with the steak about as good as you'll get anywhere in town. Daily 10am–late.

12

SICHUAN OPERA

Sichuan opera – **chuanxi** – is a rustic variant on Beijing's, based on everyday events and local legends. Most pieces are performed in Sichuanese, a rhythmic dialect well suited to theatre, which allows for humour and clever wordplay to shine through. As well as the usual bright costumes, stylized action and glass-cracking vocals, *chuanxi* has two specialities: **fire-breathing** and **rapid face-changing**, where the performers – apparently simply by turning around or waving their arms across their faces – completely change their make-up.

Today, *chuanxi* has gone into a decline as a form of popular entertainment, though there are several places around town to catch tourist-oriented **variety shows** featuring short opera scenes, fire-breathing and face-changing, comedy skits, puppetry, shadow-lantern play and storytelling. These are pretty enjoyable and you might even catch occasional full-length operas. Venues include **Shufeng Yayun** (蜀风雅韵, shǔfēng yǎyùn) in the Cultural Park (enter off Qintai Lu); the Ming-style open-air stage at the end of **Jin Li**, near Wuhou Ci; and the downtown **Jinjiang Theatre** (锦江川戏馆, jǐnjiāng chuānxìguǎn) in a lane north of Shangdong Jie. Seats cost ¥160–240, depending on the venue and row; most easily booked through your accommodation.

Underground Bar 隧道酒吧, suìdào jiǔbā. 6 Taipingnanxi Jie ☎028 885294142, ⓦunderground chengdu.com. Hidden down a tunnel, behind a cigar shop, this British pub, owned and run by Mancunian landlord Gary, is an oasis of calm amid the raucous Jiuyan Bridge bar district. More than fifty beers on offer, though no food beyond snacks; they'll help order some in for you though. Daily 7pm–2.30am.

SHOPPING

There are around half-a-dozen branches of the international **supermarket** Carrefour dotted around central Chengdu, including a large store at the junction of Dongcheng Lu and Qinglong Jie.

12

Blue Sheep 岩羊, yán yáng. 35 A Qu, Gaoshengqiao Bei Lu (behind the Walmart at Roman Holiday Plaza) ☎158 82462959, ⓦbluesheepcrafts.com. Ethically sourced handicrafts such as clothing, jewellery, leatherwork and embroidery. The profits return more fairly to the disadvantaged producers. Mon–Sat 10am–9pm.
Sanfo Outdoor 三夫户外, sānfū hùwài. 243 Wuhouci Jie ☎028 85079586. If you're heading to Tibet, western Sichuan or elsewhere in China's wilds, this is the best place to pick up good-quality camping supplies, though they are quite pricey. If you don't want to shell out so much, look for cheaper knockoffs from the many other camping stores in the area, with more on Yihuan Lu, just west of the intersection with Renmin Nan Lu. Daily 9am–6pm.

Sichuan Province Antique Store 四川省古董店, sìchuān shěng gǔdǒng diàn. Corner of Dongchenggen Lu and Shaocheng Lu ☎028 86124787. Reliable (though expensive) shop for genuine fixed-price antique snuff bottles, jewellery, birdcages and porcelain. Daily 10am–6pm.
Song Xian Qiao Antique City 宋县桥古城, sòng xiàn qiáo gǔchéng. 22 Huan Hua Bei Lu. This curio market near Sichuan Museum is good for "Mao-morabilia", wooden screens and all sorts of old-looking knick-knacks, though you'll have to haggle hard, and should be wary of buying expensive "genuine" antiques here. Daily 9am–7pm.

DIRECTORY

Consulates Australia, 11F 18 Dongyu St (☎028 64663880, ⓦchengdu.china.embassy.gov.au); France, 30F, Times Plaza, 2 Zongfu Lu (☎028 6666060); Germany, 25F, Western tower, 19 Renmin Nan Lu, Section 4 (☎028 85280800); US, 4 Lingshiguan Lu, Renmin Nan Lu (☎028 85583992, ⓦchengdu.usembassy-china.org.cn).
Hospitals and medical centres For English-speaking doctors and international-standard medical treatment, try Global Doctors, 62 Kehua Beilu, 2F Lippo Tower (☎028 85283660, ⓦwww.globaldoctor.com.au).
Left luggage Accommodation will look after excess gear while you're off in the wilds for around ¥5–10/item/day.
Visa extensions The PSB branch dealing with visa extensions and foreigners' problems is bang in the middle of town in Tianfu Square, directly behind the Mao statue; 3F, 2 Renmin Xi Lu (Mon–Fri 9am–noon & 1–5pm; ☎028 86407067).

Around Chengdu

Chengdu's surrounding attractions all make worthy day-trips from the capital, and most can be used as first stops on longer routes. Just to the northeast, the **Sanxingdui Museum** is stuffed with prehistoric bronzes, while unpretentious Qing architecture graces the picturesque market town of **Huanglongxi** southwest of Chengdu. Northwest, **Dujiangyan** sports a still-functional two-thousand-year-old irrigation scheme surrounded by wooded parkland, and nearby forested **Qingcheng Shan** is peppered with Taoist shrines.

Sanxingdui Museum

三星堆博物馆, sānxīngduī bówùguǎn • Guanghan town (广汉, guǎnghàn) • Daily 8am–6pm • ¥80 • ☎ 0838 5500349, ⓦ sxd.cn/en • City bus #1 from Renmin Nan Lu or Renmin Dong Lu to Chengdu's Zhaojue Temple bus station, then bus to Guanghan (¥50), from where local bus #10 (¥2) runs 8km out to the museum (total travel time around 90min)

In 1986, an archeological team, investigating what appeared to be a Shang-dynasty town 25km northeast of Chengdu, made an extraordinary discovery: a set of rectangular **sacrificial pits** containing a colossal trove of jade, ivory, gold and **bronze** artefacts, all of which had been deliberately broken up before burial. Subsequent excavation revealed a settlement that from 2700 BC is believed to have been a major centre for the shadowy Ba-Shu culture, until it was upstaged by Jinsha (see p.736) and abandoned around 800 BC.

All this is covered at the excellent **Sanxingdui Museum**, with two main halls and English captions. The thousands of artefacts on display are both startling and nightmarish, the products of a very alien view of the world: a 2m-high bronze figure with a hook nose and oversized, grasping hands standing atop four elephants; metre-wide masks with obscene grins and eyes popping out on stalks; a 4m-high "spirit tree" entwined by a dragon with knives and human hands instead of limbs; and finely detailed bronzes, jade tools and pottery pieces.

12

Huanglongxi

黄龙溪古城, huánglóngxī gǔchéng • Buses leave Chengdu from Xinnanmen station (every 30min 6.30am–6pm), and Chadianzi bus terminal platform 32 (every 15–20min) which both take around 90min; from Huanglongxi station, turn right as you exit and it's a 10min walk

HUANGLONGXI, 40km south of Chengdu, is a riverside village with a half-dozen **Qing-dynasty streets**, all narrow, flagstoned and lined with rickety wooden shops. Tourism aside – visitor numbers are frankly overwhelming at weekends or during holidays – it's a pretty place to wander around for an hour and then have lunch or a cup of tea at one of the many riverside restaurants; it's also popular with old ladies coming to pray for grandchildren to Guanyin, to whom all the village's **temples** are dedicated.

From the old village gate, take the left-hand lane, which is almost narrow enough to touch either side as you walk down the middle. You soon reach the 500m-long main street; turn left for two tiny **nunneries** (one on the left, the other at the end of the street beside a beribboned banyan tree), both containing brightly painted statues of Guanyin, Puxian and Wenshu. At the opposite end of town, larger **Gulong Temple** (古龙寺, gǔlóng sì; ¥5) is in a wobbly state of repair: one of the halls features a dog-headed guillotine for executing criminals, while another contains an unusually three-dimensional, fifty-armed Guanyin statue.

Dujiangyan

都江堰, dūjiāngyàn • High-speed train from Chengdu's East train station (30min) or Qingcheng Shan, then bus #4 to the Lidui Park gate (20min)

DUJIANGYAN is a large town 60km northwest of Chengdu, where in 256 BC the provincial governor, **Li Bing**, set up the **Dujiangyan Irrigation Scheme** to harness the notoriously capricious Min River. Li used a central dam and artificial islands to split the Min into an inner flow for irrigation and an outer channel for flood control, and the scheme has been maintained ever since, the present system of dams, reservoirs and pumping stations irrigating 32,000 square kilometres – even though the project's flood-control aspects became redundant when the **Zipingpu Dam**, 9km upstream, began operation in 2006.

DUJIANGYAN AND QINGCHEN SHAN BY TRAIN

High-speed trains to Dujiangyan and Qingcheng Shan depart Chengdu's East train station (daily 6.48am, 4.20pm & 7.16pm; 50min); if you get the first, the two can be combined in a single day-trip. The last regular train back to Chengdu departs Dujiangyan at 10.29pm.

Lidui Park

离堆公园, lídui gōngyuán • Daily 8am–6pm • ¥90

The scheme's **entrance** is at **Lidui Park**, which encloses the original heart of the project. An ancient, 3m-high stone statue of Li Bing graces **Fulong Guan** (伏龙观, fúlóng guān), a 1600-year-old temple flanked with vertical nanmu trees, which sits right at the tip of the first channel. From here the path crosses to the midstream artificial islands, before arriving at the **Anlan Suspension Bridge**, which spans the width of the river. Crossing to the east side brings you to steps ascending to **Erwang Miao** (二王庙, èrwáng miào), an ornate Taoist hall dedicated to Li Bing and his son, where temple volunteers provide lunch (¥7.5). Look out here for a Qing-era mural showing a bird's-eye view of the whole scheme. Heading back in a loop, follow signs for the wooded **Songmao Road**, a fragment of the ancient route from Dujiangyan to Songpan, which passes through two stone gateways and the old **Town God's Temple** at the park exit on Xingfu Lu, about 500m east of the main entrance.

Qingcheng Shan

青城山, qīngchéng shān • ¥90 • Shuttle from ticket office to base of the mountain ¥10 • 3 high-speed trains head here from Chengdu's East train station (50min), via Chengdu Xipu station (metro line #2) and Dujiangyan, then from the train station bus #101 to the ticket office; or bus from Lidui Park in Dujiangyan

Covered in verdant forest and amazingly fresh after Chengdu's smog, **Qingcheng Shan** is a smaller, easier version of Emei Shan. The mountain's many **Taoist shrines** are all set in courtyards with open-fronted halls, at the back of which are ornate, glassed-in cases containing painted statues of saints. Most have restaurants, and though the food isn't great, the mountain's tea is worth trying.

The return walk from Qingcheng Shan's main gates to the 1200m summit takes around three hours, following 450 stone steps through the forest; there's also a **cable car** (¥50 return). Pick of the shrines are **Ci Hang Dian**, dedicated to Ci Hang, the Taoist version of Guanyin; **Tianshi Dong**, a complex surrounding a small cave where the Taoist hermit Zhang Ling lived before his death at the age of 122; and **Shangqing Gong** (上青宫, shàngqīng gōng), whose attractions include gateway calligraphy by the Guomindang leader Chiang Kai-shek. At the top you'll find a six-storey **tower** containing a 12m-high golden statue of Laozi and his buffalo, with views from the balconies of back-sloping ridges and lower temples poking out of the forest.

Northeastern Sichuan

The fertile valleys of **northeastern Sichuan** wind through hilly, heavily farmed countryside, terminating around 400km from Chengdu at severe escarpments marking the border with Shaanxi. Originally, the sole way through these ranges was provided by **Shudao**, the "Road to Sichuan", linking Chengdu with the former imperial capital Xi'an, along which culture and personalities flowed over the centuries. The region contains the hometowns of the great poet **Li Bai** at **Jiangyou** and the country's only empress; it was the escape route along which the Tang emperor Xuan Zong fled the An Lushan rebellion of 756 AD (see p.928); while Shudao itself breaks out of the region through a sheer cleft in the ranges known as **Jianmenguan**, the Sword Pass. Shudao can also serve as the first stage in a journey to Jiuzhaigou (see p.773); given the seemingly permanent roadworks under way on the Chengdu–Songpan highway, it's sometimes the only viable route.

Well east from Shudao, a large grid of old streets at the pleasant riverside town of **Langzhong** is one of the few places in Sichuan where you can still see substantial areas of archaic architecture – a welcome refuge from the country's frenzied demolition of its past.

Jiangyou

江油, jiāngyóu

JIANGYOU is a pleasantly leafy town on the north bank of the Fu River some 170km from Chengdu, within sight of the steep line of hills slanting northeast towards the Shaanxi border. It's famed as the hometown of the Tang poet Li Bai, but what really justifies a visit is a side trip to quirky **Doutuan Shan**, whose monks perform some bizarre acrobatic stunts. Largely destroyed in the terrible 2008 earthquake, Doutuan's temples have now been restored to their former glory.

Li Bai's Former Home

李白故居, lǐbái gùjū • Daily 9am–5.30pm • ¥40 • Bus #9 from a depot on Taiping Lu, near Jiangyou's bus station

Li Bai was born in a period when China's arts, stimulated by unparalleled contact with the outside world, reached their height. He became China's most highly regarded romantic poet, his works masterpieces of Taoist, dream-like imagery, often clearly influenced by his notorious **drunkenness** – he drowned in the Yangzi in 762 AD, allegedly while trying to grasp the moon's reflection in the water. **Li Bai's Former Home** sits on a hill above **Qinglian** township (青莲, qīnglián), some 10km south of Jiangyou; rebuilt many times, the quiet Ming-era halls and courtyards are filled with statues and paintings illustrating his life, and a shrine to his ancestor, the Han-dynasty general Li Xin.

Doutuan Shan

窦团山, dòutuán shān • ¥67 • Direct bus (every 15min; 45min) from Jiangyou's bus station; minibus or taxi ¥100 one-way

Doutuan Shan is a little twin-peaked ridge 26km northwest of Jiangyou, famed for its martial arts and covered in historic temples. It underwent extensive sympathetic **reconstruction** after the 2008 earthquake, and though the whole site is something of a tourist trap, with monks offering to tell your fortune for a fee, it's definitely worth watching the famed wire-walking performances (¥10) between sheer pinnacles, now carried out with safety harnesses attached. It all makes for a fun day out, and the views over the surrounding countryside are fantastic.

ARRIVAL AND DEPARTURE | JIANGYOU

By train Jiangyou's train station (江油火车站, jiāngyóu huǒchē zhàn) is on the Chengdu–Xi'an line some 5km east of Jiangyou, from where city bus #2 will carry you via the centre to the bus station on Taiping Lu.
CRH destinations Chengdu East (9 daily; 1hr 4min–1hr 30min).
Other destinations Chengdu (13 daily; 2hr 9min–2hr 40min); Guangyuan (14 daily; 2hr 46min–3hr 42min);

Xi'an (10 daily; 11hr–15hr 17min).
By bus Jiangyou's South bus station (南汽车站, nán qìchēzhàn) – the town's major depot – is just south of the centre on Taiping Lu.
Destinations Chengdu (hourly; 2hr); Doutuan Shan (every 30min; 1hr); Guangyuan (8 daily; 2hr 30min); Jianmenguan (hourly; 1hr 30min).

ACCOMMODATION

Jindu Binguan 金都宾馆, jīndū bīnguǎn. Taiping Lu, over the road from the Jinxin ☏0816 3258133. Budget rival for its neighbour across the street but actually not all that much cheaper. Small, basic rooms with a/c, 24hr hot water and breakfast included. **¥120**

Jinxin Binguan 金鑫宾馆, jīnxīn bīnguǎn. Taiping Lu, next to the bus station ☏0816 3277222. This modern hotel has wi-fi access in the lobby, clean en-suite rooms with a/c, TV and wired internet, plus a great restaurant. Convenient and excellent value. **¥148**

12

Jianmenguan

剑门关, jiànménguān · ¥100 · Bus from Guangyuan (¥10); buses from Jiangyou drop 14km short on the Jiangyou–Guangyuan expressway; walk down a sliproad for 1km to waiting minibuses (¥40 for the vehicle)

Jianmenguan, the "Sword Pass" 100km from Jiangyou and 50km from Guangyuan, commands a strategic position along Shudao as the only break in a line of 72 imposing peaks. The pass itself is marked by a heavy stone **gateway** and watchtower, around which progress is slowed by the number of restaurants. A **cable car** (¥50) heads up to a viewing area and tea terrace, or you can get here from the gateway by following Shudao's original route – a very narrow, steep and slippery stone path along the base of the cliffs – for a couple of kilometres. Building work, both in recovery from the 2008 earthquake and to simply develop tourism, unfortunately detracts from historic associations, but the location is impressive nonetheless, and you'll certainly still be able to appreciate the sentiment behind Li Bai's poem, *Hard is the Road to Shu*.

Guangyuan

广元, guǎngyuán

GUANGYUAN, on the Jialing River halfway between Chengdu and Xi'an, is the last town before Shaanxi and seems to have picked up its neighbour's penchant for industrial sprawl. An unattractive manufacturing town, and home to a plutonium production plant, Guangyuan's main attraction is as a jumping-off point for **Jiuzhaigou** buses, but it is also the birthplace of China's only acknowledged empress, the Tang-dynasty ruler **Wu Zetian** (see box, p.214).

Huangze Temple

皇泽寺, huángzé sì · ¥50

About 2km south along the river from the train station, Tang-dynasty rock sculptures at **Huangze Temple** give a positive spin on Wu Zetian's reign after centuries of censure as a result of her perceived challenge to Confucian values (mostly just by being a woman in a position of authority). Carvings here include portraits of Wu Zetian and an elegant, Indian-influenced sculpture of Guanyin. It's generally a quiet spot, but is packed each September 1 when families come to celebrate "Daughters' Day".

ARRIVAL AND DEPARTURE   GUANGYUAN

By train The train station (广元火车站, guǎngyuán huǒchē zhàn) sits at the back of a huge square, about 1.5km northwest from the centre over the Jialing River.
Destinations Chengdu (21 daily; 4hr 34min–5hr 30min); Xi'an (10 daily; 8–11hr 44min).
By bus The main bus station (客运中心, kèyùn zhōngxīn) is next to the train station in the northwest of

town. The Nanhe bus station (南河汽车站, nánhé qìchēzhàn), for travel to Chengdu, is at the southern end of town, just over the river on Shumen Nan Lu.
Destinations Chengdu (6 daily; 3–4hr); Jiangyou (4 daily; 1hr); Jianmenguan (daily 7.40am & 8.40am; 1hr); Jiuzhaigou (daily 6.30am & 1pm; 6–7hr); Langzhong (daily 10am; 2hr 30min); Xi'an (daily 9.30am & 10.30am; 7hr).

GETTING AROUND

By bus Bus #6 runs from the train and main bus stations, down central Shumen Bei Lu.

By taxi A taxi anywhere in the centre shouldn't cost more than ¥10.

ACCOMMODATION AND EATING

The train station is surrounded by hostels charging ¥30–40 a bed. Hotpot stalls and restaurants fill the town's backstreets. More substantial options are available near the Nanhe bus station at the Shumen Bei Lu/Lizhou Lu crossroads.

Zhongyuan 中源宾馆, zhōngyuán bīnguǎn. 32 Lizhou Xi Lu ☎ 0839 3217026. Near the Nanhe bus station, this is a smart, straightforward and comfortable

place with small but well-furnished en suites equipped with a/c and TVs. There are plenty of other options nearby too. **¥198**

Langzhong

阆中, làngzhōng

About 225km northeast of Chengdu, **LANGZHONG** occupies a broad thumb of land around which the Jialing River loops on three sides. The town once played a pivotal role in provincial history, even becoming the **Sichuanese capital** for seventeen years at the start of the Qing. Notable people associated with Langzhong include the Three Kingdoms general **Zhang Fei**, who is buried here, and Luo Xiahong, the Han-dynasty inventor of the Chinese calendar and armillary sphere – a spherical framework of interconnecting hoops mapping the movement of celestial bodies. About a quarter of Langzhong comprises a protected **old town**, Sichuan's largest collection of antique architecture, whose streets, houses and temples provide a fascinating wander. A very few small industries, elderly canteens and teahouses survive alongside the countless touristy shops selling souvenirs, locally produced Baoning vinegar and preserved Zhangfei beef.

The old town

古城, gǔchéng • Most sights daily 8.30am–6pm • Free, but combined tickets for sights available from ¥120

Langzhong's **old town** covers about a square kilometre southwest of the centre. Orient yourself near the river at **Huaguang Lou** (华光楼, huáguāng lóu; ¥20), a three-storey, 36m-high Tang-style gate tower on Dadong Jie, last reconstructed in 1867. From the top, there are views south over the river, north to the modern town, and down over the grey-tiled roofs and atriums of Langzhong's classical buildings.

Gongyuan

贡院, gòngyuàn • ¥55

An unusual target in the north of the old town is the seventeenth-century **Gongyuan**, one of only a very few surviving imperial examination halls in China. Single-storey cells

12

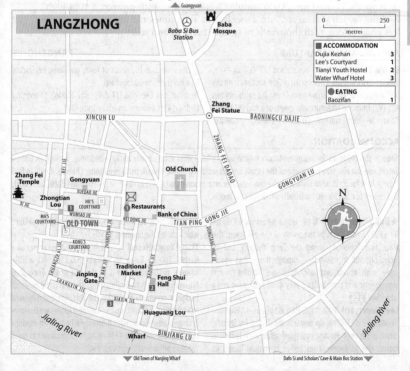

SIHEYUAN

Many of Langzhong's *siheyuan*, or **courtyard houses**, are open to the public (around 9am–6pm; ¥10) and are house museums or accommodation. There's no need to see more than a couple to get the idea of a central hall divided up by wooden screens opening into a courtyard, decorated with potted flower gardens. You can poke around inside both the ancient *Du Jia* hotel and *Water Wharf Inn* for free; they don't seem to mind.

surround a long courtyard where prospective candidates lived and elaborated on their knowledge of the Confucian classics, on which the exams were based and according to which the country was governed.

Zhang Fei Temple

张飞庙, zhāngfēi miào • Xi Jie • ¥58

Langzhong's most popular sight is the **Zhang Fei Temple**, a shrine to the ferocious Three Kingdoms general who was murdered in 221 AD by his own troops while campaigning at Langzhong. Four courtyards of Ming halls, full of painted statuary and interlocking roof brackets, lead through to the grassy mound of his **tomb**, in front of which a finally triumphant Zhang Fei sits between two demons who are holding his cringing assassins **Zhang Da** and **Fan Qiang** by the hair.

East of the river

Taxi from the centre about ¥10–15

As well as the old town, it's worth heading east across the river below a prominent Ming-dynasty pagoda to **Scholars' Cave** (状元洞, zhuàngyuán dòng; ¥4), a peaceful grotto laid with ponds and willows where two students, both later court officials, studied in their youth. Behind here, **Dafo Temple** (大佛寺, dàfó sì; ¥40) protects a 10m-high Buddha, which was carved into a rockface in Tang times and has survived more or less intact, along with thousands of smaller carvings and reliefs.

ARRIVAL AND DEPARTURE   LANGZHONG

By bus Langzhong's main bus station (阆中客运中心, làngzhōng kèyùn zhōngxīn) is 5km southeast on the highway, where you'll arrive from Chengdu; catch city bus #89 (¥2) from the forecourt into town, or a taxi (¥12). The Baba Si bus station (巴巴寺汽车站, bābāsì qìchēzhàn), in the north of town on Zhang Fei Dadao, handles traffic to Guangyuan.

Destinations Chengdu (11 daily; 3hr 30min); Chongqing (5 daily; 4hr); Guangyuan (daily 1pm; 4hr).

ACCOMMODATION

Head to the old town for accommodation, where many places offer rooms inside antique buildings. As well as formal hotels, you can also stay in any one of the family hostels scattered about, though you'll need some Chinese, if only to find them – look for small neon signs with the characters for accommodation (住宿, zhùsù) or guesthouse (客栈, kèzhàn), and expect to pay ¥50–60 for usually small but cosy rooms.

★**Dujia Kezhan** 杜家客栈, dùjiā kèzhàn. 63 Xiaxin Jie ☎0817 6221102. In the south of the old town, this place was founded during the Tang dynasty and is, incredibly, still in business – though these days rooms come with toilets and a/c. Staff are helpful, rooms atmospheric and there's also a very good restaurant and a lobby bar. **¥148**

Lee's Courtyard 李家大院, lǐjiā dàyuàn. 47 Wumiao Jie ☎0817 6236500. Up towards the Zhang Fei Temple, this is a superior vintage courtyard affair with luxurious rooms, and an excellent restaurant to match. There's no sign in English but there is for the Tong Nian Bookstore which shares the building. **¥410**

Tianyi Youth Hostel 天一青年旅舍, tiānyī qīngnián lǚshě. 100 Da Dong Jie ☎0817 6225501. It's a little strange as the reception is at the exit of the Feng Shui Museum (which is basically a shop), but this is the only real budget accommodation within the old town, and is housed in a beautiful old building. The cheapest rooms are the low-ceilinged attic rooms with futon-style beds, with modern outside bathrooms. The ¥198 en-suite rooms aren't as good value as other nearby options. **¥98**

Water Wharf Inn 水码头客栈, shuǐmǎtóu kèzhàn. 61 Xiaxin Jie ☎0817 6233333. Right next door to the *Dujia*, this is a similarly labyrinthine old courtyard building. Though claims to be a museum are a slight overstatement, there are some nice old pictures on the wall and it's worth having a look in even if you're not staying. En-suite rooms are a little cramped, but clean. **¥120**

EATING

For local food, there are a string of excellent canteens on Yanshikou, running north from Nei Dong Jie, selling noodles and rice meals for ¥8–16. The local cuisine is heavily influenced by Hunnanese food, and while much lighter on the Sichuan pepper, is much heavier on the spicy green chillies. For anything fancier, head further into the new town, along Dongtang Jing Jie, or across the river on the ferry (¥5) to the Old Town of Nanjing Wharf development, where there is a raft of restaurants, coffee shops, bars and KTVs all housed in gleaming, newly built "old" buildings.

Baozifan 煲仔饭, bāo zǎi fàn. Nei Dong Jie (no English sign). Best of the cheap eateries along here. The clay pot rice meals of its name are amazingly tasty for the price (¥16–20), as are the other inexpensive and mostly spicy local dishes (from ¥10) which can be chosen from photos on the wall. They're very friendy too, though don't speak English. Daily 8am–10pm.

Southern Sichuan

Southwest of Chengdu, fast-flowing rivers converge at **Leshan**, where more than a thousand years ago sculptors created a **giant Buddha** overlooking the waters, one of the world's most imposing religious monuments. An hour away, **Emei Shan** rises to more than 3000m, its forested slopes rich in scenery and temples. As Sichuan's most famous sights, the Buddha and Emei Shan have become tourist black holes thanks to easy access – don't go near either during holidays, when crowds are so awful that the army is sometimes called in to sort out the chaos – but at other times they are well worth the effort.

 If you're on your way down south to Yunnan, you might also want to break your journey at **Xichang**, a Yi minority town with a back-road route to **Lugu Lake**, right on the Yunnanese border. Emei and Dafo are best reached on buses, but it's easier to get to Xichang via the Chengdu–Emei Shan–Kunming rail line.

12

Leshan

乐山, lèshān

Set beside the wide convergence of the Qingyi, Min and Dadu rivers, 180km from Chengdu and 50km from Emei Shan, **LESHAN** is a dull, spread-out market town with a modern northern fringe and older riverside core, a transit point for visiting the Big Buddha, carved deep into a niche in the facing cliffs.

The Big Buddha

大佛, dàfó • Daily: April–Sept 7.30am–6.30pm; Oct–March 8am–5.30pm • ¥90 • Boat from jetty #3 on Binjiang Nan Lu, tickets (¥70) can be bought from the yellow booth on the road

Impassive and gargantuan, the **Big Buddha** peers out from under half-lidded eyes, oblivious to the swarms of sightseers trying to photograph his bulk. In 713 AD the monk **Haitong** came up with the idea of carving the Buddha into the riverside's red sandstone cliffs, using the rubble produced to fill in dangerous shoals below. The project took ninety years to complete and, once construction started, temples sprang up on the hills above the Buddha. At 71m tall, this is the world's largest Buddhist sculpture – his ears are 7m long, his eyes 10m wide, and around six small people at once can stand on his big toenail – though statistics can't convey the initial sight of this squat icon, comfortably seated with his hands on his knees,

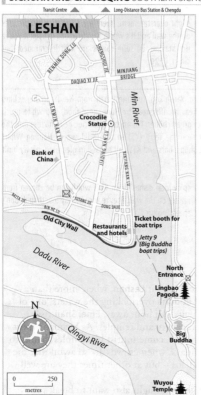

looming over you. The best view of the statue, however, is on the river from one of the **boats** that leave from Binjiang Nan Lu, which take ten minutes to chug out to the statue, wait ten minutes while everyone takes a photo, and chug back. This is probably the best option as frankly the crowds inside the park can often make a visit unbearable, especially in the sweltering summer. You only really need an hour to see everything in the park, though on weekends and public holidays, and pretty much any day during August, just queuing to descend the stairs past the Buddha can take an hour.

The easiest route in is via the **north entrance** (大佛北门, dàfó běimén), from where you walk up to the crowded terrace around the Buddha's ears; there's an insane-looking statue of Haitong here, and the one-way **staircase of nine turns** down to the Buddha's toes, after which you return to the top via the 500m-long **cliff road** cut into the rocks. From here you can press on to Maohao Mu, a set of Han-dynasty tombs, and then, via a covered bridge to **Wuyou Temple** (乌优寺, wūyōu sì), a warm pink-walled monastery – don't miss the grotesque gallery of saints in the Luohan Hall.

ARRIVAL AND DEPARTURE

By bus Leshan has at least three large bus stations, but you're most likely to arrive at the transit centre (乐山客运中心站, lèshān kèyùn zhōngxīnzhàn) on Baichang Xi Lu, around 8km northwest of the sights; buses #9 and #12 run from here to near the boat dock on Binjiang Lu, while #3 or #13 will get you to Dafo's north entrance.

Destinations Chengdu (every 30min; 2hr); Chongqing (daily 10.40am; 3hr); Dazu (daily 1.10pm; 3hr); Emei (every 10min; 30min); Xichang (daily 9.30am & 1pm; 13hr); Yibin (6 daily; 3hr); Zigong (10 daily; 2hr 30min).

GETTING AROUND

By taxi A taxi from arrival points to the ferry or the north gate shouldn't cost more than ¥15–20, or for the same price you can take a more sedate cycle rickshaw.

ACCOMMODATION AND EATING

There's no real reason to stay in Leshan, as even if you decide to enter the park, you'll still only be about four hours here maximum, and it's best to push onto Emei Shan so you can get an early start up the mountain. The best options are the mid-range **hotels** overlooking the river on Binjiang Nan Lu (around ¥150–200). It's not really worth heading into Leshan proper **to eat**, and there are plenty of options by the boat jetty on Binjiang Nan Lu, and a string of Sichuanese and Muslim restaurants by the north gate of the Buddha Scenic Area. The local Xiba tofu is reckoned to be some of the best in the country, thanks to the region's high-quality water.

Emei Shan

峨眉山, éméi shān • Trails daily 7am–6pm • Ticket ¥185, entry valid for two days, though you can stay as long as you want once you're inside

Some 160km southwest of Chengdu, **Emei Shan**'s thickly forested peaks and dozens of **temples**, all linked by exhausting flights of stone steps, have been pulling in pilgrims (and tourists) ever since the sixth-century visit of **Bodhisattva Puxian** and his six-tusked elephant, images of whom you'll see everywhere. Religion aside, the pristine natural environment is a major draw, and changes markedly through the year: lush, green and

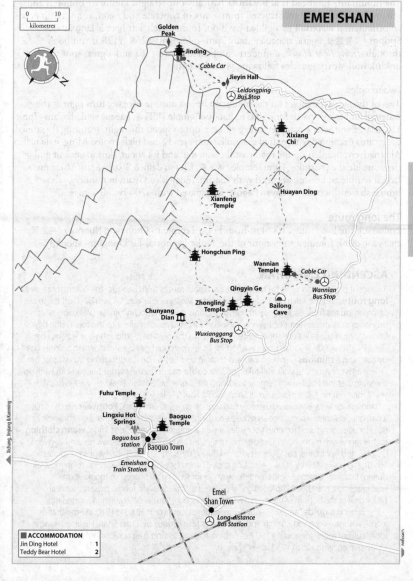

EMEI SHAN

0   10
kilometres

Golden
Peak

Jinding

Cable Car

Jieyin Hall

Leidongping
Bus Stop

Xixiang
Chi

Huayan Ding

Xianfeng
Temple

Hongchun Ping

Wannian
Temple   Cable Car

Qingyin Ge   Wannian
Bus Stop

Zhongling
Temple   Bailong
Cave

Chunyang
Dian

Wuxianggang
Bus Stop

Fuhu Temple

Lingxiu Hot
Springs   Baoguo
Temple

Baguo bus
station   Baoguo Town

Emeishan
Train Station

Emei
Shan Town

Long-distance
Bus Station

■ ACCOMMODATION
Jin Ding Hotel   1
Teddy Bear Hotel   2

Xichang, Jinjiang & Kunming

12

wet in the summer; brilliant with reds and yellows in autumn; white, clear and very cold in winter.

You can see something of the mountain in a single day, but three allows you to experience more of the forests, spend a night or two in a temple, and perhaps assault Emei's summit. It's only worth climbing this high if the weather's good, however: for a richer range of views, temples, streams and vegetation, you won't be disappointed with the lower paths.

Baoguo

报国, bàoguó • Mountain ticket not needed to visit the town and nearby temples

The mountain's trailhead is at **BAOGUO**, basically one straight kilometre of hotels and restaurants, apparently constructed from a mix of concrete and neon, running up past an ornamental **waterfall** to a gilded pavilion. Immediately left here is **Lingxiu Hot Springs** (灵秀温泉, língxiù wēnquán; daily 2pm–midnight; ¥268, ¥128 if you book through *Teddy Bear Hotel*), a modern, professionally run spa and a great spot to unkink trail-weary muscles following your descent.

Two temples

Two of the liveliest temples on the mountain lie just outside Baoguo: turn right at the waterfall and follow paths for 250m to **Baoguo Temple** (报国寺, bàoguó sì; daily 7am–7pm; ¥8), a large and serene complex where you can opt to spend the night, featuring flagstoned courtyards decorated with potted magnolias and cycads, and high-roofed Ming-style halls. Alternatively, bear left up the road past the waterfall and it's about 1km to ancient ginkgo trees outside the charming **Fuhu Temple** (伏虎寺, fúhǔ sì; daily 6.30am–8pm; ¥6). Emei's largest temple and once associated with Taoism, today it's a Guanyin nunnery, whose bronze sixteenth-century **Huayan Pagoda** is engraved with 4700 Buddha images.

The long route

Following the long route, it's 5km from Fuhu Temple to **Chunyang Nunnery** (纯阳殿, chúnyáng diàn), founded in honour of the Taoist Immortal Lü Dongbin, spookily

---

ASCENDING EMEI SHAN

An ascent of Emei Shan can be tackled via two main routes from Baoguo: the 60km, three-day **long route**; and the 40km, two-day **short route**. Most people knock 15km or so off these by catching **buses** from Baoguo to alternative starting points near Qingyin Ge (Wuxianggang bus stop) or Wannian Temple; leaving early enough, you could make it to the top in one day from either of these via the short route, descending the next day – though your legs will be like jelly afterwards. If you're really pushed for time, you could get up and down in a single day by catching a **minibus** between Baoguo Temple and Jieyin Hall (Leidongping bus stop), from where a twenty-minute walk will take you to a **cable car** up to the summit or you can walk up the stairs behind the Jieying Temple following the signs for "Golden Peak". However, this way you'll miss out on what makes Emei Shan such a special place.

Bring a torch in case you unexpectedly find yourself on a path after dark. **Footwear** needs to have a firm grip; in winter, when stone steps become dangerously icy, straw sandals and even iron cleats (sold for a few yuan and tied onto your soles) are an absolute necessity. Don't forget **warm clothing** for the top, which is around 15°C cooler than the plains and so liable to be below freezing between October and April; lower paths are very humid during the summer. You'll also want some protection against the near certainty of rain. A walking stick is handy for easing the pressure on thigh muscles during descent – a range is sold along the way – or for fending off aggressive monkeys (the macaques here have been known to go for people, particularly when food is present). Store any heavy gear at the bottom of the mountain, or in Chengdu if you're contemplating a round trip.

If you need a **guide**, an excellent choice is Patrick Yang (☎0137 08131210, ⓦemeiguides .com), who speaks good English and often takes tour groups up Emei Shan. He also arranges local "culture tours" for about ¥150 per person, touring a kung-fu school, noodle factory and kindergarten, with lunch in a farmer's house.

surrounded by mossy pine trees. A further 5km lands you at **Qingyin Ge** (清音阁, qīngyīn gé), a pavilion built deep in the forest where two streams converge and tumble through a small gorge down **Niuxin Shi** (牛心石, niú xīnshí), the ox-heart rock. It's a charming spot with a small **temple** to spend the night in, though being also just a short walk from the Wuxianggang bus stop, it can get busy with guests.

Qingyin Ge to Xixiang Chi

Qingyin Ge is just 3km from Wannian Temple (see below), but to continue the long route, follow the path up past the left side of Qingyin; this takes you along a riverbed and past a **monkey-watching area**, before starting to climb steeply through a series of gorges. About 6km further on, **Hongchun Ping** (洪椿坪, hóngchūn píng) is an eighteenth-century temple named after surrounding *hongchun* (toona) trees, which has accommodation and is about as far as you'd make it on the first day.

From here it's a very tough 15km of seemingly unending narrow stairs to **Xianfeng Temple** (仙峰寺, xiānfēng sì), a strangely unfriendly place, though well forested with pine and dove trees and planted with camellia and rhododendrons. The following 12.5km are slightly easier, heading partly downhill to a dragon-headed bridge, then up again to where the trail joins the north route near Xixiang Chi (see below), around 43km from Fuhu Temple and two-thirds of the way to the summit.

The short route

Most people start their ascent by catching a bus (every 30min) from Baoguo to the Wannian Temple bus stop at the start of Emei's short route. From here a 3km path or cable car (¥50) leads to **Wannian Temple** (万年寺, wànnián sì; daily 7.30am–7pm; ¥10), where a squat brick pavilion out back, built in 1601, houses a life-sized enamelled bronze **sculpture of Puxian**, riding a gilt lotus flower astride his great six-tusked white elephant – note the gold spots on the elephant's knees, which people rub for good luck.

From Wannian, a steady 14km hike through bamboo and pine groves should see you to where the two routes converge just south of **Xixiang Chi** (洗象池, xǐxiàng chí). This eighteenth-century monastery sits on a ridge where Puxian's elephant stopped for a wash, and on cloudy days – being more or less open to the elements and prowled by monkeys – it's amazingly atmospheric, though somewhat run-down and frigid in winter. It's a popular place to rest up, however, so get in early to be sure of a bed.

On to the summit

Beyond Xixiang Chi the path gets easier, but you'll encounter gangs of fearless and very aggressive **monkeys**; keep a good grip on your bags. The path continues for 9km past some ancient, gnarled rhododendrons to **Jieyin Hall** (接引殿, jiēyǐn diàn) where the 50km-long road from Baoguo, which has snaked its way round the back of the mountain, ends at **Leidongping bus stop** (雷洞坪车站, léidòngpíng chēzhàn) and a cable car to the summit (¥65 up, ¥55 down). The peak is somewhat of a disappointment, and the area is thick with minibus tour parties fired up for their one-day crack at the peak. The chances of a clear view are usually quite slim – although if it is clear the views are gobsmackingly good. There are a few brand-new gleaming golden temples and a massive golden Buddha towering over them all, but the crowds, food courts, restaurants and the many buildings that make up the *Jin Ding Hotel* really make the peak itself not that great an experience; but climbing Emei Shan is about the journey, not the destination.

Jinding

金顶, jīndǐng

Whether you take the cable car or spend the next couple of hours hoofing it, 3077m-high **Jinding**, the Golden Summit, is most people's final stop. There are two temples: the friendly **Woyun Nunnery** (卧云庵, wòyún ān) and the oversized **Huazang Temple** (华藏寺, huázàng sì), crowned by a massive gilded statue of a multifaced Puxian on four elephants.

12

In the afternoon, the sea of clouds below the peak sometimes catches rainbow-like rings known as **Buddha's Halo**, which surround and move with your shadow, while in clear conditions you can even make out Gongga Shan (see p.778), 150km to the west.

ARRIVAL AND DEPARTURE   EMEI SHAN

Access to the region is largely via Emei Shan town (峨眉山市, éméi shān shì), a transit hub 150km southwest of Chengdu and 7km short of the mountain.

BY TRAIN

Emei Shan train station (峨眉山火车站, éméishān huǒchē zhàn) is the new high-speed train station for the area and just a couple of km from the mountain trailhead at Baoguo; catch green bus #5A or take a taxi for less than ¥10.
Destinations Chengdu (11 daily; 1hr 9min–1hr 38min); Jiangyou (7 daily; 3hr).

Emei train station (峨眉火车站, éméi huǒchē zhàn) is a bit further away, to the east of Emei town and 10km from Baoguo; take bus #8, then change to bus #5A, or a taxi costs ¥20–30.
Destinations Beijing (daily 9.22pm; 31hr); Chengdu (5 daily; 2hr 12min–2hr 50min); Jiangyou (daily 10.30am; 5hr 13min); Kunming (3 daily; 15hr 33min–17hr); Panzhihua (3 daily; 10–11hr); Xichang (4 daily; 7hr–7hr 25min).

BY BUS

Emei Shan bus station (峨眉山气车站, éméi shān qìchēzhàn), is one of the largest in the region and where to find most long-distance transport, though it's a fair way from Baoguo; catch blue city bus #1 to the Tian Xia Ming Shan (天下名山, tiānxià míngshān) stop, then green bus #5A to the mountain trailhead at Baoguo, or a taxi costs around ¥40.
Destinations Chongqing (every 90min; 5hr); Xichang (4 daily; 12hr).

Baoguo bus station (报国汽车站, bàoguó qìchēzhàn), a decent-sized depot in the middle of Baoguo, has long-distance transport to Chengdu and Leshan until 6pm.
Destinations Chengdu (hourly; 2hr); Leshan (every 10min; 30min).

GETTING AROUND

By bus Baoguo bus station is where to catch transport up the mountain (every 30min; 6am–5pm) to Wuxianggang (for Qingyin Ge; ¥40 return); Wannian Temple (¥40 return); and Leidongping (for Jieyin Hall and the summit; ¥90 return).

ACCOMMODATION AND EATING

There are some hotels on the mountain, but it can't be stressed enough that temples offer far more interesting lodgings; all charge from ¥30–50 for a basic dorm bed to more than ¥150 for a double room with air conditioning and toilet. It's a good idea to reach your intended temple accommodation by 3pm; popular places such as Xixiang Chi can fill up early on. Food on the mountain tends to be overpriced and ordinary; stir-fries and noodle soups are available either at roadside stalls or vegetarian temple restaurants.

Jin Ding Hotel 金顶酒店, jīndǐng jiǔdiàn. At the summit of the mountain ☎ 0833 5098088, ⓦ emsjdjd .com. New with three buildings, two immediately outside the cable-car station, and a luxury annexe at the bottom of the steps to the golden Buddha (¥1000); the rooms at the former are clean and newly refurbished, but the cheapest are without bathrooms, and you'll pay another ¥300 for an en suite. The luxury annexe's rooms are pretty swanky but poor value. ¥300

Teddy Bear Hotel 玩具熊酒店, wánjùxióng jiǔdiàn. In a side street next to Baoguo bus station ☎ 0833 5590135, ⓦ teddybear.com.cn. Family-run, English-speaking hostel which is by far the best place for foreigners, it has a very wide range of accommodation from dorm beds to "five star" rooms. All are comfortable, well-furnished and share a teddy-bear-themed decor. Also has a decent restaurant serving good Western and Chinese food (slightly more pricey than outside) as well as offering excellent travel info and maps of the area. Dorms ¥35, doubles ¥100

Xichang

西昌, xīchāng

XICHANG, seven hours south from Emei Shan by train, is a surprisingly bustling place, focus for southwestern China's eight-million-strong **Yi** minority – whose **torch festival** in August is one of the largest ethnic events in all Sichuan. Xichang is also a **satellite launching site** for China's Long March space programme, and a staging post for a couple of back-road trips into Yunnan, if the straightforward train ride to Kunming doesn't appeal.

The old town

Xichang's partially walled **old town** is just northeast of the centre, a fifteen-minute walk north from central Yuechang Plaza. The old quarter's streets form a cross, of which the southern extension, **Nan Jie**, is the most interesting, running 150m through a busy market and past rickety wooden teahouses to the heavy stone **south gate** and attached battlements.

Liang Shan

凉山, liángshān • Bus #106 • Museum daily 8.30am–5pm • Free

The area around Xichang, known as **Liang Shan**, the Cool Mountains, is the heartland of the Yi community. Until the 1950s, the Yi here lived pretty much any way they wanted to, owning slaves, raiding the lowlands and conducting clan warfare. Some 5km south from town by bus, **Qionghai Lake** (邛海湖, qiónghǎi hú) is where the **Museum of Liangshan Yi Slave Society** (凉山彝族奴隶社会博物馆, liángshān yízúnúlì shèhuì bówùguǎn) exhibits Yi festival clothing and household items, and books written in the Yi script – you'll also see this on official signs around town.

ARRIVAL AND DEPARTURE
XICHANG

BY TRAIN

There's a train ticket office on Chang'an Dong Lu, just west of central Shengli Lu, but be warned that Xichang is a tough place from which to get reserved berths – or even hard seats. **Xichang train station** (西昌火车站, xīchāng huǒchē zhàn) is on the city's western outskirts, from where bus #12 (turn left out the station exit for the stop) will get you to main street Chang'an Dong Lu and both bus stations.

Destinations Chengdu (11 daily; 9–11hr 21min); Emei (6 daily; 6hr 34min–9hr 35min); Kunming (4 daily; 8hr 12min–9hr 23min); Panzhihua (9 daily; 3–5hr).

BY BUS

Bus tickets are easily available at the stations; aside from obvious destinations there are services to Lugu Lake in Yunnan, and to Kangding in western Sichuan (see p.777).

Xichang Tourist Transport Center (西昌旅游集散服务中心, xīchāng lǚyóu jísàn fúwù zhōngxīn) is a couple of km northwest of the centre on the main highway and the last stop on the #12 bus route from the train station. Destinations Chengdu (every 30min daily; 5hr 50min); Kangding (daily 6am & 6.30am; 5hr); Kunming (10am & 3pm daily; 6hr);

Central bus station (中心汽车站, zhōngxīn qìchēzhàn), in the south of the centre on Huoba Square and also on the #12 bus route, handles buses travelling the expressway to Panzhihua – where you can catch transport to Lijiang in Yunnan (see p.688) – and the rough road west to Lugu Lake, on the Yunnanese border (see p.694). Destinations Lijiang (daily 7.50am; 6hr 40min); Lugu Lake (4 daily, last at 9.20am; 3hr 40min); Panzhihua (4 daily, last 11am; 3hr).

ACCOMMODATION AND EATING

Inexpensive restaurants and hotels are scattered throughout the old town.

Hotel Pretty 美丽华大酒店, měilì huá dàjiǔdiàn. 79 Sancha Xi Lu ☎0834 6187777. Down near the main Bank of China, this place provides clean, modern budget en-suite rooms and is nowhere near as tacky as the name suggests, though they have squeezed a surprising amount of fake marble into the petite lobby. ¥180

Ziwei 紫葳酒店, zǐwēi jiǔdiàn. 56 Chang'an Dong Lu ☎0834 3286888. Modern hotel in the middle of town, well presented, with the usual trimmings, but just a cut above the normal Chinese business hotel. Smart and clean with wi-fi and a/c throughout. ¥318

Southeastern Sichuan

Surrounding the fertile confluence of the Yangzi and Min rivers 250km from Chengdu, where Sichuan, Yunnan and Guizhou provinces meet, southeastern Sichuan has some intriguing attractions. The town of **Zigong** is a treat, with some well-preserved

12

architecture, one of the world's top dinosaur museums and salt mines, especially worth checking out during its Spring Festival lantern displays. Some 80km farther south, **Yibin** offers access to the aptly named **Shunan Bamboo Sea**; and, further eastwards towards Chongqing, you shouldn't miss the carved gallery of comic-book-like Buddhist rock art at **Dazu**.

Zigong

自贡, zìgòng

ZIGONG, a thriving industrial centre, has long been an important source of **salt**, tapped for thousands of years from artesian basins below the city. In the fourth century, the Sichuanese were sinking 300m-deep boreholes here using bamboo-fibre cables attached to massive stone bits; by the 1600s, bamboo buckets were drawing brine from wells bored almost 1km beneath Zigong, centuries before European technology (which borrowed Chinese techniques) could reach this deep. **Natural gas**, a by-product of drilling, was used from the second century to boil brine in evaporation tanks, and now also powers Zigong's buses and taxis.

Xiqin Guildhall

西秦会馆, xīqín huìguǎn • Jiefang Lu • Daily 8.30am–5.30pm • ¥60

The splendid **Xiqin Guildhall**, built in the Qing dynasty by merchants from Shaanxi, is now an absorbing salt museum. Photos and relics, with plenty of English captions,

chart Zigong's mining history, from pictorial Han-dynasty tomb bricks showing salt panning, to the bamboo piping, frightening metal drills and wooden derricks used until the 1980s. All this is overshadowed by the building itself, whose curled roof corners, flagstone-and-beam halls and gilded woodwork date to 1872.

Other guildhalls

Of Zigong's many other scattered period buildings, the most notable are **Wangye Miao** (王爷庙, wángyé miào), a former guildhall-temple which sits high over the river on Binjiang Lu; and **Huanhou Gong** (桓侯宫, huánhóu gōng), a guildhall for pork butchers – or rather their patron, the Three Kingdoms' general Zhang Fei (see box, p.396) – whose beautifully carved stone gateway overlooks the junction of Jiefang Lu and Zhonghua Lu. Both are now highly atmospheric teahouses.

Shenhai Salt Well

燊海井, shēnhǎi jǐng • Daily 9am–5pm • ¥22 • Bus #5 or #35 from the riverside "Shawan" bus stop on Binjiang Lu

About 3km northeast from the city centre is **Shenhai Well**, which in 1835 reached a fraction over 1000m, the deepest ever drilled using traditional methods. Operational until 1966, the 20m-high wooden tripod minehead still overlooks the site, where you can inspect bamboo-fibre cables and the tiny well shaft itself, corked, reeking of gas, and barely 20cm across. Eight shallow vats in the building behind are still-functioning evaporation pans, where the muddy brine is purified by mixing in tofu and skimming off the resultant scum as it rises, leaving a thick crust of pure salt when the liquid has been boiled off.

12

Zigong dinosaur museum

恐龙博物馆, kǒnglóng bówùguǎn • 235 Dashanpu • Daily 8.30am–5pm • ¥42 • ⓦ zdm.cn/en • Bus #35 from the riverside "Shawan" bus stop on Binjiang Lu via Shenhai Salt Well

Right on the city's northeastern outskirts, about 45 minutes from the centre by bus, Zigong's **dinosaur museum** is built over the site of excavations carried out during the 1980s, and one of the best of its kind in the world. Near-perfect skeletal remains of dozens of Jurassic fish, amphibians and dinosaurs – including monumental thigh bones, and Sichuan's own **Yangchuanosaurus**, a toothy, lightweight velociraptor – have been left partially excavated *in situ*, while others have been fully assembled for easy viewing, posed dramatically against painted backgrounds. Fossils are for sale in the museum's shop. Visit in the morning to avoid the massive crowds.

ARRIVAL AND DEPARTURE
ZIGONG

By train Zigong is on a side-spur of the Guangzhou–Chengdu rail line, with the train station 1.5km east of the river on Jiaotong Lu, from where bus #34 heads to the central "Shawan" bus stop.
Destinations Chengdu (7 daily; 4hr 38min–7hr); Chongqing (daily 3.09am; 8hr 41min); Guangzhou (daily 3.12pm; 38hr); Guiyang (3 daily; 14hr); Kunming (3 daily; 14hr 14min–17hr); Yibin (8 daily; 1hr 27min).
By bus Zigong's long-distance bus station (自贡客运中心, zìgòng kèyùn zhōngxīn) is about 3km south of town on Dangui Dajie; turn right out of the station and it's

100m to the city bus stop. Bus #33 travels via the central "Shawan" bus stop, continuing to the bottom of Ziyou Lu; taxis charge about ¥8–10.
Destinations Chengdu (13 daily; 2hr 20min); Chongqing (every 30min; 3hr 30min); Dazu (daily 8.30am & 2.50pm; 2–3hr); Leshan (14 daily; 2hr); Yibin (7 daily; 1hr 20min).
By taxi If you're heading to the Shunan Bamboo Sea (see p.759), a new expressway means that you can get there from Zigong in just 3hr in a cab – contact the *Xiongfei Holiday Hotel* or the CITS at the *Chang Shan* about hiring one for the day for about ¥350–400.

ACCOMMODATION

Chang Shan 长闪远景宾馆, chángshǎn yuǎnjǐng bīnguǎn. 133 Ziyou Lu ☎ 0813 5390666. If you absolutely, positively need to stay at the cheapest place in town, this is it.

Shabby, tile-clad rooms come with a/c and an en suite with a squat toilet, though no English is spoken. You might be better off at the *7 Days Inn* just down the hill for ¥25 more. **¥98**

Jingu Garden 雄飞锦绣花园酒店, xióngfēi jǐnxiù huāyuán jiǔdiàn. Jiari Guangcheng ☎ 0813 2118266. Budget sister of luxury *Xiongfei* just up the road, but rooms here are still up to a good standard, though of varying quality – they have three types. Carpets are a little worn and it's worth checking to make sure your room doesn't smell too smoky. **¥159**

Xiongfei Holiday Hotel 雄飞假日酒店, xióngfēi jiàrì jiǔdiàn. 193 Jiefang Lu ☎ 0813 2118888. The only slice of luxury you're likely to find in central Zigong is this four-star pile in the town centre. Marble-clad on the outside and easy to find, the en-suite rooms come with bathtub, a/c, TV and a sit-down toilet. Good value, but not much in the way of facilities. **¥289**

EATING

For eating, street food is the order of the day (there's little else in the centre), with dumpling and noodle vendors surrounding the southern entrance to Caideng Park in a pedestrianized area known as Dongfang Guangchang, where you'll also find an alright sit-down Sichuanese restaurant, and average "steakhouse". For anything else you'll need to head to one of the modern places way out in the new town, especially in the area around the Walmart – around 20min by taxi.

Yibin

宜宾, yíbīn

A crowded, grubby port with a modern veneer, the city of **YIBIN** sits 50km south of Zigong where the Jinsha and Min rivers combine to form the **Chang Jiang**, the main body of the Yangzi River. Aside from **Daguan Lou**, an old bell tower just east off central Minzhu Lu, there's nothing to do here in between organizing transport to the nearby **Shunan Bamboo Sea**, though Yibin produces three substances known for wreaking havoc: enriched plutonium; Wuliangye *bai jiu*, China's second-favourite spirit; and *ranmian*, "burning noodles", whose chilli content has stripped many a stomach lining.

ARRIVAL AND DEPARTURE   YIBIN

BY BUS

Beimen bus station (北门汽车客运站, běimén qìchē kèyùnzhàn), 250m northwest of the centre off Zhenwu Lu. Mostly short-range regional traffic from Zigong and elsewhere; worth checking out departures here first before hauling out to the main station.
Destinations Chengdu (5 daily; 3hr 20min).

Main bus station (川高客运中心, chuāngāo kèyùn zhōngxīn) is a few km north of town, covering the largest number of regional and long-distance destinations including Chongqing, Chengdu, Zigong and Luzhou (for connections to Chishui in Guizhou province).
Destinations Chengdu (9 daily; 3hr 20min); Chongqing (10 daily; 3hr 20min); Luzhou (8 daily; 1hr 40min); Zigong (7daily; 1hr 20min).

South bus station (南岸汽车客运站, nán'àn qìchē

kèyùn zhàn), about 2km southeast of the centre on the #4 city bus route, or ¥10 by taxi. There's one scheduled daily bus to the Shunan Bamboo Sea around lunchtime; it's usually quicker to aim first for Changning (长宁, chángníng; last bus at 7.30pm; ¥10), from where you can organize transport into the park (see opposite).
Destinations Changning (roughly hourly; 1hr 30min); Dazu (daily 2.05pm; 3hr).

BY TRAIN

Yibin train station (宜宾火车站, yíbīn huǒchē zhàn), is just 1km east of the centre on Qianjin Lu. There are also less frequent services to Guangzhou and Hangzhou.
Destinations Caohai in Guizhou (7 daily; 6hr 36min–7hr 10min); Chengdu (7 daily; 6hr 10min–9hr 14min); Kunming (3 daily; 12hr 40min–15hr 37min).

ACCOMMODATION AND EATING

There's no shortage of inexpensive (under ¥100) accommodation near the train and bus stations, as well as several slightly more expensive *7 Days Inns*.

Jiudu Fandian 酒都饭店, jiǔdū fàndiàn. 50 Zhuanshu Jie ☎ 0831 8188888. If only every Chinese business hotel was up to the standard of this imposing place out east towards the river. A wide range of trim rooms of various categories, with decent carpets and an excellent restaurant. **¥298**

Ranmian Fandian 燃面饭店, ránmiàn fàndiàn. Next to the crossroads at 19 Renmin Lu ☎ 0831 8228047. Typical of the town's canteens, a tidy place where a bowl of cold *ranmian* noodles dressed in chopped nuts, coriander, vinegar and chillies costs just ¥8. Lots of other snacks too. Daily 8am–9pm.

12

The Shunan Bamboo Sea

蜀南竹海国家公园, shǔ'nán zhúhǎi guójiā gōngyuán · ¥112; cable cars ¥30 & ¥40

Some 75km southeast of Yibin, the extraordinary **Shunan Bamboo Sea** covers more than forty square kilometres of mountain slopes with feathery green tufts, and makes for a refreshing few days' rural escape. It's a relatively **expensive** one, however, as you'll need to charter a taxi for the day to see much. The two settlements inside the park, **Wanling** (万岭, wànlǐng), 1.5km inside the main West Gate entrance, and **Wanli** (万里, wànlǐ), 20km inside, are tiny but have plenty of places to stay.

Around the park

Shunan is a beautiful spot, if a bit spooky given the graceful 10m-high stems endlessly repeating into the distance. There's pleasure in just being driven around, but make sure you have at least one walk along any of the numerous paths – the trail paralleling the cable car just outside Wanling is steep but superb, taking in a couple of waterfalls – and get a look down over the forest to see the bowed tips of bamboo ripple in waves as breezes sweep the slopes. The park is a favourite film location for martial-arts movies and TV series, so don't be too surprised if you encounter Song-dynasty warriors galloping along the roads, which all enhances the place's surreal atmosphere.

ARRIVAL AND DEPARTURE   SHUNAN BAMBOO SEA

By bus Although there's an erratic direct Yibin–Shunan bus service, the main transport hub is Changning (长宁, chángníng), a small town 15km short of Shunan's West Gate, which has a bus station and minibuses into the park. There's only one direct bus back to Yibin from the West Gate at 2pm.

GETTING AROUND

By public minibus In theory, public minibuses shuttle between Changning, the West Gate, Wanling and Wanli through the day; you stand by the road and wave them down. In practice, service is patchy, tourists tend to be outrageously overcharged, and while useful for reaching accommodation they don't service the park sights.

By taxi The only way to comfortably see much of the Bamboo Sea is to hire a cab for the day; you can do this through accommodation and should expect to pay ¥200–250 for a day or ¥120–150 for a half-day, depending on where you want to go.

ACCOMMODATION AND EATING

Accommodation is available inside the park with the cheapest charging about ¥50 a bed, though most are mid-range and aimed at tour groups. Food in the park is universally good and not too expensive, featuring lots of fresh bamboo shoots and mushrooms.

Joan's Guest House (Jing Xin Yuan) 晶鑫园农家乐, jīngxīnyuán nóngjiālè. Wanling ☎ 135 47717196, ✉ 332704543@qq.com. The only really viable option for foreigners – Joan is a friendly and welcoming host, speaks English (a rarity in the area), can organize taxis, guides, onward travel, and will even send a complementary car to pick you up from the West Gate. Rooms and dorms are clean and comfortable enough, though the bathrooms leave a little to be desired. Also has a decent restaurant, run by Joan's mother and serving local food. Dorms **¥60**, doubles **¥160**

Dazu

大足, dàzú

About 200km east of Chengdu and 100km west of Chongqing, sleepy **Dazu town** is the base for viewing some fifty thousand Tang- and Song-dynasty **Buddhist cliff sculptures**, which are carved into caves and overhangs in the surrounding lush green hills – most notably at **Baoding Shan**. What makes these carvings so special is not their scale – they cover very small areas compared with better-known sites at Luoyang or Dunhuang – but their quality, state of preservation and variety of subject and style. Some are small, others huge, many are brightly painted and form comic-strip-like narratives, their characters portraying religious, moral and historical tales. While most are set fairly deeply into rock faces or are protected by galleries, all can be viewed in natural light, and are connected by walkways and paths.

12

Baoding Shan

宝顶山, bǎodǐng shān • Daily 8.30am–5pm • ¥135 • Bus #205 from over the road from the old bus station on Linguan Lu (and also stopping on Longzhong Lu) in Dazu every 30min 8am–4pm (30min; ¥3); on the return, it also stops at the south of Longzhong Lu by the new bus station; minibus from ticket office to the mountain ¥5

The carvings at **Baoding Shan**, 16km to the northeast of Dazu town, are exciting, comic and realistic by turns. The project was the life work of the monk **Zhao Zhifeng**, who raised the money and designed and oversaw the carving between 1179 and 1245, explaining the unusually cohesive nature of the ten thousand images depicted here.

The bus drops you about 500m from the Tourist Reception Centre, from where you can walk or take a minibus 2km to the main site, **Dafowan**, whose 31 niches are naturally incorporated into the inner side of a broad, horseshoe-shaped gully. As every centimetre is carved with scenes illustrating Buddhist and Confucian moral tales, intercut with asides on daily life, you could spend an hour walking the circuit here, though it's only around 700m long. Don't miss the fearsome 6m-high sculpture of a demon holding the segmented **Wheel of Predestination** (look for the faint relief near his ankles of a cat stalking a mouse); or the Dabei Pavilion, housing a magnificent gilded **Guanyin**, whose 1007 arms flicker out behind her like flames.

Further around, a 20m-long **Reclining Buddha** features some realistic portraits of important donors, while the **Eighteen Layers of Hell** is a chamber-of-horrors scene interspersed with amusing cameos such as the Hen Wife and the Drunkard and His Mother. The final panel, illustrating the **Life of Liu Benzun**, a Tang-dynasty ascetic from Leshan, is a complete break from the rest, with the hermit surrounded by multifaced Tantric figures, showing a very Indian influence. The bus stop for the return journey to Dazu is just after the noodle stands outside the exit.

ARRIVAL AND DEPARTURE   DAZU

By bus Dazu has two bus stations. The old station (老站, lǎozhàn), in the south of the town on Linguan Lu, handles Chongqing traffic; while the new station (新站, xīnzhàn), on Nanhuan Lu 1km further south, is where to

catch services to Chengdu.
Destinations Chengdu (10 daily; 4hr); Chongqing (16 daily; 2hr 30min); Leshan (daily 8.10am; 3hr); Yibin (daily 8.30 & 9am; 3hr); Zigong (4 daily; 2hr).

ACCOMMODATION

Fragrant Begonia 海棠香酒店, Hǎitáng xiāng jiǔdiàn. 35–37 Nanhuan Lu ☎023 43735555. About the best you'll find in town, and literally round the corner from the bus stop to Baoding Shan and the old bus station, it's a standard mid-ranger, and although a wee bit worn, the rooms are certainly clean and the beds

pretty comfy – prices are negotiable. **¥188**
Jinye 金叶宾馆, jīnyè bīnguǎn. 18 Longzhong Lu ☎023 43775566. A decent, inexpensive option that is central to the town, but a good 15min walk from the bus station. Although the rooms are large, the beds are hard and bathrooms fairly basic. **¥138**

EATING

For food, there are plenty of hotpot restaurants and cheap canteens around the bus stations and along the main street of Longzhong Lu, at the north end of which is the cental park that is surrounded by the town's nightlife zone of restaurants, bars and KTVs. If you have a hankering for Western food, try the shopping mall (and cinema) at the corner of Longzhong Lu and Longgang Lu (the main pedestrian street), where you can be disappointed by the overpriced pizza and steak restaurants, and a *KFC*.

Chongqing and around

重庆, chóngqìng

Based around a hilly, comma-shaped peninsula at the junction of the Yangzi and Jialing rivers, **CHONGQING** is southwestern China's dynamo, its largest city both in scale and population. Formerly part of Sichuan province and now the heavily industrialized core of **Chongqing Municipality**, which stretches 300km east to the Hubei border, the city is also a busy port, whose location 2400km upstream from Shanghai at the gateway

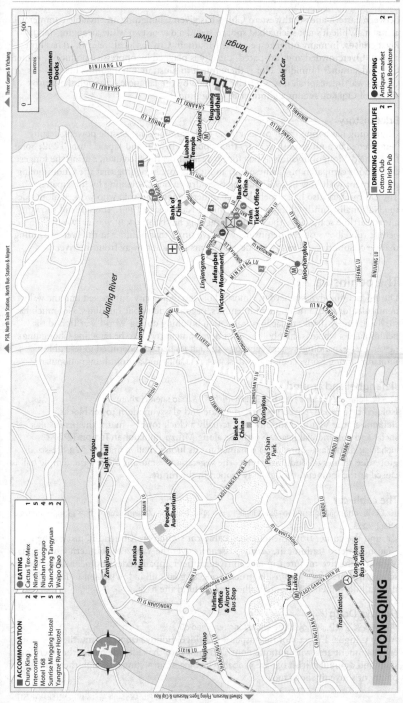

▲ Three Gorges & Yichang

▲ PSB, North Train Station, North Bus Station & Airport

Chaotianmen Docks

BINJIANG LU

Yangzi River

Cable Car

Huguang Guildhall

SHAANXI LU

XINHUA LU

SHAANXI LU

Xiaoshenzi

Ⓜ

Luohan Temple

WUYI LU

Bank of China

Bank of China

JIEFANG BEI LU

XINHUA LU

JIEFANG BEI LU

Train Ticket Office

DOUFU LU

MINQUAN LU

ZOURONG LU

MINSHENG LU

BINJIANG LU

Ⓜ **Jiaochangkou**

JIEFANG BEI LU

Linjiangmen

Jiefangbei (Victory Monument)

BEIQU LU

HUAYLU LU

ZHONG XING LU

HEPING LU

ZHONGXING LU

Jialing River

Huanghuayuan

Doxigou

Light Rail

BEIQU LU

ZHONGSHAN YI LU

DASIXIANG LU

Ⓜ **Qixinggou**

Bank of China

Pipa Shan Park

MANVU LU

NANQU LU

NANQU LU

BINJIANG LU

Zengjiayan

RENHE JIE

RENMIN LU

GANXIA XIAN JIE

ZONGSHAN SAN LU

People's Auditorium

Sanxia Museum

RENMIN LU

Airlines Office & Airport Bus Stop

ZHONGSHAN SAN LU

ZHONGSHAN ER LU

Liang Lukou
Ⓜ

CHANGJIANG YI LU GANXIA XHEN JIE

ZHONGSHAN SI LU

ZHONGSHAN ER LU

Niujiaotuo

SIXIN LU

SHANGQINGSI LU

Long-distance Bus Station

CHANGJIANG ER LU

Train Station

CHANGJIANG YI LU

CHANGJIANG ER LU

CHONGQING

▼ Stilwell Museum, Flying Tigers Museum & Ciqi Kou

N

0 — 500 metres

12

between eastern and southwestern China has given Chongqing an enviable commercial acumen. While it's not such a bad spot to spend a day or two while arranging **Yangzi River cruises**, in many other respects the Mountain City (as locals refer to it) has little appeal. Overcrowded and fast-paced, the city is plagued by oppressive pollution, winter fogs and summer humidity. Nor is there much to illustrate Chongqing's history – as China's wartime capital, it was heavily bombed by the Japanese – though the nearby village of **Ciqi Kou** retains a glimmer of Qing times.

Brief history

Chongqing has a long tradition as a place of defiance against hostile powers, despite being ceded as a nineteenth-century **treaty port** to Britain and Japan. From 1242, Song forces held Mongol invaders at bay for 36 years at nearby Hechuan, during the longest continuous campaign on Chinese soil, and it was to Chongqing that the Guomindang government withdrew in 1937, having been driven out of Nanjing by the Japanese. The US military also had a toehold here under **General Stilwell**, who worked alongside the Nationalists until falling out with Chiang Kai-shek in 1944. Though still showing a few wartime scars, since the 1990s Chongqing has boomed; now over two million people rub elbows on the peninsula, with five times that number in the ever-expanding mantle of suburbs and industrial developments spreading away from the river.

The peninsula

12

During its Qing-dynasty heyday, almost all of Chongqing city was packed into the walled **peninsula**, forming a rich port with temples, pagodas and public buildings. Not much has survived, largely thanks to Japanese saturation bombing during World War II, and the peninsula as a whole is shambolic – most development seems to be targeting Chongqing's newer, ever-expanding western suburbs – though it's being modernized to resemble a miniature Hong Kong, complete with skyscrapers, hills and a profit-hungry populace.

Jiefangbei and around

解放碑, jiěfàngbēi • Metro line #1 to Xiaoshizi station (小什字站, xiǎo shén zì zhàn)

Isolated by a broad, paved pedestrian square and glassy modern tower blocks, **Jiefangbei**, the Victory Monument – actually a clock tower – marks the peninsula's social and commercial heart. Northeast along Minzu Lu, **Luohan Temple** (罗汉寺, luóhàn sì; daily 8am–6pm; ¥10) is named for its **luohan hall**, a maze of 524 life-sized, grotesque statues of Buddhist saints. The vegetarian restaurant behind the temple hall is closed at the moment, though may reopen in the future.

The cable car

长江索道, chángjiāng suǒdào • Daily 8.30am–10pm • ¥10 • Metro line #1 to Xiaoshizi station (小什字站, xiǎo shén zì zhàn), exit 5B

Around the corner from the temple, a **cable-car station** on Xinhua Lu, just by the Xiaoshizi metro station exit, carries passengers over the Yangzi to southern Chongqing. Views on the five-minute trip take in river traffic, rampant redevelopment along the southern shore of the peninsula, trucks collecting landfill in low-season mud, and distant hills – merely faint grey silhouettes behind the haze.

Hongya Dong

洪崖洞传统风貌区, hóngyádòng chuántǒng fēngmào qū

Along Cangbai Lu, west of the suspension bridge, **Hongya Dong** is a multilevel entertainment area with antique flourishes built into the cliff-side facing the river; food stalls and a popular Irish bar are probably its biggest attractions, though there are plenty of souvenir shops too.

OPPOSITE PUXIAN STATUE AT SUMMIT, EMEI SHAN (P.751) >

Chaotianmen

朝天门码头, cháotiānmén mǎtóu • Metro line #1 to Chaotianmen station (朝天门站, cháotiān mén zhàn)

To spy on more waterfront activity, head down to **Chaotianmen docks**, a five-minute walk downhill from the Luohan Temple along Xinhua Lu. The paved **viewing area** on the high bank overlooking the tip of the peninsula makes a great perch to look down on Yangzi ferries and barges moored along the river.

Huguang Guildhall

湖广会馆, húguǎng huìguǎn • Daily 9am–5pm • ¥30 • Metro line #1 to Xiaoshizi station (小什字站, xiǎo shén zì zhàn) then walk 300m down Datong Jie

The **Huguang Guildhall**, uphill in the backstreets off Binjiang Lu, was built in 1759 as a hotel and meeting point for merchants from Jiangxi, Hunan and Hubei. Surrounded by a high, warm yellow wall, the complex comprises a dozen or more halls, atriums, ornate gateways and florid roof designs, now converted into a museum of Qing-dynasty trade. Cross the road in front and walk down to the river, and you pass through a surviving fragment of Chongqing's **old city wall**, via a heavy stone gateway and staircase.

Sanxia Museum

三峡博物馆, sānxiá bówùguǎn • Tues–Sun 9am–5pm • Free • Zengjiayan metro station

Facing the vast People's Auditorium, the **Sanxia Museum** commemorates Chongqing's regional history over four floors. Picks here include the Three Gorges Hall, with beautifully arranged dioramas of gorge scenery and a range of archeological finds; the Ba-Yu Hall, which covers everything from pre-human fossils to a marvellous array of Eastern Han tomb bricks; and the Li Chunli Hall, a donated collection of exquisite antique porcelain and paintings.

West along the Jialing River

Two worthwhile sights lie west of Chongqing's peninsula along a 12km strip of the Jialing River: the wartime US command centre at the **Stilwell Museum**, and antique streets at the one-time port town of **Ciqi Kou**. Both can be tied into a single trip using the light rail and city buses, but give yourself enough time – it can take well over an hour to get to Ciqi Kou from the centre.

The Stilwell Museum

史迪威将军博物馆, shǐdíwēi jiāngjūn bówùguǎ • Jialingxin Lu • Daily 9am–5pm • ¥15 • Metro line #2 to Fotuguan station (佛图关站, fótúguān zhàn), then walk 250m downhill to the museum

The **Stilwell Museum** occupies the former home of General Joseph Stilwell, Chief Commander of the US forces' China, Burma and India operations from 1942 until 1944. Stilwell had served as a military attaché in China during the 1930s, and during the war had to coordinate the recapture of Burma and the re-establishment of overland supply lines into China from India. He was also caught up in keeping the shaky Nationalist–Communist alliance together, and his insistence that equal consideration be given to both the Guomindang and CCP caused him to fall out with Chiang Kai-shek. The modernist 1930s building has been decked out in period furniture, with informative photo displays charting Stilwell's career.

Flying Tigers Museum

飞虎队展览馆, fēihǔduì zhǎnlǎnguǎn • March–Oct only • ¥10 • Metro line #2 to Fotuguan station (佛图关站, fótúguān zhàn), then walk 250m downhill to the museum

Directly opposite the Stilwell Museum, the little **Flying Tigers Museum** is dedicated to the "American Volunteer Group of the Chinese Air Force", better known as the Flying Tigers, which formed under General Chennault in 1941 to protect supply flights over the "hump" of the Himalayas between Burma and China. There are maps and photos of pilots and their P-40 Tomahawk fighter planes painted with tigers' eyes and teeth, and the rear of the building has been turned into a pricey gallery selling contemporary Chinese paintings.

Ciqi Kou

磁器口, cíqì kǒu • Metro line #1 to Ciqikou station (磁器口站, cíqì kǒu zhàn)

Though well within the modern city's boundaries, **Ciqi Kou**, a former porcelain production centre and port, incredibly retains a handful of flagstoned, one-hundred-year-old streets and wooden buildings. At weekends and holidays the place reaches critical mass with visitors; try to come midweek. Near the entrance, **Zhongjia Yuan** (¥4) is an old courtyard house, worth a quick browse for its antique furniture, clothing and carvings in each room. Then you're into Ciqi Kou's crowded alleys and lanes, thronged with touristy crafts shops (selling embroideries and romantic paintings of Ciqi Kou), old-style teahouses featuring traditional music recitals, snack stalls and small restaurants. On sunny days, many people head down to the river, where there's a beach of sorts and thousands of deckchairs.

ARRIVAL AND DEPARTURE   CHONGQING

BY PLANE

Chongqing Jiangbei International airport (重庆江北飞机场, chóngqìng jiāngběi fēijīchǎng) is 20km northeast of Chongqing, connected to the city by metro (¥7), by shuttle bus to the airline offices on Shangqingsi Lu (40min; ¥15), and taxi (40min; around ¥85). Terminal 1 is for international flights (including Seoul, Bangkok, Da Nang, London, Helsinki, Rome and Phnom Penh) while terminal 2 handles domestic flights to over a hundred destinations.

BY TRAIN

Chongqing train station (重庆火车站, chóngqìng huǒchēzhàn), located on the south side of the peninsula, has regular train services to Kunming, Guiyang, Xi'an, Beijing, Shanghai and beyond. Bus #503, #120 or #68 will get you to Chaotianmen at the peninsula's tip.

Destinations Beijing (7 daily; 19hr–31hr 18min); Chengdu (6 daily; 3hr–4hr 48min); Guangzhou (9 daily; 21hr 38min–31hr); Guiyang (currently suspended; 9–11hr); Shanghai (3 daily; 19hr 26min–28hr 45min); Wuhan (8 daily; 8–18hr 27min); Xi'an (7 daily; 9hr 16min–10hr 30min).

North train station (重庆火车北站, chóngqìng huǒchē běizhàn), 5km north of the peninsula, is the terminal for high-speed trains, as well as a handful of regular services. From here catch bus #141 to Chaotianmen bus station or hop on the metro towards Jiefangbei.

CRH destinations Beijing (9 daily; 12hr); Chengdu (45 daily; 1hr 27min–2hr 30min); Guangzhou (3 daily; 11hr

38min–11hr 56min); Shanghai (5 daily; 12hr 30min–13hr); Wuhan (29 daily; 6hr 9min–7hr 35min).

BY BUS

Chongqing has four main bus stations and a multitude of smaller ones, all of which confusingly serve the same destinations as others. All the major bus stations are some way out of the centre (30–40min) except the long-distance bus station, so below are listed only the services from there. Ask at your accommodation about services from other stations. Note that the Yibin bus leaves from the bus stand across the road.

Main long-distance bus station (重庆长途汽车站, chóngqìng chángtú qìchēzhàn) is on a complex traffic flow near river level at the western end of the peninsula. There are services from here to cities all over Chongqing, Sichuan and the rest of China as well as Changning (for the Shunan Bamboo Sea) and beyond; it's a frenetic place but buying tickets is easy enough.

Destinations Changning (3 daily; 4hr); Chengdu (4 daily; 4hr); Dazu (4 daily, 12.40–9pm; 1hr 30min); Emei Shan (daily 9am & 11am; 6hr 30min); Langzhong (4 daily; 5hr); Leshan (6 daily; 6hr); Yibin (every 30min; 3hr 30min); Zigong (every 30–40min; 3hr).

BY BOAT

Cruise boats With the demise of the public ferries, cruise boats and luxury cruise boats are the only way to now get down the river from Chongqing (see box, p.769).

GETTING AROUND

By bus City buses (¥1–2) are comprehensive if slow, and, with the growth of the metro, only necessary if venturing beyond central Chongqing.

By metro Chongqing's nippy metro network covers virtually all the sights in the city centre, with its four lines running along the north side of the peninsula and through the middle. Trains run every 6min (7am–7pm) and cost ¥2–7 a

ride, depending on distance; finding stations can be tricky, though, as they're often not well marked or signposted.

By taxi Taxis cost ¥10 to hire and, while drivers aren't too unscrupulous, it won't hurt to be seen studying a map along the way.

By bicycle Chongqing's gradients and horrendous road interchanges mean that nobody uses bicycles.

12

ACCOMMODATION

Given that the ferry is the main reason to come to Chongqing, it makes sense to stay near the dock up in the peninsula's eastern end around Jiefangbei and Chaotianmen. There are plenty of chain motels near the stations.

Chung King 重庆饭店, chóngqìng fàndiàn. 41–43 Xinhua Lu ☏023 63916666. Art Deco building with rooms that are the standard urban Chinese model, comfy enough and currently under renovation to make them equal to the better (more expensive) ones at its more modern and less charismatic sister hotel, the *Shengming* next door. **¥268**

Intercontinental 重庆洲际酒店, chóngqìng zhōujì jiǔdiàn. 101 Minzu Lu ☏023 89066888, ⓦintercontinental.com. Business hotel with good-sized, extremely well turned out rooms, coolly professional service, and a lobby café with piano and cream cakes. As well as the gym, spa and swimming pool it also has a Western restaurant with a buffet (also open for non-guests) for lunch (¥160) and dinner (¥230). **¥940**

Motel 168 莫泰连锁旅店, mòtài liánsuǒ lǚdiàn. 52 Cangbai Lu ☏0236 3849999, ⓦmotel168.com. The usual friendly deal with spacious rooms at lowish rates, though cheapest rooms are subterranean and only the pricier ones have windows. If the *168* doesn't grab

you, try the slightly pricier *Home Inn* in the same building. **¥190**

Sunrise Mingqing Hostel 尚悦明清客楼, shàngyuè míngqīng kèlóu. 23 Xiahongxue Xiang ☏0236 3931 579, ⓦcqsunrisemingqing.hostel.com. Hidden at the top of the stairs on the west side of the Huguang Guildhall, this hostel in an atmospheric, 200-year-old courtyard building has a great deal of charm. The rooms are comfortable and clean, if a little dark, and staff can help with the usual tours and travel advice. Dorms **¥45**, doubles **¥168**

Yangtze River Hostel 玺院国际青年旅舍, xǐyuàn guójì qīngnián lǚshè. 80 Changbin Lu ☏0236 3104208, ⓦchongqinghostels.com. Faux-antique building on the main waterfront road. Has a bar which also serves very nice food, and all the usual facilities. Rooms are on the small side but comfortable enough and the location is good. Staff are helpful with information and tours. Ten percent discount with WeChat. Dorms **¥50**, doubles **¥160**

EATING

Chongqing's centre is alive with canteens and food stalls, and at meal times already busy side-streets and markets become obstacle courses of plastic chairs, low tables and wok-wielding cooks. Local tastes lean towards snacks; a local speciality is the use of puréed raw garlic as a dressing, which only the Sichuanese could get away with. Hotpot is believed to have originated here, with the basic ingredients arriving on plates, not skewers, so the pots are divided up into compartments to prevent everyone's portions getting mixed up. For a wide range of light meals and snacks, head to Hongya Dong on Cangbai Lu (see p.762); café chains such as *Shangdao* are your best bet for non-Sichuanese food. Chongqing Beer is the local brew, served in squat, brown-glass bottles.

Cactus Tex-Mex 小天鹅火锅城, xiǎo tiān'é huǒguō chéng. 9F Hongya Dong, Cangbai Lu ☏139 83873702. A taste of home for Yanks, this bar-restaurant is owned by the same people as the *Harp Irish Pub*, and serves good Tex-Mex as well as burgers, steaks and salads (¥60–80) with a good range of beers including Samuel Adams and Guinness. Daily 11am–11pm.

Ninth Heaven 九重天饭店, jiǔchóngtiān fàndiàn. 29F, Yudu Hotel, 168 Bayi Lu ☏023 63830383. The Sichuanese food from the photo menu here is competent and tasty, if a little expensive – try the "rabbit threads" (¥48) in cut buns and mountain mushrooms with cold bamboo shoots – but the bonus is that the restaurant revolves, with the city looking its best after dark. Count on ¥100–150 for two people. Daily 7.30am–midnight.

Niushan Huoguo 牛山火锅, niúshān huǒguō. 248 Wuyi Lu. One of the last of the fast-and-furious

hotpot shacks that once lined this street, where you bump elbows with your fellow diners while dipping skewers into boiling hot, chilli-laced oil. Looks downmarket but expect to pay ¥70–80 per person. Daily 11am–10pm.

Shancheng Tangyuan 山城汤圆, shānchéng tāngyuán. 175 Bayi Lu. In two holes in the wall on Bayi Lu, these tiny establishments are famed city-wide for their inexpensive glutinous rice dumplings, noodles and buns, for ¥5–12/serving. Daily 9am–8pm.

★**Waipo Qiao** 外婆桥, wàipó qiáo. 7F Metropolitan Tower, 68 Zourong Lu ☏0236 3835988. On top of one of the city's swishest shopping malls, this excellent restaurant has three separate rooms, an inexpensive one for snacks, one for hotpot (with the ingredients floated past you in little boats) and a smart one for proper dining. They're all good and have bilingual photo menus. ¥30–150/person. Daily 11am–10pm.

12

DRINKING AND NIGHTLIFE

Chongqing's nightlife has grown, and drinking holes and nightclubs have spread throughout the town centre. As with elsewhere, places often open and close pretty quickly, so for the latest listings and what's on visit ⊚ cqexpat.com.

Cotton Club 棉花酒乐吧, huājiǔ lèba. In the slightly seedy entertainment complex opposite the Ritz-Carlton ☎ 023 63810028. A reliable nightspot which has been going for years. Drinks are pricey with bottles of beer ¥40 and up (¥50–60 for imported draught beers), but there are four house bands playing nightly, and the boss is an interesting and informative character (and every inch a classical Chinese club hostess). Daily 7pm–very late.

Harp Irish Pub 9F Hongya Dong, Cangbai Lu ☎ 139 83873702, ⊚ harpcq.com. A standard, but popular Irish bar with friendly clientele, drinks from ¥30, showing big-screen sports including English Premier League. Also has a terrace outside overlooking the river and owns the *Cactus Tex-Mex*, two doors down (you can order in). Daily 4pm–late.

SHOPPING

Antiques market 收藏品市场, shōuzángpǐn shìchǎng. 75 Zhongxin Lu. Best market for a mooch: try inside what looks like an abandoned 1960s department store where there are four floors of wooden screens, Mao-era mementos, comics, pottery and ceramics. Daily 10am–6pm.

Xinhua Bookstore 新华书店, xīnhuá shūdiàn. 121 Zourong Lu, just west of Jiefangbei. Huge bookstore with Chinese-language maps and guides on the first floor, and a small stock of English-language titles on the fourth floor. Daily 9.30am–9.30pm.

DIRECTORY

Consulates UK, Suite 28, Metropolitan Tower, 68 Zourong Lu (☎ 023 63691500); Cambodia, 10F, #1902, Building A, No 9, Yang He Road, Jiang Bei District (☎ 023 89116416); Canada, Suite 1705, Metropolitan Tower, Wuyi Lu (☎ 023 63738007); Denmark, Metropolitan Tower, 31/F, 68 Zourong Road (☎ 023 63726600).
Medical Global Doctor International Clinic, Room 701

Business Tower, *Hilton Chongqing*, 139 Zhongshan San Lu (☎ 023 89038837, ⊚ www.globaldoctor.com.au).
Visa extensions The PSB is a long way north of the centre at 555 Huanglong Lu, Yubei District (☎ 023 63961944), and its reputation for granting visa extensions is not good – best go elsewhere if possible.

12

Wulong

武隆, wǔlóng

Some 250km southeast of Chongqing along the Guizhou border, **Wulong** is a national park enclosing a massive, rugged area of limestone sinkholes, caves and river systems. The place to aim for at present is **Natural Three Bridges** (天生三桥, tiānshēng sān qiáo; daily 8am–7pm; entry, including transport inside the park, Nov–March ¥95; April–Oct ¥135), about thirty minutes away. Once inside the park, buses drop you off at a two-hour circuit walk through a system of colossal, collapsed tunnels and caves; the Tang-style buildings at the bottom of one sinkhole are sets from Zhang Yimou's period bodice-ripper *Curse of the Golden Flower*.

ARRIVAL AND GETTING AROUND

WULONG

By train The access point for Wulong national park is little Wulong town (武隆县, wǔlóng xiàn), on the Chongqing–Huai Hua rail line with regular services to and from Chongqing.
Destinations Chongqing (7 daily; 2hr 22min–5hr 22min).
By bus Wulong's Chaotianmen bus station is on Baiyang

Lu. Buses to Chongqing run 7.30am–6.30pm.
Destinations Chongqing (every 30min; 2hr).
Getting around Minibuses from Wulong town (¥20) run north into the national park headquarters every half-hour through the day; buses from the park headquarters carry you to various locations inside.

ACCOMMODATION

Aside from the following, touts around the bus and train stations can lead you to cheaper places.

Hongfu Fandian 宏福饭店, hóngfú fàndiàn. Wulong town, on the corner of main street Wuxian Lu and Baiyang Lu ☎ 023 64501666. Modern, impressively ugly edifice

offering clean, sparsely furnished en-suite rooms with a/c. Despite its aesthetic shortcomings, the rooms inside are a decent size, if a bit gloomy, and they have a restaurant. **¥258**

The Yangzi River: Chongqing to Yichang

Rising in the mountains above Tibet, the **Yangzi** links together seven provinces as it sweeps 6400km across the country to spill its muddy waters into the East China Sea, making it the third-longest flow in the world. Appropriately, one of the Yangzi's Chinese names is **Chang Jiang**, the Long River, though above Yibin it's generally known as **Jinsha Jiang** (River of Golden Sands).

Although people have travelled along the Yangzi since recorded history, it was not, until recently, an easy route to follow. The river's most dangerous stretch was the 200km-long **Three Gorges** (三峡, sānxiá) where the waters were squeezed between vertical limestone cliffs over fierce rapids: well into the twentieth century, nobody could negotiate this stretch of river alone; boats had to be hauled literally bit by bit through the rapids by teams of **trackers**, in a journey that could take several weeks, if the boat made it at all.

All this is very much academic today, however, as the **Three Gorges Dam** above Yichang (see p.421) has raised water levels through the gorges by up to 175m, effectively turning the Chongqing–Yichang stretch into a huge lake and allowing **cruise boats** easy access to the scenery. While rising waters have submerged some of the landscape – not to mention entire towns – many settlements and historical sites have been relocated in the interests of preservation and much of the scenery retains its grandeur.

Chongqing to Wanzhou

The cruise's initial 250km, before the first of the Three Gorges begins at Baidicheng, takes in hilly farmland along the river banks, with the first likely stop 172km from Chongqing at south-bank **FENGDU** (丰都, fēngdū), the "Ghost City". On the opposite side of the Yangzi, **Ming Shan Park** (名山公园, míngshān gōngyuán; ¥80) is a hillside covered in monuments to Tianzi, King of the Dead; the main temple here, **Tianzi Dian** (天子殿, tiānzǐ diàn), is crammed full of colourful demon statues and stern-faced judges of hell.

Shibaozhai

石宝寨, shíbǎozhài · Daily 8am–5pm · ¥50

A further 70km along the Yangzi from Fengdu, **Shibaozhai** is a 220m-high rocky buttress a few kilometres downstream from Zhongxian county town. Grafted onto its side – and protected from new water levels by an embankment – is the twelve-storey, bright-red **Lanruo Dian** (兰若殿, lánruò diàn), a pagoda built in 1819. The temple above dates to 1750, famed for a hole in its granary wall through which poured just enough rice to feed the monks; greedily, they tried to enlarge it, and the frugal supply stopped forever.

The Three Gorges

The **Three Gorges** themselves begin 450km from Chongqing 18km past **FENGJIE** (奉节, fèngjié) at **Baidi Cheng** (白帝城, báidì chéng), a fortified island strategically located right at the mouth of the first gorge. Baidi Cheng is closely associated with events of the *Romance of the Three Kingdoms* (see box, p.396); it was here in 265 AD that **Liu Bei** died after failing to avenge his sworn brother Guan Yu in the war against Wu. These events are recalled at the **Baidi temple** (白帝庙, báidì miào; ¥70), where there's a waxworks tableau of Liu Bei on his deathbed, and paths up to lookout points into the narrow, vertical-sided Qutang Gorge.

Qutang Gorge

瞿塘峡, qútáng xiá

Beyond Baidi Cheng, the river pours through a narrow slash in the cliffs and into **Qutang Gorge**, the shortest at just 8km long, but also the narrowest and fiercest, its once-angry waters described by the Song poet Su Dongpo as "a thousand seas in one

CRUISING THE YANGZI

Chongqing is the departure point for the two-day cruise downriver through the **Three Gorges** to Yichang. There are two main **cruise options** for those on a budget, both of which run year-round. The best option is the four-day/three-night **foreign tourist cruises** that leave daily from the wharves in Chongqing, have English-speaking staff and guides, and cost ¥2350–2950 depending on which cabin you share. The second, slightly cheaper, option is the **Chinese tourist cruises**, which cost from ¥1110 for a six-bed dorm to ¥1350 for a shared twin-cabin, though of course they are usually a lot rowdier than the former. Both of these cruises can be easily booked through your accommodation in Chongqing (or indeed an agent anywhere in China), or if you speak Chinese at one of the many booking offices opposite the wharves on Chong Bin Lu.

If you're not on a budget, you can book a berth on one of the **luxury international cruises**, which is probably best done through an agent in your own country, with prices starting at around ¥3000. These cruise boats are graded from one-star to five-star, and to enjoy your time, relax and have good meals, it is suggested you sail on a four- or five-star river cruiser.

cup". The vertical cliffs, rising to a sharp peak on the north bank, are still impressive despite the new water levels.

Little Three Gorges

小三峡, xiǎo sānxiá • Cruise from Wushan in a modern, glass-topped canal boat ¥300

On the far side of Qutang, **WUSHAN** (巫山, wūshān) marks a half-day detour north up the Daning River through the **Little Three Gorges**. This 33km excursion offers narrower, tighter and steeper scenery than along the Yangzi, particularly through the awesome **Longmen Gorge**.

Wu Gorge

巫峡, wūxiá

Wushan also sits at the mouth of 45km-long **Wu Gorge**, where the goddess **Yao Ji** and her eleven sisters quelled some unruly river dragons and then turned themselves into mountains, thoughtfully positioned to help guide ships downriver.

Zigui and Xiling Gorge

Out the other side of Wu Gorge and in Hubei province, **ZIGUI** (秭归, zǐguī) was the birthplace of the poet **Qu Yuan**, whose suicide a couple of millennia ago is commemorated throughout China by dragon-boat races. Zigui is also where 76km-long **Xiling Gorge** (西陵峡, xīlíng xiá) begins. The Xiling stretch was once the most dangerous: Westerners passing through in the nineteenth century described the shoals as forming weirs across the river, the boat fended away from threatening rocks by trackers armed with iron-shod bamboo poles, as it rocked through into the sunless, narrow chasm. Nowadays vessels cruise through with ease, sailing on to a number of smaller gorges, some with splendid names – Sword and Book, Ox Liver and Horse Lung – suggested by the rock formations.

The Three Gorges Dam and Yichang

At the eastern end of the gorges, cruises terminate at the monstrous **Three Gorges Dam** (三峡坝, sānxiá bà), from where there are minibus tours of the dam site and buses onwards to Yichang, 30km downstream (see p.421).

Western Sichuan

Sichuan's western half, sprawling towards Gansu, Yunnan and Tibet, is in every respect an exciting place to travel. The countryside couldn't be farther from the Chengdu plains, with the western highlands forming some of China's most imposing scenery – broad grasslands grazed by yaks and horses, ravens tumbling over snowbound gullies and passes, and unforgettable views of mountain ranges rising up against crisp blue skies.

How you explore western Sichuan will depend on your long-term travel plans. If you're heading north out of the province **to Gansu**, you first want to aim for the walled town of **Songpan**, horse-trekking centre and base for excursions to the nearby scenic reserves of **Huanglong** and **Jiuzhaigou**. Beyond Songpan, the road continues north via the monastery town of **Langmusi**, and so over into Gansu province.

Sichuan's immense **far west** is reached from the administrative capital **Kangding** – itself worth a stopover for easy access to the nearby scenery, or as a springboard north to pretty **Danba**. Alternatively, you can either weave northwest to Tibet via the monastery towns of **Ganzi** and **Dêgê**, with a faith-inducing mountain pass and Dêgê's Scripture Printing Hall as the pick of the sights along the way; or head due west to the high-altitude monastic seat of **Litang**, from where you can continue down into Yunnan.

Brief history

Though larger towns throughout the west have to a certain extent been settled by Han and Hui (Muslims) – the latter spread between their major populations in adjoining provinces – historically the region was not part of Sichuan at all but was known as **Kham**, a set of small states which spilled into the fringes of Qinghai and Yunnan. The Tibetans who live here, the **Khampas**, speak their own dialect, and see themselves as distinct from Tibetans further west – it wasn't until the seventeenth century, during the aggressive rule of the Fifth Dalai Lama, that monasteries here were forcibly converted to the dominant Gelugpa sect and the people brought under Lhasa's thumb. The Khampas retain their tough, independent reputation today, and culturally the region remains emphatically Tibetan, containing not only some of the country's most important lamaseries, but also an overwhelmingly Tibetan population – indeed, statistically a far greater percentage than in Tibet proper.

Songpan

松潘, sōngpān

SONGPAN, 320km north of Chengdu, was founded in Qing times as a garrison town straddling both the Min River and the main road to Gansu. Strategically, it guards the neck of a valley, built up against a stony ridge to the west and surrounded on the remaining three sides by 8m-high stone **walls**. These have been partially restored, and you can walk between the north and east gates and above the south gate. Though increasingly touristed, Songpan's **shops**, stocked with handmade woollen blankets, fur-lined jackets, ornate knives, saddles, stirrups, bridles and all sorts of jewellery, cater to local Tibetans and **Qiang**, another mountain-dwelling minority. In spring, Songpan – along with every town in western Sichuan – becomes a marketplace for **caterpillar fungus** (虫草, chóngcǎo), a peculiarly popular product (see box, p.807).

GETTING AROUND WESTERN SICHUAN

Travel in western Sichuan requires stamina: journey times between towns are long, roads twist interminably, breakdowns are far from uncommon, and landslides, ice or heavy snow can block roads for days at a time. However, a major road-building programme has been under way for some time, affecting almost all main routes through the region. Many highways feature a seemingly endless alternation of enormous bridges and lengthy tunnels, which has massively reduced journey times; this, however, has led to a great increase in tourist traffic, especially during the summer. Traffic jams are now fairly common, especially on the main G318 that runs from Chengdu, through Garzê and Kanding, then up to Litang; and the G317 that heads up from the Aba grasslands at Wenchuan (on the road to Songpan northwest of Chengdu) and up to Ganzi and Dêgê; both continue to the Tibetan border. If you're not short of cash, you can also use one of the several new or nearly completed **airports** in the region, including three of the four highest civilian airports in the world, all of which connect with Chengdu. These are Kanding, Ganzi (at Dêgê) and Daocheng, which at 4411m is the highest in the world.

Almost all of western Sichuan rises above 2500m – one pass exceeds 5000m – and you'll probably experience the effects of **altitude** (see p.46). You'll need to carry enough **cash** to see you through, as there are no cash machines taking international cards beyond Kangding, and it's better to get it in Chengdu to be on the safe side. **Horse-trekking** is a popular pastime in the region, too, with well-established operations at Songpan, Tagong and Langmusi, and plenty of ad-hoc opportunities elsewhere. As for the **seasons**, the area looks fantastic from spring through to autumn – though warm, weatherproof clothing is essential whatever the time of year. Note that some places in the region (especially near the Tibet border) can be **closed to foreigners through March**, anniversary of various uprisings in Tibet – check in Chengdu before heading off.

DOG WARNING

Western Sichuan's wild, open countryside makes for good hiking, but you need to beware of **dogs**. Some of these are just the scrawny mongrels that roam around all Tibetan settlements, including monasteries; carry a pocketful of stones and a good stick, and you should be fine. Guard dogs, however, you need to keep well clear of: you don't want an encounter with a Tibetan mastiff. These are kept chained up as a rule, but don't go near isolated houses or, especially, nomad tents without calling out so that people know you're there and will check that their dogs are secure.

Inside the walls

Songpan itself forms a small, easily navigated rectangle: the main road, partially pedestrianized, runs for about 750m from the **north gate** (北门, běimén) straight down to the **south gate** (南门, nánmén) – both mighty stone constructions topped with brightly painted wooden pavilions. Around two-thirds of the way down, covered **Gusong Bridge** (古松桥, gǔsōng qiáo) has a roof embellished with painted dragon, bear and flower carvings. Side roads head off to the **east gate** (东大门, dōng dàmén) – another monumental construction – and west into a small grid of market lanes surrounding the town's main **mosque** (古清真寺, gǔ qīngzhēn sì), an antique wooden affair painted in subdued yellows and greens, catering to the substantial Muslim population (there's another mosque north of town). Just outside the south gate is a **second gateway**, with what would originally have been a walled courtyard between the two, where caravans were inspected for dangerous goods before entering the city proper.

ARRIVAL AND DEPARTURE   SONGPAN

Note that a rail line to Songpan is also under construction, though completion dates are unknown. Check in Chengdu about the current situation before booking bus tickets.

By plane Jiuhuang airport (九黄机场, jiǔhuáng jīchǎng) is 30km to the northeast of Songpan, and you'll need to take a taxi into town which costs ¥120–200 depending on how delayed the flight is – at 3448m this is

HORSE-TREKKING AT SONGPAN

The reason to stop in Songpan is to spend a few days **horse-trekking** through the surrounding hills, which harbour hot springs and waterfalls, grassland plateaus and permanently icy mountains. Shunjiang Horse Treks (☎0837 17231161 or ☎0139 09043513), on the main road between the bus station and the north gate, charge ¥220/person per day, including everything except entry fees to reserves. Accommodation is in tents, and the guides are generally attentive, though may not speak much English. Prepare for extreme cold and tasteless food. Note that the friendly veneer of the company's staff disappears rapidly if they're presented with a complaint, so be sure to agree beforehand on exactly what your money is buying, and be aware that local ideas of animal welfare might be radically different to your own.

the world's fourth highest airport so delays are common. Tickets can be bought at travel agencies and hotels in Songpan, or online, though fares are extortionate; it costs around ¥1200 to Chengdu, for example. There's at least one daily flight to Beijing, Chengdu, Chongqing, Guangzhou, Hangzhou, Shijiazhuang, Xi'an and Zhengzhou.

By bus Songpan's bus station is about 250m outside the north gate. For Langmusi, catch the 10am Zöigê bus, and

with luck you'll just make the 2.30pm Zöigê–Langmusi service (2hr).

Destinations Chengdu (daily 6am, 6.30am & 7am; 7–8hr); Huanglong (daily 6am; 2hr); Jiuzhaigou (daily 9am & 1pm; 2hr); Zöigê (daily 10am; 4hr).

By minibus *Emma's Kitchen* can organize shared taxis to various destinations, including Huanglong (¥400–500) and Langmusi (¥1800).

ACCOMMODATION

Room rates can double July to September, when domestic tourism peaks, although the industry is up and down so equally you can pay less if it's not busy if you haggle. There's actually a glut of decent rooms in town since the heavy development of Rewa as the new tour-group dormitory for Huanglong, and it's possible to get a real bargain if you follow one of the many touts.

Emma's Guesthouse 松潘小歐洲青年旅舍, sōngpān xiǎo ōuzhōu qīngnián lǚshě. Reception at Emma's Kitchen ☎0837 7231088, ✉emmachina @hotmail.com. A quiet location down an alley between the bus station and *Emma's Kitchen*, this well-run hostel has simple but immaculately clean rooms and four-person dorms with Western toilets. A bit overpriced for what you get, but you're paying more for the the good English-

speaking service. Dorms ¥68, doubles ¥180

★**Guyun Kezhan** 古韵客栈, gǔyùn kèzhàn. Opposite the bus station ☎0837 17231368. This charming little guesthouse is very handy for the early departures from the bus station and has nicely done traditional wooden galleries around a central atrium. Clean, cosy – some might say small – rooms and 24hr hot water, though nobody speaks English. Dorms ¥40, doubles ¥140

EATING AND DRINKING

Songpan's places to eat revolve around the numerous noodle joints between the north gate and the bus station; *maoniurou gan* (yak jerky) is sold in shops around town; you should also try sweet *qingke jiu*, local barley beer.

★**Emma's Kitchen** South of the bus station, on the main road ☎0837 7231088, ✉emmachina@hotmail .com. Foreigners' café, serving tasty Western food such as sandwiches and burgers (¥22–42), steaks (¥68) and pizzas (¥48–75), local specialities like yak stew (¥58), as well as less expensive regular Chinese options (¥22–48). It doubles as a bar too, serving beers, wine and cocktails as well as excellent espresso coffees. Emma is also the best source of tour and transport information, and can

book onward tickets. Daily 8am–11pm.

Qing Zhen Mei Shi 清真美食, qīngzhēn měishí. 150m south of the bus staion. A large, green-coloured restaurant with a modern, clean interior, this Muslim restaurant serves a wide range of delicious rice and noodle dishes (¥11–22), with a handy picture menu on the wall. They also bake their own bread and do a lamb, doner-like kebab sandwich (¥40). Daily 8am–10pm.

DIRECTORY

Massage There's a blind masseur (¥78/hr) next door to *Emma's* – good if you're stiff after a tour in the saddle. They

also do cupping (¥25) and other treatments.

Huanglong

黄龙, huánglóng • Daily 9am–4pm • April–Oct ¥200; Nov–March ¥60; optional cable car ¥80

Huanglong, a 4km-long glacial valley, lies at an altitude of 3000m in the mountains 60km northeast of Songpan. Limestone-rich waters flowing down the valley have left yellow calcified deposits between hundreds of shallow blue ponds, and their scaly appearance gives Huanglong – "Yellow Dragon" – its name. The reserve here is fairly small and can be walked around in a couple of hours (though the altitude can easily wear you out); note that public transport in and out is limited and you'll want to make sure you know when the last bus is leaving and time your visit accordingly. It's best to arrive at the park before 9am, queue up straight away, and get into the park as soon as it opens: that way you can stay ahead of the crowds; avoid the cable car too, it's like a metro at rush hour.

Around the reserve

An 8km circuit track on well-made boardwalks over the fragile formations ascends east up the valley from the main-road **park gates**, through surprisingly thick deciduous woodland, pine forest and, finally, rhododendron thickets. At the first junction of the path, take the "short route" rather than the "scenic route" as you'll avoid the crowds – the former is used mostly by porters carrying unfeasibly large packs on their backs. Pick of the scenery includes the broad **Golden Flying Waterfall** and the kilometre-long calcified slope **Golden Sand on Earth**, where the shallow flow tinkles over innumerable ridges and pockmarks. Around 3km along, the small **Middle Temple** (中寺, zhōngsì) was once an important centre for **Bon**, Tibet's original religion; today they seem somewhat embarrassed by it, it's mislabelled and largely unmaintained, its doors locked and prayer wheels broken. There's a canteen restaurant opposite.

12

Huanglong Ancient Temple

黄龙古寺, huánglóng gǔsì

At the head of the valley, **Huanglong Ancient Temple** is a Qing building, featuring an atrium and two small Taoist halls, dedicated to the local guardian deity. Here there has been too much maintenance and it feels like you've stepped into a boutique hotel rather than a place of worship. Behind here, a 300m-long valley bowl is filled with multihued blue pools, contrasting brilliantly with the drab olive vegetation; the best views are from the small platforms on the slopes above.

ARRIVAL AND DEPARTURE   HUANGLONG

By bus In theory, buses travelling directly between Songpan and Pingwu can drop you off en route, though in reality this road is seldom used and there is, at best, only one bus a day in each direction, leaving Songpan at 6am, with the return bus going back a bit too late at 3pm – take a taxi (¥100–150) or hitch to Rewa where there are frequent local buses to Songpan.

By minibus taxi Eight-seater minibuses for day-trips to Huanglong can be rented in Songpan for ¥400–600 (including a couple of hours waiting time).

ACCOMMODATION

Seercuo 瑟尔嵯国际大酒店, sè ěr cuó guójì dà jiǔdiàn. Up from the park gates ☎ 0837 4249156. While Huanglong has a handful of overpriced high-end hotels near the entrance, this traditional-looking place at least has a little bit of charm. Rooms are modern, clean, and recently refurbished; it is also overpriced (and can be noisy), but the best of a bad bunch. **¥591**

Jiuzhaigou

九寨沟 jiǔzhàigōu • Daily 7am–7pm • April to mid-Nov ¥220/day; mid-Nov to March ¥80 • Unlimited bus use around the park ¥90

Around 100km northeast of Songpan, the perpetually snow-clad Min Shan range encloses **Jiuzhaigou** – "Nine Stockades Valley" – named as such after it was settled by

Tibetans several hundred years ago. The reserve forms a Y-shaped series of valleys clothed in thick alpine forests and strung with hundreds of impossibly toned **blue lakes** – said to be the scattered shards of a mirror belonging to the Tibetan goddess Semo. Jiuzhaigou's landscape looks spectacular in the autumn when the gold and red leaves contrast brilliantly with the water, or at the onset of winter in early December, when everything is dusted by snow.

Despite its remote location, Jiuzhaigou is the target of **intense tourism** – packages are offered by every travel agent in Sichuan – so don't come here expecting a quiet commune with nature, as the park clocks up over a million visitors annually, which can mean over forty thousand others with you on a weekend during the summer. Get here when the gates open at 7am and try to stay one step ahead of the hordes.

The reserve entrance

The entrance is at **JIUZHAIGOU KOU** (九寨沟口, jiŭzhàigōu kŏu), a kilometre-wide blob of services either side of the park gates. It's 14km from here to the centre of the reserve around Nuorilang, a journey that passes a marshy complex of pools at the foot of imposing Dêgê Shan that forms the **Shuzheng Lakes** (树正海, shùzhèng hăi), the largest group in the reserve and cut partway along by the 20m **Shuzheng Falls**.

Nuorilang

诺日朗, nuòrìlăng

Nuorilang is a tourist village where you can don Tibetan garb and pose on horseback for photos; there's also a **visitors' centre**, and Jiuzhaigou's most famous cascades, the **Nuorilang Falls** (诺日朗瀑布, nuòrìlăng pùbù). They look best from the road, framed by trees as water forks down over the strange, yellow crystalline rock faces.

The Primeval Forest and Five-coloured Lake

The road forks east and west at Nuorilang, with both forks around 18km long. The **eastern branch** first passes Pearl Beach Falls (珠滩瀑布, zhūtān pùbù), where a whole hillside has calcified into an ankle-deep cascade similar to Huanglong; but the main attraction here is the **Primeval Forest** (原始森林, yuánshǐ sēnlín), a dense and very atmospheric belt of ancient conifers right at the end of the road. There's less to see along the **western branch** from Nuorilang, but don't miss the stunning **Five-coloured Lake** (五彩池, wŭcăi chí) which, for sheer intensity, if not scale, is unequalled in the park.

ARRIVAL AND DEPARTURE   JIUZHAIGOU

Via Jiuzhaigou town Jiuzhaigou town, 40km east of the reserve entrance at Jiuzhaigou Kou, has a large long-distance bus station where some traffic travelling via Pingwu might terminate. Shared taxis shuttle back and forth between Jiuzhaigou town and the park gates all day long, charging ¥10 per person.
Destinations Chengdu (2 daily; 6hr).

Via Jiuzhaigou Kou Jiuzhaigou Kou's bus station (九寨沟口汽车站, jiŭzhàigōukŏu qìchēzhàn) lies just east of the park entrance; all its services depart between 7am and 8am and you need to buy tickets from the booth here at least a day in advance. Aside from long-distance routes, there is also one bus daily each way between Jiuzhaigou and Huanglong.
Destinations Chengdu (6 daily; 8hr); Guangyuan (6.30am daily; 7hr); Lanzhou (7am daily; 9hr); Songpan (3 daily; 1hr 30min).

JIUZHAIGOU ECOTOURS

If you're fairly fit and want to escape Jiuzhaigou's tourist overload, it's possible to organize **three-day treks** through the otherwise inaccessible Zharu valley with Jiuzhaigou's ecotourism department (¥1580, including entry fees, guides, food and all camping gear; ☎0837 7737070, ⚭en.jiuzhai.com); the route circuits 4500m-high Zhayi Zhaga mountain.

GETTING AROUND

By bus Buses run around the park all through the day; ticket holders have unrestricted use of them. The best plan is to head to the more distant sights and work your way back towards the entrance, as services begin to thin out after 3pm.
On foot Some people plan to save on the bus fare by

hiking everywhere, but given the distances involved – over 30km from the gates to either end of the "Y" – this isn't a realistic option. However, there's quite a network of under-used, erosion-resistant boardwalks around each stop, which will soon take you away from the crowds.

ACCOMMODATION

Note that there is no official accommodation inside the park, though some people have stayed there – illegally – with Tibetan families.

Friendship Hostel 豆豆客栈, dòu dòu kèzhàn. Pengfeng Village, 1.5km west of the park gates ☎ 158 28201354, ⊚ doudouhostel.com. Not a looker on the outside, but this clean and well-run hostel has large, comfortable rooms and tidy dorms as well as providing free minibus transportation to the park every morning. Has a restaurant and bar on site, a travel desk and very friendly English-speaking staff. Dorms ¥50, doubles ¥178
Sheraton 喜来登国际大酒店, xǐláidēng guójì dàjiǔdiàn. On the main road just north of the park gates ☎ 0837 7739988, ⊚ starwoodhotels.com. Characterless luxury accommodation in an enormous

faux Tibetan complex, complete with a giant stupa outside. Certainly the best-quality rooms in the area, but also the most expensive by far. ¥1025
★**Zhuo Ma's** 卓玛, zhuómǎ. 13km west of the park ☎ 1356 8783012, ⊚ zhuomajiuzhaigou.hostel.com. Best option in the whole area is this, a Tibetan homestay in a beautiful traditional family home, run by the welcoming Zhuo Ma. Rooms are not en suite, but there is a Western-style toilet on the ground floor. Call ahead and she'll pick you up from the park gates. Price includes breakfast and dinner. Per person ¥220

EATING

For lunch a set meal is available at the Nuorilang visitor centre for around ¥60–80; alternatively, there are plenty of other options scattered around outside the gates.

★**Abuluzi** 阿布穋孜风情藏餐吧, ābùluzī fēngqíng zàngcānba. East of the park gates, by the MCA and Sheraton ☎ 139 90421118. Run by Zhou Ma's brother, this traditional Tibetan restaurant serves generous portions of

genuine local food (plenty of yak dishes) served in comfortable and friendly surroundings. They have an English menu, though it's more expensive than other nearby restaurants; expect around ¥250 for two people. Daily 11am–10pm.

The Aba grasslands

Songpan sits just east of the vast, marshy **Aba grasslands**, which sprawl over the Sichuan, Gansu and Qinghai borders. Resting at around 3500m and draining into the headwaters of the Yellow River, the grasslands are home to nomadic herders and birdlife – including black-necked cranes and golden eagles – and form a corridor between Sichuan and Gansu province. Buses from Songpan run north to the grassland town of **Zöigê** and over the border, with Tibetan monasteries at **Langmusi** offering a prime reason to stop off along the way.

Zöigê

若尔盖, ruò'ěrgài
Around 150km northwest of Songpan at the grasslands' northernmost edge, **ZÖIGÊ** is a fairly squalid collection of markets and shops along Shuguang Lu and parallel Shangye Jie. The town's low-key **Daza monastery** (达扎寺, dázā sì) is worth a visit – not least for the small hall here whose galleried porch is hung with badly stuffed yaks, deer and blood-spattered wolves – but most people only spend time in Zöigê because they've missed the bus out.

ARRIVAL AND DEPARTURE   ZÖIGÊ

By bus The bus station (若尔盖汽车站, ruò'ěrgài qìchēzhàn) on Shuguang Lu has dawn departures for Songpan (daily 6.30am & 10am; 6hr), Jiuzhaigou,

Chengdu, and Hezuo (in Gansu); there's also one morning (6.30am) and one afternoon bus (2pm) to Langmusi (1hr).

ACCOMMODATION AND EATING

For food, there are plenty of places to grab a simple meal, or you can just hang out at the *A-Lang* teahouse across from the post office on Shangye Jie.

Ruoergai 若尔盖大酒店, ruò'ěrgài dàjiǔdiàn. Shangye Jie ☎0837 2291998. The town's most upmarket option, a short, squat building painted on the outside to look like something traditionally Tibetan. Inside, rooms are good quality, clean and nicely furnished with reproduction traditional furniture. **¥480**

Zangle 藏乐宾馆, zànglè bīnguǎn. Shangye Jie ☎0837 2298685. A clean, basic, concrete block, the building is hardly pretty and staff perfunctory, but en suites have a ready and plentiful supply of hot water, as well as a/c, and prices can be bargained. **¥180**

Langmusi
郎木寺, lángmùsì

Just off the Songpan–Hezuo highway, 90km from Zöigê, you'll find the scruffy, single-street village of **LANGMUSI**, whose surrounding forests, mountain scenery and **lamaseries** give an easy taster of Tibet.

Langmusi's two small eighteenth-century **lamaseries** (¥30) sit at the western end of the village. Walk up the main street and bear right over a bridge, and the road leads uphill to **Saizu Gompa**, whose main hall's walls are covered in pictures of meditating buddhas and where you might see monks debating in the courtyard outside. For **Gaerdi Gompa**, bear left along the main road and then aim for the temple buildings in the back lanes; this is the larger complex with several sizeable, tin-roofed halls, but seems almost totally deserted.

12

ARRIVAL AND DEPARTURE   LANGMUSI

By bus If you can't find direct transport to Langmusi, buses travelling the Songpan–Gansu highway might agree to drop you off at the intersection with the Langmusi road, where jeeps wait to take you the 3km to the village itself (¥5). The easiest way to get to Songpan, is take the Zöigê bus and get the 10am onwards from there (a total of 10hr). There's no bus station at Langmusi; buses deliver and collect from along the single main street. Leaving, vehicles assemble at dawn; ask at your accommodation the night before for times.
Destinations Zöigê (daily 7am; 2hr).

By minibus *Leisha's* can help charter minibuses to Jiuzhaigou and elsewhere (about ¥1200 for a five-seater).

ACCOMMODATION

Langmusi 郎木寺宾馆, lángmùsì bīnguǎn. Just south of the main crossroads ☎0941 6671541, ⓦlangmusi.net. Probably the smartest place in town (not saying much), this concrete place doesn't look much from the outside, but rooms are well presented, have 24hr hot water (eventually), and there's a roof-top terrace. You need to bargain doubles down as it's a little overpriced. They organize taxis, and tours including hot-air ballooning. **¥420**

Nomad's Youth Hostel 旅朋青年旅舍, lǚpéng qīngnián lǚshè. On the main street ☎0941 6671460. Standard Chinese youth hostel, popular with domestic students who are used to dormitory living – for those who aren't, the rooms here can feel cramped and in need of a clean. But staff are friendly enough and can help with treks and onward travel. Closed in winter, when you can try the *Tibetan Barley Youth Hostel* way out in the west of town. Dorms **¥30**

EATING

For food, there are several simple Muslim and Chinese restaurants along the main street, though foreigners tend to gravitate towards *Leisha's*.

TREKKING AT LANGMUSI

There's immense **hiking** potential up to ridges and peaks above Langmusi, but make sure you're equipped for dogs (see box, p.771) and changeable weather. To arrange longer guided hikes or **horse-trekking**, contact Langmusi Tibetan Horse Trekking (☎138 93991541, ⓦlangmusi.net), near the bus stop, a very organized operation whose one- to four-day trips take in nomad camps and mountain scenery (¥270–300 /person per day, ¥400 for solo travellers). Be aware that horse-trekking is not possible for those weighing over 85kg.

Leisha's 丽莎饭馆, lìshā fànguǎn. On the main road through town ☎189 19417143. This traveller-style café has been serving apple pie (¥20) and yak burgers (¥30) to

contented clientele for years, but as well as the Westernized dishes they also do an excellent range of Chinese, Tibetan and Muslim cuisine for a similar price. Daily 6.30am–11pm.

Kangding

康定, kāngdìng

KANGDING, 250km from Chengdu at the gateway to Sichuan's far west, is a crowded, expanding collection of artless modern white-tiled blocks packed along the fast-flowing **Zheduo River**. Visually this is a very Chinese town, but the deep gorge that Kangding is set in is overlooked by chortens and the frosted peaks of **Daxue Shan** (the Great Snowy Mountains) and, whatever the maps might say, this is where Tibet really begins.

The town is the capital of huge **Ganzi prefecture** and bus schedules mean that a stopover here is likely, but with a couple of temples to check out, a huge, communal evening dancing in the central square, and an immensely friendly and welcoming population it's not the worst of fates. Kangding is also a stepping stone for day-trips to the **Hailuogou Glacier Park**, which descends **Gongga Shan**.

Monasteries

Kangding's most central monastery is the little **Anjue Temple** (安觉寺, ānjué sì), just off Yanhe Xi Lu; it was built in 1654 at the prompting of the Fifth Dalai Lama. Following the main road southwest out of town brings you to the short stone arch of the **Princess Wencheng Bridge** (文成公主桥, wénchéng gōngzhǔ qiáo); on the other side, a path runs uphill to **Nanfu Temple** (南甫寺, nánfù sì), built in 1639. Check out the murals of Buddha in all his incarnations here – with their typically Tibetan iconography of skulls, demons and fierce expressions, they paint a far less forgiving picture of Buddhism than the mainstream Chinese brand.

The markets and Paoma Shan

Kangding's **markets** – mostly selling clothing and household knick-knacks of all descriptions – surround the old town **spring** (水井子, shuǐjǐngzi) and a **mosque** off Yanhe Dong Lu. A lane opposite the mosque heads up to the entrance of pine-clad **Paoma Shan** (跑马山, pǎomǎ shān; ¥50), the mountain southeast of town,

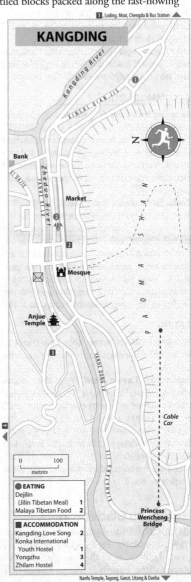

KANGDING

EATING
| Dejilin (Jilin Tibetan Meal) | 1 |
| Malaya Tibetan Food | 2 |

ACCOMMODATION
Kangding Love Song	2
Konka International Youth Hostel	1
Yongzhu	3
Zhilam Hostel	4

Nanfu Temple, Tagong, Ganzi, Litang & Danba

which hosts a **horse-race festival** in the middle of the fourth lunar month. It's a half-hour walk up stone steps to lookouts with so-so views and a Roman-theatre-style racetrack (where sad horses plod with the tourists once around the track for ¥100), or you can catch a **cable car** (¥50 return) from near the Princess Wencheng Bridge.

ARRIVAL AND DEPARTURE   KANGDING

By plane At 4280m, Kangding airport (康定机场, kāngdìng jīchǎng) is the world's third highest. It's some 40km northwest of the centre, and has flights (not always daily) to Chongqing, Daocheng, Hangzhou, Kunming and Lhasa.

By bus Kanding's bus station (康定汽车站, kāngdìng qìchē zhàn) is 1km from town towards Chengdu, a ¥6–7 cab ride or 20min walk to anywhere central.
Destinations Chengdu (hourly till 2pm; 6–8hr); Danba (daily 6am & 2pm; 4hr); Daocheng (daily 6am; 14hr); Dêgê (daily 6am; 10hr); Ganzi (daily 6am & 7am; 10–12hr); Litang (daily

7am; 9hr); Tagong (daily 8am; 3hr); Xichang (daily 7am; 8hr).
By minibus and taxi Minibuses touting for Danba, Litang, Tagong and Chengdu, and taxis to Luding, cruise the streets outside the main bus station, and while journey times will be considerably less than the buses, the driving can be less safe – choose a reliable-looking one.

ACCOMMODATION

Kangding Love Song 康定情歌大酒店, kāngdìng qínggē dàjiǔdiàn. 156 Dong Lu ☏0836 2813333. Probably the best (and certainly the most expensive) hotel in town, this place sports an air of slightly bad-taste opulent luxury, and the rooms are certainly clean and comfortable with good beds, and not quite as gaudy as the public areas. ¥480
Konka International Youth Hostel 贡嘎国际青年 旅舍, gònggā guójì qīngnián lǚshě. Qingge Da Dao ☏0836 2817788. Conveniently located on the third floor of a block a minute's walk west of the bus station (turn left, then left again at the bridge), this place is aimed at Chinese students and is correspondingly basic. They do speak English, though, and have excellent travel information. It fills up quickly, but the hotel on the floor below can take overflow and its rooms are arguably better value at ¥80.

Beds ¥35, doubles ¥150
Yongzhu 拥珠驿栈, yōngzhū yìzhàn. On an alley running uphill from Guangming Lu ☏0836 2832381 or ☏159 83738188. Basic but central hotel, clean and run by a cheery Tibetan proprietor who speaks only a little English but is always delighted to welcome Western faces through the door. Only two of her colourful and comfortable rooms have Western toilets, however. Dorms ¥40, doubles ¥160
★**Zhilam Hostel** 汇道客栈, huìdào kèzhàn. ☏0836 2831100, ⌨zhilamhostel.com. A tiring 10min hike uphill from town up from the Yongzhu, this foreign-owned venture is far and away the best place to stay, with Tibetan-style decor, a good café serving Western and Tibetan food (including home-baked cakes), and excellent travel advice. Book ahead, however – it's often full. En suites cost ¥60 more. Dorms ¥35, doubles ¥160

EATING

From the bus station to the town centre, Xinshi Qian Jie hosts heaps of cheap Sichuan and Tibetan restaurants, while for a Western food-fix the Zhilam Hostel can serve up a passable pizza among other dishes.

Dejilin (Jilin Tibetan Meal) 德吉林藏餐, déjílín zàngcān. Xinshi Qian Jie. If the colourful murals, laquered benches and mantra-chanting waitress aren't enough of a giveaway, the fact that the first item on the menu is "lumps of beef" (¥48) tells you that you're in a down-to-earth Tibetan joint. Butter tea (¥20/kettle), beef jiaozi dumplings (¥20), yak stew (¥38), beef rice (¥28), communal bench tables and a windswept rural clientele all complete the look. Daily 8am–9pm.

Malaya Tibetan Food 玛拉亚藏餐, mǎlāyà zàngcān. Yan He Dong Lu ☏0836 2877111. On the sixth floor above Dico's (take the lift or you'll end up in a KTV), this has a more sophisticated ambience but still authentic Tibetan. There's a wide choice, with dishes such as beef cooked on hot rocks (¥68), or yak meat burgers made with Tibetan bread (¥68). They even have a vegetarian dish of yoghurt baka (¥38), a rich mix of bread soaked in butter and sugar then covered in yoghurt. Daily 11am–10pm.

Hailuogou Glacier Park

海螺沟冰川公园, hǎiluógōu bīngchuān gōngyuán • ¥75 • Park bus ¥80
Hailuogou Glacier Park encloses an alpine backdrop of deep valleys forested in pine and rhododendron, with the four glaciers in question descending **Gongga Shan** (贡嘎山, gònggā shān), known as Minya Konka in Tibetan. At 7556m, this is western China's

highest point – a stunning sight on the rare mornings when the near-constant cloud cover and haze of wind-driven snow above the peak suddenly clear. Warm, weatherproof **clothing** is advisable whatever time of year you visit.

Moxi and the camps

The **park entrance** is 100km from Kangding at **MOXI** (磨西, móxī), a group of hotels, restaurants and souvenir stalls centred around a crossroads where buses cluster. A road runs 25km from the gates here to the main glacier, via three **camps** along the way at the 8-, 15- and 22km marks. There are **hot springs** (¥65) at the first two, while *Camp 2*, near where the thicker pine forests begin, is the nicest spot to stay.

The glacier

It's 3.5km from *Camp 3* to the glacier, from where you can reach a **viewing platform** by cable car (¥150 return) or by simply hiking up along a small path (2hr). From the platform, the glacier is revealed as a tongue of blue-white ice scattered with boulders and streaked in crevasses edged in black gravel, with – if you're lucky – Gongga Shan's peak rising in the distance.

ARRIVAL AND DEPARTURE   HAILUOGOU GLACIER PARK

By bus A single daily bus leaves from Chengdu's Xinnanmen bus station, taking around 5hr to arrive at the park entrance.

By taxi Shared taxis between Moxi and Kangding, via Luding (3hr), charge ¥50/person. If you don't have a full van-load you'll need to negotiate or wait for additional passengers.

ACCOMMODATION

Hailuogou No 2 Camp Hot Spring Resort 海螺沟二号营地, hǎiluógōu èrhào yíngdì. Inside the park near Buzi village ☎ 0836 3266171. This is a well-put-together place, with much-vaunted "European style" rooms, which basically means pine furniture and a sit-down toilet. Very comfortable and cosy, and considering the location it's a fair deal, though at busy times prices can rise to ludicrous levels. **¥822**

Hamu Hostel 哈姆青年旅舍, hāmǔ qīngnián lǔshè. 150m northeast of the main gate, Moxi ☎ 152 81572918. Another basic hostel, with five floors of simple but decent en-suite rooms (and no lift). Though they don't have dorms, they do have one triple on the fifth floor with no bathroom for ¥160. The owner speaks a little English. **¥168**

Milan Youth Hostel 米兰青年旅舍, mǐlán qīngnián lǔshè. Southeast of the church, Moxi ☎ 0836 3266518. Friendly place with a mix of four-bed dorms, with the female dorm (¥35) having its own toilet and shower, as do the twins and doubles. Popular with domestic backpackers. Dorms **¥30**, doubles **¥120**

Mingzhu Huayuan 明珠花园酒店, míngzhū huāyuán jiǔdiàn. Near the park gates, Moxi ☎ 0836 3266166. Top-notch accommodation for wealthy Chinese tourists, very conveniently situated. Traditional-style modern building with marble lobby, and interior furnished in beige, cream and gold. Rooms are getting a bit aged, but good value for the price. **¥280**

Danba

丹巴, dānbā

Around 120km north of Kangding, **DANBA** is a 2km-long service town for surrounding Tibetan hamlets. These feature distinctive stone towers (碉楼, diāolóu), used in former times as watchtowers and safe havens from attack. Some reach up to 35m high and are hundreds of years old – the use of stone for construction in the area has been dated back to 1700 BC.

Jiaju

甲居, jiǎjū · ¥50

The most accessible hamlet is **JIAJU**, just 7km up into the hills above Danba town. Jiaju occupies a relatively flat terrace on an otherwise steep mountainside, all dotted with traditional stone houses surrounded by their fields and farm animals. Well-formed paths link clusters of buildings, which you can spend a couple of hours exploring – bring a camera.

By bus Danba's bus station is at the west end of the town; buy tickets here the day before if possible.
Destinations Ganzi (6.50am daily; 9hr); Kangding (daily 8.30am & 2.30pm; 3hr).
By minibus Minibuses to Bamei (for connections to Tagong) leave when full from a depot at Danba's eastern side near the Caihong Bridge (彩虹桥, cǎihóng qiáo), though often called Xiansan Sancha Hedaqiao (三八线三叉河大桥, sānbāxiàn sānchā hé dàqiáo). Kangding minibuses depart until late afternoon from the bus station. Accommodation should be able to arrange a shared minibus from Danba to Jiaju for ¥80 return, including waiting time.

Jiaju Homestays There are numerous private homestays at Jiaju, though you can't really arrange these in advance. It's well worth the experience, however; facilities are extremely basic but rates include a huge evening meal. Per person **¥50**
Zaxi Zhoukang Hostel 扎西桌康游客之家, zhāxī zhuōkāng yóukè zhíjiā. Near the Caihong Bridge, Danba ☎ 0836 3521806. Spotless rooms and friendly staff make this a good option – as do 24hr hot water and wi-fi. Management can also help organize trips out to villages, though very little English is spoken. Dorms **¥25**, doubles **¥80**

Tagong

塔公, tǎgōng

Some 110km northwest of Kangding, the single-street Tibetan township of **TAGONG** is a popular stop for **horse-trekking** opportunities on the surrounding grasslands. Tagong itself is oriented around the modest **Tagong Temple** (塔公寺, tǎgōng sì; ¥20), built to honour Princess Wencheng but now busy with monks chatting on their mobile phones during morning prayers. The seventeenth-century main hall houses a sculpture of Sakyamuni as a youth, said to have been brought here by the princess in Tang times. Behind the monastery is **Fotalin**, an overgrown and under-tended forest of a hundred 3m-high stupas, each built in memory of a monk.

The golden stupa

金色佛塔, jīnsè fó tǎ • ¥10

Just 500m along the main road past Tagong Temple is the spectacular **golden stupa**, fully 20m tall and backed by snowy peaks, surrounded by a colonnade of prayer wheels – though according to the monks, this recent construction is less of a religious site than an excuse to collect tourist revenue.

The Tagong grasslands

Spreading out from behind the golden stupa, the **Tagong grasslands** occupy a string of flat-bottomed valleys on a 3700m-high plateau, all surrounded by magnificent snowy peaks. Hiking and riding possibilities are legion: **Shedra Gompa**'s monastery and Buddhist college is only a couple of kilometres away; **Shamalong** village is two hours along a track from the stupa; and **Ani Gompa** is a valley nunnery with a sky-burial site some two hours' hike cross-country. Get full directions for these routes from *Himalayak* or the *Khampa Nomad Ecolodge* – and beware of dogs.

By bus There's no bus station at Tagong, so buses drop off along the Kangding–Ganzi highway, which forms the town's main street. Leaving, you can stand on the road and flag down passing traffic – accommodation can advise on likely times – or there should be a steady supply of minibuses from Kangding looking for passengers (¥50). There are no buses to Danba, so you'll have to take a share taxi or minibus (¥70).
Destinations Bamei (many 8–8.30am; 1hr); Ganzi (daily 6am; 8hr); Kangding (daily 8am & 2pm; 2hr).
By plane Tagong is about 70km north of Kanding airport (see p.778), and a taxi from there costs around ¥300 and is best arranged through your accommodation before arrival.
Tour guides For horse treks, bike, motorbike and camping gear rental, contact long-established foreign-run Chyoger Treks at the *Khampa Nomad Ecolodge* (☎ 136 84493301, ⓦ definitelynomadic.com). Treks can also be arranged through *Himalayak*.

ACCOMMODATION

Himalayak 雪域旅社, xuěyù lǚshè. Main square ☎ 187 83671271. Formerly called *Snowlands*, this is one of Tagong's original hostels and is still going strong. The interior has very colourful decorations and there's a pleasant glass-enclosed balcony with a great view. Rooms are somewhat spartan but have their own bathrooms. They also hand out good travel advice, as does the connected *Sally's* café. Beds ¥30, rooms ¥80

Jya Drolma & Gayla's Guesthouse 甲志玛大姐家, jiǎzhìmǎ dàjiějiā. Facing the temple, it's the building behind you in the left corner of the square ☎ 0836 2866056. The hospitality and traditional Tibetan home here are almost worth the trip in themselves, though the combination of altitude and steep stairs could leave you out of breath. Dorms ¥30, doubles ¥80

★**Khampa Nomad Ecolodge** Gunong "village", 11km to the northwest of Tagong ☎ 136 84493301, ⓦ definitelynomadic.com. This off-grid ecolodge housed in a converted Tibetan farmhouse and powered by solar, wind and biogas, is run by an American–Tibetan couple, has fantastic views of the winter pastures along a valley, and features a sauna and hot tub. Price is for two people sharing one of their cosy, wooden double rooms and includes breakfast and dinner. Phone ahead and they may be able to arrange free transport from Tagong. ¥400

EATING

Sally's Kham Café Ground floor of the Himalayak Guesthouse ☎ 187 83671271, ✉ tagongsally@yahoo .com. A foreigners' hangout with Tibetan, Chinese and Western staples and plenty of helpful information, with a meal costing around ¥20–40/person. They also have the best coffee in town. Often closed Nov–March; otherwise daily 8am–10pm.

Ganzi

甘孜, gānzī

12

GANZI (also known as Garzê) sits at 3500m in a broad, flat-bottomed river valley some 300km northwest of Kangding, with the long, serrated Que'er Shan range rising to the south. The dusty, noisy town owes its importance to the adjacent **Kandze monastery**, founded by the Mongols after they invaded in 1642 and once the largest Gelugpa monastery in the Kham region. A bit empty today, it nevertheless remains an important cultural centre, especially for the teaching of religious dances and musical instruments.

Ganzi town itself acts as a transport and social focus, with blue trucks rumbling through at all hours, wild crowds cruising the streets, and markets throughout the back lanes; the kilometre-long main road is lined with shops selling knives, rugs, silverware, all sorts of jewellery, saddles, religious accessories, copper and tin kitchenware.

Kandze monastery

甘孜寺庙, gānzī sìmiào · ¥20

The **Kandze monastery** is 2km north of town – follow Jiefang Lu uphill from the bus station – and for such an obvious complex the entrance is not easy to find, being hidden behind mud-brick homes among medieval backstreets. The renovated buildings are splendid, and just wandering around fills in time, though there's little specific to seek out

---

VISITING MONASTERIES

Among the draws of many towns in western Sichuan are their Tibetan Buddhist **monasteries**, most of which belong to the yellow-hat Gelugpa sect. Monasteries form huge medieval-looking complexes sprawling over hillsides, with a central core of large, red-walled, gold-roofed **temples** surrounded by a maze of smaller buildings housing monks and staff. Monasteries are **free** to enter, except where noted in the text; if there are no signs to the contrary, assume that **photography** is forbidden inside temples. Monks are generally friendly, encouraging you to explore, steering you firmly away from closed areas, and sometimes offering **food and accommodation** – though don't take these for granted. Most importantly, remember to orbit **clockwise** around both individual temples and the complex as a whole (the only exception to this rule being at the region's few Bon temples).

aside from the **main hall** – covered in gold, murals and prayer flags, and with an incredible view of the valley and town from its roof. The large adobe walls below the monastery are remains of the Mazur and Khangsar **forts**, built by the Mongols after they took the region.

ARRIVAL AND DEPARTURE   GANZI

By bus Ganzi's bus station is central, on the crossroads of east–west Chuanzang Lu and Jiefang Lu. Staff here are helpful enough with information but you might have to buy tickets on the bus. If you're aiming for Litang and want to avoid going all the way back to Kangding, there's a morning bus south to Xinlong (新龙,

xīnlóng), from where minibuses run to Litang if they get enough people (¥80 each, or about ¥400–500 for the whole van).

Destinations Chengdu (daily 6.10am; 20hr); Dêgê (daily 6am; 6–8hr); Kangding (daily 1am; 12hr); Xinlong (4 daily; 3hr).

ACCOMMODATION AND EATING

Almost every other business in town is a restaurant, though don't expect much beyond noodles and dumplings.

Golden Yak 金牦牛宾馆, jīnmáoniú bīnguǎn. Inside the bus station compound ☏0836 6816999 or ☏150 82317222. Convenient and relatively comfy, this place has simple basic double-bed "dorm" rooms and en-suite doubles, and is the best of the lower-budget options, with a/c, hot water and balconies. Dorms **¥100**, doubles **¥200**

Hotel Himalaya 喜马拉雅宾馆, xǐmǎlāyǎ bīnguǎn. Dong Da Jie ☏0836 7521878. The pick of Ganzi's fairly down-to-earth accommodation, with clean doubles, en suites with sit-down toilets and hot water – and some with balconies. Not much English spoken, but they're very friendly. **¥150**

12 Dêgê

德格, dégé

Eight hours from Ganzi via the crossroads town of **Manigange** (马尼干戈, mǎnígàngē) and the scary, 5500m-high Chola Shan mountain pass, **DÊGÊ** initially appears to be no more than a small cluster of ageing concrete buildings squeezed into a narrow gorge. Dêgê was, however, once the most powerful Kham state, and the only one to resist the seventeenth-century Mongol invasion – hence the absence of Gelugpa-sect monasteries in the region.

Gongchen Gompa

笻庆寺庙, gàngqìng sìmiào • ¥50; cameras forbidden

At the top of Dêgê's main street is **Gongchen Gompa**, which you'll find encircled by peregrinating pilgrims busy thumbing rosaries. These red-walled buildings form one of three hubs of Tibetan culture (the other two are Lhasa, and Xiahe in Gansu). The first building encountered is the **Bakong Scripture Printing Hall** (印经院, yìnjīng yuàn); built in 1729, the four-storey hall houses 290,000 **woodblocks** of Tibetan texts, stored in racks on the second floor like books in a library, and covering subjects ranging from scriptures to scientific treatises – some seventy percent of all Tibetan literary works. You can watch the **printing process** on the third floor: though all done by hand, the printers work at a furious pace, and it's not unusual to watch ten of them turning out a hundred pages a minute.

ARRIVAL AND DEPARTURE   DÊGÊ

By plane Garze Gesar Airport (甘孜格萨尔机场, gānzī gé sà ěr jīchǎng), is being built near the town (scheduled to open 2017/2018), which will make access to the area (at least from Chengdu) a lot easier.

By bus Dêgê's modern, concrete bus station is located where the single street crosses the stream. Leaving, you'll

need to buy Ganzi or Kangding tickets a day in advance. If there are no tickets available, then you can get a minibus to most destinations, which usually leave between 6am and 8am.

Destinations Ganzi (7am daily; 6–8hr); Kangding (6am daily; 14–16hr).

ACCOMMODATION AND EATING

The road to the monastery is lined with shops, a supermarket and dozens of stir-fry restaurants.

Dêgê Binguan 雀儿山宾馆, què'érshān bīnguǎn.
Zheng Jie ☎ 0836 8222167. The primary source of beds,
try to go for one of their newer rooms; they're still

overpriced, but a little less so than the older ones. The
comfortable tearoom here, however, is a treat after the
journey. **¥280**

Litang

理塘, lǐtáng

LITANG, 300km west of Kangding, is a lively, gruff place with a large Tibetan population
and an obvious Han presence in its businesses, army barracks and expanding spread of
concrete-and-tile architecture. It's the latest town along the highway to Tibet to get a
tourist makeover, and there's a bit of a strange dichotomy between the gleaming new
streets that have livestock wandering around, while monks and dreadlocked Khampa
toughs tear around the windy streets on motorbikes. Litang is also inescapably **high** – at
4014m above sea level, it actually beats Lhasa by over 300m – so don't be surprised if
you find even gentle slopes strangely exhausting. As usual, the main distraction here is
people-watching: the shops are packed with Tibetans bargaining for temple accessories,
solar-power systems for tents and practical paraphernalia for daily use, while Muslim
smiths are busy in workshops along the main street, turning out the town's renowned
knives and jewellery. A couple of kilometres east of town, there's also the popular new
33m-high **Qudenggabu stupa**, while the Buddhist **holy mountain** of Zagashershan is a
three-hour trek to the north and can be done as a day-trip.

Ganden Thubchen Choekhorling (Chang Qing Chun Ke'er) monastery

理塘寺庙, lǐtáng sìmiào • Taxi ¥5

12

A fifteen-minute walk north of town, Litang's **Ganden Thubchen Choekhorling monastery**,
founded in 1580 at the behest of the Third Dalai Lama, has been undergoing many years
of steady renovation (twice thanks to being damaged in the 2008 earthquake) and is today
populated by over a thousand monks. The complex is entirely encircled by a wall, the four
main halls (two of them brand new) gleaming among an adobe township of monks'
quarters. At the entrance is a large stupa and pile of brightly painted mani stones left by
pilgrims for good luck, whose inscriptions have been carved to resemble yaks.

The **upper temple** (Tsengyi Zhatsang) is the most interesting, its portico flanked by
aggressively postured statues of guardians of the four directions, along with a typical,
finely executed mural of a three-eyed demon wearing tiger skins and skulls, holding the
Wheel of Transmigration. Side gates in the wall allow you to hike up to the hills behind
the monastery, sharing the flower-filled pasture with yaks, or join pilgrims circuiting
the walls to the **sky-burial ground** to the right of the main gates – do not enter or take
photos if a burial is in progress.

ARRIVAL AND DEPARTURE   LITANG

Aside from routes back to Kangding, the road south of Litang runs right down to Zhongdian in Yunnan, and you might want
to detour along the way to take in Yading (see p.785).

By bus Litang's bus station is at the eastern end of town on
main street Xingfu Lu. While there is a daily early-morning
service to Kangding leaving from here, most buses are
through services and only able to pick you up if other
passengers have got off.
Destinations Daocheng (daily noon; 2hr 30min); Kangding
(daily 7am; 7–9hr); Shangri-La (daily 6.30am; 8–9hr).
By minibus Minibuses or taxis to Chengdu (10–12hr)
Daocheng (2hr), Xinlong (6–7hr; for Ganzi), and anywhere
they can get enough customers for, hang around opposite the
bus station. Long-distance routes leave when full (6–8am).

LITANG'S HORSE FESTIVAL

Litang's week-long **horse festival** kicks off each year in late July/early August on the plains 15km (¥70 by taxi) outside town. Horsemen from all over Kham descend to compete, decking their stocky steeds in bells and brightly decorated bridles and saddles. As well as the four daily **races**, the festival features amazing demonstrations of horsemanship, including acrobatics, plucking silk scarves off the ground, and shooting (guns and bows) – all performed at full tilt. In between, you'll see plenty of **dancing**, both religious (the dancers wearing grotesque wooden masks) and for fun, with both men and women gorgeously dressed in heavily embroidered long-sleeved smocks. The exact date varies each year: contact the *Potala Inn* or *Summer Youth Hostel* (in Chinese) before you arrive, for confirmation.

ACCOMMODATION

In addition to the following, there is a vast swath of new high-end hotels currently being built to the east of the bus station towards the highway.

Potala Inn 布达拉大酒店, bùdálā dàjiǔdiàn. West and uphill from the bus station ☎0836 8322533. This Tibetan-run hotel has rooms which are of variable quality and some are in need of a bit of attention, so have a look at a few before choosing, especially since they're all the same price. They are very knowledgable about local travel, and can book tours and taxis. **¥120**

Summer International Youth Hostel 夏天国际青年旅舍, xiàtiān guójì qīngnián lǚshè. Aimin Jie ☎ 180 15791574. Hostel with the cleanest rooms in town and a friendly bar area with a pool table. Young reception staff are enthusiastic, but lack the local travel information and contacts of the *Potala Inn*. They don't speak English either. Dorms **¥35**, doubles **¥140**

EATING

Stir-fry restaurants, some of which have English menus and all serving much the same food, line Xingfu Lu.

Tian Tian 天天饮食, tiāntiān yīnshí. 126 Xingfu Dong Lu, a 10min walk west of the bus station ☎1354 1467941. The Western food here is not fantastic, though the yak steak and chips (¥80) is good comfort food, but the Chinese and Tibetan dishes (¥15–30) are much better. The main reason to come here, however, is to talk to the owner, Mr Zheng, who is the best source of local travel information and guide contacts, and has plastered the walls with useful maps. Daily 8.30am–10pm.

Tibetan Special Dishes 藏人家特餐, zàngrénjiā tècān. 302 Xingfu Dong Lu ☎ 182 83670582. Just west of the junction for the *Summer Youth Hostel*, this place has the best Tibetan food in town and boasts an English menu to boot – the potato *momos* (dumplings; ¥20) and yak meat fried rice (¥18) are a particular treat. Daily 8am–10pm.

Daocheng

稻城, dàochéng

DAOCHENG (or Dabpa) is a small, touristy T-intersection of low buildings and shops some 150km south of Litang; the main reason to come here is to catch onwards transport to Yading or Yunnan. Some 5km north of town is a collection of **hot springs** (茹布查卡温泉, rúbùchákǎ wēnquán) set among a tiny village at the head of a valley, where bathhouses ask ¥10 for a soak. From the springs, you can cross the valley and hike along a ridge back into town – tiring, given the 3500m altitude.

ARRIVAL AND DEPARTURE

DAOCHENG

By plane UFO-shaped Daocheng Yading airport (稻城亚丁机场, dàochéng yàdīng jīchǎng), at 4411m, is the highest civilian airport in the world and has flights to Chengdu, Luzhou, Xi'an, Chongqing, Hangzhou, Kangding and Kunming, though not all run daily. They can also be quite pricey, with flights to Chengdu starting at around ¥800–1200, though up to ¥4000 if booked last minute.

Flights are often cancelled during the winter months. It's located 50km north of Daocheng. Share taxis cost around ¥50/person; the airport bus costs ¥35.

By bus Daocheng's bus station is just off the main street, with several daily departures, all things being equal – but they often aren't. Come to the ticket office around 2pm the day before you need to leave and be prepared to fight for a place in the queue. Although there is a daily bus from Chengdu, it's not advised to take it as it's not only gruelling, but it's probably better to get acclimatized to the altitude by making a stopoff in Kangding.

Destinations Chengdu (daily 8am; 21–24hr); Kangding (daily 6am; 10hr); Litang (3 daily; 5hr); Shangri-La in Yunnan (daily 7am; 8–10hr).

By minibus Minibuses outside the bus station tout for customers heading to Yading or Litang.

ACCOMMODATION AND EATING

Dao Cheng International Youth Hostel 道城国际青年旅舍, dào chéng guójì qīngnián lǚshè. 500m from the bus station across Xingfu Bridge on Dexi Jie ☎0836 5727772, ⓦyhachina.com. Occupying a wood and stone Tibetan building on the edge of town, the interior is very colourful, and the communal areas as well as the rooms are clean and recently refurbished. Has a restaurant and good travel info too. Dorms ¥35, doubles ¥100

Plateau Inn 高原客栈, gāoyuán kèzhàn. 78 Gongga Lu, just north of the bus station ☎0836 5721555 or ☎138 80854911, ⓦinoat.com. The rooms here are well maintained and the location – in a renovated old Tibetan house – is wonderful. There is hot water and a café serving excellent coffee. ¥280

Yading Scenic Area

亚丁, yàdīng • ¥150, plus ¥120 for the sightseeing bus from the entrance to Yading Village; horses generally ¥250–350/day; electric carts in the park around ¥50–80/trip

Around 76km south of Daocheng, **Yading Scenic Area** is a beautiful reserve of alpine meadows, lakes and 6000m peaks. The entry point is the village formerly known as **Riwa**, which like so many places in the Himalayas has started calling itself **Shangri-La** (香格里拉镇, xiāng gé lǐlā zhèn), though since James Hilton based his fictional place on photos of this area, which he saw in **National Geographic**, it's probably got more right to than most. There's accommodation here and you can organize trips into the rest of the reserve, though you'll have to take the sightseeing bus from here 35km to the trailheads at **Yading Village** (亚丁村, yàdīng cūn). Some sights can be reached by electric cart, but ideally you'll be prepared to hike or travel on horseback. While most visitors are simply drawn by the immense natural beauty of the place, for Tibetans, the three 6000m peaks the reserve is focused around represent the Buddhas of wisdom, power and compassion; coming here and not completing the *kora* (pilgrim circuit) of the tallest mountain, **Chenresig**, would be a serious missed opportunity.

12

ARRIVAL AND DEPARTURE
YADING SCENIC AREA

By airport bus It's possible to skip Daocheng entirely, and take the Daocheng Yading airport bus 130km directly to Riwa Town (3hr 30min).

By minibus Everybody with a vehicle in Daocheng will offer to take you to Yading Village (about ¥50/ person, ¥300 for the whole vehicle); the trip takes around 2hr.

ACCOMMODATION

There is limited and extremely basic Tibetan-style guesthouse accommodation near the trailheads in Yading Village, and none at all beyond. The best hotels are in Daocheng or Riwa.

Tibetan Buddhism Cultural Theme Hotel 稻城亚丁藏迦主题文化酒店, dàochéng yàdīng zàng jiā zhǔtí wénhuà jiǔdiàn. 11 Chituhe Lu. If you don't fancy the traditional but basic ¥100–150-a-room guesthouses, and can't afford the modern luxury of *The Holyland Hotel*, this atmospheric, modern-ish place will fit the bill. Housed in an old Tibetan farmhouse, the rooms are cosy and comfortable and there's also a restaurant and bar. ¥329

The Northwest

甘肃 / 青海 / 新疆

MOGAO CAVES

13

The Northwest

Gansu, Qinghai and Xinjiang spread across the Chinese northwest in a dizzying agglomeration of deserts, grasslands, rivers and mountains. Despite the region's impressive size, which alone would form the eighth-largest country in the world, it contains just four percent of China's population – a baffling statistic considering the ethnic variety found here. Lowland Xinjiang is home to the Uyghur, predominantly Muslim people who speak a language closer to Turkish than Chinese. In Xinjiang's mountains live communities of Kazakh, Kyrgyz and Tajik, making for the curious existence of occasional blond-haired, blue-eyed holders of Chinese passports. Qinghai forms the northern edge of the Tibetan Plateau; with transport to Lhasa often restricted, the province is popular with travellers looking for an accessible window into Tibetan culture. In Gansu, there are large communities of Mongolians – also keen adherents of Tibetan Buddhism – and Hui (Muslims), as well as lesser-known groups such as Bao'an and Salar.

The Chinese of old believed that these *saiwairen* – "peoples from beyond the pale" – threatened the safety of the Empire itself; today, the relatively unrestricted use of **local languages and religions** in these areas could be taken as a sign of China's desire to restore goodwill and nurture patriotism in minorities. However, the degree of actual autonomy in the "autonomous" regions is strictly controlled, and relations between Han China and these more remote corners of the People's Republic remain fractious in places, most notably in Xinjiang.

Tourism across the Northwest focuses on the **Silk Road**, a series of historic towns and ruins running from Xi'an in Shaanxi, through Ningxia, Gansu and Xinjiang, and into Central Asia. The Northwest also offers opportunities to enjoy China's last great wilderness – the grasslands, mountains, lakes and deserts of the interior – far from the teeming population centres of the east. **Gansu**, the historical periphery of ancient China, is a rugged region of high peaks and barren deserts, spliced from east to west by the **Hexi Corridor**, which was once the most important route from China to the West.

JIAYUGUAN FORT

Highlights

❶ Labrang Monastery Explore the most imposing Lamaist monastery outside of Tibet, set in a beautiful mountain valley. **See p.804**

❷ Qinghai Lake China's largest lake is a magnet for birdwatchers and waterfowl, including rare black-necked cranes. **See p.816**

❸ Jiayuguan Fort Discover an ancient stronghold at the western end of the Great Wall, symbolically marking the limit of China proper. **See p.820**

❹ Dunhuang Travel across the sands by camel for an unforgettable adventure or discover ancient Buddhist art at the Mogao Caves. **See p.823**

❺ Turpan Relax under grape trellises or investigate Muslim Uyghur culture and ancient Silk Road relics, such as the intriguing ruins of Jiaohe. **See p.842**

❻ Kashgar's Sunday markets Join crowds haggling for goats, carpets and spices in China's most westerly and wild city. **See p.853**

HIGHLIGHTS ARE MARKED ON THE MAP ON P.790

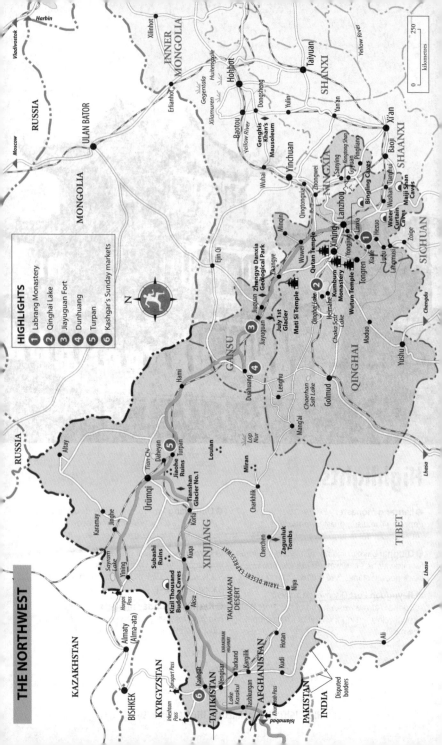

It's still the main route today – marked along its length by the Great Wall – and it terminates magnificently at the fortress of **Jiayuguan**, passing through a string of Silk Road towns including **Dunhuang**, with its Buddhist cave art.

Qinghai, the remote borderland plateau between Tibet and China proper, has monasteries, mountains, the colossal **Qinghai Lake** and a **route to Tibet** via the highest railway in the world. Qinghai is also the source of China's greatest rivers: the Yellow, Yangzi and Mekong rivers all originate in the mountains here.

THE SILK ROAD

The Khunjerab and Torugart passes that link China with Central Asia were, a thousand years ago, on well-trodden trade routes between eastern China and the Mediterranean. Starting from Chang'an (Xi'an), the **Silk Road** curved northwest through Gansu to the Yumen Pass, where it split. Travellers could follow one of two routes across the deserts to Kashgar: the **southern route** ran through Dunhuang, Miran, Niya, Hotan and Yarkand; the **northern route** through Hami, Turpan, Kuqa and Aksu. Beyond Kashgar, merchants traded their goods with middlemen who carried them south to Kashmir and Bactria, or north to Ferghana and Samarkand. Then, laden with Western goods, the Chinese merchants would turn around for the 3000km journey home. **Oases** along the route prospered as caravans sought rest and traded on their way through, becoming wealthy in their own right. When Chinese domination periodically declined, many of these cities turned into self-sufficient statelets, or **khanates**.

The foundations of this **road to the West**, which was to become one of the most important arteries of **trade and culture** in world history, were laid over two millennia ago. In 139 BC, the imperial court at Chang'an dispatched a man called **Zhang Qian** to investigate the world to the west and to seek possible allies in the struggle against nomadic marauders from the north. Zhang set out with a party of a hundred men; thirteen years later he returned, with only one member of his original expedition – and no alliances. Nevertheless, the news he brought of the lands to the west set Emperor Wu Di and his court aflame. Further **expeditions** purchased horses in Central Asia for military purposes, and from these beginnings trade developed.

By 100 BC, a dozen immense caravans were heading into the desert each year. From China emerged **silk** – of course – along with jade, porcelain, peaches, roses, cast iron, gunpowder and paper; the West sent back cucumbers, figs, sesame, walnuts, grapes (and wine-making), wool, ivory and **religion** – including Nestorian Christianity and **Buddhism**. The first Buddhist missionaries appeared in China in the first century AD, and by the fourth century Buddhism had become the official religion of much of northern China. Along the Silk Road, monasteries, stupas and grottoes proliferated, often sponsored by wealthy traders. The remains of this early flowering of **Buddhist art** are among the great attractions of the Northwest for modern-day travellers. History has taken its toll – zealous Muslims, Western archeologists, Red Guards and the forces of nature have all played a destructive part – but some sites have survived intact, above all the cave art at **Mogao** outside Dunhuang.

The Silk Road flourished for centuries, reaching its zenith under the Tang dynasty (618–907 AD) and bringing immense wealth to the Chinese nobility and merchants. But it remained a dangerous, expensive and slow route, taking at least five months from Chang'an to Kashgar, with whole caravans occasionally disappearing into the deserts or in the high mountain passes.

There was a final surge of trade in the thirteenth century, when the whole Silk Road came temporarily under Mongol rule. But with the arrival of silk farming in Europe and the opening of sea routes between China and the West, the Silk Road had had its day. The road and its cities were slowly abandoned to the wind and the blowing sands.

This was the end of the story for almost 800 years, until the turn of the millennium when China began looking to reopen the centuries-old intercontinental trade route. In spring 2016, the first Chinese freight train along the proposed New Silk Road arrived in western Russia, delivering parts to a Samsung electronics factory – proof of concept for a US$900-billion infrastructure project linking China with Europe via Central Asia. A new Southern Silk Road is also in the offing, with Chinese development of Pakistan's Gwadar Port, and improvement of the road and rail networks through Southern Xinjiang and the Karakoram, giving China access to the Indian Ocean and important markets beyond. Cheap Chinese goods, infrastructure know-how and construction funding will flow one way, and gas, oil and raw materials the other.

13

Guarding China's westernmost passes is **Xinjiang**, where China ends and Central Asia – once known as Chinese Turkestan – begins; a vast, isolated region of searing deserts and snowy peaks, formerly the most arduous section of the Silk Road. Here Turkic Uyghurs outnumber Han Chinese, mosques trade places with temples and lamb kebabs replace steamed dumplings. Highlights include the desert town of **Turpan** and, in the far west, fabled **Kashgar**, a city that until recent decades few Westerners had ever reached.

Travel can be hard going, with **enormous distances** and an unforgiving climate. **Winter** is particularly severe, with average temperatures as low as -30°C in Qinghai and Xinjiang. Conversely, in **summer** Turpan is China's hottest city, with temperatures exceeding 40°C. Despite the rugged terrain and the great expanses, however, facilities for visitors have developed considerably in recent years. The rail network has been expanded, roads improved and new airports constructed. Finally, there is the possibility of **travel** between China and its Central Asian neighbours – Kazakhstan, Kyrgyzstan and Pakistan are all connected by road or rail from Xinjiang.

Gansu and Qinghai

甘肃, gānsù / 青海 qīnghǎi

The gigantic, naturally splendid provinces of **Gansu** and **Qinghai** sit side-by-side, far west of Beijing and the Chinese seaboard. Together they form an incredibly diverse expanse, with everything from **colossal mountains** in the south to vast tracts of **desert** in the northwest. On a map, these provinces appear to be at the very centre of China, but this is only true in a geographical sense. Traditionally, the Chinese have regarded Gansu, the "closer" of the pair, as marking the outer limit of Chinese cultural influence.

The population of **Gansu** is relatively small (around 30 million people), but it comprises an extraordinary ethnic mix, including Hui, Kazakhs, Mongols and Tibetans. The province's remarkable geography encompasses stretches of the great **Yellow River**, its waters dense with silt, and the **Hexi Corridor**, a 1000km passage sandwiched between the Tibetan Plateau and Gobi Desert that narrows to a 16km-wide bottleneck at its skinniest point. Silk Road caravans trudged through the corridor, the Great Wall was built through it and even today Gansu's main rail lines and highways are funnelled along it. Here too you'll find some of the region's most spectacular historic sites: the **Mogao Caves** at **Dunhuang** house the finest examples of Buddhist art in all of China; there's the country's largest reclining Buddha at **Zhangye**; plus more rock art at **Bingling Caves**, near Lanzhou, and cave paintings at **Maiji Shan**, near **Tianshui**. The Great Wall snakes across Gansu to its end at the great Ming fortress at **Jiayuguan**, and in Gansu's mountainous southwest are the fascinating **Labrang Monastery** and the Tibetan town of **Xiahe**.

A huge, empty landscape with a population of less than six million, **Qinghai** is in many respects a part of Tibet, covering the northern section of the **Tibetan Plateau** with a strong minority presence – as well as Tibetans and Hui, there are Salar, Tu, Mongol and Kazakh people all living here. Qinghai's unspoiled natural wilderness incorporates the enormous **Qinghai Lake**, which offers opportunities for hiking and birdwatching. Only the eastern part of the province around **Xining** has a long-established Han presence, though the splendid **Kumbum Monastery**, one of the four great Tibetan lamaseries, is located just outside the city.

Brief history

China made its first serious effort to expand into the western deserts, primarily as a means to ensure control over the Silk Road trade, during the Han dynasty (206 BC–220 AD). Prefectures were established even though Gansu did not officially become a Chinese province for another millennium; during several periods, however, Chinese control extended well beyond here and into Xinjiang. Nevertheless, right into the nineteenth century the primarily Muslim inhabitants of this region were considered little better than barbarians, and the great revolts of 1862–77 were ruthlessly quashed.

Given that agriculture is barely sustainable in arid Gansu, since 1949 the central government has tried to develop heavy industry in the province. The exploitation of mineral deposits, including oil and coal, had a tentative beginning, and this was followed by Mao's paranoid "Third Line" policy in the 1960s, when factories were built in remote areas to save them from possible Soviet attack.

Qinghai has for centuries been a frontier zone, contested between the Han Chinese, Tibetans and Muslims who dwelled on its pastures and thin snatches of agricultural land. Significant Han migration didn't occur until the late nineteenth century, when it was encouraged by the Qing dynasty. However, effective Han political control was not established until 1949 when the Communists defeated **Ma Bufang**, a Hui warlord who had controlled the area since 1931. The area is still perceived by the Han Chinese as a frontier land for pioneers and prospectors, and, on a more sinister note, a dumping ground for criminals and political opponents to the regime, with hundreds of thousands held in Qinghai **prison and labour camps**.

Tianshui and around

West of the border with Shaanxi, the first significant Silk Road city is **Tianshui**, with the spectacular **Maiji Shan** complex just a few kilometres to the southeast. Maiji Shan – literally "Haystack Mountain", a name derived from its shape – is set amid beautiful wooded hills, and easily accessed from Tianshui, which is about halfway along the Lanzhou–Xi'an rail line. You will probably need to spend at least one night at Tianshui, the nearest transport hub to the caves, though the town is of limited interest. A little to the west, toward Lanzhou, are some more fascinating Silk Road relics, near the town of **Wuhan**.

Tianshui

天水, tiānshuǐ

The area around **TIANSHUI** was first settled back in Neolithic times, though today the city is a long industrial strip with two distinct centres, known as **Qincheng** (also called Qinzhou) in the west and **Beidao** (also known as Maiji – not to be confused with Maiji Shan) 20km to the east. Tianshui's only notable sights are in Qincheng, but where you stay will probably be determined by whether you arrive at the Beidao train station or the Qincheng bus station. If your only interest is a trip to Maiji Shan, you should stay in Beidao, from where all the Maiji Shan buses depart, though this is the grottier of the two ends of town.

Fuxi Miao and Tianshui City Museum

伏羲庙, fúxī miào • Fuxi Lu Pedestrian Street • Tues–Sun: May–Oct 8am–6pm; Nov–April 9am–5.30pm • ¥30 • ☎ 0938 8227304, ⓦ www.fuximiao.com (Chinese only) • Bus #21 from Qincheng bus station or bus #26 (both ¥1) from the Long-distance bus station

13

Qincheng's premier sight is **Fuxi Miao**, a Ming-dynasty complex commemorating the mythological figure Fuxi, who is credited with introducing the Chinese to fishing, hunting and animal husbandry. There is a statue of him, looking startled and clad in leaves, in the main hall. The temple is notable for its beautiful cypress trees; there is a thousand-year-old tree in the first courtyard.

To the rear of the same complex is the **Tianshui City Museum**, home to a small but varied collection that includes Tang statues and a two-thousand-year-old bronze money tree, created to ensure a wealthy afterlife for its owner. Sadly, Fuxi Miao's excellent English captions disappear once in the museum.

Nanzhaizi Folk Museum

南宅子, nán zháizi • Minzhu Lu • Daily: May–Oct 8am–6pm; Nov–April 8.30am–5.30pm • Free • ☎ 0938 8229253 • Bus #23 (¥1) from Long-distance bus station

Central Qincheng's **Nanzhaizi Folk Museum** is housed in a sprawling Ming-dynasty mansion that formerly belonged to a high-ranking imperial official. Half of the complex's courtyards have been furnished as they would have been when in use, while the remaining courtyards are given over to exhibits of local handicrafts. Of particular interest are occasional performances at the small shadow puppet theatre, and the family vault (used as an air-raid shelter in the 1970s) – just make sure you take a torch.

Yuquan Guan

玉泉观, yùquán guàn • Off Chengji Dadao • Daily: May–Oct 8.30am–8pm; Nov–April 8.30am–6pm • ¥20 • Bus #24 (¥1) from the Long-distance bus station runs past a path to the entrance

Yuquan Guan, a 700-year-old Taoist temple complex, is about ten minutes' walk northwest of Qincheng's main square. Pavilions dot an attractive hillside park and offer good views over the city. If you work up a thirst climbing the hill, head for the Jade Spring in the park's northeast corner – locals drink the spring water, claiming that it aids digestion.

ARRIVAL AND INFORMATION   TIANSHUI

By train Tianshui's train station (天水火车站, tiānshuǐ huǒchēzhàn) is in Beidao on Longchang Lu. The ticket office at the station is open 24hr; tickets are also available from a ticket office in the Hengtong Dasha (9am–noon and 1–5pm), 150m west of the Bank of China on Minzhu Lu. Hard-seat tickets are easy to buy for the same day, while sleeper tickets will need to be purchased a few days in advance. The #6 bus shuttles between the train and long-distance bus stations (6am–10pm; 30min; ¥3).

Destinations Dunhuang (2 daily; 19hr); Jiayuguan (17 daily; 10–16hr); Lanzhou (45 daily; 4–6hr); Turpan (17 daily; 20–28hr); Ürümqi (15 daily; 20–30hr); Xi'an (38 daily; 4–6hr); Xining (16 daily; 6–11hr); Zhangye (19 daily; 8–13hr).

By bus Qincheng's Long-distance bus station (秦城长途 汽车站, qínchéng chángtú qìchēzhàn) is on Xinhua Lu. Tickets are only available from the station ticket hall (6am–10pm). The station services destinations across southern Gansu, Ningxia and Shaanxi.

Destinations Guyuan (daily; 10hr); Lanzhou (hourly; 6hr); Linxia (daily; 8hr); Pingliang (9 daily; 5hr); Wushan (half-hourly; 2hr); Xi'an (12 daily; 7hr); Yinchuan (3 daily; 12hr).

Travel agents CITS (☎ 0938 8287337) is on the northwest corner of the Hezuo Lu/Minzhu Lu intersection in Qincheng. English-speaking staff here can organize tours to Maiji Shan for ¥200 (car-only) or ¥400 with an English-speaking guide – tickets not included.

GETTING AROUND

By bus Buses are the cheapest way to get around town, but slow – there are often long gaps between services. There is a city bus depot on Dazhong Zhong Lu, 200m south of the central square in Qincheng. Services cost ¥1, except those between Qincheng and Beidao (¥3) and the bus to

Maiji Shan (¥5).

By taxi Taxis are plentiful. Flag fall is ¥5; between Qincheng or Beidao it will cost ¥40, or ¥10 if you share with others – to do the latter, stand by a stop for the #1 or #6 buses and look interested and a cab ought to stop and help.

ACCOMMODATION

There's adequate accommodation in both Beidao and Qincheng, but as there's little to detain you in town after a visit to Maiji Shan, you might consider getting a late train out instead.

BEIDAO

Garden 花园酒店, huāyuán jiǔdiàn. 1 Longchang Lu, opposite the train station ☎ 0938 2651111. Easily the glitziest hotel in the train station area, the *Garden* offers pleasant – if smoky – rooms with baroque flourishes, as well as an in-house sauna and karaoke lounge. **¥208**

Maiji 麦积大酒店, màijī dàjiǔdiàn. West side of the train station plaza off Longchang Lu ☎ 0938 4920000. Beidao's oldest hotel, *Maiji* is gently dilapidated and features worn, furnished rooms and has friendly staff. Conveniently located for the train station and buses to Maiji Shan. **¥170**

U House 悦居精品酒店, yuèjū jīngpǐn jiǔdiàn. 1 Longchang Dong Lu ☎ 0938 2923388. Incredibly brightly lit "boutique" hotel near the train station plaza with enthusiastic staff, low rates and clean, modern rooms. **¥188**

QINCHENG

Golden Sun 阳光饭店, yángguāng fàndiàn. On pedestrianized Zhonghua Lu ☎ 0938 8277777. The most upmarket option in town, with a bar, a Western restaurant and English-speaking staff. A taxi from the nearby bus station costs ¥5. **¥468**

★**Tianjia** 天嘉商务酒店, tiānjiā shāngwù jiǔdiàn. Xinhua Lu, east side of the Long-distance bus station ☎ 0938 8319333. Newly opened, this is one of the region's nicest bus station hotels with a sunny teahouse on the fifth floor. Clean, modern rooms, all with 24hr hot water. **¥148**

Tianshui 天水大酒店, tiānshuǐ dàjiǔdiàn. 1 Dazhong Zhong Lu ☎ 0938 8289999. A basic hotel on the south side of Qincheng's central square – not far from Nanzhaizi. The hotel's slightly grotty double rooms are spacious, if spartan. **¥138**

EATING

Tianshui's local specialities include *shaguo*, a soup of glass noodles and vegetables or meat served sizzling in an earthen-ware pot, or *guagua*, a snack of boiled buckwheat starch served with chilli oil, sesame sauce and garlic. *KFC* has also reached Tianshui – there's a branch on the southeast side of the central square.

Shaguo Laodian 砂锅老店, shāguō lǎodiàn. Qingnian Nan Lu, Qincheng ☎ 0938 8296831. This popular restaurant is a great place to try *shaguo*, and their Chinese-only menu has some interesting variations; try the quail egg (鹌鹑蛋, ānchún dàn) version for ¥10. Standard fried dishes also available for around ¥25. Daily 11am–9pm.

Shangbu Lu Pedestrian Street 商埠路步行街,

shāngbù lù bùxíngjiē. Shangbu Lu, Beidao. This busy street in Beidao is home to most of the area's restaurants – a mix of steamy Sichuanese restaurants and Muslim barbecue joints – that really comes alive in the evenings. None of them has an English menu, so head to the busier restaurants, point at what you'd like and expect to pay under ¥20 for a dish.

DIRECTORY

Banks and exchange Beidao's Bank of China (Mon–Fri 8.30am–5pm) is at the end of the street running south from the train station, but can exchange cash only. There are also Bank of China ATMs that accept international cards in Qincheng, at the branch on Minzhu Lu and on Dazhong Zhong Lu.

Post office Beidao's post office (daily 8.30am–5.30pm) is just southwest of the train station. Qincheng's post office (daily 8.30am–5pm) is in an obscure alleyway in the northeast corner of the central square – look for the Suning shop and the alley is on the right.

Maiji Shan

麦积山, màijī shān • Daily 8am–5pm • ¥90; 2km sightseeing bus ride up the mountain ¥15; additional ¥500–600 for access to the most interesting caves • ☎ 0938 2731407 • Bus #34 to Maiji Shan from outside Tianshui train station (45min–1hr; ¥5); last bus returns at 6.30pm

The trip to **Maiji Shan**'s Buddhist grottoes is the highlight of eastern Gansu. As is often the case with similar sites in China, the natural setting is spectacular: although the whole area is hilly, the sheer, sandstone cliffs of Maiji Shan, rising out of the forest, make this hill a complete anomaly. The centrepiece of the statuary, a **16m-high Buddha** (complete with birds nesting in one of its nostrils), is visible from far away, flanked by two Bodhisattvas high up on the cliff. The combination of rickety walkways across the cliff face and the beautiful scenery opposite adds charm to the site.

The caves

The cliffs were split apart by an earthquake in the eighth century, leaving a total of 194 surviving **caves**, dating from the northern Wei (the earliest inscription is dated 502 AD) right through to the Qing. The wall paintings are fading due to rain erosion, but the statues are worth visiting. The caves on the western cliff are particularly well

13

preserved, and date mainly from the fourth to the sixth century AD. You are free to explore on your own, climbing higher and higher up the narrow stairways. Unfortunately, you'll find that many of the caves are locked, though several can be accessed with a guide for an additional fee. It's worth bringing a torch, as peering through the locked gates at the artwork and statuary is probably adequate for the nonspecialist.

Water Curtain Caves

水帘洞, shuǐlián dòng • Daily 8am–6pm, occasionally shut after wet weather • ¥30; additional ¥10 for a bus up the final 1km to the caves • Buses and trains between Lanzhou and Tianshui pass through Wushan, from where you can get bus #1 to Luomen – other caves are a ¥30 taxi ride from here

Accessible along a dry riverbed some 30km north of **WUSHAN** (武山, wǔshān) – a small town between Tianshui and Lanzhou – the **Water Curtain Caves** contain a number of important relics, including the **Lashao Temple** (拉稍寺, lāshāo sì) and the **Thousand Buddha Cave**. This extraordinary area is all the better preserved for being so inaccessible – the temple itself, set into a natural cave in a sandstone cliff, is not visible from the ground. Digging at the grottoes began during the Sixteen States period (304–439 AD). There is a 40m-high relief of Sakyamuni on the mountain cliff, flanked by Bodhisattvas and with wild animals like lions, deer and elephants at his feet. This kind of imagery is derived from the Hinayana branch of Buddhism, and very rarely found in northern Chinese religious art.

Kongtong Shan

崆峒山, kōngtóng shān • Daily: April–Oct 7am–8pm; Nov–March 8am–7pm • April–Oct ¥120; Nov–March ¥60 • ☎0933 8510202

Kongtong Shan is 15km west of the small city of Pingliang (平凉, píngliáng), 200km northeast of Tianshui. Buses from Pingliang deliver visitors to the entrance at the bottom, from where you then catch a shuttle bus (¥32 each way), take a cable car (¥50 each way) or walk to the top – there's a steep but scenic footpath that leads 4km straight up the mountain from the ticket office. On arrival, you're rewarded with spectacular views over an azure lake, the ribbed landscape dotted with Taoist temples. Maps of the mountain are available from kiosks at the top, and you're free to hike off in any direction – head up for the best buildings, or down toward the lake for the best scenery. Allow at least half a day to see it all.

ARRIVAL AND DEPARTURE | PINGLIANG AND KONGTONG SHAN

The access point for Kongtong Shan is Pingliang, where all long-distance transport terminates.

TO PINGLIANG
By train Pingliang's train station (平凉火车站, píngliáng huǒchēzhàn) is 2km northeast of the town centre on the Baoji–Baotou line and handles only a dozen or so services per day including midnight trains to Yinchuan and Xi'an. Hard-seat tickets are easy to buy, sleepers less so – tickets are available from the train station, or from a ticket booth at 54 Hongqi Jie, just southeast of the *Pingliang Hotel*. From the train station, bus #1 runs past the East bus station and the *Pingliang Hotel* to the West bus station.
Destinations Baoji (4 daily; 4–6hr); Lanzhou (2 daily; 11hr 30min–13hr); Xi'an (4 daily; 5hr 30min–6hr 30min); Yinchuan (7 daily; 7hr–11hr 30min).
By bus Pingliang has two bus stations. The West bus station (西车站, xichēzhàn), just beyond the western

end of Xi Dajie, is the busiest, with buses to Kongtong Shan as well as long-distance services. The East bus station (东车站, dōngchēzhàn) is just over 1km southwest of the train station on Jiefang Lu and has buses to Xi'an and Lanzhou, as well as to Guyuan and Tianshui – the last services to both of these destinations depart at 2pm.
Destinations Guyuan (3 daily; 2hr); Lanzhou (hourly; 5hr); Tianshui (hourly; 5hr); Xi'an (hourly; 5hr).

PINGLIANG TO KONGTONG SHAN
Once at Pingliang, you need to catch local transport to get to Kongtong Shan.
By bus Bus #13 (¥1) runs from Pingliang's West bus station to Kongtong Shan; allow up to an hour for the journey.
By taxi A cab to the mountain entrance from Pingliang costs about ¥30.

ACCOMMODATION AND EATING

The most interesting option is to spend the night on Kongtong Shan, although this tends to be quite basic so Pingliang may be the more comfortable choice. Once on Kongtong Shan, eating options are limited to a few vegetarian restaurants and monks' canteens.

KONGTONG SHAN

Juxian Zhai 聚贤斋, jùxián zhāi. *Kongtong Shan Main Village*. This is a simple vegetarian restaurant that's popular with tour groups – try to get there ahead of the hoards to avoid a long wait. Mains cost around ¥30.

Kongtong Shanzhuang 崆峒山庄, kōngtóng shānzhuāng. *Kongtong Shan Main Village* ☏ 0933 8353511. This hotel, owned by the people who run the vegetarian restaurant next door, has nicely furnished rooms set around a pleasant courtyard. The only rooms with en-suite bathrooms are the suites (¥400); otherwise, you'll need to use the grotty communal washrooms. Closed Nov–April. **¥260**

Taihe Gong 太和宫, tàihé gōng. *Offspring Temple,*
Kongtong Shan ☏ 1529 4031090. The most atmospheric – if the least comfortable – place to stay on Kongtong Shan. The welcoming monks at this hostel have a few simple twin-bed rooms available. To get there, head to the highest point on the mountain and follow signs to "Offspring Temple" (子孙宫, zǐsūn gōng), which is known locally as *Taihe Gong*. Meals included. **¥50**

PINGLIANG

Pingliang Hotel 平凉宾馆, píngliáng bīnguǎn. 86 Xi Dajie ☏ 0933 8253361, ✉ plbgzb@163.com. This is the best of the very few hotels where foreigners are allowed to stay in Pingliang itself. This is fortunately a very pleasant option, with comfortable doubles. **¥280**

Lanzhou and around

兰州, lánzhōu

Squeezed 1600m up into a narrow valley along the Yellow River, and stretching out for nearly 30km east to west, newly regenerated **LANZHOU** sits at the head of the Hexi Corridor (see p.818), which means that almost everyone heading to Xinjiang will pass through at some point. Many travellers break their journey here, and most head on before too long.

While many cities in China can feel diminished by recent development, Lanzhou is one that has been markedly improved. It was once the holder of the "World's Most Polluted City" title, but massive government investment, the arrival of high-speed rail, closure of dirty factories, and construction of Shanghai-esque skyscrapers has seen Lanzhou's character (and air quality) change markedly. Hemmed in by mountains and

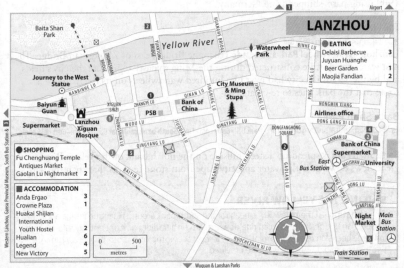

13

with ever-growing traffic, it's never going to be alpine, but the improved environment, development of riverside parks and general atmosphere of optimism that now pervades mean a stay here is one that can be enjoyed, not merely endured.

Aside from the city itself, there are a number of good day-trip possibilities, including the **Bingling Caves**, and Lanzhou forms the start and finish line for the fascinating **Xiahe Loop** (see p.802). Lastly, this is the best place in China to slurp down a bowl of **Lanzhou beef noodles** – a ubiquitous dish across the country.

Brief history

On the map, Lanzhou appears to lie very much in the middle of China, though this is misleading. For years, the city – despite being both the Gansu provincial capital and the largest industrial centre in the Northwest – has been culturally and politically remote, and recent central-government investment was very much an attempt to bring the strategically important city and region closer to Beijing.

At the head of the Hexi Corridor, it was a vital stronghold along the Silk Road and the principal crossing point of the mighty Yellow River. It has been a transportation hub for centuries, first for caravans, then shallow-draft boats and now rail lines. Not until the city became a base for imperial military operations against the Tungan Muslim rebels in the 1870s, however, did it become a large population centre as well. Today, the city has close to four million people, the vast majority of them Han Chinese.

The Yellow River

Running right past the city centre, Lanzhou's greatest sight is the **Yellow River**, which is already wide despite still being 1500km from its mouth in Shandong. In summer, the water is a rich, muddy-brown colour, a legacy of the huge quantity of silt it picks up upstream – in some years the river runs dry, leaving boats stranded on the sandbanks.

Nanbinhe Lu, on the south bank, has a paved promenade from where you can watch the river slide by, with large *Journey to the West* statues featuring Xuanzang, Monkey, Pigsy, Sandy and the horse (see box, p.844); across the road, **Baiyun Guan** (白云观, báiyún guàn; daily 8am–8pm) is a small Taoist temple that provides some respite from the hubbub. **Zhongshan Bridge** (中山桥, zhōngshān qiáo), 500m east of Baiyun Guan, was the first permanent bridge across the Yellow River, constructed between 1907 and 1909 using parts shipped from Germany.

The Waterwheel Park

水车园, shuǐchē yuán · Daily 8am–6pm · ¥6

Lanzhou's **Waterwheel Park** sits beside Huanghe Bridge, east of Zhongshan Bridge. The first waterwheels were constructed during the Ming dynasty to irrigate the city's fields, and by the 1950s the city had over two hundred waterwheels on its riverbanks – a scene that the park tries to re-create.

Baita Shan Park

白塔山公园, báitǎ shān gōngyuán · **Park** Daily 6am–6pm · Free · **South bank cable car** Daily 8.30am–6pm · ¥35 one-way; ¥45 return

Baita Shan Park is spread up a steep hillside on the north bank of the Yellow River, with great views down over the water and cityscape from stone terraces that span the park's

---

SAILING THE YELLOW RIVER

To go **boating** on the Yellow River, head for the south bank around Huanghe Bridge and Zhongshan Bridge. Here, you can ride downstream on a traditional, if not entirely safe-looking, inflated sheepskin raft (¥80/15min), or take a short scenic trip on a motorboat (¥20/10min; two-person minimum). Life vests are provided.

13

leafy heights. The Baita (White Pagoda), a 17m-tall pale brick pagoda, was raised in 1228 to honour a Tibetan monk who died here en route to pay his respects to Genghis Khan. If you fancy walking up, the entrance to the park is just north of Zhongshan Bridge. Alternatively, you can catch the cable car from the south bank of the river, west of Zhongshan Bridge on the #34 bus route.

Lanzhou City Museum

兰州市博物馆, lánzhōu shì bówùguǎn • 240 Qingyang Lu • Daily: summer 8.30am–6pm; winter 9am–5.30pm • Free • Bus #1, between Lanzhou's main train station and Lanzhou West station, passes the museum

Undergoing renovation at the time of writing, **Lanzhou City Museum** is housed in a former Buddhist temple built in 1629, complete with its own stupa. The complex's location is rather poignant; with dusty high-rises looming above it, it looks as alien as a spaceship. The highlight of its permanent collection is some amazing photos of Lanzhou from the late 1800s.

Gansu Provincial Museum

甘肃省博物馆, gānsù shěng bówùguǎn • 3 Xijin Xi Lu • Tues–Sun 9am–5pm, last admission 4pm • Free • ☎ 0931 2339133, ⓦ www.gansumuseum.com • Bus #1, #31 or #106 from the main train station or Xiguan Shizi

The **Gansu Provincial Museum** is the one sight worth visiting in western Lanzhou and occupies a Stalinist edifice on the area's main artery, Xijin Lu. It has an interesting collection including some remarkable **ceramics** dating from the Neolithic age, as well as a huge collection of **wooden tablets and carvings** from the Han dynasty – priceless resources for studying the politics, culture and economy of the period. The bronze **Flying Horse of Wuwei**, two thousand years old and still with its accompanying procession of horses and chariots, is the highlight – note the stylish chariots for top officials with round seats and sunshades. The 14cm-tall horse, depicted with one front hoof stepping on the back of a flying swallow, was discovered in a Han-dynasty tomb in Wuwei in 1969. Most of the exhibits are well labelled in English.

Wuquan and Lanshan parks

Daily 6am–6pm • ¥6 • Bus #8 to its terminus at Wuquan Park gates from anywhere along Jiuquan Lu in the town centre

In the hills bordering the south of the city, **Wuquan Park** (五泉公园, wǔquán gōngyuán) is a nice place to wander with the locals on weekends, and is full of Qing pavilions, teahouses, ponds and convoluted stairways up the mountainside. One of the oldest buildings, the **Jingang Palace**, contains a 5m-high bronze Buddha – though first cast in 1370, it was restored after being smashed into pieces in the late 1940s. From Wuquan Park, **Lanshan Park** (兰山公园, lánshān gōngyuán) can be reached by chairlift (¥20) – it's about twenty minutes to the very top, from where you'll have superb views of the city 600m below.

ARRIVAL AND DEPARTURE
LANZHOU

BY AIR

Lanzhou Zhongchuan International Airport (兰州 中川飞机场, lánzhōu zhōngchuān fēijīchǎng) lies about 70km north of the city, a 1hr 30min drive along a purpose-built expressway. Airport buses (every 30min 5.30am–8pm; ¥30) run to the Gainan Lu/Tianshui Lu intersection in town, and return from the main airlines' ticketing office just around the corner on Dong Gang Xi Lu (daily 8am–8pm; ☎ 0931 8166058). The aiport is also now connected to the city by train, with hourly departures to and from Lanzhou Station, stopping at Lanzhou West station en route. The fifty-minute journey costs ¥21.5.

Destinations Beijing (2hr 30min); Chengdu (1hr 30min); Chongqing (1hr 30min); Dunhuang (1hr 40min); Guangzhou (3hr); Jiayuguan (1hr 10min); Kunming (2hr); Shanghai (2hr 30min); Shenzhen (3hr 20min); Ürümqi (2hr 30min); Xi'an (1hr).

BY TRAIN

CRH The new Lanzhou West station (兰州西站, lánzhōu xīzhàn) lies around 8km west of the city centre, and its enormous marble-clad terminal off Xijin Xi Lu is reachable on buses #1 and #302 from Lanzhou train station (¥1), or with a taxi from town (¥30). At the time of writing,

13

Lanzhou West was purely the arrival and departure point for trains along the Lanzhou–Ürümqi high-speed line, a development that has seen the journey time between the two terminal cities almost halved. Projects are in place to join this northwestern section of the line with the rest of the national high-speed network, linking specifically with Chongqing to the south and Bejing to the east. These projects are scheduled from 2017 onwards.

Destinations Hami (Kumul) (5 daily; 7hr 30min); Jiayuguan (10 daily; 4hr 30min); Turpan (5 daily; 10hr); Ürümqi (5 daily; 11hr); Xining (15 daily; 1hr 15min); Zhangye (10 daily; 3hr)

Lanzhou Station Southwest of the town centre on Huochezhan Lu, Lanzhou Station (兰州火车站, lánzhōu huǒchēzhàn) remains the central hub for services stretching the length and breadth of the country. A huge number of the city's buses also call in or terminate here, notably the #1 and #302 shuttles between the two train stations.

Destinations Beijing (7 daily; 17–26hr 30min); Chengdu (5 daily; 22hr); Dunhuang (3 daily; 12–15hr); Guangzhou (4 daily; 29hr 30min–37hr); Guyuan (3 daily; 10hr); Hohhot (3 daily; 19hr); Jiayuguan (39 daily; 5hr 30min–11hr); Lhasa (4 daily; 24hr); Shanghai (7 daily; 24–29hr); Tianshui (49 daily; 5hr); Turpan (25 daily; 15–22hr); Ürümqi (12 daily; 16–26hr); Wuwei (27 daily; 3hr–5hr 30min); Xi'an (42 daily; 8hr 30min–10hr 30min); Xining (38 daily; 3hr 45min); Yinchuan (5 daily; 9hr); Zhangye (42

daily; 5hr 30min–8hr); Zhongwei (11 daily; 5hr 30min).

BY BUS

Main bus station (兰州客运中心, lánzhōu kèyùn zhōngxīn) Just 200m east of the main train station on Huochezhan Dong Lu, this serves most major long-distance termini.

Destinations Pingliang (11 daily; 5hr); Tianshui (22 daily; 4hr); Xining (27 daily; 3hr).

East bus station (汽车东站, qìchē dōngzhàn) About 1km north of the main train station on Pingliang Lu, this station hosts long-distance buses through the Hexi Corridor.

Destinations Jiayuguan (2 daily; 15hr); Zhangye (4 daily; 10hr)

South bus station (汽车南站, qìchē nánzhàn) All traffic to southwest Gansu – including Xiahe and Hezuo – uses this station on Langongping Lu. City bus #111 outside can take you to Xiguan Shizi and the East bus station.

Destinations Hezuo (27 daily; 4hr); Langmusi (2 daily; 8hr); Xiahe (5 daily; 4hr).

West bus station (汽车西站, qìchē xīzhàn) 1km east of the Provincial Museum on Xijin Lu, the West bus station is only useful for its frequent service to Liujiaxia for the Bingling Caves. City bus #1 runs past the front.

Destinations Liujiaxia (8 daily; 2hr).

GETTING AROUND

By bus All buses charge a flat fare of ¥1 (no change given), and run from 6am–9pm. Useful services include the #1 and #6 buses, which go from the Lanzhou train station to more central parts of town and on to the west side of the city, and #111, which runs between the East and South bus stations.

By taxi Cabs are not easy to hail in Lanzhou, especially during rush hour. Drivers often pick up additional passengers en route, so you may end up sharing your taxi with others. Fares start at ¥7 for the first 3km – most drivers use the meter, although you may need to bargain for longer journeys.

By motorbike taxi Not for the faint of heart, this is one of the best ways to beat Lanzhou's horrible traffic. Expect to bargain hard and pay roughly the same as a regular taxi.

By metro At the time of writing, a two-line metro system was under construction. Line One, scheduled for completion by 2017, will run east to west along the route of Xinjin Lu and Dong Gang Lu. Line Two will run along the north bank of the river west of Lanzhou West train station, before crossing over and linking with Line One in the city centre. The current deadline for completion of Line Two is 2020.

INFORMATION

Travel agents As most sights are within relatively easy reach, there is not much call for agency assistance; that said, there is a China Travel Service desk in the *Airlines Hotel*, next

to the airlines office on Dong Gang Xi Lu (☎0931 8883046). Many of the more upscale hotels also host travel agencies who can help with booking transport, guides and tickets.

ACCOMMODATION

Truly budget accommodation in Lanzhou used to be thin on the ground, as places where foreign travellers could stay were strictly controlled, but many of the national chains have now moved in. Today, it's unlikely you'll have to break the bank to stay somewhere clean.

Anda Ergao 安达尔高务宾馆, āndá ěrgāo wù bīnguǎn. Opposite South bus station ☎0931 2659500.

Anda Ergao is among the clutch of new cheap hotels in a block directly opposite the main gate of the South bus station. En-suite rooms are clean and super convenient if arriving late or leaving early, and staff are friendly. **¥128**

Crowne Plaza 皇冠假日酒店, huángguàn jiàrì jiǔdiàn. 1 Beibinhe Dong Lu ☎ 0931 8711111, ⓦ crowneplaza.cn. Lanzhou's newest luxury option, this outpost of the international chain in east Lanzhou is particularly nice, with enthusiastic, English-speaking staff, a big swimming pool, a great breakfast buffet and non-smoking rooms. It's located next to a conference centre on the quiet north bank of the Yellow River. **¥1100**

Huakai Shijian International Youth Hostel 花开时间国际青年旅舍, huàkāi shíjiàn qīngnián lǚshè. Building 1, F1, Motomori Estate, Tongwei Lu ☎ 1891 9050870. At the time of writing this was the only hostel in Lanzhou with dormitories officially open to foreigners, and it's pleasant even if some of the decor is overly cutesy. Dorms and private rooms all use adequate shared toilets and shower rooms, but the biggest drawback is how hard it is to find – it's unmarked on the ground floor of the first residential tower block across the new Yuantong Bridge. Dorms **¥50**, doubles **¥115**

Hualian 华联宾馆, huálián bīnguǎn. 1 Tianshui Lu ☎ 0931 4992101, ⓦ lzhlbg.com. As you emerge from the train station, you can't miss this tinted-windowed hotel. The lobby seems pretty plush for the price, though the rooms don't quite match up and can smell of drains. Still, it's good value, conveniently located and there's an on-site travel service. **¥198**

Legend 飞天大酒店, fēitiān dàjiǔdiàn. 529 Tianshui Lu ☎ 0931 8532888, ⓦ www.lanzhoulegendhotel .com. One of the most appealing hotels in town, with international-standard rooms, three restaurants, a quiet bar and friendly staff. Rates go down by ¥100 if you forgo breakfast. **¥552**

New Victory 新胜利宾馆, xīnshènglì bīnguǎn. 285 Qingyang Lu ☎ 0931 8465221. Between the eastern and western halves of the city, this hotel is handily placed for the restaurants downtown, though the rooms are showing their age and the public areas of this formerly state-owned hotel feel a little tired. The #1 and #111 buses stop nearby. **¥260**

EATING

Famed around China for its **beef noodles** (牛肉面, niúròumiàn) and delicious **summer fruits**, Lanzhou has plenty of good places to eat. You can try the noodles even if you're not staying: the train station plaza is lined with such restaurants. Otherwise, Nongmin Xiang, north of the *Legend* hotel off Tianshui Lu, is a good place to find inexpensive Chinese restaurants, and Tianping Jie, running west off Tianshui Lu about 600m north of the train station, is lined with cheap hole-in-the-wall eateries. The south bank of the Yellow River has a few overpriced "floating" fish restaurants, and branches of the usual fast-food and coffee outlets abound in Lanzhou's shopping malls.

Delaisi Barbecue 德莱斯烤肉, délàisī kǎoròu. 33 Zhongshan Lu ☎ 1391 9089223. This garrulous barbecue and noodle restaurant spills onto the pavement outside, with beer (¥15) and lamb skewers (¥2) served late into the night along with increasingly rowdy conversations. Daily 4pm–4am.

Juyuan Huanghe Beer Garden 剧院黄河啤酒广场, jùyuàn huánghé píjiǔ guǎngchǎng. Zhongshan Lu. Just south of the junction with Linxia Lu, this place can be found as easily from the noise emanating from it as the large blue sign at the entrance. Essentially a car park filled

with garden furniture and surrounded by barbecue joints, this is the place to come to grab a lamb skewer (¥2) and become embroiled in inevitably raucous cultural exchange over a beer (¥15). Daily 3pm–midnight.

Maojia Fandian 毛家饭店, máojiā fàndiàn. 90 Gannan Lu ☎ 0931 8410066. This restaurant is slightly kitsch, but has excellent spicy Hunanese food and an English picture menu. Try the house special Chairman Mao Pork (¥58), or if you're feeling particularly brave, the delicious-looking Changsha stinky tofu (¥28). Daily 11am–10.30pm.

SHOPPING

Lanzhou has traditionally specialized in manufacturing petroleum products, so there's little here in the way of must-buy souvenirs. That said, as the city moves away from its industrial past, commerce has bloomed and there are now plenty of opportunities for shopping, particularly along **Zhangye Lu** which is pedestrianized between Jiuquan Lu and Zhongshan Lu.

Fu Chenghuang Temple Antiques Market 府成隍庙, fǔ chénghuáng miào. Zhangye Lu. This temple has been converted into an antiques market and is filled to the rafters with paintings, stone carvings, calligraphy, ceramics and a head-spinning variety of beads. Daily 10am–6pm.

Gaolan Lu Nightmarket 皋兰路夜市, gāolánlù yèshì. Gaolan Lu. In the evenings, stalls pop up all along this street, hawking everything imaginable from clothes to mobile phone accessories as well as watches and all manner of cheap knick-knacks. Daily 6pm–10pm.

13

Banks and exchange Bank of China's main branch (daily 8.30am–6pm) is on Tianshui Lu, just south of the *Legend* hotel; foreign exchange is on the second floor. Other branches are scattered all over town and have ATMs that accept foreign cards.

Post offices The central Post and Telecommunications Office (daily 8.30am–7pm) stands at the junction of Pingliang Lu and Minzhu Dong Lu.

Visa extensions Visas can be extended upstairs at Lanzhou's Exit & Entry Administration Centre on Wudu Lu, a couple of hundred metres west of Jiuquan Lu – look for the yellow sign (Mon–Fri 8.30–11.30am & 2.30–5.30pm).

The Bingling Caves

炳灵寺石窟, bǐnglíngsì shíkū • April–Oct Tues–Sat 8.30am–6.30pm • ¥50 • ☎0930 8879070

The excursion from Lanzhou to the Buddhist **Bingling Caves**, which are carved into a canyon on the Yellow River, provides an introduction to both the monumental **religious art** that's spread along the Silk Road, and also to the Yellow River itself. The caves are among the earliest significant Buddhist monuments in China – started in the Western Jin dynasty and extended by the Northern Wei, the Tang, Song, Yuan and Ming. Though the earliest wall paintings here have been virtually all washed away, a considerable number of exquisite carvings have survived and are mostly in good condition – some impressive restoration work is in progress.

The caves

Water levels rose 20m after the nearby Liujiaxia Hydroelectric Dam was completed in 1969, covering the lower-level caves in mud – fortunately, the best sculptures were saved and have been moved to caves higher up. Cut into the western escarpment of **Dasi Gou** (Big Temple Gully), the remaining 183 caves stretch for 200m amid stunning scenery. The centrepiece is a huge 27m-high **seated Buddha** (cave 172), which was carved under the Tang and is currently covered in scaffolding for restoration. The majority of the caves, some little more than hollows in the rock face, are protected behind wooden doors that are opened each morning. The oldest and largest cave, number 169, is tucked away at the top of a dizzying network of stairs and ramps – if you want to see it, you will need to shell out an additional ¥300 at the entrance for a guide with the key. If you have time, it's also possible to climb to the **Upper Temple**, a further 45-minute hike up the gully, which is home to a quiet community of Tibetan lamas, who live in huts against the cliff and tend a small, modern temple.

ARRIVAL AND DEPARTURE
BINGLING CAVES

The caves are only accessible by boat, and even then only between April and early October when water levels are sufficiently high. Getting here is all part of the adventure; you'll need to take a two-hour bus journey out of Lanzhou, and then board a speedboat at the Liujiaxia Hydroelectric Dam. The ride there offers excellent views of fishermen busy at work and farmers cultivating wheat, sunflowers and rice on the steep riverbanks. Towards the end of the trip, the boat enters a dramatic gorge where the river froths and churns between jagged hills.

By bus and boat The frequent buses (¥20) depart Lanzhou's West bus station from 7am to Liujiaxia Hydroelectric Dam near Yongjing (永靖, yǒngjìng), 75km southwest of Lanzhou. At the bus stop there's an arch with a Chinese-only map, where you can pick up a speedboat for the return trip to the caves (¥150 per person or ¥700 per boat). On the way back you may need to stay the night in Yongjing if the last public bus back to Lanzhou has left without you (at around 6.30pm).

On a tour Day-trips from Lanzhou are offered by CTS and other tour operators (see p.800). An all-inclusive price (with car, speedboat and entry ticket) usually comes to around ¥500 per person for a group of four.

The Xiahe Loop

The verdant, mountainous area surrounding Lanzhou, stretching into Qinghai to the west and Sichuan to the south, is one of enormous scenic beauty, relatively untouched by the scars of industry and overpopulation. The people who live in the **Xiahe Loop** are

THE OLD ROAD TO XIAHE

Though direct buses and a highway connect Lanzhou to Xiahe, you'll get a better feel for the region by hopping slowly between towns along the more scenic **old road**, which travels via Yongjing and Liujiaxia (the jumping-off points for the Bingling Caves), and then traverses **Dongxiang Autonomous County**. Such is the beauty of this trip that you may find yourself wanting to stop off at one of the ridge towns en route, whose populations are almost entirely Muslim. Women wear a square veil of fine lace, which is black if they are married and green if they are not. The largest ridge town goes by a few different names, but is generally referred to as **Dongxiang** (东乡, dōngxiāng) and makes for a fascinating stay, with its regular bustling livestock market.

In the mountains around Dongxiang, the Islamic and Tibetan Buddhist worlds begin to overlap and villages are interspersed with ancient communities of some of China's lesser-known ethnicities. The **Dongxiang people**, numbering nearly two hundred thousand, are Muslims of Mongol origin and are descended from troops garrisoned in Linxia under Genghis Khan in the thirteenth century. These days, to outsiders at least, they are indistinguishable from the Hui except at certain celebrations when old Mongol customs re-emerge. The **Bao'an**, who number barely eight thousand, are similar to the Dongxiang in that they, too, are of Mongolian origins – while their language is written in Chinese, it contains a high percentage of Mongolian words. The **Salar** are a Turkic-speaking people whose origins lie, it's thought, in Samarkand in Central Asia; they live primarily in Xunhua County in neighbouring Qinghai province.

Regular buses ply the 25km route between Dongxiang and **Linxia** (临夏, línxià), a strongly Muslim town. Linxia's Hui are inveterate traders, and their enterprises, together with burgeoning local industry, have seen factories, tower blocks and impressive new mosques sprouting up all along the valley. The town is rather ugly, but nevertheless it's an interesting enough place to spend a few hours should you get stuck between buses. The main **Nanguan Mosque** (南关清真寺, nánguān qīngzhēn sì) is immediately south of the square at the intersection of central Tuanjie Lu and Jiefang Lu. From Linxia, there are regular buses on to Xiahe.

diverse in culture and ethnicity, including a very strong Hui and Tibetan presence. **Xiahe**, in particular, is a delightful place to visit, and is the site of the major **Labrang Monastery**, one of the largest Lamaist institutions in China, which attracts monks and pilgrims from across the Tibetan Plateau. From Xiahe, you can loop back to Lanzhou via **Tongren** – which is itself home to a large Tibetan population – and **Xining** in Qinghai province, or follow the route south towards **Sichuan** province and **Hezuo**, a small town that's experiencing something of a boom thanks to a blossoming trade in aphrodisiac caterpillars (see box, p.807).

Note that towns along the loop are mostly small affairs with few ATMs or exchange facilities – it's best to take enough **cash** to cover the entire trip.

Xiahe

夏河, xiàhé

A small but growing rural town tucked away 3000m up in the remote hills of southern Gansu, **XIAHE** is right on the edge of the Tibetan Plateau. The town's **Labrang Monastery** is one of the six major centres of the Gelugpa, or Yellow Hat Sect – of the others, four are in Tibet and one, Kumbum Monastery, is just outside the Qinghai capital in Xining (see p.813). Tibetans come here on pilgrimages in traditional dress (equipped with mittens, kneepads and even leather aprons to cushion themselves during their prostrations), and the constant flow of monks in bright purple, yellow and red, alongside seminomadic herdsmen wrapped in sheepskins and anorak-swathed Chinese tour groups, makes for an endlessly fascinating scene.

Xiahe also offers visitors the chance to spend some time in open countryside, set as it is in a sunny, fresh valley surrounded by green hills. There are a number of superb walks around town, though you should check with your accommodation before heading off, as some nearby peaks are off limits.

13

Brief history

Labrang Monastery was founded in 1709 by E'ang Zongzhe, a Living Buddha latterly recognized as the first **Jamyang**, who was born in Xiahe in 1648. Upon the death of each Jamyang a new one is born, supposedly representing the reincarnation of the previous incumbent – the present Jamyang is the sixth incarnation.

Although Labrang may seem a peaceful haven today, ferocious battles took place here in the 1920s between Muslim warlords and Tibetans, with atrocities committed by both sides. The **Cultural Revolution** brought further disaster: persecution for the monks and the virtual destruction of the monastery. It was not until 1980 that it reopened, and although it is flourishing once again it is nevertheless a smaller place than before. There are now around nine hundred registered lamas and two thousand unofficial monks, about half their former number.

Protests and rioting flared in 2008, as they did across the Tibetan Plateau, in the run-up to the Beijing Olympics, resulting in the deployment of troops and mass arrests. Scattered small and individual protests, including self-immolations, occurred over the following years, but security crackdowns, the development of Xiahe as a tourist site, the growth of the town's Han population, and increased surveillance and government control within the monastery have all worked to effectively subdue open resistance.

Labrang Monastery

拉卜楞寺, lābǔlèng sì · Daily 8am–6pm · ¥40

Phenomenally beautiful and surrounded by mountains on all sides, **Labrang Monastery** sits just west of Xiahe's centre. There's no wall separating the town from the monastery – previously the two communities just merged together with the main road running through them uninterrupted, though these days there are some bollards and a security guard posted to check tickets. With the monastery and town so interlinked, opening hours and ticket requirements are largely notional, though you will definitely need to pay to join one of the twice-daily guided tours (see opposite).

Beyond the enormous new visitor centre and coach park, the long lines of roofed **prayer wheels** trace a near-complete circle around the monastery. To the south side, along the north bank of the river, you can follow the prayer wheels to the west end of the monastery. It's mesmerizing to walk clockwise alongside the pilgrims, who turn each prayer wheel they pass.

The majority of the important **monastery buildings** are north of the road bisecting the monastery. The buildings include six colleges, prayer halls, sutra-printing workshops and mud-brick dormitories for the monks. At the colleges monks study towards degrees in astronomy, esoteric Buddhism, law, medicine and theology (higher and lower). There are also schools for dance, music and painting. The **Gongtang Pagoda** (贡唐宝塔, gòngtáng bǎotǎ; daily 8am–6pm; ¥20), first built in 1805,

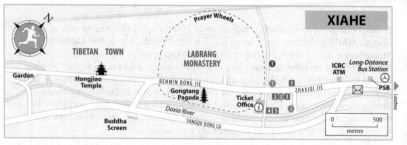

■ ACCOMMODATION				● EATING		● SHOPPING	
Labrang Baoma	1	Red Rock		Everest Café	2	Norlha Textiles	1
Nirvana	4	International Hostel	5	Nomad Restaurant	1		
Overseas Tibetan Hotel	3	Tara Guesthouse	2	Zao An Korean	3		

is the only major monastery building south of the main thoroughfare – on the prayer wheel circuit – and is worth climbing for spectacular views over the shining golden roofs of the monastery.

While there is nothing to stop you from wandering around the monastery complex by yourself (just be sensitive, use your discretion and move clockwise), it's a good idea to take a guided tour at some stage, given the bewildering wealth of architecture, art and statuary around. The hour-long tours are held roughly at 10am and 3pm, though it's recommended to arrive at the visitor centre a good thirty minutes early, particularly if an English-speaking guide is required.

ARRIVAL AND INFORMATION   XIAHE

By bus Xiahe's bus station (夏河客运站, xiàhé kèyùn zhàn) is towards the eastern end of town, and served by frequent buses from Linxia and Hezuo; there are also regular services to Lanzhou, as well as early-morning departures to Tongren and Xining in Qinghai, and Langmusi on the border with Sichuan. It's a good idea to purchase tickets at least a day in advance, particularly for the Langmusi, Tongren and Xining buses. The station ticket office is open daily 6.30am–5pm.

Destinations Hezuo (22 daily; 2hr); Langmusi (daily; 4hr); Lanzhou (4 daily; 4hr); Linxia (22 daily; 2hr); Tongren (daily; 3hr); Xining (daily; 7hr).
Travel agencies A few agencies can arrange local tours and onward travel, including Norden Tours (☏ 151 09418170, ⓦ nordentravel.com) which operates from a café opposite the main gate of the visitor centre, and OT Travels (☏ 139 0941 9888, ✉ amdolosang@hotmail.com), which runs out of the *Overseas Tibetan Hotel* (see p.806).

GETTING AROUND

By bicycle You can rent bikes from Norden Tours or the *Overseas Tibetan* and *Labrang Baoma* hotels for ¥10/hour or ¥50/day.

By taxi Shared taxis shuttle up and down Xiahe's main street, Zhaxiqi Jie. A trip anywhere in town will cost you around ¥5.

ACCOMMODATION

The east end of town has plenty of comfy, Chinese-style hotels. However, it's more fun to try one of the charismatic **Tibetan-owned guesthouses** farther up Zhaxiqi Jie towards the monastery, which attract a mixed clientele of pilgrims and budget travellers.

13

Labrang Baoma 拉卜楞宝马宾馆, lābǔlèng bǎomǎ bīnguǎn. In a courtyard off Zhaxiqi Jie, 100m northeast of the prayer wheel circuit ☏ 0941 7121078. Offering traditionally decorated rooms and 24hr hot water, this place is very popular with tour groups. Good discounts are available outside the peak summer season. **¥220**

★**Nirvana** 德吉园, déjí yuán. 247 Yagetang, 400m southeast of the monastery entrance ☏ 0941 7181702, ⓦ nirvana-hotel.net. Run by Clary from the Netherlands and her Tibetan partner Wandhikar, this smart new venture has the best dorms in town, as well as some excellent private en suites. Take into account the bar, restaurant, travel service and laundry facilities and you have one of the best accommodation options in the region, let alone Xiahe. Dorms **¥60**, doubles **¥300**

Overseas Tibetan Hotel 华侨饭店, huáqiáo fàndiàn. Zhaxiqi Jie ☏ 0941 7122642, ⓦ overseas tibetanhotel.com. This is a clean, well-maintained hotel offering private rooms that are pleasantly decorated in a vaguely Tibetan style, as well as a couple of nice dorms with communal bathrooms. Well staffed with English-speaking employees and a wide range of services. Dorms **¥50**, doubles **¥280**

Red Rock International Hostel 红石国际青年旅馆, hóngshí guójì qīngnián lǚshè. 253 Yagetang, in a courtyard next to the river just south of town ☏ 0941 7123698, ⓔ labranghongshi@yahoo.com.cn. Away from the hubbub of the main street, this hostel is centred around the lobby, which has an alpine feel and is a good place to meet fellow travellers (although most guests are Chinese and staff don't speak English). The communal showers are poor, but rooms are well maintained. Dorms **¥50**, doubles **¥170**

Tara Guesthouse 才让卓玛旅舍, cáiràng zhuómǎ lǚshè. On the south side of Zhaxiqi Jie, just east of the prayer wheel circuit ☏ 0941 7121274. The young Tibetan owners are a little eccentric (some say in a good way, others aren't so impressed) and the rooms are shabby, but this is perfect for those on a tight budget. The 11pm curfew shouldn't matter too much – this is Xiahe, after all. Dorms **¥20**, doubles **¥50**

EATING

As with accommodation, Chinese restaurants are concentrated in the east end of town, Tibetan restaurants in the west. Locals head for the cheap Tibetan canteens offering *momos* (dumplings filled with yak meat or mutton) and *thukpa* (noodle soup) that dot Renmin Xi Jie, but few have menus – ordering your meal can be a challenge.

Everest Café 华侨餐厅, huáqiáo cāntīng. Overseas Tibetan Hotel, Zhaxiqi Jie ☏ 0941 7122642. This café specializes in breakfasts: eggs, toast, yoghurt, juice and a coffee will set you back around ¥30. The friendly, English-speaking staff can also prepare you a picnic packed lunch (¥30), as well as plenty of Tibetan standards (from ¥25). Daily 8am–10pm.

★**Nomad Restaurant** 牧民齐全饭庄, mùmín qíquán fànzhuāng. 3F, corner of Zhaxiqi Jie and Tengzhi Lu, opposite Tara Guesthouse on Renmin Xi Jie ☏ 0941 7121897. This is a bustling Tibetan restaurant with great views (head for the rooftop in good weather) and an English menu. Western breakfast and main options are limited, but their expertise lies in their delicious Tibetan standards – *momos* (¥18), yak kebabs (¥45) and sweet tea (¥6). Daily 8am–10pm.

Zao An Korean 早安景福宫, zǎo'ān jǐngfú gōng. Fengqing Pedestrian Street, southeast off Zhaxiqi Jie. Offering a welcome alternative to *momos* and banana pancakes, this homely place is run by a friendly Tibetan school teacher who has learned to cook a host of delicious Korean staples, including sushi rolls (¥20) and hotpots (¥40). Veggie versions of pretty much everything on the menu are also available. Daily 8am–9pm.

SHOPPING

The vast majority of souvenir shops in town along Zhaxiqi Jie focus on **cheap reproductions** of Tibetan antiques and clothing. Haggling for these can be fun, but don't expect to uncover any genuine hidden treasures. The growing tourist boom that's bringing in increasingly well-heeled Chinese people has also signalled a small but steady growth in more exclusive boutiques, which are marketing themselves as something akin to a Tibetan Burberry.

Norlha Textiles Tengzhi Lu, northwest up the hill from the monastery entrance ⓦ norlhatextiles.com. The exquisite yak wool shirts, jackets, scarves, dresses and blankets on sale here – which can be quite pricey – are made by a nomads' cooperative near Hezuo.

DIRECTORY

Banks and exchange There is no Bank of China in Xiahe, but the *Overseas Tibetan Hotel* can exchange cash (euros and US dollars only), and you may sometimes get lucky with the ATM at the Industrial & Commercial Bank of China

(ICBC) near the post office.
Internet Most hotels and backpacker cafés have wi-fi.
Visa extensions Visas can be renewed with relative ease at the government office in a courtyard just west of the bus

station, on the same side of the road. Open Mon–Fri 8.30am–noon and 2.30–6pm.
Post offices The main post office (Mon–Fri 8am–6pm) stands 100m west of the bus station on Renmin Xi Jie.

Hezuo
合作, hézuò

About 70km southeast of Xiahe on the road to Langmusi and the Sichuan border, **HEZUO** is a trading post for Tibetan nomads, and you'll see some fairly wild-looking types in this town. If you're here in summer, don't miss Hezuo's **Caterpillar Fungus Market** (虫草批发市场, chóngcǎo pīfā shìchǎng), an ad hoc street market for an odd herbal remedy (see box below) that gathers daily in the early summer on the western side of the junction of Panxuan Lu and the G213 main road.

Milarepa Palace
米拉日巴佛楼阁, mǐlārìbāfó lóugé • Daily 7am–6pm • ¥20

Hezuo's main attraction is the **Milarepa Palace**, in the north of the city. You'll see it as you drive into town from Xiahe – indeed, you can hardly miss the impressive nine-storey structure. From town, walk north until you reach the main road to Lanzhou and Xiahe, then head east until you reach the pavilion and monastery on the left. The exterior of the tower may look stern and robust but the interior is dazzling, with each room gaudy with paintings and sculpture. Provided you take your shoes off at the door, you are free to ascend eight of the nine floors – from the roof, you can gaze out over hills dotted with prayer flags.

ARRIVAL AND INFORMATION   HEZUO

By bus Hezuo's Central bus station (合作汽车站, hézuò qìchē zhàn) serves Lanzhou, Xiahe and Xining, and is located at the northern end of Nawu Lu. The ticket office is open 6am–6pm, and also houses a booth selling train tickets (although the nearest train station is in Lanzhou). All buses heading south into Sichuan depart from the South bus station (合作汽车南站, hézuò qìchē nán

zhàn) 1km south of the centre on the corner of Tongqin Jie and Zhuoni Dong Lu; your first stop in this direction is 80km south at Luqu (碌曲, lùqū), halfway to Langmusi (see p.776).
Destinations Langmusi (3 daily; 3hr); Lanzhou (20 daily; 4hr); Linxia (20 daily; 2hr); Luqu (daily; 2hr); Xiahe (20 daily; 2hr); Xining (10 daily; 6hr); Zoige (daily; 4hr).

CHONGCAO – HIMALAYAN VIAGRA

Over the past three decades, the impoverished edges of the Tibetan Plateau have remained stubbornly resistant to the economic development that has transformed the rest of China. However, this is finally changing, thanks to an unlikely commodity: *chongcao* caterpillar fungus.

The caterpillars of the ghost moth live underground in high-altitude regions (between 3000–5000m elevation). While feeding on roots, the subterranean larva is attacked by a parasitic fungus, **Cordyceps sinensis**, which kills the caterpillar and erupts from its forehead in a stalk-like growth. When hand-collected and dried by nomads, the bizarre-looking fungus – half caterpillar, half stalk and known as **chongcao** ("insect grass") in Chinese, or *yertse kumbu* ("winter insect, summer grass") in Tibetan – is used in traditional Tibetan and Chinese medicine, where it is reputed to act as an aphrodisiac and improve a range of conditions from asthma to cancer.

As China's middle class has grown, demand for **caterpillar fungus** has increased and prices have soared (they can reach well over US$100 per gram – more expensive than gold). The profits from this booming trade have started to improve the livelihoods of people across the Himalayan region. The practice of harvesting the fungus before it has released its spores has decimated the harvest elsewhere on the plateau – pushing prices ever higher in the places where the fungus is still relatively plentiful, as it is in the Tibetan fringes of Gansu, Qinghai and Sichuan – encouraging locals to cash in while the boom lasts.

13

Services The Agricultural Bank (Mon–Fri 8.30am–5.30pm), just south of the Caterpillar Fungus Market junction on the east side of the main road, is the only place in town that will change foreign currency and has an ATM that accepts international cards.

ACCOMMODATION AND EATING

Foreigner-friendly, budget accommodation is sparse in Hezuo – attempt to check in at any of the cheaper places in the town centre and you'll be pointed towards one of the smart, new hotels shooting up across town. If you're looking for something to eat, most of Hezuo's restaurants are cheap Muslim canteens.

Gangnuo'er Restaurant 岗诺尔美食府, gǎngnuò'ěr měishífǔ. Next to the Gele Hotel, west of the Milarepa Palace. A popular place for Tibetan wedding banquets, this restaurant offers authentic Tibetan dishes like sizzling yak meat with onions, and *tsampa* – barley meal with yak butter. Daily 11am–9pm.

Gele Hotel 格乐宾馆, gélè bīnguǎn. 200m west of the Milarepa Palace ☏ 0941 8231118. This Tibetan hotel has a collection of slightly ragged rooms, friendly but chaotic service and 24hr hot water. Broadband is only available in the more expensive rooms. **¥100**

Kaibin Hotel 凯宾大酒店, kǎibīn dàjiǔdiàn. Panxuan Lu ☏ 0941 8226888. This centrally located hotel near the Caterpillar Fungus Market is better value than some of Hezuo's other upmarket options, with adequate standard rooms. **¥229**

Muslim Restaurant 清真餐厅, qīngzhēn cāntīng. On the northeast side of the Caterpillar Fungus Market junction. You'll spot this inexpensive canteen by the picture menu covering one wall. It's equally popular with Muslims and Tibetans, who come here to fill up on enormous plates of noodles. Daily 8am–8pm.

Yinxing Hotel 银星宾馆, yínxīng bīnguǎn. 8 Xishan Po ☏ 0941 8237777. This hotel is in a convenient location for the North bus station and monastery, with pleasant enough rooms and 24hr hot water. **¥158**

Tongren
同仁, tóngrén

Just across the Qinghai border from Gansu, and approximately 170km south of Xining, is the autonomous Tibetan region of **Tongren**, with a small but growing city of the same name at its centre. Known as "Repkong" in Tibetan, this makes an excellent base for exploring the nearby sights, including **Wutun Temple**, the source of Tibet's famed **thangka** paintings.

Longwu Monastery
隆务寺, lóngwù sì • Daily 9am–5pm • ¥60

In Tongren is the Yuan-dynasty Tibetan lamasery **Longwu Monastery**. Locally known as Gonchen Gompa, the monastery's temple buildings have been spruced up and it's worth keeping an eye out for the bustling kitchens. There's an official tourist trail leading around the complex, but it's better to follow the fascinating flow of worshippers around the busiest chapels. The temple is an easy walk from Zhongshan Lu in the centre of Tongren – turn left at the T-junction at the top end of the road, and it'll appear on your left after 1km or so.

Wutun
吾屯, wútún • Public minibus from Tongren ¥2; taxi ¥10

The superbly detailed pieces of Buddhist art known as *thangka* started life 8km northeast of Tongren in the incredibly scenic village of **Wutun**. They continue to be produced to this day in a number of artists' houses surrounding **Wutun Temple**. Some travellers choose to walk the whole way here from Tongren, and the village's dirt lanes are also well worth a wander – this is the Tibet people pay hundreds of dollars to see.

Wutun Temple
吾屯寺, wútún sì • Daily 9am–5pm

The Wutun Temple complex is split into upper (上, shàng) and lower (下, xià) sections that are about ten minutes from each other on foot. **Wutun Lower Temple** (¥30) is the larger and showier of the two, although this isn't saying much – both are pleasantly quiet. Keep an eye out for the beautiful old *thangka* outside the Maitreya Hall. During the Cultural Revolution these panels survived by being reversed and covered with newspaper and political slogans. Small *thangka* can usually be acquired for several hundred yuan from the monastery shop, while full-size versions – which take well over a month to make – will set you back thousands.

When visiting the **Upper Temple** (free) you'll need to find a monk to open the halls for you. Of particular interest here is a narrow chapel at the rear of the main prayer hall, containing an enormous rolled-up *thangka* that the monks display on festival days, and thousands of miniature bronze statues of the Gelugpa sect's revered founder, Tsongkhapa.

ARRIVAL AND DEPARTURE — TONGREN

By bus Buses from Xining to the north and Xiahe to the south arrive at a small station (黄南汽车站, huángnán qìchēzhàn) in the centre of town, just downhill from Zhongshan Lu; there are plenty of services heading to Xining, but the single departure to Xiahe leaves at 8am sharp every morning.

Destinations Xiahe (daily; 4hr); Xining (6 daily; 3hr).
By taxi Shared taxis (¥50 per person) drive between Tongren and a stop on Bayi Lu in Xining. They're handy if you're travelling in a group and in a hurry, but if you're a solo traveller you may find yourself waiting for ages until the car fills up with people.

ACCOMMODATION AND EATING

Qingyalou 清雅楼, qīngyǎlóu. 69 Zhongshan Lu ⊕ 0973 8726997. This Muslim hotpot restaurant is one of the many places to eat around the centre of town – *qiangguo yu*, a fish dish, is their speciality. Look for "Restaurant" in large white letters on the sign outside. Daily 11am–9.30pm.
Regong 热贡宾馆, règòng bīnguǎn. 1 Donggeer Lu ⊕ 0973 8727088. While it's not the most central of Tongren's hotels – located on the opposite side of the

Longwu River to the main town – this is one of the best, with clean rooms, 24hr hot water and only slightly grotty bathrooms. **¥160**
Yongqing 永庆宾馆, yǒngqìng bīnguǎn. Dehalong Zhong Lu ⊕ 0973 8798888. On the corner of Zhongshan Lu just uphill from the bus station, this basic hotel is convenient both for Longwu Temple and onward transport. Rooms are on the small side and can be noisy, so get one facing away from the street if possible. **¥100**

Xining and around

西宁, xīníng

Qinghai's provincial capital, **XINING** contains few tourist sights, but is increasingly a jumping-off point for Chinese backpackers heading to Qinghai Lake and deeper into the Tibetan foothills. The superb **Xiahe Loop**, which curves south from Xining (see p.802), and the nearby **Kumbum Monastery** (see p.813) and **Qutan Temple** (see p.814) make the city a worthwhile place to stay. Enclosed on all sides by mountains, Xining has a cosy feel, and its location on the outermost edge of the Tibetan Plateau means it experiences cool weather in summer, though bitter cold in winter.

Brief history

Although a largely Han Chinese city today, Xining retains a significant and highly visible minority of Hui and Tibetans. Settled during the Han dynasty and having served as a stopover on a minor branch of the Silk Road, Xining has a long history and has been a regional trading centre since at least the sixteenth century. It became the **provincial capital** when Qinghai was elevated to proper provincial status in 1928. Today, connected by train to Lanzhou and other Chinese cities, Xining is a firmly established part of the network of Han China.

Dongguan Great Mosque

东关清真大寺, dōngguān qīngzhēn dàsì • Dongguan Dajie • Mon–Thurs, Sat & Sun 8am–8pm, Fri 8–10am & 2–8pm • ¥25 • Buses #1 & #2 run past the Central Square and Ximen
Xining's major site is the **Dongguan Great Mosque**. Originally built in 1378, it encloses a large public square for worshippers to congregate – tens of thousands gather here for

13

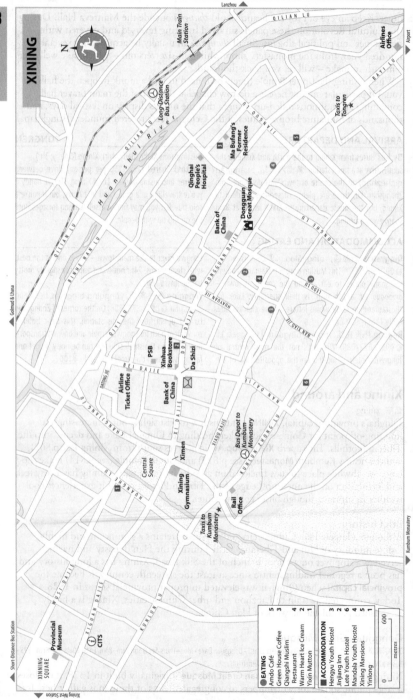

XINING

Lanzhou

QILIAN LU

Airlines Office

Airport

Main Train Station

BAXI LU

QILIAN LU

Long-Distance Bus Station

Huangshui River

BINHE NAN LU

Taxis to Tongren

Ma Bufang's Former Residence

JIANGUO LU

Qinghai People's Hospital

Dongguan Great Mosque

Bank of China

DONGGUAN DAJIE

GONGHE LU

Golmud & Lhasa

QILIAN LU

HUAYUAN JIE

TEDU LU

NAN XIAO JIE

QIYI LU

DONG DAJIE

NAN DAJIE

PSB
Xinhua Bookstore

Da Shizi

Airline Ticket Office
Bank of China
BEI DAJIE

DATONG JIE

XI DAJIE

XIAO DAJIE

KUNLUN ZHONG LU

Bus Depot to Kumbum Monastery

CHANGJIANG LU

Ximen

Central Square

Xining Gymnasium

HUANGHE LU

Rail Office

Short-Distance Bus Station

Taxis to Kumbum Monastery

Kumbum Monastery

WEST DAJIE

XINING SQUARE

Provincial Museum

CITS

XIGUAN DAJIE

KUNLUN LU

Xining West Station

● **EATING**
Amdo Café 5
Green House Coffee 3
Qiangshi Muslim
Restaurant 4
Warm Heart Ice Cream 2
Yixin Mutton 1

■ **ACCOMMODATION**
Hengyu Youth Hostel 3
Jinjiang Inn 2
Lete Youth Hostel 6
Mandala Youth Hostel 4
Xining Mansions 5
Yinlong 1

0 — 600
metres

Friday prayers (during which time the mosque is closed to visitors). Its architecture is a synthesis of Arabic and Chinese styles, and its exterior is adorned with the old Chinese favourite – white tile. Fortunately, the beautiful main prayer hall has escaped this treatment. The Tibetan prayer wheels on the roof were gifts from the monks of Labrang Monastery (see p.804).

Qinghai Provincial Museum

省博物馆, shěng bówùguǎn • Xiguan Dajie • Mon–Sat 9am–4.30pm • Free • Bus #9 runs to Jiaotong Xiang on Wusi Dajie via Xining Mansions and the Central Square

The provincial **museum** lies on the southeast side of Xinning Square (新宁广场, xīnníng guǎngchǎng), in the west of the city. The most interesting permanent exhibition displays artefacts that illustrate Qinghai's history, ranging from prehistoric rhinoceros skulls to a copy of a beautiful Qing-dynasty drum mounted on a stone elephant – the original is housed in Qutan Temple (see p.814) with English captions. Ignore signs pointing you to the carpet-weaving exhibition around the side of the building – it's a showroom.

Ma Bufang's Former Residence

马步芳公馆, mǎbùfāng gōngguǎn • 13 Weimin Xiang • Daily 8.30am–6.30pm • ¥30 • Bus #26 runs to the nearby Qinghai People's Hospital from the eastern side of the Central Square via Dongguan Mosque

Ma Bufang, one of the most prominent members of the Ma family of warlords who ruled Qinghai, Gansu and Ningxia in the first half of the twentieth century, built this luxurious house in 1942 while he was Governor of Qinghai. Having fought the communists through the 1930s, Ma was chased out of China in 1949 and finally ended up in Saudi Arabia as the Taiwanese ambassador. Today his former home – recently restored after decades of use as a vegetable market – is a fascinating example of how upper-class families lived during the Republican era, and the walls of its many rooms are faced with jade tiles and filled with imported luxuries.

ARRIVAL AND DEPARTURE   **XINING**

By plane Xining's international airport (西宁曹家堡机场, xīníng cáojiābǎo jīchǎng) is 30km east of town; the airport shuttle bus (¥21) can drop you at the airlines office (daily 8.30am–noon & 2–5.30pm; ☎0971 8133333) on Bayi Lu, 1500m south of the train station. Shuttles from the city to the airport depart hourly, while taxis cost around ¥100. Flight tickets are available from booths and hotels across town, as well as at the central post office.

Destinations Beijing (2hr 30min); Chengdu (1hr 45min); Chongqing (2hr); Guangzhou (3hr 30min); Shanghai (2hr 45min); Shenzhen (3hr 25min); Ürümqi (2hr 30min); Xi'an (1hr 30min).

By train Xining's recently rebuilt main train station (西宁火车站, xīníng huǒchēzhàn) hosts high-speed and standard east-to-west services, as well as the Lanzhou–Lhasa line. While it's easy enough to get sleeper tickets for services originating in Xining, you may have difficulty getting on trains from elsewhere. Tickets are available from the station, upstairs at the main post office, and from ticket offices at 70 Wusi Dajie, the *Tiedao Hotel* at 14 Jianguo Lu, and near the Kunlun Zhong Lu/ Chiangjiang Lu roundabout.

CRH destinations Hami (Kumul) (5 daily; 6hr 30min); Jiayuguan (14 daily; 2hr 45min–3hr 30min); Lanzhou (19 daily; 1hr–1hr 30min); Turpan (6 daily; 8hr 30min); Ürümqi (6 daily; 9hr 30min); Zhangye (12 daily; 1hr 45min).

Standard destinations Beijing (4 daily; 19–27hr); Chengdu (2 daily; 25hr); Chongqing (daily; 22hr); Golmud (9 daily; 6–8hr 30min); Hami (Kumul) (daily; 10hr); Jiayuguan (daily; 4hr); Lanzhou (25 daily; 3hr); Lhasa (6 daily; 22hr); Shanghai (2 daily; 25–31hr 30min); Shenzhen (daily; 34hr); Turpan (daily; 13hr); Ürümqi (daily; 14hr 30min); Xi'an (16 daily; 10–15hr).

By bus Xining's new Long-distance bus station (西宁汽车站, xíníng qìchēzhàn) is 200m northwest of the main train station. Tickets are only available from the station itself and same-day tickets are easy to buy. Buses to Ledu (for Qutan Temple) leave from the Short-distance bus station north of Xinning Square.

Destinations Golmud (2 daily; 14hr); Lanzhou (22 daily; 4hr); Ledu (22 daily; 1hr 30min); Linxia (daily; 6hr); Tongren (8 daily; 4hr); Zhangye (daily; 7hr).

13

INFORMATION

Travel agents For buying train or plane tickets, and for organizing trips to Qinghai Lake (see p.816), call the English-speaking staff at CITS (14F, Tower B, 49 Xiguan Dajie; ☎0971 6133844). For more interesting trips to remote parts of Qinghai and into Tibet, Tibetan Connections (☎189 97200974, ⒲tibetanconnections.com), which operates from the *Lete Youth Hostel* (see below), is the best option. Their friendly and knowledgeable staff can help organize entry permits for Tibet (which you will need if you plan to continue to Lhasa), as well as wildlife-watching trips and horse trekking.

ACCOMMODATION

The amount of accommodation in Xining is increasing as tourism in Qinghai becomes more established, and the city now boasts a number of good hostels.

Hengyu Youth Hostel 恒裕国际青年旅舍, héngyù guójì qīngnián lǚshè. 13 Weimin Xiang ☎0971 5223399, ⒲yhachina.com. A sociable hostel in a quiet location next to Ma Bufang's Former Residence. Cramped dorms and faded doubles open onto a sunny courtyard; bike rental and travel advice also available. Dorms ¥55, doubles ¥218

Jinjiang Inn 锦江之星, jǐnjiāng zhī xīng. 30 Dong Dajie ☎0971 4928333, ⒲www.jinjianginns.com. Adjoining a new shopping mall, this hotel is spotlessly clean with bright and impersonal rooms, as you'd expect from one of the leading chains in the country. If this branch is full, there's another thirty metres east along Dong Dajie – look for the large red-and-white neon sign above the courtyard entrance. ¥259

Lete Youth Hostel 理体青年旅舍, lǐtǐ qīngnián lǚshè. Jiancai Xiang ☎0971 8202080. One of the better hostels in western China, even if the shared bathrooms are a bit oversubscribed. Its sixteenth-floor location makes for superb city views, beds are comfy and the on-site bar/restaurant is a great place to eat or drink. It's a little hard to find, though, on the top of a nondescript tower block. Dorms ¥40, doubles ¥120

★Mandala Youth Hostel 曼荼罗青年旅舍, màntúluó qīngnián lǚshè. 41 Nan Xiao Jie ☎0971 5229053. This is another hostel that's tricky to find, but it's worth the effort. Situated in a gated community and looking from the outside like a family home, this is one of the most pleasant hostels in the area with pristine rooms and a bright bar and eating area. That said, basement rooms are not the pick of the bunch, and you may need to book ahead as this place fills up quickly in summer. Dorms ¥68, doubles ¥180

Xining Mansion 西宁大厦, xīníng dàshà. Dongguan Dajie/Jianguo Lu intersection ☎0971 8164999. Once upon a time, this was Xining's swankiest hotel – today, it's fallen well down the rankings, but rates are now extremely reasonable for the admittedly tired, but still entirely serviceable, rooms. ¥200

Yinlong 西宁银龙酒店, xīníng yínlóng jiǔdiàn. 38 Huanghe Lu, northwest side of Central Square ☎0971 6166666, ⒲www.ylhotel.net. Xining's poshest hotel, the *Yinlong* offers seven different restaurants (including a good Western buffet), a spa and a gym. The luxurious rooms are pricey, but if you're heading west it might be the last five-star hotel you'll see for a while. ¥900

EATING

There's an abundance of food on offer in multiethnic Xining. Local staples include kebabs, bowls of spicy noodles, mutton hotpots and *zasui* soup, made with ox and sheep entrails.

Amdo Café 安多咖啡, ānduō kāfēi. 19 Ledu Lu ☎0971 8213127, ⒲www.amdocraft.com/amdo-café -xining. This cute café – with a sister branch in Langmusi – sells handmade souvenirs and handicrafts and serves up good coffee (¥25) and fresh bakes (from ¥15). Mon–Sat 9am–8pm.

Green House Coffee 古林坊, gǔlín fāng. Xiadu Dadao ☎0971 8209376. This café is the best along Xiadu Dadao, and is popular with both locals and expats. Expect excellent coffee (¥28 a cup), tasty snacks including pizza (¥50) and a smattering of Mexican-inspired dishes (¥40), as well as expensive cakes (¥38) and a lot of passive smoking if you sit upstairs. Daily 8am–9.30pm.

Qiangshi Muslim Restaurant 强氏喜阿婆粥饼店, qiáng shì xǐ āpó zhōubǐng diàn. Dongguan Dajie ☎1329 9762301. The pick of a string of barbecue and noodle places along Dongguan Dajie, east of the junction with Gonghe Lu. As well as the ubiquitous mutton skewers (¥7) and pulled noodles (¥15), Qiangshi also has a range of good Chinese standards and a picture menu to boot. Daily 10am–10pm.

Warm Heart Ice Cream 暖心冰淇淋店, nuǎnxīn bīngqílín diàn. Qingzhen Xiang ☎0971 8185445. This shop, tucked away just south of the Dongguan Dajie/Nan Xiao Jie junction, serves up delicious ice cream in a range of flavours for ¥10 a scoop. Daily 10am–7.30pm.

Yixin Mutton 益鑫羊肉手抓馆, yìxīn yángròu shǒuzhuāguǎn. Baiyu Xiang ☎0971 8179336. One of Xining's top Muslim restaurants, bustling *Yixin* is renowned for its tender yellow-stewed mutton (*huangmen yangrou*; ¥86) and deep-fried potato slices (¥16). No English on the menu or on the signs outside – you can spot it by the gold characters on a green background. Daily 9am–9.30pm.

DIRECTORY

Banks and exchange The main Bank of China is in a huge building on Dongguan Dajie; this is the only branch that will change travellers' cheques (Mon–Fri 8.30am–5.30pm). Banks with ATMs accepting international cards can be found all along Dongguan Dajie.

Post offices The main post office (Mon–Sat 8.30am–6pm) is on the southwest corner of Da Shizi. Send parcels from the EMS office on the ground floor (entrance on Nan Dajie), and buy stamps and train/plane tickets from the first floor (entrance facing the crossroads).

Kumbum Monastery

塔尔寺, tǎ'ěr sì • Daily: 8am–5pm • ¥80, including access to nine temples; English audio-guides ¥30 from the visitor centre

Twenty-five kilometres southwest of Xining, **Kumbum Monastery** is one of the most important monasteries outside Tibet. Set in the cleft of a valley, the **walled complex** is an imposing sight and is an active place of worship for over six hundred monks, as well as the constant succession of pilgrims from Tibet, Qinghai and Mongolia who present a startling picture with their rugged features, huge embroidered coats and chunky jewellery. There are plenty of tourists too (not to mention a hulking great **military base** right next door), but Kumbum remains a good introduction to Tibetan culture.

The monastery dates from 1560, when building began in honour of **Tsongkhapa**, founder of the Gelugpa sect of Tibetan Buddhism, who was born on the Kumbum Monastery estates. Legend tells how, at Tsongkhapa's birth, drops of blood fell from his umbilical cord causing a tree with a thousand leaves to spring up; on each leaf was the face of the Buddha (the trunk is now preserved in one of the stupas). During his lifetime, Tsongkhapa's significance was subsequently borne out: his two major disciples were to become the greatest living Buddhas, the Dalai and Panchen Lamas.

The great halls

The most attractive of the temples is perhaps the **Great Hall of Meditation** (大经堂, dàjīngtáng), an enormous, very dimly lit prayer hall that is colonnaded by dozens of carpeted pillars and hung with long silk tapestries. Immediately adjacent to this is the **Great Hall of the Golden Roof** (大金瓦殿, dàjīnwǎ diàn), which has gilded tiles, red-billed choughs nesting under the eaves, wall paintings of scenes from the Buddha's life and a brilliant silver stupa containing a statue of Tsongkhapa. The grooves worn into the wooden floor in front of the temple have been made by the hands of prostrating monks and pilgrims. Built in 1560, this hall was built on the site of the pipal tree that grew with its Buddha imprints. You will still see pilgrims studying fallen leaves here, apparently searching for the face of the Buddha.

Other temples

Other noteworthy temples include the **Lesser Temple of the Golden Roof** (护法殿, hùfǎ diàn) and the **Hall of Butter Sculpture** (酥油花馆, sūyóuhuā guǎn). The former is dedicated

---

KUMBUM'S FESTIVALS

During the year, four major **festivals** are held at Kumbum, each fixed according to the lunar calendar. In January or February, at the end of the Chinese New Year festivities, there's a large ceremony centred on the lighting of yak-butter lamps. In April or May is the festival of Bathing Buddha, during which a giant *thangka* is unfurled on a hillside facing the monastery. In July or August the birthday of Tsongkhapa is celebrated with a nine-day carnival of nonstop chanting and impressive butter-lamp displays, and in September or October there's one more festival commemorating the nirvana of Sakyamuni.

13

to animals, thought to manifest characteristics of certain deities – from the central courtyard you can see stuffed goats, cows and bears on the balcony, wrapped in scarves and flags. The Hall of Butter Sculpture contains a display of colourful painted yak-butter tableaux, depicting Tibetan and Buddhist legends. After touring the temples, you can climb the steep steps visible on one side of the monastery to get a good view over the temples and hills behind.

ARRIVAL AND DEPARTURE   KUMBUM MONASTERY

Private tour buses start rolling up at the monastery around 10am, after which the place gets crowded.

By bus or minibus Buses for Kumbum (¥3) depart Xining from a depot on Xiguan Dajie near the roundabout for Kunlun Bridge. These run frequently from around 7.20am until late afternoon and take approximately forty minutes to reach the temple area; on arrival, you may be dropped at the bus station 1km short of the monastery, or taken right up to the complex itself. From the bus station, walk uphill past the trinket stalls and

rug-sellers until you pass through a gate and see a row of eight stupas at the monastery entrance. Returning to Xining, exit the monastery and grab a cab, or hang around on the street by the bus station until the bus arrives. In summer the last bus leaves around 7pm.
By taxi Shared taxis to the monastery from the roundabout on Kunlun Zhong Lu in Xining cost ¥20, or ¥80 for a cab all to yourself.

ACCOMMODATION

Most visitors just come up to Kumbum for a few hours, but it is also possible to stay the night and appreciate the monastery in peace.

Sipo Hotel 寺坡宾馆, sìpō bīnguǎn. Jinta Lu ☎ 0971 2237184. This compact and cheap little hostel is not easy to find – look for an anonymous doorway on the road between the town and temple, opposite the only junction. Once you find it, the friendly Muslim owners will make you feel at home – the basic rooms are spotless and pleasant, although the shared bathrooms are a bit grim. **¥60**

Tsongkha Hotel 宗喀宾馆, zōngkā bīnguǎn. Downhill from the Kumbum Monastery main entrance ☎ 0971 2236761. In a great location close to the monastery and with friendly staff, this hotel offers Chinese-style and Tibetan-style rooms – it's worth paying for the more attractive Tibetan rooms, which have prettier decor and feel a bit better tended to (¥280). **¥260**

Qutan Temple
瞿昙寺, qútán sì • Daily 8am–5pm • ¥50

Qutan Temple, 65km to the east of Xining in Ledu County, is much less frequented by tourists than Kumbum Monastery – which is reason enough to hunt it down. Built in 1387, this was once among the most important Buddhist centres in China and remains impressive, with plenty of original Ming-dynasty temple halls and a fascinating corridor around the edge of the main courtyard that is lined with exceptional murals illustrating the life of Sakyamuni. Inside, you'll find more paintings as well as a beautiful 3m-high Qing-dynasty drum in the shape of a kneeling elephant, which is used today to call the monks to prayer. Qutan owes its survival to generations of politically flexible abbots – reflected in the monastery's enormous stone stelae, which were presented to the monastery by various Ming and Qing emperors.

ARRIVAL AND DEPARTURE   QUTAN TEMPLE

By train, bus and taxi Access to Qutan Temple is via Ledu (乐都, lèdū), which can be reached by train (12 daily; 1hr; ¥12.50) or bus from Xining – hourly fast buses (1hr; ¥20) leave from the Short-distance bus station near Xinning Square, while more frequent slow buses (2hr; ¥12.50) leave from the southeast corner of the

Kunlun Bridge intersection. The last bus back to Xining leaves at 6pm. Between Ledu and Qutan you can take a minibus (¥7 one-way) for the 22km-long ride to the temple – these leave from a courtyard behind the *Dazhong Hotel* near the bus station. A return taxi fare should cost around ¥80.

13

West of Xining

West of Xining, Qinghai for the most part comprises a vast empty expanse. The 3000m plateau is too high to support agriculture, and the only people who traditionally have managed to eke out a living here have been nomadic yak-herders. The real highlight of the area is the huge and virtually unspoiled **Qinghai Lake**, whose shores are home to thousands of birds. A few hours beyond, **Chaka Salt Lake** is an interesting stop for those wishing to break the long journey to **Golmud**, the only town of note for hundreds of kilometres. Once there, you can catch trains to Lhasa as well as onward transport to Dunhuang and southern Xinjiang.

Qinghai Lake

青海湖, qīnghǎi hú

Situated in an extraordinarily remote location – 150km west of Xining, at 3100m above sea level on the Tibetan Plateau – **Qinghai Lake** is the largest in China, occupying an area of over 4000 square kilometres. Its cold and briny waters teem with fish (mainly the endemic **naked carp**) and are surrounded by nesting migratory birds, particularly at **Bird Island**, which, along with several man-made scenic spots, has become the lake's main tourist attraction.

If you don't have time to stop here, you can simply admire the view as you travel between Golmud and Xining; it's worth scheduling your journey to pass by during daylight hours. The train spends hours running along the northern shore, while buses skirt the southern shore instead.

Be aware that access for foreigners to certain parts of the lakeshore is restricted, particularly around the "nuclear town" of **Xihai** on the northeast edge of the lake, where China's first nuclear weapons were developed.

Bird Island

鸟岛, niǎodǎo • Daily 7am–6pm • ¥100; optional tour bus ¥15

Bird Island is in fact a peninsula, on the far western side of Qinghai Lake. A variety of migratory birds spend time here – gulls, cormorants, bar-headed geese and rare **black-necked cranes**. The main **birdwatching season** is from April to June, although the cranes stop by in February and March. Sadly, bird numbers have been dropping as visitor numbers increase, and the site has been identified as a potential nexus in the spread of bird flu. While noisy cormorants still squabble on top of **Cormorant Rock**, Bird Island's future is looking increasingly uncertain.

ARRIVAL AND DEPARTURE   **QINGHAI LAKE**

The easiest way to reach Qinghai Lake is on a tour from Xining. Although it's possible to visit independently on public transport, you may end up hitchhiking or stranded en route for a night.

By bus, taxi and hitching From Xining's Long-distance bus station, take any westbound service for Dulan (都兰, dūlán) or Wulan (乌兰, wūlán). Both routes pass along the lake's southern shore, and will be able to drop you off – the grubby little Tibetan town of Heimahe (黑马河, hēimǎhé), about four hours out of Xining, is a convenient place to aim for. From here you will need to hitch a lift to Bird Island – walk to the western end of town and flag down vehicles heading around the lake. Alternatively, take the 7.30am bus from Xining around the southern side of

the lake to Niaodao Zhen (鸟岛镇niǎodǎo zhèn), where pricey accommodation is available, and then hitch or take a taxi (¥25) for the last 10km or so out to Bird Island.
On a tour Xining's travel services (see p.812) charge in the region of ¥600 to provide a car and driver for a return day-trip to Qinghai Lake's main scenic spots, including Bird Island. It's a very long day out, leaving at 7am and returning at 10pm, but travelling this way will give you maximum flexibility to enjoy the lake scenery.

ACCOMMODATION

Camping If you have a tent, and really want a wilderness experience in China, Qinghai Lake may be the place to get

it, although frigid winter temperatures mean that the summer months – particularly July, when swaths of yellow rapeseed cover the lakeshore – are the best time to camp. Even during the summer months it's wise to bring warm clothing and enough drinking water if you're planning to stop over.

Heimahe 黑马河商务宾馆, hēimǎhé shāngwù bīnguǎn. Heimahe ⊙0974 8519377. Cheerful hotel with a nod to local aesthetics with Tibetan-style coloured trim around the windows. Rooms are basic but comfortable

enough, though (other than scarcity of alternatives) there is no justification for the exorbitant summer rates. **¥788**

Niaodao 鸟岛宾馆, niǎodǎo bīnguǎn. Niaodao Zhen ⊙0970 8655012. A bizarre, mock-Palladian facade fronts this huge hotel in the middle of nowhere; inside, it's a standard Chinese effort with clean and tidy en suites but very little beyond a modicum of comfort, despite the steep price. Good restaurant, however. **¥480**

Chaka Salt Lake

茶卡盐湖, chákǎ yánhú · Daily 7am–6.30pm · ¥50

Eighty kilometres beyond Qinghai Lake is **Chaka Salt Lake**, which has recently become something of a tourist attraction for its dazzling expanse of gleaming white salt crystals, which are visible from far away. At the site, you can ride a small train across the lake (¥35) or take a short ride on the salt-excavating ship (¥45), and cart off a hunk of the stuff with you afterwards.

ARRIVAL AND DEPARTURE   CHAKA SALT LAKE

By bus Buses heading to Dulan and Wulan from Xining's Long-distance bus station pass through the small town of Chaka Zhen (茶卡镇, chákǎ zhèn), near the lake – the earliest bus leaves at 8am (6hr; ¥50). To return to Xining, flag down local buses to Heimahe, from where there are

more frequent buses back to Xining. To continue westwards from the lake to Golmud is tricky, as there are no direct buses – you'll need to take the daily bus to Dulan, and stay overnight before catching an early bus to Golmud.

ACCOMMODATION

Qingyan 青盐宾馆, qīngyán bīnguǎn. North side of the G109 highway ⊙0977 8240254. The only hotel in Chaka Zhen that accepts foreigners, this is a decent option

in the centre of town opposite the compact square. Rooms in the new building are the best, but more expensive than the older rooms (¥580) at the rear of the hotel. **¥700**

Golmud

格尔木, gé'ěrmù

Nearly 3000m up on the Tibetan Plateau, **GOLMUD** is an incredibly isolated city, even by the Northwest's standards. The airport provides a link to Xining, but otherwise it lies at least nine hours away overland from the nearest sizeable population centre in Lhasa. In spite of this, Golmud is still the second-largest city in Qinghai, with 200,000 residents – mainly Han Chinese employed at the local potash plants.

Geographically, Golmud is located between the massive **Kunlun Mountains** to the south, and the **Chaerhan Salt Lake** to the north. The Kunlun Mountains are a major source of jade, and Golmud has a fascinating **open-air jade market** (昆仑玉批发市场, kūnlún yù pīfā shìchǎng; daily during summer) near the junction of Jiangyuan Zhong Lu and Bayi Lu, where huge lumps of stone change hands for millions of yuan.

Golmud's main draw is as somewhere to catch the train to Lhasa, as buying tickets here is easier than in Beijing (though the normal restrictions still apply). There are also bus routes north to Dunhuang (see p.823) or west to Charkhlik in Xinjiang (see p.861).

ARRIVAL AND INFORMATION   GOLMUD

By air Golmud's domestic airport (格尔木机场, gé'ěrmù jīchǎng) is 15km west of downtown Golmud. Taxis there cost around ¥30; at present there is no airport bus service.

Destinations Xi'an (2hr); Xining (1hr).

By train Golmud's train station (格尔木火车站, gé'ěrmù huǒchēzhàn) is to the south of the city centre. A taxi to anywhere in town, including the station,

costs ¥5. The ticket office is open 24hr a day, and tickets to Lhasa are relatively easy to buy. Tickets to other destinations need to be purchased a few days in advance. The Golmud–Lhasa section of the Qinghai–Tibet railway is the world's highest track, peaking at over 5000m. Note that Lhasa-bound travellers need to arrange Tibet entry permits ahead of time through a tour operator in Xining or Lhasa, and

13

have them before boarding the train.
Destinations Lhasa (8 daily; 14hr); Xining (10 daily; 8hr).
By bus The Long-distance bus station shares the square with the train station, and the ticket office is open 7am–7pm. Again, a taxi into town costs ¥5.

Destinations Charkhlik (daily; 14hr); Dunhuang (daily; 10hr); Korla (daily; 24hr); Xining (daily; 14hr).
Travel agents CITS, 60 Bayi Zhong Lu ☎0979 8496150. Erratically staffed, this office can supply permits, tours and tickets to Tibet, along with local tours to Cai Erhan Salt Lake.

ACCOMMODATION

Golmud Mansion 格尔木大厦, gé'ěrmù dàshà. 33 Yingbin Lu ☎0979 8450876. Conveniently located for the bus and train stations on the eastern side of the station plaza, this hotel is aged but clean and there's a life-sized Mao statue welcoming you into the foyer. **¥180**
Salt Lake Hotel 盐湖大酒店, yánhú dàjiǔdiàn. 26

Huanghe Zhong Lu ☎0979 8436888, ⓦqhyh-hotel .com. A 10min walk north of the train station plaza, this upmarket option has comfy rooms – and there's even an in-house bowling alley. The most luxurious rooms are in the "executive wing" next door (¥680). **¥168**

EATING

Guxiangwei 故乡味, gùxiāngwèi. Huanghe Xi Lu, opposite the Salt Lake Hotel ☎0979 8432827. This restaurant serves up tasty Chinese standards, with a focus on Hunanese and Sichuanese dishes. Vegetables from ¥20, meat from ¥40 – try the pumpkin with jujubes or *jiachang chaoji* (home-style fried chicken). Daily 11am–9.30pm.
Ma Yihei 马义黑, mǎ yìhēi. Opposite the police

station on Zhanqian Er Lu ☎1399 7398605. Take the second road on the left as you walk north from the station and you will find *Ma Yihei*, one of Golmud's most popular Muslim restaurants, serving up immense (and inexpensive) piles of excellent roast lamb every day. There's no English or picture menu, so be prepared to mime. Daily 11am–4am.

DIRECTORY

Banks and exchange The main Bank of China (Mon–Fri 9am–5.30pm), at the junction of Kunlun Lu and Chaidamu Lu, has ATMs accepting international cards, and you can exchange cash and travellers' cheques here.

Visa extensions You can extend your visa 300m east of the junction between Jiangyuan Lu and Chaidamu Lu (Mon–Fri 8.30am–noon & 2.30–6pm) – look for the huge, white complex with a red and gold badge on top.

The Hexi Corridor

For reasons of simple geography, travellers entering or leaving China from the west have always been channelled through the narrow strip of land that stretches 1000km northwest of Lanzhou. With the Qilian Mountains soaring up to the south, and a merciless combination of waterless desert and bone-dry mountains to the north, the road known as the **Hexi Corridor** offers the only feasible route through the physical obstacles that crowd in west of Lanzhou.

Historically, whoever controlled the corridor could operate a stranglehold on the fabulous riches of the Silk Road trade. The Chinese took an interest early on, and initial Great Wall-building efforts were taking place along the Hexi Corridor under Emperor Qin Shi Huang in the third century BC. Subsequently, the powerful Han dynasty incorporated the region into their empire, though the central government's influence remained far from constant for centuries, as Tibetans, Uyghurs and Mongols vied for control. Not until the Mongol conquests of the thirteenth century did the corridor finally become a settled part of the Chinese empire, with the Ming consolidating the old wall and building its magnificent last fort at **Jiayuguan**.

Further west along the corridor, **Zhangye** offers a convenient point to rest on the long journey between Lanzhou and the extraordinary Buddhist sculptures at **Dunhuang**.

Zhangye and around
张掖, zhāngyè
About 500km northwest of Lanzhou and 200km southeast of Jiayuguan, on the edge of the Loess Plateau, **ZHANGYE** has long been an important stopover for travellers on the Silk Road. Indeed, Marco Polo spent a whole year here. During the Ming period,

Zhangye was a garrison post for soldiers guarding the **Great Wall**, and it can still be seen today outside the town as a crumbling line of mud ramparts, a fascinating contrast to the restored sections elsewhere.

Zhangye itself is not especially attractive, and though there are a number of places in town that can fill a day's sightseeing, it is primarily the surrounding scenery that draws tourists to the area.

Mati Si

马蹄寺, mǎ tí sì • Daily 8am–8pm • ¥35

Situated 60km south of Zhangye, Mati Si is a network of Buddhist sites where hundreds of grottoes have been carved into the sides of sandstone cliffs. The **Thousand Buddha Caves** (千佛洞石窟, qiān fó dòng shíkǔ) complex is the easiest to reach from Zhangye, and features all the temples, statues, narrow passageways and vertigo-inducing staircases you could wish for, all carved into sheer cliff-faces. Now a well-established tourist site, the caves are thought to date back to the Jin dynasty.

To get to Mati Si, catch the early-morning bus from Zhangye's South bus station (1hr; ¥13), and keep in mind that the last buses returning to Zhangye usually leave before 5pm – plan accordingly. A taxi will cost around ¥200 for a return trip.

Zhangye Danxia Geological Park

张掖丹霞, zhāngyè dān xiá • Daily: May–mid-Oct 6am–8pm; mid-Oct–April 7am–7pm • ¥40; sightseeing bus ¥20

These so-called "rainbow mountains" can be found around 30km west of town. Here, contrasting layers of sedimentary rock have been shaped into peaks and folds by millennia of weathering, creating 320 kilometres of psychedelic rock formations. There are four official viewing areas throughout the park, which can be reached by sightseeing bus or on foot. The fourth and best viewpoint is also the furthest, around a forty-minute walk away, and this can be an arduous trek in the heat of a Gansu summer. The rocks are at their prettiest at sunrise, sunset and after a rain shower – the water making the colours particularly vivid.

The Geological Park can be reached easily from Zhangye's West bus station (30min; ¥10) while a taxi will cost around ¥180 for a half-day trip.

ARRIVAL AND DEPARTURE
ZHANGYE

BY TRAIN

Zhangye now boasts two train stations. The original, for low-speed services (张掖火车站, zhāngyè huǒchēzhàn), is 7km away to the northeast, and bus #1 (¥1) runs from here to the South bus station via the Drum Tower; a taxi costs ¥15. The new West station (张掖火车西站, zhāngyè huǒchēxīzhàn) for high-speed services is 3km west of town; a taxi there should cost between ¥5–10. You can buy train tickets at the rail office off Mingqing Jie, southeast of the Marco Polo statue (Mon–Fri 8am–noon and 1–6pm).

Zhangye Station
Destinations Dunhuang (6 daily; 8hr); Hami (19 daily; 8–11hr); Jiayuguan (25 daily; 2–3hr); Kashgar (daily; 32hr); Lanzhou (20 daily; 5hr 30min–7hr 30min); Turpan (19 daily; 11hr 30min–16hr); Ürümqi (16 daily; 13–19hr).

Zhangye West
Destinations Hami (12 daily; 4hr 40min–11hr); Jiayuguan

(20 daily; 1hr 30min–2hr 30min); Lanzhou (21 daily; 3–6hr); Turpan (12 daily; 6hr 30min–16hr); Ürümqi (12 daily; 8hr–17hr 30min); Xining (20 daily; 2–3hr).

BY BUS

Despite trains now offering cheaper and quicker services across the region, for now Zhangye still has three bus stations. The West station (西站, xīzhàn) is the busiest, with frequent services to all major destinations in Lanzhou and eastern Qinghai. The quieter South station (南站, nánzhàn) and East station (东站, dōngzhàn) operate buses to destinations in the south and east respectively, as well as the odd long-distance route. Tickets can be bought at the respective station ticket offices.

Destinations Dunhuang (2 daily; 10hr); Jiayuguan (3 daily; 5hr); Lanzhou (2 daily; 10hr); Xining (2 daily; 7hr).

ACCOMMODATION AND EATING

Bean Sprout Hostel 豆芽旅舍, dòuyá lǚshè. 113 Changshou Jie ☎ 0936 8246688. South of the junction

with Qingnian Dong Jie, the *Bean Sprout* has an English-speaking owner who is a mine of information on the local

13

sights. The establishment itself is spotlessly clean and a good place to hang out, but still struggles to justify its high prices. Dorms **¥120**

Honghao 泓昊宾馆, hónghào bīnguǎn. 141 Xianfu Jie ☎0936 8252222. Close to Zhongxin Square, this budget business hotel has good-value rooms that are neat and spacious, with tiny en-suite bathrooms. **¥158**

Ji Xiang Cun 冀乡村春饼屋, jìxiāngcūn chūnbǐng wū. Mingqing Jie ☎0936 8221958. This restaurant specializes in thin and crispy savoury pancakes, which you roll up and dip into a plum sauce (¥6); it also serves good home-style fried dishes starting from ¥20. Daily 11am–2.30pm & 4.30–9.30pm.

Rongtai 荣态大酒店, róngtài dàjiǔdiàn. 26 Xida Jie ☎0936 8865088. This is an excellent-value new hotel in the centre of town. While it may lack character, the clean en-suite rooms and convenient location more than make up for it. **¥208**

DIRECTORY

Banks and exchange The main Bank of China (daily 8.30am–6pm) is at 386 Dong Dajie. Head here to cash travellers' cheques – there are also ATMs accepting international cards here and around town.

Post offices The post office is on Xi Dajie, just west of the Drum Tower (Mon–Fri 8am–6pm).

Travel agents CITS is based at the south end of Nan Dajie, near the junction with Huancheng Nan Lu (daily 9am–5pm).

Visa extensions Zhangye's visa office is on Huancheng Nan Lu, southwest of Xilai Temple.

Jiayuguan
嘉峪关, jiāyùguān

One more cup of wine for our remaining happiness. There will be chilling parting dreams tonight.

Ninth-century poet on a leave-taking at Jiayuguan

To some Chinese, the very name **JIAYUGUAN** is synonymous with sorrow and ghastly remoteness. The last **fortress** of the Great Wall was built here by the Ming in 1372, over 5000km from the wall's easternmost point at Shanhaiguan, from which time the city made its living by supplying the needs of the fortress garrison. This was literally the final defence of the empire, the spot where China ended and beyond which lay a terrifying wilderness. Everything that travelled between the deserts of Central Asia and China's central plain – goods, traders and armies – had to go through this pass. The desolation of the landscape only adds to the melancholy: being forced to leave China altogether was a citizen's worst nightmare, and it was here that disgraced officials and condemned or fleeing criminals had to make their final, bitter farewells. The perfectly restored fort, just west of nondescript **Jiayuguan town**, is one of the highlights of northwest China, with a number of additional Wall-related sights scattered in the desert nearby.

JIAYUGUAN

0   250
metres

N

FUDIANG DONG LU

Night Market

Entertainment Park

WUYI BEI LU

Airport

XIONGGUAN DONG LU

WUYI ZHONG LU

Travel Service ② ①

XIONGGUAN XI LU

Fort

Xinhua Bookstore

SHENGLI NAN LU

Rail Office

Bank of China

XINHUA NAN LU

● EATING
Jiayuguan   2
Oriental Parkson
Food Court   1
Yuan Zhong Yuan   3

Fort

LANXIN XI LU

② JINGTIE LU

③ LANXIN DONG LU

Ⓜ Long-Distance Bus Station

■ ACCOMMODATION
7 Days Inn   3
Jiayuguan   1
Jinye   2

Main Bank of China

Train Station ▼   South Train ▼ Station

The fort
城楼, chénglóu • Daily: May–Oct 8.30am–8pm; Nov–April 8.30am–6pm • ¥120, including entry to the First Beacon Tower, Overhanging Wall, Underground Gallery and Heishan rock carvings • Bus #4 (¥1) runs from the train station past the *Jiayuguan* hotel to the fort; taxi from town ¥15

Jiayuguan's **fort** is the most important sight in the Hexi Corridor. Its location, between the permanently snowcapped Qilian Mountains to the south and the black humps of the Mazong (Horse's Mane) Mountains to the north, could not

DESERT SIGHTS AROUND JIAYUGUAN

Several other attractions around Jiayuguan could be combined with a trip to the fort: 15km north of town are the ruins of the **First Beacon Tower** (第一墩, dìyīdūn; ¥21). Built on the Great Wall in the sixteenth century, the long-abandoned tower lies crumbling on a clifftop overlooking the Taolai River at the foot of the Qilian Mountains.

The **Overhanging Wall** (悬壁长城, xuánbì chángchéng; ¥21), 8km northwest of the fort, is a section of the Great Wall connecting the fort to the Mazong range, originally built in the sixteenth century and recently restored. The ramparts afford excellent views of the surrounding land; it was more atmospheric before they built a crass tourist village nearby, but is still worth a visit to gaze out west and imagine what it was like when this place represented the end of China's civilized world.

The desert also harbours a couple of unusual collections of ancient Chinese art. One is the **Underground Gallery** (新城魏晋墓, xīnchéng wèijìnmù; ¥31), 20km northeast of Jiayuguan. This is actually a burial site from the Wei and Jin periods, more than eighteen hundred years ago, and the brick-built graves contain vivid paintings of contemporary life.

A kilometre beyond the fort are the **Heishan rock carvings** (黑山岩画, hēishān yánhuà). These look more like classic "cave man" art: there are a hundred or so pictures of hunting, horseriding and dancing dating from the Warring States Period (476–221 BC), etched into the cliffs of the Heishan range. Visiting the First Beacon Tower and the two art sites in conjunction with a tour of the fort and Overhanging Wall takes a full day. Hiring a taxi to get you around will cost ¥200–250.

Finally, one stupendous but rather inaccessible natural sight is the **July 1st Glacier** (七一冰川, qīyī bīngchuān; ¥51), which is an 80m-thick permanent ice cap 4300m up in the Qilian Mountains, named for the day it was discovered in 1958. Some 120km from Jiayuguan – remarkably close considering how toasty Jiayuguan is in summer – a day-trip by taxi costs around ¥600. Travel agents (see p.822) in town provide tours with an English guide for ¥700. It's a long day, involving a three-hour drive, five hours climbing up and down, and three hours driving back. The do-it-yourself option is to take a train to **Jingtieshan** (京铁山, jīngtiěshān), then a taxi – around ¥140 return.

be more dramatic – or more strategically valuable. As you climb the walls and survey the bleached and shimmering desert beyond, it's still possible to evoke the foreboding felt by earlier visitors to Jiayuguan.

Some kind of fort may have occupied this site as early as the Han dynasty, but the surviving building is a Ming construction, completed in 1372. Sometimes referred to as the "Impregnable Defile under Heaven", it is comprised of outer and inner walls, the former more than 700m in circumference and about 10m high. At the east and west ends of the inner wall stand symbolic gates, the Guanghua Men (Gate of Enlightenment) and the Rouyuan Men (Gate of Conciliation), respectively. Inside each are sloping walkways that lead to the top of the wall, enabling soldiers on horseback to climb up and patrol the turrets. In between the Gate of Enlightenment and the outer wall stand a pavilion, a temple and an open-air theatre, once used to entertain troops. Few of the buildings are permanent, leaving a haunting vacuum at the heart of the fort.

The Great Wall Museum

长城博物馆, chángchéng bówùguǎn • Daily 9am–5pm • Free

Right beside the fort entrance, the **Great Wall Museum** reviews the history of the Wall from the Han to the last frenzied spurt of construction under the Ming. The highlights are photos and scale models of the Great Wall taken from points across northern China, places that for the most part lie well away from tourist itineraries. In front of the museum is a gnarled old Euphrates poplar hung with red ribbons. This is the sole survivor of a Qing-dynasty greening project organized by Zuo Zongtang, a Chinese general posted to the area in the 1870s to put down the Tungan Muslim revolt.

BY AIR

Jiayuguan's domestic airport (嘉峪关机场, jiāyùguān jīchǎng) is 10km north of town. At the time of writing there was no airport bus; a taxi should cost ¥30, but you're essentially at the mercy of the drivers.

Destinations Dunhuang (daily; 45min); Lanzhou (daily; 1hr 10min); Xi'an (daily; 2hr).

BY TRAIN

Jiayuguan is another of several cities out west now boasting two train stations – one fast, one slow. The original station (嘉峪关火车站, jiāyùguān huǒchēzhàn) is in the southwest of the city linked by bus #1 and #4 (¥1) to the centre. All slow trains running between Ürümqi and eastern China (火车南站, huǒchē nánzhàn) stop here, and it's also where you'll need to come for trains to Dunhuang. The new South station (火车南站, huǒchē nánzhàn) hosts all high-speed services west to Ürümqi and east to Xining and Lanzhou. It's 10km south of the city centre, and bus #10 (¥1) runs very slowly from here into town, departing from behind the large building on the west side of the station square.

Jiayuguan Station

Destinations Dunhuang (7 daily; 4–6hr); Hami (22 daily;

5hr 30min–8hr); Kashgar (daily; 30hr); Lanzhou (27 daily; 6–10hr); Tianshui (21 daily; 10–15hr); Turpan (21 daily; 8–13hr); Ürümqi (20 daily; 10–15hr); Xining (6 daily; 4–6hr); Zhangye (37 daily; 2–3hr).

Jiayuguan South station

Destinations Hami (6 daily; 3hr); Lanzhou (15 daily; 4–5hr); Turpan (6 daily; 5hr); Ürümqi (6 daily; 6hr); Xining (14 daily; 3–4hr); Zhangye (14 daily; 1–2hr).

BY BUS

The Long-distance bus station (客运中心, kèyùn zhōngxīn) is conveniently located on Lanxin Xi Lu, 1km south of the central roundabout.

Destinations Dunhuang (3 daily; 6hr); Hami (2 daily; 11hr); Lanzhou (daily; 14hr); Zhangye (3 daily; 5hr).

SERVICES

Banks and exchange To cash travellers' cheques, you'll need to go to the main Bank of China office on Xinhua Zhong Lu. For ATMs or to exchange cash, use this branch or the smaller branch further north on the same road (both Mon–Fri 9am–5pm).

Travel agents The *Jiayuguan* hotel travel desk can supply plane tickets for a small commission and organize local tours.

ACCOMMODATION

7 Days Inn 七天连锁酒店, qītiān liánsuǒ jiǔdiàn. 29 Xinhua Zhong Lu ☎ 0937 5986888. Characterless standard motel, but central, clean, convenient and cheap. **¥160**
Jiayuguan 嘉峪关宾馆, jiāyùguān bīnguǎn. 1 Xinhua Bei Lu ☎ 0937 6226983, ⊛ www.jiayuguanhotel .com. This is the poshest hotel in town, based on the central roundabout with ticket booking services and a fancy restaurant on site. Rooms are pleasant, with sofas and

computers as standard, but the cheaper rooms are in need of a refurb. **¥380**
Jinye 金叶宾馆, jīnyè bīnguǎn. 12 Lanxin Xi Lu, diagonally opposite the bus station ☎ 0937 5941118, ⊜ jinyehotel@126.com. Its rooms are cramped and the bathrooms are tiny, but this hotel is basically clean and its location in the centre of town is convenient. Decent value. **¥120**

EATING

Jiayuguan is a migrant town, and nowhere is this more obvious than when it comes to food. There's little in the way of local cuisine, but instead you'll have a chance to try dishes from across the country. The **night market** north of the *Jiayuguan* hotel on the road to the Entertainment Park has the highest concentration of eateries in the city, although hygiene standards can be dubious – try one of the restaurants below for a sit-down meal.

Jiayuguan 嘉峪关餐厅, jiāyùguān cāntīng. *Jiayuguan* hotel ☎ 0937 6225932. This is a typical hotel restaurant, and specialities include expensive but tasty Cantonese and Sichuanese dishes – expect to pay ¥50 and up per dish. Daily 11am–1.30pm & 4.30–8.30pm.
Oriental Parkson Food Court 东方百盛, dōngfāng bǎishèng. Xinhua Bei Lu. Jiayuguan's most modern department store has a *KFC* at ground level – if you make it past that, you can join hordes of local schoolchildren and head up to the top-floor food court,

which has a range of interesting Chinese snacks and simple meals starting from around ¥10. Daily 9am–9pm.
Yuan Zhong Yuan 苑中苑酒店, yuànzhōngyuàn jiǔdiàn. Opposite the bus station ☎ 0937 6232699. This restaurant pulls in the crowds with a good-value selection of Chinese standards and efficient service. It even has an English menu, and you can't go wrong with the spicy chicken with peanuts (¥38) or home-style tofu (¥30). Daily 10.30am–10pm.

Dunhuang
敦煌, dūnhuáng

An oasis town surrounded by inhospitable desert, **DUNHUANG** has been a backpacker favourite for decades, with two main claims to fame: its colossal **sand dunes** – among the world's largest, reaching hundreds of metres in height – rising along its southern flank, and the nearby **Mogao Caves**, boasting a veritable encyclopedia of Chinese artwork on their walls. These days, the town is firmly on the main tourist trail, with heavy investment in transport and infrastructure turning Dunhuang into a shiny new desert resort, though there's little to see in the town itself bar the well-presented **City Museum** (敦煌市博物馆, dūnhuángshì bówùguǎn; Tues–Sun May–Sept 8.30am–6.30pm and Oct–April 9am–6pm; free) on Mingshan Lu, which houses a small collection of scrolls, pottery and statues that survived the twentieth-century depredations of foreign archeologists and domestic cultural revolutionaries.

ARRIVAL AND DEPARTURE   DUNHUANG

By air Dunhuang's domestic airport (敦煌机场, dūnhuáng jīchǎng) is 12km east of town; you can buy tickets at the airline office (daily 8am–10pm; ☎ 0937 8800000) on Yangguan Zhong Lu. A minibus (¥8) runs between the airport and the *Silk Road Hotel*, otherwise it's around ¥30 in a cab.

Destinations Beijing (3hr); Jiayuguan (45min); Lanzhou (1hr 30min); Ürümqi (1hr 30min); Xi'an (2hr 30min); Zhangye (1hr).
By rail Dunhuang Station (敦煌火车站, dūnhuáng huǒchēzhàn) is inconveniently located 12km from town, next to the airport. Bus #12 runs from the station square

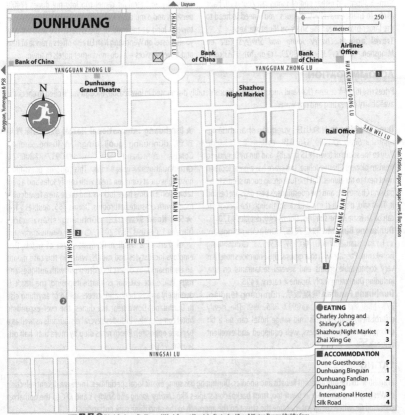

13

into town (¥1) via the bus station. Dunhuang sits on a branch of the Ürümqi–Xi'an line, and while it's relatively well connected for services heading east, if you want to go west you're best off taking a bus (¥20) or shared taxi (from ¥150/car) to Liuyuan (柳园, liǔyuán), about 150km to the north, which has a high-speed rail line. Train tickets for departures from both Dunhuang and Liuyuan stations can be booked from the booth on Yangguan Zhong Lu.

Destinations from Dunhuang Jiayuguan (10 daily; 4–6hr); Lanzhou (4 daily; 11–15hr); Xi'an (2 daily; 24hr); Zhangye (7 daily; 7hr 30min).

Destinations from Liuyuan Hami (27 daily; 3–4hr);

Jiayuguan (27 daily; 3–4hr); Kashgar (daily; 26hr); Lanzhou (20 daily; 9–14hr); Turpan (27 daily; 6–9hr); Ürümqi (24 daily; 7–12hr); Xi'an (16 daily; 17–25hr); Xining (11 daily; 5–11hr); Zhangye (27 daily; 5–7hr).

By bus The bus station is 1km east of the town centre on Sanwei Lu. While the availability of trains and the poor state of roads around Dunhuang make bus travel in and out of the town unappealing, the buses are still useful – particularly if you're heading to Qinghai or Xinjiang.

Destinations Golmud (2 daily; 10hr); Hami (3 daily; 6hr); Jiayuguan (4 daily; 5hr); Lanzhou (daily; 17hr); Turpan (2 daily; 12hr); Zhangye (2 daily; 13hr).

GETTING AROUND

By bus Private minibuses to the Mogao Caves, the airport and the train station depart from outside the *Silk Road Hotel* (all ¥8). Bus #3 (¥1) runs from the post office roundabout to Crescent Moon Lake.

By taxi There are probably more cabs in Dunhuang than all other vehicles put together – ¥5 should cover the ride to almost anywhere central, while ¥15 will get you to the sand dunes.

INFORMATION

Services Both Bank of China branches (Mon–Fri 8am–5.30pm), at either end of Yangguan Zhong Lu, have ATMs. To change travellers' cheques, you'll need to head to the larger branch near the Shazhou Night Market.

Travel agents *Charley Johng and Shirley's Café* on Mingshan Lu (☎1389 3763029, ✉dhzhzh@163.com)

comes recommended for organizing transport and tours – especially an overnight camel trip into the dunes (¥400/person), and a multiday trek west to two Han-dynasty gate towers, long abandoned in the desert. The *International* youth hostel on Wenchang Nan Lu also offers a range of trips and travel services – as do most other hotels in town.

ACCOMMODATION

Prices rise in peak season (July and August), and are considerably discounted in low season, though you'll need to check the availability of heating and hot water.

Dune Guesthouse 月泉山庄, yuèquán shānzhuāng. Mingsha Shan ☎1389 3763029, ✉dhzhzh@163.com. Way to the south of town (¥15 by cab), and run by Dunhuang tourism pioneer Charley Johng, this place has a great location right next to the dunes. But the tour group boom seems to be passing Charley by, and the guesthouse's best days are behind it. That said, it's still cheap and clean, though the lack of a/c can be an issue in the summer. Dorms ¥40, doubles ¥120

Dunhuang Binguan 敦煌宾馆, dūnhuáng bīnguǎn. 151 Yangguan Zhong Lu ☎0937 8859128, ⓦdunhuang hotel.com. Popular with tour groups, this enormous hotel has very comfortable rooms and several restaurants on site, including Dunhuang's only Japanese eatery. ¥498

Dunhuang Fandian 敦煌饭店, dūnhuáng fàndiàn. 373 Mingshan Bei Lu ☎0937 8852999. The newly refurbished rooms in this mid-range hotel can be a bit pokey, but they are spotless, well equipped and excellent value. ¥288

★**Dunhuang International Hostel** 敦煌国际青年旅舍, dūnhuáng guójì qīngnián lǚshě. Zhongzi Gongsi, Wenchang Nan Lu ☎0937 8800021, ✉dunhuangyha@gmail.com. This bright, plant-filled hostel has great common areas with comfy sofas and a pool table. Dorm rooms have lockers and there are a few double rooms with en-suite bathrooms. Dorms ¥55, doubles ¥180

★**Silk Road** 敦煌山庄, dūnhuáng shānzhuāng. Dunyue Lu ☎0937 8882088, ⓦwww.dunhuangresort .com. Part of a small nationwide chain of hotels that employs local styles and motifs, which in this case means an enormous faux desert fort kitted out with antiques and rugs. While the exterior is a little imposing, the inside is genuinely atmospheric and streets ahead of anything else in Dunhuang. Down near the dunes, the ever-expanding hotel complex also includes several restaurants as well as a bar (see opposite). Room rates drop by more than half off-season. ¥800

EATING

In addition to the omnipresent kebabs and noodles, Dunhuang has some exotic local specialities. There is a decent selection of Western food available in town too, from backpacker staples like *Charley Johng* and *Shirley's* and *KFC* to the upmarket *Zhai Xing Ge*, while cheap eateries line the street on the approach to the sand dune park entrance.

Charley Johng and Shirley's Café 风味餐厅, fēngwèi cāntīng. 21 Mingshan Lu ☎0937 88333039. A joint venture by two of Dunhuang's longest-serving hosts, this little café offers excellent pancakes and banana fritters, as well as more expensive Chinese dishes and local delicacies like braised camel paw (¥200) and donkey meat noodles (¥30). The café also organizes camel tours into the desert (see opposite). Daily 8am–10pm.

Shazhou Night Market 沙州夜市场, shāzhōu yèshìchǎng. Yangguan Zhong Lu. Unquestionably the most atmospheric place to eat in Dunhuang, with staff competing to pull punters into a string of identical open-air kebab restaurants. Spicy lamb skewers (¥7) and noodles (¥15) can be washed down with local beer (¥15). Daily 4–10pm.

Zhai Xing Ge 摘星阁, zhāixīng gé. Silk Road Hotel ☎0937 8882088. This rooftop restaurant has stunning views of the sand dunes, and ¥30 will seem like a small price to pay for a coffee or light meal while admiring the sunset. The restaurant serves Western food – expect to pay ¥50 for a pizza, ¥128 for a full steak dinner. Daily 8am–8.30pm.

THE MOGAO CAVE TREASURES

Before the arrival of Buddhism from India, Chinese religious activities had been performed in wooden buildings. Cave temples were introduced to China from India, where they were developed in response to poverty, heat and scarce building materials.

The emergence of the **Mogao** cave complex dominated early Chinese Buddhism, as pilgrims, monks and scholars passing along the Silk Road settled here to translate sutras. Merchants stopped too, endowing temples to ensure the success of their caravans and to benefit their souls. Huge numbers of **artists and craftsmen** were employed at Dunhuang, often lying on high scaffoldings in the dim light of oil lamps. The workers were paid a pittance – one document discovered at the site is a bill of indenture signed by a sculptor for the sale of his son.

The monastic community reached its peak under the Tang, with more than a thousand cave temples. Later, as ocean-going trading links supplanted the Silk Road, Mogao became increasingly provincial, until eventually the caves were **sealed and abandoned** in the fourteenth century.

In 1900, a wandering Taoist priest, **Wang Yuanlu**, stumbled upon Mogao and decided to make it his life's work to restore the site, excavating caves full of sand, touching up the murals, and even building a guesthouse, which he financed through alms. His efforts might have continued in obscurity save for his discovery of a bricked-up chamber (cave 17), which revealed an enormous collection of **manuscripts**, **sutras** and **silk and paper paintings** – some 1000 years old and virtually undamaged. The Dunhuang authorities, having first appropriated a fair amount, had the cave resealed and so it remained until the arrival of Central Asian explorer **Aurel Stein** in 1907. Stein, a Hungarian working for the British Indian Survey, had heard rumours of the caves and persuaded Wang to reopen the chamber. This is how Stein later described what he saw:

Heaped up in layers, but without any order, there appeared in the dim light of the priest's little lamp a solid mass of manuscript bundles rising to a height of nearly 10 feet and filling, as subsequent measurement showed, close on 500 cubic feet – an unparalleled archeological scoop.

This was no exaggeration. Among other manuscripts, Stein found original sutras brought from India by the Tang monk and traveller **Xuanzang** (see box, p.844), Buddhist texts in many languages (even in some unknown to the scholar) and dozens of original Tang-dynasty paintings on silk and paper – all crushed but untouched by damp.

Donating the equivalent of £130 to Wang's restoration fund, Stein left Mogao with some seven thousand manuscripts and five hundred paintings. Later the same year a Frenchman, Paul Pelliot, negotiated a similar deal, shipping thousands more scrolls back to Paris. And so, virtually overnight, the British Museum and the Louvre had acquired the core of their Chinese manuscript and painting collections.

Today, the Chinese are pressing for the **return** of all paintings and manuscripts in foreign collections. It is hard to dispute the legitimacy of these claims, though had the treasures not been removed, more would almost certainly have been lost in the chaotic years of the twentieth century. Fortunately, despite the massive loss in terms of manuscripts and scrolls, the artwork at the caves themselves is still fabulously preserved.

ENTERTAINMENT

Dunhuang Grand Theatre 敦煌大剧院, dūnhuáng dàjùyuàn. Yanguan Zhong Lu ⊙0937 8832959. This popular theatre puts on 1hr 30min dance and acrobatic performances (¥200). May–Sept daily from 8.30pm.

The Mogao Caves

莫高窟, mògāo kū • Daily: May–Oct 8am–6pm; Nov–April 9am–5.30pm; last entry 4pm • May–Oct ¥220; Nov–April ¥120; includes English-speaking guide • Minibus from Dunhuang ¥8; taxi one-way ¥50 or over ¥100 return

The **Mogao Caves**, carved out of a stretch of desert cliffs 25km southeast of Dunhuang, are one of China's greatest archeological sites – it is from here that Buddhism and Buddhist art radiated across the Chinese empire. Work started on the caves in 366 AD, and continued up until the fourteenth century. The earliest artwork shows considerable artistic influence from Central Asia, India and Persia, though you can see how these foreign styles waned over time as the iconography slowly adapted to Chinese aesthetics.

Of the original thousand-plus caves, over six hundred survive in recognizable form, but many are off-limits – either no longer considered to be of significant interest or containing murals that the Chinese consider too sexually explicit for visitors. Of the thirty caves open to the public, you are likely to manage only around fifteen in a single visit. A limited grasp of the caves' history is essential to appreciate them properly, but restorations and replacements in the modern era have complicated the picture, and many of the statues, in particular, are not original. The caves are all clearly labelled with numbers above the doors, but the interiors are unlit to preserve the murals – bring a flashlight if you have one. Photography at the caves is prohibited.

Research and exhibition centre

石窟文物研究陈列中心, shíkū wénwù yánjiū chénliè zhōngxīn • Daily 9am–5pm

The **Research and Exhibition Centre**, the modern building opposite the car park, provides a history of Mogao in English and showcases photos of off-limits caves as well as reproductions of some of the plundered frescoes that are now in Europe. There are full replicas of eight caves, and the big advantage here is that the lights are on, the colours are fresh and you can study the murals up close. The most impressive is a statue of the one-thousand-hand and one-thousand-eye Bodhisattva Guanyin – the original piece is no longer on view, due to its deteriorating condition. Upstairs are a few surviving silk scrolls and manuscripts, and there's a film about the caves.

The Northern Wei caves

The earliest caves were hewn in the fourth and fifth centuries AD during the **Northern Wei** (386–581). The Wei caves are relatively small in size, and are often supported in the centre by a large column – a feature imported from India. A statue of the Buddha is usually central, surrounded in tiers on the walls by a **mass of tiny Buddhas** brilliantly painted in black, white, blue, red and green. The statues are made of terracotta: the rock inside the caves was too soft for detailed carving, so craftsmen would first carve a rough outline of the figure, then build it up with clay.

The style of the murals in these caves shows a great deal of foreign influence. **Cave 101**, decorated towards the end of the fifth century, provides a good example: the Buddha, flanked by Bodhisattvas, is essentially a Western figure and recognizably Christ-like.

Though originally designed as a focus of devotional contemplation, the murals soon move towards a wider subject matter, their narrative sequences arranged in long horizontal strips. **Cave 135** (early sixth century) illustrates a *jataka* story – concerning a former life of the Buddha – in which he gave his own body to feed a starving tigress, unable to succour her cubs.

The Sui caves

Sixth-century China had been wracked by civil war for decades, but with the founding of the short-lived but dynamic **Sui dynasty** in 581 came a boom in Buddhist art. In the four decades up to the emergence of the Tang, more than seventy caves were carved at Mogao.

Structurally, the Sui Caves dispense with the central column, while artistically they replace the bold, slightly crude Wei brushwork with intricate, flowing lines and an increasingly extravagant use of colour that includes gilding and washes of silver. Sui-period statuary also shows change, with the figures stiff and dressed in Chinese robes, with short legs, long bodies (indicating power and divinity) and big, square heads – Cave 427 contains some good examples.

The Tang caves

The caves at Mogao reached their artistic zenith during the **Tang dynasty** (618–906). The classic Tang cave has a square floor, tapering roof and a niche set into the back wall. The statuary includes **warriors** – a new theme – and huge depictions of the **Buddha**, including a 34m-high seated example in **Cave 96**, dressed in the traditional dragon robe of the emperor – possibly designed deliberately to remind pilgrims of the Tang empress Wu Zetian. In **Cave 148** there's yet another huge Buddha, this time reclining and surrounded by acolytes.

Tang murals range from hugely scaled scenes from the sutras – now contained within one composition rather than the earlier cartoon-strip convention – to vivid paintings of individuals. One of the most popular and spectacular themes was that of the *Visit of the Bodhisattva Manjusri to Vimalakirti*. **Cave 1** contains perhaps the utmost expression of this story. Vimalakirti, on the left, is attended by a great host of heavenly beings, eager to hear the discourse of the ailing old king. The most developed Tang mural in the caves is **Cave 139A**'s depiction of the *Western Paradise of the Amitabha Buddha*, a supremely confident painting, showing the souls of the reborn rising from lotus flowers, while heavenly scenes surround the Buddha above.

Later caves

Later work, executed during the **Five Dynasties**, **Song and Western Xia** (906–1227), shows little real progression from the Tang. Much, in any case, is simply restoration or repainting of existing murals. Song work is perhaps the most interesting, tending toward a heavy richness of colour, and with many of its figures displaying the features of minority races.

Towards the end of the Mongol **Yuan dynasty** (1260–1368), before Mogao was abandoned, the standard niche in the caves' back wall gave way to a central altar, creating more surface space for murals. Tibetan-style Lamaist and Tantric figures were introduced, and occult diagrams and mandalas became fashionable.

The most interesting Yuan art is in **Cave 465**, set apart from the main body of grottoes. You could ask the guides if they will open this up for you, though they will probably only do so for a huge fee. The cave's murals include Tantric figures in the ultimate state of enlightenment, graphically represented by the state of sexual union.

Crescent Moon Lake and the Singing Sand Dune

Daily 5.30am–9pm, closed in wet weather • May–Oct ¥160; Nov–April ¥80; optional bus ride to lake ¥20; camel ride ¥100 • Bus #3 from Mingshan Lu in Dunhuang ¥1; taxi ¥10–15

A few kilometres to the south of Dunhuang is the much-touted Crescent Moon Lake (月牙泉, yuèyá quán) and Singing Sand Dune (鸣沙山, míngshā shān), the attractions on which Dunhuang's tourist future has been staked. Set amid the most impressive sand-dune scenery in China, with mounds 200 to 300m high, the sands around it hum in windy weather, hence the name. The Crescent Moon Lake is not much to look at, but is curious for its permanence – despite being surrounded by shifting sands, it was first recorded some two thousand years ago. Recent development of the area has created the air of a desert-themed amusement park, with a number of activities, including tobogganing (¥15) and quad-biking (¥120) on offer. The truly adventurous (and

13

THE UYGHUR

The **Uyghur** are the easternmost branch of the extended family of **Turkic peoples** who inhabit most of Central Asia. Around ten million Uyghurs live in Xinjiang, with another 300,000 in Kazakhstan. Despite centuries of domination by China and some racial mingling along the way, the Uyghur remain culturally distinct from the Han Chinese, and many Uyghurs look decidedly un-Chinese – stockily built, bearded, with brown hair and round eyes. Although originally Buddhists, Uyghurs have been **Muslim** for at least a thousand years and Islam remains the focus of their identity in the face of relentless Han penetration.

For the most part, Uyghurs are unable to speak fluent Chinese, and have difficulty finding well-paid work – their prospects for self-improvement within China are generally bleak. Many Han Chinese look down on Uyghurs as unsophisticated ruffians, and are wary of their supposedly short tempers and love of knives. Perhaps as a consequence of this, at times Uyghurs seem to extend their mistrust of Han Chinese to all foreigners, tourists included. Nevertheless, gestures such as trying a few words of their language or drinking tea with them will help to break down the barriers, and invitations to Uyghur homes frequently follow.

TRAVELLERS' UYGHUR

The **Uyghur language** is essentially an Eastern Turkish dialect (spoken Uyghur can be understood by Uzbek-, Kazakh- and Kyrgyz-speakers). There are several dialects, of which the Central Uyghur (spoken from Ürümqi to Kashgar) is the most popular and hence given here, including commonly used alternatives. Unlike Chinese, Uyghur is not a tonal language. It involves eight vowels and 24 consonants and uses a modified Arabic script. The only pronunciations you are likely to have difficulties with are **gh** and **kh**, but you can get away by rendering them as **g** and **k** with a light **h** at the end. **X** is pronounced "ksh", while **q** is a "ch" sound.

USEFUL WORDS AND PHRASES

Hello	*Yahximusiz*	Sunday	*Yekxembe*
Goodbye/Cheers	*Hosh*	Monday	*Doxembe*
Thank you	*Rhamat sizge*	Tuesday	*Sixembe*
Please/Sorry	*Kequrung*	Wednesday	*Qarxembe*
Yes	*He'e*	Thursday	*Peyxembe*
No	*Yakh*	Friday	*Jume*
Very	*Bek*	Saturday	*Xembe*
What is your name?	*Ismingiz nime?*		
My name is…	*Mening ismim…*	**NUMBERS**	
How much is it?	*Bahasi khange?*	1	*bir*
OK	*Bolidu*	2	*ikki*
Good	*Yahxi*	3	*uq*
Where is the…?	*…nede?*	4	*tort*
toilet	*Hajethana*	5	*bash*
hospital	*Duhturhana*	6	*alte*
temple	*Buthana*	7	*yet'te*
tomb	*Khebre*	8	*sekkiz*
I don't have	*Yenimda yeterlik*	9	*tokh'khuz*
enough money	*pul yokh*	10	*on*
Please stop here	*Bu yerde tohtang*	11	*on bir*
This is delicious	*Temlik/lezzetlik*	12	*on ikki* etc
Cold	*Soghukh*	20	*yigrime*
Hot	*Issikh*	30	*ottuz*
Thirsty	*Ussitidighan*	40	*khirkh*
Hungry	*Ag khusakh*	50	*ellik*
When?	*Vakhitta?*	60	*atmix*
Now	*Emdi/hazir*	70	*yetmix*
Today	*Bugun*	80	*seksen*
Yesterday	*Tunogun*	90	*tokhsen*
Tomorrow	*Ete*	100	*yuz*

financially flush) can splash out on microlight (¥380) and helicopter flights (¥1280). Climbing the dune in the first place, however, is incredibly hot, exhausting work; you can pay to ride up on a camel or to use the wooden steps. Note that in the summer the only sensible time to come is either before 8.30am or after 5pm.

13

Xinjiang

新疆, xīnjiāng

Xinjiang is an extraordinary region more than 3000km from any coast which, despite all the upheavals since the collapse of the Silk Road trade, still comprises the same oasis settlements strung out along the ancient routes, many producing the silk and cotton for which they were famed in Roman times (see box, p.860). Geographically, Xinjiang – literally "New Territories", and more fully the **Xinjiang Uyghur Autonomous Region** – occupies an area slightly greater than Western Europe, and yet its population is just 24 million. With ethnic minorities comprising almost sixty percent of the total population, Xinjiang is perhaps the least "Chinese" part of the People's Republic.

The **Tian Shan** range bisects Xinjiang from east to west. South of this dividing line is **Nanjiang** (southern Xinjiang), a predominantly Uyghur region that encompasses the **Tarim Basin** and the scorching Taklamakan Desert, its sands covering countless forgotten cities and another buried treasure – **oil**. China estimates that three times the proven US oil reserves are under the Taklamakan alone. The cooler forests and steppes north of the Tian Shan, in **Beijiang** (northern Xinjiang) are home to populations of Kazakhs and Mongols living a partially nomadic existence. Beijiang's climate is warm in summer, but virtually Siberian from October through to March.

Regional **highlights** include the mountain pastures outside Ürümqi, where you can hike in rare solitude and stay beside **Tian Chi** (Heavenly Lake) with Kazakhs in their yurts, but it is the old **Silk Road** that will attract most travellers, predominantly the oasis towns of **Turpan** and **Kashgar**. It is possible to follow either the Northern Silk Road from Turpan to Kashgar via Kuqa, or the virtually forgotten southern route via Hotan. There's also the possibility of continuing the Silk Road journey out beyond the borders of China itself, via the relatively well established **Karakoram Highway** into Pakistan, or over less-well-known routes into Kazakhstan or Kyrgyzstan (see box, p.732).

Brief history

While Xinjiang's past has been coloured by such great personalities as Tamerlane, Genghis Khan, Attila the Hun and Alexander the Great, the region's fortunes have waxed and waned throughout history. Likewise, China's influence has been far from constant. The area first passed under Han control in the second century BC, under Emperor Wu Di, but it was not until the **Tang dynasty** (650–850 AD) that this control amounted to more than a vague military presence. Xinjiang enjoyed something of a golden age under the Tang, with the culture and Buddhist art of the **Silk Road** oases at their zenith.

From Tang dynasty to twentieth century

The ninth century saw the gradual rise of the **Uyghurs**, and their conversion to **Islam**. Subsequent centuries saw the **Mongol conquests** under Genghis Khan and Tamerlane. Both brought havoc and slaughter in their wake, though the brief period of Mongol rule (1271–1368) hugely facilitated Silk Road trade – for the first and only time in history, east and west Asia were under a single government.

After the fall of the Mongols, Xinjiang began to split into oasis kingdoms or **khanates** and suffered a succession of religious and factional wars. Nonetheless, the Qing **reassertion** of Chinese domination in the eighteenth century was fiercely contested. A century later, in 1864, full-scale **Muslim rebellion** broke out, led by the ruler of Kashgaria, **Yakub Beg**. Ultimately, the revolt failed and by the beginning of the

XINJIANG TIME

For travellers, the classic illustration of Xinjiang's remoteness from the rest of the country is in the fact that all parts of China set their clocks to Beijing time. The absurdity of this is at its most acute in Xinjiang, 3000–4000km from the capital – which means that in Kashgar, in the far west of the region, the summer sun rises at 9am or 10am and sets around midnight. Locally, unofficial **"Xinjiang time"** (新疆时间, xīnjiāng shíjiān), two hours behind Beijing time, is used more frequently the further west you travel; when buying bus, train or plane tickets, you should be absolutely clear about which time is being used. In general, Uyghurs are more likely to use Xinjiang time, while Han Chinese prefer Beijing time. All times given in this section use Beijing time.

twentieth century, Xinjiang was a Chinese backwater controlled by a succession of warlords who acted virtually independently of the central government.

Since 1949, the Chinese government has made strenuous attempts to stabilize the region by **settling Han Chinese** from the east. The Uyghur proportion of Xinjiang's population slipped from ninety percent in 1949 to below fifty percent in the 1980s, and is still on the way down.

Modern Xinjiang

Today, the Chinese government remains nervous about Xinjiang, especially given its enormous **economic potential**. Uyghur dissent reached a peak in July 2009, when Ürümqi witnessed Xinjiang's worst-ever clashes between its Uyghur and Han populations in recent times. Official sources put the number of dead at just under 200, the majority of them Han; Uyghur groups claim that the overall figure was much higher, and that hundreds of their own people's deaths had been covered up. Security was tightened across the region, and hundreds of Uyghur men were arrested in huge sweeps of the main cities; an unknown number have since been executed.

With numerous **incidents** since 2009 targeting government authorities and Han Chinese both inside and outside Xinjiang – including a mass stabbing at Kunming train station, a car attack in Beijing's Tiananmen Square, and multiple attacks on police stations – vigilance has increased and tourist numbers, understandably, have taken a tumble. Visitors will notice a heavy police presence across Xinjiang, but especially in the strongly Uyghur regions surrounding Hotan and Kashgar. Allow extra time for **baggage scans and pat-downs** at train stations, and long-distance road journeys may also turn out longer than expected due to multiple checkpoints.

While the increased security is perhaps understandable given the threat, it is not hard to imagine that the often heavy-handed harassment of Uyghurs by an overwhelmingly Han police and military is as likely to fuel long-term discontent as it is to prevent imminent attack.

Ürümqi

乌鲁木齐, wūlǔmùqí

Well connected by road, rail and plane to the rest of China, as well as a smattering of cities abroad, **ÜRÜMQI** forms the introduction to Xinjiang for many. But the city is hardly representative of the region: the vast majority of the city's two-million-strong population are Han Chinese, and while you'll get to see Uyghur people and eat a bit of their food, you'll have a far more authentic experience elsewhere even in Turpan, just a few hours away by bus (see p.842). Ürümqi means "Beautiful Pastures", yet the name hardly applies these days: this is a political, industrial and economic capital, and there are few reasons to stay in town for more than a few days unless you're applying for Kazakh or Kyrgyz **visas**.

That said, for travellers arriving from Central Asia, Ürümqi will be the first truly Chinese city on your route – modern Han culture can be just as interesting as that of the Uyghurs. If you're heading the other way, there are also lively bazaars and food markets, as well as a vibrant nightlife – its businesspeople, gold- and oil-miners also lend the city a certain pioneering feel.

Brief history

Under the name of **Dihua**, Ürümqi became the capital of Xinjiang in the late nineteenth century. During the first half of the twentieth century, the city was a battleground for

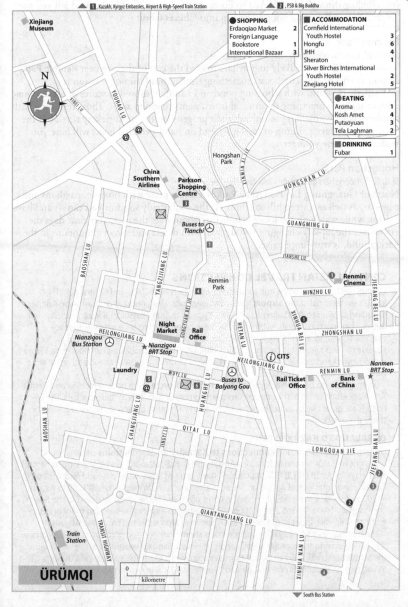

▲ 1 Kazakh, Kyrgyz Embassies, Airport & High-Speed Train Station   ▲ 2 , PSB & Big Buddha

● **SHOPPING**
Erdaoqiao Market   2
Foreign Language
  Bookstore   1
International Bazaar   3

■ **ACCOMMODATION**
Cornfield International
  Youth Hostel   3
Hongfu   6
JHH   4
Sheraton   1
Silver Birches International
  Youth Hostel   2
Zhejiang Hotel   5

● **EATING**
Aroma   1
Kosh Amet   4
Putaoyuan   3
Tela Laghman   2

■ **DRINKING**
Fubar   1

Xinjiang Museum

N

YOUHAO LU
XIBEI LU

Hongshan Park

JIANJUN LU

HONGSHAN LU

China Southern Airlines
Parkson Shopping Centre

GUANGMING LU

BAOSHAN LU

Buses to Tianchi

JIANSHE LU

YANGZIJIANG LU

Renmin Park

MINZHU LU

Renmin Cinema

JIEFANG BEI LU

XINHUA BEI LU

GONGYUAN BEIJIE

ZHONGSHAN LU

HEILONGJIANG LU

Night Market
Rail Office

Nianzigou Bus Station

HETIAN LU

Nianzigou BRT Stop

HEILONGJIANG LU

CITS

Nanmen BRT Stop

Laundry

WUYI LU

Buses to Baiyang Gou

RENMIN LU

Rail Ticket Office

Bank of China

HUANGHE LU

BAOSHAN LU

JINGTU LU

CHANGJIANG LU

QITAI LU

LONGQUAN JIE

JIEFANG NAN LU

XINHUA NAN LU

QIANTANGJIANG LU

TRANSIT HIGHWAY

Train Station

0   1
kilometre

ÜRÜMQI

▼ South Bus Station

13

feuding warlords – in 1916 Governor Yang Zengxin invited all his personal enemies to a dinner party here and had them beheaded one by one during the course of the banquet. Later, shortly before the outbreak of World War II, **Soviet troops** entered the city to help quell a Muslim rebellion; they stayed until 1960. Ürümqi began to modernize only with the completion of the Lanzhou–Ürümqi **rail line** in 1963. More than anything, this helped to integrate the city, economically and psychologically, into the People's Republic. The opening of the Ürümqi–Almaty rail line in 1991 created a direct route from Beijing through Central Asia to Europe, and the arrival of high-speed rail and the "New Silk Road" further bound Ürümqi into China's fabric.

Renmin Park

人民公园, rénmín gōngyuán • Daily 8am–10.15pm • Free

Visitors to Ürümqi are likely to gravitate toward the east of the city near **Renmin Park**. Almost every Chinese city boasts something similar, but Ürümqi's version is particularly pleasant, with a boating pond and a funfair, as well as scores of locals doing everything from practising on musical instruments to group *tai ji*. Those travelling with children may be unwilling to unleash their progeny on the most rickety rides, but the sight of kids finger-painting or racing around on hand-pedalled boats will have you wishing you were younger.

Hongshan Park

红山公园, hóngshān gōngyuán • Daily 7am–11pm • Free

North of Guangming Lu, **Hongshan Park** is a lovely place with boating, pavilions and pagodas, as well as a steep hill to climb. At the cool, shady summit you can sit and have a drink while watching the locals clambering about over the rocks; on clear days the views over the rapidly changing city skyline, with desert and snowy mountains in the background, is truly impressive.

CENTRAL ASIAN TRAVEL CONNECTIONS

Ürümqi has become a travel hub for those heading between China and Central Asia. The lovely new terminal at the **airport** handles an ever-increasing number of international flights, including services to Azerbaijan, Kazakhstan, Kyrgyzstan, Iran, Pakistan, Tajikistan and Siberian Russia. Third-party nationals will, in many of these cases, need to have **visas** in advance – check with your local embassy for details. The two visas that you can get in Ürümqi are for Kazakhstan and Kyrgyzstan (see box, p.851), although many nationalities can now get a Kyrgyz visa on arrival and visa situations are always subject to change – check ahead and arrive at the embassy as early as possible.

Ürümqi has also become a popular pit stop on the **bicycle** route between China and Central Asia – at certain times of the year, cyclists seem to outnumber "normal" backpackers. The city's hostels are great places to swap useful information with other cycle nuts, either in person or through guestbooks.

OVERLAND TO KAZAKHSTAN

Ürümqi has a couple of land **connections to Kazakhstan**. Sleeper **trains** depart around midnight on Saturday and Monday for **Almaty** (阿拉木图, ālāmùtú), and at the same time on Thursdays for Astana (阿斯塔娜, āsītǎnà). Returning trains leave Almaty around midnight on Tuesday and Sunday, and Astana on Saturday afternoons. In Ürümqi, tickets (¥1100 to Almaty, ¥1300 to Astana) can be bought from the ticket office inside the *Ya'ou Hotel* next to the South station (daily 10am–1pm & 3.30–7.30pm). The journey to Almaty takes around thirty hours, eight of which are spent at the border changing the carriages' wheels to fit Kazakh rails.

The bus journey to Almaty is around ten hours shorter. Services run from Ürümqi's International Bus station, next to the Nianziou bus station on Heilongjiang Lu, most days of the week – again, the schedule is continually changing. Tickets cost around ¥400. These services pass through Yining (see p.839), and it's possible to head there first on local transport to break the journey.

Xinjiang Museum

新疆博物馆, xīnjiāng bówùguǎn • Xibei Lu • Tues–Sun: mid-April–mid-Oct 10am–6pm; mid-Oct–mid-April 10.30am–6pm; last entry 4.30pm • Free • Five-minute walk from Ming Yuan BRT station on Line #1

A must-see sight, the **Xinjiang Museum** focuses on the lives, culture and history of the peoples of the region, and includes everything from ancient, desiccated **corpses** retrieved from desert burial sites to dioramas of ethnic minority homes. The star exhibit is the so-called "Loulan Beauty", a woman with long fair hair, allegedly 3800 years old, recovered in the ruined city of Loulan on the Southern Silk Road (see p.856). Of distinctly un-Chinese appearance, Uyghur nationalists have taken the Loulan Beauty to heart as a symbol of the antiquity (and validity) of their claims for sovereignty; a counterclaim of sorts is made by the museum, with an exhibit making it clear that Xinjiang is "together with the motherland forever".

ARRIVAL AND DEPARTURE ÜRÜMQI

BY AIR

Diwopu International Airport (地窝堡国际机场, diwōbǎo guójì jīchǎng; ⓦ xjairport.com) is 15km northwest of the city. You can get into town on the airport bus (¥10), which delivers to various airline offices, terminating at the *Ya'ou Hotel* near the train station. The budget option is to take bus #51 (¥1), which runs between Nianzigou, Hongshan Park BRT stations and the airport. A taxi will set you back around ¥40. To purchase flight tickets, the best prices are available online or from one of Ürümqi's numerous independent ticket offices. As a last resort, try the China Southern office at 576 Youhao Nan Lu, although their prices are often higher than elsewhere. Ürümqi is now only a direct flight away from virtually every major city in China, and there are also international flights linking Ürümqi with Almaty, Astana, Bishkek, Dushanbe, Islamabad, Moscow, Novosibirsk, Osh, Seoul and Tehran.

Destinations Beijing (3hr 30min); Chengdu (3hr); Chongqing (4hr); Dunhuang (1hr 40min); Guangzhou (4hr 50min); Hotan (2hr); Kashgar (1hr 50min); Korla (1hr); Lanzhou (2hr 30min); Shanghai (4hr 45min); Xi'an (3hr 15min); Xining (2hr 15min); Yinchuan (3hr); Yining (1hr).

BY TRAIN

Ürümqi South (乌鲁木齐南站, wūlǔmùqí nánzhàn). This station lies in the southwest of the city, and was for decades the main point of arrival and departure with services from as far afield as Beijing and Shanghai in the east, and Kashgar in the west, not to mention Almaty and Astana in Kazakhstan (see box opposite). It still operates, but the arrival of high-speed rail has also brought the city a new main station: Ürümqi Station (乌鲁木齐火车站, wūlǔmùqí huǒchēzhàn), northwest of the city centre. This terminus opened in late 2016; however prior to this the South station had also been known simply as Ürümqi Station, creating plenty of scope for confusion. At the time of writing, the new station was being phased in and services (including expanded high-speed services to the rest of the country) will be subject to regular change as it becomes fully operational; triple-checking which station

you need to depart from is strongly recommended.

Long distances and the Ürümqi–Lanzhou high-speed line make trains easily the most attractive option for travel in the region. Sadly, everyone else has realized this too, and you will need to book tickets well in advance – particularly for the sleeper train to Kashgar – or get ready to travel hard-seat. The station is easy to reach at the southern end of BRT #1 and served by several bus routes (including #2, #10, #16, #20). Crowds and tight security in the station itself mean that it is often better to purchase tickets from one of the ticket booths around town (all daily 9.30am–9pm) – the ones at 176 Renmin Lu and 245 Jianshe Lu are the most centrally located, though some are reluctant to issue tickets to foreigners.

International destinations Almaty (2 weekly; 34hr); Astana (weekly; 40hr).

Domestic CRH destinations Hami (10 daily; 3hr); Jiayuguan (6 daily; 6hr); Lanzhou (5 daily; 11hr); Turpan (10 daily;1hr); Xining (6 daily; 10hr); Zhangye (6 daily; 8hr).

Other domestic destinations Beijing (2 daily; 30–40hr); Chengdu (2 daily; 46hr); Hami (23 daily; 4–6hr 30min); Jiayuguan (23 daily; 10–15hr); Kashgar (4 daily; 17–24hr); Kuqa (6 daily; 8–13hr); Lanzhou (16 daily; 16–24hr); Shanghai (2 daily; 40–45hr); Tianshui (16 daily; 21–30hr); Turpan (33 daily; 2hr); Xi'an (15 daily; 24–35hr); Xining (6 daily; 14–21hr); Zhangye (23 daily; 12–18hr).

BY BUS

Nianzigou bus station (碾子沟客运中心, niǎnzigōu kèyùn zhōngxīn). 500m west of the Nianzigou BRT station, this bus station deals with traffic to northern Xinjiang, including Saryam Lake, Yining and Altai, as well as regular buses to Korla and occasional departures for Hami and into Gansu. The ticket office is open daily 7am–9pm.

South bus station (南郊客运站, nánjiāo kèyùnzhàn). 2km south of the centre at the southern end of Xinhua Nan Lu, serving destinations south of Ürümqi, including Turpan, Korla, Kuqa, Hotan and Kashgar. Bus routes #1 and #7 stop here and a taxi costs around ¥10 from the city centre. The ticket office opens daily 7am–9pm.

13

International destinations Almaty (daily; 24–36hr). Domestic destinations Hami (3 daily; 7hr); Hotan (10 daily; 24hr); Kashgar (10 daily; 24hr); Kuqa (10 daily; 12hr); Turpan (20 daily; 2hr 30min); Yining (10 daily; 12hr).

GETTING AROUND

By BRT (Bus Rapid Transit) Ürümqi's traffic can be awful, especially during rush hour – and this is just one reason to learn to love the BRT (¥1) ⓦ chinabrt.org. These special bus services escape the worst of the traffic by shooting up and down dedicated lanes in the middle of the busiest roads. Line #1 is particularly useful, running from the train station north up Changjiang Lu to Hongshan Park and on towards the museum. Line #3 runs between Erdaoqiao Market and Nanmen.

By bus City buses serve more destinations than the BRT. Buses #1 and #102 both run from Youhao Lu to the South bus station via Erdaoqiao. Bus #8 goes between the train station and Xinhua Bei Lu via Nianzigou BRT stop.

By taxi Cabs cost ¥6 for the first three kilometres – it can be difficult to find one during rush hour, but enterprising locals might stop and offer lifts for around 50 percent above the taxi fare.

INFORMATION

Travel agencies Ürümqi's helpful, English-speaking CITS office is at 16F, 33 Renmin Lu (☎0991 2821426, ⓦwww .xinjiangtour.com), and you can find CTS and CITS desks in the *Hongfu* and *Zhejiang* hotels; the youth hostels can also provide up-to-date travel advice.

ACCOMMODATION

Cornfield International Youth Hostel 麦田国际青年旅舍, màitián guójì qīngnián lǚshè. Youhao Nan Lu, next to the Parkson department store ☎0991 4591488, ⓦxjmaitian.net. Popular hostel with good beds, tiny communal bathrooms – verify the facilities for your room before checking in – and indifferent staff. Also known as the *Maitian*. Dorms **¥45**, doubles **¥160**

Hongfu 鸿福大饭店, hōngfú dàfàndiàn. 160 Wuyi Lu ☎0991 5881988, ⓦhongfuhotel.com. Get away from the chains at this swanky, upper-class hotel, which has a small on-site shopping centre and several excellent restaurants. Rooms are very pretty, with curved floor-to-ceiling windows, thick carpets and enormous beds. **¥600**

★**JHH** 俊和盒酒店, jùnhéhé jiǔdiàn. 140 Gongyuan Bei Jie ☎0991 5590666, A smartly rebranded outpost of the *Super 8* chain, offering excellent, well-equipped, refurbished rooms. Prices are bargainable based on whether you take up their breakfast and dinner packages. **¥218**

Sheraton 喜来登酒店, xǐláidēng jiǔdiàn. 669 Youhao Bei Lu ☎0991 6999999, ⓦsheraton.com. Excellent, modern hotel providing all the comfort you'd expect from this chain. Food, service standards and room quality are as good as you'll get in Xinjiang, and some rooms have tremendous mountain views. The only downside is a slightly out-of-the-way location on the airport road. **¥800**

Silver Birches International Youth Hostel 白桦林国际青年旅舍, báihuálín guójì qīngnián lǚshè. 186 Nanhu Nan Lu ☎0991 4881428. Like the *Cornfield*, this gets patchy reviews, mostly due to the pervasive smell of drains, but this out-of-the-way hostel has pleasant common areas and friendly staff. Dorms **¥50**, doubles **¥150**

Zhejiang Hotel 浙江大酒店, zhèjiāng dàjiǔdiàn. 196 Changjiang Lu ☎0991 5617888. This newly opened hotel is good value with comfortable beds, marble-covered bathrooms and helpful staff. Foregoing wi-fi and breakfast will save you ¥100 per night. **¥338**

EATING

Ürümqi has a good variety of places to eat, and whether you're after Uyghur specialities or Cantonese favourites, you'll be able to find them here.

Aroma 啊偌玛西餐厅, āruòmǎ xīcāntīng. 196 Jianshe Lu, ☎0991 2835881. Bizarrely, there's an excellent Maltese restaurant in one of the most landlocked cities on earth, specializing in delicious Mediterranean food. Tuck in to pizza, pasta or risotto from ¥60 or go all out with the steak for ¥158. Daily 11am–midnight.

Kosh Amet 库西阿买提大盘鸡, kùxi āmǎití dàpánjī. Lingguan Xiang, 200m west of the Yan'an Lu BRT station. *Kosh Amet* specializes in the Hui dish *dapanji* – "big plate of chicken". Simply decide if you want a medium dish (*zhongpanji*; ¥50) or a large one (¥85) and join the crowds of diners who flock here from the mosque on nearby Shengli Lu. Daily 11am–midnight.

Putaoyuan 葡萄园, pútáo yuán. Jiefang Nan Lu, just north of the International Bazaar. A wonderful place to rest on hot days, this is less a restaurant and more an open-air food court. Join Uyghur families in the shade of the grape vines for cold noodles, fried pastries and an exquisite concoction of yogurt and rose syrup mixed with crushed ice. Daily in summer 10am–2am.

UYGHUR FOOD

Uyghur food, unsurprisingly, has far more of a Central Asian than a Chinese flavour. The most basic staple – which often seems to be the only food available – is **laghman**, known in Chinese as *lamian*, literally "pulled noodles". Watching these being made to order is greatly entertaining: the cook grabs both ends of a roll of elastic dough and pulls it into a long ribbon before slapping it down onto a floured counter, and joining the ends of the dough, forming two ribbons. The process is repeated again and again, doubling the number of ribbons each time. Eventually a mass of thin, metre-long noodles is strung between the cook's hands. The "handles" of surplus dough are torn off either end, and the noodles dropped into boiling water to cook for a couple of minutes. The speed at which a skilled cook transforms the raw dough into a bowlful of noodles, banging, pulling, and managing to keep all the strands separate, is incredible.

In Xinjiang, *laghman* is served with a stew of mutton, tomatoes, chilli and other vegetables – rather different from the soupier version sold elsewhere in China. For the same spicy sauce but without the noodles, try *tohogish* (known in Chinese as *dapan ji*), a chicken served chopped up in its entirety, head, feet and all, or *jerkob*, a beef stew – both are served in smarter restaurants. Coriander leaf is used as a garnish on everything.

In summer, apart from *laghman*, street vendors also offer endless cold noodle soup dishes, usually very spicy. Rice is rare in Xinjiang, though it does appear in the saffron-coloured **pilau**, comprising fried rice and hunks of mutton. More familiar to foreigners are the skewers of grilled mutton **kebabs**, dusted with chilli and cumin powder – buy several of them at once, as one skewer does not make much more than a mouthful – they are often eaten with delicious glasses of ice-cold **yoghurt** (known in Chinese as *suannai*), which are available everywhere in Xinjiang. Tea often comes flavoured with cinnamon, cardamom and rose hips.

Oven-baked **breads** are also popular in markets: you'll see bakers apparently plunging their hands into live furnaces to stick balls of dough onto the brick-lined walls; these are then withdrawn minutes later as bagel-like bread rolls and naan flat breads, or sometimes *permuda* (known in Chinese as *kaobao*), which are tasty baked dough packets of mutton and onions. The latter can also be fried – as *samsa* – rather than baked. The steamed version of this, known as *manta*, recalls Chinese dumplings or *mantou*.

A couple of other specialities are worth trying: *madang* is nougat thick with walnuts, raisins and dried fruit, and sold by pedlars who carve the amount you want (or usually, more than you want – it's sold by weight) off massive slabs of the stuff. More refreshing is that characteristic Central Asian fruit, the **pomegranate**, known as *shiliu* in Chinese. You can find them whole at markets, or buy the juice off street vendors – look for the piles of skins and the juicing machines, which resemble large, spiky torture implements.

Tela Laghman 特拉快餐, tèlā kuàicān. Aiguo Xiang. There's no menu at this popular restaurant, but then there's only one thing on the menu: *laghman* (hand-pulled noodles fried with diced mutton, tomatoes and peppers). Join crowds of local diners and slurp up some of the tastiest noodles (¥17) in the city. No English sign – you can spot it by its dark wood interior. Daily 11am–8pm.

DRINKING

Fubar 福吧, fúbā. 40 Gongyuan Bei Jie ☏0991 5844498. Almost every traveller who passes through Ürümqi seems to end up here; the decor, pub atmosphere, imported beers and fair approximations of Western food can be a nice reminder of home. Daily 11am–2am.

SHOPPING

Erdaoqiao Market 二道桥市场, èrdàoqiáo shìchǎng. Jiefang Nan Lu. Hone your haggling skills in this sixth-floor market, which is jam-packed with ornamental knives, musical instruments, jade trinkets, carpets, hats, clothes, herbal medicines and various ornate handicrafts. The stalls are so plentiful they spill out onto the streets. Daily 10am–8pm.

Foreign Language Bookstore 外语书店, wàiyǔ shūdiàn. 14 Xinhua Bei Lu. This is mostly stocked with children's textbooks, though there are a few shelves on the first floor dedicated to Chinese and Western classics in English. Daily 10am–8pm.

13

KAZAKHS AT HEAVENLY LAKE

The **Kazakhs** at Heavenly Lake have recently seen massive changes to their livelihoods. Originally, they led a seminomadic herding existence in these hills, selling lambs in spring if the winter spared them – a hard, unpredictable business. However, in 2011 livestock grazing inside scenic areas was banned across Xinjiang, and overnight their traditional way of life disappeared. While this sea change has challenged the herders to adapt centuries-old habits, the natural environment has undeniably benefited, and the meadows of wild flowers around the lake have now returned to their former glory.

Today, tourism has largely replaced herding as the chief source of local revenue, with the Kazakhs providing food and accommodation for visitors to Heavenly Lake, as well as working and performing in the "Kazakh Village" that you'll pass through en route to the lake. The sheep may have gone, but some traditions are still adhered to: visit in May – considered the most beautiful time – and you may get to try the alcoholic *kumiss*, fermented mare's milk, a rare delicacy.

International Bazaar 国际大巴扎, guójì dàbāzhā. Jiefang Nan Lu. Standing opposite the Erdaoqiao Market, this bazaar isn't quite as interesting as its neighbour but houses a Carrefour supermarket and a string of music shops selling CDs of traditional Uyghur music. Daily 10am–8pm.

DIRECTORY

Banks and exchange The main Bank of China is at the junction of Renmin Lu and Jiefang Lu (Mon–Fri 10am–6.30pm); it's the only branch where you can change travellers' cheques.

Embassies Kazakhstan, 216 Kunming Lu (Mon–Thurs 9am–1pm; ☎0991 3815857); Kyrgyzstan, 58 Hetan Bei Lu (closed Wed, call to check opening hours; ☎0991 5189980). Note that services at both of these embassies ranges from offhand to wretched – try not to make any firm travel plans until you have your visa in hand. Many nationalities can now get visa-free entry to both Kazakhstan and Kyrgyzstan – check current requirements before travelling.

Post offices The main post office (daily 10am–7pm) is west of the northern end of Renmin Park. For long-distance phone calls you can buy and use phone cards from the lobbies of upmarket hotels, post offices or *Fubar* (see p.835).

Tian Chi

天池, tiānchí • Daily May–Sept 8.30am–8pm • ¥125; bus between the ticket office and the lake ¥90

Tian Chi means "Heavenly Lake", and this natural haven 100km east of Ürümqi – the starting point of Vikram Seth's book *From Heaven Lake* – almost lives up to its name, especially for travellers who have spent a long time in the deserts of northwest China. At the cool, refreshing height of 2000m, the lake is surrounded by grassy meadows, steep, dense pine forests and jagged snow-covered peaks, including the mighty **Bogda Feng**, which soars to over 6000m. The best feature of the area is that you can wander at will; there are no restrictions on accommodation (most people stay in yurts, with the seminomadic Kazakh population), and there is virtually limitless hiking. You need only to watch the **weather** – bitterly cold in winter, the lake is really only accessible during the summer months, May to September.

Tian Chi is Xinjiang's premier tourist destination, and attracts thousands of visitors every day in the summer. Most opt for day-trips by coach; independent travellers have to fit in where they can, with the buses stopping en route for various manufactured "attractions". The upside of the tour groups is that, once at the lake, the majority of people seldom stray beyond the cluster of scenic spots on the north shore. If you're prepared to hike beyond this, or to stay overnight, then you can experience the beauty of the lake in near solitude. There is a wide range of **trails** in the lake area, from a 3km path that leads steeply downhill past a pretty **waterfall** to the visitor centre (from where you can catch a bus back to the ticket office), to a 9km climb up "**Horse Tooth Mountain**" (马牙山, mǎyá shān). It takes five hours or so to hike around the lake itself. All trails are well signed from the lakeshore.

ARRIVAL AND DEPARTURE
TIAN CHI

By public transport Take a bus to Fukang (阜康, fùkāng) from Ürümqi's Nianzigou bus station, and then hop in a taxi from there to the Tian Chi ticket office (¥40).

By tour bus Booths around the northern entrance of Renmin Park in Ürümqi run good-value buses to the Tian Chi ticket office each morning (¥50 return). You can sign up for their day-trip package for an additional fee (typically including entry to the park, a boat ride and lunch at the Kazakh Village), or simply do your own thing until the allotted departure time. If you stay overnight, you'll need to pay another ¥50 or make your own way back.

By taxi A taxi from Ürümqi generally costs around ¥350 for the return journey and a few hours' waiting time.

ACCOMMODATION AND EATING

Drinks and snacks are available from kiosks inside the park, but for proper food you will need to depend on the Kazakhs or be prepared for self-catering.

Yurts To find a yurt to stay in, head around the lake anticlockwise after arriving at the main viewpoint and walk uphill at the first junction – accommodation is clustered along the road. The price per bed varies, depending on how many meals are included and the conditions inside the yurts. **¥50**

Nanshan

南山, nánshān • Daily in summer 8.30am–8.30pm • ¥15

South of Ürümqi spreads the **Nanshan** area of the Tian Shan range: these thickly forested hills, dotted with waterfalls, lakes and glaciers, are the traditional summering place for the region's Kazakh and Uyghur herders. Nanshan's most accessible part is **Xi Baiyang Gou** (西白杨沟, xi báiyáng gōu), easily reached by public bus from Ürümqi, with a pretty waterfall (5km gently uphill from the entrance) and horseriding opportunities – it's also a popular spot with couples taking wedding photographs. Further afield are several similar scenic spots, the most interesting of which is **Tianshan Glacier No. 1** (天山 一号冰川, tiānshān yīhào bīngchuān), the source of the Ürümqi River and the world's closest glacier to a major population centre, just 125km south of the city.

ARRIVAL AND DEPARTURE
NANSHAN

By bus and tour bus The tour operators outside the north gate of Renmin Park organize tours to Xi Baiyang Gou and elsewhere in Nanshan, although it's easy enough to get to Xi Baiyang Gou by bus (4 daily 9.30am–4.30pm; ¥14.50) from the depot hidden in Hotan Jie, a lane off Heilongjiang Lu.

ACCOMMODATION AND EATING

There are a few simple restaurants at Xi Baiyang Gou, concentrated near the car park where the bus stops.

Yurts Xi Baiyang Gou is the best place to stay overnight in the Nanshan area, with plenty of yurts by the roadside near the car park – haggling is expected, and be sure to ask whether the price includes meals (which you should also check the price of before tucking in). Yurt per person **¥80**

The Ili Valley

The pretty **Ili Valley** is centred on the city of **Yining**, just 60km east of the border with Kazakhstan and 600km northwest of Ürümqi. Being well off the principal Silk Road routes, not many people make the detour to get here, but it's a worthwhile trip: Ili is one of the three so-called **Kazakh Autonomous Prefectures** within Xinjiang (the other two are Karamay and Altai), which form a block along the northwest frontier. Despite the name, the Uyghurs are the more dominant minority group in the city, and there have been occasional protests against Beijing's rule. Today, however, after years of Han migration, the "frontier" character of Yining is fast disappearing.

The **climate** in the valley is cool and fresh even at the height of summer (and very chilly sometimes – make sure you have warm clothes whatever the time of year), and the views of Tian Shan – from all routes into Yining, but especially if you're coming up

13

from Kuqa to the south – are fabulous. The road climbs out of the harsh, rocky landscape of the northern Taklamakan, before entering pure alpine scenery with pine forests and azure skies, before drifting into vast grasslands ringed by snowy peaks. Another draw, north of Yining, is beautiful **Sayram Lake**, where you can find accommodation in Kazakh yurts.

Brief history

The **history** of the Ili Valley is one of intermittent Chinese control. During the Han dynasty, the area was occupied by the **Wusun**, ancestors of today's Kazakhs, who kept diplomatic relations with the Han court and introduced them to the region's tough Ferghana horses. By the eighth century, however, Ili's value as a staging post on the Silk Road had become too great a temptation, and the Tang dynasty invaded the area. Throughout the thirteenth and fourteenth centuries, the area was controlled first by Genghis Khan and then Tamerlane. This tug of war has gone on ever since, with the Qing seizing the area in the eighteenth century, only for the Russians to march in, in 1871, under the cover of protecting the territory against Yakub Beg's

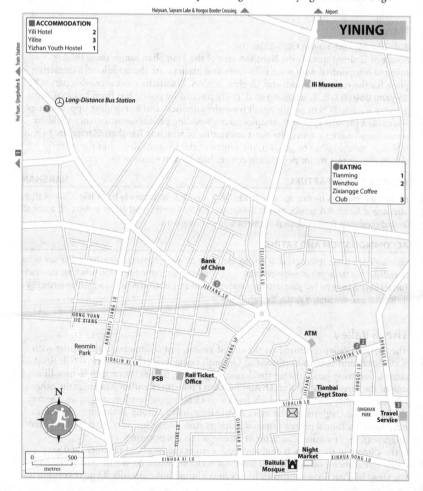

YINING

Huiyuan, Sayram Lake & Horgos Border Crossing ▲   ▲ Airport

■ ACCOMMODATION
Yili Hotel	2
Yilite	3
Yizhan Youth Hostel	1

Hui Yuan, Qingshuihe & Train Station

Ili Museum

Ⓝ Long-Distance Bus Station

● EATING
Tianming	1
Wenzhou	2
Zixiangge Coffee Club	3

Bank of China

JIEFANG LU

FEIJICHANG LU

GONG YUAN JIE XIANG

ANEMAITI JIANG LU

ATM

Renmin Park

SIDALIN XI LU

FEIJICHANG LU

YINGBING LU

SHENGLI LU

HONGQI LU

PSB

Rail Ticket Office

Tianbai Dept Store

SIDALIN LU

QINGNIAN LU

TILIHE LU

QINGNIAN PARK

Travel Service

N

Night Market

XINHUA XI LU

XINHUA DONG LU

Baitula Mosque

0   500
metres

rebellion (see p.829). There remained a significant Russian presence in one form or another until 1949, and traces of this can still be seen in the architecture of Yining.

Yining

伊宁, yīníng

Known to the Uyghurs as Ghulja, booming **YINING** is growing quickly, with older buildings rapidly being replaced by shiny office blocks and fancy shops. While still a small city by Chinese standards, with around 500,000 inhabitants, Yining is developing into an urban sprawl – outside of the eastern and southern districts it is not a rewarding place to walk around. The centre of town isn't readily obvious – most of the action seems to be in the area between **Jiefang Lu**, and **Qingnian Park** in the southeast of the city. The main Uyghur areas are south and east of Qingnian Park, and it is these areas that are most interesting to walk through and poke around, peppered as they are with mosques, street markets and traditional adobe buildings.

ARRIVAL AND DEPARTURE YINING

By air Yining's small domestic airport (伊宁机场, yīníng jīchǎng) is located 7km north of town. It's served by bus route #8 (¥1), while a taxi will set you back ¥15. Yining's airline office (☏ 0999 8044000) is in the *Yilite* hotel.
Destinations Altay (1hr); Ürümqi (1hr).
By rail Yining's station is 6km northwest of the city centre. Bus routes #4 and #401 run out there from Sidalin Lu. Tickets can be purchased from the office at 89 Sidalin Xi Jie (Mon–Fri 9.30am–5.30pm) – you'll need to buy sleeper tickets at least two days before you travel, as everything gets booked up quickly. Note that trains from Ürümqi to Kazakhstan go via Alashankou, 300km from Yining, and not

via Horgos.
Destinations Ürümqi (5 daily; 11hr 45min).
By bus The bus station is in the northwest of the city, well concealed on Jiefang Lu – bus #1 comes out here from the Xinhua Bookshop on Sidalin Lu. The station hosts both international services to Kazakhstan and domestic routes, though for most destinations in China the best option is to head to Ürümqi and catch a connection there.
International destinations Almaty (daily; 12hr).
Domestic destinations Kuqa (2 daily; 15hr); Ürümqi (12 daily; 12hr).

ACCOMMODATION

Accommodation in Yining is tightly restricted – unless a hotel has a permit to host foreign guests, you'll be turned away at the door.

Yili Hotel 伊犁宾馆, yīlí bīnguǎn. 8 Yingbin Lu ☏ 0999 8023126. An old-fashioned place set in huge leafy grounds, with a number of small blocks offering rooms of varying comfort and price – building no. 4 has respectable, if small, doubles with a bath. Bus #9 from Renmin Park stops right outside. **¥628**
★**Yilite** 伊力特大酒店, yīlitè dàjiǔdiàn. 98 Shengli Lu ☏ 0999 8035600. A range of smart, sizeable rooms at

reasonable prices are available at this straightforward place, which has friendly staff. **¥248**
Yizhan Youth Hostel 伊栈青年旅舍, yīzhàn qīngnián lǚshè. Jiu Xi Xiang off Liqun Lu ☏ 182 999 63632. This hostel's friendly, helpful English-speaking staff, laundry facilities and decent location help make up for the somewhat ambivalent approach to cleanliness and obligatory thin mattresses. Dorms **¥55**, doubles **¥160**

EATING

Street food is particularly good in Yining, although some of the best markets have fallen victim to the city's modernization. One of the liveliest surviving street eating spots is outside the Baitula Mosque on Jiefang Nan Lu – naan, kebabs, iced yoghurt and excellent, locally made *kurut* (hard, dry little cheeses) are on sale here each evening.

Tianming 天明餐厅, tiānmíng cāntīng. Opposite the bus station, on the south side of Jiefang Lu ☏ 0999 8131987. This basement restaurant is where Yining's bus drivers come to load up on fried dishes served over rice and noodles – a whole *dapanji* (spicy chicken stew) will set you back ¥60, but noodles start at a more reasonable ¥15. Daily 10am–midnight.

Wenzhou 温州酒店 wēnzhōu jiǔdiàn. Wenzhou Hotel, Jiefang Lu ☏ 0999 8217888. On the first floor of the *Wenzhou Hotel*, this restaurant looks much fancier than it really is. Good Sichuanese and Hunanese standards are served up for very reasonable prices (¥30 a dish) – order from the enormous picture menu covering one wall. Daily 11am–10pm.

13

Zixiangge Coffee Club 紫香阁, zǐxiānggé. Inside the grounds of the Ili Hotel ☏ 0999 8039388. This rather swish coffee house also serves up decent pizza (¥48) and pricey steaks. It's not cheap, but is a pleasant place to sit and drink in the evening. Mon 2pm–4am, Tues–Sun 11am–4am.

Huiyuan

惠远, huìyuǎn • Trip from Yining ¥350 by taxi or through travel agency

HUIYUAN, 40km west of Yining, is a small but historic town with a three-storey **drum tower** (鼓楼, gǔlóu; ¥10) dating from the nineteenth century. Another 20km north of here is the pretty Persian-style tomb of fourteenth-century Muslim leader **Telug Timur** (吐虎鲁克铁木尔墓, tǔhǔ lǔkè tiěmù'ěr mù; ¥10), located just outside the small town of **Qingshuihe** (清水河, qīngshuǐhé). You can climb a staircase to the upper floor and even onto the roof to take in the view.

Sayram Lake

赛里木湖, sàilǐmù hú • ¥70 for access to western shore • Buses between Yining and Ürümqi (14hr; ¥70) can drop you off, or take a local bus to Bole (博乐, bólè) and get off at the lake; shared taxi from Yining ¥200

About 120km north of Yining on the road to Ürümqi, **Sayram Lake** occupies a fantastic location between mountains and grassy banks. Over 20km across, more than 2000m above sea level and decidedly chilly for most of the year, Sayram is a great place to escape the urban hustle, with accommodation and food provided by Kazakhs or Mongols in their **yurts**. The road follows the southeast shore, and it is here that tourist facilities are concentrated. An entry fee is payable for access to the quieter western shore – it's not yet possible to drive right around the lake. Every year from July 13–15, thousands of nomads congregate here for traditional games and entertainment.

Horgos border crossing

霍果斯口岸, huòguǒsī kǒu'àn • Bus from Yining bus station ¥20; shared taxi ¥30

About 100km west of Yining is the Horgos **border crossing into Kazakhstan**. While it's not a major destination in itself (unless you're Kazakhstan-bound), the little border town of **Horgos** is an interesting place to look around, as it's home to a thoroughly bizarre shopping mall full of imported goods – from Russian chocolate and cigarettes to stuffed wolves.

The Northern Silk Road

Tracing a vague southern parallel to the **Tian Shan** range, the Northern Silk Road from Dunhuang in western Gansu to Turpan covers some of the harshest terrain in all of China – little water ever reaches this area of scorching depressions, which was dreaded by traders as one of the most hazardous sections of the entire cross-Asia trip.

The first major city you'll hit on crossing from Gansu is **Hami**, though most visitors skip this and head straight to **Turpan**, which is famed for its grapes and intense summer heat – despite which it can still be one of the most relaxing and enjoyable places in all China. The route then skirts along the Tarim Basin to **Kuqa**, with its preserved Uyghur old town and Silk Road relics in the surrounding deserts. There's then a long journey to **Kashgar**, via **Aksu** – the scene of a major terrorist bombing in 2010.

The **road** is in fairly good condition all the way, though given the vast distances involved, it makes more sense to travel by **train**.

Hami

哈密, hāmì

The city of **HAMI** is often overlooked, located as it is between better-known Dunhuang and Turpan. While it's not northwest China's most thrilling destination, the fast-expanding town itself is pleasant and relaxed, with plenty of good food, a clutch of interesting sights and arguably the most famous **melons** in the world.

Brief history

Known to the Uyghurs as Kumul, Hami's fertile oasis was tussled over for centuries, as Chinese and Turkic rulers invaded in search of ways to keep their armies fed and watered – the region was already famous for its fruit and wine by the time of the Han dynasty. Hami has hosted two of China's most famous travellers: the monk Xuanzang (see box, p.844), who stopped here in 644 to recover after a near fatal crossing of the Taklamakan Desert on his way back to Chang'an; and Marco Polo, who rested here on his way to the court of Kublai Khan. Much to his delight, Polo discovered a particularly hospitable local custom, where a host would share his wife with guests for the duration of their stay.

Between the seventeenth century and 1930, Hami was nominally ruled by the Muslim **Hami kings**, a family of local chiefs elevated to the rank of kings by a grateful Qing emperor after they helped put down a local rebellion. Their initial allegiance to the Qing dynasty eventually dissolved when they were caught up in the Muslim rebellions that swept across Xinjiang in the nineteenth and early twentieth centuries.

Tombs of the Hami Kings

哈密回王墓, hāmì huíwáng mù • Daily: summer 9am–8pm; winter 10am–7pm • ¥40 • Bus #10 from Dashizi stops outside (¥1)

Next to the bus station in the south of town are the **Tombs of the Hami Kings**, a group of attractive mausoleums built in different styles (one still clad in its original blue tiles), set in a leafy park. Particularly attractive is the **Id Kah Mosque** inside the complex, with Quranic verses painted on the walls, swallows nesting in the rafters and 108 red pillars holding up the roof. The building was built by the first Hami King in the early eighteenth century and expanded by his successors.

Muqam Heritage Centre

哈密木卡姆传承中心, hāmì mùkǎmǔ chuánchéng zhōngxīn • Daily: summer 9am–1pm & 4–7pm • ¥15; ¥40 including performance • Bus #10 from Dashizi stops outside (¥1)

Across the road from the tombs, the run-of-the-mill Hami Museum is best skipped in favour of the adjacent **Museum of Muqam**. This newly developed complex displays a wide range of traditional instruments, both antique and new, and there are regular thirty-minute performances of music and dancing – this might be your only opportunity to see *muqam* (see box, p.856) performed live.

ARRIVAL AND DEPARTURE   HAMI

By train Hami's main train station (哈密火车站, hāmì huǒchēzhàn) is at the north end of town at the junction of Tianshan Bei Lu and Qianjin Lu, and hosts both standard and high-speed services between Ürümqi and Lanzhou. Buses #1, #10 and #14 run between here and the South bus station.

CRH destinations Jiayuguan (5 daily; 3hr); Lanzhou (5 daily; 8hr); Turpan (11 daily; 2hr); Ürümqi (11 daily; 3hr); Xining (5 daily; 7hr); Zhangye (5 daily; 5hr).

Other destinations Jiayuguan (26 daily; 6–9hr); Kashgar (daily; 22hr); Kuqa (daily; 12hr); Lanzhou (19 daily;

12–18hr); Turpan (27 daily; 2–4hr); Ürümqi (24 daily; 5–7hr); Xining (6 daily; 10–14hr); Zhangye (26 daily; 8–12hr).

By bus Hami's bus station (哈密南郊客运站, hāmì nánjiāo kèyùnzhàn) is 2km southwest of Dashizi on Zhongshan Bei Lu; bus #10 (¥1) runs along this route. The ticket office is open daily 8am–8pm, and tickets are easy to get hold of.

Destinations Dunhuang (2 daily; 8hr); Turpan (daily; 7hr); Ürümqi (3 daily; 10hr).

ACCOMMODATION

Hami Hotel 哈密宾馆, hāmì bīnguǎn. 4 Yingbin Lu ☎ 0902 2233140. A stalwart of Hami's tourism industry, this was the first hotel in town. Rooms range from shabby rooms in building 1 to fancy modern doubles with wi-fi in building 6 (¥558). **¥200**

Seven Days Inn 七天连锁酒店, qītiān liánsuǒ jiǔdiàn. 4 Xin Min Si Lu/Ba Yi Bei Lu ☎ 0902 640577. Handy for the train station and close to the string of restaurants along Ba Yi Bei Lu, this budget chain's rooms are well equipped, clean and excellent value. **¥150**

13

EATING AND DRINKING

Hami's lively restaurant scene is focused on Zhongshan Bei Lu between Xiaoshizi and Dashizi (i.e. the junctions with Wenhua Lu and Jiefang Lu). Each evening stalls selling fragrant lamb kebabs, *pilau* and chilled *kvass* (a sweet, lightly fermented beverage) set up along the street.

Avzal Southern end of Zhongshan Bei Lu. This pavement café near the night market makes a brilliant place to people-watch. Come here to enjoy their creamy ice cream and a frosty glass of home-made *kvass* (¥5) – owner Shukrat has been brewing his own here for the past twenty years. Daily noon–midnight.

Shandong Jiaozi 山东饺子馆, shāndōng jiǎoziguǎn. Southeast corner of Xiaoshizi. This restaurant serves up traditional northern Chinese dishes, specializing in dumplings. You can fill up here on pork and cabbage dumplings (¥1 each – around 15 make a meal) washed down with a bowl of broth (served here instead of tea). Daily 9.30am–11pm.

DIRECTORY

Banks and exchange There's a branch of Bank of China at 11 Zhongshan Bei Lu (Mon–Fri 9am–12.40pm & 4–7pm); the ATMs accept credit cards and you can also exchange cash.

Post offices The post office is at the northern end of Zhongshan Bei Lu (Mon–Fri 9.30am–7.30pm), on the same side as the Bank of China.

Turpan

吐鲁番, tùlǔfān

The small oasis town of **TURPAN** is an absolute must-see if you're in Xinjiang, as this former Silk Road outpost has long been a travellers' favourite. Fascinating sites from ruined cities to Buddhist caves surround the town – testimony to its historical importance.

Located in a depression 80m below sea level, Turpan's climate is extreme – above 40°C in summer and well below freezing in winter. In summer, the **dry heat** is so soporific you may be hard-pushed to do anything but sleep or sip cool drinks under shady grapevines.

Despite its bone-dry surroundings, Turpan is an agricultural centre, famed across China for its **grapes**. Virtually every household has a hand in the business, and a **Grape Festival** is held at the end of August each year to celebrate the harvest.

If you come out of season (November to March), Turpan is cold and uninspiring, with the vines cut back and many businesses closed; but the sights remain interesting and are, at these times, almost devoid of other tourists.

Brief history

Turpan is a largely **Uyghur-populated** area and, in Chinese terms, an obscure backwater, but it has not always been so. As early as the Han dynasty, the oasis was a crucial point along the Northern Silk Road, and the cities of **Jiaohe** and later **Gaochang**, both of whose ruins can be visited from Turpan, were important and wealthy centres of power. On his way to India, Xuanzang spent more time than he had planned here, when the king virtually kidnapped him in order to have him preach to his subjects. This same king later turned his hand to robbing Silk Road traffic, and had his kingdom

TURPAN

■ ACCOMMODATION		● EATING	
Dap Youth Hostel	2	Herembag	1
Jiaohe Manor	3	Kadinastaamliri	2
Jiaotong	4		
Turpan	5		
Xizhou Grand	1		

annexed by China in 640 as a result. From the ninth to the thirteenth century, a rich intellectual and artistic culture developed in Gaochang, and it was not until the fourteenth century that the Uyghurs of the Turpan region converted to Islam.

The town centre

Turpan's downtown area doesn't amount to much, with most of the services near the bus station on Laocheng Lu. Pedestrianized Qingnian Lu is protected from the baking summer sun by vine trellises. There is a **museum** on Laocheng Dong Lu (吐鲁番博物馆, tǔlǔfān bówùguǎn; daily 10.30am–6.30pm; free), with a smallish collection of dinosaur fossils, silk fragments, tools, manuscripts and preserved corpses recovered from the nearby Silk Road sites. Other than this, the **bazaars** off Laocheng Lu are worth a casual look, though they are not comparable to anything in Kashgar. You'll find clothes, hats and boots on sale, while the most distinctively local products include delicious sweet raisins, as well as walnuts and almonds.

ARRIVAL AND DEPARTURE   TURPAN

By train Turpan's North train station (吐鲁番北站, tǔlǔfān běi zhàn) on the Ürümqi-to-Lanzhou high-speed line is about 10km northwest of town and is easily reached on the #202 bus (¥1) from the town centre. For slower services, and those running direct to Kuqa and Kashgar, you'll need to head to Daheyan (大河沿 dàhéyán), an hour by bus (55km) away. Advance train tickets can be purchased in town from the booth at 856 Qingnian Lu, opposite the *Xizhou Grand Hotel* (daily 9.30am–7pm).
CRH destinations Jiayuguan (5 daily; 5hr); Lanzhou (5 daily; 10hr); Ürümqi (11 daily; 1hr); Xining (5 daily; 9hr); Zhangye (5 daily; 7hr).

Other destinations Jiayuguan (27 daily; 9–13hr); Kashgar (5 daily; 15–24hr); Kuqa (7 daily; 6–11hr); Lanzhou (20 daily; 15–23hr); Ürümqi (34 daily; 2hr); Xining (6 daily; 13–19hr); Zhangye (27 daily; 11–16hr).
By bus Turpan's bus station is southwest of the town centre on Chunshu Lu, with buses every 20min to Ürümqi, as well as less regular services to major destinations in Xinjiang and Dunhuang in Gansu. The ticket office is open daily 6.30am–8.30pm, and it's best to buy tickets a day in advance.
Destinations Dunhuang (daily; 12hr); Hami (2 daily; 6hr); Hotan (daily; 20hr); Kashgar (daily; 20hr); Ürümqi (20 daily; 3hr).

GETTING AROUND AND INFORMATION

By bicycle and car You can rent a bike from *Dap Youth Hostel* for ¥5/hr, and they can also arrange a car and driver for you for around ¥300–¥500/day.
Travel agents CITS, on the first floor of the *Jiaotong Hotel* (☏0995 8535809), can help with transport bookings for

around ¥20 commission (including flights out of Ürümqi), as well as local tours. Friendly, English-speaking driver and guide Tahir Tomur (☏150 26261388), a local agent for Kashgar's Old Road Tours (see box, p.854), is also able to arrange tours to local sights.

ACCOMMODATION

Turpan has a good range of accommodation and most places have air conditioning – just make sure that yours is working when you check in.

★**Dap Youth Hostel** 达卜青年旅舍, dábǔ qīngnián lǚshè. 8 Xiang, Shahezi Lu Dado ☏0995 6263193, ⓦdaphostel.com. A lovely little youth hostel in a traditional courtyard house. Friendly English-speaking staff can help arrange visits to the nearby sights, and will also guide you in when you arrive, as this place is a little hard to find. Dorms **¥40**, doubles **¥200**
Jiaohe Manor 交河庄园酒店, jiāohé zhuāngyuán jiǔdiàn. 2 Jiaohe Dado, 2km west of the centre of town ☏0995 7685999. Built in the style of an old fort, this venture lies right in the heart of the old Uyghur district and all its vineyards. Rooms are tidy, and there are big price

reductions out of season. **¥180**
Jiaotong 交通宾馆, jiāotōng bīnguǎn. 230 Laocheng Xi Lu ☏0995 6258666. Originally the bus station hotel, *Jiaotong* has morphed into a smart mid-range business affair offering comfortable en-suite rooms. **¥220**
Turpan 吐鲁番宾馆, tǔlǔfān bīnguǎn. Qingnian Nan Lu ☏0995 8568888. This used to be the main tourist hotel in town, but new developments have left it a sad echo of its former self. That said, it's still central, clean and cheap. Dorms **¥50**, doubles **¥160**
Xizhou Grand 西州大酒店, xīzhōu dàjiǔdiàn. 882

13

Qingnian Lu ☎0995 8554000. With an unmistakeable bulging brown front, the imposing *Xizhou* is at the very least easy to find. It's perfectly comfortable, with clean rooms and pleasant staff, but the carpets have seen better days and the bathrooms are a bit pokey. Still, you do get an enormous TV. **¥380**

EATING

The most atmospheric option is to wait until evening and go for one of the pavement restaurants that pop up once the heat of the day subsides. These cluster particularly at the western ends of Wenhua Lu and Laochung Lu, and around the bus station on Chunshu Lu. If you're after somewhere with a permanent roof, every other shopfront along Bezeklik Lu is a restaurant of some kind, ranging from Muslim canteens to Western ice cream parlours, and even Japanese teppanyaki restaurants.

★**Herembag** 海尔巴格, hǎi'ěr bāgé. 21 Laoshahezi Lu, just west of Xinhua Park ☎0995 8555111, ⓦherembag.net Part of a chain of fancy Uyghur restaurants with branches throughout Xinjiang, this is a meat-eaters paradise that gets particularly festive at the weekends when family groups descend. If you're feeling particularly gluttonous, go for their speciality "one metre kebab" (¥218). They also specialize in ice cream (¥18), and you can enjoy one out on the terrace overlooking the lake in Xinhua Park. Daily 10.30am–10pm.

Kadinastaamliri 凯蒂娜美食, kǎidìnà měishí. Bezeklik Lu. A fairly standard Muslim restaurant, *Kadinastaamliri* has a picture menu that also features Chinese standards – and some of them are vegetarian. Kebabs from (¥15). Daily 10.30am–10pm.

XUANZANG AND THE JOURNEY TO THE WEST

Goods were not the only things to travel along the Silk Road; it was along this route that **Buddhism** first arrived in China at some point in the first century AD. Cities on the Silk Road became bastions of the religion (hence their abandonment and desecration following the introduction of Islam after 1000), and from early on, Chinese pilgrims visited India and brought back a varied bag of Buddhist teachings. The most famous was the Tang-dynasty monk **Xuanzang**, who undertook a seventeen-year pilgrimage from the then capital, Chang'an (Xi'an), to India.

Born in 602, Xuanzang was schooled in Mahayana Buddhism but became confused by its contradictory texts, and in 629 decided to visit India and study Buddhism at its source. He went without official permission, narrowly avoiding arrest in western Gansu; Turpan's king detained him for a month to hear him preach but eventually provided a large retinue, money and passports for safe passage through other kingdoms. Xuanzang crossed the Tian Shan into modern Kyrgyzstan, where his religious knowledge greatly impressed the Khan of the Western Turks, before he continued, via the great Central Asian city of **Samarkand**, through modern-day Afghanistan, over the Hindu Kush and into **India**, arriving about a year after he set out.

Xuanzang spent fifteen years in India visiting holy sites, studying Buddhism in its major and esoteric forms, lecturing, and debating with famous teachers. If he hoped to find ultimate clarity he was probably disappointed, as the interpretation of Buddhist lore in India was even more varied than in China. However, he amassed a vast collection of Buddhist statues, relics and **texts**, and in 644 decided that it was his responsibility to return to China with this trove of knowledge. The journey back via Kashgar took Xuanzang another year, not counting eight months spent at Hotan, waiting for imperial permission to re-enter China, but he arrived at Chang'an in 645 to find tens of thousands of spectators crowding the roads. The emperor became his patron, and he spent the last twenty years of his life translating part of his collection of Buddhist texts.

Xuanzang wrote an autobiography, but highly coloured accounts of his travels also passed into folklore, becoming the subject of plays and the sixteenth-century novel *Journey to the West*. In it, Xuanzang is depicted as terminally naive, hopelessly dismayed by the various disasters that beset him. Fortunately, he's aided by the Bodhisattva of Compassion, **Guanyin**, who sends him spirits to protect him in his quest: the vague character of **Sandy**; the greedy and lecherous **Pigsy**; and **Sun Wu Kong**, the brilliant Monkey King. A good abridgement in English is Arthur Waley's *Monkey* (see p.969).

THE FLAMING MOUNTAINS

Along the way to the Bezeklik Caves and other destinations northeast of Turpan, you'll pass the **Flaming Mountains**, made famous in the sixteenth-century Chinese novel *Journey to the West* (see p.969). It's not hard to see why the novel depicts these sandstone mountains as walls of flame, with the red hillsides lined and creviced as though flickering with flame in the heat haze. The plains below are dotted with dozens of small "nodding donkey" **oil wells**, all tapping into Xinjiang's vast reserves.

DIRECTORY

Banks and exchange There's a Bank of China (Mon–Fri 9.30am–12.30pm & 4.30–7pm) with ATMs accepting credit cards on Laocheng Xi Lu – you can change travellers' cheques here as well.

Post office The post office is located on Laocheng Xi Lu (Mon–Fri 9.30am–8pm).

Around Turpan

Nearly all visitors to Turpan end up taking the customary **tour** of the historical and natural sights outside town. These are quite fun, as much for the chance to get out into the desert as for the sights themselves, which usually include the two ancient cities of **Jiaohe** and **Gaochang**, the **Emin Minaret**, the **Karez irrigation site**, the **Bezeklik Caves** and **Astana Graves**. Only Jiaohe is indisputably worth the cost – and, in fact, you can get good views of Gaochang and the Emin Minaret without actually entering the sites. Entry fees are typically not included in tour packages.

The Emin Minaret is within **cycling** distance, and if you're a healthy sort then Jiaohe will be too. For sights further afield, you'll have to arrange a **car** or **minibus**, with prices dependent upon exactly what you wish to see. Be aware that, however you travel, you'll be in blistering heat for the whole of the day, so sun cream, a hat, water bottle and sunglasses are essential.

The Emin Minaret

苏公塔, sūgōng tǎ • Daily dawn to dusk • ¥50

You can walk to the eighteenth-century **Emin Minaret**, 2km southeast of Turpan, by following Jiefang Jie east out of town for about thirty minutes. The minaret is built in a very simple style – slightly bulging and potbellied – and erected from sun-dried bricks arranged in differing patterns. The tower tapers its way 40m skyward to a rounded tip, and adjoins a mosque with a splendidly intricate latticework ceiling. You can see the complex without visiting the site, but entry allows an ascent of the tower to gain good views over the green oasis in the foreground and the distant snowy Tian Shan beyond.

Jiaohe

交河, jiāohé • Daily dawn to dusk • ¥40; bilingual booklet *The Ruins of Jiaohe* ¥10

About 11km west of Turpan, and occupying a spectacular defensive setting on top of a 2km-long, steep-sided plateau carved out by the two halves of a forking river, the ruined city of **Jiaohe** is just about within cycling range on a hot day. Although for large parts of its history Jiaohe was under the control of Gaochang (see p.846), it became the regional administrative centre during the eighth century.

What sets Jiaohe apart from all other ruined cities along the Silk Road is that although most of the buildings comprise little more than crumbling, windswept mud walls, so many have survived, and there's such a variety – gates, temples, public buildings, graveyards and ordinary dwellings – that Jiaohe's **street plan** is still evident; there's a real feeling of how great this city must have been. A **Buddhist monastery** marked the town centre, and its foundations – 50m on each side – can still be seen. Another feature is the presence of ancient **wells** still containing water. Make sure you walk to the far end of the site, where the base of a former **tower**, dated to around 360 AD, overlooks the river.

Karez

坎儿井, kǎn'ér jǐng · Daily dawn to dusk · ¥30

Minibus drivers returning from Jiaohe usually drop you off at a dolled-up **Karez irrigation site**, an intrinsically interesting place unfortunately turned into an ethnic theme park, complete with regular Uyghur dance shows, presumably to justify the entry fee. Karez irrigation taps natural underground channels carrying water from the source – in this case glaciers at the base of the Tian Shan – to the point of use. Strategically dug wells then bring water to small surface channels that run around the streets of the town. From modern Xinjiang as far as Iran, many ancient Silk Road cities relied on this system, and Karez systems are still in use throughout Xinjiang – there are plenty of opportunities to see them for free on the way to Kashgar.

The Bezeklik Caves

柏孜克里克石窟, bózīkèlǐkè shíkū · Daily dawn to dusk · ¥20; camel rides along the Flaming Mountains ¥80

The **Bezeklik Caves**, in a valley among the Flaming Mountains some 50km northeast of Turpan, are disappointing, offering mere fragments of the former wealth of Buddhist cave art here, dating back to 640 AD. The location is nonetheless striking, with stark orange dunes behind and a deep river gorge fringed in green below, but most of the murals were cut out and removed to Berlin by Albert von Le Coq at the beginning of the twentieth century, and the remainder painstakingly defaced by Red Guards during the 1960s. The Allied bombing of Berlin in World War II subsequently destroyed a number of the murals removed by Le Coq.

Astana Graves

阿斯塔娜古墓区, āsītǎnà gǔmùqū · Daily dawn to dusk · ¥20

South of the Bezeklik Caves, the **Astana Graves** mark the burial site of the imperial dead of Gaochang from the Tang dynasty. Unfortunately, the graves have had most of their interesting contents removed to museums in Ürümqi and Turpan, and little remains beyond a couple of preserved corpses and some murals.

Gaochang

高昌, gāochāng · Daily dawn to dusk · ¥40

Adjacent to the Astana Graves, the ruins of **Gaochang** are impressive for their huge scale, despite having suffered from the ravages of both Western archeologists and the local population, who for centuries have been carting off bits of the city's 10m-high adobe walls to use as soil for their fields. Walk to the centre of the site, which is marked by a large square building, to see the remains of a monastery. Its outer walls are covered in niches, in each of which a Buddha was originally seated; just a few bare, broken traces of these Buddhas remain, along with their painted haloes. If you have time you can strike off on your own and listen to the hot wind whistling through the mud-brick walls.

Grape Valley

葡萄沟, pútáo gōu · Daily dawn to dusk · ¥75

Some 13km north of Turpan at the western end of the Flaming Mountains, **Grape Valley** makes a pleasant refuge in the middle of a stark desert, covered in shady trellises bulging with fruit (which you have to pay for if you want to eat). It's best between mid-July and September – at other times, the scenery here is not much different from that of downtown Turpan – and your ticket includes a Uyghur dance performance.

Aiding Lake

艾丁湖, àidīng hú · ¥30 · Return 2hr taxi trip along a rough road ¥200

About 50km south of Turpan, the bleak but dramatic **Aiding Lake** is located in a natural depression 154m below sea level, making this the second-lowest lake in the world after

CARVED GOURDS AND SPICES, KASHGAR MARKET (P.853) >

13

the Dead Sea. You won't actually see any water here except in spring – the rest of the year the lake is a flat plain of dried mineral deposits. The land around the lake is crusted with salt and dotted with bright yellow-green pools of saturated water that feels like oil on the skin. Locals rub it over themselves enthusiastically, claiming that it's good for you. The area around the lake is very muddy, so don't take your best shoes.

Kuqa
库车, kùchē

Roughly halfway on the 1500km journey from Ürümqi to Kashgar, **KUQA** was once a cosmopolitan town full of Silk Road traders and travellers. It was described as the "land of jewels" in Xuanzang's journal, and the fourth-century linguist and scholar **Kumarajiva**, one of the most famous of all Chinese Buddhists, came from here. Having travelled to Kashmir for his education, he later returned to China as a teacher and translator of Buddhist documents from Sanskrit into Chinese. It was in large measure thanks to him that Buddhism came to be so widely understood in China, and by the early Tang Kuqa was a major centre for the religion, with giant monasteries and its own Indo-European language. With the arrival of Islam in the ninth century, however, this era drew to a close, and today only a few traces of Kuqa's ancient history remain. The small city is sharply divided in two: the swiftly expanding new town to the east and the old, remarkably intact, Uyghur town to the west.

The New City
新城, xīnchéng

The **New City**, largely Han-populated, contains all the facilities you'll need and a few sights of marginal interest. One is the remains of the ruined city of **Qiuci** (龟兹古城, qiūcí gǔchéng gǔchéng), and the overgrown rammed-earth walls lie on the edge of the new town, 1km west of Wenhua Square along Wenhua Xi Lu. The **Tomb of Molena Ashidinhan** (莫拉纳俄仕丁坟, mòlānà'é shídīng fén), also on Wenhua Xi Lu, is a simple shrine built in 1867 in honour of an Arab missionary who visited here in the fourteenth century. There's also a daily **bazaar** along pedestrianized Xinghua Lu, which houses Xinjiang's second-largest **goldsmiths' quarters** after Kashgar.

The Old City
古城, gǔchéng • Bus route #1 from the bus station on Tianshan Lu in the New City along Renmin Lu to the bridge across the river

The largely Uyghur **Old City** is peppered with mosques and bazaars, and has a Central

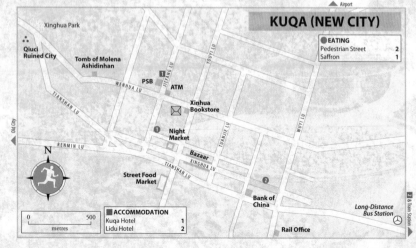

KUQA (NEW CITY)

Airport

Xinghua Park

Qiuci Ruined City

Tomb of Molena Ashidinhan

PSB

ATM

Xinhua Bookstore

Night Market

Bazaar

Street Food Market

Bank of China

Rail Office

Long-Distance Bus Station

& Train Station

WENHUA LU
TIANSHAN LU
RENMIN LU
JIEFANG LU
WULI LU
TIANJIE LU
XINGHUA LU
TIANSHAN LU
WULI LU

EATING
Pedestrian Street — 2
Saffron — 1

ACCOMMODATION
Kuqa Hotel — 1
Lidu Hotel — 2

0 — 500
metres

N

Asian atmosphere. Right by the bridge over the Kuqa River, the **bazaar** is the main venue for the highly enjoyable **Sunday market**. Here, the Uyghur population are out in force, buying and selling leather jackets, carpets, wooden boxes, goats and donkeys; livestock are traded on the river banks below.

Beyond the bridge, you can soon lose yourself in the labyrinth of narrow streets and adobe houses. Right in the heart of this, approximately fifteen minutes northwest of the bridge, is the **Kuqa Mosque** (清真大寺, qīngzhēn dàsì; daily 9.30am–8pm; ¥15), built in 1923. Neat and compact, with an attractive green-tiled dome, this mosque is of wholly arabesque design, displaying none of the Chinese characteristics of mosques in more eastern parts of the country. Beyond the mosque, on Linji Lu, the King's Palace Museum (王俯博物馆, wángfǔ bówùguǎn; daily 9.30am–7.30pm; ¥60) houses interesting collections of archeological relics. Also on Linji Lu, you can see fragments of the original **town wall**.

ARRIVAL AND INFORMATION   KUQA

By air Kuqa's domestic airport (库车机场, kùchē jīchǎng) is 20km from the New City. A taxi will set you back ¥40, while the airport bus only costs ¥10 and runs between the *International Hotel* at 337 Tianshan Lu and the airport terminal. Plane tickets can be purchased from the Kuqa Yinyan Travel Service (see below).
Destinations Ürümqi (1hr).

By train The train station (库车火车站, kùchē huǒchēzhàn) is 5km southeast of the New City (¥10 in a taxi or ¥1 if you take the #6 and #8 buses from Tianshan Lu). Tickets can be purchased from the advance ticket booth in town (59 Wuyi Nan Lu; 9.30am–1pm & 3–7pm), or from the station itself (6am–5.30pm & 6–8pm).
Destinations Kashgar (5 daily; 9hr–12hr); Lanzhou (2 daily; 31hr); Turpan (7 daily; 6–10hr); Ürümqi (6 daily; 8–13hr).

By bus Kuqa's bus station (库车客运中心, kùchē kèyùn zhōngxīn) is in the southeast of the New City on Tianshan Lu. Given the vast distances involved, trains should be the preferred option, though the road routes south through the middle of the desert to Hotan and north to Yining are ones which short-cut the rail alternative.
Destinations Hotan (2 daily; 9hr); Kashgar (daily; 16 hours); Ürümqi (7 daily; 10hr); Yining (daily; 24hr).

Tours For a tour of the sights outside the city, call on the friendly Kuqa Yinyan Travel Service (☎ 0997 7233228, ✉ qiuci_lingyan@hotmail.com) at 226 Tianshan Lu. A day-trip to the nearby Subashi Ruins and Kizil Thousand Buddha Caves (see p.850) will cost ¥600 including car and driver and entry tickets.

ACCOMMODATION

As with most places in Xinjiang, accommodation for foreigners is tightly controlled in Kuqa, with budget options decidedly thin on the ground.

Kuqa Hotel 库车宾馆, kùchē bīnguǎn. 17 Jiefang Bei Lu, north of the PSB ☎ 0997 7123500. This is a very standard and rather uninspiring state-owned hotel, but the rooms are large and bright and the location is convenient for most places in the New City. **¥140**

Lidu Hotel 丽都大酒店, lìdū dàjiǔdiàn. Tianshan Zhong Lu ☎ 0997 7233222. With the smartest rooms in Kuqa, this hotel is close to the train station but perhaps a bit inconveniently located for everything else, way out in the far east of town. **¥268**

EATING

In addition to the places below, there are numerous food stands around the Youyi Lu/Xinghua Lu intersection and south of the Youyi Lu/Tianshan Lu intersection, where you can tuck into delicious baked *kaobao*, *samsa*, bowls of *laghman* and Uyghur tea with great rough sticks and leaves floating in the cup. One thing definitely worth trying is the giant naan bread, served – unlike elsewhere in Xinjiang – thin and crispy and covered with onion, sesame and carrot.

Pedestrian Street 步行街, bùxíngjiē. The eastern end of Xinghua Lu. The epicentre of Kuqa's restaurant scene, Pedestrian Street is a bustling strip of Chinese and Muslim restaurants. Busiest on summer evenings, this is a fun place to sit out, drink beer and tuck into the wide range of regional cuisines on offer, which shouldn't cost more than ¥20. Daily noon–late.

Saffron 再帕尔美食, zàipà'ěr měishí. Behind the

Ihlas supermarket, close to the southern end of Jiefang Lu in the New City ☎ 0997 7133088. Decorated in classic Xinjiang style with lots of dark wood and ornate chandeliers, this place serves Uyghur dishes including a delicious *pilau* with pomegranate (¥18) and a variety of vegetable and meat dishes. No Chinese or English spoken, but thankfully there's a picture menu. Daily 9am–10pm.

13

Kizil Thousand Buddha Caves

克孜尔千佛洞, kèzī'ěr qiānfódòng • Daily during daylight • ¥55; ¥400 by taxi or tour from Kuqa

Around 75km northwest of Kuqa, the **Kizil Thousand Buddha Caves** were once a Central Asian treasure-trove, a mixture of Hellenistic, Indian and Persian styles with not even a suggestion of Chinese influence. Sadly, the caves suffered the ravages of the German archeologist and art thief **Albert von Le Coq** who, at the beginning of the twentieth century, cut out and carried away many of the best frescoes. However, it is still an intriguing place to visit and even older than the more extensive Mogao Caves in Gansu. Your ticket covers eight caves but you can pay extra to be guided round others, including no. 38 – the "cave of musicians" – which depicts Bodhisattvas playing musical instruments on the ceiling.

Subashi ruins

苏巴什佛寺遗址, sūbāshí fósì yízhǐ • Daily during daylight • ¥25; ¥100 by taxi or tour from Kuqa

Twenty-five kilometres north of Kuqa along a good paved road, the ancient **Subashi Buddhist complex**, abandoned in the thirteenth century, comprises fairly extensive ruins from east to west, intercepted by a river. Today, only the more interesting western parts of the ruins are open to visitors – these contain various pagodas and temples, and the remains of some wall paintings. The entire site looks very atmospheric with the bald, pink and black mountain ranges rising up behind. Along the way there, look out for the **irrigation channels** carrying runoff from the mountains to villages.

Kashgar

喀什, kāshí

The remoteness of Uyghur-dominated **KASHGAR** is palpable. Set astride overland routes to Pakistan and Kyrgyzstan, the city is over 4000km from Beijing, with the last thousand kilometres from Ürümqi for the most part uninhabitable desert: indeed, part of the excitement of Kashgar lies in the experience of reaching it. The distinctively Central Asian air to the old city's mosques and markets makes it a visible bastion of old **Chinese Turkestan** – the muezzin's call booms out across the city, and each evening the desert air is scented and blurred by the smoke of roasting lamb.

Increasingly, however, this is a bastion under siege. Han Chinese have relocated here in their thousands, and much of the old town has been ripped up and rebuilt – just a few small areas of the original buildings remain. The locals are understandably angry: Kashgar has been the focal point of **tensions** between the Han and Uyghur peoples as made painfully clear by the city's ubiquitous **security personnel** – both in uniform and undercover.

Nonetheless, the city remains well worth a visit; its population remains overwhelmingly Muslim, a fact you can hardly fail to notice with the great **Id Kah Mosque** dominating the central square, the Uyghur bazaars and teashops and, above all, the faces of the Turkic people around you. If you can choose a time to be here, aim for the Uyghur Corban **festival** at the end of the Muslim month of Ramadan, which involves activities such as dancing and goat-tussling. Whatever time of year you visit, don't miss Kashgar's **Sunday market**, for which half of Central Asia seems to converge on the city.

Brief history

Kashgar's **strategic position** has determined its history and, although a Chinese military governor was stationed here as early as the Tang dynasty, the region was only ever loosely under imperial control. By the early twentieth century, Kashgar had become a nexus between Chinese, Soviet and British **spheres of influence**, with both foreign powers maintaining consulates here: the British with an eye to their interests across the frontier in India; the Soviets with the intention of absorbing Xinjiang into their Central Asian orbit. The tangled conspiracies of this period are brilliantly evoked in

Peter Fleming's *News from Tartary* (see p.966). At the time of Fleming's visit in 1935, Kashgar was effectively run by the Soviets; Kashgar swung back under Chinese control during World War II, and with the break in Sino-Soviet relations in the early 1960s, the Soviet border (and influence) firmly closed.

The old town

Despite the fact that most of the buildings have been reconstructed since 2009, Kashgar's **old town**, north of Renmin Lu, remains the city's focal point for foreign travellers. The main attractions here are the ordinary streets, the bazaars, the restaurants, the teahouses and the people in them. Roads radiate out from **Id Kah Square**, marked by a clock tower and huge mosque, with the main markets in neighbouring lanes; while you're in the area, keep an eye open for a couple of substantial fragments of Kashgar's **old city walls**, most easily viewed south of Seman Lu and west off Youmulake Xiehai'er Lu. And don't miss out on the **old consulates** either: the British had theirs behind the *Royal Qinibagh* hotel, while the Russian headquarters survive as a fun restaurant in the courtyard behind the *Seman* hotel.

TO KYRGYZSTAN AND PAKISTAN

The **international bus station** handles traffic to Sust in Pakistan, as well as two different routes into Kyrgyzstan. Note that you're charged **excess baggage** rates for every kilo over 20kg on international buses.

THE ROAD TO KYRGYZSTAN

The 720km-long road due north from Kashgar via the Torugart Pass to **Bishkek** in **Kyrgyzstan** has been open to Westerners since the 1990s, though this trip is complicated by the fact that foreign travellers are not allowed through the border in either direction on public transport, and must be delivered and met by official guides. While, in theory, the border crossing is open Mon–Fri 10am–5pm, in practice you need to cross before noon and be prepared for sudden closure of the border post for national holidays, bad weather (the pass lies at 3750m and snow is frequent even in summer) and random political reasons. You'll have to organize the trip through an agent in Kashgar or Bishkek and expect to pay upward of US$200 per car from Kashgar to the border, and US$150 per car for onward transport to Bishkek.

An alternative, and easier, option is to head across the southern **Irkeshtam Pass**, 210km west of Kashgar, by bus (currently Mon and Thurs; US$50), proceeding on to the southern Kyrgyz city of Osh on a rough road. This route has become popular with **cyclists**; although there are five major 2400m-plus climbs before the border, there are petrol stations about every 40km for water, and towns or villages no more than 65km apart. Note that Osh has long been the centre of interethnic tensions, flaring in violence that killed hundreds in both 1990 and 2010, so check the current situation before heading in this direction.

Whichever way you take to Kyrgyzstan, check and double-check the **visa requirements** in advance before you rely on visa-free entry or on-arrival application. You can look up the current situation for most nationalities on Kyrgyzstan's US embassy website ⓦkgembassy.org. If visas are required, these can be secured at the Kyrgyz embassy in Beijing or the consulate in Ürümqi (see p.836).

THE ROAD TO PAKISTAN

The fabled **Karakoram Highway** (see p.862) heads from Xinjiang to Pakistan over the **Khunjerab Pass**. It would be a shame to do this all in one go (see p.862 for places to stop en route), but there are direct buses – in theory every day, in practice whenever there are enough people – from Kashgar to the Pakistani city of **Sust** (¥290). It may make more sense to go to Tashkurgan and take the bus from there, as there are occasional buses from Tashkurgan to Sust and all the Kashgar buses stop in Tashkurgan anyway. Despite the gradient (the pass tops out at 4693m), the stunning scenery and (mostly) decent roads mean this route is popular with **bikers** and **cyclists**. Note that the border is only open from May 1 until October (the exact closure date varies), and third-party nationals will need to have organized their **visa** in advance, something usually only possible in their home countries.

KASHGAR

Tomb of
Abakh Hoja

N

Tuman River

#23 Bus Stop
to Livestock
Market

Bank
of China

Big
Bazaar

Id Kah
Mosque

PSB
Old
City
Wall

Gaotai
Old Town

Mao Statue

Xinhua
Bookshop

RENMIN
SQUARE

Bank
of China

Renmin
Park

Dong Hu
Park

Bank
of China

Xinjiang
Airlines

Livestock Market, Shufu & International Bus Station

Moor Pagodas, Train Station & Long-Distance Bus Station

0   1
kilometre

● **EATING**
Altun Orda	4
Avral	2
John's Café	1
Mengyol	3

■ **ACCOMMODATION**
Kashgar Camel Youth Hostel	3
Old Town Youth Hostel	4
Pamir Youth Hostel	2
Royal Qinibagh	1
Seman	5

One small area of original buildings in the east of the old town, now known as **Gaotai** (高台民居, gāotái mínjū), charges an **entrance fee** of ¥30 – although you may be able to wander around without paying up.

Id Kah Mosque

艾提尕尔清真寺, àitígǎ'ěr qīngzhēnsì • Mon–Thurs, Sat & Sun 9am–4pm, Fri 9am–1pm • ¥20

Kashgar's main historical sight is the **Id Kah Mosque**, occupying the western side of Id Kah Square. Originally built in 1442, it has been restored many times – most recently in 2009 – and is today one of the biggest and most active mosques in the country. That said, this is one place where political control over religious activity is at its strongest, a situation which has not passed without protest: in 2014, the Communist Party-appointed, vocally pro-China imam of the mosque was stabbed to death after leading morning prayers.

Although visitors are allowed in, tourists are sometimes shooed away by zealous worshippers – note that visitors of either sex should have their arms and legs fully covered when entering this (or any other) mosque. While admission is curtailed on Fridays, the main Muslim prayer day, it's still worth a look as some ten thousand people crowd the mosque and square; the quietest time, when your presence will cause least disturbance, is probably early to mid-morning on any other day. Inside are pleasant poplar-lined courtyards and rose gardens where worshippers assemble.

Around Id Kah Square

A small road east of Id Kah Square, parallel to Jiefang Lu, is good for Central Asian **hats**. As well as the green-and-white square-shaped variety so beloved of old Uyghur men, there are prayer caps, skullcaps, furry winter hats and plain workmen's caps. Following this lane south you can turn right, where a large, semi-underground market occupies the space between the square and the hat lane. Here you will find a large selection of **clothes**, carpets and **crockery**, as well as Uyghur nuts, sweets and spice stands, and the occasional blacksmith hammering at his trade. Further south down the hat lane, you will come to a **woodcraft** area.

Running parallel to the north side of Id Kah Square, you'll find Kashgar's **gold market** inside a covered arcade, along with some jewellers' workshops. The road directly south of Id Kah Mosque, heading due west, sells a mixture of hats, jewellery, and large **chests** inlaid with brightly coloured tin (purpose-built for carrying gifts for brides-to-be). Further west, running south towards the main post office, you'll find an interesting street of workshops along with some stalls selling handmade **musical instruments**. The two-stringed *dutah* is the most common. The *tanber* is similar but has an even longer stem and a round bowl shaped like half a gourd, while the *rawap* has five strings and a snakeskin drum.

Tomb of Abakh Hoja

阿巴克霍加麻扎, ābākè huòjiā mázhā or 香妃墓, xiāngfēi mù • Daily 9am–8pm • ¥30 • Bus #20 from Renmin Square

The most impressive of all Kashgar's tombs is the **Tomb of Abakh Hoja**, 5km northeast of the centre. A large, mosque-like building with blue and white tiles, a green dome and tiled minarets, it was constructed in the seventeenth century and is the resting place of a large number of people – the most famous being religious and political leader Abakh Hoja. Considered by some to be a descendant of the Prophet Mohammed, Hoja is credited with overthrowing Mongol rule in Kashgar and the surrounding region.

KASHGAR'S SUNDAY MARKETS

Like many aspects of life in Kashgar, the famous **Yekshenbe Bazaar** (Sunday Market) is evolving. While it's still one of Kashgar's top sights, and a fascinating place to people-watch, it has lost some of its former chaotic charm. The first change was the departure of the **livestock market** from Ulagh Bazaar (牛羊市场, niúyáng shìchǎng), which, due to the chaos it caused in the city centre each Sunday, was relocated 10km northwest to Pamir Dadao – to get there, you can take a ¥30 cab ride from downtown or catch bus #23 (¥1) from outside the main bazaar. Once there, you'll still find a colourful bunch of traders haggling over cattle, sheep and the occasional camel, surrounded by an abundance of food stalls on the periphery.

The second wave of change saw the rest of the market rehoused in a permanent structure just northeast of Dong Hu Park, now simply called the "Big Bazaar" (大巴扎, dà bāzhā or 中西亚巴扎, zhōngxīyà bāzhā). Some stalls open every day, but it really gets going on Sundays when side markets spring up in the surrounding streets. Hats, pots, carpets, pans, fresh fruit and vegetables, clothes, boots and every kind of domestic and agricultural appliance – often handmade in wood and tin – are available, and some produce, such as Iranian saffron, has come a very long way to be sold here. The market goes on all day and into the early evening, and food and drink are widely available around the site.

To get to the main bazaar take bus #20 from Renmin Square; from the Id Kah Mosque, you can take a fascinating thirty-minute walk through the old city with its lanes full of traders, coppersmiths and blacksmiths. A taxi from the centre of town costs around ¥8.

While they may not be as impressive as Kashgar's, it might be worth heading out to one of the smaller markets in the region – the little town of **Shufu** (疏附, shūfù), 17km southwest of Kashgar, plays host to a good candidate. Today, these have a more authentic feel about them, and you're almost guaranteed to be the only one with a camera.

TOURS AROUND KASHGAR

One of the most convincing reasons to visit Kashgar is, a little paradoxically, the opportunity to get out of town. Distances can be huge, public transport nonexistent and the weather unrelenting, so it's usually best to go through a **tour operator**. Among the tours on offer – other than those to places nearby – are **mountaineering expeditions**, trips to **Tibet**, day- to week-long **camel treks** across the Taklamakan Desert, and visits to remote villages of minority peoples.

TOUR OPERATORS

CITS ☎ 0998 2980473, ⓦ www.kscits.com.cn. This Chinese tourist staple has a branch inside the *Royal Qinibagh*. Staff are friendly, speak English and are experienced in organizing visits to sights in the surrounding desert.

Elvis Ablimit ☎ 1389 9136195, ⓔ elvisablimit@ yahoo.com. Elvis is a long-time freelance operator organizing trips around Kashgar. His English is good and he knows the area well, but at heart he remains – as he started out – an expert in Kashgar's carpet markets.

Kashgar Mountaineering Adventures ☎ 0998 2821832, ⓦ www.kashgaralpine.com. Outside the

Royal Qinibagh on Jiefang Lu, this tour operator's helpful, English-speaking staff can organize a range of adventure activities including climbing and rafting trips. Contact them well in advance if you want to plan something ambitious, as many activities require some equipment and paperwork preparations.

★ **Old Road Tours** ☎ 138 99132103, ⓦ oldroadtours .com. Formerly Abdul Wahab Tours, this local company is run by six friendly brothers and marshalled by Abdul himself, who is a real fountain of local knowledge. They can organize any trip imaginable, big or small, in a number of languages including French, German and Russian.

Also buried in the mausoleum is his granddaughter Ikparhan, who is known in Chinese as **Xiang Fei**, "Fragrant Concubine". Myths have grown around the character of Xiang Fei in both Chinese and Uyghur culture, the narratives of which diverge greatly. The Chinese story tells of a woman of great beauty and alluring aroma, brought from Kashgar to Beijing, who falls in love with the emperor, while the Uyghur version portrays a ferocious young woman kidnapped from Kashgar who violently resists the evil Chinese emperor's advances before being treacherously poisoned. Make of it what you will.

On the same site is a small **exhibition of historic relics** (¥10), the highlight of which is an Iron Age mummy recovered from the nearby desert, still dressed in felt hat and fur-lined jacket, woollen trousers, leather boots, and a belt with herbs and knife attached.

Mor Pagodas

莫尔佛塔, mò'ěr fótǎ · ¥30 · Return taxi around ¥150

Accessible only by car, the **Mor Pagodas** are part of the **ancient city of Hanoi** down a rough road about 30km east of Kashgar. The pagodas have been worn to rough stumps about a dozen metres high, but the remains of ruined Buddhist temples make quite a dramatic scene in what is a virtual desert.

Shipton's Arch

天洞, tiāndòng · 4WD and driver through tour agency ¥800

One unusual attraction outside Kashgar is **Shipton's Arch**, just over two hours' drive to the west; at a height of around 400m (just topping the Empire State Building), this may be the tallest **natural rock arch** in the world. Though discovered in the 1940s by the former British consul to Kashgar, Eric Shipton, its remoteness meant that it was only accurately surveyed in 2000. Visiting the site involves a thirty-minute hike from the road and scaling a series of fixed ladders.

ARRIVAL AND DEPARTURE   KASHGAR

By plane Kashgar International Airport (喀什机场, kāshí jīchǎng) is 10km north of town; bus #2 (¥2) drives between the airport and Renmin Square. A taxi from the city centre should cost ¥20, though drivers will ask for more. For tickets, China Southern are at 152 Seman Lu (daily May–Oct 9am–8pm, Nov–April 10am–7.30pm; ☎ 0998 2985118), although you'll find cheaper prices online.

Destinations Ürümqi (1hr 45min).

By train Kashgar train station (喀什火车站, kāshí huǒchēzhàn) is 7km east of town, where minibuses and taxis, as well as bus #28 to the Id Kah Mosque and heavily armed security, await new arrivals. Tickets can be purchased from the station itself, or you can ask the travel agencies or your accommodation for assistance – buy as far in advance as possible if you want a sleeper to Ürümqi. Direct services from Kashgar to more distant locations in China are available, but slow. It makes more sense to change to high-speed connections in Turpan.

Destinations Hotan (2 daily; 6–8hr); Kuqa (5 daily; 8–11hr); Turpan (5 daily; 14–21hr); Ürümqi (5 daily; 16–24hr); Yarkand (2 daily; 2–3hr).

By bus Kashgar is served by two main bus stations: the new Long-distance bus station (新长途客运站, xīn chángtú kèyùnzhàn) out by the train station reached on the #28 bus, for all destinations north of Kashgar, and the New international bus station (新国际客运站, xīn guójì kèyùnzhàn) – thirty minutes southwest of town on the #20 bus (¥1) in a newly developing area confusingly called Guangzhou New City (广州新城, guǎngzhōu xīn chéng) – for everywhere else including buses south to Tashkurgan and Pakistan, and east to Yarkand and Hotan.

International destinations Sust (2 weekly; 36hr).

Domestic destinations Hotan (4 daily; 11hr); Kargilik (8 daily; 4hr); Kuqa (4 daily; 12hr); Lake Karakul (2 daily; 5hr); Tashkurgan (2 daily; 6hr); Yarkand (8 daily; 3hr).

GETTING AROUND

By taxi Cabs are cheap, ubiquitous and easy to hail, with the starting price a reasonable ¥5. Expect to agree a price in advance and haggle for trips to more distant destinations.

By bicycle Kashgar's youth hostels all have bicycles to rent for around ¥5/hr.

ACCOMMODATION

Thanks to Kashgar's rising popularity with Chinese backpackers, the city now has several excellent youth hostels, plus a few more luxurious options.

Kashgar Camel Youth Hostel 喀什骆驼青年旅舍, kāshí luòtuó qīngnián lǚshè. 148 Tuman Lu ☎ 1838 3056061. Not far from the big bazaar, this hostel has attractive dorms and double rooms covered with murals by a local artist, as well as pleasant common areas, though it can feel a bit out of the way. Dorms **¥40**, doubles **¥200**

★ Old Town Youth Hostel 老城青年旅舍, lǎochéng qīngnián lǚshè. 233 Wusitangboyi Lu ☎ 0998 2823262, ☺ kashgaroldcity.hostel.com. At the western end of the old town, this hostel has decent rooms, helpful staff and a courtyard that's great for meeting other travellers. Dorms **¥45**, doubles **¥160**

Pamir Youth Hostel 帕米尔青年旅舍, pàmǐ'ěr qīngnián lǚshè. Level 3, Id Kah Bazaar ☎ 0998 2823376, ☺ www.pamirhostel.com. This hostel, in a great but tricky-to-find location on the top floor of a shopping centre on the north side of the Id Kah Mosque square, has airless dorms but a fantastic rooftop café

– come here to smoke shisha and listen to the call to prayer. Dorms **¥40**, doubles **¥140**

★ Royal Qinibagh 其尼瓦克皇家大酒店, qíníwǎkè huángjiā dàjiǔdiàn. 144 Seman Lu ☎ 0998 2982103. The mother of all of Kashgar's tourist hotels, this towering giant can be seen from across town and is a favourite with tour groups. While it may not represent the authentic Xinjiang experience, the rooms here are luxurious, the views from the upper floors across the city, desert and mountains are fantastic, and the rates are extremely good value. **¥388**

Seman 色满宾馆, sèmǎn bīnguǎn. Seman Lu ☎ 0998 2582129. This rambling, historic hotel with flamboyant interior decor is a popular choice, with cheap rooms complemented by the old Russian embassy out back. There are also some useful tour agencies in the lobby. While you can save around ¥80 by going for a room without a/c, it's not worth it. **¥180**

EATING

Kashgar has a slew of excellent places to eat. Uyghur restaurants are concentrated around Id Kah Square, while street vendors sell *pilau*, kebabs and cold spicy noodles; *laghman* is also available almost everywhere.

★ Altun Orda 金奥尔达饮食, jīn'àoěrdá yǐnshí. 320 Ren Min Xi Lu ☎ 0998 2583555. Walking in here feels like stepping into a 1930s Hollywood movie, and despite being one of the classiest restaurants in town, there are enough simple ¥20–50 dishes hidden away on the picture

menu to make it affordable. The ¥88 "tower kebab" and walnut ice cream comes especially recommended. Daily 10am–midnight.

★ Avral 阿普拉乐奶油冰淇淋, āwúlālè nǎiyóu bīngqílín. Seman Lu, just west of the Bank of China. If

13

there's even one sweet tooth in your mouth, be sure to head to this inconspicuous café. The owners blew US$1000 on a special Arabic ice cream machine, and the results are rather dreamy: ¥8 will buy you a little bowlful of heaven. The menu is in Uyghur and Chinese only, but all bowls are based on their signature sweet cream – particularly good when served with the home-made cherry syrup. Daily 11am–11pm.

John's Café Royal Qinibagh Hotel ☎ 1389 9166056. Recently relocated from behind the *Seman*, and well hidden in its new location, this backpacker-friendly, open-air café doles out Sino-Western food as well as coffees, juices and beer. Pancakes in plain (¥15), banana (¥18) or chocolate (¥18) varieties are good for breakfast. This is a pleasant place to relax over a book or catch up on emails using the wi-fi. Daily 8am–midnight.

Mengyol 明邀乐饮食, míngyāolè yīnshí. South side of Id Kah Square ☎ 0998 2844000. Climb up to this fourth-floor venue overlooking the mosque to feast on Uyghur dumplings, *pilau* and meat dishes. Try to time your visit with sunset, when you'll hear the muezzin – sit mosque-side if at all possible. Daily 10am–midnight.

DIRECTORY

Banks and exchange The main Bank of China, in the northeast corner of Renmin Square (Mon–Fri: summer 9.30am–1.30pm & 4–7pm; winter 10am–2pm & 3.30–6.30pm), can change foreign currency (both cash and travellers' cheques). Their ATMs accept foreign cards.

Bookshops Xinhua Bookshop is at 32 Jiefang Bei Lu, on the east side of the road and just north of the intersection with Renmin Lu.

Post offices The main post office is at 40 Renmin Xi Lu, a short walk west of Jiefang Lu (Mon–Sat: summer 9.30am–8pm; winter 10am–7.30pm).

Visa extensions The visa office on Youmulake Xiehai'er Lu (Mon–Fri 10.30am–1.30pm & 4–8pm, closed Wed & Fri afternoons), near the end of Wusitangboyi Lu, theoretically issues visa extensions, but not for tourist L visas.

The Southern Silk Road

The **Southern Silk Road** splits off from the northern route at Kashgar, skirting the southern rim of the **Taklamakan** and curving north at **Charkhlik** on the desert's eastern edge before rejoining the northern route near Dunhuang in Gansu (see p.823). In modern times this path has fallen into obscurity, thanks in part to punishing distances, forlorn and dusty towns, and sparse transport connections. However, this is actually the older and historically more important of the two branches. The most famous Silk Road travellers used it, as well as Marco Polo and the British journalist Peter Fleming in the 1930s. The ancient settlements along the way were desert oases, kept alive by streams flowing down from the snowy peaks of the Kunlun Shan, which border the southern edge of this route.

Following the southern Silk Road opens up the possibility of travelling overland from Dunhuang to Kashgar one way and returning another, thus circumnavigating the entire Taklamakan Desert. The road from Kashgar runs for 1400km to the town of Charkhlik, from where it's still a fair way either up and around to Dunhuang, or on to Golmud in Qinghai (see p.817). The ancient city of **Hotan** is the pick of places to get off the bus and explore; it's also linked to Kuqa via the splendid 522km-long **Tarim Desert Expressway**, one of the longest desert roads in the world.

UYGHUR MUSIC – MUQAM

Song and dance is at the core of Uyghur cultural identity and is commonly presented at all social gatherings. The most established form of Uyghur music, **muqam**, has developed since the sixth century into a unique collection of songs and instrumentals, quite separate from Arabic and Persian influence. A *muqam* must open with a flowing rhythm that complies with strict modal constraints, followed by a suite of pieces that tie into this opening. In the late sixteenth century scholars and folk musicians gathered to collate this music into a definitive collection of twelve *muqams*. The entire collection takes **24 hours** to play and involves around fifteen traditional instruments such as the plucked mandolin-like *rawap*, metal-stringed *dutah* and large *dumbak* drums. Sadly, few people can play *muqam* nowadays, but recordings are popular and sold on CD and DVD throughout Xinjiang.

Yengisar

英吉沙, yīngjí shā

A mere 70km from Kashgar, the town of **YENGISAR** has for centuries been known for supplying the Uyghur people with handcrafted knives. Recent (and understandable) curbs on the open production and sale of knives have hit what was once one of the region's most widespread cottage industries. Most of the knives you'll see on sale in Xinjiang today are display pieces, manufactured at the **Anarguli Knife Factory** (阿娜尔古丽小刀厂, anà'ěrgǔlì xiǎodāochǎng) 1km south of Yengisar on the G315 national road. A few craftsmen still ply their old skills, inlaying handles with horn or silver alloy; some of the more decorative examples take nearly a fortnight to forge. Before being tempted into buying anything, be aware that travelling in the region with any kind of blade is likely to be extremely troublesome – your best bet would be to post any purchases home immediately.

Yarkand

莎车, shāchē

The town of **YARKAND**, 130km southeast of Yengisar, has been a strategically important staging post for at least the last thousand years, and is following Kashgar in becoming ever more developed and sanitized. Some of the old character remains in the northeastern backstreets, a warren of muddy lanes lined with willows and traditional adobe homes with wooden-framed balconies, but these areas are shrinking in time with the inexorable eastward march of the more ordered new town. Sundays are the best time to visit Yarkand, when a huge rustic **market** along the same lines as the more famous one in Kashgar is held in the main bazaar behind the fort – though this area has plenty of interest most days.

The old town

You'll find the town's major sights close together on Aletun Lu running north off Laocheng Lu – the immaculately restored **old fort** is opposite Yarkand's **Altunluq Mosque** (阿勒屯清真寺, ālètún qīngzhēnsì) and **Amannisahan Tomb** (阿曼尼莎汗纪念陵, āmànníshāhàn jìniànlíng; ¥15). The tomb, built for the wife of a sixteenth-century khan, is a beautiful white- and blue-tiled affair; Amannisahan was also the most influential contributor to **muqam** music (see box opposite).

The adjacent **cemetery** contains the mausoleums of several of Yarkand's former rulers, including Amannisahan's husband, and is crowded with more ordinary cylindrical Muslim tombs and ancient trees.

ARRIVAL AND INFORMATION
YARKAND

By bus The bus station (莎车客运站, shāchē kèyùnzhàn) is on Gulebage Lu, just south of the main thoroughfare Xincheng Lu.
Destinations Hotan (4 daily; 7hr); Kargilik (10 daily; 1hr); Kashgar (10 daily; 3hr); Yengisar (10 daily; 1hr 30min).

Services The Bank of China (with ATMs accepting credit cards), post office and China Telecom are all clustered around the central Qini'aibage Lu–Laocheng/Xincheng Lu intersection, known locally as Dashizi.

ACCOMMODATION

Shache Hotel 莎车宾馆, shāchē bīnguǎn. East along Xincheng Lu from the bus station ☎0998 8522365. This is a pleasant place (albeit in the standard Chinese business hotel style) that accepts foreigners – which is fortunate, as almost nowhere else in Yarkand does. ¥180

Yarkand Youth Hostel 莎车国际青年旅舍, shāchē guójì qīngnián lǚshè. West along Xincheng Lu from the bus station ☎0998 8510080. This is the only budget option in town that's open to foreigners. It feels slightly young-offenders institute, but it's cheap and staff can help with tours and onward travel. Dorms ¥40

EATING

Meraj Restaurant 米热吉快餐, mǐrèjí kuàicān. 16 Xincheng Lu. Extremely popular with locals, *Meraj* serves stuffed naan bread and all kinds of noodle dishes (¥15–20), but the real delicacy here is pigeon meat (¥25).

13

Daily 9am–midnight.

Yurtum Restaurant 尤土木, *yóutǔmù*. Overlooking the Altunluq Mosque. This Uyghur restaurant's location is brilliant – take a table upstairs overlooking the square outside the mosque and fortify yourself with their incredibly strong coffee (¥15) and tasty *pilau* (¥18). Daily 10am–midnight.

Kargilik

叶诚, yèchéng

Sixty kilometres south of Yarkand, **KARGILIK** is a long, straggling town, stretching along the highway. Every Wednesday there's a fantastic **market** about 1km towards Hotan, which is far more authentic and colourful than the Kashgar Sunday market, and well worth your time.

The road divides at Kargilik, with one fork running southwest into **Tibet**; this used to be a prime target for hardy travellers attempting to sneak to Ali in the back of a truck, but, quite aside from the appalling rigours of the trip, heavy-handed security these days makes that inadvisable, not to mention virtually impossible – you'll have to arrange a tour through an agent in Lhasa (see box, p.880).

ACCOMMODATION KARGILIK

Jiaotong Hotel 交通宾馆, *jiāotōng bīnguǎn*. Beside the bus station ☎ 0998 7285540. With its dingy but clean doubles, the accommodation here might be a bit unappealing, but this bus station hotel is convenient for transport links and surrounded by busy restaurants. **¥120**

Hotan

和田, hétián

Five hundred kilometres southeast of Kashgar, predominantly Uyghur **HOTAN** has for centuries enjoyed countrywide fame for its **carpets**, **silk** and **white jade**. A bleak and dusty grid of wide streets punctuated with growing numbers of tower blocks, the town is pretty ordinary, but the people are hospitable, and there are rare opportunities to see traditional silk production.

The town centre

Hotan centres on **Tuanjie Square**, from where the city is partitioned by Beijing Lu (running east to west) and Ta'naiyi Lu (north to south). The giant sculpture in the middle of the square shows Chairman Mao shaking hands with an elderly Uyghur man, who went to Beijing to congratulate the Communist Party on its victory in the 1950s – the symbol still serves its function, though the hostility of the local Uyghurs towards Han Chinese is no secret. The square comes alive on summer evenings, when line-dancing clubs take over the vast paved expanse.

Jade Dragon Kashgar River

玉龙喀什河, yùlóng kāshíhé

About 4km east of the city centre, following Beijing Dong Lu, is the **Jade Dragon Kashgar River**, which still yields the odd jade nugget for casual searchers. The river flows through a wide, stony plain; it's easy to get down here and forage, but you'll need to find one of the locals – who rake for stones with garden forks – to show you what you are looking for, or you may end up with a pocketful of pretty but

---

HOTAN'S BAZAAR

Hotan's fascinating **bazaar** takes place every Sunday, although there's some action here every day. Silk, carpets, leather jackets, fruit and spices are all on sale, with innumerable blacksmiths, tinsmiths, goldsmiths and carpenters hard at work among the stalls. The bazaar stretches across the northeast part of town; the easiest way to reach it is to head east along Aiyitika'er Lu, off Wenhua Lu near the centre. Follow the stalls south toward Jiamai Lu, along which you can see the pretty Jiamai mosque.

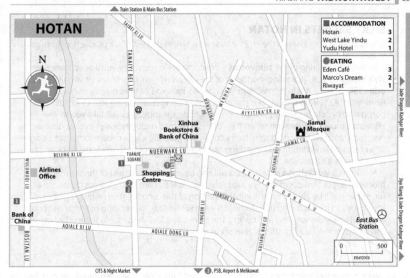

worthless quartz. Jade-hunting peaks in spring and autumn, when the water level is at its lowest.

Melikawat

米力克瓦特古城, mǐlìkèwǎtè gǔchéng • ¥20 • Taxi from town around ¥100 – make sure your driver knows the way

Silk Road specialists should visit the ruined city of **Melikawat**, out in the desert 30km to the south of Hotan beside the Jade Dragon Kashgar River. This city, formerly an important Buddhist centre on the Silk Road, was abandoned well over a thousand years ago, and the arrival of Islam in the region did nothing to aid its preservation. The site is a fragmentary collection of crumbling walls set among the dunes and tamarisk bushes, with thousands of wind-polished potshards littering the ground – you might find odd bits of glass or wood poking out of the ruins.

ARRIVAL AND DEPARTURE
HOTAN

By plane Hotan's domestic airport (和田机场, hétián jīchǎng) lies 10km southwest of town. You can reach the centre by taxi (¥25) – there's no airport bus. Buy flight tickets in the airline office at 14 Wulumuqi Lu (daily 9.30am–9pm; ☎0903 2518999), a few minutes north of the *Hetian Binguan* hotel.
Destinations Ürümqi (1hr 45min).

By train The massive station complex is about 6km north of town, with stopping services running west to Kashgar. It can be reached on bus #410 (¥1) from town or by taxi (¥10–15).
Destinations Kargilik (2 daily; 2hr 30min–3hr 30min); Kashgar (2 daily; 6–7hr); Yarkand (2 daily; 3hr 30min–4hr 30min); Yengisar (2 daily; 5–6hr 15min).

By bus The Main bus station (和田客运中心, hétián

kèyùn zhōngxīn) is north of the city alongside the train station. There are daily services to Kuqa and Ürümqi across the Taklamakan Desert, and to all destinations west of Hotan. East of Hotan along the Southern Silk Road, as well as to Jiya Xiang, you would need to use the East bus station (东车站, dōng chēzhàn) on Taibei Dong Lu; however at the time of writing these services were likely to soon be absorbed by the Main bus station.
Destinations Cherchen (daily; 12hr); Kashgar (10 daily; 8hr); Kuqa (2 daily; 9hr); Niya (4 daily; 5hr); Ürümqi (10 daily; 20hr); Yarkand (10 daily; 6hr).

By taxi At both bus stations there are official shared taxis running along some long-distance bus routes, although the prices are roughly double that of regular tickets and you'll need to wait for the taxis to fill up.

INFORMATION

Travel agents All main hotels have travel services for booking plane and bus tickets and arranging tours. Local

excursions with a guide, taking in the carpet and silk factories, should set you back around ¥100, and it's possible

13

SILKY SECRETS IN HOTAN

One of Hotan's best assets is the chance to see the whole process of silk production, from grub to garment.

To see the nurturing of the **silkworms** – only possible in summer – you'll need to explore **Jiya Xiang** (吉亚乡, jíyà xiāng) northeast of the city, a tiny Uyghur settlement specializing in **atlas silk**, which is made in small, family-run workshops. You can get here by minibus (9am–9pm; ¥2.5) from the East bus station on Taibei Dong Lu. If you are able to explain your purpose to people (a drawing of a silkworm might do the trick), they will take you to see silkworms munching away on rattan trays of fresh, cleaned mulberry leaves in cool, dark sheds. Eventually each worm should spin itself a cocoon of pure silk; each cocoon comprises a single strand about 1km in length. The hatching and rearing of silkworms is unreliable work, and for most farmers it's a sideline.

At the small **workshops** near Jiya you will also be able to see the rest of the silk-making process – about 5km down the Jiya road Atlas Silk (daily 9.30am–8pm) is a good place to aim for. Inside, you'll be able to see the initial unpicking of the cocoons, the twisting together of the strands to form a thread (ten strands for each silk thread), the winding of the thread onto reels and finally the weaving and dyeing. There are also a few shops along the road where you can pick up a vivid scarf or shirt of atlas silk as a souvenir.

to organize lengthier jeep or camel trips around the region, using routes not necessarily covered by public transport. Expect to pay ¥400 per day for a jeep, ¥150 for a camel. Camping gear is around ¥50 per person, and a guide will cost ¥100 a day. If your accommodation can't help, try Hotan's helpful, English-speaking CITS (☎0903 2516090), which is inconveniently located at 49 Tunken Lu, in the south of the city.

ACCOMMODATION

Unfortunately there is very little in the way of budget accommodation available to foreigners in Hotan, though there are plenty of decent mid-range options that can open their doors to those not from the Middle Kingdom.

Hotan 和田宾馆, hétián bīnguǎn. 57 Wulumuqi Nan Lu ☎0903 7828999. An old-school option on the edge of the town centre, this hotel has a tranquil feel, and is decorated with some local touches. The pleasant rooms come with bathtubs. ¥340

West Lake Yindu 西湖银都国际酒店, xīhú yíndū guójì jiǔdiàn. 111 Ta'naiyi Nan Lu ☎0903 2521365. This hotel is one of the most luxurious options in Hotan,

and the beds here are among the most comfortable in Xinjiang. Your fellow guests are likely to be a mix of Chinese businessmen and wealthy Uyghurs. ¥318

Yudu Hotel 玉都大酒店, yùdū dàjiǔdiàn. Southwest corner of Tuanjie Square ☎0903 2023456. The staff here may be uninterested, but the location is right in the heart of the action, making this a good central option. Rooms are recently renovated, though wi-fi is patchy. ¥198

EATING

There's a wide range of street eats in Hotan, although development work in the city centre means that locations keep changing – failing all else, check out the southern end of Tuanjie Square, and the streets running south from here.

Eden Café 伊甸咖啡, yīdiàn kāfēi. 360 Yingbin Lu ☎0903 2518888. This is a smart restaurant that's full of middle-class Uyghur families enjoying leisurely meals and a combination of Uyghur, Turkish and Western dishes. Try their delicious mint tea (¥36) and, if you're seriously hungry, the huge mixed grill (¥98). Daily 1pm–midnight.

★**Marco's Dream** 马克驿站, mǎkè yìzhàn. In a residential courtyard just north of the Xihu Hotel, 100m west along Jianshe Lu ☎0903 2025741. This café serves a range of Western and Asian dishes, from Malaysian chicken rice (¥30) to sticky toffee pudding (¥15), and will

do vegetarian meals on request. The owners speak English and are only too happy to share travel information about the region. Can be tricky to find, but give them a call and they can send out a search party. Daily 1.30–9.30pm.

Riwayat 生态餐厅, shēngtài cāntīng. 39–43 Youyi Lu ☎0903 2032230. A fun restaurant, somewhat bizarrely decked out like a tropical jungle complete with a papier-mâché crocodile and a working waterwheel. The menu is nothing if not eclectic, running from kebabs (¥8) to burgers (¥13) and from gong bao ji ding (¥32) to pizza (¥68). Daily 11am–11.30pm.

DIRECTORY

Banks and exchange The main Bank of China (9.50am–12.30pm & 4.20–7.20pm) is on Wulumuqi Nan Lu – this is the place to come to exchange travellers' cheques, and the ATMs here accept international cards.
Post office On Nuerwake Lu (Mon–Fri 9.30am–8pm).

Visa extensions For visa-related issues, head to the PSB on the corner of Yingbin Lu and Tunken Lu (Mon–Fri 9.20am–1.30pm & 4–8pm), although this is not a good place to apply for an extension.

Niya
民丰, mínfēng

On the way to **NIYA**, 300km east of Hotan, you'll pass through some of the most vividly empty landscapes you will ever see, a formless expanse of sky and desert merging at a vague, dusty yellow horizon. The modern town is 100km south of **Niya Ancient City**, first discovered by Aurel Stein in 1901; ongoing excavations have uncovered the remains of pagodas, orchards, and over a hundred dwellings beneath the desert sands. The most important artefacts have been removed to museums in Ürümqi, although there is still a small **museum** (尼雅文物馆, níyǎ wénwùguǎn) in the town.

Cherchen
且末, qiěmò

CHERCHEN, 300km east of Niya, is another small, surprisingly modern town, famed for the frequency of its sandstorms (especially in April). There is a group of 2600-year-old **tombs** about 5km to the southeast at **Zagunluk** (扎滚鲁克古墓群, zhāgǔnlǔkè gǔmùqún; daily 8am–8pm; ¥30). While only one tomb is open to view, it's been carefully reconstructed, and the taxi ride (¥30) out here through attractive villages is interesting as well. Closer to town is the **Tohlaklek Manor** (地主庄园, dìzhǔ zhuāngyuán; daily 9.30am–1.30pm & 4–7.30pm; ¥20), a former landlord's house built in 1911. There's not much inside, but it's a good example of local architecture all the same.

Charkhlik
若羌, ruòqiāng

CHARKHLIK, 360km east of Cherchen, is a small, busy place, notable for being the jumping-off point for treks by camel or jeep out to two little-known ruined cities of Silk Road vintage, Miran and Loulan (see box, p.862). It's also one final long push across the desert from Charkhlik to **Kuqa** (see p.848), or, for a hardy few, a tough bus trip across the Qaidam Basin to **Golmud** (see p.817) in Qinghai province, through a corner of China that few foreigners ever see.

CROSSING THE TAKLAMAKAN

The cities of Hotan and Kuqa – respectively on the Southern and Northern silk routes – can be linked in three different ways. The most painless option is to take the new **cross-desert highway** from Hotan to **Kuqa** on the Northern Silk Route, from where you'll at least have the option of continuing on by train; the 500km journey across the desert takes around eight hours, though it would be considerably shorter were it not for the numerous security checkpoints. There's another such highway several hundred kilometres to the east of Hotan – the Tarim Desert Expressway – with its southern terminus at the town of **Niya**; this is longer at 522km, but will save you a little time if you're heading directly to Turpan or Ürümqi. Both roads cross the **Taklamakan Desert**, and will give you a close-up view of why the Uyghurs call this the "Sea of Death". Unfortunately, many buses travelling in either direction make the crossing at night, so you don't get much of a view of the impressive ever-shifting desert sands.

For a more interesting trip back to the Northern Silk Road, you'll want to catch a bus east from Hotan to Charkhlik; from here, you can either head north towards Ürümqi or east again towards Dunhuang, Golmud or Qinghai Lake.

13

LOST CITIES: MIRAN AND LOULAN

Two remote, ruined cities make intriguing targets from Charkhlik, if you have time and plenty of cash. **Miran** (米兰古城, mǐlán gǔchéng) – subject of Christa Paula's book *Voyage to Miran* – is relatively accessible, approximately 75km northeast of Charkhlik; a far more ambitious trip would be to **Loulan** (楼兰古城, lóulán gǔchéng), 250km from town on the western edge of Lop Nur. Loulan's very existence had been completely forgotten until the Swedish explorer Sven Hedin rediscovered the site, which had been buried in sand, in the early twentieth century; it wasn't until the 1980s that the first Chinese archeological surveys were undertaken, during which distinctively un-Chinese mummified remains, including the "Loulan Beauty", were found (see p.833).

There's a **Loulan Museum** (10.30am–12.30pm & 4.30–6.30pm) in Charkhlik, but the most interesting remains have already been removed to Ürümqi. In order to visit the sites themselves, you'll need to make an application to the local department of cultural heritage whose office is in Charkhlik's Loulan Museum. The fees and permits required will depend upon the trip you have in mind, but can run to thousands of dollars for official expeditions, and nonspecialists may simply be refused entry.

ARRIVAL AND DEPARTURE   CHARKHLIK

By bus The Main bus station (若羌客运中心, ruòqiāng kèyùn zhōngxīn) is on Shengli Lu, just north of Charkhlik's centre. The ticket office is open daily 8.30am–6.30pm, and tickets are easy to buy.
Destinations Cherchen (4 daily; 4hr); Golmud (daily; 14hr); Korla (2 daily; 7hr).

ACCOMMODATION AND EATING

Longdu Business Hotel 龙都商务宾馆, lóngdū shāngwù bīnguǎn. On the corner of Shengli Lu and Jianshe Lu ☎0996 7010111. This is the only place close to the bus station that takes foreigners, although the staff might be a bit rusty at the registration process. Rooms are adequate and very large, but beds are rock hard. **¥120**
Shudu Restaurant 蜀都食府, shǔdū shífǔ. 388 Jianshe Le ☎0996 7105467. A reasonably priced Sichuanese restaurant with friendly staff and a picture menu of their chilli-laden fare. Daily 11am–10pm.

The Karakoram Highway

For millennia the 4700m-high **Khunjerab Pass**, 400km south of Kashgar, has been the nexus between the Chinese world and the Indian subcontinent. Today, the entire 1300km route from Kashgar over the mountains to Rawalpindi in northern Pakistan is known as the **Karakoram Highway** (中巴公路, zhōngbā gōnglù) and, while it's not without its perils (rock falls and snow storms are far from rare), it's hard to think of a more exciting route out of China.

The journey takes a minimum of four days, though the pass is open only from the beginning of May until the end of October, and can close without notice in bad weather. Travellers have to spend a night on the Chinese side, either in Tashkurgan or camping out by the wintry but beautiful **Lake Karakul**. You'll also need to have already arranged Pakistan visas in your home country unless you live in China, in which case you can apply through the Pakistani embassy in Beijing.

Lake Karakul

喀拉库勒湖, kālākùlē hú

Southwest of Kashgar, the road climbs out of the city's flat valley, and leaves the mud-brick buildings and irrigated wheat and rice plantations behind. Climbing through river gorges strewn with giant boulders, it creeps into a land of treeless, bare dunes of sand and gravel, interspersed with pastures scattered with grazing yaks and camels. The appearance of **Lake Karakul** by the roadside, some 200km out of Kashgar, is dramatic: right under the feet of the Pamir Mountains and the magnificent 7546m Mount Muztagata, whose vast snowy flanks have been split open by colossal glaciers, the waters of the lake are luminous blue. Don't get this mixed up with the incredible, and much larger, reservoir at the confluence of the Bulunkou, Kangxiwa and Muji rivers, about half as far outside Kashgar. While the scenery here is staggering, hiking would be a harsh proposition and accommodation is nonexistent.

At Lake Karakul there's a small **official scenic spot** (喀拉库勒湖观景台, kālākùlè hú guānjǐng tái; ¥50) on the west side of the lake, but there's really no need to come here unless you're desperate for somewhere to stay (see below).

ARRIVAL AND DEPARTURE   LAKE KARAKUL

By bus and taxi From the Kashgar International Bus Station there are two buses daily from May–Oct, leaving at 10am and 4pm (¥50), with the journey taking about six hours. Buy tickets in advance if you plan to travel to the lake on a Monday – an exodus of foreigners from Kashgar after the Sunday market can make tickets scarce. It's also possible to take a shared taxi (¥120) from a spot on Xiyu Dadao (ask for 老塔县办事处, lǎotǎxiàn bànshìchù). From Tashkurgan you can

take the Kashgar bus and get off at the lake. Leaving the lake requires slightly more ingenuity – in either direction you will need to flag down the passing buses or taxis, which may involve standing assertively in the middle of the road. Fortunately hitchhiking is relatively common along this stretch, and ought to be straightforward. Taxis back to Kashgar cost a minimum of ¥100 per person.

ACCOMMODATION

Hikers will almost certainly encounter amenable Kyrgyz yurt dwellers on their way around the lake – especially along the west side of the lake beside the road. There is some food available at the scenic spot, but otherwise you'll need to eat with the herders or bring your own food.

★**Apudi's** 400m north of the scenic spot ☎1377 9617293. While this small house looks unprepossessing from outside, it's very cosy inside and Apudi and his wife are welcoming and experienced at dealing with hikers stricken by altitude sickness. Dinner included. **¥50**

Official Yurt Camp Inside the scenic spot. The only formal accommodation around the lake, this is aimed at tour groups, and has regular rooms in addition to unappealing concrete yurts. Yurts **¥90**, doubles **¥180**

Tashkurgan
塔什库尔干, tǎshí kù'ěrgān or 塔县, tǎ xiàn

The last town before the border, **TASHKURGAN** lies 280km southwest of Kashgar, and about 220km north of the Pakistani town of **Sust** (苏斯特, sūsītè). Its primary importance for travellers is as a staging post between the two settlements, and all travellers passing through, in either direction, must stay the night here. It's a tiny place, comprising a couple of tree-lined streets with a bus station, market and a sprinkling of hotels – the uniform concrete construction is disappointingly banal considering the town's incredible location and fascinating history.

The native population is mainly **Tajik**, whose customs differ markedly from both Uyghur and Chinese – keep an eye out for the elaborate way they greet each other on the street – as well as intrepid Pakistanis setting up shop.

> ## HIKING AROUND LAKE KARAKUL
> The opportunities for hiking over the surrounding green pasture are extensive. While the walk around the lake takes around half a day, for anything more ambitious you should take a tent and warm clothing; at 3800m, the weather can be extremely cold even in summer, with snow showers occurring well into June. Whatever your plans, make sure to take plenty of food and water, as there's little available at the lake. Tour agencies in Kashgar (see box, p.854) can help to organize more ambitious treks around Mount Muztagata and beyond.

13

Stone City
石头城, shítou chéng • Daily 9.30am–8pm • ¥30

Few visitors bother to stop at Tashkurgan longer than necessary, but worth a look, especially at sunset, is the six-hundred-year-old, crumbling, mud-brick **Stone City**, which found fame as a location in the film adaptation of **The Kite Runner**. If you clamber to the top, the scenes of snowy mountains running parallel on both flanks, and woods and wetlands dotted around, are more than picturesque. To reach it, walk east from the bus station right to the end of town and the compound is on the left. Beyond this is an area of **grassland** used by Tajik herders in the summer months.

ARRIVAL AND INFORMATION   TASHKURGAN

BY BUS
Tashkurgan's tiny bus station (汽车站, qìchē zhàn) is right in the middle of town. There are morning buses to Kashgar as well as an unreliable daily service to Sust in Pakistan. If you plan to get off at Lake Karakul (see p.862) en route to Kashgar, you may be asked to pay the full ¥51 Kashgar fare anyway.

BY TAXI
Taxis and minivans also run the route between Tashkurgan and Kashgar and both wait outside the bus station to fill up before heading off, taking around six hours to complete the journey to Kashgar. For a taxi, you should expect to pay

¥120 per person; for minivans, it'll be around ¥70.

SERVICES
Banks and exchange An Agricultural Bank of China (Mon–Fri 9.30am–1.30pm & 4.30–7.30pm) lies 300m to the south of the bus station. Cash (and sometimes travellers' cheques) can be changed here at official exchange rates, but the ATMs only accept Chinese cards. If arriving from Pakistan, you can easily change your rupees with the local Pakistanis if the banks are closed.
Post offices The post office is just southeast of the bus station, open Mon–Fri 10am–1.30pm & 3–6.30pm.

ACCOMMODATION

Crown Inn 皇冠大酒店, huángguàn dàjiǔdiàn. 23 Pamir Lu, on the southern edge of town ⊕0998 3422888. This modern, bright hotel with a slightly out-of-the-way location is Singaporean-owned and very comfortable, but seems out of kilter with its surroundings. **¥450**

Jiaotong Hotel 交通宾馆, jiāotōng bīnguǎn. 385 Tashkurgan Lu, next to the bus station ⊕0998 3421192. This convenient option in the middle of town is clean and simple, with equally basic bathrooms and 24hr

hot water. Open May–Oct only. **¥150**
K2 Youth Hostel 凯途国际青年旅社, kǎi tú guójì qīngnián lǚshè. Hongqilafu Lu, at the northern end of town ⊕0998 3492266. This is a surprisingly good hostel in such a remote place, with a sunny common area and enormous windows looking out over the mountains. Dorms are huge, as are the private rooms, and the only grumble is the total lack of heating or insulation – luckily, it's only open in summer. Dorms **¥45**, doubles **¥160**

EATING

Most accommodation in Tashkurgan offers food – both *K2 Youth Hostel* and *Crown Inn* provide a selection of Chinese and Western dishes. There are also some good hotpot restaurants in the square beside the *K2*.

Shanhua 山花快餐, shānhuā kuàicān. Tashkurgan Lu ⊕151 60869270. For something other than Chinese food, try this Pakistani barbecue-influenced garden

restaurant near the bus station, which doles out excellent kebabs (¥10) and *pilau* (¥15). Daily 9am–midnight.

The Khunjerab Pass
红其拉甫口岸, hóngqí lāfǔ kǒu'àn

Khunjerab means "River of Blood" in the Tajik language – which may refer to the rusty colour of local rivers, or to the long tradition of banditry in these areas. The trip across the border at the **Khunjerab Pass** is not a totally risk-free affair – people are killed almost every year by falling rocks on the highway, and you should be aware that if your bus departs in rainy weather, you can almost certainly expect mud slides.

TASHKURGAN TO PAKISTAN

Bring **warm clothing** and plenty of **snacks and water** on your Karakoram journey. Travellers heading to Pakistan do not need to buy onward bus tickets – the ticket from Kashgar covers the whole route right through to Sust. Western tourists should be aware that they'll need to have arranged a Pakistani **visa** beforehand in their home country, though it's worth checking the current state of play at the Beijing embassy (W pakbj.org.pk). Stamp in hand, the entry and exit formalities are dealt with a few hundred metres south from the bank, and are straightforward. At **Sust**, there's plenty of accommodation to go around, as well as places in which to change yuan for rupees.

Through the pass

From Tashkurgan, the road climbs into a vast, bright plain, surrounded by breathtaking mountains. Emerging onto the top of the pass at 4693m, you're greeted by a silent, windswept space of frozen streams, protruding glaciers and bright green pastures in the sunshine. About the only creatures you'll see here are comically chubby ginger Himalayan marmots, which are easily spotted from the bus. At these heights many travellers experience some form of altitude sickness (see p.46). The journey between Tashkurgan and the small town of Sust, where Pakistani customs and immigration procedures occur, takes about seven hours. Travellers in both directions have to spend a night here, and accommodation is plentiful. From Sust there are direct daily buses to Gilgit, from where frequent buses cover the sixteen-hour route to Rawalpindi and Islamabad.

Tibet
西藏

THE FRIENDSHIP HIGHWAY

Tibet

西藏, xīzàng

14

Tibet (Bod to Tibetans), the "Roof of the World" or "Third Pole", has exerted a magnetic pull over travellers for centuries. This vast, high-altitude desert has spawned myths and legends since the dawn of time. Its mountains are home to the Hindu gods, the scenery is awe-inspiring, its monasteries are filled with art and treasure, and the religious devotion of its people is humbling. On the surface it can seem as if there is perhaps no other place on Earth that can conjure up so many exotic impressions. However, dig down, and it is all too apparent that Tibet's past has been tragic, its present painful and the future bleak: Tibet is a subjugated colony of China. While foreign visitors are perhaps more worldly than to expect a romantic Shangri-La, there is no doubt that many are shocked by the heavy military presence and authoritarian restrictions. The growing presence of Chinese immigrants, the buses full of snap-happy Han tourists, the construction of ugly apartments and factories, the damming of rivers, the digging up of mineral wealth and a programme of resettling nomads en-masse to permanent new towns are all further causes of disquiet to Tibetans. But don't stay away: many people, the Dalai Lama included, believe travellers should visit Tibet to learn all they can of the country.

One of the most isolated parts of the world, the massive **Tibetan Plateau** sits at an average height of 4500m above sea level, guarded on all sides by towering **mountain ranges**. To the south, the Himalayas separate Tibet from India, Nepal and Bhutan; to the west lie the peaks of the Karakoram and Pakistan; while to the north the Kunlun range forms a barrier to Xinjiang. Eastwards, dividing Tibet from Sichuan and Yunnan, a further series of ranges stretches for a thousand kilometres. Some of Asia's greatest **rivers** are born up on the plateau, including the Yangzi, Mekong, Yellow, Salween, Indus and Brahmaputra.

Following the centuries of self-imposed isolation which ended with Tibet being forcibly annexed by China in 1950, Tibet has become increasingly accessible, with approaches eased by plane links, paved roads and the Qinghai–Lhasa railway. Each new route has accelerated heavy, government-sponsored migration into the region, and although it is impossible to know how many Han Chinese actually live here, it is likely

Highlights

❶ The Jokhang, Lhasa Shrouded in juniper smoke and surrounded by prostrating pilgrims, it's hard not to be affected by this, one of the world's most venerated sites. **See p.888**

❷ Samye Remote walled town encapsulating Tibet's first Buddhist monastery. **See p.900**

❸ Namtso Lake A dream image of Tibet lies bright as a jewel beneath muscular peaks. **See p.906**

❹ Gyantse Explore the chapels and admire the fabulous wall murals of the Gyantse Kumbum in this laidback town. **See p.908**

❺ Everest Base Camp Breathe deep and gaze up at the jagged, snow-blown peak of the world's highest mountain. **See p.918**

❻ Mount Kailash Erase a lifetime of sins on the three-day *kora* (pilgrimage) around the world's holiest mountain. **See p.920**

HIGHLIGHTS ARE MARKED ON THE MAP ON P.870

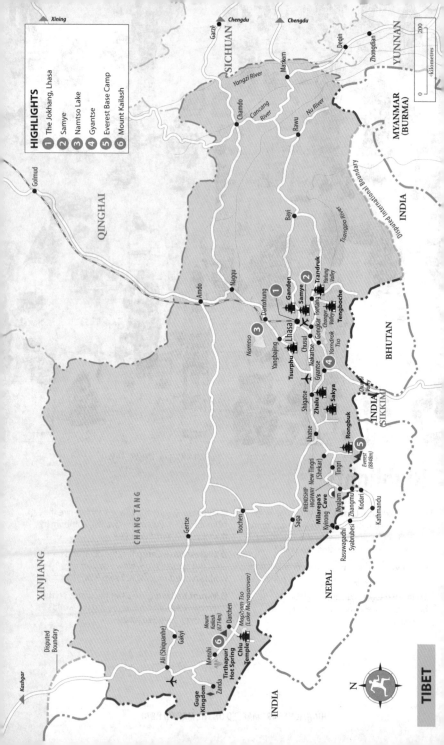

TIBET

that, at least in urban areas, they now outnumber ethnic Tibetans and have become economically dominant.

There are, of course, two sides to every story. The pre-Chinese Tibetan administration was a xenophobic religious dictatorship that tolerated slavery; when the Chinese arrived, the monied and the ruling classes escaped to India, leaving behind an uneducated working class. China has spent billions bringing modern infrastructure to the region, giving Tibetan people the chance to make a better life for themselves. Meanwhile, the Chinese migrating into Tibet are not demons. Most are people simply trying to make a life for themselves and their families, with little understanding of the implications of their presence. As with Taiwan and Xinjiang, all Chinese are taught almost from birth that Tibet is an "inalienable part of China", and to suggest otherwise is heresy.

As part of their Beijing Olympic bid, the Chinese government promised increased freedom for Tibetans, but a confluence of events — the unfurling of a Tibetan flag at Everest Base Camp by some American students in 2007, mass protests and rioting by Tibetans in spring 2008 – ended those dreams. Since 2008, an ongoing campaign in Tibet, Sichuan and even across the border in Nepal has seen scores of Tibetan protesters set themselves ablaze. Today, extremely **strict travel regulations** are in place, and temporary bans on all foreign travellers from visiting the region are regularly imposed (see p.878). Any visit to Tibet will be **expensive**, with transport and accommodation options for foreigners limited, on the whole, to the higher end of the market, though Tibetan organizations abroad ask visitors to try, wherever possible, to buy from Tibetans and to hire Tibetan guides. At all times, you should avoid putting Tibetans – and yourself – at risk by bringing up **politically sensitive issues**: you can go home; Tibetans have to live here. There are cameras, police, military and, if rumours are true, undercover informers, everywhere in urban Tibet. The Chinese authorities monitor internet activity here more strictly than in the rest of the Republic so, again, avoid sensitive topics and mentioning people by name in your emails.

Where to go

Today's **Tibetan Autonomous Region** (**TAR**), while still a massive 1.2 million square kilometres, is but a shadow of the former "Greater Tibet" carved up by China in the 1950s, when the Amdo and Kham regions were absorbed into Qinghai, Sichuan, Gansu and Yunnan provinces. The current TAR comprises only the former West and Central regions of Greater Tibet, and is itself divisible into four distinct geographical areas. The northern and largest portion is the almost uninhabited **Chang Tang**, a rocky desert at an average altitude of 4000m, where winter temperatures can fall to -44°C. South of this is the **mountainous grazing area**, inhabited by wide-ranging nomads tending herds of yaks, sheep and goats. **Eastern Tibet**, occupying around a quarter of the TAR, is heavily forested. The relatively temperate **southern valleys**, sandwiched between the nomad areas and the Himalayas along the southern border, is the most hospitable and populated area, and where most visitors spend the majority of their time.

Tourist-friendly Lhasa, **Shigatse** and **Gyantse** offer the most accessible monasteries and temples – the Jokhang, Tashilunpo and Kumbum, respectively. The **Potala Palace** in Lhasa remains an enduring image of Tibet in the Western mind, and should on no account be missed. Farther afield, the **Yarlung** and **Chongye** valleys to the southeast boast temples and ancient monuments, with a visit to the ancient walled monastery of **Samye** easily combined with these. The route along the "Friendship Highway" between Zhangmu, on the Nepalese border, and Lhasa has long been well established, with stops along the way at the Mongolian-style monastery at **Sakya** and **Everest Base Camp**. However, at the time of writing in late 2016, the actual **Nepalese border** remained closed following the 2015 Nepal earthquake; it may well be open by the time you read this, but check before travelling. Further west lie the sacred peak of **Mount Kailash**; its nearby, and similarly holy, neighbour **Lake Manasarovar**; and the mysterious cave dwellings of the **Guge Kingdom**, burrowed into the walls of an enormous, crumbling canyon.

14

Brief history

According to legend, the **earliest Tibetans** came from the union of the ogress, Sinmo, and a monkey, reincarnation of the god Chenresi, on the mountain of Gangpo Ri near Tsetang. Ethnographers, who aren't so taken with tales of primates and monsters, think it more likely that Tibetans descend from the nomadic Qiang, who roamed eastern Central Asia several thousand years ago. The first Tibetan king, Nyatri Tsenpo, who legend has it came to Earth via a magical "sky-cord", was the first of 27 kings who ruled in the pre-Buddhist era when the indigenous, shamanistic **Bön religion** held sway. Each of the **early kings** held power over a small area; the geographical isolation of Tibet made outside

---

TIBETAN BUDDHISM

Tibetan Buddhism is divided into several schools that have different philosophical emphases rather than fundamental differences. The **Nyingma**, the Old Order, traces its origins back to Guru Rinpoche, Padmasambhava, who brought Buddhism to Tibet. The **Kagyupa**, **Sakya** and **Kadampa** all developed during the eleventh-century revival of Buddhism, while the now-dominant **Gelugpa** (Virtuous School) was founded by Tsongkhapa (1357–1419) and includes the Dalai Lama and Panchen Lama among its adherents. Virtually all monasteries and temples are aligned to one or other of the schools, but, apart from an abundance of statues of revered lamas of that particular school, you'll spot little difference between the religious buildings. Tibetan people are pretty eclectic – they will worship in temples that they feel are particularly sacred, and seek blessings from lamas they feel are endowed with special powers, regardless of which school they belong to.

VISITING TEMPLES

There is little ceremony attached to **visiting temples**. Most smaller monasteries are open in the mornings (9am–noon), when pilgrims do the rounds, and again after lunch (around 2pm or 3pm, till 5pm). Larger monasteries tend to be open to foreign tourists daily from around 9am–6pm, but, regardless of monastery size, opening hours are something of a fluid concept. Smaller places may well be locked, but ask for the caretaker and the chances are you'll be let in.

There is no need to remove your shoes, but you should always circulate in a **clockwise** direction (unless it's a rare Bön monastery, in which case go anticlockwise), and you shouldn't eat, drink or smoke inside. Ask before taking **photographs**. Nowadays, in the more tourist-popular monasteries, photography is generally banned inside the buildings (outside in the courtyards it's still allowed), due to large volumes of Chinese tourists taking entirely inappropriate selfies. Foreign tourists are occasionally given special permission, sometimes for a fee, to take photos. If this is granted, be discreet and don't photograph monks. **Entrance fees** collected from tourists are often claimed by local authorities, so if you want to give to the institution itself, leave an offering on an altar.

If you've visited Tibetan Buddhist temples in neighbouring Himalayan regions, you'll know that the **monks** can be very friendly and chatty with tourists. Don't expect the same reaction in Tibet's large, touristy monasteries, where it's rare even to get eye contact with a monk. As Tibetan monks are firmly opposed to the Chinese presence here, and are often at the forefront of protests, many of the larger monasteries now have police stations; it's said that there are even informer monks. Not surprisingly then, most monks are nervous to be seen speaking with a foreigner.

The range of **offerings** Tibetans make to their gods is enormous, and religious observances include: juniper smoke sent skyward in incense burners; prayer flags erected on rooftops and mountains; tiny papers printed with religious images (*lungda*) and cast to the wind on bridges and passes; white scarves (*katag*) presented to statues and lamas; butter to keep lamps burning on altars; repetitious mantras invoking the gods; and the spinning of prayer wheels that have printed prayers rolled up inside. The idea of each is to gain merit in this life and hence affect **karma**. If you want to take part, watch what other people do and copy them; nobody is at all precious about religion in Tibet. Giving **alms to beggars** is another way of gaining merit, and most large Tibetan temples have a horde of beggars who survive on charity from pilgrims. Whether or not you give money is up to you, but, if you do, it's wise to give a few small denomination notes or so, the same amount as Tibetans give.

contact difficult. While pens, ink, silk, jewels and probably tea reached Tibet from China in the seventh century, for many centuries Tibet looked to India for religious teaching.

Arrival of Buddhism

Expansion began in the time of **King Songtsen Gampo**, born in 617 AD. Songtsen Gampo's twenty-year rule saw the unification of the country and the aggressive spread of his empire from northern India to China. China and Nepal each offered Songtsen Gampo a wife: in 632, he married Princess Bhrikuti (also known as Tritsun) of Nepal, and in 641 Princess Wencheng arrived from the Tang court, sent by her father, Emperor

14

GODS AND GODDESSES

Tibetan Buddhism has an overwhelming number of **gods and goddesses**, and each deity in turn has different manifestations or forms. For example, there are 21 forms of the favourite goddess Tara, and even the most straightforward image has both a Sanskrit and Tibetan name. Below are some of the most common you will encounter:

Amitayus (Tsepame) and **Vijaya** (Namgyelma), often placed with White Tara to form the Three Gods of Longevity.

Avalokiteshvara (Chenresi in Tibetan, Guanyin in Chinese temples), patron god of Tibet, with many forms, most noticeably with eleven faces and a thousand arms.

Maitreya (Jampa), the Buddha of the Future.

Manjusri (Jampelyang), the God of Wisdom.

Padmasambhava, with eight manifestations, most apparent as Guru Rinpoche. You may see him with his consorts, Yeshe Tsogyel and Mandarava.

Sakyamuni, Buddha of the Present.

Tara (Dolma), Goddess of Compassion. Green Tara is associated with protection and White Tara with long life.

FESTIVALS

Festival dates are calculated using the Tibetan lunar calendar, and as a result correspond to different dates on the Western calendar each year. There is a list of festival dates in the Western calendar at ⓦ www.exploretibet.com/festivals.

FEBRUARY/MARCH

Driving out of evil spirits. Twenty-ninth day of the twelfth lunar month, the last day of the year.

Losar, Tibetan New Year. First day of the first lunar month.

Monlam, Great Prayer Festival, Lhasa. Eighth day of the first lunar month.

Butter Lamp Festival, on the final day of Monlam. Fifteenth day of the first lunar month.

MAY/JUNE

Birth of Buddha. Seventh day of the fourth lunar month.

Saga Dawa (Buddha's Enlightenment). Fifteenth day of the fourth lunar month.

Gyantse Horse Festival. Fifteenth day of the fourth lunar month.

JULY

Tashilunpo Festival, Shigatse. Fifteenth day of the fifth lunar month.

JULY/AUGUST

Buddha's First Sermon. Fourth day of the sixth lunar month.

Drepung Festival. Thirtieth day of the sixth lunar month.

AUGUST/SEPTEMBER

Shotun (Yoghurt Festival), Lhasa. First to the seventh day of the seventh lunar month.

Bathing Festival, Lhasa. Twenty-seventh day of the seventh lunar month.

SEPTEMBER

Damxhung Horse Festival. Thirtieth day of the seventh lunar month.

SEPTEMBER/OCTOBER

Harvest Festival. First to the seventh day of the eighth lunar month.

NOVEMBER

Lhabab (Buddha's descent from heaven). Twenty-second day of the ninth lunar month.

NOVEMBER/DECEMBER

Palden Lhamo Festival, Lhasa. Fifteenth day of the tenth lunar month.

Taizong. They both brought their **Buddhist faith** and magnificent statues of the Buddha, which are now the centrepieces of Ramoche Temple and the Jokhang in Lhasa. Songtsen Gampo himself embraced Buddhism and established temples throughout the country, although the indigenous Bön faith remained the religion of the ordinary people. Following his death in 650, his descendants strengthened the kingdom politically, and in 763 Tibetan armies even took the Chinese capital Chang'an (modern Xi'an).

In 838, having assassinated his brother, **Langdarma** came to the throne. A fervent supporter of the by-then marginalized Bön faith, he set about annihilating Buddhism. Temples and monasteries were destroyed, monks fled, and Tibet broke up into a number of small principalities. A century later, the arrival of **Atisha** (982–1054), the most famous Indian scholar of his time, sparked a Buddhist revival involving monastery construction, the translation of scriptures into Tibetan and the establishment of several of the schools of Tibetan Buddhism. Politically, the country was divided, with the various independent principalities having little contact with China.

Mongol period

Absorbed in domestic events, the Tibetans were largely unaware of the Muslim surge across India in the twelfth and thirteenth centuries, which destroyed the great Buddhist centres of teaching. Meanwhile, to the north and east, Mongol leader **Genghis Khan** was beginning his assault on China. In 1207, he sent envoys to Tibet demanding submission, which was given without a fight, and the territory was largely ignored until his grandson, Godan Khan, sent raiding parties to explore the country. Hearing from his troops about the spirituality of the Tibetan lamas, Godan invited the head of the Sakya order, Sakya Pandita, to his court. In exchange for peace, Sakya Pandita again offered Tibetan submission and was created regent of Tibet at the Mongolian court, effectively making the Sakya lamas rulers of the country. This lasted through the generations, with Godan's son **Kublai Khan** deeply impressed by Sakya Pandita's nephew, Phagpa.

When the Chinese Ming dynasty overcame the Mongols in the fourteenth century, Tibet began a long period of independence, which ended in 1642 with the Mongols intervening directly in support of the Fifth Dalai Lama, Lobsang Gyatso (1617–82), of the **Gelugpa order**. Often referred to as "**the Great Fifth**", he united the country under Gelugpa rule and within fifteen years established authority from Kham to Kailash – the first time that one religious and political leader had ruled the country. He invited scholars to Tibet, expanded religious institutions and began work on the Potala Palace.

Regency period

One disadvantage of the **reincarnation system** of succession (in which a newborn child is identified as a new manifestation of the dead lama) is that an unstable regency period of fifteen or twenty years inevitably follows the death of a Lama while his latest incarnation grows up. For two centuries after the death of the Fifth Dalai Lama in 1682, the most influential figures in Tibet were these regents, and the representatives of China's Manchu rulers, whose influence – despite Tibet's official continuing status as a Chinese protectorate until 1912 – waned to the extent that Tibet became, to all intents and purposes, self-governing.

British invasion

During the **nineteenth century**, Tibet became increasingly isolationist, fearing Russian plans to expand their empire south and British plans to expand theirs north. But Indian and Tibetan traders continued to do business along the borders: in 1904, British patience with this one-sided arrangement ran out, and a force under Colonel Francis Younghusband was dispatched to extract favourable trading terms.

Younghusband advanced into the country, slaughtering Tibet's poorly armed peasant soldiers – largely reliant on invulnerability charms for protection – along the way.

Having cut their way through to Lhasa (where they were expecting, but failed, to find evidence of Russian influence), the British faced disappointment. One accompanying journalist wrote:

If one approached within a league of Lhasa, saw the glittering domes of the Potala and turned back without entering the precincts one might still imagine an enchanted city. It was in fact an unsanitary slum. In the pitted streets pools of rainwater and piles of refuse were everywhere: the houses were mean and filthy, the stench pervasive. Pigs and ravens competed for nameless delicacies in open sewers.

14

The invaders forced a treaty on the Tibetans which the Dalai Lama – who had fled their advance – did not ratify, and which was rejected too by China's representative. Britain then washed its hands of the whole affair, principally because of the public outcry against the first battle of the campaign, in which seven hundred Tibetans were machine-gunned as they walked away from the battlefield.

Chinese invasion

The **Thirteenth Dalai Lama**, Tubten Gyatso (1876–1933), realized that Tibet's political position needed urgent clarification. But he had a difficult rule, fleeing into exile twice, and was much occupied with border fighting against the Chinese and tensions with conservatives inside the country. Following his death, the **Fourteenth Dalai Lama** was identified in Amdo in 1938 and was still a young man when world events began to close in on Tibet. The British left India in 1947, withdrawing their representative from Lhasa. In 1950, the Chinese government declared their intention "to liberate the oppressed and exploited Tibetans and reunite them with the great motherland". The venture, however, probably had more to do with pre-empting growing Indian and Russian influence in the region than with any high-minded ideals of emancipation. In October 1950, the People's Liberation Army took the Kham region of eastern Tibet before proceeding to Lhasa the following year. Under considerable duress, Tibet signed a seventeen-point treaty in 1951, allowing for the "peaceful integration of Tibet" into China.

Early Communist era

Initially, the Chinese offered goodwill and modernization. Tibet had made little headway into the twentieth century; there were few roads, no electricity or lay education, and glass windows, steel girders and concrete were all recent introductions. While some Tibetans viewed modernization as necessary, the opposition was stiff, with the religious hierarchy seeing changes within the country as a threat to their own power. In March 1959, underground resistance to Chinese rule flared into a public confrontation. Refugees from eastern Tibet fled to Lhasa complaining of the brutality of Chinese rule, including the sexual humiliation of monks and nuns, arbitrary executions and even crucifixions. In Lhasa, the Chinese invited the Dalai Lama to a theatrical performance at the Chinese military HQ. It was popularly perceived as a ploy to kidnap him; huge numbers of Tibetans mounted demonstrations and surrounded

---

BOOKS BEWARE

If you're interested in doing some background **reading** on Tibet (see p.964), it's best to begin at home before you leave, as much that would be considered essential reading by Western audiences is simply not allowed or available in China – this includes almost all guidebooks (including this one), with their bourgeois imperialist references to Tibetan independence.

But beware: **searches** of luggage do take place – particularly at the Nepal–Tibet border at Zhangmu – where any literature deemed unpatriotic to China, anything remotely resembling a Tibetan flag and anything containing images of the Dalai Lama (though, with all pictures of him banned, it's worth pondering how the guards looking for the pictures know what he looks like) will be confiscated.

14

the Norbulingka where the Dalai Lama was staying. On the night of March 17, the Dalai Lama and his entourage fled into **exile** in India where they have since been joined by tens of thousands of refugees.

Crushing of the rebellion

The **uprising in Lhasa** was ferociously suppressed within a couple of days, the Tibetan rebels massively outgunned by Chinese troops. Recriminations and further consolidation of Chinese power, however, were to continue: between March 1959 and September 1960 the Chinese killed an estimated 87,000 people. All pretence of goodwill vanished, and a huge military force moved in, with a Chinese bureaucracy replacing Tibetan institutions. Temples and monasteries were destroyed, and Chinese **agricultural policies** proved particularly disastrous. During the years of the Great Leap Forward (1959–60), it is estimated that ten percent of Tibetans starved – harrowing accounts tell of parents mixing their own blood with hot water and *tsampa* to feed their children.

Cultural Revolution and aftermath

In September 1965, the U-Tsang and western areas of Tibet officially became the **Xizang Autonomous Region** of the People's Republic of China, but more significant was the **Cultural Revolution** (1966–76), during which mass eradication of religious monuments and practices took place. In 1959, there were 2700 monasteries and temples in Tibet; by 1978, there were just eight. Liberalization followed Mao's death in 1976, leading to a period of relative openness and peace in the early 1980s when monasteries were rebuilt, religion revived and tourism introduced. However, by the end of the decade, martial law was again in place – thanks to Hu Jintao, later China's president – following riots in Lhasa in 1988–89. In the early 1990s, foreigners were allowed back into the region, and as the decade progressed it appeared the Chinese government was loosening their heavy-handed authoritarian approach to Tibet, and were keen to exploit Tibet's potential for international tourism.

Olympic recriminations

All this fell apart during the build-up to the 2008 Beijing Olympics: pre-Games riots and protests in Tibet, Sichuan, Gansu and Qinghai focused international attention on underlying tensions in Tibet; the Chinese government, embarrassed and angry, resealed borders and introduced all-but martial law. Since then, thousands have been arrested and any open dissent – or even discussion – has been almost entirely stifled, arguably resulting in an ongoing campaign of **self-immolation** by Tibetan monks which began in 2009.

A Chinese future

The **Tibetan Government in Exile**, meanwhile, based at Dharamsala in northern India, represents some 130,000 refugees. Its leader, the Dalai Lama – known to the Tibetans as Gyalwa Rinpoche and regarded as the earthly incarnation of the god Chenresi – has never faltered from advocating a peaceful solution for Tibet, a stance that led to his being awarded the 1989 Nobel Peace Prize. The Chinese government, however, has consistently denounced the Dalai Lama as being responsible for dissent, branding him "a devil with the face of a human but the heart of a beast". His increasing age and frailty, the certainty of his death and the challenge of finding a successor pose serious questions for both China and the Tibetan authorities in exile.

In the meantime, brave Tibetans make the month-long trek every year to India, an arduous and dangerous journey over the mountains, due to ever more sophisticated border patrols. There's perhaps a weary resignation among a new generation of Tibetans and this number has fallen significantly, from a several thousand a few years ago to some hundreds now. Pilgrims have been picked off by Chinese snipers as they crossed

TRAVELLERS' TIBETAN

Although most tour guides are now conversant in several languages, including English, most Tibetans speak only their native tongue, with a smattering of Mandarin. A few words of Tibetan from a foreigner will always be greeted enthusiastically, and the further off the beaten track you get, the more useful they'll be. **Tibetan** belongs to the small Tibeto-Burmese group of languages and has no similarity at all to Mandarin. Tibetan script was developed in the seventh century and has thirty consonants and five vowels, which are placed either beside, above or below other letters when written down. There are obvious inaccuracies when trying to render this into the Roman alphabet, and the situation is further complicated by the many dialects across the region; the Lhasa dialect is used in the vocabulary below. Word order is back-to-front relative to English, and verbs are placed at the ends of sentences – "this noodle soup is delicious" becomes "tukpa dee shimbo doo", literally "noodle soup this delicious is". The only sound you are likely to have trouble with is "**ng**" at the beginning of words – it is pronounced as in "sa**ng**".

14

USEFUL WORDS AND PHRASES

Hello	tashi delay
Goodbye, to someone staying	kalay shu
Goodbye, to someone going	kalay pay
Thank you	tuk too jay
Sorry	gonda
Please	coochee
How are you?	kusu debo yinbay? or kam sangbo dugay?
I'm…	nga…
Fine	debo yin
Cold	kya
Hungry	throko-doe
Thirsty	ka gom
Tired	galay ka
I don't understand	nga ha ko ma-song
What is your name?	kayranggi mingla karay ray?
My name is…	ngeye mingla…sa
Where are you from?	kayrang kanay ray?
I'm from…	nga…nay yin
America	Amerika
Australia	Otaleeya
Britain	Injee
Ireland	Irilenda
New Zealand	Niudzilendi
How old are you?	kayrang lo katsay ray?
I'm…	nga lo…yin
Where are you going?	kaba drogee yin?
I'm going to…	nga…la drogee yin
Where is the…?	…kaba doo?
hospital	menkang
monastery	gompa
temple/chapel	lhakhang
restaurant	sakang
convent	ani gompa
caretaker	konyer
Is there…?	…doo gay?
hot water	chu tsa-bo
a candle	yangla
I don't have…	nga…mindoo
Is this OK/can I do this?	deegee rebay?
It's (not) OK	deegee (ma)ray

(Not) Good	yaggo (min)doo
This is delicious	dee shimbo doo
Do you want…?	kayrang…gobay?
I want tea	nga cha go
I don't want this	dee me-go
What is this/that?	dee/day karray ray?
How much is this?	gong kadso ray?
When?	kadoo?
Now	danta
Today	dering
Yesterday	kezang
Tomorrow	sangnyee
Monday	sa dowa
Tuesday	sa mingma
Wednesday	sa lagba
Thursday	sa purbur
Friday	sa pasang
Saturday	sa pemba
Sunday	sa nima

NUMBERS

1	chee
2	nyee
3	soom
4	zhee
5	nga
6	droo
7	doon
8	gyay
9	goo
10	chew
11	chew chee
12	chew nyee
20	nyi shoo
21	nyi shoo chee etc
30	soom chew
40	shib chew
50	ngab chew
60	drook chew
70	doon chew
80	gyay chew
90	goop chew
100	gya
200	nyee gya
1000	dong

14

the Himalayas, though increasingly those who escape stay only for a few years before heading back home. For the Tibetans who remain, life in Tibet is harsh. Per capita annual income in rural areas is pitiful and the rate of adult literacy has been described by the UN as "horrendous". It is estimated that China subsidized the TAR between 1952 and 1998 to the tune of ¥40 billion, yet Tibetans are among the poorest people in China, with some of the lowest life expectancies. As Tibet provides the Chinese with land for their exploding population along with a wealth of natural resources, the influx of more educated and better-skilled Chinese settlers, with considerable financial resources, threatens to swamp the Tibetan population, culture and economy.

ARRIVAL AND DEPARTURE   TIBET

Since 2008, strict **travel restrictions** have been in place for Tibet, and there seems no sign of a thaw for the time being. In fact, every year it seems to get that little bit harder and more expensive for a foreign tourist to visit Tibet. **No independent travel** by foreign visitors is allowed; you must be booked on a **fixed-itinerary guided tour**, though you can tailor this yourself (remembering, of course, that some areas of Tibet are permanently off-limits). You cannot do much to change your route during the trip; new destinations cannot be added to your **itinerary**, though you don't have to visit everywhere listed on your itinerary or travel permit if you don't feel like it. (Though keep in mind that tour companies

TIBET TRAVEL PERMITS

In order to enter Tibet – in fact, even to board a plane or train to Lhasa – foreign travellers must have a **Tibet Travel Permit**. Issued by the TAR authorities, this lists a full travel itinerary and provides evidence of having booked a car, driver and guide for every day you are in the region. Available through registered travel agencies only, the permit should be included as part of your travel package by whichever agency you book with. Though the permit officially carries no cost, agencies arranging permits will charge a significant **handling fee** for the service, covering the huge amount of paperwork and "other costs" involved. You must have the original permit with you, and not a printout or photocopy, when you board your transport from the rest of China to the TAR. Your tour company will send it by courier to your hotel (or your home address) before you fly to Tibet.

Be aware that until the permit is issued you will not be able to independently book flights or trains into the region. The agency you have booked your tour through, safe in the knowledge of your full itinerary and in possession of a fair-sized deposit, is likely be willing to make reservations on your behalf, or you can wait to book travel yourself at the last minute; either way, don't expect discounted tickets. While it may be tempting to try to sidestep the regulations, all foreign travellers coming from inside China will have their permits checked at point of purchase, on departure, and on arrival; hotels will not let foreigners stay unless accompanied at check-in by an official tour guide with a valid permit, and they are required to be shown again when visiting the Potala Palace and other tourist sights. Add the regular checkpoints along roads outside Lhasa and it would take a serious, concerted effort, and a massive slice of luck, for a permitless traveller to get very far.

Once in Tibet, **further permits** are needed for specific areas. Travel along the Friendship Highway to Everest (¥180), and to Mount Kailash (¥150), requires permits that are most often secured from the Public Security Bureau in Shigatse. Getting these permits is the responsibility of your tour guide but costs, for Everest in particular, might not have been included in the overall agency fee. Anyone caught without permits or overstaying their allotted time faces fines and deportation from the region. The agency that applies for the permit on your behalf may also face stiff penalties, so your guides will also be anxious for you to stick to the leaving dates set out on the permit. Bear in mind that regulations have shifted fairly regularly in the past, so it's best to check the latest requirements with tour agencies before booking.

Journalists, photographers, writers, publishers or anyone else with a job that could be considered "undesirable" by the Chinese authorities – usually anything in the media – will be automatically denied a travel permit. If you fall into this category, get creative when asked to state your job on your visa and permit forms. Norwegian passport holders are also currently banned from travelling in Tibet. For most people though, getting a travel permit isn't as hard as is sometimes made out.

themselves are not familiar with change.) You are also not allowed to stay on after the tour ends. The situation does ebb and flow: travellers have occasionally made it through to Tibet on their own – usually in winter, when the security forces let their guard down a bit – while you're unlikely to be allowed into Tibet at all from mid-Feb to early April. The anniversary on March 30 of the Dalai Lama's flight into India, as well as other politically sensitive dates during that spring period, often make it a time of unrest. Contact one of the more established **agencies** (see box, p.880) to arrange **tours** and to get the latest on the situation. Despite this, very basic public transport information is included in some of the accounts through this chapter, in the hopes that independent travel may one day again be possible. However, all foreigners would be advised against attempting these routes without first establishing whether they are permitted to do so.

14

BY PLANE

From China Planes operate between Lhasa and Chengdu (¥1300), Beijing (¥3000) and Kunming (¥2200); not direct) – prices quoted are the lowest available one-way fares. The easiest option is to fly from Chengdu, where plenty of tour operators offer tickets, tours and permits. In the July–Sept high season, flights to and from Lhasa can be heavily booked, so it's best to reserve as far in advance as you can.

From Nepal It is possible to fly in to Lhasa from Kathmandu (¥2200), but you will need to ensure you have a Chinese visa and Tibet Travel Permit (see box opposite) before attempting the journey. Permits cannot be printed out – you must have the original with you when boarding the flight. Your tour agent will be able to meet you off the plane in Lhasa.

BY TRAIN

Qinghai–Lhasa line The largest threat to the traditional Tibetan way of life – and the biggest promise of modernization, and therefore rising living standards – comes from the Qinghai–Lhasa railway line. This extraordinary feat of engineering opened in 2006 at a cost of US$4 billion; more than 1200km of new track was laid by 11,000 migrant workers, much of it at an altitude of over 4000m and on permafrost, with more than 30km of tunnels. Passengers hoping to be protected from the effects of altitude by the much-vaunted "pressurized carriages" will be disappointed – with toilet windows left open and some passengers experiencing altitude sickness, the carriages are not all they're cracked up to be. The journey itself, however, provides fantastic vistas of the plateau, with herds of yak and fascinating glimpses of human life that exists – against the odds – in this thinly oxygenated environment.

Tickets Tickets to Lhasa go on sale ten days before departure; demand is high, particularly during the summer when sleeper tickets are incredibly hard to come by. Mysteriously, travel agencies don't seem to have the same problems and can usually supply any tickets you need, but with a mark-up of several hundred percent. Hard-seat tickets are easier to secure yourself, but with a forty-hour journey time between Beijing and Lhasa, this is not for the faint of heart (or tender of bottom). Prices quoted below are for a single in a hard-sleeper berth.

Destinations from Lhasa Beijing (40hr; ¥796); Chengdu (43hr; ¥736); Chongqing (43hr; ¥749); Golmud (14hr; ¥398); Guangzhou (55hr; ¥955); Lanzhou (24hr; ¥577); Shanghai (48hr; ¥875); Xining (22hr; ¥550).

OTHER OVERLAND

From China Aside from the train, regulations bar foreigners from independent travel overland from China into Tibet, for instance on bicycle, foot or public buses from adjoining provinces. Private tours to Lhasa from places like Chengdu, Shangri-La in Yunnan, or Kashgar in Xinjiang are theoretically possible but expensive, require considerable organizing and inevitably involve spending days on end cooped up in a jeep.

From Nepal Kathmandu to Lhasa is – or rather was – a popular route, but since the 2015 Nepal earthquake the border and Tibetan roads leading to it have been closed due to severe damage along the route. A new route, linking Tingri with Nepal via the Tibetan town of Kyirong and the Nepalese town of Rasuwagadhi is expected to open to foreign tourists in 2017. The following is based on pre-earthquake information and may change once the new border crossing opens.

You can travel up to the Nepal–Tibet border from Kathmandu by bus and cross into Tibet on foot, provided you've arranged for a tour guide to collect you on the Tibet side. To get a Chinese visa in Nepal and secure the necessary Tibet Travel Permit, you will have to be booked on an organized tour. This requirement can make independent travel from Tibet on into the rest of China complicated. Visas issued in Kathmandu are often only valid for three weeks, so if you plan on crossing from Nepal into Tibet and on to the rest of China, it's worth getting your Chinese visa elsewhere. Expect to pay around US$800–1000 for an organized seven-day overland trip to Lhasa, or around US$400–500 for a three-day trip – but make sure you are clear on exactly what is and isn't included in terms of accommodation, food and entry tickets. The best advice is to spend some time in Kathmandu to get a feel for the current situation and check out your options. Beware of your guides offering money-changing services, citing a dearth of options in Tibet. This is untrue, and once you're in Tibet you'll find plenty of places to change cash at more competitive rates.

KATHMANDU TOUR OPERATORS

Himalayan Glacier Amrit Marg, Thamel ☎977 14411387, ⓦhimalayanglacier.com.

Kamzang Journeys 543/29 Nil Saraswatithan Marg, Lazimpat ☎977 9803414745, ⓦkamzang.com.
Nature Trail Trekking Chaksibari Marg, Thamel ☎977 14701925, ⓦallnepal.com.

Social Tours Tridevi Marg, Thamel ☎977 14412508, ⓦsocialtours.com.
Trekking Team Group Chaksibari Marg, Thamel ☎977 9851075681, ⓦtrekkingteamgroup.com.

GETTING AROUND

By tour vehicle One side-effect of the current travel regulations is that getting around in-country is easy – you just get in your allotted 4WD and go wherever your guide and driver take you. The vehicles provided are generally ageing Toyota Landcruisers or similar, though larger groups sticking to the well-surfaced Friendship

ARRANGING TOURS

With independent travel in Tibet currently impossible for foreign tourists, the only option is to book a **guided tour** – including a private vehicle, driver and guide – through an agency before you arrive. Despite the huge number of travel agencies in Chengdu, Xining, Golmud and Lhasa, all claiming to offer a unique service, most operate through CITS or FIT in Lhasa, hiring drivers and tour guides who are registered with the Lhasa authorities and work as freelancers. That you are forced to book from outside the region, preventing you from meeting the tour guide or seeing the vehicle before signing up, means it pays to be cautious – try to get a recommendation from a fellow traveller if possible, and go through your itinerary with a fine-tooth comb working out exactly what is covered and what you will have to pay extra for. Getting a group of four or five together to fill a **jeep** will ensure the per-person cost is as low as it can be, though if you are on your own or in a couple, most agencies will be able to match you up with a group which has spaces that need filling.

Despite the requirement to book a tour, regulations do not stipulate that **accommodation** reservations are made in advance. As a result, not all tour agencies include accommodation in their prices – clarify whether accommodation is included and, if so, where. You may be able to bring down the price of your tour, or ensure you're not bedding down in the worst place in every town, by negotiating where you stay.

Until the earthquake in Nepal and subsequent closure of the border, the **most popular tour** was along the Friendship Highway from Lhasa, across into Nepal and up to Everest Base Camp and back. When the border reopens, most people will once again arrive or leave overland via Nepal, but at the moment there's little option but to fly in and out of Lhasa from Kathmandu. Generally these tours include two to three days in Lhasa and five on the road taking in Gyantse, Shigatse and Everest Base Camp. It costs around ¥5500 per person including accommodation. However, as you need to book a driver, guide and vehicle anyway, there is no reason why you should stick to the set tours offered – you can draw up your own itinerary and negotiate costs with the agency. Expect to pay around ¥1300 per day to hire a Land Cruiser. For driver and guide fees, you're best off haggling prices as low as you can with the agency, and tip heavily at the end of the tour to ensure the money goes where you want it to.

ESTABLISHED AGENCIES

In the event of a misunderstanding, you may wish to complain to the Tour Service Inspection Office of Lhasa's Tibet Tourism Bureau, 208 Luobulingka Lu (☎0891 6333476 or ☎0891 6334193).

Himalaya Journey ☎001 (0)2532 899166, ⓦhimalayajourney.com. Run by Jamin, an American expert on Tibet, Himalaya Journey is a very professional and helpful agency.
Khampa Caravan 17 Beimen Jie, Shangri-la Diqing, Yunnan ☎887 8288648, ⓦkhampacaravan .com As well as the standard treks and tours, educational and cultural immersion tours are also on offer.
Tibetan Expeditions 100 Beijing Dong Lu, Lhasa ☎01351 8984 224, ⓦtibetanexpeditions.com.

Australian–Tibetan-run agency with a solid reputation.
Tibet Highland Tours 1 Dangayling Lu, Lhasa ⓦtibethighlandtours.com. With an office bang in the centre of Lhasa, this is a very enthusiastic and helpful agency.
Tibet Vista Jia Cuo No. 3-070, Beijing Xi Lu, Lhasa ☎28 85552138, ⓦtibettravel.org. One of the longest established of the local agencies.
Wind Horse ⓦwindhorsetour.com. One of the better regarded agencies, with offices in the US, Europe, India, Nepal and Bhutan.

WHAT TO WEAR

Despite the plateau's altitude and the perennially snowcapped mountains, not everywhere in Tibet is constantly beset by ice and freezing temperatures. In **summer**, Lhasa and the valleys across the region reach temperatures well above 20°C. During the day, T-shirt and shorts are perfectly adequate, though a hat and serious sun cream are advisable to fend off the UV rays. (Note that long trousers are required for entry into most temples, and hats should be removed once inside.) Summer evenings and nights can be chilly, however, and a jumper is the minimum requirement. Everest Base Camp, Kailash and all other high mountain areas can fall below zero even in the summer – thermals, winter jacket, gloves and a warm hat are recommended for summer nights, and from **autumn to spring** you'll need serious cold-weather clothing.

All hotels, including the guesthouse tents at Everest, supply their own bedding, but bringing your own **sleeping bag** is not a bad idea for hygiene as well as thermal considerations. If you don't want to lug your full winter wardrobe around until you get to Tibet, don't worry; there's a good supply of cheap fake-brand anoraks, winter jackets and general hiking and camping gear available in Lhasa, although most of it is certainly not of the same quality and warmth as the real thing.

14

Highway may be given people carriers or even minibuses. Tour companies (see box opposite) used to use their own transport, but in mid-2016 the rules suddenly changed, and it became compulsory to use a government-approved vehicle and driver. The government added on a significant mark-up for using these vehicles, which added about thirty percent to the cost of tours – making an already very costly part of the world even more expensive to visit. At the time of writing, tour agencies were still hoping that the new rules would be abandoned in the near future. When travelling outside Lhasa, your vehicle will stay with you at all times, and while in Lhasa will ferry you to sites listed on your itinerary too far to walk to. For extra travel within Lhasa, you'll need to take a taxi or agree an additional fee with your driver. Tour companies submit your itinerary to the vehicle providers and pay a per-kilometre rate. This means that even a very slight detour of a few kilometres off the designated route, or a random drive around a town, can be frowned upon by drivers.

By public transport The public transport system in Tibet, such as it is, consists of large buses and smaller, nippier minibuses. In-town use of public transport by foreigners is generally tolerated, though only in Lhasa might it be actually necessary. Intercity travel by bus is not permitted, and even if you can find someone willing to sell you a ticket and a driver happy to take you, you are unlikely to make your destination without running into a checkpoint of some kind, where you will be fined and ordered to leave Tibet; worse would await your guide and tour company. Nevertheless, very basic public transport information is included through this chapter for reference.

By bike Long-distance cycling is not technically illegal, but even cyclists have to hire a guide, jeep and driver while they are on the road. Authorities (and the tour agency) will do their best to make sure you stay in hotels, even if you come equipped with camping and cold-weather gear. To be fair, having a backup team can prove helpful: though most of the traditional route from Kathmandu to Lhasa is level and the road in decent condition, dogs and weather can be a hazard, and there are five 5000m-high passes to contend with. The route is covered by a few cycle tour companies, such as the UK-based Red Spokes (☎ 0207 502 7252, ⍫ redspokes.co.uk) and Path Finder Cycling in Kathmandu (☎ 977 14700468, ⍫ tibetbiking.com), or you can negotiate with any of the Lhasa-based tour companies (see box opposite) on prices for your required chaperone.

ACCOMMODATION

Hotels The widest choice of accommodation is found in the main tourist centres of Lhasa, Shigatse, Gyantse, Tsetang and Zhangmu, where tourist-class hotels provide comfortable rooms with attached bathrooms and at least some hours of hot water. In most cases, breakfast is included in room rates in all but the cheapest hotels and guesthouses. We mention in individual reviews where breakfast is not included in the rate.

Guesthouses In most Tibetan towns, simple guesthouses offer accommodation to foreigners, pilgrims and truck drivers. You can expect a basic dormitory experience, with bedding (of variable cleanliness) provided. The communal toilets are often pit latrines and are likely to be some of the most horrendous toilets you'll ever find. Most places have bowls and washstands, though not much more in the way of washing facilities. Hot water in vacuum flasks, for drinks and washing, can be found everywhere. Accommodation gets steadily more basic the further west you go, although a few new developments have meant sleeping in a warm bed is becoming more common, even way out west.

14

Camping and homestays If you are trekking, you can camp, although many trekkers find accommodation in village houses or with nomadic yak-herders. You should not expect them to feed you, and should pay ¥50 or so per night.

EATING AND DRINKING

The traditional **Tibetan diet** – constrained by what little will grow at over 4000m – consists in large part of **butter tea**, a unique mixture of yak butter, tea and salt, all churned into a blend that many Westerners find undrinkable, but which Tibetans consume in huge quantities. Into this is stirred **tsampa** (roasted barley flour) to make dough with the consistency of raw pastry and a quite pleasant nutty flavour. Yak meat, yoghurt and cheese (often dried into bite-sized cubes to preserve it), and sometimes a soup of a few vegetables, supplement this. **Thukpa** (pronounced "tukpa") is a noodle soup with a few bits and pieces of whatever is available thrown in. If you're lucky, you'll find **momos**, tiny steamed or fried dough parcels containing meat, vegetables or cheese (a *thri momo* is a solid dough parcel without a filling). In Lhasa and most stops along the Friendship Highway, restaurants have Nepali cooking staff churning out very decent curries and *dhals*, but indifferent approximations of Tibetan and Chinese cuisine. Don't get too excited when you come across menus listing all kinds of varied dishes; quite often many items on menus aren't actually on offer. The local brew, **Lhasa Beer**, is widely available – and very drinkable.

HEALTH

Altitude sickness Almost every visitor is affected by altitude sickness, as most of Tibet is over 3000m, with plenty of passes over 5000m. For your first two or three days, rest as much as possible and drink plenty of water.

TREKKING TIBET

For the experienced hiker, Tibet offers plenty of enticing **trekking routes**. The popular Ganden–Samye trek (see box, p.899) has the advantages that start and finish points are relatively accessible from Lhasa and that it takes only four to five days. Also worth considering are treks to the cave hermitage of **Drak Yerpa** from Lhasa (allow a full day and be prepared to camp), and the five-day trek from Tingri to **Everest Base Camp** via Rongbuk although much of this is now along, or close to, a road busy with tour buses. More challenging options include: the epic sixteen-day mammoth trek to the **Kangshung** face of Everest, exploring the valleys east of the mountain (the trip to second base camp and beyond on the mountain itself should only be tackled by experienced climbers); the 24-day circumnavigation of **Namtso Lake**, including the arduous exploration of the Shang Valley to the southwest; and the great thirty-day circuit from Lhatse to **Dangra Lake** up on the Chang Tang plateau. Finally, there's the sin-erasing three day *kora* around the legendary **Mount Kailash** out in the far west.

Spring (April–June) and autumn (Sept–Nov) are the best **seasons** in which to trek, though cold-weather threats such as hypothermia and frostbite should be taken seriously even in these months. While trekking is possible at any time in the valleys, high altitudes become virtually impossible in the winter; anyone contemplating trekking at this time should be sure to check information about the terrain and likely conditions. During the wettest months (June–Sept), rivers are in flood, and crossing them can be difficult, sometimes impossible. Once you start trekking, you get off the beaten track extremely quickly, and (except for the Kailash *kora*) there is no infrastructure to support trekkers and no rescue service; you therefore need to be fit, acclimatized, self-reliant and prepared to do some research before you go. There are two essential books: *Tibet Handbook: a Pilgrimage Guide* by Victor Chan (Moon), and *Trekking in Tibet* by Gary McCue (Cordee) – the latter is especially good for shorter day-treks that anyone can do without all the gear.

One of the main problems with hiking in Tibet, and the reason it's not on a par with Nepal as a trekking destination, is that many of the more accessible treks are quite **short** – two to four days is normal – and Tibet is a long way to come for such a short time trekking. Another, bigger, issue is **cost**. As a foreign trekker, you will be under the same restrictions as any other tourist, and will thus have to pay for a fully organized tour, including paying for a jeep and driver for the entire duration of your trek, even though you won't be using either. And lastly, apart from the Kailash *kora*, there are no baggage **porters**, as you would expect to find in other parts of the Himalayas. Instead, you will have to pay for a minimum of two yaks (yaks won't walk on their own) and a yak driver, all of which further adds to the expense.

You can buy oxygen canisters in most hotel receptions (¥20), though whether they're much use is debatable. A few painkillers should help to relieve any aches and pains and headaches, but more serious problems can develop; altitude sickness can be fatal, and you should never ignore persistent symptoms (see p.46).

Giardiasis A small but significant number of travellers to Tibet suffer from giardiasis, an unpleasant and debilitating intestinal complaint. The treatment is Tinadozol or Flagyl, neither or which is reliably available in Lhasa; bring a course along with you if you're planning an ambitious or lengthy trip. They can both be purchased cheaply and easily in big cities across China.

Rabies Travellers to Tibet should seriously consider rabies immunization before they travel. The dogs can be aggressive, bites are relatively common and, if you get bitten, Kathmandu is the nearest place stocking rabies serum. Be especially careful when trekking in the vicinity of nomad tents, as the Tibetan mastiffs often used as guard dogs are definitely not friendly.

WHEN TO VISIT

Bad times to visit Chinese authorities are much pricklier around festival times (see p.873) and the week before and after certain historically significant dates, when they may stop issuing permits for foreigners. Dates to bear in mind include March 5 and 10 (the anniversaries of uprisings in 1959, 1988, 1989 and 2008), March 30 (the anniversary of the Dalai Lama's escape to India), July 6 (the Dalai Lama's birthday), September 27 and October 1 (the anniversaries of protests in 1987), and December 10 (International Human Rights Day, and the anniversary of the Dalai Lama's Nobel Peace Prize). Normally, travel permits are not issued at all in, or for travel in, the period from mid-Feb to early April. Note that Aug is especially popular with domestic tour groups, so you might want to avoid that month.

Weather The best time to visit Tibet is April–Oct, outside the coldest months. June–Sept is the wettest period, when blocked roads and swollen rivers can make travel difficult, but the countryside will be at its greenest. Health considerations should be taken seriously at any time of the year, and even in relatively balmy Lhasa, temperatures fall below freezing on a regular basis. In winter, as long as you come fully prepared for the cold (most hotels have no heating) and possible delays due to snow-covered passes, the lack of tourists and the preoccupation of the security forces with staying warm can make for a pleasant trip.

Lhasa

拉萨, lāsà

Situated in a wide, mountain-fringed valley, lies the city of **LHASA** (Ground of the Gods), 3700m above sea level on the north bank of the Kyichu River. Once known as the "Forbidden City", it attracted numerous explorers, many of whom died in vain efforts to reach it. Today, for many people, just rolling the word Lhasa off the tongue still brings to mind a city shrouded in exotica. As you follow chanting pilgrims pacing the Barkhor circuit, or when you first set eyes on the huge Potala Palace, it's easy to believe you've stumbled into some kind of Shangri-La. But glance the other way and you'll find a sprawling modern city where the wide boulevards, shopping centres and ugly concrete-and-glass high-rises reveal the architectural stamp of China at its worst.

An important settlement for well over a thousand years, it was not until the seventeenth century, with the installation of the Fifth Dalai Lama as ruler by Mongolian emperor Gushri Khan, that Lhasa became the seat of government. It continues now as the **capital** of the TAR, with a population of around 250,000. Despite the passing of sixty years, Lhasa is still palpably under **imposed rule**; the armed soldiers may have taken a lower profile, with much of the security work now falling to large numbers of police and plain-clothes officers on street corners and rooftops, but the air of occupation remains.

There are enough sights in and around Lhasa to keep visitors occupied for at least a week (even if most tours cram them into a couple of days): the **Potala Palace**, **Jokhang** and the **Barkhor** district are not to be missed, and at least one trip to an outlying monastery is a must. It's also worth taking time to see some of the smaller, less showy temples and simply to absorb the atmosphere of the Forbidden City.

14

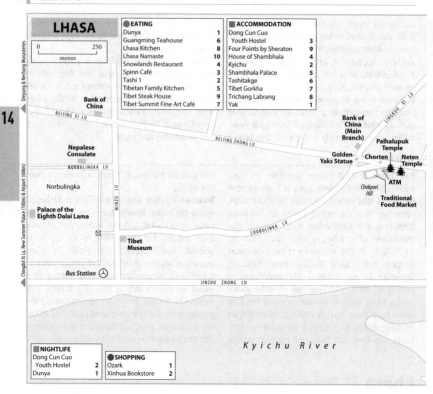

LHASA

● EATING	
Dunya	1
Guangming Teahouse	6
Lhasa Kitchen	8
Lhasa Namaste	10
Snowlands Restaurant	4
Spinn Café	3
Tashi 1	2
Tibetan Family Kitchen	5
Tibet Steak House	9
Tibet Summit Fine Art Café	7

■ ACCOMMODATION	
Dong Cun Cuo Youth Hostel	3
Four Points by Sheraton	9
House of Shambhala	4
Kyichu	2
Shambhala Palace	5
Tashitakge	6
Tibet Gorkha	7
Trichang Labrang	8
Yak	1

■ NIGHTLIFE	
Dong Cun Cuo Youth Hostel	2
Dunya	1

● SHOPPING	
Ozark	1
Xinhua Bookstore	2

The Potala Palace

布达拉宫, bùdálāgōng • Entrance on Beijing Dong Lu • Daily 8.30am–6pm, last entry 3.30pm • Courtyard: May–Oct ¥200, Nov–April ¥100 • interior: May–Oct ¥200, Nov–April ¥100 • Bus #8 from Beijing Dong Lu passes the front gate; taxi from the city centre ¥10 • Photography is prohibited inside

Perched 130m above Lhasa atop Marpo Ri (Red Mountain) – and, so it's said, named after India's Riwo Potala (Holy Mountain of the God Chenresi) – the **Potala Palace** is dazzling inside and out, an enduring landmark of the city and Tibet. As you revel in the views from the roof, gaze at the glittering array of gold and jewels and wend your way from chapel to chapel, you'll rub shoulders with excited, awestruck pilgrims from all over ethnic Tibet, making offerings at each of the altars. But be aware that, beyond the areas approved for tourists and pilgrims, the Potala is a shadow of its former self: most of the rooms are off limits; part of a UNESCO World Heritage grant was spent on a CCTV system; and the caretaker monks are not allowed to wear their robes.

Though close enough from town to reach on foot, don't tackle the Potala on your first day at altitude – it's a long climb, and even the Tibetans huff and puff on the way up; you'll enjoy it more once you've acclimatized. Morning is certainly the best time to visit, when the place bustles with pilgrims. **Photography** is banned inside, and, bizarrely, you aren't supposed to take pictures of the fabulous views from the roof. Snapping away in the palace's courtyards is tolerated, however.

Brief history

Rising thirteen storeys and consisting of over a thousand rooms, the Potala took some 8500 builders and craftsmen over fifty years to complete. The main mass of

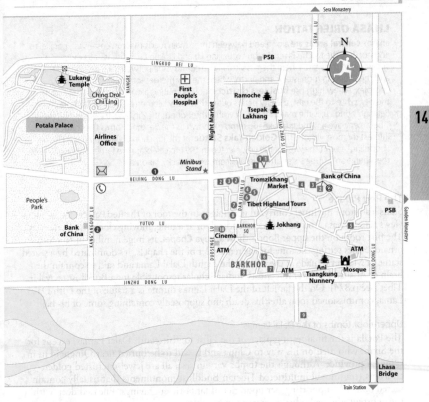

the Potala is the **White Palace** (Potrang Karpo); the building rising from its centre is the **Red Palace** (Potrang Marpo). Though founded back in the seventh century, today's White Palace (1645–48) was built during the reign of the Fifth Dalai Lama, who took up residence in 1649; the Red Palace, begun at the same time, was completed in 1693. Built for several purposes, the Potala served as administrative centre, seat of government, monastery, fortress and the home of all the Dalai Lamas from the Fifth to the Fourteenth – although from the end of the eighteenth century, when the Norbulingka was built as the Summer Palace, they stayed here only in winter.

The White Palace

The tour-group entrance is on the western side of the huge compound, and after a permit check and bag X-ray you'll find yourself standing in the grounds of the Dalai Lama's former winter home. Follow the path up to the inner courtyard of the **White Palace**, flanked by monks' rooms and stores and with the **Quarters of the Dalai Lama** at its eastern end. The opulently carved and painted **Official Reception Hall** beyond is dominated by the bulk of the high throne and hung with fabulous brocade and *thangkas* (embroidered or painted religious scrolls), with a small doorway leading into the private quarters of the Fourteenth Dalai Lama next door. There's a small audience chamber, a chapel, a hallway and finally the bedroom, with an extremely well-painted mural of Tsongkhapa, founder of the Gelugpa school to which the Dalai Lama belongs, over the bed. On the other side of the Official Reception Hall are the private quarters of the previous Dalai Lamas, but these are closed to the public.

14

The Red Palace

Stairs lead from the inner courtyard up straight to the roof of the **Red Palace**, for fabulous views across Lhasa. You can then descend a floor at a time, moving clockwise all the way. The first room on the **upper floor** is the **Maitreya Chapel**, its huge number of fabulously ornate statues setting the tone for the remainder of the chapels. It's dominated by a seated statue of Maitreya, made at the time of the Eighth Dalai Lama and said to contain the brain of Atisha, the eleventh-century Indian scholar responsible for a Buddhist revival in Tibet (see p.874). On the far left of the Dalai Lama's throne is a statue of the Fifth Dalai Lama, commissioned soon after his death and supposedly containing some of his hair.

Upper-floor tombs of the Dalai Lamas

The Potala is the final resting place of the Fifth to Thirteenth Dalai Lamas, except for the Sixth, who died on his way to China and is said to be buried near Qinghai Hu in Qinghai province. Although the **tombs** vary in size, all are jewel-encrusted golden **chortens** (traditional multitiered Tibetan Buddhist monuments that usually contain sacred objects), supporting tier upon tier of fantastic engravings. Encased deep within the chortens are the bodies, preserved in dry salt.

The tombs of the Thirteenth and the Eighth Dalai Lamas are near the Meitreya Chapel on the **upper floor**. The other chortens are on the lower floor, in the Chapel of the Dalai Lamas' Tombs (see below).

Lokeshvera Chapel and Practice Chamber of the Dharma King

Considered the oldest and holiest shrines in the Potala, the **Lokeshvara Chapel**, on the upper floor, and the **Practice Chamber of the Dharma King**, directly below on the upper middle floor, date back to Songtsen Gampo's original construction, and are the focus of all Potala pilgrims. It's easy to miss the Practice Chamber, entered from a small corridor from the balcony. King Songtsen Gampo supposedly meditated in this dark, dingy room now dominated by statues of the king and his ministers, Tonmi Sambhota and Gawa. At the base of the main pillar is a stove, apparently used by Songtsen Gampo himself.

The other floors

You have to pass through the **lower middle floor**, though the chapels here are all closed. The remainder of the open rooms are on the **lower floor**, leading off the large, many-columned Assembly Hall. The highlight down here is the grand **Chapel of the Dalai Lamas' Tombs**, containing the awesome golden chorten of the Fifth Dalai Lama, which is three storeys high and made from 3700kg of gold. To the left and right are smaller chortens with the remains of the Tenth and Twelfth Dalai Lamas, and the chortens on either side of these main ones are believed to contain relics of Buddha himself. Visitors leave by a door behind the altar in the **Chapel of the Holy Born**, from where the path winds down the west side of the hill to the western gate.

Peoples' Park

人民公园, rénmín gōngyuán • Beijing Dong Lu • Daily 5.30am–11pm • Free

Opposite the front of the Potala Palace, **People's Park** is a mini Tian'anmen Square, built in an effort to reinforce China's claim to the region; there is a Chinese flag and a monument celebrating Tibet's "liberation". Each night in summer, Chinese tourists congregate to perform traditional Tibetan circle dances to the strains of nationalistic Chinese pop songs – it's quite a sight, but not a patch on the floodlit palace opposite.

14

Palhalupuk Temple

鲁普岩寺, lǔpǔyán sì • Beijing Zhong Lu • ¥20

From just east of the public toilets at the chorten to the west of the Potala Palace, a path leads a couple of hundred metres past some busy stone-carvers to the fabulously atmospheric but under-visited **Palhalupuk Temple**, built around an ancient cave. You'll spot the less interesting ochre-and-maroon **Neten Temple** (净寺, jìng sì) on the cliff first; Palhalupuk is the smaller, white building below. Entered from an antechapel, the cave, about five square metres, was **King Songtsen Gampo**'s retreat in the seventh century and is lined with rock carvings, many of which date from that time. The most important altar is in front of the huge rock pillar that supports the roof, where the main image is of Sakyamuni, flanked by his chief disciples. At the far right-hand corner stands a jewel- and *katag*-bedecked statue of Pelden Lhamo, the fierce protective deity of Tibet, on a tiny altar. The back wall has been left untouched, and it's said that the jewels of Songtsen Gampo's Nepalese wife, Princess Bhrikuti, are hidden behind.

Ching Drol Chi Ling

宗角禄康公园, zōngjiǎo lùkāng gōngyuán • Free; boat rides ¥40–60 per 30min • Bus #8 from Beijing Dong Lu

Around the north side of the Potala Palace is **Ching Drol Chi Ling** park, which has fine views of the north facade of the Potala. The park sports a large area of trees and two boating lakes, formed by the removal of earth during the construction of the palace.

Lukang Temple

禄康寺, lùkāng sì • Daily 8am–5pm • ¥10

On an island in the westernmost of the park's two lakes is the small, pleasant **Lukang Temple** (Dragon King Temple), built by the Sixth Dalai Lama. Legend tells that the king of the **nagas**, subterranean creatures who resemble dragons, allowed earth to be excavated for the Potala's construction only as long as this chapel was built in their honour. The temple is famed for the very old and detailed **murals** on the middle and top floors, but you'll need a torch if you want to study them in detail – the protective wire in front doesn't help. The top-floor pictures are somewhat esoteric; they show the

---

POTALA TICKETS

Potala tickets have to be bought one or two days in advance. Foreign tourists must be accompanied by a **guide**, but as a visit will certainly be part of any tour to Tibet, your travel agency will normally supply tickets as part of the package. A major downside of this is that registered tour groups are – ludicrously, given the scale of the complex – limited to just **one hour** inside. Some visitors have reported being able to buy their own time-unlimited tickets the day before, but with only 2300 tickets issued per day – and 1600 of these reserved for tour groups – you'll need to get to the ticket office early and be prepared for disappointment.

Note that if you are buying your own tickets, although you pay ¥200 (¥100 Nov–April) at the ticket office at the base of the Potala, this is actually just for the courtyards, not for entry to the building itself (though nobody will inform you of this). You will then be required to pay the same fee again halfway up the steps into the complex, making the total fee quite a sting.

stages of human life, the journey of the soul after death, and various legends. The middle-floor murals, depicting the construction of the great monasteries of Sera and Drepung among others, are far more comprehensible.

Jokhang

大昭寺, dàzhāo sì • Barkhor Square • Daily 8.30am–6.30pm • ¥85 • Bus #7 from the southwest of town or #8 from the Potala Palace will drop you at Beijing Dong Lu, which is a few hundred metres north of the entrance at Barkhor Square • Photography is prohibited inside the chapels

The **Jokhang** – sometimes called Tshuglakhang (Cathedral), and the holiest temple in the Tibetan Buddhist world – can be unprepossessing from afar, but get closer and you'll be swept up by the anticipation of the pilgrims and the almost palpable air of veneration. Built in the seventh century (see box below), it stands 1km east of the Potala Palace, in the centre of the only remaining Tibetan enclave in the city, the Barkhor area (see p.890), a maze of cobbled alleyways between Beijing Dong Lu and Jinzhu Dong Lu.

Inside, you're in for one of the most unforgettable experiences in Tibet. Devout **pilgrims** turn left to move clockwise and enter each chapel in turn to pray and make offerings, though they don't hang around; stand still to admire anything and you'll be trampled in the rush. As with all temples in Tibet, it's often difficult to know exactly what you are looking at. Some of the statues are original, others were damaged during the Cultural Revolution and have been restored either slightly or extensively, and others are replicas; in any event, all are held in deep reverence by the pilgrims. The best time to visit is in the morning, when most pilgrims do the rounds.

Barkhor Square

八角街广场, bājiǎojiē guǎngchǎng

The **main entrance** to the Jokhang is from **Barkhor Square**, which is to the west of the temple. Two bulbous incense burners in front of the temple send out juniper smoke as an offering to the gods, and the two walled enclosures here contain three ancient engraved pillars. The tallest is inscribed with the Tibetan–Chinese agreement of 821 AD and reads: "Tibet and China shall abide by the frontiers of which they are now in occupation. All to the east is the country of Great China; and all to the west is, without question, the country of Great Tibet. Henceforth on neither side shall there be waging of war or seizing of territory".

JOKHANG: SUPPRESSING DEMONS

King Songtsen Gampo built the Jokhang in the seventh century to house the **dowry** brought by his Nepalese bride, Princess Bhrikuti, including the statue known as the Akshobhya Buddha. This later changed places with the Jowo Sakyamuni statue from Princess Wencheng's dowry, which was initially installed in Ramoche Temple (see p.891), and which is now regarded as Tibet's most sacred object. The **site** of the temple was decided by Princess Wencheng after consulting astrological charts, and confirmed by the king following a vision while meditating. However, construction was fraught with problems. Another vision revealed to the king and his queens that beneath the land of Tibet lay a huge, sleeping **demoness** with her head in the east, feet to the west and heart beneath Lhasa. Only by building monasteries at suitable points to pin her to the earth could construction of the Jokhang succeed. The king embarked on a scheme to construct twelve **demon-suppressing temples**: four around Lhasa, which included Trandruk (see p.903), to pin her at hips and shoulders; a set of four farther away, to pin her elbows and knees; and four even more distant, to pin her hands and feet. When these were finished, construction of the Jokhang began.

NAMTSO LAKE (P.906) >

14

The lower chapels

In front of the huge temple doors, a constant crowd of pilgrims prostrate themselves – you can hear the clack of the wooden protectors on their hands and the hiss as the wood moves along the flagstones when they lie flat on the ground. Head round the southern side to the visitors' entrance to enter the main courtyard, where ceremonies and their preparations take place. Rows of tiny butter lamps burn on shelves along the far wall; it's a bustling scene as monks make butter statues and dough offerings and tend the lamps. Through a corridor in the north wall, with the small **lower chapels** to left and right – many of whose wooden door frames and columns are original, carved by Nepalese craftsmen – you pass into the inner area of the temple. The central section, **Kyilkhor Thil**, houses statues galore, six of them considered particularly important. The most dramatic are the 6m-high Padmasambhava on the left, which dates from 1955, and the half-seated figure of Maitreya, the Buddha of the Future, to the right.

Chapel of Jowo Sakyamuni

It's easy to feel overwhelmed, but if you manage only one chapel it should be the **Chapel of Jowo Sakyamuni** in the middle of the eastern, back wall of the temple. The 1.5m-high Sakyamuni (Buddha) is depicted at twelve years of age, with a sublimely beautiful golden face; draped in heavy brocade and jewels, this is the most deeply venerated statue in Tibet. Although the Jokhang was originally built to house the statue, it first stood in the temple of Ramoche until rumours of a Tang invasion late in the seventh century led to its removal to a hiding place in the Jokhang. During the reign of Trisong Detsen, the Bön opponents of Buddhism buried the statue, but it was found and sent out of Lhasa for safety; it was again buried during King Langdarma's attempt to annihilate Buddhism, but eventually returned to the Jokhang. Although there is a rumour that the original was destroyed in the eighteenth century by Mongol invaders, most Tibetans regard this as the original. Monks here keep the butter lamps topped up while the pilgrims move around the altar, bowing their heads to Jowo Sakyamuni's right leg and then his left.

The upper floor and roof

By the time you reach the **upper floor**, you'll probably be punch-drunk; fortunately perhaps, there is less to detain you up here, although most of the chapels are now open after restoration. Of most interest is the **Chapel of Songtsen Gampo**, directly above the main entrance in the west wall and featuring a large statue of the king flanked by his two queens. Continue up the stairs in the southwest corner of the chapel to one fierce and one peaceful image of **Pelden Lhamo**, who is regarded as the protective deity of Tibet and is particularly popular with pilgrims.

From the temple **roof**, the views over Barkhor Square, into the temple courtyard and as far as the Potala Palace in the distance are wonderful, and the golden statues even more impressive.

The Barkhor

八角街, bājiǎojiē

Traditionally, pilgrims to Lhasa circled the city on two clockwise *kora* (pilgrimage) routes: an outer circuit called the Lingkhor, now vanished under two-lane highways and rebuilding, and the shorter **Barkhor circuit** through the alleyways a short distance from the Jokhang walls. This maze of picturesque streets, a world away from the rest of Lhasa, is now largely a market selling all manner of goods – saddles and stirrups, Chinese army gear, *thangkas*, jewellery, blankets, DVDs, carpets, tin trunks and pictures of lamas, and many other trinkets.

Yet the atmosphere here is the real attraction. Spend an evening swirling clockwise around the *kora* circuit and you'll quickly find yourself falling for Tibet. The hundreds of pilgrims walking or prostrating beside you are an incredible sight: statuesque Khampa men with their traditional knives and red-braided hair, decorated with huge chunks of turquoise; Amdo women dripping jewels with their hair in 108 plaits; and old ladies spinning their tiny prayer wheels and intoning mantras. The Barkhor *kora* is most impressive in the early hours of the morning, before the sun has risen, and in the early evening when a feeling of devotion is prevalent, and the constant mumble of prayer and shuffle of prostrations emanate from the shadows.

Tromzikhang market

冲赛康市场, zhōngsàikāngshìchǎng • To the north of the Jokhang; take the main alleyway into the Barkhor that leads off Beijing Dong Lu just east of Ramoche Lu, and it's just down on your left • Daily roughly 7am–dusk

The whole Barkhor area is worth exploring – with its huge wooden doors set in long, white walls and leading into hidden courtyards – but try not to miss **Tromzikhang market**. The two-storey modern building is a bit soulless, but nowhere else in the world can you see (or smell) so much yak butter in one place.

Sela Daguo Xiang

色拉达果巷, sèlā dáguǒ xiàng

Rubbing up against the Jokhang's back wall, though easily missed in the throng, are a further **three temples** hidden along **Sela Daguo Xiang**, a narrow and fantastically preserved alleyway. The first temple, closest to the Barkhor, houses a single giant prayer wheel – you'll hear the ringing of its bell before you see it – eagerly turned by a devoted scrum.

Ani Tsangkung Nunnery

仓姑寺, cānggū sì • Daily 7am–6pm • ¥40

It's well worth seeking out the **Ani Tsangkung Nunnery** to the southeast of the Jokhang; you'll probably need to ask the way. With over a hundred nuns in residence, several of whom speak good English, there is a lively but devout atmosphere, especially around prayer time at 11am. A fabulous statue of the god Chenresi in a glass case dominates the main chapel. From the back of the chapel, facing the main door, head right, round the outside, to visit the long, narrow room containing King Songtsen Gampo's meditation chamber in a pit at the end. Supposedly his meditation altered the course of the Kyichu River when it looked likely to flood the construction of the Jokhang.

If for nothing else, it's worth a visit here to sit and relax among the flowers.

Ramoche

小昭寺, xiǎozhāo sì • Xiao Zhaosi Lu, between Beijing Dong Lu and Linkuo Bei Lu • Daily 7.30am–8pm • ¥20

The three-storey, robust **Ramoche temple** is small but intriguing, and second only in importance to the Jokhang. A short walk north of the Barkhor, it was built in the seventh century by Songtsen Gampo's Chinese wife, Princess Wencheng, to house the Jowo Sakyamuni statue that she brought to Tibet. The statue later ended up in the Jokhang and was replaced by the Akshobhya Buddha, a representation of Sakyamuni at the age of eight, a version of which sits here today. This much-revered statue was broken in two during the Cultural Revolution, with one part taken to China and the other later discovered on a factory scrapheap in Tibet. The statue in position today in the main shrine, at the rear of the temple, is probably a copy.

Tsepak Lhakhang

Daily 9am–4.30pm • Free

To the south of Ramoche, call in on the tiny **Tsepak Lakhang**. The entrance is just beside a huge incense burner, and, once inside, you pass along an alley lined with a row of prayer wheels. There are two small chapels in this hugely popular temple, and the friendly monks in residence chant their daily prayers around noon. You can walk the brief circuit around the temple walls, where the murals have been newly painted.

Norbulingka

罗布林卡, luóbùlínkǎ • Minzu Lu • Daily 9am–6.30pm • ¥60 • Bus #7 from Beijing Dong Lu; taxi from the city ¥10

Situated in the west of town, the **Norbulingka** (Jewel Park), the Summer Palace of the Dalai Lama, is not in the top league of Lhasa sights, but is worth a look during the festivals of the Worship of the Buddha (雪顿节, xuēdōng jié) in July or during Shotun, the Yoghurt Festival (雪顿节, xuēdùn jié) in August/September, when crowds flock here for picnics and to see masked dances and traditional opera. The park was used as a recreation area by the Dalai Lamas since the time of the Seventh incarnation.

Palace of the Eighth Dalai Lama

The first palace to be built on the Norbulingka site was the Palace of the Seventh Dalai Lama, constructed in the mid-eighteenth century. However, his successor's work, the **Palace of the Eighth Dalai Lama**, was the most famed for its splendour and became the official summer residence to which all Dalai Lamas moved, with due ceremony, on the eighteenth day of the third lunar month.

New Summer Palace

The **New Summer Palace** was built in 1956 by the Fourteenth Dalai Lama; it was from here that he fled to India in 1959. Visitors pass through the audience chamber, via an anteroom, to the meditation chamber, on to his bedroom and then into the reception hall dominated by a fabulously carved golden throne, before passing through to the quarters of the Dalai Lama's mother. Western plumbing and a radio sit beside fabulous *thangkas* and religious murals. It's profoundly moving; the forlorn rooms bring home the reality of exile.

Tibet Museum

西藏博物馆, xīzàng bówùguǎn • Tues–Sun 10am–5pm • Free • Bus #7 from Beijing Dong Lu; taxi from the city ¥10

Opposite the Norbulingka, the **Tibet Museum** offers curiosities to anyone who's had enough of religious iconography; there are some fascinating *thangkas* illustrating theories from Tibetan medicine, as well as stuffed Tibetan wildlife, Neolithic tools and the like. Its primary purpose, however, is propaganda emphasizing China's claim to the region, so take the captions with a pinch of salt.

ARRIVAL AND DEPARTURE LHASA

By plane Gongkhar airport (贡嘎机场, gònggā jīchǎng) is 60km southwest of the city. Airport buses (¥30) run to the airline office on Niangre Lu in about an hour and a half, though foreigners coming on tours should be met by guides with transport – a direct car or taxi will take around an hour.

Destinations Beijing (1 daily; 4hr 30min); Chengdu (8–10 daily; 2hr); Chongqing (4 daily; 2hr); Kathmandu (2 daily; 1hr 15min).

By train Lhasa train station (拉萨火车站, lāsà huǒchē zhàn) is an enormous building about 3km south of the centre. Every travel agency will drop you off at the station, but should you need one then bus #15 runs to and from the city for ¥2; a taxi costs ¥10 from the station to Lhasa, but ¥20 in the opposite direction. Tickets out of Lhasa are generally easy to secure, and can be bought at the Tibet Tourism Office on Luobulingka Lu, at the station itself, or from any of the travel agencies or hotels. In 2015, a new Lhasa–Shigatse rail line came into service, which foreign tourists can also use. All quoted prices below are for a hard sleeper.

Destinations Beijing (1 daily; 40hr; ¥796); Chengdu (every 2 days; 43hr; ¥736); Chongqing (every 2 days; 43hr; ¥749); Golmud (1 daily; 14hr; ¥398); Guangzhou (1 daily; 55hr; ¥955); Lanzhou (1 daily; 24hr; ¥577); Shanghai (1 daily; 48hr; ¥875); Shigatse (1 daily; 3hr).

By bus The main bus station (拉萨气车站, lāsà qìchēzhàn) is west of the centre at the junction of Jinzhu Zhong Lu and Minzu Lu. A taxi from the centre costs ¥10. However, note that all travel by foreigners on public transport outside of Lhasa is currently forbidden.

GETTING AROUND

As the main sights are all walkable from the old town and tour operators provide airport and rail station pick-up, as well as transport to outlying monasteries as part of tour itineraries, there is generally no need to take public or other transport within Lhasa. Possible exceptions include trips to the Norbulingka and Tibet Museum, which are a little out of the centre.

By bus Numbered buses run fixed routes around the city and its environs. From the old town, the most useful buses are #15 and #8 which run to the train station and Potala Palace respectively (daily 7am–10pm; ¥2).

By taxi Cabs have a ¥10 basic rate that should cover most destinations in town, but finding an empty taxi is something of a challenge – you can't book one in advance, and there are no dedicated taxi ranks.

By cycle-rickshaw You'll have to haggle to use these, and invariably you'll be charged more than the same journey in a taxi, for a slower, less comfortable ride.

INFORMATION

Maps English maps can be purchased at hotels and news stands for around ¥10. For an alternative view of the city, the *On This Spot Lhasa Map*, published by the International Campaign for Tibet and including the notorious Drapchi

Prison, security facilities and army bases, can be found outside China — needless to say, carrying it inside Tibet is risky.

ACCOMMODATION

Whether you require **budget** or **luxury accommodation**, the old town area around the Barkhor is the place to stay. **Mid-range hotels** are springing up west of the centre, and with the sustained cranking up of investment in China, Western brands have started to re-enter the market (*Holiday Inn* withdrew in 1997 under pressure from rights groups), but, however comfortable, they simply cannot compete with the charm of the labyrinthine old town.

Dong Cun Cuo Youth Hostel 正昌东措国际青年旅馆, zhèngchāng dōngcuò guójì qīngnián lǚguǎn. 10 Beijing Dong Lu ☎0891 6273388, ⓦyhachina.com. Hugely popular with Chinese students, this well-located, spacious establishment has graffiti-covered walls and eight-bed dorms. En-suite private rooms are also available, and the whole place is efficiently run. The courtyard behind is home to a clutch of popular bars, a restaurant and a couple of craft shops. Dorms ¥50, doubles ¥160

Four Points by Sheraton 福朋喜来登酒店, fúpéng xǐláidēng jiǔdiàn. 10 Bolinka Lu ☎0891 6348888, ⓦstarwoodhotels.com. One of the first Western-backed hotels to re-enter the Tibetan market, this is a reliable and fairly typical business-class hotel, but don't expect service to be quite up there with international standards just yet. ¥500

★House of Shambhala 香巴拉宫, xiāngmǎlā gōng. Jiri Erxiang ☎0891 6326533, ⓦshambhalaserai .com. Gorgeous traditional Tibetan-style boutique hotel decorated with multiple colours and patterns, and with alcoves filled with Buddhas and prayer flags. There's a lovely carved wooden bar and cosy restaurant, and the manager is friendly. Right in the heart of the Barkhor district, it's just a couple of minutes' walk from the Jokhang. ¥680

★Kyichu 拉萨吉曲饭店, lāsà jíqū fàndiàn. 149 Beijing Dong Lu ☎0891 6331541, ⓦlhasakyichuhotel .com. Centrally located, good value, with friendly Tibetan and Nepalese staff, this is the pick of the mid-range choices. *Kyichu* has practical, large and simply decorated rooms in

two buildings around a pleasant, grassy courtyard restaurant. The mattresses on the beds are soft – a rare thing indeed in Tibet. ¥480

Shambhala Palace 香巴拉宫, xiāngbālā gōng. 7 Jiri Erxiang ☎0891 6307779, ⓦshambhalaserai.com. Under the same management as the *House of Shambala*, this place has a near-identical style of traditional Tibetan decor laced in Buddhist iconography. However, the atmosphere here isn't as warm and convivial as at its sister hotel, and it lacks a restaurant. It is a bit cheaper though. ¥580

Tashitakge 八宝宾馆, bābǎo bīnguǎn. 7 Lupu, Lane 1 ☎0891 6342191, ⓦwww.babao-hotel.com. You can't fault the price of this smart and welcoming hotel in the heart of the old quarter. Penny, the English-speaking manageress, goes out of her way to ensure that guests are happy, and the small but spotless rooms are pleasingly decorated with local artwork. At the time of writing, there was talk of the hotel having a major renovation, so things might be different by the time you get there. ¥320

Tibet Gorkha 廓尔喀酒店, kuòěrkā fàndiàn. 47 Linkuo Nanlu ☎0891 6391333. The entrance might be dowdy, but inside this standout choice you'll find a peaceful courtyard garden and traditional painted bedheads. You can even choose between a shower and a relaxing soak in a bathtub. Great value. ¥280

Trichang Labrang 赤江拉让藏式宾馆, chìjiāng lāràng bīnguǎn. 11 Lugu Wu Xiang ☎0891 6309555. A lovingly restored townhouse of whitewashed walls and flapping prayer flags set around a shady courtyard garden.

Sadly, the rooms themselves are a little plain and disappointing compared to similar-priced places nearby, but it's still pleasant enough. Excluding breakfast. **¥428**
Yak 亚宾馆, yà bīnguǎn. 100 Beijing Dong Lu ☎0891 6323496, ⓦchinayak.com. Rooms at this very central place, with a slightly old-fashioned feel, are a bit hit-and-miss, but good ones include a bathtub and heavy wooden furniture. Avoid the noisy road-facing rooms. Very popular with international tour groups. **¥650**

EATING

Besides the vast number of **restaurants** in Lhasa, there are **noodle places** near Tromzikhang market, and **bakeries** outside the mosque in Barkhor selling *naan* breads. For trekking food, try one of the **supermarkets** at the west end of Linkuo Bei Lu – thanks to Lhasa's large military presence, army rations of tinned beef and high-calorie energy bars crop up on many shelves. There's also a **traditional food market** – complete with live produce, fruit, vegetables, tins and an impressive array of spices – just west of the chorten by the Potala Palace. For a more upmarket picnic, *Dunya* turns out excellent lunchboxes.

Dunya 东尼亚餐厅, dōngníyà cāntīng. 100 Beijing Dong Lu ☎0891 6333374, ⓦwww.dunyarestaurant.com. Dutch-run and very civilized, but not particularly Tibetan. A diverse range of specials, good Western, Indian and Nepali food, and even half-decent Australian wine. Expect to pay around ¥60 a head for a main meal. A choice of breakfasts is also available for ¥40, while the bar upstairs has a good selection of drinks and a terrace looking out towards the old town. Daily 8am–10pm.

★**Guangming Teahouse** 光明港琼甜茶馆, guāngmínggǎng qióngtián cháguǎn. Dongjielin Lu. A classic spit-and-sawdust teahouse close to the Barkhor entrance, always packed with Lhasans quaffing tea and playing cards. It can be tricky finding a seat, but as long as you're not precious about personal space, they'll cram you in somewhere. Tea ¥0.8 and noodle soup ¥5. Daily 7.30am–7.30pm.

Lhasa Kitchen 拉萨厨房, lāsà chúfáng. Danjielin Lu ☎0891 6848855. Friendly English-speaking staff, but service can be temper-stretchingly slow when busy. The food is good though, particularly the Nepali options, and there is a decent range of Tibetan cuisine, such as soup with *shaphali* (meat-and-vegetable patties) followed by *deysee* (rice, raisins and yoghurt). Mains around ¥15–30. Daily 8am–10pm.

Lhasa Namaste 纳姆斯蒂餐厅, lāsà nāmǔsīdì cāntīng. Yutok Lu 30 ☎0891 6324669. Catch a film at the cinema next door and then come here for the standard mix of Tibetan, Nepalese and Western staples. It's on the first floor of a down-at-heel shopping centre. Mains around ¥25–50. Daily 11am–9.30pm.

Snowlands Restaurant 雪域餐厅, xuěyù cāntīng. Danjielin Lu ☎0891 6337323. This classic old travellers' hangout has moved a few doors down from its old home, and become more flashpacker than backpacker in the process – though it still feels like it could have been lifted straight from Kathmandu. Great curries, Tibetan dishes and, dare we say it, the best apple pie in Tibet. Mains ¥20–30. Daily 11.30am–10.30pm.

Spinn Café 风转, fēngzhuǎn. Qingu Xiang, Beijing Donglu ☎0891 6361163, ⓦcafespinn.com. Run by two cycling-mad expats – Kong from Hong Kong and Oat from Thailand – this is a relaxed spot for a decent cup of coffee (¥20), though there is virtually nothing available in the way of food. The owners are a fount of knowledge, and their website is regularly updated with the latest travel situation. Daily 10am–10pm.

Tashi 1 扎西1号餐厅, zhāxīyīhào cāntīng. Cnr Beijing Dong Lu & Danjielin Lu. A mainstay for budget travellers in Lhasa, *Tashi 1* serves up mains from their limited Tibetan menu starting at ¥15. Their special is the *bobbi* – a kind of Tibetan tortilla – which comes with a delicious garlic and yoghurt sauce. Daily 11.30am–10pm.

Tibetan Family Kitchen 更潘藏藏厨房, gèng pān zàngjiā chúfáng. Danjielin Lu ☎138 8901 5053. Climb the dark stairwell, pass through the low doorway and straight into the kitchen of this family home where you'll be welcomed with open arms to what is, hands down, the best eating experience in Tibet. The husband-and-wife team will pause from their slicing of onions, frying of meat and kneading of *momos* to lead you into the dining area, where all the guests sit down together in an unbeatably amicable atmosphere. The food is filled with creativity, spice and all things nice; if you want to know how they make it, join one of their on-demand cookery classes (¥20–30). The restaurant is tricky to find: opposite the extraordinarily tacky *Shampala Hotel* is a small, dark alleyway, between shopfronts; walk down here to a dingy courtyard – steps up to the restaurant are on the right. Mains ¥20–30. Daily 12.30–9pm.

Tibet Steak House 西藏牛排餐厅, xīzàng niúpái cāntīng. Yutok Lu ☎0891 6343777. This large, well-managed place has fast service and is more popular with locals than tourists. The namesake steaks are carefully prepared and cooked, and they also do a range of Tibetan and Nepalese dishes. The spicy *shaptak*, a mix of fried yak meat, onion, chilli and pepper, eaten with a huge sheet of naan bread, is especially good. Mains ¥25–50. Daily 12pm–10pm.

Tibet Summit Fine Art Café 顶蜂美艺术咖啡店,

dǐngfēngměi yìshù kāfēidiàn. 1 Danjielin Lu ⊕0891 6913884, ⓦthetibetsummitcafe.com. American-owned venture serving teas, coffees and cakes in a typical glossy coffee-shop chain style. Admire the works of local artists that adorn the walls as you sip a frothy cappuccino. Expect to pay ¥40 for a drink and a bite to eat. Daily 8.30am–9pm.

DRINKING, NIGHTLIFE AND ENTERTAINMENT

While Lhasa is world-renowned for its wealth of religious cultural heritage sights, it is not well known for the quality of its **nightlife**. And rightly so. Likely due to a combination of the effects of altitude, the lack of disposable income among Tibetans and the strict security, after-dark entertainment is limited. Sadly, there's not much chance to see traditional Tibetan music, dance or opera, unless you're here during a festival, though occasional shows are put on for tourists; ask in your hotel or at a travel agency. It can also make for a pleasant post-prandial stroll to head up towards People's Park where you'll find fountains, ad-hoc group dancing, plenty of Chinese tourists with selfie sticks and stunning floodlit views of the Potala Palace.

14

Dong Cun Cuo Youth Hostel 正昌东措国际青年旅馆, zhèngchāng dōngcuò guójì qīngnián lǚguǎn. 10 Beijing Dong Lu. Yes, it's a youth hostel, but behind is a courtyard boasting three bars, live music and, in summer, a large scrum of Chinese students up for fun. Beers from ¥15. Daily 5.30–10pm.

Dunya 100 Beijing Dong Lu ⊕0891 6333374, ⓦwww .dunyarestaurant.com. Upstairs from the restaurant (see opposite), this Dutch-run bar is a favourite for Westerners in search of a familiar tipple and pub ambience. A good selection of drinks, friendly owner, an excellent terrace for people-watching over sundowners, and beers from ¥20. Daily 5.30–10pm.

SHOPPING

BOOKS

Tibet is pretty much the worst place in the world you could possibly go to find books about Tibet; much that would be considered essential reading in the West is well entrenched on China's banned list. However, coffee-table books featuring sumptuous photos of the sites around Lhasa and beyond are plentiful and much easier to find here than back home.

Xinhua Bookstore 新华书店, xīnhuá shūdiàn. Cnr Yutuo Lu & Kang'angduo Lu. Probably the best bookshop in Lhasa, the Xinhua has a few titles in English. Daily 10am–8pm.

SOUVENIRS

There are endless souvenir-buying opportunities in Lhasa. The main area is the Barkhor and the street market stretching west from there along Yutuo Lu; prices here are generally higher than elsewhere, and during peak tourist season (July–Sept), market traders hawk their wares until well after 10pm. Generally traders aren't too aggressive with their sales technique. A string of gift shops on Danjielin Lu sells jewellery, handmade paper and the like. The search for postcards can be frustrating, and sets on offer at the main sights are generally pricey; those at the post office and the Xinhua Bookstore are the best value.

TAILOURED CLOTHES

There are plenty of tailors in town, both Chinese and Tibetan, who can make traditional Tibetan or Western clothes; look on Beijing Dong Lu west of the *Yak Hotel*. A huge range of materials is available, from light, summer-weight stuff, to heavier, warmer textiles. Prices depend on the material, but light jackets start at around ¥100, while skirts, trousers or a floor-length Tibetan woman's dress (*chuba*) cost ¥80 and up. Many places have samples made up and you can simply shop around until you find the style and material you want. From first measuring to collecting the finished item usually takes 24hr.

THANGKAS

Tibetan *thangkas* (religious scrolls) would appear to be obvious souvenirs, but many are of poor quality – best to spend some time browsing before you buy. The better-quality, higher-priced ones have a hand-painted central image, with finely drawn and highly detailed backgrounds. Asking prices are high (from ¥3000 for a good piece) – bargain hard.

TREKKING GEAR

Ozark 奥կ奥卡户外运动品店, àosuōkǎ hùwàiyùndòngpǐndiàn. Beijing Lu. Plenty of places sell shoes, boots, fleeces and jackets of dubious lineage near the junction of Dongjielin Lu and Beijing Dong Lu, but for hiking gear you need to actually rely on, try Ozark. Here you'll find genuine coats, rucksacks, footwear and sleeping bags – though don't come here for knock-off prices, as they are very similar to, or even higher than, those at home. Daily 9am–6pm.

DIRECTORY

Banks and exchange Lhasa's main Bank of China (Mon–Fri 9am–1pm & 3.30–6pm) is on Linkuo Bei Lu, north of the Golden Yaks Statue, and there's a branch on Beijing Dong Lu in the Barkhor (Mon–Fri 9.30am–6pm, Sat & Sun 11am–3pm). Around the old town you'll find ATM kiosks which take foreign bank cards.

Hospital First People's Hospital, 18 Linkuo Bei Lu (emergencies only ⊕0891 6371571 or ⊕0891 6371265).

It's better to go in the morning when more staff are available, and you'll need to take a Chinese translator.

Pharmacies Most are along Yutuo Lu around the junction with Dosengge Lu.

Post office The main post office is on Beijing Dong Lu, just east of the Potala Palace (daily 9am–8pm).

Visas The Nepalese Consulate, 13 Norbulingka Lu (Mon–Fri 10am–noon; ☎0891 6815744), has a next-day visa service, for which you'll need to submit one passport photograph. At the time of writing, the land border to Nepal was closed; as tourist visas for most nationalities are available on arrival at Kathmandu airport, there is currently little reason to visit this consulate.

14

Around Lhasa

Just outside Lhasa, the major monasteries of **Sera**, **Drepung**, **Nechung** and **Ganden** are easily accessible from the city as half-day or day-trips. Indeed, Sera and Drepung have virtually been gobbled up in the urban sprawl that now characterizes Lhasa, while a trip to Ganden or to **Samye** – the latter slightly further out to the southeast – is a good chance to get out into the countryside. Morning visits to any of them are likely to be in the company of parties of devout pilgrims who'll scurry around the temples making their offerings before heading on to the next target. Follow on behind them and you'll visit all the main buildings; don't worry too much if you aren't sure what you are looking at – most of the pilgrims haven't a clue either. The monasteries – Ganden and Samye in particular – are generally peaceful and atmospheric places where nobody minds you ambling at will.

Sera Monastery

色拉寺, sèlā sì • Mon–Sat 9am–5pm; debates 3.30pm • ¥50 • Taxi from Lhasa ¥10–15 • Photography is prohibited in the chapels; only phone cameras allowed in the debating courtyard

Sera Monastery, 4km north of central Lhasa, will be included on most tour itineraries and is easily the most touristy and therefore perhaps the least rewarding of the big Lhasa area monasteries. Established in 1419 by Sakya Yeshe, one of the main disciples of Tsongkhapa, founder of the Gelugpa order, Sera is situated below a hermitage where the great man spent many years in retreat. Spared during the Cultural Revolution, the buildings are in good state, although there is always a fair amount of ongoing building work. Pilgrims proceed on a clockwise circuit, as usual, visiting the three main **colleges** – Sera Me, Sera Ngag-Pa and Sera Je – and the main assembly hall, Tsokchen. All are constructed with chapels leading off a central hall and more chapels on an upper floor. They're great places to linger and watch the pilgrims rushing about their devotions. Photography is not allowed in the chapels.

Tsokchen

If you just want to catch the flavour of Sera's most dramatic buildings, head straight up the hill from the main entrance. After a couple of hundred metres, you'll reach the **Tsokchen**, Sera's largest building, built in 1710. The hall is supported by over a hundred columns, and it's here, between statues of the Fifth and Thirteenth Dalai Lamas, that you'll find the main **statue of Sakya Yeshe**, the founder of the monastery. The statue is a reproduction of the original one in Sera Ngag-Pa college. When there were plans to move the original to the Tsokchen, the story goes that the statue itself said that it wished to stay in the college, so a copy was made.

Debating courtyard

At the top of the path uphill from the entrance, the walled and shady **debating courtyard** is worth a visit at 3.30pm, when the monks assemble in small animated groups to practise their highly stylized debating skills, involving much posturing, clapping and stamping. They're used to visitors – indeed, masses of Chinese tourists

LIFE IN THE GREAT MONASTERIES

Sixty years ago, there were still six great, functioning **Gelugpa monasteries**: Sera, Drepung and Ganden near Lhasa, plus Tashilunpo in Shigatse (see p.911), Labrang (see p.804) and Kumbum (see p.813). They each operated on a similar system to cope with the huge numbers of monks who were drawn to these major institutions from all over Tibet. In their heyday, Sera and Ganden had five thousand residents each and Drepung had between eight and ten thousand – possibly the largest monastery the world has ever known.

Each monastery was divided into colleges, **dratsang**, which differed from each other in the type of studies undertaken. Each college was under the management of an abbot (*khenpo*), and a monk responsible for discipline (*ge-kor*). Attached to every college were a number of houses or *khangsten*, where the monks lived during their time at the monastery. Usually, these houses catered for students from different geographical regions. Each college had its own assembly hall and chapels, but there was also a main assembly hall where the entire community could gather.

Not every member of the community spent their time in scholarly pursuits. Communities the size of these took huge amounts of organization, and the largest monasteries also maintained large estates worked by serfs. About half the monks might be engaged in academic study while the other half worked at administration, the supervision of the estate work and the day-to-day running of what was essentially a small town.

The most obvious feature of these **monasteries today** is their emptiness; hundreds of monks now rattle around in massive compounds built for thousands. Such has been the fate of religious establishments under the Chinese and the flow of lamas into exile that there are now questions about the quality of the Buddhist education available at the monasteries inside Tibet. Monks and nuns need to be vetted and receive Chinese-government approval before they can join a monastery or convent, and although there are persistent rumours of tourists being informed on by monks, it's also apparent that both monks and nuns have been, and continue to be, at the forefront of open political opposition to the Chinese inside Tibet.

14

turn up for it, and it's hard not to feel as if the whole circus is put on for them. Only mobile phones can be used to take photos.

Sera Je college

To the left of the debating courtyard, is the impressive **Sera Je college**. Its spacious assembly hall is hung with fine *thangkas*, but the focus for pilgrims here is the **Hayagriva Chapel** (Hayagriva or Tamdrin, "the Horse-Headed One", is the protective deity of Sera), reached via an entrance in the left-hand wall.

Choding Khang

If you're feeling energetic, take the path up the hillside, from behind the Tsokchen (follow the telegraph wires) to **Choding Khang** (Tsongkhapa's Hermitage), which is a reconstruction of the founder of the Gelugpa school's original home; his meditation cave is a bit farther up. There are splendid views over Lhasa from here.

Drepung Monastery

哲蚌寺, zhébàng sì • Daily 9am–5.30pm • ¥60, including Nechung Monastery • Taxi from Lhasa ¥30–35

Just 8km west of Lhasa, **Drepung Monastery** was founded in 1416 by Jamyang Choje, a leading disciple of Tsongkhapa. Once the largest monastery in the world, it was an immediate success; a year after opening there were already two thousand monks in residence, and ten thousand by the time of the Fifth Dalai Lama (1617–82). Although it has been sacked three times – in 1618 by the king of Tsang, in 1635 by the Mongols, and in the early eighteenth century by the Dzungars – there was relatively little damage during the Cultural Revolution.

Drepung is a huge place, and it's easy to attempt to see everything and get overloaded. Make sure you go up onto the **roofs** – the views across the Kyichu Valley are splendid –

> ## STATE ORACLE AT NECHUNG
>
> Nechung was, until 1959, the seat of the **state oracle of Tibet**. By means of complex ritual and chanting, a monk entered a trance and the oracle would speak through him. The Nechung oracle was the mouthpiece of the main spiritual protector of Tibet, **Dorje Drakden**, an aspect of the guardian spirit Pehar Gyalpo. No important decisions were made by the Dalai Lama or his government without reference to Drakden. The original shrine on the site was built in the twelfth century, and the Fifth Dalai Lama built the temple later. The state oracle fled Tibet in the footsteps of the Dalai Lama in 1959, having questioned Dorje Drakden himself as to what he should do.

and you should make sure you spend a bit of time just wandering the alleyways, through courtyards, and past ancient doorways.

Ganden Palace

The easiest way to find your way around is to follow the clockwise pilgrim circuit. This leads left from the entrance up to the grand and imposing **Ganden Palace**, built in 1530 by the Second Dalai Lama, and home to the Dalai Lamas until the Fifth incarnation moved to the Potala Palace. The private quarters of the Dalai Lama are behind the balcony at the top right-hand side of the building, but there's little to see inside.

Tsokchen

The **Tsokchen**, the main assembly hall, is entered via a small door on the left-hand side, facing the building. Its roof supported by over 180 solid wooden columns, the hall is the highlight of Drepung, a space of awesome size and scale. The *thangkas* and brocade hangings add to the ambience, with dust motes highlighted by the rays of the sun slanting down from the high windows. At the rear is the **Buddha of the Three Ages Chapel**, the most impressive in Drepung, with statues crammed together in such profusion the mind reels. The central figures are Sakyamuni with his two main disciples, Shariputra and Maudgalyayana. The main steps of the Tsokchen, looking across the huge courtyard in front of the building, are a good place to sit and admire the view and watch the comings and goings of the other visitors.

The upper storeys

There are two upper storeys, both definitely worth a visit. On the next floor up, the **Maitreya Chapel** contains the head and shoulders of a massive statue of Maitreya at a young age, commissioned by Tsongkhapa himself, while the **Tara Chapel** contains a version of the Kanjur, sacred Buddhist scriptures, dating from the time of the Fifth Dalai Lama. In the middle of the volumes, which are loose leaves stored between wooden planks and wrapped in brocade, sits a statue of the incarnation of Prajnaparamita, the Mother of Buddhas; the amulet on her lap is said to contain a tooth of Tsongkhapa's. Of the three chapels on the top floor, the highlight is the stunning statue of the head of Maitreya, boasting exquisite gold ornamentation.

Outlying buildings

Behind the Tsokchen, there's a tiny **Manjusri Temple**, obligatory for the pilgrims who make offerings to the image of the Bodhisattva of Wisdom, carved out of a large rock. The remainder of the circuit is taken up with the **Ngag-Pa College**, to the northwest of the Tsokchen, and **Loseling**, **Gomang** and **Deyang colleges** to the southeast. They all have items of interest – the stuffed goat at the entrance to the Protector Chapel on the upper storey of Loseling, the cosy Deyang, and the wonderful array of statues in the central chapel of Gomang – but don't feel too bad if you've had enough by now.

Nechung Monastery

乃琼寺, nǎiqióng sì • Daily 9am–6pm; chapels closed noon–3pm • Included in Drepung Monastery ticket

Easily combined with a trip to Drepung is the eerie **Nechung Monastery**, once the seat of the state oracle (see box opposite), less than 1km southeast via a recently renovated, smooth walking trail. Try to visit on the 8th, 15th or 30th days of the Tibetan lunar month, when the faithful seek special favour.

The lower halls

Nechung has a reputation as a dark and forbidding place. As soon as you arrive at the entrance gates to the **lower halls**, you are confronted by a panoply of gore – the doors are decorated with images of flayed human skins and the murals in the courtyard depict torture by devils and people drowning in a sea of blood. In the chapels, unusually subdued supplicants are more likely to offer booze than apples. Bloodshot eyes sunk into the sockets of grinning skulls seem to follow you around.

Upstairs

Upstairs, the main room is the audience chamber, where the Dalai Lama would come to consult the oracle. The inner chapel is dedicated to Tsongkhapa, whose statue is between those of his two main disciples, Gyeltsab Je and Khedrup Je. In the only chapel at roof level is the statue of Padmasambhava that, though it dates from the early 1980s, is gloriously bedecked in old Chinese brocade.

Ganden Monastery

甘丹寺, gāndān sì • Daily 9am–4pm • ¥50 • Chartered jeeps only (around 2hr); foreigners are barred from public transport out here

Further than the other main temples, **Ganden Monastery** is 45km east of Lhasa – the final 6km of the journey is along a spectacular switchbacking road off the Lhasa–Sichuan Highway. Located high up on the Gokpori Ridge with excellent views over the surrounding countryside, this is the most dramatically situated of the Lhasa area monasteries and the one that best retains a sensation of the Tibet of old.

Founded by Tsongkhapa himself in 1410 on a site associated with King Songtsen Gampo and his queens, the main hall was not completed until 1417, two years before Tsongkhapa died after announcing his disciple, Gyeltsab Je, as the new **Ganden Tripa**, the leader of the Gelugpa order. The appointment is not based on reincarnation but on particular academic qualifications.

The Chinese have always particularly targeted Ganden, possibly because it is the main seat of the Dalai Lama's order, and what you see today is, sadly, all reconstruction.

THE GANDEN–SAMYE TREK

Though touted as the most popular trek in Tibet, you'd be unlucky to meet any other groups of trekkers while walking the four- or five-day **Ganden–Samye trek**. The route crosses the mountains that divide the **Kyichu Valley** from that of the **Tsangpo**, and takes you over two mountain passes more than 5000m high, across alpine pastures grazed by nomads' yaks (watch out for the vicious guard dogs), past glacial lakes, down a steep gorge, through pretty rhododendron forests, and finishes in the dry, almost desert-like countryside around Samye.

In the past, people started trekking from right outside **Ganden Monastery** and finished at Samye. Today, following increased road construction, most trekkers begin from the pretty village of **Hebu**, where yaks can be hired (¥120/day each) to carry gear, and finish at **Yamalung Monastery**. Count on three nights / four days, which will allow time to see Ganden Monastery before you begin walking. You must be fully self-sufficient – take camping and cooking gear and all the food you might need (including enough for your guides and yak handlers) – and be prepared for cold conditions and possible snow, even in summer.

14

Serdung Lhakhang

While it is possible to follow the pilgrims through the various buildings on their circuit, the highlight here is really the imposing **Serdung Lhakhang**, on the left side as you follow the main path north from the car park. This temple contains a huge gold and silver chorten. The original contained the body of Tsongkhapa, who was said to have changed into a 16-year-old youth when he died. The body was embalmed and placed in the chorten and, when the Red Guards broke it open during the Cultural Revolution, they supposedly found the body perfectly preserved, with the hair and fingernails still growing. Only a few pieces of skull survived the destruction; these are in the reconstructed chorten.

Sertrikhang

Up the hill and to the right, the **Sertrikhang** houses the golden throne of Tsongkhapa and all later Ganden Tripas; behind the throne you'll see images of the Tsongkhapa flanked by two of his most senior students. The bag on the throne contains the yellow hat of the present Dalai Lama.

Ganden kora

Perhaps the best reason for visiting Ganden is to walk the short and sweet **Ganden kora**, the pilgrimage path around the monastery. The views are astonishing, and it takes about an hour to follow the circuitous route. Along the way are various auspicious points, some of which are signed. These include miraculously appearing sacred images and narrow gaps in the rock where you can test your karma by squeezing through the gap.

ACCOMMODATION	GANDEN MONASTERY

Monastery Guesthouse 桑耶寺宾馆, sāng yē sì bīnguǎn. This simple guesthouse at the monastery is used mostly by people starting the Ganden–Samye trek (see box, p.899). It has large, clean rooms, though the toilets are a hundred metres or so away and used by half the residents of Ganden. ¥200

Samye

桑木耶寺, sāngmùyē sì

A visit to **SAMYE**, on the north bank of the Tsangpo River around 50km southeast of Lhasa, is a highlight of Tibet. A unique monastery and walled village rolled into one, it's situated in wonderful scenery and, however you arrive, the journey is splendid. You can climb the sacred **Hepo Ri** to the east of the complex for excellent views (1hr); it was here that Padmasambhava is said to have subdued the local spirits and won them over to Buddhism.

Brief history

Tibet's first monastery, Samye was founded in the eighth century during King Trisong Detsen's reign, with the help of the Indian masters **Padmasambhava** and **Shantarakshita**, whom he had invited to Tibet to help spread the Buddhist faith. The first Tibetan Buddhist monks were ordained here and are referred to as the "Seven Examined Men". Over the years, Samye has been associated with several of the schools of Tibetan Buddhism – Padmasambhava's involvement in the founding of the monastery makes it important in the Nyingma school, and later it was taken over by the Sakya and Gelugpa traditions. Nowadays, followers of all traditions worship here, and Samye is a popular destination for Tibetan pilgrims, some of whom travel for weeks to reach it.

14

Utse

Daily 8am–6pm • ¥40 • Photography prohibited inside

A grand, six-storey construction, **the Utse** – the main temple – normally needs a couple of hours to be seen thoroughly, but at the time of writing, much of it was closed for renovations. It's worth taking a torch, as there are some good murals tucked away in shadowy corners.

The first floor

The main assembly hall dominates **the first floor**, with fine, old mandalas on the high ceiling. On either side of the entrance to the adjoining main chapel are statues of historical figures associated with the monastery. Those on the left include Shantarakshita, Padmasambhava (said to be a good likeness of him), Trisong Detsen and Songtsen Gampo. The impressive main chapel, **Jowo Khang**, is reached through three tall doorways and is home to a Sakyamuni statue showing the Buddha aged 38. To the left of the assembly hall, a small temple, **Chenresi Lhakhang**, houses a gorgeous statue of Chenresi with an eye meticulously painted on the palm of each of his thousand hands – if you look at nothing else in Samye, search this out. To the right is the **Gonkhang**, a protector chapel, with all the statues heavily and dramatically draped. Most of the deities here were established as the demons of the Bön religion and were adopted by Buddhism as the fierce protectors – the chapel is an eerie place, imbued with centuries' worth of fear.

The upper storeys

Although the first floor is the most striking, **the upper storeys** are also worth a look, though these were closed for renovations at the time of writing. The **second floor** is an open roof area, where monks and local people carry out the craftwork needed for the temple. The highlight of the **third floor** is the **Quarters of the Dalai Lama**, consisting of a small anteroom, a throne room and a bedroom. A securely barred, glass-fronted case in the bedroom is stuffed full of fantastic relics, including Padmasambhava's hair and walking stick; a Tara statue that is reputed to speak; and the skull of the Indian master Shantarakshita. The Tibetan pilgrims take this room very seriously, and the crush of bodies may mean you can't linger as long as you would like. From the **fourth floor** up, you'll see only recent reconstruction, but the views from the balconies are extensive.

The surrounding buildings

Large buildings roughly 8am–6pm; buildings of lesser importance might close earlier • Free

The **surrounding buildings** in the complex are in varying stages of renovation. Unashamedly modern, the four coloured **chortens** are each slightly different, and visitors love or hate them. Inside, you can climb stairways and explore chapels, but generally the chortens are more dramatic from a distance. It's difficult to locate the outer temples accurately, and many are still awaiting renovation – some serve as barns and stables, others show the effects of the Cultural Revolution. The most finely worked murals in Samye are in **Mani Lhakhang**, now a chapel in a house compound in the northwest of the complex, where the occupants are happy for visitors to look around.

14

As with all destinations outside Lhasa's city limits, Samye can only be accessed by foreign tourists when accompanied by a guide in a chartered vehicle; the excursion must be listed on your official tour itinerary. Tibetans and Chinese tourists can take one of the regular buses from Lhasa.

ACCOMMODATION

Friendship Snowland Restaurant-Hotel 友谊雪域餐厅, yǒuyì xuěyù cāntīng. East gate of the Utse ☎013 659584773. Very simple guesthouse with a handful of small rooms above a popular restaurant. There are no (functioning) showers, and there is a not-quite-clean toilet. **¥180**

Samye Monastery Hotel 桑耶寺宾馆, sāngyēsì bīnguǎn. Northeast of the Utse ☎0891 7836666. This large, tour-group-friendly place has little in the way of local character, but it does have hot showers and the most comfortable rooms in town, with mattresses that aren't rock hard. **¥240**

EATING

Friendship Snowland Restaurant 友谊雪域餐厅, yǒuyì xuěyù cāntīng. East gate of the Utse ☎013 618932819. Serving a basic range of Chinese and Tibetan dishes, as well as Western pancakes, this place has good food and a tonne of Tibetan character. Mains ¥15. Daily 8am–8pm.

Samye Monastery Hotel 桑耶寺宾馆, sāngyēsì bīnguǎn. Northeast of the Utse ☎0891 7836666. The restaurant of the *Samye Monastery Hotel* has a menu offering an extensive range of mainly Chinese dishes such as bamboo and yak-meat stir-fries. Unusually most items listed on the menu are, for once, actually available rather than a figment of menu imagination. Mains ¥25. Daily 7am–10pm.

Southeast from Lhasa

The region around **Tsetang**, southeast of Lhasa and just south of the Tsangpo River, is steeped in ancient history. Legend has it that the first Tibetans originated on the slopes of Gongpo Ri to the east of Tsetang, and that the **Yarlung Valley** (where the country's earliest Buddhist scriptures magically appeared) was where the first king of Tibet descended from the heavens on a sky-cord, to father the original royal dynasty – many members of which are buried in the nearby **Chongye Valley**.

Tsetang and around

泽当, zédāng

There is little to recommend an extended stay in the thoroughly modern and unattractive town of **TSETANG**. However, the town, located 60km southeast of Lhasa as the crow flies (double this by road), is largely unavoidable as a base for explorations of **Lhoka** province, which stretches from the Tsangpo down to the Bhutan border. South from Tsetang's main traffic intersection along Naidong Lu, take a left and head east along Bare Jie into the **Tibetan area** of town, a typical jumble of walled compounds swarming with dogs and children.

Ganden Chukorlin

甘丹确廓林, gāndān què kuò lín • Daily 10am–6pm • ¥45

The first – and largest – monastery you'll encounter in Tsetang's Tibetan area is **Ganden Chukorlin**, now bright and gleaming from restoration, after being used as a storeroom for many years. It was founded in the mid-eighteenth century on the site of an earlier monastery, and there are good views of the Tibetan quarter from the roof.

Narchu Monastery and Sanarsensky Nunnery

楚寺, nàchǔsì / 萨纳斯克尼姑寺, sànàsīkè nígūsì

The fourteenth-century **Narchu Monastery** is worth stopping by for the three unusual, brown-painted Sakyamuni statues on the altar. A little farther up the hill, the

Sanarsensky Nunnery was one of the first of its kind in Tibet. It was founded in the fourteenth century in the Sakya tradition, later becoming a Gelugpa establishment. Both sites are in the old town.

Lhamo Lhatso

拉姆拉措湖, lāmǔlācuò hú • 115km northeast of Tsetang • 2hr drive

Tsetang is the base for a trip to **Lhamo Lhatso**, a small sacred lake where it's reputed that visions appearing on the surface of the water contain prophecies. Regents searching for the next incarnations of high lamas come here for clues, and Dalai Lamas have traditionally visited for hints about the future.

From the nearest town, **Gyatsa**, it's a five-hour walk up to the lake, so you'll have to negotiate with your guide whether to camp or make the long return journey in a single day. You can also continue driving beyond Gyatsa along a twisting and bumpy mountain trail to a point just short of the mountain pass that overlooks the lake; from here, it's an hour-and-a-half walk down to the lake.

14

ARRIVAL AND DEPARTURE

TSETANG

By jeep Currently the only way for foreign visitors to reach Tsetang is by chartered jeep (2.5hr from Lhasa), and you'll need to have the excursion listed on your trip itinerary.

By bus Tsetang's bus station is about 500m west of the main traffic intersection in town.

By minibus Direct minibuses leave Lhasa's main bus station for Tsetang from 8am onwards (frequent; 3hr).

ACCOMMODATION AND EATING

While there are some decent accommodation options in Tsetang, none of them is particularly cheap or good value, though for a small town the standard is surprisingly high.

Bus Station Hotel 客运宾馆, kèyùn bīnguǎn. Gesang Lu ☎ 138 89036880. Offering great value for Tsetang, this smart and friendly place, right next to the bus station, has spacious rooms with desks, TVs and overly hard beds. Get one on the upper floors to try and cut down on bus station noise. The sign is in Chinese only. Breakfast not included. **¥280**

Tibet Yulong Holiday Hotel 裕奢假日大酒店, yùlóng jiàrì dàjiǔdiàn. 16 Naidong Lu ☎ 0893 7832888. The *Yulong* makes a memorable impression, with its glitzy lobby and rooms dripping in over-the-top

decorations. It's still a fairly reasonable place to stay, if you can deal with the tackiness. **¥680**

Tsetang Hotel 泽当饭店, zédāng fàndiàn. 21 Naidong Lu ☎ 0893 7825555. The most upmarket place in town has all the trimmings you'd expect of a top-end hotel in Tibet: grand lobbies and entrances, a surfeit of gold paint, and comfortable, rather stately bedrooms that come with their own oxygen tank – naturally. There's an excellent in-house Chinese restaurant too (daily 7am–10pm; mains ¥40). **¥880**

Yarlung Valley

雅鲁鲁流域, yǎlǔlǔ liúyù

Though the 100km-long **Yarlung Valley**, just 40km south of Lhasa, is renowned as the seat of the first Tibetan kings, these days it is the dramatically sited and picturesque **Yumbulakhang**, the first Tibetan palace, which draws visitors to the area.

Trandruk Monastery

昌珠寺, chāngzhū sì • Daily dawn till dusk • ¥70

The small but significant **Trandruk Monastery**, 7km south of Tsetang, is a grand and imposing structure. One of the earliest Buddhist temples in Tibet, Trandruk was built in the seventh century during the reign of King Songtsen Gampo. It is one of the twelve **demon-suppressing temples** (see box, p.888) – Trandruk anchors the demoness's left shoulder to the earth. Legend tells how the site chosen for Trandruk was covered by a large lake containing a five-headed dragon. King Songtsen Gampo emerged from a period of meditation with such power that he was able to summon a supernatural falcon to defeat

14

the dragon and drink up all the water of the lake, leaving the earth ready for Trandruk (meaning Falcon-Dragon).

Pearl Thangka

Damaged during the Bön reaction against Buddhism in the ninth century, and again by Dzungar invaders in the eighteenth century, Tandruk then suffered the loss of many highly prized religious relics and objects following the Chinese invasion. Its remaining glory is the **Pearl Thangka**, an image of King Songtsen Gampo's wife, Princess Wencheng, as the White Tara, created from thousands of tiny pearls meticulously sewn onto a pink background. This is in the central chapel upstairs, which also houses an original statue of Padmasambhava at the age of eight.

Yumbulakhang

雍布拉康, yōngbùlākāng • Daily 7am–7pm • ¥30, only payable if you enter the chapel

From afar, the fortress temple of **Yumbulakhang**, 12km south of Tsetang, appears dwarfed by the scale of the Yarlung Valley. But once you get close and make the twenty-minute climb up the spur on which it is perched, the drama of the position and the airiness of the site are apparent. Widely regarded as the work of the first king of Tibet, Nyatri Tsenpo, the original Yumbulakhang would have been over two thousand years old – the oldest building in Tibet – when it was almost totally destroyed during the Cultural Revolution. The present building is a 1982 reconstruction in two parts, with a small, two-storey chapel and an 11m-high tower.

The chapel

The lower floor of the **chapel** is dedicated to the early Tibetan kings: Nyatri Tsenpo is to the left and Songtsen Gampo to the right of the central Buddha statue. The delightful and unusual upper-storey chapel, with Chenresi as the central image, is built on a balcony. Some of the modern murals up here show legendary events in Tibetan history; look out on the left for King Nyatri Tsenpo and for the Buddhist scriptures descending from heaven.

The tower

The energetic can ascend by ladders almost to the top of the **tower** where King Nyatri Tsenpo supposedly meditated. The deep, slit windows at knee level mean the views aren't that wonderful, however. For the best scenery, take a walk up to the ridge behind the temple to where countless prayer flags tinge the hill in all the colours of the rainbow.

Chongye Valley

崇业谷, chóng yè gǔ

From Tsetang, it's 27km south through the attractive **Chongye Valley** to the village of **CHONGYE** (阱结, jīngjié), a sleepy little place but expanding with plenty of new buildings; you can also get here via side roads from the Yarlung Valley. There are a couple of restaurants and a basic guesthouse in the village, which you'll need to ask to find. Just outside the village is the **Tangboche Monastery**, but the target for most visitors is the **Tombs of the Kings**, around 1km further south from the monastery. The entire valley is an agricultural development area, and the patchwork of fields is interspersed with irrigation work.

Tangboche Monastery

汤普齐寺, tāngpǔjí sì • Daily dawn till dusk • Free

On the east side of the valley, about 20km southeast of Tsetang, **Tangboche Monastery** sits at the base of the hill and is somewhat difficult to spot among the village houses.

Founded in the eleventh century, it was said to have hosted the great Tsongkhapa, originator of the Gelugpa tradition, three centuries later. Take a torch so you can really appreciate the most interesting features – genuinely old murals, commissioned in 1915 by the Thirteenth Dalai Lama. Look out in particular for Pelden Lhamo on the left as you enter, and, on the right-hand wall, Padmasambhava, Trisong Detsen and Shantarakshita. The artistry and detail of subject and background make an interesting comparison with some of the more modern painting you'll see in Tibet.

Atisha's hermitage

A couple of hundred metres up the hill from the monastery is the **hermitage** where the scholar **Atisha** spent some time in the eleventh century. It's small, recently renovated and, not surprisingly, dominated by rather lurid images of the Indian master.

Tombs of the Kings

藏王墓群, zàngwáng mùqún • 1km south of Chongye • Daily 8am–6pm • ¥30

The **Tombs of the Kings** are scattered over a vast area on and around the slopes of Mura Ri. Some are huge, up to 200m in length and 30m high. The body of each king was buried along with statues, precious objects and, some sources suggest, live servants. Some of the greatest kings of the Yarlung dynasty were interred here, although there is disagreement over the precise number of tombs – some sources claim it's 21, but far fewer are visible, and there is uncertainty about which tomb belongs to which king.

Songtsen Gampo's tomb

藏王墓, zàngwáng mù • Chapel ¥30

For the best view of the entire area, climb the largest tomb, **Bangso Marpo** (Red Tomb), which belongs to **Songtsen Gampo**. Just beside the road that heads south along the valley, it's easily identifiable by the chapel on the top. Songtsen Gampo, supposedly embalmed and incarcerated in a silver coffin, was entombed with huge numbers of precious gems, gifts from neighbouring countries (India sent a golden suit of armour), his own jewelled robes and objects of religious significance, all of which were looted long ago. The cosy **chapel**, originally built in the twelfth century, has central statues of Songtsen Gampo, his wives and principal ministers, Gar and Thonmi Sambhota. However, if you're templed out, give the chapel a miss.

Other tombs

Looking east from Songtsen Gampo's tomb, the large tomb straight ahead belongs to his grandson, **Mangsong Mangtsen** (646–76), who became king at the age of four. The tomb some distance to the left is that of **Tri Ralpachan** (805–36); the nearby enclosure contains an ancient pillar that records the events of his reign and is constructed on top of a stone turtle, symbolizing the foundation of the universe. Originally, every tomb had one of these pillars on top, but the others have long since disappeared.

Chingwa Tagtse Dzong

其哇达孜宗, qíwādázì zōng

The ruins of **Chingwa Tagtse Dzong**, perched high on the mountainside to the west of the tombs, give an idea of the scale of the fortress and capital of the early Yarlung kings before Songtsen Gampo moved to Lhasa. To the left, the monastery of **Riwo Dechen** is visible, and a rough road means you can drive virtually right up to this thriving Gelugpa community of around eighty monks. Originally founded in the fifteenth century, it was later expanded by the Seventh Dalai Lama and restored in the mid-1980s. There are three main chapels, the central one dominated by a large Tsongkhapa figure. A number of other chapels and monasteries on this hillside were being completely rebuilt at the time of writing.

Tsurphu and Namtso

One of the most rewarding and popular trips in Tibet is to **Namtso Lake**, around 230km northwest of Lhasa, taking in **Tsurphu Monastery** on the way. This can be done on a three-day/two-night jaunt from Lhasa by jeep. You can just see the lake in a rushed two-day/one-night trip, but the area rewards those who linger for longer.

14

Tsurphu Monastery

楚布寺, chǔbù sì • Daily 9am–1pm • ¥60

Some 70km or so northeast of Lhasa, **Tsurphu Monastery**, at an altitude of 4480m, is the seat of the **Karmapa Lama**, though it's a seat that's pretty cold these days as the present incumbent, **Urgyen Trinley Dorge**, fled to India in 1999. The questionable standing of the current Panchen Lama (see box, p.913) makes Urgyen the second-holiest Tibetan after the Dalai Lama. Urgyen seems charismatic and able and is regarded by many in exile as a natural successor for the role of leader when the Dalai Lama dies. The festival of **Saga Dawa**, on the fifteenth day of the fourth lunar month, usually in May or June, is especially fine at Tsurphu, as the massive *thangka* is displayed at this time.

Zhiwa Tratsang

直吾达昌, zhíwǔdáchāng

The solid **Zhiwa Tratsang** has a splendidly ornate gold roof and houses the main assembly hall, dominated by statues of Sakyamuni and a chorten containing the relics of the Sixteenth Karmapa Lama, who played a major part in establishing the order overseas and died in Chicago in 1981. The murals here depict the successive Karmapa lamas.

The kora circuit

A visit to the monastery can be exhausting, as it's at a considerably higher altitude than Lhasa. The clockwise path, the **kora**, climbs steeply up the hill behind the monastery from the left of the temple complex and circles around high above and behind the monastery before descending on the right. The views are lovely, and the truly fit can even clamber to the top of the ridge, but you need to allow two to three hours for the walk.

ACCOMMODATION

Monastery guesthouse 楚布寺宾馆, chǔbùsì bīnguǎn. There's little reason to stay at Tsurphu unless you're trekking in the area. There is a basic monastery guesthouse here that offers few amenities beyond a place to lie down – bring your own sleeping bag, food and candles/lamp. Dorms <u>¥50</u>, doubles <u>¥250</u>

Namtso

纳木错, nàmùcuò • ¥85

Set at 4700m and frozen over from November to May, **Namtso** (Sky Lake) is 70km long and 30km wide, the second-largest saltwater lake in China (Qinghai Lake is the largest; see p.816). The scenery comes straight from a dream image of Tibet, with snowcapped

---

BLACK HAT LAMAISM

Founded in the twelfth century by Dusun Khenyapa, the **Karmapa order** is a branch of the Kagyupa tradition, where members are known as the **Black Hats** after the Second Karmapa was presented with one by Kublai Khan. Most powerful during the fifteenth century, when they were close to the ruling families of the time, they were eventually eclipsed in 1642 when the Fifth Dalai Lama and the **"Yellow Hat" Gelugpa order**, aided by the Mongol army, gained the ascendancy. The Karmapa were the first order to institute the system of reincarnated lamas, *tulkus*, a tradition later adopted by the Gelugpa school.

mountains towering behind the turquoise-tinged lake, and yaks grazing on the bleak surrounding plains. Most people only stay one night here in a hurried trip from Lhasa. If possible, devote another day to the lake and spend some time walking around it or hiking across the open grasslands that stretch between the water and mountains.

At the lake

The final approach to **the lake** is spectacular. From the grimy and depressing truck stop town of Damxhung, it takes around two hours to pass through the Nyanchen Tanglha mountain range at Lhachen La (5150m) and descend to **Namtso Qu**, the district centre, with just a couple of houses at the eastern end of the lake. The lake is very popular with Chinese package tours, often on long day-trips from Lhasa. Groups arrive around 11am in a flurry of selfie-sticks, before hopping back on the buses.

14

Tashi Dor Monastery

扎西多寺, zhāxīduō sì

The target of most visitors is **Tashi Dor Monastery**, 42km from Lhachen La, tucked away behind two massive red rocks, on a promontory jutting into the lake. This small Nyingma monastery is built around a cave; around it, a ramshackle, wind-blown, rubbish-strewn seasonal tourist village has emerged, somewhat haphazardly. Follow the *kora* around the end of the peninsula to visit the monastery as well as several smaller cave shrines along the route; allow a couple of hours.

An almost compulsory activity for every visitor to Namtso is to **climb the hill** towering above Tahsi Dor for beautiful sunrise and sunset views. Those few with enough energy can try the neighbouring, much higher peak, which offers better views. For true devotees, a circuit of the lake can be attempted, though this takes at least eighteen days and involves camping on the way.

ARRIVAL AND INFORMATION NAMTSO

By minibus Minibuses from Lhasa to Namtso depart just east of the *Yak Hotel* around 7am each morning (4hr).

Banks Damxhung, around a 2hr drive away, has the closest ATMs to the lake.

ACCOMMODATION

Yang's Hostel 羊宾馆, yáng bīnguǎn. Near the chapels at Tashi Dor Monastery. All the accommodation in Namtso is overpriced and very basic; this place, also known as *Namtso Sheep Hotel*, is no exception, but is still the best option. The cheaper rooms are cold, depressing prefabs, not dissimilar to those used by Chinese migrant workers on building sites. The more expensive rooms are essentially the same, just a little cosier and more colourful. There's an overpriced restaurant with a big, warming stove around which everyone huddles at night to eat noodles and other basics (mains ¥40). **¥240**

To Everest and the Nepal border

Roads run southwest of Lhasa to **Mount Everest and the Nepal border**, past some of the region's most historically significant **monasteries**: Gyantse, site of a shameful episode in Britain's colonial past; Shigatse, spiritual seat of the Panchen Lamas; and spectacular Sakya, home to one of the foremost orders of Tibetan Buddhism. Then comes Everest itself, though – given the surprising urbanity of the base camp "village" here – the mountain's rugged splendour is perhaps best appreciated from afar.

Yamdrok Tso

羊卓雍错, yángzhuó yōngcuò

From Chusul Bridge, on the western outskirts of Lhasa, the southern road climbs steeply up to the Kampa La pass (4794m); at the top, a car park offers stunning views

14

of the turquoise waters of the sacred **Yamdrok Tso**, the third-largest lake in Tibet. It's a good place to take a picture, and there are plenty of Tibetans armed with baby goats, yaks and Tibetan mastiffs – dogs traditionally used by nomads to fend off wolves – who will be only too happy to pose with you, for a small fee of ¥10–20. It is said that if Yamdrok Tso ever dries up, Tibet itself will no longer support life – a tale of heightened importance now that the lake, which has no significant in-flowing rivers to keep it topped up, is powering a controversial hydroelectric scheme and the lake waters are reportedly dropping. From the pass, the road descends to Yamtso village before skirting the northern and western shores amid wild scenery dotted with a few tiny hamlets, yaks and small boats on the water.

The western shore

On the western side of the lake, 57km beyond the Kampa La pass, the dusty village of **Nakartse** (浪卡子, yángzhuóyōngcuò hú; 4500m) is the birthplace of the mother of the Great Fifth Dalai Lama. There is basic accommodation in the village, but few tours overnight here, preferring to push on to Gyantse or Shigatse.

The lake circuit trek

Yamdrok Tso has many picturesque islands and inlets visible from the road, and there's a seven-day **circular trek** from Nakartse exploring the major promontory into the lake. The climb up from Nakartse to the glacier-topped **Karo La pass** (5045m) is long and dramatic, with towering peaks on either side as the road heads south and then west toward apparently impenetrable rock faces. From the pass, the road descends gradually, via the mineral mines at Chewang, and the stunning reservoir at the **Simila Pass** (4717m) to the broad, fertile and densely farmed **Nyang Chu Valley** leading to Gyantse.

EATING   YAMDROK TSO

Tibetan restaurant Nakartse, on the western shore. This pleasant place has tables in a tiny courtyard, hidden away in the middle of the village, where you can eat rice with potato and meat curry (they fish out the meat for vegetarians) under the hungry, hopeful eyes of local dogs. Jeep drivers usually come here; otherwise, look for the tourist vehicles parked outside. Mains ¥15. Daily 8am–8pm.

Gyantse

江孜, jiāngzī

On the eastern banks of the Nyang Chu River, at the base of a natural amphitheatre of rocky ridges, **GYANTSE** is one of the most attractive and relaxed towns in Tibet. Its big draw is the splendid compound of **Gyantse Kumbum** (pronounced goom-boom) – famous among scholars of Tibetan art throughout the world – and the old fort, **Gyantse Dzong**.

Brief history

Little is known about the history of any settlement at Gyantse before the fourteenth century, when it emerged as the capital of a small kingdom ruled by a lineage of princes claiming descent from the legendary Tibetan folk hero, **King Gesar of Ling**. Hailing originally from northeast Tibet, they allied themselves to the powerful Sakya order. Also at this time, Gyantse operated as a staging post in the **wool trade** between Tibet and India, thanks to its position between Lhasa and Shigatse. By the mid-fifteenth century, the Gyantse Dzong, Pelkor Chode Monastery and the Kumbum had been built, although decline followed as other local families increased their influence.

The Younghusband Expedition

Gyantse rose to prominence again in July 1904 when Younghusband's machine-gun-equipped **British** expedition approached the town via the trade route from Sikkim, killing over half of the 1500 Tibetans sent to stop them. The British later took the Dzong; in doing so they suffered just four casualties, and killed three hundred more Tibetans. As part of the ensuing agreement between Tibet and Britain, a British Trade Agency was established in Gyantse allowing the route from Calcutta up through Sikkim and on to Gyantse to become increasingly busy.

GYANTSE

ACCOMMODATION
Gyantse Hotel	3
Jianzang	2
Yeti	1

EATING
Gyantse Kitchen	3
Tashi	2
Yeti Hotel	1

Gyantse Dzong

江孜古堡, jiāngzī gǔbǎo · Daily 9am–6pm · ¥30

The original **Gyantse Dzong** dates from the mid-fourteenth century, though the damage caused by the British in 1904 means much of what you see is a reconstruction. After climbing up to the fort, visitors are allowed into the **Meeting Hall**, which houses a waxworks tableau, and the aptly-named **Anti-British Imperialist Museum**, where weapons, used by the defenders against the British, are on display. Climb higher and you reach the upper and lower chapels of the **Sampal Norbuling Monastery**. A few of the murals in the upper chapel probably date from the early fifteenth century, but most of the other artefacts are modern. The best views are from the top of the tallest tower in the north of the complex. You'll need to climb some very rickety ladders, but the scenery is well worth it.

Gyantse Kumbum

江孜孔崩塔, jiāngzībēng tǎ · Daily 9am–6pm · ¥60; photography up to ¥20/chapel

At the northern edge of town, the rather barren monastic compound that now contains the glorious **Gyantse Kumbum** was once home to religious colleges and temples belonging to three schools of Tibetan Buddhism: the Gelugpa, Sakya and Bu (the last of these is a small order whose main centre is at Zhalu; see p.911).

Constructed around 1440 by Rabten Kunsang, the Gyantse prince most responsible for the town's fine buildings, the Gyantse Kumbum is a remarkable building. It's a huge **chorten**, crowned with a golden dome and umbrella, and with chapels bristling with **statues** and smothered with **paintings** at each level. This style is unique to Tibetan architecture and, while several such buildings have survived, Gyantse is the best preserved (despite some damage in the 1960s) and most accessible. The word *kumbum* means "a hundred thousand images" – which is probably an overestimate, but maybe not by much. Many of the statues have needed extensive renovation, and most of the murals are very old – take a torch if you want a good look.

The chapels

Some of the lesser chapels close between around 12.30pm and 2.30pm

The structure has eight levels, decreasing in size as you ascend; most of the **chapels** within, except those on the uppermost floors, are open. With almost seventy chapels on the first four levels alone, there's plenty to see. The highlights, with the densest, most lavish decoration, include the two-storey chapels at the cardinal points on the first and third levels and the four chapels on the fifth level. The views of the town and surrounding area get better the higher you go, and some of the outside stuccowork is especially fine. At the sixth level, you'll emerge onto an open platform, level with the eyes of the chorten that look in each direction.

Pelkor Chode Monastery

白居寺, báijū sì

In the same compound as Gyantse Kumbum, the **Pelkor Chode Monastery** was built by Rabten Kunsang some twenty years earlier and used for worship by monks from all the surrounding monasteries. Today, the main assembly hall contains two thrones, one for the Dalai Lama and one for the main Sakya Lama. The glitter and gold, sunlight and flickering butter lamps in the chapels make a fine contrast to the gloom of much of the Kumbum. The main chapel, **Tsangkhang**, is at the back of the assembly hall and has a statue of Sakyamuni flanked by deities amid some impressive wood carvings – look for the two peacocks perched on a beam. The second floor of the monastery contains five chapels, and the top level just one, **Shalyekhang** (Peak of the Celestial Mansion), with some very impressive, 2m-wide mandalas.

ARRIVAL AND DEPARTURE   GYANTSE

By jeep Gyantse is a 6–7hr drive with stops from Lhasa (263km) on the old southern road, and 90km (1hr 30min) southeast of Shigatse.

By bus There is a bus station along Yingxiong Nan Lu, near the junction with Guofang Lu, with regular departures to both Lhasa and Shigatse.

ACCOMMODATION

Gyantse Hotel 江孜饭店, jiāngzī fàndiàn. 2 Shanghai Dong Lu ☏ 0892 8172222. East of the main crossroads, this cavernous three-star affair lacks character but is fairly comfortable, spacious, and generally clean, plus has 24hr hot water and a tub in every bathroom. ¥385

Jianzang 建藏饭店, jiànzàng fàndiàn. 14 Yingxiong Nan Lu ☏ 0892 8173720. Built around an old courtyard, this centrally located, family-run place is clean, well-managed and has some pretty Tibetan decoration. All things considered, it's one of the better hotels in small-

town Tibet. ¥320

Yeti 雅迪花园酒店, yǎdí huāyuán jiǔdiàn. 11 Weiguo Lu ☏ 0892 8175555, ⓦ yetihoteltibet.com. Smart, central and very popular place at the top of town near the Gyantse Dzong. The rooms come with writing desks and armchairs, and the bathrooms have hot water but somewhat erratic plumbing. Staff are very used to dealing with foreign tourists and mostly speak English. The breakfast spread might be the best outside of Lhasa. ¥360

EATING

Gyantse Kitchen 江孜橱房, jiāngzī chúfáng. Shanghai Dong Lu ☏ 0892 8176777. Opposite the Gyantse Hotel, this place is popular with tour groups and churns out pretty decent Chinese, Nepali, Western and Tibetan food. The evening buffet is good value at ¥40 if you're hungry, but service can be slow. Daily 7am–10pm.

Tashi 达西餐厅, dáxī cāntīng. Yingxiong Zhong Lu ☏ 0892 8172793. An unashamedly Nepalese restaurant

and all the better for it. This friendly place knocks out excellent curries as well as the standard *momos*, pizzas and pancakes. You can get breakfast here, but you should let them know the night before. Around ¥35 per head for a main meal. Daily 8am–10.30pm.

Yeti Hotel 雅迪花园酒店, yǎdí huāyuán jiǔdiàn. 11 Weiguo Lu ☏ 0892 8175555, ⓦ yetihoteltibet.com. Modern, clean restaurant inside the hotel (see above), with an English picture menu for ease of ordering and an enormous list of food available including Chinese, Tibetan and Western options – though don't expect everything on the menu to be in the kitchen. Mains around ¥40. Daily 8am–10pm.

Zhalu Monastery

夏鲁寺, xiàlǔ sì • Around 22km from Shigatse, 75km from Gyantse and 4km south of Tsungdu village, between kilometre-markers 18 and 19 on the Gyantse–Shigatse road • Daily 8.30am–6pm • ¥40

Zhalu Monastery (also spelled Shalu Monastery) was originally built in the eleventh century and rose to prominence as the seat of the **Bu tradition** of Tibetan Buddhism founded by Buton Rinchendrub in the fourteenth century. Buton's claim to fame is as the scholar who collected, organized and copied the Tengyur commentaries by hand into a coherent whole, comprising 227 thick volumes, though the originals were destroyed during the Cultural Revolution. There were once about 3500 monks living here, but the tradition never had as many followers as the other schools. It did, however, have a fair degree of influence: **Tsongkhapa**, among others, was inspired by Buton's teachings. The monastery has a finely colonnaded courtyard decorated with luck symbols, but is most remarkable for the green-glazed **tiles** that line the roof.

Riphuk

热布, rèbù

For the energetic, it's a one- to two-hour walk up in the hills southwest of Zhalu to the hermitage of **Riphuk**, where Atisha (see p.874) is supposed to have meditated during his journey from Sakya to Samye. Here you'll find a clutch of rebuilt temples and a stupa inside the ruined walls of a complex that was once home to some three hundred monks. Residents will probably dispense with administering the traditional blessing of three pitchers of cold spring water over the head of visitors.

Gyankhor Lhakhang

江廓拉康, jiāngkuòlākāng

About 1km north of Zhalu, **Gyankor Lhakhang** dates from 997. Sakya Pandita, who established the relationship between the Mongol Khans and the Sakya hierarchy in the thirteenth century (see p.874), was ordained here as a monk, and the stone bowl over which he shaved his head prior to ordination is in the courtyard. Just inside the entrance is a conch shell, said to date from the time of Buton Rinchendrub and reputedly able to sound without human assistance.

Shigatse

日喀则, rìkāzé

Traditionally the home of the Panchen Lamas – religious and political rivals to the Dalai Lamas – Tibet's second city, **SHIGATSE**, is used by travellers as an overnight stop on the way to or from Lhasa. One day is long enough to see the two main sights, **Tashilunpo Monastery** and **Shigatse Dzong**, but if you're not pressed for time it's worth spending at least an extra night here simply to do everything at a more leisurely pace, take in the market, wander the attractive, tree-lined streets and absorb the buzz provided by the huge numbers of Tibetan pilgrims and foreign visitors. Although most of the city is modern, you'll find the traditional Tibetan houses concentrated in the old town west of the market, where you can explore the narrow alleyways running between high, whitewashed walls.

Tashilunpo Monastery

扎什伦布寺, zhāshílúnbù sì • Mon–Sat 9am–6.30pm • ¥80; photography ¥70–200 per chapel

Something of a showcase for foreign visitors, the large complex of **Tashilunpo Monastery** is situated on the western side of town just below the Drolma Ridge –

14

14

the gleaming, golden roofs will lead you in the right direction. Tashilunpo was founded in 1447 by **Gendun Drup**, Tsongkhapa's nephew and disciple, who was later recognized as the First Dalai Lama. It rose to prominence in 1642 when the Fifth Dalai Lama declared that Losang Chokyi Gyeltsen, who was his teacher and the abbot of Tashilunpo, was a manifestation of the Amitabha Buddha and the Fourth reincarnation of the **Panchen Lama** (Great Precious Teacher), in what has proved to be an ill-fated lineage (see box opposite). The Chinese have consistently sought to use the Panchen Lama in opposition to the Dalai Lama, beginning in 1728 when they gave the Fifth Panchen Lama sovereignty over western Tibet.

The monastery has some of the most fabulous **chapels** outside of Lhasa, and it takes several hours to do it justice. Though photography is allowed inside most of the chapels, the fees can be extortionate, so make sure you check the price before snapping away.

Jamkhang Chenmo

西藏最大未来佛, xīzàng zuìdà wèiláifó

The **temples** and shrines of most interest in Tashilunpo stand in a long line at the northern end of the compound. From the main gate, head uphill and left to the **Jamkhang Chenmo**. Several storeys high, this was built by the Ninth Panchen Lama in 1914 and is dominated by a 26m gold, brass and copper statue of Maitreya, the Buddha of the Future. Hundreds of small images of Maitreya and Tsongkhapa and his disciples are painted on the walls.

Tomb of the Tenth Panchen Lama

世班禅喇嘛灵塔, shìbānchán lǎmalíng tǎ

To the east of the Jamkhang Chenmo, the next main building contains the gold and jewel-encrusted **Tomb of the Tenth Panchen Lama**, which was consecrated in 1994 and cost US$8 million. Near the top is a small window cut into a tiny niche, containing his picture.

SHIGATSE

■ ACCOMMODATION
Ganggyan	2
Gesar	3
Shigatse Hotel	4
Tashi Tshuta	1

Shigatse Dzong
Market
OLD TOWN
Tashilunpo Monastery
Entrance
Bank of China
Fruit and Vegetable Market
Shigatse Hospital
Gang-Gyen Carpet Factory
FIT Office
Bus Station
Bank of China
Dechen Phodrang

TOMZIGANG LU
DE QIANG LU
QINGDAO LU
JIGEZI LU
SHANDONG LU
ZHUFENG LU
BHANGCAR LU
PUZHANG LU
FIT TRAIL
SHANDONG LU
SHANGHAI LU

Lhasa & B (1km)
Lhasa
PSB
Gyantse

● EATING
Songtsen Tibetan Restaurant	1
Third Eye Nepali Restaurant	3
Tibetan Family Restaurant	2

0   500
metres

Palace of the Panchen Lamas

德钦颇章, dé qīn pō zhāng

Past the Tenth Panchen Lama's tomb, the **Palace of the Panchen Lamas**, built in the eighteenth century, is closed to the public, but the long building in front houses a series of small, first-floor chapels. The **Yulo Drolma Lhakhang**, farthest to the right, is worth a look and contains 21 small statues showing each of the 21 manifestations of Tara, the most popular goddess in Tibet.

Tomb of the Fourth Panchen Lama

世班禅喇嘛灵塔, shìbānchán lǎmalíng tǎ

The **Tomb of the Fourth Panchen Lama** lies to the east of the Palace of Panchen Lamas, and contains an 11m-high chorten, with statues of Amitayus, White Tara and Vijaya, the so-called Three Gods of Longevity, in front. His entire body

THE PANCHEN LAMA CONTROVERSY

The life of Choekyi Gyaltsen, the **Tenth Panchen Lama** (1938–89), was a tragic one. Selected by the Nationalist authorities in 1949 – without approval from the government in Lhasa – he fell into Communist hands and was for years China's highest-profile Tibetan collaborator. In 1959, however, his role changed when he openly referred to the Dalai Lama as the true ruler of Tibet. Ordered to denounce the Dalai Lama, Gyaltsen refused and was barred from speaking in public until 1964, when, to an audience of ten thousand people, he again proclaimed support for the exiled leader. He spent the following fourteen years in jail. Released in 1978, Gyaltsen never again criticized the Chinese in public, arguing for the protection of Tibetan culture at all costs, even if it meant abandoning independence. Some saw him as a sellout; others still worship him as a hero. He died in 1989, officially from a heart attack, though rumours of poisoning persist.

The **search for a successor** was always likely to be fraught, with the Dalai Lama and the Chinese government both claiming authority to choose the next incarnation. The search was initially led according to tradition by checking on reports of "unusual" children, and in January 1995 the Dalai Lama identified the Eleventh Panchen Lama but, concerned for the child's safety, delayed a public announcement. The Chinese authorities, meanwhile, decreed selection should take place by drawing of lots from a golden urn.

In May, the Dalai Lama publicly identified his choice, and within days the boy and his family had disappeared. Fifty Communist Party officials moved into Tashilunpo to root out monks loyal to the Dalai Lama and his choice of Panchen Lama. In July, riot police quelled an open revolt by the monks, but by the end of 1995 dissent was suppressed enough for the drawing of lots to take place. The lucky winner, **Gyaincain Norbu**, was enthroned at Tashilunpo and taken to Beijing for publicity appearances, where he has since stayed to complete his studies. Two decades later, the fate of the Dalai Lama's choice and his family remains unknown, though Beijing claims they are free and voluntarily opting to remain anonymous.

As for Gyaincain Norbu, despite Beijing's best efforts, his returns to Tibet are rare and lacklustre affairs; when he does come home, the authorities often close the region to foreigners. His predecessor, the rotund Choekyi Gyaltsen, is usually the figure you'll see smiling beatifically down from pictures on Tibetan living-room walls.

14

was supposedly interred in the chorten in a standing position, together with an ancient manuscript and *thangkas* sent by the second Manchu emperor.

Kelsang Lhakhang

格桑拉康, gésānglākāng

The largest, most intricate and confusing building in Tashilhunpo, the **Kelsang Lhakhang** stands in front of the Tomb of the Fifth Panchen Lama. The Lhakhang consists of a courtyard, the fifteenth-century assembly hall and a whole maze of small chapels, often interconnecting, in the surrounding buildings. The flagged **courtyard** is the setting for all the major temple festivals; the surrounding three-level colonnaded cloisters are covered with murals, many recently renovated. The huge throne of the Panchen Lama and the hanging *thangkas*, depicting all his incarnations, dominate the **assembly hall**. If you've got the energy, it's worth trying to find the **Thongwa Donden Lhakhang**, one of the most sacred chapels in the complex, containing burial chortens, including that of the founder of Tashilunpo, the First Dalai Lama, Gendun Drup, as well as early Panchen Lamas and abbots of Tashilunpo.

The kora

Spare a couple of hours to walk the 3km **kora**, the pilgrim circuit, which follows a clockwise path around the outside walls of the monastery. Turn right on the main road as you exit the monastery and continue around the walls; a stick is useful, as some of the dogs are aggressive. The highlight of the walk is the view of the glorious golden roofs from above the top wall. The massive, white-painted wall at the top northeast corner is where the 40m appliquéd *thangka* is displayed annually at the festival on the fifteenth day of the fifth lunar month (usually in July). At this point, instead of returning downhill to the main road, you can follow the track that continues around the hillside above the Tibetan part of town and eventually leads to the old Shigatse Dzong.

Shigatse Dzong

日喀则宗, rìkāzézōng

The fort of **Shigatse Dzong** was built in the seventeenth century by Karma Phuntso Namgyel when he was king of the Tsang region and held sway over much of the country. It's thought that its design was used as the basis for the later construction of the Potala Palace in Lhasa. The structure was initially ruined by the Dzungars in 1717, and further damage took place in the 1950s. At the time of writing, visitors were not allowed inside, but you can walk around the exterior of the *dzong* and marvel at the views.

The market

Opposite the *Tenzin Hotel*, Tomzigang Lu • Daily dawn till dusk

The **market** is worth a browse for souvenirs, jewellery, fake antiques and religious objects (if not for its most obvious product, whole dead sheep). You'll need to brush up on your bargaining skills and be patient – the stallholders are used to hit-and-run tourists, so the first asking prices can be sky-high.

Gang-Gyen Carpet Factory

刚坚地毯厂, gāngjiān dìtǎn chǎng • Zhufeng Lu • Mon–Fri 9am–1pm & 3–6pm

Even if you're not interested in rugs, it's worth dropping into the **Gang-Gyen Carpet Factory**, a few minutes' walk from the entrance of Tashilunpo. You can see the whole carpet-making process – from the winding of the wool through to the weaving and finishing – and the dexterity of the women working here is mind-boggling. There's also a shop with a good range of traditional and modern designs, but even with prices well below what you'd find in the West there's still nothing on offer for under a couple of hundred dollars. If you do take the plunge, the factory can arrange shipping, and they take credit cards.

ARRIVAL AND DEPARTURE

SHIGATSE

By jeep Shigatse to Gyantse takes around 3hr, to Lhasa at least 7hr, and Sakya around 4hr.

By bus Shigatse's bus station is in the centre of town on

Shanghai Lu, south of its junction with Zhufeng Lu. Buses to Lhasa leave in the morning (8am & 9am). Those to and from Gyantse run until around 4pm.

INFORMATION AND GETTING AROUND

Tourist permits Shigatse's PSB, on Zhufeng Dong Lu (Mon–Fri 9.30am–1pm & 3.30–7pm; ☎0892 8829803), is used to dealing with tour groups and is where permits for Everest (¥50) are issued – though such formalities should be handled by your tour guide.

Banks and exchange The Bank of China (Mon–Sat

10am–4pm), south of the *Shigatse Hotel*, and on Zhufeng Lu, east of the Gang Gyan, gives advances on Visa cards. If you're heading west, stock up here on local currency, as there are no more facilities until Zhangmu.

By taxi Taxis are ¥10 for any destination in town.

THE FRIENDSHIP HIGHWAY

From Shigatse, the **Friendship Highway** is surfaced all the way to Zhangmu on the Nepalese border, closed at the time of writing. The only public buses in this direction are the Shigatse to Sakya, Lhatse and Tingri services, but as usual, foreigners cannot take these. From the broad plain around Shigatse, the road gradually climbs to the pass of Tsuo La (4500m) before the steep descent to the Sakya Bridge and the turnoff to Sakya village – well worth detouring to (see opposite). Further south, the journey to **Everest Base Camp** is a once-in-a-lifetime experience (see p.918).

ACCOMMODATION

Ganggyan 刚坚宾馆, gāngjiān bīnguǎn. 77 Zhufeng Xi Lu ☏ 0892 8820777. Run as a business by the Tashilunpo Monastery, which is only a couple of hundred metres away, the *Ganggyan* has plainly decorated en-suite rooms that could do with a makeover. Service is indifferent, and you're better off going elsewhere for breakfast – the one here is pretty dismal. The main reason to stay is for proximity to the monastery. ¥250

★**Gesar** 格萨尔大酒店, gésà'ér jiǔdiàn. Longjiang Lu ☏ 0892 8800088. Ignore the uninspiring mirrored exterior of this large and fairly new four-star hotel, and head inside for one of the best hotels outside of Lhasa. The rooms, with plenty of Tibetan colour and decoration, have excellent wi-fi signal, above-average bathrooms with

piping-hot water and unusually comfortable beds. Staff are professional and keen to help. ¥450

Shigatse Hotel 日喀则饭店, rìkāzé fàndiàn. 12 Shanghai Zhonglu ☏ 0892 8822525. This tour-group hotel, a bit out of the centre, is rather cavernous if there aren't many people around. Choose between the heavily decorated Tibetan-style rooms and the cookie-cutter Chinese options. ¥500

Tashi Tshuta 扎西曲塔大酒店, zhāxī qūtā dàjiǔdiàn. 2 Xuechang Lu ☏ 0892 8830111. Four-star luxury option in a central location, with good service and plain but well-maintained, comfortable rooms. Rather overpriced though. ¥700

EATING

There's no shortage of restaurants in Shigatse, including several aimed at the stuttering flow of Western tourists. If you're getting a picnic, visit the fruit and vegetable market south off Qingdao Lu.

Songtsen Tibetan Restaurant 松赞西藏餐厅, sōngzàn xīzàng cāntīng. 19 Xigezi Lu ☏ 0892 8832469. Cosy place turning out a good mix of tourist-friendly Tibetan, Nepali, Western and Chinese favourites. Great location, though not particularly cheap; mains around ¥40. Daily 9am–10pm.

Third Eye Nepali Restaurant 尼泊尔雪莲餐厅, níbó'ěr xuělián cāntīng. Zhufeng Xi Lu, upstairs next to the Ganggyan Hotel ☏ 0892 8838898. Very well turned out Nepali dishes and average Chinese standards, particularly good for vegetarians who can opt for *paneer*

curry or a vegetable *thali*. Popular with tour groups; expect ¥50 per head. Daily 9am–10pm.

Tibetan Family Restaurant 丰盛藏式餐厅, fēngshèng zàngshì cāntīng. 62 Xigezi Lu ☏ 1390 8929222. Friendly and usually full of Tibetan tea-drinkers, this place also has a small balcony for sitting outside and people-watching. The food, all hearty Tibetan fare and heavy on the yak-meat side (yak steak is a particular favourite), is tasty and very reasonably priced, with mains from ¥20. Daily 9am–10pm.

Sakya

萨迦, sàjiā

The small but rapidly growing village of **SAKYA**, set in the midst of an attractive plain, straddles the small Trum River and is highly significant as the centre of the Sakya school of Tibetan Buddhism. The main reason to visit is to see the remaining **monastery**, a unique, Mongol-style construction dramatically visible from far away. The village around is now a burgeoning Chinese community, full of ugly concrete, and can be crowded with coach parties in peak season. But, while it's not a place to linger, the monastery makes this a more than worthwhile side-trip from the Friendship Highway.

The Southern Monastery

萨迦南寺, sàjiānán sì • Mon–Sat 9am–5.30pm • ¥45; photography ¥100–350 per chapel

A massive fortress, the **Southern Monastery** was built in the thirteenth century on the orders of **Phagpa**, nephew of Sakya Pandita. The entrance is in its east wall; on the way there, note the unusual decoration of houses in the area – grey, with white and red vertical stripes – which dates back to a time when it denoted their taxable status within the Sakya principality.

Photography is allowed in some chapels; always check the price first, as fees can be extortionate.

14

Puntsok Palace

平措宫, píncuògōng

The five main temples in the complex are surrounded by a huge wall with turrets at each corner. On the left of the entrance is the tall, spacious chapel on the second floor of the **Puntsok Palace**, the traditional home of one of the two main Sakya lamas, who now lives in the US. The chortens contain the remains of early Sakya lamas.

As you move clockwise around the courtyard, the next chapel is the **Phurkhang** (普康, pǔkāng), with statues of Sakyamuni to the left and Manjusri to the right of Sakya Pandita. The whole temple is stuffed with thousands of small statues and editions of sacred texts with murals on the back wall.

The Great Assembly Hall

大雄宝殿, dàxióngbǎodiàn

Facing the entrance to the courtyard, the **Great Assembly Hall** is an imposing chapel, with walls 3.5m thick. Its roof is supported by forty solid **wooden columns**, one of which was said to be a personal gift from Kublai Khan and carried by hand from China; another was supposedly fetched from India on the back of a tiger; a third was brought in the horns of a yak; and yet another is said to weep the black blood of the naga water-spirit that lived in the tree used for the column. The chapel is overwhelmingly full of brocade hangings, fine statues, butter lamps, thrones, murals and holy books. The grandest statues, of Buddha, are against a golden, carved background, and contain the remains of previous Sakya lamas.

Silver Chorten Chapel

萨迦银塔殿, sàjiāyíntǎ diàn

Next along, the **Silver Chorten Chapel** houses eleven chortens; there are yet more in the chapel behind. Completing the circuit, the **Drolma Lhakhang** (卓玛拉康, zhuómǎlākāng) is on the second floor of the building to the right of the entrance. This is the residence of the other principal Sakya Lama, the **Sakya Trizin**, currently residing in India, where he has established his seat in exile in Rajpur. Be sure to take time to walk around the top of the walls for fine views, both into the monastery and over the surrounding area.

ARRIVAL AND DEPARTURE   SAKYA

Situated 150km southwest of Shigatse, Sakya is an easy side-trip off the Friendship Highway; most tours call in here on the way to Everest.

By jeep Everest (7hr); Lhatse (45min); Saga (7hr); Shigatse (3hr).

By bus Public buses run Mon–Fri to Sakya from Shigatse, though foreigners are not permitted to take these, as usual. It's a surprisingly slow trip – at least 6hr.

Destinations Lhatse (daily; 1hr); Shigatse (daily; 6hr).

SAKYA'S NORTHERN MONASTERY

Originally, there were two monasteries at Sakya: the imposing, Mongol-style structure of the Southern Monastery that visitors come to see today, and a **Northern Monastery** across the river, which was a more typical complex containing 108 chapels. The Northern Monastery was founded in 1073 by Kong Chogyal Pho, a member of the Khon family, whose son, Kunga Nyingpo, did much to establish Sakya as an important religious centre. He married and had four sons; three became monks, but the fourth remained a layman and continued the family line. The **Sakya order** has remained something of a family affair, and, while the monks take vows of celibacy, their lay brothers ensure the leadership remains with their kin.

The Northern Monastery was completely destroyed during the Cultural Revolution and has been largely replaced by housing. Prior to the Chinese occupation, there were around five hundred monks in the two monasteries; there are now about a hundred.

ACCOMMODATION AND EATING

Manasarovar Sakya Hotel 神湖萨迦宾馆, shénhú sàjiā bīnguǎn. 1 Kelsang Xi Lu ☎ 0892 8242222. The main hotel in town and owned by the same people as the *Yak* hotel in Lhasa (see p.894), so many tour groups end up here. Rooms are clean, but can feel cold – though you do get an electric blanket – and there's often not enough hot water to go round. The adjoining restaurant turns out steaming platefuls of Chinese, Tibetan and Western food (of sorts). ¥350

Lhatse

拉孜, lāzī

Just 24km west of Sakya Bridge, the truck-stop town of **Lhatse** (4050m) sits alongside the Friendship Highway. With plenty of restaurants and some basic accommodation, it used to be an almost compulsory overnight stop for travellers heading to Everest. However, with ever-improving roads speeding up journey times, most people only pause here for a quick bite to eat.

ACCOMMODATION AND EATING   LHATSE

Both of Lhatse's hotels have restaurants, and there are numerous good-value places – Sichuanese, especially – to eat along the main drag.
Shanghai Hotel 上海大酒店, shànghǎi dàjiǔdiàn. ☎ 0892 8323678. Top billing in town goes to this Chinese-run establishment which dominates the central square. Cavernous and totally lacking character, but with smart, clean rooms it's a sensible choice, though hardly inspiring.

¥350
Tibetan Farmers' Adventure Hostel 西藏拉孜农民娱乐旅馆, xīzàng lāzī nóngmín yúlè lǚguǎn. At the western end of town ☎ 0892 8322858. Proudly proclaims itself "Tibet's first hotel by peasants": enjoy the charm of the ramshackle cells at the front, but do your best to stay in one of the new, decidedly un-peasant-like en-suite rooms at the back. ¥280

Approaching Everest

Entry fee ¥180 per person, vehicle fee ¥400; most tour companies do not include entry to the Everest region in their fees, so you will need to cover this, as well as your guide's entry fee (also ¥180) and the vehicle fee

Approaching Everest along the Friendship Highway from Lhatse, allow about four hours in a good jeep to get up over the Lhakpa La pass (5220m) to **NEW TINGRI** (新定日, xīndìngrì; also known as **Shekar**). Almost entirely constructed from concrete blocks, it's not the nicest place, but it holds the ticket office for entry to the Mount Everest area and represents the last chance to stock up on provisions before the mountain.

There's a checkpoint on the highway about 5km further on, where some visitors have reported guards being particularly assiduous in confiscating printed material specifically about Tibet (books on China that include Tibet seem to be fine). Just 7km west of this checkpoint, the small turning to **Rongbuk Monastery** and on up to **Everest Base Camp** is on the south side of the road.

Through Pang La pass

It's a long, windy, spellbinding 90km to Rongbuk – and worth every tortured minute of the three-hour drive. The road zigzags steeply up to the **Pang La pass** (5150m), from where the glory of the Everest region is laid out before you – the earlier you go in the day, the better the views, as it clouds over later. There's a lookout spot with a plan to help you identify individual peaks such as Cho Oyu (8153m), Lhotse (8501m) and Makalu (8463m), as well as the mighty **Mount Everest** (8848m; Chomolungma in Tibetan, Zhumulangma in Chinese). From here the road descends into a network of fertile valleys with small villages in a patchwork of fields. You'll gradually start climbing again and pass through **Peruche** (19km from Pang La), **Passum** (10km further) and **Chodzom** (another 12km), before the scenery becomes rockier and starker and you eventually reach Rongbuk Monastery, 22km farther on.

14

Rongbuk Monastery

绒布寺, róngbù sì • No set hours, but the monks and nuns usually open the chapels around 8.30/9am–5.30pm • ¥25

Rongbuk Monastery – at 4980m, the highest in the world – was founded in 1902 by the Nyingma Lama, **Ngawang Tenzin Norbu**, although a hardy community of nuns had used meditation huts on the site for about two hundred years before this. The chapels themselves are of limited interest; Padmasambhava is in pride of place, and the new murals are attractive, but the position of the monastery, perched on the side of the Rongbuk Valley leading straight towards the north face of Everest, is stunning. Just to sit outside and watch the play of light on the face of the mountain is the experience of a lifetime.

ACCOMMODATION AND EATING   RONGBUK MONASTERY

Campsite Around 2km past Rongbuk Monastery is a large horseshoe of tents pitched around what is presumably the world's highest car park. Each of the tents, which are only available mid-April to mid-Oct, claims the status of a "guesthouse", offering relatively comfortable dormitory accommodation on camp-beds for the single night most people stay. Basic meals are a pricey ¥30–50 per dish. Even by Tibetan standards, the communal toilets are remarkably dirty. In the corner of the car park is a post office from where you can send Everest-stamped postcards. Tent dorms **¥60**

Rongbuk Monastery Hotel 绒布寺饭店, róngbùsì fàndiàn. ☎189 08925152. Traditional-style single-storey building directly opposite the monastery, with basic but clean rooms around a small courtyard/car park. They advertise 24hr hot water, but don't get too excited by the thought: it all comes via a flask rather than pipes and taps, and the toilets are communal long-drops. The highlight is its teahouse/restaurant which has windows facing down the valley – a perfect place to sit and watch the mountain play peek-a-boo, over a tankard of hot, sweet, milky tea. Dorms **¥60**

Everest Base Camp

珠峰大本营, zhūfēng dàběnyíng • Bus from the campsite ¥25

Everest Base Camp (5150m) is 4km south of Rongbuk Monastery. There's a bus, but the walk alongside the river through the boulder-strewn landscape and past a small monastery on the cliff is glorious, and the route fairly flat. Base camp is often a bit of a surprise, and not a very pleasant one, especially during the climbing seasons (March–May and Sept–Oct), when you'll find a colourful and untidy tent city festooned with Calor gas bottles and satellite dishes. Throughout the summer, there's a constant stream of Chinese package tourists waving selfie-sticks. At other times of year it's almost completely deserted, save for a perpetual detachment of Chinese troops keeping an eye out for potential "trouble".

Don't be surprised if you suffer with the **altitude** here – breathlessness and headaches are the norm. Base camp is around 1500m higher than Lhasa, so even if you acclimatized well in the city, you could be in trouble here. Be sensible and don't contemplate a trip to base camp immediately after arrival up on the Tibetan plateau.

Tingri

From the Rongbuk and Everest Base Camp turning on the Friendship Highway, it's a fast 50km south to **TINGRI** (定日, dìngrì; 4342m). The road is good, and you should allow about an hour in a jeep. A convenient stop on the final day's drive to Zhangmu, Tingri has some good restaurants and excellent views south towards Everest. To get the best of these, climb up to the old fort that stands sentinel over the main part of the village.

ACCOMMODATION AND EATING   TINGRI

Kangar 康嘎宾馆, kānggá bīnguǎn. ☎152 08027313. It's not saying much, but the *Kangar* is your best bet for accommodation in Tingri. Rooms are spartan, and it gets extremely cold at night, but it's all kept clean enough, and the restaurant (mains ¥40) is a popular place to tuck into basic noodle-based dishes. **¥320**

To the Nepalese border

The traditional way to travel overland between Tibet and Nepal has been via the border town of **ZHANGMU** (2300m). However, the April 2015 **earthquake** that so devastated parts of Nepal also almost completely destroyed Zhangmu and the surrounding areas. All cross-border traffic was shut down, and the road between Tingri and Zhangmu has been **closed to tourist vehicles** since the earthquake.

In 2016, a **new main border crossing** was announced, some 50km west of Zhangmu. At the time of writing, this new route was still closed to foreign tourists, though parts of the Nepalese side were open. The road will take travellers from Tingri or Saga to **Kyirong** on the Chinese side of the border. From here, via an enormously ostentatious gateway with piped patriotic music, travellers will cross into the Nepalese town of **Rasuwagadhi**, with its much less flamboyant garden-shed-sized old stone fort. Currently tiny and with few facilities, Rasuwagadhi will likely develop very quickly once the border has opened. The 160km journey from Rasuwagadhi to Kathmandu used to take nine torturous but spectacular hours. However, due to significant road upgrades that were under way when this guide was being written, travel times should speed up considerably.

Half an hour or so after crossing into Nepal, the road runs past **Syabrubesi**, the traditional starting point of the fabulous and very popular **Langtang trek**. Sadly, the Langtang region suffered severe damage during the earthquake; the trekking route was closed at the time of research, but is likely to reopen within the next few years.

Western Tibet

Travellers spend huge amounts of time and money plotting and planning trips to **Western Tibet**, with its key sights of **Mount Kailash**, **Lake Manasarovar** and the remains of the tenth-century **Guge kingdom**. However, this is no guarantee of reaching any of these destinations – regulations change frequently and weather can be a factor. Access to Mount Kailash generally isn't a problem – you just need to find a tour agency running the trip. Cost is likely to be the largest obstacle, as tours from Lhasa to the mountain and back take at least two weeks.

Saga

萨嘎, sàgā

From Sakya or Lhatse it's a solid day's journey to the dusty town of **SAGA**. There's a military garrison here and not much else, but Saga, already a well-established stopover for pilgrims from Tibet, is growing quickly, with increasing numbers of visitors from China, Nepal and India heading to Kailash.

ACCOMMODATION   SAGA

Norling Hotel 落福岭宾馆, luòfúlǐng bīnguǎn. 8 Lunzhu Lu ☏ 1828 9128885. At the south end of town, along a street running parallel to the highway, this place has en suites with hot showers, 24hr electricity and erratic wi-fi. The rooms themselves would be standard anywhere else in China; here they are luxury. There's a restaurant serving typical Tibetan and Chinese staples (mains ¥30–40). Breakfast not included. **¥360**

Saga Grand Hotel 萨嘎大厦, sàgā dàshà. Cnr Deji Lu & Gesang Lu ☏ 1388 9025676. The *Saga Grand* is the newest hotel in town and by far the most appealing, but don't get too excited – if this hotel were anywhere but western Tibet, you probably wouldn't look twice at it. As it is, the bathrooms (with temperamental hot water), clean bedrooms and (admittedly unreliable) wi-fi make it an easy winner. The in-house restaurant serving Chinese and Tibetan staples (mains ¥35–40) is the best place to eat in town, but that's not saying much. Breakfast not included. **¥400**

14

Darchen

塔钦, tǎqīn • Private tourist vehicles are not allowed to drive to Darchen; jeeps must be left in Hor Qu, where you board an "eco" bus to take you into Darchen (¥150 return)

Access to the Mount Kailash and Lake Manasarovar area is via **DARCHEN**, 450km northwest of Saga. Aside from at one recently opened hotel, facilities here are spartan – there's little running water and no mains electricity. Explorers who prefer to wash in hot water can always visit the **Holy Shower and Bathing Centre** public baths (daily dawn till dusk; ¥30) in the centre of the village.

ACCOMMODATION   DARCHEN

Himalaya Kailash 喜马拉雅凯拉斯宾馆, xīmǎlāyǎ kǎilāsī bīnguǎn. At the southern end of town, on the east side of the road ☎ 139 89974987. Brand new and turning the accommodation scene around Kailash on its head, this sizeable hotel almost verges on designer. The large plate-glass windows give partial views of the mountain, while the rooms are warm and very comfortable, with inviting bathrooms and big beds covered in thick,

clean duvets. Expensive it may be, but after walking the Kailash *kora*, it's a very tempting prospect. It also has by far the best restaurant in town (mains ¥40). **¥600**

Lhasa Holy Land Guesthouse 拉萨圣地宾馆, lāsà shèngdì bīnguǎn. ☎ 139 89070818. Very basic dorm-style accommodation set around a cosy Tibetan-style teahouse. Dorms **¥100**

Mount Kailash

冈仁波齐峰, gāngrénbōqí fēng • Joint ticket for Mount Kailash and Lake Manasarovar ¥300; yaks from ¥160/day each, porters ¥180/day

Top of most Western Tibet itineraries is **Mount Kailash** (6714m; Gang Rinpoche to the Tibetans), the sacred mountain at the centre of the universe for Buddhists, Hindus and Jains. The 58km *kora* around the mountain takes three days (though Tibetans usually do it in one); you might consider hiring a porter and/or yak, as it's a tough walk and you need to carry all your gear and at least some food. On the first day you should reach **Drirapuk Monastery**; on the second day you climb over the Dolma La pass (5636m) to **Zutrulpuk Monastery**; and the third day you arrive back in Darchen.

ACCOMMODATION AND EATING   MOUNT KAILASH

Guesthouses At each stop on the mountain there are basic guesthouses which also turn out simple food for breakfast and in the evenings, but you'll need to bring lunches with you, plus trekking snacks. Dorms **¥60**

Mapham Tso (Lake Manasarovar)

玛旁雍错, mǎpáng yōngcuò • Joint ticket for Mount Kailash and Lake Manasarovar ¥300; bus around the lake ¥280

After the exertions of Mount Kailash, most tours head south 30km to **Mapham Tso (Lake Manasarovar)**, the holiest lake in Asia for Hindus and Tibetan Buddhists alike. It's a four-day, 90km trek to circumnavigate the lake, but plenty of travellers and pilgrims relax lakeside for another day or two. You can stay at one of the cluster of

---

ROUTES THROUGH WESTERN TIBET

The **southern route**, a well-surfaced highway running parallel to the Himalayas all the way to Western Tibet's main town, **ALI** (also known as **Shiquanhe**), passes through Saga, and on to Darchen, and makes for a stunningly picturesque journey. From Lhasa to Mount Kailash is around 1400km.

The alternative **northern route** via Tsochen, Gertse and Gakyi is longer: it's over 1700km to Ali, and then another 300km or so southeast to Mount Kailash. It's a much wilder route across the edge of the vast Changtang plateau, where sightings of Tibetan antelope are fairly common. Some tours plan to take one route out, and the other on the way back – expect around a week's-travelling time on either.

guesthouses along the northwest shore, overlooked by the **Chiu Temple** (极物寺, jíwù sì), a popular haunt. Those not in the mood for more walking can take an eight-hour bus from the **visitors' centre**, on the northern shore, around the lake.

ACCOMMODATION AND EATING	LAKE MANASAROVAR
Guesthouses Guesthouses near the Chiu Temple offer extremely basic beds and simple meals; have a look round a	few before making your choice, though don't expect anything like clean linen, running water or flush toilets. **¥60**

Menshi

门石, ménshí

Truck-stop town **MENSHI**, around 100km west from Mount Kailash, is a common stopoff on the way to and from Guge Kingdom sites near Zanda, a further four hours' drive west. The whole town stretches little more than 200m along the road, but the backstreets are picturesque, the sunsets beautiful and – hundreds of kilometres from the nearest city – the stars breathtaking.

Tirthapuri Hot Springs

扎达布日, zhādá bùrì • ¥20

The third major pilgrimage site in Western Tibet is **Tirthapuri Hot Springs**, which are closely associated with Padmasambhava; they're situated less than 10km south of Menshi and accessible by road. Pilgrims immerse themselves in pools here before visiting the nearby monastery containing Padmasambhava's footprint and the cave that he used, and digging for small, pearl-like stones believed to have healing properties.

ACCOMMODATION AND EATING	MENSHI
Guesthouses There's no accommodation at the springs themselves, but a handful of very basic guesthouses in Menshi, with no washing facilities and a shared hole in the	ground for a toilet, will rustle up basic noodle-based meals for guests. Dorms **¥80**

Zanda and the Guge Kingdom

扎达, zhādá

These days just another arid army town, **ZANDA** (also known as **Tholing**; 托林, tuōlín) was once capital of the **Guge Kingdom**. Today only Tholing Monastery, some chortens, and ruins just outside town remain, but it is still the best place to base yourself to visit the Guge sites.

Guge Kingdom sites

古格王国, gǔgé wángguó • ¥200 including Tsaparang, Piyang, Tholing Monastery and five other sites

The major remains of the tenth-century **Kingdom of Guge** (pronounced to rhyme with "cougar"), where Buddhism survived while being eclipsed in other parts of Tibet, are the monastery of **Tholing** in Zanda; the crumbling ancient capital of **Tsaparang** (古格王国遗址, gǔgé wángguó yízhǐ), 20km to the west; and the cliff-top settlement of **Piyang** (皮央石窟群, píyāng shíkū qún), 30km to the north. The whole area – an incredible two-and-a-half-thousand square kilometres of sand-stone canyons, now protected as **Zanda Earth Forest National Park** – is littered with ancient caves dug out of cliff walls and crumbling ruins, some of which are around a thousand years old. Views from the edge of the park, the vast canyons in the foreground and the Himalayas behind, defy description.

ACCOMMODATION	ZANDA
Transportation Hotel 扎达运输宾馆, zhādá yùnshū bīnguǎn. ☎ 139 89973914. It's hardly the height of luxury, but the rooms here are of a decent size and	are kept clean enough. The big news, if you've just been sharing filthy communal toilets for the past week or two, is that rooms have private bathrooms. **¥350**

BEIJING OPERA

Contexts

History

As modern archeology gradually confirms ancient records of China's earliest times, it seems that, however far back you go, Chinese history is essentially the saga of the country's autocratic dynasties. Although this generalized view is inevitable in the brief account below, bear in mind that, while the concept of being Chinese has been around for over two thousand years, the closer you look, the less "China" seems to exist as an entity – right from the start, regionalism played an important role. And while concentrating on the great events, it's easy to forget that life for the ordinary people wavered between periods of stability, when writers, poets and artisans were at their most creative, and dire times of heavy taxation, war and famine. While the Cultural Revolution, ingrained corruption and clampdowns on political dissent may not be a good track record for the People's Republic, it's also true that since the 1980s – only yesterday in China's immense timescale – the quality of life for ordinary citizens has vastly improved.

Prehistory and the Three Dynasties

Chinese legends relate that the creator, **Pan Ku**, was born from the egg of chaos and grew to fill the space between Yin, the earth, and Yang, the heavens. When he died his body became the soil, rivers and rain, and his eyes became the sun and moon, while his parasites transformed into human beings. A pantheon of semidivine rulers known as the **Five Sovereigns** followed, inventing fire, the calendar, agriculture, silk-breeding and marriage. Later, a famous triumvirate included **Yao the Benevolent** who abdicated in favour of **Shu**. Shu toiled in the sun until his skin turned black and then he abdicated in favour of **Yu the Great**, the tamer of floods. Yu was said to be the founder of China's first dynasty, the **Xia**, which was reputed to have lasted 439 years until its last degenerate and corrupt king was overthrown by the **Shang** dynasty. The Shang was in turn succeeded by the **Zhou**, whose written court histories put an end

---

HISTORY TODAY: THE THREE DYNASTIES

Hubei Museum Wuhan (see p.417). A collection of relics from the Warring States Period.
Luoyang Museum Luoyang (see p.258). Luoyang was one of the largest cities in the world during the Three Dynasties; its wonderful museum is, accordingly, one of the best places to see treasure from those days.
The Tomb of Confucius Qufu (see p.305). Confucius was born in this small Shandong town, and his burial place sits just to the north in a pleasant, forest-like area.

4800 BC	21C–16C BC	16C–11C BC
First evidence of human settlement. Banpo in the Yellow River basin build Bronze Age town of Erlitou in Henan. Yin in Anyang boasts a rich and developed culture	Xia dynasty	Shang dynasty. First extant writing in China

to this legendary era. Together, the Xia, Shang and Zhou are generally known as the **Three Dynasties**.

As far as archeology is concerned, **Homo erectus** remains indicate that China was already broadly occupied by human ancestors well before modern mankind began to emerge 200,000 years ago. Excavations of more recent Stone Age sites show that agricultural communities based around the fertile Yellow River and Yangzi basins, such as **Banpo** in Shaanxi and **Homudu** in Zhejiang, were producing pottery and silk by 5000 BC. It was along the Yellow River, too, that solid evidence of the bronze-working Three Dynasties first came to light, with the discovery of a series of large rammed-earth palaces at **Erlitou** near Luoyang, now believed to have been the Xia capital in 2000 BC.

Little is known about the Xia, though their territory apparently encompassed Shaanxi, Henan and Hebei. The events of the subsequent Shang dynasty, however, were first documented just before the time of Christ by the historian **Sima Qian**. Shang society, based over much the same area as its predecessors and lasting from roughly 1750 BC to 1040 BC, had a king, a class system and a skilled **bronze technology** which permeated beyond the borders into Sichuan, and which produced the splendid vessels found in today's museums. Excavations on the site of Yin, the Shang capital, have found tombs stuffed with weapons, jade ornaments, traces of silk and sacrificial victims – indicating belief in **ancestor worship** and an afterlife. The Shang also practised divination by incising questions onto tortoiseshell or bone and then heating them to study the way in which the material cracked around the words. These **oracle bones** provide China's **earliest written records**, covering topics as diverse as rainfall, dreams and ancestral curses.

Around 1040 BC a northern tribe, the **Zhou**, overthrew the Shang, expanded their kingdom west of the Yellow River into Shaanxi and set up a capital at Xi'an. Adopting many Shang customs, the Zhou also introduced the doctrine of the **Mandate of Heaven**, a belief that heaven grants ruling authority to leaders who are strong and wise, and takes it from those who aren't – a justification of successful rebellion that remains integral to the Chinese political perspective. The Zhou consequently styled themselves "Sons of Heaven" and ruled through a hierarchy of vassal lords, whose growing independence led to the gradual dissolution of the state from around 600 BC.

The decline of the Zhou

Driven to a new capital at Luoyang, later Zhou rulers exercised only a symbolic role; real power was fought over by some two hundred city-states and kingdoms during the four hundred years known as the **Spring and Autumn** and the **Warring States** periods. This time of violence was also an era of vitality and change, with the

---

HISTORY TODAY: THE QIN

The Terracotta Army Xi'an (see p.212). Standing silently in their thousands, these famed clay warriors rank among China's most important historical sights.

The Tomb of Qin Shi Huang Xi'an (see p.214). The unexcavated mound that the terracotta soldiers were built to protect.

11C–771 BC	770–476 BC	457–221 BC
Zhou dynasty. Concept of Mandate of Heaven introduced	Spring and Autumn period. Kong Fuzi or Confucius (c.500 BC) teaches a philosophy of adherence to ritual and propriety	Warring States Period. The Great Wall "completed"

HISTORY TODAY: THE HAN

Famen Temple Shaanxi (see p.216). 120km west of Xi'an, this stunning temple houses the legendary finger of the Buddha.

Jingzhou Museum Hubei (see p.421). A superb collection of Western Han tomb remains.

Mao Ling and Qian Ling Shaanxi (see p.215). The resting places of two Han-dynasty emperors, respectively 40km and 80km west of Xi'an.

Shaanxi Museum Xi'an (see p.202). Look for some great Han-dynasty funerary ceramics, most notably a clutch of model houses.

---

rise of the ethics of **Confucianism** (see p.942) and **Taoism** (see p.943). As the warring states rubbed up against one another, agriculture and irrigation, trade, transport and diplomacy were all galvanized; iron was first smelted for weapons and tools, and great discoveries were made in medicine, astronomy and mathematics. Three hundred years of war and annexation reduced the competitors to seven states, whose territories, collectively known as Zhong Guo, the **Middle Kingdom** (China's present name in Mandarin), had now expanded west into Sichuan, south to Hunan and north to the Mongolian border.

The Qin dynasty (221–207 BC)

The Warring States Period came to an end in 221 BC, when the **Qin** armies overran the last opposition and united China as a single centralized state for the first time, introducing systems of currency and writing that were to last two millennia. The rule of China's first emperor, **Qin Shi Huang**, was absolute and harsh, his advisers favouring the philosophy of **Legalism** – the idea that mankind is inherently bad, and needs to be kept in line by draconian punishments. Ancient literature and historical records were destroyed and peasants were forced off their land to work as labourers on massive construction projects, including his tomb outside Xi'an (guarded by the famous **Terracotta Army**) and an early version of the **Great Wall**. Determined to rule the entire known world, Qin Shi Huang gradually pushed his armies west and southeast beyond the Middle Kingdom. But when he died in 210 BC the provinces rose in revolt, and his heirs proved to lack the authority that had held his empire together.

The Han dynasty (206 BC–220 AD)

In 206 BC the rebel warlord **Liu Bang** took Xi'an and founded the **Han dynasty**. Lasting some four hundred years and larger at its height than contemporary imperial Rome, the Han was China's first great empire, one that experienced a flowering of culture and a major impetus to push out frontiers. In doing so it defined the national identity to such an extent that the main body of China's population still style themselves "**Han Chinese**".

While Liu Bang maintained the Qin model of central government, to prevent others from repeating his own military takeover he handed out large chunks of land to trustworthy relatives. This secured a period of stability, with effective taxation financing

221–207 BC

Qin dynasty. Emperor Qin Shi Huang founds first centralized empire. Terracotta Army guard Qin's tomb

206 BC–220 AD

Han dynasty. Han emperors bring stability and great advances in trade; leave Han tombs near Xi'an. Confucianism and Buddhism ascendant. Silk Road opens up first trade with Central Asia

a growing civil service and the construction of a huge and cosmopolitan capital, **Chang'an**, at today's Xi'an. Growing revenue also refuelled the expansionist policies of a subsequent ruler, **Wu**. From 135 to 90 BC he extended his lines of defence well into Xinjiang and Yunnan, opening up the **Silk Road** for trade in tea, spices and silk with India, west Asia and Rome. At home Wu stressed the Confucian model for his growing civil service, beginning a two-thousand-year institution of Confucianism in government offices.

By 9 AD, however, the empire's resources and supply lines were overstretched: increased taxation led to unrest, and the ruling house was split by political intrigue. Following fifteen years of civil war, the dynasty re-formed as the **Eastern Han** at a new capital, Luoyang. But the Han had passed their peak, and were unable to stem the civil strife caused by local authorities setting themselves up as semi-independent rulers. Despite everything, Confucianism's ideology of a centralized universal order had crystallized imperial authority; and **Buddhism**, introduced into the country from India, began to enrich life, especially in the fine arts and literature, while also being absorbed and changed by native beliefs.

The Three Kingdoms to the Sui (220–581)

Nearly four hundred years separate the collapse of the Han in about 220 AD from the return of unity under the Sui in 589. However, although China was under a single government for only about fifty years of that time, the idea of a unified empire was never forgotten.

From 200 AD the three states of **Wei**, **Wu** and **Shu** struggled for supremacy in a complex war, later immortalized in the saga *Romance of the Three Kingdoms* (see box, p.396), that ruined central China and encouraged mass migrations southwards. The following centuries saw China's regionalism become entrenched: the **Southern Empire** suffered weak and short-lived dynasties, but still saw prosperity and economic growth, while the capital at **Nanjing** became a thriving trading and cultural centre. Meanwhile, with the borders unprotected, the north was invaded in 386 by the **Tobas**, who established the **Northern Wei dynasty**: at their first capital, **Datong**, the Tobas created a wonderful series of Buddhist carvings, but in 534 their empire fell apart.

The period was a dark age of war, violence and genocide, but it was also a richly formative one, and when the dust had settled, a very different society had emerged. For much of this time, many areas produced sufficient **food surpluses** to support a rich

---

HISTORY TODAY: THE THREE KINGDOMS TO THE SUI

The Longmen Caves Henan (see p.259). Just south of Luoyang, these caves feature some imposingly monumental Buddhist art.

The Mogao Caves Gansu (see p.826). Southeast of Dunhuang, these caves are remote and quite spectacular; the earliest were hewn out during the Northern Wei.

The Yungang Caves Shanxi (see p.242). A series of caves built just before the Longmen ones, containing art that's every bit as beautiful.

Wuhou Ci Chengdu (see p.735). The burial place of Liu Bei, a Three Kingdoms emperor, and a memorial to his chief strategist, Zhuge Liang.

220–280

Three Kingdoms period; influence of Buddhist India and Central Asia enlivens a Dark Age

265–420

Jin dynasty. Northern barbarians absorbed into Chinese culture

and leisured ruling class in the cities and the countryside, as well as large armies and burgeoning Buddhist communities. So culture developed, literature flourished, and calligraphy and sculpture – especially Buddhist carvings, all enriched by Indian and Central Asian elements – reached new levels.

The Sui (581–618)

After grabbing power from his regent in 581, General **Yang Jian** unified the fragmented northern states, conquered southern China and founded the **Sui dynasty**. Yang Jian (**Emperor Wen**) was an active ruler who simplified and strengthened the bureaucracy, brought in a new legal code, recentralized civil and military authority and made tax collection more efficient. Near Xi'an, his architects designed a new capital, **Da Xing Cheng** (City of Great Prosperity), with an outer wall over 35km round – the largest city in the world at that time.

Following Wen's death in 604, **Yang Di** elbowed his elder brother out to become emperor. Yang encouraged a revival of Confucian learning but is generally remembered for his use of forced labour to complete vast engineering projects – half the total workforce of five million died during the construction of the 2000km **Grand Canal**, built to transport produce from the southern Yangzi to his capital at Xi'an. Yang was assassinated in 618 after popular hatred inspired a military revolt.

Medieval China (618–1271)

The seventh century marks the beginning of the medieval period of Chinese history. This was the age in which Chinese culture reached its peak, a time of experimentation in literature, art, music and agriculture, and one which unified seemingly incompatible elements.

Tang dynasty

Li Yuan consolidated his new **Tang dynasty** by spending the rest of his eight-year reign eliminating rivals. Under his son **Tai Zong**, Tang China broadened its horizons: the Turkic peoples of the Northwest were crushed, the Tibetans brought to heel and relations established with Byzantium. China kept open house for traders and travellers of all races and creeds, who settled in the mercantile cities of Yangzhou and Guangzhou, bringing with them their religions, especially **Islam**, and influencing the arts, cookery, fashion and entertainment. Chinese goods flowed out to India, Persia, the Near East and many other countries, and China's language and religion gained currency in Japan and Korea. At home, **Buddhism** remained the all-pervading foreign influence, with Chinese pilgrims travelling widely in India. The best known of these, **Xuanzang** (see box, p.844), set off in 629 and returned after sixteen years in India with a mass of Buddhist sutras, adding greatly to China's storehouse of knowledge.

Within a decade after Tai Zong's death in 649, China's only empress, **Wu Zetian**, had consolidated the Tang empire's direct influence on neighbouring nations. Though widely unpopular, Wu Zetian was a great patron of Buddhism, commissioning the famous Longmen carvings outside Luoyang; she also created a

420–581

581–618

Southern and Northern dynasties: rapid succession of short-lived dynasties brings disunity. Earliest Longmen caves near Luoyang

Sui dynasty. Centralization and growth under Wen Di. Extension and strengthening of Great Wall; digging of Grand Canal

civil service selected on merit rather than birth. Her successor, **Xuan Zong**, began well in 712, but his later infatuation with the beautiful concubine **Yang Guifei** led to the **An Lushan rebellion** of 755, his flight to Sichuan and Yang's ignominious death at the hands of his mutinying army. Xuan Zong's son, **Su Zong**, enlisted the help of Tibetan and Uyghur forces, and recaptured Xi'an from the rebels; but though the court was re-established, it had lost its authority, and real power was once again shifting to the provinces.

Five Dynasties and Ten Kingdoms

The following two hundred years saw the country split into regional alliances. From 907 to 960, all the successive **Five Dynasties** were too short-lived to be effective. China's northern defences were permanently weakened, while her economic dependence on the south increased and the dispersal of power brought social changes. The traditional elite whose fortunes were tied to the dynasty gave way to a military and merchant class who bought land to acquire status, alongside a professional ruling class selected by examination. In the south, the **Ten Kingdoms** (some existing side by side) managed to retain what was left of the Tang civilization, their greater stability and economic prosperity sustaining a relatively high cultural level.

The Song

Eventually, in 960, a disaffected army in the north put a successful general, **Song Tai Zu**, on the throne. His new ruling house, known as the **Northern Song**, made its capital at **Kaifeng** in the Yellow River basin, well placed at the head of the Grand Canal for transport to supply its million people with grain from the south. By skilled politicking rather than military might, the new dynasty re-established civilian primacy. However, northern China was occupied by the **Jin** in 1115, who pushed the imperial court south to **Hangzhou** where, guarded by the Yangzi River, their culture continued to flourish from 1126 as the **Southern Song**. Developments during their 150-year dynasty included gunpowder, the magnetic compass, fine porcelain and moveable-type printing. In due course, however, the Song were overrun by their aggressive northern "barbarian" neighbours, who launched the thirteenth-century **Mongol Invasion**.

HISTORY TODAY: TANG TO SONG

Baoding Shan Dazu (see p.760). A series of delightful carvings, created between 1179 and 1245.
Dafo Leshan (see p.749). Built from 713, and still one of the world's largest Buddhist sculptures after all these years.
Kaifeng Henan (see p.270). Pleasant city which maintains a small array of Song-dynasty sights.
Kaiyuan Temple Quanzhou (see p.471). A gigantic temple founded in 686.
Mausoleums of the Western Xia Ningxia (see p.225). Monuments to the nine kings of the Xi Xia kingdom, just west of Yinchuan.
The Small and Big Goose pagodas Xi'an (see p.202 & p.203). Two splendid towers just to the south of the walled city.
Suzhou Jiangsu (see p.318). Some of this city's many enchanting gardens date back to the Song.

618–907	907–960	960–1271
Tang dynasty. Arts and literature reach their most developed stage. Great Buddha at Leshan completed	Five dynasties. Decline of culture and the northern defences. Cliff sculptures of Dazu	Song dynasties. Consolidation of the lesser kingdoms

HISTORY TODAY: THE MING
Ancient Observatory Beijing (see p.88). An underrated sight, this old observatory boasts a clutch of beautiful Ming-dynasty astrological instruments.
Chengde Hebei (see p.147). A wonderful small city, featuring an old imperial retreat, and a series of stunning temples.
The Forbidden City Beijing (see p.70). One of China's most famous tourist sights, this old imperial stomping ground goes back to the Mongol era, but its present structure is essentially Ming.
The Great Wall Beijing (see p.119). Another Chinese icon, the wall also predates the Ming, but it's work from this period that's most visible.
The Imperial Palace Shenyang (see p.171). A miniature Forbidden City, constructed by the Mongols before their takeover of the country.
The Jinjiang Princes' Palace Guilin (see p.612). Another mini-Forbidden City, though actually 34 years older than the one in Beijing.
The Ming Tombs Nanjing (see p.316). The resting place of the first Ming emperor.
The Temple of Heaven Beijing (see p.89). Justly regarded as the epitome of Ming design, the centre of annual agricultural rituals.
Yixian Anhui (see p.407). A collection of antique villages dating back to the Ming.

The Yuan dynasty (1271–1368)

In fact, Mongolian influence had first penetrated China in the eleventh century, when the Song emperors paid tribute to separate Mongolian states to keep their armies from invading. These individual fiefdoms were unified by **Genghis Khan** in 1206 to form an immensely powerful army, which swiftly embarked upon the conquest of northern China. By 1271 the **Yuan dynasty** was on the Chinese throne at Khanbalik – modern **Beijing** – with **Kublai Khan**, Genghis Khan's grandson, at the head of an empire that stretched way beyond the borders of China. The country was thrown open to foreign travellers, traders and missionaries; the Grand Canal was extended; while in Beijing the Palace of All Tranquillities was built inside a new city wall, later known as the **Forbidden City**. Descriptions of much of this were brought back to Europe by **Marco Polo**, who recorded his impressions of Yuan lifestyle and treasures after he'd served in the government of Kublai Khan.

The Yuan only retained control over all China until 1368. Their power was ultimately sapped by the combination of becoming too Chinese for their northern brethren to tolerate, and too aloof from the Chinese to assimilate. After northern tribes had rebelled, and famine and disastrous floods brought a series of uprisings in China, a monk-turned-bandit-leader from the south, **Zhu Yuanzhang**, seized the throne from the last boy emperor of the Yuan in 1368.

The Ming dynasty (1368–1644)

Taking the name **Hong Wu**, Zhu proclaimed himself the first emperor of the **Ming dynasty**, with Nanjing as his capital. Zhu's extreme despotism culminated in two appalling purges in which thousands of civil servants and literati died, and he initiated a course of **isolationism** from the outside world which lasted throughout the Ming and Qing eras. Nowhere is this more apparent than in the Ming construction of the

1271–1368

1368–1644

Yuan dynasty. Genghis Khan invades. Trade with Europe develops under Kublai Khan. Forbidden City built. Marco Polo visits China 1273–92

Ming dynasty. Imperial investigative fleet under Admiral Zheng He reaches Africa. Later isolationist policies restrict contact with rest of world

current Great Wall, a grandiose but futile attempt to stem the invasion of northern tribes into China, built in the fifteenth century as military might and diplomacy began to break down.

Yet the period also produced fine artistic accomplishments, particularly **porcelain** from the imperial kilns at Jingdezhen. Nor were the Ming rulers entirely isolationist. During the reign of **Yongle**, Zhu's 26th son, the imperial navy (commanded by the Muslim eunuch, Admiral **Zheng He**) ranged right across the Indian Ocean as far as the east coast of Africa on a fact-finding mission. But stagnation set in after Yongle's death in 1424, and the maritime missions were cancelled as being incompatible with Confucian values, which held contempt for foreigners. Thus the initiative for world trade and exploration passed into the hands of the Europeans, with the great period of world voyages by Columbus, Magellan and Vasco da Gama. In 1514, **Portuguese** vessels appeared in the Pearl River at Guangzhou (Canton) and Portugal was allowed to colonize nearby **Macau** in 1557. Although all dealings with foreigners were officially despised by the imperial court, trade flourished as Chinese merchants and officials were eager to milk the profits.

In later years, a succession of less able Ming rulers allowed power to slip. By the early seventeenth century, frontier defences had fallen into decay, and the **Manchu tribes** in the north were already across the Great Wall. A series of uprisings against the Ming began in 1627, and when rebel forces led by **Li Zicheng** managed to break into the capital in 1644, the last Ming emperor fled from his palace and hanged himself – an ignoble end to a three-hundred-year-old dynasty.

The Qing dynasty (1644–1911)

The Manchus weren't slow to turn internal dissent to their advantage. Sweeping down on Beijing, they threw out Li Zicheng's army, claimed the capital as their own and founded the **Qing dynasty**. It took a further twenty years to capture the south of the country, but on its capitulation China was once again under foreign rule. The Qing initially did little to assimilate domestic culture, ruling as separate overlords. Manchu became the official language, the Chinese were obliged to wear the Manchu **pigtail**, and intermarriage between a Manchu and a Chinese was strictly forbidden. Under the Qing dynasty the distant areas of Inner and Outer Mongolia, Tibet and Turkestan were fully incorporated into the Chinese empire, uniting the Chinese world to a greater extent than during the Tang period.

Three outstanding early Qing emperors brought an infusion of new blood and vigour to government. **Kangxi**, who began his 61-year reign in 1654 at the age of six, assiduously cultivated his image as the Son of Heaven by making royal progresses throughout the country. His fourth son, the emperor **Yungzheng** (1678–1735), ruled over what is considered one of the most efficient and least corrupt administrations ever enjoyed by China. This was inherited by **Qianlong** (1711–99), whose reign saw China's frontiers widely extended and the economy stimulated by peace and prosperity. In 1750 the nation was perhaps at its apex, one of the strongest, wealthiest and most powerful countries in the world.

During the late eighteenth century, however, problems began to increase. Settled society had produced a **population explosion**, causing a land shortage. This in turn saw

1644	Mid- to late 17C	Late 18C
Qing dynasty begins. Manchus gain control over China and extend its boundaries	Potala Palace in Lhasa rebuilt by Fifth Dalai Lama	East India Company monopolizes trade with Britain. Summer Palace in Beijing completed

trouble flaring as migrants from central China tried to settle the remoter western provinces, dispossessing the original inhabitants. Meanwhile, Portuguese traders in Guangzhou had been joined by the British **East India Company**, who were eager to be granted a trade monopoly. Convinced of their own superiority, however, China's immensely rich and powerful rulers had no desire to deal directly with foreigners. When **Lord Macartney** arrived in 1793 to propose a political and trade treaty between Britain and China, he found that the emperor totally rejected any idea of alliance with one who, according to Chinese ideas, was a subordinate.

The Opium Wars

Foiled in their attempts at official negotiations with the Qing court, the East India Company decided to take matters into their own hands and create a clandestine market in China for Western goods. Instead of silver, they began to pay for tea and silk with **opium**, cheaply imported from India. As demand escalated during the early nineteenth century, China's trade surplus became a deficit, as silver drained out of the country to pay for the drug. The emperor intervened in 1840 by ordering the confiscation and destruction of over twenty thousand chests of opium – the start of the first **Opium War**. After two years of British gunboats shelling coastal ports, the Chinese were forced to sign the **Treaty of Nanking**, whose humiliating terms included a huge indemnity, the opening of new ports to foreign trade, and the **cession of Hong Kong**. The war was later reignited and, in 1860, Britain – joined by other Western powers – destroyed Beijing's Summer Palace and forced further concessions on the country.

The Taiping Uprising

The Opium Wars brought anti-Manchu feeling, economic hardship and internal **rebellions**. While serious unrest occurred in Guizhou, Gansu and Yunnan, the most widespread revolt was the **Taiping Uprising**, which stormed through central China in the 1850s to occupy much of the rich Yangzi Valley. Having captured Nanjing as their "Heavenly Capital", the Taipings began to make military forays towards Beijing, and European powers decided to step in, worried that the Taipings' antiforeign government might take control of the country. With their support, Qing troops defeated the Taipings in 1864, leaving twenty million people dead and five provinces in ruins.

HISTORY TODAY: THE QING

Pingyao Shanxi (see p.251). Perhaps the most convincing of China's many walled cities, and justifiably popular with international tourists.

The Potala Palace Lhasa (see p.884). The most recognizable symbol of Tibet, and the traditional seat of power for the Dalai Lama.

The Puppet Emperor's Palace Changchun (see p.176). A forlorn full-stop to China's rich dynastic history, this is where the last emperor lived during the Japanese annexation of Manchuria.

The Summer Palace Beijing (see p.95). Though it dates back to the eleventh century, this park-like area is inextricably connected to the follies of the Dowager Empress Cixi.

St Sofia's Cathedral Harbin (see p.184). China's most beautiful Christian place of worship.

1839–62	1851–64	1899
Opium Wars. As part of the surrender settlement, Hong Kong is ceded to Britain	Taiping Uprising. Conservative policies of Dowager Empress Cixi allow foreign powers to take control of China's industry	Boxer Rebellion

The late nineteenth century

It was during the Taiping Uprising that the **Empress Dowager Wu Cixi** first took control of the country, ruling from behind various emperors from 1861 until 1908. Certain that reform would weaken the Qings' grasp on power, she pursued a deep conservatism at a time when China needed desperately to overhaul its political and economic structure. Her stance saw increased foreign ownership of industry, rising Christian missionary activity that undermined traditional society, and the disintegration of China's **colonial empire**. France took the former vassal states of Laos, Cambodia and Vietnam in 1883–85; Britain gained Myanmar (Burma); and **Tibet**, which had nominally been under China's control since Tang times, began to assert its independence. Even worse, a failed military foray into Korea in 1894 saw China lose control of **Taiwan** to Japan, while a Russian-built rail line into the northeast effectively gave Russia control of Manchuria.

The Boxer Movement

By the late 1890s, popular antiforeign feeling crystallized into the **Boxer Rebellion**, a quasi-spiritual martial arts movement that set itself loose to slaughter missionaries and Christian converts. During the summer of 1900 the Boxers took control of Beijing, besieging the foreign legation compound, though they were routed when an international relief force arrived on August 14. In the massacre, looting and confusion which followed, Cixi and the emperor disguised themselves as peasants and fled to Xi'an in a cart, leaving her ministers to negotiate a peace.

Though they clung feebly on for another decade, this was the end of the Qing, and internal movements to dismantle the dynastic system and build a new China proliferated. The most influential of these was the **Tong Meng Hui** society, founded in 1905 in Japan by the exile **Sun Yatsen**, a doctor from a wealthy Guangdong family. Cixi died three years later, and, in 1911, opposition to proposals to nationalize railways drew events to a head in Wuchang, Hubei province, igniting a popular uprising which finally toppled the dynasty. As two thousand years of dynastic succession ended, Sun Yatsen returned to China to take the lead in the provisional **Republican Government** at Nanjing.

From republic to communism

Almost immediately the new republic was in trouble. Though a **parliament** was duly elected in 1913, northern China was controlled by the former leader of the Imperial Army, **Yuan Shikai**. Faced with a choice between probable civil war and relinquishing his presidency at the head of the newly formed Nationalist People's Party – the **Guomindang** – Sun Yatsen stepped down. Yuan promptly dismissed the government, forced Sun into renewed exile, and attempted to establish a new dynasty. But his plans were stalled by his generals, who wanted private fiefdoms of their own, and Yuan's sudden death in 1916 marked the last time in 34 years that China would be united under a single authority. As civil war erupted, Sun Yatsen returned once more, this time to found a southern Guomindang government.

Thus divided, China was unable to stem the increasingly bold territorial incursions made by Japan and other colonial powers as a result of **World War I**. Siding with the

1911	1921	1927
End of imperial China. Sun Yatsen becomes leader of the Republic	Chinese Communist Party founded in Beijing	Chiang Kai-shek orders massacre of Communists in Shanghai. Mao Zedong organizes first peasant-worker army

Allies, Japan had claimed the German port of Qingdao and all German shipping and industry in the Shangdong Peninsula on the outbreak of war, and in 1915 presented China with **Twenty-One Demands**, many of which Yuan Shikai, under threat of a Japanese invasion, was forced to accept. After the war, hopes that the 1919 **Treaty of Versailles** would end Japanese aggression (as well as the unequal treaties and foreign concessions) were dashed when the Western powers, who had already signed secret pacts with Japan, confirmed Japan's rights in China. This ignited the antiforeign **May 4 Movement**, a series of demonstrations and riots which slowly forced the return of the foreign concession areas to Chinese control.

The rise of the CCP
Against this background, the **Chinese Communist Party** (**CCP**) was formed in Shanghai in 1921; its leadership included the young **Mao Zedong** and **Zhou Enlai**. Though the CCP initially listened to its Russian advisers and supported the Guomindang in its military campaigns against the northern warlords, this alliance became untenable after Sun Yatsen died in 1925 and his brother-in-law **Chiang Kai-shek** took over the Guomindang. Chiang was a staunch nationalist who had no time for the CCP or its plans to end China's class divisions. In 1927, a general strike organized by left-wing elements in Shanghai was brutally suppressed by Chiang's henchmen: around five thousand striking workers were massacred, including much of the original Communist hierarchy. Those who escaped the purge regrouped in remote areas across the country, principally at **Jinggang Shan** in Jiangxi province, under the leadership of Mao Zedong.

Mao Zedong, the Red Army and the Long March
Son of a well-off Hunanese farmer, **Mao** believed social reform lay in the hands of the peasants who still had few rights and no power base. Drawing upon the analyses of Karl Marx, Mao argued that a mass armed rebellion was the only way the old order could be replaced, and organized what was later to be called the **Autumn Harvest Uprising** in Changsha. Moving with other Communist forces to the Hunan–Jiangxi border in 1927, this **Red Army** of peasants, miners and Guomindang deserters achieved unexpected successes against the Nationalist troops sent against them until **Li Lisan**, the overall Communist leader, ordered Mao out of his mountain base to attack the cities. After the ensuing open assaults against the superior Guomindang forces proved disastrous, Chiang Kai-shek mobilized half a million troops, and encircled Jinggang Shan with a ring of concrete block-houses and barbed-wire entanglements.

Forced to choose between fight or flight, in October 1934 Mao organized eighty thousand troops in an epic 9500km retreat which became known as the **Long March**. By the time they reached safety in **Yan'an** in Shaanxi province a year later, the Communists had lost three-quarters of their followers to the rigours of the trip, but had also started their path towards victory: Mao had become undisputed leader of the CCP at the **Zunyi Conference**, severing the Party from its Russian advisers.

Japanese invasion and the United Front
Meanwhile, **Japan** had taken over Chinese Manchuria in 1933 and installed Pu Yi (last emperor of the Qing dynasty) as puppet leader. The Japanese were obviously preparing to invade eastern China, and Mao wrote to Chiang Kai-shek advocating an end to civil

1932	1936–41	1945
Japan invades Manchuria	The Nationalist Guomindang and the People's Liberation Army form the United Front against the Japanese	Surrender of Japan. Civil war between the Guomindang and the People's Liberation Army

war and a **United Front** against the threat. Chiang's response was to move his Manchurian armies, under **Zhang Xueliang**, down to finish off the Reds in Shaanxi. Zhang, however, saw an alliance as the only way to evict the Japanese from his homeland, and so secretly entered into an agreement with the Communists. On December 12, 1936, Chiang was kidnapped by his own troops and forced to sign his assent to the Communist–Nationalist United Front, an alliance to fight the Japanese.

Full-scale war broke out in July 1937 when the Japanese attacked Beijing, and by the end of the year they controlled most of eastern China. With a capital-in-occupation at Nanjing, the Japanese concentrated their efforts on routing the GMD, leaving a vacuum in the north that was filled by the Communists, establishing what amounted to stable government of a hundred million people across the North China Plain.

The outbreak of war in Europe in September 1939 soon had repercussions in China. Nazi Germany stopped supplying the weaponry upon which the GMD relied, while the bombing of Pearl Harbor two years later put an end to all military aid from the United States to Japan. With the country's heavy industry in Japanese hands, China's United Front government, having withdrawn to **Chongqing** in Sichuan province, became dependent on supplies flown over the Himalayas by the Americans and British.

The end of the war and the Communist victory

By the time the two atom bombs ended the Japanese empire and World War II in 1945, the Red Army was close on a million strong, with a widespread following throughout the country. It was not, however, that secure. Predictably enough, the US sided with Chiang Kai-shek and the GMD; more surprisingly, so did the Soviet Union – Stalin believed that with American aid, the GMD would easily destroy the CCP. All the same, **peace negotiations** between the Nationalist and Communist sides were brokered by the US in Chongqing, where Chiang Kai-shek refused to admit the CCP into government, knowing that its policies were uncontrollable while the Red Army still existed. For their part, it was evident to the CCP that without an army, they were nothing.

In 1948 the Communists' newly named **People's Liberation Army** (**PLA**) rose against the GMD, decisively trouncing them that winter at the massive battle of **Huai Hai** in Anhui province. With Shanghai about to fall before the PLA in early 1949, Chiang Kai-shek packed the country's entire gold reserves into a plane and took off for **Taiwan** to form the **Republic of China**. Here he was to remain until his death in 1975, forlornly waiting to liberate the mainland with the two million troops and refugees who later joined him. Mopping-up operations against mainland pockets of GMD resistance would continue for several years, but in October 1949 Mao was able to proclaim the formation of the **People's Republic of China** in Beijing. The world's most populous nation was now Communist.

The People's Republic under Mao

With the country laid waste by over a century of economic mismanagement and war, massive problems faced the new republic. By the mid-1950s, however, all industry had

1949	1957
Communist takeover. Chiang Kai-shek flees to Taiwan. The newly proclaimed People's Republic of China supports North Korea in the Korean War	The Hundred Flowers campaign unsuccessfully attempts liberalization

been nationalized and output was back at prewar levels, while, for the first time in Chinese history, land was handed over to the peasants as their own. A million former landlords were executed, while others were enrolled in "**criticism and self-criticism**" classes, a traumatic re-education designed to prevent elitism or bourgeois deviancy from contaminating the revolutionary spirit.

With all the difficulties on the home front, the government could well have done without the distraction of the **Korean War**. After Communist North Korea invaded the south in 1950, US forces intervened on behalf of the south and, despite warnings from Zhou Enlai, continued through to Chinese territory. China declared war in June, and sent a million troops to push the Americans back to the 38th parallel and force peace negotiations. As a boost for the morale of the new nation, the campaign could not have been better timed. Meanwhile, China's far western borders were seen to be threatened by an uprising in **Tibet**, and Chinese troops were sent there in 1951, swiftly occupying the entire country and instituting de facto Chinese rule. Eight years later, a failed coup by Tibetan monks against the occupation saw a massive clampdown on religion, and the flight of the **Dalai Lama** and his followers to Nepal.

The Hundred Flowers

By 1956 there were signs that the euphoria driving the country was slowing. Mao – whose principles held that constant struggle was part of existence, and thus that acceptance of the status quo was in itself a bad thing – felt that both government and industry needed to be prodded back into gear. In 1957 he decided to loosen restrictions on public expression, and following the slogan "Let a hundred flowers bloom, and a hundred schools of thought contend", people were encouraged to voice their complaints. The plan backfired: instead of picking on inefficient officials as Mao had hoped, the **Hundred Flowers** campaign resulted in attacks on the Communist system itself. As Mao was never one to take personal criticism lightly, those who had spoken out found themselves victims of an **anti-rightist** campaign, confined to jail or undergoing heavy bouts of "re-education". From this point on, intellectuals as a group were mistrusted and scrutinized.

The Great Leap Forward

Agriculture and industry were next to receive a shake-up. In August 1958 it was announced that all farmland was to be pooled into 24,000 self-governing **communes**, with the aim of turning small-scale farming units into hyperefficient agricultural areas. Industry was to be fired into activity by the co-option of seasonally employed workers, who would construct heavy industrial plants, dig canals and drain marshes. Propaganda campaigns promised eternal wellbeing in return for initial austerity; in a single **Great Leap Forward**, China would match British industrial output in ten years.

From the outset, the Great Leap Forward was a disaster. Having been given their land, the peasants now found themselves losing it once more, and were not eager to work in huge units. This, combined with the problem of ill-trained commune management, led to a slump in agricultural and industrial production. In the face of a stream of ridiculous **quotas** supplied by Beijing – one campaign required that all communes must produce steel, regardless of the availability of raw materials – no one

1958	1964	1966–68
Agricultural and industrial reform in the shape of the commune system and the Great Leap Forward. Widespread famine results	China explodes its first atomic weapon	In the Cultural Revolution, Red Guards purge anti-Maoist elements along with "ideologically unsound" art and architecture

had time to tend the fields. The 1959 and 1960 harvests both failed, and millions starved. As if this wasn't enough, a thaw in US–USSR relations in 1960 saw the Soviet Union stopping all aid to China.

With the economy in tatters, the commune policy was abandoned, but the incident had ruined Mao's reputation and set members of the Communist Party Central Committee against his policies. One critic was **Deng Xiaoping**, who had diffused the effects of commune policy by creating a limited free-market economy among the country's traders. Behind this doctrine of material incentives for workers was a large bureaucracy over which Mao held little political sway.

The Cultural Revolution

Mao sought to regain his authority. Using a campaign created by Communist Party Vice-Chairman **Lin Biao**, he began in 1964 to orchestrate the youth of China against his moderate opponents in what became known as the **Great Proletarian Cultural Revolution**. Under Mao's guidance, the movement spread in 1966 to Beijing University, where the students organized themselves into a political militia – the **Red Guard** – and within weeks were moving out onto the streets.

The enemies of the Red Guard were the **Four Olds**: old ideas, old culture, old customs and old habits. Brandishing copies of the *Quotations of Chairman Mao Tsetung* (the famous **Little Red Book**), the Red Guard attacked anything redolent of capitalism, religion or foreign influence. Academics were assaulted, books were burned, temples and ancient monuments desecrated. Shops selling anything remotely Western were destroyed along with the gardens of the "decadent bourgeoisie". As under the commune system, quotas were set, this time for unearthing and turning in the "Rightists", "Revisionists" and "Capitalist Roaders" corrupting Communist society. Officials who failed to fill their quotas were likely to fall victim themselves, as were those who failed to destroy property or denounce others enthusiastically enough. Offenders were paraded through the streets wearing placards carrying humiliating slogans; tens of thousands were humiliated, beaten to death or driven to suicide. On August 5, 1966, Mao proclaimed that reactionaries had reached the highest levels of the CCP: Deng Xiaoping and his followers were dismissed from their posts and imprisoned, condemned to wait on tables at a Party canteen, or given menial jobs.

Meanwhile, the violence was getting completely out of control, with Red Guard factions attacking foreign embassies and even turning on each other. In August 1967 Mao ordered the arrest of several Red Guard leaders and the surrender of all weapons to the army, but was too late to stop nationwide street fighting, which was halted only after the military stormed the Guard's university strongholds. To clear them out of the way, millions of Red Guards were rounded up and shipped off into the countryside, ostensibly to reinforce the Communist message among the rural community.

Ping-pong diplomacy

The US, its foreign policy determined by business and political interests that stood to gain from the collapse of communism, had continued to support Chiang Kai-shek's Guomindang in Taiwan during the postwar period, while also stirring up paranoia over the possibility of a Sino-Soviet pact. After China exploded its first **atomic bomb** in 1964, however, the US began to tread a more pragmatic path. In

1971	1972	1976
People's Republic replaces Taiwan at the United Nations	US president Nixon visits Beijing	The Tian'anmen Incident reveals public support for moderate Deng Xiaoping. Mao Zedong dies, and the Gang of Four are arrested shortly afterwards

1970, envoy Henry Kissinger opened communications between the two countries, cultural and sporting links were formed (the latter gave rise to the phrase "**ping-pong diplomacy**"), and in 1971 the People's Republic became the official representative at the UN of the nation called China, displacing Taiwan. The following year US president **Richard Nixon** was walking on the Great Wall and holding talks with Mao, trade restrictions were lifted and China began commerce with the West. The "bamboo curtain" had parted, and the damage caused by the Cultural Revolution began slowly to be repaired.

The Gang of Four

This new attitude of realistic reform derived from the moderate wing of the Communist Party, headed by Premier Zhou Enlai – seen as a voice of reason – and his protégé Deng Xiaoping, now in control of the day-to-day running of the Communist Party Central Committee. Zhou's tact had given him a charmed political existence which for fifty years kept him at Mao's side despite policy disagreements. But with Zhou's death early in 1976, the reform movement immediately succumbed to the **Gang of Four**, who, led by Mao's third wife **Jiang Qing**, had become the radical mouthpiece of an increasingly absent Mao. In early April, at the time of the **Qing Ming** festival commemorating the dead, the Heroes Monument in Beijing's Tian'anmen Square was filled with wreaths in memory of Zhou. On April 5 radicals removed the wreaths and moderate supporters flooded into the square in protest; a riot broke out and hundreds were attacked and arrested. The obvious scapegoat for what became known as the **Tian'anmen Incident**, Deng Xiaoping, was publicly discredited and thrown out of office for a second time.

The death of Mao

In July 1976 the catastrophic **Tangshan earthquake**, centred on Hebei province, killed half a million people. The Chinese hold that natural disasters always foreshadow great events, and no one was too surprised when Mao himself died on September 9. Deprived of their figurehead, and with memories of the Cultural Revolution clear in everyone's mind, Jiang Qing and the other members of the Gang of Four were arrested. Deng returned to the political scene for the third time and was granted a string of positions that included Vice-Chairman of the Communist Party, Vice-Premier and Chief of Staff to the PLA; titles aside, he was now running the country. The move away from Mao's policies was rapid: in 1978 anti-Maoist **dissidents** were allowed to display wall posters in Beijing and elsewhere, and by 1980 Deng and the moderates were secure enough to sanction officially a cautious condemnation of Mao's actions. His ubiquitous portraits and statues began to come down, and his cult was gradually undermined.

"One Party" capitalism

Under **Deng Xiaoping**, China became unrecognizable from the days when the Red Guards enforced ideological purity. Deng's legacy was the "open door" policy, which brought about new social freedoms as well as a huge rise in the trappings of Westernization, especially in the cities. The impetus for such sweeping changes was economic. Deng's statement, "I don't care whether the cat is black or white as long as it

1977	1980	1981	1989
Deng Xiaoping rises to become Party Chairman	Beginning of the "open door" policy	Trial of the Gang of Four	Suppression of the democracy movement in Tian'anmen Square

catches mice", illustrates the pragmatic approach he took to the economy, one which has largely guided policy ever since. Deng **decentralized production**, allowing more rational decision-making based on local conditions, and the production and allocation of goods according to market forces; factories now contracted with each other instead of with the state. In agriculture, the collective economy was replaced, and farming households, after meeting government targets, were allowed to sell their surpluses on the free market. On the coast, **Special Economic Zones** (SEZs) were set up, where foreign investment was encouraged and Western management practices, such as the firing of unsatisfactory workers, were cautiously introduced.

Tian'anmen Square

Economic reform did not precipitate **political reform**, and was really a way of staving it off, with the Party hoping that allowing the populace the right to get rich would halt demands for political rights. However, dissatisfaction with corruption, rising inflation, low wages and the lack of freedom was vividly expressed in the demonstrations in **Tian'anmen Square** in 1989. These started as a mourning service for former Party General Secretary **Hu Yaobang**, who had been too liberal for Deng's liking and was dismissed in 1987; by mid-May there were nearly a million students, workers and even Party cadets around the square, demanding free speech and an end to corruption. On May 20, **martial law** was declared, and by the beginning of

---

HOW CHINA IS GOVERNED

Since 1949 the Chinese state has been controlled by the **Communist Party**, which brooks no dissent or rival, and which, with 66 million members, is the biggest political party in the world. It has a pyramid structure resting on millions of local organizations, and whose apex is formed by a Politburo of 24 members controlled by a nine-man standing committee. The Party's workings are opaque; personal relations count more than job titles, and a leader's influence rests on the relations he builds with superiors and protégés, with retired Party elders often retaining a great deal of influence. Towards the end of his life, for example, Deng Xiaoping was virtually running the country when his only official title was head of a bridge club. The country's head of state is its president, while the head of government is the premier. Politburo members are supposedly chosen by the three thousand delegates of the National People's Congress: officially a parliament though it in fact serves largely as a rubber stamp for Politburo decisions.

The Party owes its success, of course, to the **military**, and links with the PLA remain close, though the army has lost power since Jiang Zemin stripped its huge business empire in the 1990s. There is no PLA representative on the standing committee, but the military has a strong influence on policy issues, particularly over Taiwan and relations with the US, and generally maintains a hard line.

The law in China is a mix of legislation based on Party priorities and new statutes to haul the economy into line with those of major foreign investors. The National People's Congress is responsible for drafting laws covering taxation and human rights, among other subjects. In other areas, the State Council and local governments can legislate. Even after laws have been passed there is no guarantee they will be respected; provincial governments and state-owned enterprises view court decisions as negotiable, and for the Party and the state, the rule of law is not allowed to supersede its own interests.

1992	1995	1997
Major cabinet reshuffle puts Deng's men in power	Death of Chen Yun, last of the hardline Maoists in the Politburo. Work begins on the Three Gorges Dam	Hong Kong returns to the mainland. Death of Deng Xiaoping

age of peace and social virtues, he preached adherence to **ritual and propriety** as the supreme answer to the horrifying disorder of the world as he found it. No one paid much attention while he was alive; after his death, however, his writings were collected as the **Analects**, and this book became the most influential and fundamental of Chinese philosophies.

Never a religion in the sense of postulating a higher deity, Confucianism is rather a set of **moral and social values** designed to bring the ways of citizens and governments into harmony with each other. Through proper training in the scholarly classics and rigid adherence to the rules of propriety, including ancestor-worship, the superior man could attain a level of moral righteousness that would, in turn, assure a stable and righteous social order. As a political theory, Confucianism called for the **"wisest sage"**, the one whose moral sense was most refined, to be ruler. A good ruler who exemplified the **five Confucian virtues** – benevolence, righteousness, propriety, wisdom and trustworthiness – would bring society naturally to order. As Confucius said:

Just as the ruler genuinely desires the good, the people will be good. The virtue of the ruler may be compared to the wind and that of the common people to the grass. The grass under the force of the wind cannot but bend.

Instead of God, **five hierarchical relationships** are the prerequisites for a well-ordered society; given proper performance of the duties entailed in these, society should be "at ease with itself". The five relationships outline a structure of duty and obedience to authority: ruler to ruled, son to father, younger brother to older, wife to husband, and – the only relationship between equals – friend to friend. In practice, adherence to the unbending hierarchy of these relationships, as well as to the precepts of filial piety, has been used to justify totalitarian rule throughout Chinese history. The supreme virtue of the well-cultivated man and woman was always **obedience**.

During the time of the Han dynasty (206 BC–220 AD), Confucianism became institutionalized as a **system of government** that was to prevail for two thousand years. With it, and with the notion of the scholar-official as the ideal administrator, came the notorious Chinese **bureaucracy**. Men would study half their lives in order to pass examinations on Confucian thought and attain a government commission. Right until the start of the twentieth century, power was wielded through a bureaucracy steeped in the rites and rituals written five hundred years before Christ.

The ideal ruler, of course, never quite emerged (the emperor was not expected to sit the exams), and today, Confucian rituals are no longer practised. However, just as Protestantism is seen as having provided the underpinning to the advance of the West, so Confucianism, with its emphasis on order, harmony and cooperation, has been regarded as providing the ideological foundations for the recent successes of Asian culture.

Taoism

Taoism is the study and pursuit of the ineffable "Way", as outlined in the fundamental text, the **Daodejing** (often written as *Tao Te Ching*) or "The Way of Power". This obscure and mystical text comprises the wise sayings of the semi-mythical hermit **Lao Zi**, a contemporary of Confucius, compiled three centuries after his death.

The Tao is never really defined – indeed by its very nature it is undefinable. To the despair of the rationalist, the first lines of the *Daodejing* read:

The Tao that can be told
is not the eternal Tao.
The name that can be named
is not the eternal name.

GETTING AROUND A CHINESE TEMPLE

Whether Buddhist or Taoist, Chinese temples share the same broad features. Like cities, they **face south** and are surrounded by walls. Gates are sealed by **heavy doors**, guarded by paintings or statues of warrior deities to chase away evil. Further protection is ensured by a **spirit wall** that blocks direct entry; although easy enough for the living to walk around, this foils spirits, who are unable to turn corners. Once inside, you'll find a succession of **halls** arranged in ornamental courtyards. In case evil influences should manage to get in, the area nearest the entrance contains the least important rooms or buildings, while those of greater significance – living quarters or main temple halls – are set deeper inside the complex.

One way to tell Buddhist and Taoist temples apart is by the colour of the **supporting pillars** – Buddhists use bright red, while Taoists favour black. **Animal carvings** are more popular with Taoists, who use decorative good-luck and longevity symbols such as bats and cranes; some Taoist halls also have distinctive raised octagonal cupolas sporting the black-and-white *yin–yang* symbol.

In essence, however, it might be thought of as the underlying principle and source of all being, the bond that unites man and nature. Its central principle, **Wu Wei**, can crudely be translated as "no action", though it is probably better understood as "no action which runs contrary to the laws of nature". Whereas Confucianism is concerned with repairing social order and social relationships, Taoism is interested in the relationship of the individual with the natural universe.

Taoism's second major text is a book of parables written by one ideal practitioner of the Way, **Zhuang Zi**, another semi-mythical figure. In the famous butterfly parable, Zhuang Zi examines the many faces of reality:

Once upon a time Zhuang Zi dreamed he was a butterfly. A butterfly flying around and enjoying itself. It did not know it was Zhuang Zi again. We do not know whether it was Zhuang Zi dreaming that he was a butterfly, or a butterfly dreaming he was Zhuang Zi.

In its affirmation of the irrational and natural sources of life, Taoism has provided Chinese culture with a balance to the rigid social mores of Confucianism. In traditional China it was said that the perfect lifestyle was to be Confucian during the day – a righteous and firm administrator, upholding the virtues of the gentleman ruler – and a Taoist when relaxing. If Confucianism preaches duty to family and to society, Taoism champions the sublimity of withdrawal and non-committedness. The **art and literature** of China have been greatly enriched by Taoism's notions of contemplation, detachment and freedom from social entanglement, and the Tao has become embedded in the Chinese soul as a doctrine of yielding to the inevitable forces of nature.

Buddhism

The first organized religion to penetrate China, **Buddhism** enjoyed a glorious period of ascendancy under the Tang dynasty (618–907 AD). In the eighth century there were over 300,000 Buddhist monks in China, and this period saw the creation of much of the country's **great religious art** – above all the cave shrines at **Luoyang** (Henan), **Datong** (Shaanxi) and **Dunhuang** (Gansu), where thousands of carvings of the Buddha and paintings of holy figures attest to the powerful influence of Indian art and religion.

Gradually, though, Buddhism was submerged into the native belief system. Most contemporary schools of Indian Buddhism taught that life on Earth was essentially one of suffering, an endless cycle in which people were born, grew old and died, only to be born again in other bodies; the goal was to break out of this by attaining nirvana, which could be done by losing all desire for things of the world. This essentially individualistic doctrine was not likely to appeal to the regimented Chinese, however, and so it was the relatively small **Mahayana school** of Buddhism that came to dominate

Chinese thinking. The Mahayana taught that perfection for the individual was not possible without perfection for all – and that those who had already attained enlightenment would remain active in the world as **Bodhisattvas**, to help others along the path. In time Bodhisattvas came to be ascribed miraculous powers, and were prayed to in a manner remarkably similar to conventional Confucian ancestor-worship. The mainstream of Chinese Buddhism came to be more about maintaining harmonious relations with Bodhisattvas than about attaining nirvana.

Another entirely new sect of Buddhism also arose in China through contact with Taoism. Known in China as **Chan** (and in Japan as Zen), it offered a less extreme path to enlightenment. For a Chan Buddhist, it was not necessary to become a monk or a recluse in order to achieve nirvana – instead this ultimate state of being could be reached through life in accord with, and in contemplation of, the Way.

In short, the Chinese managed to marry Buddhism to their pre-existing belief structures with very little difficulty. This was facilitated by the general absence of dogma within Buddhist thought. Like the Chinese, the **Tibetans**, too, found themselves able to adapt the new belief system to their old religion, **Bön** (see p.872), rather than simply replacing it. Over the centuries, they established their own schools of Buddhism, often referred to as **Lamaism**. The now dominant **Gelugpa** (or Yellow Hat) school, of which the Dalai and Panchen Lamas are members, dates back to the teachings of Tsongkhapa (1357–1419).

Minority faiths and popular beliefs

Though Buddhism was the only foreign religion to leave a substantial mark on China, it was not the only one to enter China via the Silk Road. Both **Islam** and **Christianity** also trickled into the country this way, and to this day a significant minority of Chinese, numbering in the tens of millions, are Muslim. Unlike much of the rest of Asia, however, China did not yield wholesale to the tide of Islam, and thoroughly rejected it as a political doctrine.

When Jesuit missionaries first arrived in China in the sixteenth and seventeenth centuries, they were astounded and dismayed by the Chinese **flexibility of belief**. One frustrated Jesuit put it thus: "In China, the educated believe nothing and the uneducated believe everything". For those versed in the classics of Confucianism, Taoism and Buddhism, the normal belief was a healthy and tolerant scepticism. For the great majority of illiterate peasants, however, **popular religion** offered a plethora of ghosts, spirits, gods and ancestors who ruled over a capricious nature and protected humanity. If Christian missionaries handed out rice, perhaps Christ too deserved a place alongside them. In popular Buddhism the hope was to reach the "Pure Land", a kind of heaven for believers ruled over by a female deity known as the Mother Ruler. Popular Taoism shared this feminine deity, but its concerns were rather with the sorcerers, alchemists and martial-arts aficionados who sought solutions to the riddle of immortality; you may see some of these figures depicted in Taoist temples.

Modern China

During the twentieth century, confronted by the superior military and technical power of the West, the Chinese have striven to break free from the shackles of superstition. Since the imperial examinations were abolished at the start of the twentieth century, Chinese intellectuals have been searching for a modern yet essentially Chinese philosophy. The **Cultural Revolution** can be seen as the culmination of these efforts to repudiate the past. Hundreds of thousands of temples, ancestral halls and religious objects were defaced and destroyed. Monasteries were burnt to the ground, and their monks imprisoned. The classics of literature and philosophy – the "residue of the reactionary feudal past" – were burned. In 1974, towards the end of the Cultural Revolution, a campaign was launched to "criticize Lin Biao and Confucius", pairing the general with the sage to imply that both were equally reactionary in their opposition to the government.

Yet the very fact that Confucius could still be held up as an object for derision in 1974 – nearly 2500 years after his death – reveals the tenacity of traditional beliefs. With the Cultural Revolution now long gone, religion and philosophy are again being accepted as an essential part of the cultural tradition that binds the Chinese people together. Despite a lifetime of commitment to the Marxist revolution, the older generation are comforted and strengthened by their knowledge of the national heritage, while the young are rediscovering the classics, the forbidden fruit of their school days. The result is that Chinese temples of all descriptions are once more prosperous, busy places, teeming with people who have come to ask for grandchildren or simply for money. The atmosphere may not seem devout or religious, but then perhaps it never did.

Traditional Chinese Medicine

As an agricultural society, the Chinese have long been aware of the importance of the balance of natural, elemental forces: too much heat causes drought; too much rain, floods; while the correct measure of both encourages farmers' crops to grow. The ancient Chinese saw heaven, earth and humankind existing as an integral whole, such that if people lived in harmony with heaven and earth, then their collective health would be good. The medical treatise *Huang Di Neijing*, attributed to the semi-mythical Yellow Emperor (2500 BC), mentions the importance of spiritual balance, acupuncture and herbal medicine in treating illnesses, and attests to the venerable age of China's medical beliefs – it may well be a compilation of even earlier texts. Acupuncture was certainly in use by the Han period, as tombs in Hebei dated to 113 BC have yielded acupuncture needles made of gold and silver, as well as illustrations of therapeutic exercises, similar to those still practised today.

The belief in universal balance is known as **Dao** (or Tao) – literally "the Way". As an extension of Daoist principles, life is seen as consisting of opposites – man and woman, sun and moon, right and left, giving and receiving – whereby all things exist as a result of their interaction with their opposites. This is expressed in the black-and-white Daoist diagram which shows two interacting opposites, the **yin** ("female", passive energy) and the **yang** ("male", active energy). At the core of Traditional Chinese Medicine lies the belief that in order for a body to be healthy, its opposites must also be in a state of dynamic balance; there is a constant fluctuation, for example, between the body's heat, depending on its level of activity and the weather, and the amount of water needed to keep the body at the correct temperature. An excess of water in the system creates oedema, too little creates dehydration; too much heat will cause a temperature, and too little cause chills. Chinese medicine therefore views the body as an integrated whole, so that in sickness, the whole body – rather than just the "ill" part of it – requires treatment.

Qi and acupuncture

An underlying feature of Chinese medical philosophy, **qi** (or *chi*) is the energy of life: in the same way that electricity powers a light bulb, *qi*, so the theory goes, enables us to move, see and speak. *Qi* is said to flow along the body's network of **meridians**, or energy pathways, linking the surface tissues to specific internal **organs** that act as *qi* reservoirs; the twelve major meridians are named after the organ to which they are connected. The meridians are further classed as *yin* or *yang* depending on whether they are exposed or protected. In the limbs, for instance, the channels of the outer sides are *yang*, and important for resisting disease, while the channels of the inner sides are *yin*, and more involved with nourishing the body.

Mental and physical tensions, poor diet, anger or depression, even adverse weather, are said to inhibit *qi* flow, causing illness. Needles inserted in the body's **acupuncture points** reinforce or reduce the *qi* flow along a meridian, in turn influencing the activities of the organs. When the *qi* is balanced and flowing smoothly once more, good health is regained; acupuncture is specifically used to combat inflammation, to regenerate damaged tissue and to improve the functional power of internal organs.

That said, despite some acceptance of acupuncture in the West, there remains no good evidence for its efficacy. Studies have found that patients treated by acupuncturists had the same recovery rate as patients poked with needles at random positions. Sceptics argue that the act of sticking needles in the body produces pain-killing endorphins, which, combined with the placebo effect, aids recovery.

Herbal medicine

In the 2200 years since the semi-mythical Xia king **Shennong** compiled his classic work on **medicinal herbs**, a vast amount of experience has been gained to help perfect their clinical use. Approximately seven thousand herbs, derived from roots, leaves, twigs and fruit, are today commonly used in Chinese medicine, with another thousand or so of animal or mineral origin (also classified as "herbs"). Each is first processed by cleaning, soaking, slicing, drying or roasting, or even stir-frying with wine, ginger or vinegar, to influence its effects; the brew is then boiled down and drunk as a tea (typically very bitter and earthy tasting).

Herbs are used to prevent or combat a wide variety of diseases. Some are used to treat the underlying cause of the complaint, others to treat symptoms and help strengthen the body's own immune system, in turn helping it to combat the problem. An everyday example is in the treatment of flu: the herbal formula would include a "cold action" herb to reduce the fever, a herb to induce sweating and thus clear the body-ache, a purgative to clear the virus from the system, and a tonic herb to replenish the immune system. In all treatments, the patient is re-examined regularly, and as the condition improves the herbal formula is changed accordingly.

Just as Western aspirin is derived from willow bark, many Chinese drugs have been developed from herbs. One example is the antimalarial herb *qinghaosu*, or artemisinin, which has proved effective in treating certain strains of malaria with minimal side effects.

Art

Chinese art objects have had a difficult modern history: in the nineteenth century many were acquired by Westerners; then the greatest collections were taken by the Nationalists to Taiwan, where they are now in the National Palace Museum; many more art objects were destroyed during the Cultural Revolution; and today destruction – or dubious appropriation – of cultural relics continues as a consequence of modern development. Yet an astonishing wealth of treasures remains in China, mostly in local museum collections.

Pottery, bronzes and sculpture

The earliest Chinese objects date back to the Neolithic farmers of the **Yangshao** culture – **pottery** vessels painted with geometric designs. The decoration is from the shoulders of the pots upwards, as what has survived is mostly from graves and was designed to be seen from above when the pots were placed round the dead. From the same period come decorated clay heads, and pendants and ornaments of polished stone or jade – a simplified sitting bird in polished jade is a very early example of the Chinese tradition of animal sculpture. Rather later is the Neolithic **Longshan** pottery – black, thin and fine, wheel-turned and often highly polished, with elegant, sharply defined shapes.

The subsequent era, from around 1500 BC, is dominated by **Shang and Zhou bronze vessels** that were used for preparing and serving food and wine, and for ceremonies and sacrifices. One of the most common shapes is the *ding*, a three- or four-legged vessel that harks back to the Neolithic pots used for cooking over open fires. Casting methods were highly sophisticated, using moulds, while design was firm and assured and decoration often stylized and linear, featuring geometric and animal motifs, as well as grinning masks of humans and fabulous beasts. There are some naturalistic animal forms among the vessels, too – fierce tigers, solid elephants and surly rhinoceroses. Other bronze finds include weapons, decorated horse harnesses and sets of bells used in ritual music.

Later, under the **Zhou**, the style of the bronzes becomes more varied and rich: some animal vessels are fantastically shaped and extravagantly decorated; others are simplified natural forms; others again seem to be depicting not so much a fierce tiger, for example, as utter ferocity itself. You'll also see from the Shang and Zhou small objects – ornaments, ritual pieces and jewellery pendants – bearing highly simplified but vivid forms of tortoises, salamanders and flying birds. Some painted clay funeral figures and a few carved wooden figures also survive from the end of this period.

Although the Shang produced a few small sculpted human figures and animals in marble, **sculptures** and works in stone begin to be found in great quantities in **Han-dynasty** tombs. The decorated bricks and tiles, the bas-reliefs and the terracotta figurines of acrobats, horsemen and ladies-in-waiting placed in the tombs to serve the dead, even the massive stone men and beasts set to guard the Spirit Way leading to the tomb, are all lifelike and reflect concern with everyday activities and material possessions. The scale models of houses with people looking out of the windows and of farmyards with their animals have a spontaneous gaiety and vigour; some of the watchdogs are the most realistic of all.

It was the advent of **Buddhism** that encouraged stone carving on a large scale in the round, using mallet and chisel. **Religious sculpture** was introduced from India; in the fourth-century caves at **Datong** (see p.242), and the earlier caves at **Longmen**, near Luoyang (see p.259), the Indian influence is most strongly felt in the stylized Buddhas and attendants. Sometimes of huge size, these have an aloof grace and a rhythmic quality in their flowing robes, but also a smooth, bland and static quality. Not until the **Tang** do you get the full flowering of a native Chinese style, where the figures are rounder, with movement, and the positions, expressions and clothes are more natural and realistic. Some of the best examples are to be seen at **Dunhuang** (see p.826) and in the later caves at Longmen. The **Song** continued to carve religious figures, and at **Dazu** in Sichuan (see p.759), you'll find good examples of a decorative style that had broadened its subject matter to include animals, ordinary people and scenes of everyday life; the treatment is down-to-earth, individual, even comic. As the Dazu carvings are well preserved, they can still be seen painted, as they were meant to be. In later years, less statuary was produced until the **Ming** with their taste for massive tomb sculptures. You can see the best of these in **Nanjing** and **Beijing**.

Ceramics

From Neolithic painted pottery onwards, China developed excellent **ceramics**, a pre-eminence recognized even in the English language, which took the word "china" to mean fine-quality ceramic ware. In some of the early wares you can see the influence of shapes derived from bronzes, but soon the rise of regional potteries using different materials, and the development of special types for different uses, led to an enormous variety of shapes, textures and colours. This was really noticeable in the **Tang dynasty**, when an increase in the production of pottery for daily use was stimulated by the spread of tea drinking, and by the restriction of the use of valuable copper and bronze to coinage. The Tang also saw major technical advances; the production of true **porcelain** was finally achieved, and Tang potters became skilled in the delicate art of polychrome glazing. You can see evidence of this in the *san cai* (three-colour) statuettes of horses and camels, jugglers, traders, polo players, grooms and court ladies, which have come in great numbers from imperial tombs, and which reflect in vivid, often humorous, detail and still-brilliant colours so many aspects of the life of the time.

The **Song** dynasty witnessed a refinement of ceramic techniques and of regional specialization. The keynote was simplicity and quiet elegance, in both colour and form. There was a preference for using **single pure colours**, and for incised wares made to resemble damask cloth. In the museums you'll see the famous green celadons, the thin white porcelain *ding* ware and the pale grey-green *ju* ware reserved for imperial use. The Mongol **Yuan** dynasty, in the early fourteenth century, enriched Chinese tradition with outside influences – notably the introduction of **cobalt blue underglaze**, early examples of the blue and white porcelain that was to become so famous.

The **Ming** saw the flowering of great potteries under imperial patronage, especially **Jingdezhen**. Taste moved away from Song simplicity and returned to the liking for the vivid, almost gaudy, colour previously displayed by the Tang – deep **red**, **yellow** and **orange** glazes, with a developing taste for pictorial representation. From the seventeenth century onwards, Chinese export wares flowed in great quantity and variety to the West to satisfy a growing demand for chinoiserie, and the efforts of the Chinese artists to follow what they saw as the tastes and techniques of the West produced a style of its own. The early **Qing** created delicate enamel wares and *famille rose* and *verte*. So precise were the craftsmen that some porcelain includes the instructions for the pattern in the glaze.

Painting and calligraphy

While China's famous ceramics were made by craftsmen who remained anonymous, **painting and calligraphy** pieces were produced by famous scholars, officials and poets.

It has been said that the four great treasures of Chinese painting are the brush, ink, inkstone and paper. The earliest **brush** to have been found dates from about 400 BC, and is made out of animal hairs glued to a hollow bamboo tube. **Ink** was made from pine soot, mixed with glue and hardened into a stick that would be rubbed with water on a slate **inkstone**. The first known painting on silk was found in a **Han** tomb; records show that a great deal of such painting was created, but in 190 AD the vast imperial collection was destroyed in a civil war, when soldiers used the silk to make tents and knapsacks. All we know of Han painting comes from decorated tiles, lacquer, painted pottery and a few painted tombs, enough to show a great sense of movement and energy. The British Museum holds a scroll in ink and colour on silk from around 400 AD, attributed to **Gu Kaizhi** and entitled *Admonitions of the Instructress to Court Ladies*, and it's known that the theory of painting was already being discussed by then, as the treatise *The Six Principles of Painting* dates from about 500 AD.

The Sui and Tang

The **Sui–Tang** period, with a powerful stable empire and a brilliant court, was the perfect moment for painting to develop. A great tradition of **figure painting** grew up, especially of court subjects – portraits and pictures of the emperor receiving envoys, and of court ladies, can be seen in Beijing. Although only a few of these survived, the walls of Tang tombs, such as those near Xi'an, are rich in vivid frescoes that provide a realistic portrayal of court life. Wang Wei in the mid-eighth century was an early exponent of monochrome **landscape painting**, but the great flowering of landscape painting came with the **Song dynasty**. An academy was set up under imperial patronage, and different schools of painting emerged which analysed the natural world with great concentration and intensity; their style has set a mark on Chinese landscape painting ever since. There was also lively **figure painting**, as epitomized by a famous horizontal scroll in Beijing that depicts the Qing Ming River Festival. The Southern Song preferred a more intimate style, and such subjects as flowers, birds and still life grew in popularity.

The Yuan

Under the **Mongols**, many officials found themselves unwanted or unwilling to serve the alien Yuan dynasty, and preferred to retire and paint. This produced the **"literati" school**, in which many painters harked back to the styles of the tenth century. One great master, **Ni Can**, also devoted himself, among many others, to the ink paintings of bamboo that became important at this time. In this school, of which many examples remain extant, the highest skills of techniques and composition were applied to the simplest of subjects, such as plum flowers. Both ink painting as well as more conventional media continued to be employed by painters during the next three or more centuries. From the **Yuan** onwards, a tremendous quantity of paintings has survived.

The Ming and Qing

The **Ming dynasty** saw a great interest in collecting the works of previous ages, and a willingness by painters to be influenced by tradition. There are plenty of examples of bamboo and plum blossom, and bird and flower paintings being brought to a high decorative pitch, as well as schools of landscape painting firmly rooted in traditional techniques. The arrival of the Manchu **Qing dynasty** did not disrupt the continuity of Chinese painting, but the art became wide open to many influences. It included the Italian **Castiglione** (Lang Shining in Chinese) who specialized in horses, dogs and flowers; the Four Wangs, who reinterpreted Song and Yuan styles in an orthodox manner; and individualists such as the Eight Eccentrics of Yangzhou and certain Buddhist monks who objected to derivative art and sought a more distinctive approach to subject and style.

CONTEMPORARY ART

Contemporary art is flourishing in China. There are hundreds of private galleries and every major city has an arts centre, often an old factory converted into studios and exhibition spaces – 798 in Beijing (see p.98) and 50 Moganshan Lu (see p.371) in Shanghai are the biggest examples, but it's also worth noting Nordica in Kunming (see p.670) and OCT in Shenzhen, among others. Fairs such as the Shanghai Biennale and Guangzhou's triennial have become enormous events. Chinese art is seen as hot by investors, and there's plenty of money sloshing around; it helps that art is less easy to counterfeit than other cultural forms, and, because "meaning" in art can be nebulous, trickier for the government to censor.

However, the first crop of modern Chinese artists, who emerged in the 1990s, worked in obscurity with, it seemed, no prospects of exhibition. They banded together for survival in artists' villages, most famously at the **Yuanmingyuan Artists' Community** outside Beijing. The artists here developed a school of painting that expressed their individualism and their sceptical, often ironic and sometimes jaundiced view of contemporary China; this was, of course, the generation that had seen its dreams of change shot down at Tian'anmen Square. Nurtured by curator **Li Xianting**, as well as sympathetic foreign collectors, they built the foundations of the art scene as it is today. The most famous of these so-called "cynical realists" is **Fang Lijun**, whose paintings of disembodied bald heads against desolate landscapes are now some of the most characteristic images of modern Chinese art. Look out too for **Yue Minjun**'s Goya-esque paintings and sculptures of grinning, naked men; **Yang Shaobin**'s slickly painted sinister figures; the bitingly satirical caricatures of **Wang Yinsong** and **Song Yonghong**; **Zhang Xiaogang**'s disturbing, blurred paintings of 1950s family photos; and pigeonhole-phobic **Wang Xingwei**'s impressively diverse range of paintings.

Artists such as **Wang Guangyi** developed another school of distinctly Chinese contemporary art, "political pop". Here, a mocking twist is given to the iconography of the Cultural Revolution in order to critique a society that has become brashly commercial; Red Guards are shown waving iPods instead of Little Red Books, for example. This has become rather a hackneyed genre, though every artist seems to go through a phase of it, and it's enthusiastically collected in the West.

Although it's hard to pick out trends amid such a ferment of activity, many artists these days are, unsurprisingly, preoccupied with documenting the destruction of the Chinese urban landscape and the gut-wrenching changes that have accompanied modernization. As spaces for viewing art have grown, artists have diversified into new media such as **performance and video**; exciting new faces to look out for include **Cui Xiuwen**, whose videos of women in a toilet at a karaoke bar are shocking and memorable; and **Xu Zhen**, whose video *Rainbow* shows his back turning red from unseen slaps. **Documentary photography** is also popular; among its finest exponents is **Yang Fudong**, notable for his wistful images of city life. **Wu Gaozhong** first drew attention for a performance piece in which he climbed into the belly of a slaughtered cow, but his recent work, involving giant props implanted with boar hair, is more subtle, and has a creepy beauty. And it's always worth looking out for a show curated by *enfant terrible* **Gu Zhenqing**, who has a reputation for gleefully pushing the limits.

Calligraphy

Calligraphy – the word is derived from the Greek for "beautiful writing" – was crystallized into a high art form in China, where the use of the brush saw the development of handwriting of various styles, valued on a par with painting. Of the various different scripts, the **seal script** is the archaic form found on oracle bones; the **lishu** is the clerical style and was used in inscriptions on stone; the **kaishu** is the regular style closest to the modern printed form; and the cursive **cao shu** (grass script) is the most individual handwritten style. Emperors, poets and scholars over centuries have left examples of their calligraphy cut into stone at beauty spots, on mountains and in grottoes, tombs and temples all over China; you can see some early examples in the caves at Longmen (see p.259). At one stage during the Tang dynasty, calligraphy was so highly prized that it was the yardstick for the selection of high officials.

Other arts

Jade and lacquerware have also been constantly in use in China since earliest times. In Chinese eyes, **jade**, in white and shades of green or brown, is the most precious of stones. It was used to make the earliest ritual objects, such as the flat disc **Bi**, symbol of Heaven, which was found in Shang and Zhou graves. Jade was also used as a mark of rank and for ornament, in its most striking form in the jade burial suits to be seen in the country's museums.

Lacquer, made from the sap of a specific tree which dries to a tough, shiny coat, is also found as early as the Zhou. Many layers of the stuff were painted on a wood or cloth base that was then carved and inlaid with gold, silver or tortoiseshell, or often most delicately painted. Numerous examples of painted lacquer boxes and baskets survive from the Han, and, as with jade, the use of this material has continued ever since.

Music

The casual visitor to China could be forgiven for thinking that the only traditional style of music to compete with bland pop is that of the kitsch folk troupes to be heard in hotels and concert halls. But an earthy traditional music still abounds throughout the countryside; it can be heard at weddings, funerals, temple fairs and New Year celebrations – and even downtown in teahouses. A very different, edgier sound can be heard in certain smoky city bars – the new Chinese rock, with its energetic expressions of urban angst.

Traditional music

Chinese musical roots date back millennia – archeological finds include a magnificent set of 65 bronze bells from the fifth century BC – and modern forms can be directly traced to the Tang dynasty. Traditional Han music, like Irish music, is **heterophonic** – the musicians play differently decorated versions of a single melodic line. Percussion plays a major role, both in instrumental ensembles and as accompaniment to opera, narrative-singing, ritual music and dance.

But in the turbulent years after 1911, some intriguing **urban forms** sprang up from the meeting of East and West, such as the wonderfully sleazy Cantonese music of the 1920s and 1930s. As the movie industry developed, people in Shanghai, Guangzhou and Hong Kong threw themselves into the craze for Western-style dance halls, fusing the local traditional music with jazz, and adding saxophone, violin and xylophone to Chinese instruments such as the *gaohu* (high-pitched fiddle) and the *yangqin* (dulcimer). Composers **Lü Wencheng** and **Qiu Hechou** (Yau Hokchau), the violinist **Yin Zizhong** (Yi Tzuchung), and **He Dasha** ("Thicko He"), guitarist and singer of clown roles in Cantonese opera, made many wonderful commercial recordings during this period. While these musicians kept their roots in Cantonese music, the more Westernized (and even more popular) compositions of **Li Jinhui** and his star singer **Zhou Xuan** subsequently earned severe disapproval from Maoist critics as decadent and pornographic.

New "**revolutionary**" music, composed from the 1930s onwards, was generally march-like and optimistic, while in the wake of the Communist victory of 1949, the whole ethos of traditional music was challenged. Anything "feudal" or "superstitious" – which included a lot of traditional folk customs and music – was severely restricted, while Chinese melodies were "cleaned up" with the addition of rudimentary harmonies and bass lines. The Communist anthem "**The East is Red**", which began life as a folksong from the northern Shaanxi province, is symptomatic. Its local colour was ironed out as it was turned into a conventionally harmonized hymn-like tune. It was later adopted as the unofficial anthem of the Cultural Revolution, during which time musical life was driven underground, with only eight model operas and ballets permitted on stage.

The **conservatoire style** of **guoyue** (national music) was an artificial attempt to create a pan-Chinese style for the concert hall, with composed arrangements in a style akin to Western light music. There are still many conservatoire-style chamber groups – typically including *erhu* (fiddle), *dizi* (flute), *pipa* (lute) and *zheng* (zither) – playing evocatively titled pieces, some of which are newly composed. While the plaintive pieces for solo *erhu* by musicians such as **Liu Tianhua** and the blind beggar **Abing** (also a Daoist priest), or atmospheric tweetings on the *dizi*, have been much recorded by *guoyue* virtuosos like **Min Huifen** or **Lu Chunling** respectively, there is much more to Chinese music than this. Folk music has a life of its own, and tends to follow the Confucian ideals of moderation and harmony, in which showy virtuosity is out of place.

The qin and solo traditions

The genuine solo traditions date back to the scholar-literati of imperial times, and live on in the conservatoires today, in pieces for the *pipa, zheng* and *qin*.

The **qin** (also known as *guqin*) is the most exalted of these instruments. A seven-string plucked zither, it is the most delicate and contemplative instrument in the Chinese palette. It's also the most accessible, producing expressive slides and ethereal harmonics. Modern traditions of the **pipa** (lute) and **zheng** (zither) derive from regional styles, transmitted from master to pupil, although "national" repertoires developed during the twentieth century. For the *zheng*, the northern styles of Henan and Shandong, and the southern Chaozhou and Hakka schools, are best known. The *pipa*, on the other hand, has thrived in the Shanghai region. It makes riveting listening, with its contrast between intimate "civil" pieces and the startlingly modern-sounding martial style of traditional pieces such as "Ambush from All Sides" (*shimian maifu*), with its frenetic percussive evocation of the sounds of battle.

The north: blowers and drummers

Classical traditions derived from the elite of imperial times live on today in **folk ensembles**, which are generally found in the north of the country. The most exciting examples are to be heard at **weddings** and **funerals**.

These occasions usually feature raucous **shawm** (a ubiquitous instrument in China, rather like a crude clarinet) and percussion groups called **chuigushou** – "blowers and drummers". While wedding bands naturally tend to use more jolly music, funerals may also feature lively pieces to entertain the guests. The blowers and drummers play not only lengthy and solemn suites but also the latest pop hits and theme tunes from TV and films. They milk the audience by sustaining notes, using circular breathing, playing even while dismantling and reassembling their *shawms*, or by balancing plates on sticks on the end of their instruments while playing.

Mentioned as far back as the tenth century BC, the **sheng** ranks among the oldest Chinese instruments. It comprises a group of bamboo pipes of different lengths bound in a circle and set in a wooden or metal base into which the player blows. Frequently used for ceremonial music, it adds an incisive rhythmic bite. Long and deafening strings of firecrackers are another inescapable part of village ceremony. Some processions are led by a Western-style brass band with a *shawm*-and-percussion group behind, competing in volume, oblivious of key. In northern villages, apart from the blowers and drummers, ritual **shengguan** ensembles are also common, with their exquisite combination of mouth organs and oboes, as well as darting flutes and the shimmering halo of the *yunluo* gong-frame, accompanied by percussion. Apart from this haunting melodic music, they perform some spectacular ritual percussion – the intricate arm movements of the cymbal players almost resemble martial arts.

Around Xi'an, groups performing similar wind and percussion music, misleadingly dubbed **Xi'an Drum Music** (**Xi'an guyue**), are active for temple festivals not only in the villages but also in the towns, especially in the sixth moon, around July. If you remember the tough *shawm* bands and haunting folksong of the film *Yellow Earth*, or the harsh falsetto narrative in *The Story of Qiuju*, go for the real thing among the barren hills of northern Shaanxi. This area is home to fantastic folk singers, local opera (such as the Qinqiang and Meihu styles), puppeteers, *shawm* bands and folk ritual specialists. Even *yangge* dancing, which in the towns is often a geriatric form of conga dancing, has a wild power here, again accompanied by *shawms* and percussion.

The south: silk and bamboo

In southeast China, the best-known instrumental music is that of **sizhu** ("silk and bamboo") ensembles, using flutes (of bamboo) and plucked and bowed strings (until recently of silk). More mellifluous than the outdoor wind bands of the north, these provide perhaps the most accessible Chinese folk music.

The most famous of the many regional styles is that of **Shanghai**, where enthusiasts get together in the afternoons, sit round a table and take it in turns to play a set with Chinese fiddles, flutes and banjos. The most celebrated meeting place is the teahouse in the **Chenghuang Miao** (see p.360), a picturesque two-storey structure on an island in the old quarter, where there are Monday-afternoon gatherings. The contrasting textures of plucked, bowed and blown sounds are part of the attraction of this music, each offering individual decorations to the gradually unfolding melody. Many pieces consist of successive decorations of a theme, beginning with the most ornate and accelerating as the decorations are gradually stripped down to a fast and bare final statement of the theme itself. Above the chinking of tea bowls and subdued chatter of the teahouse, enjoy the gradual unravelling of a piece like "Sanliu", or feel the exhilarating dash to the finish of "Xingjie", with its breathless syncopations.

Amateur *sizhu* clubs can be found throughout the lower Yangzi area, including Nanjing and Hangzhou. Although this music is secular and recreational in its urban form, the *sizhu* instrumentation originated in ritual ensembles and is still so used in the villages and temples of southern Jiangsu. In fact, amateur ritual associations exist all over southern China, as far afield as Yunnan, punctuating their ceremonies with sedate music reminiscent of the Shanghai teahouses, albeit often featuring the *yunluo* gong-frame of northern China.

Another fantastic area for folk music is the coastal region of **southern Fujian**, notably the cities of Quanzhou and Xiamen. Here you can find not only opera, ritual music and puppetry, but the haunting **nanguan ballads**. Popular all along the coast of southern Fujian, as in Taiwan across the strait, *nanguan* features a female singer accompanied by end-blown flute and plucked and bowed lutes. The ancient texts depict the sorrows of love, particularly of women, while the music is mostly stately and the delivery restrained yet anguished.

Still further south, the coastal regions of **Chaozhou** and **Shantou**, and the **Hakka** area (inland around Meixian and Dabu), also boast celebrated string ensembles that feature a high-pitched *erxian* (bowed fiddle) and *zheng* (plucked zither), as well as large and imposing ceremonial percussion bands, sometimes accompanied by shrill flutes.

The temples

All over China, particularly on the great religious mountains such as **Wutai Shan**, **Tai Shan**, **Qingcheng Shan**, **Wudang Shan** and **Putuo Shan**, temples are not just historical monuments but living sites of worship. Morning and evening services are held daily, and larger rituals on special occasions. The priests mainly perform vocal liturgy accompanied by percussion. They intone sung hymns with long melismas, alternating with chanted sections accompanied by the relentless and hypnotic beat of the woodblock.

Melodic instrumental music tends to be added when priests perform rituals outside the temples. These styles are more earthy and accessible even to ears unaccustomed to Chinese music. The Daoist priests from the Xuanmiao Guan in **Suzhou**, for example, perform wonderfully mellifluous pieces for silk-and-bamboo instruments, gutsy blasts on the *shawm*, music for spectacularly long trumpets, and a whole battery of percussion.

Opera and other vocal music

Chinese musical drama became overwhelmingly popular from the Yuan dynasty onwards. Of the several hundred types of regional opera, **Beijing Opera**, a rather late

CHINESE ROCK

Although often connected to the Hong Kong/Taiwanese entertainment industry, China's indigenous **rock** is a different beast, one which has its traditions in passionate and fiery protest, and which still possesses a cultural and political self-awareness. The rock scene was nonexistent in China until the mid-1980s, when foreign students on cultural exchange brought tapes of their favourite rock and pop music (and their own electric guitars) to the Chinese mainland, and shared them with their fellow students. Their music quickly caught the imagination of Chinese university youth and the urban vanguard.

Chinese **protest-rock** really began with singer-trumpeter-guitarist Cui Jian, who was influenced by the Taiwanese singer **Teresa Teng** (known to the Chinese by her original name, Deng Lijun; 1953–95). Teng's singing style can be directly traced to Zhou Xuan and 1930s Shanghai. Probably the most popular Chinese singer of her time, her recordings were circulated in China on the black market from the late 1970s onwards, when such music was officially banned.

A Beijinger born to parents of Korean descent, **Cui Jian** studied the trumpet at an early age, trained as a classical musician and joined the Beijing Symphony Orchestra in 1981. After being introduced to Anglo-American rock in the mid-1980s, however, he forged an independent path and his gritty voice became the primary reference point of Chinese rock. His love song "Nothing To My Name" became an anthem of the democracy movement, evoking a memorable complaint from General Wang Zhen, a veteran of the Long March: "What do you mean, you have nothing to your name? You've got the Communist Party, haven't you?"

Notable **1980s bands** that followed in Cui Jian's wake include Black Panther (*Hei Bao*) and Tang Dynasty, though their long hair and leathers were perhaps more influential than their soft rock. They were followed by Cobra, China's first all-female rock band, folk-rocker Zhang Chu, bad boy He Yong, Compass, Overload, and Breathing, among others. Unsigned, these bands would perform for very little money as part of vaudeville shows, until 1990, when China's first domestic full-scale rock concert took place. Six bands, including Tang Dynasty and Cobra, played at the Beijing Exhibition Centre Arena and were immediately signed by Japanese and Taiwanese labels, who then brought their music to the mainstream. They paved the way for home-grown labels such as Modern Sky, Scream, New Bees Records and Badhead, which now specialize in Chinese rock, hip-hop and alternative music.

The rock scene these days remains healthy, with hundreds of bands, and though it does centre heavily on **Beijing**, the **Shanghai** and **Shenzhen** scenes continue to grow apace. For visitors, this slice of Chinese culture is well worth exploring, and surprisingly accessible, as most bands sing at least half of their songs in English. Acts to look out for include Sex Pistols wannabes Joyside; Shanghainese folk punk showmen Top Floor Circus; long-running ska punk outfit Brain Failure; and Joy Divisionistas, the Retros. For dance and electronica you can't beat Queen Sea Big Shark, while Snapline produce a fusion of post-punk and electronica. Car Sick Cars and Residence A are the indie shoegazers to catch, and Beijing low-fi rockers Mr. Graceless are always worth a listen. If you're tired of hearing Western-style music, hunt down the Mongolian folk stylings of Hanggai, or Xiban's quirky mix of Beijing opera, Tibetan mantras and good old rock.

To immerse yourself fully in the scene, look for various events hosted through the year and around the country by **Midi Festival** – see ⓦfacebook.com/midifestival for current information.

hybrid form dating from the eighteenth century, is the most widely known – now heard throughout China, it's the closest thing to a "national" theatre. Many librettos now performed date back to the seventeenth century and describe the intrigues of emperors and gods, as well as love stories and comedy. Northern "clapper operas" (*bangzi xi*), named after the high-pitched woodblock that insistently runs through them, are earthy in flavour – for example, the "Qinqiang" of Shaanxi province. **Sichuan opera** is remarkable for its female chorus. **Ritual masked opera** may be performed in the countryside of Yunnan, Anhui and Guizhou. Chaozhou and Fujian also have beautiful ancient styles of opera: **Pingju** and **Huangmei Xi** are genteel in style, while

Cantonese opera is funkier. If you're looking for more music and less acrobatics, try to seek out the classical but now rare **Kunqu**, often accompanied by the sweet-toned *qudi* flute. There are also some beautiful **puppet operas**, often performed for ritual events; Quanzhou in Fujian boasts a celebrated marionette troupe, and other likely areas include northern Shaanxi and the Tangshan and Laoting areas of eastern Hebei.

While Chinese opera makes a great visual spectacle, musically it is frankly an acquired taste, resembling to the uninitiated the din of cats fighting in a blazing firework factory. The singing style is tense, guttural and high-pitched, while the music is dominated by the bowed string accompaniment of the *jinghu*, a sort of sawn-off *erhu*. It also features plucked lutes, flutes and – for transitional points – a piercing *shawm*. The action is driven by percussion, with drum and clappers leading an ensemble of gongs and cymbals in an assortment of set patterns. Professional opera troupes exist in the major towns, but rural opera performances, which are given for temple fairs and even weddings, tend to be livelier. Even in Beijing you may come across groups of old folk meeting in parks to go through their favourite Beijing Opera excerpts.

Narrative-singing also features long classical stories. You may find a teahouse full of old people following these story-songs avidly, particularly in Sichuan, where one popular style is accompanied by the *yangqin* (dulcimer). In Beijing, or more often in Tianjin, amateurs sing through traditional *jingyun dagu* ballads, accompanied by drum and *sanxian* banjo. In Suzhou, *pingtan*, also accompanied by a plucked lute, is a beautiful genre.

Film

Film came early to China. The first moving picture was exhibited in 1896 at a "teahouse variety show" in Shanghai, where the country's first cinema was built just twelve years later. By the 1930s, cinema was playing an important role in the cultural life of Shanghai, though the huge number of resident foreigners ensured a largely Western diet of films. Nevertheless, local Chinese films were also being made, mainly by the so-called May Fourth intellectuals (middle-class liberals inspired by the uprising of May 4, 1919), who wanted to modernize China along Western lines. Naturally, Western influence on these films was strong, and they have little to do with the highly stylized, formal world of traditional performance arts such as Beijing Opera or shadow-puppet theatre. Early film showings often employed a "storyteller", who sat near the screen reading out the titles for the benefit of those who could not read.

The Shanghai studios

Of the handful of important **studios** in Shanghai operating in the 1920s and 1930s, the most famous was the **Mingxing**, whose films were left-leaning and anti-imperialist. *Sister Flower* (1933) tells the story of twin sisters separated at birth, one of whom ends up a city girl living in Shanghai, while the other remains a poor villager. Another film from the same year, *Spring Silk Worm*, portrays economic decline and hardship in Zhejiang province, and levels the finger of accusation at Japanese imperialism. Finally, *The Goddess* (1934), from the **Lianhua** studio, depicts the struggle of a prostitute to have her son educated. The improbably glamorous prostitute was played by China's own Garbo, the languorous Ruan Lingyu. Despite the liberal pretensions of these films, it was inevitable – given that audiences comprised a tiny elite – that they would later be derided by the Communists as bourgeois.

When the **Japanese occupied** Shanghai in 1937, "subversive" studios such as the Mingxing and Lianhua were immediately closed, and much of the film-making talent fled into the interior. The experience of war put film-makers in touch with their potential future audiences, the Chinese masses. China's great wartime epic, **Spring River Flows East** (1947–48), was the cinematic result of this experience. The story spans the duration of the anti-Japanese war – and the ensuing civil war – through the lives of a single family torn apart by the conflict. The heroine, living in poverty, contrasts with her husband, who has abandoned his wife for a decadent existence in Shanghai. Traumatized by a decade of war, the Chinese who saw this film appreciated it as an authentic account of the sufferings through which the nation had lived. Over 750,000 people saw the film at its release, a remarkable figure given that the country was still at war.

Communism and the cinema

The story of Chinese film-making under the **Communists** really dates back to 1938, when Mao Zedong and his fellow Long Marchers set up their base in **Yan'an**. No world could have been further removed from the glamour of Shanghai than this dusty, poverty-stricken town, but it was the ideal location for the film-makers of the future

People's Republic to learn their skills. Talent escaping through Japanese lines trickled through in search of employment, among them the actress **Jiang Qing**, later to become Mao's wife and self-appointed empress of Chinese culture. One thing upon which all the leading Communists in Yan'an were agreed was the importance of film as a **centralizing medium**, which could be used to unify the culture of the nation after the war had been won.

The immediate consequence of the Communist victory in 1949 was that the showing of foreign films was curtailed, and the private Shanghai studios wound down. A **Film Guidance Committee** was set up to decide upon film output for the entire nation. The first major socialist epic, **Bridge**, appeared in 1949, depicting the mass mobilization of workers rushing enthusiastically to construct a bridge in record time. Although predictably dull in terms of character and plot, the cast still contained a number of prewar Shanghai actors to divert audiences. At the end of the film the entire cast gathers to shout "Long live Chairman Mao!", a scene that was to be re-enacted time and again in the coming years.

A year after *Bridge*, one of the very last nongovernment Shanghai studio films appeared, **The Life of Wu Xun**, a huge project that had started well before 1949, and, surprisingly, was allowed to run to completion. Its subject was the famous nineteenth-century entrepreneur, Wu Xun, who started out as a beggar and rose to enormous riches, whereupon he set out on his lifetime's ambition to educate the peasantry. Despite the addition of a narrator's voice at the end of the film, pointing out that it was revolution and not education that peasants needed, the film was a disaster for the Shanghai film industry. Mao wrote a damning critique of it for idolizing a "Qing landlord", and a campaign was launched against the legacy of the entire Shanghai film world – studios, actors, critics and audiences alike.

The remains of the May Fourth movement struggled on. The consolation for the old guard was that newer generations of Chinese film-makers had not yet solved the problem of how to portray life in the contemporary era. The 1952 screen adaptation of Lao She's short story *Dragon's Beard Ditch*, for example, was supposed to contrast the miserable pre-1949 life of a poor district of Beijing with the prosperous life that was being lived under the Communists. The only problem, as audiences could immediately see, was that the supposedly miserable pre-1949 scenes actually looked a good deal more heart-warming than the later ones.

Nevertheless, the Communists did achieve some of their original targets during the **1950s**. The promotion of a universal culture and language was one of them. All characters in all films – from Tibetans to Mongolians to Cantonese – were depicted as speaking in flawless **Mandarin Chinese**. Above all, there was an explosion in audiences, from around 47 million tickets sold in 1949, to 600 million in 1956, to over 4 billion in 1959. The latter figure should be understood in the context of the madness surrounding the Great Leap Forward, a time of crazed overproduction in all fields, film included. Film studios sprouted in every town in China, though with a catastrophic loss of quality – a typical studio in Jiangxi province comprised one man, his bicycle and an antique stills camera. The colossal output of that year included uninspiring titles such as *Loving the Factory as One's Home*.

The conspicuous failure of the Great Leap Forward did, however, bring certain short-lived advantages to the film industry. While Mao was forced temporarily into the political sidelines during the late 1950s, the cultural bureaucrats signalled that in addition to "revolutionary realism", a certain degree of "**revolutionary romanticism**" was to be encouraged. Chinese themes and subjects, as opposed to pure Marxism, were looked upon with more favour. A slight blossoming occurred, with improbable films such as *Lin Zexu* (1959), which covered the life of the great Qing-dynasty official who stood up to the British at the time of the Opium Wars. There was even a tentative branching out into comedy, with the film *What's Eating You?* based on the relatively un-socialist antics of a Suzhou waiter. Unusually, the film featured local dialects, as well as a faintly detectable parody of the government's campaign to encourage greater sacrifices by promoting the mythical hero worker Lei Feng.

The Cultural Revolution

Sadly, this bright period came to a swift end in 1966 with the **Cultural Revolution**. No interesting work was made in China for nearly fifteen years – indeed, no film was produced anywhere in the whole country between 1966 and 1970. The few films that did subsequently appear before Mao's death were made under the personal supervision of Jiang Qing, and all were on the revolutionary model, a kind of ballet with flag waving. Attendance at these dreadful films was virtually **compulsory** for people who did not wish to be denounced for a lack of revolutionary zeal. Ironically, Jiang Qing herself was a big fan of Hollywood productions, which she would watch in secret.

Recovery from the trauma of the Cultural Revolution was bound to take time, but the years 1979 and 1980 saw a small crop of films attempting to assess the horror through which the country had just lived. The best known, *The Legend of Tianyun Mountain*, made in Shanghai in 1980, featured two men, one of whom had denounced the other for "Rightism" in 1958. The subsequent story is one of guilt, love, emotions and human relationships, all subjects that had been banned during the Cultural Revolution. Understandably, the film was an enormous popular success, though before audiences had time to get too carried away, a subsequent film, *Unrequited Love* (1981), was officially criticized for blurring too many issues.

Modern cinema

In **1984** the Chinese film industry was suddenly brought to international attention for the first time by the arrival of the so-called "**fifth generation**" of Chinese film-makers. That year, director **Chen Kaige** and his cameraman **Zhang Yimou**, both graduates from the first post-Cultural Revolution class (1982) of the Beijing Film School, made the superb art-house film **Yellow Earth**. The film was not particularly well received in China, either by audiences, who expected something more modern, or by the authorities, who expected something more optimistic. Nevertheless, it set the pattern for a series of increasingly overseas-funded (and overseas-watched) films comprising stunning images of a "traditional" China, irritating the censors at home and delighting audiences abroad.

Chen Kaige's protégé Zhang Yimou was soon stealing a march on his former boss with his first film **Red Sorghum**. This film was not only beautiful, and reassuringly patriotic, but it also introduced the world to heart-throb actress **Gong Li**. Zhang and Gong worked together on a string of hits, including *Judou*, *The Story of Qiu Ju*, *Raise the Red Lantern*, *Shanghai Triad* and *To Live*. None of these could be described as art-house in the way that *Yellow Earth* had been, and the potent mix of Gong Li's sexuality and figure-hugging dresses with exotic, mysterious locations in 1930s China was clearly targeted at Western rather than Chinese audiences.

Zhang Yimou has since been warmly embraced by the authorities, though his films have become worse. His most recent Hollywood-friendly martial-arts spectaculars **Hero** (2002), **The House of Flying Daggers** (2004) and **Curse of the Golden Flower** (2007) are commercial successes, and beautifully shot, but they are shallow and soulless.

Contemporary realism

The best Chinese films of the modern age are those that have turned their back on the frigid perfection on offer from Zhang Yimou and are raw, gritty reflections of Chinese life. Inevitably, the fifth generation was followed by a sixth, which produced **underground movies**, generally shot in black-and-white, depicting what they consider to be the true story of contemporary China – ugly cities, cold flats, broken and depressed people. **Beijing Bastards** (1993) is a good example. Many of the finest

MAINLAND MOVIES AVAILABLE FOR DOWNLOAD OR ON DVD

★**24 City** (2009). Film by Chollywood bad-boy Jia Zhangke, following three generations of a Chengdu family as their factory closes down, and gives way to a modern apartment complex. Very well received by international critics.

Beijing Bastards (1993). A story of apathetic, fast-living youths, this was one of China's first independently produced films; it stars rock singer and rebel Cui Jian, who is depicted drinking, swearing and playing the guitar.

Beijing Bicycle (2001). Told in a social-realist aesthetic, this is the story of a lad trying to get his stolen bike back – a lot more interesting than it may sound.

★**Blind Shaft** (2003). Sharply directed by Yang Li, this is about two coal miners who kill colleagues, make it look like an accident, then collect the mine owner's hush money. As well as a telling indictment of runaway capitalism, it's a great piece of film noir.

Cell Phone (2003). Perhaps the most successful work of Feng Xiaogang, one of China's most revered directors, this satirical comedy revolves around two men having affairs.

Devils on the Doorstep (2000). Set during the anti-Japanese war, this black farce concerns a group of peasants who get a couple of hostages dumped on their farm by the local Communists. It was banned in China, having failed to demonize the Japanese.

★**Farewell My Concubine** (1994). Chen Kaige's superb summation of modern Chinese history, although the main protagonist – a homosexual Chinese opera singer – is hardly typical of modern China.

The Grandmaster (2013). Almost totally mythical biopic of Yip Man, Bruce Lee's real-life kung fu teacher. Plenty of stylishly shot fight sequences, but the plot is thinner than Chinese soup.

Ke Ke Xi Li (2004). Chuan Lu's hard-boiled true story about a volunteer gang fighting against ruthless antelope poachers on the high Tibetan plateau. It was filmed using nonprofessional local actors and has the feel of a Western, but is entirely unsentimental.

Let the Bullets Fly (2010). A Chinese "Noodle" Western starring Chow Yun-fat and set in 1920s Sichuan; it broke all sorts of box-office records on release.

Lost in Thailand (2014). Three-Stooges-style slapstick about a trio of hapless travellers staggering from one disaster to another during a nightmare business trip. Unexpectedly, this was the first Chinese film to earn over a billion yuan at the box office.

★**Raise the Red Lantern** (1991). Beautifully-shot Gong Li vehicle set in the 1920s, and directed by Zhang Yimou. This time she plays the concubine of a wealthy businessman, vying for his affection with her fellow mistresses.

Red Cliff (2008/09). The tangled schemes and set-piece battles surrounding China's break-up at the end of the Han dynasty receive lavish treatment from legendary Hong Kong action director John Woo. Avoid cut-down versions and settle in for the full four-hour feature.

Red Sorghum (1987). Set in a remote wine-producing village of northern China at the time of the Japanese invasion, this film was based on parts of *The Red Sorghum Clan*, a novel which contributed heavily towards writer Mo Yan's 2012 Nobel Prize.

Still Life (2007). Extremely controversial Jia Zhangke film about the search for people who have gone missing in the mass displacements caused by the Three Gorges Dam project.

Tuya's Marriage (2006). Wang Quan'an employed nonprofessional actors and grand scenery to great effect with this story of a Mongolian herdswoman's search for a new husband. Like much good contemporary Chinese art of all genres, its subject is people struggling to cope with vast social change.

Xiao Wu (1997). Too controversial for domestic release, this Jia Zhangke film is the intimate portrayal of a pickpocket whose life is falling apart.

Yellow Earth (1984). The story of a soldier who travels north from Yan'an, tasked with rewriting local folk songs with Communist lyrics. Still shots predominate, recalling traditional Chinese scroll painting, with giant landscapes framed by hills and the distant Yellow River.

modern movies turn a baleful eye on the recent past; see **Lei Feng is Gone** (1997), **In the Heat of the Sun** (1995) and **Devils at the Doorstep** (2000).

Many recent films are simply too controversial for domestic release, but if they garner attention abroad they then become available at home to download or buy on DVD (see box above).

Hong Kong

The movies that have the least difficulty with the Chinese censors are those produced in **Hong Kong**, the world's fourth-largest movie producer behind India, the US and Nigeria. Its popular appeal is made easier by the content: generally easy-to-digest romances, comedies or high-speed action, with little interest in deeper meanings or the outside world – and certainly not in politics.

World interest in Hong Kong's film industry dates back to 1970s martial-arts legend **Bruce Lee**. Although Lee was better known overseas for the Hollywood-financed *Enter the Dragon* (1973), the success in Hong Kong of his earlier films *Fist of Fury* and *The Big Boss* launched a domestic **kung-fu movie boom**, off the back of which sprang **Jackie Chan** and a much-needed element of slapstick comedy – best seen in Chan's early works, such as *Drunken Master* (1978). As the genre faltered in the 1980s, directors mixed in a supernatural aspect, pioneered by **Tsui Hark** in *Zu: Warriors from the Magic Mountain* (1983) and *Chinese Ghost Story* (1987). The kung-fu genre was later revived by director **Stephen Chow**, whose *Kung Fu Hustle* (2004) sported uniquely surreal humour and visuals, and **Wilson Yip**'s fictionalized biopic of Bruce Lee's teacher, *Ip Man* (2008).

Martial arts remain an inevitable component of Hong Kong's modern **action movies** and **police thrillers**. This genre can largely be attributed to **John Woo**'s influential hits *A Better Tomorrow* (1986) and *Hard Boiled* (1992), which feature Chow Yun-fat shooting his way through relentless scenes of orchestrated violence. Woo's many imitators have mostly succeeded only in making pointless, bloody movies whose plots inevitably conclude with the massacre of the entire cast, though above-average efforts such as *Infernal Affairs* (2002; remade in the US as *The Departed*) at least add a little depth to the heroes' moody characters.

At present, Hong Kong's only director interested in anything but light entertainment is **Wong Karwai**, whose early works such as *Chungking Express* (1994) and *Fallen Angels* (1995) depict Hong Kong as a crowded, disjointed city where people, though forced together, seem unable to communicate. His subsequent films added a European sense of style, which worked in the sensuous *In the Mood for Love* (2000) but overwhelmed the plot in the obscure, self-referential *2046* (2004). His most recent film, *The Grandmaster* (2013) – another martial-arts epic – was a box-office hit but divided the critics.

Books

The last few years have seen a glut of excellent writing coming out of China, from international commentators' views on current economic and social upheavals, to translated journalism and popular novels, and often eccentric – or jaundiced – expat memoirs. Classics aside, few of the titles below are available in China (though you might get lucky in Hong Kong), so it's best to locate them before your trip.

Note that the Chinese put surnames before first names, and we've listed authors here in alphabetical order accordingly (though Westernized Chinese names follow the English format).

HISTORY

Patricia Ebrey *Cambridge Illustrated History of China*. An up-to-date, easy-going historical overview, excellently illustrated and clearly written.

Peter Fleming *The Siege at Peking*. An account of the events that led up to June 20, 1900, when the foreign legations in Beijing were attacked by the Boxers and Chinese imperial troops. The 55-day siege marked a watershed in China's relations with the rest of the world.

Peter Frankopan *The Silk Roads*. Thorough, detailed epic about the history of the trade routes which once connected Europe to China through Central Asia, the Middle East and India, and the way that goods – and cultures – flowed along them in both directions. Something to pack for a long train journey.

Paul French *Midnight in Peking*. A real-life murder mystery, revolving around the search for the killer of Pamela Warner, an English girl whose body was found in Beijing, minus its heart and blood, in 1937.

Jacques Gernet *Daily Life in China on the Eve of the Mongol Invasion 1250–1276*. Based on assorted Chinese sources, this is a fascinating survey of southern China under the Song, focusing on the capital, Hangzhou, then the largest and richest city in the world. Gernet also deals with the daily lives of a cross section of society, from peasant to leisured gentry, covering everything from cookery to death.

★ **Larry Gonick** *The Cartoon History of the Universe vols II and III*. A masterwork setting world history in cartoon format, full of verve, great visuals and awful puns, but also accurate – the bibliography shows how much research has gone into this manic project. About the only textbook that attempts to set Chinese history in a world context.

★ **Peter Hopkirk** *The Great Game*. Hugely entertaining account of the nineteenth-century struggle between Britain and Russia for control of Central Asia. In tracing the roots of the Chinese occupations of Tibet and Xinjiang, and also detailing the invariable consequences for foreign powers who meddle with Afghanistan, it's also disturbingly topical.

Ann Paludan *Chronicle of the Chinese Emperors*. Lively stories on the lives of all 157 of those strangest of characters, the Chinese emperors. Well illustrated and a good starting point for getting to grips with Chinese history.

Sima Qian *Historical Records* aka *Records of the Historian*. Written by the Han-dynasty court historian, *Records* is a masterpiece, using contemporary court documents and oral tradition to illuminate key characters – everyone from emperors to famous con men – from early Chinese history. Although long discredited, Sima Qian's accounts have now been partially corroborated by recent archeology.

Edgar Snow *Red Star Over China*. The definitive first-hand account of the early days of Mao and the Communist "bandits", written in 1936 after Snow, an American journalist, wriggled through the Guomindang blockade and spent months at the Red base in Yan'an.

★ **Jonathan Spence** *The Gate of Heavenly Peace; The Search for Modern China*. The first of these traces the history of twentieth-century China through the eyes of the men and women caught up in it – writers, revolutionaries, poets and politicians – and is among the best books for getting to grips with China's complex modern history. Though quite hard for a straight-through read, *The Search for Modern China* is authoritative and probably the best overall history of China available.

TIBET

John Avedon *In Exile from the Land of Snows*. A detailed and moving account of modern Tibetan history, covering both those who remained in the country and those who fled into exile. Required reading for anyone contemplating a trip.

Michael Buckley *Meltdown in Tibet*. The latest in a long line of passionate, morally outraged books detailing the threats facing Tibetan culture – mostly from China. Buckley's theme is "ecocide", ecological warfare, from the fallout from industrial pollution generated in neighbouring countries to the construction of hydroelectric dams across rivers that are vital to local irrigation and agriculture.

Edmund Candler *The Unveiling of Lhasa*. China was not the first country to invade Tibet: in 1904, a British military expedition marched on Lhasa, using modern machine guns against the peasant armies sent to stop them. Candler, a journalist embedded with the expedition, paints an honest and ultimately disillusioned picture of the events, which were to open the country up to colonization.

Victor Chan *Tibet Handbook: a Pilgrimage Guide*. A hugely detailed guide to Tibet's pilgrimage sites and treks, and how to reach them. Absolutely essential if you're considering a trek.

Graham Coleman (ed) *A Handbook of Tibetan Culture: a Guide to Tibetan Centres and Resources Throughout the World*. The subtitle says it all; the book exhaustively documents cultural organizations, teaching centres and libraries across the globe that have a Tibetan focus. It also includes biographies of major Tibetan lamas, brief histories of the major schools of Tibetan Buddhism and an illustrated glossary.

★**Heinrich Harrer** *Seven Years in Tibet*. A classic account of a remarkable journey to reach Lhasa and of the years there prior to the Chinese invasion, when Harrer was tutor to the Fourteenth Dalai Lama.

Isabel Hilton *The Search for the Panchen Lama*. The whole sorry story of the search for the Eleventh Panchen Lama, and how the Tibetans' choice ended up as the world's youngest political prisoner (see p.913).

Thubten Jigme and Colin Turnbull *Tibet, Its History, Religion and People*. The best account around of the traditional everyday lives of the Tibetan people, co-authored by the brother of the Fourteenth Dalai Lama.

CULTURE AND SOCIETY

Alex Ash *Wish Lanterns*. Coming-of-age in millennial China: through the well-crafted stories of six disparate youngsters from across the country, the author examines the struggles facing China's modern generation, whose aspirations are often both strikingly familiar and Westernized and yet, conflictingly, utterly Chinese.

★**Jasper Becker** *The Chinese*. An incisive portrait of modern China at both government and individual level by one of the great Sinologists. Becker draws intriguing parallels between modern rulers and ancient emperors.

David Bonavia *The Chinese: a Portrait*. A highly readable introduction to contemporary China, focusing on the human aspects as a balance to the sociopolitical trends.

Ian Buruma *Bad Elements*. Interviews with dissident exiles abroad tell an (inevitably antigovernment) story of modern China.

Gordon Chang *The Coming Collapse of China*. A detailed and well-informed overview of what's wrong with contemporary Chinese society by an influential prophet of doom – though his thesis, that a popular revolution will eventually destroy the Communist Party, is overstretched.

Leslie T. Chang *Factory Girls*. This tells the personal stories of a couple of migrant workers, giving the story of wrenching change and development in modern China a human face. Good for general readers.

Chen Guidi and Wu Chuntao *Will the Boat Sink the Water?* Modern China was founded to improve the lot of its peasant majority, but the journalist authors show how – and how badly – the country's officials are failing them. Banned in China, it reputedly sold ten million copies on the black market.

Tim Glissold *Mr China*. The eye-opening story of how the author went to China to make a fortune and instead lost US$400 million. A great first-person account of the eccentric Chinese business environment, and a must for anyone thinking of investing there.

Alexandra Harney *The China Price*. This powerful exposé of the true environmental and social costs of manufacturing in China makes a compelling, if uncomfortable read, especially for anyone thinking of outsourcing production.

★**Duncan Hewitt** *Getting Rich First*. Written by a long-term foreign resident and journalist, this excellent book moves beyond commonplace Western views of China – all dynastic history, Cultural Revolution and economic boom – with an informed look at the major social themes shaping the nation.

Mark Kitto *That's China*. A roller-coaster read recalling the heady 1990s when China's new socialist economy was still opening up. Written by a British metals-trader-turned-media-mogul, this is a warts-and-all account of trying to do big business at a time when the rules were, to say the least, unpredictable.

Jen Lin-Liu *Serve the People*. Equal parts travelogue and cookbook, which tries to understand the Chinese by heading in through the stomach. Light, witty and entertaining.

Michael Myer *In Manchuria*. Elegantly written portrait of modern China, told through the lives of the inhabitants of an utterly unimportant, ordinary town in the middle of nowhere. There's plenty of background to put things in context, with a good look at Manchuria's relatively unknown history told by people who lived through the Japanese occupation and postwar period.

★**Jason Y. Ng** *Umbrellas in Bloom*. Firsthand account of Hong Kong's 2014 democracy protests, which perhaps first brought to international attention the territory's growing anger at creeping "mainlanderization". Ng covers everything from the rent hikes caused by Chinese property speculation, to enforced Mandarin language classes at schools, "birth tourism" and Beijing's unsympathetic, heavy-handed meddling in local politics. Offers an impressive insight into Hong Kong's future.

Rob Schmitz *Street of Eternal Happiness*. Another in the growing genre of "foreign resident interviews ordinary Chinese", this is a light but very readable mosaic of life in modern Shanghai. Schmitz taps the usual parade of characters and situations: a squabbling middle-aged couple, aspirant youths, government inefficiencies and rogues who dare to break with convention.

Joe Studwell *The China Dream*. Mandatory reading for foreign businesspeople in China, this is a cautionary tale, written in layman's terms, debunking the myth that there's easy money to be made from China's vast markets. A great read for anyone interested in business, economics or human greed.

Robert Temple *The Genius of China*. Condensed from Joseph Needham's epic work *Science and Civilization in China*, this thoroughly illustrated compendium covers hundreds of important Chinese inventions through the ages – though the text does browbeat readers over how little credit the West gives China's creative talent.

Lin Yutang *My Country and My People*. An expatriate Chinese scholar writes for Western audiences in the 1930s about what it means to be Chinese. Obviously dated in parts, but overall remarkably fresh and accessible.

★**Zhang Xinxin and Sang Ye** *Chinese Lives*. This Studs Terkel-like series of first-person narratives from interviews with a broad range of Chinese people is both readable and informative, full of fascinating details of day-to-day existence that you won't read anywhere else.

TRAVEL WRITING

Mildred Cable with Francesca French *The Gobi Desert*. Cable and French were missionaries with the China Inland Mission in the early part of the twentieth century. *The Gobi Desert* is a poetic description of their life and travels in Gansu and Xinjiang, without the sanctimonious and patronizing tone adopted by some of their contemporary missionaries.

Austin Coates *Myself a Mandarin*. Despite dated views and the changing times, this humorous account of the author's time as a Hong Kong magistrate during the 1950s still rings true.

★**Rachel DeWoskin** *Foreign Babes in Beijing*. Wry, witty snapshot of 1990s Beijing as a place of untested, unexpected opportunities: the author arrives to manage a PR firm and ends up as a bohemian soap-opera star.

Peter Fleming *One's Company: a Journey to China* and *News from Tartary*. The former is an amusing account of a journey through Russia and Manchuria to China in the 1930s. En route, Peter Fleming (brother of Ian) encounters a wild assortment of Chinese and Japanese officials, and the puppet emperor Henry Pu Yi himself. *News from Tartary* records an epic journey of 5600km across the roof of the world to Kashmir in 1935.

Rob Gifford *China Road: a Journey into the Future of a Rising Power*. An interesting look into China's future, from the eyes of a traveller on Route 312 – China's own Route 66, which zips from the eastern seaboard to the Gobi Desert.

Peter Hessler *River Town – Two Years on the Yangtze*. One of the best of the mini-genre "how I taught English for a couple of years in China and survived". The book accepts

China's positive aspects and avoids cynicism when dealing with social problems and contradictions.

Somerset Maugham *On a Chinese Screen*. Brief, sometimes humorous, and often biting sketches of European missionaries, diplomats and businessmen whom Maugham encountered in China between 1919 and 1921; worth reading for background detail.

★**Matthew Polly** *American Shaolin*. A stereotypical weakling, Polly dropped out of a US college to spend two years studying kung fu at the legendary Shaolin temple. Not just the macho romp you'd expect, the book is self-deprecating, funny and steers clear of cultural cringe.

Marco Polo *The Travels*. Said to have inspired Columbus, *The Travels* is a fantastic read, full of amazing details picked up during Polo's 26 years of wandering in Asia between Venice and the court of Kublai Khan. It's not, however, a coherent history, having been ghost-written by a novelist from Marco's notes.

Vikram Seth *From Heaven Lake: Travels through Sinkiang and Tibet*. A student for two years at Nanjing University, Seth set out in 1982 to return home to Delhi via Tibet and Nepal. This account of how he hitched his way through four provinces – Xinjiang, Gansu, Qinghai and Tibet – is in the finest tradition of the early travel books.

Colin Thubron *Behind the Wall*. A thoughtful and superbly poetic description of an extensive journey through China just after it opened up in the early 1980s. The single best piece of travel writing to have come out of modern China.

GUIDES AND REFERENCE BOOKS

Kit Chow and Ione Kramer *All the Tea in China*. Everything you need to know about Chinese teas, from variations in growing and processing techniques to a rundown of fifty of the most famous brews. Good fun and nicely illustrated.

Mackinnon, Showler and Phillipps *A Field Guide to the Birds of China*. By far the best book on the subject, with over 1300 species illustrated (mostly in colour), plus outline text descriptions and distribution maps.

Jessica Rawson *Ancient China: Art and Archaeology*. By an oriental antiquities specialist at the British Museum, this scholarly introduction to Chinese art puts the subject in historical context. Beginning in Neolithic times, the book explores the technology and social organization that shaped its development up to the Han dynasty.

Derek Sandhaus *Baijiu*. Useful handbook for anyone trying to get beyond their first mouthful of China's favourite raw spirits, with the history and individual characteristics of dozens of brands laid out in thumbnail sketches. Everything you need to know, from *baijiu* drinking culture to separating rotgut *ergoutou* (literally "two-pot-head") from the subtleties of the finest Maotai. Don't miss the useful cocktail recipes at the back.

George Schaller *Wildlife of the Tibetan Steppe*. Reference book on the mammals – especially the rare Tibetan antelope – that inhabit the inhospitable Chang Tang region, by a zoologist who spent over thirty years studying China's wildlife.

Mary Tregear *Chinese Art*. An authoritative, clearly written and well-illustrated summary of the main strands in Chinese art from Neolithic times, through the Bronze Age and up to the twentieth century.

COOKERY

★**Fuchsia Dunlop** *Sichuan Cookery*. The best available English-language cookbook on Chinese cuisine, from a talented writer who spent three years honing her skills at a Chengdu cookery school. Dishes smell, look and taste exactly as you find them in Sichuan.

★**Hsiang Ju Lin and Tsuifeng Lin** *Chinese Gastronomy*. A classic work, relatively short on recipes but strong on cooking methods and philosophy – essential reading for anyone serious about learning the finer details of Chinese cooking. Wavers in and out of print, sometimes under different titles; look for Lin as the author name.

Kenneth Lo *Chinese Food*. Good general-purpose cookbook covering a wide range of methods and styles, from Westernized dishes to regional specialities.

Wei Chuan Cultural Education Foundation *Vegetarian Cooking* and *Chinese Dim Sum*. Two in a series of excellent, easy-to-follow cookbooks published by the Taiwanese Wei Chuan cooking school; simplified versions of classic dishes that produce good results. Not available in China, but easy enough to find in major bookshops in the West.

RELIGION AND PHILOSOPHY

★**Asiapac** These entertaining titles, available in Hong Kong and Beijing, present ancient Chinese philosophy in comic-book format, making it accessible without losing its complexity. Particularly good are the *Book of Zen*, a collection of stories and parables, and the *Sayings of Confucius*.

Kenneth Chen *Buddhism in China*. Very helpful for tracing the origin of Buddhist thought in China, the development of its many different schools and the four-way traffic of influence between India, Tibet, Japan and China.

★**Chuang Tzu** *The Book of Chuang Tzu*. Wonderful Taoist parables, written in antiquity by a philosopher who clearly had a keen sense of humour and a delight in life's very inexplicability.

Confucius *The Analects*. Good modern translation of this classic text, a collection of Confucius's teachings focusing on morality and the state.

Lao Zi *Tao Te Ching*. The collection of mystical thoughts and philosophical speculation that form the basis of Taoist philosophy.

★**Bill Porter** *Road to Heaven*. Clear and fascinating account of Porter's journeys around eastern China's mountain ranges, as he interviews the area's few remaining modern-day hermits. Without being in the slightest bit preachy, it sheds a good deal of light on Buddhist practices and the history of the hermit tradition in China.

Arthur Waley *Three Ways of Thought in Ancient China*. Translated extracts from the writings of three of the early philosophers – Zhuang Zi, Mencius and Han Feizi. A useful introduction.

BIOGRAPHIES AND AUTOBIOGRAPHIES

Dalai Lama *Freedom in Exile*. The autobiography of the charismatic, Nobel Prize-winning Fourteenth Dalai Lama.

Jung Chang *Wild Swans*. Enormously popular in the West, this three-generation family saga was banned in China for its honest account of the horrors of life in turbulent twentieth-century China. As well as being a good read, it serves as an excellent introduction to modern Chinese history.

David Leffman *The Mercenary Mandarin*. Set against a late Qing-dynasty backdrop, this lively biography, by our very own Rough Guides author, documents the unlikely life of British adventurer William Mesny. After jumping ship at Shanghai in 1860, Mesny spent the rest of his 59 years in China as a gun-runner, smuggler, customs official, arms instructor, botanist, explorer, journalist and decorated general in the Chinese military.

Li Kunwu and Philippe Ôtié *A Chinese Life*. Manga-format autobiography, written from street level, about the changes China has undergone since the postwar period. The book takes readers through the disastrous social experimentation of the 1950s and 60s and into the post-Maoist, "socialist capitalism" of today. The unheroic author is unapologetically pro-Party and doesn't attempt to pander to Western sensibilities; this is an honest and sometimes ugly tale of an ordinary person living in difficult times.

★**Ma Jian** *Red Dust*. Facing arrest for spiritual pollution, writer and artist Ma Jian fled Beijing to travel around China's remotest corners in the 1980s, often in extreme poverty. This picaresque tale of China in the first phase of its opening up is told in lively prose and offers the kind of insights only an alienated insider could garner.

John Man *Genghis Khan*. Lively and readable biography of the illiterate nomad who built the biggest empire the world has ever seen, intercut with Man's travels to Mongolia and China to find his tomb.

Naisingoro Pu Yi *From Emperor to Citizen*. The autobiography of the young boy who was born into the Qing imperial family and chosen by the Japanese to become the puppet emperor of the state of Manchukuo in 1931.

Philip Short *Mao: a Life*. Despite its length, an extremely readable account of Mao and his times – even if the Great Helmsman's ideologies are becoming ever less relevant in contemporary China.

★ **Hugh Trevor-Roper** *Hermit of Peking: the Hidden Life of Sir Edmund Backhouse*. Intrigued by Backhouse's thoroughly obscene memoirs, Trevor-Roper used external sources to uncover the facts behind the extraordinarily convoluted life of Edmund Backhouse – Chinese scholar, eccentric recluse and phenomenal liar – who lived in Beijing from the late nineteenth century until his death in 1944.

Marina Warner *The Dragon Empress*. An exploration of the life of Cixi, one of only two female rulers of China, that lays bare the complex personality whose conservatism, passion for power, vanity and greed had such a great impact on the events that culminated in the collapse of the imperial ruling house and the founding of the republic.

LITERATURE

MODERN WRITING

J.G. Ballard *Empire of the Sun*. This, the best literary evocation of old Shanghai, is a compelling tale of how the gilded life of expat Shanghai collapsed into chaos with the onset of war, based on the author's own experience growing up in a Japanese internment camp. It was made into a pretty decent film by Steven Spielberg.

★ **Pearl S. Buck** *The Good Earth*. The best story from a writer who grew up in China during the early twentieth century, *The Good Earth* follows the fortunes of the peasant Wang Lung from his wedding day to his dotage, as he struggles to hold onto his land for his family through a series of social upheavals.

Louis Cha *The Book and the Sword*. Northwestern China becomes a battleground for secret societies, evil henchmen, Muslim warlords and sword-wielding Taoists as a quest to save a valuable copy of the Quran uncovers a secret that threatens to topple the Qing emperor. Written in the 1950s by China's foremost martial-arts novelist, it has inspired numerous films and TV shows.

Chen Yuanbin *The Story of Qiuju*. A collection of four tales, of which the title story, about a peasant woman pushing for justice after her husband is assaulted by the village chief, was made into a film by award-winning director Zhang Yimou.

Chi Zijian *The Last Quarter of the Moon*. A tender tale revolving around the Evenki people, reindeer herders who live along China's northern frontier. Imagery-rich, it highlights what the encroaching world is doing to one of China's last isolated minority peoples.

Guo Xiaolu *A Chinese English Dictionary for Lovers*. A Chinese girl's journey of self-discovery when she comes to London, this is a bright, lively book, daringly written in Chinglish.

James Hilton *Lost Horizon*. The classic 1930s novel of longevity in a secret Tibetan valley, which gave the world – and the Chinese tourist industry – the myth of Shangri-La.

Lao She *Rickshaw Boy*. Lao She was driven to suicide during the Cultural Revolution for his belief that all politics were inherently unjust. The story is a haunting account of a young rickshaw-puller in pre-1949 Beijing.

Lu Xun *The Real Story of Ah Q*. Widely read in China today, Lu Xun is regarded as the father of modern Chinese writing. *Ah Q* is one of his best tales, short, allegorical and cynical, about a simpleton who is swept up in the 1911 revolution.

★ **Mo Yan** *The Red Sorghum Clan*, *The Garlic Ballads*. China's only winner of the Nobel Prize for Literature, Mo Yan (whose name, meaning "don't speak", says volumes about how popular he is with the regime) is most famed for *The Garlic Ballads*, a hard-hitting novel of rural life; and *The Red Sorghum Clan*, parts of which were turned into *Red Sorghum*, a Zhang Yimou film (see p.962). Both books were banned in China.

Murong *Dancing Through Red Dust*. Often dubbed "China's poet laureate of corruption", Murong's third novel delves deep into the country's murky legal system. Fluid prose infused with trademark black humour make this a compelling, if unnerving, read.

Qian Zhongshu *Fortress Besieged*. Scathing satire, set in the 1930s, about a failed student who uses a fake degree to win a teaching post and a wife. Now highly influential, it was banned for years in both mainland China and Taiwan.

Qiu Xiaolong *When Red Is Black*, *A Loyal Character Dancer*, *A Case of Two Cities*, *The Mao Case*. Procedural detective stories set in Shanghai, featuring the poetry-loving Inspector Chen. Though sometimes Qiu seems more interested in examining society and morals than in weaving a mystery, his stories of corrupt officials, sharp operators and compromised cops are some of the best evocations of modern China in contemporary English-language fiction.

Sheng Keyi *Northern Girls*. A fine debut novel chronicling the trials and tribulations of female migrant workers from Hunan province. Set in the southern boom town of Shenzhen, the narrative marks a refreshing break from male-centric stories set in Shanghai or Beijing.

Robert Van Gulik *The Judge Dee Mysteries*. Sherlock Holmes-style detective stories set in the Tang dynasty and starring the wily Judge Dee, who gets tough on crime as detective, judge and jury. Recommended are *The Red Pavilion*, *Murder in Canton* and *The Chinese Nail Murders*. Fun, informative and unusual.

Wang Shuo *Playing for Thrills* and *Please Don't Call Me Human*. Wang Shuo writes in colourful Beijing dialect about the city's wide boys and chancers. *Playing for Thrills* is fairly representative – a mystery story whose boorish narrator spends most of his time drinking, gambling and chasing girls. *Please Don't Call Me Human* is a satire of modern China as a place where greed is everything, as the Party turns a dignified martial artist into a vacuous dancer in order to win an Olympic gold medal.

Wei Hui *Shanghai Baby*. Salacious chick-lit about a Chinese girl who can't decide between her Western lover and her drug-addled Chinese boyfriend (though her real love seems to be for designer labels). Notable for the Chinese authorities' attempts to ban it and for spawning a genre in modern Chinese writing, the urban girl's saucy confessional.

Yiyun Li *A Thousand Years of Good Prayers; Gold Boy, Emerald Girl*. Two short stories looking at how China's rapid changes have affected the lives of ordinary folk, from a Beijinger now living in the States.

CLASSICS

Asiapac Chinese classics and folk tales entertainingly rendered into cartoon format. Titles include *Journey to the West*, *Tales of Laozhai* and *Chinese Eunuchs*.

Cyril Birch (ed) *Anthology of Chinese Literature*. Two volumes that cover three thousand years of poetry, philosophy, drama, biography and prose fiction, with interesting variations of translation.

Cao Xueqing and Gao E *Dream of Red Mansions/Story of the Stone*. This intricate eighteenth-century tale of manners

follows the fortunes of the Jia clan through the emotionally charged adolescent lives of Jia Baoyu and his two girl cousins, Lin Daiyu and Xue Baochai. The full translation fills five paperbacks, but there's also a much simplified English version available in China.

★**Li Bai and Du Fu** *Li Po and Tu Fu*. Fine translations of China's greatest Tang-dynasty poets, with a detailed introduction that puts them in context. Li Bai was a drunken spiritualist, Du Fu a sharp-eyed realist, and their surprisingly accessible and complementary works form an apex of Chinese literature.

★**Luo Guanzhong** *Romance of the Three Kingdoms*. Despite being written 1200 years after the events it portrays, this tale vividly evokes the battles, political schemings and myths surrounding China's turbulent Three Kingdoms period. One of the world's great historical novels.

Pu Songling *Strange Tales from a Chinese Studio*. Born during the early Qing dynasty, Pu Songling spent his life amassing these contemporary folk tales, which range from the almost believable to downright weird stories of spirits, ghosts and demons.

Shi Nai'an and Luo Guanzhong *Outlaws of the Marsh* aka *The Water Margin*. A heavy dose of popular legend, as a group of Robin Hood-like outlaws takes on the government in feudal times. Wildly uneven, and hard to read right through, but some amazing characters and set pieces.

Sun Zi *The Art of War*. "Lure them with the prospect of gain, then take them by confusion". This classic on strategy and warfare, told in pithy maxims, is as relevant today as when it was written around 500 BC. A favourite with the modern business community.

★**Wu Cheng'en** *Journey to the West*. Absurd, lively rendering of the Buddhist monk Xuanzang's pilgrimage to India to collect sacred scriptures, aided by Sandy, Pigsy and the irrepressible Sun Wu Kong, the monkey king. Arthur Waley's version, *Monkey*, retains the spirit of the tale while shortening the hundred-chapter opus to paperback length.

Chinese

As the most widely spoken language on earth, Chinese can hardly be overlooked. Chinese is, strictly speaking, a series of dialects spoken by the dominant ethnic group within China, the Han. Indeed, the term most commonly used by the Chinese themselves to refer to the language is hanyu, meaning "Han-language", though zhongyu, zhongwen and zhongguohua are frequently used as well. However, non-Han peoples such as Uyghurs and Tibetans speak languages which have little or nothing to do with Chinese.

The dialects of *hanyu* are diverse, having about as much in common as, say, German and English. The better-known and most distinct dialects include those spoken around China's coastal fringes, such as **Shanghainese** (*shanghai hua*), **Fujianese** (*minnan hua*) and **Cantonese** (*guangdong hua* or *yueyu*). Cantonese and Fujianese are themselves languages of worldwide significance, being the dialects spoken by the people of Hong Kong and among Overseas Chinese communities, particularly those in Southeast Asia.

What enables Chinese from different parts of the country to converse is **Mandarin Chinese**. Historically based on the language of Han officialdom in the Beijing area, Mandarin has been promoted over the past hundred years or so to be the official, unifying language of the Chinese people. It is known in mainland China as **putonghua** – "common language". As the language of education, government and the media, Mandarin is understood to a greater or lesser extent by the vast majority of Han Chinese, and by many non-Han as well.

Another element tying the various dialects together is the Chinese **script**. No matter how different two dialects may sound when spoken, once they are written down in the form of Chinese characters they become mutually comprehensible again, as the different dialects use the same written characters.

From the point of view of foreigners, the main distinguishing characteristic of Chinese is that it is a **tonal** language: in order to pronounce a word correctly, it is necessary to know not only its sound but also its correct tone. Accuracy in **pronunciation** is particularly important in Chinese, for which an understanding of the **pinyin** phonetic system is vital (see opposite).

Chinese characters

There are tens of thousands of **Chinese characters**, though the vast majority are obsolete – you need about 2500 to read a newspaper, and even educated Chinese are unlikely to know more than ten thousand. The characters themselves originated as **pictograms**, each representing a **concept** rather than a specific pronunciation. Chinese speakers have to memorize the sounds of individual characters, and the meanings attached to them.

THERE'S AN APP FOR THAT

Travellers are increasingly using their mobile phones to counter linguistic difficulties faced during their time in China. One of the most useful apps is the free **Waygo Visual Translator**, which allows the steady-handed to scan Chinese characters, which it then translates for you – particularly handy in restaurants with no English-language menu. Better for word-to-word translation is the excellent **Pleco** app, which also has scanning facilities if you're prepared to pay extra fees; the **DianHua** app is similar, and nearly as good.

Although to untrained eyes many Chinese characters seem impossibly complex, there is a logic behind their structure which helps in their memorization. Firstly, each character is written using an exact number of brush (or pen) **strokes**: thus the character for "mouth", which forms a square, is always written using only three strokes: first the left side, then the top and right side together, and finally the base. Secondly, characters can (very broadly) be broken up into two components, which often also exist as characters in their own right: a **main** part, which frequently gives a clue as to the pronunciation; and a **radical**, which usually appears on the left side of the character and which vaguely categorizes the meaning. As an example, the character for "mother" (妈, mā) is made up of the character for "horse" (马, mǎ; note the similar sound), combined with the radical "女, nǚ" which means "female". In some cases, the connection between the pictogram and its meaning is obvious – the character for wood (木, mù) resembles a tree. Others require some lateral thinking, or have become so abstract or complex that the meaning is hidden.

Given the time and difficulty involved in learning characters, and the negative impact this has had on the general level of literacy, in 1954 a couple of thousand of the most common characters were **simplified**, making them easier to learn and quicker to write. For example, the traditional version of "dragon" is written 龍, while the simplified version is 龙. The simplified characters were adopted in mainland China and Singapore, but Hong Kong and Taiwan continue to use the older, traditional forms.

Grammar

Chinese **grammar** is relatively simple. There is no need to conjugate verbs, decline nouns or make adjectives agree – being attached to immutable Chinese characters, Chinese words simply cannot have different "endings". Instead, context and fairly rigid rules about word order are relied on to make those distinctions of time, number and gender that Indo-European languages are so concerned with. Instead of cumbersome tenses, the Chinese make use of words such as "yesterday" or "tomorrow"; instead of plural endings they simply state how many things there are, or use quantifier words equivalent to "some" or "many".

For English speakers, **Chinese word order** follows the familiar subject-verb-object pattern, and you'll find that by simply stringing words together you'll be producing fairly grammatical Chinese. Just note that adjectives, as well as all qualifying and describing phrases, precede nouns.

Pronunciation and pinyin

Back in the 1950s it was hoped eventually to replace Chinese characters with a regular alphabet of Roman letters, and to this end the **pinyin** system was devised. Basically, *pinyin* is a way of using the Roman alphabet to write out the sounds of Mandarin Chinese, with Mandarin's four tones represented by **accents** above each syllable. Other dialects of Chinese, such as Cantonese – having nine tones – cannot be written in *pinyin*.

The aim of replacing Chinese characters with *pinyin* was abandoned long ago, but in the meantime *pinyin* has one very important function, that of helping foreigners to pronounce Chinese words. However, in *pinyin* the letters do not all have the sounds you would expect, and you'll need to spend an hour or two learning these. You'll often see *pinyin* in China, on street signs and shop displays, but only well-educated locals know the system well. Occasionally, you will come across **other systems** of rendering Mandarin into Roman letters, such as **Wade-Giles**, which writes Mao Zedong as Mao Tse-tung. These forms are no longer used in mainland China, but you may see them in Western books about China.

The Chinese terms in this book have been given both in characters and in *pinyin*; the pronunciation guide below is your first step to making yourself comprehensible. Don't get overly paranoid about your tones: with the help of context, intelligent listeners should be able to work out what you are trying to say. If you're just uttering a single word, however, for example a place name – without a context – you need to hit exactly the right tone, otherwise don't be surprised if nobody understands you.

The tones

There are **four tones** in Mandarin Chinese, and every syllable of every word is characterized by one of them, except for a few syllables which are considered toneless. This emphasis on tones does not make Chinese a particularly musical language – English, for example, uses all of the tones of Chinese and many more. The difference is that English uses tone for effect – exclaiming, questioning, listing, rebuking and so on. In English, to change the tone is to change the mood or the emphasis; in Chinese, to change the tone is to change the word itself.

First or "High" ā ē ī ō ū. In English this level tone is used when mimicking robotic or very boring, flat voices.

Second or "Rising" á é í ó ú. Used in English when asking a question showing surprise, for example "eh?". Try raising your eyebrows when attempting to make a sound with this tone – it never fails.

Third or "Falling-rising" ǎ ě ǐ ǒ ǔ. Used in English when echoing someone's words with a measure of incredulity. For example, "John's dead." "De-ad?!"

Fourth or "Falling" à è ì ò ù. Often used in English when counting in a brusque manner – "One! Two! Three! Four!" Try stamping your foot lightly when attempting to make a sound with this tone.

Toneless A few syllables do not have a tone accent. These are pronounced without emphasis, much like that lovely word "meh".

Note that if there are two consecutive characters with the third tone, the first character is pronounced as though it carries the second tone.

Consonants

Most consonants are pronounced in a similar way to their English equivalents, with the following exceptions:

c as in ha**ts**

g is hard as in **g**od (except when preceded by "n", when it sounds like sa**ng**)

q as in **ch**eese

x has no direct equivalent in English, but you can make the sound by sliding from an "s" sound to a "sh" sound and stopping midway between the two

z as in su**ds**

zh as in fu**dge**

Vowels and diphthongs

As in most languages, the vowel sounds are rather harder to quantify than the consonants. The examples here give a rough description of the sound of each vowel followed by related combination sounds.

a usually somewhere between f**a**r and m**a**n

ai as in **eye**

ao as in c**ow**

e usually as in f**ur**

ei as in g**ay**

en is an unstressed sound as at the end of hyph**en**

eng as in s**ung**

er as in f**ur** (ie with a stressed "r")

i usually as in t**ea**, except in *zi, ci, si, ri, zhi, chi* and *shi*, when it is a short clipped sound like the American military "sir"

ia as in y**a**k

ian as in y**en**

ie as in y**eah**

o as in b**ore**

ou as in sh**ow**

ü as in the German ü (make an "ee" sound and glide slowly into an "oo"; at the mid-point between the two sounds you should hit the ü sound); in *pinyin* it's sometimes written as a V

u usually as in f**oo**l except where u follows j, q, x or y, when it is always pronounced **ü**

ua as in s**ua**ve

uai as in wh**y**

ue as though contracting "you" and "air" together, **you'air**

ui as in w**ay**

uo as in w**ore**

Useful words and phrases

Chinese put their **family names first** followed by their given names, the reverse of Western convention. The vast majority of Chinese family names comprise a single character, while given names are either one or two characters long. So Zuo Zongtang has the family name of Zuo, and the given name of Zongtang.

When asked for their name, the Chinese tend to provide either just their family name, or their whole name. In **formal situations**, you might come across the terms "Mr" (*xiansheng*), "Mrs" (*taitai*, though this is being replaced by the more neutral term *airen*) or "Miss" (*xiaojie*), which are attached after the family name: for example, Mr Zuo is *zuo xiansheng*. In more casual encounters, people use familiar terms such as "old" (*lao*) or "young" (*xiao*) attached in front of the family name, though "old" or "young" are more relative terms of status than indications of actual age in this case: Mr Zuo's friend might call him "Lao Zuo", for instance.

BASICS

I	我	wǒ
You (singular)	你	nǐ
He	他	tā
She	她	tā
We	我们	wǒmén
You (plural)	你们	nǐmén
They	他们	tāmén
I want...	我要	wǒ yào...
No, I don't want...	我不要...	wǒ bú yào...
Is it possible...?	可不可以...?	kěbùkěyǐ...?
It is (not) possible	(不)可以	(bù) kěyǐ
Is there any/Have you got any...?	有没有...?	yǒuméi yǒu...?
There is/I have	有	yǒu
There isn't/I haven't	没有	méiyǒu
Please help me	请帮我忙	qǐng bāng wǒ máng
Mr...	...先生	xiānshēng
Mrs...	...太太	tàitài
Miss...	...小姐	xiǎojiě

COMMUNICATING

I don't speak Chinese	我不会说中文	wǒ bú huì shuō zhōngwén
My Chinese is terrible	我的中文很差	wǒ de zhōngwén hěn chà
Can you speak English?	你会说英语吗?	nǐ huì shuō yīngyǔ ma?
Can you get someone who speaks English?	请给我找一个会说英语的人	qǐng gěiwǒ zhǎoyíge huìshuō yīngyǔ de rén?
Please speak slowly	请说得慢一点	qǐng shuōde mànyìdiǎn
Please say that again	请再说一遍	qǐng zài shuōyíbiàn
I understand	我听得懂	wǒ tīngdedǒng
I don't understand	我听不懂	wǒ tīngbùdǒng
I can't read Chinese characters	我看不懂汉字	wǒ kànbùdong hànzì
What does this mean?	这是什么意思?	zhè shì shénme yìsi?
How do you pronounce this character?	这个字怎么念?	zhègezì zěnme niàn?

GREETINGS AND BASIC COURTESIES

Hello/How do you do?	你好	nǐhǎo!
How are you?	你好吗?	nǐ hǎo ma?
I'm fine	我很好	wǒhěnhǎo
Thank you	谢谢	xièxie

Don't mention it/You're welcome	不客气	búkèqì
Sorry to bother you...	麻烦你	máfan nǐ
Sorry/I apologize	对不起	duìbùqǐ
It's not important/No problem	没关系	méiguānxi
Goodbye	再见	zàijiàn
Chitchat	聊天	liáotiān
What country are you from?	你是哪个国家的？	nǐ shì nǎge guójiā de?
Britain	英国	yīngguó
Ireland	爱尔兰	ài'ěrlán
America	美国	měiguó
Canada	加拿大	jiā'nádà
Australia	澳大利亚	àodàlìyà
New Zealand	新西兰	xīnxīlán
China	中国	zhōngguó
Outside China	外国	wàiguó
What's your name?	你叫什么名字？	nǐ jiào shénme míngzi?
My name is...	我叫...	wǒ jiào...
Are you married?	你结婚了吗？	nǐ jiéhūnle ma?
I am (not) married	我(没有)结婚(了)	wǒ (méiyǒu) jiéhūn le
Have you got (children)?	你有没有孩子？	nǐ yǒu (méiyǒu) háizi?
Do you like...?	你喜不喜欢...？	nǐ xǐbùxǐhuān...?
I (don't) like...	我不喜欢...	wǒ (bù)xǐhuān...
What's your job?	你干什么工作？	nǐ gàn shénme gōngzuò?
I'm a foreign student	我是留学生	wǒ shì liúxuéshēng
I'm a teacher	我是老师	wǒ shì laǒshī
I work in a company	我在一个公司工作	wǒ zài yí ge gōngsī gōngzuò
I don't work	我不工作	wǒ bùgōngzuò
Clean/dirty	干净/脏	gānjìng/zāng
Hot/cold	热/冷	rè/lěng
Fast/slow	快/慢	kuài/màn
Pretty	漂亮	piàoliàng
Interesting	有意思	yǒuyìsi

NUMBERS

Zero	零	líng
One	一	yī
Two	二/两	èr/liǎng*
Three	三	sān
Four	四	sì
Five	五	wǔ
Six	六	liù
Seven	七	qī
Eight	八	bā
Nine	九	jiǔ
Ten	十	shí
Eleven	十一	shíyī
Twelve	十二	shí'èr
Twenty	二十	èrshí
Twenty-one	二十一	èrshíyī
One hundred	一百	yībǎi
Two hundred	二百	èrbǎi
One thousand	一千	yīqiān
Ten thousand	一万	yīwàn
One hundred thousand	十万	shíwàn

One million	一百万	yībǎiwàn

*liǎng is used when enumerating; for example "two people" is liǎng ge rén. èr is used when counting.

TIME

Now	现在	xiànzài
Today	今天	jīntiān
(In the) morning	早上	zǎoshàng
(In the) afternoon	下午	xiàwǔ
(In the) evening	晚上	wǎnshàng
Tomorrow	明天	míngtiān
The day after tomorrow	后天	hòutiān
Yesterday	昨天	zuótiān
Week/month/year	星期/月/年	xīngqī/yuè/nián
Monday	星期一	xīngqī yī
Tuesday	星期二	xīngqī èr
Wednesday	星期三	xīngqī sān
Thursday	星期四	xīngqī sì
Friday	星期五	xīngqī wǔ
Saturday	星期六	xīngqī liù
Sunday	星期天	xīngqī tiān
What's the time?	几点了?	jǐdiǎn le?
10 o'clock	十点钟	shídiǎn zhōng
10.20	十点二十	shídiǎn èrshí
10.30	十点半	shídiǎn bàn

TRAVELLING AND GETTING ABOUT TOWN

North	北	běi
South	南	nán
East	东	dōng
West	西	xī
Airport	机场	jīchǎng
Ferry dock	船码头	chuánmǎtóu
Left-luggage office	寄存处	jìcún chù
Ticket office	售票处	shòupiào chù
Ticket	票	piào
Can you buy me a ticket to...?	可不可以给我买到 ...的票?	kěbùkěyǐ gěi wǒ mǎi dào ... de piào?
I want to go to...	我要去...	wǒ yào qù ...
I want to leave at (8 o'clock)	我想(八点钟)离开	wǒ xiǎng (bā diǎn zhōng) líkāi
When does it leave?	什么时候出发?	shénme shíhòu chūfā?
When does it arrive?	什么时候到?	shénme shíhòu dào?
How long does it take?	路上得多长时间?	lùshàng děi duōcháng shíjiān?
CITS	中国国际旅行社	zhōngguó guójì lǚxíngshè
Train	火车	huǒchē
(Main) Train station	主要火车站	(zhǔyào) huǒchēzhàn
Bus	公共汽车	gōnggòng qìchē
Bus station	汽车站	qìchēzhàn
Long-distance bus station	长途汽车站	chángtú qìchēzhàn
Express train/bus	特快车	tèkuài chē
Fast train/bus	快车	kuàichē
Ordinary train/bus	普通车	pǔtōngchē
Minibus	小车	xiǎochē
Sleeper bus	卧铺车	wòpùchē
Lower bunk	下铺	xiàpù

Middle bunk	中铺	zhōngpù
Upper bunk	上铺	shàngpù
Hard seat	硬座	yìngzuò
Soft seat	软座	ruǎnzuò
Hard sleeper	硬卧	yìngwò
Soft sleeper	软卧	ruǎnwò
Soft-seat waiting room	软卧候车室	ruǎnwò hòuchēshì
Timetable	时间表	shíjiān biǎo
Upgrade ticket	补票	bǔpiào
Unreserved ticket	无座	wúzuò
Returned ticket	退票	tuìpiào
Platform	站台	zhàntái

GETTING ABOUT TOWN

Map	地图	dìtú
Where is…?	…在哪里?	…zàinǎlǐ?
Go straight on	往前走	wǎng qián zǒu
Turn right	往右拐	wǎng yòu guǎi
Turn left	往左拐	wǎng zuǒ guǎi
Taxi	出租车	chūzū chē
Please use the meter	请打开记价器	qǐng dǎkāi jìjiàqì
Underground/Subway station	地铁站	dìtiě zhàn
Bicycle	自行车	zìxíngchē
I want to rent a bicycle	我想租自行车	wǒ xiǎng zū zìxíngchē
How much is it per hour?	一个小时得多少钱?	yí gè xiǎoshí děi duōshǎo qián?
Bus	公共汽车	gōnggòngqìchē
Which bus goes to…?	几路车到...去?	jǐlùchē dào…qù?
Number (10) bus	(十)路车	(shí)lùchē
Does this bus go to…?	这车到...去吗?	zhèchē dào…qù ma?
When is the next bus?	下一班车几点开?	Xiàyìbān chē jǐdiǎn kāi?
The first bus	头班车	tóubān chē
The last bus	末班车	mòbān chē
Please tell me where to get off	请告诉我在哪里下车	qǐng gàosù wǒ zài nǎlǐ xià chē
Museum	博物馆	bówùguǎn
Temple	寺院	sìyuàn
Church	教堂	jiàotáng
Mosque	清真寺	qīngzhēn sì
Toilet (men's)	男厕所	nán cèsuǒ
Toilet (women's)	女厕所	nǚ cèsuǒ

ACCOMMODATION

Accommodation	住宿	zhùsù
Hotel (upmarket)	宾馆	bīnguǎn
Hotel (downmarket)	招待所，旅馆	zhāodàisuǒ, lǚguǎn
Hostel	旅社	lǚshè
Foreigners' guesthouse (at a university)	外国专家楼	wàiguó zhuānjiālóu
Is it possible to stay here?	能不能住在这里?	néngbùnéng zhùzài zhèlǐ?
Can I have a look at the room?	能不能看一下房间?	néngbùnéng kànyíxià fángjiān?
I want the cheapest bed you've got	我要你最便宜的床位	wǒ yào nǐ zuìpiányi de chuángwèi
Single room	单人房	dānrénfáng
Twin room	双人房	shuāngrénfáng
Three-bed room	三人房	sānrénfáng
Dormitory	多人房	duōrénfáng
Suite	套房	tàofáng

(Large) bed	(大)床	(dà)chuáng
Passport	护照	hùzhào
Deposit	押金	yājīn
Key	钥匙	yàoshi
I want to change my room	我想换一个房间	wǒ xiǎng huàn yíge fángjiān
Laundry (the action)	洗衣服	xǐyīfu
Laundry (the place)	洗衣店	xǐyīdiàn
Washing powder	洗衣粉	xǐyīfěn

SHOPPING, MONEY AND BANKS, AND THE POLICE

How much is it?	多少钱?	duōshǎo qián?
That's too expensive	太贵了	tàiguìle
Have you got anything cheaper?	有没有便宜一点的?	yǒuméiyǒu piányi yìdiǎn de?
Department store	百货商店	bǎihuò shāngdiàn
Market	市场	shìchǎng
¥1 (RMB)	一块(人民币)	yíkuài (rénmínbì)
US$1	一块美金	yíkuài měijīn
£1	一个英磅	yígè yīngbàng
HK$1	一块港币	yíkuài gǎngbì
Change money	换钱	huànqián
Bank of China	中国银行	zhōngguó yínháng
Travellers' cheques	旅行支票	lǚxíngzhīpiào
PSB	公安局	gōng'ān jú

COMMUNICATIONS

Post office	邮电局	yóudiànjú
Envelope	信封	xìnfēng
Stamp	邮票	yóupiào
Airmail	航空信	hángkōngxìn
Surface mail	平信	píngxìn
Telephone	电话	diànhuà
International telephone call	国际电话	guójì diànhuà
Reverse charges/collect call	对方付钱电话	duìfāng fùqián diànhuà
Fax	传真	chuánzhēn
Telephone card	电话卡	diànhuàkǎ
I want to make a telephone call to (Britain)	我想给(英国)打电话	wǒ xiǎng gěi (yīngguó) dǎ diànhuà
I want to send a fax to (US)	我想给(美国) 发一个传真	wǒ xiǎng gěi (měiguó) fā yíge chuánzhēn
Can I receive a fax here?	能不能在这里 收传真?	néngbùnéng zàizhèlǐ shōu chuánzhēn?
Internet café	网吧	wǎngbā

HEALTH

Hospital	医院	yīyuàn
Pharmacy	药店	yàodiàn
Medicine	药	yào
Chinese medicine	中药	zhōngyào
Diarrhoea	腹泻	fùxiè
Vomit	呕吐	ǒutù
Fever	发烧	fāshāo
I'm ill	我生病了	wǒ shēngbìng le
I've got flu	我感冒了	wǒ gǎnmào le
I'm (not) allergic to	我对...(不)过敏	wǒ duì... (bù) guòmǐn

Antibiotics	抗生素	kàngshēngsù
Condom	避孕套	bìyùntào
Mosquito coil	蚊香	wénxiāng
Mosquito	蚊帐纱	wénzhàngshā

A food and drink glossary

The following lists should help out in deciphering the characters on a Chinese menu – if they're written clearly. If you know what you're after, try sifting through the staples and cooking methods to create your order, or sample one of the everyday or regional suggestions, many of which are available all over the country. Note that some items, such as seafood and *jiaozi*, are ordered by weight.

GENERAL

Restaurant	餐厅	cāntīng
House speciality	拿手好菜	náshǒuhǎocài
How much is that?	多少钱?	duōshǎoqián?
I don't eat (meat)	我不吃(肉)	wǒ bùchī(ròu)
I'm Buddhist/I'm vegetarian	我是佛教徒/我只吃素	wǒshì fójiàotú/wǒ zhǐchī sù
I would like...	我想要....	wǒxiǎngyào...
Local dishes	地方菜	dìfāngcài
Snacks	小吃	xiǎochī
Menu/set menu/English menu	菜单/套餐/英文菜单	càidān/tàocān/yīngwén càidān
Small portion	少量	shǎoliàng
Chopsticks	筷子	kuàizi
Knife and fork	刀叉	dāochā
Spoon	勺子	sháozi
Waiter/waitress	服务员/小姐	fúwùyuán/xiǎojiě
Bill/cheque	买单	mǎidān
Cook these ingredients together	一块儿做	yīkuài'er zuò
Not spicy/no chilli please	请不要辣椒	qǐng búyào làjiāo
Only a little spice/chilli	一点辣椒	yìdiǎn làjiāo
500 grams	斤	jīn
1 kilo	公斤	gōngjīn

DRINKS

Beer	啤酒	píjiǔ
Sweet fizzy drink	汽水	qìshuǐ
Coffee	咖啡	kāfēi
Milk	牛奶	niúnǎi
(Mineral) water	(矿泉)水	(kuàngquán) shuǐ
Wine	葡萄酒	pútaojiǔ
Spirits	白酒	báijiǔ
Soya milk	豆浆	dòujiāng
Yoghurt	酸奶	suānnǎi

TEAS

Tea	茶	chá
Black tea	红茶	hóngchá
Chrysanthemum	菊花茶	júhuāchá
Green tea	绿茶	lǜchá
Iron Buddha	铁观音	tiěguānyīn
Jasmine	茉莉花茶	mòlìhuā chá
Pu'er	普洱茶	pǔ'ěr chá

STAPLE FOODS

Aubergine	茄子	qiézi
Bamboo shoots	笋尖	sǔnjiān
Bean sprouts	豆芽	dòuyá
Beans	豆	dòu
Beef	牛肉	niúròu
Bitter gourd	葫芦	húlu
Black bean sauce	黑豆豉	hēidòuchǐ
Bread	面包	miànbāo
Buns (filled)	包子	bāozi
Buns (plain)	馒头	mántou
Carrot	胡萝卜	húluóbo
Cashew nuts	腰果	yāoguǒ
Cauliflower	菜花	càihuā
Chicken	鸡	jī
Chilli	辣椒	làjiāo
Chocolate	巧克力	qiǎokèlì
Coriander (leaves)	香菜	xiāngcài
Crab	蟹	xiè
Cucumber	黄瓜	huángguā
Duck	鸭	yā
Eel	鳝鱼	shànyú
Eggs (fried)	煎鸡蛋	jiānjīdàn
Fish	鱼	yú
Fried dough stick	油条	yóutiáo
Garlic	大蒜	dàsuàn
Ginger	姜	jiāng
Green pepper (capsicum)	青椒	qīngjiāo
Green vegetables	绿叶素菜	lǜyè sùcài
Jiaozi (dumplings, steamed or boiled)	饺子	jiǎozi
Lamb	羊肉	yángròu
Lotus root	莲心	liánxīn
MSG	味精	wèijīng
Mushrooms	磨菇	mógu
Noodles	面条	miàntiáo
Omelette	摊鸡蛋	tānjīdàn
Onions	洋葱	yángcōng
Oyster sauce	蚝油	háoyóu
Pancake	摊饼	tānbǐng
Peanut	花生	huāshēng
Pork	猪肉	zhūròu
Potato (stir-fried)	(炒)土豆	(chǎo) tǔdòu
Prawns	虾	xiā
Preserved egg	皮蛋	pídàn
Rice, boiled	白饭	báifàn
Rice, fried	炒饭	chǎofàn
Rice noodles	河粉	héfěn
Rice porridge (aka "congee")	粥	zhōu
Salt	盐	yán
Sesame oil	芝麻油	zhīma yóu
Sichuan pepper	四川辣椒	sìchuān làjiāo
Snails	蜗牛	wōniú
Snake	蛇肉	shéròu
Soup	汤	tāng

Soy sauce	酱油	jiàngyóu
Squid	鱿鱼	yóuyú
Sugar	糖	táng
Tofu	豆腐	dòufu
Tomato	蕃茄	fānqié
Vinegar	醋	cù
Water chestnuts	马蹄	mǎtí
White radish	白萝卜	báiluóbo
Yam	芋头	yùtóu

COOKING METHODS

Boiled	煮	zhǔ
Casseroled (see also "Claypot")	焙	bèi
Deep-fried	油煎	yóujiān
Fried	炒	chǎo
Poached	白煮	báizhǔ
Red-cooked (stewed in soy sauce)	红烧	hóngshāo
Roast	烤	kǎo
Steamed	蒸	zhēng
Stir-fried	清炒	qīngchǎo

EVERYDAY DISHES

Braised duck with vegetables	炖鸭素菜	dùnyā sùcài
Cabbage rolls (stuffed with meat or vegetables)	卷心菜	juǎnxīn cài
Chicken and sweetcorn soup	玉米鸡丝汤	yùmǐ jīsī tāng
Chicken with bamboo shoots and baby corn	笋尖嫩玉米炒鸡片	sǔnjiān nènyùmǐ chǎojīpiàn
Chicken with cashew nuts	腰果鸡片	yāoguǒ jīpiàn
Claypot/sandpot (casserole)	沙锅	shāguō
Crispy aromatic duck	香酥鸭	xiāngsūyā
Egg flower soup with tomato	蕃茄蛋汤	fānqié dàntāng
Egg-fried rice	蛋炒饭	dànchǎofàn
Fish-ball soup with white radish	萝卜鱼蛋汤	luóbo yúdàn tāng
Fish casserole	焙鱼	bèiyú
Fried shredded pork with garlic and chilli	大蒜辣椒炒肉片	dàsuàn làjiāo chǎoròupiàn
Hotpot	火锅	huǒguō
Kebab	串肉	chuànròu
Noodle soup	汤面	tāngmiàn
Pork and mustard greens	芥末肉片	jièmò ròupiàn
Pork and water chestnut	马蹄猪肉	mǎtí zhūròu
Pork and white radish pie	白萝卜肉馅饼	báiluóbo ròuxiànbǐng
Prawn with garlic sauce	大蒜炒虾	dàsuàn chǎoxiā
"Pulled" noodles	拉面	lāmiàn
Roast duck	烤鸭	kǎoyā
Scrambled egg with pork on rice	滑蛋猪肉饭	huádàn zhūròufàn
Sliced pork with yellow bean sauce	黄豆肉片	huángdòu ròupiàn
Squid with green pepper and black beans	豆豉青椒炒鱿鱼	dòuchǐ qīngjiāo chǎoyóuyú
Steamed eel with black beans	豆豉蒸鳝	dòuchǐ zhēngshàn
Steamed rice packets wrapped in lotus leaves	荷叶蒸饭	héyè zhēngfàn
Stewed pork belly with vegetables	回锅肉	huíguōròu

Stir-fried chicken and bamboo shoots	笋尖炒鸡片	sǔnjiān chǎojīpiàn
Stuffed bean-curd soup	豆腐汤	dòufutāng
Stuffed bean curd with aubergine and green pepper	茄子青椒煲	dòuu qiézi qīngjiāobǎo
Sweet-and-sour spareribs	糖醋排骨	tángcù páigǔ
Sweet bean-paste pancakes	赤豆摊饼	chìdòu tānbǐng
White radish soup	白萝卜汤	báiluóbo tāng
Wuntun soup	馄饨汤	húntun tāng

VEGETABLES AND EGGS

Aubergine with chilli and garlic sauce	大蒜辣椒炒茄子	dàsuàn làjiāo chǎoqiézi
Aubergine with sesame sauce	拌茄子片	bànqiézipiàn
Bean curd and spinach soup	菠菜豆腐汤	bōcài dòufu tāng
Bean-curd slivers	豆腐花	dòufuhuā
Bean curd with chestnuts	马蹄豆腐	mǎtí dòufu
Braised mountain fungus	炖香菇	dùnxiānggū
Egg fried with tomatoes	蕃茄炒蛋	fānqié chǎodàn
Fried bean curd with vegetables	豆腐素菜	dòufu sùcài
Fried bean sprouts	炒豆芽	chǎodòuyá
Monks' vegetarian dish (stir-fry of mixed vegetables and fungi)	罗汉斋	luóhànzhāi
Pressed bean curd with cabbage	卷心菜豆腐	juǎnxīncài dòufu
Spicy braised	香茄子条	xiāngqiézitiáo
Stir-fried bamboo shoots	炒冬笋	chǎodōngsǔn
Stir-fried mushrooms	炒鲜菇	chǎoxiān'gū
Vegetable soup	素菜汤	sùcài tāng

NORTHERN DISHES

Aromatic fried lamb	炒羊肉	chǎoyángròu
Beijing (Peking) duck	北京烤鸭	běijīng kǎoyā
Fish with ham and vegetables	火腿素菜鱼片	huǒtuǐ sùcài yúpiàn
Fried prawn balls	炒虾球	chǎoxiāqiú
Lion's head (pork rissoles casseroled with greens)	狮子头	shīzitóu
Mongolian hotpot	蒙古火锅	ménggǔ huǒguō
Red-cooked lamb	红烧羊肉	hóngshāo yángròu

EASTERN DISHES

Beggars' chicken (baked)	叫花鸡	jiàohuājī
Brine duck	盐水鸭	yánshuǐ yā
Crab soup	蟹肉汤	xièròu tāng
Dongpo pork casserole (steamed in wine)	东坡焙肉	dōngpō bèiròu
Drunken prawns	醉虾	zuìxiā
Five flower pork (steamed in lotus leaves)	五花肉	wǔhuāròu
Fried crab with eggs	蟹肉鸡蛋	xièròu jīdàn
Pearl balls (rice-grain-coated, steamed rissoles)	珍珠球	zhēnzhūqiú
Shaoxing chicken	绍兴鸡	shàoxīng jī
Soup dumplings (steamed, containing jellied stock)	汤包	tāngbāo
Steamed sea bass	清蒸鲈鱼	qīngzhēnglúyú
Stuffed green peppers	馅青椒	xiànqīngjiāo

West Lake fish (braised in a sour sauce)	西湖醋鱼	xīhúcùyú
"White-cut" beef (spiced and steamed)	白切牛肉	báiqiē niúròu
Yangzhou fried rice	杨州炒饭	yángzhōu chǎofàn

WESTERN CHINESE DISHES

Boiled beef slices (spicy)	水煮牛肉	shuǐzhǔ niúròu
Carry-pole noodles (with a chilli-vinegar-sesame sauce)	担担面	dàndànmiàn
Crackling-rice with pork	爆米肉片	bàomǐ ròupiàn
Crossing-the-bridge noodles	过桥面	guòqiáomiàn
Deep-fried green beans with garlic	大蒜刀豆	dàsuàn dāodòu
Dong'an chicken (poached in spicy sauce)	东安鸡子	dōng'ān jīzǐ
Doubled-cooked pork	回锅肉	huíguōròu
Dried yoghurt wafers	乳饼	rǔbǐng
Dry-fried pork shreds	油炸肉丝	yóuzhá ròusī
Fish-flavoured aubergine	鱼香茄子	yúxiāng qiézi
Gongbao chicken (with chillies and peanuts)	宫保鸡丁	gōngbǎo jīdīng
Green pepper with spring onion and black bean sauce	豆豉青椒	dòuchǐ qīngjiāo
Hot and sour soup (flavoured with vinegar and white pepper)	酸辣汤	suānlà tāng
Hot-spiced bean curd	麻婆豆腐	mápódòufu
Rice-flour balls, stuffed with sweet paste	汤圆	tāngyuán
Smoked duck	熏鸭	xūnyā
Strange flavoured chicken (with sesame-garlic-chilli)	怪味鸡	guàiwèijī
Stuffed aubergine slices	馅茄子	xiànqiézi
Tangerine chicken	桔子鸡	júzijī
"Tiger-skin" peppers (pan-fried with salt)	虎皮炒椒	hǔpí chǎojiāo
Wind-cured ham	火腿	huǒtuǐ

SOUTHERN CHINESE DISHES

Baked crab with chilli and black beans	辣椒豆豉焙蟹	làjiāo dòuchǐ bèixiè
Barbecued pork ("char siew")	叉烧	chāshāo
Casseroled bean curd stuffed with pork mince	豆腐煲	dòufubāo
Claypot rice with bean-curd-stuffed sweet sausage	香肠饭	xiāngchángfàn
Crisp-skinned pork on rice	脆皮肉饭	cuìpíròufàn
Fish-head casserole	焙鱼头	bèiyútóu
Fish steamed with ginger and spring onion	清蒸鱼	qīngzhēngyú
Fried chicken with yam	芋头炒鸡片	yùtóu chǎojīpiàn
Honey-roast pork	蜂蜜烤猪肉	fēngmì kǎo zhūròu
Kale in oyster sauce	蚝油白菜	háoyóu báicài
Lemon chicken	柠檬鸡	níngméngjī
Litchi (lychee) pork	荔枝肉片	lìzhīròupiàn
Salt-baked chicken	盐鸡	yánjī
White fungus and wolfberry soup (sweet)	枸杞炖银耳	gǒuqí dùnyín'ěr

DIM SUM

Dim sum	点心	diǎnxīn
Barbecued pork bun	叉烧包	chāshāo bāo
Crab and prawn dumpling	蟹肉虾饺	xièròu xiājiǎo
Custard tart	蛋挞	dàntǎ
Doughnut	炸面饼圈	zhá miànbǐngquān
Fried taro and mince dumpling	蕃薯糊饺	fānshǔ hújiǎo
Lotus-paste bun	莲蓉糕	liánrónggāo
Moon cake (sweet bean paste in flaky pastry)	月饼	yuèbǐng
Paper-wrapped prawns	纸包虾	zhǐbāoxiā
Pork and prawn dumpling	烧麦	shāomài
Prawn crackers	虾片	xiāpiàn
Prawn dumpling	虾饺	xiājiǎo
Prawn paste on fried toast	芝麻虾	zhīmaxiā
Shanghai fried meat and vegetable dumpling ("potstickers")	锅贴	guōtiē
Spring-roll spareribs and chilli	春卷	chūnjuǎn
Steamed	排骨	páigǔ
Stuffed green peppers with black bean sauce	豆豉馅青椒	dòuchǐ xiànqīngjiāo
Stuffed rice-flour roll	肠粉	chángfěn
Sweet sesame balls	芝麻球	zhīma qiú
Turnip-paste patty	萝卜糕	luóbo gāo

FRUIT

Fruit	水果	shuǐguǒ
Apple	苹果	píngguǒ
Banana	香蕉	xiāngjiāo
Durian	榴莲	liúlián
Grape	葡萄	pútáo
Honeydew melon	哈密瓜	hāmì guā
Longan	龙眼	lóngyǎn
Lychee	荔枝	lìzhī
Mandarin orange	橘子	júzi
Mango	芒果	mángguǒ
Orange	橙子	chéngzi
Peach	桃子	táozi
Pear	梨	lí
Persimmon	柿子	shìzi
Plum	李子	lǐzi
Pomegranate	石榴	shíliu
Pomelo	柚子	yòuzi
Watermelon	西瓜	xīguā

Glossary

Arhat Buddhist saint

Bei North

Binguan Hotel; generally a large one, for tourists

Bodhisattva A follower of Buddhism who has attained enlightenment, but has chosen to stay on earth to teach rather than enter nirvana; Buddhist god or goddess

Boxers The name given to an antiforeign organization which originated in Shandong in 1898 (see p.932 & p.96)

Chorten Tibetan stupa

CITS China International Travel Service. Tourist organization primarily interested in selling tours, though they can help with obtaining train tickets

CTS China Travel Service. Tourist organization similar to CITS

Concession Part of a town or city ceded to a foreign power in the nineteenth century

Cultural Revolution Ten-year period beginning in 1966, characterized by destruction, persecution and fanatical devotion to Mao (see p.936)

Dagoba Another name for a stupa

Dong East

Dougong Large, carved wooden brackets, a common feature of temple design

Fandian Restaurant or hotel

Feng Peak

Feng shui A system of geomancy used to determine the positioning of buildings

Gang of Four Mao's widow and her supporters who were put on trial immediately after Mao's death for their role in the Cultural Revolution, for which they were convenient scapegoats

Ge Pavilion

Gong Palace; usually indicates a Taoist temple

Guan Pass; in temple names, usually denotes a Taoist shrine

Guanxi Literally "connections": the reciprocal favours inherent in the process of official appointments and transactions

Guanyin The ubiquitous Buddhist Goddess of Mercy, the most popular Bodhisattva in China

Gulou Drum tower; traditionally marking the centre of a town

Guomindang (GMD) The Nationalist Peoples' Party. Under Chiang Kai-shek, the GMD fought Communist forces for 25 years before being defeated and moving to Taiwan in 1949, where it remains a major political party

Hai Sea; in western China, also lake

Han Chinese The main body of the Chinese people, as distinct from other ethnic groups such as Uyghur, Miao, Hui or Tibetan

He River

Hu Lake

Hui Muslim minority, mainly based in Gansu and Ningxia. Visually they are often indistinguishable from Han Chinese

Hutong A narrow alleyway

I Ching The Book of Changes, an ancient handbook for divination that includes some of the fundamental concepts of Chinese thought, such as the duality yin and yang

Inkstones Decoratively carved blocks traditionally used by artists and calligraphers as a palette for mixing ink powder with water

Jiang River

Jiao (or **mao**) A tenth of a yuan

Jiaozi Crescent-shaped, ravioli-like dumpling, usually served fried by the plateful for breakfast

Jie Street

Kang A raised wooden platform in a Chinese home, heated by the stove, on which the residents eat and sleep

Kazakh A minority, mostly nomadic, in Xinjiang

Lamian "Pulled noodles", a Muslim speciality usually served in a spicy soup

Legalism In the Chinese context, a belief that humans are intrinsically bad and that strict laws are needed to rein in their behaviour

Ling Tomb

Little Red Book A selection of "Quotations from Chairman Mao Zedong", produced in 1966 as a philosophical treatise for Red Guards during the Cultural Revolution

Long March The Communists' 9500km tactical retreat in 1934–35 from Guomindang troops

Lu Street

Luohan Buddhist disciple

Mandala Mystic diagram which forms an important part of Buddhist iconography, especially in Tibet

Mantou Steamed bread bun (literally "bald head")

Men Gate/door

Miao Temple, usually Confucian

Middle Kingdom A literal translation of the Chinese words for China

Nan South

PLA The People's Liberation Army

PSB Public Security Bureau, the branch of China's police force which deals directly with foreigners

Pagoda Tower with distinctively tapering structure, often associated with pseudoscience of feng shui

Pinyin The official system of transliterating Chinese script into Roman characters

Putonghua Mandarin Chinese; literally "Common Language"

Qianfodong Literally, "Thousand Buddha Cave", the name given to any Buddhist cave site along the Chinese section of the Silk Road

Qiao Bridge

RMB Renminbi. Another name for Chinese currency literally meaning "the people's money"

Red Guards The unruly factional forces unleashed by Mao during the Cultural Revolution to find and destroy brutally any "reactionaries" among the populace

Renmin The people

SEZ Special Economic Zone. A region in which state controls on production have been loosened and Western techniques of economic management are experimented with

Sakyamuni Name given to future incarnation of Buddha

Shan Mountain

Shi City or municipality

Shui Water

Shuijiao Similar to *jiaozi* but boiled or served in a thin soup

Si Temple, usually Buddhist

Siheyuan Traditional courtyard house

Spirit wall Wall behind the main gateway to a house, designed to thwart evil spirits, which, it was believed, could move only in straight lines

Spirit Way The straight road leading to a tomb, lined with guardian figures

Stele Freestanding stone tablet carved with text

Stupa Multitiered tower associated with Buddhist temples that usually contains sacred objects

Sutra Buddhist texts, often illustrative doctrines arranged in prayer form

Ta Tower or pagoda

Taiping Uprising Peasant rebellion against Qing rule during the mid-nineteenth century

Tian Heaven or the sky

Uyghur Substantial minority of Turkic people, living mainly in Xinjiang

Waiguoren Foreigner

Xi West

Yuan China's unit of currency. Also a courtyard or garden (and the name of the Mongol dynasty)

Yurt Round, felt tent used by nomads. Also known as *ger*

Zhan Station

Zhao Temple; term used mainly in Inner Mongolia

Zhong Middle; China is referred to as *zhongguo*, the Middle Kingdom

Zhonglou Bell tower, usually twinned with a *gulou*.

Zhou Place or region

Small print and index

Rough Guide credits

Editors: Helen Abramson, Samantha Cook, Lucy Kane, Tim Locke, Alice Park, Georgia Stephens
Layout: Jessica Subramanian
Cartography: Rajesh Mishra
Picture editor: Mark Thomas
Proofreader: Diane Margolis
Chinese proofreader: Shan Sun
Managing editor: Andy Turner

Assistant editor: Payal Sharotri
Production: Jimmy Lao
Cover photo research: Marta Bescos Sanchez
Editorial assistant: Aimee White
Senior DTP coordinator: Dan May
Programme manager: Gareth Lowe
Publishing director: Georgina Dee

Publishing information

This eighth edition published June 2017 by
Rough Guides Ltd,
80 Strand, London WC2R 0RL
11, Community Centre, Panchsheel Park,
New Delhi 110017, India
Distributed by Penguin Random House
Penguin Books Ltd, 80 Strand, London WC2R 0RL
Penguin Group (USA), 345 Hudson Street, NY 10014, USA
Penguin Group (Australia), 250 Camberwell Road,
Camberwell, Victoria 3124, Australia
Penguin Group (NZ), 67 Apollo Drive, Mairangi Bay,
Auckland 1310, New Zealand
Penguin Group (South Africa), Block D, Rosebank Office
Park, 181 Jan Smuts Avenue, Parktown North, Gauteng,
South Africa 2193
Rough Guides is represented in Canada by DK Canada, 320
Front Street West, Suite 1400, Toronto, Ontario M5V 3B6
Printed in Singapore
© Rough Guides, 2017
Maps © Rough Guides

The publishers and authors have done their best to
ensure the accuracy and currency of all the information
in **The Rough Guide to China**, however, they can accept
no responsibility for any loss, injury, or inconvenience
sustained by any traveller as a result of information or
advice contained in the guide.
1 3 5 7 9 8 6 4 2

MIX
Paper from
responsible sources
FSC   FSC™ C018179
www.fsc.org

Help us update

We've gone to a lot of effort to ensure that the eighth
edition of **The Rough Guide to China** is accurate and up-
to-date. However, things change – places get "discovered",
opening hours are notoriously fickle, restaurants and
rooms raise prices or lower standards. If you feel we've got
it wrong or left something out, we'd like to know, and if
you can remember the address, the price, the hours, the
phone number, so much the better.

Please send your comments with the subject line
"**Rough Guide China Update**" to mail@uk.roughguides
.com. We'll credit all contributions and send a copy of the
next edition (or any other Rough Guide if you prefer) for
the very best emails.

Readers' updates

Thanks to all the readers who have taken the time to write in with comments and suggestions (and apologies if we've
inadvertently omitted or misspelt anyone's name):

Geoff Brown; Chris Coe; Justin Fisch; J Griffin; Celia Jenkins; Sasha FA Levy-Andersson; Martin Lewis; Matthew Newton;
Simon Triller.

ABOUT THE AUTHORS

Thomas Bird has been wandering East Asia for so long, he's forgotten how long. He's concerned with everything from tea culture to environmental issues to contemporary art. On completing this guidebook he intends to spend less time sipping craft ale in Beijing rock dives and more time studying *tai ji*. He especially enjoys the teachings of Zhuangzi. Monitor his progress at: ⊚thomasbird.info.

Stuart Butler is a writer and photographer who has been travelling in, hiking through and writing about the Himalaya region for over twenty years and was delighted to research Tibet for this book. He is based in southwest France with his wife and two young children. His website is: ⊚stuartbutlerjournalist.com.

Joanna James started her career as a commodity broker in London before a dislike of commuting and a chronic case of wanderlust intervened. She escaped to Asia and worked in a series of very odd jobs before settling into life as a freelance writer. When she's not somewhere else, Jo lives on a small island in Hong Kong with her husband and son, and tries not to offend anyone with her awful Cantonese.

David Leffman first visited in China in 1985 and has since clocked up over five years there in total, mostly working as a travel writer. Among other things, he has written guidebooks to China, Hong Kong, Australia, Indonesia and Iceland. Find out more at: ⊚davidleffman.com.

Simon Lewis is a screenwriter and novelist. He's particularly proud of his crime thriller *Bad Traffic* – a novel about a Chinese policeman looking for his missing daughter – which has been translated into eight languages. The sequel will be published soon.

Mark South first visited Asia in 1980. After a twenty-year gap while he learned to walk, talk, read and – eventually – write, he returned in 2000. Having lived in Taipei, Beijing and Shanghai, he can currently be found in Kathmandu laying plans for a smog-free life in Connemara.

Charles Young has been travelling since university and, as well as working on over a dozen Rough Guide titles, has taught English in Catalunya, run a coffee shop in Hong Kong, was a publican in South Korea and worked in the spice trade in India. He currently lives in deepest, darkest China.

Martin Zatko has been in China most years since his first visit in 2003, and feels privileged to have witnessed the country's astonishing transformation first hand. He has written or contributed to almost thirty Rough Guides, including those to Korea, Japan, Vietnam, Myanmar, Turkey, Morocco and Europe.

Acknowledgements

Thomas Bird: In China it can be difficult to operate without noble comrades devoted to aiding and abetting my many farfetched and far-reaching endeavors. In no particular order I would like to raise a glass of *baijiu* to: Mathias Daccord; Harvey Thomlinson; Bruce Humes; Mike Bossick; David Sivell; Sarah Griffiths; Helder Beja; Ricardo Pinto; Peter Fenton; Danny Parrott; Richard Lloyd; Yan Qing Qing; Wu Tiao Ren; Leo Lee; Li Zhengde; Chen Jin; the artists of Songzhuang; the people at Old Heaven Books; Wu Qiang; A'Lan; Wu Liao and my "*niubi*" godson Wu Dian, to whom my chapters of this book are dedicated. Thanks also to my family in Wales for understanding my compulsion to wander.

Stuart Butler: First and foremost I must once again thank my wife, Heather, and my children, Jake and Grace, for their patience and understanding as I disappeared off into the mountains of Tibet. Jake, I promise I will bring a yeti home next time. Without the generous help and time of Jamin York from Himalaya Journey and Tenzin Gelek from Tibet Highland Tours, this project could never have happened. I would also like to thank my ever-patient guide in Tibet, Jamyang. Thank you also to Dan Royse for being a great travel companion. Finally, thanks to all at Rough Guides for their help and input.

Joanna James: Many thanks to everyone who helped me, knowingly or unknowingly, and in particular to Dave, David, Jerry and – most of all – to my understanding Research-Partner-in-Chief, Theo.

David Leffman: For companionship, information and punches, thanks to Narrell; Paul Andrews; Peter Goff; Oscar Holland; Pete and Sue; Derek Sandhaus; Shan Shan; Paul Tomic; and Yao Chengrong. Also thanks to Lucy Kane and Helen Abramson for smooth editing.

Simon Lewis: Thanks to Kathrine; Sam; Du; Cici; Olivia; Polly; and Ivy.

Mark South: Thanks to Siobhan; Simons Lewis and Farnham; David L; Charles Y; Hsuan-Fen; Nina; Ari; Jyunge; my parents for not yet having asked when I'm going to get a proper job; and everyone at the Red Cross.

Charles Young would like to thank Qing Qing for all her help and company; my family for support; authors David and Simon; Chris; Jake; Arius; Gerry; Jill; Catherine; Shin Miao and the Guiyang crew; Golden Dragon and Jessica in Bama; all the folk at the DMZ bar; Sean in Kunming; as well as Alice and Helen at Rough Guides.

Martin Zatko would like to thank father Ludvik for dropping by; Michael Spavor for his North Korean border hospitality; Jingwen Cheung for the tour around Nanjing; Amber Yin for her company in Ji'nan and Tai'an; Yeongae Min for popping across the sea to Qingdao; Daniel at Fly by Knight; Jun and Lorimer for their assistance with accommodation; and the baby sparrow who joined the journey for a while, and managed to survive for a week (including three high-speed train journeys in a converted Pringles tube) between Kaifeng and Xi'an.

A ROUGH GUIDE TO ROUGH GUIDES

Published in 1982, the first Rough Guide – to Greece – was a student scheme that became a publishing phenomenon. Mark Ellingham, a recent graduate in English from Bristol University, had been travelling in Greece the previous summer and couldn't find the right guidebook. With a small group of friends he wrote his own guide, combining a contemporary, journalistic style with a thoroughly practical approach to travellers' needs.

The immediate success of the book spawned a series that rapidly covered dozens of destinations. And, in addition to impecunious backpackers, Rough Guides soon acquired a much broader readership that relished the guides' wit and inquisitiveness as much as their enthusiastic, critical approach and value-for-money ethos. These days, Rough Guides include recommendations from budget to luxury and cover more than 120 destinations around the globe, from Amsterdam to Zanzibar, all regularly updated by our team of roaming writers.

Browse all our latest guides, read inspirational features and book your trip at **roughguides.com**.

Photo credits

All photos © Rough Guides, except the following:
(Key: t-top; c-centre; b-bottom; l-left; r-right)

Index

Maps are marked in grey

O

P

N

Q

Map symbols

The symbols below are used on maps throughout the book

International boundary	Zoo	MTR station
State/province boundary	Tourist office	Subway
Motorway	Hospital	Beijing subway
Road	Place of interest	Metro
Pedestrianized road	Ruins	Bus station/depot
Steps	Golf course	Embassy
Path	Mosque	Mountain peak
Railway	Tower	Mountain range
Funicular	Arch	Ski area
Cable car	Monument	Bridge
Ferry route	Border crossing	Cave
Wall	Fountain	Mountain pass
International airport	Viewpoint	Church
Domestic airport	Waterfall	Building
Transport stop	Temple	Pedestrianized area
Dock	Dagoba	Market
Spring/spa	Pagoda	Stadium
Swimming/pool	Statue	Park/national park
Internet café/access	Museum	Beach
Post office	Gate	Pine tree
		Christian cemetery

Listings key

- Accommodation
- Eating
- Drinking/nightlife
- Shopping